FUNDAMENTALS

OF

LEGAL RESEARCH

By

J. MYRON JACOBSTEIN
Professor of Law Emeritus and Law Librarian Emeritus
Stanford University

ROY M. MERSKY
William Stamps Farish Professor of Law and Director of Research
University of Texas, Austin

DONALD J. DUNN
Dean and Professor of Law
Western New England College

SEVENTH EDITION

New York, New York
FOUNDATION PRESS
1998

ISBN 1–56662–613–7

 TEXT IS PRINTED ON 10% POST CONSUMER RECYCLED PAPER

Dedications

J. Myron Jacobstein dedicates this book to his family:
Bennett, Ellen, and Belle

Roy M. Mersky dedicates this book to his granddaughters:
Grace, Rebekah, and Sophie

Donald J. Dunn dedicates this book to his family:
Kevin and Cheryl

He [or She] Who Cites His [or Her] Source, Begins
Deliverance to the World

Mishnah, Avot. VI

PREFACE

The processes and sources used in legal research are always in a state of flux. New sources emerge, existing ones are remodeled, and still others are discontinued. The skills and methodology employed in conducting research are also evolving. The greatest challenge of legal research is to remain current in order to resolve legal issues in the most thorough and efficient way. Today, print and various forms of electronic media collectively represent the means for conducting traditional legal research.

In preparing this edition of *Fundamentals of Legal Research*, we have been conscious of the many changes relating to legal research that have occurred in recent years and have tried to incorporate those changes into this 7th edition. To make the changes essential for a contemporary text, all chapters have been updated and enhanced. Several have been substantially revised or had major portions rewritten. Of the more than two hundred Illustrations in this text, over one hundred of them are new. Many of these new Illustrations are to Internet sources. Illustrations are numbered by chapter and then by their order of appearance within that chapter. For example, Illustration 12-3 means that this is the third Illustration in Chapter 12. This numbering enables us to easily reference to an Illustration in one chapter that might be contained in a different chapter.

We have retained for this edition the features that have proven so popular over the years. We have used the same organizational arrangement of the chapters and the familiar outline format for use in identifying and explaining individual sources and concepts. As most law students begin the study of law with the reading and analysis of cases, we have consistently found it most effective to begin legal research instruction with an examination of the process of publication of court cases and the methods of locating these cases. The examination of court cases is followed by chapters on other sources of primary law, then chapters on secondary sources useful in legal research, and, finally, by specialized chapters on international law, English legal research, computer-assisted legal research, citation form, and federal taxation. The text is organized, however, to allow an instructor to begin instruction with any of the sources examined in this book. Summaries, included at the end of most chapters, continue to highlight the major points made in the detailed discussions within the text.

We continue to resist, for pedagogical reasons, the temptation to make this work *the* definitive source for legal bibliography. Rather, we intend it to be primarily a basic text for students learning to do legal research. The text is organized in a format that enables law students and lawyers, as well as other researchers, to locate and to use the legal resources necessary to solve their research problems. In addition, the text includes footnotes to sources beyond those examined, so that research may be pursued in greater depth, if desired. The Appendices, which include a new and selective listing of law-related Internet sources, offer additional detailed information on legal abbreviations and coverage of various legal research sources.

Assignments to Accompany Fundamentals of Legal Research is available as a separate pamphlet. These assignments are designed to help the student understand and examine in detail the research tools described in the book. Unique to *Fundamentals of Legal Research* since 1977 is the *Noter Up*, a newsletter issued in August and January to coincide with the start of the fall and spring semesters and provided on a complimentary basis to instructors who adopt the main text for classroom use. This publication, in addition to providing updating and supplementation for the main text, also discusses recent developments and events of special interest to those involved in legal research.

Collectively, *Fundamentals of Legal Research*, the accompanying *Assignments*, and the semiannual *Noter Up* enable users to learn the essentials of legal research and to remain current with respect to new sources and research methodologies.

J. MYRON JACOBSTEIN
ROY M. MERSKY
DONALD J. DUNN

June 1998

ACKNOWLEDGMENTS

We are pleased to have this opportunity to express our gratitude to the many people who have helped in the preparation of *Fundamentals of Legal Research, Seventh Edition.*

The law library staffs at The University of Texas Jamail Center for Legal Research and Western New England College School of Law have earned our most sincere thanks for their collective expertise. A special note of thanks to Gwyn Anderson, Senior Administrative Associate, at The University of Texas for her advice and help in the preparation of this book.

At Western New England College, where much of this revision took place, we are especially grateful to Bonnie L. Koneski-White, Law Librarian; Michele Dill LaRose, Head of Reader Services; Christine Archambault, Head of Technical Services; Patricia Newcombe, Reference Librarian; Nancy Johnson, Catalog Librarian; and Susan Drisko, Collection Services Librarian. The research assistance of Margaret B. Easton, '97, was both enormous and indispensable. Thanks also goes to Marie E. Irzyk, Administrative Assistant to the Dean, for her help and patience.

We are happy that for this edition Mary Ann Nelson, Executive Law Librarian of the University of Iowa Law School, assumed responsibility for the Assignments and the Instructor's Manual.

In the body of the text, credit is given to those who prepared individual chapters or sections. We want to acknowledge again these contributors: Steven M. Barkan, Director of the Law Library and Professor of Law, University of Wisconsin Law School; David Gunn, Head of Reference Services at the University of Texas at Austin, Jamail Center for Legal Research, Tarlton Law Library; Bonnie L. Koneski-White, Law Librarian at Western New England College School of Law; Daniel W. Martin, Director of the Law Library and Associate Professor of Law at Pepperdine University School of Law; Robert J. Nissenbaum, Director of the William M. Rains Library and Professor of Law at Loyola Marymount University School of Law; Jonathan Pratter, Foreign and International Law Librarian at the University of Texas at Austin, Jamail Center for Legal Research, Tarlton Law Library; Gail Levin Richmond, Associate Dean, Academic Affairs and Professor of Law, Nova Southeastern Shepard Broad School of Law; Fred R. Shapiro, Associate Librarian for Public Services and Lecturer in Legal Research at Yale Law School; Keith A. Stiverson, Deputy Law Librarian, The University of Texas at Austin University of Texas at Austin, Jamail Center for Legal Research, Tarlton Law Library; and Stephen E. Young, Collection

ACKNOWLEDGMENTS

Management Librarian and Lecturer, at The University of Texas at Austin, Jamail Center for Legal Research, Tarlton Law Library. To all our contributors through the seven editions of this work, we are most grateful.

We want to thank the many publishers who provided updated information on their materials. Also we want to pay special tribute to the staff at Foundation Press for their courtesy, patience, advice, and publication expertise, and to the West Group and its parent company, Thomson Law Publishing, for their support.

We again wish to express our deep appreciation to the many instructors who have adopted *Fundamentals of Legal Research* for classroom use. Their suggestions about possible additions to the text have been most useful.

Finally, we thank all the law students who read and use the book. It is gratifying when lawyers indicate that the book they used in their first year legal research class or in an advanced course in legal research is still in their personal library, and that they continue referring to it. All of these comments truly give us a sense of pride and humility. Ultimately, we are grateful for having the opportunity to make our contribution to the body of legal literature.

SUMMARY OF CONTENTS

APPENDICES

*

TABLE OF CONTENTS

TABLE OF CONTENTS

TABLE OF CONTENTS

TABLE OF CONTENTS

TABLE OF CONTENTS

GLOSSARY OF TERMS USED
IN LEGAL RESEARCH

This glossary of terms* is limited in scope, and the definitions of words are restricted in meaning to their legal or legal research context. Words whose meanings conform to general usage and are obvious are omitted from the list, e.g., Index.

ACQUITTAL—

the verdict in a criminal trial in which the defendant is found not guilty.

ACT—

an alternative name for statutory law. When introduced into the first house of the legislature, a piece of proposed legislation is known as a bill. When passed to the next house, it may then be referred to as an act. After enactment the terms law and act may be used interchangeably. An act has the same legislative force as a joint resolution but is technically distinguishable, being of a different form and introduced with the words Be it enacted instead of Be it resolved.

ACTION—

the formal legal demand of one's rights from another person brought in court.

ADJUDICATION—

the formal pronouncing or recording of a judgment or decree by a court.

ADMINISTRATIVE AGENCY—

a governmental authority, other than a legislature or court, which issues rules and regulations or adjudicates disputes arising under its statutes and regulations. Administrative agencies usually act under authority delegated by the legislature.

ADMINISTRATIVE LAW—

law that affects private parties, promulgated by governmental agencies other than courts or legislative bodies. These administrative agencies derive their power from legislative enactments and are subject to judicial review.

* Revised for this edition by Fred R. Shapiro, Associate Librarian for Public Services and Lecturer in Legal Research, Yale Law School; Editor, *Oxford Dictionary of American Legal Quotations* (Oxford University Press, 1993) and *Trial and Error: An Oxford Anthology of Legal Stories* (Oxford University Press, 1997).

ADVANCE SHEETS—

current pamphlets containing the most recently reported opinions of a court or the courts of several jurisdictions. The volume and page numbers usually are the same as in the subsequently bound volumes of the series, which cover several numbers of the advance sheets.

ADVISORY OPINION—

an opinion rendered by a court at the request of the government or an interested party and indicates how the court would rule on a matter should adversary litigation develop. An advisory opinion is thus an interpretation of the law without binding effect. The International Court of Justice and some state courts will render advisory opinions; the Supreme Court of the United States will not.

AFFIDAVIT—

a written statement or declaration of facts sworn to by the maker, taken before a person officially permitted by law to administer oaths.

AMICUS CURIAE—

means, literally, friend of the court. A party with strong interest in or views on the subject matter of the dispute will petition the court for permission to file a brief, ostensibly on behalf of a party but actually to suggest a rationale consistent with its own views.

ANNOTATIONS—

(1) Statutory: brief summaries of the law and facts of cases interpreting statutes passed by Congress or state legislatures that are included in codes; or (2) Textual: expository essays of varying length on significant legal topics chosen from selected cases published with the essays.

ANSWER—

the pleading filed by the defendant in response to plaintiff's complaint.

APPEAL PAPERS—

the briefs and transcripts of records on appeal filed by attorneys with courts in connection with litigation. A brief consists of a summary of the facts and circumstances or legal propositions as presented by a party to a pending action.

APPELLANT—

the party who requests that a higher court review the actions of a lower court. Compare with APPELLEE.

APPELLEE—

the party against whom an appeal is taken (usually, but not always, the winner in the lower court). It should be noted that a party's status as appellant or appellee bears no relation to his or her status as plaintiff or defendant in the lower court.

ARBITRATION—

the hearing and settlement of a dispute between opposing parties by a third party. This decision is often binding by prior agreement of the parties.

ASSAULT—

an unlawful, intentional show of force or an attempt to do physical harm to another person. Assault can constitute the basis of a civil or criminal action. See also BATTERY.

ASSAULT AND BATTERY—

See BATTERY.

ATTORNEY GENERAL OPINIONS—

opinions issued by the government's chief counsel at the request of some governmental body interpreting the law for the requesting agency in the same manner as a private attorney would for his or her client. The opinions are not binding on the courts but are usually accorded some degree of persuasive authority.

AUTHORITY—

that which can bind or influence a court. Case law, legislation, constitutions, administrative regulations, and writings about the law are all legal authority. See PRIMARY AUTHORITY; SECONDARY AUTHORITY; MANDATORY AUTHORITY; PERSUASIVE AUTHORITY.

AUTOCITE—

a computerized citation verification service of Reed Elsevier PLC. AUTOCITE provides parallel citations and case-history information.

BAIL—

security given, in the form of a bail bond or cash, as a guarantee that released prisoners will present themselves for trial. This security may be lost if the released person does not appear in court at the appointed time.

BATTERY—

an unlawful use of force against another person resulting in physical contact (a tort); it is commonly used in the phrase assault and battery, assault being the threat of force, and battery the actual use of force. See also ASSAULT.

BILL—

a legislative proposal introduced in the legislature. The term distinguishes unfinished legislation from directly enacted law.

BLACK LETTER LAW—

an informal term indicating the basic principles of law generally accepted by the courts and/or embodied in the statutes of a particular jurisdiction.

BLUEBOOK—

a manual of legal citation form published by the Harvard Law Review, Yale Law Journal, Columbia Law Review, and University of Pennsylvania Law Review.

BOOLEAN LOGIC—

a form of search strategy used in databases such as LEXIS–NEXIS and WESTLAW. In a Boolean search, connectors such as AND, OR, and NOT are used to construct a complex search command. The LEXIS command fungible and gasoline for example, retrieves documents in which the term fungible and the term gasoline both appear. Compare with NATURAL LANGUAGE.

BREACH OF CONTRACT—

the failure to perform any of the terms of an agreement.

BRIEF—

(1) in American law practice, a written statement prepared by the counsel arguing a case in court. It contains a summary of the facts of the case, the pertinent laws, and an argument of how the law applies to the facts supporting counsel's position; (2) a summary of a published opinion of a case prepared for studying the opinion in law school.

BRIEFS AND RECORDS—

See APPEAL PAPERS.

CALENDAR—

can mean the order in which cases are to be heard during a term of court. Martindale-Hubbell Law Directory contains calendars for state and federal courts, and includes the name of the court, the name of the judge, and the date of the term's beginning.

CALR—

an acronym for Computer-Assisted Legal Research. LEXIS–NEXIS and WESTLAW are CALR systems.

CAPTION—

See STYLE OF A CASE.

CASE IN POINT—

a judicial opinion which deals with a fact situation similar to the one being researched and substantiates a point of law to be asserted. (Also called Case on All Fours.)

CASE LAW—

the law of reported judicial opinions as distinguished from statutes or administrative law.

CASEBOOK—

a textbook used to instruct law students in a particular area of law. The text consists of a collection of court opinions, usually from appellate courts, and notes by the author(s).

CAUSE OF ACTION—

a claim in law and in fact sufficient to bring the case to court; the grounds of an action. (Example: breach of contract.)

CD–ROM—

an abbreviation for "compact disk/read only memory." A compact disk is a disk approximately 4 inches in diameter on which data is coded to be scanned by a laser beam and transmitted to a computer monitor. A large volume of data can be stored on such a disk.

CERTIORARI—

a writ issued by a superior to an inferior court requiring the latter to produce the records of a particular case tried therein. It is most commonly used to refer to the Supreme Court of the United States, which uses the writ of certiorari as a discretionary device to choose the cases it wishes to hear. The term's origin is Latin, meaning to be informed of.

CHARTER—

a document issued by a governmental entity that gives a corporation legal existence.

CHATTEL—

any article of personal property, as opposed to real property. It may refer to animate as well as inanimate property.

CHOSE—

any article of personal property. See PROPERTY.

CITATION—

the reference to authority necessary to substantiate the validity of one's argument or position. Citation to authority and supporting references is both important and extensive in any form of legal writing. Citation form is also given emphasis in legal writing, and early familiarity with *The Bluebook: A Uniform System of Citation* will stand the law student in good stead.

CITATORS—

a set of books and online sources that provide the subsequent judicial history and interpretation of reported cases or lists of cases and legislative enactments construing, applying, or affecting statutes. In America, the most widely used citators are Shepard's Citations and KeyCite.

CITED CASE—

a case that is referred to by other cases.

CITING CASE—

the case that refers to the cited case.

CIVIL LAW—

(1) Roman law embodied in the Code of Justinian, which presently prevails in most countries of Western Europe other than Great Britain and that is the foundation of Louisiana law; (2) the law concerning noncriminal matters in a common law jurisdiction.

CLAIM—

(1) the assertion of a right, as to money or property; (2) the accumulation of facts that give rise to a right enforceable in court.

CLASS ACTION—

a lawsuit brought by a representative party on behalf of a group, all of whose members have the same or a similar grievance against the defendant.

CODE—

in popular usage, a compilation of statutes. Technically, in a code, the laws in force and judicial decrees having the force of law, are rewritten and arranged in classified order. Repealed and temporary acts are eliminated and the revision is reenacted.

CODIFICATION—

the process of collecting and arranging systematically, usually by subject, the laws of a state or country.

COMMON LAW—

the origin of the Anglo-American legal systems. English common law was largely customary law and unwritten, until discovered, applied, and reported by the courts of law. In theory, the common law courts did not create law but rather discovered it in the customs and habits of the English people. The strength of the judicial system in preparliamentary days is one reason for the continued emphasis in common law systems on case law. In a narrow sense, common law is the phrase still used to distinguish case law from statutory law.

COMPILED STATUTES—

in popular usage, a code. Technically, it is a compilation of acts printed verbatim as originally enacted but in a new classified order. The text is not modified; however, repealed and temporary acts are omitted.

COMPLAINT—

the plaintiff's initial pleading. Under Federal Rules of Civil Procedure, it is no longer full of the technicalities demanded by the common law. A complaint need only contain a short and plain statement of the claim upon which relief is sought, an indication of the type of relief requested, and an indication that the court has jurisdiction to hear the case.

CONNECTOR—

See BOOLEAN LOGIC.

CONSIDERATION—

something to be done, or abstained from, by one party to a contract in order to induce another party to enter into a contract.

CONSOLIDATED STATUTES—

in popular usage, a code. Technically, it is a compilation of acts rewritten, arranged in classified order and reenacted. Repealed and temporary acts are eliminated.

CONSTITUTION—

the system of fundamental principles by which a political body or organization governs itself. Most national constitutions are written; the English and Israeli constitutions are unwritten.

CONVERSION—

the wrongful appropriation to oneself of the personal property of another.

CONVEYANCE—

the transfer of title to property from one person to another.

COUNT—

a separate and independent claim. A civil petition or a criminal indictment may contain several counts.

COUNTERCLAIM—

a claim made by the defendant against the plaintiff in a civil lawsuit; it constitutes a separate cause of action.

COURT DECISION—

the disposition of the case by the court. See OPINION.

COURT RULES—

rules of procedure promulgated to govern civil and criminal practice before the courts.

DAMAGES—

monetary compensation awarded by a court for an injury caused by the act of another. Damages may be actual or compensatory (equal to the amount of loss shown), exemplary or punitive (in excess of the actual loss given to punish the person for the malicious conduct that caused the injury), or nominal (a trivial amount given because the injury is slight or because the exact amount of injury has not been determined satisfactorily).

DATABASE—

(1) a collection of information organized for rapid retrieval by computer. In legal research, it usually refers to a commercial service searched online by a user at a terminal connected to a communications network. A full-text database provides the complete text of documents such as court cases or newspaper articles. LEXIS–NEXIS and WESTLAW are full-text databases. A bibliographic database provides citations or abstracts of articles, books, reports, or patents. DIALOG is an example of a service with many bibliographic databases.

(2) in WESTLAW, a collection of documents that can be searched together.

DECISION—

See COURT DECISION.

DECREE—

a determination by a court of the rights and duties of the parties before it. Formerly, decrees were issued by courts of equity and distinguished from judgments, which were issued by courts of law. See EQUITY.

DEFENDANT—

the person against whom a civil or criminal action is brought.

DEMURRER—

a means of objecting to the sufficiency in law of a pleading by admitting the actual allegations made, but disputing that they frame an adequate legal claim.

DIALOG—

the information retrieval service of DIALOG Information Services, a subsidiary of Knight-Ridder Information, Inc. DIALOG is composed of hundreds of individual databases providing indexing, abstracting, or full text of publications relating to a wide range of academic, business, news, and law-related subjects.

DICTUM—

See OBITER DICTUM.

DIGEST—

an index to reported cases, providing brief, unconnected statements of court holdings on points of law, which are arranged by subject and subdivided by jurisdiction and courts.

DOCKET NUMBER—

a number, sequentially assigned by the clerk at the outset to a lawsuit brought to a court for adjudication.

DUE CARE—

the legal duty one owes to another according to the circumstances of a particular case.

DUE PROCESS OF LAW—

a term found in the Fifth and Fourteenth Amendments of the Constitution and also in the constitutions of many states. Its exact meaning varies from one situation to another and from one era to the next, but basically it is concerned with the guarantee of every person's enjoyment of his or her rights (e.g., the right to a fair hearing in any legal dispute).

EN BANC—

a session in which the entire bench of the court will participate in the decision rather than the regular quorum. In other countries, it is common for a court to have more members than are usually necessary to hear an appeal. In the United States, the Circuit Courts of Appeals usually sit in groups of three judges but for important cases may expand the bench to nine members, when they are said to be sitting en banc.

ENCYCLOPEDIA—

a work containing expository statements on principles of law, topically arranged, with supporting footnote references to cases in point.

EQUITY—

justice administered according to fairness as contrasted with the strictly formulated rules of common law. It is based on a system of rules and principles that originated in England as an alternative to the harsh rules of common law and that were based on what was fair in a particular situation. One sought relief under this system in courts of equity rather than in courts of law.

ESTATE—

(1) the interest or right one has in real or personal property; or (2) the property itself in which one has an interest or right.

EXECUTIVE AGREEMENT—

an international agreement, not a treaty, concluded by the President without senatorial consent on the President's authority as Commander-in-Chief and director of foreign relations. The distinction between treaty and executive agreement is complicated and often of questionable constitutionality, but the import of such agreements as that of Yalta or Potsdam is unquestionably great.

EXECUTIVE ORDERS—

an order issued by the President under specific authority granted to the President by Congress. There is no precise distinction between presidential proclamations and executive orders; however, proclamations generally cover matters of widespread interest, and executive orders often relate to the conduct of government business or to organization of the executive departments. Every act of the President authorizing or directing the performance of an act, in its general context, is an executive order. See PRESIDENTIAL PROCLAMATIONS.

FICHE—

See MICROFICHE.

FORM BOOKS—

include sample instruments that are helpful in drafting legal documents.

FORMS OF ACTION—

governed common law pleadings and were the procedural devices used to give expression to the theories of liability recognized by the common law. Failure to analyze the cause of the action properly, to select the proper theory of liability and to choose the appropriate procedural mechanism or forms of action could easily result in being thrown out of court. A plaintiff had to elect his or her remedy in advance and could not subsequently amend the pleadings to conform to his or her proof or to the court's choice of another theory of liability. According to the relief sought, actions have been divided into three categories: real actions were brought for the recovery of real property; mixed actions were brought to recover real property and damages for injury to it; personal actions were brought to recover debts or personal property, or for injuries to personal, property, or contractual rights. The common law actions are usually considered to be eleven in number: trespass, trespass on the case, trover, ejectment, detinue, replevin, debt, covenant, account, special assumpsit, and general assumpsit.

FRAUD—

a deception that causes a person to part with his or her property or a legal right.

FREESTYLE—

is an associative retrieval natural language search protocol for use on LEXIS–NEXIS. FREESTYLE analyzes a natural language search strategy, eliminates irrelevant terms, and then ranks in importance the remaining terms in the strategy.

FULL TEXT—

See DATABASE.

GRAND JURY—

a jury of six to twenty-three persons that hears criminal accusations and evidence, and then determines whether indictments should be made. Compare with PETIT JURY.

HEADNOTE—

a brief summary of a legal rule or significant facts in a case, which, among other headnotes applicable to the case, precedes the printed opinion in reports.

HEARINGS—

proceedings extensively employed by both legislative and administrative agencies. Adjudicative hearings of administrative agencies can be appealed in a court of law. Investigative hearings are often held by congressional committees prior to enactment of legislation, and are important sources of legislative history.

HOLDING—

the declaration of the conclusion of law reached by the court as to the legal effect of the facts of the case.

HOLOGRAPH or OLOGRAPH—

a will, deed, or other legal document that is entirely in the handwriting of the signer.

HORNBOOK—

the popular reference to a series of treatises published by West Group each of which reviews a certain field of law in summary, textual form, as opposed to a casebook that is designed as a teaching tool and includes many reprints of court opinions.

INDEMNITY—

a contractual arrangement whereby one party agrees to reimburse another for losses of a particular type.

INDICTMENT—

a formal accusation of a crime made by a grand jury at the request of a prosecuting attorney.

INFORMATION—

an accusation based not on the action of a grand jury but rather on the affirmation of a public official.

INJUNCTION—

a judge's order that a person do or, more commonly, refrain from doing, a certain act. An injunction may be preliminary or temporary, pending trial of the issue presented, or it may be final if the issue has already been decided in court.

INSTACITE—

a computerized citation verification service of Group. This service, which is available through WESTLAW, provides parallel citations and case-history information.

INTERNET—

a worldwide system of thousands of interconnected computer networks using the TCP/IP protocols. The Internet facilitates various data communication services.

INTESTATE—

not having made a valid will.

JUDGMENT—

See COURT DECISION.

JURISDICTION—

the power given to a court by a constitution or a legislative body to make legally binding decisions over certain persons or property, or the geographical area in which a court's decisions or legislative enactments are binding.

JURISPRUDENCE—

(1) the science or philosophy of law; (2) a collective term for case law as opposed to legislation.

KEY NUMBER—

a building block of the major indexing system devised for American case law, developed by West Group. The key number is a permanent number given to a specific point of this case law.

KEYCITE—

the computerized citator service of West Group, available through WESTLAW. KeyCite traces the history of a case, retrieves a list of cases and secondary sources citing the case, and characterizes citations according to the legal issues decided in the case.

LAW REVIEW or LAW JOURNAL—

a legal periodical. The term law review usually describes a scholarly periodical edited by students at a law school.

LEGISLATIVE HISTORY—

that information embodied in legislative documents that provides the meanings and interpretations (intent) of statutes. Citations and dates of legislative enactments, amendments, and repeals of statutes are sometimes imprecisely identified as legislative histories. More accurate designations of these citations of legislative changes, as included in codes, are historical notes or amendatory histories.

LEXIS–NEXIS—

a subsidiary of Reed Elsevier PLC. LEXIS–NEXIS is a database providing the full text of court decisions, statutes, administrative materials, ALR annotations, law review articles, reporter services, Supreme Court briefs, and other items. Documents are organized into libraries that are subdivided into files. Natural language searches, key-word searches, and segment searches are available.

LIABILITY—

the condition of being responsible either for damages resulting from an injurious act or for discharging an obligation or debt.

LIBEL—

(1) written defamation of a person's character. Compare with SLANDER; (2) in an admiralty court, the plaintiff's statement of the cause of action and the relief sought.

LIEN—

a claim against property as security for a debt, under which the property may be seized and sold to satisfy the debt.

LITIGATE—

to bring a civil action in court.

LOOSELEAF SERVICES AND REPORTERS—

contain federal and state administrative regulations and decisions or subject treatment of a legal topic. They consist of separate, perforated pages or pamphlet-sized inserts in special binders, simplifying frequent insertion or substitution of new material.

MALPRACTICE—

professional misconduct or unreasonable lack of skill. This term is usually applied to such conduct by doctors and lawyers.

MANDATORY AUTHORITY—

authority that a given court is bound to follow. Mandatory authority is found in constitutional provisions, legislation, and court cases. Compare with PERSUASIVE AUTHORITY.

MEMORANDUM—

(1) an informal record; (2) a written document that may be used to prove that a contract exists; (3) an exposition of all the points of law pertaining to a particular case (referred to as a memorandum of law); (4) an informal written discussion of the merits of a matter pending in a lawyer's office, usually written by a law clerk or junior associate for a senior associate or partner (referred to as an office memorandum).

MICROFICHE—

a sheet of film, usually 4 x 6 inches or 3 x 5 inches in size, containing miniaturized photographic images of printed text. The term fiche is synonymous with microfiche. Ultrafiche is a type of microfiche containing images that are reduced by a factor of 90 or more.

MICROFILM—

a film containing miniaturized photographic images of printed text. This is usually in a reel, but may also be in a cartridge or cassette form.

MICROFORM—

a general term describing miniaturized reproduction of printed text on film or paper. Microfilm and microfiche are specific types of microform.

MODEL CODES—

codes formulated by various groups or institutions to serve as model laws for legislatures, intended to improve existing laws or unify diverse state legislation.

MOOT POINTS—

points that are no longer subjects of contention and that are raised only for purposes of discussion or hypothesis. Many law schools conduct moot courts where students gain practice by arguing hypothetical or moot cases.

MOTION—

a formal request made to a judge pertaining to any issue arising during the pendency of a lawsuit.

NATIONAL REPORTER SYSTEM—

the network of reporters published by West Group, which attempt to publish and digest all cases of precedential value from all state and federal courts.

NATURAL LANGUAGE—

an online database search strategy using normal English-language sentences or phrases instead of Boolean commands. See BOOLEAN LOGIC. WESTLAW's natural language searching is called WIN (WESTLAW is Natural); LEXIS–NEXIS's natural language is called FREESTYLE.

NEGLIGENCE—

the failure to exercise due care.

NEXIS—

the general and business news database of LEXIS–NEXIS, a subsidiary of Reed Elsevier PLC. NEXIS provides the full text of newspaper, magazine and newsletter articles, wire-service stories, and other items.

NISI PRIUS—

generally, a court where a case is first tried, as distinguished from an appellate court.

NOTERUP—

the term used in the British Commonwealth countries for a citator.

OBITER DICTUM—

an incidental comment, not necessary to the formulation of the decision, made by the judge in his or her opinion. Such comments are not binding as precedent.

OFFICIAL REPORTS—

court reports directed by statute. Compare with UNOFFICIAL REPORTS.

OPINION—

an expression of the reasons why a certain decision (the judgment) was reached in a case. A majority opinion is usually written by one judge and represents the principles of law that a majority of his or her colleagues on the court deem operative in a given decision; it has more precedential value than any of the following. A separate opinion may be written by one or more judges in which he, she, or they concur in or dissent from the majority opinion. A concurring opinion agrees with the result reached by the majority, but disagrees with the precise reasoning leading to that result. A dissenting opinion disagrees with the result reached by the majority and thus disagrees with the reasoning and/or the principles of law used by the majority in deciding the case. A plurality opinion (called a judgment by the Supreme Court) is agreed to by less than a majority as to the reasoning of the decision, but is agreed to by a majority as to the result. A per curiam opinion is an opinion by the court that expresses its decision in the case but whose author is not identified. A memorandum opinion is a holding of the whole court in which the opinion is very concise.

ORAL ARGUMENT—

a spoken presentation of reasons for a desired decision directed to an appellate court by attorneys for the parties.

ORDINANCE—

the equivalent of a municipal statute, passed by the city council and governing matters not already covered by federal or state law.

PAMPHLET SUPPLEMENT—

a paperbound supplement to a larger bound volume usually intended to be discarded eventually.

PARALLEL CITATION—

a citation reference to the same case printed in two or more different reports.

PER CURIAM—

literally, by the court. Usually a short opinion written on behalf of the majority of the court. It may be accompanied by concurring or dissenting opinions.

PERIODICAL—

a publication appearing at regular intervals. Legal periodicals include law school publications, bar association publications, commercially published journals, and legal newspapers.

PERMANENT LAW—

an act that continues in force for an indefinite time.

PERSONAL PROPERTY—

See PROPERTY.

PERSUASIVE AUTHORITY—

that law or reasoning which a given court may but is not bound to follow. For example, decisions from one jurisdiction may be persuasive authority in the courts of another jurisdiction. Compare with MANDATORY AUTHORITY.

PETIT JURY—

a group of six, nine, or twelve persons that decides questions of fact in civil and criminal trials. Compare with GRAND JURY.

PETITION—

a formal, written application to a court requesting judicial action on a certain matter.

PETITIONER—

the person presenting a petition to a court, officer, or legislative body; the one who starts an equity proceeding or the one who takes an appeal from a judgment.

PLAINTIFF—

the person who brings a lawsuit against another.

PLEA BARGAINING—

the process whereby the accused and the prosecutor in a criminal case work out a mutually satisfactory disposition of the case. It usually involves the defendant's pleading guilty to a lesser offense or to only one or some of the counts of a multi-count indictment in return for a lighter sentence than that possible for the graver charge.

PLEADINGS—

technical means by which parties to a dispute frame the issue for the court. The plaintiff's complaint or declaration is followed by the defendant's answer; subsequent papers may be filed as needed.

POCKET SUPPLEMENT or POCKET PART—

a paper-back supplement to a book, inserted in the book through a slit in its back cover. Depending on the type of publication, it may have textual, case, or statutory references keyed to the original publication.

POPULAR NAME TABLE—

a table listing popular names by which some cases and statutes have become known, and identifying for each popular name the official name and citation of the case or statute.

POWER OF ATTORNEY—

a document authorizing a person to act as another's agent.

PRECEDENT—

See STARE DECISIS.

PRELIMINARY PRINTS—

the name given to the advance sheets of the official United States Reports.

PRESENTMENT—

in criminal law, a written accusation made by the grand jury without the consent or participation of a prosecutor.

PRESIDENTIAL PROCLAMATIONS—

a declaration issued under specific authority granted to the President by Congress. Generally, they relate to matters of widespread interest. Some proclamations have no legal effect but merely are appeals to the public, e.g., the observance of American Education Week. See EXECUTIVE ORDERS.

PRIMARY AUTHORITY—

statutes, constitutions, administrative regulations issued pursuant to enabling legislation, and case law. Primary authority may be either mandatory or persuasive. All other legal writings are secondary authority and are never binding on courts. See MANDATORY AUTHORITY; PERSUASIVE AUTHORITY.

PRIVATE LAW—

an act that relates to a specific person.

PROCEDURAL LAW—

that law which governs the operation of the legal system, including court rules and rules of procedure, as distinguished from substantive law.

PROPERTY—

ownership or that which is owned. Real property refers to land; personal property refers to moveable things or chattels; chose in action refers to a right to personal property of which the owner does not presently have possession but instead has a right to sue to gain possession (e.g., a right to recover a debt, demand, or damages in a contractual action or for a tort or omission of a duty).

PUBLIC LAW—

an act that relates to the public as a whole. It may be (1) general (applies to all persons within the jurisdiction), (2) local (applies to a geographical area), or (3) special (relates to an organization that is charged with a public interest).

RATIO DECIDENDI—

the point in a case that determines the result—the basis of the decision.

REAL PROPERTY—

See PROPERTY.

RECORD—

the documentation, prepared for an appeal, of the trial court proceedings (pleadings, motions, transcript of examination of witnesses, objections to evidence, rulings, jury instructions, opinion, etc.

RECORDS AND BRIEFS—

See APPEAL PAPERS.

REGIONAL REPORTER—

a unit of the National Reporter System that reports state court cases from a defined geographical area.

REGULATIONS—

rules or orders issued by various governmental departments to carry out the intent of the law. Agencies issue regulations to guide the activity of their employees and to ensure uniform application of the law. Regulations are not the work of the legislature and do not have the effect of law in theory. In practice, however, because of the intricacies of judicial review of administrative action, regulations can have an important effect in determining the outcome of cases involving regulatory activity. United States Government regulations appear first in the *Federal Register*, published five days a week, and are subsequently arranged by subject in the *Code of Federal Regulations*.

RELIEF—

the remedy or redress sought by a complainant from the court.

REMAND—

to send back for further proceedings, as when a higher court sends back to a lower court.

REPORTS—

(1) court reports—published judicial cases arranged according to some grouping, such as jurisdiction, court, period of time, subject matter, or case significance; and (2) administrative reports or decisions—published decisions of an administrative agency.

RESOLUTION—

a formal expression of the opinion of a rule-making body adopted by the vote of that body.

RESPONDENT—

the party who makes an answer to a bill in an equity proceeding or who contends against an appeal.

RESTATEMENTS OF THE LAW—

systematic restatements of the existing common law in certain areas, published by the American Law Institute since 1923. The Restatements are valuable secondary research sources, but are not binding as law.

REVISED STATUTES—

in popular usage, a code. Technically, it is a compilation of statutes in the order and wording originally passed by the legislature, with temporary and repealed acts deleted.

RULES OF COURT—

the rules regulating practice and procedure before the various courts. In most jurisdictions, these rules are issued by the individual courts or by the highest court in that jurisdiction.

SANCTION—

(1) to assent to another's actions; (2) a penalty for violating a law.

SCOPE NOTE—

a notation appearing below a topic heading in a publication, that delimits and identifies the content of the topic.

SECONDARY AUTHORITY—

See PRIMARY AUTHORITY.

SECTION LINE—

the subject of a key number in West's Key Number digests, printed after the key number.

SESSION LAWS—

laws of a state enacted that are published in bound or pamphlet volumes after adjournment of each regular or special session.

SHEPARDIZING—

a trade-mark of Shepard's Citations, Inc., descriptive of the general use of its publications.

SLANDER—

oral defamation of a person's character. Compare with LIBEL.

SLIP LAW—

a legislative enactment published in pamphlet or single sheet form immediately after its passage.

SLIP OPINION—

an individual court case published separately soon after it is decided.

SQUIB—

a very brief rendition of a single case or a single point of law from a case. Compare with HEADNOTE.

STAR PAGINATION—

a scheme in reprint editions of court reports, that is used to show where the pages of the text of the official edition begin and end.

STARE DECISIS—

the doctrine of English and American law that states that when a court has formulated a principle of law as applicable to a given set of facts, it will follow that principle and apply it in future cases where the facts are substantially the same. It connotes the decision of present cases on the basis of past precedent.

STATUS TABLE—

gives the current status of a bill or court decision.

STATUTES—

acts of a legislature. Depending upon its context in usage, a statute may mean a single act of a legislature or a body of acts that are collected and arranged according to a scheme or for a session of a legislature or parliament.

STATUTES AT LARGE—

the official compilation of acts passed by the Congress. The arrangement is currently by Public Law number, and by chapter number in pre-1951 volumes. This is the official print of the law for citation purposes where titles of the *United States Code* have not been enacted into positive law.

STATUTES OF LIMITATIONS—

laws setting time limits after which a dispute cannot be taken to court.

STATUTORY INSTRUMENTS—

English administrative regulations and orders. The term applies especially to the administrative rules published since 1939, supplementing the English administrative code, Statutory Rules and Orders.

STATUTORY RULES AND ORDERS—

English administrative regulations and orders.

STYLE OF A CASE—

the parties to a lawsuit as they are written in the heading at the beginning of a written case. Also known as the caption of a case.

SUBPOENA—

a court order compelling a witness to appear and testify in a certain proceeding.

SUBSTANTIVE LAW—

that law which establishes rights and obligations, as distinguished from procedural law, which is concerned with rules for establishing their judicial enforcement.

SUMMONS—

a notice delivered by a sheriff or other authorized person informing a person that he or she is the defendant in a civil action, and specifying a time and place to appear in court to answer to the plaintiff.

SUPERSEDE—

to displace or to supplant one publication or its segment with another.

SUPREME COURT—

(1) the court of last resort in the federal judicial system (the Supreme Court of the United States also has original jurisdiction in some cases); (2) in state judicial systems, except New York and Massachusetts, the highest appellate court or court of last resort.

SYLLABUS—

See HEADNOTE.

TABLE OF CASES—

a list of cases, arranged alphabetically by case names, with citations and references to the body of the publication where the cases are found or treated.

TABLE OF STATUTES—

a list of statutes with references to the body of the publication where the statutes are treated or construed.

TEMPORARY LAW—

an act that continues in force for a limited period of time.

TERM OF COURT—

signifies the space of time prescribed by law during which a court holds session. The court's session may actually extend beyond the term. The October Term of the Supreme Court of the United States is now the only term during which the Court sits, and lasts from October to June or July.

TORT—

a civil wrong that does not involve a contractual relationship. The elements of a tort are a duty owed, a breach of that duty, and the resultant harm to the one to whom the duty was owed.

TRANSCRIPT OF RECORD—

the printed record as made up in each case of the proceedings and pleadings necessary for the appellate court to review the history of the case.

TREATISE—

an exposition, which may be critical, evaluative, interpretative, or informative, on case law or legislation. Usually it is more exhaustive than an encyclopedia article, but less detailed and critical than a law review article.

TREATY—

an agreement between two or more sovereign nations.

TRESPASS—

an unlawful interference with one's person, property, or rights. At common law, trespass was a form of action brought to recover damages for any injury to one's person or property or relationship with another.

ULTRAFICHE—

See MICROFICHE.

UNIFORM LAWS—

statutes drafted for adoption by the several states in the interest of uniformity. A considerable number of uniform laws on various subjects have been approved by the National Conference of Commissioners on Uniform State Laws, and have been adopted in one or more jurisdictions in the United States and its possessions. The Uniform Commercial Code is now the law in forty-nine states.

UNIFORM SYSTEM OF CITATION—

See BLUEBOOK.

UNOFFICIAL REPORTS—

court reports published without statutory direction. They are not distinguished from official reports on grounds of varying quality or accuracy of reporting.

URL—

an abbreviation for Uniform Resource Locator. A URL is a standard address for a resource or site on the Internet. A URL such as http://www.tiddlywinks.com describes the access method used (http) and the location of the server hosting the site (www.tiddlywinks.com). The most common use of a URL is to enter into a World Wide Web browser program such as Netscape.

VENUE—

the particular geographical area where a court with jurisdiction may try a case.

WAIVER—

the voluntary relinquishment of a known right.

WEB—

See WORLD WIDE WEB.

WESTLAW—

the computerized legal research system of West Group. WESTLAW provides the full text of court decisions, statutes, administrative materials, ALR annotations, law review articles, reporter services, Supreme Court briefs, and other items. Documents are organized into databases. Natural language searches, key-word searches, field searches, and key-number searches are available. See NATURAL LANGUAGE.

WORLD WIDE WEB or WEB—

a subset of the Internet using hypertext links and mixing text, graphics, sound files, multimedia, etc. The Web has become the major medium for publishing information on the Internet.

WRIT—

a written order, of which there are many types, issued by a court and directed to an official or party, commanding the performance of some act.

WRONGFUL DEATH—

a type of lawsuit brought by or on behalf of a deceased person's beneficiaries, alleging that the death was attributable to the willful or negligent act of another.

FUNDAMENTALS

OF

LEGAL RESEARCH

*

Chapter 1

AN INTRODUCTION TO LEGAL RESEARCH[1]

Legal research is the investigation for information necessary to support legal decision-making. In its broadest sense, legal research includes each step of a process that begins with analyzing the facts of a problem and concludes with applying and communicating the results of the investigation.

Many types of information are needed to support legal decision-making. Although this book focuses on information sources that are concerned explicitly with law, legal decisions cannot be made out of their economic, social, historical, and political contexts. In a modern complex society, legal decisions are often dependent on business, scientific, medical, psychological, and technological information. Consequently, the process of legal research often involves investigation into other relevant disciplines.

This chapter is an introduction to legal research that is intended to explain why researchers seek certain types of information. After explaining the basic jurisprudential model upon which legal resources are designed, created, and collected, the chapter presents an introductory discussion of the materials of legal research that are discussed extensively in this book.

SECTION A. SOURCES OF LAW

American law, like the law of other countries, comes from a variety of sources. In the context of legal research, the term "sources of law" can refer to three different concepts that should be distinguished. One, sources of law can refer to the origins of legal concepts and ideas. Custom, tradition, principles of morality, and economic, political, philosophical, and religious thought may manifest themselves in law. On occasion, legal research must extend to these areas, especially when historical or policy issues are involved.

Two, sources of law can refer to the governmental institutions that formulate legal rules. The United States incorporates one national (federal) government, fifty autonomous state governments, and the local government of the District of Columbia. Although there are some variations in their structures, each of these governments has legislative, executive, and judicial components that interact with each other. Because all three branches of government "make law" and create legal

---

[1] This chapter was written by Steven M. Barkan, Director of the Law Library and Professor of Law, University of Wisconsin Law School.

1

information that is the subject of legal research, researchers must understand the types of information created by each branch.

Three, sources of law can refer to the published manifestations of the law. The books, electronic databases, microforms, optical disks, and other media that contain legal information are all sources of law.

1. The Nature of Legal Authority

Legal authority is any published source of law setting forth legal rules, legal doctrine, or legal reasoning that can be used as a basis for legal decisions.[2] In discussions about legal research, the term *authority* is used to refer both to the types of legal information and to the degree of persuasiveness of legal information.

When the term is used to describe types of information, legal authority can be categorized as *primary* or *secondary*.[3] Primary authorities are authorized statements of the law by governmental institutions. Such documents include the written opinions of courts (*case law*); constitutions; legislation; rules of court; and the rules, regulations, and opinions of administrative agencies. Secondary authorities are statements about the law and are used to explain, interpret, develop, locate, or update primary authorities. Treatises, articles in law reviews and other scholarly journals, *American Law Reports (A.L.R.)* annotations, Restatements of the Law, and looseleaf services are examples of secondary authorities.[4]

When the term is used to describe the degree of persuasiveness of legal information, authority is an estimation of the power of information to influence a legal decision. In this sense, authority can be termed *binding* (also called *mandatory*), meaning that a court or other decision-maker believes the authority applies to the case before it and must be followed; or authority can be considered *persuasive*, meaning that a decision-maker can, if so persuaded, follow it. Only primary authority can be binding; but some primary authority will be merely persuasive, depending on the source of the authority and its content. Secondary authority can never be binding, but can be persuasive. Of course, the application of legal authority to individual problems is a complex and controversial process. Variations in the factual content of individual cases give judges, influenced by their own philosophies and perspectives, wide discretion in interpreting and applying legal authority.[5]

---

[2] Thomas B. Marvell, Appellate Courts and Lawyers 129 (1978).

[3] When used in this sense, the terms *authority* and *source* are interchangeable.

[4] Other types of relevant information, such as historical, economic, and social science information, are sometimes referred to as secondary authorities. Such materials are often sources of law and thus used in legal argument.

[5] For an excellent, but dated, explanation of why courts cite authority and a discussion of the authority of various legal sources, see John Henry Merryman, *The Authority of Authority*, 6 Stan. L. Rev. 613 (1954). For an examination of how one noted jurist used authority, see William H. Manz, *Cardozo's Use of Authority: An Empirical Study*, 32 Cal. W. L. Rev. 31 (1995).

2. The Common Law Tradition

The American legal system, like those of most English-speaking countries, is part of the *common law* tradition. The common law is the body of law that originated and developed in England and spread to those countries that England settled or controlled. Historically, the common law was considered to be the "unwritten law" and was distinguished from the "written," or statutory, law. The common law was an oral tradition derived from general customs, principles, and rules handed down from generation to generation and was eventually reflected in the reports of the decisions of courts. The colonists carried the English common law with them to America and used it as a basis for developing their own law and legal institutions.[6] English common law is still cited as authority in American courts.[7]

The common law tradition should be contrasted with the *civil law* tradition, which is based on Roman law and predominates in continental Europe and other western countries. Common law and civil law systems differ in their theories about the sources of law, the relative persuasiveness of the sources, and the ways the sources are used in legal reasoning. For example, in legal systems that are part of the civil law tradition, the legislature creates a comprehensive code of legal principles that represents the highest form of law, and there is a presumption that code provisions apply to every legal problem.[8] In common law systems, there is no presumption that statutes or codes cover all legal problems; many legal principles are discoverable only through the "unwritten," or common law.

3. Case Law and the Doctrine of Precedent[9]

a. *Structure of the Court System.* On the federal level, and in the states, there are hierarchical judicial systems in which some courts have jurisdiction, or control, over other courts. The typical court structure consists of three levels,[10] and it is important to understand what types of information are created at each level and where that information may be found.

Trial courts are courts of original jurisdiction that make determinations of law and of fact, with juries often making the determinations of fact. Documents prepared by the parties called *pleadings* (complaint, answer, interrogatories, among others) and *motions* are filed before and during a trial; *exhibits* are submitted into evidence during the trial; and

---

[6] For general histories of American law, see LAWRENCE M. FRIEDMAN, A HISTORY OF AMERICAN LAW (2d ed. 1985) and KERMIT L. HALL, THE MAGIC MIRROR: LAW IN AMERICAN HISTORY (1989).

[7] *See* Chapter 21, *infra,* for a discussion of basic English legal research.

[8] JOHN HENRY MERRYMAN, THE CIVIL LAW TRADITION 22–24 (2d ed. 1985).

[9] Case law is discussed extensively in the following chapters, *infra:* Chapter 3, Court Reports; Chapter 4, Federal Court Cases; Chapter 5, State Court Cases and the National Reporter System; Chapter 6, Digests for Court Reports; Chapter 7, Annotated Law Reports.

[10] A chart included in Chapter 3, *infra,* depicts the federal judicial system and a typical state judicial system.

a *record* (or transcript) is made. Pleadings, motions, exhibits, and records are usually only available directly from the court in which the litigation was conducted; these documents are usually not collected by law libraries. The trial court issues a judgment or decision and sometimes a written opinion, which, however, is rarely published (or reported) or made generally available to the public.[11]

Intermediate appellate courts, often called circuit courts or courts of appeal,[12] have authority over lower courts in a specified geographical area or jurisdiction. Appellate courts will not review factual determinations made by lower courts, but will review claimed errors of law that are reflected in the record created in the lower courts. Appellate courts accept written *briefs* (statements prepared by the counsel arguing the case) and frequently hear *oral arguments*. Some large law libraries collect copies of the briefs filed in appellate courts. Intermediate appellate courts often issue written opinions that are sometimes published in volumes found in law libraries.

A court of last resort, often called the supreme court, is the highest appellate court in a jurisdiction. State courts of last resort are the highest authorities on questions of state law, and the Supreme Court of the United States is the highest authority on questions of federal law and federal constitutional law. Many libraries collect copies of the briefs and records filed in the Supreme Court of the United States and of the court of last resort in the state in which they are located. Transcripts of the oral arguments in these courts also are available in many law libraries. Courts of last resort usually issue written opinions that are almost always published and collected by libraries.

b. *Federal and State Jurisdiction.* There are some matters over which a state or federal court has exclusive jurisdiction and some matters over which a state court has concurrent jurisdiction with the federal courts. Federal courts can, in some instances, decide questions of state law; state courts can, in some instances, decide questions of federal law. For both the beginning law student and the experienced attorney, it can be difficult to determine which matters are questions of federal law, which are questions of state law, and which can be subjects of both. The point to be made here is that, with any particular problem, legal information of various types may be needed from both state and federal sources.

c. *Precedent.* In the early history of English law, the custom developed of considering the decisions of courts to be *precedents* that would serve as examples, or authorities, for decisions in later cases with similar questions of law. Under what has come to be called the *doctrine of precedent,* the decision of a common law court not only settles a

---

[11] Many inexperienced legal researchers are surprised to learn that written opinions are not issued in all cases, and that only a small percentage of written opinions are reported and published. For a more complete discussion of this subject, see Chapter 3, *infra.*

[12] Some states have no intermediate appellate courts; appeals go directly to the courts of last resort in these states.

dispute between the parties involved but also sets a precedent to be followed in future cases among other litigants.[13] According to an older, now discredited, theory, judges merely declared what had always been the law when they decided a case. It is now generally acknowledged that judges often create new law when applying precedent to current problems.

The doctrine of precedent encompasses three closely related concepts represented by the Latin terms *stare decisis, ratio decidendi,* and *dictum.*

Stare decisis, literally "to stand on what has been decided," is the principle that the decision of a court is binding authority on the court that issued the decision and on lower courts in the same jurisdiction for the disposition of factually similar controversies. In the hierarchical federal and state court systems, therefore, the decisions of a trial court can bind future decisions of that trial court, but they cannot bind other trial courts or appellate courts. Appellate courts can bind themselves and

---

[13] "The bare skeleton of an appeal to precedent is easily stated: The previous treatment of occurrence X in manner Y constitutes, *solely because of its historical pedigree,* a reason for treating X in manner Y if and when X again occurs." Frederick Schauer, *Precedent,* 39 STAN. L. REV. 571 (1987). For a discussion of the early development of the doctrine of precedent, see M. ETHAN KATSH, THE ELECTRONIC MEDIA AND THE TRANSFORMATION OF LAW 33–39 (1989).

For the views of a former U.S. Supreme Court Justice regarding the importance of *stare decisis,* see Lewis F. Powell, Jr., *Stare Decisis and Judicial Restraint,* 47 WASH. & LEE L. REV. 281 (1990). *See also* William N. Eskridge, Jr., *The Case of the Amorous Defendant: Criticizing Absolute Stare Decisis for Statutory Cases,* 88 MICH. L. REV. 2450 (1990); Lawrence C. Marshall, *Contempt of Congress: A Reply to the Critics of an Absolute Rule of Statutory Stare Decisis,* 88 MICH. L. REV. 2467 (1990). David K. Koehler, *Justice Souter's "Keep–What–You–Want-and–Away-the-Rest" Interpretation of* Stare Decisis, 42 BUFF. L. REV. 859 (1994); Amy L. Padden, *Overruling Decisions in the Supreme Court: The Role of a Decision's Vote, Age, and Subject Matter in the Application of Stare Decisis After* Payne v. Tennessee, 82 GEO. L.J. 1689 (1994); Robert C. Wigton, *What Does It Take to Overrule? An Analysis of Supreme Court Overrulings and the Doctrine of Stare Decisis,* 18 LEGAL STUD. F. 3 (1994). For an empirical study of why justices of the Supreme Court of the United States chose to alter precedent during a 47 year period, see SAUL BRENNER & HAROLD J. SPAETH, STARE INDECISIS: THE ALTERATION OF PRECEDENT ON THE SUPREME COURT, 1946–1992 (1995). For an article that argues that justices are not influenced by landmark precedents with which they disagree, see Jeffrey A. Segal & Harold J. Spaeth, *The Influence of* Stare Decisis *on the Votes of United States Supreme Court Justices,* 40 AM. J. POL. SCI. 971 (1996), which is a portion of an entire issue devoted to *stare decisis.*

For an extensive sociological inquiry into the importance of precedent, including the need for attention to computer technology, see Susan W. Brenner, *Of Publication and Precedent: An Inquiry into the Ethnomethodology of Case Reporting in the American Legal System,* 39 DE PAUL L. REV. 461 (1990). *But see* Michael Wells, *The Unimportance of Precedent in the Law of Federal Courts,* 39 DE PAUL L. REV. 357 (1990). For an attempt to describe precedent and its applications, see Ruggero J. Aldisert, *Precedent: What It Is and What It Isn't, When Do We Kiss It and When Do We Kill It?* 17 PEPPERDINE L. REV. 605 (1990). *See also* Lawrence C. Marshall, *"Let Congress Do It": The Case for an Absolute Rule of Statutory Stare Decisis,* 88 MICH. L. REV. 177 (1989); Note, *Constitutional Stare Decisis,* 103 HARV. L. REV. 1344 (1990); SUSAN W. BRENNER, PRECEDENT INFLATION (1991). See also, Evan H. Caminker, *Why Must Inferior Courts Obey Superior Court Precedents?,* 46 STAN. L. REV. 817 (1994).

lower courts over which they have appellate jurisdiction, but appellate courts cannot bind each other by their decisions.

The *ratio decidendi* is the holding or the principle of law on which the case was decided. It is the *ratio decidendi* that sets the precedent and is binding on courts in the future. Unlike legislatures, American courts do not state general propositions of law, nor do they respond to hypothetical questions. Rather, courts decide actual cases and controversies, and they announce rules that are tied to specific fact situations. Therefore, the *ratio decidendi,* or rule of the case, must be considered in conjunction with the facts of the case.

In contrast, *dictum* (or *obiter dictum*) is language in an opinion that is arguably not necessary to the decision. *Dictum* comes from the Latin verb *decere,* "to say," and refers to what is "said by the way," specifically, that which is not essential to the holding of the decision. Although language categorized as *dictum* is not binding on future courts, it might be persuasive. It is common for yesterday's *dictum* to develop into today's doctrine.

The *ratio decidendi* and *dictum* are sometimes easily identified, but more often the distinction is subject to interpretation. The determination of what is the *ratio decidendi,* and what is *dictum,* is a focus of legal analysis and is often the critical point of legal argument.

Courts have much leeway in interpreting cases put forth as binding precedent.[14] No two cases are exactly the same, and at some point every case can be distinguished from all others. Generally, a case will be considered binding if it shares the same significant facts with the case at issue and does not differ in any significant facts from the instant case. Furthermore, the issues presented in the two cases must be the same and must have been necessary to the decision in the previous case (otherwise, the words of the court would be *dictum*). Courts can reject cases put forth as binding authority by distinguishing the cases on their facts or issues, thus finding that the previous cases are different from the instant case in some significant way.[15] In some situations, a court can avoid being bound by a previous case by finding that the rule put forth in the previous case is no longer valid and by overruling it.

The doctrine of precedent assumes that decisions of common law courts should be given consideration even if they are not binding. It is for this reason that researchers often look for the relevant decisions of

---

[14] In a chapter entitled "The Leeways of Precedent," Karl Llewellyn presented "a selection of [sixty-four] available impeccable precedent techniques" used by courts to follow, avoid, expand, or redirect precedent. KARL N. LLEWELLYN, THE COMMON LAW TRADITION: DECIDING APPEALS 77–91 (1960).

[15] *See generally* Kent Greenawalt, *Reflections on Holding and Dictum,* 39 J. LEGAL EDUC. 431 (1989). The practice of judges writing separately, generally in the hopes of laying the groundwork for a reversal or to demonstrate why one rationale may be better than another, is becoming commonplace. For some observations on this trend, see Laura Krugman Ray, *The Justices Write Separately: Uses of the Concurrence by the Rehnquist Court,* 23 U.C. DAVIS L. REV. 777 (1990); Ruth Bader Ginsburg, *Remarks on Writing Separately,* 65 WASH. L. REV. 133 (1990).

other states, jurisdictions, and even other common law countries. Cases that are not directly on point can contain principles on which to build legal arguments. Decisions that are not binding, either because they have different fact situations or because they are from another jurisdiction, can be persuasive because of the depth of analysis and quality of reasoning in the opinion. Among the other factors that can determine the persuasiveness of a non-binding opinion are the location and position of the court that issued the opinion, whether the opinion was issued by a unanimous or split court or written by a well-respected jurist, as well as subsequent judicial and academic approval of the opinion.

Policy considerations in favor of the doctrine of precedent are that it results in fairness because it encourages similar cases to be treated alike; it leads to predictability and stability in the legal system; and it saves time and energy because it enables us to make use of previous efforts and prior wisdom.[16] Critics argue that a reliance on precedent can result in a rigid and mechanical jurisprudence that can force us to treat unlike cases as if they were similar; that it can perpetuate outmoded rules; and that its inherently conservative nature can impede the law from being responsive to new social needs.[17]

Notwithstanding these criticisms, the doctrine of precedent remains the foundation upon which our models of legal research are constructed. The written opinions of courts, particularly appellate courts, are the "stuff" of legal argument and the major source of legal doctrine. Consequently, they are the primary, but certainly not the only, objects of legal research. Law libraries are filled with published court opinions, along with secondary sources and index tools to help researchers find, interpret, and update opinions that are relevant to particular fact patterns.

4. Legislation and the Interpretation of Statutes[18]

a. *Legislation.* A *statute,* sometimes referred to as legislation, is a positive statement of legal rules enacted by a legislature. In comparison, a constitution is the fundamental body of principles, most often written, by which a political body such as a nation or state governs itself. Because many of the basic concepts and techniques of statutory and constitutional research are similar, they can be discussed together at an introductory level. However, American constitutional law, both federal and state, is a pervasive and specialized subject; and including it in a general discussion of legislation should not obscure either its importance or its uniqueness.

In English law, the earliest statutes were enacted by the king with the concurrence of his council; later the role of statute-maker was

---

[16] *See* John Henry Merryman, *The Authority of Authority, supra* note 5, for a discussion of the benefits of following precedent.

[17] *See* Steven M. Barkan, *Deconstructing Legal Research: A Law Librarian's Commentary on Critical Legal Studies,* 79 Law Libr. J. 617 (1987).

[18] Constitutions and legislation are discussed in the following chapters, *infra:* Chapter 8, Constitutions; Chapter 9, Federal Legislation; Chapter 10, Federal Legislative Histories; Chapter 11, State and Municipal Legislation.

assumed by Parliament. In America, statutes are enacted by the legislative branch and signed into law by the executive. The growth of statutory law reflected the impact of the industrial revolution, as it became apparent that a jurisprudence based only on judicial decisions could not meet the needs of a growing, dynamic society. Situations developed in which answers were needed that were not found in court reports, or the answers found in court reports no longer met current needs, or resulted in actions that were considered unjust.

Statutes, and collections of statutes arranged by subject called *codes,* have become very important in common law systems; and American law is a combination of statutory law and case law. Statutes are used to create new areas of law, to fill gaps in the law, and to change court-made rules. However, unlike civil law systems, the American legal system has no presumptions that a statute will apply to every legal problem or that codes are comprehensive statements of the law.

b. *Statutory Interpretation.* Courts play predominant roles in interpreting and applying statutes and in extending the law to subjects not expressly covered by statutes. Judicial interpretations of statutes have the greatest authority for present controversies. In other words, the legislature can state a general legal rule in the form of a statute, but it is the judiciary that interprets the general rule and applies it to specific cases. Under the doctrine of precedent, it is the statute as *interpreted by the courts* that is applied in the next case. In theory, if the legislature disagrees with the way a court has interpreted a statute, the legislature must revise the statute.[19]

Statutory interpretation is an important part of legal research.[20] Researchers must not merely find the statutes applicable to a problem, but must also find information that will help determine what the statutes mean and how they should be applied. After looking for the "plain meaning" of the words of a statute,[21] and applying traditional canons or principles of statutory interpretation to the text of the statute,[22] researchers resort to a number of approaches to statutory interpretation.

An important method of statutory interpretation is to look for judicial opinions that have construed the specific statute. The persuasiveness of interpretive opinions will depend on the similarity of facts involved and on the courts issuing the opinions. Legislatures sometimes

---

[19] Guido Calabresi, A Common Law for the Age of Statutes 31–34 (1982).

[20] On statutory construction in general see Norman J. Singer, Statutes and Statutory Construction (5th ed. 1992).

[21] Some states have "plain meaning" statutes that attempt to limit courts in their interpretation of statutes that are unambiguous on their face. For an example, see Or. Rev. Stat. § 174.010 *et seq.* (1987).

[22] Karl Llewellyn provided an extensive listing of canons of construction to demonstrate that, since legal arguments suggest that there can be only one correct meaning of a statute, there are two opposing canons on every point. Karl N. Llewellyn, The Common Law Tradition: Deciding Appeals 521–35 (1960).

enact common law rules into statutes, and in such situations judicial opinions that pre-date the statute might be useful aids to interpretation.

Researchers often attempt to identify the legislature's purpose in passing the statute and the legislature's intended meaning for specific provisions of the statute. To do this, researchers will look at the *legislative history* of the statute—the documents such as revised versions of bills and legislative debates, hearings, and reports, among other materials, created by the legislature while the statute was under consideration—for evidence of legislative purpose and intent.[23] Although controversy exists over the proper uses of legislative histories,[24] legislative histories are often consulted by lawyers and judges and are frequently used in legal argument.

Researchers also search for cases from other jurisdictions that have interpreted similar statutes. Although these opinions are not binding authority, well-reasoned opinions from other courts can be very persuasive. This approach is consistent with the doctrine of precedent, under which the decisions of other common law courts may be considered, even if they are not binding.

5. Administrative Law[25]

The third major institutional source of law is the executive branch of government. The President of the United States and the governors of the states issue orders and create other documents with legal effect. Executive departments and offices, and administrative agencies, establishments, and corporations all create legal information.

Administrative agencies, which exist on the federal and state levels, are created by the legislative branch of government and are usually part of the executive branch. A number of independent agencies, establishments, and corporations exist that are within the executive branch but are not considered to be executive departments.[26] For the most part, federal agencies handle matters of federal law and state agencies handle matters of state law, but there is often interaction between federal and state agencies. Administrative agencies conduct activities that are in nature legislative and adjudicative, as well as executive. Under the

[23] The usual components of a legislative history are described in detail in Chapter 10, *infra.*

[24] *See* Peter C. Schanck, *An Essay on the Role of Legislative Histories in Statutory Interpretation,* 80 LAW LIBR. J. 391, 414 (1988); Philip P. Frickey, *From the Big Sleep to the Big Heat: The Revival of Theory in Statutory Interpretation,* 77 MINN. L. REV. 241 (1992); James J. Brudney, *Congressional Commentary on Judicial Interpretations of Statutes: Idle Chatter or Telling Response?,* 93 MICH. L. REV. 1 (1994). *But see* J. Myron Jacobstein & Roy M. Mersky, *Congressional Intent and Legislative Histories: Analysis or Psychoanalysis?,* 82 LAW LIBR. J. 297 (1990). *See also* Chapter 10, *infra.*

[25] Administrative law is discussed in Chapter 13, *infra.*

[26] *See* 5 U.S.C. § 104 (1988). The Federal Communications Commission, the Interstate Commerce Commission, and the Securities and Exchange Commission are among the many independent federal establishments and corporations. The *United States Government Manual* contains a complete list of executive agencies, independent establishments, and government corporations.

authority of a statute, they often create and publish rules and regulations that further interpret the statute. Agencies may also make determinations of law and fact in controversies arising under the statute and, like courts, publish opinions.

Administrative law can be a very complex area to research. Not only will researchers need to find, interpret, and update the rules, regulations, and decisions created by the administrative agency, but they will also need to find, interpret, and update the legislation the agency is administering and the judicial opinions interpreting the rules, administrative adjudications, and legislation.

SECTION B.   THE MATERIALS OF LEGAL RESEARCH

Published legal resources can be divided into three broad categories: (1) primary sources or authorities,[27] (2) secondary sources, and (3) index, search, or finding tools. All of these "published" legal resources can appear in various media. They include printed books, online databases, microforms, compact disks (CD–ROM), video and audio cassettes, the Internet, and other media. Many resources contain more than one type of information and serve more than one function. For example, some electronic databases and looseleaf services include both primary authority and secondary materials; and they are, at the same time, designed to be finding tools. Regardless of the media in which they are published, an understanding of how legal materials are structured and organized will contribute to effective legal research.

1.   Primary Sources

As noted earlier in this chapter, primary sources are authoritative statements of legal rules by governmental bodies. They include opinions of courts, constitutions, legislation, administrative regulations and opinions, and rules of court. Because many primary sources are published in the order they are issued with little or no subject access, secondary sources and indexing tools are needed to identify and retrieve them.

2.   Secondary Sources[28]

Secondary sources are materials about the law that are used to explain, interpret, develop, locate, or update primary sources. The major types of secondary sources are treatises, Restatements, looseleaf services, legislative histories, law reviews and other legal periodicals, legal encyclopedias, *American Law Reports (A.L.R.)* annotations, and legal dictionaries. Secondary sources can be interpretive and contain textual analysis, doctrinal synthesis, and critical commentary of varying degrees of per-

---

[27] As noted earlier, the terms *authorities* and *sources* are interchangeable when referring to types of legal materials.

[28] Secondary sources are discussed in the following chapters, *infra:* Chapter 7, Annotated Law Reports; Chapter 10, Federal Legislative Histories; Chapter 14, Looseleaf Services; Chapter 16, Legal Encyclopedias; Chapter 17, Legal Periodicals and Indexes; Chapter 18, Treatises, Restatements, Model Codes, and Uniform Laws; Chapter 19, Other Legal and General Research and Reference Aids.

suasiveness. Some secondary sources, such as Restatements, scholarly treatises, and journal articles, might be persuasive to a court, depending on the reputation of the author.[29] On the other hand, practice manuals and legal encyclopedias have little persuasive value but are useful for basic introductions to subjects, for concise or "black letter" statements of legal rules, and for practical advice. Secondary sources can be used as finding tools to locate other information. For example, cases cited in treatises, law review articles, and encyclopedias can lead to other cases.

3. Index, Search, and Finding Tools[30]

Index, search, and finding tools are intended to help locate or update primary and secondary sources. The major types of finding tools are *digests* (to locate cases discussing similar points of law), *annotations* in annotated statutes and codes,[31] *Shepard's Citators,* and legal periodical indexes. Index, search, and finding tools are *not* authority and should never be cited as such.

Looseleaf services and computer-assisted legal research systems such as WESTLAW and LEXIS are among the most valuable finding tools. They must be distinguished from other finding tools because they contain the full text of primary sources which, of course, can be cited as authority, as well as secondary information, which might also be cited as persuasive authority.

4. American Law Publishing

a. *Proliferation of Materials.* In the colonial period of American history, law books were extremely scarce and consisted mostly of English law reports. The most extensive law book collections numbered from fifty to one hundred volumes.[32] The situation did not continue for long. As the country spread westward and the economy changed from agrarian to industrial, greater demands were made upon courts and legislatures; and the body of American legal literature grew proportionately.[33]

---

[29] It should be noted, however, that the writings of legal scholars are generally not held in the same high levels of esteem in common law systems as in civil law systems. See JOHN HENRY MERRYMAN, THE CIVIL LAW TRADITION 56–60 (2d ed. 1985).

[30] In this book, index, search, and finding tools are discussed in conjunction with the resources they are designed to locate. The following chapters, *infra,* however, are devoted to specific finding tools: Chapter 6, Digests for Court Reports; Chapter 15, Citators.

[31] Do not confuse annotated statutes, which have brief annotations, or "squibs," describing cases that interpret statutory provisions, and annotated reports, such as *A.L.R.,* which have lengthy interpretive annotations of cases.

[32] ALBERT J. HARNO, LEGAL EDUCATION IN THE UNITED STATES 19 (1953); LAWRENCE M. FRIEDMAN, A HISTORY OF AMERICAN LAW 621–29 (2d ed. 1985). For thorough discussions of early American law book publishing, see ERWIN C. SURRENCY, A HISTORY OF AMERICAN LAW PUBLISHING (1990); Jenni Parrish, *Law Books and Legal Publishing in America, 1760–1840,* 72 LAW LIBR. J. 355 (1979).

[33] For an indication of the growth in size of academic law libraries, see J. Myron Jacobstein & Roy M. Mersky, *An Analysis of Academic Law Library Growth Since 1907,* 75 LAW LIBR. J. 212 (1982).

There has been extraordinary growth in the quantity of primary legal materials. During the period from 1658 to 1896 American courts reported 500,000 decisions,[34] and by 1990 there were 4,000,000 reported decisions. In 1950, 21,000 cases were published, and it is estimated that over 140,000 cases are now published annually. Congress and the state legislatures produce about 50,000 pages of statutory law per year, and federal and state administrative agencies produce thousands of pages of rulings and regulations.[35] Many of these primary materials are reproduced in multiple sources. The quantities of secondary sources and other law-related materials have expanded proportionately. The flood of legal publications has caused concern to the legal profession for over one hundred years; but the numbers continue to proliferate.[36]

b. *Official and Unofficial Publications.* American legal resources, whether books, electronic databases, or other media, can be divided into those that are *official,* and those that are *unofficial.* This distinction is important but often misunderstood. An official publication is one that has been mandated by statute or governmental rule. It might be produced by the government, but does not have to be. Citation rules[37] may require both official and unofficial citations, but the authority of official and unofficial publications is equivalent.

Unofficial publications of cases, statutes, and regulations are often more useful than official publications. Unofficial publications of primary authorities are published more quickly and usually include editorial features and secondary information that help interpret the primary sources, along with important locating or finding tools.

c. *Law Publishers.* American law publishing traditionally has been dominated by the private publishing industry, and the decade of the 1990's was a period of mergers, acquisitions, and consolidation for the industry. Although the law publishing industry is now dominated by a relatively small number of large publishers, many of the trade names under which resources were originally published have been retained.

The largest private publisher of legal information is West Group of Eagan, Minnesota, formerly known as West Publishing Company. West produces the *National Reporter System* (the largest and most comprehensive collection of federal and state judicial opinions), the *American Digest System,* a computerized research system called WESTLAW, annotated statutes, treatises, legal encyclopedias, law school textbooks, and many other resources. The company, which developed its resources around a theory of comprehensive reporting, has played such an important role in legal publishing that some scholars claim West influenced

---

[34] 1 CENTURY DIGEST iii (1897).

[35] Recently, volumes of the *Federal Register* have exceeded 60,000 pages annually.

[36] For a discussion of the problems of excessive reporting, see J. Myron Jacobstein, *Some Reflections on the Control of the Publication of Appellate Court Opinions,* 27 STAN. L. REV. 791 (1975).

[37] For an explanation of how to read legal citations, see Chapter 23, *infra.*

the development of American law.[38] Among the trade names published by West Group are: Bancroft Whitney; Banks Baldwin; Barclays; Carswell; Clark Boardman Callaghan; Foundation Press; Information Access Corporation; Lawyers Cooperative Publishing Company; Research Institute of America; Sweet & Maxwell; Warren Gorham & Lamont; Thomson & Thomson; and West.

Other major commercial legal publishers and some of the trade names under which they publish include: Reed Elsevier (Butterworths; Congressional Information Service (CIS); LEXIS–NEXIS; Marquis; Michie; Praeger; and University Publications of America); Kluwer (Aspen; Commerce Clearing House (CCH); Kluwer; Little Brown; Nijhoff; Panel; and, Prentice Hall); Times–Mirror (Matthew–Bender; Shepard's Citations); Bureau of National Affairs (BNA); Wiley; and Anderson.[39]

5. Evaluating Legal Resources

When inspecting and evaluating legal resources, it is important to determine and understand the purposes the resources were designed to serve. The author or editor should be noted along with the types of authority (primary and secondary) included and the potential persuasiveness of the authority. Is the resource part of a set, or is it designed to be used with other resources? Does it have finding tools or special features, such as indexes and tables? When was the resource last updated, and how is the resource brought up to date? An awareness of the functions, features, interrelationships, strengths, and weaknesses of available resources will prove valuable for conducting legal research effectively.

SECTION C. AN ESSENTIAL SKILL

In 1992, a special task force of the American Bar Association on law schools and the legal profession issued a report that stated that "[i]t can hardly be doubted that the ability to do legal research is one of the skills that any competent practitioner must possess."[40] That report also stated: "[i]n order to conduct legal research effectively, a lawyer should have a working knowledge of the nature of legal rules and legal institutions, the fundamental tools of legal research, and the process of devising and implementing a coherent and effective research design."[41]

Furthermore, the ABA's *Model Rules of Professional Conduct* provide:

---

[38] *See* GRANT GILMORE, THE AGES OF AMERICAN LAW 58–59 (1977); Robert C. Berring, *Full-Text Databases and Legal Research: Backing into the Future,* 1 HIGH TECH. L.J. 27 (1986); Steven M. Barkan, *Can Law Publishers Change the Law?* LEGAL REFERENCE SERVICES Q., Nos. 1/2, 1991, at 29.

[39] The reliance of lawyers on private law book publishers led the Federal Trade Commission to promulgate standards for the law book trade. *See* 16 CFR § 256 (1993).

[40] LEGAL EDUCATION AND PROFESSIONAL DEVELOPMENT: AN EDUCATIONAL CONTINUUM, REPORT OF THE TASK FORCE ON LAW SCHOOLS AND THE PROFESSION: NARROWING THE GAP 163 (1992). The full text of the section of the report discussing legal research is reproduced in Appendix D, *infra.*

[41] *Id.*

A lawyer shall provide competent representation to a client. Competent representation requires the legal knowledge, skill, thoroughness, and preparation reasonably necessary for the representation.[42]

Clearly, a lawyer must be able to research the law to provide competent representation. In addition to issues of professional responsibility, questions relating to competency in legal research may arise in legal malpractice actions in which an attorney is sued for failing to know "those plain and elementary principles of law which are commonly known by well-informed attorneys, and to discover the additional rules which, although not commonly known, may readily be found by standard research techniques."[43] Issues relating to the competency of legal research are also raised in claims for malicious prosecution,[44] and in claimed violations of the Sixth Amendment right to effective assistance of counsel.[45]

The knowledge and ability to use fundamental legal research tools and to implement an effective and efficient research plan must become part and parcel of every lawyer's training if she or he is to provide competent representation and uphold the standards of the legal profession.

[42] MODEL RULES OF PROFESSIONAL CONDUCT, Rule 1.1 (1983).

[43] Smith v. Lewis, 13 Cal. 3d 349, 530 P.2d 589, 118 Cal. Rptr. 621 (1975). In this case the plaintiff received a judgment of $100,000 in a malpractice action based on the negligence of the defendant lawyer in researching the applicable law.

[44] *See, e.g.,* Sheldon Appel Co. v. Albert & Oliker, 765 P.2d 498, 509 (Cal. 1989), a case in which the plaintiff in a malicious prosecution action unsuccessfully argued, among other things, that lack of probable cause for an action may be established by showing that the former adversary's attorney failed to perform reasonable legal research before filing a claim.

[45] *See, e.g.,* People v. Ledesma, 43 Cal. 3d 171, 729 P.2d 839, 233 Cal. Rptr. 404 (1987).

Chapter 2

THE LEGAL RESEARCH PROCESS[1]

Legal research is as much an art as a science. There are many approaches to legal research, and there is no single, or best, way to do legal research. Methods will vary according to the nature of the problem and will depend on the researcher's subject expertise and research skills.

Approaches to legal research may also be shaped by where the research is conducted. A knowledge of alternative research tools will prove to be valuable because every law library will not have all of the resources described in this book. Furthermore, sometimes the preferred resources do not produce the expected results.

The capacity to solve legal problems rapidly and accurately can best be developed by constructing a systematic approach to legal research. No matter how sophisticated you become in a field of law, you will encounter problems necessitating research into unfamiliar subjects. At these moments your basic approach developed as a novice becomes the artful technique of a trained professional.

The processes of legal research and legal writing are closely related. Legal research is often futile if the results are not communicated effectively. Legal research informs legal writing, and legal writing is meaningless unless its content is accurate. There are many differing viewpoints about how legal research and legal writing interrelate. Some researchers prefer to conduct most of their research before they begin to write. Others prefer to write as they conduct their research.

This chapter presents a general approach to legal research that can be modified and applied to most problems and can be merged with various approaches to legal writing. In the end, you must develop the research and writing methodology that you find most effective.

A GENERAL APPROACH TO LEGAL RESEARCH

A general approach to legal research, which can be modified to accommodate most problems, can be broken down into four basic steps. These are:

STEP 1. Identify and analyze the significant facts.

STEP 2. Formulate the legal issues to be researched.

STEP 3. Research the issues presented.

STEP 4. Update.

[1] This chapter was written by Steven M. Barkan, Director of the Law Library and Professor of Law, University of Wisconsin Law School.

This discussion will focus on each of these steps individually; however, each step is closely interrelated with the others. In the process of executing any one of the steps it will be necessary to revise and refine the work done in previous steps.

1.   STEP 1: Identify and Analyze the Significant Facts

The researcher's first task is to identify and analyze the facts surrounding the particular problem. Some facts have legal significance; others do not. The process of legal research begins with compiling a descriptive statement of legally significant facts. It is often difficult for a beginner to identify the significant facts and to discard the insignificant ones. Consequently, when researching a problem in an unfamiliar area of the law, it is usually best to err on the side of over-inclusion rather than on the side of exclusion.

Factual analysis is the first step in formulating the legal issues to be researched. Another important purpose of factual analysis is to identify access points to the available resources. Which volumes do we pull off the shelf? Which subjects should be consulted in indexes and tables of contents? Which words should be used in an initial computer search? An experienced researcher will be able to identify issues and take a subject approach to the resources; but the beginning researcher, who does not have the experience to examine a fact pattern and readily categorize it and formulate legal issues, will need to devote more time and attention to this activity.

Inexperienced legal researchers tend to skim over the facts and begin researching. No productive research can be done outside a particular fact pattern. Most research, and controversy, is over facts, not law; and cases are most often distinguished on the facts. The rules stated by courts are tied to specific fact situations, and, in the future, must be considered in relation to those facts. Because the facts of a legal problem will control the direction of research, the investigation and analysis of facts must be incorporated into the research process. You will save time, and will achieve more accuracy, if you initially take the time to identify the relevant facts and write them down in some narrative form.

The TARP Rule. A useful technique is to analyze your facts according to the following factors:

T—**Thing** or subject matter;

A—Cause of **action** or ground of defense;

R—**Relief** sought;

P—**Persons** or **parties** involved.

Thing or subject matter. The place or property involved in a problem or controversy may be a significant element. Thus, when a passenger is injured in a skidding automobile, the automobile becomes an essential fact in the dispute.

Cause of action or ground of defense. Identify the claim that might be asserted or the defense that might be made. For example, the cause of action might be a breach of contract, negligence, or some other claim.

Relief sought. What is the purpose of the lawsuit? It might be a civil action in which the party bringing the suit is seeking monetary damages for an injury, or an action in which a party is asking the court to order another party to do a specific act or to refrain from doing a specific act; or it might be a criminal action brought by the state.

Persons or parties involved in the problem; their functional and legal status and relationship to each other. The parties or persons might be individuals, or might be a group that is significant to the solution of the problem or the outcome of the lawsuit. Similarly, the relationship between the parties, such as exists between husband and wife or employer and employee, might be of special importance.

2.   STEP 2: Formulate the Legal Issues to Be Researched

This is the initial intellectual activity that presumes some knowledge of the substantive law. It is, therefore, the point at which inexperienced legal researchers are most likely to have trouble. The goal is to classify or categorize the problem into general, and increasingly specific, subject areas and to begin to hypothesize legal issues. For example, is this a matter of civil or criminal law? Federal or state law? Are we generally in the area of contracts or torts, or both? If torts, is it products liability or negligence? It should be noted that problems are not easily categorized and compartmentalized, problems can fall into more than one category, and categories affect each other.

a.   *Get an Overview.* To assist in formulating issues, it is useful to consult general secondary sources for an overview of all relevant subject areas. These sources can include national legal encyclopedias, a state encyclopedia, treatises, looseleaf services, or one or more subject periodicals or journals. The best choice will vary according to your background, but start with the most general and work to the more detailed and specific. These sources can provide valuable background reading and can direct you to issues and to primary resources. Be sure to note any constitutional provisions, statutes, administrative regulations, and judicial and administrative opinions cited by these sources. The point to remember is that, at this stage, these secondary sources are used to provide background information and to help you formulate issues; they are the tools, not the objects of research.

Writing a clear, concise statement of each legal issue raised by the significant facts is an important and difficult task. Failure to frame all of the issues raised by a particular set of facts results in incomplete and inadequate research. It is better, when framing the issues, for a beginner to err on the side of too many issues. Insignificant issues can always be eliminated after they have been thoroughly investigated, and overlapping issues can be consolidated.

b.   *Create an Outline.* Once statements of the issues have been drafted, they should be arranged in a logical pattern to form an outline.

Logically related issues may be combined as sub-issues under a broader main issue. Issues which depend upon the outcome of other issues should be arranged accordingly. Your outline should be expanded, modified, and revised as your research progresses. As a particular issue is researched, it is often discovered to be overly broad, and it becomes evident that the statement of the issue should be narrowed. It may also be necessary at times to split an issue into two, or to divide an issue into two sub-issues. Similarly, it may develop that the original issue is too narrow and does not lead to any relevant information. In such instances, the issue should be broadened. Many times, during the process of research, it becomes apparent that issues not originally considered are relevant. For this reason, the task of framing issues may not be completed until the research project is finished.

3. STEP 3: Research the Issues Presented[2]

After the facts have been analyzed and the issues have been framed, it is time to begin researching the first issue.

a. *Organize and Plan.* Although serendipity can play an important role in legal research, good legal researchers, as a rule, are systematic, methodical, and organized; and they keep good records. Every researcher must develop a system for taking notes.

For each issue, it is important to decide which sources to use, which sources not to use, and the order in which sources should be examined. The best practice is to write down all sources to be searched under each issue to be researched, even if sources are repeated. As you find information, record where you found it and why it is relevant. Expand your outline to include the information that you discover. Maintaining an accurate list of sources consulted, sources to be consulted, terms and topics checked, and updating steps taken will help prevent wasting time and overlooking crucial information.

As a general practice, it is best to research each issue completely before moving to the next issue. It will be necessary to revise issues along the way, but it is best to follow through with each issue before moving on, rather than moving back and forth from issue to issue. Dealing with each issue separately helps avoid backtracking or excessive interplay of issues, helps ensure that each issue and sub-issue will be distinct and logically complete, and helps avoid the temptation to stray into interesting but irrelevant areas.

There is sometimes a great temptation to include information that has taken many hours to develop but which you later determine is irrelevant to a proper analysis of the issues. You should expect to investigate a number of leads during the research process that prove to be irrelevant, and you must avoid the temptation to retain irrelevant information that detracts from, and often masks, the legal analysis which is directly on point.

---

[2] After reading Step 3 it might also be useful to consult the "Chart on Legal Research Procedure" in Appendix F.

b. *Identify, Read, and Update All Relevant Constitutional Provisions, Statutes, and Administrative Regulations.* Identifying and reading relevant constitutional provisions, statutes, and administrative regulations will provide you with the framework on which the rest of your research will be built. These primary sources can be identified in several ways.

● *Statutory Compilations.* Statutory compilations almost always have tables of contents and indexes that list the subjects and topics covered by the statutes. Because relevant statutory provisions are often found in several places in the compiled statutes, consult both the table of contents and the index.

● *Computer–Assisted Legal Research.* The United States Code, the Code of Federal Regulations, the Federal Register, and the statutes of many states are available on LEXIS–NEXIS, WESTLAW, and other electronic sources. It is possible to search the full text of these sources for statutes and regulations that apply to your problem.

● *Secondary Sources.* Secondary sources such as encyclopedias, treatises, looseleaf services, and law review articles, commonly cite relevant constitutional provisions, statutes, and administrative regulations, particularly if those secondary sources focus on the law of one state or on federal law.

It will not always be easy to identify all relevant statutes at the onset of your research. Indexing problems sometimes make it difficult to match concepts with indexing terms. Sometimes your issues will be too vague or underdeveloped for you to realize that a statute applies. Accordingly, continue searching for relevant constitutional provisions, statutes, and administrative regulations as your research progresses; and be prepared to modify your issues and strategies accordingly.

c. *Identify, Read, and Update All Relevant Case Law.* After you have identified and read the relevant constitutional provisions, statutes, and administrative regulations, you must identify, read, and update the case law that has interpreted and applied those forms of enacted law, as well as other case law that is relevant to your fact situation.

Do not limit your search to cases that support your position. A competent researcher will anticipate both sides of an argument and identify the cases that indicate contrary conclusions. In many situations, these will be the same cases, and the argument will be over how the cases are to be interpreted, *e.g.,* whether the holding is to be broadly or narrowly applied, or whether the facts of the cases can be distinguished. Frequently, however, both sides will argue that entirely different lines of cases are controlling.

Your goal, at this stage of research, is to compile a comprehensive, chronological list of relevant opinions for each issue. Because no two cases are exactly alike, you should not expect to find cases with fact patterns identical to yours. The most relevant judicial opinions will come from the same court or superior appellate courts in your jurisdiction because they are the only ones that are potentially binding. Next in importance will be judicial opinions, which might be persuasive, from other courts and jurisdictions dealing with similar facts, statutes, and issues. Even if you find cases that you consider to be binding authority, persuasive authority from other jurisdictions might help bolster your argument, particularly if the opinions you find are from well-known and respected judges. Reading the cases chronologically can reveal background information that is not necessarily repeated in each case, can show the development of the case law, and can point to the "lead" case that will be cited in other opinions.

Cases that interpret statutes can be identified in several ways.

● *Annotated Statutes and Codes.* Annotated statutes and codes list interpretive cases after each statutory provision.

● *Treatises and Looseleaf Services.* Treatises and looseleaf services, particularly if they are devoted to the law of one state or to federal law, cite cases that interpret the statutes they discuss.

● *Citators.* Citation services such as Shepard's Citations and Key-Cite can provide a list of cases that have cited the statute.

● *Computer–Assisted Legal Research (CALR).* Both WESTLAW and LEXIS–NEXIS can be searched for cases that have cited the statute.

Other relevant cases can be identified by subject searches of secondary sources and finding tools. Digests provide a subject arrangement of brief abstracts of cases that can be accessed through a table of contents and a descriptive word index. Also, the full text of court opinions can be searched in LEXIS–NEXIS and WESTLAW; treatises, *A.L.R.* annotations, looseleaf services, and encyclopedias should provide relevant case citations.

Once you have identified a relevant case, there are several techniques that can help you identify other cases on the same subject. These techniques include tracing the key numbers used in that case through the digests to find other cases with the same key numbers, shepardizing or KeyCiting the case and using the CALR systems as citators to find other citing cases, and consulting the tables of cases in treatises, looseleaf services, encyclopedias, and digests.

As you read and brief each case, be sure to note its full citation, parallel citations, the judge and court issuing the opinion, the date of the decision, the relevant facts, the holding, a summary of the court's reasoning, key numbers assigned, and the sources cited by the court. Each of the sources cited should be read, briefed, and shepardized or KeyCited, and new cases should be added to your list. Each case you brief should be incorporated into your outline. There will likely be a great deal of redundancy, particularly when courts list a "string" of citations for each point of law.

d.　*Refine the Search.* After you have identified, read, and organized the primary sources, go to secondary sources to refine the search and expand your argument. Invariably, new cases and lines of argument will appear. Treatises, law review articles, and Restatements of the Law are not binding authority, but they can be persuasive and can provide ideas on how best to utilize the primary sources you have found. If the problem involves a statute, the legislative history might suggest the legislature's intent in passing the act and the problem the law was intended to remedy. Historical, social, economic, and political information can put legal arguments in their proper context and can support policy arguments.

4. STEP 4: Update

Although updating was discussed earlier as an integral part of researching the issues, its importance warrants special attention. Law changes constantly. Legislatures pass new statutes and modify old ones. Each appellate court decision either adds new law, refines the law, reaffirms the law, or changes the law; and researchers must be aware of the most recent decisions on the subject being researched. Research that is current today can be out of date tomorrow. Few lawyers would disagree that failure to update legal research is careless and negligent, sometimes leading to disastrous results.

Shepardize cases, statutes, and regulations; consult electronic databases such as WESTLAW, LEXIS–NEXIS, KeyCite, Insta–Cite, and Auto–Cite; and check pocket parts and supplements, looseleaf services, and advance sheets to determine whether the authorities have been interpreted or altered in any way, or whether new cases, statutes, or regulations have been published.

5. When to Stop

The question of when to stop researching is a difficult one. Obviously, there is no easy answer to the question: "Can I safely stop here?" With experience, researchers develop insight into when they can safely terminate their research. In many instances an obvious repetition of citations or absence of information will suggest that enough research has been done. However, there is no uniform rule on how extensive research should be, and knowing when to terminate research is a skill that can only be developed over time.

In some instances, carrying a problem through all the sources can be needless, unwarranted, or repetitious. It is possible to over-research your problem. All cases are not of equal importance; much information is redundant. Including too much information can obscure the important points you are trying to make. Furthermore, many simple problems do not call for exhaustive research. Common sense and professional insight, therefore, play significant roles in legal research.

In the last analysis, the skills of sophisticated researchers are measured as much by the knowledge of what can be omitted as by which research materials are used and how they are used. The attorney's stock in trade is time; a skilled legal researcher knows how to use it wisely.[3]

---

[3] For an in-depth discussion of when to stop researching, see Christina L. Kunz, *Terminating Research,* 2 Perspectives: Teaching Legal Res. & Writing 2 (1993).

Chapter 3

COURT REPORTS

SECTION A. THE REPORTING OF COURT CASES

1. Introduction

The doctrine *stare decisis,* as discussed in Chapter 1, Section A–3, has as its premise that courts are to adhere to judicial precedent. Reliance on judicial precedent in American jurisprudence is derived from the common law. Researchers and the courts are expected to turn to established judicial authorities and rules of law as the foundation for formulating legal arguments and issuing opinions. Access to "case law"—the aggregate of reported cases that form a body of jurisprudence, as distinguished from statutory and administrative law—is, therefore, often crucial when one is asked to research a legal issue. Consequently, the editing, publishing, and ready availability of court cases have special characteristics in American law.

Court reports are compilations of judicially-decided cases, most often from state and federal appellate courts, arranged according to some grouping, such as jurisdiction, court, period of time, subject matter, or case significance. Today, the word "reporter" is often used synonymously with court reports.

When a court reaches a determination as to the outcome of a case, it issues an opinion in which it states the reason for its decision. Technically speaking, the *decision* of a court only signifies the action of the court and is indicated by the words *Affirmed,* or *Reversed,* or *Remanded,* or similar words and phrases. The *opinion* provides the explanation for the decision. In actual practice, the terms *opinion* and *decision* are often used interchangeably.[1]

The first volume of state appellate court reports was published in 1789, with the reports of the Supreme Court of the United States commencing officially in 1817. The numbers of published reports have proliferated dramatically since that time. Because these past court cases play such an important role in our law, the tremendous growth and inclusiveness of court reports are quite understandable.

Approximately 5,000,000 reported United States judicial cases are now in published form, and over 140,000 new American cases are reported each year from more than 600 courts. Most of these published

---

[1] For a discussion of the difference between *decision of the court* and *opinion of the court,* see Rogers v. Hill, 289 U.S. 582, 587 (1933). *See also* Towley v. King Arthur Rings, Inc., 40 N.Y.2d 129, 351 N.E.2d 728, 386 N.Y.S.2d 80 (1976).

cases are from the federal and state appellate courts. Justice Holmes observed that, "It is a great mistake to be frightened by the ever-increasing number of reports. The reports of a given jurisdiction in the course of a generation take up pretty much the whole body of law, and restate it from the present point of view. We could reconstruct the corpus from them if all that went before were burned."[2]

Computer technology has added yet another dimension to the storage and retrieval of legal information. The development and rapid expansion of two major electronic storage and retrieval systems, LEXIS–NEXIS and WESTLAW, both launched in the 1970s, allow full-text searching of court cases and numerous other databases of law-related materials. Even more recent technology, such as the Internet, CD–ROMs (compact disk-read only memory), and electronic imaging, also provide computerized access to the full text of cases and to other materials for legal research. At times, a researcher's needs can be satisfied by relying exclusively on either computer-retrievable sources or bound court reporters; at other times the best results can be achieved by using both. Computer-assisted legal research (CALR) is discussed in detail in Chapter 21.

The massive quantity of available court cases in both bound volumes and computer-retrievable sources in turn creates problems for the legal profession—problems relating to locating relevant information within the published reports, keeping current in one's field, publication and subscription costs, space and technological considerations, and related issues.

Not all appellate court cases are published and publication procedures differ in the various appellate courts.[3] Justice Holmes' comments notwithstanding, the tremendous growth in the number of recently-decided cases has increased the attempts to restrict the number of those that are reported.[4] Many judges and lawyers believe that far too many

---

[2] Oliver W. Holmes, *The Path of the Law, in* Collected Legal Papers 167, 169 (1920 & photo. reprint 1985).

[3] George M. Weaver, *The Precedential Value of Unpublished Judicial Opinions,* 39 Mercer L. Rev. 477 (1988). *See also* William L. Reynolds & William M. Richman, *An Evaluation of Limited Publications in the United States Courts of Appeals: The Price of Reform,* 48 U. Chi. L. Rev. 573 (1981).

[4] The practice of selective reporting of appellate court opinions has caused considerable debate as to its value. For an historical survey, see J. Myron Jacobstein, *Some Reflections on the Control of the Publication of Appellate Court Opinions,* 27 Stan. L. Rev. 791 (1975). For more recent views, see Richard L. Neumeir, *Unpublished Opinions: Their Threat to the Appellate System,* Brief (A.B.A.), Spring, 1988, at 22; Keith H. Beyler, *Selective Publication Rules,* 21 Loy. U. Chi. L.J. 1 (1989); Jenny Mockenhaupt, Comment, *Assessing the Nonpublication Practice of the Minnesota Court of Appeals,* 19 Wm. Mitchell L. Rev. 787 (1993); Elizabeth M. Horton, Comment, *Selective Publication and the Authority of Precedent in the United States Courts of Appeals,* 42 U.C.L.A. L. Rev 1631 (1995).

For the current practice for some state supreme courts to "depublish" opinions of intermediate appellate courts, see Philip L. Dubois, *The Negative Side of Judicial Decision Making: Depublication as a Tool of Judicial Power and Administration of State Courts of Last Resort,* 33 Vill. L. Rev. 469 (1988); Steven R. Barnett, *Making Decisions Disappear: Depublication and Stipulated Reversal in the California Supreme Court,* 26 Loy. L.A. L. Rev. 1033 (1993); Gerald F. Uelman, *Publication and Depublication of California Court of*

opinions that do not merit the treatment of permanent publication are, nevertheless, written and reported. They argue that a significant number of reported cases relate merely to prosaic problems and make no doctrinal advancements. Although of value to the parties involved in the litigation, these cases add little or nothing to the existing law.

Ordinarily, cases decided by state trial courts are not reported. A few states, such as New York, Ohio, and Pennsylvania, do publish some trial court cases, but those selected are few in number and represent only a very small portion of the total cases heard by the trial courts. Moreover, cases decided by trial courts do not serve as mandatory precedents, and they do not play an important role in legal research.

2. The Structure and Operation of the Court System

Each jurisdiction has its own system of court organization, and although there may be differences in detail, the typical structure is the same. In general, there are trial courts and appellate courts. The former are the courts where the trial is held (courts of first instance). It is here the parties appear, witnesses testify, and the evidence is presented. The trial court usually determines any questions of fact in dispute and then applies the applicable rules of law.

Once the trial court reaches its decision, the losing party has a right of appeal to an appellate court. Each state has a final court of appeals or court of last resort. Forty-two states also have intermediate courts of appeals.[5] [See Illustration 3–1.] Generally, the appellate court can only decide questions of law and its decision in each case is based on the trial record from below, *e.g.,* pre-trial proceedings and trial transcript. Appellate courts do not receive new testimony or decide questions of fact, and in most jurisdictions only the appellate courts issue written opinions.

When a case is appealed to an appellate court, both parties submit written briefs that contain a summary of the facts and arguments on the points of law involved, and the court may hear oral arguments by the attorneys. The court then issues an opinion in which it states the reasons for its decision. If the case is decided by an intermediate appellate court and the losing party believes his or her position is legally correct, this lower court decision can frequently be appealed again, this time to the court of last resort for a further determination.

SECTION B. THE SEGMENTS OF COURT CASES

An American court case typically includes the following segments: [See Illustrations 3–2 and 3–3.]

Appeals Opinions: Is the Eraser Mightier Than the Pencil, 26 Loy. L.A. L. Rev. 1077 (1993); William H. Manz, *The Citation Practices of the New York Court of Appeals, 1850–1993,* 43 Buff. L. Rev. 121 (1995). *See infra* Chapter 4, note 12 for information on the federal court practices in this regard.

[5] For detailed information on the activities of state courts, see State Court Caseload Statistics: Annual Report, produced jointly by the Conference of State Court Administrators and the National Center for State Courts. *See also* the latest Council of State Governments, Book of the States (biennial).

1. Name or Title of the Case

Cases generally are identified by the names of the parties to a lawsuit. This is sometimes referred to as the "caption." Examples are:

Heidi Bauer, Plaintiff v. Richard M. Green, Defendant—in table of cases (a listing of cases typically arranged in alphabetical order) as *Bauer v. Green.*

In re Bauer—in table of cases as *Bauer, In re.* These are judicial proceedings in which there are no adversarial parties. Such designations usually denote a bankruptcy case, a probate case, a guardianship matter, a contempt case, a disbarment, or a *habeas corpus* case.

Ex parte Bauer—in table of cases as *Bauer, Ex parte.* This is a special proceeding for the benefit of one party only.

State on the relation of Bauer v. Green—in table of cases as *State ex rel. Bauer v. Green.* These cases involve extraordinary legal remedies, *e.g., mandamus,* prohibition, *certiorari, quo warranto,* or *habeas corpus.*

State v. Bauer—in table of cases as *State v. Bauer.* Suit by the state in its collective capacity as the party wronged by a criminal act. In some reporters the criminal cases are arranged in alphabetical order under the names of the respective states. *People* or *Commonwealth* is used in some states instead of *State.* If the United States brings the suit, it is captioned, for example, as *United States v. Bauer.* To aid with location, a case of this nature may also be listed in the table of cases as *Bauer, State v.* or *Bauer, United States v.*

In maritime law, a suit may be brought against the ship, *e.g., The Caledonia.*

Cases involving the seizure of commodities use the commodity as a party, *e.g., United States v. 37 Photographs.*

Usually the plaintiff-defendant names remain in that order when cases are appealed by the defendant; however, in some states, they are reversed, and the defendant on appeal becomes the plaintiff in error.

2. Citation

The citation to the case frequently appears near the name of the case in a published reporter. Often the parallel citation to another reporter in which the case is published is also provided.

3. Docket Number

A docket number is the numerical designation assigned to each case by a court, *e.g.,* No. 98–1145, or some similar numbering sequence. It is the means of identifying the case as the suit is in progress. Also, it is a convenient method commonly used by law libraries to organize the appellate briefs in the libraries' collections.

4. Date of Decision

This is the date on which the decision was rendered, and generally it appears after the docket number in the reported case.

5. Prefatory Statement

The prefatory statement explains the nature of the case, its disposition in the lower court, the name of the lower court and sometimes its judge, and the disposition of the case in the appellate court, *e.g., Affirmed* or *Reversed.*

6. Syllabus or Headnote

Headnotes, or syllabi, are brief summaries of the rules of law or significant facts in a case. They are usually drafted by editors or reporters employed by the court, although in a few states they are prepared by the judges who rendered the decisions. Each headnote represents a point of law extracted from the case, and the number of headnotes will vary from case to case. However, headnotes cannot be relied on as authority; the actual case must be consulted.

The syllabi or headnotes are useful in allowing the reader to grasp quickly the legal issues discussed within the case and then to locate these issues within the case. They also serve a very useful function in the process of locating other cases on the same or similar points of law. This feature will be discussed in more detail in Chapter 6. [See Illustrations 3–2 and 3–4 for examples of headnotes.]

7. Names of Counsel

The names of counsel for both parties to a suit precede the opinion of the court.

8. Statement of Facts

A statement of the facts in the case usually follows the names of counsel.

9. Opinions of the Court

As previously mentioned, most court cases that are published are those of the appellate court. Every appellate court has at least three judges,[6] and in some jurisdictions the courts may have five, seven, nine, or more judges. The *opinion* of the court is the explanation of the court's decision, the latter being the conclusion or result in a controversy. The *majority opinion* is written by one member of the court and represents the principles of law that a majority of his or her colleagues on the court deem operative in a given decision.

A member of the majority, while agreeing with a decision, may disagree with its reasoning. He or she then may write a *concurring opinion* elaborating his or her reasoning. When more judges join an opinion than any concurring opinion, but yet not a majority of the court, it is known as a *plurality opinion.*

---

[6] Many appellate courts sit in panels smaller than the full court. When the full court meets, it is referred to as an *en banc* proceeding. *See* Neil D. McFeeley, *En Banc Proceedings in the United States Courts of Appeals,* 24 IDAHO L. REV. 255 (1987–1988).

The views of the minority generally are expressed by a *dissenting opinion,* which is written by one of the dissenting judges. An opinion, in *accord* with the dissent, is written by a dissenting judge when he or she agrees with the conclusions and results of the dissent, but disagrees with its reasoning. Or several dissenting opinions may be rendered independently by the judges, each expressing different views.

Dissenting opinions are not the law in a case; nor are they binding as precedent. They assume the characteristics of *dicta* and serve merely as persuasive or secondary authority. However, not infrequently the controlling opinion may later be overruled and the dissenting opinion might then be accepted as the correct statement of the law.

A *per curiam* opinion is an opinion of the entire majority as distinguished from an opinion written by a specific judge. In some courts, *e.g.,* New York Court of Appeals, a *per curiam* opinion may present a lengthy or a brief discussion of the issues in the case. In other courts, *e.g.,* Supreme Court of the United States, this type of opinion may only give the conclusion without any reasoning.[7] A *memorandum opinion* is a brief holding of the whole court in which the opinion is limited or omitted.

Two additional elements, mentioned in Chapter 1, merit reiteration. The first is the *ratio decidendi,* or the point in a case that determines the result. In other words, it is the basis of the decision, explicitly or implicitly, stated in the opinion. The second is *obiter dictum.* This is a collateral statement contained in the opinion that does not relate directly to the issues raised in the case. *Dictum,* therefore, is an official, incidental comment made by a judge in his or her opinion not necessary to the formulation of the decision and that is not binding as precedent.

10. Decision, with Judgment or Decree

This refers to the actual disposition of the case by the court. Thus, a decision is noted by such terms as *Affirmed, Reversed, Modified,* etc. Often the words *decision* and *judgment* are used synonymously. A decree, typically issued in equity or admiralty actions, announces the legal consequences of the facts found.

SECTION C. OFFICIAL AND UNOFFICIAL REPORTS

If the publication of a set of court reports is sanctioned by statute or court rule, the set is referred to as *official reports.* [See Illustration 3–2.] In some instances, these publications are produced under government supervision; in others the official report may have ceased and an existing commercial publication designated as the official source. This is discussed in more detail in Chapter 5. Those published without legislative or judicial authority are referred to as *unofficial reports, i.e.,* commercial or private publications. Neither term reflects superior quality or accura-

---

[7] For discussion of the decline in the use of the *per curiam* opinion by the Supreme Court of the United States, see Stephen L. Wasby et al., *The Per Curiam Opinion: Its Nature and Functions,* 76 JUDICATURE 29 (1992). *See also* Stephen L. Wasby et al., *The Supreme Court's Use of Per Curiam Dispositions: The Connections to Oral Argument,* 13 No. ILL. U.L. REV. 1 (1992).

cy, because the language of the opinions reported in both is identical. [See Illustrations 3–2 through 3–6.]

1. Unofficially Reported Cases as Authority

Because court cases are not copyrighted,[8] numerous sets of court reports have been, or are currently, published by commercial publishers. These sets either duplicate the opinions in the official reports, or include cases not officially published, or both. Since the early nineteenth century, legal scholars have warned against the proliferation of court reports. In the past, courts and legislatures have attempted to control the publication of court cases by limiting the publication of cases in the official reports to those that (1) lay down a new rule of law or alter or modify an existing rule; (2) involve a legal issue of continuing public interest; (3) criticize existing law; or (4) resolve an apparent conflict of authority. But, inevitably, each such attempt has resulted in those cases that do not appear in the official reports being published in unofficial sets of reports. Furthermore, the availability of unreported cases has increased with the expansion of online legal databases.[9]

Only fairly recently have some courts attempted to control this proliferation by prohibiting the citing of opinions not specifically marked "For Publication."[10] This practice in turn has been severely criticized by some members of the bar. The final solution to the proliferation of court cases has still not been found. It is reasonable to conclude that so long as precedent plays a dominant role in American law, the number of published court cases will continue to grow. Always check local court rules before using unpublished cases as authority.

2. National Reporter System

The most exhaustive collection of bound court cases is in West's *National Reporter System.* The *National Reporter System,* which began in approximately 1880, is composed of numerous units that group together cases from the federal courts, state courts, and specialized courts. The *National Reporter System* is discussed in detail in Chapter 5.

---

[8] Wheaton v. Peters, 33 U.S. (8 Pet.) 591 (1834). *See also* Banks v. Manchester, 128 U.S. 244 (1988).

[9] The issue of copyright has also arisen between the two leading providers of online legal databases, particularly as it relates to the page numbers used in West Publishing Company's reporters. West Publishing Co. v. Mead Data Central, Inc., 616 F. Supp. 1571 (D. Minn. 1985) (grant of preliminary injunction on copyright issue), *aff'd,* 799 F.2d 1219 (8th Cir. 1986), *cert. denied,* 479 U.S. 1970 (1987). At the time of this litigation, the West Group was known as West Publishing Company and Mead Data Central, Inc. was the owner of LEXIS.

The issue of copyright of page numbers continues to be a hotly-contested issue with two recent decisions being at odds. Oasis Publishing Co., Inc. v. West Publishing Co., 924 F. Supp. 918 (D.Minn. 1996) (granting partial summary judgment for West's claim that it has a protectable copyright interest in the arrangement of the decisions in *Florida Cases*); Hyperlaw, Inc. v. West Publishing Co., No. 94 Civ. 0589, 1997 WL 266972 (S.D.N.Y. May 19, 1997) (copying of opinions from West's reporters does not violate West's copyright).

[10] *E.g.,* CAL. R. P. 977. The treatment on non-publication of cases in the federal courts of appeals is discussed in Chapter 4.

3. Cases on the Internet

The rapid development of the Internet provides an entirely new way to access court cases. In many instances, courts make their opinions available via the Internet simultaneously with their release to publishers. This enables individuals to obtain these cases at little or no cost and offers an exciting new means for obtaining legal information. Links to these sources are proliferating on web sites throughout the country, and any listing of them would be immediately outdated. It is best to read the professional literature relating to cases available on the Internet and to consult local libraries, especially law libraries, for the best sources to use.

A note of caution is appropriate when dealing with cases located using the Internet. These cases lack the editorial enhancements and the sophisticated search engines found with other electronic sources. Most often only the most recent cases are available, as there has been very little effort to provide retrospective coverage. Some Internet sources containing court cases are entirely reliable. However, there are also sources where the cases have not been carefully proofread, the arrangement is difficult to discern, and a newer, recently-edited version will replaced an older one. When citation to legal authority is critical, the Internet, in general, is not yet reliable or stable enough to assure lasting accuracy. Still it is a wonderful development that will, most certainly, improve over time. Chapters 4 and 5 contain more detailed discussion of court cases available on the Internet.

SECTION D. THE ELEMENTS OF JUDICIAL REPORTING

Several methods are used in publishing court cases. Generally, the order of their release is determined by their decision dates and not by other arrangements, such as subject. In states that still publish official reports, cases may be published separately as *slip opinions* soon after they are decided. Usually, each *slip opinion* is paged separately, contains no syllabus, and is not indexed.

The more common method of publishing cases is first as *advance sheets*. These pamphlets contain numerous recently-decided cases, are consecutively paged, are published as quickly as they can be assembled after the decisions are rendered, and when sufficient in size (typically three to five issues) are cumulated into a bound volume that uses the same page numbers as the *advance sheets*. These techniques permit prompt, permanent citations to cases. The features of the cases in the *advance sheets* are identical with those included in bound volumes. Some jurisdictions do not publish *advance sheets*. Online sources, of course, merge new cases with existing ones and, thus, can often eliminate the need for *slip opinions* and *advance sheets*.

1. Features of Bound Volumes of Reports

As indicated previously, cases are ultimately cumulated in bound volumes or incorporated into online versions. The bound volumes include most of the following significant features:

a. A table of cases contained in the volume.

b. A table of statutes interpreted in the cases reported in the volume.

c. Various types of opinions: (1) written by a judge (majority, plurality, dissenting, or concurring); (2) *per curiam;* and (3) memorandum.

d. The cases are cumulated from advance sheets and have the same volume and page numbers as the advance sheets.

e. Table of cases decided without opinions.

f. Subject index or digest of the cases reported.

g. Judicial definition of words and phrases used in the cases reported.

h. Changes in court rules.

i. A list of all judges sitting on the courts covered by the volume.

j. Unofficial reports generally contain cross-reference tables to the official reports.

SECTION E. ORGANIZATION OF COURT REPORTS

Court reports are organized in several different ways:

1. By Jurisdiction

The cases of a particular court are issued chronologically in a numbered series, such as the *New York Reports* or the *Illinois Appellate Court Reports* or the *United States Reports*. In some instances, the reports of both the highest state court and its intermediate appellate court are published in the same set of reports, such as in the *California Reporter*.

2. By Geography

The cases of a group of geographically adjacent states are published in one set of reports such as the *North Western Reporter,* which includes cases from the appellate courts of Iowa, Michigan, Minnesota, Nebraska, North Dakota, South Dakota, and Wisconsin. These various geographical groupings are discussed in Chapter 5.

3. By Subject

Standard sets of law reports contain cases arranged chronologically, and each volume may contain cases on subjects ranging from A to Z. Examples of these subject reports are *Labor Law Reports, United States Tax Reporter,* and *United States Patents Quarterly.*

SECTION F.　ILLUSTRATIONS

[Illustration 3–1]

BASIC COURT STRUCTURE IN THE UNITED STATES

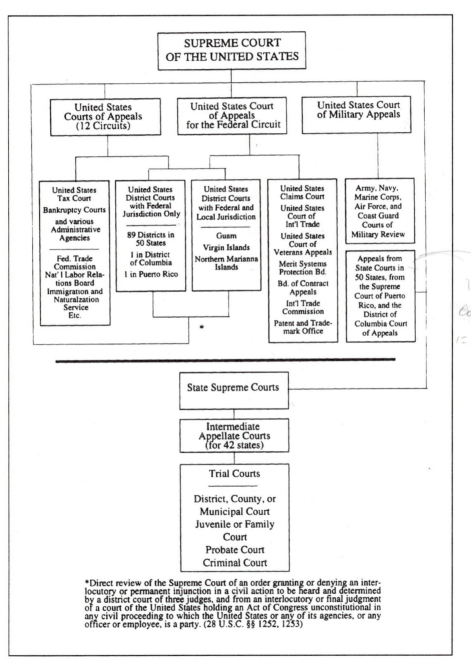

[Illustration 3–2]

A TYPICAL CASE AS REPORTED IN AN OFFICIAL SET
OF STATE COURT REPORTS (308 ARK. 439)

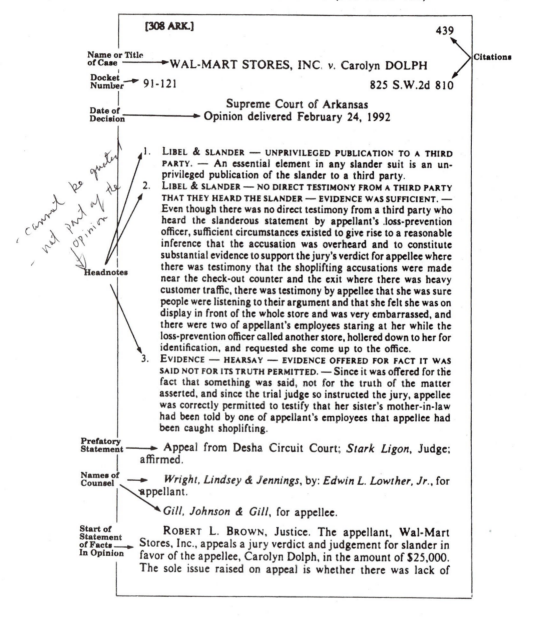

[308 ARK.]   439

Name or Title of Case → WAL-MART STORES, INC. *v.* Carolyn DOLPH   Citations

Docket Number → 91-121   825 S.W.2d 810

Supreme Court of Arkansas

Date of Decision → Opinion delivered February 24, 1992

— cannot be quoted — not part of the opinion

1. LIBEL & SLANDER — UNPRIVILEGED PUBLICATION TO A THIRD PARTY. — An essential element in any slander suit is an unprivileged publication of the slander to a third party.

2. LIBEL & SLANDER — NO DIRECT TESTIMONY FROM A THIRD PARTY THAT THEY HEARD THE SLANDER — EVIDENCE WAS SUFFICIENT. — Even though there was no direct testimony from a third party who heard the slanderous statement by appellant's loss-prevention officer, sufficient circumstances existed to give rise to a reasonable inference that the accusation was overheard and to constitute substantial evidence to support the jury's verdict for appellee where there was testimony that the shoplifting accusations were made near the check-out counter and the exit where there was heavy customer traffic, there was testimony by appellee that she was sure people were listening to their argument and that she felt she was on display in front of the whole store and was very embarrassed, and there were two of appellant's employees staring at her while the loss-prevention officer called another store, hollered down to her for identification, and requested she come up to the office.

Headnotes →

3. EVIDENCE — HEARSAY — EVIDENCE OFFERED FOR FACT IT WAS SAID NOT FOR ITS TRUTH PERMITTED. — Since it was offered for the fact that something was said, not for the truth of the matter asserted, and since the trial judge so instructed the jury, appellee was correctly permitted to testify that her sister's mother-in-law had been told by one of appellant's employees that appellee had been caught shoplifting.

Prefatory Statement → Appeal from Desha Circuit Court; *Stark Ligon*, Judge; affirmed.

Names of Counsel → *Wright, Lindsey & Jennings*, by: *Edwin L. Lowther, Jr.*, for appellant.

Gill, Johnson & Gill, for appellee.

Start of Statement of Facts In Opinion → ROBERT L. BROWN, Justice. The appellant, Wal-Mart Stores, Inc., appeals a jury verdict and judgement for slander in favor of the appellee, Carolyn Dolph, in the amount of $25,000. The sole issue raised on appeal is whether there was lack of

[Illustration 3–3]

LAST PAGE OF OPINION, 308 ARK. 439, 443

[308 ARK.]   WAL-MART STORES, INC. v. DOLPH   443
Cite as 308 Ark. 439 (1992)

the testimony of Ms. Dolph as to what someone else told her — and you heard the linkage of where it came from — is not being offered for the truth of what Ms. Dolph said was told to Ms. Dolph, but merely for the purpose of showing that she did, in fact, receive some information, whether true or not. And my instruction to you is, you are not to consider it as being given or stated here for the truth of what Ms. Dolph said, but merely to show that she heard something.

Wal-Mart argues that the circuit court erred in permitting what amounted to triple hearsay into evidence. We do not agree.

Portion of Opinion

The Eighth Circuit Court of Appeals resolved a similar question in a libel case and held that the testimony in question was not hearsay. *See Luster* v. *Retail Credit Company*, 575 F.2d 609 (8th Cir. 1978). In *Luster*, the plaintiff sued Retail Credit for a false statement made in a credit report which suggested arson on the plaintiff's premises. To prove publication, plaintiff used the testimony of a third-party insurance agent who heard from a deceased agent that a Dallas insurance firm believed Retail Credit's report implied arson. A hearsay objection was made and rejected by the trial court which gave a limiting instruction at the time of the disputed testimony. The Eighth Circuit affirmed the trial court's ruling on the basis that the testimony was admitted solely to prove the fact that the words were said — not to prove that they were true.

[3]   The Eighth Circuit's reasoning in *Luster* is persuasive in this case which involves a comparable publication issue. Here, the testimony of the sister's mother-in-law about what the Wal-Mart employee said was not offered to prove the truth of what was said. It was offered to prove *the fact* that it was said, which then became some evidence of publication. The distinction is an important one, and we hold that the circuit court's ruling with the corollary instruction to the jury was appropriate in this case.

Decision ➤ Affirmed.

DUDLEY, J., not participating.

= "Justice"

[Illustration 3–4]

A TYPICAL CASE AS REPORTED IN A SET OF UNOFFICIAL REPORTS, 825 S.W.2d (SAME CASE AS 308 ARK. 439)

810 Ark.   **825 SOUTH WESTERN REPORTER, 2d SERIES**

308 Ark. 439

WAL–MART STORES, INC., Appellant,

v.

Carolyn DOLPH, Appellee.

No. 91–121.

Supreme Court of Arkansas.

Feb. 24, 1992.

Customer brought suit against store for slander. The Desha County Circuit Court, Stark Ligon, J., rendered judgment for customer, and store appealed. The Supreme Court, Brown, J., held that: (1) there was sufficient evidence of publication, and (2) trial court did not permit inadmissible hearsay to support publication argument.

Affirmed.

1. Libel and Slander ⟲1

Central element in any slander suit is unprivileged publication of slander to third party.

2. Libel and Slander ⟲112(1)

Although there was no direct testimony from any third party who heard slanderous statement by store's loss-prevention officer that customer had been apprehended for shoplifting in another town the week before, sufficient circumstances existed to give rise to reasonable inference that officer's accusation was overheard and thus "published"; there was testimony of shoplifting accusations made by officer within a few feet of check-out counter and exit where there was heavy customer traffic and further testimony by customer that she was sure people were listening to the argument.

3. Evidence ⟲267

In customer's slander suit against store, customer's testimony that her sister's mother-in-law had been told by store employee that customer had been caught shoplifting was not hearsay; testimony was not offered to prove truth of what was said, but to prove fact that it was said, which then became some evidence of publication.

Edwin Lowther, Jr., Samuel Bird, Monticello, for appellant.

Brooks A. Gill, Dumas, for appellee.

BROWN, Justice.

The appellant, Wal–Mart Stores, Inc., appeals a jury verdict and judgment for slander in favor of the appellee, Carolyn Dolph, in the amount of $25,000. The sole issue raised on appeal is whether there was lack of sufficient proof of publication of the slander. We hold that there was substantial evidence of publication to support the judgment, and we affirm it.

The events leading to the complaint occurred on June 16, 1989, at the Wal–Mart

> This is the same case as shown in Illustrations 3-2 & 3-3 as it appears in the *South Western Reporter 2d*, an unofficial set of court reports.
>
> The prefatory statement and headnotes to the left in this Illustration are prepared by the publisher's editorial staff. Note that these are *not* the same as in the official *Arkansas Reports*.
>
> Although the material preceding the opinion of the court may vary in the unofficial hard copy reports and computer-retrievable versions from that in the official reports, the text of the opinion itself is identical. [See Illustration 3-5.]
>
> The differences between the official and unofficial reports, as well as other features of court reports, are further discussed in Chapters 4, 5, and 6.
>
> See Appendix B for a list of states that have discontinued their official reports.

that she was not free to leave. McNeely then requested that Dolph come up to the office, but she refused and asked to see the manager. It turned out that McNeely was in error and that Dolph's sister—not

[Illustration 3–5]

LAST PAGE OF 825 S.W.2d 810, 812

812 Ark.   825 SOUTH WESTERN REPORTER, 2d SERIES

heavy customer traffic. There was further testimony by Dolph that she was sure people were listening to the argument between McNeely and her. She was on display in front of the whole store, Dolph stated, and was very embarrassed. Two Wal–Mart employees were specifically staring at her, Dolph testified, while McNeely was contacting the McGehee store and, then, hollering down at her for identification, and requesting that she come up to the office. We can make no clear distinction between this case and the foreign authorities cited above. The circumstances here were both sufficient to raise a reasonable inference of publication and also constitute substantial evidence to support the jury's verdict.

[3] Wal–Mart also raises a collateral hearsay issue relating to publication. At trial, Dolph testified that her sister's mother-in-law had been told by one of the Wal–Mart employees that Dolph had been caught shoplifting. The circuit court permitted the testimony into evidence but gave the following cautionary instruction:

However, I need to instruct you that in this particular case, the testimony of Ms. Dolph as to what someone else told her— and you heard the linkage of where it came from—is not being offered for the truth of what Ms. Dolph said was told to Ms. Dolph, but merely for the purpose of showing that she did, in fact, receive some information, whether true or not. And my instruction to you is, you are not to consider it as being given or stated here for the truth of what Ms. Dolph said, but merely to show that she heard something.

Wal–Mart argues that the circuit court erred in permitting what amounted to triple hearsay into evidence. We do not agree.

The Eighth Circuit Court of Appeals resolved a similar question in a libel case and held that the testimony in question was not hearsay. *See Luster v. Retail Credit Company,* 575 F.2d 609 (8th Cir.1978). In *Luster,* the plaintiff sued Retail Credit for a false statement made in a credit report which suggested arson on the plaintiff's premises. To prove publication, plaintiff used the testimony of a third-party insur-

ance agent who heard from a deceased agent that a Dallas insurance firm believed Retail Credit's report implied arson. A hearsay objection was made and rejected by the trial court which gave a limiting instruction at the time of the disputed testimony. The Eighth Circuit affirmed the trial court's ruling on the basis that the testimony was admitted solely to prove the fact that the words were said—not to prove that they were true.

The Eighth Circuit's reasoning in *Luster* is persuasive in this case which involves a comparable publication issue. Here, the testimony of the sister's mother-in-law about what the Wal–Mart employee said was not offered to prove the truth of what was said. It was offered to prove *the fact* that it was said, which then became some evidence of publication. The distinction is an important one, and we hold that the circuit court's ruling with the corollary instruction to the jury was appropriate in this case.

Affirmed.

DUDLEY, J., not participating.

> **Compare this Illustration with Illustration 3-3. Note that all of page 443 of the *Arkansas Reports* (vol. 309) is contained on page 812 of the *South Western Reporter 2d* (vol. 825) and that the opinion in both sources is identical.**

[Illustration 3–6]

TYPICAL STATUTORY PROVISIONS FOR PUBLICATION OF COURT REPORTS

Excerpts from West's Ann. Calif. Gov't Code

§ 68902. Publication of reports: Supervision by Supreme Court

Such opinions of the Supreme Court, of the courts of appeal, and of the appellate departments of the superior courts as the Supreme Court may deem expedient shall be published in the official reports. The reports shall be published under the general supervision of the Supreme Court.

Excerpts from McKinney's Consol. Laws of N.Y. Ann. Judiciary Law

§ 430. Law reporting bureau; state reporter

There is hereby created and established the law reporting bureau of the state of New York. The bureau shall be under the direction and control of a state reporter, who shall be appointed and be removable by the court of appeals by an order entered in its minutes. The state reporter shall be assisted by a first deputy state reporter and such other deputy state reporters and staff as may be necessary, all of whom shall be appointed and be removable by the court of appeals.

§ 431. Causes to be reported

The law reporting bureau shall report every cause determined in the court of appeals and every cause determined in the appellate divisions of the supreme court, unless otherwise directed by the court deciding the cause; and, in addition, any cause determined in any other court which the reporter, with the approval of the court of appeals, considers worthy of being reported because of its usefulness as a precedent or its importance as a matter of public interest.

Excerpts from Vernon's Ann. Mo. Stat.

§ 477.231. Designation of private publication as official reports

The supreme court may declare the published volumes of the decisions of the supreme court as the same are published by any person, firm or corporation, to be official reports of the decisions of the supreme court, and the courts of appeals may jointly make a similar declaration with respect to published volumes of the opinions of the courts of appeals. Any publication so designated as the official reports may include both the opinions of the supreme court and the courts of appeals in the same volume.

SECTION G. ABBREVIATIONS AND CITATIONS OF COURT REPORTS

Court reports are published in numbered sets,[11] with the name of the set reflected in its title; for example, *Illinois Reports* (opinions of the

---

[11] The first American cases were reported by private reporters and are cited to the name of the reporter. In Michigan, for example, the first volume of court reports was reported by

Illinois Supreme Court) or *United States Reports* (opinions of the Supreme Court of the United States) or *Oil and Gas Reporter* (opinions from all U.S. jurisdictions dealing with the law of oil and gas). In all legal writing it is customary when referring to a court case to give both the name of the case and its citation in the appropriate court reports. But rather than citing to, for example, *Volume 132 of the Illinois Reports for the case starting at page 238,* a citation is given using a standard format and a standard abbreviation for the set of reports, *e.g.,* 132 Ill. 238, or 498 U.S. 103, or 18 Oil & Gas Rep. 1083.

It is extremely important in any legal writing to give a complete citation to the source or sources relied on in reaching one's conclusions. Tables of Abbreviations should be consulted for the proper method of abbreviation; and citation manuals for proper form of citation.[12]

To enable researchers to find and give citations to slip opinions and unreported cases, both WESTLAW and LEXIS–NEXIS provide a standard format for citation to recent cases and administrative decisions contained in their databases. These formats are called WESTLAW Cites and LEXIS–NEXIS Cites, respectively. In addition, WESTLAW includes in its online version of cases *star pagination* to the page numbers of cases appearing in West's *National Reporter System* and in the official *United States Reports*. Through a licensing agreement with West, LEXIS–NEXIS also has added *star pagination* to its databases for West's *National Reporter System*. *Star pagination* enables one to find where the language in the print version appears in the online version.

An extensive Table of Abbreviations with reference to the full name of court reports is set forth in Appendix A. Legal citation form is the subject of Chapter 23; computer-assisted legal research is discussed in Chapter 22.

SECTION H. SUMMARY

To facilitate learning the essential features of the significant publications described in this and subsequent chapters, a summary is provided in the last section of some chapters. The summaries are generally arranged with the following points in mind: (1) scope—indicating coverage by subject matter and chronology, if any; (2) arrangements—for example, alphabetically by subject, by names or titles, or by chronology (following a time sequence); (3) index; and (4) supplementation.

Douglass and is cited as 1 Doug. The practice of citing to names or nominative reporters ceased in most jurisdictions during the middle of the nineteenth century.

[12] There is no universally accepted table of abbreviations or manual of citations. In addition to those abbreviations contained in Appendix A, tables of abbreviations may be located in law dictionaries and in other books on legal bibliography. The most widely used citation manual is *The Bluebook: A Uniform System of Citation* (16th ed. 1996), published by the Harvard Law Review Association, Columbia Law Review, University of Pennsylvania Law Review, and Yale Law Journal. The current edition provides guidance on citing sources in electronic formats. This manual is revised every five years.

1. Reporting of Court Cases

a. Court reports are compilations of judicial cases.

b. Most court reports contain only appellate court cases; trial court cases are rarely reported.

c. Court cases are available in both hard copy and computer-retrievable versions.

d. Not all appellate court cases that are decided are published.

2. Segments of a Court Case

a. Name of the case.

b. Citation.

c. Docket number.

d. Date of decision.

e. Prefatory statement—Synopsis, or summary, of the case.

f. Syllabus or headnote—brief summary of the legal rule or significant facts in a case.

g. Names of counsel.

h. Statement of facts.

i. Opinion or opinions and elements therein.

(1) Opinion of the court—explanation of the court's decision written by a judge in the majority.

(2) Concurring opinion—opinion that agrees with the decision of the majority but disagrees with the reasoning.

(3) Plurality opinion—opinion where less than a majority join an opinion than any concurring opinion.

(4) Dissent—expressed disagreement of one or more judges of a court with the decision reached by the majority.

(5) Accord—opinion by a dissenting judge that agrees with the conclusions and results of the dissent, but not with its reasoning.

(6) *Per curiam* opinion—opinion of the majority of the court as distinguished from an opinion written by a specific judge.

(7) Memorandum opinion—a brief holding of the whole court in which the opinion (explanation) is very concise or totally absent.

(8) *Ratio decidendi*—the point in a case that determines the result.

(9) *Obiter dictum*—incidental comment made by a judge in his or her opinion, which is not necessary to the formulation of the decision nor binding as precedent.

j. Decision of the court—disposition of the case by the court.

3. Official and Unofficial Reports

a. Official reports—court reports authorized by statute or court rule.

b. Unofficial reports—court reports published without statutory authority or court direction, the most comprehensive being West's *National Reporter System*. The Internet is an increasingly important source for court cases.

4. Elements of Judicial Reporting

a. *Slip opinion*—an individual court case published separately soon after it is decided.

b. Advance sheets—pamphlets that contain the most recently decided cases by a court or the courts of several jurisdictions.

c. Order of release of cases is determined by their decision dates and not by other arrangements, such as subject.

d. A bound volume includes:

(1) Table of cases contained in the volume.

(2) Table of statutes interpreted in the cases reported in the volume.

(3) Cases cumulated from preceding advance sheets—written, *per curiam,* or memorandum.

(4) Subject index or digest of the cases reported.

(5) Judicial definitions of words and phrases used in the cases reported.

(6) Changes in court rules.

(7) A list of judges sitting on the court covered by the volume.

(8) Unofficial reports generally contain cross-reference tables to official reports and *star pagination* that show where pages in the official version appear in the unofficial version.

5. Organization of Court Reports

a. By jurisdiction. Cases of a specific court or several courts from the same state or jurisdiction and generally reported in chronological order.

b. By geography. Cases of the courts of adjacent states are reported in the same set of reports.

c. By subject. Cases only on a specific subject are included.

Chapter 4

FEDERAL COURT CASES

Section 1 of Article III of the Constitution of the United States provides that "The judicial Power of the United States, shall be vested in one supreme Court, and in such inferior Courts as the Congress may from time to time ordain and establish." Since the adoption of the Constitution in 1789, Congress has provided for various arrangements of the federal courts.[1]

Since 1880 the federal court system can be described as consisting of three main divisions: the Supreme Court of the United States (the highest court); the courts of appeals (intermediate courts); and the district courts (courts of original jurisdiction or trial courts).[2] [See Illustration 4–1 for a map of the lower federal courts.]

All written opinions of the Supreme Court of the United States are published in both official and unofficial reports. Most of its *per curiam* cases also are reported. All written opinions designated *for publication* by the courts of appeals are published in unofficial reports. Only selected cases of the federal district courts are reported unofficially. Unreported cases of the district courts generally are available through the court clerks, although the local court rules should be consulted before relying on any unreported cases as authority.

[1] CHARLES ALAN WRIGHT, THE LAW OF FEDERAL COURTS 1–8 (5th ed. 1994).

[2] For a description of the federal court system, see JAMES WILLIAM MOORE ET AL., MOORE'S FEDERAL PRACTICE §§ 0.1, 0.2 (2d ed. 1989) [hereinafter MOORE'S FEDERAL PRACTICE]. *See also* ERWIN C. SURRENCY, HISTORY OF THE FEDERAL COURTS (1987); ADMINISTRATIVE OFFICE OF THE UNITED STATES COURTS, THE UNITED STATES COURTS: THEIR JURISDICTION AND WORK (1989) [hereinafter THE UNITED STATES COURTS].

[Illustration 4–1]

GEOGRAPHICAL BOUNDARIES OF U.S. COURTS OF APPEALS AND U.S. DISTRICT COURTS
as set forth by 28 U.S.C. §§ 41, 81–131

US court of appeal   12 circuits + 1
Fed distric   district.

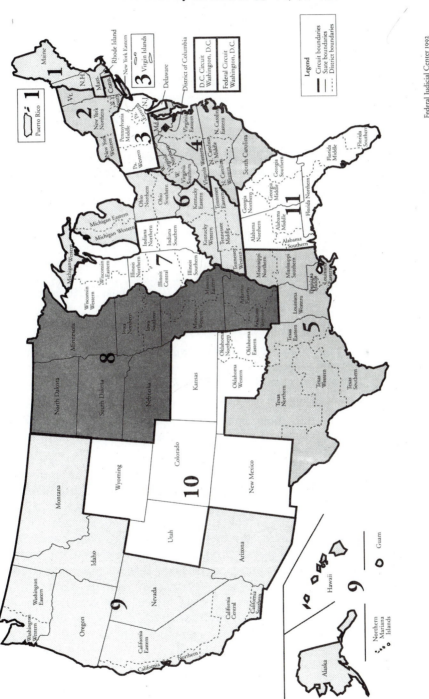

Federal Judicial Center 1992

SECTION A.   UNITED STATES SUPREME COURT REPORTS

Because of the preeminent role the Supreme Court of the United States holds in our system of jurisprudence, its discretion as to which cases it will review, and the significance of the limited cases it decides each year, access to the Court's cases is crucial. These cases are available in five current, printed sets and the two major computer-assisted legal research (CALR) services.

Bound reporters:

1. *United States Reports* (official edition) (Government Printing Office), cited *U.S.*

2. *West's Supreme Court Reporter* (West Group, formerly West Publishing Company), cited *S. Ct.* or *Sup. Ct.*

3. *United States Supreme Court Reports, Lawyers' Edition* (LEXIS Law Publishing, formerly Lawyers Cooperative Publishing), cited *L. Ed.* and *L. Ed. 2d.*

Looseleaf Reporters:

4. *United States Law Week* (Bureau of National Affairs), cited *U.S.L.W.*

Electronic Services:

5. WESTLAW, database identifier SCT for cases 1945 to date; SCT–OLD for cases 1790–1944.

6. LEXIS–NEXIS, GENFED Library, US file.

7. Internet (various sources and various scope of coverage)

1.   United States Reports (Official Edition)

The *United States Reports* are the official reports for cases decided by the Supreme Court of the United States. Prior to 1817, the *United States Reports* were published by private reporters. Since that date they have been published by official reporters.

The first 90 volumes are cited by the name of the individual ("reporter"), from Dallas through Wallace, who compiled the cases for publication. There were seven of these early reporters, and each time a new reporter was named the volume numbering began anew. Later, these volumes were renumbered consecutively from 1–90. Commencing with volume 91 (1875), the use of the name of the Reporter of Decisions of the Supreme Court for citation purposes was discontinued and consecutive numbering continued. 1 Dallas, although a volume of the *United States Reports,* contains only Pennsylvania cases. The other three volumes of Dallas contain both Supreme Court of the United States and Pennsylvania cases.[3] The seven early reporters, with their abbreviations and volumes and years of coverage, are as follows:

---

[3] Arthur John Keefe, *More Than You Want to Know About Supreme Court Reports,* 62 A.B.A. J. 1057 (1976). *See also* Craig Joyce, Wheaton v. Peters: *The Untold Story of the*

Dallas (Dall.)	4 v.	v. 1–4 U.S.	(1789–1800)
Cranch (Cranch)	9 v.	v. 5–13 U.S.	(1801–1815)
Wheaton (Wheat.)	12 v.	v. 14–25 U.S.	(1816–1827)
Peters (Pet.)	16 v.	v. 26–41 U.S.	(1828–1842)
Howard (How.)	24 v.	v. 42–65 U.S.	(1843–1860)
Black (Black)	2 v.	v. 66–67 U.S.	(1861–1862)
Wallace (Wall.)	23 v.	v. 68–90 U.S.	(1863–1874)

Until fairly recently, it was the custom of the Supreme Court of the United States to have one term that started in October and ordinarily adjourned in June or July, with special terms held "whenever necessary." The current rule, effective January 1, 1990, requires the Court to "hold a continuous annual Term commencing on the first Monday in October."

The cases decided by the Supreme Court are officially printed and sold by the United States Government Printing Office and are issued in three formats. Initially, the cases are issued separately as *slip opinions*. Typically, each includes a syllabus and summary of facts prepared by the Reporter of Decisions, is individually paged, contains no index, and is subject to correction by the Court. These *slip opinions* are subsequently compiled, assigned a volume number, and published in consecutively-paged advance sheets known as *preliminary prints*, to which an index is added.

After two or three *preliminary prints* are published, they are cumulated into a bound volume using the same volume and page numbers as in the *preliminary prints*. Three or four bound volumes are issued per term. Due to lengthy publication delays by the Government Printing Office, the *preliminary prints* are usually two to three years behind schedule. Even worse, the bound volumes run four or five years behind schedule. As a result of the slower publication schedule for the *United States Reports,* and the editorial features in the unofficial reports discussed next, most researchers prefer the unofficial versions to the official one.

Sample pages from a case in the *United States Reports* are shown in Illustrations 4–2 through 4–5.

2. West's Supreme Court Reporter

This set, a unit of West's *National Reporter System,* reproduces verbatim the text of the opinion or opinions for each Supreme Court case. The publisher then adds the many editorial features common to its other sets of law reports, *e.g.,* syllabus, headnotes, topics, and key

Early Reporters, 1985 Sup. Ct. Hist. Soc'y Y.B. 35. For a description of these early reports and the early reporters, see Morris L. Cohen & Sharon Hamby O'Connor, A Guide to the Early Reports of the Supreme Court of the United States (1995). For a listing of the opinions by individual justices, see Linda A. Blandford & Patricia Russell Evans, Supreme Court of the United States, 1789–1980: An Index to Opinions Arranged by Justice (1983). This two-volume set and a 1994 supplement lists opinions of all justices from October 1980 through 1990.

numbers. These various features are discussed in Chapters 5 and 6. *West's Supreme Court Reporter* begins with volume 106 (1882) of the official set; therefore, it does not contain the cases reported in volumes 1–105 of the official reports.

Cases are first issued in advance sheets biweekly while the Court is in session and then compiled into interim volumes while the Court is making final corrections in its opinions. Once the corrections are made, these interim volumes are replaced by three bound, permanent volumes containing all the cases of the term.[4] The volume and page numbers used in the advance sheets and the interim volumes are the same as in the later permanent volumes. Because this set uses smaller type than is used in the official reports, two or three volumes of official reports are contained in one volume of *West's Supreme Court Reporter*.

Sample pages from *West's Supreme Court Reporter* are shown in Illustrations 4–6 through 4–8.

3.   United States Supreme Court Reports, Lawyers' Edition

This set is privately published by LEXIS Law Publishing and formerly by Lawyers Cooperative Publishing and is in two series. The first series, which covers 1 U.S. through 351 U.S. (1789–1956), is in 100 volumes; the second series, which restarts its numbering with volume one, commences coverage with 350 U.S. (1956). Current cases are published twice a month in advance sheets while the Court is in session. The volume number and pagination of the advance sheets are the same as in subsequent bound volumes.

Until volume 78 of *Lawyers' Edition 2d,* two to three volumes of the official reports were in one volume of the unofficial set. The publisher then began to issue a single bound volume each time a volume of the official set was completed in advance sheet form. Both series reprint the opinions and syllabi in the *United States Reports*. These are supplemented with the editorial treatment given the cases by the publisher, including its own summary of cases and headnotes that precede the opinions.

In addition, and for selected important cases only, summaries of attorneys' briefs submitted to the Court and annotations written by the publisher's editorial staff are included in an appendix to each bound volume. Advance sheets do not contain annotations. Annotations are articles or essays on significant legal issues discussed in the reported cases. These are very useful in gaining an understanding of the impact and meaning of the cases. An increase in the number of annotations per volume occurred with volume 93 of the first series of *Lawyers' Edition.* Annotations are discussed in more detail in Chapter 7.

---

[4] Through volume 79 of *West's Supreme Court Reporter,* the volumes of the *United States Reports* covering a Term of the Court could be published in one volume of the West version. As the Court's opinions lengthened, commencing with the October 1959 Term, West began publishing the coverage of a Term in two books, *e.g.,* volumes 80 and 80A. Commencing with the October 1985 Term, coverage expanded to three books, *e.g.,* volumes 106, 106A, and 106B, owing in great part to the separate concurring and dissenting opinions issued by the justices.

A two-volume *Later Case Service* for volumes 1–31 of *Lawyers' Edition 2d,* updated with annual, cumulative pocket supplements, provides later cases relevant to the annotations in these 31 volumes. Beginning with volume 32, each volume of *Lawyers' Edition 2d* is updated with an annual pocket supplement in the back of each volume.

This supplement is in three parts: (1) *Citator Service,* consisting of brief summaries of the pertinent holdings from Supreme Court opinions subsequent to those reported in the volume; (2) *Later Case Service,* supplementing the annotations in the volume; and (3) *Court Corrections,* consisting of any corrections made by the Court after the bound *Lawyers' Edition* volumes were published.

Starting with volume 114, an interim edition of each bound volume of L. Ed. 2d is issued. These interim volumes, bound in black, replace the corresponding advance sheet pamphlets. The interim volumes are updated by pocket supplements, including *Citator Service* material for the cases in each volume and *Later Case Service* materials for the annotations. The interim volumes then are replaced by final bound volumes after about two years. These final bound volumes, three per term, include all court-approved corrections, official reporter pagination, summaries of the briefs, and full listing of counsel. The *Citator Service* and the *Later Case Service* is transferred from the interim volume to the final volume when the final volume is published.

A six-volume *General Index* (also published as part of *United States Supreme Court Digest, Lawyers' Edition* discussed in Chapter 6) provides a comprehensive topical index to cases decided by the Supreme Court of the United States. This index also includes a Table of Justices, statutory table, and a history table of past annotations. An annual *Quick Case Table* pamphlet contains an alphabetically-arranged table of cases for all the Court's decisions accompanied by opinions. It also includes references to annotations in *Lawyers' Edition 2d*[5] and the various *A.L.R.* series.

Sample pages from the *United States Supreme Court Reports, Lawyers' Edition 2d* are shown in Illustrations 4–9 and 4–10.

4. United States Law Week

Because cases decided by the Supreme Court of the United States are *the law of the land* and must be followed as precedent by all other American courts, both federal and state, it is obvious that lawyers, as well as lay persons, need immediate access to the Court's most recently-decided cases. Before cases can be published in the advance sheets mentioned previously, they must receive editorial treatment, such as preparation of the summary and the headnotes and then await enough cases to constitute a pamphlet, resulting in a delay of several weeks from the date a case is decided until it appears in an advance sheet.

---

[5] The *ALR Index,* discussed in Chapter 7, also indexes these annotations.

More rapid access to current Supreme Court of the United States cases is available through the *United States Law Week*, published by the Bureau of National Affairs. The publisher receives the slip opinions on the day they are handed down, reproduces them, and mails them promptly to subscribers. These Supreme Court cases have few editorial features added to them, but they do allow cases to become available within a week or less after they are released by the Court and are most helpful for use during the current term. For older cases, it is preferable to use one of the three other sets previously discussed. *Law Week* consists of two looseleaf binders, and in July 1997 this publication underwent a complete redesign.

The heart of *Law Week* is the "Case Alert," which contains in the first two pages access to the issue's entire contents in alphabetic topical abstracts. This is followed by one paragraph case descriptions complemented by context and analysis provided by the publisher's editorial staff of each selected case. Full-text access is provided through a link to BNA's Web site. The "Legal News" component gives analysis of selected pre-decisional developments and non-judicial, non-case-oriented legal news utilizing information in more than 100 specialized publications. A "General Topical Index" is provided for these two components.

The third component is "Supreme Court Today." It includes a print edition of each week's Supreme Court proceedings and opinions, with a separate "Supreme Court Index." A supplemental electronic component provides both "near real time notice and text" of every Supreme Court action, including opinions, and a powerful, fully-searchable archive. The "Supreme Court Today" component includes the following valuable features:

(a) Summary of Orders: A summary of cases acted upon, as well as the lower court holdings that the Supreme Court consented to review, together with the questions presented for review by those cases.

(b) Journal of Proceedings: The minutes of all sessions of the Court held during the week.

(c) Cases Docketed: Includes citations to cases decided in the lower courts and to be heard by the Supreme Court, and the general subject matter of the cases.

(d) Summary of Cases Recently Filed.

(e) Hearings Scheduled: Includes docket number, caption, and brief statement of issues presented.

(f) Arguments Before the Court: A summary of the oral arguments of the more important cases argued each week.

(g) Table of Cases and Case Status Report: Issued every three to four weeks. For most cases the user can determine the status of a case by consulting this table.

(h) Topical Index: Published at the outset of the Court's term and cumulated at frequent intervals, with a final cumulative index published shortly after the Court's last session of the term.

5. Electronic Access to Opinions

Both WESTLAW and LEXIS–NEXIS provide online access to the text of cases decided by the Supreme Court of the United States much faster than any of the publications discussed previously. The text of each case decided by the Court is transmitted electronically from the Court to these two information vendors almost simultaneously with the decision being announced from the bench. These cases frequently are available in these online sources within a day, and typically within a few hours, after being decided.

Later, when the *United States Reports* and *West's Supreme Court Reporter* are published, both vendors add *star pagination* to the text of the opinions in order for users to locate where the exact pages of these reporters appear on the screen. WESTLAW and LEXIS–NEXIS both provide comprehensive coverage dating from the Court's first term in 1790 to the present. In addition, *West's Supreme Court Reporter,* a part of the West CD–ROM Libraries family, covers from 1789 forward by including both the official *United States Reports* (volumes 1–105) and the complete *West's Supreme Court Reporter.* LEXIS Law Publishing also provides a CD–ROM product, *Federal Law on Disc,* which includes complete Supreme Court coverage. Both CD–ROM products can be updated through a subscription to the corresponding CALR service.

Project Hermes, begun by the Supreme Court of the United States in 1990, transmits opinions to WESTLAW and LEXIS–NEXIS, wire services, and an educational consortium simultaneous with issuance of the opinion from the bench. As a result of the consortium arrangement, these Supreme Court cases are available through the Internet from *lii hermes,* a project of the Legal Information Institute of Cornell University [See Illustration 4–11], *Federal Court Locator,* a joint initiative of the Villanova University School of Law and the Illinois Institute of Technology's Chicago–Kent College of Law [See Illustration 4–12], and numerous other sites often with links from the two sources just mentioned.

6. Chambers Opinions of the Supreme Court Justices

Each Supreme Court Justice is assigned at the beginning of each term the supervision of one or more federal judicial circuits. Frequently, when the Supreme Court is not in session, a petition may be directed to a Justice in his or her capacity as Circuit Justice. An opinion resulting from such a petition is known as a *Chamber Opinion.* Before the 1970 Term, these chambers opinions appeared only in *Lawyers' Edition* and *West's Supreme Court Reporter.* Starting with the 1970 Term, they also appear in the official *United States Reports.*[6] They are included as well in *United States Law Week* and WESTLAW and LEXIS–NEXIS.

---

[6] Robert L. Stern et al., Supreme Court Practice 647–48 (7th ed. 1993) [hereinafter Supreme Court Practice]. *See also* Frederick Bernays Wiener, *Opinions of Justices Sitting*

7. Preview of United States Supreme Court Cases

The *Preview of United States Supreme Court Cases,* published by the American Bar Association's Public Education Division, is not a reporter, but rather is composed of essays written by scholars on selected cases pending on the Court's calendar, but not yet argued. These essays provide excellent background and analysis of the cases the Court subsequently will decide.

8. Citing United States Supreme Court Cases

Proper citation practice calls for citing only to *United States Reports* after these are published. Therefore, the unofficial reporters, *West's Supreme Court Reporter* and *United States Supreme Court Reports, Lawyers' Edition,* which have their own distinct pagination, also show the pagination of the official reports in order for the proper citation to be made to the *United States Reports.* Like that used by the online services, this is known as *star pagination.* Both the *Supreme Court Reporter* and *Lawyers' Edition* include in each volume a cross-reference table listing the cases in the *United States Reports* and showing where they are reported in their volumes.

SECTION B. LOWER FEDERAL COURT REPORTS

Although the Supreme Court of the United States is our country's highest court, it deals with only a small fraction of the total litigation within the federal court system. With certain exceptions, the Supreme Court selects only the cases it wishes to hear on appeal,[7] and these are relatively few in number. The bulk of the work of the federal courts occurs in the trial courts, *i.e.,* the federal district courts, and in the appeals from them to the United States courts of appeals. These appellate courts are divided geographically into twelve circuits, plus the United States Court of Appeals for the Federal Circuit. Each state and U.S. territory has one or more federal district courts. [See Illustration 4–1.]

In addition, there are federal courts with limited or specialized jurisdiction. The more important of these are the United States Court of Federal Claims,[8] the United States Court of Appeals for the Federal Circuit (mentioned above),[9] and the United States Tax Court.[10]

---

in Chambers, 49 Law Libr. J. 2 (1956); Marian Boner, *Index to Chambers Opinions of Supreme Court Justices,* 65 Law Libr. J. 213 (1972).

[7] Technically, cases reach the Supreme Court either by writ of *certiorari* or by appeal. *See* Supreme Court Practice, *supra* note 6.

[8] This court, originally named the United States Claims Court, was created by the Federal Courts Improvement Act of 1982, Pub. L. No. 97–164, 96 Stat. 25, effective on October 1, 1982. The United States Claims Court was renamed the United States Court of Federal Claims, as a result of certain provisions of the Federal Courts Administration Act of 1992, Pub. L. No. 102–572, 106 Stat. 4506, effective October 29, 1992.

[9] This court was created by Pub. L. No. 97–164, 96 Stat. 25, effective on October 1, 1982. It is a merger of the Court of U.S. Customs and Patent Appeals and the appellate division

1. Privately Published Editions of the Lower Federal Court Reports

Only a few sets of official reports are published for lower federal court cases, and these are for specialized courts only. No official reports are published exclusively for cases of the federal district courts and the United States courts of appeals. West assumed the responsibility for publishing cases decided by these courts, primarily through the federal units of its *National Reporter System,* and until the arrival of CALR systems, West's reporters were the only comprehensive sources for these cases. These various West publications are discussed in this section. Additional information as to coverage is provided in Appendix C.

a. *Federal Cases.* Prior to 1880 and the development of the *National Reporter System,* the cases decided by the district courts and the circuit courts of appeals were published in many different sets of law reports. In the mid–1890s, West reprinted all previously reported lower federal court cases in one set of 31 volumes called *Federal Cases.* This set contains 18,313 cases reported between 1789 and 1879, accompanied by brief notes (annotations) to the cases. Unlike most sets of court reports, where the cases are arranged chronologically, the cases in this set are arranged alphabetically by case name and are numbered consecutively. Cases are cited by number. Volume 31 is the Digest volume and includes Blue Tables that cross reference from the citations of the original volumes of reports to *Federal Cases.*

Approximately 15 years before the compilation of *Federal Cases,* West commenced publication of its *National Reporter System,* which has grown to several units over the years. The features of these various units include the use of topic and key numbers and the issuance of cases first in advance sheets that are later cumulated into bound volumes that have the same volume and page numbers as the advance sheets. The remaining portions of this Section B–1 detail the content of the various federal units and an alerting service valuable for most recent case information. Broad discussion of the uses of and features in the *National Reporter System* are discussed in Chapter 5.

b. *Federal Reporter.* The *Federal Reporter* began in 1880. Although the *Federal Reporter* has contained cases from various federal courts over the years, it is most important to remember that it contains the cases of the United States Courts of Appeals (formerly the U.S. Circuit Courts of Appeals) from their organization in 1891, federal district court cases until 1932 when the *Federal Supplement* was started, and the Temporary Emergency Court of Appeals from 1972 to 1993. Cases from other federal courts that have since been abolished or reorganized are also included in the *Federal Reporter,* namely the United States Circuit Court, Commerce Court of the United States, United States Emergency

of the U.S. Court of Claims. For additional information on this court, see THE UNITED STATES COURT OF APPEALS FOR THE FEDERAL CIRCUIT: A HISTORY 1982–1990 (1991).

[10] For a more detailed description of specialized federal courts, see THE UNITED STATES COURTS, *supra* note 2; MOORE'S FEDERAL PRACTICE §§ 0.1, 0.2, *supra* note 2.

Court of Appeals, the United States Court of Claims, and the United States Court of Customs and Patents Appeals.[11]

The *Federal Reporter* is in three series. The First Series stopped with Volume 300 in 1924. The Second Series, consisting of volumes 1–999, covers cases reported in 1924 and continues coverage into 1993. The Third Series began in the fall of 1993.[12]

Under current practice, only those cases that are ordered to be published by the federal courts of appeals are included in the *Federal Reporter 2d* and *3d*. All of these courts have rules restricting the number of published cases.[13] To let researchers know the cases that were decided without written published opinions, the *Federal Reporter 2d* and *3d* periodically contain a list of *Decisions without Published Opinions*. [See Illustration 4–13.]

c. *Federal Supplement*. This set began in 1932 when West decided to cease including the federal district court cases and United States Court of Claims cases (from Volumes 1 to 181) in the *Federal Reporter* and to include them in this additional reporter. Coverage of United States Court of Claims cases returned to the *Federal Reporter* in 1960.

Since these are the trial courts within the federal court system, the cases reported in the *Federal Supplement* are exceptions to the general rule that only appellate court cases are reported. It must be emphasized, however, that only a very small percentage of the cases heard in the federal district courts are ever reported in the *Federal Supplement*. The

---

[11] Cases from the United States Court of Customs and Patents Appeals were reported in the *Federal Reporter,* beginning with volume 34 of the Second Series, until the court was abolished October 1, 1982. The function of that court, as well as that of the appellate division of the former United States Court of Claims, was transferred to the United States Court of Appeals for the Federal Circuit, whose cases are included in the *Federal Reporter. See supra* note 9 for additional information pertaining to this particular court.

[12] West provided very little by way of explanation as to why a *Federal Reporter 3d* started after almost seventy years and volume 999 of *Federal Reporter 2d*, other than to say it was "to avoid potential confusion that could arise from a four-digit case volume citation." Matthew Goldstein, *68 Years, 999 Volumes of F.2d End as New Era of F.3d Begins*, N.Y. L.J., October 14, 1993, at 1. No change in format or coverage occurred in this new series. Obviously, having volume numbers that are less than four digits in length saves, over an extended period of time, a tremendous amount of space in both printed citations and electronic storage.

[13] For discussion of these policies, see David Dunn, Note, *Unreported Decisions in the United States Courts of Appeals*, 63 CORNELL L. REV. 128 (1977); William L. Reynolds & William M. Richman, *The Non–Precedential Precedent—Limited Publication and No-Citation Rules in the United States Courts of Appeals*, 78 COLUM. L. REV. 1167 (1978); William L. Reynolds & William M. Richman, *An Evaluation of Limited Publication in the United States Courts of Appeals: The Price of Reform*, 48 U. CHI. L. REV. 573 (1981); Donald R. Songer, *Criteria for Publication of Opinions in the U.S. Courts of Appeals: Formal Rules Versus Empirical Reality*, 73 JUDICATURE 307 (1990); Martha J. Dragich, *Will the Federal Courts of Appeals Perish If They Publish? Or Does the Declining Use of Opinions to Explain and Justify Judicial Decisions Pose a Greater Threat?*, 44 AM. U.L. REV. 757 (1995); Ellen Platt, *Unpublished vs. Unreported: What's the Difference?*, 5 PERSPECTIVES: TEACHING LEG. RES. & WRIT. 26 (1996). *See also supra* Chapter 3, notes 3 and 4.

decision whether or not to publish is made by the judge writing the opinion.

The *Federal Supplement,* in addition to its federal district court coverage, also reports cases of the United States Court of International Trade since 1980, from the United States Customs Court from 1956 to 1980 when it was replaced by the United States Court of International Trade, the Special Court under the Regional Rail Reorganization Act of 1973, and the Judicial Panel on Multidistrict Litigation since its inception in 1969.

Some cases not reported in the *Federal Supplement* may be printed in the subject reporters of other publications (discussed in Chapter 14) or may be available online.

d. *Federal Rules Decisions.* This set contains cases of the federal district courts since 1939 that construe the Federal Rules of Civil Procedure and cases since 1946 decided under the Rules of Criminal Procedure. These cases are not published in the *Federal Supplement.* Similar to other units of the *National Reporter System, F.R.D.* is issued in advance sheets and bound volumes, with headnotes that are classified to West's *Key Number System.* In addition to court cases, it also includes articles on various aspects of federal courts and federal procedure. A cumulative index to these articles is in every tenth volume, and a consolidated index for volumes 1–122 is in volume 122.

e. *Military Justice Reporter.* This set, which began in 1975, is the successor to the U.S. Court of Military Appeals *Decisions* and the *Court–Martial Reports* (1951–1975) by other publishers. This reporter includes cases of the United States Court of Military Appeals and the Courts of Military Review of the Army, Navy–Marine Corps, Air Force, and Coast Guard.

f. *Bankruptcy Reporter.* This set began in 1980 as a result of major changes in the bankruptcy laws enacted in 1978.[14] It reports cases from the United States Bankruptcy Courts and those cases from the federal district courts that deal with bankruptcy matters, no longer including these in the *Federal Supplement.* The *Bankruptcy Reporter* also reprints bankruptcy cases appearing in *West's Supreme Court Reporter* and *Federal Reporter 2d* and *3d,* retaining the paginations of these reporters.

g. *Federal Claims Reporter.* This set is a continuation of the *United States Claims Court Reporter,* which began in 1983 as a reporter of cases of the United States Claims Court, a trial-level federal court created in 1982. When the name of the United States Claims Court was changed to the United States Court of Federal Claims in 1992,[15] the *United States Claims Court Reporter* was renamed the *Federal Claims Reporter,* commencing with volume 27. This reporter also includes reprints from the *Federal Reporter 2d* and *3d* and *West's Supreme Court Reporter* of those cases that have reviewed cases of the United States Claims Court.

[14] Bankruptcy Reform Act of 1978, Pub.L. No. 95–598, 92 Stat. 2549.

[15] *See supra* note 8.

h. *West's Veterans Appeals Reporter.* Begun in October 1991, this set contains cases decided in the United States Court of Veterans Appeals[16] and cases of the United States Court of Appeals, Federal Circuit and the Supreme Court of the United States, which hear appeals from the decisions of the Court of Veterans Appeals.

I. *West's Federal Case News.* This is a weekly pamphlet, not a reporter, that summarizes recently-decided federal cases even before they are published in advance sheets. This alerting service includes the case name, court, judge deciding the case, filing date, docket number, and the essential points of the case.

2.   Officially Published Reports of Special Federal Courts

Cases Decided in the United States Court of Claims. Washington, Government Printing Office, 1863–1982. v. 1–231.

United States Court of International Trade Reports. Washington, Government Printing Office, 1980 to date. v. 1 *et seq.* This court was formerly the United States Customs Court, and its cases were reported in *United States Custom Court Reports,* 1938–1980, v. 1–85.

Reports of the United States Tax Court. Washington, Government Printing Office, Oct. 1942 to date. v. 1 *et seq.*

Cases Decided in the United States Court of Appeals for the Federal Circuit. Washington, Government Printing Office, 1982 to date. v. 1 *et seq.*

3.   Electronic Access

Both WESTLAW and LEXIS–NEXIS provide comprehensive, full-text coverage of published federal cases, including the various specialized federal courts. These cases are made available online with ever-increasing speed, and always prior to their publication in advance sheets. In addition, these two services include many cases found in looseleaf services and other publications but that may never be published in a West reporter. For these cases, the two services note at the start of the online version that this case may not be appropriate to rely on as authority. Both the West Group and LEXIS Law Publishing also make available a library collection of federal court opinions on CD–ROM.

In mid–1993, all federal courts of appeals began offering electronic public access via a bulletin board to their slip opinions through a system known either as Appellate Court Electronic Services (ACES) or Electronic Dissemination of Opinions System (EDOS). More recently, several Web sites have been created that provide access to federal courts of appeals opinions. Two of the better sources are *The Federal Court Locator* [See Illustration 4–12] and the *Federal Courts Finder* of Emory

---

[16] Veterans' Judicial Review Act of 1988, Pub.L. No. 100–687, 102 Stat. 4105. *See* Laurence R. Helfer, *The Politics of Judicial Structure: Creating the United States Court of Veterans Appeals,* 25 Conn. L. Rev. 155 (1992). For additional information about this court, see *Veterans Law Symposium,* 46 Me. L. Rev. 1 (1994).

Law library. [See Illustration 4–14.] The opinions found in these two sites are typically from the mid–1990s forward.

SECTION C. ILLUSTRATIONS

The case of *Hercules, Inc. v. United States* [516 U.S. 417, 116 S. Ct. 981, 137 L. Ed. 2d 47 (1996)] as it is published in:

[Illustration 4–2]

HERCULES, INC. V. UNITED STATES, AS REPORTED IN THE PRELIMINARY PRINTS (ADVANCE SHEETS) OF THE UNITED STATES REPORTS, 516 U.S. 417 (1996)

OCTOBER TERM, 1995 **417**

Syllabus

HERCULES, INC. ET AL. *v.* UNITED STATES

CERTIORARI TO THE UNITED STATES COURT OF APPEALS FOR THE FEDERAL CIRCUIT

No. 94–818. Argued October 30, 1995—Decided March 4, 1996

Petitioner chemical manufacturers produced the defoliant Agent Orange under contracts with the Federal Government during the Vietnam era. After they incurred substantial costs defending, and then settling, tort claims by veterans alleging physical injury from the use of Agent Orange, petitioners filed suits under the Tucker Act to recover such costs from the Government on alternative theories of contractual indemnification and warranty of specifications provided by the Government. The Claims Court granted summary judgment against them and dismissed the complaints. The Court of Appeals consolidated the cases and affirmed.

Held: Petitioners may not recover on their warranty-of-specifications and contractual-indemnification claims. Pp. 422–430.

(a) The Tucker Act's grant of jurisdiction to the Claims Court to hear and determine claims against the Government that are founded upon any "express or implied" contract with the United States, 28 U.S.C.

This page is taken from the *Preliminary Prints* (advance sheets) to the *United States Reports.* As customary, indication is given to the court from which the case is being appealed.

Note that docket number, date of argument, and date of decision are also given.

that petitioners allege. Pp. 422–424.

(b) Neither an implied contractual warranty of specifications nor *United States* v. *Spearin,* 248 U.S. 132, the seminal case recognizing a cause of action for breach of such a warranty, extends so far as to render the United States responsible for costs incurred in defending and settling the veterans' tort claims. Where, as here, the Government provides specifications directing how a contract is to be performed, it is logical to infer that the Government warrants that the contractor will be able to perform the contract satisfactorily if it follows the specifications. However, this inference does not support a further inference that would extend the warranty beyond performance to third-party claims against the contractor. Thus, the *Spearin* claims made by petitioners do not extend to postperformance third-party costs as a matter of law. Pp. 424–425.

[Illustration 4–3]

SAMPLE PAGE FROM 516 U.S.

418   HERCULES, INC. *v.* UNITED STATES

Syllabus

(c) Although the Government required petitioner Thompson to produce Agent Orange under authority of the Defense Production Act of 1950 (DPA) and threat of civil and criminal fines, imposed detailed specifications, had superior knowledge of the hazards, and, to a measurable extent, seized Thompson's processing facilities, these conditions do not give rise to an implied-in-fact agreement to indemnify Thompson for losses to third parties. The Anti-Deficiency Act, which bars federal employees from entering into contracts for future payment of money in advance of, or in excess of, an existing appropriation, 31 U. S. C. § 1341,

---

Each case is preceded by a summary and syllabus prepared by the Reporter of Decisions. See also previous Illustration.

Note the indication as to which Justice wrote the majority opinion, which Justices joined the opinion, which Justices dissented, and which Justice did not participate in the case.

Note also how the names of the attorneys who were involved in the case before the Supreme Court of the United States are given.

---

not reveal an intent to indemnify contractors. Likewise, since Thompson claims a breach of warranty by its customer rather than its seller and supplier, it misplaces its reliance on *Ryan Stevedoring Co.* v. *Pan-Atlantic S. S. Corp.*, 350 U. S. 124. Finally, petitioners' equitable appeal to "simple fairness" is considerably weakened by the fact that the injured veterans could not recover from the Government, see *Feres* v. *United States*, 340 U. S. 135, and, in any event, may not be entertained by this Court, see *United States* v. *Minnesota Mut. Investment Co.*, 271 U. S. 212, 217–218. Pp. 426–430.

24 F. 3d 188, affirmed.

REHNQUIST, C. J., delivered the opinion of the Court, in which SCALIA, KENNEDY, SOUTER, THOMAS, and GINSBURG, JJ., joined. BREYER, J., filed a dissenting opinion, in which O'CONNOR, J., joined, *post,* p. 431. STEVENS, J., took no part in the consideration or decision of the case.

Carter G. Phillips argued the cause for petitioners. With him on the briefs were *James S. Turner, Alan Dumoff, Jerold Oshinsky, Gregory W. Homer, Rhonda D. Orin,* and *Walter S. Rowland.*

Edward C. DuMont argued the cause for the United States. With him on the brief were *Solicitor General Days, Assistant Attorney General Hunger, Deputy Solicitor Gen-*

[Illustration 4–4]

SAMPLE PAGE FROM 516 U.S.

Cite as: 516 U. S. 417 (1996)   419

Opinion of the Court

eral Bender, David S. Fishback, Alfred Mollin, and *Michael T. McCaul.* *

CHIEF JUSTICE REHNQUIST delivered the opinion of the Court.

Petitioners in this case incurred substantial costs defending, and then settling, third-party tort claims arising out of their performance of Government contracts. In this action under the Tucker Act, they sought to recover these costs from the Government on alternative theories of contractual indemnification or warranty of specifications provided by the Government. We hold that they may not do so.

When the United States had armed forces stationed in Southeast Asia in the 1960's, it asked several chemical manu-

> This is the third page of the *Hercules* case illustrating the start of the majority opinion.

facture and sell it a specific phenoxy herbicide, code-named Agent Orange. The Department of Defense wanted to spray the defoliant in high concentrations on tree and plant life in order to both eliminate the enemy's hiding places and destroy its food supplies. From 1964 to 1968, the Government, pursuant to the Defense Production Act of 1950 (DPA), 64 Stat. 798, as amended, 50 U. S. C. App. § 2061 *et seq.* (1988 ed. and Supp. V), entered into a series of fixed-price production contracts with petitioners. The military prescribed the formula and detailed specifications for manufacture. The contracts also instructed the suppliers to mark the drums containing the herbicide with a 3-inch orange band with "[n]o

---

Herbert L. Fenster, Ray M. Aragon, and *Robin S. Conrad* filed a brief for the Chamber of Commerce of the United States of America as *amicus curiae* urging reversal.

Robert M. Hager filed a brief for the Agent Orange Coordinating Council as *amicus curiae* urging affirmance.

Gershon M. Ratner filed a brief for the National Veterans Legal Services Program as *amicus curiae.*

[Illustration 4–5]

SAMPLE PAGE FROM 516 U.S.

Cite as: 516 U. S. 417 (1996)   431

BREYER, J., dissenting

JUSTICE BREYER, with whom JUSTICE O'CONNOR joins, dissenting.

The petitioners, two chemical companies, have brought this breach-of-contract action seeking reimbursement from the Government for their contribution to the settlement of lawsuits brought by Vietnam veterans exposed to their product Agent Orange. The companies argue that their contracts with the Government to produce Agent Orange contain certain promises or warranties that, in effect, hold them harmless. To win this case, as in the most elementary breach-of-contract case, the companies must show that the Government in fact made the warranties or promises, that the Government breached them, and that the Agent Orange settlement contribution was a consequent foreseeable harm.

First page of dissenting opinion.

(1979); 5 A. Corbin, Contracts §§ 997, 1001, 1002 (1964).

The companies concede that the promises, or warranties, are not written explicitly in their contracts; but, the companies intend to prove certain background facts and legal circumstances, which, they say, will show that these promises, or warranties, are an *implicit* part of the bargain that the parties struck. See 3 *id.*, §§ 538, 551 (common and trade usage, course of dealings, and existing statutes and rules of law are always probative as to the meaning of the parties).

The background facts alleged include the following:

• In the 1960's the Government, by exercising special statutory authority, required the companies to enter into the Agent Orange production contracts over the explicit objection of at least one of the companies. See Defense Production Act of 1950 (DPA), 50 U. S. C. App. § 2061 *et seq.* (1988 ed. and Supp. V); App. 8–9, 23–24.

• The Government required the companies to produce Agent Orange according to precise, detailed production specifications. *Ibid.*

• At that time the Government knew but did not reveal that Agent Orange was defective, or unsafe, to the point

[Illustration 4–6]

HERCULES, INC. v. UNITED STATES AS REPORTED IN 116 S. Ct. 981 (1996) INTERIM VOLUME

HERCULES INC. v. U.S. **981**
Cite as 116 S.Ct. 981 (1996)

**HERCULES INCORPORATED,
et al., Petitioners,**

v.

UNITED STATES.

No. 94–818.

Argued Oct. 30, 1995.

Decided March 4, 1996.

Chemical manufacturers that produced defoliant "Agent Orange" brought action against federal government to recover litigation expenses and settlement costs incurred in Agent Orange litigation. The United States Court of Federal Claims, Yock, J., 25 Cl.Ct. 616; 26 Cl.Ct. 17, granted government's motion for summary judgment, and manufacturers appealed. The United States Court of Appeals for the Federal Circuit, 24 F.3d 188, affirmed. Certiorari was granted. The Supreme Court, Chief Justice Rehnquist, held that: (1) neither warranty of specification nor *Spearin* extended so far as to render United States responsible for costs incurred in defending and settling tort claims; (2) conditions of contracting did not give rise to implied-in-fact agreement to indemnify manufacturers; and (3) Defense Production Act (DPA) did not provide for indemnity of manufacturers.

Affirmed.

Justice Breyer filed dissenting opinion in which Justice O'Connor joined.

Justice Stevens took no part in consideration or decision of case.

2. United States ⊕125(3)

United States, as sovereign, is immune from suit save as it consents to be sued and terms of its consent to be sued in any court define that court's jurisdiction to entertain suit.

3. Federal Courts ⊕1072

Congress created Claims Court to permit special and limited class of cases to proceed against United States and court can take cognizance only of those claims which by terms of some act of Congress are committed to it.

4. Federal Courts ⊕1076, 1077

Claims Court's jurisdiction, conferred by Tucker Act, to hear and determine claims against United States founded upon any "express or implied" contract with United States extends only to contracts either express or implied in fact, and not to claims on contracts implied in law, and each material term or contractual obligation, as well as contract as whole, is subject to this jurisdictional limitation. 28 U.S.C.A. § 1491(a).

5. Contracts ⊕27

Agreement "implied in fact" is founded upon meeting of minds, which, although not embodied in express contract, is inferred, as fact, from conduct of parties showing, in light of surrounding circumstances, their tacit understanding.

> See publication Words and Phrases for other judicial constructions and definitions.

6. Implied and Constructive Contracts ⊕1

Agreement "implied in law" is fiction of law where promise is imputed to perform legal duty, as to repay money obtained by

---

> This is the first page of the *Hercules* case as it appears in West's *Supreme Court Reporter*, an unofficial set. The summary is prepared by its editors.
>
> The headnotes shown in the right column were prepared by West's editorial staff. The significance of headnotes is discussed in Chapter 6.

---

with Government specifications, if contractor warned United States about any hazards known to contractor but not to Government.

> See publication Words and Phrases for other judicial constructions and definitions.

specifications nor *Spearin* case recognizing cause of action for breach of such warranty, extended so far as to render United States responsible for costs incurred by chemical manufacturers in defending and settling veterans' tort claims involving defoliant "Agent

[Illustration 4–7]

HERCULES, INC. v. UNITED STATES AS REPORTED
IN 116 S. Ct. 981 (1996) INTERIM VOLUME

982   **116 SUPREME COURT REPORTER**

Orange"; *Spearin* claims made by chemical manufacturers did not extend to postperformance third-party costs as matter of law.

8. United States ⊂⊃69(6), 78(17)

Although Government required chemical manufacturer to produce defoliant "Agent Orange" under authority of Defense Production Act (DPA) and threat of civil and criminal fines, imposed detailed specifications, had superior knowledge of hazards, and, to measurable extent, seized manufacturer's processing facilities, those conditions did not give rise to implied-in-fact agreement to indemnify manufacturer for costs incurred in defending and settling veterans' tort claims involving "Agent Orange." Defense Production Act of 1950, § 1, 50 App.U.S.C.A. § 2061.

9. United States ⊂⊃69(6)

Anti-Deficiency Act's limitation upon authority to impose contract obligations upon United States is as applicable to contracts by implication as it is to those expressly made, and it applies equally to capped and open-ended indemnification agreements. 31 U.S.C.A § 1341.

10. United States ⊂⊃69(6)

Implied agreements to indemnify should not be readily inferred from circumstances of contracting with United States.

11. United States ⊂⊃78(17)

Chemical manufacturer was not entitled

defending and settling veterans' tort claims involving "Agent Orange" on theory of "simple fairness"; Supreme Court was constrained by limited jurisdiction and could not entertain claim based on merely equitable considerations.

Syllabus *

Petitioner chemical manufacturers produced the defoliant Agent Orange under contracts with the Federal Government during the Vietnam era. After they incurred substantial costs defending, and then settling, tort claims by veterans alleging physical injury from the use of Agent Orange, petitioners filed suits under the Tucker Act to recover such costs from the Government on alternative theories of contractual indemnification and warranty of specifications provided by the Government. The Claims Court granted summary judgment against them and dismissed the complaints. The Court of Appeals consolidated the cases and affirmed.

Held: Petitioners may not recover on their warranty-of-specifications and contractual-indemnification claims. Pp. 985–989.

(a) The Tucker Act's grant of jurisdiction to the Claims Court to hear and determine claims against the Government that are founded upon any "express or implied" contract with the United States, 28 U.S.C. § 1491(a), extends only to contracts either

> The left column of this Illustration shows a continuation of the headnotes. The right column shows the syllabus as it appears in the official *United States Reports.* The remaining pages of the case (not shown) contain the majority, concurring, and dissenting opinions set forth exactly as in the official reports.

damages for any act resulting directly or indirectly from compliance with order issued pursuant to DPA, despite fact that production of "Agent Orange" was done in compliance with DPA order; statute provided immunity, not indemnity. Defense Production Act of 1950, § 707, 50 App.U.S.C.A § 2157.

12. United States ⊂⊃78(17)

Chemical manufacturers were not entitled to recover, from United States, costs of

tioners must establish that, based on the circumstances at the time of contracting, there was an implied agreement between the parties to provide the undertakings that petitioners allege. Pp. 985–986.

(b) Neither an implied contractual warranty of specifications nor *United States v. Spearin,* 248 U.S. 132, 39 S.Ct. 59, 63 L.Ed. 166, the seminal case recognizing a cause of action for breach of such a warranty, extends

* The syllabus constitutes no part of the opinion of the Court but has been prepared by the Reporter of Decisions for the convenience of the reader.

See *United States v. Detroit Lumber Co.,* 200 U.S. 321, 337, 26 S.Ct. 282, 287, 50 L.Ed. 499.

[Illustration 4–8]

HERCULES, INC. v. UNITED STATES AS REPORTED
IN 116 S. Ct. 981 (1996) INTERIM VOLUME

HERCULES INC. v. U.S.
Cite as 116 S.Ct. 981 (1996)
989

DPA. Petitioner reads the provision too broadly. The statute plainly provides immunity, not indemnity. By expressly providing a defense to liability, Congress does not implicitly agree that, if liability is imposed notwithstanding that defense, the Government will reimburse the unlucky defendant.[14] We think petitioner's reliance on *Ryan Stevedoring Co. v. Pan–Atlantic S.S. Corp.,* 350 U.S. 124, 76 S.Ct. 232, 100 L.Ed. 133 (1956), is likewise misplaced; there, in an action between private parties, we held that the stevedore was liable to the shipowner for the amount the latter paid in damages to an injured employee of the former. Here petitioner claims a breach of warranty by its customer, not by its seller and supplier.

[12] Perhaps recognizing the weakness of their legal position, petitioners plead "simple fairness," Tr. of Oral Arg. 3, and ask us to "redress the unmistakable inequities." Brief f...

> **This is the last page of the majority opinion in *Hercules*. All opinions in West's *Supreme Court Reporter* are identical to those in the official *United States Reports*. Only the editorial material preceding the majority opinion differs.**
>
> **Note the smaller type used in the West reporter compared with that of the *United States Reports*. This allows the unofficial reporter to reproduce cases of each Term in fewer volumes.**

the Court of Appeals is

Affirmed.

Justice STEVENS took no part in the consideration or decision of this case.

Justice BREYER, with whom Justice O'CONNOR joins, dissenting.

The petitioners, two chemical companies, have brought this breach of contract action

seeking reimbursement from the Government for their contribution to the settlement of lawsuits brought by Vietnam veterans exposed to their product Agent Orange. The companies argue that their contracts with the Government to produce Agent Orange contain certain promises or warranties that, in effect, hold them harmless. To win this case, as in the most elementary breach of contract case, the companies must show that the Government in fact made the warranties or promises, that the Government breached them, and that the Agent Orange settlement contribution was a consequent foreseeable harm. See Restatement (Second) of Contracts §§ 346, 347, 351 (1979); 5 A. Corbin, Contracts §§ 997, 1001, 1002 (1964).

The companies concede that the promises, or warranties, are not written explicitly in their contracts; but, the companies intend to prove certain background facts and legal circumstances, which, they say, will show that these promises, or warranties, are an *implicit* part of the bargain that the parties struck. See 3 *id.,* §§ 538, 551 (common and trade usage, course of dealings, and existing statutes and rules of law are always probative as to the meaning of the parties).

The background facts alleged include the following:

• In the 1960's the Government, by exercising special statutory authority, required the companies to enter into the Agent Orange production contracts over the explicit objection of at least one of the companies. See Defense Production Act of 1950 (DPA), 50 U.S.C.App. § 2061 *et seq.* (1988 ed. and Supp. V); App. 8–9, 23–24.

• The Government required the companies to produce Agent Orange according to precise, detailed production specifications. *Ibid.*

• At that time the Government knew but did not reveal that Agent Orange was defective, or unsafe, to the point where its use

14. The United States urges us to interpret § 707 as only barring liability to customers whose orders are delayed or displaced on account of the priority accorded Government orders under § 101 of the DPA, which authorizes the President to require contractors to give preferential treatment to contracts "necessary or appropriate to

promote the national defense." 50 U.S.C.App. § 2071(a)(1) (1988 ed., Supp. V). We need not decide the scope of § 707 in this case because it clearly functions only as an immunity, and provides no hint of a further agreement to indemnify.

[Illustration 4–9]

HERCULES, INC. v. UNITED STATES AS REPORTED IN 134 L. Ed. 2d

HERCULES INCORPORATED, et al., Petitioners

v

UNITED STATES

516 US —, 134 L Ed 2d 47, 116 S Ct —

[No. 94-818]

Argued October 30, 1995. Decided March 4, 1996.

Decision: Government contractor manufacturers held not entitled to recover from United States on implied-contract theories for costs of defending and settling third-party tort claims alleging injuries from Agent Orange.

SUMMARY

Two chemical manufacturers—which, pursuant to the Defense Production Act of 1950 (DPA) (50 USCS Appx §§ 2061 et seq.), had during the 1960's entered fixed-price contracts to manufacture, under a formula and detailed specifications prescribed by the military, the herbicide Agent Orange for use in the Vietnam War—entered into a settlement agreement with respect to tort claims brought against the manufacturers to recover for Vietnam

ve
Su
U:
ur
ri:
in
th
cl:
er

> This is the first page of the *Hercules* case as it appears in an advance sheet of L. Ed. 2d. Formerly published by Lawyers Cooperative Publishing, this set is now published by LEXIS Law Publishing. The Summary is prepared by the publisher's editorial staff.
>
> Note the citations to the other sets of reports. The page numbers will be added when the case is part of the permanent bound volume. The publisher also prepares its own headnotes.

The United States Court of Appeals for the Federal Circuit, in affirming, rejected the theory of implied warranty of specifications, which was asserted by both manufacturers, and the theory of implied promise to indemnify for liabilities incurred in performing the contracts, which was asserted by only one manufacturer (24 F3d 188).

On certiorari, the United States Supreme Court affirmed. In an opinion by REHNQUIST, Ch. J., joined by SCALIA, KENNEDY, SOUTER, THOMAS, and GINSBURG, JJ., it was held that (1) the two manufacturers were not entitled to recover from the United States on the theory of breach of an implied

47

[Illustration 4–10]

HERCULES, INC. v. UNITED STATES AS REPORTED IN 134 L. Ed. 2d

HERCULES INC. v UNITED STATES
(1996) 134 L Ed 2d 47

ing circumstances, their tacit understanding, while (2) by contrast, an agreement implied in law is a fiction of law where a promise is imputed to perform a legal duty, as to repay money obtained by fraud or duress.

United States § 146 — implied warranty of specifications

~~8. When the Federal Government~~

F
a
b
r
t

The headnotes in this set are prepared by LEXIS Law Publishing and differ from those in West's *Supreme Court Reporter*.
"**Research References**" direct the user to related sources in other publications of this publisher.

ls
u-
ge
ie
id
c-

~~if the contractor follows the specifi-~~
cations; the specifications will not frustrate performance or make performance impossible.

United States § 174 — government contractor — indemnification agreements

9a, 9b. The Anti-Deficiency Act (31 USCS § 1341), which bars a federal employee or agency from entering into a contract for future payment of money in advance of, or in excess of, an existing appropriation, applies equally to capped indemnification agreements as the Act applies to open-ended indemnification agree-

ments. (Breyer and O'Connor, JJ., dissented in part from this holding.)

Claims § 73 — equity jurisdiction — Supreme Court

10. With respect to two chemical manufacturers' pleading for "simple fairness" and asking the United States Supreme Court to "redress the unmistakable inequities"—in a case

ture, are not entitled to recover from the United States on implied-contract theories for the costs of defending and settling third-party tort claims alleging that Vietnam veterans incurred physical injuries as a result of exposure to Agent Orange—(1) the fact that the veterans could not recover against the government considerably weakens the manufacturers' equitable appeal, and (2) in any event, the Supreme Court is constrained by the court's limited jurisdiction and may not entertain claims based on merely equitable considerations.

RESEARCH REFERENCES

32B Am Jur 2d, Federal Courts §§ 2266, 2284; 63A Am Jur 2d, Public Funds § 53; 77 Am Jur 2d, United States § 67

7A Federal Procedure, L Ed, Court of Claims (Claims Court) § 19:58; 15A Federal Procedure, L Ed, Government Contracts §§ 39:828, 39:857

6A Federal Procedural Forms, L Ed, Claims Court § 18:75

14 Am Jur Trials 437, Representing the Government Contractor

28 USCS § 1491; 31 USCS § 1341; 50 USCS Appx § 2157

Am Law Prod Liab 3d §§ 20:1, 52:42

L Ed Digest, United States §§ 146, 152

L Ed Index, Implied Warranty; Public Works and Contracts; Restitution and Implied Contracts; Tucker Act

51

[Illustration 4–11]

CORNELL'S LEGAL INFORMATION INSTITUTE LII HERMES WEB SITE

---

http://supct.law.cornell.edu/supct/   http://supct.law.cornell.edu/supct/

current | historic | court | search

The LII and Hermes: overview and recent developments

The Legal Information Institute offers Supreme Court opinions under the auspices of Project Hermes, the court's electronic-dissemination project.   This archive contains (or will soon contain) all opinions of the court issued since May of 1990.   In addition, our collection of over 580 of the most important historical decisions of the Court is available on CD-ROM and (with reduced functionality) over the Net.

During our first four years of operation, the LII simply built finding aids -- such as tables of party names and searching tools -- which in turn pointed to the Hermes archive at Case Western Reserve University. We have now acquired our own Hermes subscription and begun streamed conversion of the decisions into HTML at the time of release. We have also converted the entire CWRU backlist to HTML, and have begun working to fill some long-standing gaps in the Hermes collection.

As the foregoing implies, there are still some omissions and errata in this collection, and a high likelihood that in the process of conversion we've missed a few links here and there. If you run into a problem which is not mentioned in our list of errata and items under construction, do let us know.

 new! At the start of the current term in October, 1997, the Court changed the file formats used in its Hermes distribution. Previously, opinions, syllabi, and order lists were distributed in WordPerfect 5.1 and flat ASCII formats. Current practice is to distribute the opinions in Adobe Acrobat (PDF) format and in a special, SGML-ish tagged ASCII format which is a hybrid of structural and presentational markup. There is no distribution of files in any word-processing format. See our section on the nuts and bolts of PDF distribution for details. In order to view the opinions in the proprietary Acrobat format, you will need to get Acrobat Reader software from Adobe.

Decisions in the LII collection (from May 1990)

[Illustration 4–12]

THE CENTER FOR INFORMATION LAW AND POLICY'S
THE FEDERAL COURT LOCATOR WEB SITE

The Federal Court Locator   http://www.law.vill.edu/Fed-Ct/fedcourt.html

The Center for Information Law and Policy

Search Cases   S.Ct. FLITE Database   Map Jumps   Table of Contents

"The Home Page for the Federal Courts on the Internet"™

The Federal Court Locator is a service provided by the Center for Information Law and Policy. It is intended to give net citizens a means to access information related to the federal judiciary, including slip opinions. This information can be viewed on-line or it can be downloaded. If you learn of a federal court site on the Internet, please mail us so that we can add a link to it and continue to improve the access to federal judicial information. Also, please visit our page dedicated to *Friends of CILP*, who have helped keep this the most up-to-date Web page concerning the federal courts.

©1994-1997 Center for Information Law and Policy

CLICK ON THE MAP TO RETRIEVE THE COURT HOME PAGE
(Text Links Below Map)

[Illustration 4–13]

PAGE FROM 133 FEDERAL REPORTER, 3d SERIES

UNITED STATES COURT OF APPEALS
Second Circuit

DECISIONS WITHOUT PUBLISHED OPINIONS

Title	Docket Number	Date	Disposition	Appeal from and Citation (if reported)
Amaker v. Lacy	96–2737	10/8/97	Affirmed	E.D.N.Y., 941 F.Supp. 1340
Barry v. U.S.	97–6114	1/27/98	Affirmed	E.D.N.Y.
Bartel v. Eastern Airlines	96–5105	1/6/98	Affirmed	S.D.N.Y.
Bowe v. Barkley	97–2294	1/27/98	Affirmed	N.D.N.Y.
Brewer v. Schatz	97–7571	1/27/98	Affirmed	D.Conn.
Brumer v. Paul Revere Life Ins. Co.	96–9362	1/12/98	Affirmed	E.D.N.Y., 874 F.Supp. 60
Campfield v. C.I.R.	96–4187	10/31/97	Affirmed	U.S.T.C.
Candelaria v. Coughlin	96–2794	12/31/97	Affirmed	S.D.N.Y.
Cerniglia v. U.S.	96–2998	10/31/97	Affirmed	S.D.N.Y.
Chisman v. J.J. Cassone Bakery,				

> **A table illustrating how cases without published opinions that are decided in a Federal Court of Appeals is included in each volume and advance sheet of the *Federal Reporter 2d* and *3d*.**

Title	Docket Number	Date	Disposition	Appeal from and Citation (if reported)
can Centennial Ins. Co.	97–7097	10/31/97	Affirmed	S.D.N.Y.
Comrie v. Bronx Lebanon Hosp.	97–7484	1/27/98	Reversed	S.D.N.Y.
Control Data Systems, Inc. v. Computer Power Group, Ltd.	97–7777	1/21/98	Vacated	S.D.N.Y.
Cook v. CBS, Inc.	97–7728	12/31/97	Affirmed	S.D.N.Y.
Cowell v. Artuz	97–2537	1/14/98	Vacated	S.D.N.Y.
Cruz v. Artuz	97–2303	12/8/97	Affirmed	E.D.N.Y.
Cucina Classica Italiana, Inc. v. Banco Nazionale Del Lavoro	97–7087	10/9/97	Affirmed	S.D.N.Y.
Curran v. All-Waste Systems, Inc.	97–7393	10/31/97	Affirmed	S.D.N.Y.
Davis v. Artuz	96–2911	1/27/98	Reversed	S.D.N.Y.
Davis v. Chater	97–6065	1/27/98	Affirmed	S.D.N.Y.
Delfyett v. Brown	96–6347	10/28/97	Affirmed	E.D.N.Y.
Dickerson v. State Farm Fire & Cas. Co.	97–7262	10/31/97	Affirmed	S.D.N.Y.
Dilger v. Consolidated Rail Corp.	97–7237	10/31/97	Affirmed	S.D.N.Y.
Dorman & Wilson, Inc. v. General Acc. Ins. of America	97–7375	10/31/97	Affirmed	E.D.N.Y.
Dow Jones & Co., Inc. v. WSJ Inc.	97–7690	1/6/98	Affirmed	S.D.N.Y.
Fadeyi v. U.S.	97–2053	1/6/98	Affirmed	E.D.N.Y.
Ferguson v. McDonnell Douglas Corp.	97–7179	1/30/98	Affirmed	N.D.N.Y.

[Illustration 4–14]

EMORY LAW LIBRARY FEDERAL COURTS LOCATOR

U.S. Federal Courts Finder　　　　　　　　　　http://www.law.emory.edu/FEDCTS/

U.S. Supreme Court | **U.S. Court of Appeals for the Armed Forces**
Federal Circuit | **D.C. Circuit** | **First Circuit** | **Second Circuit** | **Third Circuit** | **Fourth Circuit** |
Fifth Circuit | **Sixth Circuit** | **Seventh Circuit** | **Eighth Circuit** | **Ninth Circuit** | **Tenth Circuit** |
Eleventh Circuit

SECTION D.   SUMMARY

1.   United States Supreme Court Reports

　　a.   *United States Reports* (Official Edition)

(1) Text of all cases of the Supreme Court of the United States.

(2) First 90 volumes are cited frequently by named reporter, because originally these volumes were not separately numbered.

(3) *Slip opinions* are published first, followed by advance sheets (*preliminary prints*).

(4) Bound volumes and advance sheets have the same volume and page numbers.

(5) Include syllabi; no summaries of briefs of counsel.

(6) Bound volumes are two to three years behind in publication schedule.

b. *West's Supreme Court Reporter*

(1) Part of the *National Reporter System;* Key Numbered sections of headnotes.

(2) Begins coverage with volume 106 of official *United States Reports*.

(3) A bound volume contains several volumes of the official reports.

(4) Advance sheets, interim volumes, and bound volumes have same volume and page numbers.

(5) Cross-reference table from the official citations to *West's Supreme Court Reporter* volume and pages.

(6) Star pagination.

(7) No summaries of briefs of counsel; contains West's standard editorial features.

c. *United States Supreme Court Reports, Lawyers' Edition*

(1) Includes all cases decided by the Supreme Court—two series.

(2) Bound volume once contained several volumes of the official reports; starting with volume 78 a new bound volume is published when each official volume is complete.

(3) Bound volumes and advance sheets have the same volume and page numbers.

(4) Cross-reference table from the official citations to *Lawyers' Edition* volume and pages.

(5) Briefs of counsel are summarized; contains the publisher's other standard editorial features.

(6) Annotations of cases reported discussing significant issues in increasing numbers since volume 93 of the first series of *Lawyers' Edition*.

(7) Volumes 1–31 of *Lawyers' Edition 2d* are updated by *Later Case Service* volumes; beginning with volume 32 updating is with annual pocket supplementation.

(8) *General Index* provides topical access to cases; *Quick Case Table* provides an alphabetically-arranged table of cases that are accompanied by opinions.

(9) Star pagination.

    d.   *United States Law Week*

(1) Speedy, looseleaf publication of Supreme Court cases and journal of cases.

(2) Includes discussion of federal statutes, lower state and federal court cases and agency rulings, and legal news.

    e.   *LEXIS–NEXIS and WESTLAW*

(1) Comprehensive, online coverage of Supreme Court cases that is faster than print versions.

(2) Star pagination.

    f.   Supreme Court opinions are available on several Web sites.

    g.   *Chambers Opinions of the Supreme Court.*   Until 1969, published only in *West's Supreme Court Reporter* and *Lawyers' Edition.*   Since 1970, also published in *United States Reports.*   Included in *United States Law Week* and online services.

    h.   *Preview of United States Supreme Court Cases.*   Essays written by scholars on selected cases pending on the Supreme Court's docket, but not yet argued.

2. Federal Cases

    a.   Reprinted reports of all available U.S. circuit and district court cases, 1789–1879.

    b.   Cases are arranged alphabetically by case names and consecutively numbered.

    c.   Cases are cited by number.

    d.   Annotations are brief notes to the cases.

    e.   Digest volume, volume 31, includes Blue Tables that cross-reference from the original reporter citations to the *Federal Cases* numbers.

3. National Reporter System (Federal Units)

All of the following reporters, federal units of the *National Reporter System,* include topics, key numbers, headnotes, and other standard West Group features.   Cases reported are issued first in advance sheets that are later cumulated into bound volumes.   The advance sheets and bound volumes have the same volume and page numbers.   These cases are also included in WESTLAW and LEXIS–NEXIS.

    a.   *Federal Reporter*

(1) Only current reporter for United States courts of appeals cases. It is in its third series.

(2) Reports cases from 1879 to date.

(3) Prior to 1932 included district court cases.

(4) Now reports cases of the circuit courts of appeals, plus those of the United States Temporary Emergency Court of Appeals. Has also reported cases from specialized federal courts at various times during these courts' existence, specifically, the U.S. Circuit Court, Commerce Court of the U.S., U.S. Emergency Court of Appeals, U.S. Court of Claims, and the U.S. Court of Customs and Patents Appeals.

b. *Federal Supplement*

(1) Only current reporter of federal district court cases.

(2) Reports cases since 1932.

(3) Includes *selected* cases of the federal district courts, plus those of the U.S. Court of International Trade (formerly U.S. Customs Court), the Special Court under the Regional Rail Reorganization Act, and the Judicial Panel on Multidistrict Litigation.

(4) From 1932 to 1960, included U.S. Court of Claims cases.

c. *Military Justice Reporter*

(1) Reports cases since 1975.

(2) Includes cases from U.S. Court of Military Appeals and the Courts of Military Review of the Army, Navy–Marine Corps, Air Force, and Coast Guard.

d. *Bankruptcy Reporter*

(1) Reporter for cases of the United States Bankruptcy Courts.

(2) Reports cases since 1980 from the U.S. Bankruptcy Courts and those cases from the federal district courts that deal with bankruptcy matters.

(2) Reprints bankruptcy cases in *West's Supreme Court Reporter* and *Federal Reporter 2d* and *3d,* retaining the paginations of these reporters.

e. *Federal Claims Reporter,* volume 27 to date (*United States Claims Court Reporter,* volumes 1–26).

(1) Only current reporter for cases of the United States Court of Federal Claims.

(2) Reports cases of the United States Claims Court from October 1982 through October 1992 (as *United States Claims Court Reporter*) and of the United States Court of Federal Claims since October 1992.

(3) Includes reprints from the *Federal Reporter 2d* and *3d* and *West's Supreme Court Reporter* of those cases that have reviewed cases of the United States Claims Court and the United States Court of Federal Claims, retaining the pagination of these reporters.

f. *West's Veterans Appeals Reporter*

(1) Only current reporter for cases of the U.S. Court of Veterans Appeals.

(2) Reports cases since the Court's creation in October 1991.

(3) Includes cases of the U.S. Court of Veterans Appeals, plus cases of the U.S. Court of Appeals, Federal Circuit, and the Supreme Court of the United States in review of the Court of Veterans Appeals.

4. Federal Case News

A weekly pamphlet that summarizes recently-decided federal cases prior to publication in advance sheets.

5. Unpublished Opinions

Not all opinions of the federal courts of appeals and the federal district courts are published. Both WESTLAW and LEXIS–NEXIS include in their database cases that are not in the federal units of the *National Reporter System*. One must check local court rules before relying on these cases as authority.

6. Internet Access

Web sites are available for accessing recent federal courts of appeals cases.

Chapter 5

STATE COURT CASES AND THE NATIONAL REPORTER SYSTEM

SECTION A. STATE COURT REPORTS

As has been indicated in earlier chapters, the laws or court rules of the individual states provide for the method of publishing state court cases. Case reporters sanctioned by statutes are called *official reports.* [See Illustration 3–6.] Private companies also publish court cases, with or without legislative directives. The private publications of cases that are not legislatively endorsed are called *unofficial reports,* although they are no less accurate than the official reports. The unofficial reports may duplicate the opinions in the official reports or may be the only source of publication.

The unofficial reports fall into three categories. The first consists of those sets that were or are published to compete directly with the officially-published state reports. These reports, which collect cases decided by the courts and publish them in chronological order, usually have more helpful editorial features and a faster publication schedule than the official reports. In most states, the unofficial sets are units of the *National Reporter System,* which is discussed in the next section of this chapter. The other categories are annotated reports, discussed in Chapter 7, and special or subject reports, discussed briefly in this chapter and in more detail in subsequent chapters.

At one time, all states published their court cases in bound volumes of reports, such as the *Michigan Reports.*[1] Those states having intermediate courts of appeals[2] also may have separately bound sets of reports, such as the *Illinois Appellate Reports.* The cases are published chronologically by terms of court. An increasing number of states, however, have discontinued publishing official state reports and rely solely on the *National Reporter System* or reports of another commercial publisher as the official source.[3] In a few instances, a state will not have a designated

---

[1] For additional references to early law reporting in America, see 1–3 CHARLES EVANS, AMERICAN BIBLIOGRAPHY (1903); 4 ISAIAH THOMAS, HISTORY OF PRINTING IN AMERICA (2d ed. 1874); 1 CHARLES WARREN, HISTORY OF THE HARVARD LAW SCHOOL AND OF EARLY LEGAL CONDITIONS IN AMERICA 203–14 (1908); 1784 Conn. Pub. Acts 267; MARY R. CHAPMAN, BIBLIOGRAPHICAL INDEX TO THE STATE REPORTS PRIOR TO THE NATIONAL REPORTER SYSTEM (1977); Daniel R. Coquillette, *First Flower—The Earliest American Law Reports and the Extraordinary Josiah Quincy, Jr. (1744–1775),* 30 SUFFOLK U.L.REV. 1 (1996).

[2] For a listing of states with intermediate courts of appeals, see the latest edition of *Book of the States.*

[3] See Appendix B for a list of states that have discontinued their state reports and for a Table showing the year of the first case decided for each state or territory. For a state-by-state guide to published court reports and how they interrelate with the *National Reporter System,* see KEITH WIESE, HEIN'S STATE REPORT CHECKLIST (2d ed. 1990) [A.A.L.L. Legal Research Series, Title #2, updated annually].

official set of reports. Increasingly, states are using the Internet to make available their court cases.

Advance sheets or slip opinions often precede the publication of official bound reports in several states. The unofficial print publications always include advance sheets as part of the subscription.

A court or its reporter of decisions may have the power to select the cases for publication in the official state reports. In the exercise of that power some less important cases may be eliminated from the official reports.[4]

In a general survey, such as this, it is not possible to present a detailed study of the reporting system for each state. Legal research guides have been published for many states. These guides typically discuss a state's case law research in depth.[5]

SECTION B. NATIONAL REPORTER SYSTEM

The *National Reporter System,* which began in 1879, is published by West Publishing Company and is the largest and most comprehensive collection of state and federal cases in printed form. It consists of three main divisions: (1) cases of state courts; (2) cases of federal courts; and (3) cases of special courts. There are also subject reporters that extract cases from the various *National Reporter System* units. See Appendix E for a chart showing coverage of the *National Reporter System.*

The development of the *National Reporter System* has had a profound impact on the method of finding court cases and indeed on the development of American law.[6] At the inception of the *National Reporter System,* the states and territories in existence at the time, the various federal circuit courts, and the Supreme Court of the United States were all publishing court reports. In fact, some of these publications had been ongoing for almost a century. In the absence of a coherent, uniform means of accessing these materials, the difficulty of finding cases with similar points of law became immense. The *National Reporter System* brought organization to the chaos resulting from the rapid growth in published court reports by numerous sources. It continues to do so today.

---

[4] Leah F. Chanin, *A Survey of the Writing and Publication of Opinions in Federal and State Appellate Courts,* 67 LAW LIBR. J. 362 (1974). *See also supra,* Chapters 3 and 4, notes 4 and 12, respectively, and accompanying text.

[5] A list of these state guides is published in Appendix A.

[6] See Thomas A. Woxland, *"Forever Associated with the Practice of Law": The Early Years of the West Publishing Company,* LEGAL REFERENCE SERVICES Q., Spring, 1985, at 115; Joe Morehead, *All Cases Great and Small: The West Publishing Company Saga,* SERIALS LIBRARIAN, 1988, at 3. *See also* Robert C. Berring, *Full–Text Databases and Legal Research: Backing into the Future,* 1 HIGH TECH. L.J. 27, 29–38 (1986); Robert C. Berring, *Legal Research and Legal Concepts: Where Form Molds Substance,* 75 CAL. L. REV. 15 (1987); Robert C. Berring, *Chaos, Cyberspace and Tradition: Legal Information Transmogrified,* 12 BERKELEY TECH. L.J. 189 (1997).

1. State Court Coverage

The original idea of the *National Reporter System* was to group together the cases from several adjacent states. The first of these geographical groupings was the *North Western Reporter* begun in 1879. By 1887, an additional six groupings, *Pacific, North Eastern, Atlantic, South Western, Southern,* and *South Eastern* in that order, had been added and coverage was nationwide. [See Illustration 5–1 for a map of the regional groupings of the *National Reporter System.*]

These seven units are often referred to as regional reporters, although the states included in some groupings are not always what one might expect to find there, *e.g.,* Oklahoma in *Pacific Reporter,* Michigan in *North Western Reporter.* These early geographical groupings were likely based on the country's population at the time and with it the expectation that each regional unit would grow at approximately the same pace. Certainly this did not occur, but the regional groupings have remained unchanged since they were originally established. Today, each regional unit contains several hundred volumes and all are in a second series.

Population growth has, however, altered the coverage of two of the regional reporters. This occurred first in 1888 with the establishment of a separate reporter for New York, the *New York Supplement.* This reporter includes cases from the New York Court of Appeals, which is New York's court of last resort, as well as cases from the lower courts. The only New York cases currently reported in the *North Eastern Reporter* are those of the New York Court of Appeals. In 1960, West began publishing the *California Reporter.* It includes cases from the California Supreme Court and its intermediate appellate court. These intermediate appellate court cases from California are no longer in the *Pacific Reporter.* Both of these state units of the *National Reporter System* are in their second series.

The *National Reporter System* has, since its beginning, reported cases from each state's highest court. While it now also reports cases from all state intermediate appellate courts, the inclusion of these cases began at different times. For example, Missouri appellate cases are included in the *South Western Reporter,* beginning with 93 Mo. App. (1902); Illinois appellate cases are contained in the *North Eastern Reporter,* beginning with 284 Ill. App. (1936). The publisher notes that the *National Reporter System* also contains over 130,000 cases that are not in the official reports.

Often it is impractical for attorneys to acquire a regional reporter when what they most often need is access to cases from their particular state. Consequently, West publishes "offprint" reporters for individual states by reprinting a state's cases from a regional reporter and rebinding them under a new name, *e.g., Texas Cases, Missouri Decisions.* There are approximately 30 publications of this type. These offprints retain the volume number and pagination of the regional reporter. The exception to this is the third state unit, *Illinois Decisions,* in which each volume is paged consecutively. Many states that no longer publish official state reports have adopted the regional reporter that covers their state and the offprint version as their official reports.

Both WESTLAW and LEXIS–NEXIS provide extensive state court case coverage. While there is no uniform date as to how far back this coverage extends, it is fair to say that coverage for most states is at least since the 1940s. For many states, the coverage is much more exhaustive, often dating from the late 1800s. Information as to the scope of coverage is available online and through publications of these two vendors. In addition, both the West Group and LEXIS Law Publishing have developed collections of state cases on CD–ROM. These products allow for hypertext linking whereby a researcher can highlight a case citation and jump automatically to a screen displaying the cited case. These CD-ROM products can be updated through a subscription to the corresponding CALR service.

2. Federal Court and Special Court Coverage

West's federal court coverage began only a year after its first regional reporter in 1879. Today, four units of the *National Reporter System* cover the various federal courts—*West's Supreme Court Reporter, Federal Reporter* (F., F.2d, F.3d), *Federal Supplement,* and *Federal Rules Decisions*. Another four units contain cases from specialized federal courts—*Bankruptcy Reporter, Military Justice Reporter, Federal Claims Reporter,* and *Veterans Appeals Reporter*. Like the regional reporters, the federal units are available online in both WESTLAW and LEXIS–NEXIS. These various federal units of the *National Reporter System* are discussed in Chapter 4.

3. Ultra Fiche Edition

West also publishes an ultra fiche edition of the *National Reporter System*. The reduction ratio is 75x and is compatible with lenses covering a range of 67x to 92x. The First Series and Second Series are available in this format. The Third Series is being filmed as the hard copy volumes are published, with very little lag time between issuance of the two formats. The shelf space savings allowed by the ultra fiche edition are enormous.

4. Coverage of Specialized Subjects

In addition to the federal, state, and regional reporters mentioned above, West also publishes the *Education Law Reporter, Social Security Reporting Service,* and *United States Merit Systems Protection Board Reporter*. While not units of the *National Reporter System,* these sets often reprint cases found in it.

5. Features of the National Reporter System

As has been shown, the full texts of cases decided by the various state and federal appellate courts are contained in the *National Reporter System*. West adds numerous enhancements in its reporters that facilitate use. These common features, discussed below, make possible a relatively simple method for researchers to find cases for all the states as well as those decided in the federal courts on the same or similar points of law.

When West receives cases decided by the courts, its editors prepare headnotes for these cases, which are Key Numbered to its *American Digest System,* and then issues these cases first in advance sheets, which are later cumulated into bound volumes. This Key Numbering is the crux of the *National Reporter System*'s indexing method, the nature of which is described in Chapter 6. Bound volumes retain the same volume and page numbers as the advance sheets.[7]

In addition to the opinions and headnotes, the advance sheets and bound volumes of the *National Reporter System* also include a synopsis of the case, a digest section containing the Key Numbered headnotes of the cases covered,[8] a Table of Cases arranged by state, a Table of Statutes interpreted by cases covered, a list of Words and Phrases defined in the cases reported, and a table showing cases that have cited the second edition of the American Bar Association's *Standards for Criminal Justice.* For all West reporters, except the *Military Justice Reporter,* there are tables listing all Federal Rules of Civil Procedure, Federal Rules of Criminal Procedure, Federal Rules of Appellate Procedure, and Federal Rules of Evidence that are interpreted by the cases covered. From time to time the various units also include proposed changes to or newly-approved versions of court rules.

The advance sheets to the reporters contain several current awareness features that are not incorporated into the bound volumes. For example, the state and regional reporters contain summaries of federal cases arising in each state covered by that reporter. "Judicial Highlights" and "Congressional and Administrative Highlights," found in all *National Reporter System* units except the *Federal Rules Decisions* and the *Bankruptcy Reporter* respectively, are monthly features that briefly describe cases, legislation, and administrative agency activities of special interest or significance.

---

[7] Occasionally after a case has been published in an advance sheet, the judge who wrote the opinion may, for one reason or another, decide it should not be published, and will recall the opinion. In such instances, another case is published in the appendix of a subsequent advance sheet with the same pagination as the withdrawn case. By this means, the original pagination is preserved in the bound volume.

[8] Features such as the digest section in individual volumes are current awareness devices and are repeated in the cumulations of digests on the state, regional, and national levels. Consequently, West does not reproduce these digest sections and some other features when reprinting older volumes.

[Illustration 5–1]

MAP OF THE NATIONAL REPORTER SYSTEM*
Showing the States in each Regional Reporter Group

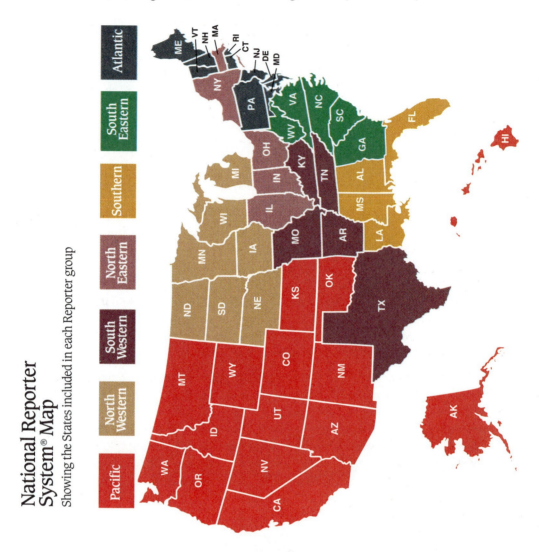

* The National Reporter System also includes:

Supreme Court Reporter
Federal Supplement
West's Bankruptcy Reporter
West's California Reporter
West's Military Justice Reporter
Federal Claims Reporter

Federal Reporter
Federal Rules Decisions
New York Supplement
West's Illinois Decisions
Veterans Appeals Reporter

SECTION C. METHODS OF CITING

1. State Cases

a. *Name of Case.* Depending upon the court rules, a case when cited, should contain the name of the case followed by the citation to the case either in the official reports if available, the citation to the corresponding unit or units of the *National Reporter System,* or both.[9] When both the official and unofficial citation are used, this is referred to as *parallel citation.* The full name of the case appears at its beginning, and then there is usually a short form of the case name at the top of each subsequent page of the case. Typically, it is the short form (or a slight variation) that is used in the citation, *e.g.,*

Josephine RAVO, an Infant, by Her Father and Natural
Guardian, Antonio RAVO, Respondent

v.

Sol RAGATNICK, Respondent, and Irwin L. Harris,
Appellant

Its short form title is *Ravo v. Ragatnick.*

b. *Parallel Citations.* When a case has been reported in an official state reporter and in a regional reporter, the citation to the state report is given first, followed by the parallel citation to the appropriate regional reporter or reporters, and, when available, its citation in the *American Law Reports.*[10] The year the case was decided is then given in parenthesis. Examples are:

Ravo v. Ragatnick, 70 N.Y.2d 305, 514 N.E.2d 1104, 520 N.Y.S.2d 533, 9 A.L.R. 5th 1170 (1987).

Izazaga v. Superior Court, 54 Cal. 3d 356, 285 Cal. Rptr. 231, 815 P.2d 304 (1991).

Commonwealth v. DiBenedetto, 413 Mass. 37, 605 N.E.2d 811 (1992).

When there is no official set of state reports, citation is given first to where it is reported in the *National Reporter System* and then, if available, to the *American Law Reports,* with an indication of the court and year of decision in parenthesis. Examples are:

Tussey v. Commonwealth, 589 S.W.2d 215 (Ky. 1979).

Thompson v. State, 318 So. 2d 549, 90 A.L.R. 3d 641 (Fla. Dist. Ct. App. 1975).

c. *Early State Reporters.* Where the name of a reporter is used in citing an early state report, the favored practice is to indicate the state and the date. An example is:

Day v. Sweetser, 2 Tyl. 283 (Vt. 1803).

---

[9] For state court documents, the 16th edition of *The Bluebook: A Uniform System of Citation* requires parallel citations only for cases decided by courts of the state in which the documents are being submitted. For all other states, only the unofficial citation is required. However, courts do not necessarily follow *The Bluebook.* It is essential, therefore, to check the court rules to ascertain the proper citation form to be used.

[10] The *American Law Reports* are discussed in Chapter 7.

2. Federal Court Cases

a. *Supreme Court of the United States.* Since both *West's Supreme Court Reporter* and the *United States Supreme Court Reports, Lawyers' Edition* give cross references to the pages of the official *United States Reports*, it is customary to cite only to the official set, *e.g., University of California Regents v. Bakke,* 438 U.S. 265 (1978). If the case is so recent that it is not yet in the official reporter, the preferred practice is to cite to *West's Supreme Court Reporter.* For cases even more recent than *West's Supreme Court Reporter,* the preferred cite is to *U.S. Law Week.*

b. *Courts of Appeals and District Courts.* Since there are no official reports for the cases of these courts, citations are given to the appropriate unit of the *National Reporter System.* Examples are:

To find Parallel Citation

United States v. One 1987 27 Foot Boston Whaler, 808 F. Supp. 382 (D.N.J. 1992).

In re Ostaco, Inc., 981 F.2d 1166 (10th Cir. 1992).

SECTION D. CROSS–REFERENCE TABLES

1. State Court Citations

Frequently, a researcher has only the citation to a case in an official state report or a regional or state unit of the *National Reporter System* and needs to find the parallel citation. This can be accomplished in several ways.

a. *State Citation to National Reporter System Citation.* When only the state citation is available, refer to one of the following:

(1) *National Reporter Blue Book.* This set, published by West Group, lists all state citations, alphabetically by state, and gives for each state citation its parallel citation in the appropriate unit or units of the *National Reporter System.* This set consists of bound volumes that are kept current by annual cumulative pamphlets. [See Illustration 5–2.]

(2) *Shepard's Citations* for the state.

(3) The *Table of Cases* in the appropriate state or regional digest.

b. *National Reporter System Citation to State Citation.* When only the citation is available to a volume of the *National Reporter System,* refer to one of the following:

(1) *[State] Blue and White Book.* Another West publication, this volume is only sent to subscribers for the state in which the subscriber is located and is not available for all states. The blue pages repeat for the state the information available in the *National Reporter Blue Book* described above. The white pages give citations for the regional reporter or reporters to the official state reports. [See Illustration 5–2.] This publication is useful in locating state citations for the state where the research is taking place.

(2) *Shepard's Citations* for the appropriate regional and state reporter unit.

(3) *Table of Cases* in the appropriate state or regional digest, or *Table of Cases* volumes in the appropriate unit of the *American Digest System.*

(4) *Star Pagination in the National Reporter System.* As early as 1922, West provided star pagination or parallel pagination from the texts of opinions in its *New York Supplement* to the corresponding pages in the official *New York Reports.* This use of star pagination allows the researcher not only to find the official version of the case, but also to provide "jump cites" or "pinpoint cites" to textual matter within the body of the case. While this feature is still included for a few official reports in the unofficial reports, the delay of most states in publishing their official reports when coupled with West's speed in publishing their own, often renders star pagination impossible.

2. Federal Court Citations

a. *Supreme Court of the United States.* The general practice is to cite only to the official *United States Reports* because the unofficial sets include the official citations in their unofficial publications. When, however, the only citation available is to *West's Supreme Court Reporter* or the *United States Supreme Court Reports, Lawyers' Edition,* the citation to the other two sets can be obtained by referring to:

(1) *Shepard's United States Citations: Cases volumes.*

(2) *Table of Cases* in one of the digests for federal cases.

Tables of Cases and the American Digest System are discussed in Chapter 6. *Shepard's Citations* are discussed in Chapter 15.

b. *Lower Federal Court Cases.* Since there are no official reports for the federal courts of appeals and the federal district courts, citations are to the three series of the *Federal Reporter* and to the *Federal Supplement,* respectively.

3. Insta–Cite and Auto–Cite

Insta–Cite is an electronic case history and citation verification service available on WESTLAW. Auto–Cite, a similar service developed by Lawyers Cooperative Publishing, is available on LEXIS–NEXIS and displays citations with *The Bluebook* punctuation and abbreviations. Each service can be used to locate a parallel citation when only the official or unofficial citation is known. [See Illustration 5–3.] Both of these systems are discussed in more detail in Chapter 15.

SECTION E.   INTERNET RESOURCES

The Internet has spawned remarkable growth in the ready availability of state case law resources. Several wonderful Web sites provide links to judicial opinions. Among the best are The Center for Information Law and Policy's *The State Court Locator* (similar in format and at the same

URL address as Illustration 4–12) and *Hieros Gamos* [See Illustration 5–4], a source that is striving to be the most comprehensive law-related Web site. These sites are being updated frequently as new state court materials become available. The amount of information for each state varies greatly depending upon the speed with which these various governments are entering the electronic age.

SECTION F. ILLUSTRATIONS

[Illustration 5–2]

AN EXCERPT FROM THE NATIONAL REPORTER BLUE BOOK

20 CALIFORNIA REPORTS, THIRD SERIES

Cal.3d Page	Vol.	Parallel Citation Page	Cal.3d Page	Vol.	Parallel Citation Page	Cal.3d Page	Vol.	Parallel Citation Page	Cal.3d Page	Vol.	Parallel Citation Page
1	141 CalRptr	28	232	142 CalRptr	171	457	143 CalRptr	215	679	143 CalRptr	865
	569 P2d	133		571 P2d	628		573 P2d	433		574 P2d	1237
10	141 CalRptr	20	238	142 CalRptr	279	476	143 CalRptr	205	→ 694	144 Cal.Rptr.	751
	569 P2d	125		571 P2d	990		573 P2d	423		576 P.2d	466
25	141 CalRptr	315	251	142 CalRptr	414	489	143 CalRptr	212	708	144 CalRptr	133
	569 P2d	1303		572 P2d	28		573 P2d	430		575 P2d	285
55	141 CalRptr	146	260	142 CalRptr	411	500	143 CalRptr	240	717	144 CalRptr	214
	569 P2d	740		572 P2d	25		573 P2d	458		575 P2d	757
73	141 CalRptr	169	267	142 CalRptr	418	512	143 CalRptr	247	725	144 CalRptr	380
	569 P2d	763		572 P2d	32		573 P2d	465		575 P2d	1162
90	141 CalRptr	157	285	142 CalRptr	429	523	143 CalRptr	609	765	144 CalRptr	758
	569 P2d	751		572 P2d	43		574 P2d	425		576 P2d	473
109	141 CalRptr	177	300	142 CalRptr	286	550	143 CalRptr	253	788	144 CalRptr	404
	569 P2d	771		571 P2d	997		573 P2d	472		575 P2d	1186
130	141 CalRptr	447[1]	309	142 CalRptr	439	552	143 CalRptr	408	798	144 CalRptr	408
	570 P2d	463[2]		572 P2d	53		573 P2d	852		575 P2d	1190
142	141 CalRptr	542	317	142 CalRptr	443	560	143 CalRptr	625	813	144 CalRptr	905
	570 P2d	723		572 P2d	57		574 P2d	441		576 P2d	945
150	141 CalRptr	698	327	142 CalRptr	904	567	143 CalRptr	542	844	143 CalRptr	695
	570 P2d	1050		572 P2d	1128		573 P2d	1240		574 P2d	761

The *National Reporter Blue Book* consists of a main bound volume, bound volume supplements, and an annual cumulative pamphlet. This *Blue Book* contains tables showing volume and page of the *National Reporter* volume for every case found in the corresponding state reports.

In this example, if one had only the citation to 20 Cal. 3d 694, the table may be used to locate the citation of this case in the *California Reporter* and the *Pacific Reporter 2d.*

AN EXCERPT FROM THE WHITE TABLES IN CALIFORNIA BLUE AND WHITE BOOK

1190......20 Cal.3d 798	**579 P.2d** Parallel
144 Cal.Rptr. 408	Page Citation
	1........21 Cal.3d 337
576 P.2d Parallel	146 Cal.Rptr. 352
Page Citation	7........21 Cal.3d 471
92 [1]	146 Cal.Rptr. 358
Not officially published	441........21 Cal.3d 322
92 [2].....20 Cal.3d 878	146 Cal.Rptr. 550
144 Cal.Rptr. 609 [3]	449........21 Cal.3d 386
93......20 Cal.3d 888	146 Cal.Rptr. 558
144 Cal.Rptr. 610	476........21 Cal.3d 431
→ 466......20 Cal.3d 694	146 Cal.Rptr. 585
144 Cal.Rptr. 751	495........21 Cal.3d 349
473......20 Cal.3d 765	146 Cal.Rptr. 604
144 Cal.Rptr. 758	505........21 Cal.3d 497
945......20 Cal.3d 813	146 Cal.Rptr. 614
144 Cal.Rptr. 905	514........21 Cal.3d 482
963......20 Cal.3d 893	146 Cal.Rptr. 623
145 Cal.Rptr. 1	1043........21 Cal.3d 513
971......20 Cal.3d 906	146 Cal.Rptr. 727
145 Cal.Rptr. 9	1048........21 Cal.3d 542
1342......21 Cal.3d 1	146 Cal.Rptr. 732
145 Cal.Rptr. 176	1053........21 Cal.3d 523
	146 Cal.Rptr. 737

[Illustration 5–3]

USING INSTA–CITE OR AUTO–CITE TO FIND A PARALLEL CITATION

```
Insta-Cite          AUTHORIZED FOR EDUCATIONAL USE ONLY        Page   1
                                                Date of Printing: MAR 05,1998


                               INSTA-CITE
CITATION: 516 U.S. 417

                             Direct History

         1 Hercules Inc. v. U.S., 25 Cl.Ct. 616, 60 USLW 2684,
               37 Cont.Cas.Fed. (CCH) P 76,291 (Cl.Ct., Apr 02, 1992)
               (NO. 90-496C)
               Judgment Affirmed by
         2 Hercules Inc. v. U.S., 24 F.3d 188, 40 Cont.Cas.Fed. (CCH) P 76,778
               (Fed.Cir., May 04, 1994) (NO. 92-5124, 92-5138), rehearing denied,
               in banc suggestion declined (Jul 07, 1994)
               Certiorari Granted by
         3 Hercules, Inc. v. U.S., 514 U.S. 1049, 115 S.Ct. 1425, 131 L.Ed.2d 308,
               63 USLW 3717, 63 USLW 3720 (U.S., Apr 03, 1995) (NO. 94-818)
               AND Judgment Affirmed by
     => 4 Hercules Inc. v. U.S., 516 U.S. 417, 116 S.Ct. 981, 134 L.Ed.2d 47,
               64 USLW 4117, 40 Cont.Cas.Fed. (CCH) P 76,894,
               96 Cal. Daily Op. Serv. 1403, 96 Daily Journal D.A.R. 2395
               (U.S., Mar 04, 1996) (NO. 94-818)

         5 Wm. T. Thompson Co. v. U.S., 26 Cl.Ct. 17,
               38 Cont.Cas.Fed. (CCH) P 76,311 (Cl.Ct., Apr 22, 1992)
               (NO. 90-391C)
               Judgment Affirmed by
         6 Hercules Inc. v. U.S., 24 F.3d 188, 40 Cont.Cas.Fed. (CCH) P 76,778
               (Fed.Cir., May 04, 1994) (NO. 92-5124, 92-5138), rehearing denied,
               in banc suggestion declined (Jul 07, 1994)
               Certiorari Granted by
         7 Hercules, Inc. v. U.S., 514 U.S. 1049, 115 S.Ct. 1425, 131 L.Ed.2d 308,
               63 USLW 3717, 63 USLW 3720 (U.S., Apr 03, 1995) (NO. 94-818)
               AND Judgment Affirmed by
     => 8 Hercules Inc. v. U.S., 516 U.S. 417, 116 S.Ct. 981, 134 L.Ed.2d 47,
               64 USLW 4117, 40 Cont.Cas.Fed. (CCH) P 76,894,
               96 Cal. Daily Op. Serv. 1403, 96 Daily Journal D.A.R. 2395
               (U.S., Mar 04, 1996) (NO. 94-818)


                            Secondary Sources

     Corpus Juris Secundum (C.J.S.) References
               91 C.J.S. United States Sec.89 Note 42.5+ (Pocket Part)
               91 C.J.S. United States Sec.118 Note 54 (Pocket Part)

     (C) Copyright West Group 1998
```

```
Auto-Cite (R) Citation Service, (c) 1998 LEXIS-NEXIS. All rights reserved.

516 US 417:                                       Screen 1 of 65

CITATION YOU ENTERED:

 <=1> Hercules Inc. v. United States*1, 516 U.S. 417, 134 L. Ed. 2d 47, 1996
U.S. LEXIS 1557, 116 S. Ct. 981, 64 U.S.L.W. 4117, 96 C.D.O.S. 1403, 96 Daily
Journal D.A.R. 2395, 40 Cont. Cas. Fed. (CCH) P 76894, 9 Fla. L. Weekly Fed. S
422 (1996)

PRIOR HISTORY:

 <=2> In re "Agent Orange" Product Liability Litigation*2, 475 F. Supp. 928,
1979 U.S. Dist. LEXIS 10418, 206 U.S.P.Q. (BNA) 378 (E.D.N.Y. 1979)

   later proceeding, <=3> In re "Agent Orange" Product Liability
   Litigation, 506 F. Supp. 737, 1979 U.S. Dist. LEXIS 8474 (E.D.N.Y. 1979)

-------------------------------------------------------------------------
Alternate presentation formats are available.
For further explanation, press the H key (for HELP) and then the ENTER key.
To return to LEXIS, press the EXIT SERV key.
```

[Illustration 5–4]

HIEROS GAMOS WEB SITE

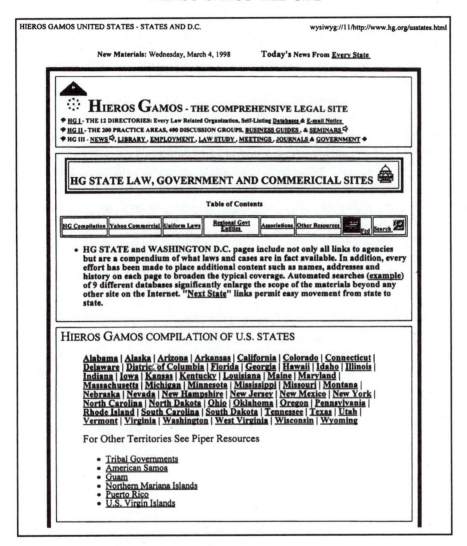

SECTION G.   SUMMARY

1.   State Court Reports

a.   Official reports are court reports published by statutory or court authority.

b.   Unofficial reports are court reports published without statutory or court authority and often are available sooner than official publications.

c.   Slip opinions and advance sheets are published officially for several states. Advance sheets are published for all unofficial reports.

d.   Many states rely on unofficial advance sheets and bound volumes, *e.g., National Reporter System* or other commercial publications. Some states have adopted a commercial publication as their state's official publication.

e.   Extensive coverage is provided in WESTLAW and LEXIS–NEXIS.

2. National Reporter System

a.   Cases of all state appellate courts, arranged geographically into seven regional reporters and three state reporters.

b.   Cases of the federal courts in four reporters, plus four reporters for special courts.

c.   Three subject reporters that include cases reprinted from the *National Reporter System.*

d.   Bound volumes retain the same pagination and volume number as the advance sheets.

e.   Contains many editorial features, including headnotes, table of cases reported, table of statutes construed, words and phrases judicially defined, and key number digest section. Advance sheets often provide current awareness information.

3. Citations and Cross–Reference Tables

a.   Depending upon the court rules, a citation may require inclusion of both the official and unofficial report.

b.   *National Reporter Blue Book* refers the user from the official citation to the unofficial *National Reporter System* citation.

c.   White Tables in *[State] Blue and White Book* refer the user from the unofficial *National Reporter System* citation to the official citation.

d.   *Shepard's Citations* refer the user from the official citation to the unofficial citation and vice versa.

4. Insta–Cite and Auto–Cite

These are electronic case history and citation verification services that can be used to locate parallel citations in different sets of court reports.

5. Internet Web Sites

State court cases are increasingly available on state Web sites and are easily located by referring to larger, more comprehensive sites.

Chapter 6

DIGESTS FOR COURT REPORTS

SECTION A. DIGESTS: IN GENERAL

Because our system of law follows the doctrine of *stare decisis,* the ability to locate earlier cases on the same or similar points of law is essential to sound legal research. As has been noted, cases are published in court reports in chronological order rather than being arranged by subject. For example, although a given volume of reports may contain cases dealing with diverse subjects ranging from *Abatement* to *Zoning,* their arrangement corresponds to the date of the decision. Without a method to search cases by subject, locating those cases with the same or similar points of law as the legal issue being researched would become unwieldy and unmanageable.

After cases are decided, editors for commercial publishers analyze the cases and write brief descriptive abstracts of the various points of law in the cases. These abstracts are typically referred to as headnotes or digest paragraphs. Later, these descriptive paragraphs are arranged by subject and published in sets known as *digests.* Digests are a very important means used in case finding. To demonstrate how digests can be used to research legal issues, assume the following problem, which will serve as the basis for discussion and most of the Illustrations used later in this chapter:

> Leslie was under a physician's care for the treatment of insomnia. Her physician prescribed the drug Halcion to treat Leslie's condition. The drug had certain adverse effects including psychosis and homicidal compulsion, unknown to either Leslie or her physician. One day Leslie took the manufacturer's recommended dose of the drug and then fatally shot her mother.

Before beginning to research this inquiry, the researcher first must determine the important issues involved. One issue may be whether the pharmaceutical company that manufactured the drug is negligent for failure to warn Leslie of the adverse side effects of the drug. Another issue may be whether the pharmaceutical company should be held liable for a design defect in the drug. A third may be whether any statutory exemption from strict liability applies because the drug is unavoidably unsafe. Certainly, if liability against Leslie's physician is possible, one would also want to learn about the measure of damages that could be sought.

In order to find the law applicable to this situation, the researcher must search for appellate court cases with the same or similar facts.

From these cases, the rules of law should be determined. If this incident had happened, for example, in Utah, and all that was available to the researcher were volumes of the reports of the Utah appellate courts, it would be necessary to examine individually hundreds of volumes of the Utah reports to determine if any cases were on point. If a Utah case on point could not be located, it then would be necessary to search for cases from other states. Because of their subject arrangement, digests alleviate the laborious task of having to search for cases in court reports volume by volume.

Digests provide various types of coverage. Some include only cases from the courts of a single state, one court, or a system of courts; others include cases from a group of neighboring states; some include only federal cases; and some include cases on only one broad subject. One includes cases from all appellate courts, federal and state.

In this chapter we will describe digests published primarily by the West Group. West's *Key Number Digests* consist of national, regional, state, federal, and subject units as is shown in Section I. Our focus will be on the *American Digest System,* the most extensive and comprehensive and also the most cumbersome of the many West's *Key Number Digests.* Since the methodology used in conducting research in the *American Digest System* is similar to that used with the other West's *Key Number Digests,* an understanding of the *American Digest System* can be transferred readily to the smaller, specialized West digests. This knowledge is also extremely helpful in conducting WESTLAW research. Other digests, as well as different techniques for locating cases, are discussed in subsequent chapters.

SECTION B. WEST'S KEY NUMBER DIGESTS

1. Key Number System

When the *National Reporter System* began in the late-nineteenth century, West Publishing Company, as it was then known, realized that users of its reporters needed a means to locate by subject the thousands of points of law made in the chronologically-arranged cases. To answer this need, West developed its own unique classification of law, created digest paragraphs containing the points of law made in the cases, and classified these digest paragraphs from all the cases to its system of classification.

West's classification system divides the subject of law into seven main classes: Persons; Property; Contracts; Torts; Crimes; Remedies; and Government. Each class is divided into subclasses and each subclass into Topics. Each of the over 400 Topics corresponds to a legal concept. [See Illustration 6–1.] The Topics are then divided into subdivisions in a given paragraph number called a Key Number. The Key Numbers vary from Topic to Topic from a few to many hundreds within a Topic. These digest paragraphs with their Topic and Key Numbers are cumulated and published in multi-volume sets of digests.

With this background in mind, it is necessary to examine the actual steps involved in developing West's *Key Number Digests*. Essentially, the process starts with a slip opinion or more frequently with an electronic version transmitted directly from the court. After a court case is decided, a copy of the opinion goes to the West Group and is assigned to an editor. Assume the editor receives the opinion for *Grundberg v. Upjohn Co.,* a case with facts similar to the one used in our problem. The editor reads and analyzes the case and writes the headnotes, each headnote representing a particular point of law addressed in the case. Over 275,000 new headnotes are written each year. The editor takes each point of law that has been made into a headnote and assigns to it one or more Topics and Key Numbers, and determines the appropriate unit or units of the *National Reporter System* in which the case and its corresponding headnotes, Topics, and Key Numbers will be published.

For example, an editor decides that a particular headnote deals with products liability. The editor consults the list of over 400 Topics and assigns to the headnote the Topic *Products Liability*. The next step is the assignment of a particular Key Number or Key Numbers. The editor examines a detailed outline (subdivisions) under the Topic *Products Liability*. This outline, discussed more fully in Section D of this chapter, is referred to as the *Analysis*.

After consulting this outline, the editor determines that the headnote deals with acts or omissions constituting liability on part of the manufacturer and specifically with the second subdivision in the *Analysis*—duty to warn. The Topic *Products Liability* receives Key Numbers 8 and 14. The same steps are followed for the next two paragraphs, both of which are assigned the Topic *Drugs and Narcotics* and Key Number 18. Once the editorial work is complete, the case is published in the appropriate unit or units of the *National Reporter System*. [See Illustration 6–2.]

A set of brackets surrounding a number in the text of the published opinion, e.g., [4], indicates the language that corresponds to the headnote. [See Illustration 6–3.] This enables a researcher interested in the point of law discussed in a particular headnote to go directly to that headnote's origin in the case. As indicated above, at times a headnote is classified to more than one Topic. In such instances, all appropriate Topics and Key Numbers are shown.

2. The American Digest System

The *American Digest System* is a massive set of materials in several units and is described by West as a "master index to all of the case law of our country." It contains the headnotes, with their corresponding Topics and Key Numbers, from every unit of the *National Reporter System*. Once the process of creating headnotes for a case and assigning the case to a reporter is completed, the editors take the headnotes with their Topics and Key Numbers in the reporters and merge them into the proper locations in the appropriate sets of West's *Key Number Digests*.

In the *American Digest System,* this process of merging begins with a publication named the *General Digest.* This publication is issued in bound volumes, with a new volume issued approximately once a month. Each volume consists of *all* the headnotes taken from *all* the units of the *National Reporter System* for the period covered. These headnotes are arranged alphabetically by Topic, and then under each Topic numerically by Key Number.

If no further cumulation took place, digests of all the cases, arranged topically, would be in the bound volumes of the *General Digest.* Therefore, to find all the cases dealing with a particular Topic, e.g., *Drugs and Narcotics,* it would be necessary to examine each one of hundreds of bound volumes. Since this obviously is not practical, in 1906 West cumulated into one alphabetical arrangement all the Topics for all the *General Digest* volumes from 1897 to 1906. This set is called the *First Decennial Digest.* By examining a volume of the *First Decennial* containing a particular Topic and Key Number, all cases decided on that point during 1897–1906 can be located.

This process of systematically cumulating a set of the *General Digest* into a *Decennial* has taken place since 1897, with a new *Decennial* compiled every ten years. The latest complete set is the *Tenth Decennial Digest, Part 1,*[1] covering 1986–1991, with the *Tenth, Part 2,* covering 1991–1996 in the process of being compiled. The fact that the *Tenth, Part 2* is not yet complete makes for an even more cumbersome search process than usual. All digest paragraphs of cases decided from late 1991 through 1996 will be found either in the *General Digest, 8th Series* or in the *Tenth, Part 2,* and those from the end of 1996 forward in the *General Digest, 9th Series.*

Thus, given a Topic and a Key Number, one can start with the *First Decennial* and proceed through the *Tenth, Part 1,* the *General Digest, 8th Series* and *9th Series,* and the available volumes of the *Tenth, Part 2* to locate all cases on a point of law under a particular Topic and Key Number from 1897 to several weeks ago.[2] [See Illustrations 6–4 and 6–5.] When the *Tenth, Part 2* is complete it will be necessary to consult only the *General Digest, 9th Series* for later digest paragraphs.

It is possible to find all cases from 1658, the date of the first reported American case, since cases from 1658 to 1896 are digested in a publication named the *Century Edition.* Since the *National Reporter*

---

[1] Starting with the *Ninth Decennial,* the publisher decided to issue it in two parts: *Part 1* covering 1976–81; *Part 2* covering 1981–86. This process of cumulating cases every five years has continued with the *Tenth Decennial.* One advantage of this new arrangement is that a researcher has fewer volumes of the *General Digest* to examine since it now ends, starts to be superseded by new part of a *Decennial,* and commences anew in five-year increments rather than the previous ten.

[2] In the *Decennials* and the *General Digest* cases are arranged hierarchically, beginning with those of the Supreme Court of the United States and followed by the lower federal courts, with the most recent case listed first in each grouping. These cases are followed by cases relating to the individual states. These cases are arranged alphabetically by state and hierarchically by court, with the most recent case listed first in each grouping.

System did not exist during this period, the *Century Edition* does not contain Key Numbers. A different topical arrangement was used. For example, the Topic *Drugs and Narcotics* Key Number 18 in the *Decennials* stands for *Civil Liability of Manufacturers,* whereas in the *Century Edition, Drugs and Narcotics* 18 was listed under the heading of Druggists, and more specifically, under the sections *Persons Purchasing or Using Articles Sold or Dispensed* and *Actions for Damages* are digested under Section Numbers 8 and 9.[3]

Century digest	1658–1896	50 vols.
First Decennial	1897–1906	25 vols.
Second Decennial	1907–1916	24 vols.
Third Decennial	1916–1926	29 vols.
Fourth Decennial	1926–1936	34 vols.
Fifth Decennial	1936–1946	52 vols.
Sixth Decennial	1946–1956	36 vols.
Seventh Decennial	1956–1966	38 vols.
Eighth Decennial	1966–1976	50 vols.
Ninth Decennial, Part 1	1976–1981	38 vols.
Ninth Decennial, Part 2	1981–1986	48 vols.
Tenth Decennial, Part 1	1986–1991	44 vols.
Tenth Decennial, Part 2	1991–1996	in progress
General Digest (8th Series)	1991–1996	complete
General Digest (9th Series)	1996–2001	in progress

3. Digest Paragraphs in WESTLAW

The West Group includes the equivalent of its *American Digest System* in WESTLAW, the largest of its computer-assisted legal research services. It is, therefore, possible to search, for example, the Topic *Drugs and Narcotics,* Key Number 18 and retrieve all cases digested under this point of law, to restrict the search to a particular period of time, or to add a specific search term, such as *manufacturer,* to the query. Key Number searching in WESTLAW eliminates the often laborious task of searching in the *Decennials.*[4]

WESTLAW and companion CD–ROM product includes the powerful hypertext feature in its headnotes. A researcher can "jump" directly to the related text in the opinion or jump from the text directly to the related headnote. [See Illustration 6–6, Figure 1.] Computer-assisted legal research is discussed in more detail in Chapter 21.

---

[3] In both the first and second *Decennials*, cross-references are made from the Decennial Key Numbers used in the *Century Edition*, with the one in the second being more complete. If one locates a point of law in the *Century Edition*, Key Numbers for later cases on the same point of law can be located by consulting a pink reference table in volume 21 of the *First Decennial*.

[4] In WESTLAW Topics are converted to a numerical equivalent that corresponds to the alphabetically-arranged Topics used in West digests. [See Illustration 6–1.] The Key number symbol is converted to the letter "k." [See Illustration 6–6, Figures 1 and 2.] Information showing the corresponding WESTLAW Topic number equivalent to use when searching WESTLAW is available online and in numerous print publications.

4. Keeping the Key Number System Current

Law, of course, is constantly expanding or changing. For example, when the original Key Number classification was prepared in 1897, no provisions were made for cases dealing with damages resulting from a jet breaking the sound barrier or for the control and regulation of nuclear energy. Consequently, to cover new areas of the law, at times West adds new Topics to the Key Number classification. In recent years these newly-added Topics include *Commodity Futures Trading Regulation* and *Racketeer Influenced and Corrupt Organizations* (RICO).

In addition to adding new Topics, Key Numbers are sometimes reclassified (revised) in order to adapt to changing circumstances. For example, the Topics *Bankruptcy* and *Federal Civil Procedure* were recently reclassified, i.e., the existing Key Number classifications were changed to newly-renumbered ones to accommodate recent changes in the federal laws governing these areas. When this reclassification occurs, Key Number Translation Tables are provided near the start of the topic in the digest to show where the former Key Number is located in the new Key Number classification and vice versa. [See Illustration 6–7.] WESTLAW updates this information automatically for all Key Numbers since 1932. A researcher can retrieve all relevant cases under a current Key Number even though some of those cases may have been previously classified under a different Key Number. [See Illustration 6–6, Figure 2.]

At still other times, existing Topics are expanded as additional issues emerge in the area over time. For example, until approximately 30 years ago all headnotes dealing with issues concerning liability of sellers of prescription drugs, an issue relevant to our research problem, received the Topic *Druggists* and the Key Number 9.

EXAMPLE FROM TOPIC *DRUGGISTS*, SEVENTH DECENNIAL DIGEST (1956–1966)

7.	Liabilities to persons purchasing of using article sold or dispensed.
8.	—— In general.
9.	—— Negligence.
10.	Actions for damages.
11.	Penalties for forfeitures and actions therefor.
12.	Criminal prosecutions.

The *Eighth Decennial Digest* changed the Topic *Druggists* to *Drugs and Narcotics* and divided the Topic into two main categories: *Drugs and Druggists In General* and *Narcotics and Dangerous Drugs*.

EXAMPLE FROM TOPIC *DRUGS AND NARCOTICS,* EIGHTH DECENNIAL DIGEST (1966–1976)

> I. DRUGS AND DRUGGISTS IN GENERAL
> 　　17. Civil liability
> 　　18. ____ Manufacturers.
> 　　19. Retailers or dispensers.
> 　　20. Actions for damages.
> 　　21. ____ Evidence.
> 　　22. ____ Questions for jury.
> II. NARCOTICS AND DANGEROUS DRUGS

Thus, by adding new Topics, reclassifying older ones, and expanding existing ones, West's Key Number System attempts to keep current with the changing and dynamic aspects of law.

5. Table of Key Numbers

For cases more recent than those in the *Decennials,* it is necessary to examine the digest paragraphs under the same Topic and Key Number in the individual volumes of the latest *General Digest.* Since each volume contains digest paragraphs covering only a short period of time, there may be as many as sixty volumes to search before they are cumulated and replaced by a new *Decennial.* To avoid the necessity of examining a volume of the *General Digest* that does not include a particular Key Number, the publisher includes a *Table of Key Numbers* in every tenth volume of the *General Digest.* These tables indicate in which volumes of the *General Digest* cases are digested for a particular Key Number for that ten volume increment. [See Illustration 6–8.]

Illustrations in Section C show the development of headnotes from reported cases, the assignment of Topics and Key Numbers to the headnotes, how headnotes become a part of the various units of the *American Digest System,* and headnotes as they appear in WESTLAW.

Methods of determining under what Topics and Key Numbers to search are described in Sections D and E, *infra.*

SECTION C. ILLUSTRATIONS: KEY NUMBER CLASSIFICATION AND UNITS OF THE AMERICAN DIGEST SYSTEM

6–1.　　**Sample page from List of Digest Topics**
6–2—　**Pages from volume of Southern Reporter 2d**
　6–3.
6–4.　　**Page from General Digest, 8th Series**
6–5.　　**Page from Tenth Decennial Digest, Part 1**
6–6.　　**Sample Screens from WESTLAW**
6–7.　　**Example of Key Number Translation Table**
6–8.　　**Page from Table of Key Numbers in General Digest, 8th Series**

[Illustration 6–1]

SAMPLE PAGE FROM ALPHABETICAL LIST OF DIGEST
TOPICS USED IN KEY NUMBER SYSTEM

DIGEST TOPICS

The topic numbers shown below may be used in WESTLAW searches for cases
within the topic and within specified key numbers.

1	Abandoned and Lost Property	40	Assistance, Writ of	77	Citizens
2	Abatement and Revival	41	Associations	78	Civil Rights
		42	Assumpsit, Action of	79	Clerks of Courts
3	Abduction	43	Asylums	80	Clubs
4	Abortion and Birth Control	44	Attachment	81	Colleges and Universities
		45	Attorney and Client		
5	Absentees	46	Attorney General	82	Collision
6	Abstracts of Title	47	Auctions and Auctioneers	83	Commerce
7	Accession			83H	Commodity Futures Trading Regulation
8	Accord and Satisfaction	48	Audita Querela	84	Common Lands
		48A	Automobiles	85	Common Law
9	Accoı	48B	Aviation		

There are over 400 Topics in the *American Digest System*. These Topics are used in creating headnotes. See next Illustration.

The numbers to the left of the Topics are used in accessing the Topics on WESTLAW. This is discussed in B–3 of this chapter.

15A	Administrative Law and Procedure	58	Bonds	92B	Consumer Credit
		59	Boundaries	92H	Consumer Protection
16	Admiralty	60	Bounties	93	Contempt
17	Adoption	61	Breach of Marriage Promise	95	Contracts
18	Adulteration			96	Contribution
19	Adultery	62	Breach of the Peace	97	Conversion
20	Adverse Possession	63	Bribery	98	Convicts
21	Affidavits	64	Bridges	99	Copyrights and Intellectual Property
22	Affray	65	Brokers		
23	Agriculture	66	Building and Loan Associations	100	Coroners
24	Aliens			101	Corporations
25	Alteration of Instruments	67	Burglary	102	Costs
		68	Canals	103	Counterfeiting
26	Ambassadors and Consuls	69	Cancellation of Instruments	104	Counties
				105	Court Commissioners
27	Amicus Curiae	70	Carriers	106	Courts
28	Animals	71	Cemeteries	107	Covenant, Action of
29	Annuities	72	Census	108	Covenants
30	Appeal and Error	73	Certiorari	108A	Credit Reporting Agencies
31	Appearance	74	Champerty and Maintenance		
33	Arbitration			110	Criminal Law
34	Armed Services	75	Charities	111	Crops
35	Arrest	76	Chattel Mortgages	113	Customs and Usages
36	Arson	76A	Chemical Dependents	114	Customs Duties
37	Assault and Battery	76H	Children Out-of-Wedlock	115	Damages
38	Assignments			116	Dead Bodies

VII

1–

[Illustration 6–2]

SAMPLE PAGE FROM 813 P.2d 89

GRUNDBERG v. UPJOHN CO.   Utah **89**
Cite as 813 P.2d 89 (Utah 1991)

L.Ed.2d 328 (1980), sustained the federal government's statutory right to appeal a sentence on the ground that the policies underlying the double jeopardy clause are not offended by such a procedure. 449 U.S. at 136, 101 S.Ct. at 437. The Court also held in *DiFrancesco* that the increased punishment which could be imposed by an appellate court on review did not constitute multiple punishment in violation of the double jeopardy clause. *See id.* at 137, 101

> **This is the first page of *Grundberg v. Upjohn Co.*, a case relevant to our research problem. Four headnotes have been assigned to this case. Notice how each headnote has been assigned a Topic and a specific Key Number.**
> **See next Illustration.**

though the question of double jeopardy was not directly at issue, the Court, quoting *Bryant v. United States*, 214 F. 51, 53 (8th Cir.1914), stated: " 'It is well settled that it is not double jeopardy to resentence a prisoner who had his first sentence vacated by writ of error....' " 79 Utah at 80, 7 P.2d at 829.

Affirmed.

HALL, C.J., HOWE, Associate C.J., and DURHAM and ZIMMERMAN, JJ., concur.

Ilo Marie GRUNDBERG, individually, and Janice Gray, as personal representative of the Estate of Mildred Lucille Coats, deceased, Plaintiffs,

v.

The UPJOHN COMPANY, a Delaware corporation, Defendant.

No. 900573.

Supreme Court of Utah.

May 14, 1991.

Rehearing Denied June 26, 1991.

Insomniac brought products liability action against prescription drug manufac-

turer alleging, in part, that she shot her mother as result of ingesting a defectively designed drug. The United States District Court for the District of Utah, J. Thomas Greene, J., certified question. The Supreme Court, Durham, J., held that: (1) FDA-approved prescription drugs are unavoidably unsafe products; and (2) manufacturer of FDA-approved prescription drugs is immune from strict liability claims based on design defects.

Question answered.

Howe, Associate C.J., dissented and filed opinion in which Stewart, J., joined.

Stewart, J., dissented and filed opinion.

1. **Products Liability** ⚖=8, 14

Seller of unavoidably unsafe product is not strictly liable for unfortunate consequences of use of product if product is properly prepared and marketed and distributed with appropriate warnings.

2. **Products Liability** ⚖=8, 14

Seller may be liable if unavoidably unsafe products are mismanufactured or unaccompanied by adequate warnings, even if plaintiff cannot establish seller's negligence.

3. **Drugs and Narcotics** ⚖=18

FDA-approved prescription drugs are unavoidably dangerous in design; thus, manufacturers are immune from strict liability claims for alleged design defect.

4. **Drugs and Narcotics** ⚖=18

If prescription drug manufacturer knows or should know of risk associated with its product, it is directly liable to patient if it fails to adequately warn medical profession of that danger, even though all FDA-approved prescription drugs are unavoidably unsafe products.

Gary W. Pendleton, St. George, Earle F. Lasseter, Thomas R. Vuksinick, H. Ross

[Illustration 6–3]

SAMPLE PAGE FROM 813 P.2d

GRUNDBERG v. UPJOHN CO.   Utah   97
Cite as 813 P.2d 89 (Utah 1991)

FDA, regardless of whether the physician, the manufacturer, or others believe the reaction to be drug-related. 21 C.F.R. § 314.80(b). The manufacturer must also periodically submit reports as to what actions it took in response to ADRs and must submit data from any post-marketing studies, reports in the scientific literature, and foreign marketing experience. 21 C.F.R. §§ 314.80(b), .80(c). The FDA has authority to enforce these reporting requirements; any failure to comply may subject a manufacturer to civil and criminal penalties. 21 U.S.C. §§ 332–34 (1972 & Supp.1991). In response to its surveillance findings, the FDA may require labeling changes or if necessary withdraw NDA approval and

---

This is another page from *Grundberg v. Upjohn Co.* It illustrates how headnotes are developed. The bracketed numbers are inserted by the editors. Each section so bracketed has been condensed into a corresponding headnote for the point of law in each bracketed section.

See next Illustration.

---

drugs are not placed on the market without continued monitoring for adverse consequences that would render the FDA's initial risk/benefit analysis invalid. Allowing individual courts and/or juries to continually reevaluate a drug's risks and benefits ignores the processes of this expert regulatory body and the other avenues of recovery available to plaintiffs.

We note that the Utah Legislature has recognized the value of the FDA approval process and the public interest in the availability and affordability of prescription drugs by restricting the extent of liability

for injuries resulting from the use of those drugs. Utah Code Ann. § 78–18–2(1) (Supp.1990) states that "punitive damages may not be awarded if a drug causing the claimant's harm: (a) received premarket approval or licensure by the Federal Food, Drug, and Cosmetic Act, 21 U.S.C. Section 301 et seq...." This policy, designed to avoid discouraging manufacturers from marketing FDA-approved drugs, applies even to drugs marketed with inadequate warnings.

[4] The legislature has also acknowledged the important role of governmental standards in Utah Code Ann. section 78–15–6(3).[7] In that section, the legislature declared that there is a rebuttable presumption that a product which fully complies with the applicable government standards at the time of marketing is not defective.[8]

Our prior case law supports this approach as well. In *Barson v. E.R. Squibb & Sons, Inc.*, 682 P.2d 832 (Utah 1984), we addressed the sufficiency of evidence for a claim that a drug manufacturer negligently failed to warn of risks associated with its product. We held that even after meeting governmental requirements, if there are dangers about which the drug manufacturer knew or should have known, the manufacturer may be subject to liability. *Id.* at 836. Thus, consistent with our holding in this case, if a manufacturer knows or should know of a risk associated with its product, it is directly liable to the patient if it fails to adequately warn the medical profession of that danger. *Id.* at 835.

---

7. Section 3 of the Utah Products Liability Act, Utah Code Ann. §§ 78–15–1 to –6, was held unconstitutional by this court in *Berry v. Beech Aircraft Corp.*, 717 P.2d 670 (Utah 1985), as a statute of repose. Because section 78–15–3 was not severable from the other sections of the Act, we ruled that the remainder of the Products Liability Act was invalid. The legislature repealed and amended certain sections in an apparent effort to comply with the court's concerns. Although section 78–15–6 was neither repealed, amended, nor specifically reenacted, there is no indication that the legislature has changed its policy regarding deference to governmental standards.

8. Plaintiffs argue that immunizing drug manufacturers from strict liability for design defects is contrary to this statute, because that conclusion would establish an "irrebuttable presumption" that the drug was not defective or unreasonably dangerous. We disagree. Plaintiffs may still recover under a strict liability claim by demonstrating that the product was unreasonably dangerous due to an inadequate warning, a manufacturing flaw, mismarketing, or misrepresenting information to the FDA. We cite these statutes only to demonstrate the legislature's similar deference to the expertise of certain governmental agencies, particularly that of the FDA.

[Illustration 6–4]

SAMPLE PAGE FROM GENERAL DIGEST, 8TH SERIES

477   **DRUGS & NARCOTICS** ⟸20

question for the jury, failure to timely raise the issue waives the right to rely on the defense. U.S.C.A Const.Amend. 5.—People v. Sering, 283 Cal.Rptr 507.

⟸202. Plea of guilty, or nolo contendere.

C.A.7 (Ill.) 1991. Defendant could not collaterally attack on double jeopardy grounds convictions based on voluntary guilty pleas through motion for correction of illegal sentence; defendant did not claim that his plea was involuntary or that he had received ineffective assistance of counsel and no facial double jeopardy violation existed. Fed.Rules Cr.Proc.Rule 35(a), 18 U.S.C.A; U.S.C.A Const.Amend. 5.—U.S. v. Makres, 937 F.2d 1282.

DOWER AND CURTESY

I. IN GENERAL. ⟸1–28.

II. INCHOATE INTEREST. ⟸29–53

III RIGHTS AND REMEDIES OF SURVIVING SPOUSE, ⟸54–118.

II. INCHOATE INTEREST.

(A) RIGHTS AND REMEDIES OF CLAIMANT.

owned solely by other spouse is to merely release inchoate rights of dower and nothing more. I.C.A. § 633.238.—Id.

Wife who joins her husband on mortgage concerning property owned by him in fee simple is presumed to do so only for purpose of relinquishing her dower right.—Id.

DRAINS

[NO PARAGRAPHS]

DRUGS AND NARCOTICS

I. DRUGS AND DRUGGISTS IN GENERAL. ⟸1–40.

II. NARCOTICS AND DANGEROUS DRUGS, ⟸41–198.

I. DRUGS AND DRUGGISTS IN GENERAL.

⟸12. Registration, certificate, or license.

⟸15. — Revocation or suspension.

Colo.App. 1990. State Board of Pharmacy

directly of potential risks and required only that manufacturer warn medical community.—Reaves v. Ortho Pharmaceutical Corp., 765 F.Supp. 1287.

"Learned intermediary doctrine" allows manufacturers of prescription drugs to assume that patients rely on physician to evaluate benefits and risks of using drug for particular purpose and, thus, such manufacturers discharge their duty to warn by properly warning prescribing physicians of risks and harmful side effects associated with use of prescription drug.—Id.

Learned intermediary doctrine was cognizable under Michigan law.—Id.

Under Michigan law, learned intermediary doctrine applies to oral contraceptives, which do not differ significantly from other prescription drugs.—Id.

Utah 1991. FDA-approved prescription drugs are unavoidably dangerous in design; thus, manufacturers are immune from strict liability claims for alleged design defect.—Grundberg v. Upjohn Co., 813 P.2d 89.

If prescription drug manufacturer knows or should know of risk associated with its product, it is directly liable to patient if it fails to adequately warn medical profession of that danger, even though all FDA-approved prescription drugs are unavoidably unsafe products.—Id.

⟸20. Actions for damages.

Cl.Ct. 1991. Special master did not act arbitrarily, capriciously, with an abuse of discretion, or contrary to law when she ordered payment of damages for lost earning capacity as part of lump sum award in Vaccine Act case. Public Health Service Act, §§ 2112(e)(2)(B), 2115(a)(3)(B), (f)(4)(A), as amended, 42 U.S.C.A. §§ 300aa–12(e)(2)(B), 300aa–15(a)(3)(B), (f)(4)(A).—Stotts v. Secretary of Dept. of Health and Human Services, 23 Cl.Ct. 352.

Special master's award of damages under Vaccine Act for child's pain and suffering was not arbitrary or capricious, although it was contended that child was unable to experience any pain and suffering due to severity of his initial vaccine-related injury; there was evidence that child was presently able to experience positive and negative feelings and that it was likely child would continue to experience those feelings, and there was no probative counterveiling evidence to support government's position. Public Health Service Act, § 2115(f)(4)(A), as amended, 42 U.S.C.A. § 300aa–15(f)(4)(A).—Id.

Special master did not abuse her discretion in awarding Vaccine Act pain and suffering damages as part of lump sum instead of funding it through annuity which would purportedly preserve limited Act funds for distribution to other persons suffering from vaccine-related injuries. Public Health Service Act, § 2115(f)(4)(A), as amended, 42 U.S.C.A. § 300aa–15(f)(4)(A).—Id.

Special master abused her discretion in Vaccine Act case in failing to reduce lump-sum award for future pain and suffering to its net present value. Public Health Service Act, § 2115(a)(4), (f)(4)(A), as amended, 42 U.S.C.A. § 300aa–15(a)(4), (f)(4)(A).—Id.

Special master's decision in Vaccine Act case to include in lump-sum award damages for architectural modifications required for child suffering from vaccine-related injury was not arbitrary or capricious; there was no statutory obligation that compensation for that element of damages be funded through purchase of annuity. Public Health Service Act, § 2115(f)(4)(A), as amended, 42 U.S.C.A. § 300aa–15(f)(4)(A).—Id.

Special master's Vaccine Act award of compensation for special education and special therapy services without offset for any services

[Overlay box:]

> When the Topic and Key Number are known, sets of digests can be consulted to locate cases with the same or similar points of law. The text of these cases should then be read. The digest paragraphs from the *Grundberg* case were first published in the *General Digest 8th* and will later be cumulated into the *Tenth Decennial, Part 2.* In these sets of digests, federal court cases are listed first, followed by state court cases arranged alphabetically by state and starting with the most recent case.
>
> Notice how digest paragraphs are reprinted as they originally appeared as headnotes in the reported cases. Notice also how citations are given after the digest paragraph to where the case is reported.
>
> After selecting the relevant paragraphs and noting citations, one should then check under the same Topic and Key Number in other *General Digest* volumes for additional cases. One can check the prior *Decennials* under this Topic and Key Number for earlier cases.

more, burden is upon challenger to show special language in contract or deed entitling nonowner spouse to payments, or evidence of some other agreement between spouses regarding ownership of proceeds.—Id.

Mere fact that purchaser made payments jointly to both spouses is insufficient to overcome presumption that presence of spouse's name as grantor in conveyance of property

dition with predicted condition had vaccine not been administered. Public Health Service Act § 2101 et seq., as amended, 42 U.S.C.A § 300aa–1 et seq.—Misasi v. Secretary of Dept of Health and Human Services. 23 Cl.Ct. 322

⟸18. — Manufacturers.

Under Michigan law learned intermediary doctrine relieved oral contraceptive manufacturer of duty to warn patient

For subsequent case history information see Table of Cases Affirmed, Reversed or Modified

[Illustration 6–5]

SAMPLE PAGE FROM TENTH DECENNIAL DIGEST, PART 1

☞17   **DRUGS & NARCOTICS**   18 10th D Pt 1—650

the particular type of DES taken by plaintiff's mother, that they did not market DES in geographic area where plaintiff's mother obtained drug, or that the relevant period for injuries that utero on "mark "enterprise liabil ry.—Id.

Ill.App. 1 Dist. unreasonably da adequate warnin companying product.—Batteast by Batteast v. Wyeth Laboratories, Inc., 122 Ill.Dec. 169, 526 N.E.2d 428, 172 Ill.App.3d 114, appeal allowed 128 Ill.Dec. 887, 535 N.E.2d 398, 123 Ill.2d 556, reversed 148 Ill.Dec. 13, 560 N.E.2d 315, 137 Ill.2d 175.

Kan. 1990. Diagnostic drugs can be entitled to the unavoidably unsafe product exception to strict liability in tort.—Savina v. Sterling Drug, Inc., 795 P.2d 915, 247 Kan. 105.

La.App. 1 Cir. 1988. Detailmen who were employed by drug manufacturers and whose duties included distribution of product samples, delivery of package inserts, and communication of warnings contained in inserts to physicians in territory were not negligent in failing to warn physician about tooth staining side effects of tetracycline, and thus, detailmen could not be held personally liable to those who suffered side effects; detailmen delivered and explained new package inserts to plaintiffs' physician and detailmen testified that they were unaware of danger at time in question.—Wallace v. Upjohn Co., 535 So.2d 1110, writ denied 539 So.2d 630.

Mo.App. 1987. Pharmaceutical firm was not liable for consumer's alleged injury from drug given uncontradicted evidence that firm never supplied drug to hospitals where woman was treated.—Ahearn v. Lafayette Pharmacal, Inc., 729 S.W.2d 501.

N.Y.A.D. 3 Dept. 1989. Fact that drug distributor distributed drug with instructions for dispensing did not show that it represented the drug as its own so as to permit it to be held liable for death of user who shot himself, allegedly as a result of severe depression induced by the drug.—Martin v. Hacker, 550 N.Y.S.2d 130, 156 A.D.2d 914.

Ohio 1990. There is no private cause of action for monetary recovery based upon alleged violations of Federal Food, Drug, and Cosmetic Act. Federal Food, Drug, and Cosmetic Act, § 1 et seq., 21 U.S.C.A. § 301 et seq.—Renfro v. Black, 556 N.E.2d 150, 52 Ohio St.3d 27, rehearing denied 559 N.E.2d 1368, 53 Ohio St.3d 710.

Pa.Super. 1990. There was no evidence that birth control clinic routinely distributed contraceptives without physician prescription, as required to support patient's negligence claim.— Taurino v. Ellen, 579 A.2d 925, 397 Pa.Super. 50, appeal denied 589 A.2d 693, 527 Pa. 603.

Pa.Super. 1990. Information supplied by drug manufacturer is only one source that physician must consult when deciding whether to prescribe drug, and physician is expected to make independent medical judgment in determining whether given drug is appropriate for particular patient.—Brecher v. Cutler, 578 A.2d 481, 396 Pa.Super. 211.

Pa.Super. 1987. In case of prescription drugs, warning required is not to general public or to consumer but rather to prescribing doctor.—Makripodis by Makripodis v. Merrell-Dow Pharmaceuticals, Inc., 523 A.2d 374, 361 Pa.Super. 589.

R.I. 1988. Cause of action exists for personal injuries caused by prescription drugs based on theory of strict liability in tort.—Castrignano v.

E.R. Squibb & Sons, Inc., 546 A.2d 775, on subsequent appeal 900 F.2d 455, rehearing denied.

One can check the *Decennials* under Drugs and Narcotics 18 for cases with the same or similar points of law that were earlier than those in the *General Digest.*

---

to warn.—Id.

☞18. — **Manufacturers.**

C.A.D.C. 1988. Under law of Maryland and District of Columbia, women who were exposed to DES prior to their birth could not recover from drug manufacturer for injuries allegedly caused by DES, under "concert of action" or "market share" theories of liability, absent showing that manufacturer produced drug ingested by their mothers.—Tidler v. Eli Lilly and Co., 851 F.2d 418, 271 U.S.App.D.C. 163.

Under law of Maryland and District of Columbia, women who were exposed to DES prior to their birth could not recover from drug manufacturer under "bulk supply" theory of liability, even if manufacturer produced 95% of bulk DES sold in area during relevant period, absent evidence that manufacturer produced DES consumed by the plaintiffs' mothers.—Id.

C.A.8 (Ark.) 1989. Under Arkansas law, "CU–7" intrauterine device was not within scope of "unavoidably unsafe" products exception to strict liability rule, and manufacturer of that device could be required to bear risk of injury caused by product if it was defective and unreasonably dangerous; alternative methods of birth control were available, and manufacturer had made no showing that its device, or IUDs in general, were exceptionally beneficial to society.—Hill v. Searle Laboratories, a Div. of Searle Pharmaceuticals, Inc., 884 F.2d 1064, rehearing denied.

"Learned intermediary rule" assumes that it is reasonable for manufacturer of drug products to rely on prescribing physician to forward to patient, the ultimate user of those products, any warnings regarding their possible side effects.— Id.

Under Arkansas law, manufacturer did not adequately warn ultimate users of intrauterine device of its potential side effects by warning prescribing physicians; "learned intermediary rule" was inapplicable as treating physician was not intervening party between user and manufacturer, it was feasible to warn ultimate user, and such warning was required by FDA regulation.— Id.

C.A.11 (Ga.) 1988. Parents whose child died after receiving DTP vaccine were not entitled to proceed in products liability action against all three possible manufacturers of vaccine under theory of alternative liability under Georgia law.—Chapman v. American Cyanamid Co., 861 F.2d 1515.

C.A.7 (Ill.) 1988. Manufacturer of synthetic estrogen used by plaintiff's mother during her pregnancy would be liable for injuries plaintiff allegedly sustained as result of mother's ingestion of drug, even though it could not have foreseen specific type of injury plaintiff sustained, as long as it should have known that estrogen could cause some harm to fetus.— Needham v. White Laboratories, Inc., 847 F.2d 355.

C.A.7 (Ill.) 1986. Manufacturer of swine flu vaccine could not be liable to vaccinee who had contracted paralytic and degenerative nervous system condition as a result of being vaccinated; vaccinee had been fully informed of that risk of

vaccine, any failure to warn would have been attributable solely to Government and Government was not liable as a matter of law, so ...ent-con ...S., 803

...r design ...nsas law ...ry found ...d that a ...ologically ... Labora ...ts Corp., 90b F.2d 1399 certiorari denied 111 S.Ct. 511, 112 L.Ed.2d 523, on remand 760 F.Supp.1410.

Federal law did not preempt Kansas tort claims alleging improper manufacture of DTP (diphtheria, tetanus and pertussis) vaccine, despite Food and Drug Administration's (FDA) regulation of the area.—Id.

C.A.5 (La.) 1987. Manufacturer of prescription medication discharged its duty to consumers, under Louisiana law, when it informed prescribing physicians of dangers of harm from such drug through package inserts listing in physician's desk reference, and broadcast letters to physicians which repeatedly warned against prescribing medications for persons who suffer from aspirin sensitivity; thus, consumer could not maintain action against manufacturer for adverse reaction she allegedly suffered.—Anderson v. McNeilab, Inc., 831 F.2d 92.

C.A.4 (Md.) 1991. Pharmaceutical manufacturer must warn physicians or other medical personnel authorized to prescribe drugs by state law of risks known or reasonably foreseeable at time product is administered.—Miles Laboratories, Inc. Cutter Laboratories Div., 927 F.2d 187.

C.A.4 (Md.) 1988. Woman who sustained injury as result of her mother's ingestion of diethylstilbestrol (DES) could not maintain action under agency theory against pharmaceutical manufacturer which did not manufacture particular brand of DES ingested by mother but which had issued franchise to retail pharmacy where mother's DES was purchased; manufacturer franchisor was not responsible for sale of other manufacturer's medication by its franchise given absence of showing of express or apparent agency.—Hofherr v. Dart Industries, Inc., 853 F.2d 259.

Manufacturer of prescription drug which had franchise agreement with retail pharmacy did not have obligation to warn consumer or franchisee of dangers associated with particular drug; any obligation on part of pharmaceutical manufacturer to warn was strictly to physician who prescribed medication.—Id.

C.A.5 (Miss.) 1987. "Unavoidably unsafe" drug will be deemed unreasonably dangerous per se, and its producer held liable, only if potential harmful effects of product outweigh legitimate public interest in its availability.—Swayze v. McNeil Laboratories, Inc., 807 F.2d 464, rehearing denied 812 F.2d 1405.

Drug manufacturer whose language of warnings for fentanyl, printed in package inserts and published in reference books, was adequate, was not required to provide warnings to consumers regarding danger of narcotic anesthetic, where fentanyl was administered only within a physician-patient relationship.—Id.

Drug manufacturer was not required to police individual operating rooms to determine whether doctors adequately supervised surgical teams to avoid unsupervised administration of narcotic anesthetic for which adequate warnings were given in package inserts and published in reference books.—Id

Drug manufacturer was not required to remove its narcotic anesthetic fentanyl from mar

---

For references to other topics, see Descriptive-Word Index

[Illustration 6–6]

SAMPLE SCREENS FROM WESTLAW SHOWING HEADNOTES

Figure 1. Headnote 4 from *Grundberg v. Upjohn Co.*

```
                    Copr. (C) West 1998 No Claim to Orig. U.S. Govt. Works
AUTHORIZED FOR EDUCATIONAL USE ONLY
813 P.2d 89        FOUND DOCUMENT           P 8 OF 55         UT-CS        Page
(Cite as: 813 P.2d 89)
Grundberg v. Upjohn Co.
   [4]         KeyCite this headnote
   138    DRUGS AND NARCOTICS
   138I      Drugs and
   138k17     Civil L
```

   138k18   k. Manufac
Utah,1991.
If prescription drug
its product, it is d
medical profession c
drugs are unavoidabl

> This is the fourth headnote in *Grundberg v. Upjohn Co.* as it appears in WESTLAW. Note that in WESTLAW the Topic name is replaced with a number and the Key Number symbol is replaced with the letter "k." Hypertext links enable the user to "jump" directly to the related text of the opinion.

Figure 2. Case Headnote with *Formerly* Line

```
                    Copr. (C) West 1998 No Claim to Orig. U.S. Govt. Works
AUTHORIZED FOR EDUCATIONAL USE ONLY
619 F.2d 216       FOUND DOCUMENT           P 8 OF 25         CTA         Page
(Cite as: 619 F.2d 216)
In re Adamo
   [5]         KeyCite this headnote
   51     BANKRUPTCY
   51I       In General
   51I(B)       Constitutional and Statutory Provisions

   51k2026  k. Repeal.
Formerly 51k8
```

C.A.N.Y., 1980.
Premature repeal of t
dischargeability of s
commenced prior to th
Education Act of 1965

> The Topic Bankruptcy was recently revised. This headnote illustrates how a search of a new Key Number also identifies the Topic's former Key Number. See next Illustration.

   11 U.S.C.A. s 523(a)(8); s 402(a), 11 U.S.C.A. note preceding section
101.

[Illustration 6–7]

KEY NUMBER TRANSLATION FROM THE TENTH
DECENNIAL DIGEST, PART 1

4 10th D Pt 1—943   **BANKRUPTCY**

TABLE 3

KEY NUMBER TRANSLATION TABLE

FORMER KEY NUMBER TO PRESENT KEY NUMBER

The topic BANKRUPTCY has been extensively revised in consideration of the Bankruptcy Reform Act of 1978.

This table indicates the location, in the revised topic, of cases formerly classified to the earlier key numbers.

In many instances there is no one-to-one relation between the key numbers, new and old. This table recognizes only significant correspondence, and the user who has found a particular case classified to an old key number is advised to consult the Table of Cases, where its present classification may be found.

The absence of a key number indicates that there is no useful parallel.

Former Key Number	Present Key Number	Former Key Number	Present Key Number
1	2012–2018	44.5	2255, 2256, 2311
2, 3	2013–2025	47	2258
4	2001, 2021, 2022	48	2252–2254, 2259–2264
5	2023	49	2264(1)
6	2023–2025	50	2252–2254, 2259–2264
7	2023	51	2251
8	2026	52	2281, 2293
9	2002, 2513, 2534, 2762–2765, 2826	54	2234
		55–64	2281
10	2341	65	2282, 2284, 2288
11(1)	2001, 2016, 2041–2082, 2102, 2104, 2122–2126,	67	2222–2231, 2311
		68	2229

> This illustrates one of the ways the Key Number classification is kept current. The Topic *Bankruptcy* has been revised. This table translates an old key number to a new one. For example, if one had reference to Key Number 8 from an older *Decennial*, the point of law covered by that Key Number is now digested under Key Number 2026. See previous Illustration, Figure 2.
>
> A similar Table translates the current Key Numbers to older ones.

Former	Present	Former	Present
24	2127	81	2290, 2293
25	2201	82, 83	2290
27	2321–2325	84(1)	2204, 2292
28	2321	85, 86	2290
29	2322	87	2131
30	2323	88	2204
31	2324	89	2294
32	2325	90	2290
33	2127	91	2294
35	2127, 2131	91(1, 2)	2296
36	2133	92	2282–2289, 2295
37	2121	93	2130; Jury ⬅19(9)
38	2001, 2251	94–96	2295
39	2235	97	3040–3048
41	2222–2231	98	3761 et seq.
42	2227	99	2295
43	2224–2228	100	2297
44	2257, 2311	101	3061

[Illustration 6–8]

TABLE OF KEY NUMBERS FROM VOLUME 10
OF THE GENERAL DIGEST, 8TH SERIES

DOUBLE JEOPARDY—Cont'd	DOUBLE JEOPARDY—Cont'd	DRUGS AND NARCOTICS —Cont'd	DRUGS AND NARCOTICS —Cont'd
5—1, 3, 4, 5, 6, 8, 9, 10	143—2, 3, 8, 9	41—8	184(1)—1, 3, 4, 6, 8
6—1, 2, 3, 4, 5, 6, 7, 8, 9	144—1, 2, 5, 7, 9, 10	42—2, 6	184(2)—1, 2, 4, 5, 8, 10
7—6, 9	145—1, 3, 5, 6, 9, 10	43—1, 2, 3, 4, 5, 6, 7, 8, 9, 10	184(3)—1, 3, 4, 6
21—2, 4, 5, 7	146—1, 3, 4, 5, 6, 7, 8, 9	44—8	184(4)—3, 4, 5, 6, 7
22—1, 2, 3, 6, 8	147—1, 5	45—1, 2, 4, 5, 6, 7, 8	184(5)—1, 3, 4, 5, 6, 9
23—2, 5, 6, 7, 8, 9, 10	148—1, 2, 3, 4, 5, 6, 9	46—1, 2, 3, 4, 5, 6, 7, 8, 9	184(6)—6, 10
24—3, 5, 9	149—2, 3, 5, 6, 7, 8, 9	47—2, 8	185(1)—1, 3, 4, 7, 8, 9
25—1, 2, 5, 7, 8, 9, 10	150(1)—1, 2, 3, 4, 5, 6, 7, 8, 9	61—1, 2, 3, 4, 5, 6, 7, 8, 10	185(2)—3, 4, 7, 8
26—2, 6, 7, 8, 9	150(2)—3, 6, 8	62—2	185(3)—1, 2, 3, 4, 5, 6, 7, 8, 9
27—6, 9, 10	151(1)—4, 6	63—1, 2, 3, 6, 7, 8, 9, 10	185(4)—1, 2, 3, 5, 6, 8
28—2, 3, 4, 5, 7, 8, 9	151(2)—2, 6, 7, 8, 9	64—1, 2, 3, 5, 6, 8, 9, 10	185(5)—4, 5
29—2, 3, 4, 5, 6, 7, 8, 9	151(3)—2	65—1, 2, 3, 4, 5, 6, 7, 8, 9, 10	185(6)—8, 9
30—1, 4, 5, 6, 7, 8, 9	151(4)—2, 3, 4, 5, 7, 8	66—1, 2, 3, 4, 5, 6, 7, 8, 9, 10	185(7)—3, 5, 6, 7, 8
31—1, 2, 5, 6, 7, 8	151(5)—2, 3, 6, 7, 8, 9	67—1, 2, 3, 4, 5, 6, 7, 8, 9	185(8)—2, 3, 4, 10
32—2, 6, 9	152—2, 3, 7, 8, 9, 10	68—9	185.5—1, 2, 3, 4, 6, 7, 8, 9, 10
33—2, 3, 6, 8	161—2, 3, 4, 5, 6, 7, 8, 9	69—1, 2, 4, 5, 6, 7, 8, 9, 10	185.10—1, 2, 3, 4, 5, 6, 7, 8, 9
34—3, 5, 10	162—2, 3, 6	70—2, 4, 5, 6, 9, 10	187(1)—4, 7, 9
51—3, 4, 6, 8	163—1, 6, 10	72—2	187(2)—2, 5, 6, 7, 9, 10
52—3, 8	164—2, 5	73—1, 2, 3, 4, 6, 7, 8, 9, 10	188(1)—1, 3, 4, 5, 6, 8, 9, 10
54—1, 5, 6, 8	165—6, 9	74—10	188(2)—1, 2, 4, 5, 6, 7, 8, 9, 10
55—3	166—2, 4, 6, 7, 9	76—1, 2, 3, 4, 5, 7, 8, 9, 10	188(3)—1, 4, 5, 6, 7, 8, 9
56—5	167—1, 2, 9	78—1, 2, 3, 7, 8	188(4)—1, 3, 4, 5, 6, 7, 8
57—1, 7, 8, 9	181—5	101—6	188(5)—1, 2, 3, 6, 8
59—1, 2, 3, 4, 5, 7, 8, 9, 10	182—2, 3, 4, 6, 8	102—1, 2, 4, 8, 9, 10	188(6)—1, 2, 3, 4, 5, 6, 7, 8, 9,
60—3, 5, 6, 8, 9	183—1, 2, 3, 5, 8		)
81—1, 4, 6, 9			)—1, 2, 3, 4, 5, 6, 7, 8, 9

(overlaid text box:)

> This Table, published in every tenth volume of the *General Digest*, allows a researcher to determine which of the volumes 1-10 contain a particular Topic and Key Number.
>
> In this example, one would only have to consult seven of the 10 volumes for cases dealing with the Topic *Drugs and Narcotics* and Key Number 18.

82—2			—1, 2, 3, 4, 5, 6, 7, 9, 10
83—1			—1, 2, 3, 4, 6, 7, 8, 9
84—1, 2, 4,			—1, 8
85—9, 10			—3, 5, 6, 8, 9, 10
86—7, 9			—1, 3, 4, 5, 7, 9
87—1, 8			—2
88—1, 4, 8,			1, 2, 3, 4, 5, 6, 7, 8, 9, 10
89—7, 9			2, 3, 4, 6, 7, 8, 10
90—9			1, 3, 4, 5, 6, 7, 8, 9
91(1)—1, 5,			2, 3, 5, 7, 9
92—4			1, 2, 3, 4, 5, 6, 7, 8, 9, 10
94—9		118—1, 2, 3, 4, 5, 6, 7, 8, 9, 10	195—1, 2, 3, 4, 5, 6, 7, 8, 9, 10
95—1, 2, 3, 4, 6, 7, 8, 9, 10	35—10	119—1, 2, 3, 4, 5, 6, 7, 8, 9, 10	196—1, 2, 3, 6, 7, 8, 9
96—1, 2, 3, 4, 6, 7, 8, 9, 10	37—10	120—2, 3, 8	197—1, 5, 9
97—3, 4, 5, 6, 7, 8, 10	49—1	121—1, 2, 4, 5, 6, 8, 9, 10	198—2, 8
98—1, 2, 3, 4, 5, 6, 9, 10	65—10	123(1)—1, 2, 3, 4, 7, 9, 10	
99—1, 2, 3, 4, 5, 7, 8, 9, 10		123(2)—1, 2, 3, 4, 5, 6, 7, 8, 9,	EASEMENTS
100—1, 2, 5, 7, 8, 9	DRAINS	10	
101—9		123(3)—1, 2, 3, 4, 5, 8	1—1, 2, 3, 4, 5, 6, 7
102—1, 9, 10	50—9	123(4)—2, 9	2—1, 9
103—1, 2, 4, 5, 6, 7, 8	66—9	124—1, 3, 5, 8	3(1)—3, 4, 6, 9
104—3, 4, 6, 7, 9, 10	76—9	125—3, 7	3(2)—3, 4
105—1, 3, 5, 6, 8, 9		126—1, 2, 3, 4, 5, 6, 8, 9, 10	5—2, 3, 4, 5, 6, 7, 8, 9, 10
106—4		127—2, 3, 4, 7, 8, 10	6—2, 3, 7
107—1, 3, 4, 5, 6, 9	DRUGS AND NARCOTICS	128—8	7—4, 8, 9
108—1, 2, 3, 5, 6, 7, 8, 9		129—1, 4, 6, 7	7(1)—1, 3
109—1, 3, 4, 6, 7, 9	2—8	130—1, 2, 3, 4, 5, 6, 7, 9, 10	7(3)—3, 7
110—5	3—3, 6, 8	131—1, 2, 4, 6, 7, 8, 9, 10	7(5)—5, 6, 7, 8
112—2, 4, 5, 6, 7, 8, 9	9—2, 9	132—2, 6, 8, 9, 10	8(1)—2, 5, 6, 7, 8
114—1, 2, 3, 7, 8, 9, 10	10—2, 9	133—1, 2, 4, 5, 6, 7, 8, 9, 10	8(2)—4, 5, 6, 8, 10
115—1, 2, 3, 6	11—2, 8	181—2, 7, 10	8(4)—3, 4, 7
116—3, 7	14—9	182(1)—7	9(1)—4, 7
117—9	15—1, 2, 8	182(2)—4, 6, 8, 9	10(4)—8
118—3	17—1, 2, 3, 5, 6, 7, 8, 9, 10	182(3)—2, 6	12(1)—1, 4, 5, 6, 7, 10
131—2, 4, 6, 7, 8, 9, 10	18—1, 2, 4, 5, 6, 7, 8	182(4)—2, 6, 9	12(2)—1, 7
132—2, 3, 4, 5, 6, 7, 8, 9	19—2, 4, 9	182(5)—3	12(3)—4, 7
133—2, 3, 4, 5	20—1, 2, 3, 4, 6, 8, 9	183(1)—1, 4, 6	14(1)—3
134—1, 2, 3, 4, 5, 6, 7, 8, 9	21—1, 2, 3, 5, 6, 7, 8, 9, 10	183(2)—1, 2, 4, 5, 7, 9	14(3)—8
135—1, 2, 4, 5, 6, 7, 8, 9, 10	22—5, 6	183(3)—1, 2, 3, 7, 8, 9	15—1, 4, 5, 6, 8
136—1, 2, 3, 4, 5, 6, 7, 10	25—1	183(4)—1, 4, 5, 6, 8, 9, 10	16—2, 3, 4, 6
137—3	26—1, 6, 10	183(5)—1, 2, 3, 4, 5, 6, 7, 8, 9,	17(4)—1, 4, 6, 9
138—1, 3, 4, 8, 9, 10	27—5	10	17(5)—3, 5
139—3, 4, 6, 7, 8, 9	28—1	183(6)—1, 2, 4, 5, 6, 8, 9	18(1)—1, 2, 3, 4, 5, 7, 8, 10
140—1, 2, 4, 5, 7, 8, 9	29—2, 5	183(7)—1, 2, 5, 7	18(2)—5
141—1, 4, 6, 7, 9	30—5, 10	183.10—5	18(3)—1, 2, 5, 7
142—1, 2, 3, 4, 5, 6, 7, 8, 10	31—2, 5, 10		

SECTION D. FINDING TOPICS AND KEY NUMBERS

The *American Digest System,* as classified to the *Key Number System,* provides a means to locate all cases on the same or similar point of law. Once it is determined to what Topic and Key Number a particular point of law has been classified, searching for cases can commence in the various units of the *American Digest System.*

Learning how to find the appropriate Topics and Key Numbers is very important for successful case finding. Four common methods are provided for finding Topics and Key Numbers within the *American Digest System*.

1. The Descriptive Word Method

The *Descriptive–Word Index* is a highly-detailed, alphabetically-arranged subject index to the contents of the digests. This index is often the best starting point for research, unless a relevant case or the particular Topic and Key Number being researched is already known. It includes *catch words* or descriptive words relating to the legal issues digested and all the Topics of the digest classification system. There is a separate *Descriptive–Word Index,* often in several volumes, for each of the *Decennial* units. Each volume of the *General Digest* contains its own *Descriptive–Word Index,* which is cumulated in every tenth volume.

Using the *Descriptive–Word Indexes* successfully requires analysis of the legal issues and often the ability to think in both broad and narrow terms or from the general to the specific. It might prove helpful at this point to review the *TARP Rule* discussed in Chapter 2.

Let us examine the problem described in Section A to see how the *Descriptive–Word Indexes* to the *Decennial* units of the *American Digest System* are used to locate Topics and Key Numbers for finding cases dealing with the liability of a manufacturer for drugs that cause injury.

In starting the search, it is best to begin in a recent *Decennial* or in the *General Digest*. When using an index, the first entry to consult should be a specific word or phrase relevant to the fact situation under research.

In our fact situation, the most specific word is *manufacturer*. An examination of this word in the *Tenth Decennial, Part 1* reveals the following entry:

MANUFACTURERS AND MANUFACTURING COMPANIES

DRUGS AND MEDICINE, CIVIL LIABILITY

Drugs & N 18

[See Illustration 6–9.]

Be sure to check the cumulative volumes of the *General Digest* for additional entries.

These references indicate that under the Topic *Drugs and Narcotics,* Key Number 18 in both the *Tenth Decennial Digest, Part 1* and the *General Digest* are digest paragraphs that address the legal issue being researched.

2. Analysis or Topic Method

As mentioned in Section B–1, over 400 Topics are used in West's *Key Number Digests*. Once an editor assigns a Topic to a headnote, the next step is assignment of the Key Number. Each Topic is arranged in outline form with main heading and subdivisions. Often these subdivisions are further subdivided into minute detail. These various breakdowns under a broad Topic are assigned Key Numbers. After analyzing the legal issue contained in a particular headnote, the editor uses these outlines to establish the most specific Key Number for the point of law in the headnote. On occasion, and in order to assure that a headnote receives the necessary topical coverage, it may be assigned to more than one Topic.

These outlines are published at the start of each Topic in the *American Digest System.* Two preliminary sections, "Subjects Included" and "Subjects Excluded and Covered in Other Topics," are published immediately before the detailed outline. Reading this "scope note" is often helpful in determining if the research is being conducted in the proper Topic. The topical outline that follows immediately thereafter, actually West's Key Number classification scheme, is entitled the *Analysis.*

The *Analysis* sections under the Topics *Products Liability* and *Drugs and Narcotics* were used in establishing the Key Numbers for the headnotes in *Grundberg v. Upjohn Co.,* the case used in our problem. By rereading these headnotes, one can see that the headnote pertaining to products liability covers a broad general principle of law, whereas the two relating to drugs and narcotics are much more specific. By carefully scanning the *Analysis,* a researcher can often see details in coverage that might not have come to mind in initial assessment of a legal issue and, thus, identify the most specific Key Number to use. [See Illustration 6–10.]

Use of the *Analysis* method generally requires certainty that the Topic selected is the proper one, as well as a thorough understanding of West's Key Number classification. Therefore, use of this method is often most successful when used in connection with the *Descriptive–Word Index* method.

3. Table of Cases Method

Each *Decennial* unit and each volume of the *General Digest* have an alphabetical *Table of Cases* by plaintiff. The *Table of Cases* is cumulated in every tenth volume of the *General Digest*. Each case listing includes the citation and the Topics and Key Numbers under which the case has been digested. For example, if one knows that the case of *Grundberg v. Upjohn Co.* is pertinent to the issue being researched and the case citation is not available, the *Table of Cases* will provide both the citation and the Topics and Key Numbers assigned to that case. [See Illustration 6–11.] Once the Topic and Key Numbers are known, the *Analysis* can be consulted for other relevant Key Numbers.

Defendant–Plaintiff volumes are published for the *Decennials* commencing with the *Ninth Decennial Digest, Part 1.* These volumes enable a researcher to locate a case when only the name of the defendant, e.g., *Upjohn Co.*, is known.

4. An Alternative Method for Locating Topics and Key Numbers

Frequently, in the course of one's research, a citation to a case will be located that suggests that it contains a relevant point of law. Such citations may be found in almost any legal source, e.g., a law review article, another case, a set of annotated statutes, a treatise, an encyclopedia. Rather than attempting to find similar cases using any of the three methods described *supra,* it is sometimes more practical to go immediately to the unit of the *National Reporter System* containing the cited case that has been identified. If after reading the case, a determination is made that it is important to the research being conducted, one should note all relevant Topics and Key Numbers. A researcher can then go directly to any of West's *Key Number Digests* and look under the same Topics and Key Numbers and find other digest paragraphs with these same Topics and Key Numbers.

SECTION E.   ILLUSTRATIONS: FINDING TOPICS AND KEY NUMBERS

[Illustration 6–9]

PAGE FROM DESCRIPTIVE–WORD INDEX TO THE TENTH DECENNIAL DIGEST, PART 1

39-10th D Pt 1—115   **MAPS**

MANDAMUS—Cont'd
SURETY bonds. **Mand 171**
TAX assessments, see this index **Tax Assessments**
TAX levy. **Mand 112–116**
TAXATION, see this index **Taxation**
TAXPAYERS' actions, see this index **Tax-payers' A**
TIME to sue.
TITLE to offic
TOLLS of cor
TRANSFER o
TRIAL—
    In mandam
        173
    Subject of r
UNITED State
        64
UNITED State
    Courts of A
    State's imm
VARIANCE.
VENUE—
    Change of,
    In mandam
VERDICT, rece
    purpose of
VIOLATION of
WAGES compelling payment. **Mand 107**
WATER—
    Compelling supplying of. **Mand 89**
WITNESSES as subject or purpose of relief. **Mand 40**
ZONING as subject of relief. **Mand 87, 99**
    Rezoning. **Mand 99**

MANDATE
APPELLATE court mandate on appeal or other proceedings for review. **App & E 1186–1216**
    Compliance with—
        Failure to obey. **App & E 1216**
        New trial. **App & E 1198**
        Powers and duties of lower court. **App & E 1210(2)**
    Courts of Appeals of United States. **Fed Cts 949–957**
    Criminal case. **Crim Law 1192**
    Filing in lower court. **App & E 1191**
    Form and requisites. **App & E 1190**
    Issuance. **App & E 1188**
    Necessity. **App & E 1186**
    Operation and effect. **App & E 1192**
    Payment of fees and costs. **App & E 1189**
    To justice of the peace. **J P 190**
    CONTEMPT by—
        Abuse. **Contempt 11**
        Disobedience. **Contempt 18–26**
        Interference with execution. **Contempt 17**
    MANDAMUS, see this index **Mandamus**

MANDATORY INJUNCTION
See generally, this index **Injunction**

MANGOES
TOLERANCE for ethylene dibromide, judicial review—
    Admin Law 229
    Food 5

MANHOLES
OBSTRUCTION. **Mun Corp 777**
STREETS and highways—
    Injuries. **Mun Corp 783**

MANIFEST
CUSTOMS duties, see this index **Customs Duties**
MANN ACT
PROSTITUTION, see generally, this index **Prostitution**

This page illustrates how Topics and Key Numbers can be located by using the Descriptive–Word Index to a unit of the American Digest System. In this instance, we begin with the most specific word in our fact situation, "manufacturer." Notice in the sub–entry "Drugs and medicine, civil liability" that we should consult "Drugs and Narcotics," Key Number 18.

Many times, one will not find an index entry under a particular word or phrase. In such instances, one should search in the Index under another appropriate word or phrase.

BAILMENT, goods delivered for manufacture. **Bailm 14(2)**
BOUNTIES for manufacturing. **Bounties 4, 7**
COMBINATIONS to control. **Monop 14**
CONDEMNATION of property for mill. **Em Dom 37**
CONSTITUTIONAL and statutory provisions. **Manuf 1**
CONTRACTS—
    Construction. **Contracts 201**
    Implied contract to manufacture for United States. **U S 69(4)**
    Mutuality of obligation. **Contracts 10(2)**
DRUGS and medicine, civil liability. **Drugs & N 18**
EXCISE tax on manufacturers, see this index **Excise**
EXPLOSIVES. **Explos 3, 8**
    Illegal or negligent manufacture causing injuries. **Explos 8**
FOOD, illegal manufacture. **Food 13**
INCORPORATION and organization. **Corp 14(3)**
INTOXICATING liquors, see this index **Intoxicating Liquors**
LABOR relations acts—
    Employments included. **Labor 49**
LIABILITY and indemnity insurance, liability for personal injuries. **Insurance 435.24**
LIBEL or slander in words tending to injure business. **Libel 9(7)**
LICENSE tax. **Licens 12**
    Exemption from license or tax. **Licens 19(4)**
    Food manufacturer. **Food 3**
    Sale of goods by manufacturer. **Licens 15(3)**
MONOPOLIES, see generally, this index **Monopolies**
NEGLIGENCE, liabilities of manufacturers of goods or articles causing injury, see generally, this index **Products Liability**
NUISANCE. **Nuis 3(5)**
OLEOMARGARINE, see this index **Oleomargarine**
PATENTS, see this index **Patents**

MANUFACTURERS AND MANUFACTURING COMPANIES—Cont'd
PLACE for work. **Labor 11**
RIGHTS, privileges, and regulations of public mills. **Manuf 2**
SALES, use and service taxes. **Tax 1245**
SALES of goods to be manufactured. **Sales**
        Sales 71(4)
        ompanies.
        of manufac-
        :nerally, this
        es
        .ct to manu-
        see this in-
        ulations
        this index
        ncy
        y mills and
Public water supply for manufacturing purposes, see this index **Public Water Supply**
Riparian rights to use water for manufacturing purposes. **Waters 46**
WEAPONS. **Weap 4**
    Liability for injuries from illegal or negligent manufacture. **Weap 18**
WORKERS' compensation—
    Application of compensation acts. **Work Comp 133, 139**
ZONING regulations—
    Construction and operation. **Zoning 286**

MANUMISSION
SLAVES. **Slaves 22**

MANURE
LEASED premises. **Land & Ten 138**

MAPS
ASSESSMENT for public improvements. **Mun Corp 479**
BOUNDARIES, description of. **Bound 3(8), 10**
    Admissibility of evidence. **Bound 36(3, 5)**
CONDEMNATION proceedings. **Em Dom 186**
COPYRIGHTS. **Copyr 6**
    Infringement. **Copyr 64**
DEDICATION by designation in maps. **Dedi 19**
    Statutory dedication. **Dedi 22–28**
DEEDS or other conveyances, description of property by reference to map—
    Deeds 40, 112
    Mtg 127
    Ven & Pur 64
EMPLOYMENT of surveyor to make map. **Mun Corp 214(1)**
EVIDENCE—
    Best and secondary evidence of contents. **Evid 161(4)**
    Documentary evidence, see this index **Documentary Evidence**
    Private maps. **Evid 358**
HEARSAY evidence. **Crim Law 419(12)**

[Illustration 6–10]

TOPIC: DRUGS AND NARCOTICS FROM TENTH
DECENNIAL DIGEST, PART 1

18 10th D Pt 1—627

DRUGS AND NARCOTICS

SUBJECTS INCLUDED

Regulation of the manufacture, dispensing, and sale of medicines and other drugs and
    devices by pharmacists or others

Civil and criminal liabilities relating to drugs in general

Regulation of the sale, use, etc., of narcotics and hallucinogenic, depressant, and
    stimulant drugs

Violation of laws relating to such drugs and criminal liability and prosecution
    therefor

Searches, seizures, and forfeitures relating to such drugs

SUBJECTS EXCLUDED AND COVERED BY OTHER TOPICS

Commitment and treatment of addicts, see CHEMICAL DEPENDENTS.

Insecticides and fungicides, see POISONS

Internal revenue acts generally, offenses and prosecutions under, see INTERNAL
    REVENUE

Poisons, regulations relating to, see POISONS

For detailed references to other topics, see Descriptive-Word Index

---

I. DRUGS

II. NARCOT

  (A) RE

  (B) OF

    1

    2

  (C) SE

> This illustrates the "Analysis" method of locating Topics and Key
> Numbers. If a researcher knows that a particular issue deals with *Drugs
> and Narcotics*, that Topic can be consulted immediately in the appropriate
> volume or volumes of a digest. After reading the "scope note" for
> information included, excluded, or covered elsewhere, the next step is to
> find a relevant Key Number.
>
> Note that the initial outline under "I. Drugs and Druggists In
> General" includes the civil liability of manufacturers, Key Number 18.

I. DRUGS AND DRUGGISTS IN GENERAL.

1. Power to regulate.
2. Federal regulation.
3. —— Drugs or devices within regulations.
4. —— Adulteration and misbranding in general.
5. —— False or misleading labeling as misbranding.
6. —— What constitutes labeling.
7. —— Labeling requirements.
8. —— Prescription drugs.
9. —— New drugs.
10. —— Administrative action and judicial review or
    enforcement.
11. State and municipal regulation in general.
12. Registration, certificate, or license.
13. —— Necessity.
14. —— Eligibility and right; licensing boards.
15. —— Revocation or suspension.

16. Conduct of business.
17. Civil liability.
18. —— Manufacturers.
19. —— Retailers or dispensers.
20. Actions for damages.
21. —— Evidence.
22. —— Questions for jury.
23. Injunction.
24. Penalties.
25. Seizure and forfeiture.
26. —— Property subject and grounds.
27. —— Proceedings.
28. —— Evidence.
29. Offenses.
30. Criminal prosecutions.
31. —— Evidence and questions for jury.

[Illustration 6–11]

PAGE FROM TABLE OF CASES IN VOLUME 10
OF THE GENERAL DIGEST, 8TH SERIES

GROVER

TABLE OF CASES 984
References are to Digest Topics and Key Numbers

Grover v. State, FlaApp 4 Dist, 581 So2d 1379.—Cons Prot 50; Crim Law 1159.6; Larc 57.

Groves v. Alabama State Bd. of Educ., MDAla, 776 FSupp 1518.—Civil R 126, 127.

Groves v. Illinois Dept. of Professional Regulation, IllApp 4 Dist, 164 IllDec 539, 583 NE2d 93, 221 IllApp3d 689.—Licens 20; Statut 188.

Groves v. Land's End Housing Co., Inc., NYAD 1 Dept, 573 NYS2d 181.—Judgm 181(33).

Groves v. U.S., DDC, 778 FSupp 54.—Autos 175(1), 175(2), 175(3), 210; Death 81, 84, 95(2), 99(1).

Growers Packing Co. v. Community Bank of Homestead, SDFla, 134 BR 438.—Bankr 2130; Jury 19(9).

Growth Horizons, Inc. v. Delaware County, Pa., EDPa, 784 FSupp 258.—Fed Cts 29, 34, 178, 221.

Grubb, Matter of, NCApp, 405 SE2d 797, 103 NCApp 452.—Infants 153, 202.

Grubb v. State, Miss, 584 So2d 786.—Crim Law 980(1), 998(3), 998(11), 998(14), 1083.

Grubb v. Zakaib, WVa, 413 SE2d 112. See Garlow v. Zakaib.

Grubbs v. Brown, KyApp, 818 SW2d 616. See Pendleton v. Centre College of Kent

Grubbs   1459.— Double 490(3), 357(9).

Grubbs v. 78.—Armed S 155, 160.

Grubbs v. Hannigan, DKan, 771 FSupp 1159.—Const Law 266(7); Crim Law 339.7(1), 388(2); Hab Corp 493(2).

Grubbs, Inc. v. Suncoast Excavating, Inc., FlaApp 5 Dist, 594 So2d 346. See John G. Grubbs, Inc. v. Suncoast Excavating, Inc.

Grubel, In re, BkrtcyEDNY, 132 BR 242.—Bankr 3152, 3190.

Gruber v. Price Waterhouse, EDPa, 776 FSupp 1044.—Fed Civ Proc 1809; Sec Reg 60.30, 60.48(1), 60.48(3).

Gruber v. State, TexApp–Corpus Christi, 812 SW2d 368.—Autos 355(6); Const Law 268(8); Crim Law 412(4), 412(6), 412.1(1), 414, 643, 660, 700(9), 995(1), 995(8), 1134(3), 1134(8), 1144.13(2), 1158(4).

Gruetzke v. City of Gresham, OrApp, 815 P2d 228, 108 OrApp 325.—Review 16, 20.

Grumet v. New York State Educ. Dept., NYSup, 579 NYS2d 1004, 151 Misc2d 60.—Const Law 42.3(1), 42.3(2), 84.5(3); Schools 22.

Grund v. Grund, NYSup, 573 NYS2d 840.—Divorce 252.3(1), 252.3(4).

Grundberg v. Upjohn Co., DUtah, 140 FRD 459.—Fed Civ Proc 1271, 1635, 1693; Records 32, 50.

Grundberg v. Upjohn Co., DUtah, 137 FRD 372.—Copyr 31, 36, 41, 50.25, 50.30, 75.5, 83(3), 83(4), 83(5), 84, 85, 86; Fed Civ Proc 1935.

Grundberg v. Upjohn Co., DUtah, 137 FRD 365.—Evid 128, 220(1), 220(6), 267, 351, 370(1), 555.4(1), 560; Fed Civ

Grundberg v. Upjohn Co., Utah, 813 P2d 89.—Drugs & N 18; Prod Liab 8, 14

Grunsfeld v. State, TexApp–Dallas, 813 SW2d 158.—Crim Law 388(1), 396(2), 650, 749, 986.1, 986.2(1), 986.6(3), 1042,

1144.13(2), 1152(1), 1159.2(1), 1159.2(7), 1159.2(9), 1159.4(2), 1162, 1169.1(10), 1177, 1208.1(6); Rape 51(1), 51(4); Statut 181(1), 205, 208, 217.2, 230, 241(2).

Grunwald v. Bronkesh, NJSuperAD, 604 A2d 126, 254 NJSuper 530.—Atty & C 105, 129(1); Const Law 69; Lim of Act 1, 55(2), 106; Neglig 1.

Grupo Protexa, S.A. v. All American Marine Slip, a Div. of Marine Office of America Corp., CA3 (NJ), 954 F2d 130.—Fed Cts 864, 941; Insurance 488, 505; Intern Law 10.8.

Gruskin v. Edelstein, NYAD 2 Dept, 571 NYS2d 511.—Insurance 603.

Grussing v. Kvam Implement Co., MinnApp, 478 NW2d 200.—Const Law 42.2(2), 55, 213.1(2), 251.3, 275(2); Witn 216(1).

G.S., People in Interest of, ColoApp, 820 P2d 1178. See People in Interest of G.S.

G.S. v. State, FlaApp 3 Dist, 586 So2d 501.—Infants 153.

G.S.F. Corp., In re, CA1 (Mass), 938 F2d 1467.—Bankr 2053, 2058, 2368, 3767, 3782, 3786; Inj 26(5).

G.S.L. Enterprises, Inc. v. Commissioner of Finance, NYSup, 580 NYS2d 828. See Goldman, Estate of v. Commissioner of Finance.

G.S., State ex rel., Ex parte, AlaCivApp, 591 So2d 890. See State ex rel. G.S., Ex parte.

G.S., State ex rel., v. J.A.S., AlaCivApp, 591 So2d 890. See State ex rel. G.S., Ex parte.

G.T., Appeal of, PaSuper, 597 A2d 638. See G.T., In Interest of.

G.T., In Interest of, PaSuper, 597 A2d 638.—Com Law 11; Crim Law 20, 328; Infants 66, 153, 172, 173, 176.

GT & MC, Inc. v. Texas City Refining, Inc., TexApp–Hous [1 Dist], 822 SW2d 252.—App & E 961, 969, 977(5), 1024.3, 1050.1(1), 1056.1(1); Contracts 148(2), 147(1), 152, 176(1), 206, 303(3); Evid 351, 355(3); Judgm 199(3.7), 199(3.10); New Tr 6; Pretrial Proc 44, 45; Sales 284(1), 426, 442(1); Trial 182, 349(2).

GTE Communications Systems Corp. v. Curry, TexApp–San Antonio, 819 SW2d 652.—Costs 2; Courts 85(2).

GTE North Inc. v. Iowa State Utilities Bd., Div. of Dept. of Commerce, State of Iowa, Iowa, 473 NW2d 48.—Pub Ut 102, 123; Statut 184, 188.

GTE Northwest Inc. v. Eachus, OrApp, 813 P2d 46, 107 OrApp 539. See Pacific Northwest Bell Telephone Co. v. Eachus.

GTE Products Corp. v. Kennametal, Inc., WDVa, 772 FSupp 907.—Fed Cts 685; Pat 99, 112.1, 168(2), 226.6, 237, 312(1), 312(3), 312(5), 312(6), 312(10), 314(1), 328(2).

GTE Products Corp. v. Unemployment Compensation Bd. of Review, PaCmwlth, 596 A2d 1172.—Admin Law 763, 791; Social S 387, 561, 567, 588.5, 651, 659, 662.

GTE Sprint Communications Corp. v. State Bd. of Equalization, CalApp 1 Dist, 2 CalRptr2d 441.—Statut 268, 270; Tax 493.8.

G.T.T., In Interest of, GaApp, 405 SE2d 750, 199 GaApp 706.—Infants 17a, 179, 210, 252.

Guadalupe A., In re, CalApp 5 Dist, 291 CalRptr 570. See Guadalupe A v Superior Court of Fresno County (Davis).

Guadalupe A. v. Superior Court of Fresno County (Davis), CalApp 5 Dist, 285 CalRptr 570, reh den, opinion mod.—App & E 837(1); Infants 154, 173, 205; Refer 45; Trial 20(4), 31, 367.

Guadalupe–Blanco River Authority, City of Lytle, CA5 (Tex), 937 F2d 184.—Rem of C 21.

Guam Hakubotan, Inc. v. Furukawa Inv. Corp., CA9 (Guam), 947 F2d 398.—Fed Cts 776; Mtg 323(3), 326(1), 294, 593, 596; Statut 226.

Guam Soc. of Obstetricians and Gynecologists v. Ada, DGuam, 776 FSupp 1422.—Civil R 262; Const Law 274(5), Territories 8, 9, 15, 32.

Guaranty Nat. Ins. Co. v. International Ins. Co., NDIll, 780 FSupp 546. See International Ins. Co v. Guaranty Nat Ins. Co.

Guardala Mouthpieces, Inc. v. Sugal Mouthpieces, Inc., SDNY, 779 FSupp 335. See Dave Guardala Mouthpieces, Inc. v. Sugal Mouthpieces, Inc.

Guardian Moving & Storage Co., Inc. v.   2d 1428.—Admin   merce 108, 153.

  nge Assur., Ltd   yn, P.I.C., Tex   st Law 305(5);   1212.5), 1522.16.

Insurance 26.

Guardianship and Custody of Lindsy E., Matter of, NYAD 1 Dept, 574 NYS2d 15.—Infants 157.

Guardianship and Custody of Tracey Q.T., Matter of, NYSur, 576 NYS2d 783.—Guard & W 9%; Infants 1930.

Guardianship and Custody of Veronica Jonice N., Matter of, NYAD 1 Dept, 581 NYS2d 11.—Infants 156, 254.

Guardianship No. 89–CA–9865 in Circuit Court for Howard County, In re, MdApp, 594 A2d 606, 88 MdApp 191.—Appear 11; Costs 194.46; Parties 3; Refer 47.

Guarnier v. American Dredging Co., NYAD 1 Dept, 577 NYS2d 542.—Seamen 29(5.14)

Gubler v. Boe, Idaho, 815 P2d 1034.—Phys 18.80(2); Trial 26; Witn 37(2), 262.

Gude v. Sullivan, CA8 (Mo), 956 F2d 791.—Social S 140.20, 143.60, 143.85, 149.5, 175.25.

Gudmundson v. State, Alaska, 822 P2d 1328.—Const Law 44, 258(3); Crim Law 1030(2); Game 7.

Gudachinsky v. State, Alaska, 815 P2d 851.—App & E 1177(8); Ex & Ad 110, 219, 221(10), 496(1), 501.

Guebara v. Green–Glo Turf Maintenance, Inc., KanApp, 819 P2d 135.—Work Comp 821, 825, 1946, 1956.

Guenther v. C.I.R., CA9, 939 F2d 758.—Const Law 314; Fed Civ Proc 1969, 2333; Int Rev 4655.

Guenzer, In re, DCApp, 601 A2d 83.—Atty & C 58.

Guerra v. SAIF Corp., OrApp, 826 P2d 1034, 111 OrApp 579.—Statut 219(9); Work Comp 1319, 1687.

Guerra v. Scruggs, CA4 (NC), 942 F2d 270.—Armed S 22; Const Law 213.1(2), 242.1(3), 277(1), 277(2), 278.4(1), 278.6(3).

When a case is known to deal with a topic of law, Key Numbers assigned to that Topic can be located by use of the Table of Cases. See, for example, the listing for Grundberg v. Upjohn Co.

For Later Case History Information, see INSTA-CITE on WESTLAW

SECTION F. OTHER WEST'S KEY NUMBER DIGESTS

1. In General

As has been noted, the *American Digest System* with its Key Number classification is made up of the headnotes from all the units of the *National Reporter System*. Because it is all-inclusive, it is most useful when one is interested in locating cases from all American jurisdictions. More typically, however, when one is engaged in legal research, the interest is primarily in locating cases from a particular state or group of states, or in only those cases decided in the federal courts. In such instances, it is better and easier to use a specialized West's *Key Number Digest* that is less comprehensive than the *American Digest System.* These consist of state, regional, federal, and subject digests.

Before describing the actual contents of these specialized digests, it is important to understand how their content is determined and to realize that a Topic and Key Number that appear in the *American Digest System* also appear in identical form in at least one of the other West's *Key Number Digests*. For example, assume that a state appellate case is appealed to the Supreme Court of the United States and a decision is issued. The digest paragraphs and Topics and Key Numbers used for the Supreme Court case are published in identical form in the appropriate state digest, the appropriate regional digest (if one is published covering that state), the most recent federal digest, a digest dealing with only Supreme Court of the United States cases, and possibly in subject matter digests as well.

2. Common Features

West's *Key Number Digests* have the following common features in addition to Topics and Key Numbers:

a. *Descriptive–Word Index* volume(s) used in the same manner as was described for the *American Digest System.*

b. *Table of Cases* volume(s) for plaintiff-defendant and used in the same manner as was described for the *American Digest System.*

c. *Words and Phrases* volume(s) that contain in alphabetical order words and phrases that have been judicially defined. Volumes of this type are not provided for the units of the *American Digest System* or for the regional digests.

d. *Defendant–Plaintiff* volume(s) used to locate a case when only the name of the defendant is known. Volumes of this type are not provided for the regional digests, except for the latest *Pacific Digest.* They were first provided for the *American Digest System* commencing with the *Ninth Decennial Digest, Part 1.*

e. Updating, consisting of replacement volumes, pocket supplements, interim pamphlet supplements, and later bound volumes and advance sheets of the West reporters.

f. References in the pocket supplements and recently published volumes to Topics that may be used in WESTLAW searches for cases with the Topic and within specified Key Numbers.

3. State Digests

West Group publishes a *Key Number Digest* for almost every state.[5] A typical state Key Number digest consists of digest paragraphs for all reported appellate cases of the particular state, including federal court cases that arose in or were appealed from that jurisdiction. [See Illustrations 6–11 and 6–12 for examples of a state digest.] Some of the West state digests have special features unique to a particular state, such as a reference to law review articles from law schools within the state. Researchers should examine carefully the state digest available for their state and familiarize themselves with any special features.

4. Regional Digests

Four sets of regional digests are published that correspond to four sets of the regional reporters of the *National Reporter System*. Other regional digests have ceased over time, likely due to an inadequate subscription base. Regional digests are arranged under the Key Number classification and include digests of all reported cases for each of the states in the region. The digest paragraphs under each Key Number are arranged alphabetically by the states included within the digest. The regional digests still being published are:

Atlantic Digest, First and Second Series

North Western Digest, First and Second Series

Pacific Digest, Five series[6]

South Eastern Digest, First and Second Series

5. Digests for Federal Court Cases

Whenever a researcher is aware that the problem being researched is one under the jurisdiction of a federal court, it is quicker and more accurate to confine the research to a federal digest. Numerous digests are published for federal court cases.

a. *West's Federal Practice Digest, 4th.*[7] This set includes digests of cases from December 1975 to date for all federal courts. Its special features are:

---

[5] West publishes Key Number digests for every state except Delaware, Nevada, and Utah. Additionally, a few states have digests available from other publishers.

[6] Volumes in these series are not connoted as 1st, 2d, etc. Rather each series shows the first volume of the *Pacific Reporter* or *Pacific Reporter 2d* included in the set.

[7] Publication of West's *Federal Practice Digest, 4th* began in 1989 and was completed in 1993. There is no "bright line" as to its scope of coverage or to West's *Federal Practice Digest, 3rd,* which it continues. For example, some volumes of the *3rd,* issued in 1975 when this set began, covered cases through November 1975 and were never revised. These volumes contained pocket supplementation that included cases decided from December 1975 and into 1983. Other volumes of the *3rd* were revised at various times, the last being

(1) Under each Key Number, cases are arranged chronologically, first for the Supreme Court of the United States, then the courts of appeals, and then the district courts arranged alphabetically by jurisdiction.

(2) The digest paragraphs include information as to whether a case has been *affirmed, reversed,* or *modified.*

(3) A complete numerical listing of all patents adjudicated for the period covered by this digest is found under the Topic, *Patents,* Key Number 328.

(4) An alphabetical table of all *Trade–Marks and Trade Names Adjudicated* is included in the *Trade Regulations* volume at Key Number 736.

(5) References to Topics that may be used in WESTLAW searches for cases with the Topic and within specified Key Numbers.

b. *Earlier Federal Digests.* Federal cases prior to 1984 are available in the following:

(1) *West's Federal Practice Digest, 3rd,* December 1975 to *West's Federal Practice Digest 4th.*

(2) *West's Federal Practice Digest, 2nd,* 1961–November 1975.

(3) *Modern Federal Practice Digest,* 1939–1960.

(4) *Federal Digest,* all federal cases prior to 1939.

c. *U.S. Supreme Court Digest.* Because the Supreme Court of the United States plays such a significant role within the American legal system, a digest that contains only its cases is extremely useful. West publishes a multi-volume set for this purpose. It duplicates the Supreme Court digest paragraphs in the *American Digest System* and in the various West federal digests.

6. Other Specialized West Digests

a. *West's Bankruptcy Digest.* This Key Number digest includes cases from *West's Bankruptcy Reporter* and selected bankruptcy cases from the *Federal Reporter 2d* and *3d* and the West's *Supreme Court Reporter.*

b. *West's Military Justice Digest.* This set digests cases from *West's Military Justice Reporter* and is a Key Number digest.

c. *United States Federal Claims Digest.* This is a Key Number digest that includes cases from volumes 1–26 of the *United States Claims Court Reporter* and volume 27 and forward of the *Federal Claims Reporter.*

issued in 1983. As new volumes of the *4th* were published, they incorporated the supplementation to the *3rd.* This means that some volumes in the *4th* contain cases from December 1975, while others have coverage commencing in 1983. Therefore, specifically for the period December 1975 through 1983, both the *3rd* and *4th must* be consulted to assure comprehensive coverage. For cases from 1984 forward, only the *4th* needs to be consulted.

d. *West's Education Law Digest.* This publication provides Key Number digest paragraphs from all cases in the *National Reporter System* on Topics relating to education law.

e. *United States Merit Systems Protection Board Digest.* This publication digests cases involving federal employees and the federal merit system. It uses a classification scheme different from the Key Number digests.

SECTION G. UPDATING WEST'S KEY NUMBER DIGESTS

Because digest paragraphs originate as headnotes in the advance sheets of the *National Reporter System,* to update paper research to its most current point one must engage in a systematic process. After locating an appropriate Topic and Key Number in the bound volume of a digest, next check under the same Topic and Key Number in the pocket supplement in that volume and in any interim pamphlets. Note the information in the table usually entitled *Closing with Cases Reported in* located in the front of the latest supplementation, typically on the back of the title page. This "closing table" indicates the last volume from each *National Reporter System* unit covered.

For example, a recent closing table in *West's Federal Practice Digest 4th* might include references similar to the following:

Closing with Cases Reported in

Supreme Court Reporter	117 S.Ct. 1730
Federal Reporter, Third Series	113 F.3d 218
Federal Supplement	961 F.Supp. 281
Federal Rules Decisions	171 F.R.D. 329
Bankruptcy Reporter	208 B.R. 607
Federal Claims Reporter	37 Fed.Cl. 722
Military Justice Reporter	46 M.J. 128; 714
Veterans Appeals Reporter	10 Vet.App. 208

Once you have determined the coverage of the digest, the next step is to check under this Topic and Key Number in the digest section found in the *back* of any later bound volumes of reporters covering the jurisdiction being researched. The last step is to check the digest paragraphs found in the *front* of each advance sheet to these reporters. Only *West's Supreme Court Reporter* cumulates its digest paragraphs in the last advance sheet for a volume.

SECTION H. ILLUSTRATIONS USING A STATE DIGEST

6–12. **Page from Descriptive–Word Index to Massachusetts Digest 2d**

6–13. **Page from Massachusetts Digest 2d**

[Illustration 6–12]

SAMPLE PAGE FROM DESCRIPTIVE–WORD INDEX
TO MASSACHUSETTS DIGEST 2d

27 Mass D 2d—135   **DRUNKARDS**

References are to Digest Topics and Key Numbers

DRUGS AND MEDICINE—Cont'd
CONTRACEPTIVES—Cont'd
Distribution, statute permitting to married but not single persons, equal protection. Health & E 21
Limiting to delivery by physician or pharmacist to married person. Health & E 21
CRIMINAL law—
Drug use affecting capacity. Crim Law 46
CRIMINAL prosecutions. Drugs & N 30
Evidence and questions for jury. Drugs & N 31
DAMAGES—
Actions for. Drugs & N 20–22
DANGEROUS drugs—

Frequently, when engaged in legal research, the researcher is interested in finding cases from the courts of a particular state. In such instances, it may be best to start the research in a state digest. Suppose the researcher is interested in determining whether cases similar to the Utah case of *Grundberg v. Upjohn Co.* have been decided in Massachusetts. As this Illustration indicates, this is much less complex than using the *Descriptive-Word Index* as shown in Illustration 6-9.

State digests are kept current with replacement volumes, annual pocket supplements, interim pamphlets, and later bound volumes and advance sheets of West reporters covering cases from the particular state for which research is being conducted.

FEDERAL preemption—
State laws or regulations. States 18.65
FEDERAL regulation. Drugs & N 2–10
FORFEITURE—
Seized drugs and medicine. Drugs & N 25–28
GROUNDS for seizure and forfeiture. Drugs & N 26
IMITATIONS. Food 7
INJUNCTION. Drugs & N 23
INTOXICATING ingredients. Int Liq 135, 136
Prescription by physician as offense. Int Liq 155
JUDICIAL review—
Federal administrative action. Drugs & N 10
LABELS—
False or misleading labeling as misbranding. Drugs & N 5
Requirements. Drugs & N 7
What constitutes labeling. Drugs & N 6
MANUFACTURERS—
Civil liability. Drugs & N 18
MISBRANDING in general—
Drugs & N 4
Food 8
False or misleading labeling. Drugs & N 5
MUNICIPAL regulation in general. Drugs & N 11
NARCOTICS, see generally, this index Narcotics
NARCOTICS and dangerous drugs, see generally, this index Narcotics and Dangerous Drugs
NEW drugs. Drugs & N 9
OFFENSES. Drugs & N 29
PENALTIES. Drugs & N 24
POISONS, see generally, this index Poisons
POWER to regulate. Drugs & N 1
PRESCRIPTION drugs. Drugs & N 8
PROPERTY subject to seizure and forfeiture. Drugs & N 26
QUESTIONS for jury—
Criminal prosecutions. Drugs & N 31
Damages, actions for. Drugs & N 22
REGULATION—
Federal regulation. Drugs & N 2–10
State and municipal regulation in general. Drugs & N 11
RETAILERS—
Civil liability. Drugs & N 19

DRUGS AND MEDICINE—Cont'd
SEARCHES and seizures, drug seized during search for another product. Searches 3.8(2)
SEIZURE and forfeiture. Drugs & N 25–28
SELF-INCRIMINATION, unregistered person dealing in depressant or stimulant drugs. Crim Law 393(1)
STATE regulation in general. Drugs & N 11
TESTAMENTARY capacity, see this index Testamentary Capacity
TRADEMARKS and trade names—
Infringement. Trade Reg 353
Misrepresentation as defense. Trade Reg 382

INDICTMENT and information—
Bill of particulars. Ind & Inf 121.2(7)
Certainty and particularity. Ind & Inf 71.4(7)
Following language of statute. Ind & Inf 110(3)

DRUGSTORE
ZONING regulations—
Permits and certificates, evidence. Zoning 645

DRUMMERS
See this index—
Hawkers and Peddlers
Salesmen

DRUNKARDS AND DRUNKENNESS
In general. Chem Dep 1
AGGRAVATION of offense. Crim Law 54
ARREST without warrant. Arrest 63.3
Violence in arresting, evidence of condition in justification. Evid 132
ASSAULT on drunken person. Assault 2
AUDITOR'S finding of intoxication of automobile passengers as evidence. Refer 99(6)
AUTOMOBILES, contributory negligence of intoxicated person injured by automobile. Autos 226(2), 245(73, 90)
AUTOMOBILES, driving while intoxicated—
Arrest without warrant—
Arrest 63.3
Autos 349
Arrested persons, right of access to doctor. Const Law 321
Chief of police as ground for removal. Mun Corp 182
Contributory negligence. Autos 224(8)
Question for jury. Autos 245(71, 73)
Contributory negligence of guest—
Gross negligence. Autos 244(4)
Remaining in automobile as jury question. Autos 245(87)
Riding with motorist under influence of liquor as question for jury. Autos 245(87, 88)
Evidence. Autos 244(4, 20)
Breath of driver. Autos 243(3)
Hospital record as evidence. Evid 351

[Illustration 6–13]

SAMPLE PAGE FROM MASSACHUSETTS DIGEST 2d

10 Mass D 2d—431   **DRUGS & NARCOTICS** ☞18

For references to other topics, see Descriptive-Word Index

and items contained therein may be shown by testimony of any observer thereof.

> 7 Op.Atty.Gen.1923, p. 33.

In view of explicit provision of G.L., c. 94, § 198 (M.G.L.A.), a copy of a prescription or original prescription for narcotic drugs cannot be taken from the files of a retail pharmacy for purpose of evidence prosecution of a violator of chapter and the druggist may not be permitted or required to make a copy of the prescription for narcotic drugs sold by him in the course of his business and give the copy to any of the authorities specified in chapter at their requ̲

mother ingested DES during pregnancy which resulted in plaintiff's birth, that DES caused plaintiff's subsequent injuries, and that drug companies produced or marketed the type of DES taken by mother and that they acted negligently in so doing; individual drug companies may exculpate themselves by proving by preponderance of the evidence that they did not produce or market the particular type of DES taken by mother, or that they did not market DES in relevant geographic market or distribute drug during time period of mother's pregnancy.

, 617

sen̲
ano
ny,
anc
the

> After locating a Topic and Key Number as demonstrated in the previous Illustration, the next step is to consult the digest paragraphs under the appropriate Key Number.
>
> Cases from other jurisdictions may be located by switching to other sets of Key Number digests and consulting the same Topic and Key Number.

at de-
ly in
drug,
any
ıot to
rs, or

of a registered pharmacist.

> 5 Op.Atty.Gen.1919, p. 318.

Atty.Gen. 1907. R.L., c. 76, § 23, required that an unregistered member of a copartnership engaged in the practice o̲ ' ̲armacy, who compounded for sale or dispen̲ d for medicinal purposes drugs, medicines, chemicals or poisons, should do so only under the personal supervision of a registered pharmacist.

> 3 Op.Atty.Gen.1907, p. 92.

Atty.Gen. 1906. A registered pharmacist could, under St.1906, c. 281, fill a prescription written by a registered physician practising medicine in the city or town where such registered pharmacist was engaged in practice, without regard to place of residence of such physician.

> 3 Op.Atty.Gen.1906, p. 50.

☞**17. Civil liability.**

Library references

> C.J.S. Drugs and Narcotics §§ 49, 50, 52, 57.

D.C.Mass. 1982. No private right of action for remedial equitable relief could be implied under Federal Food Drug and Cosmetic Act. Federal Food, Drug, and Cosmetic Act, § 1 et seq., 21 U.S.C.A. § 301 et seq.

> National Women's Health Network, Inc. v. A. H. Robins Co., Inc., 545 F.Supp. 1177.

☞**18. ⸺ Manufacturers.** ◄

D.C.Mass. 1985. Under Massachusetts law, plaintiff in action against drug manufacturers for injuries resulting from mother's ingestion of diethylstilbestrol (DES) who cannot meet traditional identification requirements of products liability action can avail herself of market share theory of liability by alleging that

that defendants engaged in mutual assistance in marketing the drug, could not recover damages from defendants under theories of "concert of action," "aiding and abetting," or "joint venture" under Massachusetts law.

> Payton v. Abbott Labs, 512 F.Supp. 1031.

Mass. 1985. Manufacturer of birth control pills owes direct duty to consumer to warn of dangers inherent in use of the pills.

> MacDonald v. Ortho Pharmaceutical Corp., 475 N.E.2d 65.

Manufacturer of oral contraceptives is not justified in relying on warnings to medical profession to satisfy its common-law duty to warn ultimate user of dangers inherent in their use in light of heightened participation of patients in decisions relating to use of the pill, substantial risks affiliated with use of the pill, feasibility of direct warnings by manufacturer to user, limited participation of physician who generally writes only annual prescriptions, and possibility that oral communications between physician and user may be insufficient or too scanty standing alone fully to apprise user of the dangers.

> MacDonald v. Ortho Pharmaceutical Corp., 475 N.E.2d 65.

In instances where trier of fact could reasonably conclude that compliance of oral contraceptives manufacturer with FDA labeling requirements or guidelines did not adequately apprise users of inherent risks, manufacturer should not be shielded from liability by its compliance; thus, compliance with FDA requirements, though admissible to demonstrate lack of negligence, is not conclusive on issue of whether manufacturer's warnings were adequate, just as violation of FDA requirements is

see Massachusetts General Laws Annotated
10 Mass.Dig.2d—15

SECTION I.   CHART ILLUSTRATING WEST'S KEY NUMBER DIGESTS

MASTER INDEX TO ALL CASE LAW	STATE COURT COVERAGE
American Digest System	**Individual State Digests**
Cases from: U.S. Supreme Court, all lower federal courts, all specialized federal courts, and all state courts.	Coverage corresponds to regional digest in which the state appears. <u>Note</u>: Some state digests are in a 2d, 3d, or 4th series.
	Published for all states except: Del. (<u>Use</u>: *Atlantic Digest*); Nev. and Utah (<u>Use</u>: *Pacific Digest*)

<u>Use</u>:	Chronological Coverage
*Century Digest	1658-1896
First Decennial	1896-1906
Second Decennial	1907-1916
Third Decennial	1916-1926
Fourth Decennial	1926-1936
Fifth Decennial	1936-1946
Sixth Decennial	1946-1956
Seventh Decennial	1956-1966
Eighth Decennial	1966-1976
Ninth Decennial (Part 1)	1976-1981
Ninth Decennial (Part 2)	1981-1986
Tenth Decennial (Part 1)	1986-1991
Tenth Decennial (Part 2) (in progress)	1991-1996
General Digest (8th Series)	1991-1996
General Digest (9th Series) (in progress)	1996-2001

*The Century Digest indexes cases prior to the start of the National Reporter System. Therefore, digest coverage is more inclusive than reporter coverage.

Regional Reporter Digests

Cases from: The seven regional reporters, Calif. & N.Y., plus pre-reporter cases

<u>Use</u> as appropriate:

Atlantic (CT, DE, MD, ME, NH, NJ, PA, RI, VT, DC)
  1st (to 1938)
  2d (1938 to date)
North Western (IO, MI, MN, NE, ND, SD, WI)
  1st (to 1941)
  2d (1941 to date)
Pacific (AK, AZ, CA*, CO, HI, ID, KA, MT, NM, NV, OK, OR, UT, WA, WY)
  1850-1931 (California & Pacific)
  1-100 P.2d
  101-366 P.2d
  367-584 P.2d
  585-to date
South Eastern (GA, NC, SC, VA, WV)
  1st (to 1938)
  2d (1938 to date)
    *   *   *   *   *
North Eastern (IL, ID, MA, NY, OH)
  (to 1968)
  CEASED PUBLICATION
  <u>Use</u>: appropriate state digest
Southern (AL, FL, LA, MS)
  (to 1988)
  CEASED PUBLICATION
  <u>Use</u>: appropriate state digest
South Western
  NOT PUBLISHED
  <u>Use</u>: state digests for AR, KY, MO, TN, TX

*Covers all Calif. courts to 1960 and only Cal. Sup. Ct. thereafter. For full coverage since 1960, use *California Digest* Series.

FEDERAL COURT COVERAGE

Complete Supreme Court coverage

Cases from: *Supreme Court Reporter*

<u>Use</u>: *U.S. Supreme Court Digest*

Complete Federal Court coverage

Cases from: U. S. Supreme Court, all lower federal courts, and all specialized federal courts.

<u>Use</u>: *Federal Practice Digest, 4th*
    (Dec. 1975 to date)
  Federal Practice Digest, 3rd
    (Dec. 1975 to Fed. Prac. Dig. 4th)
  Federal Practice Digest, 2nd
    (1961 - Nov. 1975)
  Modern Federal Practice Digest
    (1939 - 1960)
  Federal Digest

SECTION J.   OTHER DIGESTS

Digests are not unique to the West Group. In fact, digests on a variety of topics are prepared by numerous publishers. Researchers frequently will encounter these in the course of their research and should take the time to become familiar with their format and special features. Some deserve special mention and are discussed below.

(1) *Digest of United States Supreme Court Reports, Lawyers' Edition* (LEXIS Law Publishing; formerly Lawyers Cooperative Publishing). This is a multi-volume digest, with annual pocket supplements, to all cases of the Supreme Court of the United States. The digest paragraphs used are collected from those published in the *U.S. Supreme Court Reports, Lawyers' Edition*. This digest provides references to this publisher's other publications.

(2) *Digests for Looseleaf Services, Topical Reporters, and Other Types of Publications.* Frequently looseleaf services, topical reporters, multi-volume treatises, and, on occasion, legal periodicals, provide digests of particular subjects or of cases arranged alphabetically. At other times, materials are grouped under state or federal code sections. Still others use a hybrid of these methods. Since digests are useful finding aids for identifying like-kind materials, it is always useful to check sets for separate bound digest volumes and for digest sections within volumes.

(3) *A.L.R. Digests.* These publications are discussed in Chapter 7.

(4) *Taxes.* See Chapter 24.

SECTION K.   CITING DIGESTS

Because digests are finding aids that serve as a means of locating cases by subject, they have no legal authority and are never cited for such. Do not rely on the text of the digest paragraphs for the theory of a case, but merely as a means for obtaining citations to cases. Digest paragraphs are necessarily brief and can fail to suggest a nuance or shading of a case or may omit an element that may have a specific bearing on the problem being researched.

In all instances, the actual opinion from which the digest paragraph was obtained should be read.

SECTION L.   WORDS AND PHRASES
AND POPULAR NAME TABLES

1. Words and Phrases

Sometimes a problem in legal research involves the definition of certain words or phrases as, for example, *income* or *reasonable attorney's fee*. Courts frequently must define the meaning of such words and phrases. In cases reported in the units of the *National Reporter System*, these definitions are often included as headnotes, as in the following example from 111 S. Ct. 2597 (1991):

> **17. Courts ⟸89**
>
> "Stare decisis" is the preferred course because it promotes evenhanded, predictable and consistent development of legal principles, fosters reliance on judicial decisions, and contributes to the actual and perceived integrity of judicial process.
>
> **See** publication Words and Phrases for other judicial constructions and definitions.

Headnotes that contain judicial definitions are subsequently reprinted in *Words and Phrases,* a multi-volume set containing approximately 550,000 alphabetically-arranged judicial definitions of legal and non-legal terms. *Words and Phrases* is kept up to date by annual cumulative pocket supplements, which are further supplemented by *Words and Phrases* tables in later bound volumes and advance sheets of the various units of the *National Reporter System.* Many of the digests discussed in Section F also contain such tables. [See Illustration 6–14 for an example of a page from *Words and Phrases.*]

2. Popular Name Tables

Frequently, a case becomes better known by a popular name rather than by its actual name. For example, *Cruzan v. Director, Missouri Dept. of Health* is popularly known as the *"Right to Die" Case.* At other times, a group of cases may come to be known collectively by a popular name, such as the *Right to Counsel Cases.* When only the popular name of a case or a group of cases is known, it is necessary to consult a table of cases by popular name in order to obtain citations to the actual case or cases. These tables may be located in the following sources:

a. *First through Sixth Decennial Digests.* The Table of Cases volume contains a cumulative *List of Popular Name Titles* in the *American Digest System.* This feature was discontinued with the *Seventh Decennial.*

b. *Tables of Cases by Popular Names* in the various special digests.

c. *Shepard's Acts and Cases by Popular Names.* [See Illustration 6–15.]

SECTION M. ILLUSTRATIONS

6–14. Page From Words and Phrases
6–15. Page From Shepard's Acts and Cases by Popular Name

[Illustration 6–14]

SAMPLE PAGE FROM VOLUME OF WORDS AND PHRASES

35 W & P—5

PSYCHOCALISTHENICS

PSYCHIATRIC EVIDENCE

Statute defining psychiatric evidence as evidence of a mental disease or defect which is offered in connection with the affirmative defense of lack of criminal responsibility [McKinney's CPL § 250.10, subd. 1(a)] does not limit "psychiatric evidence" to opinions of psychiatrists and psychologists and may be read as including opinions of certified social workers. People v. Scala, 491 N.Y.S.2d 555, 562, 128 Misc.2d 831.

Properly qualified certified social workers appointed to examine a defendant in relation to a potential defense of lack of criminal responsibility may provide expert opinions that may serve as the sole "psychiatric evidence" in relation to the affirmative defense. Id.

PSYCHIATRIC EXAMINATION

Requiring a criminal defendant to undergo an involuntary "psychiatric examination" once the question of insanity is raised as a defense is not inconsistent with the Standards for Criminal Justice, Discovery and Procedure Before Trial of the American Bar Association providing that a judicial officer may require the accused to submit to a reasonable physical or "medical inspection" of his body. State v. Seehan, Iowa, 258 N.W.2d 374, 378.

PSYCHIATRIC EXAMINER

A properly qualified certified social worker may act as a "psychiatric examiner" under the dangerousness statute [McKinney's CPL § 330.20 . . .]

PSYCHIATRIC THERAPY

For purpose of determining whether medical expenses exceeded the $500 threshold under the Insurance Law, neurological evaluation, X rays and laboratory procedures did not constitute excludable "psychiatric therapy"; fact that procedures were performed at the request of a psychiatrist or in a psychiatric hospital did not change their nature. Shorey v. LaRocca, 399 N.Y.S.2d 771, 772, 59 A.D.2d 1030.

PSYCHIATRIST

See, also,

Competent Psychiatrist.
Qualified Psychiatrist.

"Psychiatrist" specializes in the treatment of mental, emotional and behavioural disorders. Nick v. Colonial Nat. Bank of Garland, Tex.Civ.App., 517 S.W.2d 375, 377.

A "psychiatrist" is a medical doctor who usually has completed at least three years of post graduate training in psychiatry (the branch of medicine concerned with the diagnoses and treatment of mental illness) at a recognized training hospital. U.S. v. Cortes-Crespo, ACMR, 9 MJ 717, 721.

PSYCHIATRY

"Psychiatry" is branch of medicine that relates to mental diseases. Wallach v. Monarch Life Ins. Co., 295 N.Y.S.2d 109, 111, 58 Misc.2d 202.

A page from *Words and Phrases*. The paragraphs are essentially the same as they appeared as headnotes in the volumes of the *National Reporter System*. The pocket supplements of the volumes of *Words and Phrases* should always be checked.

This Illustration shows definitions that could be important to our research problem.

---

misconduct, that principal's damages included lost reputation, humiliation, stress, loss of sleep, and impaired enjoyment of life, did not rise to level of "psychiatric impairment" caused by willful conduct, but instead were more in nature of humiliation and other emotional harm which were incidental claims in action, and therefore principal's action did not implicate statute stating that district court shall order that personal injury tort and wrongful death claims shall be tried in district court in which bankruptcy case is pending. Bertholet v. Harman, Bkrtcy.D.N.H., 126 B.R. 413, 415.

PSYCHIATRIC OR MEDICAL EVIDENCE

For purposes of proceeding brought by county department of social services seeking guardianship and custody of child on ground that mother was unable, by reason of mental illness, to provide proper and adequate care for child, proof proposed by mother dealing with competence and expertise of psychiatrists constituted "psychiatric or medical evidence" as provided in statute giving parent "the right to submit other psychiatric, psychological or medical evidence" in such a proceeding. Matter of Roth, 412 N.Y.S.2d 568, 569, 97 Misc.2d 834.

PSYCHOANALYSIS

"Psychoanalysis" is a specialized form of psychotherapy. Markham v. U.S., D.C.N.Y., 245 F.Supp. 505, 507.

PSYCHOCALISTHENICS

Term "psychocalisthenics," as employed by defendant in brochures, advertisements, and promotions for its courses in a series of physical exercises combining various yoga systems, dance, and calisthenics, was not merely "descriptive" but was sufficiently fanciful to be entitled to registration as a "suggestive term" without proof of a secondary meaning, where it was an odd and unusual term which suggested a number of things, but which did not describe any one thing in particular and, though it could indicate a system of purely mental exercises such as those employed by plaintiff, it could also indicate a system of physical exercises such as defendant's which was designed to create specific mental, emotional, and physical results, or even a traditional exercise program merely designed to improve mental fitness and alertness. West & Co., Inc. v. Arica Institute, Inc., C.A.N.Y., 557 F.2d 338, 342.

[Illustration 6–15]

SAMPLE PAGE FROM SHEPARD'S ACTS
AND CASES BY POPULAR NAMES

FEDERAL AND STATE CASES CITED BY POPULAR NAME	Rol

Rights of Pretrial Detainees Case
441 US 520, 60 LE2d 447, 99 SC 1861

Right to Appoint Counsel Case
440 US 367, 59 LE2d 383, 99 SC 1158

Right to be Heard Case
415 US 452, 39 LE2d 505, 94 SC 1209

Right to Counsel Cases
315 US 791, 86 LE 1194, 62 SC 639; 316 US 455,
86 LE 1595, 62 SC 1252
469 US 91, 83 LE2d 488, 105 SC 490
51 LE2d 424, 97 SC 1232
116 F2d 690; 313 US 551, 85 LE 1222, 61 SC 835;
315 US 60, 86 LE 680, 62 SC 457; 315 US 827,
86 LE 1222, 62 SC 629, 62 SC 637

'Right to Die" Case
111 LE2d 224, 110 SC 2841

Right-To-Reply Case

Roane-Anderson Case
192 Tenn 150, 239 SW2d 27; 342 US 847, 96 LE
639, 72 SC 74; 342 US 232, 96 LE 257, 72 SC
257

Roanoke Rapids Case
345 US 153, 97 LE 918, 73 SC 609; 191 F2d 796;
343 US 941, 96 LE 1346, 72 SC 1034

Robertson Case
89 Fed 504

Rochester Telephone Case
307 US 125, 83 LE 1147, 59 SC 754; 23 FS 634; 59
SC 252

Rochin Case
342 US 165, 96 LE 183, 72 SC 205; 101 CalApp2d
140, 225 P2d 1, 225 P2d 913

Rockaway Rolling Mill Case
101 NJEq 192, 137 At 650; 103 NJEq 297, 143 At

This is a typical page from the "Cases" section of *Shepard's Acts and Cases by Popular Names*. This set is kept current by publication of a periodic pamphlet supplement.

Other Tables of Popular Names are in many of the state, regional, and other special digests.

---

20 F2d 873; 275 US 552, 72 LE 421, 48 SC 115; 275
US 555, 72 LE 423, 48 SC 116
121 Tex 515, 50 SW2d 1065; 25 SW2d 706

River Rights Cases
199 AppDiv 539, 192 NYSupp 211; 235 NY 351,
139 NE 474; 236 NY 579, 142 NE 291; 271 US
364, 70 LE 992, 46 SC 569
199 AppDiv 552, 192 NYSupp 222; 235 NY 364,
139 NE 477; 236 NY 578, 142 NE 291; 271 US
403, 70 LE 1009, 46 SC 581

River Road Case
353 US 30, 1 LE2d 622, 77 SC 635; 353 US 948, 1
LE2d 857, 77 SC 823; 229 F2d 926

Riverside Mills Case
168 Fed 987; 168 Fed 990; 219 US 186, 55 LE 167,
31 SC 164

Million Dollar Road Bond Case
207 Iowa 923, 223 NW 737

Road Cases
30 Tex 503
30 Tex 506

294 US 648, 79 LE 1110, 55 SC 595

Rockne Case
115 US 600, 29 LE 477, 6 SC 201

Rodin's Hand of God Case
177 FS 265, 394 FS 1390

Rogers Lumber Company Case
117 NLRB 1732, No. 230

Rogers Silverware Cases
285 US 247, 76 LE 740, 52 SC 387
11 Fed 495
70 Fed 1017
110 Fed 955
17 PQ 32
39 Conn 450
66 NJEq 119, 57 At 1037; 66 NJEq 140, 57 At 725;
67 NJEq 646, 60 At 187; 71 NJEq 560, 63 At
977; 72 NJEq 933, 67 At 105

Roller Miller Patent Case
43 Fed 527; 156 US 261, 39 LE 417, 15 SC 333

SECTION N. SUMMARY

1. Digests in General

Digests give brief, unconnected statements of court holdings or facts of the cases, and are classified by subject. Digests are seldom, if ever, cited.

2. Types of West Digests

    a. All appellate courts, federal and state.

    b. Regional digests (four) for a group of adjacent states.

    c. State.

    d. Specific court or court system.

    e. Specific subject.

3. American Digest System

    a. *Scope*

    (1) Digest series that purports to cover every reported case, federal and state, from 1658 to date.

    (2) Consists of a *Century Digest* (1658–1896), nine complete *Decennial Digests,* the *Tenth, Part 1* (1986–1991), the *Tenth, Part 2* (1991–1996) and the *General Digest, 9th Series* (for cases 1996–2001).

    b. *Arrangement*

    (1) All reported cases are assigned headnotes, including Topics, that are then classified to the Key Number classification system. The headnotes then become digest paragraphs.

    (2) Corresponding Key Numbers used in all *Decennial Digests, General Digests,* and other West Key Number digests.

    (3) Scope note (delimits and identifies the content of a Topic).

    (4) Analysis (conceptual breakdown of a Topic).

    (5) Section lines, preceded by the Key Numbers, indicate the content of each Key Number under a Topic.

    (6) Digest paragraphs arranged under Key Numbers by: Supreme Court of the United States, other federal courts, and state cases listed alphabetically by names of states. The name and citation of each case follow the digest paragraph.

    (7) Periodically, Topics are expanded or reclassified (revised) and new Topics are added.

    c. *Century Edition* (1658–1896)

    (1) Not classified by Key Number System.

    (2) To refer from the *Century Edition* to the *Decennials,* use the pink reference table in volume 21 of the *First Decennial.*

(3) When a Key Number is known and one needs to locate the corresponding section in the *Century Edition,* refer to the cross references in the *First* or *Second Decennials.* Those in the *Second Decennial* are more complete.

    d. *Use of Indexes with the American Digest System*

(1) Each *Decennial* and the *General Digest* have a *Descriptive–Word Index.*

(2) Since recent cases are preferred, begin research with the latest *Decennial's Descriptive–Word Index.* After locating a Key Number, check it in all *Decennials* and the *General Digest* on point and then convert Key Number to section number in *Century Edition* for earlier cases. This process will disclose cases on point from 1658 to date.

    e. *Digest Paragraphs in WESTLAW*

(1) Includes the online equivalent of the *American Digest System.*

(2) Provides the ability to hypertext from a headnote to its point of origin in the case and vice versa.

(3) Automatically updates reclassified headnotes from the old headnote for cases from 1932 forward.

    f. *Using the Analysis or Topic Method*

(1) Examine the scope note and analysis under the appropriate Topic. Select the Key Number and proceed as in d. (2) above.

(2) Requires careful analysis and knowledge of West's Key Number classification.

4. Supreme Court of the United States Reports

    a. *Two publishers digest the cases of the Supreme Court of the United States.*

(1) West's *U.S. Supreme Court Digest* uses the West *Key Number System* and provides references to other West publications.

(2) LEXIS Law Publishing's *Digest of United States Supreme Court Reports, Lawyers' Edition* uses its own classification system and provides references to its other publications.

    b. *Word Indexes and Tables of Cases.* Both of these digests contain word indexes and tables of cases.

5. West's Federal Practice Digest, 4th

    a. *Scope*

(1) Digests federal cases from December 1975 to date.

(2) Covers cases of the Supreme Court of the United States and other federal court cases reported in the various federal reporters published by West.

(3) Kept up to date with replacement volumes, cumulative pocket supplements, interim pamphlets, and later bound volumes and advance sheets of the various West reporters covering federal cases.

(4) Both the *4th* and the *3rd* must be consulted for cases from December 1975 through 1983. Only consult the *4th* for cases from 1984 forward.

6. West's Federal Practice Digest, 3rd

a. *Scope*

(1) Digests federal cases from December 1975 to the point coverage begins in *West's Federal Practice Digest, 4th*. Consult both the *3rd* and *4th* for cases from December 1975 through 1983.

(2) Covers cases of the Supreme Court of the United States and other federal court cases reported in the various federal reporters published by West.

7. Earlier Federal Digests

a. *Federal Practice Digest, 2nd,* 1961 through November 1975.

b. *Modern Federal Practice Digest,* 1939–1960.

c. *Federal Digest,* all federal cases through 1938.

8. West's Regional Digests

a. Segments of the *American Digest System,* grouped by states that form the regional units of the *National Reporter System.*

b. Some *regional digests* include cases prior to the corresponding unit of the regional reporter. Four regional digests are presently published.

c. Kept up to date with replacement volumes, cumulative pocket supplements, interim pamphlets, and later bound volumes and advance sheets of the regional reporters.

d. Classified under the *Key Number System.*

e. Contain standard digest features, e.g., *Descriptive–Word Index, Table of Cases, Words and Phrases.*

9. West's State Digests

a. West's state digests follow the *Key Number System* and are components of the *American Digest System.*

b. Standard features common to many state digests.

(1) Cover all reported state cases and federal cases arising in each state or applying state law from the earliest period to date.

(2) Contain standard digest features, e.g., *Descriptive–Word Index, Table of Cases.*

(3) Kept up to date by replacement volumes, cumulative pocket supplements, interim pamphlets, and later bound volumes and advance sheets of corresponding units of the regional reporters.

10. Other Digests

(1) A few state digests are produced by publishers other than West. These are not Key Number digests.

(2) Looseleaf services, topical reporters, and multi-volume treatises frequently contain digests.

11. Words and Phrases

a. Contains judicially-defined words and phrases, both legal and non-legal.

b. Definitions often originate as headnotes that are later incorporated into the set.

12. Popular Names of Cases

a. In *Table of Cases* volumes of *First* through *Sixth Decennials,* in state digests, and in some speciality digests.

b. In *Shepard's Acts and Cases by Popular Names.*

Chapter 7

ANNOTATED LAW REPORTS

As has been shown in the previous three chapters, one means of case finding is through the comprehensive publishing of court reports, together with the sophisticated digest methodology used for locating these cases by subject. *Annotations,* as the term is used in this chapter, are encyclopedic essays or memoranda that collect cases germane to a particular point of law and then, through use of these cases, discuss and analyze in depth that particular point of law.

The leading publisher of *annotations* for many decades was Lawyers Cooperative Publishing (and its related company Bancroft–Whitney Company). During this time it was one of West's leading competitors. In 1996, Lawyers Cooperative Publishing and several other companies came under the umbrella of the West Group, thus expanding West's approaches to case reporting.

Obviously, not all cases decided each year are of interest to most lawyers. Many deal with either strictly local matters or cover an area of the law so well settled that they add very little to the understanding of the law. Originally, the West philosophy was to publish all reported cases and provide finding aids to help one locate all cases on point. When the West Group was formed and Lawyers Cooperative Publishing became a part of the larger entity, West continued its tradition of comprehensive reporting and also Lawyers Cooperative's tradition of identifying points of law not previously resolved, or that indicate a change in the law, or that indicate an emerging trend in legal thinking.

To produce its annotated series, the publisher selects and reports one contemporary case representative of a particular legal issue, collects all the relevant cases, and uses them in providing a detailed critique of that point of law. By providing this method of *selective law reporting,* the publisher feels that lawyers have a choice between a comprehensive collection represented by the various units of the *National Reporter System* and one which selectively reports and annotates those cases considered to be most important.

Although selective law reporting was the basis for Lawyers Cooperative Publishing's first venture into publishing court reports, this publisher also realized that researchers must be able to locate cases not reported in its publications and to have a method of locating current cases. It began to publish auxiliary sets, all related to each other, and all aimed to assist researchers in finding answers to legal questions through these publications. These sets gradually grew into what came to be called the *Total Client–Service Library (TCSL),* consisting of several distinctive units national in scope. These *TCSL* units serve as additional reference sources in the series. In addition to the publisher's national units, there are numerous state units and several specialized publications that interrelate by means of extensive cross referencing. This chapter discusses various annotated law reports.

SECTION A.   AMERICAN LAW REPORTS

1. Introduction

The *American Law Reports (A.L.R.)* series, which began in 1919 through the efforts of Lawyers Cooperative Publishing and which is now published by the West Group, is a selective reporter of appellate court cases. Its attorney-editors scan all current cases looking for points of law that warrant *Annotations*. Once they identify a point of law deserving of an *Annotation,* they then select a case to illustrate the point of law to be annotated. This case and the accompanying monographic *Annotation* are published in *A.L.R.*

2. A.L.R. and its Series

The *American Law Reports* are in six series.[1]

(a) Federal (cited *A.L.R. Fed.*), 1969 to date. This series discusses federal topics only and is a consequence of the increasing importance and growth of federal case law. From volumes 1–110 the illustrative case immediately preceded the related *Annotation.* Commencing with volume 111 (1993), the illustrative cases reported in the volume follow all the *Annotations* in that volume. Also starting with volume 111, this set includes for the first time references to West's *Key Number System* and to West's legal encyclopedia *Corpus Juris Secundum (C.J.S.),* electronic search queries compatible with LEXIS–NEXIS and WESTLAW, a jurisdictional table of cited statutes and cases, and references to secondary sources such as law reviews and texts and looseleaf services from other publishers. Commencing with volume 128, a Special Commentaries feature at the beginning of the each volume contains an analysis by expert practitioners on a chosen subject in their area of speciality. An annual three-volume pamphlet set, the *ALR Federal Tables*, lists cases, statutes, and regulations covered in the set and provides a volume-by-volume listing of annotation titles.

(b) Fifth Series (cited *A.L.R.5th*), 1992 to date. This series covers state topics only and includes numerous enhancements not found in some of the earlier series discussed below. For example, it includes references to West's *Key Number System* and to *C.J.S.,* electronic search queries, a jurisdictional table of cited statutes and cases, and references to secondary sources such as law reviews and texts and looseleaf services from other publishers. It also includes the features traditional in most

---

[1] The *American Law Reports* replace the *Lawyers' Reports Annotated (L.R.A.).* For information about this set, three sets collectively known as the *Trinity Series,* and other earlier sets of annotated reports, see ERVIN H. POLLACK, FUNDAMENTALS OF LEGAL RESEARCH 116–17 (3d ed. 1967).

A.L.R. series, such as the illustrative cases, outlines, *Annotations* and their various sections, indexes, and references to other West Group publications. The illustrative cases reported in the volume follow all the *Annotations* in that volume.

(c) Fourth Series (cited *A.L.R.4th*), 1980–1992, 90 volumes. This set covers state topics only and contains the traditional *A.L.R.* series features, including the illustrative cases, outlines, *Annotations* and their various sections, indexes, and references to related publications. The illustrative case immediately precedes the related *Annotation.* The same enhancements included in *A.L.R.5th* and in *A.L.R. Fed.* are being added to the pocket supplements of *A.L.R.4th. Electronic Search Queries and West Digest Key Numbers for Annotations in ALR 4th* is provided as a separate paperback book.

(d) Third Series (cited *A.L.R.3d*), 1965–1980, 100 volumes. For the period 1965 to 1969 this series covers both state and federal topics. After *A.L.R. Fed.* began in 1969, coverage in *A.L.R.3d* was limited to state topics. It includes the traditional features found in the more recent *A.L.R.* series.

(e) Second Series (cited *A.L.R.2d*), 1948–1965, 100 volumes. This series covers both state and federal topics and includes the traditional features found in the later *A.L.R.* series.

(f) First Series (cited *A.L.R.*), 1919–1948, 175 volumes. Coverage and features are the same as in *A.L.R.2d.*

3. The Value of A.L.R. Annotations

The usefulness of locating a relevant *A.L.R. Annotation* should be evident, since it presents in an organized fashion a commentary and discussion of all previously reported cases and saves the researcher the task of locating the cases and then analyzing and synthesizing them. Approximately 10–20 separate *Annotations* are published in each volume of *A.L.R.*

SECTION B.   FINDING A.L.R. ANNOTATIONS

Finding *A.L.R. Annotations* and demonstrating their value can best be made clear with an example and illustrations.

In the case of *Kampe v. Howard Stark Pro. Pharmacy,* decided in the Missouri Court of Appeals, Western District,[2] a customer sued her pharmacy alleging that the pharmacy failed to monitor or evaluate the customer's use of prescribed drugs. The publisher determined that this four-page case [See Illustration 7–2] was representative of the modern view with respect to whether a pharmacist can be held liable for injuries caused by prescription medications even when there is a valid and authorized prescription and it is properly filled. Thereafter, an editor prepared a 130 page *Annotation* entitled *Liability of Pharmacist Who*

---

[2] 841 S.W.2d 223, 44 A.L.R. 5th 829 (Mo. App. 1992).

Accurately Fills Prescription for Harm Resulting to User. [See Illustration 7–3.]

In preparing this *Annotation,* the editor researched the entire area of the law covered by the topic of the *Annotation,* collected all cases from all jurisdictions that related to the *Annotation,* and wrote the *Annotation,* incorporating the many editorial features common to the *A.L.R.* series. This *Annotation,* as with all *A.L.R. Annotations,* discusses all the cases and all sides of the issue, presents general principles deduced from the cases, and gives their exceptions, qualifications, distinctions, and applications. [See Illustrations 7–4 through 7–7.]

1. Index Method

The first step in locating an *A.L.R. Annotation* is to consult the multi-volume *ALR Index.* This set indexes all *Annotations* in all the *A.L.R.* series, except the First Series. (There is also a separate, one volume *ALR Federal Quick Index* and a separate, one volume *ALR Quick Index for ALR3d, 4th, and 5th* that reproduce the references found in the *ALR Index.*) The *ALR Index* is kept current by annual pocket supplements.

In our example, the terms to use would probably be "products liability" or "prescription drugs."

Under the two terms suggested are the following [see also Illustration 7–8]:

PRODUCTS LIABILITY
Pharmacist, liability of pharmacist who accurately fills prescription for harm resulting to user, 44 ALR5th 393, §§ 27–29

PRESCRIPTION DRUGS
Liability of pharmacist who accurately fills prescription for harm resulting to user, 44 ALR5th

---

2. Digest Method

There are separate sets of digests for *A.L.R.* and *A.L.R.2d.* However, *A.L.R.3d, A.L.R.4th, A.L.R.5th,* and *A.L.R.Fed.* are combined in one set of digests.

The *Digests* are classified into over four hundred topics arranged alphabetically. Under each topic are headnotes from cases reported in the entire *A.L.R.* family, along with a listing of the *Annotations* that deal with the particular subject in question. [See Illustration 7–9.]

3. Electronic Format Method

The over 13,000 *Annotations* in *A.L.R.2d* through *5th, A.L.R.Fed.,* and *Lawyers' Edition 2d* are available on LEXIS–NEXIS, in its ALR library, the ALR file, and on WESTLAW, in its ALR database. *Annotations* can be located through Boolean, FREESTYLE, and WIN searches (these techniques are discussed in Chapter 22), with additional means of access provided for the features common to the *A.L.R.* series. They are retrieved automatically when one searches all federal cases or all state cases. Updating these citations through *Auto–Cite* and *Insta-Cite* is discussed in D–3–b of this chapter.

ALR on LawDesk is a CD–ROM product containing the contents of all of *A.L.R.3d, 4th,* and *5th.* It enables a user to "jump" directly to the articles and sections needed.

4. Shepard's Citations Method

Shepard's Citations for Annotations, a set that covers *A.L.R.3d, 4th, 5th,* and *Federal,* contains references to annotations citing to cases and references to cases citing to annotations. Other units of *Shepard's Citations* also provide references to *A.L.R. Annotations. Shepard's Citations* are discussed in Chapter 15.

SECTION C.   HOW A.L.R. IS KEPT CURRENT

1. Upkeep Service

Once an *A.L.R. Annotation* is found, further steps must be taken to locate cases subsequent to those found in the *Annotation.* Over the years the publisher has developed several different ways to keep its various *A.L.R.* series up to date.

a. *A.L.R.3d, 4th, 5th, Federal.* Each volume of these series has an annual cumulative pocket supplement. After reading an *Annotation* in any of these series, it is necessary to check the pocket supplement for later cases. Digests of cases are keyed directly to each section of the *Annotation.* Also, as new volumes continue to be published for *A.L.R.5th* and *A.L.R. Federal,* to assure complete coverage it is necessary to examine the contents page or "subjects annotated" section in all bound volumes published after the pocket supplement.

b. *A.L.R.2d.* This series is kept current with a multi-volume *A.L.R.2d Later Case Service,* with each volume covering two to four volumes of the 100 volumes in *A.L.R.2d.* This *Later Case Service* provides digests of cases and then keys them directly to each section of the *A.L.R.2d Annotations.* This set is kept up to date with annual pocket supplements and occasional revised volumes. Thus, to update an *A.L.R.2d Annotation,* both the bound *Later Case Service* and its supplement must be checked.

c. *A.L.R. (First Series).* This series is kept current through a cumbersome eight volume set entitled the *A.L.R. Blue Book of Supplemental Decisions.* Each "permanent" volume covers a different span of years, with the latest being for 1990–1996. Each volume lists citations to all cases on the same topic as the *Annotations,* but provides no discussion of the cases. The set is supplemented with an annual pamphlet, making it necessary to consult nine separate sources to fully update an *Annotation* in *A.L.R. (First Series).*

2. Superseding and Supplementing Annotations

a. *Superseding Annotations.* Frequently, a topic of law of an *A.L.R. Annotation* is completely changed by later cases. For example, an *Annotation* in an early volume of *A.L.R.* might show that there is little likelihood that one would be convicted of cruelty to animals. Subsequently, statutes are enacted, cases interpret those statutes, and the law changes. The editors may then decide to rewrite and publish in a later *A.L.R.* volume a *superseding* (replacement) *Annotation*. Sometimes only a part of a previous *Annotation* will be superseded.

b. *Supplementing Annotations.* This method was used most frequently in *A.L.R.* and *A.L.R.2d.* In such instances, a new *Annotation* was written that supplemented the original one. Therefore, for comprehensive coverage both *Annotations* must be read together as if they are one *Annotation*.

3.   Locating the Most Recent Annotations

a. *Annotation History Table.* Whenever a researcher has a citation to an *A.L.R. Annotation,* to avoid a waste of time by reading an obsolete *Annotation* or one not fully covering a topic, the researcher should always first check to see if an *Annotation* has been *superseded* or *supplemented*. This is done either by checking the citation in the appropriate *A.L.R.* upkeep volume, or by using the *Annotation History Table* located in the T–Z volume of the *ALR Index*. This *Table* gives the history of *Annotations* in all of the *A.L.R.* series. Its use can best be shown with the excerpt below:

ANNOTATION HISTORY TABLE

12 ALR 111	13 ALR 17	13 ALR 1465
Supplemented 37 ALR2d 453	Supplemented 39 ALR2d 782	Superseded 3 ALR5th 370
12 ALR 333	13 ALR 151	14 ALR 240
Superseded 7 ALR2d 226	Superseded 46 ALR2d 1227	Superseded 51 ALR2d 331
12 ALR 596	13 ALR 225	14 ALR 316
Superseded 57 ALR2d 379	Superseded 13 ALR4th 1060	Superseded 11 ALR3d 1074

This example means that 12 *A.L.R.* 111 and 37 *A.L.R.2d* 453 should be read together as if they are a single *Annotation,* and then updated for later cases using the *A.L.R.2d Later Case Service* as previously described.

Suppose, however, that the researcher has found a citation to 82 *A.L.R.2d* 794, an *Annotation* on cruelty to animals. By checking the *Annotation History Table* in the *ALR Index,* it would be noted that this *Annotation* is *superseded* as indicated below:

```
┌─────────────────────────────────────────────────────────────────┐
│                 ANNOTATION HISTORY TABLE                          │
│                                                                   │
│    78 ALR2d 412          79 ALR2d 431           ┌──────────────┐  │
│  Superseded 69 ALR Fed 600   § 29, 36 Superseded 46 ALR4th 1197 │ 82 ALR2d 794 │  │
│                                                  │Superseded 6 ALR5th 733│  │
│                          § 35 Superseded 63 ALR4th 105  └──────────────┘  │
│    78 ALR2d 429          § 37 Superseded 54 ALR4th 574            │
│  Superseded 98 ALR Fed 778                       82 ALR2d 1183    │
│                             79 ALR2d 990      § 3-5 Superseded 53 ALR4th 282 │
│    78 ALR2d 446          Superseded 20 ALR3d 1127      63 ALR4th 221 │
│  Superseded 25 ALR3d 383      38 ALR4th 200                        │
│                                                  82 ALR2d 1429    │
│                             79 ALR2d 1005     Superseded 44 ALR4th 271 │
│                          Superseded 54 ALR4th 391                 │
└─────────────────────────────────────────────────────────────────┘
```

b. *Shepard's Citations for Annotations.* This volume enables the user to Shepardize *Annotations* for *A.L.R. 3d, 4th, 5th,* and *A.L.R. Fed. Shepard's Citations* are discussed in Chapter 15.

c. *Auto–Cite. Auto–Cite,* available on LEXIS–NEXIS, is an electronic citation validation and verification service. By typing an *A.L.R.* citation into *Auto–Cite* the system retrieves citations to all supplementing or superseding annotations. For example, entering 82 *A.L.R.2d* 794, the same citation as used with the *Annotation History Table,* the result reproduced below is obtained:

```
┌─────────────────────────────────────────────────────────────────┐
│ Auto–Cite (R) Citation Service, (c) 1998 LEXIS-NEXIS             │
│                                                                   │
│ 82 ALR2D 794:                              Screen 1 of 2         │
│                                                                   │
│ CITATION YOU ENTERED:                                            │
│                                                                   │
│ What constitutes statutory offense of cruelty to animals, 82 A.L.R.2d │
│ 794 (superseded by What constitutes offense of cruelty to animals— │
│ modern cases, 6 A.L.R.5th 733).                                  │
│                         *  *  *                                   │
└─────────────────────────────────────────────────────────────────┘
```

c. *Latest Case Service Hotline.* Each pocket supplement lists a toll free number that can be used to obtain citations to any relevant cases decided since the last supplement.

SECTION D.   UNITED STATES SUPREME COURT REPORTS, LAWYERS' EDITION

Chapter 4 discusses the *United States Supreme Court Reports, Lawyers' Edition.* It was pointed out that a significant aspect of this set is the *Annotations* that are provided for selected important cases. [See Illustrations 4–9 and 4–10.] These *Annotations* are published only in the bound volumes. These *Annotations* can be located using the *ALR Index* or *Auto–Cite.*

**SECTION E.   ILLUSTRATIONS: A.L.R. ANNOTATIONS
AND HOW TO FIND AND UPDATE THEM**

[Illustration 7–1]

CONTENTS OF AN A.L.R.5th VOLUME

Contents of This Volume

Near the front of each volume is the Contents, which lists the
Annotations contained within. Following this listing is "Subjects
Annotated In this Volume," an alphabetical, subject guide to the
Annotations in the volume.

xi

[Illustration 7–2]

HEADNOTES AND START OF OPINION IN A.L.R.5th

---

44 ALR5th   KAMPE V HOWARD STARK PRO. PHARMACY
841 SW2d 223, 44 ALR5th 829

enacted after the plaintiff customer's alleged cause of action accrued and was not to be applied retroactively, and (2) the statute was definitional in nature and did not purport to set forth duties, a companion statute, in fact, providing that pharmacists "may," rather than must, provide pharmaceutical consultation and advice to persons concerning the safe and therapeutic use of their prescription drugs.

[Annotated]

Drugs and Druggists § 3 — federal regulation as creating duty of pharmacist to monitor, advise, and counsel customer regarding prescribed drug

4. A federal regulation, 21 CFR § 1306.04, creates responsibility on the part of pharmacists in dispensing controlled substances, but places no affirmative duty on pharmacists to counsel a consumer regarding lawfully prescribed drugs.

[Annotated]

APPEARANCES OF COUNSEL

Thomas W. Koelling, Kansas City, for appellant.

Allan V. Hallquist, Dora E. Reid, Kansas City, for respondent.

Before LOWENSTEIN, C.J., and BERREY and ULRICH, JJ.

OPINION OF THE COURT

BERREY, Judge.

Appellant appeals the trial court's order dismissing his cause of action. He alleges the pharmacy was negligent in filling prescrip-

---

A case representative of the subject of each *A.L.R. Annotation* in a volume is also reported in that volume. When citing an *A.L.R. Annotation*, reference is to the *Annotation*, not the representative case.

---

care. Appellant alleges trial court error in granting defendant's motion to dismiss because the pharmacy failed to exercise ordinary and prudent pharmacology, which constituted actionable negligence, by its failure to warn, counsel, evaluate, or verify the appropriateness of prescriptions, including controlled substances.

Appellant alleges that between March 1987 and September 1989, the respondent accurately filled prescriptions for appellant but failed to monitor or evaluate appellant's use of the prescribed drugs. Appellant's claim is based on a theory that the pharmacist is duty bound to monitor a consumer's use of prescription drugs and failure to do so is negligence. Appellant argues that the scope of a pharmacy's duty is a question of fact and, therefore, summary judgment or dismissal is improper. Such theory is contrary to the law in most jurisdictions and is a case of first impression in Missouri.

831

[Illustration 7–3]

FIRST PAGE OF ANNOTATION, 44 A.L.R.5th 393

---

44 ALR5th 393

LIABILITY OF PHARMACIST WHO ACCURATELY FILLS PRESCRIPTION FOR HARM RESULTING TO USER

by
David J. Marchitelli, J.D., B.S. Pharmacy

In the interest of public safety and security against the grave consequences of negligence in keeping, handling, and disposing of prescription drugs; pharmacists have been traditionally held to a professional standard of conduct commensurate with the degree of knowledge, skill, and diligence ordinarily exercised by other members of the profession, as opposed to a reasonable person standard. Despite what has been described as "the highest

> This is the first page of the *Annotation* for 44 A.L.R.5th 393. This prefatory paragraph, new to *A.L.R.5th*, briefly describes the subject of the *Annotation*. For *A.L.R.5th*, the illustrative cases used with the *Annotations* are published toward the back of the volume following all *Annotations* in that volume. For earlier *A.L.R.* series, the case immediately precedes the *Annotation*.

are not limited to accurately filling a valid prescription. In most cases, courts have taken a position consistent with Kampe v Howard Stark Professional Pharmacy (1992, Mo App) 841 SW2d 223, 44 ALR5th 829, in which the court held that a pharmacist has no duty to warn a customer of the risk of harm that might be encountered from drugs which are accurately dispensed upon a valid and legal prescription. In other cases, plaintiffs have asserted claims based on negligence, strict products liability, breach of warranty, statutory provisions regulating the pharmacy profession, and pharmacy trade association standards, with successes being limited largely to cases in which the circumstances indicate that the defendant pharmacists knew or should have known that the particular plaintiff was at risk. This annotation analyzes those cases in which courts have discussed the question whether a pharmacist may be held liable for injuries arising out of use of a medication that was accurately dispensed upon a valid and legal prescription.

Kampe v Howard Stark Professional Pharmacy, is fully reported at page 829, infra.

393

[Illustration 7–4]

FIRST PAGE OF OUTLINE TO ANNOTATION, 44 A.L.R.5th 393

---

44 ALR5th   PHARMACIST LIABILITY
44 ALR5th 393

TABLE OF CONTENTS

Research References

Index

Jurisdictional Table of Cited Statutes and Cases

ARTICLE OUTLINE

This is the first page of a detailed outline of the *Annotation*. It follows the prefatory paragraph. Note that while this *Annotation* covers the point specific to the *Kampe* case, it covers numerous other issues as well. The outline enables a researcher to turn immediately to a section being researched and find relevant cases.

395

[Illustration 7–5]

PAGE SHOWING RESEARCH REFERENCES
FOR ANNOTATION, 44 A.L.R.5th 393

---

44 ALR5th   PHARMACIST LIABILITY
                         44 ALR5th 393

> Following the outline, the *A.L.R. Annotations* include references to other publications, as well as to sources by other publishers. In earlier series, these references were in a box on the first page of the *Annotation*.

Research References

TOTAL CLIENT-SERVICE LIBRARY® REFERENCES

The following references may be of related or collateral interest to a user of this annotation.

Annotations

See the related annotations listed in the body of the annotation.

Encyclopedias and Texts

25 Am Jur 2d, Drugs, Narcotics, and Poisons §§ 54–56, 60

63 Am Jur 2d, Products Liability §§ 332, 721

Practice Aids

9 Am Jur Pl & Pr Forms (Rev), Drugs, Narcotics, and Poisons, Forms 31, 33, 43

7 Am Jur Proof of Facts 3d 1, Injuries from Drugs

397

[Illustration 7–6]

PAGE SHOWING LAST PAGE OF INDEX TO ANNOTATION, 44 A.L.R.5th 393, AND START OF JURISDICTIONAL TABLE

---

44 ALR5th   PHARMACIST LIABILITY
44 ALR5th 393

Theophylline, § 13

Third parties, duties owed to, § 42

Timolol, §§ 19[b], 34[b]

Timoptic, §§ 19[b], 34[b]

Tofranil or imipramine, §§ 12, 17[b], 34[b], 42[a]

Toxic epidermal necrolysis, §§ 26, 31, 32

Trade association standards, §§ 34[b], 41

Tranquilizers, § 5[a]

Trikro...

Tymp...

28[...

Ulcer...

Unav-...

41[...

Und ...

§§ ..[c], ..

Unregistered pharmacist, § 38

Unusual or obviously erroneous prescriptions, §§ 3-8, 11[b], 12, 17[b], 40

Urgent need for medication, § 4

Urinary tract infection, §§ 9, 19[b], 34[b]

Vaccine, §§ 20[b], 27, 28[b]

Valium, §§ 12, 24, 34[b]

> *A.L.R.5th Annotations* include a detailed index that can lead to specific points in the *Annotation*. See Illustration 7-7. Lengthy Annotations in earlier series also contain an index.
>
> The jurisdictional table, found in *A.L.R.5th*, provides citations to statutes and cases relevant to the *Annotation*. This information is much more detailed than in earlier series.

Unfit or spoiled drug product, dispensing, § 21

Unreasonably dangerous product, §§ 28[b], 29

Warranty, breach of, §§ 28[b], 30-33

Willingness of pharmacists to stock certain products, effect of strict liability on, § 27

Jurisdictional Table of Cited Statutes and Cases*

ALABAMA

Watkins v Potts (1929) 219 Ala 427, 122 So 416, 65 ALR 1097—§ 8

ARIZONA

Lasley v Shrake's Country Club Pharmacy (1994, App) 179 Ariz 583, 880 P2d 1129, 162 Ariz Adv Rep 10, CCH Prod Liab Rep ¶ 13910—§§ 11[a], 41[a]

CALIFORNIA

Cal Bus & Prof Code $4046 (a). See § 27
Cal Bus & Prof Code $4046 (b). See § 27
Cal Bus & Prof Code $4046 (b, c). See § 27

Huggins v Longs Drug Stores Cal. (1993) 6 Cal 4th 124, 24 Cal Rptr 2d

---

* Statutes, rules, regulations, and constitutional provisions bearing on the subject of the annotation are included in this table only to the extent, and in the form, that they are reflected in the court opinions discussed in this annotation. The reader should consult the appropriate statutory or regulatory compilations to ascertain the current status of relevant statutes, rules, regulations, and constitutional provisions.

For federal cases involving state law, see state headings.

[Illustration 7–7]

PAGE FROM ANNOTATION, 44 A.L.R.5th 393

§ 41[b]   PHARMACIST LIABILITY   44 ALR5th
                              44 ALR5th 393

serve as a source of legal duties on the part of pharmacists extending beyond the duty to fill prescriptions accurately and correctly as written.

Rejecting a contention that a pharmacist had a duty to monitor the
plaintiff's use of medications accurately dispensed pursuant to a valid prescription, the court in Adkins v Mong (1988) 168 Mich App 726, 425
NW   no such
dut   **Notice how § 42 brings together and discusses all cases**   ards of
pra   **dealing with a pharmacist's duty to third parties. The *Kampe***   979 and
upc   **case is discussed in § 41[b] under the heading "Trade association** rve as a
sou   **standards." § 1 always gives the scope of the *Annotation* and**   rescrip-
tion   **then lists related *Annotations*.**   defendant pharmacy, on the ground that there was no liability for injuries
caused by an accurately dispensed prescription drug, the court stated that
it was unpersuaded by those nonlegal authorities, particularly in light of
the weight of contrary judicial authority.

Rejecting a contention that a pharmacist had a duty to warn or counsel
a patient in regard to several prescription medications, apparently including the addictive propensities of some controlled substances, as well as a
duty to monitor the plaintiff and evalutate and verify the appropriateness
of the prescriptions, the court in Kampe v Howard Stark Professional
Pharmacy (1992, **Mo App**) 841 SW2d 223, 44 ALR5th 829, also refused to
hold that such duties were created by the "Standards of Practice" adopted
by the American Pharmaceutical Association. Affirming an order dismissing the plaintiff's cause of action, and holding that the defendant pharmacy
incurred no liability for injuries caused by an accurately dispensed
prescripition drug, the court rejected the argument that nonlegal authorities could impose legal duties.

§ 42. Duties owed to third parties

[a] Duty supportable

In the following case, in which it was asserted that a pharmacist's failure
to warn of dangers associated with a particular prescription drug
proximately resulted in the death of someone other than the intended
user, despite otherwise filling the prescription accurately as written, the
court declined to hold, as a matter of law, that the defendant owed no
duties which extended to the decedent.

In Docken v Ciba-Geigy (1987) 86 **Or App** 277, 739 P2d 591, CCH
Prod Liab Rep ¶ 11515, review den 304 Or 405, 745 P2d 1225, later
proceeding 101 Or App 252, 790 P2d 45, review den 310 Or 195, 795
P2d 554 and review den 304 Or 405, 745 P2d 1225, the court declined to
take a position which would prevent recovery against a pharmacist for

[Illustration 7–8]

EXAMPLE FROM ALR INDEX

ALR INDEX

PRODUCE—Cont'd
Perishable Agricultural Commodities
 Act—Cont'd
  trusts, statutory trust under Perish-
   able Agricultural Commodities
   Act (7 USCS §§ 499a et seq), 128
   ALR Fed 303

PRODUCTION O
Attorney-Client Pri
Jencks Act (this ind
Pre-action, propriety

> An *ALR Index* citation to the
> *Annotation* for the problem being
> researched.

 grant or denial of application for pre-
  action production or inspection of
  documents, persons, or other evidence, 12 ALR5th 577
Subpoena duces tecum
 Supreme Court's construction and
  application of Rule 17 of Federal
  Rules of Criminal Procedure,
  pertaining to subpoena in criminal cases, 112 L Ed 2d 1237

PRODUCTS LIABILITY
Advertising and Advertisements (this
 index)
Air bag systems, defective motor vehicle
 air bag systems, 39 ALR5th 267
Automobiles and Highway Traffic (this
 index)
Danger and dangerous conditions
 presumption or inference, in
  products liability action based on
  failure to warn, that user of
  product would have heeded an
  adequate warning had one been
  given, 38 ALR5th 683
 universal symbols, failure to
  provide product warning or
  instruction in foreign language or
  to use universally accepted
  pictographs or symbols, 27
  ALR5th 697
Due process clause of Federal
 Constitution's Fourteenth Amendment as violated by amount of punitive damages awarded or by
 procedures concerning imposition or
 review of such amount—Supreme
 Court cases, 129 L Ed 2d 941

PRODUCTS LIABILITY—Cont'd
Evidence
 admissibility of government
  factfinding in product liability
  actions, 29 ALR5th 534
Explosions and Explosives (this index)
Insurance
      ering liability insurance
      e as occurring within
      of time covered by
      insurance policy where
      r damage is delayed—
  modern cases, 14 ALR5th 695
Lighters and lighter fluid, 14 ALR5th
 47
Limitation of actions
 validity and construction of statute
  terminating right of action for
  product-caused injury at fixed
  period after manufacture, sale, or
  delivery of product, 30 ALR5th 1
Pharmacist, liability of pharmacist who
 accurately fills prescription for harm
 resulting to user, 44 ALR5th 393,
 § 27-29
Presumption or inference, in products
 liability action based on failure to
 warn, that user of product would
 have heeded an adequate warning had
 one been given, 38 ALR5th 683
Punitive damages
 excessiveness or inadequacy of
  punitive damages in cases not
  involving personal injury or
  death, 14 ALR5th 242, § 21[b, c],
  22[a-c]
Safety device, products liability, defective motor vehicle air bag systems, 39
 ALR5th 267
Strict products liability
 used products, application of strict
  liability doctrine to seller of used
  product, 9 ALR5th 1
Testing and inspections
 breach of assumed duty to inspect
  property as ground for liability to
  third party, 13 ALR5th 289
Theatrical equipment, products liability,
 theatrical equipment and props, 42
 ALR5th 699

Consult Main Volume for Earlier Annotations

Index-38

[Illustration 7–9]

PAGE FROM ALR DIGEST TO 3d, 4th, 5th, Fed.

DRUGS AND DRUGGISTS

§ 1

Consult pocket part for later cases

§ 3 —Violation of statute
§ 4 —Negligence of employee
§ 5 —Contributory negligence
§ 6 Criminal liability for injuries
§ 7 Narcotics and controlled substances, generally
§ 8 —Prescription, distribution, and sale of dangerous drugs by medical practitioners and druggists
§ 9 —Possession and use of drugs, controlled substances, and drug paraphernalia

§ 10 —Sale, distribution, and manufacture of controlled substances
§ 11 —Transportation of controlled substances
§ 12 —Fraud, forgery, and falsehood in obtaining or distributing controlled substances
§ 13 —Miscellaneous offenses and violations
§ 14 —Civil commitment; rehabilitation programs

TABLE OF PARALLEL REFERENCES

The following table shows where the subject matter of changed sections in the original topic *Drugs and Druggists* is now treated in the new topic *Drugs and Druggists*. Consult the new topic scheme for detail and for matter not appearing in the original topic.

Original §	New §	Original §	New §
§ 1.5	§§ 7-13	§ 1.6	§ 14

§ 1 Generally

Text References:

21 Am Jur 2d, Criminal Law §§ 1-93; 35 Am Jur 2d, Drugs, Narcotics, and Poisons §§ 1-93; 35 Am Jur 2d, Health § 20; 43 Am Jur 2d §§ 547-551; 44 Am Jur 2d §§ 1495, 1842; 47 Am Jur 2d, Juvenile Courts and Delinquent and Dependent Children §§ 63-70; 61 Am Jur 2d, Physicians, Surgeons, and Other Healers §§ 135, 139, 204, 253-255, 393-395; 63 Am Jur 2d, Products Liability §§ 9, 28-32, 394, 491, 718-724

13 Federal Procedure, L. Ed, Food, Drugs, and Cosmetics §§ 35:1-35:111, 35:155-35:218, 35:280-35:313, 35:328, 35:375-35:378, 35:389-35:425, 35:513 et seq.

Practice References:

9 Federal Procedural Forms, L. Ed. Food, Drugs, and Cosmetics §§ 31:1 et seq.

8 Am Jur Pl & Pr Forms (Rev), Criminal Procedure, Forms 1 et seq., 255-258; 9 Am Jur Pl & Pr Forms (Rev), Drugs, Narcotics, and Poisons, Forms 1 et seq.; 12 Am Jur Pl & Pr Forms (Rev), Food, Forms 21-24; 19A Am Jur Pl & Pr Forms (Rev), Physicians, Surgeons, and Other Healers, Forms 153, 156-158, 253-257; 20A Am Jur Pl & Pr Forms (Rev), Products Liability, Forms 211, 212, 218, 219, 222

7A Am Jur Legal Forms 2d, Drugs, Narcotics, and Poisons §§ 93:1-93:5, 93:10; 8A Am Jur Legal Forms 2d, Food §§ 120:1, 120:2, 120:51, 120:52; 15 Am Jur Legal Forms 2d, Products Liability §§ 209:1, 209:2

3 Am Jur Proof of Facts 127, Cancer; 4 Am Jur Proof of Facts 549, Drugs; 7 Am Jur Proof of Facts 479, Malpractice; 13 Am Jur Proof of Facts 391, Criminal Drug Addiction and Possession; 14 Am Jur Proof of Facts 211, Cosmetics; [...] Facts 1, Side Effects of [...] of Facts 567, Negligent [...] in Diagnosis and Treat- [...] Jur Proof of Facts 723, [...] Drug Therapy; 6 Am Jur [...] Manufacturer's Duty to [...] Directly of Product— [...] Am Jur Proof of Facts 2d 425, Failure of Product to Meet Manufacturer's Specifications or Standards; 7 Am Jur Proof of Facts 3d 1, Injuries from Drugs

1 Am Jur Trials 555, Locating and Preserving Evidence in Criminal Cases; 2 Am Jur Trials 357, Locating Medical Experts; 6 Am Jur Trials 109, Basis of Medical Testimony; 7 Am Jur Trials 1, Drug Products Liability and Malpractice Cases; 8 Am Jur Trials 573, Defense of Narcotics Cases; 9 Am Jur Trials 59, Food Seizure Litigation; 12 Am Jur Trials 1, Products Liability Cases; 14 Am Jur Trials 619, Juvenile Court Proceedings; 16 Am Jur Trials 471, Defense of Medical Malpractice Cases; 17 Am Jur Trials 1, Drug Products Liability and Malpractice Cases

USCS, Constitution, Amendments 1, 5, 8, 9, and 14; 21 USCS §§ 1 et seq.

L. Ed Digest, Constitutional Law §§ 431, 458; Drugs, Narcotics and Poisons §§ 1-10; Evidence § 362; Food §§ 1, 1.5, 2, 4-10; Health § 1.5; Privacy § 1

Annotations:

State and local administrative inspection of and administrative warrants to search pharmacies, 29 ALR4th 264

Right of medical patient to obtain, or physician to prescribe, Laetrile for treatment of illness—state cases, 5 ALR4th 178

Products liability: diethylstilbestrol (DES), 2 ALR4th 1091

Notice how the outline of the topic *Drugs and Druggists* directs the researcher to the proper location in the digest. Notice also the references to other sources, including Annotations.

SECTION F. SUMMARY

1. Annotated Law Reports

a. *Annotations.* Often lengthy, encyclopedic essays on a particular point of law.

b. *Selective law reporting.* Used extensively by West Group in the *A.L.R.* series. A representative case is selected that is illustrative of a point of law discussed in an *Annotation.*

2. American Law Reports (A.L.R.)

a. *Scope*

(1) Began in 1919 and is now in six series—*A.L.R.* through *A.L.R.5th* and *A.L.R. Federal,* with *A.L.R.5th* and *A.L.R. Federal* currently being published.

(2) Federal topics are included in *A.L.R. Federal, A.L.R., A.L.R.2d,* and volumes 1–21 of *A.L.R.3d.*

(3) State topics are included in *A.L.R.* through *A.L.R.5th.*

b. *Features*

(1) *Annotations* and illustrative case; citations are to the *Annotation,* not the illustrative case.

(2) Detailed outline of topic annotated.

(3) Index accompanying each *Annotation* in *A.L.R.5th* and lengthy *Annotations* in other series.

(4) Jurisdictional references.

(5) References to other publications of this publisher, and, commencing with *A.L.R.5th,* volume 111 of *A.L.R. Fed.,* and *A.L.R.4th* pocket supplements, references to sources by other publishers, West *Key Number System* references, and electronic search queries.

3. How A.L.R. Is Kept Current

a. *Upkeep Service*

(1) *A.L.R.3d, 4th, 5th, Federal.* These sets are kept current with annual pocket supplements in which digests of cases are keyed directly to each section of the *Annotation.*

(2) *A.L.R.2d.* A *Later Case Service,* with annual pocket supplements, digests cases and keys them to each section of the *Annotation.*

(3) *A.L.R. (First Series).* A eight volume *A.L.R. Blue Book of Supplemental Decisions* and an update pamphlet lists citations to more recent cases than those in the *Annotation.* All nine sources must be used for complete updating.

b. *Superseding and Supplementing Annotations.* A superseding *Annotation* replaces an existing one; a supplementing *Annotation* updates an existing one and both must be read as if they are one *Annotation.*

c. *Locating the Most Recent Annotations.* Use the *Annotation History Table* in the T–Z volume of *ALR Index,* the appropriate *A.L.R.* upkeep service, *Auto–Cite,* or *Shepard's Citations for Annotations.*

4. United States Supreme Court Reports, Lawyers' Edition.

This set contains *Annotations* for selected important cases. These *Annotations* can be located using the *ALR Index* and the General Index to the *United States Supreme Court Reports, Lawyers' Edition,* as discussed in Chapter 4, A–3.

Chapter 8

CONSTITUTIONS

This chapter discusses the role of constitutions for the federal and state governments. As these documents are the charters adopted by the people, they are the highest primary authority.

SECTION A.   FEDERAL CONSTITUTION

The Constitution of the United States of America, in a formal sense, is the written document that was drafted at Philadelphia in the summer of 1787, plus the amendments that have since been added. The framers of the Constitution did not intend it to be a static document, but rather, as stated by Chief Justice Marshall, "to endure for ages to come, and, consequently, to be adapted to various *crises* of human affairs."[1] A noted twentieth century scholar has commented that "[t]he proper point of view from which to approach the task of interpreting the Constitution is that of regarding it as a living statute, palpitating with the purpose of the hour, reenacted with every waking breath of the American people, whose primitive right to determine their institutions is its sole claim to validity as law and as the matrix of laws under our system."[2]

It follows from these famous observations that to research problems in constitutional law, one must not only consult the document itself,[3] but also sources that assist in the interpretation of the Constitution. These sources include the background and record of the Constitutional Convention, the interpretation of the Constitution by the Supreme Court of the United States in the approximately 520 volumes of its reports, and the commentaries on the Constitution in treatises, legal periodicals, encyclopedias, and other secondary sources. This chapter discusses how to locate and use these various sources.

1. Judicial Interpretations

a. *Annotated Editions of the Federal Constitution*

[1] McCulloch v. Maryland, 17 U.S. (4 Wheat.) 316, 415 (1819).

[2] Edwin S. Corwin, *Constitution V. Constitutional Theory: The Question of the State V. the Nation,* 19 Am. Pol. Sci. Rev. 290, 303 (1925). For more recent commentary on constitutional interpretation, see *Symposium: In Celebration of Our Constitution,* 70 Marq. L. Rev. 351 (1987); *Symposium: "To Endure for Ages to Come"—A Bicentennial View of the Constitution,* N.C. L. Rev. 881 (1987).

[3] The text of the Constitution and its amendments are readily available. In addition to being included with the official *United States Code* and the annotated federal codes (discussed in this section), it is typically included in sets of state annotated codes, as well as in constitutional law texts and casebooks, law dictionaries, and in pamphlets frequently distributed at annual May 1 "Law Day" events across the country.

The courts, and especially the Supreme Court of the United States, are frequently called upon to interpret provisions of the Constitution of the United States. Some of the most useful sources for these interpretations are the various annotated editions of the Constitution. These publications set forth each article, section, and clause of the Constitution and its amendments and provide digests of the cases interpreting that part of the Constitution or its amendments and, in some instances, commentary as to the provisions and their interpretations.

(1) *United States Code Annotated, Constitution of the United States Annotated* (West Group). This set, published as part of the *United States Code Annotated (U.S.C.A.)* consists of ten unnumbered volumes,[4] supplemental pamphlets or pocket parts, and two tables volumes. An index to the Constitution is included at the end of the last volume of the set, i.e., the volume that also contains Amendments 14 to End. After each article, section, and clause of the Constitution and for each of its 27 amendments are cross references to pertinent sections in *U.S.C.A.* and references to encyclopedias, law reviews, texts, and treatises.

Notes of Decisions, which are digest paragraphs from all cases that have interpreted a constitutional provision or amendment, follow these various references. For example, Article I, Section 1 is followed by 85 notes of decisions, while Article I, Section 8, Clause 3 is followed by 1,560 notes. These notes are preceded first by references to West's *Key Number System* and relevant encyclopedia section numbers and then by numbered topics, which enable a user to go directly to the cases digested under those topics. Additional notes of decisions are in the annual pocket and subsequent pamphlet supplements. [See Illustrations 8–1 through 8–3 for the means of locating a constitutional provision and the notes of decisions that accompany it.]

(2) *United States Code Service, Constitution* (LEXIS Law Publishing). These six volumes are a separate unit of the *United States Code Service (U.S.C.S.)* and include references to this publisher's other publications. These *Constitution* volumes are organized and updated in much the same way as the *United States Code Annotated* and are used in a like manner, with the last volume containing an index.

(3) *The Constitution of the United States of America* (Library of Congress ed. 1992, and latest supplement). This annotated, one volume edition of the Constitution[5] is prepared by the Congressional Research Service of the Library of Congress, as authorized by a Joint Congressional Resolution.[6] This publication sets forth each article, section, and

---

[4] This set, published in 1987 and referred to by the publisher as the "Bicentennial Edition," is a comprehensive revision of all earlier volumes in this set.

[5] THE CONSTITUTION OF THE UNITED STATES OF AMERICA, S. DOC. No. 6, 103rd Cong., 1st Sess. (1992).

[6] 2 U.S.C. § 168 (1994). This Joint Resolution provides for a new hard-bound volume every ten years with pocket supplements to be issued biennially. The present 2,444 page edition covers to June 29, 1992. Although a biennial supplement is published, it typically only supplements the volume to within about two years of the date at the time of its

clause of the Constitution and its amendments. Immediately following each of them, in smaller typeface, is an analysis and commentary prepared by the editorial staff. Important cases decided by the Supreme Court of the United States are discussed in the analysis, and citations to the cases are given in the footnotes. [See Illustrations 8–4 and 8–5.] Frequently, the commentary quotes from the proceedings of the Constitutional Convention, the opinions of dissenting justices, and other documents. This volume, unlike the ones discussed above, does not attempt to cite or comment on all cases of the Supreme Court of the United States, but refers only to the more significant ones. This is a very useful volume and is often the preferred starting point for research on constitutional questions. It has a detailed index and includes the following useful tables:

Proposed Amendments Pending Before the States.

Proposed Amendments Not Ratified by the States.

Acts of Congress Held Unconstitutional in Whole or in Part by the Supreme Court of the United States.

State Constitutional and Statutory Provisions and Municipal Ordinances Held Unconstitutional on Their Face or As Administered.

Ordinances Held Unconstitutional.

Supreme Court Decisions Overruled by Subsequent Decisions.

Table of Cases.

b. *Digests of Federal Court Cases*

Digests of federal cases provide access to additional interpretations of the Constitution.[7] The following publications are discussed in detail in Chapter 6.

(1) *Digest of United States Supreme Court Reports, Lawyers' Edition* (LEXIS Law Publishing). Volume 17 contains the text of the Constitution together with references to this publisher's relevant headnote topics and sections.

(2) *U.S. Supreme Court Digest* (West Group).

(3) *Federal Digest, Modern Federal Practice Digest,* and *West's Federal Practice Digest, 2nd, 3rd, 4th,* and *5th* (West Group).

c. *Annotations.* The *Annotations* in *A.L.R. Federal, U.S. Supreme Court Reports, Lawyers' Edition, A.L.R., A.L.R.2d,* and *A.L.R.3d* (pre–1969) may contain discussions of constitutional issues, in which case these *Annotations* will provide case references.

d. *Online Access.* The text of the *United States Code* is available on LEXIS–NEXIS; *U.S.C.A.* is available exclusively on WESTLAW; and

---

issuance. The current edition is available from the Superintendent of Documents *GPO Access* Web Site. [See the last entry in Illustration 9–4 in the next chapter.]

[7] It is important to remember that state and regional digests also contain digest paragraphs for federal cases arising within their jurisdictional coverage.

U.S.C.S. is exclusively on LEXIS–NEXIS. All three sets contain the text of the Constitution. For the two annotated sets, search terms can be used with sections and clauses in the Constitution and with the amendments to retrieve relevant cases.

e. *Shepard's Citations. Shepard's United States Citations* and the state units of Shepard's citators provide references to cases citing or construing the Constitution. *Shepard's Citations* are discussed in Chapter 15.

2. Secondary Sources

The constitutional commentary by legal scholars is voluminous. Research in constitutional law can seldom be completed successfully without consulting the secondary sources, such as texts, treatises, encyclopedias, and periodical articles, as these sources may provide exhaustive analysis of constitutional concerns being researched. Some of these sources deserve special mention.

The 200th anniversary of the U.S. Constitution celebrated in 1987 seemed to spawn significant scholarship that is especially useful in constitutional analysis. The four volume *Encyclopedia of the American Constitution*[8] contains approximately 2,100 articles written by 262 authors, typically lawyers, historians, and political scientists. Arrangement is alphabetical with either cases or subjects forming the basis of the discussion. Some of the articles contain useful bibliographic references.

The Founders' Constitution[9] is a five volume set containing an extensive collection of documents that bear on the text of the Constitution, from the Preamble through the Twelfth Amendment. Volume 1 is arranged by theme and highlights the debate over the principles embodied in the Constitution; volumes 2–4 are arranged to correspond to the text of the Constitution; and volume 5 is devoted to Amendments I–XII.

Researchers seeking an extensive listing of sources on the Constitution will want to consult Kermit L. Hall's *A Comprehensive Bibliography of American Constitutional and Legal History, 1896–1979.*[10] This five volume set contains over 68,000 entries for books, journal articles, and doctoral dissertations. It is divided into seven chapters: general surveys and texts; institutions; constitutional doctrine; legal doctrine; biographical; chronological; and geographical. Also useful in this regard is the one volume *The Constitution of the United States: A Guide and Bibliography to Current Scholarly Research.*[11]

While all law dictionaries provide definitions of terms bearing on constitutional law, the two volume *Constitutional Law Dictionary*[12] is

[8] Leonard W. Levy, Editor-in-Chief, Macmillan Publishing Co. (1986). *Supplement I* was published in 1992.

[9] Philip B. Kurland & Ralph Lerner eds., University of Chicago Press (1987).

[10] Krauss International Pubs. (1984). A two volume supplement covers 1980–1987.

[11] Bernard D. Reams, Jr. & Stuart D. Yoak eds., Oceana Pubs. (1988). This volume is also published as volume 11 of *Sources and Documents of United States Constitutions.*

[12] Ralph C. Chandler et al., ABC–Clio Information Sources (1985 & 1987). These volumes are updated periodically with bound supplements.

intended specifically for this purpose. Volume 1 is subtitled *Individual Rights;* volume 2 *Governmental Powers.* Each volume contains a summary of approximately 300 cases organized in a subject-matter chapter format whereby cases are grouped under topics. This arrangement is followed by several hundred definitions.

The most highly-regarded contemporary treatises in the area of constitutional law are Laurence H. Tribe's one volume *American Constitutional Law,*[13] the four volume *Treatise on Constitutional Law: Substance and Procedure,*[14] by Ronald D. Rotunda and John E. Nowack, and the three volume *Modern Constitutional Law,*[15] by Chester James Antieau. Constitutional law casebooks[16] and legal periodicals[17] also often provide constitutional analysis.

3. Historical Sources

When faced with the task of interpreting the meaning of a provision or clause of the Constitution, it is frequently useful to ascertain the meaning of the words used by the framers. This may make it necessary to consult sources that preceded the adoption of the Constitution, such as documents of the Continental Congress or the Articles of Confederation. These sources can be readily located in the Library of Congress Legislative Reference Service's *Documents Illustrative of the Formation of the Union of the American States.*[18] Also useful is *Documentary History of the Constitution of the United States of America, 1786–1870.*[19] Indispensable are the essays of Madison, Jay, and Hamilton published as *The Federalist.*[20] The sources mentioned in this paragraph, as well as other sources on the historical development of the Constitution, are available

---

[13] 2d ed., Foundation Press (1988).

[14] 2d ed., West Publishing Co. (1992). An abridged version is published as *Constitutional Law* (5th ed. 1995) and is a part of West's Hornbook Series.

[15] 2d ed., West Group (1997).

[16] The best example is GERALD GUNTHER, CONSTITUTIONAL LAW (13th ed., Foundation Press, 1997). An annual supplement is published.

[17] Almost any legal periodical will, at times, publish articles on constitutional issues. Some, however, are devoted to these topics, such as the University of Minnesota's *Constitutional Commentary,* Seton Hall University's *Constitutional Law Journal, George Mason University Civil Rights Law Journal, Harvard Civil Rights–Civil Liberties Law Review, Hastings Constitutional Law Quarterly,* and *William and Mary Bill of Rights Journal.* Legal periodicals are discussed in detail in Chapter 17.

[18] H.R. DOC. No. 398, 69th Cong., 1st Sess. (1935). *See also* SOL BLOOM, FORMATION OF THE UNION UNDER THE CONSTITUTION (1935). For background on the Articles of Confederation, see William F. Swindler, *Our First Constitution: The Articles of Confederation,* 67 A.B.A. J. 166 (1961). For documents pertaining to the adoption of the Bill of Rights, see BERNARD SCHWARTZ, THE BILL OF RIGHTS: A DOCUMENTARY HISTORY, Chelsea House (2 vols., 1971), and NEIL H. COGAN ED., THE COMPLETE BILL OF RIGHTS: THE DRAFTS, DEBATES, SOURCES, AND ORIGINS, Oxford University Press (1997).

[19] U.S. Bureau of Rolls and Library of the Department of State (1894–1905; reprinted in 1965 by Johnson Reprint Corp.).

[20] *The Federalist* has been published in many editions. *See also* JAMES MADISON, THE PAPERS OF JAMES MADISON (Henry D. Gilpin ed. 1840).

on WESTLAW in the *Bicentennial of the Constitution* (BICENT) database.

While the Constitutional Convention did not keep official records of its secret sessions, the most widely-accepted source for insights into the debates that took place is Max Farrand's three volume *Records of the Federal Constitution of 1787.*[21] For understanding the ratification process by the states, a valuable source is *Elliot's Debates.*[22] When complete, by far the most comprehensive and up-to-date source of the history of the ratification of the U.S. Constitution will be *Documentary History of the Ratification of the Constitution.*[23] The courts, at times, also turn to these historical sources for support in their opinions.[24]

SECTION B. ILLUSTRATIONS: FEDERAL CONSTITUTION

Problem: In a products liability case where suit was brought against a prescription drug manufacturer, *Abbot v. American Cyanamid Co.*, 844 F.2d 1108 (4th Cir. 1988), the issue related to defective design and failure to warn. Does federal law preempt state common law liability?

Illustrations

[21] Yale University Press (1911). A supplement was prepared in 1987 by James H. Hutson. *See also* THE FOUNDERS' CONSTITUTION, *supra* note 10; WILBOURN E. BENTON, 1787: DRAFTING THE U.S. CONSTITUTION, Texas A & M University Press (2 vols., 1986).

[22] JONATHAN ELLIOT, THE DEBATES, RESOLUTIONS, AND OTHER PROCEEDINGS, IN CONVENTION, ON THE ADOPTION OF THE FEDERAL CONSTITUTION (1827). This set has appeared in many editions with different titles and somewhat different content, all known generally as *Elliot's Debates.* The most complete edition was published in five volumes in 1937.

[23] Merrill Jensen ed. (State Historical Society of Wisconsin). This set, which began in 1976 and is projected for approximately 20 volumes, is over one-half complete.

[24] *See, e.g.,* Morrison v. Olson, 487 U.S. 654, 674 (1988) (citing RECORDS OF THE FEDERAL CONVENTION OF 1787 (Max Farrand ed. 1966)); Welch v. Texas Dept. of Highways, 483 U.S. 468, 481 n. 10 (1987) (citing ELLIOT'S DEBATES, 2d ed. 1861); Atascadero State Hosp. v. Scanlon, 473 U.S. 234, 271 (1985) (Brennan, J., dissenting) (citing DOCUMENTARY HISTORY OF THE RATIFICATION OF THE CONSTITUTION).

[Illustration 8–1]

PAGE FROM VOLUME CONTAINING INDEX
TO CONSTITUTION: U.S.C.A.

CONSTITUTION OF THE UNITED STATES   **LETTERS**

JUDICIAL OFFICERS
See, also, Judges or Justices, generally, this index
Oath to support Constitution, Art. 6, cl. 3

JUDICIAL POWER
Vested in Supreme and inferior courts, Art. 3, § 1

JUDICIAL PROCEEDINGS
See Actions and Proceedings, generally, this index

JURISDICTION
Controversy to which judicial power of U.S. extends, Art. 3, § 2, cl. 1
Crime, fugitives to be removed to State having, Art. 4, § 2, cl. 2
New State not to be erected within another State, Art. 4, § 3, cl. 1
Original and appellate of Supreme Court, Art. 3, § 2, cl. 2
Supreme Court, Art. 3, § 2, cl. 2
  Ambassadors, and other public ministers and consuls, cases affecting, Art. 3, § 2, cl. 2
  Inferior courts, judicial power vested in, Art. 3, § 1
  Original jurisdiction, Art. 3, § 2, cl. 2
  Where State is party, Art. 3, § 2, cl. 2

JURY
Common law,
  No fact tried by jury shall be re-examined except according to, Am. 7
  Rules adhered to, Am. 7
  Trial by jury,
    According to rules of, suits involving certain amounts, Am. 7
    Actions exceeding certain dollar amount, Am. 7
Crimes and Offenses, this index
Criminal cases, Art. 3, § 2, cl. 3; Am. 6
  Right to jury trial, Art. 3, § 2, cl. 2; Art. 3, § 2, cl. 3; Am. 6
Grand Jury, generally, this index
Impartial, in all criminal prosecutions, Am. 6
Impeachment, jury trial not required, Art. 3, § 2, cl. 3
Re-examination after jury trial, restrictions, Am. 7
Suits at common law, Am. 7

KING
Office holder accepting present, title, etc., from, Art. 1, § 9, cl. 8

LABOR
Due in one State not to be abrogated in another, Art. 4, § 2, cl. 3

LANDS
Congress to have power over land owned by U.S., Art. 1, § 8, cl. 17
Judicial power and controversies for land claims, Art. 3, § 2, cl. 1
Private Lands or Property, generally, this index

LAWS
Bills, generally, this index
Cases arising under laws of U.S., judicial power extends to, Art. 3, § 2, cl. 1
Congress shall make necessary laws, Art. 1, § 8, cl. 18
Congress to provide,
  Call in militia to execute, Art. 1, § 8, cl. 15
  Punishing offenses against Law of Nations, Art. 1, § 8, cl. 10
President's duty regarding executing laws of U.S., Art. 2, § 3
State judges to be bound by law of the land, Art. 6, cl. 2
Supreme Court to have appellate jurisdiction as to law, Art. 3, § 2, cl. 2
What constitutes supreme law of the land, Art. 6, cl. 2

LAWYERS
Attorneys and Counselors, generally, this index

LEGAL TENDER
No State to make anything but gold and silver, Art. 1, § 10, cl. 1
States' powers restricted, Art. 1, § 10, cl. 1

LEGISLATION
See specific index headings

LEGISLATURES OF STATES
Amendments, application for or ratification, Art. 5
Consent of, required,
  By U.S. in purchasing, Art. 1, § 8, cl. 17
  In forming new States, Art. 4, § 3, cl. 1
May apply for or ratify amendments, Art. 5

The first step in researching a problem involving the U.S. Constitution is to look in the volume containing the index to the Constitution. For the problem under research, Article 1, Section 6, Clause 2 should be examined. See next Illustration.

Private property not to be taken for public use without, Am. 5

JUSTICE
Constitution to establish, **Preamble**
Fugitives From Justice, generally, this index
Judges or Justices, generally, this index

KEEPING ARMS
Right not to be infringed, Am. 2

election of, Art. 1, § 4, cl. 1
United States to protect States against invasion, Art. 4, § 4

LETTERS
Marque and reprisal,
  Power of Congress to grant, Art. 1, § 8, cl. 11
  States, prohibited from issuing, Art. 1, § 10, cl. 1

[Illustration 8–2]

PAGE FROM A CONSTITUTION VOLUME: U.S.C.A.

Art. 6   SUPREME LAW OF LAND   **Cl. 2**

WESTLAW ELECTRONIC RESEARCH

See WESTLAW guide following the Explanation pages of this volume.

Clause 2. Supreme Law of Land ✓

This Constitution, and the Laws of the United States which shall be made in Pursuance thereof; and all Treaties made, or which shall be made, under the Authority of the United States, shall be the supreme Law of the Land; and the Judges in every State shall be bound thereby, any Thing in the Constitution or Laws of any State to the Contrary notwithstanding.

LIBRARY REFERENCES

Law Reviews

Adjudication of federal causes of action in state court. Martin H. Redish and

---

This shows the text of the constitutional provision covering federal supremacy as it appears in a Constitution volume of the *United States Code Annotated.* Note the references to additional useful sources.   This set and the *United States Code Service* are kept current by annual pocket supplements and subsequent pamphlets.

---

review. Jesse H. Choper, 86 Yale L.J. 1552 (1977).

Texts and Treatises

Federal common law, see Wright, Miller & Cooper, Federal Practice and Procedure: Jurisdiction § 4514.

Federal preemption, see Rotunda, Nowak & Young, Treatise on Constitutional Law: Substance and Procedure §§ 12.1 to 12.4.

Relations of state and federal courts, see Wright, Miller & Cooper, Federal Practice and Procedure: Jurisdiction § 4201 et seq.

Treaties and executive agreements, see Tribe, American Constitutional Law § 4–4.

WESTLAW ELECTRONIC RESEARCH

See WESTLAW guide following the Explanation pages of this volume.

NOTES OF DECISIONS

I.   **GENERALLY 1–30**
II.   **FEDERAL LAWS AS SUPREME 31–90**
III. **TREATIES AS SUPREME 91–130**
IV. **STATE LAWS OR ACTS DISPLACED BY SUPREME LAW—GENERALLY 131–170**
V.   **FEDERAL INSTRUMENTALITIES AND PROPERTY GENERALLY 171–210**
VI. **TAXATION OF FEDERAL INSTRUMENTALITIES AND PROPERTY 211–260**
VII. **MISCELLANEOUS LAWS OR ACTS 261–430**
VIII. **STATE JUDGES BOUND BY SUPREME LAW 431–458**

For Detailed Alphabetical Note Index, see the Various Subdivisions.

555

[Illustration 8–3]

PAGE SHOWING NOTES OF DECISIONS (DIGEST PARAGRAPHS) FROM A CONSTITUTION VOLUME: U.S.C.A.

Cl. 2   **SUPREME LAW OF LAND**   **Art. 6**

I. GENERALLY

Subdivision Index

Constitution as supreme
   Generally 2
   Foreign relations and intercourse
     3
   Labor activities 4
Federal district courts, persons bound
   by supreme law 6
Foreign relations and intercourse, Con-
   stitution as supreme 3
International law 9
Labor activities, Constitution as su-
   preme 4
Persons bound by supreme law
   Generally 5
   Federal district courts 6
   State legislatures 7
   United States Supreme Court 8
Private rights of action 10
Purpose 1
State legislatures, persons bound by su-
   preme law 7
United States Supreme Court, persons
   bound by supreme law 8

American Digest System
   Nature and authority of constitutions,
see Constitutional Law ⟐1.

Encyclopedias
   Constitution as supreme law of the
land, see C.J.S. Constitutional Law § 3.

1. Purpose
   The purpose of this clause was to
avoid the disparities, confusions and
conflicts that would follow if the federal
government's general authority were
subject to local controls. U.S. v. Alleghe-
ny County, Pa., Pa.1944, 64 S.Ct. 908, 322
U.S. 174, 88 L.Ed. 1209.

   This clause was intended to eliminate
right of any state to regulate operations

courts for enforcement of federal law
which state deems penal. Robinson v.
Norato, 1945, 43 A.2d 467, 71 R.I. 256.

**2. Constitution as supreme—General-
ly**

   Under this clause that the Constitution
and laws made in pursuance thereof
shall be the supreme law of the land, it
is of the very essence of supremacy to
remove all obstacles to its action within
its own sphere, and so to modify every
power vested in subordinate governments as to exempt its own operations
from their own influence. Public Utilities Commission of State of Cal. v. U.S.,
Cal.1958, 78 S.Ct. 446, 355 U.S. 534, 2
L.Ed.2d 470, rehearing denied 78 S.Ct.
713, 356 U.S. 925, 2 L.Ed.2d 760.

   Federal power, which is constitutionally exerted for protection of public or
private interests, or both, becomes supreme law of land and cannot be curtailed, circumvented, or extended by a
state procedure merely because it will
apply some doctrine of private right.
Garner v. Teamsters, Chauffeurs and
Helpers Local Union No. 776 (A.F.L.)
Pa.1953, 74 S.Ct. 161, 346 U.S. 485, 98
L.Ed. 228.

   The United States Constitution and the
laws passed pursuant to it are the supreme laws of the land, binding alike
upon states, courts, and the people, anything in the Constitution or laws of any
state to the contrary notwithstanding.
Testa v. Katt, R.I.1947, 67 S.Ct. 810, 330
U.S. 386, 91 L.Ed. 967.

   This Constitution is the supreme law
of the land, and no Act of Congress is of
any validity which does not rest on authority conferred by that instrument.
U.S. v. Germaine, Me.1878, 99 U.S. 508, 9
Otto. 508, 25 L.Ed. 482. See, also, Choc-
taw Indians, 1870, 13 Op.Atty.Gen. 357;

After the text of each clause are digest paragraphs of all cases that have
interpreted the clause. These paragraphs are preceded by an index to these
paragraphs.

U.S. 1094, 34 L.Ed.2d 682.

   This clause was intended to apply only
in case of conflict between federal Constitution, acts and treaties and state Constitution and laws, and does not compel
a state to provide, at its own expense,

but, it is also, for certain purposes, a
government of the people; within the
scope of its powers, as enumerated and
defined, it is supreme and above the
states, but beyond, it has no existence.
U.S. v. Cruikshank, La.1876, 92 U.S. 550,
2 Otto. 550, 23 L.Ed. 588.

556

[Illustration 8–4]

PAGE FROM THE CONSTITUTION OF THE UNITED STATES OF AMERICA (LIBRARY OF CONGRESS, 1992 ed.)

PRIOR DEBTS, NATIONAL SUPREMACY, AND OATHS OF OFFICE

ARTICLE VI

Clause 1. All Debts contracted and Engagements entered into, before the Adoption of this Constitution, shall be as valid again

Confe

> **This one volume edition sets forth the full text of each Article, Section, and Clause of the Constitution and its amendments. Analysis and commentary immediately follow, in smaller type.**

Clause 2. This Constitution, and the Laws of the United States which shall be made in Pursuance thereof; and all Treaties made, or which shall be made, under the Authority of the United States, shall be the supreme Law of the Land; and the Judges in every State shall be bound thereby; any Thing in the Constitution or Laws of any State to the Contrary notwithstanding.

NATIONAL SUPREMACY

Marshall's Interpretation of the National Supremacy Clause

Although the Supreme Court had held, prior to Marshall's appointment to the Bench, that the supremacy clause rendered null and void a state constitutional or statutory provision which was inconsistent with a treaty executed by the Federal Government,[1] it was left for him to develop the full significance of the clause as applied to acts of Congress. By his vigorous opinions in *McCulloch v. Maryland*[2] and *Gibbons v. Ogden*,[3] he gave the principle a vitality which survived a century of vacillation under the doctrine of dual federalism. In the former case, he asserted broadly that "the States have no power, by taxation or otherwise, to retard, impede, burden, or in any manner control, the operations of the constitutional laws enacted by Congress to carry into execution the powers vested in

---

[1] Ware v. Hylton, 3 Dall. (3 U.S.) 199 (1796).
[2] 4 Wheat. (17 U.S.) 316 (1819).
[3] 9 Wheat. (22 U.S.) 1 (1824).

917

[Illustration 8–5]

PAGE FROM THE CONSTITUTION OF THE UNITED STATES OF AMERICA (LIBRARY OF CONGRESS, 1992 ed.)

918   ART. VI—PRIOR DEBTS, SUPREMACY CLAUSE, ETC.

Cl. 2—Supremacy of the Constitution, Laws, Treaties

the general government. This is, we think, the unavoidable consequence of that supremacy which the Constitution has declared."[4] From this he concluded that a state tax upon notes issued by a branch of the Bank of the United States was void.

In *Gibbons v. Ogden*, the Court held that certain statutes of New York granting an exclusive right to use steam navigation on the waters of the State were null and void insofar as they applied to vessels licensed by the United States to engage in coastal trade. Said the Chief Justice: "In argument, however, it has been contended, that if a law passed by a State, in the exercise of its acknowledged sovereignty, comes into conflict with a law passed by Congress in pursuance of the Constitution, they affect the subject, and each other, like equal opposing powers. But the framers of our Constitution foresaw this state of things, and provided for it by de-

> **Analysis of the Supremacy Clause by the editors of the volume. Footnotes contain citations to cases mentioned in the analysis.**

clause which confers the same supremacy on laws and treaties, is to such acts of the State legislatures as do not transcend their powers, but though enacted in the execution of acknowledged State powers, interfere with, or are contrary to the laws of Congress, made in pursuance of the Constitution, or some treaty made under the authority of the United States. In every such case, the act of Congress, or the treaty, is supreme; and the law of the State, though enacted in the exercise of powers not controverted, must yield to it."[5]

Task of the Supreme Court Under the Clause: Preemption

In applying the supremacy clause to subjects which have been regulated by Congress, the primary task of the Court is to ascertain whether a challenged state law is compatible with the policy expressed in the federal statute. When Congress legislates with regard to a subject, the extent and nature of the legal consequences of the regulation are federal questions, the answers to which are to be derived from a consideration of the language and policy of the state. If Congress expressly provides for exclusive federal dominion or if it expressly provides for concurrent federal-state jurisdiction, the task of the Court is simplified, though, of course, there may still be doubtful areas in which interpretation will be necessary. Where Congress is silent, however, the Court must itself decide

---

[4] 4 Wheat. (17 U.S.) 436 (1819).

[5] 9 Wheat. (22 U.S.), 210–211 (1824). See the Court's discussion of *Gibbons* in Douglas v. Seacoast Products, 431 U.S. 265, 274–279 (1977).

SECTION C. STATE CONSTITUTIONS

Each of the fifty states has adopted its own constitution, and many states have adopted several different constitutions at different times over the years. A state's constitution, except for those issues covered by the supremacy clause of the Constitution of the United States,[25] is the highest primary legal authority for the state. The procedure for adopting a new constitution is usually accomplished by the convening of a state constitutional convention. *State Constitutional Conventions, Commissions, and Amendments,* a microfiche collection of Congressional Information Service covering 1776 through 1978, is the most comprehensive source of documents for the fifty states.[26]

When doing research involving a state constitution, it also may be necessary to check the historical documents that led to its adoption and to consult the state and federal court cases interpreting it.

1. Texts of State Constitutions

a. The most common source for the text of a state constitution is the constitution volume of the state code.[27] This constitution volume ordinarily contains the current text, the text of previously-adopted versions, and digest paragraphs similar in annotated version format to those discussed in Section A–1 of this chapter. Many states also print and distribute an unannotated edition of the state constitution in pamphlet form.

b. Columbia University, Legislative Drafting Research Fund. *Constitutions of the United States: National and State* (2d ed. 1974 to date).

This multi-volume looseleaf set collects the texts of the constitutions for the United States, the fifty states, and all U.S. territories and is kept current by supplements.[28]

2. Judicial Interpretations of State Constitutions

Court cases interpreting provisions of a state's constitution can be located in ways similar to those discussed in Section A–1.[29] These include

---

[25] U.S. Const. art. VI, cl. 2. *See* digest paragraphs in *U.S.C.A.* and *U.S.C.S.* for cases on the supremacy clause.

[26] Two bibliographies provide access to this set: CYNTHIA E. BROWNE, STATE CONSTITUTIONAL CONVENTIONS FROM INDEPENDENCE TO THE COMPLETION OF THE PRESENT UNION, 1776–1959: A BIBLIOGRAPHY, Greenwood Press (1973); CONGRESSIONAL INFORMATION SERVICE, STATE CONSTITUTIONAL CONVENTIONS, 1959–1978: AN ANNOTATED BIBLIOGRAPHY (2 vols., 1981).

[27] State codes are on WESTLAW and LEXIS–NEXIS and with them the state's constitutions. This development greatly improves the ability to conduct comparative research of state constitutional provisions. State codes are discussed in Chapter 11.

[28] For a listing of over 2,100 entries relating to the literature of state constitutions, see BERNARD D. REAMS, JR. & STUART D. YOAK, THE CONSTITUTIONS OF THE STATES: A STATE-BY-STATE GUIDE AND BIBLIOGRAPHY TO CURRENT SCHOLARLY RESEARCH, Oceana Pubs. (1987). This volume is also published as volume 5 of *Sources and Documents of United States Constitutions, Second Series. See also* ROBERT L. MADDEX, CONGRESSIONAL QUARTERLY'S STATE CONSTITUTIONS OF THE UNITED STATES (1998).

[29] Recent articles have focused on the roles of state constitutions. *See, e.g.,* James A. Gardner, *The Failed Discourse of State Constitutionalism,* 90 MICH. L. REV. 761 (1992); Hans A. Linde, *Are State Constitutions Common Law?* 34 ARIZ. L. REV. 215 (1992).

the digest paragraphs accompanying the annotated version of the state constitution, state digests, state Shepard's citators, computer-assisted legal research, and *A.L.R. Annotations.* Likewise, treatises,[30] legal periodical articles, and state legal encyclopedias can assist with constitutional interpretation.

3. Historical Sources of State Constitutions

The records, journals, proceedings, and other documents relating to state constitutional conventions provide valuable information on the intended meanings and interpretations given to state constitutions by their framers. *State Constitutional Conventions, Commissions, and Amendments,* discussed earlier, makes available most of these materials. *Sources and Documents of United States Constitutions,*[31] compiled by William F. Swindler, reprints in chronological order the major constitutional documents of each state.

4. Comparative Sources of State Constitutions

Frequently, a provision of a particular state constitution may not have received any judicial interpretation. In such instances, cases on similar provisions in other state constitutions may be useful. One method of locating comparative state constitutional provisions is through *Index Digest of State Constitutions*[32] (Columbia University, Legislative Drafting Research Fund), a companion to *Constitutions of the United States: National and State,* discussed in Section C–1–b. It is arranged alphabetically by subject and under each subject are listed references to the various constitutional provisions of the states. Although this volume has only been updated through 1967, it is still useful, as many provisions of state constitutions do not change with great frequency.[33]

---

[30] *Reference Guides to the State Constitutions of the United States* is a series begun in 1990 by Greenwood Press, Westport, CT. The series covers each of the 50 states in a separate volume. Each volume contains an historical overview of the state's constitutional development, the text of the state's constitution and a section-by-section analysis, a bibliographic essay, a table of cases, and an index. A separate volume discusses common themes and variations in constitutional development. A separate index to the 51 volumes completes the set.

[31] Oceana Pubs. (11 vols. in 12, 1973–79). Volume 11, a bibliography, was added to this set in 1988. *See supra* note 12. A Second Series began in 1982. Older, but still useful titles for tracing the historical development of state constitutions are BENJAMIN PEARLEY POORE, CHARTERS AND CONSTITUTIONS (1877); FRANCIS NEWTON THORPE, FEDERAL AND STATE CONSTITUTIONS (1909); NEW YORK CONSTITUTIONAL CONVENTION COMMITTEE, 3 REPORTS: CONSTITUTIONS OF THE STATES AND UNITED STATES (1938). Although the Poore and Thorpe volumes are out of date, they are helpful for their parallel study of state constitutions. The last item, although never brought up to date, is still useful for its index volume to the constitutions of all of the states. *See also* ALBERT LEE STRUM, A BIBLIOGRAPHY ON STATE CONSTITUTIONS AND CONSTITUTIONAL REVISION, 1945–1975 (1975).

[32] Oceana Pubs. (2d ed. 1959).

[33] An attempt to provide a comprehensive subject index to all state constitutions began in 1980 when Columbia University's Legislative Drafting Research Fund issued "Fundamental Liberties and Rights: A Fifty State Index" as part of its *Constitutions of the United States: National and State.* This was followed in 1982 by "Laws, Legislature, Legislative

SECTION D. FOREIGN CONSTITUTIONS

There are occasions when it is necessary to locate the constitutions of foreign countries. This can be accomplished by consulting *Constitutions of the Countries of the World.*[34] This multi-volume set is published in looseleaf format, with a separate pamphlet for each country. The constitutions for each country are preceded by a constitutional chronology and followed by an annotated bibliography. For countries where there is not an official English version, an English translation is provided. The introduction in Chapter 1 of this set should be consulted for bibliographical references to previous compilations of constitutions. Supplements are issued periodically, keeping each constitution up to date.

A companion set is *Constitutions of Dependencies and Special Sovereignties.*[35] This multi-volume set contains pamphlets on the world's associated states, dependent territories, and areas of special sovereignty. Each pamphlet contains constitutional status data and an annotated bibliography. When a *territory* in this set achieves the status of a nation-state, its constitution is incorporated into *Constitutions of the Countries of the World.*

Also helpful is Congressional Quarterly's *Constitutions of the World* (1996), which serves as a guide to the constitutions and constitutional histories of 80 nations, selected for their political and constitutional importance.

SECTION E. SUMMARY

1. Federal Constitution

a. *Text in:*

(1) *United States Code*

(2) *United States Code Annotated "Constitution"* volumes

(3) *United States Code Service "Constitution"* volumes

(4) *Digest of United States Supreme Court Reports, Lawyers' Edition* (LEXIS Law Publishing)

(5) *Constitution of the United States of America* (Library of Congress edition)

(6) WESTLAW and LEXIS–NEXIS

b. *Interpretation*

(1) Judicial

(a) *U.S.C.A.* and *U.S.C.S. "Constitution"* volumes: (i) index to text of Constitution; (ii) topic analysis precedes digest of cases; (iii) digests of interpretive federal and state cases arranged under consti-

---

Procedure: A Fifty State Index." Since no further indexes have been published, it seems that this ambitious project has been abandoned.

[34] Albert P. Blaustein & Gisbert H. Flanz eds., Oceana Pubs. (1971 to date).

[35] Albert P. Blaustein & Eric B. Blaustein eds., Oceana Pubs. (1975 to date).

tutional provisions, subdivided by topic analysis; and (iv) cumulative annual pocket and subsequent pamphlet supplements.

(b) *The Constitution of the United States of America* (Library of Congress ed. 1992): (i) includes detailed index, table of cases, and numerous useful tables; (ii) provides commentary on the constitutional provisions and analysis of important cases of the Supreme Court; and (iii) kept up to date with a pocket supplement.

(c) *Digests* (*see* Section A–1–b)

(d) *Annotations: A.L.R. Federal, U.S. Supreme Court Reports, Lawyers' Edition, A.L.R., A.L.R.2d,* and *A.L.R.3d* (pre–1969) may discuss constitutional issues and provide case references.

(e) *Online Access* (*see* A–1–d)

(f) *Shepard's Citations* (*see* A–1–e)

c. *Secondary Sources*

(1) *Encyclopedia of the American Constitution.*

Contains over 2,100 articles.

(2) *The Founders' Constitution.*

An extensive collection of documents that bear on the Constitution.

(3) Bibliographies, texts, treatises, dictionaries, and legal periodicals can assist with constitutional analysis (*see* A–2).

d. *Historical Sources* (*see* A–3)

2. State Constitutions

a. Published with each state code and in *Constitutions of the United States: National and State;* often available on WESTLAW and LEXIS–NEXIS.

b. Annotated code volumes contain digest paragraphs.

c. Historical Sources

State Constitutional Conventions, Commissions, and Amendments (microfiche) is the most comprehensive collection (*see* C–3).

3. Sources of Comparative Information about State and Federal Constitutions

a. *See* Section C.

b. *Index Digest of State Constitutions* (2d ed.)

Comparative statement of all provisions of all state constitutions arranged by subject.

c. *Constitutions of the United States: National and State*

(1) Looseleaf publication that is a companion publication to the *Index Digest.*

(2) Texts of the constitutions of the United States and the fifty states.

(3) Index volume has two subject matter pamphlets; no new index pamphlets have been issued in recent years.

4. Foreign Constitutions

a. *Constitutions of the Countries of the World*

(1) A looseleaf publication containing the constitution for each country.

(2) Includes annotated bibliographies.

b. *Constitutions of Dependencies and Special Sovereignties.*

(1) Contains constitutional status data and an annotated bibliography on the world's associated states, dependent territories, and areas of special sovereignty.

(2) A looseleaf companion volume to *Constitutions of the Countries of the World*.

Chapter 9

FEDERAL LEGISLATION*

lists

Article I, Section 8, of the United States Constitution enumerates the powers of Congress, and provides the authority for Congress to make all laws necessary and proper for carrying into execution the enumerated powers, as well as other powers vested in Congress.

The Senate and the House of Representatives, collectively known as Congress, meet in two-year periods. Each year is a session and the two-year period is known as a Congress. The period in which Congress met, for example, during 1992–93, is known as the 102nd Congress, the 1st Congress being 1789–91. Under the Constitution, Congress must meet at least once a year.[1]

This chapter is devoted exclusively to a discussion of enacted legislation and the sources for locating these materials. Chapter 10, Federal Legislative Histories, discusses the various documents generated during the legislative process, the sources to use to locate these documents, and the sources containing the documents themselves.

SECTION A. THE ENACTMENT OF FEDERAL LAWS

Before discussing the various ways federal legislation is published, a brief description of the legislative process is necessary.[2] At the beginning of each Congress, Representatives and Senators may introduce legislation in their respective branch of Congress. Each proposed law is called a *bill* or a *joint resolution*[3] when introduced. The first bill in the House of Representatives in each Congress is labeled H.R. 1, with all subsequent

---

* Prepared for this edition by Bonnie L. Koneski–White, Law Librarian, Western New England College.

[1] U.S. CONST. art. I, § 4, cl. 2.

[2] For more detailed statements on the enactment of federal laws, see EDWARD F. WILLETT, JR., HOW OUR LAWS ARE MADE, H.R. DOC. No. 139, 101st Cong., 2d Sess. (1990) [hereinafter HOW OUR LAWS ARE MADE]; ROBERT B. DOVE, ENACTMENT OF A LAW: PROCEDURAL STEPS IN THE LEGISLATIVE PROCESS, S. DOC. No. 20, 97th Cong., 1st Sess. (1982). *See also* CONGRESSIONAL QUARTERLY, INC., CONGRESSIONAL QUARTERLY'S GUIDE TO CONGRESS (4th ed. 1991) [hereinafter CONGRESSIONAL QUARTERLY'S GUIDE]; ROBERT U. GOEHLERT & FENTON S. MARTIN, CONGRESS AND LAW-MAKING: RESEARCHING THE LEGISLATIVE PROCESS (2d ed. 1989); JUDITH MANION ET AL., A RESEARCH GUIDE TO CONGRESS: HOW TO MAKE CONGRESS WORK FOR YOU (2d ed. 1991); WANT'S HOW FEDERAL LAWS ARE MADE (3rd rev. ed. 1994).

[3] A *bill* is the form used for most legislation. A *joint resolution* may also be used, but there is no practical difference between the two, and the two forms are used indiscriminately. *Concurrent resolutions* are used for matters affecting the operations of both houses, but are not legislative. *Simple resolutions* are used for matters concerning the operation of either house and are not legislative. The first three forms are published in the *United States Statutes at Large*, the latter in the *Congressional Record*. HOW OUR LAWS ARE MADE, *supra* note 2, at 5–7.

156

bills numbered sequentially. Similarly, the first bill introduced in the Senate is labeled *S. 1*. After a bill passes the house in which it was introduced, it is sent to the other house for consideration. If approved in identical form, it is then sent to the President for signing. If the President signs it, the bill becomes a law. If the President vetoes it,[4] it becomes law only if the veto is overridden by two-thirds of both houses of Congress.[5] Under the Constitution, a bill sent to the President also becomes law if the President does not either sign or veto it within ten days of receiving it.[6] Bills introduced, but not passed during a specific Congress, do not carry over to the next Congress. If the sponsors wish the bill to be considered by the new Congress, it must be submitted as a new bill.

After a bill becomes law, it is sent to the Archivist, who is directed to publish all laws so received.[7] The Archivist classifies each law as either a public law or a private law. A *public law* affects the nation as a whole, or deals with individuals as a class and relates to public matters. A *private law* benefits only a specific individual or individuals. Such laws deal primarily with matters relating to claims against the government or with matters of immigration and naturalization.[8]

The first law to pass a Congress is designated as either Public Law No. 1, *e.g.*, Pub. L. No. 103–1, or Private Law No. 1, *e.g.*, Priv. L. No. 103–1, with 103 designating the Congress. Each succeeding public or private law is then numbered in sequence throughout the two-year life of a Congress.

SECTION B. PUBLICATION OF FEDERAL LAWS

1. Recent Public Laws

The first official publication of a law is issued by the United States Government Printing Office in the form of a *slip law.* [See Illustration 9–1.] Each law is separately published and may be one page or several hundred pages in length. Slip laws are available in all libraries that are depositories for U.S. government publications[9] and in other libraries that subscribe to these publications. Other sources that are commonly consulted for the text of recent public laws are:

a. *United States Code Congressional and Administrative News.* This set, which began in 1941 with the 77th Congress, 1st Session, is

---

[4] For a list of Presidential vetoes, see GREGORY HARNESS, PRESIDENTIAL VETOES, 1789–1988 (1992); GREGORY HARNESS, PRESIDENTIAL VETOES, 1989–1991 (1992).

[5] U.S. CONST. art. I, § 7, cl. 2.

[6] *Id.*

[7] U.S.C. § 106(a) (1994), Executive Order No. 10530, ch. 47 CODIFICATION OF PRESIDENTIAL PROCLAMATIONS AND EXECUTIVE ORDERS 935, 936 (1989 comp.). *See also* 44 U.S.C. §§ 709–711 (1994).

[8] For a complete discussion of private bills and laws, see CONGRESSIONAL QUARTERLY'S GUIDE, *supra* note 2, at 359–68.

[9] There are approximately 1,400 depository libraries. For a complete listing, see JOINT COMM. ON PRINTING, A DIRECTORY OF U.S. GOVERNMENT DEPOSITORY LIBRARIES (annual).

published by West Group. During each session of Congress, it is issued in monthly pamphlets and prints the full text of all public laws. Each issue contains a cumulative subject index and a cumulative *Table of Laws Enacted*. After each session of Congress, the pamphlets are reissued in bound volumes.

b. *United States Code Service Advance Service*. These monthly pamphlets, containing newly-enacted public laws, are published by LEXIS Law Publishing in connection with the *United States Code Service*. This *Service* contains a cumulative index arranged in alphabetical order.

c. *WESTLAW* and *LEXIS–NEXIS*. Both online systems include the text of current and retrospective public laws.

d. *Specialized Looseleaf Services*. For selected "important" legislation that relates to the subject covered by the looseleaf service, publishers often provide pamphlet reproductions of public laws.

2.   United States Statutes at Large

At the end of each session of Congress, all the slip laws, both public and private, are published in numerical order as part of the set entitled *United States Statutes at Large.* Public and private laws are in separate sections of the volumes. Thus, all the laws enacted since 1789 are contained in the many volumes of this set. [See Illustration 9–5.] The *United States Statutes at Large* (Stat.) is the source for the authoritative text of federal laws.

Because this set did not commence until 1846, it was necessary to publish retrospectively the legislation up to that point. Consequently, volumes 1–5 cover the public laws and volume 6 the private laws for the 1st through 28th Congresses (1789–1845), with volumes 7 and 8 devoted exclusively to treaties. See Chapter 19 for a discussion of treaties. The publication pattern for volumes 9 through 49 differs from the one used now. Volume 9 covers the 29th–31st Congresses; volumes 10 through 12 cover two Congresses each (32nd–37th); and volumes 13 to 49 cover one Congress each (38th–74th). The current pattern of one numbered volume per session began in 1936 with the 75th Congress, 1st Session.[10]

It is important to keep in mind that the laws in the *United States Statutes at Large* are arranged in chronological order rather than by subject. Moreover, amendments to a prior law may appear in different volumes from the law being amended. For example, a law passed in 1900 is in volume 31 of the *United States Statutes at Large*. If Congress amended it in 1905, the amendment will appear in the volume for that year. Some laws have been amended numerous times. To obtain the full and current text of such a law, the *United States Statutes at Large* volume containing the original law must be examined in conjunction with subsequent volumes in which amendments to that law appear.

---

[10] For a concise historical explanation of the development of the United States Statutes at Large, its significance, and a complete bibliographic listing of the set, see CURT E. CONKLIN & FRANCIS ACLAND, A BIBLIOGRAPHIC INTRODUCTION TO THE UNITED STATES STATUTES AT LARGE (1992). *See also* LARRY M. BOYER, CHECKLIST OF U.S. SESSION LAWS, 1789–1873 (1976).

Each volume of the *United States Statutes at Large* has its own subject index. Beginning in 1991, a popular name index was added. From 1957 through 1976, each volume contained tables listing how each public law in that volume affected previous public laws. Marginal notes since volume 33 give House or Senate bill numbers, Public Law numbers, and dates. The *United States Statutes at Large* also contain interstate compacts. Regrettably, publication of the bound *United States Statutes at Large* runs about two years, or one Congress, behind in its schedule. When published, it supersedes the slip laws for that volume.

SECTION C. CODIFICATION OF FEDERAL LAWS

The chronological method of publication of congressional laws creates obvious problems for the process of determining the statutory provisions on any given subject. Therefore, the laws passed by Congress have to be rearranged in a manner that will do three things: (1) collate the original law with all subsequent amendments by taking into consideration the deletion or addition of language made by the amendments; (2) bring all laws on the same subject or topic together; and (3) eliminate all repealed, superseded, or expired laws. This process is called codification.[11]

1. United States Revised Statutes

The first codification of the *United States Statutes at Large* resulted in the publication of the *Revised Statutes of the United States.*[12] This first codification is also known either as the Revised Statutes of 1873, reflecting the last year of laws contained in this code, as the Revised Statutes of 1874, reflecting the date of enactment of this code, or as the Revised Statutes of 1875, reflecting its date of publication. Throughout this chapter, this codification will be called the "Revised Statutes of 1875."

Because the *United States Statutes at Large* have no cumulating subject index, the difficulty in research was apparent. In 1866, President Andrew Johnson, pursuant to congressional authorization, appointed a commission to extract from the volumes of the *United States Statutes at Large* all public laws that met the following criteria: (1) they were still in force, and (2) they were of a general and permanent nature. The next step was to take each public law and all its amendments and rewrite the law in one sequence by incorporating amending language and eliminating deleted language. All the laws were then arranged by topics in chapters, or *Titles*. Title 14, for example, contained all legislation passed by Congress, and still in force, on the judiciary; Title 64, all legislation in force on bankruptcy. All the Titles were then bound in one volume, a

---

[11] For a discussion of the process involved in codification, see Charles S. Zinn, *Revision of the United States Code,* 51 Law Libr. J. 388 (1958). For an historical discussion of the codification process, see Larry Becraft, *Titles of the United States Code,* Antishyster, no. 2, 1994, at 10.

[12] Ralph H. Dwan & Ernest R. Feidler, *The Federal Statutes—Their History and Use,* 22 Minn. L. Rev. 1008, 1012–13 (1938) [hereinafter Dwan & Feidler].

subject index prepared, and the volume issued as the *Revised Statutes of 1875.*

The *Revised Statutes of 1875* was submitted to Congress, introduced as a bill, and went through the legislative process of becoming a public law. Incorporated in the bill before Congress was a Title specifically repealing each previously passed public law that had been incorporated into the *Revised Statutes of 1875.*[13]

Thus, when it passed Congress and was signed by the President, all the public laws passed between 1789 and 1873, in force and of a general and permanent nature, were codified in the *Revised Statutes of 1875.* Moreover, as the act of codification repealed all pertinent *United States Statutes at Large,* the *Revised Statutes of 1875* became *positive law,* and it was no longer necessary to refer to the *United States Statutes at Large.*

Unfortunately, this volume, known as the first edition, was subsequently discovered to contain many inaccuracies and unauthorized changes in the law.[14] In 1878, a second edition of the *Revised Statutes* was authorized to be published that would include legislation passed since 1873, delete sections that were repealed since 1873, and correct the errors inadvertently incorporated into the first edition.

The second edition indicated changes to the text of the first edition by the use of brackets and italics. It is important to note, however, that the second edition of the *Revised Statutes* was never enacted into positive law by Congress, and all changes indicated in it are only *prima facie* evidence of the law. Although several attempts were made to adopt a new codification, it was not until 1924 that Congress authorized the publication of a codification of federal laws.[15]

2. United States Code (U.S.C.)

Prior to 1926, the positive law for federal legislation was contained in one volume of the *Revised Statutes of 1875* and then in each of the twenty-four subsequent volumes of the *United States Statutes at Large.* In 1926, the *United States Code,* prepared under the auspices of special committees of the House and Senate, was published. In this codification, all sections of the *Revised Statutes of 1875* that were not repealed were extracted, and then all the public and general laws still in force from the *United States Statutes at Large* since 1873 were included.

These laws were then arranged into fifty Titles and published as the *United States Code,* 1926 edition.[16] Between 1927 and 1933 cumulated bound supplements were issued each year. In 1934 a new edition was issued that incorporated the cumulated supplements to the 1926 edition,

[13] Revised Statutes of the United States, 1873–74, Act of June 22, 1874, tit. LXXIV, §§ 5595–5601, at 1085 (1878).

[14] Dwan & Feidler, *supra* note 12, at 1014–15.

[15] For a discussion and bibliography of federal laws before 1926, see Erwin C. Surrency, *The Publication of Federal Laws: A Short History,* 79 LAW LIBR. J. 469 (1987).

[16] *See* Preface at 44, Pt. 1 Stat. at v (1926).

and this became the *United States Code,* 1934 edition. Every six years a new edition is published with cumulative supplements issued during the intervening years. The *U.S.C.* is thus the "official" edition of the codification of federal public laws of a general and permanent nature, which are in effect at the time of publication.

Unlike the *Revised Statutes of 1875,* the *U.S.C.* was never submitted to Congress and enacted into positive law in its entirety. Instead, Congress created the Office of the Revision Counsel[17] and directed that Office to revise the *U.S.C.* Title by Title. Each Title is submitted to Congress for enactment into positive law. To date, less than one half of the Titles have been enacted into law.[18] Thus, in using the *U.S.C.,* it is important to ascertain if the Title being consulted has been enacted into positive law. Those Titles not yet enacted are *prima facie* evidence of the law.[19] Should there be a conflict between the wording in the *U.S.C.* and the *United States Statutes at Large,* the latter will govern.[20] The *United States Statutes at Large* citations, the original enactment, and any amendments are provided after each section of the *U.S.C.* These parenthetical references lead to the positive law for those Titles of the *U.S.C.*

[17] The principal duty of this Office is "to develop and keep current an official and positive codification of the laws of the United States," 2 U.S.C. § 285a (1994), and "to prepare . . . one title at a time, a complete compilation, restatement, and revision of the general and permanent laws of the United States. . . ." 2 U.S.C. § 285b(1) (1994).

[18] Titles enacted into positive law are 1, 3, 4, 5, 9, 10, 11, 13, 14, 17, 18, 23, 28, 31, 32, 35, 37, 38, 39, 44, 46, 49, and the Internal Revenue Code (Title 26). Title 34 was eliminated by Title 10; and the enactment of Title 31 repealed Title 6. A list of Titles reenacted as positive law is in the following sources: (1) after the title page of, and in the preface to, the volumes of the *U.S.C.;* (2) after Section 204(e) of Title 1 in the *U.S.C.,* the *United States Code Annotated,* and the *United States Code Service (U.S.C.S.);* and (3) inside the front cover of bound volumes of the *U.S.C.S.*

[19] 1 U.S.C. § 204(a) (1994) provides that:

The matter set forth in the edition of the Code of Laws of the United States current at any time shall, together with the then current supplement, if any, establish *prima facie* the laws of the United States, general and permanent in their nature, in force on the day preceding the commencement of the session following the last session the legislation of which is included: *Provided, however,* That whenever titles of such Code shall have been enacted into positive law the text thereof shall be legal evidence of the laws therein contained, in all the courts of the United States, the several States, and the Territories and insular possessions of the United States.

[20] For an interpretation of 1 U.S.C. § 204(a), see United States v. Welden, 377 U.S. 95, 98 n. 4 (1964). *See also* North Dakota v. United States, 460 U.S. 300 (1983); United States v. Wodtke, 627 F. Supp. 1034, 1040 (N.D. Iowa 1985), *aff'd,* 871 F.2d 1092 (8th Cir. 1988).

that have not yet been enacted into positive law by the Congress. [See Illustrations 9–9 and 9–10.]

Some additional features of the *U.S.C.* are as follows:

a.   A multi-volume general index.

b.   Historical notes that provide information on amendments or other public laws' effect on sections of the *U.S.C.*

c.   Cross references to other sections of the *U.S.C.* that contain related matter or that refer to the section of the *U.S.C.* being researched.

d.   A table of "Acts Cited by Popular Name," in which public laws are listed alphabetically by either the short titles assigned by Congress or by the names by which the laws have become known. Citations are provided to the *U.S.C.* and to the *United States Statutes at Large.*

e.   Tables volumes that provide the following information:

(1) Table 1 shows where Titles of the *U.S.C.* that have been revised and renumbered since the 1926 edition appear in the current edition of the *U.S.C.*

(2) Table 2 provides references to the current edition of the *U.S.C.* from the *Revised Statutes of 1878.*

(3) Table 3 lists the public laws in the *United States Statutes at Large* in chronological order and indicates where each section of a public law is contained in the current edition of the *U.S.C.*

(4) Another table provides information on internal cross references within the *U.S.C.*

(5) There are additional tables that indicate where other documentation, *e.g.,* Presidential executive orders, are referenced in the current edition of the *U.S.C.*

The Tables volumes are updated by the annual cumulative supplements to the *U.S.C.*

3.   Annotated Editions of the United States Code

Because the *U.S.C.* is printed and sold by the U.S. Government Printing Office, it is often slow in being published, particularly in the issuance of the supplements, which are seldom available until several months after a session of Congress is over. Furthermore, the meaning of a law passed by a legislative body is not always clear and the language used must frequently be interpreted by a court. Consequently, access to the court cases interpreting statutes is frequently as important as the text of the statute itself. This has led to the publication of annotated codes where digests of court cases interpreting or deciding the constitutionality of a *Code* section are given. Two annotated editions of the *U.S.C.* are published privately.

The annotated editions have many advantages over the official edition of the *U.S.C.* and are usually consulted in preference to it. These advantages are: (1) each Title is published in one or more separate volumes; (2) the entire set is kept up to date by annual cumulative pocket supplements and, when necessary, by recompiled volumes; (3) pamphlets are issued during the year bringing the pocket supplements up to date; (4) more detailed indexing is provided in bound volumes and supplements [see Illustration 9–2]; (5) each *Code* section contains annotations of court cases that have interpreted it; and (6) when applicable, citations to the *Code of Federal Regulations*[21] are given.

a. *United States Code Annotated (U.S.C.A.).* This set is published by West Group. *U.S.C.A.* uses the text as it appears in the official version, the *U.S.C.* Thus, it contains the same features as were listed in Section C–2, *supra.*

Many enhancements have been added by the publisher to supplement those features found in the official version of the *U.S.C.* Most important are the Notes of Decisions, which provide digests of cases that have interpreted a particular section of the *Code.* This feature is popularly referred to as annotations. Notes of Decisions are organized under an alphabetical subject index, which precedes the actual annotations.

Other features of the *U.S.C.A.* are as follows:

(1) References to other West publications and to Topic and Key Numbers that can assist the users in finding additional cases and other materials pertinent to their research.

(2) A multi-volume General Index is issued annually in paperback form. In addition, each Title of the *U.S.C.A.* has a separate index in the last volume containing sections of the particular Title of the *U.S.C.A.*

(3) Public laws that have been enacted since the last supplementation was prepared for a specific Title and that affect sections of that Title can be located in *U.S.C.A.*'s supplementary pamphlets. The public laws are classified to particular *Code* sections. The most recent Notes of Decisions are included for *Code* sections that have been construed by the courts since the last pocket supplements were published. The most recent court cases that have interpreted public laws can be located by using the Tables of Statutes Construed in the bound volumes and advance sheets of the units of the *National Reporter System.*

(4) A "Popular Name Table for Acts of Congress" is located in the last volume of the General Index. [See Illustration 9–12.] The listing is alphabetical by popular name, with references provided to the *United States Statutes at Large* and to the *Code.* This Popular Name Table is cumulatively updated by means of the pamphlets discussed in 3, *supra.* Also, many Titles of the *U.S.C.A.* contain tables entitled "Popular Name Acts," which provide an alphabetical listing of public laws within that Title and references to sections of that specific Title. [See Illustration 9–13.] These tables are located in the first volume of the Title, if there is more than one volume.

[21] This publication is discussed in Chapter 13.

The General Index also includes, in the proper alphabetical location, the public law by popular name. Most frequently, the researcher is referred to the Popular Name Table for Acts of Congress in the last volume of the *U.S.C.A.*'s General Index. Occasionally, a direct reference is given to the *Code*.

(5) The *U.S.C.A.* contains many of the same tables as described for the *U.S.C.* These tables are contained in separate volumes labeled as such and are updated by means of pocket and pamphlet supplementation as described *supra*.

b. *United States Code Service (U.S.C.S.).* This set is published by LEXIS Law Publishing. Like *U.S.C.A., U.S.C.S.* provides the same features of *U.S.C.*, historical notes, cross references in a section entitled "History; Ancillary Laws and Directives," which follows each section of the *Code*.

A major difference between *U.S.C.S.* and *U.S.C.A.* is that *U.S.C.S.* follows the text of the public laws as they appear in the *United States Statutes at Large.* Therefore, if a Title has not been enacted into positive law, the user will have the language that is needed. If the editors of *U.S.C.S.* believe that clarification of the language of the public laws in the set is necessary, this information will be shown by the use of brackets (inserting words or references) or by use of explanatory notes.

Because it is an annotated *Code, U.S.C.S.* provides "pertinent" digests of not only court cases but also of federal administrative agency decisions that have interpreted or construed a public law or a particular section of a public law by means of Interpretative Notes and Decisions.

An "analytical" index, which precedes the actual digest of cases and administrative decisions, enables users to focus their research. The Later Case and Statutory Service pamphlets, issued three times a year, update the Interpretative Notes and Decisions between the time of the issuance of the annual pocket supplements.

Other features of the *U.S.C.S.* are as follows:

(1) *U.S.C.S.* provides references to other publications, including those of West Group, and to relevant law review articles. These references are in a section entitled Research Guide.

(2) A multi-volume Revised General Index, which is kept current by a General Index Update pamphlet.

(3) Public laws that have been enacted since the last supplementation has been prepared for a specific Title and that affect sections of that Title can be located in *U.S.C.S.*'s Cumulative Later Case and Statutory Service, issued three times a year. The public laws are classified to particular *Code* sections.

(4) A "Table of Acts by Popular Name," is located in the Tables volumes of *U.S.C.S.* The listing is alphabetical by popular name, with references provided to the *United States Statutes at Large* and to

U.S.C.S. This Table is updated by the *United States Code Service Advance Service* discussed in Section B–1–b, *supra.*

The General Index also includes, in the proper alphabetic location, the public law by popular name. References are given to a *U.S.C.S.* citation or a cross reference is given to a subject in the General Index when the specific sections of the public law are contained in the *U.S.C.S.*

(5) *U.S.C.S.* contains many of the same tables as described for the *U.S.C.* These tables are contained in separate volumes labeled as such and are updated by means of pocket and pamphlet supplementation as described *supra.*

c.   *Summary and Comparison: Annotated Editions of the United States Code.* Both the *U.S.C.A.* and the *U.S.C.S.* follow the same citation pattern as the official *U.S.C.* and, therefore, a citation to *U.S.C.* can be located in either of the two annotated sets.[22] As noted in Section C–2, *supra,* only certain Titles of the *U.S.C.* have been enacted into positive law. The *U.S.C.A.* uses the text as it appears in the *U.S.C.,* while the *U.S.C.S.* follows the text as it appears in the *United States Statutes at Large.* Thus, when using the *U.S.C.A.,* it may be necessary at times to check the text of the *United States Statutes at Large* for those Titles that are still only *prima facie* evidence of the law.

Both *U.S.C.A.* and *U.S.C.S.* contain digests of cases that have interpreted a section of the *U.S.C.* Each set is kept up to date by annual pocket supplements, monthly pamphlets, and, when necessary, by issuance of replacement volumes. Each has editorial matter that refers to other publications by the same publisher. The *U.S.C.A.* contains more annotations than the *U.S.C.S.;* the *U.S.C.S.* frequently cross references to *Annotations* in *A.L.R.* or in *United States Supreme Court Reports, Lawyers' Edition* for additional cases in lieu of providing annotations. Each set is easier to use, more current, and better indexed than the *U.S.C.* However, when only the text of the *Code* is needed, it may be simpler to consult the official, unannotated edition. [See Illustrations 9–2 and 9–10, which show the use of the various sets of the *Code.*]

Both annotated codes include volumes containing the United States Constitution and the various court rules. These components are discussed in Chapters 8 and 12, respectively.

4.   Access to the Code in Electronic Format

a.   *LEXIS–NEXIS.* LEXIS–NEXIS contains the *Code* as published in the *U.S.C.S* Each section of a *Code* Title contains the full text of the law, a complete history of the *Code* section showing source and derivations of the law plus any amendments, and a list of research references and interpretative notes. Each *Code* section is updated to include the new material in the paper supplementation. Information regarding each section's currency is included.

---

[22] For a discussion of these two sets, *see* Jeanne Benioff, *A Comparison of Annotated U.S. Codes,* LEGAL REFERENCE SERVICES Q., Spring 1982, at 37.

b. *WESTLAW.* WESTLAW contains the *Code* as published in the *U.S.C.A.* The USC database provides the unannotated version. A related materials directory enables the user to update the *Code* section, to view historical notes, references and tables, and to find Notes of Decisions. The USCA database contains the text of the *Code,* annotations, and a popular name table. The *Code* section can be updated and notes, references, and tables can be viewed by using the update feature.

c. *CD–ROM Products.* West Group, LEXIS Law Publishing, and the Government Printing Office each have a CD–ROM version of the *Code* they publish.

d. *Internet Sources*

(1) The Legal Information Institute at Cornell has the full text of the latest edition of the *United States Code.* [See Illustration 4–11.]

(2) FedLaw does not provide original information at its site but does contain links to more than 1,600 legal-related information sources on the World Wide Web.

(3) Meta–Index for U.S. Legal Research is a site maintained by Georgia State University College of Law. It provides an interface to searchable databases of legal information including the *United States Code,* etc.

(4) U.S. Code Gopher contains the full text of the *Code* including the table of popular names.

(5) GPO Access, available through the Home Page of the Government Printing Office, contains a wide ranging collection of useful information including the *United States Code.* [See Illustration 9–4.]

SECTION D.   ILLUSTRATIONS

9–1.   **A public law in slip form**
9–2.   **A page from a volume of the General Index to the U.S.C.A.**
9–3.   **Page from Title 43, U.S.C., 1988 ed.**
9–4.   **Page from GPO Access**
9–5.   **A page from volume 90 of United States Statutes at Large, Pub. L. No. 94–579**
9–6—   **Pages from Title 43, U.S.C.A.**
  9–8.
9–9—   **Pages from Title 43, U.S.C.S.**
  9–10.

[Illustration 9–1]

SLIP LAW—105th CONGRESS

①↴

111 STAT. 248   PUBLIC LAW 105–30—JULY 25, 1997

Public Law 105–30
105th Congress

An Act

July 25, 1997
②◄ [H.R. 1901]

To clarify that the protections of the Federal Tort Claims Act apply to the members
and personnel of the National Gambling Impact Study Commission.

*Be it enacted by the Senate and House of Representatives of
the United States of America in Congress assembled,*

SECTION 1. APPLICABILITY OF FEDERAL TORT CLAIMS PROVISIONS.

Section 6 of the National Gambling Impact Study Commission
Act (18 U.S.C. 1955 note) is amended by adding at the end the
following:

"(e) APPLICABILITY OF FEDERAL TORT CLAIMS PROVISIONS.—
For purposes of sections 1346(b) and 2401(b) and chapter 171 of
title 28, United States Code, the Commission is a 'Federal agency'
and each of the members and personnel of the Commission is
an 'employee of the Government'.".

③◄ 18 USC 1955
note.

SEC. 2. CONSTRUCTION.

The amendment made by section 1 shall not be construed
to imply that any commission is not a "Federal agency" or that
any of the members or personnel of a commission is not an
"employee of the Government" for purposes of sections 1346(b)
and 2401(b) and chapter 171 of title 28, United States Code.

③◄ 18 USC 1955
note.

SEC. 3. EFFECTIVE DATE.

The amendment made by section 1 shall be effective as of
August 3, 1996.

This is a typical *slip law.* At the end of a session, laws
are published in a bound volume of the *United States Statutes at Large.*

Marginal notes are not part of the law but editorial
aids. The *Code* citations in the margin indicate where the
text is found in the *United States Code.*

Notes: 1. *United States Statutes at Large* citation.

2. Bill number in House.

3. *United States Code* sections.

LEGISLATIVE HISTORY—H.R. 1901:

HOUSE REPORTS: No. 105–145 (Comm. on the Judiciary).
CONGRESSIONAL RECORD, Vol. 143 (1997):
   June 23, considered and passed House
   July 9, considered and passed Senate.

[Illustration 9–2]

PAGE FROM VOLUME OF GENERAL INDEX TO THE U.S.C.A.

725   **GRAZING**

GRAZING—Cont'd
→Districts—Cont'd
  Soldiers' and sailors' civil relief, remission,
    etc., of grazing fees, 50 Ap § 561
  State police power, 43 § 315m
  States,
    Appropriations, moneys received by State,
      43 § 315j
    Police power, 43 § 315n
  Stone, use for domestic purposes, 43 § 315d
→Water rights, 43 § 315b
  Wells, 43 § 315c
  Wildlife, cooperation in conservation or
    propagation, 43 § 315h
Domestic livestock on public rangelands.
  Public Lands, generally, this index
El Malpais National Conservation Area, con-
  tinuance of, 16 § 460uu–22
El Malpais National Monument, 16 § 460uu–3
Federal civil defense, applicability of section
  concerning leases of Government realty
  for grazing purposes, 50 Ap § 2285
Federal land policy and management. Public
  Lands, this index
Fossil Ridge Recreation Management Area,
  16 § 539l
Grand Canyon National Park, 16 §§ 221e,
  228f, 228l
Great Basin National Park, appropriate limit
  or control of land with respect to, 16

GRAZING—Cont'd
Lands—Cont'd
  State police power, 43 § 315n
  War, payment for use for war purposes, 43
    § 315q
  Withdrawal of grazing lands for war or na-
    tional defense purposes, 43 § 315q
Lassen Volcanic National Park, 16 § 202
Leases,
  Defined, Federal land policy and manage-
    ment, 43 § 1702
  Glen Canyon National Recreation Area, 16
    § 460dd–5
Military departments, real property transac-
  tions, applicability of section to real prop-
  erty for grazing purposes, 10 § 2662
National Parks, generally, 16 § 3
National Wilderness Preservation System, gen-
  erally, this index
Oregon and California railroad grant lands,
  lease of revested lands for grazing, 43
  § 1181d
Oregon Cascades Recreation Area, allowance
  of limited activities, etc., for livestock
  grazing, 16 § 460oo
Permits,
  Arches National Park, 16 § 272b
  Capitol Reef National Park,
    Generally, 16 § 273b
    Renewals, occupied lands, period in-

FINDING A FEDERAL LAW

Problem: Find the statutory section dealing with water rights in grazing districts.

Step 1. Check index to either *U.S.C.*, *U.S.C.A.*, or *U.S.C.S.*

This will indicate that this topic is covered at 43 U.S.C. § 315b.

Lake Mead National Recreation Area, 16
  § 460n–3
Lands,
  Coos Bay Wagon Road grant lands, recon-
    veyed lands, 43 § 1181d
  Field employees of Bureau of Land Man-
    agement to furnish horses and equip-
    ment, 43 § 315o–2
  Inapplicability, provisions concerning Feder-
    al civil defense transactions to lease of
    Government realty for grazing, 50 Ap
    § 2285
  Leases, 43 §§ 315m, 315m–1
  Mining activities causing damage, liability,
    30 § 54
  National defense, payment for use for na-
    tional defense purposes, 43 § 315q
  National Forest Administration land under,
    43 §§ 315k, 315l
  Preference right to users of withdrawn pub-
    lic lands after restoration of withdrawal,
    43 § 315m
  Public rangelands improvement. Public
    Lands, generally, this index
  Rentals, payment in advance authorized, 43
    § 315r

    generally, this index
Paiute Indian Tribe of Utah, trust lands, 25
  § 766 nt
Sequoia National Park, 16 § 45c
Suspension, violation, provisions protecting
  endangered species, 16 § 1540
Pine Ridge National Recreation Area, contin-
  uation, objective, 16 § 460rr–2
Public lands, policy and management,
  Advisory boards,
    Consultation and cooperation, allotment
      management plans, 43 § 1752
    Establishment, maintenance, 43 § 1753
    Range lands improvement. Public lands,
      generally, this index
  Appeal, allotment reductions, time, etc., 43
    § 1752 nt
  Defined, 43 § 1702
  Districts, lands acquired within to become
    part of, 43 § 1715
  Fees, disposition, 43 § 1751
  Permits and leases,
    Court ordered environmental statements,
      basis for establishing short term, 43
      § 1752
    Terms and conditions, 43 § 1752

[Illustration 9–3]

PAGE FROM UNITED STATES CODE, 1988 EDITION

§ 315a   TITLE 43—PUBLIC LANDS   **Page 48**

REFERENCES IN TEXT

The Stock Raising Homestead Act, referred to in text, is act Dec. 29, 1916, ch. 9, 39 Stat. 862, as amended, which was classified generally to subchapter X (§ 291 et seq.) of chapter 7 of this title and was repealed by Pub. L. 94–579, title VII, §§ 702, 704(a), Oct. 21, 1976, 90 Stat. 2787, 2792, except for sections 9 and 11 which are classified to sections 299 and 301, respectively, of this title. For complete classification of this Act to the Code, see Short Title note set out under section 291 of this title and Tables.

Section 471 of title 16, referred to in text, was repealed by Pub. L. 94–579, title VII, § 704(a), Oct. 21, 1976, 90 Stat. 2792.

AMENDMENTS

1954—Act May 28, 1954, struck out of first sentence provision limiting to one hundred and forty-two million acres the area which might be included in grazing districts.

1936—Act June 26, 1936, increased acreage which could be included in grazing districts from 80 million to 142 million acres.

SHORT TITLE

Act June 28, 1934, which enacted this subchapter, is popularly known as the "Taylor Grazing Act".

SECTION REFERRED TO IN OTHER SECTIONS

This section is referred to in sections 315a, 1715 of this title.

§ 315a. Protection, administration, regulation, and improvement of districts; rules and regulations; study of erosion and flood control; offenses

time in accordance with governing law. Grazing permits shall be issued only to citizens of the United States or to those who have filed the necessary declarations of intention to become such, as required by the naturalization laws, and to groups, associations, or corporations authorized to conduct business under the laws of the State in which the grazing district is located. Preference shall be given in the issuance of grazing permits to those within or near a district who are landowners engaged in the livestock business, bona fide occupants or settlers, or owners of water or water rights, as may be necessary to permit the proper use of lands, water or water rights owned, occupied, or leased by them, except that until July 1, 1935, no preference shall be given in the issuance of such permits to any such owner, occupant, or settler, whose rights were acquired between January 1, 1934, and December 31, 1934, both dates, inclusive, except that no permittee complying with the rules and regulations laid down by the Secretary of the Interior shall be denied the renewal of such permit, if such denial will impair the value of the grazing unit of the permittee, when such unit is pledged as security for any bona fide loan. Such permits shall be for a period of not more than ten years, subject to the preference right of the permittees to renewal in the discretion of the Secretary of the Interior, who shall specify from time to time numbers of stock and seasons of use. During pe-

---

Step 2. Locate the title and section referred to in the index. Ordinarily, one would consult the latest edition of *U.S.C.* and its cumulative supplement, or one of the two annotated codes.

This Illustration shows how this law appears in the *U.S.C.*

Note how at the end of § 315b (as is the case with all *U.S.C.* sections) citations are given to where the section originally appeared in the *United States Statutes at Large.* § 315b was first passed in 1934 and amended in 1947 and 1976.

---

of the range; and the Secretary of the Interior is authorized to continue the study of erosion and flood control and to perform such work as may be necessary amply to protect and rehabilitate the areas subject to the provisions of this subchapter, through such funds as may be made available for that purpose, and any willful violation of the provisions of this subchapter or of such rules and regulations thereunder after actual notice thereof shall be punishable by a fine of not more than $500.

(June 28, 1934, ch. 865, § 2, 48 Stat. 1270.)

→ **§ 315b. Grazing permits; fees; vested water rights; permits not to create right in land**

The Secretary of the Interior is authorized to issue or cause to be issued permits to graze livestock on such grazing districts to such bona fide settlers, residents, and other stock owners as under his rules and regulations are entitled to participate in the use of the range, upon the payment annually of reasonable fees in each case to be fixed or determined from time to

be hereafter initiated or acquired and maintained in accordance with such law. So far as consistent with the purposes and provisions of this subchapter, grazing privileges recognized and acknowledged shall be adequately safeguarded, but the creation of a grazing district or the issuance of a permit pursuant to the provisions of this subchapter shall not create any right, title, interest, or estate in or to the lands.

(June 28, 1934, ch. 865, § 3, 48 Stat. 1270; Aug. ◄ 6, 1947, ch. 507, § 1, 61 Stat. 790; Oct. 21, 1976, Pub. L. 94–579, title IV, § 401(b)(3), 90 Stat. 2773.)

AMENDMENTS

1976—Pub. L. 94–579 substituted provisions authorizing fees to be fixed in accordance with governing law, for provisions authorizing fees to take into account public benefits to users of grazing districts over and above benefits accruing to users of forage resources and provisions requiring fees to consist of a grazing fee and a range-improvement fee.

1947—Act Aug. 6, 1947, provided for method to be used by Secretary of the Interior in fixing amount of

[Illustration 9–4]

GPO ACCESS WEB PAGE

United States Congress   http://www.access.gpo.gov/congress/index.l

Congressional Publications	Miscellaneous House Publications	Miscellaneous Senate Publications	House Committees	Senate Committees	GPO Access Search Page

The following are official, searchable publication databases authorized for dissemination to the public via GPO Access. The origin of these databases begins with the Legislative process in both the U.S. House of Representatives and the U.S. Senate. Some of the publications listed are published by other Government entities. If Congress is not the publisher, the search page accessed by clicking on a listed publication reveals the entity with publishing responsibility.

Congressional Publications

Congressional Bills
Congressional Directory, 104th and 105th Congresses
Congressional Documents
Congressional Hearings
Congressional Pictorial Directory, 105th Congress
Congressional Record
Congressional Record Index
Congressional Reports
Economic Indicators
History of Bills
Public Laws
U.S. Code, 1994 edition
U.S. Constitution, Analysis and Interpretation: 1992 Edition and 1996 Supplement

U.S. House of Representatives

Miscellaneous House Publications and Committees

U.S. Senate

Miscellaneous Senate Publications and Committees

[Illustration 9–5]

PAGE FROM 90 UNITED STATES STATUTES AT LARGE

PUBLIC LAW 94–579—OCT. 21, 1976   90 STAT. 2773

of all moneys received by the United States as fees for grazing domestic livestock on public lands (other than from ceded Indian lands) under the Taylor Grazing Act (48 Stat. 1269; 43 U.S.C. 315 et seq.) and the Act of August 28, 1937 (50 Stat. 874; 43 U.S.C. 1181d), and on lands in National Forests in the eleven contiguous Western States under the provisions of this section shall be credited to a separate account in the Treasury, one-half of which is authorized to be appropriated and made available for use in the district, region, or national forest from which such moneys were derived, as the respective Secretary may direct after consultation with district, regional, or national forest user representatives, for the purpose of on-the-ground range rehabilitation, protection, and improvements on such lands, and the remaining one-half shall be used for on-the-ground range rehabilitation, protection, and improvements as the Secretary concerned directs. Any funds so appropriated shall be in addition to any other appropriations made to the respective Secretary for planning and

As noted in the previous Illustration, 43 U.S.C. § 315b has been amended twice, most recently in 1976. As is frequently the case, a public law may amend different Titles and sections of the same Title of the *U.S.C.*

tive Secretary may direct after consultation with user representatives. The annual distribution and use of range betterment funds authorized by this paragraph shall not be considered a major Federal action requiring a detailed statement pursuant to section 4332(c) of title 42 of the United States Code.

(2) The first clause of section 10(b) of the Taylor Grazing Act (48 Stat. 1269), as amended by the Act of August 6, 1947 (43 U.S.C. 315i), is hereby repealed. All distributions of moneys made under section 401(b)(1) of this Act shall be in addition to distributions made under section 10 of the Taylor Grazing Act and shall not apply to distribution of moneys made under section 11 of that Act. The remaining moneys received by the United States as fees for grazing domestic livestock on the public lands shall be deposited in the Treasury as miscellaneous receipts.

43 USC 1751.

43 USC 315j.

(3) Section 3 of the Taylor Grazing Act, as amended (43 U.S.C. 315), is further amended by—

43 USC 315b.

    (a) Deleting the last clause of the first sentence thereof, which begins with "and in fixing," deleting the comma after "time", and adding to that first sentence the words "in accordance with governing law".

    (b) Deleting the second sentence thereof.

GRAZING LEASES AND PERMITS

Sec. 402. (a) Except as provided in subsection (b) of this section, permits and leases for domestic livestock grazing on public lands issued by the Secretary under the Act of June 28, 1934 (48 Stat. 1269, as amended; 43 U.S.C. 315 et seq.) or the Act of August 28, 1937 (50 Stat. 874, as amended; 43 U.S.C. 1181a–1181j), or by the Secretary of Agriculture, with respect to lands within National Forests in the eleven contiguous Western States, shall be for a term of ten years subject to such terms and conditions the Secretary concerned deems appropriate and consistent with the governing law, including, but not limited to, the authority of the Secretary concerned to cancel, suspend, or modify a grazing permit or lease, in whole or in part, pursuant to the terms and conditions thereof, or to cancel or suspend a grazing permit or

43 USC 1752.

[Illustration 9–6]

PAGE FROM TITLE 43 U.S.C.A.

Ch. 8A   GRAZING LANDS   **43 § 315b**

West's Federal Practice Manual

Grazing in grazing districts, see § 5587 et seq.

Code of Federal Regulations

Criminal law enforcement, see 43 CFR 9260.0–1 et seq.
Gifts, see 43 CFR 2110.0–1 et seq.
Leases, see 43 CFR 2120.0–2 et seq.
National Wildlife Refuge System, see 50 CFR Chap. I, Subchap. C.
Off-road vehicles, see 43 CFR 8340.0–1 et seq.
Visitor service, see 43 CFR 8360.0–3 et seq.
Wild horse and burro management, see 43 CFR 4700.0–1 et seq.

Notes of Decisions

Cooperative agreements   2
Fines   3
Rules and regulations   1

1. Rules and regulations

The Federal Range Code for Grazing Districts promulgated under this chapter is the law of the range and the activities of Federal range agents are controlled by its provisions. Hatahley v. U.S., Utah 1956, 76 S.Ct. 745, 351 U.S. 173, 100 L.Ed. 1065.

Rights to the use of the public domain must be determined in accordance with provisions of this chapter and the Range Code. U.S. v. Morrell, C.A.Utah 1964, 331 F.2d 498, certiorari denied 85 S.Ct. 146, 379 U.S. 879, 13 L.Ed.2d 86.

State Grazing Dist. v. Tysk. D.C.Mont.1968, 290 F.Supp. 227.

Rules and regulations respecting issuance and effect of grazing permits as promulgated by Secretary of the Interior have the force and effect of law, and the law existing at the time and place of making of permit agreement is as much a part thereof as though it were expressed therein. Wilkinson v. U.S., D.C.Or.1960, 189 F.Supp. 413.

2. Cooperative agreements

Under agreement, authorized by this chapter, between state cooperative grazing district and federal Bureau of Land Management whereby Bureau agreed to establish and fix, in cooperation with state grazing district, grazing capacity of federal and district land,

---

> The *U.S.C.A.* has the same text as it appears in the official edition of the *Code*, the *U.S.C.*

---

did not assess adequately the individual district or area situations to provide the local decision maker with the necessary data to analyze alternatives open to him and their consequences. Natural Resources Defense Council, Inc. v. Morton, D.C.D.C.1974, 388 F.Supp. 829, affirmed 527 F.2d 1386, 174 U.S.App.D.C. 77, certiorari denied 96 S.Ct. 3201, 427 U.S. 913, 49 L.Ed.2d 1204.

Regulations issued pursuant to this chapter, have effect of law. Buffalo Creek Co-op.

Tysk, D.C.Mont.1968, 290 F.Supp. 227.

3. Fines

$500 fine limitation under this chapter refers only to the penalty which can be imposed upon a criminal prosecution for a violation of this chapter or its implementing regulations; in no way does it limit the administrative sanctions otherwise available to the Secretary of the Interior. Diamond Ring Ranch, Inc. v. Morton, C.A.Wyo.1976, 531 F.2d 1397.

§ 315b.   Grazing permits; fees; vested water rights; permits not to create right in land

The Secretary of the Interior is hereby authorized to issue or cause to be issued permits to graze livestock on such grazing districts to such bona fide settlers, residents, and other stock owners as under his rules and regulations are entitled to participate in the use of the range, upon the payment annually of reasonable fees in each case to be fixed or determined from time to time in ac-

[Illustration 9–7]

PAGE FROM TITLE 43 U.S.C.A.

43 § 315b   PUBLIC LANDS   Ch. 8A

cordance with governing law. Grazing permits shall be issued only to citizens of the United States or to those who have filed the necessary declarations of intention to become such, as required by the naturalization laws, and to groups, associations, or corporations authorized to conduct business under the laws of the State in which the grazing district is located. Preference shall be given in the issuance of grazing permits to those within or near a district who are landowners engaged in the livestock business, bona fide occupants or settlers, or owners of water or water rights, as may be necessary to permit the proper use of lands, water or water rights owned, occupied, or leased by them, except that until July 1, 1935, no preference shall be given in the issuance of such permits to any such owner, occupant, or settler, whose rights were acquired between January 1, 1934, and December 31, 1934, both dates inclusive, except that no permittee complying with the rules and regulations laid down by the Secretary of the Interior shall be denied the renewal of such permit, if such denial will impair the

> This Illustration shows the references to the *United States Statutes at Large* and the Historical Notes summarizing the effect of the amendments on the original public law.

range depletion due to severe drought or other natural causes, or in case of a general epidemic of disease, during the life of the permit, the Secretary of the Interior is hereby authorized, in his discretion to remit, reduce, refund in whole or in part, or authorize postponement of payment of grazing fees for such depletion period so long as the emergency exists: *Provided further,* That nothing in this subchapter shall be construed or administered in any way to diminish or impair any right to the possession and use of water for mining, agriculture, manufacturing, or other purposes which has heretofore vested or accrued under existing law validly affecting the public lands or which may be hereafter initiated or acquired and maintained in accordance with such law. So far as consistent with the purposes and provisions of this subchapter, grazing privileges recognized and acknowledged shall be adequately safeguarded, but the creation of a grazing district or the issuance of a permit pursuant to the provisions of this subchapter shall not create any right, title, interest, or estate in or to the lands.

(June 28, 1934, c. 865, § 3, 48 Stat. 1270; Aug. 6, 1947, c. 507, § 1, 61 Stat. 790; Oct. 21, 1976, Pub.L. 94–579, Title IV, § 401(b)(3), 90 Stat. 2773.)

Historical Note

1976 Amendment. Pub.L. 94–579 substituted provisions authorizing fees to be fixed in accordance with governing law, for provisions authorizing fees to take into account public benefits to users of grazing districts over and above benefits accruing to users of forage resources and provisions requiring fees to consist of a grazing fee and a range-improvement fee.

1947 Amendment. Act Aug. 6, 1947, provided for method to be used by the Secretary of the Interior in fixing the amount of grazing fees and by assessing a separate grazing fee and a range-improvement fee.

Savings Provisions. Amendment by Pub.L. 94–579 not to be construed as terminating any valid lease, permit, patent, etc., existing on Oct. 21, 1976, see section 701 of Pub.L. 94–579 set out as a note under section 1701 of this title.

Legislative History. For legislative history and purpose of Act Aug. 6, 1947, see 1947 U.S.Code Cong.Service, p. 1638. See, also, Pub.L. 94–579, 1976 U.S.Code Cong. and Adm.News, p. 6175.

296

[Illustration 9–8]

PAGE FROM TITLE 43 U.S.C.A.

Ch. 8A GRAZING LANDS   43 § 315b
Note 2

Cross References ◄────────

Disposition of moneys received, see section 315i of this title.

────────► West's Federal Practice Manual

Permits and licenses, see § 5588.

Library References ◄────────

Public Lands ⇐17.
C.J.S. Public Lands §§ 19 to 23.

────────► Notes of Decisions

Death of permittee, termination of permits
    11
Denial of application 4
Drought conditions, termination of permits
    10
Grazing fees 5
Grazing preference 6
Indispensable parties 17
Injunction 20
Interest in lands 7
Issuance of permits 3
Jurisdiction 14
Mandamus 23
Nature and scope of permits 2

other lands under regulation providing that transfer of base property or part thereof would entitle transferee, if qualified, to so much of grazing privilege as was based thereon, and that original license or permit would be terminated or decreased to extent of such transfer, such regulation became a part of permit agreement between Government and decedent. Wilkinson v. U.S., D.C.Or.1960, 189 F.Supp. 413.

2. Nature and scope of permits

Secretary of Interior properly granted grazing permit to extent of number of animal

───────────────────────────

The important difference in the annotated sets of the *Code* is the digest of court cases that appear after each section of the *Code*. These digests assist in interpreting the meaning of the *Code* section.

Also illustrated are other research aids available in the *U.S.C.A.*

───────────────────────────

Review 22
Rights, title, or interest in lands 7
Rules and regulations 1
Safeguard of grazing privileges
    Generally 12
    Trespass on grazing lands 13
Termination of permits
    Generally 9
    Death of permittee 11
    Drought conditions 10
Trespass on grazing lands, safeguard of grazing privileges 13
Withdrawal of permits 8

1. Rules and regulations

A regulation that permit for grazing within National Forests shall have the full force and effect of a contract between the United States and the permittee means only that the United States will regard the terms of its permit as binding between it and other permit seekers. Osborne v. U.S., C.C.A.Ariz.1944, 145 F.2d 892.

Where deceased as owner of land was issued grazing permit with respect to certain

Udall, 1964, 340 F.2d 801, 119 U.S.App.D.C. 276, certiorari denied 85 S.Ct. 1448, 381 U.S. 904, 14 L.Ed.2d 285.

The grant of grazing permits is a use of the public domain for the benefit of the United States which receives a fee from the holders of preferential permits, and of those holding grazing permits. U.S. v. Morrell, C.A.Utah 1964, 331 F.2d 498, certiorari denied 85 S.Ct. 146, 379 U.S. 879, 13 L.Ed.2d 86.

Stock raisers qualifying for grazing permits under this chapter acquire rights which are something of real value and have their source in an enactment of Congress. McNeil v. Seaton, 1960, 281 F.2d 931, 108 U.S.App. D.C. 296.

A permit, granted owners of land in grazing district by district grazer, to graze additional number of cattle after they leased adjacent state land and two ranches, did not impliedly grant them exclusive right to graze livestock on public domain simply because it decreased lessor's grazing permit by equivalent number of sheep, in view of evidence that district grazer and advisory board did not intend to grant such owners exclusive grazing

297

[Illustration 9–9]

PAGE FROM TITLE 43 U.S.C.S.

GRAZING LANDS   **43 USCS § 315b**

life of the permit, the Secretary of the Interior is hereby authorized, in his discretion to remit, reduce, refund in whole or in part, or authorize postponement of payment of grazing fees for such depletion period so long as the emergency exists: Provided further, That nothing in this Act shall be construed or administered in any way to diminish or impair any right to the possession and use of water for mining, agriculture, manufacturing, or other purposes which has heretofore vested or accrued under existing law validly affecting the public lands or which may be hereafter initiated or acquired and maintained in accordance with such law. So far as consistent with the purposes and provisions of this Act, grazing privileges recognized and acknowledged

---

This illustrates the cross references and "Research Guide" (continued next Illustration) of the *U.S.C.S.* U.S.C.S. uses the text of the public law as it appears in the *United States Statutes at Large.*

---

law. for , and in fixing the amount of such fees the Secretary of the Interior shall take into account the extent to which such districts yield public benefits over and above those accruing to the users of the forage resources for livestock purposes. Such fees shall consist of a grazing fee for the use of the range, and a range-improvement fee which, when appropriated by the Congress, shall be available until expended solely for the construction, purchase, or maintenance of range improvements."

Other provisions:

Savings provisions. Act Oct. 21, 1976, P. L. 94-579, Title VII, § 701(a), 90 Stat. 2786, located at 43 USCS § 1701 note, provided that nothing in Act Oct. 21, 1976, shall be construed as terminating any valid lease, permit, patent, right-of-way, or other land use right or authorization existing on Oct. 21, 1976.

CODE OF FEDERAL REGULATIONS

Nondiscrimination in federally-assisted programs of Department of Interior; effectuation of Title VI of Civil Rights Act of 1964, 43 CFR Part 17.
Grazing administration, exclusive of Alaska, 43 CFR Part 4100.
Grazing administration; Alaska; livestock, 43 CFR Part 4200.
Grazing administration; Alaska; reindeer, 43 CFR Part 4300.
Wild free-roaming horse and burro protection, management and control, 43 CFR Part 4700.

CROSS REFERENCES

National Environmental Policy Act, 42 USCS §§ 4321–4347.
Lease of isolated or disconnected tracts for grazing, 43 USCS § 315m.
Range management, grazing leases and permits, 43 USCS § 1752.

RESEARCH GUIDE

Am Jur:
26 Am Jur 2d, Eminent Domain § 276.

253

[Illustration 9–10]

PAGE FROM TITLE 43 U.S.C.S.

---

43 USCS § 315b   PUBLIC LANDS

Forms:

5 Federal Procedural Forms L Ed, Condemnation of Property § 13:204.

14 Federal Procedural Forms L Ed, Public Lands and Property §§ 55:2, 55:7.

15 Am Jur Legal Forms 2d, Public Lands § 212:18.

Annotations:

Construction and application of Taylor Grazing Act [43 USCS §§ 315 et seq.] 42 ALR Fed 353.

Federal Tort Claims Act: Construction of provision excepting claims involving "discretionary function or duty." 99 ALR2d 1016.

INTERPRETIVE NOTES AND DECISIONS ◄──────────

I. IN GENERAL

1. Generally
2. Relation to other laws

II. ISSUANCE, REVOCATION, RENEWAL, AND MODIFICATION OF PERMITS

3. Issuance as discretionary
4. Fees

Annotations:

Construction and application of Taylor Grazing Act [43 USCS §§ 315 et seq.] 42 ALR Fed 353 (see, especially § 4 on Federal Supremacy).

2. Relation to other laws

Congress did not desire that restrictions contained in 43 USCS § 315b should be applicable to grazing leases in 43 USCS § 315m since if it

---

This Illustration shows the remainder of the Research Guide and the annotations, which are editorial enhancements to the annotated sets of the *Code*.

III. OTHER CONSIDERATIONS AFFECTING PERMITS

10. Grazing privileges on isolated tracts
11. Binding nature of permits
12. Preferences
13. Temporary licenses
14. Protection of permit rights
15. Grazing trespass

IV. PRACTICE AND PROCEDURE

16. Jurisdiction
17. Secretary as indispensable party
18. Pleadings
19. Representation at hearings
20. Evidence, generally
21. —Grazing trespass
22. Burden of proof
23. Review

I. IN GENERAL

1. Generally

Congress intended to grant to Secretary of Interior exclusive power over granting permits to use of public domain, and this power supersedes police power or regulations of state as to right of use of federal public domain. Noh v Babcock (1937, DC Idaho) 21 F Supp 519, revd on other grounds (CA9 Idaho) 99 F2d 738.

Grazing clearly may have severe impact on local environments so that grazing permit program of Bureau of Land Management is subject to requirement of filing environmental impact statements under National Environmental Policy Act (42 USCS §§ 4321–4347), plaintiffs have standing in federal court in action alleging that Bureau of Land Management's grazing permit program does not comply with National Environmental Policy Act's requirements regarding filing of environmental impact statements where all but one of plaintiffs are environmental organizations whose general objectives are to enhance and protect environment and insure proper resource management, and where remaining plaintiff is specialist in study of bighorn sheep, whose scientific, conservation and esthetic interests are allegedly jeopardized; motion for summary judgment was granted against Department of Interior officials where Bureau of Land Management's programmatic environmental impact statement was insufficient to comply with National Environmental Policy Act in that specific environmental effects of permits issued or renewed in each district must be assessed. Natural Resources Defense Council, Inc. v Morton (1974, DC Dist Col) 388 F Supp 829, affd without op 174 App DC 77, 527 F2d 1386, and affd without op 174 App DC 77, 527 F2d 1386, cert den 427 US 913, 49 L Ed 2d 1204, 96 S Ct 3201.

254

SECTION E. POPULAR NAMES FOR FEDERAL LAWS

It is common practice to refer to a publication by a popular name. With respect to federal legislation, this is generally the name that the public or media gives to a statute and it may describe its subject matter, *e.g.*, Gold Clause Act, or refer to its authors, *e.g.*, Taft–Hartley Act.

The tables of popular names of federal laws are designed to provide citations to acts when only the popular names are known. In addition to the popular name tables already discussed in this chapter in connection with *U.S.C., U.S.C.A.*, and *U.S.C.S.*, the following sources also provide popular name tables:

1. *Shepard's Acts and Cases by Popular Names.* This source is discussed in Chapter 15. [See Illustrations 6–15 and 9–11.]

2. *United States Code Congressional and Administrative News.* Since the 77th Congress, 2d Session, 1942, this source contains a table of "Popular Name Acts" for each session of Congress.

SECTION F. TABLES FOR FEDERAL LAWS

As has been noted, federal laws are first published in chronological order in the volumes of the *United States Statutes at Large.* A particular law may be on one topic, or may include matters on several different topics. Another law may amend one or several previous laws. Some are public laws of a general and permanent nature and are codified in the *U.S.C.*

This method of enacting and publishing laws makes it necessary to have tables that enable a researcher to trace each section of a law as it appears in the *United States Statutes at Large* and find out if it has been codified and, if so, its citation in the *U.S.C.* For example, assume a researcher has a citation to Section 3(2) of Pub. L. No. 101–376 and needs to find out where this section is in the *U.S.C.* To do so, the appropriate table of public laws has to be consulted. [See Illustration 9–14.]

From time to time, a particular Title of *U.S.C.* is completely revised with entirely new section numbers. One having a citation to the old Title must then consult a table to find out the section number in the new Title. [See Illustration 9–15.]

Each of the three sets containing the *Code* described *supra* has a volume or volumes that include cross-reference tables that serve various purposes. These include the following:

1. *Revised Title.* These tables show where sections of former Titles of the *U.S.C.* that have been revised are now incorporated within the *Code.*

2. *Revised Statutes of 1878.* This table shows where *Revised Statutes* citations are found in the *Code.*

3. *United States Statutes at Large.* This table shows where public laws as they appear in the *United States Statutes at Large* are found in the *Code.*

SECTION G. ILLUSTRATIONS: POPULAR
NAMES AND TABLES

[Illustration 9–11]

PAGE FROM SHEPARD'S ACTS AND CASES BY POPULAR NAMES

FEDERAL AND STATE ACTS CITED BY POPULAR NAME Tra

Tracy-Copps Act (Vocational Rehabilitation)
Ohio Laws Vol. 109, p. 310

Trade Act (Aleutian)
See U.S. Code tables
Nov. 16, 1990, P.L. 101-595, 104 Stat. 2979, §
601 et seq.

Trade Act of 1974
U.S. Code 1988 Title 19, §2101 et seq.
Jan. 3, 1975, P.L. 93-618, 88 Stat. 1978

Trade Act (Monopoly or Restraint of)
N.Y. General Business Law (Consol. Laws Ch.
20) §340 et seq.

Trade Act (Philippine)
U.S. Code 1970 Title 22, §1251 et seq.
Apr. 30, 1946, c. 244, 60 Stat. 141

**Trade Adjustment Assistance Reform and
Extension Act of 1986**
See U.S. Code tables

Trade and Competitiveness Act
See U.S. Code tables
U.S., Aug. 23, 1988, P.L. 100-418, 102 Stat.
1107

Trade and Customs Act
See U.S. Code tables
Aug. 20, 1990, P.L. 101-382, 104 Stat. 629

Trade and Development Enhancement Act of 1983
U.S. Code 1988 Title 12, §635o et seq.
U.S. Code 1988 Title 19, §§1671a, 1671b, 1671g
Nov. 30, 1983, P.L. 98-181, 97 Stat. 1153, §1,
Subsecs. 641 to 650

**Trade and Export Policy Commission Act
(Agriculture)**
U.S., Aug. 30, 1984, P.L. 98-412, 98 Stat.
1576, §1217 et seq

**Trade and Industrial Competitiveness Act
(International)**
N.Y. Agriculture and Markets (Consol. Laws,
Ch. 69) §1

Frequently, a public law will become known by a popular name. When only
the popular name is known, popular name tables enable one to locate the actual
citation(s). *See, e.g.,* Trade Act of 1974.

See next two Illustrations.

Trade Agreements Act
U.S. Code 1988 Title 19, §1351 et seq.
June 12, 1934, c. 474, 48 Stat. 943

Trade Agreements Act of 1979
U.S. Code 1988 Title 19, §2501 et seq.
July 26, 1979, P.L. 96-39, 93 Stat. 144

Trade Agreements Extension Act
U.S. Code 1988 Title 19, §1351 et seq.
Mar. 1, 1937, c. 22, 50 Stat. 24
Apr. 12, 1940, c. 96, 54 Stat. 107
June 7, 1943, c. 118, 57 Stat. 125
July 5, 1945, c. 269, 59 Stat. 410
June 26, 1948, c. 678, 62 Stat. 1053
Sept. 26, 1949 c 585, 63 Stat. 697
June 16, 1951, c. 141, 65 Stat. 72
Aug. 7, 1953, c. 348, 67 Stat. 472
July 1, 1954, c 445, 68 Stat. 360
June 21, 1955, c 169, 69 Stat. 162
Aug 20, 1958, P.L. 85-686, 72 Stat. 673

Trade and Agricultural Development Act
See U.S. Code tables
Nov 28, 1990, P.L. 101-624, 104 Stat. 3359, §§
1501 to 1578

U.S. Code 1988 Title 25, §§177, 179, 180, 193,
194, 201, 229, 230, 251, 263
July 22, 1790, c. 33, 1 Stat. 137
Mar. 1, 1793, c. 19, 1 Stat. 329
Mar. 3, 1799, c. 46, 1 Stat. 743
June 30, 1834, c. 161, 4 Stat. 729

Trade and Investment Act
U.S. Code 1988 Title 19, §§2112, 2114, 2114a,
2138, 2155, 2171, 2241, 2411 et seq
U.S. Code 1988 Title 22, §§3101, 3103, 3104
Oct. 30, 1984, P.L. 98-573, 98 Stat. 2948, Title
3

Trade and Manufacturing Site Act
Alk. Comp. Laws Anno. 1949, §47-2-71

Trade and Tariff Act of 1984
See U.S. Code tables
Oct 30, 1984, P.L. 98-573, 98 Stat. 2948

Trade Center Act
Wash. Rev. Code 1989, 53.29.010 et seq

363

[Illustration 9–12]

PAGE FROM POPULAR NAME TABLE IN U.S.C.A.

Trade Act of 1974
See, also, Jackson-Vanik Amendment
Pub.L. 93–618, Jan. 3, 1975, 88 Stat. 1978 (5 §§ 5312, 5314, 5315, 5316; 19 §§ 160, 162 to 164, 170a, 1202, 1303, 1315, 1321, 1330, 1332, 1333, 1337, 1352, 1484, 1515 note, 1516, 1862, 1863, 1872, 1981, 2101, 2102, 2111 to 2119, 2131 to 2137, 2151 to 2155, 2171, 2191 to 2194, 2211 to 2213, 2231, 2232, 2251 to 2254, 2271 to 2275, 2291 to 2298, 2311 to 2322, 2331, 2341 to 2352, 2354, 2355, 2371 to 2374, 2391 to 2395, 2411 to 2420, 2431 to 2441, 2461 to 2466, 2481 to 2487, 2491 to 2495, 2631, 2632; 26 § 3302; See 31 §§ 1513, 1514)

Pub.L. 96–39, § 3(e), Title I, § 106(b)(3), Title II, §§ 202(c)(1), 224, Title V, §§ 502(b), (c), 503, 507, Title VI, § 601(b), Title IX, §§ 901, 902, Title XI, §§ 1101, 1103, 1104, 1106(c), 1111(a), July 26, 1979, 93 Stat. 150, 193, 202, 235, 251, 253, 268, 295, 299, 307, 308, 310, 311, 315 (19 §§ 1315, 1352, 2101 note, 2111 note, 2112, 2119, 2131, 2135 note, 2155, 2192, 2194, 2211, 2251, 2253, 2411–2416, 2432, 2434, 2462, 2463, 2464, 2481, 2486)

Pub.L. 96–417, Title VI, § 612, Oct. 10, 1980, 94 Stat. 1746 (19 § 2322)

Pub.L. 97–35, Title XXV, §§ 2501 to 2504(a), 2505(a), 2506(2), 2507 to 2511, 2513(a) to (c), (d)(6), 2521 to 2527, Aug. 13, 1981, 95 Stat. 881 to 893 (19 §§ 2272, 2274, 2275, 2291 to 2293, 2296 to 2298, 2311, 2313, 2315, 2317 to 2319, 2343 to 2347, 2353, 2355)

Pub.L. 97–164, Title I, § 163(a)(5), Apr. 2, 1982, 96 Stat. 49 (19 § 2395)

Pub.L. 97–456, § 3(a) to (d)(4), Jan. 12, 1983, 96 Stat. 2504 (5 §§ 5312, 5314; 19 § 2171)

Pub.L. 98–120, §§ 2, 3, 4, Oct. 12, 1983, 97 Stat. 809 (19 §§ 2272, 2317, 2345)

Pub.L. 98–369, Title VI, §§ 2671 to 2673, 98 Stat. 1172 (19 §§ 2293, 2297, 2298, 2355)

Pub.L. 98–573, Title II, §§ 248, 249, Title V, §§ 502 to 505, 507, Title VII, § 703, Oct. 30, 1984, 98 Stat. 2988, 3018 to 3020, 3023, 3043 (19 §§ 1330, 2171, 2192, 2251, 2253, 2461, 2462, 2464 to 2466)

Pub.L. 99–47, § 8(b), June 11, 1985, 99 Stat. 84 (19 §§ 2112, 2462, 2463, 2464)

Pub.L. 99–107, § 3, Sept. 30, 1985, 99 Stat. 479

Pub.L. 99–155, § 2(b), Nov. 14, 1985, 99 Stat. 814

Pub.L. 99–181, § 2, Dec. 13, 1985, 99 Stat. 1172

Pub.L. 99–189, § 2, Dec. 18, 1985, 99 Stat. 1184

Pub.L. 99–272, Title XIII, §§ 13002 to 13008, 13023, Apr. 7, 1986, 100 Stat. 300 to 305, 307 (19 §§ 2171, prec. 2271 note, 2271, 2272, 2291, 2292, 2293, 2296, 2297, 2311, 2317, 2319, 2341 to 2344, 2346)

Pub.L. 99–514, § 1887, Oct. 22, 1986, 100 Stat. 2923 (19 §§ 2112, 2138, 2155, 2171, 2462, 2464)

Pub.L. 99–570, Title IX, §§ 9001, 9002, Oct. 27, 1986, 100 Stat. 3207–164, 3207–166 (19 §§ 2462, 2491 to 2495, 2702)

Pub.L. 100–203, Title IX, § 9504, Dec. 22, 1987, 101 Stat. 1330–382 (19 § 2171)

Pub.L. 100–204, Title VIII, § 806(a), (b), Dec. 22, 1987, 101 Stat. 1398 (19 § 2492)

Pub.L. 100–418, Title I, §§ 1104, 1107(b), 1111(a), 1213(a), 1214(j), 1215, 1301(a), (b), 1302, 102 Stat. 1132, 1135, 1163, 1176 (19 § 1 et. seq.)

Pub.L. 100–647, Title IX, §§ 9001(a)(1), (2)(A), (8), (10), (20), Nov. 10, 1988, 102 Stat. 3806 to 3808 (19 §§ 2131, 2212, 2253, 2254, 2296)

Pub.L. 100–690, Title IV, § 4408, Nov. 18, 1988, 102 Stat. 4281 to 4284 (19 § 2492)

Pub.L. 101–179, Title III, § 301, Nov. 28, 1989, 103 Stat. 1311 (19 § 2462)

Pub.L. 101–207, § 1(a), Dec. 7, 1989, 103 Stat. 1833 (19 § 2171)

Pub.L. 101–382, Title I, §§ 103(a), 131, 132(a) to (c), 136, Title II, § 226, Aug. 20, 1990, 104 Stat. 134, 643 to 647, 652, 660 (19 §§ 2171, 2191 to 2194, 2318, 2432, 2435, 2437, 2462, 2463)

Pub.L. 102–145, § 121, as added Pub.L. 102–266, § 102, Apr. 1, 1992, 106 Stat. 95 (19 § 2487)

Pub.L. 102–318, Title I, § 106(a), July 3, 1992, 106 Stat. 294 (19 § 2291)

Pub.L. 103–66, Title XIII, ch. 2, Subchapter D, Pt. I, §§ 13802(a), (b)(1), 13803, Aug. 10, 1993, 107 Stat. 667, 668 (19 §§ 2299, 2317, 2346, 2462, 2465)

Pub.L. 103–149, § 4(b)(9), Nov. 23, 1993, 107 Stat. 1506 (19 § 2462; 22 § 5001 note)

Pub.L. 103–182, Title III, §§ 315, 317(b), Title V, §§ 502, 503(a) to (d), 504, 505, 513, Dec. 8, 1993, 107 Stat. 2107, 2108, 2149 to 2152, 2156 (19 §§ 2242, 2252, 2271, 2272, 2273, 2275, 2317, 2322, 2331, 2395)

Pub.L. 103–465, Title I, §§ 127(f), 128, 129(a)(7), Title III, §§ 301 to 303, 311 to 314, Title IV, §§ 404 (e)(3), 421(a), Title VI, §§ 601(a), 621(a)(8), (9), 108 Stat. 4836, 4837, 4909, 4932, 4934, 4937, 4938, 4949, 4961, 4964, 4990, 4993, (19 §§ 1303 note, 2135 note, 2155, 2171, 2192, 2194, 2241, 2242, 2252 to 2254, 2411, 2414, 2416, 2420, 2463, 2465)

Pub.L. 104–65, § 21(b), Dec. 19, 1995, 109 Stat. 705 (19 § 2171)

Pub.L. 104–188, Title I, Subtitle J, § 1952, Aug. 20, 1996, 110 Stat. 1917 to 1926 (19 §§ 2461 to 2467)

[Illustration 9–13]

POPULAR NAME TABLE FROM TITLE 19, U.S.C.A.

POPULAR NAME ACTS

Popular Name	Sections
Tariff Act of 1930	1490 to 1510, 1512 to 1516a, 1520, 1521, 1523, 1524, 1526 to 1528, 1551, 1552 to 1565, 1581 to 1588, 1592, 1594 to 1595a, 1599, 1602 to 1615, 1617 to 1625, 1641, 1643 to 1645, 1648, 1649, 1651 to 1653, 1654, 1671 to 1671f, 1673 to 1673i, 1675, 1677 to 1677g
Tariff Classification Act of 1962	prec. 1202 notes, 1202, 1312, 1351 note
Tariff Schedules of the United States	1202
Tariff Schedules Technical Amendments Act of 1965	prec. 1202 notes, 1202, 1981 note
Trade Act of 1974	2101, 2102, 2111 to 2119, 2131 to 2137, 2151 to 2155, 2171, 2191 to 2194, 2211 to 2213, 2231, 2232, 2251 to 2253, 2271 to 2274, 2291 to 2298, 2311 to 2322, 2341 to 2354, 2371 to 2374, 2391 to 2394, 2411 to 2416, 2431 to 2441, 2461 to 2465, 2481 to 2487
Trade Agreements Act	1351, 1352, 1353, 1354
Trade Agreements Act of 1979	1202, 1202 notes, 1303, 1303 note, 1311, 1311 note, 1315, 1332, 1336, 1337, 1351, 1352, 1352 note, 1401a, 1401a note, 1402, 1466, 1500, 1514 to 1516a, 1671 notes, 1671 to 1671f, 1673 to 1673i, 1675, 1677 to 1677g, 1872, 2033, 2102 note, 2111 notes, 2112, 2112 note, 2119, 2119 note, 2131, 2135 notes, 2155, 2192, 2194, 2211, 2251, 2253, 2411 note, 2411 to 2416, 2432, 2434, 2435, 2462 to 2464, 2464 note, 2481, 2486, 2501 note, 2501 to 2504, 2511 note, 2511 to 2518, 2531 note, 2531 to 2533, 2541 to 2547, 2551 to 2554, 2561, 2562, 2571 to 2573, 2581, 2581 note, 2582
Trade Agreements Extension Act of 1937	1352
Trade Agreements Extension Act of 1940	1352
Trade Agreements Extension Act of 1943	1351, 1352
Trade Agreements Extension Act of 1945	1351, 1352, 1354
Trade Agreements Extension Act of 1949	1351, 1352, 1354
Trade Agreements Extension Act of 1951	1352, 1354, 1360, 1361, 1366
Trade Agreements Extension Act of 1953	1330, 1352
Trade Agreements Extension Act of 1954	1352
Trade Agreements Extension Act of 1955	1351, 1352
Trade Agreements Extension Act of 1958	1333, 1335 to 1337, 1351, 1352, 1360
Trade Expansion Act of 1962	prec. 1202 note, 1323, 1351, 1352, 1352 note, 1801, 1806, 1821, 1823, 1862, 1863, 1872, 1881, 1885, 1887, 1888, 1916, 1918 to 1920, 1981, 1982
Trade Fair Act of 1959	1751 to 1756
Underwood Tariff Act	124, 128, 130, 131
Unfair Practices in Imports Acts	1337, 1337a

[Illustration 9–14]

PAGE FROM TABLES VOLUME—U.S.C.S.

103 Stat					STATUTES AT LARGE					101st Cong

Pub. L.	Section	Stat. Page	USCS Title	Section	Status	Pub. L.	Section	Stat. Page	USCS Title	Section	Status
				1990 August—Cont'd						**1990 August—Cont'd**	
101-366—Cont'd						101-371		453		Spec.	Un-class.
	102(b)	431	38	prec. 4141	Added						
			38	4141	Added	101-372		454		Spec.	Un-class.
		435	38	4142	Added						
	102(c)	436	38	4107(e)(1)	Amd.	101-373		455		Spec.	Un-class.
	102(d)		38	prec. 4101	Amd.						
	103	437	38	4107(e)(5)	Amd.	101-374	1	456	42	201 nt.	New
	104		38	4141 nt.	New		2(a)		42	290aa-12(a)	Amd.
	201(a)(1)		38	620C	Added		2(b)(1)		42	290aa-12(d)	Rpld.
	201(a)(2)	438	38	prec. 601	Amd.		2(b)(2)		42	290aa-12(e)- (g)	Redes.
	201(b)		38	620C nt.	New					[(c), (e), (f)]	
	202(a)		38	5051	Amd.		2(b)(3)		42	290aa-12(c),	
	202(b)(1)		38	5053(a)	Amd.					(d)	Added
	202(b)(2)		38	5053(b)	Amd.		2(c)(1)		42	290aa-12(g)(1)	Amd.
	203(1)	439	38	4114(a)(3)(A)	Amd.		2(c)(2)		42	290aa-12(g)(3)	Amd.
	203(2)		38	4114(a)(3)(C)	Amd.		2(c)(3)	457		Appn.	Un-class.
	204		38	612A nt.	Amd.						
	205(a)(1)		38	prec. 4351	Amd.		2(d)			Spec.	Un-class.
			38	4351	Added						
		440	38	4352	Added		2(e)		42	290aa-12 nt.	New
			38	4353	Added		3(a)		42	290cc-2	Amd.
			38	4354	Added						

> This Table lists all Public Laws and indicates where each section has been codified in the *U.S.C.*
>
> For example, Section 3(2) of Pub. L. No. 101–376 can be located in Title 5 § 7701(j) in the *U.S.C.*, or the *U.S.C.A.*, or the *U.S.C.S.*

Pub. L.	Section	Stat. Page	USCS Title	Section	Status	Pub. L.	Section	Stat. Page	USCS Title	Section	Status
	205(c)(2)		38	4302(a)(1), (b)	Amd.						class.
	205(c)(3)		38	4304(1)(A), (2) (D), (5)	Amd.						
	206(a)		38	1784A	Added				**1990 August 17**		
	206(b)	442	38	1434 nt.	New	101-376	1	461	5	7501 nt.	New
	206(c)		38	prec. 1770	Amd.		2(a)		5	7511	Amd.
	206(d)		5	552a nt.	New		2(b)	462	5	4303(e)	Amd.
	207		38	1622 nt.	New		2(c)		5	4303 nt.	New
	208(a)	443	38	1791(b)	Amd.		3(1)		5	7701(k)(j)	Redes.
	208(b)		38	1791 nt.	New		3(2)		5	7701(j)	Added
	209			Spec.	Un-class.		4	463	5	4303 nt.	New
101-367	1, 2	445		Spec.	Un-class.	101-377	1	464	16	430g-4	New
							2		16	430g-5	New
101-368	1	446	42	201 nt.	New		3	465	16	430g-6	New
	2(a)(1)		42	247b(j)(2)			4		16	430g-7	New
	2(a)(2)		42	247b(k)(2)(A)- (D)	Amd.		5	466	16	430g-8	New
							6	467	16	430g-9	New
	2(b)		42	247b(f)	Added		7		16	430g-10	New
	2(c)		42	247b(j)(2)	Amd.	101-378	Title I				
101-369	1	448	9	prec. 301	Amd.		101	468		Spec.	Un-class.
			9	301	Added		Title II				
			9	302	Added		201			Spec.	Un-class.
			9	303	Added						
		449	9	304	Added		202			Spec.	Un-class.
			9	305	Added						
			9	306	Added		203	469		Spec.	Un-class.
			9	307	Added						
	2	450	9	prec. 1	Amd.		204			Spec.	Un-class.
	3		9	301 nt.	New						
101-370	1	451	49				205(a)	470	16	1132 nt.	Amd.
			Appx.	1475(d)(4)	Added		205(b)			Spec.	Un-class.
	2		49				Title III				
			Appx.	1357(g)	Amd.		301(1)	471	43	1629c(d)(1)(A)	Amd.
	3	452	49				301(2)		43	1629c(d)(2)(B) (i)](d)(2)(B)]	Redes.
			Appx.	1482 nt.	New						

400

[Illustration 9–15]

PAGE FROM TABLES VOLUME—U.S.C.S.

T 38   REVISED TITLES

TITLE 38—VETERANS' BENEFITS

[This title was enacted into law by Act Sept. 2, 1958, P. L. 85-857, § 1, 72 Stat. 1105. This table shows where sections of former Title 38 are incorporated in revised Title 38]

Title 38 Former Sections	Title 38 New Sections	Title 38 Former Sections	Title 38 New Sections
1–3	Omitted	16b	5203
4	214	16c	5204
5–9	Omitted	16d	5205
10	215	16e	5206
11	201, 210(b)	16f	5207
11a	101(1), 210(a), 210(b)	16g	5208
11a-1	Omitted	16h	601(4), 5209
11a-2	211(a)	16i	5210
11a-3	233	16j	Omitted
11b	5006	17	5220
11c–11d-1	Omitted	17a	5221
11e	214	17b	5222
11f	Omitted	17c	5223
11g	202	17d	5224
11h	3303	17e	5225
11i	5014	17f	5226
11j	233(1), (2)	17g	5227
11k	233(4)	17h	5228
11l	3204	17i	Omitted
12	Omitted	17j	210(c)

When a Title of the *U.S.C.* is revised with new section numbering, a table similar to this one is prepared and can be consulted in the Tables Volumes of the various sets containing the *Code*.

13e	4206	34	902
13f	4207	35	Omitted
13g	4208	36	3102(b)
14	5101	37	101(4)
14a	5102	38	107(a)
14b	5103	39, 39a	505
14c	5104	41	3002
14d	5105	42–49	Omitted
14e	214	49a	3107
15	4101	50	3020
15a	4102	51–57	Omitted
15b	4103	58	See 3011
15c	4104	71–75	Omitted
15d	4105	76	111(a)–(c)
15e	4106	77	111(d)
15f	4107	91–95	Omitted
15g	4108	96	See 3021
15h	4109	97	Omitted
15i	4110	101	3402, 3403
15j	4111	102	3404
15k	4112	103	3405
15l	4113	104	Omitted
15m	4114	111	3404
15n	4115	112–116	Omitted
16	5201	121–124	Omitted
16a	5202	125	3301

92

SECTION H. FEDERAL LEGISLATION:
RESEARCH PROCEDURE

1. Public Laws in Force

To determine whether there are any *Code* sections on any given topic, the following procedures may be used:

a. *Index Method.* Check first the general index to one of the sets of the *Code.* As both *U.S.C.A.* and *U.S.C.S.* have more current indexes, it is usually better to start with either of these rather than the official *U.S.C.* The index will lead to the *Code* Title under which the subject being researched will be found. Next, check the index to the individual *Code* Title in either of the annotated editions. The individual *Code* Title indexes may provide a better guide to the subject matter of the Title than the entries located in the general index.

b. *Topic or Analytic Method.* If one is familiar with a *Code* Title that includes the topic under research, *e.g.,* bankruptcy or copyright, it may be useful to obtain the volumes covering the Title and consult the outline or "table of contents" preceding each Title. This listing will provide the headings for each section and, therefore, can narrow the research path.

c. *Definition Method.* The general indexes of all three sets of the *Code* have a main entry, "Definitions," and list under it all terms that have been defined within the *Code.* This method may be a quick entry into the *Code.* For example, if one were doing research in labor relations and wanted to determine if the term *supervisor* is defined in the *Code,* the following relevant entries would be noted in the *U.S.C.A.:*

SUPERVISOR

Labor management relations, 29 § 142.

Federal employees, 5 § 7103

Federal Service, 5 § 7101 nt, EON 11491

National Labor Relations Act, 29 § 152.

Similar information can be found in the *U.S.C.* and the *U.S.C.S.*

2. Public Laws No Longer in Force

When interested in locating public laws that are no longer in force, the following indexes should be consulted:

a. Middleton G. Beaman & A.K. McNamara, *Index Analysis of the Federal Statutes, 1789–1873* (1911).

b. Walter H. McClenon & Wilfred C. Gilbert, *Index to the Federal Statutes, 1874–1931* (1933).

To locate the text of public laws no longer in force, the superseded editions of the *U.S.C.* may be consulted. As indicated, the *U.S.C.* began in 1926 and since 1934 has been published every six years with cumulative supplements issued between editions. Many law libraries keep the superseded editions or have them in microform. A microfiche collection of historical compilations of federal laws, *Hein's Early Federal Laws* (1992–) can be consulted to locate federal laws from the 18th and 19th centuries.

3. Private, Temporary, and Local Laws

Occasionally, there is the need to locate a private or temporary or local law that was never included in the *U.S.C.* These laws are in the *United States Statutes at Large* and can be consulted if the date of enactment is known. If this date is not known, it becomes more difficult to locate such laws. The *Consolidated Index to the Statutes at Large of the United States of America from March 4, 1789 to March 3, 1903,* may be used to find laws within the time frame covered. After that period the volumes of the *United States Statutes at Large* must be checked individually.

The *United States Code Service* has a volume, *Notes to Uncodified Laws and Treaties,* that contains interpretive notes and decisions for laws that were not classified to the *U.S.C.* or that were classified to the *U.S.C.* but subsequently eliminated. The text of the law is not included.

4. Shepard's Citations

Shepard's United States Citations can be used to determine the history and treatment of a federal statute. This unit of Shepard's is discussed in detail in Chapter 15.

SECTION I. SUMMARY

1. Slip Law

This is the first official form of publication for federal legislation. Each law is separately published.

2. United States Statutes at Large

    a. Published after each session of Congress.

    b. Arrangement—chronological by date of passage of the law.

    c. Grouped into public and private laws in separate sections.

    d. Volumes 1–8 were published retrospectively. Volumes 1–5 contain public laws arranged in chronological order; volume 6 consists of private laws; volumes 7 and 8 contain treaties.

    e. Volumes 9–49 vary in the number of Congresses included in the volume; beginning with volume 50 each volume includes the laws of one session of Congress.

    f. Marginal notes, included since volume 33, indicate the House or Senate bill number, Public Law number, and date.

    g. Each volume has a subject index.

    h. From 1957 through 1976, each volume contained a table indicating how each public law in that volume affected previous public laws.

  i.   Beginning in 1991, each volume contains a popular name index.

3. Methods of Codification (see Section C)

4. Features Common to Codes

  a.   Constitutions.

  b.   Laws, or sections thereof, compiled in topical or subject arrangement.

  c.   Historical notes.

  d.   Tables.

  e.   Indexes.

  f.   Tables of popular names of laws.

  g.   Supplementation.

5. United States Revised Statutes

  a.   1875 edition—rewritten and enacted into positive law, with inaccuracies and unauthorized changes, all public laws of a general and permanent nature, then in force.

  b.   1878 edition—published to correct mistakes in 1875 edition but never reenacted into positive law.

6. United States Code, Current Edition

  a.   Current official *Code*.

  b.   Covers public laws of a general and permanent nature, in force.

  c.   Arranged alphabetically under 50 Titles.

  d.   Supplemented annually by cumulative bound volumes.

  e.   Multi-volume index.

  f.   Numerous tables.

  g.   *Prima facie* evidence of law, except for Titles listed in 1 U.S.C. § 204.

  h.   Cross references to other pertinent sections of the *Code*.

  i.   New edition every six years.

7. United States Code Annotated (West Group)

  a.   Text of public laws of a general and permanent nature, in force, as laws appear in *U.S.C.*

  b.   Arranged under the 50 Titles of the *U.S.C.*

  c.   Annotations (digests of cases interpreting sections of the *Code*) are complete, covering federal and state court cases.

  d.   Historical notes.

  e.   Kept current by cumulative pocket and pamphlet supplements and replacement volumes.

f. Multi-volume paperback General Index issued annually.

g. Popular Name Tables.

h. Title index in last volume of each Title.

i. Tables volumes.

j. References to other West publications and to Topic and Key Numbers.

k. Federal court rules.

l. Available online in WESTLAW.

8. United States Code Service (LEXIS Law Publishing)

a. Covers public laws of a general and permanent nature, in force, as the laws appear in the *United States Statutes at Large.*

b. Annotations include selected federal and state court cases and federal administrative agency decisions.

c. Historical notes.

d. Separate volume of Notes (annotations) to Uncodified Laws and Treaties.

e. Tables volumes.

f. Multi-volume Revised General Index and each Title has an index covering its subject matter.

g. References to other publications in *Total–Client Service Library* and to law review articles.

h. Federal laws by popular name.

i. Kept up to date by cumulative annual pocket and pamphlet supplements and replacement volumes.

j. Federal court rules.

k. Available online in LEXIS–NEXIS.

9. Tables for Federal Laws

Tables translating *United States Statutes at Large* or the *Revised Statutes of 1878* citations into *U.S.C.* citations are found in *U.S.C., U.S.C.A.,* and *U.S.C.S.* Tables also contain transfer tables for revised Titles.

10. Popular Names of Federal Laws

a. Tables found in *U.S.C., U.S.C.A.,* and *U.S.C.S.* Also listed under popular name in general indexes.

b. *Shepard's Acts and Cases by Popular Names—Federal and State.* Kept current by cumulative pamphlets.

c. Since 1942, *United States Code Congressional and Administrative News* includes a table of public laws by popular name.

Chapter 10

FEDERAL LEGISLATIVE HISTORIES*

SECTION A. LEGISLATIVE HISTORIES
IN LEGAL RESEARCH

A law is the means by which a legislative body expresses its intent to declare, command, or prohibit some action. In the traditional sense, a *legislative history* is the term used to designate the documents that contain the information considered by the legislature prior to deciding whether or not to enact a law. Therefore, one purpose of a legislative history is to facilitate one's understanding of the reasons behind an enactment of a law or the failure of a bill to become law. For pending legislation, researchers may need to find the current status of the proposed legislation and to locate documents generated during the progress of this legislation through Congress. Often, the status of pending legislation is important to certain groups and to their representatives to influence whether or not pending legislation becomes a public law.

Because an act of the legislature is usually prospective and is not always drafted in the most precise language, a legislative history most frequently will be used to determine the purpose of a law or to ascertain the meaning of specific language used in the law. Courts often look to certain legislative documents to determine the intent of a legislative body in passing a law or to determine the meaning of specific language used in a law.[1] Some differences of opinion exist as to the extent to which legislative histories should be used to determine the meaning of a law.[2] This conflict has led to a re-examination of legislative histories as a

---

* Prepared for this edition by Bonnie L. Koneski–White, Law Librarian, Western New England College.

[1] "But, while the clear meaning of statutory language is not to be ignored, 'words are inexact tools at best,' ... and hence it is essential that we place the words of a statute in their proper context by resort to the legislative history." Tidewater Oil Co. v. United States, 409 U.S. 151, 157 (1972).

[2] *See, e.g.,* Schwegmann Bros. v. Calvert Distillers Corp., 341 U.S. 384, 395 (1951) (Justice Jackson in a concurring opinion indicating that "we should not go beyond Committee reports"); National Small Shipments Traffic Conference, Inc. v. Civil Aeronautics Board, 618 F.2d 819, 828 (D.C. Cir. 1980) (court warns against the manufacture of legislative histories). *But see* Schwenke v. Secretary of Interior, 720 F.2d 571, 575 (9th Cir. 1983) (reversing the lower court for failure to consider legislative history of the statute in question). *See also Conference on Statutory Interpretation: The Role of Legislative History in Judicial Interpretation: A Discussion Between Kenneth W. Starr and Judge Abner J. Mikva,* 1987 Duke L.J. 361.

An increasingly vocal group of federal judges led by Justice Antonin Scalia of the Supreme Court of the United States argue that legislative history has become an unreliable

subject in law school legal research courses.[3] However, these conflicts are more academic than practical because the use of legislative histories is an essential component of contemporary litigation.

Investigation into the success or failure of a bill to become law, research to find the current status of pending legislation, and questions concerning the purpose of a law or the meaning of specific language used in legislation may be found in the language of the bill introduced into the legislature, the subsequent amendments to the bill, the reports of legislative committees to which the bill was assigned, the debates about the bill, and other documents issued in consideration of the bill.

guide to congressional intent because it is so often distorted by lobbyists and congressional staff members. *See, e.g.,* Charles Rothfeld, *Read Congress's Words, Not Its Mind, Judges Say,* N.Y. TIMES, Apr. 14, 1989, at B5, col. 3. *See generally* U.S. DEPARTMENT OF JUSTICE, OFFICE OF LEGAL POLICY, USING AND MISUSING LEGISLATIVE HISTORY: A RE-EVALUATION OF THE STATUS OF LEGISLATIVE HISTORY IN STATUTORY INTERPRETATION 120 (1989), which offers four basic principles intended to "reinforce certain traditional axioms of statutory analysis, consistent with original meaning jurisprudence." For a look at the use of legislative history during a recent Supreme Court term, *see* Stephanie Wald, *The Use of Legislative History in Statutory Interpretation Cases in the 1992 U.S. Supreme Court Term; Scalia Rails but Legislative History Remains on Track,* 23 Sw. U. L. REV. 47 (1993).

For discussions of the use, misuse, abuse, or appropriateness of legislative histories in judicial decision making, see Anthony D'Amato, *Can Legislatures Constrain Judicial Interpretation of Statutes?,* 75 VA. L. REV. 561 (1989); George Costello, *Sources of Legislative History as Aids to Statutory Construction* (1989); Jeffrey J. Soles, *Changing the Past: The Role of Legislative History in Statutory Interpretation,* United States ex rel. Bergen v. Lawrence, 6 COOLEY L. REV. 361 (1989); George A. Costello, *Reliance on Legislative History in Interpreting Statutes,* CRS REV., Jan.–Feb. 1990, at 29; Louis Fisher, *Statutory Interpretation by Congress and the Courts,* CRS REV., Jan.–Feb. 1990, at 32; Patricia M. Wald, *The Sizzling Sleeper: The Use of Legislative History in Construing Statutes in the 1988–89 Term of the United States Supreme Court,* 39 AM. U.L. REV. 277 (1990); Nicholas S. Zeppos, *Legislative History and the Interpretation of Statutes: Toward a Fact-Finding Model of Statutory Interpretation,* 76 VA. L. REV. 1295 (1990); Leigh Ann McDonald, *The Role of Legislative History in Statutory Interpretation: A New Era After the Resignation of Justice William Brennan?* 56 MO. L. REV. 121 (1991); Stephen Breyer, *On the Uses of Legislative History in Interpreting Statutes,* 65 S. CAL. L. REV. 845 (1992); William T. Mayton, *Law Among the Pleonasms: The Futility and Aconstitutionality of Legislative History in Statutory Interpretation,* 41 EMORY L.J. 113 (1992); W. David Slawson, *Legislative History and the Need to Bring Statutory Interpretation Under the Rule of Law,* 44 STAN. L. REV. 383 (1992); Jack Schwartz & Amanda Stakem Conn, *The Court of Appeals at the Cocktail Party: The Use and Misuse of Legislative History,* 54 Md. L. Rev. 432 (1995); Randall W. Quinn, *The Supreme Court's Use of Legislative History in Interpreting the Federal Securities Laws,* 22 SEC. REG. L.J. 262 (1994). For a discussion of how legislative history has been used in one specialized area of the law, see Gregory E. Maggs, *The Secret Decline of Legislative History: Has Someone Heard a Voice Crying in the Wilderness,* 1994 PUB. INTEREST L. REV. 57.

[3] *See, e.g.,* Peter C. Schanck, *An Essay on the Role of Legislative Histories in Statutory Interpretation,* 80 LAW LIBR. J. 391 (1988); J. Myron Jacobstein & Roy M. Mersky, *Congressional Intent and Legislative Histories—Analysis or Psychoanalysis?,* 82 LAW LIBR. J. 297 (1990); Peter C. Schanck, *The Only Game in Town: Contemporary Interpretive Theory, Statutory Construction, and Legislative Histories,* 82 LAW LIBR. J. 419 (1990). For references to additional sources regarding the uses of legislative histories, *see* Peter C. Schanck, *The Use of Legislative Histories in Statutory Interpretation: A Selected and Annotated Bibliography,* LEGAL REFERENCE SERVICES Q., No. 1, 1993, at 5.

In this chapter, legislative history will be discussed in terms of identifying which documents are pertinent to one's research, becoming familiar with finding aids that will provide citations and references to such documents, and obtaining the documents themselves.

Once the concept of what is contained in a legislative history is understood, the location and compilation of the history of a federal law becomes easier.[4] The techniques for identifying and locating legislative documents should provide assistance for all purposes.

As the term "legislative history" denotes, the true components of a legislative history are the documents that contain the words expressing the intent of the members of Congress. However, ancillary documents, such as Presidential messages, testimony of witnesses at hearings, etc., often provide assistance in accomplishing the purposes of doing a legislative history. Therefore, these sources are also included in the discussion in this chapter.

Chapter 9, Federal Legislation, should be consulted for a discussion of enacted legislation and for the sources containing those laws.

SECTION B. DOCUMENTS RELEVANT TO A FEDERAL LEGISLATIVE HISTORY

Before compiling a federal legislative history, it is necessary to be familiar with the documents that may be relevant to establishing legislative intent.[5] These documents can typically be found in federal government depository libraries, through commercial online vendors, through the Internet, and are available for purchase from the Government Printing Office.

1. Congressional Bills

Prior to its enactment as a law, a proposed piece of legislation is introduced as a bill or a joint resolution into either the House of Representatives, where it is assigned an H.R. or H.J. Res. number, or the Senate, where it is assigned either an S. or S.J. Res. number.[6] [See Illustration 10–8.] This number stays with the bill until it is passed or until the end of the Congress in which it was introduced. When a bill is amended, it is usually reprinted with the amending language, or the amendment or amendments are printed separately. The comparison of the language of the bill as introduced and its subsequent amendments, with the final language of the bill as passed (the public law), may reveal

---

[4] This Chapter is devoted exclusively to a discussion of federal legislative histories. The documents for compiling a state legislative history are often more difficult to obtain and rarely are as extensive as those of the federal government. Chapter 11, Section G discusses state legislative histories.

[5] Because legislative histories consist primarily of documents produced during the consideration of the bill by Congress, the sources cited in Chapter 9, note 2, should be consulted.

[6] *See* Chapter 9, note 3.

legislative intent since the insertion or deletion of language may indicate a legislative choice.[7]

Therefore, the researcher will need to identify and obtain each of the following documents that exist for the research being done:

    a.   The bill as originally introduced in the House or Senate.

    b.   The bill with any amendments.

    c.   The bill as it passed in the originating body and as introduced into the other house.

    d.   The bill as amended by the second house.

    e.   The bill as it is passed by the second chamber.

    f.   The bill as amended by a conference committee of the House and Senate.

    g.   The public law.

2. Committee Reports

After a bill is introduced into either the House or the Senate, it is assigned to one or more committees that have jurisdiction over the subject matter of the bill. The committee's obligation is to consider the bill and to decide whether or not to recommend its passage. If passage is not recommended or if no action is taken during the Congress in which the bill was introduced, the bill "dies in committee." If the committee recommends passage, it does so in a written committee report that usually sets forth: the revised text of the bill, if any; the changes made in committee; an analysis of the intent and the content of the proposed legislation; and the rationale behind the committee's recommendation.

When the bill is approved by the house in which it was introduced, it is then sent to the other house and again assigned to an appropriate committee or committees where it receives similar consideration.[8] When a bill is passed by both houses, but in different versions, a conference committee is convened, which consists of Representatives and Senators who are restricted to reconciling differing language in the respective versions of the bill. The conference committee issues a conference committee report, which contains recommendations for reconciling the differences between the two bills and a statement explaining the effect of the actions.

Committee reports are usually considered the most important documents in determining the legislative intent of Congress because the reports reflect the understanding of those members of Congress closely

---

[7] United States v. St. Paul M. & M. Ry. Co., 247 U.S. 310, 318 (1918). *See also* Donovan v. Hotel, Motel & Restaurant Employees and Bartenders Union, Local 19, 700 F.2d 539, 543, n.4 (9th Cir. 1983).

[8] After a bill passes one house, it is thereafter referred to as an *act*. An act only becomes a law when it successfully makes its way through the entire legislative process as described in this chapter.

involved in studying the subject matter of and then drafting the proposed legislation.[9] [See Illustration 10–1.]

Therefore, the researcher will need to identify and obtain each of the following documents that exist for the research being done:

a.   The reports of the committees of both houses to which the bill was assigned.

b.   The report of the conference committee of the House and Senate. This report is usually issued as a House report.[10]

3.   Committee Hearings

Hearings, which may be held by the committees of the House and Senate, are generally of two types. A hearing may be held to investigate matters of general concern, *e.g.,* AIDS. The second type is the most prevalent, that is, hearings related to proposed legislation. These hearings are held after a bill is assigned to a Congressional committee.

The primary function of this type of hearing is to provide committee members with information that may be useful in their consideration of the bill. Interested persons or experts on the subject of the bill may be requested to express their opinions on the bill's purpose or effect and may suggest changes or amendments to the bill. In most instances, transcripts of the hearings are published. When published, hearings contain the transcript of testimony, the questions of committee members and the answers of the witnesses, statements and exhibits submitted by interested parties, and occasionally the text of the bill that is the subject of the hearing.

It is important to remember that hearings are not held on all legislation and that not all hearings are published. In addition, hearings that are pertinent to the intent of a public law may have been held during a session of Congress prior to the one in which the law was enacted. Hearings also might have been held on proposed legislation that contains similar provisions to the law being researched. Therefore, it may be beneficial to extend the search for hearings beyond a particular session, or for legislation other than the law being researched. The last caveat is especially beneficial if either no hearings were held or if the hearings were not published for the legislation being researched.

Committee hearings are technically not part of a legislative history since they do not contain Congressional deliberations but rather the views of non-legislators of what the bill under consideration should accomplish. Often senators and members of the House of Representatives may present testimony. Therefore, hearings should be consulted

---

[9] Gwendolyn B. Folsom, Legislative History: Research for the Interpretation of Laws 33 (1972). *See also* Zuber v. Allen, 396 U.S. 168, 186 (1969); Stevenson v. J.C. Penney Co., 464 F. Supp. 945, 948–49 (N.D. Ill. 1979).

[10] Under the rules of Congress, the conference report is also to be printed as a Senate report. This requirement frequently is waived by the unanimous consent of the Senate. Enactment of a Law: Procedural Steps in the Legislative Process, S. Doc. No. 20, 97th Cong., 1st Sess. (1981).

when available because they frequently contain information helpful to understanding why Congress adopted or did not adopt certain language based on the testimony heard and to find the testimony of legislators.

Therefore, the researcher will need to identify and obtain each of the following documents that exist for the research being done:

a. The hearings held by the committees to which the bill was assigned.

b. The hearings from previous Congressional sessions concerning the subject matter of the bill being researched.

c. The hearings on related bills or bills containing similar provisions that may have been held in prior Congresses.

4. Congressional Debates

Debate on the floor of the House or Senate on a bill can take place at almost any time during the legislative process, but most frequently the debate occurs after a bill has been reported out of the committee to which it was assigned.[11] During the debates, amendments may be proposed, arguments for and against the pending bill and amendments are made, and discussion and explanation of ambiguous or controversial provisions occur. Some authorities claim that floor statements of legislators on the substance of a bill under discussion are not to be considered by courts as determinative of Congressional intent.[12] The courts, however, generally do give some weight to such statements, especially when they are made by the bill's sponsors, whose stated intention is to clarify or explain the bill's purpose.[13] Such statements are published in the *Congressional Record* and are usually included as an integral part of legislative histories.[14]

[11] Most public laws are passed without ever being debated on the floor of Congress. Usually, only bills of great public interest receive such debate.

[12] S. & E. Contractors, Inc. v. United States, 406 U.S. 1, 13 n.9 (1972).

[13] Federal Energy Admin. v. Algonquin SNG, Inc., 426 U.S. 548, 564 (1976). *But see* State of Ohio v. United States Environmental Protection Agency, 997 F.2d 1520, 1532 (D.C. Cir. 1993). *But see* Lori L. Outzs, *A Principled Use of Congressional Floor Speeches in Statutory Interpretation*, 28 COLUM. J. L. & SOC. PROBS. 297 (1995).

[14] The *Congressional Record* may not truly reflect what was actually said on the floor of either house of Congress, since members have the right to correct their remarks before publication. Studies have shown that this privilege generally is not abused since the majority of revisions are syntactical or otherwise within the bounds of propriety. Prior to 1978, members of Congress were allowed to insert remarks into the *Congressional Record* that were not delivered on the floor of either house without any indication that this was the process followed. Effective March 1, 1978, Congress changed its rules to provide that statements in the *Congressional Record* were to be identified when no part of them was spoken on the floor of either house of Congress. In such instances, a *bullet* symbol (•) precedes and follows the statement. If, however, any part of a statement was delivered orally, the entire statement appears without the symbol. 124 CONG. REC. 3852 (1978). *See also* Donald J. Dunn, *Letter to the Editor*, 14 GOV'T PUBLICATIONS REV. 113 (1987) (updating a part of Michelle M. Springer, *The Congressional Record: "Substantially a Verbatim Report"?*, 13 GOV'T PUBLICATIONS REV. 371 (1986)). *Note:* Commencing with vol. 132, no. 115 of the *Congressional Record* (September 8, 1986), the House of Representatives abolished

Therefore, the researcher will need to identify and obtain the debates, if any, on the floor of both houses of Congress for the research being done. [See Illustration 10–10.]

5. Committee Prints

Committee prints are special studies in specific subject areas prepared for the use and reference of Congressional committees and their staffs. These publications are of a varied nature, from bibliographies, analyses of similar bills on a subject, excerpts from hearings, etc.[15]

Therefore, the researcher will need to identify and obtain those documents that may have some relation to the present legislation under consideration for the research being done.

6. Presidential or Executive Agency Documents

Occasionally, other documents are relevant to developing a legislative history but since the documents are not developed by Congress, they are not primary sources for legislative intent. These may consist of Presidential messages[16] or reports and documents of federal agencies. The President of the United States or members of an executive agency, who usually act through the President, often send proposed legislation to Congress for consideration. Presidential messages or executive agency memoranda may accompany the proposal to Congress. These documents explain the purpose and describe the President's or agency's intent of the legislation.

After a bill passes Congress, it is sent to the President. If the President signs or vetoes the legislation, the President may add a signing statement or veto message, which incorporates the President's rationale for the action taken on the legislation.

Therefore, the researcher will need to identify and obtain each of the following documents that exist for the research being done:

a. Presidential or executive agency reports accompanying proposed legislation sent to Congress by the President.

b. Presidential signing statements or veto messages.

the *bullet* symbol and substituted instead the use of a different style of typeface to indicate material inserted or appended. The Senate, however, has retained the *bullet* symbol. *See* Joe Morehead, *Into the Hopper: Congress and the Congressional Record: A Magical Mystery Tour,* 13 SERIALS LIBR. 59 (1987).

[15] Often, only a limited number of committee prints, for the use of the committee members, are printed. Recently, they have become more available through the Depository Program, though indexing is often incomplete. See Chapter 9, note 2.

[16] The role of presidential signing statements in a legislative history is discussed in Frank B. Cross, *The Constitutional Legitimacy and Significance of Presidential Signing Statements,* 40 Admin. L. Rev. 209 (1988); Brad Waites, Note, *Let Me Tell You What You Mean: An Analysis of Presidential Signing Statements,* 21 GA. L. REV. 755 (1987); Kathryn M. Dressayer, Note, *The First Word: The President's Place in 'Legislative History',* 89 MICH. L. REV. 399 (1990); William D. Popkin, *Judicial Use of Presidential Legislative History: A Critique,* 66 IND. L.J. 699 (1990). *See also* Mark R. Killenbeck, *A Matter of Mere Approval? The Role of the President in the Creation of Legislative History,* 48 ARK. L. REV. 239 (1996).

SECTION C.   FEDERAL LEGISLATIVE
HISTORY DOCUMENTATION

The possible documents that can result as part of the legislative process and that may be relevant to a federal legislative history are illustrated on the chart that follows.

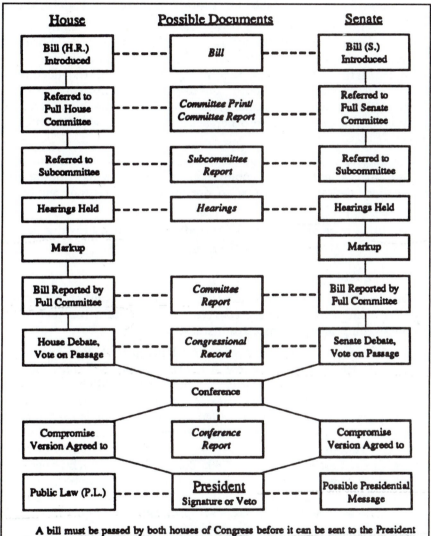

A bill must be passed by both houses of Congress before it can be sent to the President for action. A straight line shows a simple path a bill may take in Congress. At times, a bill may also go to the Rules Committee, to more than one subcommittee, and be debated more than once. A bill may be amended as it goes through these steps. A broken line leads to possible documents that can be generated in the legislative process.

SECTION D. SOURCES FOR LOCATING COMPILED FEDERAL LEGISLATIVE HISTORIES

The process of identifying and then locating the various documents that are needed for a legislative history can be a time-consuming and laborious task. As compiled legislative histories may be available for some public laws, researchers may save considerable time and effort by ascertaining if one is available for the law involved in their research.

This section is divided into three areas. The first division, Finding Aids, lists sources that provide references to print or online publications that can contain: a listing of documents that need to be obtained for a federal legislative history; the text of some or all of the documents needed; or a combination of both. These sources do not contain either the list of the necessary documents nor the documents themselves but merely alert the researcher to other sources that include this information.

The second division of this section, Finding Aids and Documents, includes sources that contain some or all of the following: finding aids; texts of documents; or citations to documents not reproduced in the source itself.

The third division, Compiled Legislative Histories, provides general informational sources for compiled legislative histories.

1. Finding Aids

The following sources provide information on whether a compiled legislative history exists. These sources do not contain the text of the documents comprising a legislative history.

a. *Sources of Compiled Legislative Histories: A Bibliography of Government Documents, Periodical Articles, and Books.*[17] This looseleaf service provides references to other publications or online services that contain compiled legislative histories for major laws. The definition of compiled legislative history, as provided by the compiler, is the collection in one place of "either the texts of legislative documents pertaining to a statute or citations to the necessary legislative documents."[18] Coverage began with the first Congress in 1789. This checklist, which is arranged chronologically by Congress and then by Public Law number, indicates which legislative documents are contained or referenced in the publication or online service listed. Indexes are provided for author-title and for Public Law by name.

b. *Union List of Legislative Histories: 47th Congress, 1881–101st Congress, 1990.*[19] This publication, compiled by the Law Librarians' Society of the District of Columbia, provides information on compiled

---

[17] Nancy P. Johnson, Sources of Compiled Legislative Histories: A Bibliography of Government Documents, Periodical Articles, and Books (1979) (updated periodically).

[18] *Id.* at i.

[19] (Rothman, 6th ed., 1991).

legislative histories commercially produced or compiled in-house by librarians in the Washington, D.C. area.

c. *Monthly Catalog of United States Government Publications.* Legislative histories may be compiled by agencies of the federal government. Access to these publications may be through *Sources of Compiled Legislative Histories, supra,* or through the *Monthly Catalog of United States Government Publications,* a comprehensive index to publications of the federal government.

d. *CIS On–Line.* The *CIS Indexes* as discussed *infra,* containing the index and abstract volumes since 1970, are available through DIALOG Information Services, Inc. and through LEXIS–NEXIS.

e. *Federal Legislative Histories: An Annotated Bibliography and Index to Officially Published Sources* (1994). Compiled by Bernard D. Reams, Jr., the 255 entries in this annotated bibliography on legislative histories covers congressional, executive agency, and special commission sources published from 1862 through 1990. The annotations describe the types of documentation in a work, contain notes about citations and paginations of original documents, and refer to the location of texts in the *United States Statutes at Large.* It includes numerous indexes.

2. Finding Aids and Documents

The sources described below contain components that list, identify, or cite to documents that are generated as a bill travels through Congress and also have a component (usually microfiche) that reproduces some of the documents themselves.

a. *Congressional Information Service, Inc. (CIS).* The publication of a set commencing in 1970 by CIS has simplified the method of compiling a federal legislative history. CIS provides indexes to locate legislation where some action has occurred after the introduction of the bill. Abstracts also are provided that give a brief synopsis of the document resulting from a specific step in the progress of the bill. If the bill is enacted as a public law, this set provides a compiled legislative history providing citations to documents comprising the legislative history. A companion microfiche component reproduces many of the documents needed to determine the intent of the public law.

Since 1970, the CIS service is the quickest and most efficient method of locating citations to and the full text of many of the documents that make up a legislative history due to the frequency of publication, the thoroughness of the indexing, the citation to all relevant documents, and the microfiche component. Each of the components of the set is described below.

(1) *CIS/Index.* This monthly component is in two parts, an abstract and an index pamphlet. The abstract pamphlet of the *CIS/Index* contains entries that briefly describe the format and scope of the hearings, reports, committee prints, and other Congressional publications such as House and Senate Documents included in the *Index.* For hearings, the abstract provides not only a synopsis of the testimony but also the name,

affiliation, and perspective of the witness. The abstract pamphlet to the *CIS Index* is cumulated yearly as the *CIS Annual/Abstracts*.

This index pamphlet contains detailed indexes by subject, title, bill, report, document, hearing, and print number. Each index entry includes an accession number that provides access to a specific publication in the abstract volume. [See Illustrations 10–3 and 10–4.] The index pamphlet of the *CIS/Index* is cumulated quarterly and annually as the *CIS Annual Index* and then quadrennially.

(2) *Legislative Histories of U.S. Public Laws*. From 1970 to 1983, each CIS Annual volume contained a section on legislative histories for public laws passed during the year. Starting in 1984 this section expanded into a separate volume, *Legislative Histories of U.S. Public Laws*. Each public law is listed and citations are given to the bill number, the committee reports, hearings, the *Congressional Record,* and other documents that may be relevant to a legislative history, such as committee prints and other Congressional documents. Through the use of indexes and the annual *Legislative Histories of U.S. Public Laws,* references to public laws may be found by the name or title of a public law, by the subject matter of the law, or by bill number.

The Legislative History volumes contain histories in two formats. For laws identified as major legislation (based on the criteria that the law may be the subject of litigation in which interpretation of its provisions may be important), the citations for Congressional committee publications also include the CIS abstracts. Additional citations are provided to all relevant bills and debates. [See Illustration 10–2.]

For the other laws, citations do not include the full abstract but instead references to the abstracts are provided. Related bills are not cited, and debate citations are limited to those provided from the slip law.

Both formats provide citations to Presidential Signing Statements or veto messages.

(3) *CIS/Microfiche Library,* 1970 to date. For bills that have become public laws, this component provides a microfiche reprint of the bills, hearings, reports, committee prints, and Congressional documents related to the enacted legislation.

(4) *Congressional Masterfile 2*. This CD–ROM product provides access to each *CIS Index, Abstract,* and *Legislative History* volume published since 1970. The *Index* and *Abstracts* are updated quarterly and the *Legislative History* component is updated annually. *Congressional Masterfile 1* is a CD–ROM product which provides access to the indexes published by CIS to locate other Congressional documents pre–1970. The CIS print indexes to hearings, the *Serial Set,* and committee prints are discussed *infra.*

(5) *Congressional Universe*. This commercial service provided by Congressional Information Service, Inc. is available through the Internet. It contains various congressional documents, hearings, bills, com-

mittee reports and prints. The *Congressional Record* from the 99th Congress forward also is provided.

b. *Public Laws—Legislative Histories on Microfiche.*[20] From the 96th Congress through the 100th Congress, this set made available the House and Senate bill as introduced; the reported House bill, Senate bill, or both; committee reports; conference reports, if any; committee prints; slip laws; and relevant legislative debate as reported in the *Congressional Record.* All enactments are indexed by subject, by Public Law number, and by bill number. This set includes a compiled legislative history for every public law.

c. *GAO Legislative History Collection.* This collection, reproduced in microfiche by Information on Demand, Inc., is comprised of selected legislative histories of public laws beginning with 1921 as compiled by the General Accounting Office. Each legislative history contains: prints of all relevant bills and amendments; committee reports; debates; hearings; and related Congressional material.

The *GAO Legislative History Collection Register of Public Laws* contains a listing by Public Law number and title of all legislative histories that are a part of the collection.

d. *United States Code Congressional and Administrative News (USCCAN).* Besides the tables in the *United States Code Congressional and Administrative News,* which are discussed *infra, USCCAN* contains a finding aid list and the text of some documents relevant to a federal legislative history.

This set is published by the West Group and is issued in monthly pamphlets during each session of Congress. After each session of Congress, it is reissued in bound volumes. It contains the public laws for each session of Congress and has separate volumes for legislative histories.

Immediately before the reprint of the selected committee reports and other documents, if applicable, *USCCAN*'s legislative history section provides the researcher with: citations to all committee and conference reports; references to the dates of consideration and passage of the bill in both houses; and to the President's Signing Statement, if any. [See Illustration 10–1.]

Prior to the 99th Congress (1985–86), *USCCAN* usually printed only a House report or a Senate report. Starting with the 99th Congress, it expanded its coverage, usually including the House or Senate report and the conference report. It also now includes any statement that the President made upon signing the law. Recently, *USCCAN* began to include joint explanatory statements and statements by legislative leaders for laws that the editors view as major legislation. These statements often contain citations to the *Congressional Record.*

[20] This set, which ceased publication in 1988, was published by Commerce Clearing House and covered 1979–1988.

USCCAN is available in many law libraries and provides a simple method of obtaining one of the most important documents of a legislative history, the committee reports.

The committee reports and Presidential Signing Statements included in *USCCAN* also are available online through WESTLAW. Coverage for committee reports begins in 1948. Presidential Signing Statements are available from 1986.

e. *The United States Congressional Serial Set.* The *Serial Set* has been known by various titles since its inception in 1789. It is published by the Government Printing Office.

Although the *Serial Set* includes numerous publications of the federal government and even from some non-governmental organizations, the relevant publications for legislative history are the committee reports and the Presidential messages relevant to legislation.

From the 84th through the 95th Congresses, House and Senate reports on public and private bills were available in bound volumes entitled "Miscellaneous Reports" for each type of bill. Beginning with the 96th Congress, all reports are compiled and arranged in numerical sequence in bound volumes. Presidential messages can be found in the House and Senate Documents section of the *Serial Set*. Occasionally, a committee print may be classified as a House or Senate document and can be found in this set.

Congressional Information Service, Inc. publishes the *CIS US Serial Set Index,* covering 1789–1969, along with microfiche files that provide access to the documents located through the *Index*. Also available is a four-volume Index by Reported Bill Numbers.

3. Compiled Legislative Histories

The following sources provide access to many documents needed for a legislative history. Because of the variety of publishers and online vendors that provide these sources, methods of gaining access to the documents vary with each source.

a. *Looseleaf Services, Treatises, and Other Compiled Legislative Histories.* Many looseleaf services and treatises dealing with specific areas of the law, *e.g.,* securities, tax, and labor, may contain compiled legislative histories for laws related to their subject. Other publications may have as their sole purpose the compilation of a federal legislative history. Some of these sources will be covered in *Sources of Compiled Legislative Histories, supra.*

b. *Online Sources.*

(1) *LEXIS(–NEXIS).* This online service provides legislative histories for selected bankruptcy, estates, tax, securities, environmental, and banking statutes and for appropriation laws for various agencies. The documents included vary with each legislative history as does the Library and File where the legislative history may be found.

(2) *WESTLAW.* WESTLAW contains selective legislative histories for major public laws. The legislative histories were prepared by the law firm of Arnold & Porter. Some areas covered are pensions, environment, banking, bankruptcy, and securities. The documents included vary with each legislative history.

(3) LEGI–SLATE is an online service of the Washington Post Company. It includes the text of bills, committee reports, and the issues of the *Congressional Record* from the current Congress.

Supplementary information is provided, including citations to articles discussing a bill in selected commercial publications, such as the *Washington Post.*

SECTION E.   HOW TO IDENTIFY/FIND CITATIONS TO DOCUMENTS RELEVANT TO A FEDERAL LEGISLATIVE HISTORY

Frequently, a legislative history has to be compiled during the course of one's research. This may be necessary because the sources described in Section C are not available, or because the public law in question does not have a previously-compiled history. As mentioned previously, it may be necessary to examine Congressional documents for a bill considered by Congress but not enacted into a public law, or to track pending legislation.

The first step in this process is to obtain a list of documents related to the public law, the legislation that was not enacted, or the pending bill.

The sources described below will provide information, references, or citations to the documents generated during the bill's progress.

1. Slip Laws/United States Statutes at Large

Since 1975, at the end of each slip law there is a legislative history summary, which provides citations to the bill that became the public law, to the committee reports, to the dates of consideration and passage of the bill by both houses of Congress, and to Presidential statements, if any. Although the volume number of the *Congressional Record* is provided for dates of consideration and passage of the bill, there are no page references. When the slip laws are compiled as the *United States Statutes at Large* this information is retained. [See Illustration 10–9.]

From 1963 to 1974, the *United States Statutes at Large* contains a Guide to Legislative History of Bills Enacted into Public Law, which includes the same references now provided at the end of the slip law, except that references to Presidential statements began to be included in 1971 for the 91st Congress, 2d Session.

Each slip law contains the bill number that was enacted into the specific public law reprinted in this format. Since the 58th Congress in 1903, each public law reprinted in the *United States Statutes at Large* gives the bill number that became the public law.[21] [See Illustration 10–9.]

The slip laws and *United States Statutes at Large* provide information for bills that have become public laws.

2. United States Code Congressional and Administrative News (USCCAN)

The monthly pamphlets of *USCCAN* contain a Legislative History Table that provides information on bills that have become public laws. The tables are cumulated in the annual bound volume. The Table, which is arranged by Public Law number, provides the citation to the *United States Statutes at Large*, the bill number, citations to the committee reports, and references to dates of consideration and passage of the bill. Beginning with the 1992 volumes, the dates of consideration of bills were eliminated. The information for committee reports includes the Committee report number and an abbreviated reference to the committees of the House and Senate, and the conference committee, if any. For dates of consideration and passage of the bill, the volume of the *Congressional Record* is provided along with the dates when the House and Senate took these actions.

3. Digest of Public General Bills and Resolutions

The *Digest of Public General Bills and Resolutions* was published by the Congressional Research Service of the Library of Congress from 1936 until publication ceased with the 102nd Congress in 1990. Thus, this resource is primarily helpful for historical research. The *Digest* was issued annually in two volumes. The *Digest* is divided into three parts.

One part provides summaries of the provisions of the legislation on which some action occurred after the bill was introduced. A brief legislative history lists, as appropriate, dates reported from committee, report numbers, dates for consideration and passage, conference actions, and the date of Presidential action. This part is further divided into Public Laws and Other Measures Receiving Action.

The second part provides digests for bills and resolutions where no action was taken after the measure was introduced and assigned to a committee. Indexes by sponsor and co-sponsor, short title, subject, and identical bills comprise the third part.

As noted above, this publication provides information on bills enacted into public law, and those that were pending, or that were not enacted as a public law.

4. Congressional Record

This publication will be discussed in detail later in this chapter, however, there are several features that are highlighted here because of

---

[21] Bill numbers for laws passed prior to 1903 may be located in EUGENE NABORS, LEGISLATIVE REFERENCE CHECKLIST: THE KEY TO LEGISLATIVE HISTORIES FROM 1789–1903 (1982).

their usefulness in identifying documents that are part of a federal legislative history.

(a) *History of Bills and Resolutions.* The *History of Bills and Resolutions* is a section of the bi-weekly index to the daily edition of the *Congressional Record.* It is divided by chamber and is arranged in order by bill number. Information available in this section includes a brief digest of the legislation, the name of the sponsor, the committee to which the legislation was referred, and references to debates, committee reports, and passage. Page references are provided to the daily *Congressional Record* where the activity is reported. Although this section only covers bills acted upon during the two weeks covered by the index, coverage is complete back to the date of the bill's introduction. A cumulative "History of Bills and Resolutions" for each session of Congress is a part of the annual Index to the bound set of the *Congressional Record.* [See Illustration 10–6.] *GPO Access* also provides the information through the Internet. [See Illustration 9–4.]

Thomas, an Internet site maintained by the Library of Congress, contains a database which provides a short description of the activity on a bill, accompanied by citations to the *Congressional Record,* where the action is recorded. The database can be searched by many access points. [See Illustration 10–11.]

(b) *History of Bills Enacted into Public Law.* This table appears in the annual Daily Digest volume of the bound *Congressional Record.* It includes the same information as the History of Bills and Resolutions, with the exception of entries for the sponsor and for the debates. As the name implies, it only covers bills that have become public laws.

Both History tables in the *Congressional Record* provide citations to bill numbers. The History table in the bi-weekly index can provide information on pending bills, on bills that have not become public law, and on bills that were enacted into public law.

5. Congressional Index

This two-volume looseleaf service is published by Commerce Clearing House, Inc. (CCH) and is updated weekly while Congress is in session and for several weeks thereafter until all public bills and resolutions sent to the President have been acted upon. New volumes are issued for each Congress.

A digest provides the contents of each bill introduced in Congress. There are status tables for pending bills in the Senate and in the House. The status tables set forth actions taken on the bill and provide committee report numbers and most importantly note if hearings were held and on what date. [See Illustration 10–5.]

Subject and sponsor indexes are provided for bills and public laws. An Enactment—Vetoes section contains tables by Public Law number and by the name of the law. The set also contains a table of companion bills, tables of voting records of Congressional members by bill and resolution number, and a list of treaties, reorganization plans, and nominations pending.

Because of its weekly supplementation, the *Congressional Index* is an excellent source to use in obtaining information about pending legislation and for those bills that became public law. Older volumes can be consulted to gather information on bills that failed to reach the enactment stage.

6. House and Senate Calendars

The *Calendars* chronicle the activity of bills as they travel through Congress.

(a) *Calendars of the United States House of Representatives and History of Legislation.* This is the "calendar" of the House of Representatives, but it actually consists of five calendars to which House bills may be assigned. It is printed each day that the House is in session. Although the *Calendars* title refers only to the House, it serves as an index to all legislation that has been reported by the committees and acted upon by either or both chambers, with the exception of Senate resolutions not of interest to the House and special House reports.

Each issue of the *Calendar* is cumulative. A subject index for both House and Senate legislation that have been reported by the committees and acted upon by either or both of the chambers is printed in the *Calendar* on the first legislative day of the week that the House is in session. It does not list hearings and debates comprehensively.

The section of this *Calendar* entitled "History of Bills and Resolutions: Numerical Order of Bills and Resolutions Which Have Been Reported to or Considered by Either or Both Houses," divides the pending legislation by chamber and then again by the form of legislation. It provides the current status and legislative history of all activity on each piece of legislation on which some action has been taken. Information on hearings is not provided. It is arranged by bill or resolution number.

(b) *Senate Calendar of Business.* This *Calendar* is less useful in tracing the current status of Senate legislation. It does not cumulate and has no index. However, a separate section entitled "General Orders" covers all legislation by bill number, title, and report number.

These sources provide bill numbers and can be used to trace action on pending legislation on public laws and on bills that did not become public laws.

The Calendars of the United States House of Representatives and History of Legislation and the *Senate Calendar* are available through the Internet site, *GPO Access.*

7. House and Senate Journals

The *Journals,* unlike the *Congressional Record,* are constitutionally mandated and as such are the official documents for the proceedings of

Congress. Both *Journals* are published at the end of each session; they have subject indexes and "History of Bills and Resolutions" actions.

SECTION F.   ILLUSTRATIONS: IDENTIFYING DOCUMENTS

Compiling legislative history for H.3680, 104th Cong., 2d Sess.

[Illustration 10–1]

PAGE FROM 1996 USCCAN LEGISLATIVE HISTORY VOLUME

WAR CRIMES ACT OF 1996

P.L. 104–192, see page 110 Stat. 2104

→ DATES OF CONSIDERATION AND PASSAGE

House: July 29, 1996

Senate: August 2, 1996

Cong. Record Vol. 142 (1996)

→ **House Report (Judiciary Committee)
No. 104–698, July 24, 1996
[To accompany H.R. 3680]**

No Senate Report was submitted with this legislation. The House Report (this page) and the President's Signing Statement (page 2181) follow

HOUSE REPORT NO. 104–698

[page 1]

The Committee on the Judiciary, to whom was referred the bill (H.R. 3680) to amend title 18, United States Code, to carry out the international obligations of the United States under the Geneva Conventions to provide criminal penalties for certain war crimes, having considered the same, report favorably thereon without amendment and recommend that the bill do pass.

Legislative Histories are in a separate section or volume in USCCAN. This is the first page of the legislative history of Pub. L. No. 104-192. Notice how at the top of the page, reference is made to a committee report and to the Dates of Consideration and Passage.

While USCCAN is useful and widely available, it does not set forth the texts of all the documents of a legislative history. USCCAN reprints the House or Senate report and the Conference report, if any. Since 1986, it includes the text of Presidential Signing Statements.

PURPOSE AND SUMMARY

H.R. 3680, as reported by the Committee, carries out the international obligations of the United States under the Geneva Conventions of 1949 to provide criminal penalties for certain war crimes. The bill provides that whoever, whether inside or outside the United States, commits a grave breach of the Geneva Conven-

[Illustration 10–2]

PAGE FROM 1996 CIS/ANNUAL LEGISLATIVE HISTORIES VOLUME

Public Law 104-192   **110 Stat. 2104**

War Crimes Act of 1996

August 21, 1996

Public Law   ③

(CIS96:H521-68   iv+88 p.)
(Y4.J89/1:104/81.)

1.1   Public Law 104-192, approved Aug. 21, 1996. (H.R. 3680)

(CIS96:PL104-192   1 p.)

P.L. 104-192 Miscellaneous   ⑥

"To amend title 18, United States Code, to carry out the international obligations of the United States under the Geneva Conventions to provide criminal penalties for certain war crimes."
Establishes criminal penalties for certain war crimes committed by or against members of the U.S. armed forces or U.S. nationals.

8.1   Weekly Compilation of Presidential Documents, Vol. 32 (1996): Aug. 21, Presidential statement.

P.L. 104-192 Reports ← ①

104th Congress   ②

2.1   H. Rpt. 104-698 on H.R. 3680, "War Crimes A[1996," July 24, 1996.

(CIS96:H523-28   1
(Y1.1/8:104–

Recommends passage of H.R. 3680, the War Crimes Act of 1996, to out international obligations of the U.S. under the 1949 Geneva Cor tions for the protection of war victims, to establish criminal penaltie certain war crimes, including murder and torture by or against men of the U.S. armed forces or U.S. nationals.
H.R. 3680 is related to H.R. 2587.

---

① → **P.L. 104-192 Debate**

142 Congressional Record
104th Congress, 2nd Session - 1996

4.1   July 29, House consideration and passage of H 3680, p. H8620.

4.2   Aug. 2, Senate consideration and passage of H 3680, p. S9648.

P.L. 104-192 Hearings ← ⑤

104th Congress

5.1   "War Crimes Act of 1995," hearings before the Subcommittee on Immigration and Claims, House Judiciary Committee, June 12, 1996.

This page is from CIS Legislative History for Pub.L. 104–192. It is important to note that CIS does not reproduce in full the various documents that are part of a legislative history. Rather, it gives only abstracts with full citations to the actual documents. But it is most useful, as it cites all relevant Congressional documents for each public law.

CIS gives the following information, either in abstract or citation to:

1. all House, Senate, and conference reports issued in reference to the enacted public laws;

2. committee reports that may have been issued that are relevant to the public law;

3. the bill that was enacted and companion bills;

4. debates on bills in the *Congressional Record*;

5. all hearings held on or related to the public law;

6. Presidential messages; and

7. committee prints (not illustrated.)

[Illustration 10–3]

PAGE FROM 1996 CIS/INDEX

Index of Subjects and Names   **Washington State**

War Crimes Act
War crimes penalties, Geneva Conventions implementation, H523–28, PL104–192
War crimes prosecution and pen..ties, Geneva Conventions implementation, H521–68

War Crimes Disclosure Act
WWII war crimes info disclosure under the Freedom of Info Act, H403–15

War games
China military exercises in Taiwan Strait, review and US policy issues, H461–77

War Powers Resolution
Haiti restoration of democracy, US military forces assistance ops review, Pres communic, H460–12
Intl peacekeeping ops in former Yugoslavia republics, US forces participation, Pres communic, H460–24

War prisoners
see Prisoners of war

Ward, Benny L.
Fed crop insurance and agric disaster assistance programs, 1994 revisions implementation issues, H161–5.3

Ward, Mike
Arm: of Engrs wa programs, funding appro H751–26.15
DOT and related agencies approp, H181–73.4
Energy and water resources dev programs, FY97 approp, H181–19.4
Fed bldgs and courthouses honorary designations, H751–2.3
Nomination of Jerome A Stricker to be Member, Fed Retirement Thrift Investment Bd, S401–9.2

Ward, Peter J.
Interior Dept and related agencies programs, FY97 approp, H181–35.1

Ward, Sara
Interior Dept and related agencies programs, FY97 approp, H181–34.1

Ward, Sylvia J.
Alaska public lands mgmt and access issues, S311–3.4

Ward Valley, Calif.
Land sale to Calif for use as radioactive waste repository site, S313–5

Ward Valley Land Transfer Act
Land sale to Calif for use as radioactive waste repository site, S313–5

Warden, Gail L.
Biomedical research and training programs, problems and issues, S541–22.1
Medicaid program revisions, H271–70.2

Wardle, Lynn D.
Marriage definition under Fed law, estab, H521–53.3, S521–33.2

Wares Creek
Flood control project in Fla, environmental impact assessments, H181–18.4, H181–19.7

Warfield, William L.
VA programs, FY97 budget proposal review, H761–11.4

Wark, Kevin
Bluefish fishery mgmt and conservation in Atlantic coastal areas, H651–28.2

Warman, Timothy W.
Agric commodity programs review, S161–19.2

Warner Brothers
Trademarks intl registration system, protocol implementation; trademarks distinctive quality dilution, trademark owner standing to sue, H521–41.2

Warner, Edward L., III
UN intl peacekeeping ops, US involvement issues review, S201–4.1

Warner, Isiah M.
Natl Inst of Standards and Technology labs R&D activities review, H701–24.2

Warner, John W.
DC area airports operating authority restructuring, S261–19.1
DC prison facility in Lorton, Va, closure and prisoner relocation, H401–3.2
Judgeship and Justice Dept nominations, S521–21.7
Va natl parks boundary revisions; Shenandoah Valley Natl Battlefields estab, S311–46.1

Warning systems
see Emergency communication systems

Warren, Andrew L.
Fed hwy and surface transportation

In the 1996 *CIS/INDEX*, the Index of Subjects and Names, one can locate references under the Title of Public Law 104-192.

DOD chemical weapons stockpile destruction programs, review, H571–6.2
DOD depot maintenance programs outsourcing issues review, H571–14.3

Warren, Melinda
Fed regulations impact on small business, review, H721–29.1

Warren, William A.
Business R&D expenditures tax credit extension and revision, H781–17.5

Warrens, Frank R.
Fishery conservation and mgmt programs, extension and revision, S261–1.1

Warrick, Thomas S.
Bosnia-Herzegovina civil conflict resolution, refugee, war crimes, and human rights issues, H461–16.1
UN mgmt and budget issues, review, H461–14.2
UN war crimes tribunal for former Yugoslavia, briefing, J892–20.1

Warrior-Tombigbee Development Association
Energy and water resources dev programs, FY97 approp, H181–18.1

Warrior-Tombigbee Waterway
Energy and water resources dev programs, FY97 approp, H181–18

Warsaw, Poland
Helsinki Agreement human rights commitments implementation, Warsaw meeting rpt, J892–2

Warships
see Naval vessels

Wasem, Ruth E.
Welfare programs reform initiatives review, H781–24.6

Washburn, Marshall V.
Employers classification of workers as independent contractors, tax issues, H721–24.1

Washington
see Washington State
see D.C. and terms beginning with D.C.

Washington Airports Task Force
DC area airports operating authority restructuring, S261–19.3

Washington Analysis Corp.
Radio spectrum mgmt technical and policy issues, review, S261–15.3

Washington Board of Rabbis
Tax treatment of persons who relinquish US citizenship or residency, revision, H781–22.3

Washington Cattle Feeders Association
North Amer Free Trade Agreement implementation, Canada trade practices effects on US agric industry in Pacific Northwest, H161–8.4

Washington County, N.Y.
Hydroelectric projects in NY State, construction deadlines extension, PL104–242

Washington County, Utah
Utah land exchange with Water Conservancy Dist of Washington Cty, Utah, PL104–333

Washington, D.C., Convention Center
Ops and new center preconstruction orization, S401–33

Judge, DC Superior

Broadcast stations saic to minorities or women, spec tax rules oversight, S361–13.3

Washington, George
Commemorative coins minting and issuance, PL104–329

Washington Humane Society
Bird imports restrictions implementation, H651–2.3

Washington Institute for Near East Policy
Palestine Liberation Organization peace agreements with Israel, implementation issues, H461–43.3

Washington Institute for Policy Studies
Fed depts and agencies reorganization proposals, State, local govt, and business methods application, H401–34.8

Washington Legal Foundation
"Government Contracts Reform: A Critical Analysis of the Administration's Proposal", H721–18.1

Washington Metropolitan Area Transit Authority, D.C.
Approp, FY97, H181–45.4
Fed hwy and surface transportation programs and policies, revision, H751–3.3
Washington Metropolitan Area Transit Regulation Compact amendments, Congressional consent, PL104–322

Washington Metropolitan Area Transit Regulation Compact
Amendments, Congressional consent, PL104–322

Washington Orientation and Mobility Association
Fed hwy and surface transportation programs and policies, revision, H751–3.3

Washington Performance Partnership
Fed depts and agencies reorganization proposals, State, local govt, and business methods application, H401–34.8

Washington State
Army Corps of Engrs programs, FY97 approp, H181–13

[Illustration 10–4]

PAGES FROM 1996 CIS/ABSTRACTS

Judiciary **H521–68.1**

sion in *Quill v. Vacco*, which struck down New York State statutes prohibiting assisted suicide on grounds of violating the 14th amendment equal protection clause.

Supplementary material (p. 3-7, 431-485) includes submitted statements and correspondence.

H521–66.1: Apr. 29, 1996. p. 9-148.

Witnesses: FOLEY, Kathleen M. (Dr.), Director, Death in America Project, Open Society Institute.
QUILL, Timothy E. (Dr.), Medicine/Psychiatry Professor, School of Medicine, University of Rochester.
COLEMAN, Diane, Executive Director, Progress Center for Independent Living.
KLAGSBRUN, Samuel C. (Dr.), Executive Medical Director, Four Winds Hospital, Katonah, N.Y.
HENDIN, Herbert (Dr.), Executive Director, American Suicide Foundation.

Statements and Discussion: Need to improve the quality of health care available to dying patients, including access to and delivery of hospice care; review of medical, legal, and ethical issues concerning physician-assisted suicide (related bibl., p. 24-34; articles, p. 43-52, 119-126).

Concerns ab[out]... plication of leg[al]... disabled individu[al]... findings of re[cent]... issues related t[o]... euthanasia in t[he]...

Insertions:

a. Coleman, [Diane]... ing Treatm[ent]... Disabilities [and]... tion Considerations" Issues in Law and Medicine, Volume 8, Number 1, 1992 (p. 76-88).

b. Gill, Carol J. (Chicago Inst of Disability Research), "Suicide Intervention for People with Disabilities: A Lesson in Inequality" Issues in Law and Medicine, Volume 8, Number 1, 1992 (p. 89-97).

c. Hendin, H., "Assisted Suicide, Euthanasia, and Suicide Prevention: The Implications of the Dutch Experience" Suicide and Life-Threatening Behavior, Spring 1995 (p. 127-138).

H521–66.2: Apr. 29, 1996. p. 149-309.

Witnesses: KRAUTHAMMER, Charles (Dr.), syndicated columnist.
LEE, Barbara C., chief petitioner of Oregon assisted suicide statute.
KAMISAR, Yale, Law Professor, University of Michigan Law School.
BARON, Charles H., Law Professor, Boston College Law School.
ROSENBLUM, Victor G., Professor, Law and Political Science, School of Law, Northwestern University.

Statements and Discussion: Criticism of recent circuit court decisions on assisted suicide; perspectives on State lawmaking regarding assisted suicide; differing views on advisability of legalizing active intervention to bring about death.

Refutation of legal arguments upholding the right of the terminally ill to physician-assisted suicide on civil liberty grounds; legal defense of upholding distinction between the right to die by refusing medical treatment and the right to die by assisted suicide.

Volume 27, Number 1-12

Refutation of arguments of assisted suicide proponents holding that court decisions in abortion cases provide a precedent for assisted suicide constitutional protection; support for State regulation of physician-assisted suicide, with review of States' rights issues; criticism of recent circuit court decisions on assisted-suicide, with constitutional analysis.

Insertions:

a. Kamisar, Y., "Against Assisted Suicide, Even a Very Limited Form" University of Detroit Mercy Law Review, Volume 72, 1995 (p. 177-211).

b. Kamisar, Y., "Some Non-Religious Views Against Proposed 'Mercy-Killing' Legislation" Minnesota Law Review, May 1958 (p. 212-249).

c. Baron, C. H., "Statute: A Model State Act To Authorize and Regulate Physician-Assisted Suicide" Harvard Journal on Legislation, Winter 1996 (p. 258-275).

H521–66.3: Apr. 29, 1996. p. 309-429.

Witnesses: BRISTOW, Lonnie R. (Dr.), President, AMA.
SPONG, John S. (Rev.), Bishop, Episcopal Diocese of Newark.

[box: ... improve quality of the care for terminally ill patients; support for legalizing physician-assisted suicide on moral grounds; feared adverse effects of legalizing assisted suicide, including concerns about involuntary euthanasia; perspectives on medical ethics issues related to assisted suicide.]

Insertions:

a. AMA, "Quality Care at the End of Life" task force report, 1995 (p. 325-339).

b. Kass, L. R., "Death with Dignity and the Sanctity of Life" Commentary, Mar. 1990 (p. 373-383).

c. Kass, L. R., "Suicide Made Easy: The Evil of 'Rational' Humaneness" Commentary, Dec. 1991 (p. 384-389).

d. Kass, L. R., "'I Will Give No Deadly Drug' Why Doctors Must Not Kill" American College of Surgeons Bulletin, Mar. 1992 (p. 390-401).

e. Kass, L. R., "Is There a Right to Die?" Hastings Center Report, Jan.-Feb. 1993 (p. 402-411).

H521–67 **ORIGINS AND SCOPE OF ROE v. WADE.**
Apr. 22, 1996. 104-2.
iii+125 p. GPO $6.00
S/N 552-070-20045-7.
CIS/MF/4
•Item 1020-A; 1020-B.
*Y4.J89/1:104/80.

Committee Serial No. 80. Hearing before the *Subcom on the Constitution* to examine legal and other issues relating to Supreme Court 1973

---

decision in *Roe v. Wade* which established a woman's constitutional right to obtain an abortion.

Hearing was held in light of President Clinton's veto of H.R. 1833, the Partial-Birth Abortion Ban Act of 1995, which would have established a ban on a certain late-term abortion procedure.

H521–67.1: Apr. 22, 1996. p. 3-42.

Witnesses: DUNSMORE, Sharon, neonatal intensive care nurse.
CALVIN, Steven E. (Dr.), Assistant Professor, Department of Obstetrics and Gynecology, University of Minnesota.
GREEN, Ronald M., Director, Ethics Institute, Dartmouth College.
JESSEN, Gianna, abortion survivor.

Statements and Discussion: Personal perspectives on the results of unsuccessful abortions; agreement with Supreme Court *Roe v. Wade* decision, citing moral and scientific considerations; views on legal and medical issues relating to abortion.

H521–67.2: Apr. 22, 1996. p. 43-125.

Witnesses: GLENDON, Mary A., Law Professor, Harvard University.

... [box obscures] ... nal Law ... Law Cen-... ional Law ... me.
... nt, Polling ... verse legal ... ion; exami-... ortion as a ... considera-... tions relating to the Ninth and Fourteenth Amendments; issues involved in identifying so-called unenumerated rights not specified in the Constitution.

Arbitrariness of *Roe v. Wade* decision, with circumstances leading to Supreme Court decision; analysis of public opinion regarding *Roe v. Wade* decision and abortion in general; perspectives on legal and other issues relating to abortion.

H521–68 **WAR CRIMES ACT OF 1996.**
June 12, 1996. 104-2.
iv+88 p. GPO $4.50
S/N 552-070-20010-0.
CIS/MF/3
•Item 1020-A; 1020-B.
*Y4.J89/1:104/81.

Committee Serial No. 81. Hearing before the *Subcom on Immigration and Claims* to consider H.R. 2587 (text, p. 3-4), the War Crimes Act of 1995, to carry out international obligations of the U.S. under the 1949 Geneva Conventions for the protection of war victims, to establish criminal penalties for certain war crimes, including murder and torture against members of the U.S. armed forces or U.S. nationals.

Supplementary material (p. 49-88) includes submitted statements, correspondence, and:
– Rubin, Alfred P. (Tufts Univ), War crimes prosecution issues book excerpt (p. 66-88).

H521–68.1: June 12, 1996. p. 7-8.
Witness: CRONIN, Michael P., Chairman, Legislative Affairs Committee, Allied Pilots Association.

CIS/INDEX 203

[Overlaid box:] By using the accession number in the *CIS/INDEX*, one can refer to the CIS/Abstract volume to find a synopsis of hearings held on Public Law 104-192. Notice that it provides the (1) names of the witness and (2) internal page references to the hearings where the specific witness' testimony may be located. See next page.

[Illustration 10–4 Cont.]

PAGES FROM 1996 CIS/ABSTRACTS

H521–68.1   **Judiciary**

Statement: Merits of H.R. 2587.

H521–68.2: June 12, 1996. p. 8-19.
Witnesses: MATHESON, Michael J., Principal Deputy Legal Adviser, Department of State.
McNEILL, John H., Senior Deputy General Counsel, International Affairs and Intelligence, Office of General Counsel, DOD.
Statements and Discussion: Support for H.R. 2587 intent, with suggested revisions.

H521–68.3: June 12, 1996. p. 20-48.
Witnesses: EVERETT, Robinson O., Senior Judge, Court of Appeals for the Armed Forces.
LEIGH, Monroe, Chairman, Task Force on War Crimes in Yugoslavia, ABA.
ZAID, Mark S., Chair, Task Force on Proposed Protocols on Evidence and Procedure for Future War Crimes Tribunals, ABA.
Statements and Discussion: Approval of H.R. 2587, with recommended revisions; issues involved in and merits of providing U.S. with criminal jurisdiction for prosecuting foreign war criminal suspects residing in the U.S.

H521–69   **FEDERAL RECORDKEEPING AND SEX OFFENDERS.**
June 19, 1996. 104-2.
iii+67 p. GPO $3.50
S/N 552-070-20194-7.
CIS/MF/3
•Item 1020-A; 1020-B.
*Y4.J89/1:104/90.

Committee Serial No. 90. Hearing before the *Subcom on Crime* to examine proposals to improve registry and tracking of information on sex offenders convicted of victimizing children.
Briefly considers H.R. 3180, the Amber Hagerman Child Protection Act, focusing on provisions to require the FBI to establish a national registry for tracking and alerting States to the interstate movements of convicted child molesters.
Includes a submitted statement (p. 67).

H521–69.1: June 19, 1996. p. 4-24.
Witnesses: FROST, Martin, (Rep, D-Tex)
HAGERMAN, Richard
WHITSON, Donna, both parents of homicide victim.
ZIMMER, Dick, (Rep, R-NJ)
GUTKNECHT, Gil, (Rep, R-Minn)
Statements and Discussion: Merits of various bills to track sex offenders, including H.R. 3180.

H521–69.2: June 19, 1996. p. 24-39.
Witness: McEWEN, Harlin R., Deputy Assistant Director, Criminal Justice Information Services Division, FBI.
Statement and Discussion: Review of progress in developing new automated information systems to track sex offenders.

H521–69.3: June 19, 1996. p. 40-66.
Witness: ALLEN, Ernest E., President, National Center for Missing and Exploited Children (NCMEC).
Statement and Discussion: Need to create national sex offender registry network from existing State registries.
Insertion:
– NCMEC, "Summary of Sex Offender Registry Statutes by State" (p. 47-62).

H522   **Prints**
JUDICIARY
Committee, House

H522–1   **PHYSICIAN-ASSISTED SUICIDE AND EUTHANASIA IN THE NETHERLANDS.**
Sept. 1996 104-2.
iii+21 p. GPO $1.75
S/N 552-070-19971-3.
CIS/MF/3

Committee Print No. 6. Report, prepared by the *Subcom on the Constitution,* examining legal developments and policy arguments in the Netherlands concerning physician-assisted suicide and euthanasia for competent patients suffering from physical or mental illness.
Includes conclusion (p. 21).

H522–2   **FEDERAL RULES OF APPELLATE PROCEDURE, With Forms.**
Dec. 1, 1996. 104-2.
xiv+42 p. GPO $4.00
S/N 052-070-07082-0.
CIS/MF/3
•Item 1020-A; 1020-B.
*Y4.J89/1-10:996.
LC 87-655653.

Committee Print No. 7. Contains rules of appellate procedure for Federal courts, as amended through Dec. 1, 1996, promulgated by the Supreme Court. Rules include provisions for appeals from district court judgments and orders, review of U.S. Tax Court decisions, review and enforcement of administrative orders, and habeas corpus proceedings.
Includes appellate procedure forms adopted by the Court (p. 39-42).

H522–3   **FEDERAL RULES OF CIVIL PROCEDURE, With Forms.**
Dec. 1, 1996. 104-2.
xxiii+124 p. GPO $9.50
S/N 052-070-07079-0.
CIS/MF/4
•Item 1020-A; 1020-B.
*Y4.J89/1-11:996.

Committee Print No. 8. Contains rules of civil procedure for U.S. district courts, as amended through Dec. 1, 1996, promulgated by the Supreme Court. Rules include provisions related to commencement of action and service of process, pleadings and motions, parties in suit, depositions and discovery, trial proceedings, judgments, provisional and final remedies, and special proceedings.
Includes civil action forms adopted by the Court (p. 91-114) and supplemental rules for certain admiralty and maritime claims (p. 115-124).

H522–4   **FEDERAL RULES OF CRIMINAL PROCEDURE.**
Dec. 1, 1996. 104-2.
xxi+54 p. GPO $5.00
S/N 052-070-07080-3.
CIS/MF/3
•Item 1020-A; 1020-B.
*Y4.J89/1-12:996.

Committee Print No. 9. Contains rules of criminal procedure for U.S. district courts, as amended through Dec. 1, 1996, promulgated by the Supreme Court. Rules include provisions relating to preliminary proceedings, indictments and information, arraignment and trial preparation, venue, trial, judgments, and supplementary and special proceedings.

H522–5   **FEDERAL RULES OF EVIDENCE.**
Dec. 1, 1996. 104-2.
xvi+25 p. GPO $3.50
S/N 052-070-07081-1.
CIS/MF/3
•Item 1020-A; 1020-B.
*Y4.J89/1-13:996.

Committee Print No. 10. Contains rules of evidence for use in U.S. courts and proceedings before U.S. magistrates, as amended through Dec. 1, 1996, promulgated by the Supreme Court.
Rules include provisions related to evidence relevancy, witnesses, opinions and expert testimony, hearsay, authentication and identification, and contents of writings, recordings, and photographs.

H522–6   **FAIR USE GUIDELINES FOR EDUCATIONAL MULTIMEDIA.**
Dec. 1996. 104-2. iii+13 p.
GPO $1.50
S/N 552-070-20263-3.
CIS/MF/3
•Item 1020-A; 1020-B.
*Y4.J89/1:C94.

Committee Print No. 11. *Subcom on Courts and Intellectual Property* report containing nonbinding fair use guidelines, drafted under the auspices of the Consortium of College and University Media Centers, for multimedia proj. , developed by educators and students using portions of lawfully acquired copyrighted works.
Under the Copyright Act of 1976, the fair use exemption places limits on the exclusive rights of copyright holders in order to promote free speech, learning, and scholarly research. The updated guidelines were formulated in response to technological developments in multimedia since 1976 which were not specifically covered by previous guidelines.

H523   **Reports**
JUDICIARY
Committee, House

H523–1   **IMMIGRATION IN THE NATIONAL INTEREST ACT OF 1995.**
Mar. 4, 1996. 104-2.
iii+545 p. GPO $20.00
S/N 052-071-01160-9.
CIS/MF/8
•Item 1008-C; 1008-D.
H. Rpt. 104-469, pt. 1.
*Y1.1/8:104-469/PT.1.
MC 96-11116.

[Illustration 10–5]

PAGE FROM HOUSE STATUS TABLE FROM CONGRESSIONAL INDEX

35,086	99 11-22-96

Status of House Bills
See also Status at pages 34,101 and 34,501.
For digest, see "Bills" and "Resolutions" Divisions.

Ref to H Resources Com 6/18/96
Hrgs by Insular Subcom 7/17/96

3673

Introduced 6/19/96
Ref to H Veterans Affairs Com 6/19/96
Ordered reptd w/amdts by Com 6/20/96
Reptd w/amdts, H Rept 104-649, by Com
. . . . 6/27/96
Passed under suspension of rules by 2/3 vote
(Voice) 7/16/96
Ref to S Veterans Affairs Com 7/17/96

3674

Introduced 6/19/96
Ref to H Veterans Affairs Com 6/19/96
Ordered reptd w/o amdts by Com 6/20/96
Reptd w/o amdts, H Rept 104-650, by Com
. . . . 6/27/96
Passed under suspension of rules by 2/3 vote
(Voice) 7/16/96
Ref to S Veterans Affairs Com 7/17/96

★ 3675

Introduced 6/19/96
Reptd w/o amdts, H Rept 104-631, by
Appropriations Com 6/19/96
Rule granted allowing amdts (H Res 460)
. . . . 6/25/96
H began consideration 6/26/96
Amdts rejected (193 to 212; H Leg 288) . 6/27/96
Amdts rejected (162 to 238; H Leg 289) . 6/27/96
Amdts rejected (123 to 280; H Leg 290) . 6/27/96
Amdts adopted (247 to 159; H Leg 291) . 6/27/96
Amdts adopted (Voice) 6/27/96
Passed by . . .
Ref to S A . . .
Approved . . .
Ordered re . . .
Reptd w/a . . .
. . . .

Amdts reje . . .
Amdts ado . . .
Amdts ado . . .
Amdts adopted (Voice) 7/31/96
Passed by S (95 to 2; S Leg 261) 7/31/96
S insisted on its amdts and requested conf (Voice)
. . . . 7/31/96
H agreed to conf (Voice) 9/5/96
H instructed its conferees (Voice) 9/5/96
Conferees reached agreement 9/11/96
Conf rept filed, H Rept 104-785 . . . . . . 9/16/96
Rule granted allowing no amdts (H Res 522)
. . . . 9/17/96
H agreed to conf rept (395 to 19; H Leg 419)
. . . . 9/18/96
S agreed to conf rept (85 to 14; S Leg 294)
. . . . 9/18/96
Sent to President 9/20/96
Signed by President 9/30/96
Public Law 104-205 (110 Stat 2951) 9/30/96

★ 3676

Introduced 6/19/96

Ref to H Judiciary Com 6/19/96
Approved w/amdts by Crime Subcom . . . 7/10/96
Ordered reptd w/amdts by Com 9/11/96
Reptd w/amdts, H Rept 104-787, by Com
. . . . 9/16/96
Passed under suspension of rules by 2/3 vote
(Voice) 9/17/96
Passed by S (Voice) 9/18/96
Sent to President 9/20/96
Signed by President 10/1/96
Public Law 104-217 (110 Stat 3020) . . . 10/1/96

★ 3680

Introduced 6/19/96
Ref to H Judiciary Com 6/19/96
Approved w/o amdts by Immigration Subcom
. . . . 6/27/96
Ordered reptd w/o amdts by Com 7/16/96
Reptd w/o amdts, H Rept 104-698, by Com
. . . . 7/24/96
Passed under suspension of rules by 2/3 vote
(Voice) 7/29/96
Passed by S (Voice) 8/2/96
Sent to President 8/9/96
Signed by President 8/21/96
Public Law 104-192 (110 Stat 2104) . . . 8/21/96

3700

Introduced 6/20/96
Ref to H Oversight Com 6/20/96
Ordered reptd w/amdts by Com 9/19/96
Amdts adopted (Voice) 9/26/96
Passed under suspension of rules by 2/3 vote
(Voice) 9/26/96

> This Status Table in the *Congressional Index* (CCH) for 1995-96 lists all bills introduced during the 104th Congress and gives citations to committee reports. Date references for hearings and debates are provided.

. . . . 6/25/96
. . . . 6/25/96
. . . . . . m
. . . . 7/31/96
. . . . 8/1/96
. . . . 8/2/96
. . . . 8/2/96
. . . . 9/24/96
Passed by S (Voice) 9/24/96
Sent to President 9/26/96
Signed by President 10/2/96
Public Law 104-230 (110 Stat 3047) . . . 10/2/96

3717

Introduced 6/25/96
Ref to H Govt Reform; Judiciary Coms . 6/25/96
Hrgs by Postal Subcom 7/10/96
Hrgs by Postal Subcom 7/18/96
Hrgs by Postal Subcom 9/17/96
Hrgs by Postal Subcom 9/26/96

3719

Introduced 6/26/96
Ref to H Small Business Com 6/26/96
Com began markup 7/10/96
Ordered reptd w/amdts by Com 7/18/96
Reptd w/amdts, H Rept 104-750, by Com
. . . . 8/2/96

H 3673

©1996, **CCH** INCORPORATED

[Illustration 10–6]

PAGE FROM 1996 CONGRESSIONAL RECORD BI–WEEKLY INDEX

HOUSE BILLS — H.B. 27

H.R. 3647—Continued
killed in the line of duty receive benefits; to the Committee on the Judiciary.
By Mr. MANZULLO (for himself, Mr. Weldon of Pennsylvania, Mr. Waxman, Mr. Solomon, Mr. Coleman, Mr. Coble, Mr. Evans, Mr. Diaz-Balart, Mr. Frost, and Mr. Jacobs), H6413 [13JN]
Cosponsors added, H8095 [22JY], H8248 [23JY], H8375 [24JY], H9706 [1AU]

H.R. 3648—A bill to reestablish the National Science Scholars Program; to the Committee on Economic and Educational Opportunities; Science, for a period to be subsequently determined by the Speaker, in each case for consideration of such provisions as fall within the jurisdiction of the committee concerned.
By Mr. MARKEY, H6413 [13JN]
Cosponsors added, H6532 [19JN], H6765 [25JN], H7155 [9JY], H7260 [10JY], H7658 [16JY], H8248 [23JY]

H.R. 3654—A bill to ensure the competitiveness of the U.S. textile and apparel industry; to the Committee on Ways and Means.
By Mr. SPRATT (for himself, Mr. Coble, Mr. Payne of Virginia, Mr. Burr, Mr. Collins of Georgia, Mr. Rangel, Mr. Rogers, Mr. Cardin, Mr. Neal of Massachusetts, Mr. Coyne, Mr. Ford, Mr. Lewis of Georgia, Mr. Levin, Mr. Matsui, Mr. Hunter, Mr. Flanagan, Mr. Baker of California, Mr. Chambliss, Mr. Browder, Mr. Frank of Massachusetts, Mr. Hefner, Mr. Quillen, Ms. Kaptur, Mr. Spence, Mr. Montgomery, Mr. Lewis of Kentucky, Mr. Orream, Mr. Deal of Georgia, Mr. Funderburk, Mr. Jones, Mr. Clyburn, Mr. Watt of North Carolina, Mr. Ballenger, Mr. Heineman, Mr. Rahall, Mr.

Presented to the President, H9704 [1AU]
H.R. 3665—A bill to transfer to the Secretary of Agriculture the authority to conduct the census of agriculture; to the Committees on Government Reform and Oversight; Agriculture, for a period to be subsequently determined by the Speaker, in each case for consideration of such provisions as fall within the jurisdiction of the committee concerned.
By Mr. ROBERTS (for himself, Mr. de la Garza, Mr. Emerson, Mr. Ross, Mr. Combest, Mr. Stenholm, Mr. Boehner, Mr. Johnson of South Dakota, Mr. Baker of Louisiana, Mr. Hilliard, Mr. Calvert, Mr. Pomeroy, Mr. Cooley, Mr. Bishop, Mr. LaHood, Mr. Baldacci, and Mr. Wise), H6508 [18JN]
Cosponsors added, H6532 [19JN], H7108 [27JN]
Reported with amendments (H. Rept. 104–653), H7105 [27JN]
Rules suspended. Passed House amended, H8052 [22JY]
Text, H8052 [22JY]
Referred to the Committee on Governmental Affairs, S9293 [31JY]

H.R. 3666—A bill making appropriations for the Departments of Veterans Affairs and Housing and Urban Development, and for sundry independent agencies, boards, commissions, corporations, and offices for the fiscal year ending September 30, 1997, and for other purposes.
By Mr. LEWIS of California, H6508 [18JN]
Amendments, H6511 [18JN], H6532, H6533, H6534, H6535 [19JN], H6691, H6692 [20JN], H6765, H6813, H6815, H6819, H6826, H6831, H6839, H6844 [25JN], H6856, H6857, H6858, H6863, H6868, H6870, H6873, H6875, H6876, H6878, H6881, H6884, H6887, H6893, H6897, H6900.

to provide criminal penalties for certain war crimes; to the Committee on the Judiciary.
By Mr. JONES (for himself, Mr. Hoke, Mr. Stump, Mr. Solomon, Mr. McHale, Mr. Hunter, Mr. Montgomery, Mr. Lewis of Kentucky, Mr. Torkildsen, Mr. Watts of Oklahoma, Mr. Everett, Mr. McHugh, Mr. Ortiz, Mr. Hostettler, Mrs. Fowler, Mr. Longley, and Mr. Kolbe), H6532 [19JN]
Cosponsors added, H6691 [20JN]
Reported (H. Rept. 104–698), H8374 [24JY]
Rules suspended. Passed House, H8620 [29JY]
Text, H8620 [29JY]
Passed Senate, S9648 [2AU]

H.R. 3687—A bill to amend Title 5 of the United States Code to provide a civil remedy for the request or receipt of protected records for a nonroutine use by any person within the Executive Offices of the President, and for other purposes; to the Committees on Government Reform and Oversight; the Judiciary, for a period to be subsequently determined by the Speaker, in each case for consideration of such provisions as fall within the jurisdiction of the committee concerned.
By Mr. BARR, H6690 [20JN]
Cosponsors added, H6915 [26JN], H7260 [10JY], H8598 [26JY]

H.R. 3688—A bill to require that 401(k)-type pension plans be subject to the same prohibited transaction rules that apply to traditional defined benefit pension plans; to the Committee on Economic and Educational Opportunities.
By Mr. WHITE, H6690 [20JN]
Cosponsors added, H7108 [27JN], H7658 [16JY], H9566 [31JY]

> Locating legislative history information using *History of Bills and Resolutions* Table in the *Congressional Record* Index.
>
> This Table gives the history of all bills introduced into each session of Congress. It refers to all relevant documents, except hearings.
>
> These Tables are located in the bound annual Index volumes of the *Congressional Record*, and in the bi–weekly index of the unbound issues. H.R. in this Illustration stand for History of Bills and Resolutions.

---

to be subsequently determined by the Speaker, in each case for consideration of such provisions as fall within the jurisdiction of the committee concerned.
By Mr. TORRICELLI (for himself and Mr. Pallone), H6414 [13JN]
Cosponsors added, H8982 [30JY]

H.R. 3660—A bill to make amendments to the Reclamation Wastewater and Groundwater Study and Facilities Act, and for other purposes; to the Committee on Resources.
By Mr. HANSEN, H6423 [17JN]
Reported with amendments (H. Rept. 104–703), H8374 [24JY]

H.R. 3663—A bill to amend the District of Columbia Self-Government and Governmental Reorganization Act to permit the Council of the District of Columbia to authorize the issuance of revenue bonds with respect to water and sewer facilities, and for other purposes; to the Committee on Government Reform and Oversight.
By Mr. DAVIS (for himself, Ms. Norton, Mr. McHugh, Mr. Gutknecht, Mr. LaTourette, Mr. Flanagan, Mr. Towns, Miss Collins of Michigan, Mr. Hoyer, Mrs. Morella, Mr. Moran, and Mr. Wynn), H6508 [18JN]
Reported (H. Rept. 104–635), H6764 [25JN]
Amended and passed House, H6982 [27JN]
Text, H6982 [27JN]
Amendments, H6983 [27JN]
Passed Senate, S9208 [30JY]
Examined and signed in the House, H9703 [1AU]
Examined and signed in the Senate, S9426 [1AU]

Reported (H. Rept. 104–631), H6531 [19JN]
Made special order (H. Res. 460), H6764 [25JN]
Amendments, H6766 [25JN], H7079, H7080, H7085, H7086, H7089, H7091 [27JN]
Debated, H6964 [26JN], H7067 [27JN]
Amended and passed House, H7099 [27JN]
Read the first and second times. Referred to the Committee on Appropriations, S7301 [28JN]
Reported with amendments (S. Rept. 104–325), S8373 [19JY]
Debated, S9118 [30JY], S9265, S9275 [31JY]
Text, S9118 [30JY]
Amendments, S9118, S9129, S9130, S9131, S9132, S9134, S9141, S9143, S9145, S9146, S9147, S9148, S9149, S9162, S9163, S9164 [30JY], S9268, S9275, S9276, S9279, S9280, S9305, S9306 [31JY]
Passed Senate as amended, S9287 [31JY]
Senate insisted on its amendments and asked for a conference, S9287 [31JY]
Conferees appointed, S9288 [31JY]

H.R. 3677—A bill to amend the Internal Revenue Code of 1986 relating to the unemployment tax for individuals employed in the entertainment industry; to the Committee on Ways and Means.
By Mr. ENGLISH of Pennsylvania (for himself, Mr. Matsui, Mr. Royce, Mr. Rangel, Mr. Bono, Mr. Gejdenson, Mr. Dornan, Mr. Torres, and Mr. Waxman), H6531 [19JN]
Cosponsors added, H7260 [10JY], H8375 [24JY]

H.R. 3680—A bill to amend title 18, United States Code, to carry out the international obligations of the United States under the Geneva Conventions

paign Act of 1971 to permit interactive computer services to provide their facilities free of charge to candidates for Federal offices for the purpose of disseminating campaign information and enhancing public debate; to the Committee on House Oversight.
By Mr. WHITE (for himself, Mr. Thomas, Ms. Dunn of Washington, Ms. Pryce, and Mr. Rohrabacher), H6691 [20JN]
Cosponsors added, H6915 [26JN], H7475 [11JY], H7533 [12JY], H7658 [16JY], H8248 [23JY], H8375 [24JY], H8982 [30JY], H9706 [1AU]

H.R. 3706—A bill to protect the retirement security of Americans; to the Committees on Economic and Educational Opportunities; Ways and Means; Government Reform and Oversight; Transportation and Infrastructure, for a period to be subsequently determined by the Speaker, in each case for consideration of such provisions as fall within the jurisdiction of the committee concerned.
By Mr. ANDREWS, H7780 [17JY], H9925 [2AU]

H.R. 3710—A bill to designate a U.S. courthouse located in Tampa, FL, as the "Sam M. Gibbons United States Courthouse"; to the Committee on Transportation and Infrastructure.
By Ms. BROWN of Florida, H6764 [25JN]
Cosponsors added, H7260 [10JY], H7658 [16JY], H8095 [22JY], H8248 [23JY], H8375 [24JY], H8557 [25JY], H8598 [26JY], H8982 [30JY], H9706 [1AU], H9925 [2AU]
Committee discharged. Amended and passed House, H9900 [2AU]

[Illustration 10–7]

U.S. HOUSE OF REPRESENTATIVES SERVERS—INTERNET

United States House of Representatives - 105th Congress   http://www.house.gov/

[text version]

U.S. House of Representatives
105th Congress, 2nd session

House
Office
Web Sites

Member Offices

What's New

House Operations

House Directory

Committee Offices

Leadership Offices

Other House Organizations,
Commissions, and Task Forces

Media Galleries ^{NEW}

1 of 2   3/17/98 10:26 AM

[Illustration 10–7 Cont.]

U.S. HOUSE OF REPRESENTATIVES SERVERS—INTERNET

United States House of Representatives - 105th Congress

http://www.house.gov/

This Week on the House Floor
The schedule the House intends to consider this week.

Currently on the House Floor
Up-to-date events on the House floor as they happen.

Today in Committee
Up-to-the-hour Committee hearing schedules.

Annual Congressional Schedule NEW

The Legislative Process
Access to information about bills and resolutions being considered in the Congress.

Roll Call Votes NEW
As compiled through the electronic voting machine by the House Tally Clerks under the direction of Robin H. Carle, Clerk of the House.

House Committee Hearing Schedules and Oversight Plans
Each committee maintains its own schedule of hearings on the web. A committee's oversight plan describes its agenda for the 105th Congress, based on the jurisdiction of the committee. The public can attend any open committee meeting listed, and some hearings are televised by C-SPAN.

THOMAS

In the spirit of THOMAS Jefferson, the Library of Congress provides you with searchable information about the U.S. Congress and the legislative process. Search bills, by topic , bill number, or title. Search through and read the text of the Congressional Record for the 104th and 105th Congress. Search and find committee reports by topic or committee name.

Write Your Representative

Constituents may identify and/or contact their elected Member to the U.S. House of Representatives.

Internet Law Library

Free public access to the basic documents of U.S. law. Full text searchable copy of the U.S. Code. Over 8,900 links to law resources on the Internet.

| Educational Links | Visiting the Nation's Capitol | Government Links |

Comments

To comment on how to improve this site, use this form or send e-mail to the Webmaster

2 of 2   3/17/98 10:26 AM

SECTION G.   ILLUSTRATIONS: DOCUMENTS

[Illustration 10–8]

H.R. 3680—104TH CONGRESS, 2D SESSION— AS PRINTED IN CONGRESSIONAL RECORDS

H8620   CONGRESSIONAL RECORD — HOUSE   *July 29, 1996*

Mr. Speaker, H.R. 740, introduced by the gen
SCHIFF]
Mexico
Pueblo
claim i
Claims
quired
States,
vised by
regard
never fl.
before t
limitati

> From the indexes or tables shown in previous Illustrations the researcher should now have citations to (1) bill number, (2) reports, and (3) *Congressional Record*. These must all be separately obtained and examined.
>
> This Illustration shows H.R. 3680 as introduced during the 104th Congress, 2d Session.

The SPEAKER pro tempore. The

The SPEAKER pro tempore. Is there equest of the gen

.ction.

..xas. Mr. Speaker, I
i time as I may

. 3680 is designed to
eva conventions for
rictims of war. Our
tleman from North
JONES, should be
troducing this bill
on to such a worthy

The Court's jurisdiction would apply only to claims accruing on or before August 13, 1946, as provided in the Indian Claims Commission Act.

The Pueblo of Isleta Tribe seeks the opportunity to present the merits of its aboriginal land claims, which otherwise would be barred as untimely. The tribe cites numerous precedents for conferring jurisdiction under similar circumstances, such as the case of the Zuni Indian Tribe in 1978.

An identical bill passed the Senate in the 103d Congress, but was not considered by the House. In the 102d Congress, H.R. 1206, amended to the current language, passed the House, but was not considered by the Senate before adjournment. On June 11, 1996, the Judiciary Committee favorably reported this bill by unanimous voice vote.

Mr. Speaker, I reserv the balance of my time.

Mr. SCOTT. Mr. Spea r, I yield myself such time as I may consume.

Mr. Speaker, I think the bill has been explained that was introduced the gentleman from New Mexico (Mr. SKEEN] and the gentleman from New Mexico [Mr. SCHIFF]. It is a fair bill, and I would just urge colleagues to support it at this time.

Mr. Speaker, I yield back the balance of my time.

Mr. RICHARDSON. Mr. Speaker, i wish to extend my strong support for H.R. 740 which deals with the Pueblo of Isleta Indian land claims. H.R. 740 comes before Congress for a vote which will correct a 45-year-old injustice. In 1951, the Pueblo of Isleta was given erroneous advice by employees of the Bureau of Indian Affairs regarding the nature of the claim the Pueblo could mount under the Indian Claims Commission Act of 1946. This is documented and supported by testimony. The Pueblo was not made aware of the fact that a land claim could be made based upon aboriginal use and occupancy. As a result, it lost the opportunity to make such a claim.

The Pueblo of Isleta was a victim of circumstances beyond its control, and this bill is an opportunity for us to correct this wrong. No expenditure or appropriations of funds are provided for in this bill: only the opportunity for the Pueblo to make a claim for aboriginal lands which the Isletas believe to be rightfully theirs. This bill may be the last chance for the United States to correct an injustice which occurred many years ago because of misinformation from the BIA.

Therefore, I urge my colleagues to support H.R. 740.

Mr. SMITH of Texas. Mr. Speaker, I have no further requests for time, and I yield back the balance of my time.

Mr. SMITH of Texas. Mr. Speaker, I move to suspend the rules and pass the bill (H.R. 3680) to amend title 18, United States Code, to carry out the international obligations of the United States under the Geneva Conventions to provide criminal penalties for certain war crimes.

The Clerk read as follows:

▶ H.R. 3680

Be it enacted by the Senate and House of Representatives of the United States of America in Congress assembled,
SECTION 1. SHORT TITLE.

This Act may be cited as the "War Crimes Act of 1996".
SEC. 2. CRIMINAL PENALTIES FOR CERTAIN WAR CRIMES.

(a) IN GENERAL.—Title 18, United States Code, is amended by inserting after chapter 117 the following:

"CHAPTER 118—WAR CRIMES

"Sec.
"2401. War crimes.

"§ 2401. War crimes

"(a) OFFENSE.—Whoever, whether inside or outside the United States, commits a grave breach of the Geneva Conventions, in any of the circumstances described in subsection (b), shall be fined under this title or imprisoned for life or any term of years, or both, and if death results to the victim, shall also be subject to the penalty of death.

"(b) CIRCUMSTANCES.—The circumstances referred to in subsection (a) are that the person committing such breach or the victim of such breach is a member of the armed forces of the United States or a national of the United States (as defined in section 101 of the Immigration and Nationality Act).

"(c) DEFINITIONS.—As used in this section, the term 'grave breach of the Geneva Conventions' means conduct defined as a grave breach in any of the international conventions relating to the laws of warfare signed at Geneva 12 August 1949 or any protocol to any such convention, to which the United States is a party."

(b) CLERICAL AMENDMENT.—The table of chapters for part I of title 18, United States Code, is amended by inserting after the item relating to chapter 117 the following new item:

"118. War crimes .... 2401".

The SPEAKER pro tempore. Pursuant to the rule, the gentleman from Texas [Mr. SMITH] and the gentleman from Virginia [Mr. SCOTT] each will control 20 minutes.

The Chair recognizes the gentleman from Texas [Mr. SMITH].

GENERAL LEAVE

Mr. SMITH of Texas. Mr. Speaker, I ask unanimous consent that all Members may have 5 legislative days to revise and extend their remarks on the bill under consideration.

□ 1445

Mr. Speaker, the Geneva Conventions of 1949 codified rules of conduct for military forces to which we have long adhered. In 1955 Deputy Under Secretary of State Robert Murphy testified to the Senate that—

The Geneva Conventions are another long step forward towards mitigating the severity of war on its helpless victims. They reflect enlightened practices as carried out by the United States and other civilized countries, and they represent largely what the United States would do, whether or not a party to the Conventions. Our own conduct has served to establish higher standards and we can only benefit by having them incorporated in a stronger body of wartime law.

Mr. Speaker, the United States ratified the Conventions in 1955. However, Congress has never passed implementing legislation.

The Conventions state that signato countries are to enact penal legislatio punishing what are called grav breaches, actions such as the deliberate kill g of prisoners of war, the subjecting of prisoners to biological experiments, the willful infliction of great suffering or serious injury on civilians in occupied territory.

While offenses covering grave breaches can in certain instances be prosecutable under present Federal law, even if they occur overseas, there are a great number of instances in which no prosecution is possible. Such nonprosecutable crimes might include situations where American prisoners of war are killed, or forced to serve in the Army of their captors, or American doctors on missions of mercy in foreign war zones are kidnapped or murdered. War crimes are not a thing of the past, and Americans can all too easily fall victim to them.

H.R. 3680 was introduced in order to implement the Geneva Conventions. It prescribes severe criminal penalties for anyone convicted of committing, whether inside or outside the United States, a grave breach of the Geneva Conventions, where the victim or the perpetrator is a member of our Armed Forces. In future conflicts H.R. 3680 may very well deter acts against Americans that violate the laws of war.

Mr. Speaker, I urge my colleagues to support this legislation, and I reserve the balance of my time.

Mr. SCOTT. Mr. Speaker, I yield myself such time as I may consume.

Mr. Speaker, as the gentleman from Texas has fully explained, H.R. 3680 implements this country's international

[Illustration 10–9]

PUB. L. NO. 104–192 AS PRINTED AS A SLIP LAW

---

110 STAT. 2104　　　　PUBLIC LAW 104–192—AUG. 21, 1996

Public Law 104–192
104th Congress

An Act

Aug. 21, 1996

[H.R. 3680]

War Crimes Act
of 1996.
18 USC 2401
note.

To amend title 18, United States Code, to carry out the international obligations of the United States under the Geneva Conventions to provide criminal penalties for certain war crimes.

Be it enacted by the Senate and House of Representatives of the United States of America in Congress assembled,

SECTION 1. SHORT TITLE.

This Act may be cited as the "War Crimes Act of 1996".

SEC. 2. CRIMINAL PENALTIES FOR CERTAIN WAR CRIMES.

(a) IN GENERAL.—Title 18, United States Code, is amended by inserting after chapter 117 the following:

> **Note how the Slip Law refers to (1) the date the bill became law and (2) the bill which became public law.**
>
> **The text of the public law as it appears here can be compared against the bill to determine legislative intent, if amendments were made.**

"(a) OFFENSE.—Whoever, whether inside or outside the United States, commits a grave breach of the Geneva Conventions, in any of the circumstances described in subsection (b), shall be fined under this title or imprisoned for life or any term of years, or both, and if death results to the victim, shall also be subject to the penalty of death.

"(b) CIRCUMSTANCES.—The circumstances referred to in subsection (a) are that the person committing such breach or the victim of such breach is a member of the Armed Forces of the United States or a national of the United States (as defined in section 101 of the Immigration and Nationality Act).

"(c) DEFINITIONS.—As used in this section, the term 'grave breach of the Geneva Conventions' means conduct defined as a grave breach in any of the international conventions relating to

---

> **Since 1975 at the end of each slip law separately-published and then cumulated in the *United States Statutes at Large* is a brief summary providing references or citations to some documents that may be relevant to the legislative history of a public law.**

---

the item relating to chapter 117 the following new item:

"118. War crimes .... 2401".

Approved August 21, 1996.

LEGISLATIVE HISTORY—H.R. 3680:

HOUSE REPORTS: No. 104–698 (Comm. on the Judiciary).
CONGRESSIONAL RECORD, Vol. 142 (1996):
　　July 29, considered and passed House.
　　Aug. 2, considered and passed Senate.
WEEKLY COMPILATION OF PRESIDENTIAL DOCUMENTS, Vol. 32 (1996):
　　Aug. 21, Presidential statement.

○

[Illustration 10–10]

PAGE FROM DEBATES ON H.R. 3680—104th CONGRESS, 2d SESSION—CONGRESSIONAL RECORD

S9648   CONGRESSIONAL RECORD — SENATE   *August 2, 1996*

The PRESIDING OFFICER. The Senator from Oklahoma.

WAR CRIMES ACT OF 1996

Mr. INHOFE. Mr. President, I ask unanimous consent that the Senate now proceed to the consideration of H.R. 3680 which was received from the House.

The PRESIDING OFFICER. The clerk will report.

The assistant legislative clerk read as follows:

A bill (H.R. 3680) to amend title 18, United States Code, to carry out the international obligations of the United States under the Geneva Conventions to provide criminal penalties for certain war crimes.

The PRESIDING OFFICER. Is there objection to the immediate consideration of the bill?

There being no objection, the Senate proceeded to consider the bill.

Mr. INHOFE. Mr. President, this particular act is known as the War Crimes Act of 1996. This was called to my attention by a very articulate young Congressman from North Carolina, Walter Jones, Jr., whose father we served with for many, many years over in the House of Representatives.

He was ve[...] something. [...] the ratificat[...] tions, that i[...] we actually[...] essary legis[...] tion within[...] ecute war crimes that we were aware of.

So this legislation will correct that after this long period of time. It is kind of inconceivable to me that we would send out to battle and to various parts of the world our young troops, trying to equip them properly—I would say properly, that if we ever get our authorization passed—and have these people ready to do the work that they are trained to do, and yet if a crime is perpetrated against them, and that criminal happens to be in the United States, we cannot even prosecute them in our Federal courts. That is all going to come to a stop.

I think also this bill might even address another problem that is taking place right now in this country. As you know, I am from Oklahoma. And one of the worst terrorist acts took place just a little over a year ago in Oklahoma City with the bombing of the Murrah Federal Office Building. And with all of the terrorist acts recently, this could act as a deterrent, this War Crimes Act of 1996, for people who may be considering perpetrating some terrorist act that could be defined as a war crime.

So I believe this is something that should have been done some 40 years ago, but was not. So we will correct that tonight. This has been cleared by both sides.

Mr HELMS. Mr. President, this bill will help to close a major gap in our Federal criminal law by permitting American servicemen and nationals,

who are victims of war crimes, to see the criminal brought to justice in the United States.

Before addressing the need for this legislation, let me thank and commend the distinguished WALTER JONES, who so ably represents the third district of North Carolina, for his commitment and hard work toward the passage of this bill. I'd also like to thank my distinguished colleague, Senator JAMES INHOFE, for his support of this important bill.

Many have not realized that the U.S. cannot prosecute, in Federal court, the perpetrators of some war crimes against American servicemen and nationals. Currently, if the United States were to find a war criminal within our borders—for example, one who had murdered an American POW—the only options would be to deport or extradite the criminal or to try him or her before an international war crimes tribunal or military commission. Alone, these options are not enough to insure that justice is done.

While the Geneva Convention of 1949 grants the U.S. authority to criminally prosecute these acts, the Congress has never enacted implementing legislation. The War Crimes Act of 1996 cor-

ican, who is charged with a war crime, to be tried in an American court and to receive all of the procedural protections afforded by our American justice system.

Mr. President, at a time when American servicemen and women serve our Nation in conflicts around the world, it is important that we give them every protection possible. I urge my colleagues to support this bipartisan bill and reaffirm our commitment to our country's servicemembers.

I ask unanimous consent that an article from the New York Times be printed in the RECORD.

There being no objection, the article was ordered to be printed in the RECORD, as follows:

[From the New York Times, June 25, 1996]

Ms MALONEY AND MR. WALDHEIM

(By A.M. Rosenthal)

For a full half-century, with determination and skill, and with the help of the law, U.S. intelligence agencies have kept secret the record of how they used Nazis for so many years after World War II, what the agencies got from these services—and what they gave as payback.

Despite the secrecy blockade, we do know how one cooperative former Wehrmacht officer and war crimes suspect was treated. We know the U.S. got him the Secretary Generalship of the U.N. as reward and base.

For more than two years, Congress has had legislation before it to allow the public access to information about U.S.-Nazi intelligence relations—a bill introduced by Representative Carolyn B. Maloney, a Manhattan Democrat, and now winding through the legislative process.

If Congress passes her War Crimes Disclosure Act, H.R. 1281, questions critical to history and the conduct of foreign affairs can be answered and the power of government to withhold them reduced. The case of Kurt Waldheim is the most interesting example—the most interesting we know of at the moment.

Did the U.S. know when it backed him for Secretary General that he had been put on the A list of war-crime suspects adopted in London in 1948, for his work as a Wehrmacht intelligence officer in the Balkans, when tens of thousands of Yugoslavs, Greeks, Italians, Jew and nonJew, were being deported to death?

If not, isn't that real strange, since the U.S. representative on the War Crimes Commission voted to list him? A report was sent to the State Department. Didn't State give the C.I.A. a copy—a peek?

And when he was running for Secretary General why did State Department biographies omit any reference to his military service—just as he forgot to mention it in his autobiographies?

If all that information was lost by teams of stupid clerks, once the Waldheim name came up for the job why did not the U.S. do the obvious thing—check with Nazi and war-crime records in London and Berlin to see if his name by any chance was among those deadly wanted?

Didn't the British know? They voted for the listing too. And the Russians—Yugoslavia moved to list him when it was a Soviet [...]

[...] Moscow?

[...] the U.S. for [...]? Twice in [...] the job. The [...] tries that [...] dy can say [...]

[...] and British?

One at a time. Or was he a big-power group. serving all?

One thing is not secret any longer, thanks to Prof. Robert Herzstein of the University of South Carolina history department. He has managed through years of perseverance to pry some information loose. He found that while Mr. Waldheim worked for the Austrian bureaucracy, the U.S. Embassy in Vienna year after year sent in blurby reports about his assistance to American foreign policy—friendly, outstanding, cooperative, receptive to American thinking. All the while, this cuddly fellow was on the A list, which was in the locked files or absent with official leave.

On May 24, 1994, I reported on Professor Herzstein's findings and the need for opening files of war-crime suspects. Representative Maloney quickly set to work on her bill to open those files to Freedom of Information requests providing safeguards for personal privacy, ongoing investigations and national security if ever pertinent.

Her first bill expired in the legislative machinery and in 1996 she tried again. She got her hearing recently thanks to the chairman of her subcommittee of the Government Reform Committee—Stephen Horn the California Republican.

If the leaders of Congress will it, the Maloney bill can be passed this year. I nominate my New York Senators to introduce it in the Senate. It will be a squeeze to get it passed before the end of the year, so kindly ask your representatives and senators to start squeezing.

If not, the laborious legislative procedure will have to be repeated next session. Questions about the Waldheim connection will go unanswered, and also about other cases that may be in the files or strangely misplaced, which will also be of interest.

Mr. INHOFE. Mr. President, I ask unanimous consent that the bill be

> The discussion of a pending bill by member of Congress may be useful in determining Congressional intent. The researcher should ascertain such discussion in both houses of Congress.

[Illustration 10–11]

THOMAS—INTERNET SITE

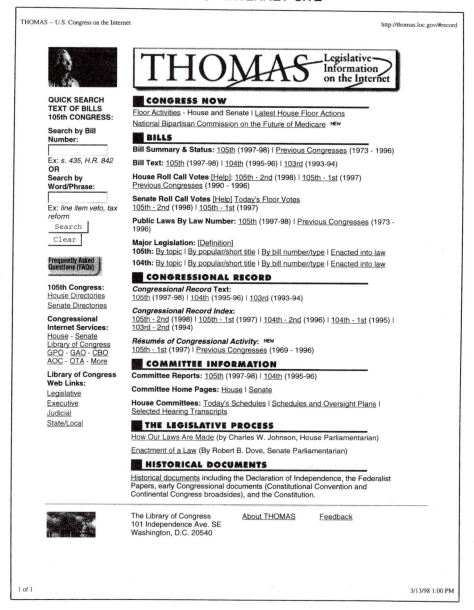

SECTION H.   HOW TO OBTAIN THE LEGISLATIVE HISTORY DOCUMENTS

After using the sources previously described, the bills with amendments, the committee reports, the debates on the bills, and the committee hearings now have to be located and examined. Ancillary sources such as committee prints, Presidential messages, and hearings on related bills should also be located and examined. In prior sections of this chapter, sources were discussed that allow a researcher to identify which documents exist and that often provide references or citations to the documents. This section explains where the full text of these documents may be located. Also, additional sources for locating hard-to-find legislative documents are highlighted.

1. Public Bills

a. *United States Congress Public Bills and Resolutions*. This microfiche set, published by the United States Government Printing Office, contains the text of all public bills and resolutions, including amendments introduced in both houses of Congress since the 96th Congress. Access to this set is provided by the *Microfiche Users Guide/Bill Finding Aid*. It should be noted that recently the *Guide* may refer to a public bill or resolution that has not yet been provided in the microfiche set.

b. *CIS/Microfiche Library*. From 1970, CIS provides reprints of the bills that have become public laws.

c. *Public Law—Legislative Histories on Microfiche*. From 1979 through 1988, bills can be located in this collection.

d. *GAO Legislative History Collection*. For selected legislation that has become public law, reprints of relevant bills and amendments are available on microfiche.

e. *Looseleaf Services*. As previously discussed, looseleaf services for specific areas of the law may issue legislative documents, including bills as introduced and as amended, as special releases (usually as pamphlets). Other publications of the government or commercial entities may include the text of bills in their compilations.

f. *Congressional Record*. Occasionally, the text of a bill, especially if amended on the floor of either house during discussion or debate, may be printed in the *Congressional Record*. However, it should be noted that this is not a usual circumstance.

g. *Committee Reports*. Often, the bill as amended by a committee will be included in a report if the bill in fact is reported out of committee.

The committee reports reprinted in the *United States Code Congressional and Administrative News* do not include the text of the bill even if it was a part of the report reprinted in that set.

h. *Online Services*.

(1) *LEXIS–NEXIS*. The text of current public bills, including amendments can be found in various LEXIS–NEXIS libraries and files. Historical material is available in the same libraries, with individual designations for each Congress.

(2) *WESTLAW*. The Congressional Quarterly's Washington Alert—Text of Congressional Bills (CQ–BILLTXT) database includes the text of all available versions of bills introduced in the 103rd Congress.

(3) *LEGI–SLATE.* The text of bills introduced in the current Congress are available through this service.

(4) *Congressional Universe.* Selected bills are provided through this Internet service.

(5) *GPO Access.* The home page of the U.S. Government Printing Office provides a database containing all bills beginning from the 103rd Congress. The database is updated each day the House or Senate is in session. [See Illustration 9–4.]

(6) *Thomas.* This Internet site is made available by the Library of Congress and provides:

(a) the full text and summaries of all bills introduced in either the House or Senate;

(b) a link to bills that are expected to be acted upon on the floor of the House or Senate during the current week;

(c) a link to bills voted on by the House or Senate during the previous week; and

(d) a link to major bills introduced in Congress. The major bills can be searched by topic, popular or short title, bill number or whether they have been passed. [See Illustration 10–11.]

(7) The Internet servers of the United States House of Representatives provide a link to the full text of Congressional bills. [See Illustration 10–7.]

2. House, Senate, and Conference Committee Reports

a. *CIS.* Reports from 1970 to date that have been issued for bills that have become public law can be found in the *CIS Microfiche Library.*

b. *United States Code Congressional and Administrative News.* From 1941, *USCCAN* selectively reprints committee reports for public bills that became law. Beginning with the 99th Congress, the House or the Senate committee reports are reprinted as are the Conference committee reports.

c. *Serial Set.* The Committee reports are reprinted in the official series and the commercial set published by CIS.

d. *GAO Legislative Histories.* For selected laws, committee reports for bills that became public laws are available.

e. *Public Laws—Legislative Histories on Microfiche.* This set makes available Senate, House, and Conference committee reports for public laws enacted during the 96th–100th Congresses.

f. *Looseleaf Services, Treatises, and Other Compiled Legislative Histories.* Committee reports for specialized areas of legal research may be available in these sources.

g. *Congressional Record.* This publication may contain committee reports, although this is not the standard method of publication.

h. *Online Services.*

(1) *WESTLAW.* As noted previously, WESTLAW, since 1948, includes all committee reports printed in USCCAN. From 1990, the database contains all committee reports, as they are available, even for bills that did not become law.

(2) *LEXIS–NEXIS.* House and Senate reports for legislation since 1990 are available.

(3) *LEGI–SLATE.* Committee reports for bills from the current Congress are available through this online service.

i.   *Internet Sources.*

(1) *Congressional Universe.* Committee reports from the 104th Congress forward are available through this commercial service.

(2) *GPO Access.* This home page offers selected House and Senate reports starting in 1995. [See Illustration 9–4.]

(3) *Thomas.* Selected House and Senate committee reports are available through this Internet site.

3.   Congressional Debates

Although the *Congressional Record* contains much more than the debates that occur on proposed legislation, it is the primary source for the transcripts of debates and votes on pending legislation. When using the *Congressional Record,* the researcher should be acquainted with its history and pattern of publication.

a.   *Predecessors to the Congressional Record.* The predecessors to the *Congressional Record* are the *Annals of Congress,* 1789–1824 (1st to 18th Cong., 1st Sess.); the *Register of Debates,* 1824–1837 (18th Cong., 2d Sess. to 25th Cong., 1st Sess.); and the *Congressional Globe,* 1833–1873 (25th Cong., 2d Sess. to 42d Cong., 2d Sess.). The early volumes of the *Congressional Globe* contain abridged versions of the proceedings of Congress. The *Congressional Record* began in 1873 with the 43d Cong., 1st Sess.

b.   *Congressional Record Daily Edition.* The *Congressional Record* is published daily while either chamber is in session. It consists of four sections: the proceedings of the House of Representatives and the Senate (including debates) in separate sections; the Extensions of Remarks (reprints of articles, editorials, book reviews, and tributes); and the Daily Digest (since the 80th Congress, each issue contains a "Daily Digest," which summarizes the day's proceedings, lists actions taken and laws signed by the President that day, and provides very useful committee information). [See Illustrations 10–8 and 10–10.]

Each section of the daily *Congressional Record* is paginated consecutively and separately during each session of Congress. Each page in each section is preceded by the following letter prefix: S–Senate; H–House; E–Extension of Remarks; and D–Daily Digest.

An index to the *Congressional Record* is published every two weeks and provides access in a single alphabetical listing by subject, name of legislator, and title of legislation. These indexes are noncumulative.

c. *Congressional Record Permanent Edition.* A permanent, bound edition of the *Congressional Record* is slated to be published after the end of each session of Congress. Due to contract problems with printers, the paper and microfiche copies of this edition are behind schedule and are often issued in the order of printing, not always in chronological order. However, the permanent edition is generally the accepted source for most research.

The permanent edition differs from the daily edition in that it does not use the same method of pagination but rather integrates all material into one sequence. Additionally, the permanent edition does not contain the Extensions of Remarks from 1955 to 1968.

The permanent edition has an index that provides access by subject, sponsor, and bill number. The "Daily Digest" section of each of the daily editions of the *Congressional Record* is cumulated in one volume of the permanent edition.

d. *Congressional Record Online.* The *Congressional Record* is available through these commercial online sources:

(1) *LEXIS–NEXIS.* Since 1985, the House and Senate debates and proceedings are available.

(2) *WESTLAW.* Coverage is available beginning in 1985.

(3) *LEGI–SLATE.* The *Congressional Record* for the current Congress is included in this online service.

e. Internet Sources. The *Congressional Record* can be located through these Internet resources:

(1) *GPO Access.* The database available through this Government Printing Office home page begins coverage in 1994. It is updated each morning that the *Congressional Record* is published. There also is an index to the *Congressional Record* dating back to 1992. [See Illustration 9–4.]

(2) *Thomas*, an Internet site made available by the Library of Congress provides access to the *Congressional Record*. [See Illustration 10–11.]

4.   Hearings

The hearings relating to bills can be difficult to locate. In addition to the references provided *supra,* the following may provide information for locating reprints of the published and unpublished texts of these documents:

a. *Congressional Information Service (CIS).*

(1) Since 1970, the CIS publications have provided citations to, and a microfiche copy of the full text of, all Senate and House hearings.

(2) *CIS US Congressional Committee Hearings Index.* This *Index* provides access to published hearings from 1833 to 1969. The microfiche component provides the text of published hearings within the time frame covered by this *Index.*

(3) *CIS Index to Unpublished US Senate Committee Hearings.* The volumes of this *Index* provide coverage for Senate hearings from 1823 to 1968 that were not published. The microfiche component to the set allows access to the text of the hearings. Supplements are planned for coverage beyond 1968.

(4) *CIS Index to Unpublished US House of Representative Hearings.* Along with the microfiche portion, this *Index* enables a researcher to find the citation to an unpublished hearing and to locate the text. Coverage is from 1833 to 1946, with planned supplementation.

b.   United States. Congress. Senate. Library. *Index of Congressional Committee Hearings (not confidential in character) prior to January 3, 1935 in the United States Senate Library.*

c.   United States. Congress. Senate. Library. *Cumulative Index of Congressional Committee Hearings (not confidential in character) from Seventy–Fourth Congress (January 3, 1935) Through Eighty–Fifth Congress (January 3, 1959) in the United States Senate Library.*

d.   United States. Congress. Senate. Library. *Shelflist of Congressional Committee Hearings (not confidential in character) in the United States Senate Library from Eighty–Sixth Congress (January 7, 1959) through Ninety–First Congress (January 2, 1971).*

e.   *Congressional Hearings Calendar: An Index to Congressional Hearings by Date, Committee/Subcommittee, Chairman, and Title,* 1985 to date. The purpose of these compilations is to provide a current means to identify recently held hearings that may not yet be covered by government document indexes. It also provides different access points than *CIS,* for example, by date of hearing, by name of committee and subcommittee, and by name of the chair presiding over the hearing. This is especially helpful for multi-part hearings, making only one look-up necessary.

f.   *Monthly Catalog of United States Government Publications.* This index provides references to hearings held on a particular piece of legislation.

5.   Committee Prints

The sources that follow can provide access to committee prints:

a.   *CIS US Congressional Committee Prints Index* and microfiche component. This multi-volume Index covers committee prints from 1830 to 1969. The microfiche component reprints these documents.

b.   *CIS.* From 1970 forward, the *CIS Index and Abstracts* volumes enable the researcher to locate committee prints published since 1970. The CIS microfiche library provides reprints of the documents.

c. *Serial Set*. If a committee print is designated as a House or Senate document, it is available in the official *Serial Set* or in the CIS commercial component of this set. The commercial series is complete through 1969 and is then continued by the CIS microfiche library, *supra*.

d. *GPO Access*. A database available through this home page provides selected Senate and House documents starting in 1995.

6. Presidential Documents

The statements that the President uses when sending proposed legislation to Congress or when signing or vetoing a bill can be located in the following sources.

a. *Weekly Compilation of Presidential Documents*. The *Weekly Compilation* is issued each Monday and includes the text of many Presidential documents. Of particular importance to compilers of legislative histories are the veto messages, signing statements, messages to Congress, and a list of acts approved by the President. Each issue contains an index to all material in the previous issues for the current quarter. Commencing with volume 31, number 1, January 9, 1995, a cumulative index is no longer published in each issue. Rather, indexes are issued quarterly and distributed separately. Semi-annual and annual cumulative indexes also are published. This publication is discussed in more detail in Chapter 13.

The *Weekly Compilation* is available through LEXIS–NEXIS.

b. *Public Papers of the Presidents of the United States*. This annual series began with the 1957 volume covering the Eisenhower administration. The series is being compiled contemporaneously and retrospectively. Prior to 1977, *Public Papers* was an edited version of the *Weekly Compilation*. However, beginning with the administration of Jimmy Carter and continuing through the volume for 1988–89, the last year of President Reagan's administration, the set includes all of the material printed in the *Weekly Compilation of Presidential Documents*. Beginning in 1989, the first year of the administration of President Bush, Proclamations and Executive Orders are not reproduced. Rather a table refers the user to the appropriate issue of the *Federal Register* in which the documents are published.

The set contains an annual index for each year of an administration. A cumulative index for each administration is commercially published under the title *Cumulated Indexes to the Public Papers of the Presidents of the United States*. This publication is discussed in Chapter 13.

Public Papers is available through LEXIS–NEXIS from 1981.

c. *United States Code Congressional and Administrative News*. Since 1986, *USCCAN* reprints the text of Presidential Signing Statements in the legislative history volumes of the set. The Signing Statements as reprinted by *USCCAN* are available through WESTLAW.

d. *Additional Sources*. Presidential messages can also be found in the *Congressional Record*, the House and Senate *Journals*, and in the *Serial Set* if considered as a House or Senate document. The White House internet site has a collection of presidential documents.

SECTION I. FINDING AIDS AND SOURCES FOR DOCUMENTS

This chart identifies a document; its finding aids; and sources where the document itself may be located. For specific information on the items in these categories, the reader should refer back to the narrative in this chapter.

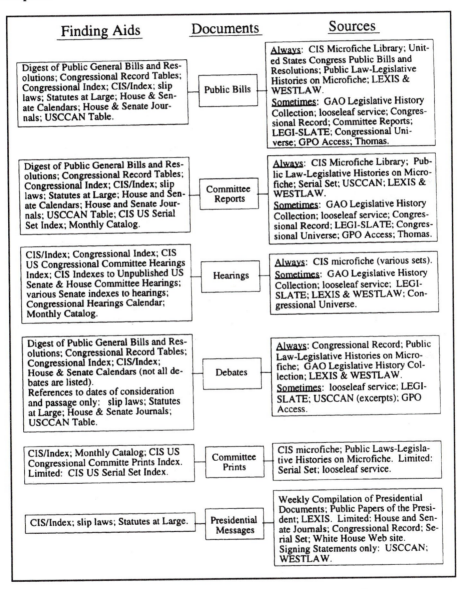

Finding Aids	Documents	Sources
Digest of Public General Bills and Resolutions; Congressional Record Tables; Congressional Index; CIS/Index; slip laws; Statutes at Large; House & Senate Calendars; House & Senate Journals; USCCAN Table.	Public Bills	**Always:** CIS Microfiche Library; United States Congress Public Bills and Resolutions; Public Law-Legislative Histories on Microfiche; LEXIS & WESTLAW. **Sometimes:** GAO Legislative History Collection; looseleaf service; Congressional Record; Committee Reports; LEGI-SLATE; Congressional Universe; GPO Access; Thomas.
Digest of Public General Bills and Resolutions; Congressional Record Tables; Congressional Index; CIS/Index; slip laws; Statutes at Large; House and Senate Calendars; House and Senate Journals; USCCAN Table; CIS US Serial Set Index; Monthly Catalog.	Committee Reports	**Always:** CIS Microfiche Library; Public Law-Legislative Histories on Microfiche; Serial Set; USCCAN; LEXIS & WESTLAW. **Sometimes:** GAO Legislative History Collection; looseleaf service; Congressional Record; LEGI-SLATE; Congressional Universe; GPO Access; Thomas.
CIS/Index; Congressional Index; CIS US Congressional Committee Hearings Index; CIS Indexes to Unpublished US Senate & House Committee Hearings; various Senate indexes to hearings; Congressional Hearings Calendar; Monthly Catalog.	Hearings	**Always:** CIS microfiche (various sets). **Sometimes:** GAO Legislative History Collection; looseleaf service; LEGI-SLATE; LEXIS & WESTLAW; Congressional Universe.
Digest of Public General Bills and Resolutions; Congressional Record Tables; Congressional Index; CIS/Index; House & Senate Calendars (not all debates are listed). References to dates of consideration and passage only: slip laws; Statutes at Large; House & Senate Journals; USCCAN Table.	Debates	**Always:** Congressional Record; Public Law-Legislative Histories on Microfiche; GAO Legislative History Collection; LEXIS & WESTLAW. **Sometimes:** looseleaf service; LEGI-SLATE; USCCAN (excerpts); GPO Access.
CIS/Index; Monthly Catalog; CIS US Congressional Committe Prints Index. Limited: CIS US Serial Set Index.	Committee Prints	CIS microfiche; Public Laws-Legislative Histories on Microfiche. Limited: Serial Set; looseleaf service.
CIS/Index; slip laws; Statutes at Large.	Presidential Messages	Weekly Compilation of Presidential Documents; Public Papers of the President; LEXIS. Limited: House and Senate Journals; Congressional Record; Serial Set; White House Web site. Signing Statements only: USCCAN; WESTLAW.

SECTION J. PENDING LEGISLATION

In addition to the sources previously described, the following online sources allow researchers to track the progress of pending legislation and in most cases to identify documents generated during the bill's progress.

1. BILLCAST

BILLCAST, published by Information for Public Affairs, Inc., provides a forecast report for public bills pending in the current Congress. The report gives a brief summary of the bill's purpose and predictions of the bill's chance of passing in committee and on the floor. BILLCAST for the current Congress is available through WESTLAW and LEXIS–NEXIS. Both online services also include archives for BILLCAST.

2. Bill Tracking Reports

a. *WESTLAW.* This database contains summaries and status information relating to current federal legislation. A public bill is covered through each step of the legislative process.

b. *LEXIS–NEXIS.* Bill tracking summaries providing an ongoing update of the status of bills pending in both houses of the current Congress are available. Each summary contains a synopsis of the bill, its introduction date, committee referrals, and a complete legislative chronology including references to the *Congressional Record.*

c. *LEGI–SLATE.* In addition to the full-text documents available through this online service, LEGI–SLATE tracks legislative action on pending bills.

d. *Electronic Legislative Search System (ELSS).* This online bill tracking service, offered by Commerce Clearing House, summarizes pending legislation and provides daily information on the progress of the legislation as it proceeds through Congress.

e. *Thomas.* This Library of Congress Internet site provides information about the status of pending legislation. It can be searched in a variety of ways including keyword, number, sponsor, and committee. [See Illustration 10–11.]

f. *United States House of Representatives Servers.* This server provides a description of major floor and committee action taken in Congress and a schedule of upcoming floor and committee actions. [See Illustration 10–7.]

SECTION K. CONGRESSIONAL QUARTERLY MATERIALS

Congressional Quarterly, Inc. is a prolific publisher of materials that provide current information and reference works that deal with all branches of the federal government. Some of these publications particularly relevant to federal legislative histories are highlighted in this section.

1. Congressional Quarterly Weekly Report

This magazine of Congressional news contains summaries of major legislation and issues. Although coverage is not as complete as the sources previously described, *CQ Weekly Report* is valuable because of its extensive analysis and background discussion of laws and legislative issues.

2. Congressional Quarterly Almanac

At the end of each session of Congress, the *CQ Almanac* is published to provide information of permanent research value on Congressional activity during that year. The *CQ Almanac* provides an excellent narrative overview of the legislative history of major bills passed. Therefore, it is a good starting point when one is not sure whether a specific section of the bill, as enacted, actually became a part of the law.

3. Congress and the Nation

Although this publication began as a project to cumulate and summarize information in individual *CQ Almanacs*, this work, which is comprised of many volumes with each covering a span of years, provides greater evaluation and assessment of the politics and legislation for the years covered by a volume.

4. Congressional Monitor

This daily reporting service provides information on active legislation before Congress. The *Monitor* does not include the in-depth analysis or coverage of the other Congressional Quarterly publications since its primary purpose is to provide up-to-date data on the daily activity of Congress.

SECTION L. SUMMARY

1. Documents Comprising a Federal Legislative History

In order to do a federal legislative history some or all of the following would need to be identified, obtained, and examined.

Bills as introduced in both houses, with any amendments.

Reports of committees to which bill was referred.

Report of the conference committee, if any.

Debates and discussions on floor of Congress, if any.

Hearings before committees considering the bill.

Hearings related to the bill held in prior Congresses.

Committee prints.

Presidential documents related to the legislation.

2. Compiled Legislative Histories

Check the following sources to determine if a legislative history may have been compiled.

    a. *Sources of Compiled Legislative Histories.*

    b. *Union List of Legislative Histories.*

    c. *Monthly Catalog of United States Government Publications.*

If these publications reference a compiled legislative history, obtain, if possible, since identifying and location information may be included as well as the documents themselves.

    d. Online Sources: LEXIS–NEXIS; WESTLAW; LEGI–SLATE.

3. Sources that assist in identifying many documents of a federal legislative history and that contain some of the documents themselves

    a. *CIS,* 1970 to date.

    (1) Indexes.

    (2) Abstracts.

    (3) Legislative History volumes.

    (4) Microfiche Library.

    (5) *Congressional Universe*

    b. *Public Laws—Legislative Histories on Microfiche,* 96th Congress–100th Congress.

    c. *GAO Legislative History Collection.*

    (1) Register of Public Laws—finding aid.

    (2) Microfiche component—documents.

    (3) selective.

    (4) coverage begins in 1921.

    d. *United States Code Congressional and Administrative News—* Legislative History volumes.

    (1) House or Senate committee report.

    (2) Conference Committee report.

    (3) Presidential Signing Statement.

    (4) Selected excerpts from the *Congressional Record* for major laws.

    e. *United States Congressional Serial Set.*

    (1) Especially important for committee reports.

    (2) Also available through 1969 as a commercial publication by CIS with microfiche component.

    f. Internet Sites.

    (1) *GPO Access.*

    (2) *Thomas.*

    (3) *U.S. House of Representatives Servers.*

4. Other methods of compiling a federal legislative history

If the sources described above are not available or do not provide assistance for the specific research, the following steps should be taken.

a. Refer to the Finding Aids listed in Section I, which are explained in detail in the chapter, to identify the documents that need to be retrieved.

b. Once the documents are identified, refer to the Sources in Section H, which are explained in greater detail in the chapter, to obtain the documents.

c. For pending legislation, additional sources can be found in Section J.

d. More than one finding aid or source may be needed to complete the process of compiling a legislative history.

Chapter 11

STATE AND MUNICIPAL LEGISLATION

The enactment, organization, and publication of federal and of state statutes are very similar. The differences that do exist among the statutes of the fifty states are mostly in nomenclature rather than substance. Each state has a state legislature and, with the exception of Nebraska, each has an upper and lower house similar to the Senate and the House of Representatives of the United States Congress. In general, the legislative process for the passage of state laws is similar to that previously described for federal laws.[1]

State legislatures meet in either annual or biennial sessions. Information for individual states as to nomenclature, frequency of session, and other pertinent information on state legislatures can be obtained by consulting the latest edition of *The Book of the States*.[2]

SECTION A. SESSION LAWS

Each state publishes all of the laws passed during each session of its legislature in volumes with the generic name, *session laws,* although in some states these may have other names, such as *acts and resolves,* or *statutes,* or *laws*.[3] These include public laws, as well as private, temporary, local, and appropriation acts. The session laws are published in chronological order comparable to those in the *United States Statutes at Large* and are issued in bound form after the session is over. Several states also publish their laws in *slip* form soon after they are passed. In addition, current laws are frequently provided by private publishers in advance sheets a part of a subscription to an annotated state code.[4] [See Illustration 11–1.] Internet access to session laws is discussed in Section C, *infra*.

SECTION B. CODIFICATION OF STATE LAWS

Each volume of the session laws for a state contains the public laws passed by the legislature during an annual, biennial, or special session.

---

[1] The primary purpose of this Chapter is to present information on how to locate state statutes. It must be noted, however, that after the relevant statute has been found, it is frequently necessary to determine its proper application. For this latter purpose, see NORMAN SINGER, STATUTES AND STATUTORY CONSTRUCTION (5th ed. 1992).

[2] COUNCIL OF STATE GOVERNMENTS, THE BOOK OF THE STATES (latest).

[3] SESSION LAWS OF AMERICAN STATES AND TERRITORIES (William S. Hein & Co., Inc.) is a comprehensive microfiche collection covering 1775 to date. It contains both operative and inoperative law. *See also infra* note 7 and accompanying text.

[4] For information pertaining to the availability of slip laws, advance legislative services, and advance annotation services, see MARY L. FISHER, GUIDE TO STATE LEGISLATIVE AND ADMINISTRATIVE MATERIALS (4th ed. 1988).

Since the laws passed are arranged chronologically in each volume, in order to facilitate access it is necessary to have the laws rearranged by title or subjects as they are in the *United States Code.* Each state does, in fact, have a set of statutes that have been extracted from the session laws and then reorganized topically for ease of use. [See Illustration 11–2.] The terms *revised, compiled, consolidated,* and *code* are often used indiscriminately to describe such sets of books.[5] Internet access to state codes is discussed in Section C, *infra.*

In some instances, compilations are accomplished under the official auspices of a state, in others by private publishers, and in some states there are both official and unofficial sets of codes.[6] Some state codes have been enacted into positive law; others are only *prima facie* evidence of the law with the positive law being in the volumes of the session laws. The important thing to note is that each state has a set of session laws and at least one current code. The set being used should be examined carefully to note its features, its method of publication, and the way it is kept up to date. Since state codes contain only public acts, the private, temporary, local, and appropriation acts must be located in the session laws.

The following features are common to many sets of state codes:

1. Constitutions

Each state code contains the constitution of the state that is currently in force, usually with annotations, as well as the text of previous constitutions. The text of the Constitution of the United States, typically unannotated, is usually included as well.

2. Tables

Each state code has tables, usually in a separate volume, that cross reference from the session law to the code section, and many will have tables that refer from the older codification to the current one. [See Illustration 11–3.]

---

[5] Methods of compilation differ from state to state. One state may simply reissue the session laws in chronological order but with temporary and repealed acts not included. A second may arrange the laws still in effect in a classified order but with the text kept intact as originally arranged. A third may rewrite, rearrange, and reenact the laws in a new classified order. For additional information, consult the sources *infra* note 6.

[6] For articles dealing with the codification of state laws, see Barbara C. Salken, *To Codify or Not to Codify—That Is the Question: A Study of New York's Efforts to Enact an Evidence Code,* 58 BROOK. L. REV. 641 (1993); Kelly Kunsch, *Statutory Compilations of Washington,* 12 U. PUGET SOUND L. REV. 285 (1989); Vincent C. Henderson, *The Creation of the Arkansas Code of 1987 Annotated,* 11 U. ARK. LITTLE ROCK L.J. 21 (1988–89); Terry A. McKenzie, *The Making of a New Code: The Official Code of Georgia Annotated: Recodification in Georgia,* 18 GA. ST. B.J. 102 (1982); Dennis R. Bailey et al., Comment, *1975—A Code Odyssey, A Critical Analysis of the Alabama Recodification Process,* 10 CUMB. L. REV. 119 (1979); Diana S. Dowling, *The Creation of the Montana Code Annotated,* 40 MONT. L. REV. 1 (1979); John H. Tucker, Jr., *Tradition and Technique of Codification in the Modern World: The Louisiana Experience,* 25 LA. L. REV. 698 (1965).

3. Indexes

All sets of state codes contain a separate subject index for use in locating materials within the entire set. [See Illustration 11–4.] These indexes will occasionally provide the popular names of state acts. In addition, most of these sets also contain an index at the completion of each subject grouping within the set.

4. Text of Statutes

Each state code contains the public laws of a general nature and still in force, arranged by subject. [See Illustrations 11–2 and 11–5.]

5. Historical Notes

Historical references, which follow the text of the statute, provide citations to the session laws from which the statute was derived. Since many states have had several codifications of their laws over time, citations frequently are given to the present provision in a previous codification.

6. Annotations

At least one annotated code is published for each state and in some instances there are two, each by a different publisher. Some are very similar in appearance to the *U.S.C.A.* or the *U.S.C.S.,* including such information as notes of decisions, citations to law review articles, legal encyclopedias, and other research aids, and cross references to related code provisions. [See Illustration 11–5.] Some codes include pamphlet "advance annotation services" containing the latest topically-arranged materials prior to their incorporation into the pocket supplements.

7. Rules of Court

State codes typically contain the rules of court, which detail the procedural requirements for presenting matters before the various courts within the state. Frequently, a separate "rules" pamphlet, issued annually, accompanies the set. Court rules are discussed in Chapter 12.

SECTION C. ELECTRONIC ACCESS TO STATE LEGISLATION

WESTLAW and LEXIS–NEXIS have comprehensive coverage for the annotated codes for the 50 states, the District of Columbia, and the territories. The unannotated versions for all states are also available online. These statutory sources can be searched individually or collectively for all states. Similarly, the advance legislative services, which contain the most recently-enacted legislation, are in these online services. State codes are also available on CD–ROM from various publishers, often in conjunction with case law databases.

The phenomenal growth of the Internet has prompted states to make available their legislation in unprecedented ways. A substantial majority of the states have their official state codes available through their home page and some states even include their session laws. Some of the sources discussed elsewhere in this text provide easy access to these state sources. For example, the Center for Information Law and Policy [See Illustration 4–12] has a separate *State Web Locator* that offers a search engine for all state offices available on the Internet; *Hieros Gamos* [See Illustration 5–4] likewise provides excellent links to all state resources. The individual home pages for the states, which can be located thorough links provided by massive sources such as those just mentioned or through the URL address for an individual state's home page if known, offer a wealth of sources of information. Coverage, however, varies greatly from state to state. The State of California seems to have set the standard for providing access to its state legal materials. [See Illustration 11–6.]

SECTION D.   FINDING STATE LEGISLATION

1.   Current State Law

When researching state legislation, one is usually attempting to ascertain if there is a current state statutory provision on a particular subject, e.g., at what age may one be issued a driver's license? The first step in the research process is to examine carefully the code for the state in question and become familiar with the way the code is organized. Consulting the index should lead to the citation of a provision in the code that sets forth the current statutory law on the subject. Next, if the set is annotated, the notes of decisions and other references set forth below the statutory provision should be consulted. The method of supplementation should also be noted, e.g., revised replacement volumes, pocket supplements, bound cumulative supplements, or advance pamphlets, and these sources should be checked for the most recent enactments.

At times, a state statute may become known by its popular name rather than by its actual name. Citations to acts can often be located in the "Table of Acts by Popular Names or Short Title" in the appropriate state unit of *Shepard's Citations* [See Illustration 11–7] or in the national *Shepard's Acts and Cases by Popular Name*. The state units of *Shepard's Citations* can also be helpful for locating citations when only the actual name of the act is known. These sources are discussed in Chapter 15.

2.   Inoperative State Law

At times the problem being researched may involve an act that has been repealed or is no longer in force. In these instances consult the code that was available when the law was in force or the session law volume that contains the text of the act as originally passed by the legislature. These sources are often available in microform.[7]

---

[7] HEIN'S SUPERSEDED STATE STATUTES AND CODES (William S. Hein & Co., Inc.) is a comprehensive microfiche collection that contains volumes of annotated codes that have been replaced by later volumes in sets that are currently being published. "Superseded," as used in this collection, does not suggest that all laws in a replaced volume are inoperative; however, some of them will be. *See also supra* note 3.

SECTION E.   ILLUSTRATIONS FOR STATE LEGISLATION

[Illustration 11–1]

PAGE FROM THE 1992 VERNON'S MISSOURI LEGISLATIVE SERVICE (SESSION LAWS)

NO. 127   **86th GENERAL ASSEMBLY** **H.B. 852**

HIGHWAY PATROL

H.B. No. 852

WEST'S No. 127

AN ACT to repeal section 43.200, RSMo 1986, relating to the highway patrol, and to enact in lieu thereof two new sections relating to the same subject.

Be it enacted by the General Assembly of the State of Missouri, as follows:

Section A.   Section 43.200, RSMo 1986, is repealed and two new sections enacted in lieu thereof, to be known as sections 43.200 and 1, to read as follows:

43.200.   1.   The members of the patrol shall ~~not~~ have the right ~~or~~ and power of search ~~nor shall they have the right or power of~~ and seizure ~~except~~ to take from any person under arrest or about to be arrested deadly or dangerous weapons in the possession of such person, and ~~except that the members of the patrol shall have the power of~~ to search and ~~seizure~~ seize on a public highway of this state, or off the public highways of this state as an incident to an arrest made following a hot pursuit from a public highway.

2.   When ordered to any county or municipality in this state by the governor because of civil disorder ~~the~~ members of the patrol during that time may exercise all powers of search and seizure in the same manner and to the same extent as any sheriff in this state ~~except that a member of the patrol shall not apply for or serve search warrants~~.

3.   The members of the highway patrol may request that the prosecuting or circuit attorney apply for, and members of the highway patrol may serve, search warrants anywhere within the state of Missouri, provided the sheriff of the county in which the warrant is to be served, or his designee, shall be notified upon application by the applicant of the search warrant. The sheriff or his designee shall participate in serving the search warrant. Any designee of the sheriff shall be a deputy sheriff or other person certified as a peace officer under chapter 590, RSMo. The sheriff shall always have a designee available.

~~2.~~4.   The superintendent of the highway patrol shall see that every member of the highway patrol is thoroughly instructed in the powers of police officers to arrest for misdemeanors and felonies and to search and seize in order that no person or citizen traveling ~~the highways~~ in this state shall be hindered, stopped, or arrested or his person or property searched or seized without constitutional grounds existing therefor.

5.   The authority of the members of the highway patrol to request that the prosecuting or circuit attorney apply for and the authority to serve search warrants shall expire on March 15, 1995.

Section 1.   Each criminal justice agency which submits criminal arrest, charge and disposition information to the central repository shall make criminal history information available on request to the investigator of the Missouri senate without charge.

Approved July 8, 1992.

Effective 90 days after adjournment.

This is a 1992 session law from Missouri. The Illustration is from *Vernon's Missouri Legislative Service*. After the end of a legislative session, all laws passed will be published in a bound volume of session laws. All public laws, such as this one, will also be incorporated into the state code. See next Illustration.

1406   Additions are indicated by underline; deletions by strikeout

[Illustration 11-2]

PAGE FROM THE 1993 POCKET SUPPLEMENT, VERNON'S ANNOTATED MISSOURI STATUTES

STATE HIGHWAY PATROL 43.200

43.200. Search and seizure powers of highway patrol—authority to serve search warrants anywhere in state on request to prosecutors or circuit attorneys—authority expires 3-15-95—sheriff to assist, duties

1. The members of the patrol shall have the right and power of search and seizure to take from any person under arrest or about to be arrested deadly or dangerous weapons in the possession of such person, and to search and seize on a public highway of this state, or off the public highways of this state as an incident to an arrest made following a hot pursuit from a public highway.

2. When ordered to any county or municipality in this state by the governor because of civil disorder members of the patrol during that time may exercise all powers of search and seizure in the same manner and to the same extent as any sheriff in this state.

3. The members of the highway patrol may request that the prosecuting or circuit attorney apply for, and members of the highway patrol may serve, search warrants anywhere within the state of Missouri, provided the sheriff of the county in which the warrant is to be served, or his designee, shall be notified upon application by the applicant of the search warrant. The sheriff or his designee shall participate in serving the search warrant. Any designee of the sheriff shall be a deputy sheriff or other person certified

> This Illustration is from the 1993 pocket supplement to *Vernon's Annotated Missouri Statutes*. Notice how the session law that was passed the year before and shown in the previous Illustration has been incorporated into the state code. Notice also how a citation is given to the session law from which § 43.200 was codified.
>
> To locate a citation to a section of a state's code when only the session law citation is available it is necessary to use a transfer table. See next Illustration.

or circuit attorney apply for, and the authority to serve, search warrants shall expire on March 15, 1995.

(Amended by L.1992, H.B. No. 852, § A.)

Historical and Statutory Notes

1992 Legislation

The 1992 amendment divided subsec. 1 into subsecs. 1 and 2; in subsec. 1, substituted "have the right and power of search and seizure" for "not have the right or power of search nor shall they have the right or power of seizure except" and substituted "to search and seize" for "ex-

cept that the members of the patrol shall have the power of search and seizure"; in subsec. 2, deleted "except that a member of the patrol shall not apply for or serve search warrants"; inserted subsec. 3; redesignated former subsec. 2 as subsec. 4; in subsec. 4, substituted "in this state" for "the highways"; and added subsec. 5.

Notes of Decisions

4. Searches

Search of defendant's vehicle was not product of "pretextual" traffic stop, where the vehicle was observed weaving within its lane of travel, sergeant observed manner in which vehicle was being operated and questioned whether operator

was sleepy or intoxicated, operator indicated that vehicle belonged to defendant, a passenger, and stories of defendant and operator were conflicting. State v. Marshell (App.1992) 825 S.W.2d 341, rehearing denied.

[Illustration 11–3]

PAGE FROM THE TABLES VOLUME, VERNON'S ANNOTATED MISSOURI STATUTES

TABLE OF SESSION LAWS

	LAWS 1992 Second Regular Session SENATE BILLS			LAWS 1992 Second Regular Session HOUSE BILLS	
S.B. No.	Sec.	V.A.M.S. Sec.	H.B. No.	Sec.	V.A.M.S. Sec.
	B	Emergency		(A)2	340.202
867	A	334.044		(A)3	340.204
	B	Emergency		(A)4	340.206
870	1	no class		(A)5	340.208
	2	no class		(A)6	340.210

| | LAWS 1992 Second Regular Session HOUSE BILLS | | | | (A)7 | 340.212 |

H.B. No.	Sec.	V.A.M.S. Sec.		
852	A	43.200	(A)8	340.214
	(A)1	43.541	(A)9	340.216
878	A	268.011	(A)10	340.218
		268.031	(A)11	340.220
		268.041	(A)12	340.222
		268.101	(A)13	340.224
		268.131	(A)14	340.226
		268.141	(A)15	340.228
		269.010	(A)16	340.230
		269.020	(A)17	340.232
		269.021	(A)18	340.234
		269.022	(A)19	340.236
		269.023	(A)20	340.238
		269.025	(A)21	340.240
		269.030	(A)22	340.244
		269.032	(A)23	340.246
			(A)24	340.248
			(A)25	340.250
			(A)26	340.252

> When only a citation to a state session law is available, a transfer table, usually included in a volume of the state's codification, must be consulted to locate where a particular section of a session law is within the state's code. For example, this Illustration shows that House Bill (H.B.) No. 852 is incorporated into Section 43.200 of *Vernon's Annotated Missouri Statutes* (*V.A.M.S.*).
>
> Sometimes an individual session law may deal with several different matters as does H.B. 878 also shown in this table. In these instances, notice how the session law may be incorporated into several sections of the code.

				(A)39	340.278
	269.140			(A)40	340.280
	269.145			(A)41	340.282
	269.150			(A)42	340.284
	269.160			(A)43	340.286
	269.170			(A)44	340.288
	269.200			(A)45	340.290
	269.210			(A)46	340.292
	269.220			(A)47	340.294
	340.010 Rep.			(A)48	340.296
	340.020 Rep.			(A)49	340.298
	340.030 Rep.			(A)50	340.300
	340.060 Rep.			(A)51	340.302
	340.080 Rep.			(A)52	340.304
	340.120 Rep.			(A)53	340.306
	340.130 Rep.			(A)54	340.308
	340.140 Rep.			(A)55	340.310
	340.141 Rep.			(A)56	340.312
	340.142 Rep.			(A)57	340.314
	340.145 Rep.			(A)58	340.316
	340.150 Rep.			(A)59	340.318
	340.160 Rep.			(A)60	340.320
	340.170 Rep.			(A)61	340.322
	340.180 Rep.			(A)62	340.324
(A)1	340.200				

307

[Illustration 11–4]

PAGE FROM AN INDEX VOLUME, MASSACHUSETTS
GENERAL LAWS ANNOTATED

EASEMENTS

EASEMENTS—Cont'd
Low-level radioactive waste management, site selection, 111H § 23
Massachusetts bay transportation authority, 161A § 1 et seq.
Massachusetts turnpike, acquisition, 81 App. § 1–7
Natural gas pipe line companies, eminent domain, requisites, 164 § 75C
Nominal damages for disturbing, allowance of costs, 187 § 4
Notice,
  Disturbance of easement, 187 § 4
  Herbicide spraying by public utilities, 132B § 6B
  Prevent acquisition of, 187 § 3
Posting notice preventing acquisition of easement, 187 §§ 3, 4
Prescription, 187 § 2
Preservation restrictions, 184 § 31 et seq.
Prevention of easements by notice, 187 §§ 3, 4
Private ways, public utilities, 187 § 5
Public Utilities, this index
Quieting title, 240 § 1
  Discharge of mortgages, 240 § 15

EASEMENTS—Cont'd
Time, acquisition by prescription, twenty year use, 187 § 2
Trails, construction and maintenance by department of natural resources, 132 § 38A
Turnarounds, way not connected with another way, subdivision control law, 41 § 81Q
Urban renewal projects, 121B § 23
Use, light and air, 187 § 1
Use for twenty years, acquisition by prescription, 187 § 2
Water companies,
  Authority to acquire, 165 § 4B
  Private ways, 187 § 5
Water resources division, impoundment sites, acquisitions of lands and waters, 21 § 9A
Watershed preservation restrictions, 184 § 31 et seq.
Waterworks, lands no longer needed, 40 § 15B
Windows, light and air, acquisition by use, 187 § 1

When research involves locating a statute, the search is started in the index volume of the state code.

Assume the problem under research is whether a property owner in Massachusetts can gain an easement to light and air through the use of windows.

This Illustration shows how the relevant statute is located in the *Massachusetts General Laws Annotated* at Chapter 187, § 1.

Registration, examination of title, fee, 262 § 39
Registry of deeds, notice to prevent acquisition of easement, 187 § 3
Sewers and drains,
  Abandonment, 83 § 4
  Construction and maintenance, 83 § 1
Solar energy, 187 § 1A
Solid waste disposal, 16 § 19
State forests,
  Public utilities, etc., 132 § 34A
  Trails, 132 § 38
State highways. Highways and Streets, this index
State recreation areas, public utilities, 132A § 3
State tidelands, access, scuba and skin diving, 91 § 10D
Subdivision Control Law, turnaround, termination, 41 § 81Q
Superior court actions, costs, 261 § 4
Tax deed, conveyance subject to benefit of easement, 60 § 45
Tax title subject to, 60 § 54
Telephone and telegraph companies, 166 § 37
  Herbicide spraying notices, 132B § 6B
  Private ways, 187 § 5

See, also, Cities and Towns, generally, this index
Brockton regional transit authority, 161B § 1 et seq.
Congressional districts, 57 § 1
District court, 218 § 1
Medical examiners, 38 § 1
Senatorial districts, 57 § 3

EAST BROOKFIELD, TOWN OF
See, also, Cities and Towns, generally, this index
Congressional districts, 57 § 1
District court, 218 § 1
Senatorial districts, 57 § 3

EAST LONGMEADOW, TOWN OF
See, also, Cities and Towns, generally, this index
Congressional districts, 57 § 1
District court, 218 § 1
Lower Pioneer Valley regional transit authority, 161B § 1 et seq.
Senatorial districts, 57 § 3

EAST NORFOLK, TOWN OF
District court,
  Assistant clerks, 218 § 10

148

[Illustration 11–5]

PAGE FROM CHAPTER 187, MASSACHUSETTS GENERAL LAWS ANNOTATED

TITLE TO REAL PROPERTY

After locating the citation to the statute in the Index, the section cited must be read carefully.

Always check any supplement that may be available. In this set, annual pocket supplements and advance annotation pamphlets are published.

Following the text of each section of a statute, citations are provided to: (1) historical and statutory sources; (2) articles from law reviews published in the state; (3) encyclopedias, digests, and treatises; and (4) notes of decisions from all federal and state cases and Attorney General opinions that have cited and interpreted this section of the statute.

---

§ 1.   Right to light and air

Whoever erects a house or other building with windows overlooking the land of another shall not, by the mere continuance of such windows, acquire an easement of light or air so as to prevent the erection of a building on such land.

Historical and Statutory Notes ◄——— ①

St.1852, c. 144.   P.S.1882, c. 122, § 1.
G.S.1860, c. 90 § 32.   R.L.1902, c. 130, § 1.

② ———► Law Review Commentaries

Air space utilization. (1971) 5 Suffolk U.L. Rev. 1009.
Easements of light and air over streets. (1901) 15 Harvard L.Rev. 305.

Solar access: Transferable development rights. (1978) 13 New England L.Rev. 835.

Library References ◄——— ③

Easements ⚷11.
WESTLAW Topic No. 141.
C.J.S. Easements § 19.

Comments.
    Conditions and covenants, see M.P.S. vol. 14A, Simpson and Alperin, § 1431 et seq.

Damnum absque injuria, see M.P.S. vol. 14A, Simpson and Alperin, § 1683; vol. 17, Bishop, § 543.
Easement of light or air, see M.P.S. vol. 28, Park, § 290.

WESTLAW Electronic Research

See WESTLAW Electronic Research Guide following the Preface.

④ ———► Notes of Decisions

In general   1
Acquisition of easements   2
Deeds and conveyances   4
Injunctions   6
Intention of parties   3
Windows overlooking another's land   5

1. In general

One has no right to have adjacent premises remain open for the admission of light and air. In re Opinion of the Justices (1911) 94 N.E. 849, 208 Mass. 603.

2. Acquisition of easements

Easement of light and air is acquired only by express grant, by covenant, or by implication. Novello v. Caprigno (1931) 176 N.E. 809, 276 Mass. 193.

Easement of light and air can be acquired only by express grant, by covenant, or by implication where light or air is actually and absolutely necessary. Hampe v. Elia (1925) 146 N.E. 730, 251 Mass. 465.

Easement of light and air can exist only by express grant, covenant, or absolute necessity, and cannot be created by prescription. Tidd v.

608

[Illustration 11–6]

SCREEN FROM STATE OF CALIFORNIA WEB SITE

CA Home Page: Your Government

http://www.ca.gov/s/govt/

Your Government

Your Elected Officials
Read about your California elected officials including the Governor, constitutional officers, Assembly Members, Senators, and members of Congress.

California Courts
Learn about the California court system; link to California court websites; read opinions of the California Supreme Court.

State Government Services & Agencies
Link directly to a California state agency or department.

Your Local Government
Find your home town's web site; link to California county information available on the Internet.

Voting & Elections
Browse voter registration information and eligibility requirements for voting; view legislative and congressional district maps; view election results for state and national elections in 1996.

Laws, Codes, and Regulations
Search California Bills and Codes, U.S. Bills and Codes, and the U.S.Code of Federal Regulations.

Useful Government Sites
Connect to the White House; find state home pages; view extensive listings of government agencies on the web.

Graphic & Photo Credits:
California State Archives; California State Library; California Department of Water Resources, and Tom Meyers - photography.

[Illustration 11–7]

PAGE FROM SHEPARD'S MISSOURI CITATIONS—TABLE OF MISSOURI ACTS (POPULAR NAMES)

TABLE OF MISSOURI ACTS   M-N

Missouri Retail Credit Sales Act
  Mo. Rev. Stat. 1986, 408.250 et seq.

Missouri-St. Louis Metropolitan Airport Authority Law
  Mo. Rev. Stat. 1986, 305.500 et seq.

Missouri Securities Act
  Mo. Rev. Stat. 1986, 409.101 et seq.

Missouri Seed Law
  Mo. Rev. Stat. 1986, 266.011 et seq.

Missouri Take Over Bid Disclosure Act
  Mo. Rev. Stat. 1986, 409.500 et seq.

Missouri Treated Timber Law
  Mo. Rev. Stat. 1986, 280.005 et seq.

Missouri Uniform Gifts to Minors Act
  Mo. Rev. Stat. 1986, 404.005 et seq.

Motor Vehicle Right of Way Act
  Mo. Rev. Stat. 1986, 304.022

Motor Vehicle Safety Responsibility Act
  Mo. Rev. Stat. 1986, 303.010 et seq.

Motor Vehicle Special Fuel Tax Act
  Mo. Rev. Stat. 1986, 142.362 et seq.

Motor Vehicle Time Sales Act
  Mo. Rev. Stat. 1986, 365.010 et seq.

Motor Vehicle Use Tax Act
  Mo. Rev. Stat. 1986, 144.440 et seq.

Motorcycle Headgear Act
  Mo. Rev. Stat. 1986, 302.020, Subsec. 3

Motorist Act (Nonresident)
  Mo. Rev. Stat. 1986, 506.200 et seq.

Motorist Violator Compact Act (Nonresident)

Each state unit of *Shepard's Citations* includes a section with a Table of Acts arranged alphabetically by popular name. For example, if one knows that Missouri has enacted a Motorcycle Headgear Act, the citation can be found using this section.

  Mo. Rev. Stat. 1986, 536.010 et seq.

Molestation Act (Minor)
  Mo. Rev. Stat. 1969, 563.160

Molesting and Indecent Liberties Act
  Mo. Rev. Stat. 1969, 559.360

Morgan-McCullogh Act (Highways)
  Laws 1917, p. 485
  Laws 1919, p. 650

Motor Bus and Truck Act
  Mo. Rev. Stat. 1986, 390.011 et seq.

Motor Carrier Act
  Mo. Rev. Stat. 1986, 390.011 et seq.

Motor Fuel Tax Law
  Mo. Rev. Stat. 1986, 142.010 et seq.

Motor Vehicle Act
  Mo. Rev. Stat. 1986, 301.010 et seq.

Motor Vehicle Financial Responsibility Act
  Mo. Rev. Stat. 1986, 303.010 et seq.

Motor Vehicle Franchise Practices Act
  Mo. Rev. Stat. 1986, 407.810 et seq.

Motor Vehicle Operators' and Chauffeurs' License Act
  Mo. Rev. Stat. 1986, 302.010 et seq.

Motor Vehicle Registration Act
  Mo. Rev. Stat. 1986, 301.010 et seq.

Municipal Annexation Act
  Mo. Rev. Stat. 1986, 71.015

Municipal Housing Act
  Mo. Rev. Stat. 1986, 99.010 et seq.

Municipal Land Reutilization Law
  Mo. Rev. Stat. 1986, 92.700 et seq.

Museum Act
  Laws 1907, p. 94

Mutual Insurance Company Act
  Mo. Rev. Stat. 1986, 380.011 et seq.

Mutual Insurance Acts
  Mo. Rev. Stat. 1986, 379.205 et seq.

N

Narcotic Drug Act
  Mo. Rev. Stat. 1986, 195.010 et seq.

National Defense Cooperation Act of 1941
  Mo. Rev. Stat. 1986, 91.620 et seq.

Neglected and Delinquent Children Act
  Mo. Rev. Stat. 1986, 211.011 et seq.

Negotiable Instruments Law
  Mo. Rev. Stat. 1959, 401.001 et seq.

Neighborhood Assistance Act
  Mo. Rev. Stat. 1986, 32.100 et seq.

305

SECTION F. COMPARATIVE STATE STATUTORY RESEARCH

State statutes do not have a comprehensive indexing service comparable to West's *Key Number System*. When one must compare a particular law of one state with that of another or must compare similar laws of all fifty states, it may be necessary to consult the indexes for all state codes being researched. This process can perhaps be circumvented through a well-constructed search query used in one of the CALR services. Regardless of whether the research is conducted in an online service or in hard copy, it is tedious and time-consuming. It is important to remember that the various state codes do not have a national thesaurus. Consequently, the words or concepts used in one state code may differ from those used by other states.

Naturally, if someone has already done the research for you, do not attempt to recreate the effort. The following sources provide citations to or digests of all state statutes on a particular subject.

1. Looseleaf Services

Many looseleaf services provide either full texts, digests, or tables of citations on a specific subject. For example, Research Institute of America's *United States Tax Reporter* provides charts and digests of comparative tax provisions; Commerce Clearing House's *Inheritance, Estate and Gift Tax Reporter* has separate volumes that provide the text of state laws from all states on wills, trusts, and estates.

2. Martindale–Hubbell Law Directory

This annual publication, discussed more fully in Chapter 19, includes a two-volume *United States Law Digest* that provides a digest of state laws on many subjects.

3. Sources for Locating State Statutory Compilations

Treatises, legal periodical articles, and other secondary sources are often good sources for multistate comparisons of state laws. Especially helpful is the subject-arranged volume by Lynn Foster & Carol Boast, *Subject Compilations of State Laws* (1981), which covers compilations published between 1960 and summer 1979, and its various supplements: Cheryl Rae Nyberg & Carol Boast, *Subject Compilations of State Laws, 1979–1983* (1984); Cheryl Rae Nyberg, *Subject Compilations of State Laws, 1983–1985* (1986); *1985–1988* (1989); *1988–1990* (1991); *1990–1991* (1992). Effective with the *1990–1991* volume, this source became an annual publication. A cumulative index is available to the first five volumes.

Also helpful is Jon S. Schultz, *Statutes Compared: A U.S., Canadian, Multinational Research Guide to Statutes by Subject* (1991) and Richard A. Leiter, *National Survey of State Laws* (2d ed. 1996). This latter title, presented in chart form, allows users to make basic state-by-state comparisons of current state laws for 43 frequently-requested and controversial legal topics in the United States.

SECTION G. STATE LEGISLATIVE HISTORIES

Attempting to compile a legislative history for a state law in a manner similar to that described in Chapter 10 for federal laws is often difficult and, at times, is impossible. As a general rule, state legislatures do not publish their debates, committee reports, or transcripts of hearings held before legislative committees. Yet the need for these sources are often just as great, since state laws can contain provisions that are vague and ambiguous.[8]

The most accessible official documents are the Senate and House Journals. These Journals usually contain only brief minutes of the proceedings and final votes on legislation.[9] A few states may have reports of a State Law Revision Commission or the reports of special committees of the legislature for selected laws. If a state has an annotated code, the notes should be carefully examined to see if reference is made to such documents.

Often, guidance for research in state legislative history is available in the state legal research guides listed in Appendix B or from librarians with extensive experience within the state. Some states maintain "working documents" or copies of legislative history materials that are only available through a visit to the state's legislative library in the capital. In many instances, however, extrinsic aids for determining legislative intent are not available and one must rely on the language of the act by using the ordinary rules of statutory construction.

SECTION H.   MUNICIPAL OR LOCAL GOVERNMENT LEGISLATION

Traditionally, the various forms of local government are known as *municipal corporations* or *municipalities*. Municipalities are instruments of the state and have only such power as is granted to them by the state. This power varies from state to state,[10] and the constitution and statutes of the state in which the municipality is located must be examined to ascertain a municipality's scope of authority.

1. Municipal Charters

In general, a municipality operates under a charter, which is the basic document setting forth its power. Usually the charter has been adopted by the voters of a municipality and is analogous to a state constitution. The form of publication varies and, in the larger cities, may include bound volumes.

2. Ordinances

Ordinances are the legislative enactments of local jurisdictions, as passed by their legislative body, e.g., the city council, county commission-

---

[8] To determine those state documents that are available, see FISHER, *supra* note 5. For information on the legislative process for each state, see LYNN HELLEBUST, STATE LEGISLATIVE SOURCEBOOK: A RESOURCE GUIDE TO LEGISLATIVE INFORMATION IN THE FIFTY STATES (annual).

[9] Maine and Pennsylvania, however, have legislative journals that record actual legislative debate and parallel the *Congressional Record* in form of content. Increasingly, these materials are becoming available on state Web sites. Alaska and California have the most comprehensive collection of legislative history materials, including online access to a majority of its documents.

[10] EUGENE MCQUILLIN, THE LAW OF MUNICIPAL CORPORATIONS §§ 2.07c, 2.08a (1987).

ers, board of supervisors. Ordinances are to municipalities what acts are to the state legislatures and the United States Congress. In larger cities, ordinances are first published in an official journal and may be separately published in *slip* form. In smaller communities, they are frequently published in the local newspaper.

3.　Codes

Municipal codes are codifications of ordinances. As with state codes, they generally contain only those ordinances in force at the time of publication and are usually classified and arranged according to a subject plan. Published municipal codes are the exception rather than the rule. To research local laws it is often necessary to go to the seat of government and examine the ordinances on file there. The municipal codes that are published are most frequently for cities, rather than townships, counties, etc., and even these are not always supplemented in a timely fashion. Most city codes have the following common features:

a.　*City Charters*. Most city codes include the text of city charters. They usually are unannotated.

b.　*Text of Ordinances*. The texts of city ordinances constitute most of the information in these codes. They are rarely annotated with digests of cases.

c.　*Topical Analysis; Historical Notes; Cross References*. In some city codes a topical analysis may precede each chapter. The history of the sections, references to pertinent state law, and cross references to related provisions in the city code may be given after the text of each ordinances or in footnotes.

d.　*Indexes*. The codes are indexed according to various schemes. Some index the charter and ordinances together, and some contain separate indexes to each of these units. For a few cities, where the codes are divided into separately-bound parts, each part may have a detailed index.

e.　*Tables*. In some municipal codes, tables are included that show the disposition of the sections of an earlier code and the location of earlier provisions in the current compilation.

4.　Interpretations of Municipal Charters and Ordinances

Most municipal codes do not include annotations of cases interpreting the charters and ordinances. The following are useful in obtaining court cases for municipal legislation:

a.　*State Digests*. The reported cases interpreting an ordinance or a charter are included in a state digest. The location of the appropriate key number or paragraph numbers under which such cases are digested may be located through the use of the index or topical outlines to the digest.

b.　*Treatises*. Both Eugene McQuillin, *The Law of Municipal Corporations* (3d ed. rev.) and Chester James Antieau, *Municipal Corpora-*

tion Law, are helpful in locating court cases. Helpful in understanding and drafting ordinances is Byron S. Matthews, *Municipal Ordinances: Text and Forms* (2d ed.).

    c. *Shepard's State Citations.*[11] These are useful for finding court cases that have cited and interpreted municipal laws. [See Illustrations 11–8 and 11–9.]

    d. *Shepard's Ordinance Law Annotations.* This multi-volume set is arranged under broad subjects, with each subject subdivided into sub-entries. Under each sub-entry, annotations of court cases are listed. This set is useful when legal research requires locating cases on the same aspect of local government law in different cities. [See Illustration 94.]

5. Internet Access

Some cities are now publishing their codes, ordinances, and charters on the Internet. It is becoming good practice to check a city's home page when conducting research on municipal law.

SECTION I. ILLUSTRATIONS FOR
MUNICIPAL LEGISLATION

---

[11] *Shepard's Citations* are discussed in Chapter 15.

[Illustration 11–8]

PAGE FROM SHEPARD'S MISSOURI CITATIONS—
INDEX TO THE ORDINANCE SECTION

INDEX TO ORDINANCES   M

Limousine Service—(Continued)

Regulations........................Waynesville
Violation—Punishment..........Waynesville

Litter

Violations...........................Lakeside

Littering

Provisions.........................Brentwood

Livestock

Location
Proximity to Neighboring Residence
Kansas City

Livery Stables

Erection
City Limits........................St. Louis
Locations
Permit............................St. Louis

Lodging House

M

Magistrate Courts

Clerks
Other Employees—Appointment.....St. Louis
—Salaries.........................St. Louis

Manufacturers

Definition...........................St. Louis
License
Fee...............................St. Louis
Form..............................St. Louis
Statement Required................St. Louis

Markets

City
Bonds—Improvements...........Kansas City
—Improvements—Payment.......Kansas City
—Payment......................Kansas City
Comptroller's Supervision—Rental...St. Louis
Control—Management.............St. Louis
Locations........................St. Louis

> • **Each state unit of *Shepard's Citations* has a section, with an index, pertaining to charters and ordinances.**
>
> **If, for example, one is interested in locating ordinances on the licensing of massage parlors, the index will indicate which cities have ordinances on this subject.**
>
> **See Chapter 15 for a detailed description of *Shepard's Citations*.**

Purpose — Promotion...........Kansas City

Lots

Uses
Restrictions—Expiration—Extension
Kansas City

Lottery

Aiding and Assisting.................St. Louis
Provisions.........................St. Louis
Springfield

Lottery Tickets

Sale
Conviction--Res judicata--State.....St. Louis

Louisiana Purchase Exposition

Construction
Power to Regulate.................St. Louis
Expiration
Restoration of Parks—Time Limit....St. Louis
Grant
Right to Occupy Park..............St. Louis

Permits
Display—Regulations........St. Louis County
Issuance—Conditions........St. Louis County
—Denial—Judicial Review...St. Louis County
Requirements...............St. Louis County
Revocation -Suspension—Grounds
St. Louis County
Transfer...................St. Louis County

Premises
Inspection—Requirements....St. Louis County

Regulations..................St. Louis County

Sanitation and Health
Regulations Promulgation..St. Louis County

Massage Parlors

Licensing
Educational Requirements..........St. Louis
Provisions........................St. Louis
Refusal to Issue-- Revocation-- Grounds
St. Louis

Operation
License Fees Requirement.........Jennings
Regulations......................Jennings
St. Louis
Special Permit -- Requirement........Jennings

Master Plumber

Bond...........................Kansas City

(Continued)

471

[Illustration 11–9]

PAGE FROM SHEPARD'S MISSOURI CITATIONS— ORDINANCE SECTION

St. Louis	ORDINANCES		
Livery Stables Erection–City Limits 194US361 48LE1018 24SC673 Locations–Permit 317Mo910 296SW993 382SW2d717 **Lodging House** Definition 283Mo79 222SW430 Fees 283Mo80 222SW430 Permit 283Mo79 222SW430 **Loitering** Prohibition 478SW2d321 710SW2d13 302FS1387 **Lottery** Aiding and Assisting 222SW2d531 222SW2d536 223SW2d847 223SW2d859 223SW2d865 Provisions 29KCR(2)187 29KCR(2)201 29KCR(2)281 **Lottery Tickets** Sale–Conviction– Res judicata–State 220SW2d780 **Louisiana Purchase**	License–Fee 318Mo104 192SW399 300SW1077 250US460 63LE1086 39SC522 8F2d447 11SLR244 —Form 311Mo11 276SW34 —Statement Required 8F2d447 **Markets** City–Comptroller's Supervision–Rental 226Mo67 125SW1134 —Control–Management 226Mo68 125SW1134 —Locations 226Mo67 125SW1134 **Massage Parlors** Licensing–Educational Requirements C596SW2d456 —Provisions C596SW2d455 —Refusal to Issue– Revocation–Grounds C596SW2d457 Operation–Regulations C596SW2d455 **Merchants** Accounts–Inspection 318Mo104 300SW1077 Definition 311Mo11	300SW1077 32SW2d283 Taxes–Rates 318Mo104 326Mo442 300SW1077 32SW2d283 **Milk** Dealers–License– Applications 295Mo83 317Mo914 243SW136 296SW995 —License–Refusal– Grounds 295Mo83 314Mo84 317Mo914 243SW136 282SW438 296SW995 Grades–Standards 307SW2d497 Inspectors–Access– Right to Samples 235Mo692 235Mo725 139SW434 139SW444 Pasteurization 314Mo84 282SW436 Permits–Nontransferable– Posted 295Mo83 243SW136 Products–Definition 307SW2d497 —Sale–Permit–Denial 307SW2d497 —Sale–Ungraded–Time 307SW2d497	—Skimmed Milk 235Mo675 235Mo688 235Mo703 235Mo736 236Mo12 295Mo84 184MA333 139SW430 139SW438 139SW443 139SW449 139SW450 168SW1138 243SW136 Sale–Adulteration– Misbranding 235Mo670 235Mo703 236Mo3 236Mo12 295Mo84 139SW429 139SW438 139SW441 139SW450 243SW136 —Grades 307SW2d497 —Permits 256Mo492 295Mo77 165SW1081 243SW134 307SW2d495 —Ungraded 307SW2d497 Whole Milk Standards 235Mo715 295Mo84 184MA333 139SW447 168SW1138

> **This Illustration shows how *Shepard's Citations* enables a researcher to locate court cases interpreting a city ordinance.**

Parks–Time Limit 200F240 Grant–Right to Occupy Park 200F240 **Magistrate Courts** Clerks–Other Employees– Appointment 356Mo831 204SW2d235 —Other Employees–Salaries 356Mo825 204SW2d235 359SW2d718 **Manufacturers** Definition 311Mo1 276SW32 8F2d447	323W2d283 License 311Mo11 318Mo103 326Mo442 276SW34 300SW1077 32SW2d283 —Assignment 326Mo442 32SW2d283 —Statements 318Mo104 326Mo442 300SW1077 32SW2d283 —Violations– Penalty 311Mo11 318Mo104 326Mo442 276SW34	—Condensed–Preserved– Evaporated 295Mo83 243SW136 —Cream Standards 295Mo84 243SW136 —Fat Content 353SW2d743 —Ice Cream 227Mo639 295Mo86 314Mo84 127SW309 243SW134 282SW438 —Penalty 235Mo678 295Mo84 139SW431 243SW136	**Motor Vehicles** Brakes–Regulation 679SW2d283 Commercial–Licenses 149SW2d888 335SW2d128 —Licenses–Failure to Pay–Penalties 149SW2d888 —Speed Limits 132SW2d1055 Commission–Driver's License–Administration 223SW2d118 Definitions 220MA606 287SW2d881

[Illustration 11–10]

PAGE FROM SHEPARD'S ORDINANCE LAW ANNOTATIONS

MASSAGE PARLORS

EDITORIAL COMMENT. The massage business appears to be one that is subject to certain abuses, and cities have accordingly enacted ordinances attempting to control such abuses. The cases hold that the business may be regulated and licensed, as long as the regulations are in promotion of the public health, morals, or welfare.

One of the more interesting regulations is the one forbidding the massage, for compensation, of a person of the opposite sex (§6). The results have been varied; however, the United States Supreme Court has determined that no constitutional question is involved.

I. REGULATING THE BUSINESS OR PERSONS

§ 1. Requiring License or Permit
§ 2. Standards of Facilities
§ 3. Citizenship Requirements
§ 4. Prohibiting Existing Business

II. LIMITING CERTAIN BUSINESS PRACTICES OR ACTIVITIES

§ 5. Medical Diagnosis or Treatment
§ 6. Massaging Persons of Opposite Sex
§ 7. Limiting Hours

I. REGULATING THE BUSINESS OR PERSONS

§1. Requiring License or Permit

Licensing of massage parlors has not been preempted by the state licensing of any professional art of healing. A massage parlor is not such an art of healing and is subject to control by the city. The control may include the right to grant and revoke licenses on notice and hearing.

NC   Smith v Keator (1974) 21 NCApp 102, 203 SE2d 411; affd (1974) 206 SE2d 203.

This multi-volume set, published by Shepard's, is actually a digest rather than a citator.

It is topically arranged and digests appellate court cases that have interpreted a provision of a city charter or ordinance.

For example, if research involved the regulation of massage parlors, this set, under that heading, digests all cases wherein such ordinance was the subject of litigation.

This set is kept current by pocket parts and annual pamphlet supplements.

Pa   Berger v Bethel Park (1974) 14 PaCmwlth 13, 321 A2d 389.

SECTION J. SUMMARY

1. Publication of State Session Laws

State session laws are published in bound, chronologically-arranged volumes after adjournment of the state legislatures for the regular or special sessions and cover the laws enacted during that period.

2. Codification of State Statutes

State statutes are compiled under a subject arrangement with the obsolete and revoked laws eliminated.

3. Features Common to Many State Codes

   a. Constitutions.

   (1) State—usually unannotated.

   (2) Federal—usually unannotated.

   b. Text of statutes.

   c. Historical notes.

   d. Annotations.

   e. Tables.

   f. Research aids.

   g. Cross references to related sections.

   h. Indexes.

   i. Rules of court.

   j. Popular names of state acts.

   k. Supplementation—cumulative annual pocket parts, pamphlet supplements, and replacement volumes.

4. Private, Temporary, Local, and Appropriation Acts

Generally, consult session laws.

5. Popular Names of State Acts

   a. In *Shepard's Acts and Cases by Popular Names* and in state units of *Shepard's Citations*.

6. Electronic Access to State Legislation

   a. An unannotated state code, as well as recently-enacted session laws, for each state are available on WESTLAW and LEXIS–NEXIS.

   b. An annotated state code is available for almost all states on both WESTLAW and LEXIS–NEXIS.

   c. Most state Web sites contain their state codes. Many also contain session laws.

7. Inoperative State Law

Consult earlier state codes, replaced volumes of current code, or session laws.

8. Comparative State Statutory Research

a. Looseleaf services often provide the text, digests, or citations to multistate legislation.

b. The annual *Law Digest* volumes of the *Martindale–Hubbell Law Directory* contain synopses of some statutory laws of all states.

c. *Subject Compilations of State Laws* and its supplements, *Statutes Compared: A U.S. Canadian, Multinational Research Guide to Statutes by Subject* provide references to secondary sources that provide comparative information on state laws. *National Survey of State Laws* provides comparisons for current state laws under 43 topics.

9. Municipal Charters—set forth the basic power of a municipality

10. Municipal Ordinances—legislative enactments of local jurisdictions

11. Municipal Codes—codifications of ordinances

12. Features Common to Most Municipal Codes

a. Arranged by subject.

b. City charters.

c. Text of ordinances.

d. Topical analysis; historical notes; cross references.

e. Indexes.

f. Tables.

g. Supplementation—not always up to date.

h. Annotations in municipal codes are rare.

12. Interpretations of Municipal Charters and Ordinances

a. State unit of *Shepard's Citations*.

b. *Shepard's Ordinance Law Annotations*.

c. Treatises and state digests.

Chapter 12

COURT RULES AND PROCEDURES

This chapter is concerned with the rules and procedures for the conduct of matters in the courts. While courts are expected to rule on the substantive rights of the parties, before this adjudication can occur the parties must follow a number of processes to assure that the court will allow dispute resolution to commence and, once begun, to continue. The sources discussed in this chapter deal with the procedures for bringing and defending a court suit, and the procedures and methods used in the appellate courts. These sources include legislation pertaining to judicial proceedings, the rules promulgated by the courts for the conduct of their business, court cases concerning these rules, and legal forms used in court proceedings.

SECTION A.   COURT RULES IN GENERAL

Rules of courts control the operation of the courts and the conduct of the litigants appearing before them. Court rules relate to such matters as the issuance of complaints, assignment of cases, method of appeal, and the proper means for making motions that are required during the many phases of a court proceeding. Some rules can be as basic as the format to follow in preparing a document; others, such as time limitations, control whether a matter can proceed. In general, the purposes of court rules are to: (1) aid the court in performing its business; (2) establish uniform procedures; and (3) provide the parties to a lawsuit with information and instructions on matters pertaining to judicial proceedings.

SECTION B.   FEDERAL COURT RULES: SOURCES, INTERPRETATIONS, ANALYSIS, AND FORMS

1. In General

The power of a court to promulgate court rules is found either in its inherent authority or in a constitutional or statutory provision. For example, Section 17 of the Judiciary Act of 1789 gave the federal courts the authority to promulgate rules relating to the orderly conduct of their business. Statutory language, found primarily in Title 28 of the *United States Code (U.S.C.)*, although legislative, mandates some procedural requirements for the courts that are not in sets of court rules.

Federal court rules and procedures are in four categories: (1) rules of general application that are national in scope; (2) individual rules of the various federal courts, such as for the Supreme Court of the United States and the bankruptcy and admiralty courts; (3) "local" rules for individual courts within the federal court system; and (4) statutory

251

requirements found in Title 28 of the *United States Code*. In practice before the federal courts, it is essential to follow all the proper requirements.

Four sets of rules of general application in the federal courts have been promulgated over time: the Federal Rules of Civil Procedure, effective September 16, 1938; the Federal Rules of Criminal Procedure, effective March 21, 1946; the Federal Rules of Appellate Procedure, effective July 1, 1968; and the Federal Rules of Evidence, effective July 1, 1975.

In addition, the various federal courts have rules specific to their operations. For example, the way one files a motion in the U.S. Court of International Trade may differ from how it is done in the U.S. Claims Court. "Local" rules often add yet another layer to the procedural process. For example, one federal district court may permit television in the courtroom; another may not. The local rules cover these situations. Finally, but most important, separate statutes and judicial interpretations of these statutes and the various federal rules also control matters of court procedure.

Court rules are available in both unannotated and annotated versions.

2. Unannotated Rules

The text of the Federal Rules of Criminal Procedure is in the Appendix to Title 18 of the *U.S.C.*, and the text of the Federal Rules of Civil Procedure, Appellate Procedure, and Evidence, as well as the rules for some of the specialized federal courts, are in the Appendix to Title 28 of the *U.S.C.* Still other sets of rules accompany the *U.S.C.* Title covering that subject, e.g., Bankruptcy, Title 11; Copyright, Title 17.

The *U.S.C.* also includes the Judicial Conference Advisory Committee Notes. These notes are provided by the committee that drafted the original rules, and also include notes by any subsequent committees that proposed changes to the original rules. These notes can prove especially helpful in interpreting the meaning and intent of the rules.

Because of the delay in publishing the *U.S.C.*, the following other sources are often more useful, especially for recent rules changes:

a. *Federal Procedure, Lawyers Edition* (West Group, formerly Lawyers Cooperative Publishing). This set reproduces in a single "National Volume" the complete text of rules of general application and the Advisory Committee notes, along with several other sets of specialized rules. Eleven other volumes contain the rules applicable to each of the circuit courts of appeals and the district courts within each circuit.

b. *Federal Rules Service* (West Group, formerly Lawyers Cooperative Publishing). This set, discussed in Section B–5, contains a "Findings Aids" volume that includes the Federal Rules of Civil and Appellate Procedure along with the rules for several specialized federal courts.

c. *Electronic Sources.* Both WESTLAW and LEXIS–NEXIS provide online access to the federal rules. WESTLAW's US–RULES database contains the most recent versions of rules appearing in the *U.S.C.* and appendices. These include not only the four sets of rules of general application, but also the various rules of the specialized courts. The latest changes can be monitored through the WESTLAW Topical Highlights—Federal Practice and Procedure database (WTH–FPP). LEXIS–NEXIS's GENFED Library, RULES file contains the four sets of rules of general application, as well as the Advisory Committee notes. Some of the other federal court rules are also included.

Court rules can frequently be found on the Internet by checking sources mentioned in earlier chapters. [See Illustrations 4–12, 5–4, and 11–6.]

d. *Cyclopedia of Federal Procedure,* 3d ed. (West Group, formerly Lawyers Cooperative Publishing). The texts of the various rules, without the Advisory Committee notes, are in Volume 16A (Parts 1 and 2), "Rules" of this set.

e. *Pamphlet Editions.* West publishes annually a pamphlet that contains various federal rules and related statutory provisions. In addition, for the state statutory compilations published by West and LEXIS Law Publishing, pamphlets are issued annually that contain the federal district court and appellate court rules for the corresponding courts in that state.

f. *Reporters of Federal Cases.* When changes to major rules are proposed or adopted, they are published in the advance sheets to *West's Supreme Court Reporter, Federal Reporter 3d, Federal Supplement,* and *Federal Rules Decisions.* The advance sheets to the *U.S. Code Congressional and Administrative News* contain amendments to the rules for all courts. The bound *Federal Rules Decisions* also include rule changes, preliminary drafts of proposed changes, proposed amendments, congressional acts, and the publisher's editorial comments.

3. Annotated Rules

Four sources provide annotated versions of the federal rules:

a. *United States Code Service.* The various court rules, except for the Federal Rules of Evidence published as an appendix to Title 28, are in 14 unnumbered volumes entitled "Court Rules." The text of the rule is given and is then followed by annotations of cases under the rule. [See Illustrations 12–1 and 12–2.] The notes include comments from the Advisory Committee, as well as references to law review articles and to appropriate sections in other sets of this publisher's *Total Client–Service Library.* This compilation of rules is especially useful for its historical references.

b. *United States Code Annotated.* The annotated rules in this set correspond to the arrangement of the *United States Code.* They follow, for example, Titles 18 and 28. Each rule is followed by editorial annotations and Advisory Committee notes. Newer volumes also contain information for WESTLAW searches and citations to law review articles and other sources. [See Illustrations 12–3 and 12–4.]

c. *U.S. Supreme Court Digest, Lawyers Edition.* This set includes several "Court Rules" volumes containing the rules for all the federal courts, the Advisory Committee notes, references to other *Total Client–Service Library* publications, and annotations for cases decided by the Supreme Court of the United States only.

d. *Moore's Rules Pamphlets* (Matthew Bender). Published annually in three volumes, these pamphlets contain the four sets of rules of general application, the rules for the Supreme Court of the United States, and a few selected statutory provisions. Excerpts from the Advisory Committee notes, annotations of leading cases, and references to the multi-volume treatise, *Moore's Federal Practice,* are also provided.

4. Statutory Provisions Relating to Court Procedure

Statutory provisions specific to court procedure are in various Titles of the *U.S.C.* Perhaps the most notable are the venue and *habeas corpus* provisions in Title 28. These various statutory provisions are referenced in treatises and often are in pamphlets that include the federal rules of general applicability.

5. Federal Rules as Interpreted by the Court

After the promulgation of rules, there frequently is litigation concerning the meaning of the rules and their applicability to specific fact situations. When involved in research on federal procedure, one must often locate court cases that interpret the rules. The following sources are useful for this purpose:

a. *Federal Rules Decisions* (West Group). *Federal Rules Decisions (F.R.D.)* is a unit of the *National Reporter System* and contains cases of the federal district courts since 1939 that construe the Federal Rules of Civil Procedure and cases since 1946 decided under the Rules of Criminal Procedure. These cases are not published in the *Federal Supplement.* Similar to other units of the *National Reporter System, F.R.D.* is issued in advance sheets and bound volumes, with headnotes that are classified to West's *Key Number System.* In addition to court cases, it also includes articles on various aspects of federal courts and federal procedure. A cumulative index to these articles is in every tenth volume, and a consolidated index for volumes 1–122 is in volume 122.

b. *Federal Rules Service* (West Group, formerly Lawyers Cooperative Publishing). This set is useful when searching for court cases construing the Federal Rules of Civil Procedure and the Federal Rules of Appellate Procedure. It is in four sections:

(1) *Federal Rules Service* reporter.

First Series, 1939–1958

Second Series, 1958–1985

Third Series, 1985 to date.

These three series contain the full text of federal court cases construing the Federal Rules of Civil Procedure and the Federal Rules of Appellate Procedure. The Third Series is kept current with monthly advance sheets.

(2) *Federal Rules Digest* (3d ed. 1973 to date). This multi-volume digest classifies all court cases from April 1954 to date that appear in the *Federal Rules Service*. Headnotes are organized using the publisher's "Findex" system of rule subdivisions, which enables a user to pinpoint a rule of interest and go directly to *Digest* sections listing pertinent cases. Digests of cases from 1938 to 1954 are located in the four volumes of *Federal Rules Digest* (2d ed.).

(3) *Federal Local Court Rules*. These volumes are discussed in Section C.

(4) *Finding Aids* volume. This volume includes a Word Index to the Federal Rules of Civil Procedure and Appellate Procedure, the full text of the rules with the "Findex" feature whereby numbered rule subdivisions are keyed to specific *Digest* sections, a cumulative table of cases, and an outline on how to use the entire *Federal Rules Service* set.

c. *Federal Rules of Evidence Service* (West Group, formerly Lawyers Cooperative Publishing). This set is useful when searching for civil and criminal cases from all federal courts that have interpreted the Federal Rules of Evidence. The format is similar to that of the *Federal Rules Service,* in that the set contains a case reporter (covering September 1975 to date), a *Digest* set, and a "Finding Aids" volume with the Findex feature. The "Finding Aids" volume includes a State Correlation Table that compares the Federal Rules of Evidence to similar state evidence provisions.

6. Treatises

Many treatises pertain to the practice and procedure of the federal courts. They generally contain the text of appropriate statutes and federal rules that are the subject of the treatise. Typically, the text of each rule is followed by an analysis of the rules, and citations to court cases are given in the footnotes. The following multi-volume sets, some of which are encyclopedic in nature, are useful in obtaining commentary on federal practice:

a. *Cyclopedia of Federal Procedure* (West Group, formerly Lawyers Cooperative Publishing)

b. *Federal Procedure, Lawyers Edition* (West Group, formerly Lawyers Cooperative Publishing)

c. Marlin N. Volz, *West's Federal Practice Manual*

d. Charles Alan Wright & Arthur R. Miller, *Federal Practice and Procedure* (West Group) [See Illustration 12–5.]

e. *Moore's Federal Practice,* 2d ed. (Matthew Bender)

f. *Federal Litigation Guide* (Matthew Bender)

g. *Orfield's Criminal Procedure under the Federal Rules,* 2d ed. (West Group, formerly Lawyers Cooperative Publishing)

h. Jack B. Weinstein, *Weinstein's Evidence: Commentary on the Rules of Evidence for the United States Courts and Magistrates* (Matthew Bender).

7. Form Books

Model instruments or forms used in federal practice also have been published and keyed to the Federal Rules. They contain proper terms, phrases, and other essential details needed by an attorney to compose formal, correct legal documents. Those discussed in this section are multi-volume practice form books. Other types of form books are discussed in Chapter 19.

a. *Bender's Federal Practice Forms.* This is a looseleaf publication with annotations and cross references to *Moore's Federal Practice,* 2d ed. The forms cover civil and criminal rules.

b. *Nichols Cyclopedia of Federal Procedure Forms* (West Group, formerly Lawyers Cooperative Publishing). The forms are annotated and cover civil and criminal rules and some administrative agencies.

c. *West's Federal Forms.* This set, covering both civil and criminal forms for use in the federal courts, is annotated and includes references to *Federal Practice and Procedure.*

d. *Federal Procedural Forms, Lawyers Edition* (West Group, formerly Lawyers Cooperative Publishing). This set provides civil and criminal forms for use in all federal courts, as well as for adversary and rulemaking proceedings before administrative agencies.

e. Additional treatises and books of forms may be located by checking the catalog in a law library.

8. Historical Sources

At times it may be necessary to go beyond the text of the rules, Advisory Committee notes, judicial interpretations, and secondary sources for one's research. The following sources are especially helpful in this regard:

a. *Records of the U.S. Judicial Conference: Committees on Rules of Practice and Procedures, 1935–1988* (Congressional Information Service). This major compilation gathers together the minutes and transcripts of meetings, deskbooks, correspondence, and comments of committees established by the Supreme Court of the United States to draft new rules of practice and procedure for the federal district and appellate courts.

This collection, consisting of over 4,000 pieces of microfiche, is organized by committee into the following groupings: Standing Committee on Rules 1935–88; Committee on Civil Procedure 1935–88; Committee on Admiralty Procedure 1952–74; Committee on Criminal Procedure 1941–88; Committee on Appellate Procedure, 1958–88; Committee on Bankruptcy 1949–1988; and Committee on Evidence 1959–84. Three hard copy indexes provide access to the set: "List of Documents;" "Index by Rule Topics;" and "Index by Names of Individuals and Organizations." The collection is updated annually.

b. *Drafting History of the Federal Rules of Criminal Procedure,* (Madeleine Wilken & Nicholas Triffin, comp., Hein, 1991) Published in seven volumes in five books, this set provides a "legislative history" of the Federal Rules of Criminal Procedure. The set includes an exact reproduction of the four volume *Comments, Recommendations, and Suggestions Concerning the Proposed Rules of Criminal Procedure* originally used by the committee members.

In addition, the set contains previously unpublished preliminary drafts, letters and Supreme Court memoranda, successive preliminary drafts of the Rules of Criminal Procedure, the Final Committee report, and final approved Federal Rules of Criminal Procedure. Various finding aids facilitate research.

c. *The Federal Rules of Evidence: Legislative Histories and Related Documents* (James F. Bailey, II & Oscar M. Trelles, III, comp., Hein, 1991). This four-volume collection contains materials from the American Law Institute, the National Conference of Commissioners on Uniform State Laws, and the Judicial Conference of the United States, as well as congressional hearings and legislation.

SECTION C. FEDERAL COURT RULES OF SPECIFIC APPLICABILITY, INCLUDING LOCAL RULES

The Supreme Court of the United States, the courts of appeals, the federal district courts, and the various specialized courts have promulgated court rules. These rules apply only to the court issuing them and are mainly concerned with its operation. These include rules for filing motions and the preparation of briefs, as well as other rules dealing with the procedure of the court. The rules for the various federal courts may be found in the following publications:

1. Rules for the Supreme Court of the United States

The Rules for the Supreme Court of the United States are widely available. They are available in all the sources previously discussed in this chapter, including the online sources, and via the Internet.[1]

2. Rules for the Courts of Appeals

a. *Federal Rules Service, Federal Local Rules* volumes. This three-volume looseleaf set contains all the rules currently in force. Rules are arranged alphabetically by state, and the volumes are kept up to date as amendments and new rules are issued.

b. *Federal Procedure, Lawyers Edition.* This set includes a "National" volume covering the rules for the various federal courts and 11

---

[1] The most widely used treatise for practice in the Supreme Court of the United States is ROBERT L. STERN ET AL., SUPREME COURT PRACTICE (7th ed. 1993), with periodic pamphlet updates.

"Local" volumes for the First through the Eleventh Circuit. These "local" volumes also include the rules for the district courts within the circuit.

c. Rules volumes following Title 18 and Title 28 for the *U.S.C.* and the *U.S.C.A.*

d. "Rules" volumes of *U.S.C.S.* and the *United States Supreme Court Reports Digest, Lawyers' Edition.*

e. Each court also issues its rules in pamphlet form.

f. Certain courts of appeals have privately published guide books that include their rules, e.g., Federal Bar Council, *Second Circuit Redbook;* George K. Rahdert & Larry M. Roth, *Appeals to the Fifth Circuit;* and George K. Rahdert & Larry M. Roth, *Appeals to the Eleventh Circuit.*

3. Rules for the Federal District Courts

a. *Federal Rules Service, Federal Local Rules* volumes. This set is discussed in C–2–a. [See Illustration 12–6.]

b. Many of the federal district courts also issue their court rules in pamphlet form.

4. Rules for the Specialized Federal Courts

a. *Federal Rules Service, Federal Local Rules* volumes. This set, also discussed in C–2–a, includes rules for the specialized courts, i.e., admiralty, bankruptcy, copyright, and international trade, and such courts as the Court of Claims and the Temporary Emergency Court.

b. Rules volumes following Title 18 and Title 28 for the *U.S.C.* and the *U.S.C.A.*

c. "Rules" volumes of *U.S.C.S.* and the *United States Supreme Court Digest, Lawyers' Edition.*

SECTION D. COURT RULES FOR STATE COURTS

The method of publication of the rules of court varies from state to state.[2] In most states, they are published in the state code, in separate rules pamphlets, or in the state reports. Many courts now publish their court rules on their state's Web site.

Treatises on state civil and criminal practice have been published for many states. They may be located in the catalog of a law library.

SECTION E. CITATORS

1. Federal Rules Citations

This unit of *Shepard's Citations* includes citations to the Federal Rules of Civil Procedure, Criminal Procedure, Appellate Procedure, and

---

[2] For a table of sources for state court rules for each state, the District of Columbia, and the territories of the United States, *see* Betsy Reidinger & Virginia Till Lemmon, *Sources of Rules of State Courts*, 82 LAW LIBR. J. 761 (1990). *See also* JACK B. WEINSTEIN, REFORM OF COURT RULE-MAKING PROCEDURES (1977). If one is available, also check the relevant state legal research manual. See Appendix B.

Evidence, the corresponding state rules of the 50 states and Puerto Rico, as well as every reported state and federal case involving procedural issues.

2. Other Shepard's Units Containing Rules Information

Shepard's compiles citations to federal court rules in *Shepard's United States Citations—Statutes*. Citations to a federal court rule that has been cited by state courts can be obtained by consulting the appropriate Shepard's state edition. Also, citations to a federal court rule cited in major law reviews and legal periodicals can be obtained by referring to *Shepard's Federal Law Citations in Selected Law Reviews*.

Shepard's Citations is discussed in detail in Chapter 15.

SECTION F. ILLUSTRATIONS

[Illustration 12–1]

PAGE CONTAINING RULE 13 FROM U.S.C.S. FEDERAL RULES OF CRIMINAL PROCEDURE VOLUME

Rule 12.3   RULES OF CRIMINAL PROCEDURE

(d) Protective procedures unaffected. This rule shall be in addition to and shall not supersede the authority of the court to issue appropriate protective orders, or the authority of the court to order that any pleading be filed under seal.

(e) Inadmissibility of withdrawn defense based upon public authority. Evidence of an intention as to which notice was given under subdivision (a), later withdrawn, is not, in any civil or criminal proceeding, admissible against the person who gave notice of the intention.

> After the text of the Rule are notes from the Advisory Committee and cross references and citations to related sources of the publisher, as well as to other secondary sources.

Federal Procedure L Ed:
9 Fed Proc L Ed, Criminal Procedure §§ 22:598.5 et seq.

Rule 13. Trial Together of Indictments or Informations

The court may order two or more indictments or informations or both to be tried together if the offenses, and the defendants if there is more than one, could have been joined in a single indictment or information. The procedure shall be the same as if the prosecution were under such single indictment or information.

HISTORY; ANCILLARY LAWS AND DIRECTIVES

Other provisions:
Notes of Advisory Committee on Rules. This rule is substantially a restatement of existing law, 18 USC former § 557 (Indictments and presentments; joinder of charges); Logan v United States, 144 US 263, 296, 12 S Ct 617, 36 L Ed 429; Showalter v United States, 260 Fed 719, CCA 4th, certiorari denied 250 US 672, 40 S Ct 14, 63 L Ed 1200; Hostetter v United States, 16 F2d 921, CCA 8th; Capone v United States, 51 F2d 609, 619–620, CCA 7th.

CROSS REFERENCES

Joinder of offenses and defendants, USCS Rules of Criminal Procedure, Rule 8.
Relief from prejudicial joinder, USCS Rules of Criminal Procedure, Rule 14.

RESEARCH GUIDE

Federal Procedure L Ed:
9 Fed Proc L Ed, Criminal Procedure §§ 22:367, 401, 616, 617, 618, 622.
20 Fed Proc L Ed, Internal Revenue § 48:1375.

Am Jur:
1 Am Jur 2d, Actions § 159.5.
32 Am Jur 2d, Federal Practice and Procedure § 425.

608

[Illustration 12–2]

PAGE OF ANNOTATIONS FOR RULE 13, U.S.C.S. FEDERAL RULES OF CRIMINAL PROCEDURE VOLUME

ARRAIGNMENT   **Rule 13, n 4**

Forms:
7 Fed Procedural Forms L Ed, Criminal Law § 20:361.

Annotations:
What constitutes "series of acts or transactions" for purposes of Rule 8(b) of Federal Rules of Criminal Procedure, providing for joinder of

> Following the explanatory notes and various references to related sources, annotations ("interpretative notes and decisions") of all cases interpreting the Rule are set forth.

Right of defendants in prosecution for criminal conspiracy to separate trials. 82 ALR3d 366.
Consolidated trial upon several indictments or informations against same accused, over his objection, under Rule 13. 59 ALR2d 841.

Texts:
Cook, Constitutional Rights of the Accused: Pretrial Rights.
Orfield, Criminal Procedure Under the Federal Rules.

⟶ INTERPRETIVE NOTES AND DECISIONS

1. Generally
2. Constitutionality
3. Relationship with other rules
4. —FRCrP 8
5. —FRCrP 14
6. Discretion of court
7. Offenses that could have been joined
8. —Prejudice
9. —Same or similar acts
10. —Connected acts or transactions
11. —Conspiracy and substantive offenses
12. —Separate offenses
13. —Consent of defendant
14. Defendants that could have been joined
15. —Same offense
16. —Common scheme
17. —Conspiracy and substantive offenses
18. Judgment and sentence
19. Appeal and review
20. —Harmless error

1. Generally

Identity of parties in both indictments is not prerequisite to consolidation. United States v Samuel Dunkel & Co. (1950, CA2 NY) 184 F2d 894, cert den 340 US 930, 95 L Ed 671, 71 S Ct 401.

Indictments that are consolidated become, in legal effect, separate counts of one indictment. Dunaway v United States (1953) 92 App DC 299, 205 F2d 23.

Rule 13 is designed to promote economy and efficiency and to avoid multiplicity of trials where this can be achieved without substantial prejudice to rights of defendants to fair trial.

Daley v United States (1956, CA1 Mass) 231 F2d 123, 56-1 USTC ¶ 9405, 49 AFTR 392, cert den 351 US 964, 100 L Ed 1484, 76 S Ct 1028.

2. Constitutionality

Trial of defendant before one jury upon indictment for unlawful sale of narcotics in which 11 separate offenses are charged is not denial of due process of law. Brandenburg v Steele (1949, CA8 Mo) 177 F2d 279.

Joint trial of defendants charged with conspiracy does not violate standards of due process. United States v Keine (1971, CA10 Colo) 436 F2d 850, cert den 402 US 930, 28 L Ed 2d 864, 91 S Ct 1531.

3. Relationship with other rules

Where joinder of offenses is improper under Rules 8 and 13, relief from joinder should be granted under Rule 14 and failure to do so is not harmless error under Rule 52. United States v Graci (1974, CA3 Pa) 504 F2d 411.

Unless indictment has been transfered under Rule 21, court may not order indictment pending in another district consolidated with case pending in court's district. United States v Sklaroff (1971, SD Fla) 323 F Supp 296.

4. —FRCrP 8

When consolidation is permissible under formal requirements of Rule 13 and Rule 8, question of severance or common trial is vested under Rule 14 in sound discretion of trial judge. Cataneo v United States (1948, CA4 Md) 167 F2d 820.

[Illustration 12–3]

PAGE CONTAINING RULE 13 FROM U.S.C.A. TITLE 18 APPENDIX, FEDERAL RULES OF CRIMINAL PROCEDURE VOLUME

Rule 12.2
Note 17   **RULES OF CRIMINAL PROCEDURE**

Error, if any, in district court's exclusion of certain expert testimony on ground that testimony came within notice requirement of this rule was harmless where excluded expert testimony bore relevance only to entrapment defense, which was properly withheld from jury consideration. U.S. v. Perl, C.A.Md.1978, 584 F.2d 1316, certiorari denied 99 S.Ct. 1050, 439 U.S. 1130, 59 L.Ed.2d 92.

In prosecution for supplying employer with fraudulent withholding exemption certificate, trial court did not err in striking testimony of defense witness who was alcoholism and drug therapist and who testified that defendant was not responsible for his actions and in refusing to instruct jury on mental capacity, in view of defendant's failure to give notice of expert testimony relating to issue of whether defendant had mental state required for the offense:

a deadly weapon, proffered testimony of a psychologist pertaining to defendant's nonaggressive nature was covered by provision of this rule pertaining to written notification of the government attorney of an intention to introduce expert testimony relating to a mental disease or defect, and although the Government should have been given notice so that it would have had an opportunity to secure its own expert witness to rebut such testimony, that fact did not mandate affirmance of the district court's decision to exclude the psychologist's testimony. U.S. v. Staggs, C.A.Ill.1977, 553 F.2d 1073.

Where timely notice has not been given of intent to rely on expert testimony relating to mental disease, etc., and where there has been no showing of cause for late filing of the

---

This set also sets forth the Rule and then provides various related references to West publications and to other secondary sources.

Olson, C.A.Ct.1976, 576 F.2d 1267, certiorari denied 99 S.Ct. 256, 439 U.S. 896, 58 L.Ed.2d 242.

Although, in prosecution under section 111 of this title for assaulting a federal officer with

that defendant made Government aware of his intention to call an expert witness two days before trial notwithstanding that a continuance was a conceivable alternative. U.S. v. Edwards, D.C.Va.1981, 90 F.R.D. 391.

Rule 13. Trial Together of Indictments or Informations

The court may order two or more indictments or informations or both to be tried together if the offenses, and the defendants if there is more than one, could have been joined in a single indictment or information. The procedure shall be the same as if the prosecution were under such single indictment or information.

Notes of Advisory Committee on Rules

This rule is substantially a restatement of existing law [former] 18 U.S.C. § 557 (Indictments and presentments, joinder of charges); Logan v. United States, 144 U.S. 263, 296, 12 S.Ct. 617, 36 L.Ed. 429; Showalter v. United

States, 4 Cir., 260 F. 719 certiorari denied, 250 U.S. 672, 40 S.Ct. 14, 63 L.Ed. 1200. Hostetter v. United States, 8 Cir., 16 F.2d 921, Capone v. United States, 7 Cir., 51 F.2d 609, 619, 620.

United States Magistrates Rules

Trial of misdemeanors in proceeding before United States Magistrate, see rule 1 et seq., this title.

Federal Practice and Procedure

Trial together of indictments or information, see Wright: Criminal 2d § 211 et seq.

West's Federal Forms

Consolidating informations, motion and order, see § 7331 et seq.
Relief from prejudicial joinder, see § 7341 et seq.

West's Federal Practice Manual

Joinder of offenses and defendants, see § 6773.

Library References

Criminal Law ⚖620(1), (2).
C.J.S. Criminal Law § 931.

90

[Illustration 12–4]

PAGE OF ANNOTATIONS FOR RULE 13 FROM U.S.C.A. TITLE 18 APPENDIX, FEDERAL RULES OF CRIMINAL PROCEDURE VOLUME

JOINT TRIAL **Rule 13**
Note 5

Notes of Decisions

Generally **3**
Abuse of discretion by court **8**
Conspiracy and substantive offenses
   Generally **10**
   Drug offenses **11**
   Fraud **12**
   Miscellaneous offenses **14**
   Transportation in interstate commerce **13**
Construction with other rules **1**
Discretion of court
   Generally **7**
   Abuse of discretion **8**
Dismissal of one indictment **9**
Drug offenses, conspiracy and substantive offenses **11**
Duty of court **6**
Fraud, conspiracy and substantive offenses **12**
Identity of parties **17**
Nature of consolidation process **4**
Power of court **5**
Purpose **2**
Same or connected transactions **16**
Similarity of consolidated charges **15**
Time for motion **19**
Transportation in interstate commerce, conspiracy and substantive offenses **13**
Use of evidence against codefendant **18**
Waiver **20**

---

1. Construction with other rules

This rule has no relation to rule 8(a) of these rules providing that more than one offense may be included in one indictment, nor does phrase "single indictment" in this rule mean

the relevant evidence by resting before that evidence was introduced. U.S. v. Polizzi, C.A. Cal.1974, 500 F.2d 856, certiorari denied 95 S.Ct. 802, 803, 419 U.S. 1120, 42 L.Ed.2d 820.

Grant of authority to consolidate charges involving connected transactions manifests intent that public considerations of economy and speed outweigh possible unfairness to the accused where charges are so closely connected that all evidence produced in court would have been admissible if any one of the indictments had been brought to trial alone. U.S. v. Smith, C.C.A.N.Y.1940, 112 F.2d 83.

3. Generally

There is substantial public interest in joint trial of persons charged with committing same offense or with being accessory to its commission. U.S. v. Camacho, C.A.Ariz.1976, 528 F.2d 464, certiorari denied 96 S.Ct. 2208, 425 U.S. 995, 48 L.Ed.2d 819.

Test as to whether separately indicted defendants may be jointly tried is whether they could have been jointly indicted. King v. U.S., C.A.Mass.1966, 355 F.2d 700.

Single joint trial of several defendants may not be had at expense of defendant's right to fundamentally fair trial. U.S. v. Echeles, C.A. Ill.1965, 352 F.2d 892.

Indictments could be consolidated only in cases where the offenses charged in separate indictments were such that they might have been embraced in separate counts in one indictment. De Luca v. U.S., C.C.A.N.Y.1924, 299 F. 741. See, also, Miller v. U.S., 1912, 38

Annotations ("notes of decisions") of all cases interpreting the Rule are set forth after the explanatory notes and various references to related sources.

This rule must be read with rule 8(b) of these rules authorizing two or more defendants to be charged in the same information, if they allegedly participated in the same transaction or series of transactions constituting the offense. Daley v. U.S., C.A.Mass.1956, 231 F.2d 123, certiorari denied 76 S.Ct. 1028, 351 U.S. 964, 100 L.Ed 1484.

Where defendants were alleged to have participated in the same act or transaction, or in the same series of acts or transactions, constituting charged offense, they might under rule 8(b) of these rules have been joined as defendants in a single indictment, and district court could, under this rule, order indictments to be tried together. Malatkofski v. U.S., C.A.Mass 1950, 179 F.2d 905.

2. Purpose

One purpose of joint trial of defendants allegedly involved in a single scheme is to facilitate the evaluation by the jury of the evidence against each defendant in light of the entire course of conduct, which purpose would be frustrated as to a particular defendant if he could bar consideration as to him of some of

time. U.S. v. Mandel, D.C.Md.1976, 415 F.Supp. 1033.

4. Nature of consolidation process

Consolidated indictments are, in legal effect, separate counts of one indictment. Dunaway v. U.S., 1953, 205 F.2d 23, 92 U.S.App.D.C. 299. See, also, Pankratz Lumber Co. v. U.S., C.C.A. Wash.1931, 50 F.2d 174.

5. Power of court

Where one indictment charged defendant with engaging in illegal distilling operations with two other named persons and another indictment charged defendant with engaging in such operations with a third named defendant, court had power to consolidate the indictments for trial. Jordan v. U.S., C.C.A.Ga 1941, 120 F.2d 65, certiorari denied 62 S.Ct. 102, 314 U.S. 608, 86 L.Ed. 489.

District court in Southern District of Florida was without authority to order indictment pending in Northern District of Georgia to be consolidated for trial with indictment pending in Florida. U.S. v. Sklaroff, D.C.Fla.1971, 323 F.Supp. 296.

[Illustration 12–5]

PAGE FROM C. WRIGHT & A. MILLER, FEDERAL PRACTICE AND PROCEDURE

§ 211
Rule 13

ARRAIGNMENT

Ch. 5

RULE 13. TRIAL TOGETHER OF INDICTMENTS OR INFORMATION

Analysis

Sec
211.   In General.
212.   Several Offenses.
213.   Several Defendants.

Text of Rule 13

The court may order two or more indictments or informations or both to be tried together if the offenses, and the defendants if there is more than one, could have been joined in a single indictment or information. The procedure shall be the same as if the prosecution were under such single indictment or information.

§ 211.   In General

Rule 13, which has never been amended since its original adoption, is a restatement of prior law that permitted the joinder of charges in an indictment and the consolidation of indictments for trial.[1] The former statute, with origins going back to 1853, provided for the consolidation of indictments charging against one defendant offenses that

---

Page from C. Wright & A. Miller, *Federal Practice and Procedure*, setting forth the text of the Rule. Thereafter, the authors present commentary regarding the Rule. Other treatises on federal rules do likewise.

---

1. **Restatement of prior law**
See generally Orfield, Consolidation in Federal Criminal Procedure, 1961, 40 Or.L.Rev. 318.

The Advisory Committee Note to the rule said: "The rule is substantially a restatement of existing law, 18 U.S.C. § 557 (Indictments and presentments; joinder of charges) [since repealed]; Logan v. United States, 144 U.S. 263, 296, 12 S.Ct. 617, 36 L.Ed. 429; Showalter v. United States, 260 Fed. 719, C.C.A.4th, certiorari denied 250 U.S. 672, 40 S.Ct. 14, 63 L.Ed. 1200; Hostetter v. United States, 16 F.2d 921, C.C.A.8th; Capone v. United States, 51 F.2d 609, 619–620, C.C.A.7th."

The full text of all Advisory Committee Notes is set out in the Appendix in vol. 3A.

2. **Former statute**
The statute, formerly 18 U.S.C.A. § 557, provided: "When there are several charges against any person for the same act or transaction, or for two or more acts or transactions connected together, or for two or more acts or transactions of the same class of crimes or offenses, which may be properly joined, instead of having several indictments the whole may be joined in one indictment in separate counts, and if two or more indictments are found in such cases, the court may order them to be consolidated. (R.S. § 1024.)"

758

[Illustration 12–6]

PAGE FROM FEDERAL RULES SERVICE,
FEDERAL LOCAL RULES VOLUME

FEDERAL LOCAL COURT RULES Florida (N.D.)

(C) Release of Information by Attorneys—Civil Cases. A lawyer or law firm associated with a civil action shall not during its investigation or litigation make or participate in making an extrajudicial statement, other than a quotation from or reference to public records, which a reasonable person would expect to be disseminated by means of public communication if there is a reasonable likelihood that such dissemination will interfere with a fair trial and which relates to:

(a) Evidence regarding the occurrence or transaction involved.

(b) The character, credibility, or criminal record of a party, witness, or prospective witness.

(c) The performance or results of any examinations or tests or the refusal or failure of a party to submit to such.

(d) His opinion as to the merits of the claims or defenses of a party, except as required by law or administrative rule.

> Rule 16 of the Federal District Court, Northern District, Florida, on television in the courtrooms.
>
> As rules are added or amended, the publisher supplies replacement pages for the new or amended rule.

rights of the accused to a fair trial by an impartial jury, the seating and conduct in the courtroom of spectators and news media representatives, the management and sequestration of jurors and witnesses, and any other matters which the Court may deem appropriate for inclusion in such an order.

Rule 16. Photographs; Broadcasting or Televising.

The taking of photographs or the broadcasting or televising of proceedings in any courtroom or hearing room of this Court, or the environs thereof, either while the Court is in session or at recesses between sessions when Court officials, attorneys, jurors, witnesses or other persons connected with judicial proceedings of any kind are present, are prohibited, except that a judge may authorize: (a) the use of electronic or photographic means for the presentation of evidence, or for the perpetuation of a record; and (b) the broadcasting, televising, recording, or photographing of investigative, ceremonial, or naturalization proceedings.

In order to facilitate the enforcement of this rule, no photographic, broadcasting, television, sound or recording equipment of any kind, except that of Court personnel or other employees of the United States government on official business in the building, will be permitted in any part of any building where federal judicial proceedings of any kind are usually conducted in this District, unless such is done with the approval of one of the Judges of this Court.

As used in this Rule, the term "environs" means the interior of the entire building in which judicial proceedings are held or conducted in any city in this District.

SECTION G. SUMMARY

1. Purposes of Court Rules

a. Aid the court in expediting and performing its business.

b. Establish uniform procedures for the conduct of the court's business.

c. Provide parties to a suit with procedural information and instructions on matters pertaining to judicial proceedings.

2. Publication, Interpretation, and Analysis of Federal Court Rules

a. *Rules of General Application* (Rules of Civil Procedure; Rules of Criminal Procedure; Rules of Appellate Procedure; Federal Rules of Evidence) and *Rules for Other Federal Courts:*

Unannotated:

Titles 18 and 28, *U.S.C.* Appendix

Federal Rules Service "National Volume"

LEXIS–NEXIS and WESTLAW

Cyclopedia of Federal Procedure, 3d ed., volume 16A

Pamphlets

Internet

Annotated:

U.S.C.S. "Court Rules" volumes (Civil, Criminal, Appellate); Title 28 Appendix (Evidence)

Titles 18 and 28, *U.S.C.A.* Appendix

United States Supreme Court Digest, Lawyers' Edition (Supreme Court only)

Moore's Rules Pamphlets (selective)

b. *Local Rules*

Federal Rules Service, Federal Local Rules volumes

Federal Procedure, Lawyers Edition (a separate volume for each federal circuit including rules for district courts within the circuit)

Pamphlets

c. *Statutory Provisions*

In various Titles of *U.S.C., U.S.C.A.,* and *U.S.C.S.*

d. *Judicial Interpretations*

Federal Rules Decisions

Federal Rules Digest

e. *Treatises*

See Section B–6

f. *Form Books*

See Section B–7

g. *Historical Sources*

Records of the U.S. Judicial Conference: Committees on Rules of Practice and Procedures, 1935–1988

Drafting History of the Federal Rules of Criminal Procedure

The Federal Rules of Evidence: Legislative Histories and Related Documents

h. *State Courts*

Check local law library catalog and Internet state Web sites

i. *Citators*

Federal Rules Citations

United States Citations—Statutes

State units of *Shepard's Citations*

Shepard's Federal Law Citations in Selected Law Reviews

Chapter 13

ADMINISTRATIVE LAW*

SECTION A. FEDERAL ADMINISTRATIVE REGULATIONS AND DECISIONS: INTRODUCTION

Administrative law has been defined as:

[T]he law concerning the powers and procedures of administrative agencies, including especially the law governing judicial review of administrative action. An administrative agency is a governmental authority, other than a court and other than a legislative body, that affects the rights of private parties through either adjudication, rulemaking, investigating, prosecuting, negotiating, settling, or informally acting. An administrative agency may be called a commission, board, authority, bureau, office, officer, administrator, department, corporation, administration, division or agency.[1]

The principal purpose of this chapter is to explain the manner in which the regulations, rules, and adjudications of federal administrative bodies are published and how they can be located. Also discussed are Presidential documents and state administrative materials.

The power to issue regulations[2] and to adjudicate disputes is delegated to administrative bodies by Congress.[3] The increasing complexity of American society, industry, and government in the last fifty years brought about a tremendous increase in the number of administrative agencies and in the documents produced by them for publication. The normal procedure is for Congress to delegate to an administrative office or agency the power to issue rules and regulations, and in some instances the power to hear and settle disputes arising from the statute. Once an administrative body has been established, the issuance of rules and regulations is fairly simple, unlike the enactment of a statute which must go through the legislative process in Congress. Some agencies, such

---

* Revised for this edition by Bonnie L. Koneski–White, Law Librarian, Western New England College.

[1] 1 KENNETH DAVIS, ADMINISTRATIVE LAW AND GOVERNMENT 6 (2d ed. 1975).

[2] A summary of all the procedures that affect the rulemaking process is contained in ADMINISTRATIVE CONFERENCE OF THE UNITED STATES, A GUIDE TO FEDERAL AGENCY RULEMAKING (2d ed. 1991).

[3] For a discussion of Congressional authority to delegate legislative power to administrative agencies, see 1 JACOB A. STEIN ET AL., ADMINISTRATIVE LAW § 3.03 (1988). For example, 16 U.S.C. §§ 1600–1687 (1994) deal with the nation's forest preserves and § 1613 provides that "[t]he Secretary of Agriculture shall prescribe such regulations as he determines necessary and desirable to carry out the provisions of this subchapter."

as the National Labor Relations Board, not only promulgate regulations, but are also authorized to adjudicate disputes between management and labor unions; the results of their adjudications are published in a format similar to court reports.

All regulations by administrative agencies are issued either under authority delegated to them by a federal statute or by a Presidential Executive Order.

The types of actions taken by federal agencies may be classified as: rules or regulations; orders; licenses; advisory opinions; and decisions. These are defined as follows:

(1) *Rules or regulations.* The words *rules* and *regulations* are used interchangeably. These are statements of general or particular applicability made by an agency and are designed to implement, interpret, or prescribe law or policy. Properly promulgated rules and regulations have the same legal effect as statutes.

(2) *Orders.* These are used to describe the final dispositions of any agency matters (other than rulemaking, but including licensing).

(3) *Licenses.* These include any permits, certificates, or other forms of permission.

(4) *Advisory opinions.* Although containing advice regarding contemplated action, these are not binding and serve only as authoritative interpretations of statutes and regulations.

(5) *Decisions.* Federal agencies authorized by law adjudicate controversies arising out of the violation or interpretation of statutes and administrative regulations or rules. The results of these adjudications are issued as decisions of the agencies. The adjudication function is performed by special boards of review, hearing examiners, or other officers.

SECTION B. PUBLICATION OF FEDERAL REGULATIONS: HISTORICAL BACKGROUND

Prior to 1936, no official source for publication of rules and regulations of federal agencies existed, nor indeed were such agencies required to make their rules and regulations available to the public. This resulted in much confusion, since there was no way to determine if a proposed action by a person or company was prohibited by some federal agency. In fact, in one well-known instance, the federal government prosecuted a corporation for violations of an administrative regulation. This case, *Panama Refining Co. v. Ryan,*[4] reached the Supreme Court of the United States before the Attorney General realized that the action was based on a regulation that had been revoked prior to the time the original action had begun.[5]

[4] 293 U.S. 388 (1935).

[5] *See* Note, *The Federal Register and the Code of Federal Regulations—A Reappraisal,* 80 HARV. L. REV. 439 (1966).

As a result of the *Panama Refining* case, in 1935 Congress passed the Federal Register Act[6] providing for the publication of the *Federal Register*. The *Federal Register* was first published in 1936. Any administrative rule or regulation that has general applicability and legal effect must be published in the *Federal Register*. The definition of a document that has "general applicability and legal effect" is as follows:

> ... [A]ny document issued under proper authority prescribing a penalty or course of conduct, conferring a right, privilege, authority, or immunity, or imposing an obligation, and relevant or applicable to the general public, members of a class, or persons in a locality, as distinguished from named individuals or organizations.... [7]

Thus, since 1936, the *Federal Register* has contained, in chronological order, every regulation having general applicability and legal effect, and amendments thereto, issued by federal agencies authorized by Congress or the President to issue rules or regulations.

Had the *Federal Register* continued year after year with no compilation of its regulations, the ability to locate regulations would have become unmanageable and researchers virtually would have been back to the point that existed at the time of the *Panama Refining* case. Fortunately, in 1937, Congress amended the Act[8] and provided for a systematic method of codification of and subject access to these regulations in a set entitled the *Code of Federal Regulations (CFR)*. The *CFR*, first published in 1939, bears the same relationship to the *Federal Register* as the *United States Code* bears to the *United States Statutes at Large*. Over the years the *CFR* has been published at different intervals and in different formats, but since 1968 the *CFR* has been issued annually, in quarterly installments.

Despite the fact that by 1937 a regular vehicle had been mandated for publication and compilation of agency rules and regulations by the Federal Register Act, as amended, the process and procedures of agency rulemaking remained an enigma to the public. In 1946, Congress remedied this situation by passing the Administrative Procedure Act,[9] which granted the public the right to participate in the rulemaking process by requiring agencies to publish notice of their proposed rulemaking in the *Federal Register* and by providing the public with the opportunity to comment on these proposed rules.

Subsequently, three additional laws were enacted to enhance the public's access to agency information. The Freedom of Information Act

---

[6] Ch. 417, 49 Stat. 500 (1935) (codified as amended at 44 U.S.C. §§ 1501–1511 (1994)).

[7] 1 C.F.R. § 1.1 (1997). It is often difficult to determine precisely which documents the government should be required to publish in the *Federal Register*. For a discussion of this problem, see Randy S. Springer, Note, *Gatekeeping and the* Federal Register: *An Analysis of the Publication Requirement of Section 552(a)(1)(D) of the Administrative Procedure Act,* 41 Admin. L. Rev. 533 (1989).

[8] Ch. 369, 50 Stat. 304 (1937) (codified as amended at 44 U.S.C. § 1510 (1994)).

[9] Ch. 324, 60 Stat. 237 (1946) (codified as amended in scattered sections of 5 U.S.C.).

of 1966[10] requires that agencies publish in the *Federal Register* (1) descriptions of their organizations including the agency employees from whom the public may obtain information, (2) rules of procedure and general applicability, and (3) policy statements and interpretations. The Government in the Sunshine Act of 1976[11] requires agencies to publish in the *Federal Register* notices of most meetings.

In 1980, the Regulatory Flexibility Act[12] was passed which dictates that agencies publish in the *Federal Register* during October and April an agenda briefly detailing (1) the subject area of any rule that the agency expects to propose or promulgate which would have a significant economic impact, (2) a summary of the rules being considered, their objectives, and the legal basis for issuance, and (3) an approximate schedule for finishing action on rules for which the agency issued notices of proposed rulemaking.

SECTION C. SOURCES OF FEDERAL REGULATIONS

1. The Federal Register[13]

The *Federal Register* is published daily (except Saturday, Sunday, and official federal holidays) and its contents are required to be judicially noticed.[14] All issues in a given year constitute a single volume with consecutive pagination throughout the year. In recent years an annual volume of the *Federal Register* has exceeded 60,000 pages. In addition to the chronologically-arranged publication of the rules and regulations of federal agencies [See Illustrations 13–11 and 13–12], issues of the *Federal Register* contain the following features.

a. *Contents.* At the front of each issue is a table of contents in which agencies are listed alphabetically. Under the name of each agency, the documents appearing in that issue are arranged by category and page references are provided. WESTLAW contains the daily *Federal Register*'s table of contents. Coverage begins in January, 1993.

b. *CFR Parts Affected In This Issue.* Discussed in Section E–1–b *infra.*

c. *Presidential Documents.* Discussed in Section H *infra.*

d. *Proposed Rules.* This section contains notices of proposed issuance of rules and regulations. Its purpose is to give interested persons an opportunity to participate in the rulemaking process prior to the adoption of final rules.

---

[10] Pub. L. No. 89–487, 80 Stat. 250 (1966) (codified as amended at 5 U.S.C. § 552 (1994)).

[11] Pub. L. No. 94–409, 90 Stat. 1241 (1976) (codified as amended at 5 U.S.C. §§ 551–52, 556–57; 5 App. U.S.C. § 10; 39 U.S.C. § 410 (1994)).

[12] Pub. L. No. 96–354, 94 Stat. 1164 (1980) (codified as amended at 5 U.S.C. §§ 601–612 (1994)).

[13] Additional information on this publication is provided in OFFICE OF THE FEDERAL REGISTER, THE FEDERAL REGISTER: WHAT IT IS AND HOW TO USE IT (1992).

[14] 44 U.S.C. § 1507 (1994).

e. *Notices.* This section of the *Federal Register* contains documents other than rules or proposed rules that are applicable to the public, *e.g.*, grant application deadlines, filing of petitions and applications.

f. *Sunshine Act Meetings.* Notices of meetings required by the Government in the Sunshine Act are in this section.

g. *Unified Agenda of Federal Regulations.* The Regulatory Flexibility Act requires that agencies publish in April and October regulatory agenda describing the regulatory actions they are developing. Each agency lists its rules in four groups: (1) Prerule Stage; (2) Proposed Rule Stage; (3) Final Rule Stage; and (4) Completed Actions.

h. *Reader Aids.* This section appears at the end of the *Federal Register* and contains telephone numbers for information and assistance, a parallel table of *Federal Register* pages for the month, a cumulative table of *CFR Parts Affected* during the month, and a List of Public Laws, which lists those bills from the current session of Congress that have recently become law. The Monday issue contains a "CFR Checklist" of the current *CFR* Parts.

i. *Special Sections.* To accommodate the duplication and distribution needs of issuing agencies, some agency documents are published in separate sections near the end of each issue rather than in the appropriate sections.

In addition to the paper and microfiche copies available from the federal government, an Internet edition of the *Federal Register* on *GPO Access* is issued under the authority of the Administrative Committee of the Federal Register as the official legal equivalent of the paper and microfiche editions. The online database is updated by 6 a.m. each day the *Federal Register* is published. The database includes both the text and graphics from Volume 59, Number 1 (January 2, 1994) forward. [See Illustrations 13–14 and 13–15.]

2. The Code of Federal Regulations (CFR)[15]

This set is a codification of rules and regulations first published in the *Federal Register,* in which all regulations and amendments in force are brought together by subject. The *Code of Federal Regulations* is *prima facie* evidence of the text of the documents.[16] The *CFR* is in fifty Titles (similar to, but not parallel to, the arrangement of the *United States Code*). Each Title is subdivided into Chapters, Subchapters, Parts, and Sections and is cited by Title and Section, *e.g.*, 42 C.F.R. § 405.501. [See Illustrations 13–14 and 13–15.] Each year the pamphlet volumes of the *Code of Federal Regulations* are issued in a different colored binding from the previous year (except Title 3, which has had a white cover since 1985) and on a quarterly basis approximately as follows:

Title 1 through Title 16 . . . . as of January 1

[15] For a detailed history of the publication of the earlier editions of the *Code of Federal Regulations,* see Ervin H. Pollack, Fundamentals of Legal Research 366–72 (3d ed. 1967).

[16] 44 U.S.C. § 1510(e) (1994).

Title 17 through Title 27 .... as of April 1
Title 28 through Title 41 .... as of July 1
Title 42 through Title 50 .... as of October 1

Each new volume contains the text of regulations in force, incorporating those promulgated during the preceding twelve months and deleting those revoked. Through this process, all regulations first published chronologically in the *Federal Register* and currently in force are rearranged by subject and agency in the fifty Titles of the *CFR*. For example, all regulations issued by the Federal Communications Commission, and still in force, are in Title 47 of the *CFR* and are up to date through October 1.

The *Code of Federal Regulations* is available through *GPO Access* [See Illustration 13–15] and through *the United States House of Representatives Internet Law Library*. [See Illustration 10–7.] The latter site also provides information on search strategies.

3. Looseleaf Services

Looseleaf services, discussed in Chapter 14, often contain documents published in the *Federal Register* and the *CFR*. These services usually are better indexed than the government publications and contain other features facilitating the location of information.

Consequently, when it is necessary to research a problem of administrative law, it is good practice to ascertain if a looseleaf service covering the topic under research exists and to use that service as a starting point rather than the official publications.

4. Electronic Research

The following electronic sources can be extremely helpful in locating regulations, especially when a particular word or phrase cannot be found in the print indexes to the *Federal Register* or the *Code of Federal Regulations*.

a. *LEXIS–NEXIS.* The *Federal Register* is available through LEXIS–NEXIS from July 1980. The current *Code of Federal Regulations* is available and the archived *CFR*s beginning in 1981 are available. The CFR and *Federal Register* files can be searched in a combined file.

b. *WESTLAW.* In WESTLAW, rules and regulations, proposed rules, notices and Unified Agenda documents published in the *Federal Register* can be accessed beginning from July 1, 1980. The current *Code of Federal Regulations* is available as is an historical database of *CFR*s beginning with 1984.

c. *LEGI–SLATE.* This service, which is published by Legislate, Inc., an information subsidiary of the *Washington Post,* contains the *Federal Register* and the *Code of Federal Regulations.* A database, DAILY, incorporates the promulgated final rules and regulations directly into the *CFR* in the appropriate Title each weekday. This service is available through dial-in lines or through the Internet.

d. *DIALOG.* The *Federal Register* is available through DIALOG from 1988.

e. *Internet.*

(1) Counterpoint Publishing Inc. provides same-day availability of the complete *Federal Register.* Backfile issues of the *Federal Register* are available from January 1993. The *Code of Federal Regulations* also is available.

(2) *Congressional Universe* includes the *Federal Register* from 1980 and the current *Code of Federal Regulations.*

(3) The *Federal Register* since 1994, the *Code of Federal Regulations* and the *Unified Agenda* are now available directly from the Government Printing Office in *GPO Access.* [See Illustrations 13–14 and 13–15.]

f. *CD–ROMS.* A number of CD–ROM products have been developed that facilitate access to federal regulations. Several are highlighted below.

(1) *Compact Disc Federal Register.* This CD–ROM product is recompiled and issued weekly and provides the complete text of the previous week's *Federal Register* and the past six months of *Federal Register*s on one disk. The disk is updated monthly, bi-monthly, quarterly, and semi-annually. Searching can be done by table of contents, agency name, page number, date, and by using Boolean logic. Coverage begins with July 1, 1990.

(2) *Federal Register.* This CD–ROM product, produced by Knight–Ridder Information, Inc., contains the full-text of the *Federal Register.* It is updated monthly and can be updated more frequently by using the *Federal Register* file on DIALOG. Historical coverage is available from 1990. DIALOG search strategy can be used.

(3) *Compact Disc Code of Federal Regulations.* The 50 Titles of the *CFR* are available on CD–ROM from Counterpoint Publishing. Update disks are provided according to the rotating publishing schedule of the Government Printing Office. A monthly update disk incorporates the final rules and regulations and presidential documents into the appropriate Titles of the *CFR*. Subscriptions for any grouping of titles can also be purchased. Titles that relate to specific areas of interest are available as "bundle" subscriptions.

(4) *CD CFR.* This CD–ROM product from CD Book Publishers, Fullerton, California, offers the 50 Titles of the *CFR*. It is updated annually.

(5) *CFR LawDesk.* This product of LEXIS Law Publishing is linked to this publisher's *USCS LawDesk*, enabling the user to go back and forth between federal statutes and regulations.

(6) *Solutions CFR Database on CD–ROM.* This CD–ROM, published by Solution Software Corp., contains the current *CFR* and is updated quarterly.

(7) *West's Code of Federal Regulations.* All fifty titles of the *CFR* are included and the most recent changes published in the *Federal Register* are incorporated. It is updated monthly and can be searched by WEST-LAW protocol or natural language.

5. Other Sources

Selected regulations also are published in the monthly pamphlets to the *United States Code Congressional and Administrative News* and in the *United States Code Service* Advance Service.

SECTION D.   FINDING FEDERAL REGULATIONS

Because the *Federal Register* and the *Code of Federal Regulations* are the official sources of agency regulations, these two sources are emphasized in this discussion.

The key to knowing whether to start one's research in the *Federal Register* or the *CFR* is the date of the regulation. If the regulation was recently issued, that is, later than the scope of the coverage of the *CFR* volume on the same subject, the research should commence in the *Federal Register*. If, however, the regulation is not very recent, or if the date is not known, the starting point is the *CFR*. These two sources are accessed differently.

1. Access to the Federal Register

a. *Federal Register Index.* This official index, arranged alphabetically by agency, is issued monthly. Each issue of this *Index* cumulates that year's previous monthly indexes, with the December issue being the final annual index. Because this *Index* is not distributed until several weeks after the month covered, the Contents in each issue of the *Federal Register* subsequent to the last *Index* should be consulted. The *Index* and Contents, however, are not adequately detailed and, at times, it is difficult to locate a regulation if one does not know the agency that issued it.

b. *CIS Federal Register Index.* This publication, which started in 1984, comprehensively indexes each issue of the *Federal Register*. It is issued weekly with monthly cumulative indexes and permanent semi-annual bound volumes. It includes indexes by subject and name, *CFR* Section numbers affected, federal agency docket number, and Calendar of Effective Dates and Comment Deadlines.

2. Access to the Code of Federal Regulations

a. *CFR Index and Finding Aids.* This single volume accompanies the *CFR* and is revised annually.[17] It provides several access points to the *CFR*.

(1) *Index.* The index includes in one alphabet both subject entries and the names of administrative agencies. Consequently, one can consult

---

[17] LEXIS Law Publishing publishes a copy of the *CFR Index and Finding Aids* volume as a part of the *United States Code Service*.

it either under the name of an agency or under a specific subject heading. Since January 1980, the subject terms used are taken from a thesaurus developed by the Office of the Federal Register.[18] This now assures that the same subject headings are used in the index if two or more agencies use different terms covering the same concept. For example, in its regulations one agency may use the word *compensation,* another *pay,* and a third *salaries.* By use of the thesaurus, references to all three of these regulations will appear in the index under the subject heading *Wages.*

The index refers to the appropriate Title of the *CFR* and then to the specific Part within the Title. [See Illustration 13–1.] Because the references are to Parts and not to Sections, specificity is reduced.

(2) *Parallel Table of Authorities and Rules.* This table appears as Table I in the *CFR Index and Finding Aids* volume. [See Illustration 13–3.] If the citation is known to a law or Presidential document that authorized an agency or administrator to issue regulations, this table indicates where administrative regulations promulgated under such authority are found in the *CFR.* The table also includes citations to laws that are interpreted or applied by regulations codified in the *CFR.* The citations in Table I are divided into four segments: U.S.C.; Statutes at Large; public law; and Presidential documents. Within each segment the citations are arranged in numerical order.

For Presidential documents included or cited in regulations in the *CFR,* one should use Table II. However, Table II has not been revised since January 1, 1976, and was last published in the *Index* for that year.

(3) *List of Agency–Prepared Indexes Appearing In Individual CFR Volumes.* This list provides information to locate agency-prepared indexes that are published in various volumes of the *CFR.*

b. *Index to the Code of Federal Regulations.*[19] Published since 1984, this annual, private publication provides access by subject and geographic location. The references are to *CFR* Title and Part. [See Illustration 13–2.]

c. The Index portion of the 1990 CFR *Index and Finding Aids* volume is available online through LEXIS–NEXIS.

3. Regulations No Longer in Force

It is often necessary to determine what regulations were in force at some prior date. Where prior editions of the *CFR* are available, one simply can consult the edition that was current at the applicable time. Some libraries keep superseded editions of the *CFR* in paper copy or in microform.[20] Regulations no longer in force can also be located in the electronic sources listed in Section C–4, *supra.*

---

[18] Thesaurus of Indexing Terms, 45 Fed. Reg. 2998 (1980).

[19] Congressional Information Service, Inc. Earlier editions of the *Index* were published by Information Handling Services (1977–79) and Capitol Services Annotated (1980).

[20] Some libraries may have a cumulation of each Title on microfilm or microfiche.

One also can begin by locating the applicable subject matter in the current edition of *CFR*, which gives the date and *Federal Register* citation for the adoption of each section, and the same information for each subsequent amendment of that section. This allows the researcher to determine whether the present language of the section was in effect at the applicable time and to find the original language in the *Federal Register* if the section has been amended.

The following official publications also provide *CFR* citations to allow one to find the precise text of regulations that were in force on any given date during the years covered: *Code of Federal Regulations List of Sections Affected, 1949–1963; List of CFR Sections Affected, 1964–1972* (2 volumes); and *List of CFR Sections Affected, 1973–1985* (4 volumes). For changes from January 1, 1986, each volume of the *CFR* contains a *List of CFR Sections Affected.* The *List* appears at the end of the volume and is arranged by year.

SECTION E.   UPDATING REGULATIONS

After one has located a regulation, further research is necessary to determine whether the regulation has been amended or revoked. If the regulation was amended or revoked or if a new regulation has been promulgated, the *Federal Register* contains the documentation. The sources described below are essential tools to locate citations to the *Federal Register* where changes to regulations are published.

1. Sources

a. *LSA: List of CFR Sections Affected.* This publication is issued monthly and indicates finalized and proposed changes made since the latest publication of the *CFR*. The December issue cumulates all changes for Titles 1–16; the March issue contains all changes for Titles 17–27; the June issue lists changes for Titles 28–41; and the September issue indicates changes for Titles 42–50. [See Illustrations 13–6 and 13–7.] For changes to regulations which have become final, the *LSA* is arranged by *CFR* Title and Section and sets forth the nature of the changes, *e.g.,* "revised," and provides page number references to the *Federal Register*. [See Illustration 13–8.] For proposed changes, the *LSA* is arranged by Title and Part with reference to the applicable *Federal Register* page numbers. [See Illustration 13–9.] A separate section of the *LSA* updates the *Parallel Table of Authorities and Rules.*

LEXIS–NEXIS contains the *LSA* from March, 1991. Changes for each Title can be searched cumulatively or by each month. The *LSA* online is not as current as the print version.

b. *CFR Parts Affected.* Each issue of the *Federal Register* contains a section near the front that lists *CFR Parts Affected in This Issue.* However, this section is incorporated in the cumulative list in the Reader Aids section. The section in the front of the *Federal Register* would be used if one must review each issue of the *Federal Register* to ascertain if any changes occur to a specific regulation being monitored.

Each issue of the *Federal Register* also includes a list of *CFR Parts Affected* in the Reader Aids section. The list is cumulative for one calendar month. [See Illustration 13–13.] Both lists give page number references to the *Federal Register*.

c. *Converting Page Number References to Specific Issues of the Federal Register.* If the regulation one is researching has been affected, a reference to the *Federal Register* is provided in the *LSA* and/or the list of *CFR Parts Affected*. This reference is to the page number of the *Federal Register* on which the amendment, proposed amendment, or removal appears. To find the issue of the *Federal Register* in which the change appears, use the conversion table in the *Federal Register Index* or the *LSA,* whichever is more current. [See Illustration 13–10.] If the page number does not appear in the *Index*'s or *LSA* 's conversion table, one must turn to the last issue of each month of the *Federal Register* published since the *Index* or the *LSA* and use the conversion tables, which appear in the Reader Aids section. [See Illustration 13–13.]

d. *Shepard's Code of Federal Regulations Citations.* To ascertain whether a federal court has ruled on the constitutionality or validity of a regulation, this unit of *Shepard's Citations* should be consulted. In addition to updating regulations, a researcher may be interested in locating cases and other materials that have cited a regulation. *Shepard's Code of Federal Regulations Citations* provides a method for locating citations to court cases, selected law review articles, and *A.L.R. Annotations* that have cited regulations published in the *CFR*. The use of *Shepard's Citations* is explained in Chapter 15.

2. Research Methodology

The need to refer to the sources to update a regulation described *supra* is dictated by where the regulation being updated was found and the recency of the publication containing the regulation.

If the regulation was found in the *CFR,* the researcher should first use the most current *LSA*. It is important to note the publication date on the cover of the *CFR* volume in which the regulation was found in order to cover the appropriate time period. Since the *LSA* is issued monthly, a further check must be made in the cumulative list of *CFR Parts Affected* in the *Federal Register* for any later changes. Therefore, note the coverage of the *LSA* used, and check the list of *CFR Parts Affected* in the last issue of each subsequent month, including the current month, of the *Federal Register*.

If the regulation was found in the *Federal Register* and if the latest issue of *LSA* is for a month *later* than the month of the issue of the *Federal Register* in which the regulation appears, first use the *LSA* that covers the period from the date of the issue of the *Federal Register* in which the regulation was found. Since the *LSA* is issued monthly, a further check must be made for any later changes in the cumulative list of *CFR Parts Affected* in the *Federal Register*. Therefore, note the coverage of the *LSA* used, and check the list of *CFR Parts Affected* in the last issue of each subsequent month, including the current month, of the *Federal Register*.

If the regulation was found in an issue of the *Federal Register* and if the latest *LSA* available is for a month *prior* to the month of the issue of the *Federal Register* in which the regulation appears, check the list of *CFR Parts Affected* in the last issue of the month of the *Federal Register* in which the regulation was found and the list of *CFR Parts Affected* in the last issue of each subsequent month, including the current month, of the *Federal Register*.

If the regulation appears in an issue of the *Federal Register* for the current month, check the list of *CFR Parts Affected* in the last available issue of the current month's *Federal Register* to be as up to date as possible.

SECTION F. ILLUSTRATIONS OF FEDERAL REGISTER AND CODE OF FEDERAL REGULATIONS

Problem: Find regulations pertaining to determination of payment rates for hospice care for the aged and disabled.

[Illustration 13–1]

EXCERPTS FROM CFR INDEX AND FINDING AIDS VOLUME

CFR Index	Health professions
Contracting by negotiation, 48 CFR 1615	Federal employees health benefits program,
Contractor qualifications, 48 CFR 1609	debarment, civil monetary penalties and
Definitions of words and terms, 48 CFR 1602	assessments imposed against providers, 5 CFR 890
Federal Acquisition Regulations System, 48 CFR 1601	Health education assistance loan program, 42 CFR 60
Forms, 48 CFR 1653	Health manpower shortage areas
Improper business practices and personal conflicts of interest, 48 CFR 1603	Designation, 42 CFR 5
Protection of privacy and freedom of information, 48 CFR 1624	National Health Service Corps, 42 CFR 23
Protests, disputes, and appeals, 48 CFR	Indian fellowship and professional development programs, 34 CFR 263

> **Step 1**
>
> Consult the Index in the current *CFR Index and Finding Aids* volume. Health insurance for the aged refers one to Medicare. See next page.

Termination of contracts, 48 CFR 1649	Health care practitioners and providers of
Types of contracts, 48 CFR 1616	health care services under Medicare,
Special programs and projects, Medicare, 42 CFR 403	imposition of sanctions by peer review organizations, 42 CFR 1004
Health insurance for aged	Introduction; general definitions, 42 CFR 1000
See Medicare	Medicaid, State-initiated exclusions,
Health maintenance organizations (HMO)	program integrity, 42 CFR 1002
Medicaid, contracts, 42 CFR 434	Medicare and State health care programs, program integrity, 42 CFR 1001
Medicare	Longshoremen's and Harbor Workers'
Health care maintenance organizations, competitive medical plans, and health care prepayment plans, 42 CFR 417	Compensation Act, administration and procedure, debarment, 20 CFR 702
Introduction; definitions, 42 CFR 400	Medicaid
Health professions	Nursing facilities and intermediate care facilities for mentally retarded, payment standards, 42 CFR 442
See also Veterinarians	Payments for services, 42 CFR 447
Alien physicians, criteria for evaluating comprehensive plan to reduce reliance on, 45 CFR 51	Program integrity, 42 CFR 455
	States and long term care facilities, requirements, 42 CFR 483
Armed forces, appointment of doctors of osteopathy as medical officers, 32 CFR 74	Medical malpractice claims against military and civilian personnel of armed forces, 32 CFR 61
Construction of teaching facilities, educational improvements, scholarships and student loans, grants, 42 CFR 57	Medicare
	Ambulatory surgical services, 42 CFR 416
Drugs used for treatment of narcotic addicts, 21 CFR 291	Appeals procedures for determinations that affect participation and for
Emergency health and medical occupations, 44 CFR 325	determinations that affect participation of ICFs/MR and certain
Family planning services, grants, 42 CFR 59	NFs in Medicaid program, 42 CFR 498
Federal Aviation Administration, representatives of Administrator to test airmen for certification, 14 CFR 183	Conditions for payment, 42 CFR 424
	Conditions of participation, home health agencies, 42 CFR 484

335

[Illustration 13–1 Cont.]

EXCERPTS FROM CFR INDEX AND FINDING AIDS VOLUME

Medicare	CFR Index

Premarket approval of medical devices, 21 CFR 814

Minority biomedical research support program, 42 CFR 52c

National Cancer Institute, construction grants, 42 CFR 52b

National Center for Health Services, research grants, 42 CFR 67

National Heart, Lung, and Blood Institute; prevention and control projects, grants, 42 CFR 52e

National Institute for Occupational Safety and Health research and demonstration grants, 42 CFR 87

National Institute of Environmental Health Sciences hazardous substances basic research and training grants, 42 CFR 65a

National Institutes of Health center grants, 42 CFR 52a

National Institutes of Health training grants, 42 CFR 63a

National Library of Medicine

Gra...

Natio...

6...

Public...

Resea...

CFR 52

Research subjects, identity protection, 42 CFR 2a

Scientific peer review of research grant applications and research and development contract projects, 42 CFR 52h

Veterans health care, 38 CFR 17

→ **Medicare**

See also Peer Review Organizations (PRO)

Exclusions from Medicare and limitations on Medicare payment, 42 CFR 411

Federal health insurance for aged and disabled, 42 CFR 405

Ambulatory surgical services, 42 CFR 416

Appeals procedures for determinations that affect participation and for determinations that affect participation of ICFs/MR and certain NFs in Medicaid program, 42 CFR 498

Conditions for payment, 42 CFR 424

Conditions of participation, home health agencies, 42 CFR 484

General administrative requirements, official records confidentiality and disclosure, 42 CFR 401

Health facilities certification, 42 CFR 491

Health maintenance organizations, competitive medical plans, and health care prepayment plans, 42 CFR 417

→ Hospice, 42 CFR 418

Hospital insurance—
Benefits, 42 CFR 409
Eligibility and entitlement, 42 CFR 406

Hospitals, conditions of participation, 42 CFR 482

Inpatient hospital services, prospective payment systems, 42 CFR 412

Intermediaries and carriers, 42 CFR 421

Introduction; definitions, 42 CFR 400

Laboratory requirements, 42 CFR 493

Payment on reasonable charge basis, end-stage renal disease, 42 CFR 414

Principles of reasonable cost reimbursement, end-stage renal disease services payment, optional ... payment ... facilities, 42 ...

... Financing ... 420

Provider agreements and supplier approval, 42 CFR 489

Services furnished by physicians in providers, supervising physicians in teaching settings, and residents in certain settings, 42 CFR 415

Special programs and projects, 42 CFR 403

Specialized providers, conditions of participation, 42 CFR 485

Specialized services furnished by suppliers, conditions for coverage, 42 CFR 486

States and long term care facilities, requirements, 42 CFR 483

Supplementary medical insurance (SMI)—
Benefits, 42 CFR 410
Enrollment and entitlement, 42 CFR 407

Supplementary medical insurance (SMI), premiums, 42 CFR 408

Survey, certification, and enforcement procedures, 42 CFR 488

Inspector General Office-Health Care, Health and Human Services Department

Step 1 con't
Note the sub-entry, Hospice, 42 CFR 418. This refers to Title 42, Part 418. See next Illustration.

438

[Illustration 13–2]

PAGE FROM THE INDEX TO THE CODE
OF FEDERAL REGULATIONS (CIS)

HEALTH INSURANCE **PROGRAM**

Requirements for Long Term Care Facilities   42 CFR 483
-ORGAN TRANSPLANTS — REIMBURSEMENT
   Conditions for Coverage Organ Procurement Organizations
                                          42 CFR 485 301-308
-OUTPATIENTS — SURGERY
   Payments to Providers   42 CFR 413 60-74
   Ambulatory Surgical Services   42 CFR 416
-PATIENT RIGHTS — HOME HEALTH AGENCIES
   Administration   42 CFR 484 10-18
-PEER REVIEW ORGANIZATIONS — PROGRAM MANAGEMENT
   Recommendations of the Administrative Conference of the United States
                                         1 CFR 305
-PHYSICIANS — CLINICAL LABORATORY SERVICES
   Physician Ownership of and Referral of Patients of Laboratory Specimens to
     Entities Furnishing Clinical Laboratory or Other Health Services
                                42 CFR 411 350-361
-PHYSICIANS — ELIGIBILITY REINSTATEMENT
   Reinstatement into the Programs   42 CFR 1001 3001-3005
   Effect and Duration of Exclusion   42 CFR 1004 110-120
-PHYSICIANS — REIMBURSEMENT
   Criteria for Determination of Reasonable Charges, Payment for Services of
     Hospital Interns, Residents, and Supervising Physicians [Tables]
                                42 CFR 405 501-535
-PHYSICIANS — REPORTING REQUIREMENTS
   Physician Certification Requirements   42 CFR 424 10-27
-PHYSICIANS — VIOLATIONS
   Imposition of Sanctions on Health Care Practitioners and Providers of Health
     Care Services by a Peer Review Organization   42 CFR 1004
-PREPAID HEALTH PLANS
   Health Maintenance Organizations, Competitive Medical Plans and Health Care
     Prepayment Plans   42 CFR 417
-PREPAID HEALTH PLANS — ELIGIBILITY
   Health Care Prepayment Plans   42 CFR 417 800-810
-PREPAID HEALTH PLANS — FINANCIAL REPORTS
   Health Care Prepayment Plans   42 CFR 417 800-810
                                42 CFR 417 800-810
-PREPAID HEALTH PLANS — REIMBURSEMENT
   Health Care Prepayment Plans   42 CFR 417 800-810
-PROGRAM MANAGEMENT — PEER REVIEW ORGANIZATIONS
   Recommendations of the Administrative Conference of the United States
                                         1 CFR 305
-PSYCHIATRIC HOSPITALS
   Requirements for Specialty Hospitals   42 CFR 482 60-66
-PSYCHIATRIC HOSPITALS — ELIGIBILITY
   Conditions of Participation for Hospitals   42 CFR 482
-PUBLIC HEALTH AGENCIES — ELIGIBILITY

Medicare Payment Risk Basis   42 CFR 417 500-580
-REIMBURSEMENT — HEALTH MAINTENANCE ORGANIZATIONS
   Medicare Payment to HMOs and CMPs General Rules   42 CFR 417 524-528
   Medicare Payment Cost Basis   42 CFR 417 530-570
   Medicare Payment Risk Basis   42 CFR 417 500-580
-REIMBURSEMENT — HEARINGS
   Provider Reimbursement Determinations and Appeals   42 CFR 405 1801-1889
-REIMBURSEMENT — HOME HEALTH AGENCIES
   Principles of Reasonable Cost Reimbursement Payment for End-Stage Renal
     Disease Services   42 CFR 413
-REIMBURSEMENT — HOSPICES
   Payment for Hospice Care   42 CFR 418 301-311
-REIMBURSEMENT — MAMMOGRAPHY
   Conditions for Coverage of Particular Services   42 CFR 494
-REIMBURSEMENT — MEDICAL EQUIPMENT
   Criteria for Determination of Reasonable Charges Payment for Services of
     Hospital Interns, Residents, and Supervising Physicians [Tables]
                                42 CFR 405 501-535
   Payment for Durable Medical Equipment and Prosthetic and Orthotic Devices
                                42 CFR 414 224-230
-REIMBURSEMENT — MEDICAL SERVICES
   Principles of Reimbursement for Services by Hospital-Based Physicians [Tables]
                                42 CFR 405 465-482
   Prospective Payment Systems for Inpatient Hospital Services   42 CFR 412
   Principles of Reasonable Cost Reimbursement Payment for End-Stage Renal
     Disease Services   42 CFR 413
   Determination of Reasonable Charges Under the ESRD Program
                                42 CFR 414 200-335
-REIMBURSEMENT — MEDICAL STUDENTS
   Criteria for Determination of Reasonable Charges Payment for Services of
     Hospital Interns, Residents, and Supervising Physicians [Tables]
                                42 CFR 405 501-535
-REIMBURSEMENT — ORGAN TRANSPLANTS
   Conditions for Coverage Organ Procurement Organizations
                                42 CFR 485 301-308
-REIMBURSEMENT — PHYSICIANS
   Criteria for Determination of Reasonable Charges. Payment for Services of
     Hospital Interns, Residents, and Supervising Physicians [Tables]
                                42 CFR 405 501-535
-REIMBURSEMENT — PREPAID HEALTH PLANS
   Health Care Prepayment Plans   42 CFR 417 800-810
-RENAL DIALYSIS — REPORTING REQUIREMENTS
   Conditions for Coverage of Suppliers of End-Stage Renal Disease (ESRD)
     Services [Tables]   42 CFR 405 2100-2184
   Payment for End-Stage Renal Disease (ESRD) Services   42 CFR 413 170-178
-RENAL DISEASE — BENEFIT LIMITATIONS

> **Step 1a**
>
>   This privately-published Index of the Congressional Information Service provides much more detailed indexing. Notice how it leads directly to reimbursement for hospices.

24-230

-REHABILITATION THERAPY SERVICES — EVALUATION
   Conditions of Participation Clinics, Rehabilitation Agencies, and Public Health
     Agencies as Providers of Outpatient Physical Therapy and/or Speech
     Pathology Services, and Conditions for Coverage, Outpatient Physical Therapy
     Services Furnished by Physical Therapists in Independent Practice
                                  42 CFR 405 1701-1737
-REHABILITATION THERAPY SERVICES — FACILITY CERTIFICATION
   Conditions of Participation and Conditions for Coverage Specialized Providers
                                42 CFR 485
-REHABILITATION THERAPY SERVICES — VECTOR CONTROL
   Conditions of Participation Clinics, Rehabilitation Agencies, and Public Health
     Agencies as Providers of Outpatient Physical Therapy and/or Speech
     Pathology Services and Conditions for Coverage Outpatient Physical Therapy
     Services Furnished by Physical Therapists in Independent Practice
                                42 CFR 405 1701-1737
-REIMBURSEMENT
   Criteria for Determination of Reasonable Charges, Payment for Services of
     Hospital Interns, Residents and Supervising Physicians [Tables]
                                42 CFR 405 501-535
   Payment for Part B Medical and Other Health Services   42 CFR 414
-REIMBURSEMENT — ANESTHETICS
   Payment for the Services of Anesthetists   42 CFR 414 450-453
-REIMBURSEMENT — HEALTH FACILITIES
   Principles of Reimbursement for Services by Hospital-Based Physicians [Tables]
                                42 CFR 405 465-482
   Prospective Payment Systems for Inpatient Hospital Services   42 CFR 412
   The Medicare Geographic Classification Review Board   42 CFR 412 230-280
   Principles of Reasonable Cost Reimbursement, Payment for End-Stage Renal
     Disease Services   42 CFR 413
   Scope of Benefits   42 CFR 415 60-75
   Payment for Facility Services   42 CFR 416 120-150
-REIMBURSEMENT — HEALTH INSURANCE COMPANIES
   Medicare Payment to HMOs and CMPs General Rules   42 CFR 417 524-528
   Medicare Payment Cost Basis   42 CFR 417 530-570

-RULE MAKING — *HEALTH CARE FINANCING ADMINISTRATION*
   Recommendations of the Administrative Conference of the United States
                                         1 CFR 305
-RURAL HEALTH FACILITIES
   Rural Health Clinic and Federally Qualified Health Center Services
                                42 CFR 405 2401-2472
-SENIOR CITIZENS — SOCIAL SECURITY BENEFITS
   Federal Health Insurance for the Aged and Disabled   42 CFR 405
-SERVICE AGREEMENTS — HEALTH FACILITIES
   Provider and Supplier Agreements   42 CFR 489
-SERVICE CONTRACTS — APPEALS
   Medicare Contract Appeals   42 CFR 417 640-694
-SERVICE CONTRACTS — INFORMATION ACCESS
   Access to Books, Documents, and Records of Subcontractors
                                42 CFR 420 300-304
-SOCIAL SECURITY BENEFITS — DISABLED PERSONS
   Federal Health Insurance for the Aged and Disabled   42 CFR 405
-SOCIAL SECURITY BENEFITS — SENIOR CITIZENS
   Federal Health Insurance for the Aged and Disabled   42 CFR 405
-SUPPLEMENTARY MEDICAL INSURANCE BENEFITS
   Special Programs and Projects   42 CFR 403
   Supplementary Medical Insurance (SMI) Enrollment and Entitlement
                                42 CFR 407
   Supplementary Medical Insurance (SMI) Benefits   42 CFR 410
-SUPPLEMENTARY MEDICAL INSURANCE BENEFITS — BENEFIT
LIMITATIONS
   Payment of SMI Benefits [Tables]   42 CFR 410 150-175
-SUPPLEMENTARY MEDICAL INSURANCE BENEFITS — BENEFIT
PAYMENTS
   Payment of SMI Benefits [Tables]   42 CFR 410 150-175
-SUPPLEMENTARY MEDICAL INSURANCE BENEFITS —
CERTIFICATION
   Medicare Supplemental Policies   42 CFR 403 200-258
-SUPPLEMENTARY MEDICAL INSURANCE BENEFITS — STATE

[Illustration 13–3]

PAGE FROM PARALLEL TABLE OF AUTHORITIES AND RULES, CFR INDEX AND FINDING AIDS VOLUME

CFR Index

42 U.S.C.—Continued	CFR
300j–9	29 Parts 1, 5, 24
	40 Parts 2, 9, 23, 25, 35, 141–143
300m–4	42 Part 124
300o–1	42 Part 124
300o–3	29 Parts 1, 5
300r	42 Part 124
300s	42 Part 124
300s–1a	42 Part 124
300u et seq	21 Part 5
300u–300u–5	21 Part 20
300v–1	7 Part 1c
	10 Part 745

42 U.S.C.—Continued	CFR
	42 Part 406
428	20 Part 404
432	20 Part 422
433	20 Part 404
501	29 Part 31
503	20 Parts 640, 650
602	20 Part 401
	45 Parts 95,
	204–206, 233, 234, 250, 255–257
603—604	45 Part 305
603	45 Parts 201,
	205, 234, 235, 240, 250, 255–257

	Part 56
	Part 224
	233, 234
	205, 233
	Part 233
	Part 205
	Part 240
	Part 235
	355–1357
	Part 405
	301–303
	Part 304
	Part 307
	s 95, 305
	Part 304
	Part 581
	350, 363

Step 1b

An alternative method of finding regulations in the *CFR.*

There are times when the U.S.C. citation to the statute that delegated the authority to issue regulations is known. In such instances, the Parallel Table of Authorities and Rules in the *CFR Index and Finding Aids* volume can be used to locate citations to regulations in the *CFR*. For example, the statutory authorization for determination of payment rates under Medicare for hospice care is found at 42 U.S.C. § 1302. See next page.

42 U.S.C.—Continued	CFR
300w e	
300w n	
300x et	
300y et	
300y–1)	
300z–7	42 Part 62a
300aa–1	21 Parts 5, 20
300aa–1 note	21 Part 5
	42 Part 100
	45 Part 4
300aa–11	42 Part 100
300aa–14	42 Part 100
300aa–15	21 Parts 5, 600
300aa–25	21 Part 5
300aa–27	21 Parts 5, 17
300aa–28	42 Part 63a
300cc–15	42 Part 52a
300cc–16	42 Part 63a
300cc–41	45 Part 233
301	20 Part 404
301 note	45 Part 1393
302—303	45 Part 201
303	42 Part 57
316	20 Part 404
401—407	42 Part 406
402	20 Part 410
404	20 Parts 401, 422
405	42 Parts 405, 1005, 1006
405 note	20 Part 404
409—418	20 Part 404
416	42 Part 424
418	20 Part 422
418 note	20 Part 404
421—431	20 Part 404
421	20 Parts 416, 422
421 note	20 Parts 404, 416
423	20 Part 416
423 note	20 Part 416
426—426a	42 Part 406
426	20 Part 404
	42 Part 405
426–1	20 Part 404

42 U.S.C.—Continued	CFR
	34 Parts 734, 818
660	45 Parts 301–303
661—662	5 Part 581
	20 Parts 350, 363
	32 Part 818
663—682	5 Part 581
663—664	45 Part 303
664	45 Parts 301, 302, 307
665	15 Part 15b
	32 Parts 54, 818
	33 Part 54
	42 Part 21
666—667	45 Parts 301–303, 307
670 et seq	45 Parts 1355–1357
681—687	45 Parts 240, 250
684	45 Part 251
701 et seq	45 Part 96
702	42 Part 51a
706	42 Part 51a
901—904	20 Part 422
901	20 Part 423
902	20 Parts 401, 404, 422, 423, 498
907	45 Part 204
1070b	34 Part 676
1102	20 Part 615
1141 note	24 Part 581
1202—1203	45 Part 1393
1202	45 Part 233
1203	45 Part 201
1232c	34 Part 676
1301	45 Parts 201, 301, 1355
1302	20 Parts 401, 404, 409, 410, 417, 601, 602, 603, 625, 640, 650
	40 Part 404
	42 Parts 51a,

768

[Illustration 13–3 Cont.]

PAGE FROM PARALLEL TABLE OF AUTHORITIES AND RULES, CFR INDEX AND FINDING AIDS VOLUME

Authorities

42 U.S.C.—Continued   CFR

400, 401, 403, 405–418, 420, 421, 424, 430–436, 440–442, 447, 455–456, 462, 466, 473, 476, 482–486, 488, 489, 491, 493, 498, 1000–1006
    45 Parts 75, 95, 201, 204–206, 212, 213, 225, 233, 235, 237, 250, 251, 255–257, 301–305, 307, 1355–1357

1302c–3	42 Part 466
1304 note	45 Part 96
1305	45 Part 96
1306	20 Parts 401, 410, 416, 422
	45 Parts 5, 205, 206
1307b–7	45 Part 205
1310	20 Part 416
	45 Parts 63, 204
1313	45 Part 212
1315	45 Part 204
1316	45 Part 201
1320–1	42 Parts 100, 405
1320a–3	42 Part 1002
1320a–5	42 Part 1002
1320a–7—1320a–7a	42 Part 1003
1320a–7	42 Parts 1001, 1002, 1005
1320a–7a	42 Parts 405, 1006
1320a–7b	42 Part 1001
1320a–8	20 Part 498
1320b–1	20 Part 422
1320b–2	45 Part 95
1320b–2 note	45 Part 95
1320b–7	42 Part 433
	45 Part 205
1320b–8	42 Part 405
	20 Part 498
1320b–10	42 Part 1003
1320b–11	20 Part 401
1320b–13	20 Part 422
1320c—1320c–2	42 Part 462
1320c	42 Part 405
1320c–1—1320c–2	42 Part 462
1320c–3—1320c–4	42 Part 405
1320c–3	42 Parts 405, 466, 476
1320c–5	42 Parts 455, 476, 1004, 1005
1320c–8	42 Part 466
1320c–9	42 Part 476
1327	20 Part 416
1331a	20 Part 416
1341	20 Part 401
1352—1353	45 Part 1393
1352	45 Part 233
1353	45 Part 201
1381—1383d	20 Part 416
1382	45 Parts 233, 1393
1382c	20 Part 404
1383	20 Part 404
	45 Parts 205, 1393
1383 note	45 Part 201
1385x	42 Part 411
1394hh	42 Part 412
1394ww	42 Part 412
1395 et seq	20 Part 404
1395	42 Parts 405, 410, 415, 421, 484, 485, 489, 498
1395–1	42 Part 421
1395a	42 Part 414

42 U.S.C.—Continued   CFR

1395d—1395f	42 Part 418
1395f—1395v	42 Part 405
1395f	42 Part 482
1395g	42 Parts 412, 413
1395h	42 Part 418
1395i—1395z	42 Part 406
1395i–2	42 Part 408
1395i–3	42 Part 489
1395i–4	42 Part 412
1395k—1395l	42 Parts 410, 416
1395k	42 Parts 415, 488
1395l	42 Parts 405, 414, 491, 494
1395m	42 Parts 410, 415
1395p—1395s	42 Part 408
1395u—1395w–4	42 Part 414
1395u	42 Parts 405, 415, 1001, 1003
1395v	42 Part 408
1395w–4	42 Parts 405, 414, 415
1395x—1395z	42 Part 405
1395x	40 Parts 413, 414, 418, 484, 494
	42 Parts 409, 410, 411, 413, 415, 417, 418, 420, 489, 493
1395y	21 Parts 5, 805
	42 Parts 415, 418, 489, 494, 1001
1395y note	21 Parts 5, 409, 805
1395z	42 Parts 416, 494
1395aa—1395cc	42 Part 405
1395aa—1395bb	42 Part 494
1395aa	42 Parts 416, 489
1395cc	42 Parts 415, 466, 489
1395dd	42 Part 1003
1395ff—1395ii	42 Part 405
1395hh—1395ll	42 Part 421
1395hh	40 Part 484
	42 Parts 400, 401, 403, 405–408, 413, 414, 417, 418, 420, 421, 424, 466, 473, 482, 483, 486, 489, 1000, 1001
1395kk	42 Parts 403, 405, 417
1395mm—1395rr	42 Part 405
1395mm	42 Part 1003
1395nn	42 Part 1003
1395pp—1395rr	42 Part 405
1395rr	42 Parts 408, 410, 415
1395ss	42 Part 1003
1395tt	42 Part 405
1395uu	42 Part 421
1395ww—1395xx	42 Part 405
1395ww note	42 Part 413
1395zz	42 Part 405
1395ccc	42 Part 405
1396—1396a	42 Part 491
	45 Part 19
1396	42 Parts 482, 488, 1002
	45 Part 95
1396a—1396b	42 Parts 405, 433, 435, 436, 447, 1002
	45 Parts 302–304
1396a	42 Part 494
1396b	42 Parts 456, 482, 483, 1003, 1007

[Illustration 13–4]

PAGE FROM TITLE 42 OF CFR

Health Care Financing Administration, HHS   **Pt. 418**

§417.940 Civil action to enforce compliance with assurances.

The provisions of §417.163(g) apply to entities that have outstanding loans or loan guarantees administered under this subpart.

[59 FR 49843, Sept. 30, 1994]

➤ PART 418—HOSPICE CARE

Subpart A—General Provision and Definitions

AUTHORITY: Secs. 1102 and 1871 of the Social Security Act (42 U.S.C. 1302 and 1395hh).

SOURCE: 48 FR 56026, Dec. 16, 1983, unless otherwise noted.

Step 2
Refer to Title 42, Part 418 of the *CFR* as located using Step 1. After each Part, a detailed list of Sections is given. In this instance, Section 418.306 seems relevant. Note how at the end of Subpart H the statutory authorization is noted.

591

[Illustration 13–5]

PAGE FROM TITLE 42 OF CFR

§ 418.306   **42 CFR Ch. IV (10–1–96 Edition)**

(c) Services of the patient's attending physician, if he or she is not an employee of the hospice or providing services under arrangements with the hospice, are not considered hospice services and are not included in the amount subject to the hospice payment limit described in § 418.309. These services are paid by the carrier under the procedures in subparts D or E, part 405 of this chapter.

§ 418.306 Determination of payment rates.

(a) *Applicability.* HCFA establishes payment rates for each of the categories of hospice care described in § 418.302(b). The rates are established using the methodology described in section 1814(i)(1)(C) of the Act.

(b) *Payment rates.* The payment rates for routine home care and other services included in hospice care are as follows:

(1) The following rates, which are 120 percent of the rates in effect on September 30, 1989, are effective January 1, 1990 through September 30, 1990 and October 21, 1990 through December 31, 1990:

Routine home care	$75.80
Continuous home care:	
Full rate for 24 hours	442.40
Hourly rate	18.43
Inpatient respite care	78.40
General inpatient care	337.20

(2) Except for the period beginning October 21, 1990, through December 31, 1990, the payment rates for routine home care and other services included in hospice care for Federal fiscal years 1991, 1992, [...]
on or afte[...] ment rat[...] graph du[...] increased [...] centage i[...] 1886(b)(3)(B)(III) of the Act, otherwise applicable to discharges occurring in the fiscal year. The payment rates for the period beginning October 21, 1990, through December 31, 1990, are the same as those shown in paragraph (b)(1) of this section.

(3) For Federal fiscal years 1994 through 1997, the payment rate is the payment rate in effect during the previous fiscal year increased by a factor

equal to the market basket percentage increase minus—

(i) 2 percentage points in FY 1994;

(ii) 1.5 percentage points in FYs 1995 and 1996; and

(iii) 0.5 percentage points in FY 1997.

(c) *Adjustment by intermediary.* The payment rates established by HCFA are adjusted by the intermediary to reflect local differences in wages.

(d) *Federal Register notices.* HCFA publishes as a notice in the FEDERAL REGISTER any proposal to change the methodology for determining the payment rates.

[56 FR 26919, June 12, 1991, as amended at 59 FR 26960, May 25, 1994]

§ 418.307 Periodic interim payments.

Subject to the provisions of § 413.64(h) of this chapter, a hospice may elect to receive periodic interim payments (PIP) effective with claims received on or after July 1, 1987. Payment is made biweekly under the PIP method unless the hospice requests a longer fixed interval (not to exceed one month) between payments. The biweekly interim payment amount is based on the total estimated Medicare payments for the reporting period (as described in §§ 418.302–418.306). Each payment is made 2 weeks after the end of a biweekly period of service as described in § 413.64(h)(5) of this chapter. Under certain circumstances that are described in § 413.64(g) of this chapter, a hospice that is not receiving PIP may request an accelerated payment.

[59 FR 36713, July 19, 1994]

[...] amount of [...] [...] paragraph [...] Medicare [...] furnished during a cap period is limited by the hospice cap amount specified in § 418.309.

(b) Until October 1, 1986, payment to a hospice that began operation before January 1, 1975 is not limited by the amount of the hospice cap specified in § 418.309.

(c) The intermediary notifies the hospice of the determination of program reimbursement at the end of the cap year in accordance with procedures

> **Step 3**
>
> Note how at the end of Part 418.306 citations are given to where the regulation and amendments appeared in the *Federal Register*. Next the researcher would read § 418.306.

[Illustration 13–6]

COVER FROM LSA: LIST OF CFR SECTIONS AFFECTED PAMPHLET

LSA

List of CFR Sections Affected

September 1997

**Save this issue for Titles
42—50 (Annual)**

Step 4
    Title 42 of the *CFR* is revised annually as of October 1.
Hence, it must be ascertained if any changes have subsequently
occurred. See next Illustration.

United States
Government
Printing Office
SUPERINTENDENT
OF DOCUMENTS
Washington, DC 20402

PERIODICALS

Postage and Fees Paid
U.S. Government Printing Office
(ISSN 0097–6326)

code of federal regulations

G C.S

[Illustration 13–7]

TITLE PAGE FROM LSA: LIST OF CFR SECTIONS AFFECTED PAMPHLET

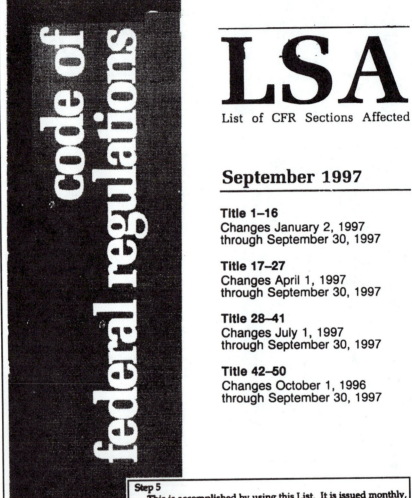

code of federal regulations

LSA

List of CFR Sections Affected

September 1997

Title 1–16
Changes January 2, 1997
through September 30, 1997

Title 17–27
Changes April 1, 1997
through September 30, 1997

Title 28–41
Changes July 1, 1997
through September 30, 1997

Title 42–50
Changes October 1, 1996
through September 30, 1997

Step 5
This is accomplished by using this List. It is issued monthly, the December, March, June, and September issues consisting of an annual cumulation as indicated on the title page.

[Illustration 13–8]

PAGE FROM LSA: LIST OF CFR SECTIONS AFFECTED PAMPHLET

104   **LSA—LIST OF CFR SECTIONS AFFECTED**

CHANGES OCTOBER 1, 1996 THROUGH SEPTEMBER 30, 1997

TITLE 42 Chapter IV—Con.

415.174 (a)(4)(iii) amended **59554**	447.31 (a) amended **63749**
417.479 (b), (f) introductory text, (5), (g)(1)(iv), (2)(ii), (h)(1)(iv), (v) and (2) revised; (g)(2)(iii) removed **69049**	473.38 Heading and (b) amended **25855**
	(a) and (b) corrected **49938**
417.600 (b)(3)(ii) revised **23374**	473.46 (a) revised **25855**
417.604 (b)(4) revised **23374**	473.48 (a)(1), (2) and (b) amended
417.606 (a)(4) added **23374**	....**25855**
417.608 (a), (b)(2) and (c) revised **23375**	485 Technical correction **49049**
	485.601—485.645 (Subpart F) Heading revised **46035**
417.609 Added **23375**	485.601 (a) and (b) amended **46037**
417.612 (a) amended **25855**	485.602 Amended **46037**
417.614 Revised **23375**	485.603 (a)(1) and (2) revised; (c) added **46035**
417.616 (a)(4) added **23375**	485.604 Introductory text amended..**46037**
417.617 Added **23375**	
417.618 Revised **23375**	485.606 Revised **46036**
417.620 (c), (d) and (e) revised **23376**	485.608 Introductory text, (a), (c) and (d) amended **46037**
417.626 Amended **25855**	
417.632 (b) amended **25855**	485.610 Revised **46036**
417.634 Revised **25855**	485.612 Revised **46036**
➡ 418.306 (c) revised..........................**42882**	485.614 Removed **46036**
424 Technical correction **49049**	485.616 Revised **46036**
424.1 (a)(1) amended **46035**	485.618 Introductory text, (b) introductory text and (e) amended **46037**
424.15 Heading and (a) revised........**46035**	
(a) and (b) amended **46037**	
424.20 Introductory text amended..**46037**	485.620 Revised **46036**
	485.623 (d)(1) and (2) amended **46036**
431.108 Added **43935**	(a), (b) introductory text, (c) introductory text, (4) and **46037**
431.151 (a)(3) added **43935**	
431.153 (b)(5) added **43935**	

Step 5a

Note that a subsection of 418.306 has been revised. This addition was first printed at page 42882 of the 1997 *Federal Register*. This should be read for the text of the addition.

440 Technical correction **49049**	(4), (b)(1), (2) introductory text, (3), (4), (c)(1) introductory text, (iii), (iv), (2), (3), (4) introductory text, (i), (ii), (d)(1) and (2) amended **46037**
440.40 Heading revised; (c) added **59188**	
440.70 (a)(2), (b)(3), (c) and (d) revised; eff. 11–10–97 ....**47902**	
Regulation at 62 FR 47902 eff. date corrected to 11–10–97 ....**49726**	485.638 (a)(1), (4), (b)(1) and (2) amended **46037**
440.167 Added; eff. 11–10–97 ....**47902**	485.639 Introductory text, (a) introductory text, (b) and (c) introductory text amended **46037**
Regulation at 62 FR 47902 eff. date corrected to 11–10–97 ....**49726**	
440.170 (g) heading, (1) and (2) amended **46037**	485.641 (a)(1) introductory text, (i), (iii), (b) introductory text, (3), (4), (5)(i), (ii) and (iii) amended **46037**
(f) removed; eff. 11–10–97 ....**47902**	
Regulation at 62 FR 47902 eff. date corrected to 11–10–97 ....**49726**	485.645 Heading, introductory text and (a) revised; (b) introductory text amended **46036**
442 Heading revised **43936**	
442.13 Revised **43936**	

NOTE: **Boldface page numbers indicate 1996 changes.**

[Illustration 13–9]

PAGE FROM LSA: LIST OF CFR SECTIONS AFFECTED PAMPHLET

SEPTEMBER 1997   **105**

CHANGES OCTOBER 1, 1996 THROUGH SEPTEMBER 30, 1997

(c) introductory text amended
....46037
488 Technical correction 49049
488.1 Amended 46037
488.6 (a) amended 46037
488.10 (d) amended 46037
488.11 Revised 43936
488.18 (d) amended 46037
488.24 (b) amended 46037
488.53 (a)(10) and (b) introductory
    text amended..............................46037
488.436 (a) amended.........................44221
489 Technical correction..................**66919**
    Technical correction 49049
489.1 (d) added...............................43936
489.2 (b)(7) amended 46037
489.11 (c)(1) and (2) amended 43937
489.13 Revised 43936
489.20 (d) and (e) amended.............46037
489.27 Regulation at 61 FR 46225
    eff. 10–1–96.................................51217
    Amended 46037
489.53 (b) heading, (c)(1) and (2)
    revised......................................43937
    (a)(14) removed..........................46037
489.102 (a) amended........................46037
493 Authori...
493.1202 Hea...
493.1203 Hea...
493.1443   (b...
    text an...
493.1834 (i)(1)(11) amended.............**63749**
498 Technical correction 49049
498.2 Amended 46037
498.3 (a) and (d) introductory
    text revised; (b)(14), (d)(14)
    and (15) added...........................43937

Chapter V—Office of Inspector General—Health Care, Department of Health and Human Services (Parts 1000—1999)

1003.103 (c) revised............................**52301**
1004.20 Revised...............................23143
1004.80 (b)(8), (c)(4) and (5) re-
    vised; (c)(6) removed.................23143
1004.100 (b), (d)(6) and (7) revised;
    (d)(8) removed...........................23143
1004.110 (d)(1)(i) and (2) revised
....23143
1008 Added; interim.........................7357

⟶ *Proposed Rules:*

68a..5953
121..**58158**

400—499 (Ch. IV)...............................**68697**
....3563, 49649
400 ....33158, 43962
405 ....33158, 43962
410.......................32715, 33158, 43962
412...**29902**
413...............................14851, 22995, 29902
414 ....33158, 43962
416 ....**46998**
424 32715
484 ....11004, 11005, 11035, 11953
489..**29902**
1000 47182
1001 ....**69060**
...........................28410, 39798, 47182, 47195
1002 47182
1005 47182

TITLE 43—PUBLIC LANDS: INTERIOR

Subtitle A—Office of the Secretary of the Interior (Parts 1—199)

10.1 (b)(3) amended........................41293

Step 5b
    This *LSA* should also be consulted to ascertain if proposed rules may be pertinent.

10.5 (e)(9) revised; (f) amended.......41293
10.6 (a) introductory text, (2)(i),
    (iii) introductory text and
    (A) amended 41293
10.8 (d)(1)(A), (B) and (C) redesig-
    nated as (d)(1)(i), (ii) and
    (iii);   (d)(3)   amended;
    (d)(4)(iii) revised.......................41293
10.9 (b)(4)(iii) and (e)(1) amended
....41293
10.10 (a)(1)(i), (3) and (b)(1)(i) re-
    vised..41294
10.12 Added; interim......................1821
10.15   Heading,   (a)(1)   and   (2)
    amended 41294
12 Authority citation revised.........**68667**
    Authority citation revised..........45944
12.2 (a) and (b) revised 45944
12.11—12.31 (Subpart B) Removed
....45945
12.66 (a), (b) introductory text
    and (1) revised...............45939, 45945
12.700 Revised **68667**
12.705 Amended **68668**
12.710 (a), (b) and (c) revised **68668**

NOTE: **Boldface page numbers indicate 1996 changes.**

[Illustration 13–10]

PAGE FROM LSA'S TABLE OF FEDERAL REGISTER ISSUE PAGES AND DATES

TABLE OF FEDERAL REGISTER ISSUE PAGES AND DATES		201	
12915–13288	19	32021–32194	12
13289–13529	20	32195–32469	13
13531–13799	21	32471–32682	16
13801–13981	24	32683–32988	17
13983–14282	25	32989–33337	18
14283–14631	26	33339–33536	19
14633–14771	27	33537–33732	20
14773–15082	28	33733–33969	23
15083–15353	31	33971–34155	24
15355–15598	Apr. 1	34157–34383	25
15599–15808	2	34385–34610	26
15809–16051	3	34611–35063	27
16053–16464	4	35065–35335	30
16465–16657	7	35337–35657	July 1
16659–17039	8	35659–35945	2
17041–17529	9	35947–36197	3
17531–17682	10	36199–36446	7
17683–18014	11	36447–36643	8
18017–18			9
18261–18			10
18505–18			11
18705–19			14
19023–19			15
19219–19			16
19473–19			17
19667–19896	23	38421–38896	18
19897–20088	24	38897–39100	21
20089–22872	25	39101–39414	22
22873–23123	28	39415–39745	23
23125–23334	29	39747–39916	24
23335–23611	30	39917–40251	25
23613–23937	May 1	40253–40425	28
23939–24323	2	40427–40726	29
24325–24558	5	40727–40910	30
24559–24795	6	40911–41247	31
24797–25105	7	41249–41803	Aug. 1
25107–25419	8	41805–42036	4
25421–25797	9	42037–42208	5
25799–26203	12	42209–42383	6
26205–26380	13	42385–42645	7
26381–26734	14	42647–42895	8
26735–26914	15	42897–43065	11
26915–27166	16	43067–43267	12
27167–27491	19	43269–43452	13
27493–27685	20	43453–43628	14
27687–27925	21	43629–43916	15
27927–28304	22	43917–44065	18
28305–28605	23	44067–44198	19
28607–28794	27	44199–44390	20
28795–28974	28	44391–44533	21
28975–29284	29	44535–44879	22
29285–29645	30	44881–45139	25
29649–30228	June 2	45141–45292	26
30229–30425	3	45293–45521	27
30427–30738	4	45523–45708	28
30739–30978	5	45709–46173	29
30979–31313	6	46175–46430	Sept. 2
31315–31506	9	46341–46663	3
31507–31700	10	46665–46865	4
31701–32019	11	46867–47136	5

Step 6
   This Table lists pages of the *Federal Register* and shows the date of the *Federal Register* in which the pages are located.
   Page 42882 is found in the August 8, 1997 *Federal Register*.

[Illustration 13–11]

PAGE FROM VOLUME 62, FEDERAL REGISTER

42882   Federal Register / Vol. 62, No. 153 / Friday, August 8, 1997 / Rules and Regulations

TABLE C.—IMPACT OF HOSPICE WAGE INDEX CHANGE—Continued

	Number of hospices (1)	Number of routine home care days in thousands (2)	Payments using old wage index in thousands (3)	Payments using new wage index first transition year blend in thousands (4)	Percent change in hospice payments (5)
Urban Hospices	1,200	14,811	1,685,552	1,686,214	0.0
Rural Hospices	634	2,368	218,497	217,835	−0.3
Region (Urban):					
New England	91	545	64,625	67,473	4.4
Middle Atlantic	157	1,687	200,376	202,123	0.9
South Atlantic	160	3,335	384,600	385,506	0.2
East North Cent	202	2,631	297,586	295,001	−0.9
East South Cent	77	639	72,432	71,261	−1.6
West North Cent	85	989	102,553	102,139	−0.4
West South Cent	158	1,883	195,386	192,709	−1.4
Mountain	73	816	101,912	100,685	−1.2
Pacific	168	2,126	253,035	257,225	1.7
Puerto Rico	29	159	13,049	12,091	−7.3
Region (Rural):					
New England	18	54	5,231	5,316	1.6
Middle Atlantic	'4	157	15,981	15,826	−1.0
South Atlantic	103	511	46,636	46,436	−0.4
East North Cent	111	455	42,290	42,203	−0.2
East South Cent	67	322	28,309	28,202	−0.4
West North Cent	131	339	31,020	30,896	−0.4
West South Cent	67	227	19,860	19,783	−0.4
Mountain	58	141	13,251	13,163	−0.7
Pacific	42	149	14,769	14,960	1.3
Puerto Rico					−8.9
Size (Routine Home Care D...					
0 - 1,551 Days					−0.2
1,551 - 4,385 Days					−0.2
4,385 -10,110 Days					0.2
10,110 + Days					0.0
Type of Ownership:					
Voluntary	1,272	12,517	1,370,153	1,372,430	0.2
Proprietary	388	4,152	482,816	480,497	−0.5
Government	151	450	45,046	45,044	0.0
Other	23	60	6,035	6,078	0.7
Hospice Base:					
Freestanding	674	9,375	1,046,456	1,042,436	−0.4
Home Health Agency	679	4,633	507,575	510,966	0.7
Hospital	464	3,058	334,128	334,891	0.2
Skilled Nurs. Fac	17	112	15,891	15,756	−0.9

> These are the pages from the *Federal Register* on which the revision to 418.306 is published.

We have concluded that this final regulation will have an impact on small hospices. However, the provisions of this regulation were determined by consensus through a negotiated rulemaking committee. Based on all of the options considered, the committee determined that the provisions in this regulation were favorable for the hospice community as a whole, as well as for the beneficiaries that they serve.

We have also determined, and certify, that this final rule will not result in a significant economic impact on a substantial number of small entities and will not have a significant impact on the operations of a substantial number of small rural hospitals. For these reasons, we are not preparing analyses for the RFA or section 1102(b) of the Act.

In accordance with the provisions of Executive Order 12866, this regulation was reviewed by the Office of Management and Budget.

VI. Collection of Information Requirements

This document does not impose information collection and recordkeeping requirements. Consequently, it need not be reviewed by the Office of Management and Budget under the authority of the Paperwork Reduction Act of 1995 (44 U.S.C. 3501 *et seq.*).

Lists of Subjects for 42 CFR Part 418

Health facilities, Hospice care, Medicare, Reporting and recordkeeping requirements.

42 CFR part 418 is amended as set forth below:

PART 418—HOSPICE CARE

1. The authority citation for part 418 continues to read as follows:

Authority: Secs. 1102 and 1871 of the Social Security Act (42 U.S.C. 1302 and 1395hh).

2. In § 418.306, paragraph (c) is revised to read as follows:;

§ 418.306 Determination of payment amounts.

*   *   *   *   *

(c) *Adjustment for wage differences.* HCFA will issue annually, in the Federal Register, a hospice wage index based on the most current available HCFA hospital wage data, including any

[Illustration 13–12]

PAGE FROM VOLUME 62, FEDERAL REGISTER

Federal Register / Vol. 62, No. 153 / Friday, August 8, 1997 / Rules and Regulations   42883

changes to the definitions of Metropolitan Statistical Areas. The payment rates established by HCFA are adjusted by the intermediary to reflect local differences in wages according to the revised wage index.

* * * * *

(Catalog of Federal Domestic Assistance Program No. 93.773, Medicare—Hospital Insurance; and Program No. 93.774, Medicare—Supplementary Medical Insurance Program)

Dated: April 16, 1997.

Bruce C. Vladeck,

Administrator, Health Care Financing Administration.

Appendix: Note This Appendix Will Not Appear in the Code of Federal Regulations

United States Department of Health and Human Services Negotiating Committee on the Medicare Hospice Wage Index

Committee Statement

April 13, 1995.

The Negotiating ~~Hospice Wage Ind~~ following recomm whole, concerning adjust Medicare p services to reflect wages:

A. Data to be Used

The wage index for hospices will be based on the wage index used by the Health Care Financing Administration (HCFA) for hospitals under the Medicare Prospective Payment System, prior to reclassification. This means that the hospital wage index will not be adjusted to take into account the geographic reclassification of hospitals in accordance with sections 1886(d)(8)(B) and 1886(d)(10) of the Social Security Act.

The hospital wage index prior to reclassification will be referred to in this statement as the Raw Index and will be adjusted as provided below to calculate what will be referred to as the Revised Wage Index.

Special provisions governing a transition period are described in paragraph D below.

B. Budget Neutrality

HCFA will determine a Budget Neutrality Factor that will be applied to achieve budget neutrality during and after the transition period. Budget neutrality means that, in a given year, estimated aggregate payments for Medicare hospice services using the Revised Wage Index will equal estimated payments that would have been made for the same services if the wage index adopted for hospices in 1983 (1983 Index) had remained in effect. HCFA will estimate aggregate payments for Medicare hospice services using the best available utilization data.

C. Adjustments

Each Raw Index value will be adjusted in one of two ways to determine the Revised Wage Index value applicable to each area.

(1) If the Raw Index value for any area is 0.8 or greater, the Revised Wage Index will be calculated by multiplying the Raw Index value for that area by the Budget Neutrality Factor.

(2) If the Raw Index value for any area is less than 0.8, the Revised Wage Index will be the greater of either:

(a) The Raw Index value for that area multiplied by the Budget Neutrality Factor; or

(b) The Raw Index value for that area multiplied by 1.15 (in effect, a 15-percent increase), but subject to a maximum index value of 0.8.

D. Transition Period

The Revised Wage Index will be implemented over a 3-year transition period beginning on or about October 1, 1996. For the first year of the transition period, a blended index will be calculated by adding two-thirds of each 1993 Index value for an ~~...~~ ~~...~~ ~~...~~ Throughout the transition period, new hospices will be treated the same as existing hospices based in the same county.

E. Annual Updates

The Revised Wage Index will be updated annually, so that it is based on the most current available data used by HCFA to construct the hospital wage index, as well as on changes by the Office of Management and Budget to Metropolitan Statistical Areas as adopted by HCFA in calculating the hospital wage index.

HCFA will use the most current hospital cost report data available that allows HCFA to publish a proposed rule containing wage index values at least 4 months in advance of the effective date of each annual update to the Revised Wage Index.

F. Effective Date

The effective date of a final rule revising the wage index as stated above should be October 1, 1997.

G. Statement to Accompany Proposed and Final Hospice Wage Index Notice

The proposed rule is based upon a Committee Statement developed by a Negotiating Committee on the Medicare hospice wage index which was convened under the Negotiated Rulemaking Act. A new hospice wage index is needed because the existing hospice wage index is based on a 1983 wage index using 1981 Bureau of Labor Statistics (BLS) data which is inaccurate and outdated.

The Committee reached consensus; however, this means only that all Committee members could "live with" the agreement, considered as a whole, even if elements of that agreement were not the preferred choice of individual Committee members. The Committee Statement reflects those issues upon which the Committee ultimately concurred, but does not address many issues that were considered by the Committee.

The Committee considered the appropriate data to be used to construct a wage index, the appropriateness of retaining a 0.8 floor, budget neutrality, and how to structure a transition to timely update the index yet ensure access to hospice care. In particular, the Committee considered the problems faced by hospices that would receive significant decreases under the new wage indices, rural hospices, hospices with low ~~wage indices, and hospices that~~ may have ~~...~~ ge costs. ~~...~~ sive ppeared the hospice nput. While ~~...~~ i, the ~~...~~ ospice data collection is maturing and encourages its continued development. In addition, while other issues were identified, the scope of the Committee's negotiations was limited by the notice of intent to negotiate.

Given these constraints, and taking into account the differing and conflicting interests that would be significantly affected, the Committee sought to develop a wage index that would be as accurate, reliable, and equitable as possible, but would not threaten access to hospice care.

The Committee recognizes that hospice care is still not universally available. The Committee further recognizes that there may be geographic or other circumstances that inhibit the provision of hospice care. The Committee strongly requests that HCFA consider options to address these access problems.

Reaching consensus was a long and deliberative process. The Committee concurred that the wage index it recommends will be better both for the hospice community, as a whole, and for the Medicare beneficiaries it serves, than a wage index developed by the traditional rulemaking process.

[FR Doc. 97–20775 Filed 8–1–97: 4:55 pm]

BILLING CODE 4120–01–P

These are the pages from the *Federal Register* on which the revision to 418.306 is published.

[Illustration 13–13]

PAGE FROM VOLUME 62, FEDERAL REGISTER—
LISTING OF CFR PARTS AFFECTED

i

Reader Aids

Federal Register

Vol. 62, No. 191

Thursday, October 2, 1997

CUSTOMER SERVICE AND INFORMATION

Federal Register/Code of Federal Regulations
General Information, indexes and other finding 202–523–5227
aids
E-mail   info@fedreg.nara.gov

Laws
For additional information   523–5227

Presidential Documents
Executive orders and proclamations   523–5227
The United States Government Manual   523–5227

Other Services
Electronic and on-line services (voice)   523–4534
Privacy Act Compilation   523–3187
TDD for the hearing impaired   523–5229

ELECTRONIC
Free Electronic
Federal Registe
inspection.

PUBLIC LAWS
Free electronic
now available.
with the messa

FAX-ON-DEMA
You may acces
There is no cha
telephone char
public inspecti
contents are available. The document numbers are 7050-Public
Inspection list and 7051-Table of Contents list. The public
inspection list is updated immediately for documents filed on an
emergency basis.

NOTE: YOU WILL ONLY GET A LISTING OF DOCUMENTS ON
FILE. Documents on public inspection may be viewed and copied
in our office located at 800 North Capitol Street, NW., Suite 700.
The Fax-On-Demand telephone number is: 301–713–6905

FEDERAL REGISTER PAGES AND DATES, OCTOBER

51367–51592 1
51593–51758 2

CFR PARTS AFFECTED DURING OCTOBER

At the end of each month, the Office of the Federal Register
publishes separately a List of CFR Sections Affected (LSA), which
lists parts and sections affected by documents published since
the revision date of each title.

3 CFR
Administrative Orders:
Memorandums:
August 5, 1997 51367
Notices:
September 30, 1997........51591
Executive Orders:
11145 (Continued by
   EO 13062)...................51755
11183 (Continued by
   EO 13062)...................51755
11287 (Continued by
   EO 13062)...................51755
12876 (Continued by
   EO 13062).................51755
12882 (Continued by
   EO 13062).................51755
12891 (Revoked by
   EO 13062).................51755
12900 (Continued by
   EO 13062).................51755
12905 ((Continued by
   EO 13062).................51755
12946 (Revoked by
   EO 13062).................51755
12964 (Revoked by
   EO 13062).................51755
12974 (Superseded by
   EO 13062).................51755
12994 (Continued by
   EO 13062).................51755
13015 (Revoked by
   EO 13062).................51755
13038 (Amended in
   part by EO
   13062) 51755
13054 (Amended in
   part by EO
   13062) 51755
13062..............................51755
13063..............................51755

12 CFR
602..............................51593
650..............................51369

14 CFR
39.........................51593, 51594
97 ....51597, 51598, 51600
187.................................51736
Proposed Rules:
39 ....51383, 51385, 51386,
                                51388
93 51564

15 CFR
744...............................51369
Proposed Rules:
700...............................51389

31 CFR
Proposed Rules:
208...............................51618

33 CFR
Proposed Rules:
334...............................51618

37 CFR
202...............................51603
Proposed Rules:
253...............................51618

38 CFR
111...............................51372

40 CFR
52................................51603
81................................51604
258...............................51606
721...............................51606
Proposed Rules:
136...............................51621
180...............................51397
745...............................51622

42 CFR
57................................51373

43 CFR
2090..............................51375

Step 7

The *LSA: List of CFR Sections Affected* as shown in Illustrations 13–8 and 13–9 indicates changes made during the year to the *CFR*. To ascertain further changes, one should check the *CFR Parts Affected* table in the last issue of the *Federal Register* for months subsequent to the most recent *LSA*. Note the table of *Federal Register* pages and dates.

........51610

........51512
........51370

........51601
........51740

........51614

[Illustration 13–14]

CONTENTS PAGES TO GPO ACCESS

U.S. Government Printing Office   http://www.access.gpo.gov/#infc

Keeping America Informed
UNITED STATES GOVERNMENT PRINTING OFFICE

About the Government Printing Office

What's New Page

Access to Government Information Products

Services Available to Federal Agencies

Business and Contracting Opportunities

Employment Opportunities

Establishing Links to Documents in GPO WAIS Databases

Navigation Aids and FAQ's

Access to Government Information Products
    Superintendent of Documents
        What Is GPO Access?
        Search Databases
        New/Noteworthy Products from GPO
        Find Government Information
        Browse Federal Bulletin Board Files
        Find Products for Sale by GPO
        Government Information at a Library Near You
    Agency for Health Care Policy and Research
    Commission on the Roles and Capabilities of the United States
    Intelligence Community
    Bureau of Land Management (Colorado Office)
    Congress of the United States
    Department of Interior Office of Inspector General
    Executive Office of the President
        Council of Economic Advisers
        Office of Management and Budget
    Federal Labor Relations Authority
    Food and Drug Administration
    General Accounting Office
    Merit Systems Protection Board
    National Archives and Records Administration's Office of the
    Federal Register
    National Bankruptcy Review Commission
    National Gambling Impact Study Commission

[Illustration 13–14 Cont.]

CONTENTS PAGES TO GPO ACCESS

U.S. Government Printing Office   http://www.access.gpo.gov/#info

       National Labor Relations Board
       Occupational Safety and Health Review Commission◄■■◄
       Office of Compliance
       Office of Government Ethics
       Office of Special Counsel
       Office of Technology Assessment
       United States Commission on Civil Rights
       United States Trade Representative
       U.S. Equal Employment Opportunity Commission
       U.S. Nuclear Waste Technical Review Board

Services Available to Federal Agencies
       Customer Service
       Electronic Prepress and Document Creation
       Training Opportunities - Institute for Federal Printing and
       Electronic Publishing
       Office of Congressional, Legislative, and Public Affairs

Business and Contracting Opportunities
       Printing Procurement
       Materials Management Service

Employment Opportunities
       Office of Personnel◄■■◄

Questions or comments regarding this service? Contact
wwwadmin@www.access.gpo.gov.

Page #INDEX March 12, 1998

2 of 2   3/23/98 1:54 PM

[Illustration 13–15]

PAGES FROM THE NATIONAL ARCHIVES AND RECORDS ADMINISTRATION ON GPO ACCESS

National Archives and Records Administration   http://www.access.gpo.gov/nara/index.html

National Archives and Records Administration

Office of the Federal Register

Code of Federal Regulations	Federal Register	Privacy Act Issuances	Public Laws	United States Government Manual	Weekly Compilation of Presidential Documents	U.S. Congress Information	GPO Access Search Page

▶ *Code of Federal Regulations* Online via *GPO Access* ◀█

   About the CFR online
   Establishing HTML links to GPO's CFR WAIS databases
   Search the entire set of CFR databases by keyword (current data)
   Retrieve CFR sections by citation (current and/or historical data)
   Search your choice of CFR titles and/or volumes (current and/or historical data)
   Search the Federal Register for related documents (current and/or historical data)

▶ *Federal Register* Online via *GPO Access* (1994 - Forward)

   The *Federal Register* is published Monday through Friday, except Federal holidays. The
   Table of Contents from the current issue is available here on the day of publication. The issue
   date is always the same as the day of publication. Table of Contents of the *Federal Register*
   also available as ASCII text

   To search the Unified Agenda, return to the list of databases for simple searches on the GPO
   Access Search Page.

   Cancellation of Legislative Items Pursuant to Line Item Veto Act (P.L. 104-130) ◀█

   Federal Register Document Drafting Handbook--April 1997 Revision (located on National
   Archives and Records Administration's website) ◀█

[Illustration 13–15 Cont.]

PAGES FROM THE NATIONAL ARCHIVES AND RECORDS ADMINISTRATION ON GPO ACCESS

National Archives and Records Administration   http://www.access.gpo.gov/nara/index.html

Federal Register documents in the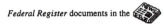

- Medicare and Medicaid Programs: Physicians' Referrals to Health Care Entities With Which They Have Financial Relationships ◀▬▬
- Medicare Program: Revisions to Payment Policies and Adjustments to the Relative Value Units Under the Physician Fee Schedule, Other Part B Payment Policies, and Establishment of the Clinical Psychologist Fee Schedule for Calendar Year 1998
- Food and Drug Administration final rule on Quality Mammography Standards, including Correction Document.
- Previous listings

▶ Privacy Act Issuances Online via *GPO Access* (1995 Compilation)

The Privacy Act Issuances, 1995 Compilation Online Database contains descriptions of Federal agency systems of records maintained on individuals and rules agencies follow to assist individuals who request information about their records.

The two sources of Privacy Act Notices are: the Privacy Act Issuances, 1995 Compilation and the Federal Register which has updates to the 1995 Compilation.

▶ *Public Laws* Online via *GPO Access* (1994 - Forward)

The *Public Laws* of the 104th Congress and the 105th Congress are prepared and published by the Office of the Federal Register (OFR), National Archives and Records Administration (NARA). Each law is first published as a slip law and then later compiled into a volume of the *Statutes-at-Large*.

▶ *United States Government Manual* Online via *GPO Access* (1995 - Forward)

As the official handbook of the Federal Government, *The United States Government Manual* provides comprehensive information on the agencies of the legislative, judicial, and executive branches. The *Manual* also includes information on quasi-official agencies; international organizations in which the United States participates; and boards, commissions, and committees.

A typical agency description includes a list of principal officials, a summary statement of the agency's purpose and role in the Federal Government, a brief history of the agency, including its legislative or executive authority, a description of its programs and activities, and a "Sources of Information" section. This last section provides information on consumer activities, contracts and grants, employment, publications, and many other areas of public interest.

[Illustration 13–15 Cont.]

PAGES FROM THE NATIONAL ARCHIVES AND RECORDS ADMINISTRATION ON GPO ACCESS

National Archives and Records Administration http://www.access.gpo.gov/nara/index.html

▶ *Weekly Compilation of Presidential Documents* Online via *GPO Access* (1995-Forward) ◀

The online edition of the *Weekly Compilation of Presidential Documents* is currently under development as a pilot project jointly authorized by the publisher, the National Archives and Records Administration's Office of the Federal Register (OFR) and the Government Printing Office (GPO). Its purpose is to provide the public with enhanced access to Presidential documents. Work is underway to create fields within the database to permit date-range searches and fielded subject categories to enable users to fine-tune their searches. We are also evaluating the possibility of creating links to related information not contained in the *Weekly Compilation of Presidential Documents*. Your suggestions for improvements to the search/navigation capabilities and the visual presentations are welcome.

The OFR publishes the *Weekly Compilation of Presidential Documents* every Monday. The publication contains statements, messages, and other Presidential materials released by the White House during the preceding week. The online edition accessible through *GPO Access* contains data from the January 9, 1995 issue to the present.

This document is sponsored by the Office of the Federal Register, National Archives and Records Administration on the United States Government Printing Office web site.

Questions or comments regarding this service? Contact the GPO Access User Support Team by Internet e-mail at gpoaccess@gpo.gov; by telephone at (202) 512-1530 or toll free at (888) 293-6498; by fax at (202) 512-1262.

GPO Home GPO INETservices

Page #NARA-INDEX March 23, 1998

3 of 3

3/23/98 1:54 PM

SECTION G. SOURCES OF ADDITIONAL INFORMATION ON ADMINISTRATIVE AGENCIES

1. The United States Government Manual

This handbook, published by the Office of the Federal Register, is revised annually and contains general information about Congress and the federal judiciary. *GPO Access*, the Government Printing Office's home page, contains editions of the *United States Government Manual*. [See Illustration 13–15.] However, the major emphasis of this publication is on the executive branch and regulatory agencies. Each department and agency is described in concise form with citations to the statutes creating the department or agency. A description of functions and authority, names and functions of officials, and listings of major publications are provided.

The *Manual* includes several appendices. One appendix lists all abolished and transferred agencies with an indication of what has happened to the functions for which they had responsibility. For example, under *Civil Service Commission, U.S.* it is noted that the agency has been redesignated as the *Merit Systems Protection Board* and its functions transferred to the *Board* and to the *Office of Personnel Management* by the Reorganization Plan No. 2 of 1978.

Other appendices list: commonly used abbreviations and acronyms; *Standard Federal Regions* and *Federal Executive Boards;* and all agencies, in alphabetical order, that appear in the *CFR.* Separate indexes for name and agency/subject also are available.

It is frequently useful to consult *The United States Government Manual* before starting research on an administrative law problem.

2. Federal Regulatory Directory[21]

The *Directory* can be used to augment the information in *The United States Government Manual.* Discussion of the topic of regulation and of the current issues involving federal administrative agencies and extensive profiles of the largest and most important agencies are included. Summary information on most of the other federal agencies is provided. The 8th edition, published in 1997, is the most recent.

SECTION H.   PRESIDENTIAL DOCUMENTS

Most rules or regulations are the result of the activities of federal agencies operating under powers delegated by Congress. The President also has the authority to issue documents that have legal effect. This authority is either constitutional, statutory, or both. This section describes the types of Presidential documents and sources in which documentation of Presidential activities may be located.

1. Proclamations and Executive Orders[22]

Proclamations and executive orders have been widely used by presidents to exercise their authority. Proclamations are generally addressed to the entire nation and their content frequently relates to ceremonial or celebratory occasions. [See Illustration 13–16.] Executive orders general-

---

[21] Published by Congressional Quarterly, Inc.

[22] For a detailed study, see HOUSE COMM. ON GOVERNMENT OPERATIONS, 85TH CONG., 1ST SESS., EXECUTIVE ORDERS AND PROCLAMATIONS: STUDY OF A USE OF PRESIDENTIAL POWERS (Comm. Print 1957). *See also* Donna Bennett & Philip Yannarella, *Locating Presidential Proclamations and Executive Orders—A Guide to Sources,* LEGAL REFERENCE SERVICES Q., Sum./Fall 1985, at 177; Mary Woodward, *Executive Orders: A Journey,* LEGAL REFERENCE SERVICES Q., No. 3, 1990, at 125. To locate Executive Orders issued prior to the publication of the *Federal Register,* see NEW YORK CITY HISTORICAL RECORDS SURVEY, PRESIDENTIAL EXECUTIVE ORDERS, NUMBERED 1–8030, 1862–1938 (1944); NEW JERSEY HISTORICAL RECORDS SURVEY, LIST AND INDEX OF PRESIDENTIAL EXECUTIVE ORDERS: UNNUMBERED SERIES (1789–1941) (1944).

ly are used by the President to direct and govern the activities of government officials and agencies. [See Illustration 13–17.]

Proclamations and Executive Orders appear in:

a. *Federal Register*

b. *Weekly Compilation of Presidential Documents*

c. Title 3 of *CFR* and compilation volumes of Title 3

d. *Public Papers of the Presidents* to January 1989

e. *United States Code Congressional and Administrative News* Advance Pamphlets

f. *United States Code Service,* Advance Service pamphlets

g. *CIS Presidential Executive Orders & Proclamations on Microfiche*

h. LEXIS–NEXIS and WESTLAW as described in Section C–4 *supra.* WESTLAW contains Executive Orders since 1936 and Proclamations, Administrative Orders, Trade Agreements, and Reorganization Plans or Designations from the *Federal Register* since 1984.

LEXIS–NEXIS has the full text of the *Weekly Compilation of Presidential Documents* and the *Public Papers of the Presidents* from January 20, 1981.

In addition, the other electronic research sources described in Section C–4 contain the Presidential documents that are in the *Federal Register* and the *CFR.*

i. Proclamations also may be found in the *United States Statutes at Large.*

j. The White House Internet site contains all White House documents released during the Clinton administration, including executive orders and proclamations in the White House Virtual Library. [See Illustrations 13–18 and 13–19.]

2. Codification of Presidential Proclamations and Executive Orders

This publication was started in 1979 by the Office of the Federal Register. Its purpose is to provide in one source Proclamations and Executive Orders that have general applicability and continuing effect. This codification takes all the previously-published Proclamations and Executive Orders still in force and arranges them by subject. Amendments to the original documents are incorporated in the text.

This codification is arranged in 50 titles corresponding to those of the *Code of Federal Regulations* and covers the period April 13, 1945—January 20, 1989. A "Disposition Table" at the back of the volume lists all Proclamations and Executive Orders issued during 1945–1989, with their amendments, and indication of their current status and chapter designations, where applicable.

3.   Reorganization Plans

By the provisions of 5 U.S.C. §§ 901–912 (1994), the President is authorized to examine the organization of all agencies and make changes that provide for the better management of the executive branch of the government. The President is authorized to submit proposed reorganization plans to both houses of Congress. Proposed reorganization plans are published in the *Congressional Record*. The reorganization plan becomes effective if the President accepts the joint resolution passed by the House and the Senate approving the plan submitted by the President.

Reorganization plans are published, as approved, in the *Federal Register*, Title 3 of the *CFR*, *United States Statutes at Large*, and in 5 *U.S.C.* Appendix. The *Congressional Record* is a source for plans not approved by Congress.

4.   Other Presidential Documents

In addition to the documents discussed *supra*, the President issues Administrative Orders, such as findings, determinations, and memoranda; Executive Agreements (discussed in Chapter 20); and messages to Congress and signing statements [see Chapter 10]. Administrative Orders are published in the *Federal Register* and in Title 3 of the *Code of Federal Regulations*.

5.   Presidential Nominations

At the end of each issue of the *Weekly Compilation of Presidential Documents* is a list of Presidential nominations submitted to the Senate. The *Congressional Record's Daily Digest* for the Senate contains in each issue the names of those nominated and of those confirmed by the Senate.

An up-to-date cumulative list of Executive branch (but not judicial) nominations is published in Volume 1 of the *CCH Congressional Index*.[23]

6.   Compilations of Presidential Documents

The following sources provide comprehensive collections of presidential documents:

a.   *Weekly Compilation of Presidential Documents.* This Office of the Federal Register publication is published every Monday and contains statements, messages, and other Presidential materials released by the White House during the preceding week. It includes an index of Contents at the beginning of each issue for documents in that issue. Each issue also contains a cumulative subject index and name index for the previous issues of the current quarter. An annual index, divided into names and subjects, is published. Commencing with Volume 31, Number 1, January 9, 1995, a cumulative index is no longer published in each issue. Rather, indexes are issued quarterly and distributed separately. Other finding

---

[23] For a directory of judicial nominations, see IRIS J. WILDMAN, FEDERAL JUDGES AND JUSTICES: A CURRENT LISTING OF NOMINATIONS, CONFIRMATIONS, ELEVATIONS, RETIREMENTS (1987, periodically supplemented).

aids are: lists of laws approved by the President; nominations submitted to the Senate; and a checklist of White House releases.

The National Archives and Records Administration site available in *GPO Access* contains the *Weekly Compilation of Presidential Documents.* [See Illustration 13–15.]

b. *Public Papers of the Presidents.* This series starts with the administration of President Hoover. It is published annually in one or more volumes and includes a compilation of the Presidents' messages to Congress, public speeches, news conferences, and public letters. The final volume for each year contains a cumulative index to the volumes published during the year. After all the volumes for an administration are published, a cumulative index for that President is published by a commercial publisher.[24] The papers of President Franklin Roosevelt and certain earlier Presidents have been published commercially.

Beginning with the 1977 volumes, which cover the first year of President Carter's administration and continuing through the volume for 1988–89, the last year of President Reagan's administration, the set includes all of the material printed in the *Weekly Compilation of Presidential Documents.* Beginning in 1989, the first year of the administration of President Bush, Proclamations and Executive Orders are not reproduced. Rather a table refers the user to the appropriate issues of the *Federal Register* in which the documents are published.

c. *Title 3 of the Code of Federal Regulations.* Presidential documents that were required to be published in the *Federal Register* are compiled in Title 3 of the *CFR.* Prior to 1976, compilation volumes of Title 3 were published covering various time periods. Since 1976, a compilation volume has been published annually. Unlike the other yearly codifications of agency regulations, each compilation of Title 3 is a unique source of Presidential documents and not an updated codification. Thus, each compilation of Title 3 is a permanent reference source. Since 1985, most yearly compilations of Title 3 have a white cover to distinguish them from other volumes of the *CFR* and to emphasize the permanent value of each edition.

d. *Inaugural Addresses of the Presidents of the United States from George Washington 1789 to George Bush 1989* [Bicentennial Edition], Washington, DC: Government Printing Office, 1989.

7. Updating Presidential Documents

The use of *Shepard's Code of Federal Regulations Citations,* described in Section E–1–d *supra,* also applies to Presidential Proclamations, Executive Orders, and Reorganization Plans. Presidential documents included in Title 3 can be updated using the *LSA.*

---

[24] THE CUMULATED INDEXES TO THE PUBLIC PAPERS OF THE PRESIDENTS OF THE UNITED STATES (KTO Press, 1977–79; Krauss International Publications, 1979).

SECTION I. ILLUSTRATIONS FOR PRESIDENTIAL DOCUMENTS

[Illustration 13–16]

EXAMPLE OF PRESIDENTIAL PROCLAMATION

Federal Register / Vol. 58, No. 197 / Thursday, October 14, 1993 / Presidential Documents   **53101**

Presidential Documents

Proclamation 6609 of October 8, 1993

National School Lunch Week, 1993

By the President of the United States of America

A Proclamation

Since 1946, the National School Lunch Program has demonstrated a partnership between Federal, State, and local officials in providing nutritious low-cost and free meals to America's schoolchildren. Our commitment to the National School Lunch Program reflects our recognition of the importance of nutrition to our children's health and to our Nation's future.

Currently, the National School Lunch Program operates in more than 90 percent of the Nation's public schools and serves about 25 million lunches a day. Many of our children receive their only nutritious meal of the day at sch[~~~~~~~~~~~~~~~~~~~~~~~~~~~~~~~~~~]ion span and l[Proclamation issued by the President   ]. School lunch[~~~~~~~~~~~~~~~~~~~~~~~~~~~~~~~~~~~~~~~]learning laboratories, putting into practice the classroom lessons learned by the students on the importance of nutrition to health and well-being.

There is no longer any question that diet is related to good health, and school meal programs should meet the Dietary Guidelines for Americans so that children get nutritious meals. Like preventive medicine, the value of school lunches will multiply and the benefits will last a lifetime. National School Lunch Week affords us the opportunity to take a fresh look at the National School Lunch Program to determine what changes are necessary in order to meet these dietary guidelines. We also can recognize health professionals, school food service personnel, teachers, principals, parents, community leaders, and others for their commitment to ensuring that the lunches served in their schools will provide the nutrition so important to young students.

In recognition of the contributions of the National School Lunch Program to the nutritional well-being of children, the Congress, by joint resolution of October 9, 1962 (Public Law No. 87–780), has designated the week beginning the second Sunday in October in each year as "National School Lunch Week" and has requested the President to issue a proclamation in observance of that week.

NOW, THEREFORE, I, WILLIAM J. CLINTON, President of the United States of America, do hereby proclaim the week beginning October 10, 1993, as National School Lunch Week. I call upon all Americans to recognize those individuals whose efforts contribute to the success of this valuable program.

IN WITNESS WHEREOF, I have hereunto set my hand this eighth day of October, in the year of our Lord nineteen hundred and ninety-three, and of the Independence of the United States of America the two hundred and eighteenth.

William J. Clinton

[FR Doc. 93–25411
Filed 10–13–93; 4:09 pm]
Billing code 3195–01–P

[Illustration 13–17]

EXAMPLE OF PRESIDENTIAL EXECUTIVE ORDER

Federal Register / Vol. 58, No. 96 / Thursday, May 20, 1993 / Presidential Documents   29517

Presidential Documents

Executive Order 12848 of May 19, 1993

Federal Plan To Break the Cycle of Homelessness

By the authority vested in me as President by the Constitution and the laws of the United States of America, including title II of the Stewart B. McKinney Homeless Assistance Act, as amended (42 U.S.C. 11311–11320), and section 301 of title 3, United States Code, and in order to provide for the streamlining and strengthening of the Nation's efforts to break the cycle of homelessness, it is hereby ordered as follows:

Section 1. Federal member agencies acting through the Interagency Council on the Homeless, established under title II of the Stewart B. McKinney Homeless Assistance Act, shall develop a single coordinated Federal plan for breaking the cycle of existing homelessness and for preventing future homelessness.

Sec. 2. The plan shall recommend Federal administrative and legislative in[...]oposed sc[...]ng any n[...]legisla- ti[...] appro- priate, existing programs designed to assist homeless individuals and families.

> **Executive Order issued by the President**

Sec. 3. The plan shall make recommendations on how current funding programs can be redirected, if necessary, to provide links between housing, support, and education services and to promote coordination and cooperation among grantees, local housing and support service providers, school districts, and advocates for homeless individuals and families. The plan shall also provide recommendations on ways to encourage and support creative approaches and cost-effective, local efforts to break the cycle of existing homelessness and prevent future homelessness, including tying current homeless assistance programs to permanent housing assistance, local housing affordability strategies, or employment opportunities.

Sec. 4. To the extent practicable, the Council shall consult with representatives of State and local governments (including education agencies), nonprofit providers of services and housing for homeless individuals and families, advocates for homeless individuals and families, currently and formerly homeless individuals and families, and other interested parties.

Sec. 5. The Council shall submit the plan to the President no later than 9 months after the date of this order.

William J. Clinton

THE WHITE HOUSE,
May 19, 1993.

[FR Doc. 93–12224
Filed 5–19–93; 12:22 pm]
Billing code 3195–01–P

[Illustration 13–18]

THE WHITE HOUSE WEB PAGE

Welcome To The White House   http://www.whitehouse.gov/WH/Welcome.htmi

[Text version]

Follow President Clinton's Historic Trip to Africa

1 of 2   03/24/98 11:29:00

[Illustration 13–18 Cont.]

THE WHITE HOUSE WEB PAGE

Welcome To The White House   http://www.whitehouse.gov/WH/Welcome.html

The President & Vice President:
Their accomplishments, their families, and how to send them electronic mail --

Interactive Citizens' Handbook: Your guide to information about the Federal government

White House History and Tours:
Past Presidents and First Families, Art in the President's House and Tours
-- Tour Information

The Virtual Library:
Search White House documents, listen to speeches, and view photos

White House Help Desk:
Frequently asked questions and answers about our service

Commonly Requested Federal Services:
Direct access to Federal Services

What's New:
What's happening at the White House -
President Clinton Participates in Social Security Discussion

Site News:
Recent additions to our site -
-President's Initiative on Race
-White House Millennium Council

The Briefing Room:
Today's releases, hot topics, and the latest Federal statistics

White House for Kids:
Helping young people become more active and informed citizens

To comment on this service, send feedback to the Web Development Team.

[Illustration 13–19]

PAGES FROM THE WHITE HOUSE VIRTUAL LIBRARY INTERNET SITE

The White House Library   http://www.whitehouse.gov/WH/html/library.html

[Text version]

You can search the White House web site for:

- All White House web features combined: Press releases, Radio Addresses, photographs and Web Pages.
  - o White House documents: Publicly-released documents since the start of the Clinton Administration.
  - o The contents of this web site: Just the pages of this service.
  - o Radio Addresses of the President: Search and listen to the President's Saturday Radio Addresses.
  - o Executive Orders: Official actions, procedural changes, and organizational changes.
  - o White House photographs: Search a public collection of photographs.

- You can also search the GovBot database all government sites

You can also browse some historic national documents:

- The Declaration of Independence
- The Constitution of the United States of America

If you wish to receive White House publications on a daily basis, you can subscribe to the publications mailing list

Presidential addresses and the White House press releases may be found in the Briefing Room.

To comment on this service,
send feedback to the Web Development Team.

[Illustration 13–19 Cont.]

PAGES FROM THE WHITE HOUSE VIRTUAL LIBRARY INTERNET SITE

Search White House Website   http://library.whitehouse.gov/cgi-bin/pr...ry_TITLE=&status=Submit+this+search+form

[Text version]

White House Virtual Library

Search White House Website

1. To search White House Website, enter a TERM or PHRASE in the box below which describes your topic of interest (for example, "social security benefits for retired people").

TERM/PHRASE

proclamation

2. In addition, you can search for keywords in the titles of the web pages.

TITLE

Reset this search form   Submit this search form

RESULTS

(1 - 10 of 77)

White House Website

Thanksgiving **Proclamation**
http://www.whitehouse.gov/WH/New/html/thanksgiving.html

What's New Archives -- November 1996
http://www.whitehouse.gov/WH/New/html/novnew96.html

What's New Archives -- November 1996

SECTION J.   FEDERAL ADMINISTRATIVE DECISIONS

1. Agency Decisions

Many federal administrative agencies also serve a quasi-judicial function and, in performing this function, issue decisions.[25] The Federal Communications Commission, for example, is authorized by statute to license radio and television stations. It also has the authority to enforce its regulations covering the operations of these stations. When stations

---

[25] Many of the mysteries about various administrative law courts are explained in Harold H. Bruff, *Specialized Courts in Administrative Law*, 43 ADMIN. L. REV. 329 (1991).

allegedly violate the terms of the statute or the regulations, the Federal Communications Commission can hear charges and issue decisions.

Decisions of administrative agencies are published, not in the *Federal Register,* but in separate sources.[26] They are often in two formats: (1) official publications of administrative agencies published by the U.S. Government Printing Office, and (2) unofficial publications of commercial publishers, including LEXIS–NEXIS and WESTLAW, CD–ROMS, and as internet documents.

a. *Official Publications of Decisions of Federal Administrative Agencies.* These are available in most law libraries and in public and university libraries that are official depositories of the U.S. Government Printing Office. Selected decisions of selected agencies also are available through the Internet. [See Illustration 13–14.] The format, frequency, and method of publication vary from agency to agency. Generally, they are issued on an infrequent schedule and are poorly indexed. Some sets have indexes and digests in the back of each volume. For other sets, separate indexes and digests are published. Some sets of federal administrative decisions have an advance sheet service.

b. *Unofficial Publications of Decisions of Federal Administrative Agencies.* Commercially published agency decisions are reproduced in looseleaf services, which often are accompanied by bound, sequentially numbered volumes. For example, Pike and Fischer's *Radio Regulations* contains decisions of the Federal Communications Commission. LEXIS–NEXIS and WESTLAW have topical databases that contain FCC decisions. CD–ROM products are being published covering the decisions. Looseleaf services are discussed in Chapter 14 and computer-assisted legal research is discussed in Chapter 21.

2. Judicial Review of Agency Decisions

After an agency has issued a decision, the decision may, in most instances, be appealed to the federal courts. The decisions resulting from these appeals may be found by consulting the following sources:

a. *West's Federal Practice Digest 4th* and its predecessor sets.

b. *United States Supreme Court Digest, Lawyers' Edition* or *U.S. Supreme Court Digest.*

c. *American Digest System* if the preceding digests are not available.

d. *Shepard's United States Administrative Citations* (discussed in Chapter 15).

e. *Treatises on administrative law* (discussed in Chapter 18).

f. *Looseleaf services* (Chapter 14 contains a general discussion).

g. *LEXIS–NEXIS and WESTLAW.*

[26] For a detailed discussion of sources (official, unofficial, and databases) to consult for decisions of 33 agencies, *see* Veronica Maclay, *Selected Sources of United States Agency Decisions,* 16 GOV'T PUBLICATIONS REV. 271 (1989).

3. Representative Examples of Currently Published Official Decisions of Federal Administrative Agencies

a. Federal Communications Commission. *Reports* [1st Series], vol. 1–45 (1934–1965); [2d Series], vol. 1–104 (1965–1986). Continued by: *FCC Record,* vol. 1 *et seq.* (1986 to date).

b. Federal Trade Commission. *Decisions,* vol. 1 *et seq.* (1915 to date).

c. Interstate Commerce Commission. *Reports* [1st Series], vol. 1–366 (1887–1983); [2d Series], vol. 1 *et seq.* (1984 to date).

d. National Labor Relations Board. *Decisions and Orders,* vol. 1 *et seq.* (1935 to date).

e. Occupational Safety and Health Review Commission. *Reports,* vol. 1 *et seq.* (1971 to date).

f. Securities and Exchange Commission. *Decisions and Reports,* vol. 1 *et seq.* (1934 to date).

As noted elsewhere in this chapter, internet sites of government agencies often contain decisions, rules and regulations and other documents pertinent to the agencies.

SECTION K.   STATE ADMINISTRATIVE REGULATIONS AND DECISIONS

1.   State Regulations

The regulations of state agencies are published in a variety of formats. In some states the administrative regulations are officially codified and published in sets similar to the *Code of Federal Regulations.*[27] These may be supplemented by a publication similar to the *Federal Register.* In other states, each agency issues its own regulations, and it is necessary that inquiries be directed to the pertinent agency. Increasingly, state regulations are being added to WESTLAW and LEXIS–NEXIS, are being produced as CD–ROM products, and are being made available through the World Wide Web.

2.   State Administrative Decisions

Many state agencies also publish their decisions. Most commonly, the decisions of unemployment compensation commissions, tax commissions, and public utility commissions are published. Increasingly, state agency decisions are being added to WESTLAW and LEXIS–NEXIS, are being produced as CD–ROM products, and are being made available through the World Wide Web.

---

[27] 27 Judith A. Miller & Kamla J. King, BNA's Directory of State Administrative Codes and Registers (2d ed. 1995), provides comprehensive coverage for the 50 states and the territories of American Samoa, Guam, Puerto Rico, Northern Mariana Islands, and Virgin Islands, including the contents pages from each published administrative code.

3. Research in State Administrative Law

a. Check the state code to determine if the state has an Administrative Procedure Act and if the method for publication of regulations is prescribed therein.

b. Check the state's organization manual to determine the agencies that issue regulations or decisions.

c. Consult a legal encyclopedia or administrative law treatise if published for a state.

d. Consult a state legal research manual, if available (see Appendix B).

e. Consult the various electronic and internet sources to determine if state regulations or agency decisions are available.

SECTION L. SUMMARY

1. Federal Register

a. Types of documents published are:

(1) Regulations and rules of federal agencies.

(2) Proposed regulations and rules of federal agencies.

(3) Agency notices.

(4) Presidential documents.

b. Indexes.

(1) *Federal Register Index.*

Cumulative index published monthly and annually.

(2) *CIS Federal Register Index.*

c. Cumulative *List of CFR Parts Affected.*

This table updates the monthly issues of the *LSA: List of CFR Sections Affected.*

d. Frequency of publication.

Began in 1936. Published Monday through Friday, except on an official federal holiday.

e. Contents of the *Federal Register* must be judicially noticed.

2. Code of Federal Regulations

a. Contains all regulations that first appeared in the *Federal Register* that are of a general and permanent nature and are still in force.

b. Arranged by subject in 50 Titles.

c. Each Title is subdivided into Chapters, Subchapters, Parts, and Sections. The *CFR* is cited by Title and Section.

d. Each Title is in a separate pamphlet or pamphlets. Each Title is republished once a year, at which time new material is added, and repealed or obsolete material is deleted.

e. Regulations published in the *CFR* are *prima facie* evidence of the official text.

f. Indexes.

(1) *CFR Index and Finding Aids.*

Annual subject and agency index. The *Finding Aids* section in the annual index volume has a *Parallel Table of Authorities and Rules* and other aids for locating regulations and Presidential documents.

(2) CIS *Index to the Code of Federal Regulations.*

g. *LSA: List of CFR Sections Affected.*

This list indicates any changes to the annual volumes of the *CFR*.

3. The United States Government Manual

a. Annual handbook.

b. Describes administrative organizations whose regulations are published in the *Federal Register*.

c. Information on Congress, the federal judiciary, and important agency personnel.

d. Subject/agency index and name/agency index.

4. Presidential Documents

a. Issued pursuant to constitutional or statutory authority, or both.

b. Types of documents:

(1) Proclamations

(2) Executive Orders

(3) Reorganization Plans

(4) Administrative orders, executive agreements, messages to Congress, and signing statements.

c. Official comprehensive sources of Presidential documents.

(1) *Weekly Compilation of Presidential Documents*

Published each Monday and contains Presidential materials released by the White House during the preceding week.

(2) *Public Papers of the Presidents*

Coverage begins with the administration of President Hoover. Papers of Franklin Roosevelt are excluded. Volumes are issued annually and from 1977 to January 1989 include all material in the *Weekly Compilation.*

(3) Title 3 of *Code of Federal Regulations*

Since 1976, an annual compilation providing Proclamations, Executive Orders, and other Presidential documents. Prior to 1976, compilation volumes for various time periods were published. Since each compilation is a unique source of one year's documents, each compilation has permanent reference value.

    d.   Sources of selective types of documents:

    (1) *Federal Register*

    (2) Codification of Presidential Proclamations and Executive Orders

Subject arrangement of all previously-published Proclamations and Executive Orders still in force.

    (3) *United States Code Congressional and Administrative News,* Advance pamphlets

    (4) *United States Code Service,* Advance Service pamphlets

    (5) *CIS Presidential Executive Orders & Proclamations on Microfiche*

    (6) LEXIS–NEXIS and WESTLAW

    (7) *United States Statutes at Large*

    (8) 5 *U.S.C.* Appendix

    (9) *Congressional Record*

    (10) CD–ROM products

    (11) Internet sites.

5. Federal Administrative Decisions

    a.   Official publications published by U.S. Government Printing Office.

    b.   Unofficial publications by commercial publishers.

    c.   Electronic resources, including WESTLAW and LEXIS–NEXIS, CD–ROMs and Internet sites.

6. State Administrative Regulations and Decisions

    a.   Some states have codified the regulations of their administrative agencies.

    b.   Some states publish the decisions of their administrative agencies.

Chapter 14

LOOSELEAF SERVICES

SECTION A. INTRODUCTION TO LOOSELEAF SERVICES

Law publishers have always been concerned with keeping their publications current. Traditionally, this has been accomplished by the issuance of pocket supplements, usually on an annual basis, together with supplemental pamphlets and occasional revised volumes. This is still the most common non-electronic method of keeping sets of statutes, digests, and encyclopedias up to date. Some other types of materials, most notably those in the area of administrative law, often require much more frequent updating, and thus a different method of supplementation.

For example, to research adequately a problem in the law of taxation, a researcher must locate not only relevant statutes and court cases but also regulations of the Internal Revenue Service and the Treasury Department, rulings of the Commissioner of Internal Revenue, news releases, technical information bulletins, U.S. Tax Court cases, and other agency documents. A researcher attempting to find the answer to a tax problem using only the *United States Code,* the digests, the *Federal Register,* and the *Code of Federal Regulations* would find it not only cumbersome but, at times impossible, to accomplish. Publishers have responded to the problems of inaccessibility, complexity, and the sheer bulk of rapidly-changing information by developing looseleaf services.

1. Special Characteristics

As the name indicates, looseleaf services consist of special binders that simplify the insertion, removal, and substitution of individual pages. This characteristic allows the publisher to update material frequently and systematically through a process of constant editing, introducing what is new, and removing what is superseded. The speed and accuracy afforded by this ongoing revision are two of the looseleaf services' greatest assets.

This looseleaf format also allows for creativity in the ways materials are organized. Most services, however, attempt to consolidate into one source the statutes, regulations, court cases and administrative agency decisions, and commentary on a particular legal topic and then facilitate access to this material through detailed indexes and other finding aids. By these means a researcher can find the relevant material, both primary and secondary, in one place. Further, most services include current awareness information, which can include news of proposed legislation, pending agency regulations and agency decisions, and even informed rumor. They also frequently contain forms, summaries of professional meetings, calendars of forthcoming events, and other news deemed relevant to the researcher or practicing attorney.

Looseleaf services are of three types: (1) those, as previously described, in which pages are *interfiled* with existing materials; (2) those in *newsletter* format whereby each issue is added to a binder sequentially and chronologically; and (3) a combination of the two formats. Traditionally, those prepared by a publisher's editorial staff, regardless of the publication's format, have a standardized publication schedule, typically weekly, biweekly, or monthly. By contrast, looseleaf services by named authors usually are updated with interfiled materials less frequently and on an "as needed" basis.

The convenience, currency, frequency, and excellent indexing of looseleaf services often make them the best place to begin researching administrative law problems. In many rapidly-developing areas of the law, such as privacy, the environment, and consumer protection, the looseleaf service may be the only exhaustive research tool available.[1]

2. Publishers of Looseleaf Services

Looseleaf services vary in content and coverage, reflecting both the subject area of the service and the editorial policy of the publisher. Historically, three publishers—Commerce Clearing House (CCH), Bureau of National Affairs (BNA), and Prentice Hall (PH)—were the leading publishers of looseleaf services prepared by editorial staffs. A few years ago, Prentice Hall was sold and subdivided and its publications were either taken over by others or discontinued, leaving CCH and BNA as dominant players.

Recently, the Research Institute of America has increased its activity in the editorial staff-produced looseleaf services market.[2] Matthew Bender & Company, Inc. continues to be the largest publisher of treatises by named authors, including such notable works as *Moore's Federal Practice, Benedict on Admiralty,* and *Powell on Real Property,* with Aspen Law & Business, formerly, Little, Brown & Company, and West Group and LEXIS Law Publishing also playing prominent roles.

Perhaps the most remarkable development in recent years with respect to looseleaf services is the extent to which they are being added

---

[1] A tremendous number of looseleaf services by various publishers on many different subjects are currently published. *See, e.g.,* LEGAL LOOSELEAFS IN PRINT (Arlene L. Eis comp. & ed.), which is an annual publication that lists approximately 3,500 titles by over 260 publishers. This source includes information on the number of volumes in a looseleaf set, price, frequency, cost of supplementation, and Library of Congress classification number. It is arranged alphabetically by title and includes publisher, subject, and electronic format indexes.

[2] For example, Research Institute of American (RIA) publishes the *United States Tax Reporter,* a remodeled version of what was once Prentice Hall's *Federal Taxes.* RIA also publishes a number of other looseleaf services in the tax, estate planning, and business areas.

full-text to the online services, WESTLAW and LEXIS–NEXIS, and being published in CD–ROM versions. This electronic availability allows precision searching of these services that heretofore was impossible.

This Chapter focuses on only those features that are common to most interfiled and newsletter looseleaf services. Particular attention is given to representative publications from CCH and BNA. When using any looseleaf service, one should be alert to its individual characteristics, and special attention should be paid to the introductory and prefatory materials supplied by the publisher. This is particularly necessary when using looseleaf services on taxation [3] or labor law because the magnitude of materials on these subjects makes the looseleaf service very complex.

SECTION B. USING LOOSELEAF SERVICES

1. Interfiled Looseleafs in General

Most topical looseleaf services in which new material replaces older pages rather than supplementing existing ones have the following common elements:

    a. Full text of the statutes on the topic, often with significant legislative history

    b. Either full text or digests of relevant court cases or administrative agency decisions

    c. Editorial comment and explanatory notes

    d. Topical indexes

    e. Tables of cases and statutes

    f. Finding lists for statutes, cases, and administrative materials

    g. Indexes to current materials and cumulative indexes

    h. Current reports summarizing recent developments

    i. A weekly, biweekly, or monthly publication schedule.

2. Newsletter Looseleafs in General

Most topical looseleaf services in the newsletter format, whereby pamphlets are filed sequentially and chronologically, have the following common elements:

    a. News and editorial comments of general interest

    b. Recent state and federal developments and recent developments in particular topics within the broad subject covered

    c. Text of or excerpts from major legislation, court cases, and administrative regulations and agency decisions

    d. Subject and table of cases indexes

    e. A weekly, biweekly, or monthly publication schedule.

---

[3] For more detailed information on federal taxation, see Chapter 24.

3. Using Commerce Clearing House Looseleaf Services

Commerce Clearing House, Inc. (CCH) is one of the leading publishers of looseleaf services, and its publications are typically of the type in which pages are interfiled. Examples of these include the *Copyright Law Reporter, Federal Securities Law Reporter, Products Liability Reporter,* and *Trade Regulation Reporter.* CCH publications range from those complete in one binder to those that fill a dozen or more.

Regardless of size, these publications begin with an introductory section that discusses the use and organization of the service. The importance of this feature cannot be over-emphasized. A careful reading of it may save the researcher both time and frustration. The volumes are divided into sections by tabcards. These offer quick access to major topic headings. Typically, there will be a comprehensive Topical Index to the entire service. In addition, some services have special indexes to particular topics or volumes. The quality of the indexing is generally quite high, as the publisher strives to provide as many access points as possible.

The indexes are made more useful by the unique, dual numbering system employed by the publisher. Under this system, in addition to normal pagination, there is a paragraph number assigned to each topic area. These numbers may encompass as little as one textual paragraph or as much as fifty or more pages. This flexibility of format allows for frequent additions and deletions to the text without a total disruption of the indexing system. Research can begin by consulting one of the indexes, which will refer to the appropriate paragraph number. By then turning to the correct paragraph number, one can locate the pertinent material. In looseleaf services, page numbers often are used only as guides for filing new pages and removing old ones. The volumes containing the CCH editorial explanations of the topic of the reporter, various reference materials, laws and regulations, and forms are typically referred to as "compilation" volumes.

The full texts of new court cases and agency rulings, often supplied as part of the looseleaf service, generally are placed in a separate volume or section from the contents of the compilation volume(s). Each case or ruling is commonly assigned its own paragraph number, and can be located in any one of several ways. Most services have tables of cases, statutes, and administrative regulations. When a citation to one of these is encountered, research can begin by consulting the appropriate table and obtaining the paragraph number where the cited material is discussed. Special indexes cross reference from materials found under the paragraph numbers to materials concerning current developments.

Materials summarizing current developments generally are presented in the form of weekly bulletins that accompany the pages to be filed. These bulletins are often retained as part of the service, and constitute valuable research tools in themselves. [See Illustrations 14–1 through 14–4 for examples of how a typical CCH looseleaf service is used.]

Some services include state laws sections. These are generally arranged by state, with the same paragraph number being assigned uniformly to the same topic for each state. In some instances, *all-state* charts are published that give citations to the various state codes. [See Illustration 14–5.]

Often a CCH service that systematically reports court cases or agency decisions will have a separate, bound reporter that results from the looseleaf subscription.[4] For example, CCH's widely-used *Standard Federal Tax Reporter* includes a binder labeled "U.S. Tax Cases— Advance Sheets." These advance sheets are cumulated into bound volumes twice a year, with the "Advance Sheet" volume always containing only the most recent materials. This set is also available on WEST-LAW.

In general, the successful use of CCH looseleaf services requires the researcher to use the following three steps:

a. Locate the topic or topics under research by consulting the Topical Index to the service.

b. Read carefully all materials under paragraph numbers referred to by the Topical Index. When digests of cases are given, note citations to cases so that the full text can be read.

c. Consult the appropriate index or indexes to current materials.

4. Using Bureau of National Affairs Looseleaf Services

The Bureau of National Affairs, Inc. (BNA) is another major publisher of looseleaf services. As a general rule, its organizational principles differ from those of CCH. BNA's typical format consists of one or more three-ring binders in which periodic issues (or releases) are filed. Unlike CCH, the issues generally do not contain individual pages to be interfiled with existing text, but instead consist of pamphlet inserts numbered sequentially and filed chronologically. Thus, there is no provision for revision of earlier issues. This format allows for the service to be issued quickly, at the expense of the comprehensiveness guaranteed by the interfiling system. Examples of these publications are *Antitrust & Trade Regulation Report, Securities Regulation & Law Report,* and *Patent, Trademark & Copyright Journal.*

A slight variation of the self-contained publications are those that include several separate components, usually including a summary and analysis of major developments, the text of pertinent legislation, and the text or a digest of court actions. Such features as important speeches, government reports, book reviews, and bibliographies also may be included. Each of these components is generally filed behind its own tabcard. Examples of these services include *United States Law Week,*

---

[4] As was noted in Chapter 4, federal district court cases are reported selectively. Some cases not reported in the *Federal Supplement* are published in one or more of the subject looseleaf services. Consequently, it is frequently worthwhile to check the Table of Cases of these services for cases not reported in the *Federal Supplement.*

Criminal Law Reporter, and *Family Law Reporter,* with the latter also including a monograph section that provides detailed treatments of timely, practice-related issues.

BNA services feature cumulative indexes that offer topical access to the material. Since current issues supplement earlier ones, there is no need for paragraph numbers, and simple pagination is used. There are also case tables for each service. For some of its sets, BNA periodically supplies special storage binders for old issues, so that the main volumes can always contain current material. Regardless of whether the service is issued as a single newsletter or in several pamphlet-type components, each is an attempt to keep the researcher fully informed of all developments in the subject area of the service.

BNA has long published one large service that differs significantly in arrangement from its other looseleaf services described above. This is its *Labor Relations Reporter.* This set has separate looseleaf volumes for the following areas of labor relations:

> *Labor Management Relations* (federal)
> *Labor Arbitration and Dispute Settlements*
> *Wages and Hours*
> *Fair Employment Practices*
> *State Labor Laws*
> *Individual Employment Rights*
> *Americans with Disabilities*

Each of the looseleaf volumes for these units of the *Labor Relations Reporter* contains relevant statutes, regulations, and court cases. Periodically, court cases are removed from the looseleaf volumes and reprinted in bound series, e.g., *Labor Arbitration Reports, Wage and Hour Cases.* Each set of cases also has its own index and digest where the cases are classified according to BNA's classification scheme.

The entire set is unified by a two-volume looseleaf "Master Index" and a two-volume looseleaf "Labor Relations Expediter." [See Illustrations 14–5 through 14–8 for how one component of the *Labor Relations Reporter* is used.]

BNA also publishes other services, including *Environment Reporter* and *Occupational Safety & Health Reporter,* in a format similar to *Labor Relations Reporter.*[5]

5. Looseleaf Services in Electronic Format

The concept of a looseleaf service as exclusively a paper product has disappeared. These services are made available on LEXIS–NEXIS and WESTLAW with increasing frequency. Having a full-text, interfiled-type version of a looseleaf service available online may provide the most

---

[5] A useful source for learning more about the various publications and services of the Bureau of National Affairs, Inc. is the latest edition of BNA's REPORTER SERVICES AND THEIR USE.

convenient means yet discovered for updating materials, while offering the most precise searching capabilities. Rather than subscribers having to file new pages, the online versions are updated electronically by the vendors as new language is added, deleted, or changed. Obviously, the sequentially-published newsletter-type looseleaf services are even easier to include in databases.

Almost all Bureau of National Affairs' publications are available online in LEXIS–NEXIS and WESTLAW, with coverage for many services dating back to 1982. Some services issued more frequently than their online counterparts are available only online. These include *Law Week Daily Edition* and *BNA Tax Updates,* the latter being updated twice daily. Several Research Institute of America publications are likewise available in the CALR services. While CCH services are less likely to be available in the two major CALR services, *Standard Federal Tax Reporter* and its companion volumes are on WESTLAW, and the state securities *Blue Sky Law Reporter* is on both LEXIS–NEXIS and WESTLAW.

In addition, numerous looseleaf treatises are in online versions. Because of their less frequent updating, these looseleaf treatises also lend themselves well to CD–ROM technology. For example, Matthew Bender has several CD–ROM products containing looseleaf treatises, and BNA publishes its *Tax Management Portfolio* series as a CD–ROM product. Matthew Bender's *Authority* is discussed in Chapter 18. The availability of looseleaf services in electronic format continues to expand.[6]

[6] The best means to determine whether a particular publication is available in electronic format is to consult the online and paper content guides of both WESTLAW and LEXIS–NEXIS or a particular publisher's catalog. Also helpful is the "Electronic Format Index" in LEGAL LOOSELEAFS IN PRINT, note 1 *supra.*

SECTION C. ILLUSTRATIONS

Illustrations Using CCH Products Liability Reports

Problem: What constitutes adequate warning about the potential dangers of a product's design?

Illustrations Using BNA Fair Employment Practices (FEP) Division of Labor Relations Reporter

Problem: Can attorneys' fees be collected for the work of paralegals and law clerks?

[Illustration 14–1]

PAGE FROM TOPICAL INDEX, CCH PRODUCTS LIABILITY REPORTS

905 3-98   **Topical Index**   **185**

References are to paragraph (¶) numbers.
See also pages 31, 51, and 101.

VIRGINIA—continued
. damages—continued
.. punitive damages...3350.48
. definition of product
.. blood products...1630.48
. demonstrative evidence
.. experiments and tests...2770.48
.. films and videos...2775.48
. design defects
.. negligence...1110.48
. government contractor defense...2820.48
.. government/industry standards...2840.40
. hearsay rule exceptions
.. learned treatises...2725.48
.. public records...2735.48
. implied warranties
.. fitness for a particular purpose...660.48
.. habitability...720.48
.. merchantability...700.48
. inspection and testing...1130.48
. jurisdiction...2420.48
. manufacturers
.. apparent or ostensible manufacturers...

WARNING DEFECTS—continued
. scope of duty...1805
. sophisticated users...1830
. unavoidably unsafe products...1835
WARNINGS
. product integrity program...30,371
WARRANTY...500
. chart of UCC jurisdictions...520
. express warranty...595
. implied warranties...645
.. fitness for a particular purpose...660
.. habitability...720
.. merchantability...700
. privity of contract
.. food products...540
.. nonfood products...550
. reliance...800
. sale requirement...745
WASHINGTON
. allergy and unusual susceptibility...3015.49
. alteration/modification of product...3060.49
. alternative theories of recovery...2460.49

Step 1

Consult the Topical Index under an appropriate term, in this instance "Warning Defects." Notice sub-entry "adequacy of warnings" which is followed by "1815." The "1815" refers to a particular paragraph.

Note that looseleaf service indexing is typically sophisticated. This same information may also be indexed under a different key word or phrase such as "Design Defects" or "Product Defects." Note also that there are separate indexes in the set for prior cases and for the most recent material not yet integrated into the larger indexes.

See next Illustration for Step 2.

. seat belt defense...3035.48
. similar occurrences...2610.48
. statutes of limitations...3130.48
. statutes of repose...3100.48
. strict liability, acceptance...1550.48
. subsequent remedial measures...2620.48
. unreasonably dangerous condition...1715.48
. warning defects
.. negligence...1150.48
. warranty
.. express warranty...595.48
.. fitness for a particular purpose...660.48
.. habitability...720.48
.. merchantability...700.48
.. privity of contract, food products...540.48
.. privity of contract, nonfood products...550.48
.. reliance...800.48
.. sale requirement...745.48
VITAMINS...4010

W

WARNING DEFECTS
. adequacy of warnings...1815
. bulk suppliers...1825
. delegation of duty/warnings to employers...1820
. learned intermediary doctrine...1840
. negligence...1150
. open and obvious danger rule...1810

. design defects
.. feasible design alternatives...1760.49
.. negligence...1110.49
.. safety devices...1770.49
.. unavoidably unsafe products...1780.49
. design defects, tests
.. consumer expectations...1725.49
.. risk/utility...1730.49
. employers...2340.49
. expert and opinion testimony...2630.49
. government contractor defense...2820.49
. government/industry standards...2840.49
. hearsay rule exceptions
.. ancient document rule...2705.49
.. learned treatises...2725.49
. implied warranties
.. fitness for a particular purpose...660.49
.. habitability...720.49
.. merchantability...700.49
. indemnity and contribution...2310.49
. inspection and testing...1130.49
. jurisdiction...2420.49
. manufacturers
.. apparent or ostensible manufacturers...2225.49
.. component suppliers...2230.49
.. control...2210.49
.. identification of tortfeasors...2240.49
.. successor corporations...2245.49
. manufacturing defects...1090.49
. misrepresentation...1190.49
. misuse of product...3050.49
. nondefective firearms...1890.49

Products Liability Reports   **WAS**

[Illustration 14–2]

PAGE FROM COMPILATION VOLUME, CCH
PRODUCTS LIABILITY REPORTS

---

897 11-97 **Warning Defects** **4221**

¶ 1815 ADEQUACY OF WARNINGS

Once a duty to warn is established, which is generally a question of law, the adequacy or sufficiency of the warning must be established. The question of adequacy is most often a question of fact for the jury.

Under strict products liability, a product carrying an inadequate warning is defective because it is unreasonably dangerous to the user or consumer in the absence of an adequate warning. The adequacy of any warning is measured by what warning would be reasonable under the circumstances, which is technically a general negligence standard.

The content of a warning that would discharge a seller's responsibility to the user is one that, if followed, would render the product safe for users. Factors that must be considered by a jury include consumer expectations as to how the product operates, how complicated the product is, the severity and likelihood of harm to which the user will be subject if the product is not properly used, and whether a warning is feasible and likely to prevent injury.

> **Step 2**
>
> Consult the paragraph number referred to in the Topical Index, e.g., "1815." Most CCH looseleaf services provide a brief discussion of the subject of the paragraph, in this instance "Adequacy of Warnings."
>
> Following the general discussion under the paragraph number, there is frequently an alphabetical listing of "Annotations by Jurisdiction" or "Annotations by Topic."
>
> **See next Illustration.**

danger is open and obvious, to conspicuous warnings where the danger might be overlooked or not appreciated by foreseeable users. Open and obvious dangers are discussed at ¶ 1810; the duty to warn sophisticated users is discussed at ¶ 1830.

When a warning is given, the seller may reasonably assume that it will be read and heeded. A product bearing such a warning, which is safe for use if it is followed, is not in a defective condition, nor is it unreasonably dangerous.

Hypersensitive or Idiosyncratic Users. Warnings by a product manufacturer or seller are not necessarily inadequate because they do not specifically warn an allergic user; it is generally sufficient to warn of known dangers. Some decisions have limited liability where there has not been an "appreciable" number of users suffering an adverse reaction. However, where the severity of the potential injury is great, even if the risk to the ordinary user is slight, a duty to warn may be imposed, and warnings may be inadequate based on failure to warn of a slight risk of severe injury.

Annotations to ¶ 1815 Appear by Jurisdiction Below, as Follows:

Alabama	.01	Idaho	.13
Alaska	.02	Illinois	.14
Arizona	.03	Indiana	.15
Arkansas	.04	Iowa	.16
California	.05	Kansas	.17
Colorado	.06	Kentucky	.18
Connecticut	.07	Louisiana	.19
District of Columbia	.09	Maine	.20
Florida	.10	Maryland	.21
Georgia	.11	Massachusetts	.22

Products Liability Reports **¶ 1815**

[Illustration 14–3]

PAGE FROM COMPILATION VOLUME, CCH
PRODUCTS LIABILITY REPORTS

4222   **Strict Liability**   897   11-97

.01 Alabama.—Whether a warning to a tester of a high-pressure vessel not to stand in front of a pipe stopper during a hydrostatic test adequately apprised the tester of the risk of injury and death presented by the mismatching of the jaws securing the stopper was a question of fact. The tester sustained a fatal head injury when the stopper became dislodged and shot off of one of the vessel's pipes during the test. [SJ]*

    Hicks v. Commercial Union Ins. Co. (AlaSCt 1994) PRODUCTS LIABILITY REPORTS ¶ 14,023, 652 So2d 211.

Manufacturer's warnings that were included on the labels, decals, instructions, and hang tag that accompanied a kerosene heater, as well as in the owner's manual and safety tips brochure furnished with the unit, were specific, comprehensive and detailed in notifying users of the potential

manuals or charts to insure that parts he was using were matching parts. [SJ]

    Reynolds v. Bridgestone/Firestone, Inc. (11thCir 1993) PRODUCTS LIABILITY REPORTS ¶ 13,477, 989 F2d 465.

Warnings on packages of cigarette lighters that the lighters should be kept out of the reach of, or away from, children were inadequate as a matter of law. An action was brought by the parents of a 4-year-old child who died in a fire she allegedly started with a lighter. Whether parents were adequately warned that small children would be attracted to a disposable butane lighter, and that the lighter could easily be operated by children, had to be determined by a jury.

    Bean v. BIC Corp. (AlaSCt 1992) PRODUCTS LIABILITY REPORTS ¶ 13,163, 597 So2d 1350.

In an action brought by the estate of a tractor

Starting with paragraph 1815.01 are digests of all cases arranged alphabetically by state dealing with "Adequacy of Warnings."

Be sure to read the relevant cases in their entirety. Notice how citations are given to both the CCH reporter and to the *National Reporter System*.

1993) PRODUCTS LIABILITY REPORTS ¶ 13,745, 628 So2d 478.

Warnings given by a manufacturer of a silicone breast implant understated the risks of the implant's rupturing during a surgical procedure.

    Toole v. McClintock (11thCir 1993) PRODUCTS LIABILITY REPORTS ¶ 13,606, 999 F2d 549.

Whether warnings by the manufacturer of a multipiece wheel assembly, which had propensity to explode when a tire was being inflated on it, were adequate was a jury question. A tire changer died when he inflated a tire. The wheel assembly exploded, and he was struck by pieces of the wheel rim. The assembly parts were not imprinted with a warning and were not color-coded to prevent mismatching. The changer was repairing a tire off the employer's premises and had no access to

A manufacturer and a seller of a one-person motorcycle adequately warned of the dangers associated with carrying passengers on the vehicle as a matter of law. Thus, a 14-year-old passenger who disregarded the manufacturer's warnings could not recover damages for a leg injury he sustained while being driven on the motorcycle. The manufacturer only had a duty to warn of the dangers when the vehicle was put to its intended use. Because the manufacturer made it clear that carrying passengers on the cycle was an unintended use, the manufacturer discharged its duty to warn.

    Gurley v. American Honda Motor Co., Inc. (AlaSCt 1987) PRODUCTS LIABILITY REPORTS ¶ 11,385, 505 So2d 358.

If the risk of explosion and spraying of hot burning paint could have been diminished or elim-

---

    * [SJ] *indicates a post-1992 summary judgment ruling.*

¶ 1815.01

[Illustration 14–4]

PAGE FROM COMPILATION VOLUME, CCH
PRODUCTS LIABILITY REPORTS

---

904   2-98   **Cumulative Index to Prior Decisions**   **11,107**
                    See also Cumulative Index to Current Decisions

From Compilation   **To Current Decisions**
Paragraph No.   **Paragraph No.**

1230	.14	Shattering of glass peanut jar created inference of negligence (7thCir)	13,784
1250	.11	Six-month use of tractor by workers who did not read manual (GaCtApp)	13,672
	.11	Res ipsa loquitur inapplicable to claim involving bun (GaCtApp)	14,571
	.14	Sufficient evidence of exclusive control over glass peanut jar (7thCir)	13,784
	.44	Res ipsa loquitur inapplicable to claim v. canned soup maker (TennCtApp)	14,157
1270	.14	Removal of label from glass peanut jar not mishandling (7thCir)	13,784
1290	.14	No evidence of extraneous circumstances in shattering of glass peanut jar (7thCir)	13,784
1310	.31	Identification of parties in catheter and tubing failure (NJSuperCtAppDiv)	14,000

Strict Liability

1550	.10	Water pipe maker not liable for purchaser's failed test (FlaDistCtApp)	15,012
1610	.14	Unbound corrugated cardboard boxes not product (IllAppCt)	15,047
	.15	Refurbishing of seam welder not provision of product (NDInd)	15,065
1715	.01	Contaminated biscuit-with-gravy meal unreasonably dangerous (AlaSCt)	15,075
	.04	Exterior wall coating not unreasonably dangerous (ArkSCt)	14,932
	.09	Design defect claim v. cigarette maker requires specific defects (DDC)	15,085

> One must also ascertain if there are any relevant cases that were decided after those that appear in the main (compilation) volume. This can be accomplished by consulting the cross-reference tables in the volume that contains current materials.

1725	.44	Loader not defective under consumer expectations test (TennCtApp)	15,056
	.45	Jury issue as to unreasonable danger posed by raw oysters (TexCtApp)	15,056
	.49	Window not defective under consumer expectations test (WashCtApp)	15,033
1730	.45	Non-childproof cigarette lighter not defectively designed (WDTex)	15,103
1735	.33	Issue as to whether tractor loader safe for intended use (WDNY)	14,944
	.33	Bullets not defective for intended use (SDNY) aff'd (2dCir)	14,592; 15,016
1750	.15	Obvious danger of shearing machine not absolute defense (IndCtApp)	14,990
	.45	Non-childproof cigarette lighter not defectively designed (WDTex)	15,103
1760	.15	Alternative design for forklift irrelevant to warning defect issue (IndCtApp)	15,112
	.19	No proof of feasible alternative design for container chassis (LaCtApp)	15,031
	.19	Alternative design for tire jack jury issue (5thCir)	15,067
	.25	No proof of feasible alternative designs for portable conveyor (5thCir)	15,074
	.31	No feasible alternative design for traffic control box (NJSuperCtAppDiv)	14,985
	.45	Non-childproof cigarette lighter not defectively designed (WDTex)	15,103
1770	.15	Shearing machine's safety device not unreasonably dangerous (IndCtApp)	14,990
	.33	Issue as to design defect in tractor loader without safety devices (WDNY)	14,944
	.33	No duty to install safety devices on forklift (NYAppDiv)	14,998
	.45	No proof of safer alternative design for cigarettes (TexSCt)	14,992
1805	.15	Refurbisher of seam welder had no duty to warn (NDInd)	15,065
	.16	Crane maker has no duty to warn of wire rope dangers (IowaSCt)	15,109
	.27	No duty to warn of auto side window's spontaneous breakage risk (MontSCt)	15,105
	.33	Computer keyboard maker has duty to warn of repetitive stress risk (EDNY)	15,041
	.37	Heeding presumption overcome in antidepressant drug case (EDOkla)	15,087
	.38	Fishbowl maker had duty to warn of carrying filled product (OrCtApp)	15,049
1815	.15	Alternative design for forklift irrelevant to warning defect issue (IndCtApp)	15,112
1850	.15	Elements of enhanced injury claim v. forklift maker (IndCtApp)	15,112

Parties

2130	.04	Horse purchaser not protected by products liability statutes (ArkSCt)	14,495
	.05	Claim for death of military pilot from jet ejection seat defect (DC Cal)	13,487
	.10	Water pipe maker not liable for purchaser's failed test (FlaDistCtApp)	15,012
	.11	Insurance company's strict liability claim against tractor maker (GaCtApp)	13,672
	.14	DES makers owed no duty to third-generation victims (IllAppCt)	13,642
	.14	No recovery for emotional distress from v. clutch housing maker (IllAppCt) aff'd (IllSCt)	14,499
	.14	Worker not ultimate user of corrugated cardboard boxes (IllAppCt)	15,047
	.15	Delivery truck driver not user/ consumer of shipping box (IndCtApp)	14,290
	.21	Asbestos distributor not liable to bystanders for punitive dmaages (MdCtApp)	14,416

Products Liability Reports

[Illustration 14–5]

PAGE FROM CCH FOOD, DRUG, COSMETIC LAW REPORTER

1520   12-2-91   **10,025**

FOOD DEFINITIONS

¶ 10,011

"Food" is defined in most state food laws to mean: (1) articles used for food or drink for man or other animals, (2) chewing gum, and (3) articles used for components of any such article.

A few states impose special restrictions on the use of "food additives," "color additives," and "pesticide chemicals" in or on food and define these terms.

Definitions of "food," "food additive," "color additive," and "pesticide chemical" that appear in the basic laws are referred to in the chart below.

State	"Food"	"Food Additive"	"Color Additive"	"Pesticide Chemical"
Ala.	¶ 11,020			
Alas.	¶ 11,624			
Ariz.	¶ 12,011	¶ 12,011	¶ 12,011	¶ 12,011
Ark.	¶ 12,512			
Cal.	¶ 13,023	¶ 13,024	¶ 13,015	¶ 13,036
Colo.	¶ 13,512	¶ 13,512	¶ 13,512	¶ 13,512
Conn.	¶ 14,012	¶ 14,012	¶ 14,012	¶ 14,012
Del.	¶ 14,511			
D.C.[1]	¶ 15,012, 15,052			
Fla.	¶ 15,513	¶ 15,513	¶ 15,513	¶ 15,513
Ga.				
Ha'	Several looseleaf services include coverage for state laws. In some,			—
Ida	the sections containing the full text of the state laws are preceded			—
Ill.	with a chart outlining where the laws on a topic may be found for the			—
Ind	various states.			—
Iowa	¶ 18,551			
Kan.	¶ 19,012	¶ 19,012	¶ 19,012	¶ 19,012
Ky.	¶ 19,512	¶ 19,512	¶ 19,512	¶ 19,512
La.	¶ 20,012			
Me.	¶ 20,542			
Md.	¶ 21,011	¶ 21,011	¶ 21,011	
Mass.	¶ 21,511			
Mich.	¶ 22,034	¶ 22,036	¶ 22,037	¶ 22,035
Minn.	¶ 22,511	¶ 22,511	¶ 22,511	¶ 22,511
Miss.	¶ 23,014			
Mo.	¶ 23,511			
Mont.	¶ 24,052	¶ 24,052	¶ 24,052	¶ 24,052
Neb.				

[1] Provisions of the Federal Act also are applicable to commerce within the District of Columbia

Food Drug Cosmetic Law Reports   **¶ 10,011**

[Illustration 14–6]

PAGE FROM BNA MASTER INDEX TO LABOR RELATIONS REPORTER CONTAINING FAIR EMPLOYMENT PRACTICES (FEP) OUTLINE OF CLASSIFICATIONS

D-I 116   FEP Cases OUTLINE OF CLASSIFICATIONS

▶ **108.81—Contd.**

.8155	—Against EEOC, etc.
.8157	—Depositions
.8158	—Interrogatories
.8160	—Records, documents, etc.
	[For interrogatories, see ▶ 108.8158.]
.8162	—Requests for admission
.8163	—Ex parte interviews; access to employees and ex-employees
	[For cases prior to FEP Vol. 53, see ▶ 108.8151.]
	—Defenses
.8165	——In general
	[For relevancy defense cases after FEP Vol. 52, see ▶ 108.8170.]
.8166	——Privilege

Step 1

Consult the Outline of Classifications for Fair Employment Practices (FEP) in the Master Index to Labor Relations Reporter. Note how 108.8908 appears to be relevant. Consult this paragraph number for digests of cases in the Consolidated Index and Digest (CDI) in the Master Index. See next Illustration.

Note: This search could have started in the FEP–Master Index using a subject approach rather than a classification approach.

.834	1866 Act
.836	Equal Pay Act
.837	Age Discrimination in Employment Act
.839	State FEP Acts
	[For cases prior to FEP Vol. 53, see ▶ 108.831.]

▶ **108.85 Sanctions**

[For sanctions in discovery proceedings, see ▶ 108.8175. For attorneys' fees for discovery proceedings, see ▶ 108.8937. For sanctions for appeals, see ▶ 108.781.]

.8501	In general
.8511	Fed.R.Civ.P. 11

▶ **108.87 Pattern-or-Practice Suits**

[For remedies, see ▶ 200.01 et seq.]

.871	In general
.873	Jurisdiction and procedure
.875	Evidence

▶ **108.89 Attorneys and Attorneys' Fees**

[For attorneys and attorneys' fees in the federal sector, see ▶ 110.8901 et seq.]

.8901	In general
.8903	Appointment
	[For petition for attorney, see ▶ 108.6915.]
.8905	Disqualification
.8908	Paralegals and law clerks
	Fees
.8911	—In general
.8912	—Factors in determining fees
	[For contingency fee cases after FEP Vol. 46, see ▶ 108.8920. For incentive fees, including bonuses, multipliers and upward adjustments of fees, see ▶ 108.8918. For delay in awarding fees, see ▶ 108.8919.]
.8914	—Discovery for purpose of determining fees
.8915	—Purpose of award
.8916	—Burden of proof
.8917	—Contingency fees
	[For cases before FEP Vol. 47, see ▶ 108.8912.]
.8918	—Incentive fee (bonus, multiplier, upward adjustment of fees, etc.)
	[For upward adjustment or multiplier due to delay in award after FEP Vol. 30, see ▶ 108.8919.]
.8919	—Delay in awarding fees
	[For cases prior to FEP Vol. 31, see ▶ 108.8912 and ▶ 108.8918.]
	Award; entitlement
.8921	—In general
	[Includes Equal Access to Justice Act cases]
.8922	—Discretion of court in awarding fees
.8924	—Discretion of court as to amount
.8926	—Rate of payment
	[For time spent in litigating fee issue, see ▶ 108.8938.]
.8927	—Calculation of hours
.8928	—Allocation of liability; award against attorneys
.8932	—Award against EEOC, US
.8933	—Award against state, local governments
.8935	—Appeals, fees for
.8937	—Discovery proceedings, fees for
.8938	—Time spent in litigating fee issue
	[For rate of payment, see ▶ 108.8926.]
.8940	Prevailing party
.8943	Interim award
.8950	Recovery by employer, union
.8960	1866 and 1871 Acts, availability of fees
.8965	Recovery by private non-profit corporation
.8967	Third parties; intervenors

[Illustration 14–7]

PAGE FROM BNA MASTER INDEX TO LABOR RELATIONS REPORTER CONTAINING FAIR EMPLOYMENT PRACTICES (FEP) CUMULATIVE DIGEST AND INDEX (CDI)

Final CDI	61 FEP Cases	D-II A765

▶ **108.875** Employer has not engaged in pattern or practice of bias in job upgrades, even though women occupy lower job classifications than men with comparable seniority, where there is no evidence that women were told not to bid for jobs, that bids went unrecognized, or that jobs were so male-dominated that women did not seek to obtain them when they were available. —Jenson v. Eveleth Taconite Co. (DC Minn) 61 FEP Cases 1252

Policy and practice of bias by facility in providing training opportunities has not been shown, despite claim that women are not trained in duties of jobs other than own to same extent as men, where there was no evidence that training de jure means of groo￼ for promotion. *Id.*

Finding that employ￼ or practice of exposin￼ hostile environment d￼ class member to pres￼ sexually harassed, but￼ remains on individu￼ show by preponderanc￼ was as affected as rea￼

▶ **108.8901** Reversib￼ when one of protecte￼ torneys testified as to ￼ tion that employer ha￼ ery to construct cha￼ showed pattern of ag￼ where chart was exc￼ grounds. —Gusman v. ￼ 61 FEP Cases 382

Employee who asked firm to withdraw as counsel should not bear costs of retaining successor counsel and learning issues in case, where it is not unheard of that lengthy litigation generates ill will within camps of contending parties, and absent showing that plaintiff acted unreasonably to undermine attorney-client relationship, it would be mistake to craft rule binding party to lawyer in whom party has lost confidence by imposing cost on seeking new counsel. —Malarkey v. Texaco Inc. (DC SNY) 61 FEP Cases 407

▶ **108.8908** Counsel for claimants properly were awarded fees incorporating 1988 rates of $110 per hour for 1985 law school graduates to $235 per hour for 1969 law school graduates, in addition to $70 per hour for paralegals. —Davis v. San Francisco, City & County of (CA 9) 61 FEP Cases 440

▶ **108.8911** Discharged police officer could have obtained attorneys' fees award

under Rehabilitation Act in state-court proceeding, and failure to do so bars him, on ground of res judicata, from seeking fees in federal court following state-court decision awarding reinstatement and back pay. —Antonsen v. Ward (CA 2) 2 AD Cases 279

Lower court properly awarded attorneys' fees to ex-employees after finding that employer improperly removed state-court action, which was based on claims of age bias and breach of contract, on theory that action raised claims under ERISA because ex-employees, in depositions, expressed concern that decision to discharge them was motivated by potential for pension savings.￼

￼ to award fees if ￼nd finding of im-￼g removal is not ￼rd of fees, which ￼ble. —Morris v. ￼c. (CA 6) 61 FEP ￼

￼can include reim-￼ket expenses like ￼ng costs that are ￼torney-client rela-￼Francisco, City & ￼P Cases 440 ￼cation was timely, ￼d within six weeks ￼ere employer filed ￼time, and counsel ￼tion in reliance on ￼uiring itemization ￼. —McKenzie v. ￼Inc. (CA 11) 61

FEP Cases 1534

Firm that withdrew from case at request of employee should not be required to pay costs associated with retaining successor counsel and learning of issues in case, absent showing that it acted in way inconsistent with professional obligations and thus caused relationship with client to deteriorate. —Malarkey v. Texaco Inc. (DC SNY) 61 FEP Cases 407

▶ **108.8912** Billing rate that attorney can obtain from paying client is presumptive rate that should be used in determining fee award under 1964 CRA, and fact that there is different average rate in community is not reason to depart from presumptive rate. —Gusman v. Unisys Corp. (CA 7) 61 FEP Cases 382

Experienced attorney for handicapped ex-NIH employee is awarded $165 per hour and junior associates between $90 and $125 per hour, where claim was not difficult to litigate, senior counsel was quite able but

---

Step 2

Note how 108.8908 digests cases dealing with the question of awarding attorney's fees to non-lawyers employed by attorneys.

The search must be updated by consulting any supplemental indexes.

Full texts of the digested cases are in the volumes of *Fair Employment Practices* (FEP) cases. Note that the case located is in volume 61 of FEP Cases. It is first published in the looseleaf "Cases" binder of the FEP volumes and later in a bound volume.

See next Illustration.

[Illustration 14–8]

PAGE FROM A VOLUME OF BNA FAIR EMPLOYMENT PRACTICES CASES

---

61 FEP Cases 440   DAVIS v. CITY & COUNTY OF SAN FRANCISCO

lows: In footnote 3, line 9 [61 FEP Cases at 111, footnote 4, line 12], delete the phrase "he relied solely on federal precedent," the period following the phrase, and the following sentence, which begins "consequently, the district court's analysis. . ." Replace the deleted text with the following: "consequently the district court's analysis

4. Attorneys' fees — Time spent on fee petition ►108.8938

Title VII claimants' counsel were properly compensated for time spent on fee petition, even though they hired additional lawyer to act as fee counsel, there being no claim that time spent by claimants' counsel on fee petition

---

Step 3

Read the full text of digested cases located through indexes. In the problem given, only one case was relevant. Note how the publisher provides headnotes that enable the researcher to go directly to the point in the case being researched, in this instance headnote 7.

See next Illustration.

---

into five subclasses because of potential conflicts of interest and that each subclass necessarily had to be represented by different attorney, and it found that hours claimed by additional attorneys with special expertise who were hired to help develop overall strategy and legal analysis reflected their contribution to case for most part.

DAVIS v. CITY & COUNTY OF SAN FRANCISCO

U.S. Court of Appeals, Ninth Circuit (San Francisco)

DAVIS, et al. v. CITY AND COUNTY OF SAN FRANCISCO, No. 91-15113, October 6, 1992

CIVIL RIGHTS ACT OF 1964

1. Attorneys' fees — Hours ►108.8927

Federal district court properly allowed counsel for Title VII claimants to supplement their time sheets with additional documentation of their efforts; it did not abuse its discretion in finding that reconstructed records, which drew on agendas and summaries of meetings and notes and time sheets of co-counsel, were extensive.

2. Attorneys' fees — Hours ►108.8927

Attorneys are not entitled to attorneys' fees for performing clerical matters, such as filing of pleadings and travel time associated with this task.

3. Attorneys' fees — Hours ►108.8927

Title VII claimants' counsel were properly allowed to claim time spent traveling to co-counsel meetings, where counsel submitted evidence establishing that local attorneys customarily bill their clients for travel time to co-counsel meetings, and city did not introduce any contrary evidence

6. Attorneys' fees — Hours ►108.8927

Title VII claimants' counsel were properly awarded fees for time spent in press conferences and other public relations work that contributed directly and substantially to attainment of claimants' litigation goals.

7. Attorneys' fees — Rate ►108.8938 ►108.8926

Counsel for Title VII claimants properly were awarded fees incorporating 1988 rates of $110 per hour for 1985 law school graduates to $235 per hour for 1969 law school graduates, in addition to $70 per hour for paralegals.

8. Attorneys' fees — Rate ►108.8926

Federal district court properly applied same hourly rate to each task performed by each attorney; private practitioners do not generally charge varying rates for different lawyerly tasks that they undertake on given case.

9. Attorneys' fees — Rate ►108.8926

Federal district court properly applied 1988 billing rates to each hour claimed by counsel regardless of year in which work was actually performed.

10. Attorneys' fees — Contingency ►108.8917

Federal district court should not have enhanced lodestar amount of attorneys' fees awarded to Title VII claimants' counsel to account for fact

[Illustration 14–9]

PAGE FROM A VOLUME OF BNA FAIR EMPLOYMENT PRACTICES CASES

---

61 FEP Cases 448   DAVIS v. CITY & COUNTY OF SAN FRANCISCO

fighting force. As of August 8, 1990 minority composition stood at 24%. In a department which hired no women before 1985 there are now 36, comprising 2.6% of the force. One of the women is a lieutenant. Minority men have registered even broader gains in the officer ranks. In a fire department that had no minority members in the ranks of lieutenant or above in 1985, there are presently 54 lieutenants, eight captains, five battalion chiefs, one assistant chief and one assistant deputy chief II." *Id.* The court also scrutinized the educational background, career history and community standing of each appellee's attorney and concluded that they possessed a "high level of experience, ability and reputation . . . ." *Id.*

[7] In light of these factors, the court turned to the evidence submitted by the appellees concerning the rates charged by San Francisco attorneys for work comparable to that performed in the SFFD litigation. We recently pronounced that declarations of

The City did not controvert this evidence below. The only evidence it presented concerning billing rates was a survey done of the California legal market as a whole which discussed a wide variety of practice areas. As the Supreme Court made clear in *Blum,* however, the proper reference point in determining an appropriate fee award is the rates charged by private attorneys in the same legal market as prevailing counsel, San Francisco in this instance, for work similar to that performed by such counsel, broad-based complex litigation here. The City's survey was properly dismissed by the district court as shedding no light on this matter.

Before this court, the City discusses several district court decisions which, in its estimation, establish that the rates claimed by appellees' counsel for work performed in the San Francisco market were excessive. In *Bernardi v. Yeutter,* 754 F.Supp. 743 [54 FEP Cases 1551] (N.D. Cal. 1990), *aff'd in part and rev'd in part,* 951 F.2d 971 [60 FEP

Bracketed numbers in the text of the cases, in this example [7], identify the location that served as the topic of the headnote.

Block, 940 F.2d 1211, 1235 [60 FEP Cases 1000] (9th Cir.), *cert. denied,* 112 S.Ct. 640 [60 FEP Cases 1896] (1991). Here, the appellees produced numerous affidavits declaring that the fees sought by appellees' counsel, which incorporated 1988 rates of $110 per hour for 1985 law school graduates to $235 per hour for 1969 law school graduates, in addition to $70 per hour for paralegals, were well within the bounds of the "prevailing market rates" that form the basis for a proper fee award. *Blum* at 895. The district court referred to several of those affidavits in granting appellees' counsel's requested rates. It pointed to the declaration of a "prominent Title VII class action attorney" in San Francisco that attorneys at his firm with credentials similar to those of appellees' counsel would, in 1988, have billed at rates ranging from $110 per hour for 1986 law school graduates to $250 per hour for 1969 graduates, with paralegal time billed at $50 to $85 per hour. It further noted the affidavit of an attorney at McCutchen, Doyle, Brown & Enersen, a well-respected San Francisco firm, that lawyers comparable to appellees' counsel at his firm would have billed at 1988 rates ranging from $150 per hour for 1985 graduates to $230 for 1971 graduates. It referred, finally, to an affidavit indicating that a third San Francisco firm billed at essentially the same rates. 748 F.Supp. at 1430-1431.

party in a sex discrimination case. One of those lawyers is also involved in this case. The court pointedly noted, however, that it did not consider "the case to have been complex litigation," 754 F.Supp. at 746, and therefore rejected evidence concerning the much higher rates which San Francisco attorneys charge for such litigation. By contrast, there is no claim here that the challenge to the SFFD's hiring and promotion policies did not amount to a complex class suit.

The City also points to the district court's decision in *Bucci v. Chromalloy,* 1989 W.L. 222441 [60 FEP Cases 405] (N.D. Cal. 1989), *aff'd* 927 F.2d 608 [61 FEP Cases 616] (9th Cir. 1991) (unpublished memorandum), where fees were awarded based on rates ranging from $175 per hour for an attorney of twenty years experience to $130 per hour for an attorney of nine years experience. While those rates are somewhat lower than the ones utilized by the district court in the present case, the district court in *Bucci* characterized the proceedings before it as having been quite simple. "This case was a straightforward discrimination action based on a flagrant pattern of abusive and insulting behavior on the part of plaintiff's supervisor. While the action vindicated significant civil rights, it did not involve complex fact patterns or novel and difficult legal questions. Indeed, plaintiff's counsel admitted in

SECTION D. SUMMARY

Looseleaf services often have the following characteristics, features, and type of content:

1. Allow for frequent, rapid, and systematic updating.

2. Include interfiled and newsletter formats.

3. Current reports summarize recent developments.

4. Excellent indexing.

5. Best place to start research for subjects governed by administrative regulations and rulings.

6. Written by a publisher's editorial staff or published as treatises with named authors.

7. Contents of a looseleaf service by a publisher's editorial staff typically include:

    a. Text of statutes on the topic, with significant legislative history.

    b. Text of relevant administrative regulations.

    c. Full texts, or digests, of court cases or agency decisions on the subject. Some services also provide permanent bound volumes for cases and agency decisions.

    d. Multiple indexes to subjects.

    e. Tables of cases, statutes, and regulations.

    f. Some services cover state law, with comparative analysis.

8. Looseleaf services are available increasingly in electronic formats.

Chapter 15

SHEPARD'S CITATIONS, KEYCITE, AND OTHER CITATOR SERVICES

Citators are sources, available in print, CD–ROM, online, and Internet format, that provide, through letter-form abbreviations, words, or symbols, the prior and subsequent history and interpretation of reported cases, and lists of cases and legislative enactments construing, applying, or affecting statutes, as well as subsequent court cases unrelated to the litigation that have referred to the cited case. Citators also often provide references to a variety of secondary sources.

Some previous chapters were directed toward enabling one to locate court cases, statutory provisions, administrative documents, and secondary sources relevant to a particular point of law. In most instances, this research is a preliminary step toward a more concrete goal—preparation of a trial or appellate brief, an opinion letter, or an article. However, before relying on any primary authority that has been located as "good law," its current status must be determined.[1]

For example, a case must be checked to make certain that it has not been reversed by a higher court, overruled by a subsequent case of the same court, or so eroded by criticism by the courts that its merit is questionable. Statutes must be checked to determine whether they have been ruled unconstitutional, amended, or repealed. It might be necessary to examine law review articles, *A.L.R. Annotations*, and other secondary sources for relevant discussion. Citators enable you to perform some or all of these important functions.

The most widely-used citators for research in the United States and its territories are the many units of *Shepard's Citations*, which are available in various formats. Until 1997, almost no real competition existed in the citator market. At that time, the West Group launched its own case law citation research system, KeyCite, an online service available exclusively on WESTLAW. The result is two systems that are vying aggressively for customers.

---

[1] A judicial trend exists towards finding it inexcusable for failure to use readily available and conveniently accessible information in presenting legal arguments on behalf of one's client. *See, e.g.*, McNamara v. United States, 867 F. Supp. 369 (E.D. Va. 1994); Whirlpool Financial Corp. v. GN Holdings, Inc., 67 F.3d 605 (7th Cir. 1995). Updating and verifying the accuracy of the legal information used is the professional responsibility of a lawyer. DeMyrick v. Guest Quarters Suite Hotels, 1997 WL 177838 (N.D. Ill. Apr. 6, 1997) (" . . . [N]o counsel ought to cite a case . . . without Shepardizing that case (or without conducting the equivalent electronic search via Westlaw or Lexis).")

SECTION A. INTRODUCTION TO SHEPARD'S CITATIONS

Verification of the validity of authority is often accomplished by the use of *Shepard's Citations,* and the process used is typically referred to as "Shepardizing."[2] Also, secondary authority relevant to the point of law being researched can frequently be located through Shepardizing.

Shepard's Citations consist of many units, and are available in book, online, CD–ROM, and Internet formats. These publications can be thought of as either "jurisdictional," e.g., those covering a state or a grouping of states and those in the federal arena, or "topical," e.g., those covering a specialized type of materials, such as law reviews or Restatements, or those devoted to a particular subject, such as labor or tax law. The type of unit or units to use depends upon the citation you have to update. KeyCite, discussed *infra,* is limited to case law.

The distinguishing feature of the print version of *Shepard's Citations* is the combination of a unique citation style, e.g., 833 F. Supp. 1028 would be shortened to 833FS1028, and editorial letters employed by the publisher, e.g., q for *questioned.* For the uninitiated, looking at a page of *Shepard's Citations* can seem as daunting as one's initial exposure to a logarithm table, but in actuality the process of "Shepardizing" is relatively simple to master. In the electronic versions, symbols or words replace the letter-form abbreviations making the information more readily understandable.

SECTION B. SHEPARD'S CASE CITATORS

1. Understanding Shepard's Citations' Print Version References, Abbreviations, and Arrangement

Shepard's Citations for cases provide a means to analyze whether any reported case has been cited by a later case and, if so, whether the case can still be relied upon as authority. A case being checked for its subsequent history, current status, and use by other courts is referred to as the "cited" case. If a case has been cited in later cases and other sources, these cases and other sources are referred to as "citing" references. In addition to providing references to sources citing your case, the print *Shepard's Citations* also provides a letter-form abbreviation preceding a citing reference if that citing reference somehow affects the case being researched.

These letter codes relate either to the *history* or the *treatment* of the case. The *history* letter-form abbreviations pertain specifically to what

---

[2] The term "Shepardizing" is the trademark property of Shepard's and is used here with reference to its publications only and with its express consent. The term is derived from the company's founder Frank Shepard, who in 1873 began the process of listing each time a case was cited or affected by a later case.

How to Shepardize: Your Guide to Complete Legal Research Through Shepard's Citations is a complimentary pamphlet issued periodically by the publisher and is an excellent source for additional detail about the technique of Shepardizing and the various units of *Shepard's Citations.* A separate pamphlet, *Questions and Answers,* with practice exercises, as well as a software tutorial, are also available.

has happened to the case during the adjudication phase and generally involve the same parties, facts, and litigation. If, for example, a higher court has "affirmed" or "reversed" the case being Shepardized, the letter "a" or "r" precedes the citing reference.

The *treatment* letters, by contrast, relate to how courts in unrelated litigation have evaluated the cited case. The value of precedent for any given case depends to a large extent on the assessment of the case by other courts, and these assessments can be of vital importance in determining the present value of the cited case as authority. For example, one court may have "criticized" the wisdom of the cited case or "followed" its soundness or reasoning. These citing references will be preceded either by the letter "c" or "f." If no letter precedes a citing reference, it simply means the citing source has included a reference to the cited case but that neither its history nor treatment was affected.

There is no need to try to learn these abbreviations as they are defined in the prefatory materials of every book. The *Shepard's Citations* in CALR systems use expanded citation styles, including symbols and words, that make them readily understandable. Increasingly, legal researchers are using the online *Shepard's* in lieu of the print versions. While print *Shepard's* are still widely available and heavily used, especially in academic law libraries, law firms in particular often rely exclusively on the online or CD–ROM versions.

The arrangement of references in print versions of *Shepard's Citations* is straightforward. Case citations are arranged in numerical order, corresponding to the order of the citation in the reporter being Shepardized. These cited case references are listed by volume and page number in black letter (**bold**) type. Each cited reference is followed by "parallel" references to the same case in a different reporter, if such a parallel reference is available. Parallel references, if any, are enclosed in parentheses. Citing references follow immediately thereafter. [See Illustrations 15–3 and 15–4.] Once a parallel citation is included in a bound volume, it is not included in the supplementary pamphlets. Addition of parallel references to electronic versions is automatic. *If no reference to a reported case is in Shepard's Citations, it means there are no parallel references and no citing references.*

A separate set of *Shepard's Citations* is published for each set of court reports. Consequently, there are sets of *Shepard's Citations* for each of the fifty states, the District of Columbia, and Puerto Rico; separate sets for each of the regional reporters of the *National Reporter System;* one set for the *Federal Reporter* and the *Federal Supplement;* and one for the reports of the Supreme Court of the United States.

Based on the foregoing discussion, an example can illustrate some of the ways *Shepard's Citations* can facilitate one's case law research. Assume the problem under research pertains to warrantless searches. During the course of the research, a Wisconsin Supreme Court case, *State v. Griffin,* 131 Wis. 2d 41, 388 N.W.2d 535 (1986) is found and is on point. Before this case can be cited as authority, one must first determine if *Griffin* has been appealed to the Supreme Court of the United States and has either been affirmed or reversed. If it has been reversed, it is no longer controlling authority and must not be cited as if it were.

Another fact to ascertain is whether the Wisconsin Supreme Court in a subsequent case overruled its decision in the *Griffin* case (assuming it had not been reversed). If this case has been overruled, it can no longer be cited as authority.

These determinations, both as to history and treatment, are made by checking the print versions of *Shepard's Wisconsin Citations* [See Illustration 15–1] or *Shepard's Northwestern Reporter Citations* [See Illustration 15–2] or the electronic counterparts [See Illustrations 15–5 and 15–6]. Because these citators list every case subsequently decided in which the cited case was mentioned, it can be determined easily if the cited case has been affirmed, reversed, overruled, etc.

Since many court cases are reported in both official and unofficial sets of court reports, one has to determine which set of *Shepard's* to use in Shepardizing a case or, in the alternative, use one of the easier electronic versions. When using the print version and because the *Griffin* case was reported in both a set of state court reports and in a regional reporter, one must determine whether to Shepardize the case in the appropriate state or regional reporter unit of *Shepard's Citations.* Each bound volume and pamphlet supplement contains a cover page that lists the sources covered by that citator. Which citator unit to select is discussed *infra.*

2. Shepard's Citations for the States and Territories

These are used in connection with state reports and are available for each of the fifty states, the District of Columbia, and Puerto Rico. They are available in print and online versions, and as CD–ROM and Internet products.

Because most reported cases cover more than one point of law, the print *Shepard's,* through the use of superscript figures, keys each citing case to the headnotes of the cited case. For example, the case of *State v. Griffin,* as published in the *Wisconsin Reports 2d,* has ten headnotes, each on a different point of law. A citing case may, for example, cite *Griffin* only for the point of law in its fourth or sixth headnotes. Therefore, *Shepard's* adds the superscript *4* or *6,* as appropriate, to the citing case. By this means, one can find in *Shepard's Wisconsin Citations* all subsequent cases that have cited *Griffin* for these points of law. [See Illustration 15–3.]

The state *Shepard's* units give citing cases only from courts within the jurisdiction or cases that originated in the federal court within the state. A state *Shepard's* also gives citations to any legal periodical in the state (plus 20 national legal journals) that cite the cited case, as well as citations to Attorney General opinions of the states in question that cite the cited case.

Shepard's follows a consistent order of arrangement of citations in the print versions of state cases. This order is listed in the prefatory material for each *Shepard's* unit.

State *Shepard's* also have a section or a separate volume arranged by the regional reporter citation. By this means, when only a state unit *Shepard's* is available, the case can be still Shepardized under both the state and regional reporter citation. In both instances, citing cases are given only for the courts within the state.

Separate companion volumes, *State Case Name Citators,* provide both plaintiff-defendant and defendant-plaintiff listings for each case decided by courts within the state being covered.

3.   Shepard's Citations for the Regional Reporters

In the example of *State v. Griffin,* this case also could be Shepardized in *Shepard's Northwestern Reporter Citations* under 388 N.W.2d 535. In such instances, that reporter volume has to be examined to determine which headnote or headnotes are of interest. In the *North Western Reporter 2d,* the *Griffin* case is given four headnotes [See Illustration 15–2], and each can be followed in the same manner as described *supra.* In our example, if the *Shepard's Wisconsin Citations* is used, all citing cases are to cases in the *Wisconsin Reports* as well as to federal cases in the jurisdictions covering Wisconsin.

By contrast, in the *Shepard's Northwestern Reporter Citations,* all citations to the same cases are to the *North Western Reporter* as well as to federal cases in the jurisdictions covering Wisconsin. [See Illustration 15–4.] The regional *Shepard's,* unlike the state *Shepard's,* also give citations to any case throughout the *National Reporter System.* Thus, if a Massachusetts case cited *State v. Griffin,* this citing reference can be found in *Shepard's Northwestern Reporter Citations.* The order of citing references is generally the same as described for state citators.

4.   Shepard's Citations for Federal Cases

a.   *Shepard's United States Citations.* This voluminous unit is divided into four separate parts:

(1) *Cases.* The cases volumes consist of main volumes and bound and pamphlet supplements that contain citations to the *U.S. Reports,* the *U.S. Supreme Court Reports, Lawyers' Edition,* and *West's Supreme Court Reporter.* When a state court cites a Supreme Court of the United States case, it is listed only under the *U.S. Reports* citation if the state case was reported prior to the summer of 1986. For state cases reported after that time, the citations are listed under all three reporters. *Slip opinions* are listed by docket number.

Where there is no single majority opinion in a case, citing cases are listed separately under the name of the justice whose opinion is being cited and only in the *U.S. Reports* section. (Citations to the syllabus of the case are listed under the heading of "First.") In the *Lawyers' Edition* and *West's Supreme Court Reporter* sections, citations to all parts of these fragmented cases are listed together.

(2) *Constitutions, Statutes, Treaties, and Court Rules.* These volumes include all cases citing the U.S. Constitution, the *United States Code,* the *U.S. Treaty Series,* and the court rules of the Supreme Court of the United States. This unit is discussed in Section E, *infra.*

(3) *Administrative.* These volumes show citations to the decisions and orders of selected federal administrative agencies, courts, boards, and commissions.

(4) *Patents and Trademarks.* These volumes of *Shepard's United States Citations* are a compilation of citations to U.S. patents, trademarks, and copyrights.

The patents section lists each patent by number and lists all citations to a patent by a court or administrative agency; the copyright section lists titles of copyrighted works and lists citations to all court cases and administrative decisions involving each title; and the trademark section lists all trademarks alphabetically and lists all citations to court cases and administrative decisions involving the trademark. A separate section contains all citations to cases published in the *United States Patent Quarterly* and *Decisions of the Commissioner of Patents.*

b. *Shepard's United States Supreme Court Case Name Citator.* This is a companion set to *Shepard's United States Citations* and is to be used in conjunction with it. It lists alphabetically both the plaintiff's and defendant's names with date of decision for all Supreme Court of the United States cases since 1900.

c. *Shepard's Federal Citations.* This multi-volume unit is divided into two separate parts:

(1) Citations to cases reported in *Federal Cases* and *Federal Reporter* (F., F.2d, F.3d).

(2) Citations to cases in *Federal Supplement, Federal Rules Decisions, Court of Claims Reports,* and *Claims Court Reporter* (now *Federal Claims Reporter*).

d. *Federal Case Names Citators.* This is a companion set to *Shepard's Federal Citations.* A separate volume or volumes is published for each of the federal circuits. Names can be checked by either plaintiff or defendant for references in the *Federal Reporter 2d* and *3d, Federal Supplement, Federal Rules Decisions,* and *Bankruptcy Reporter.*

e. *Federal Circuit Table.* This publication identifies the circuit or district of any reference shown in any edition of *Shepard's Citations* in terms of volume and page of the *Federal Reporter, Federal Supplement, Federal Rules Decisions,* and *Bankruptcy Reporter.* Each table lists for any page in such volumes the circuit or district in which that page originates.

5. Shepard's Case Citations in Electronic Format

a. *In General.* Almost all units of *Shepard's Citations* are available in the CALR services, LEXIS–NEXIS and WESTLAW. Coverage is comprehensive for cases. The screen displays from the two vendors differ, but both customized displays consolidate the references from several citators and their supplements into an integrated whole. Shepard's and LEXIS–NEXIS have formed an exclusive partnership. Daily updates to the online and Internet versions via LEXIS–NEXIS makes Shepard's in this CALR service current within six to 24 hours. While one needs to take extra steps to Shepardize parallel citations in the print and CD–ROM versions, the process is seamless when using the online and Internet versions and represents an important time-saving development. In contrast with LEXIS–NEXIS access, the Shepard's on WESTLAW is only as current as the latest print and CD–ROM versions, meaning that coverage is approximately 30 days behind that provided through LEXIS–NEXIS. One must subscribe to a Daily Update service for the most recent information.

The electronic versions of Shepard's employ several useful features impossible in print versions. In addition to being able to locate references to parallel citations [See Illustration 15–5, Figure 1], restrictions can be placed on a search, such as by circuit or by dissenting opinion. [See Illustration 15–5, Figure 2 and Illustration 15–6, Figure 1.] Shepard's on CD–ROM uses the Signal feature. Through three simple traffic-light "signals", Proceed (green), Caution (yellow), and Warning (red), users can quickly focus on cases that support or undermine their position. One can then Target negative references to find out why a case received a yellow or red signal, or check a green signal to show positive treatment. Do not rely solely on a green symbol in deciding if a case is good law. Instead, click on Underpinnings to check on the precedential value of the case. [See Illustration 15–6, Figure 1.] Shepard's on LEXIS–NEXIS also has the Signal feature, but uses words rather than graphics. The most recent cases are always listed first in the electronic versions. Headnotes can also be Shepardized, much in the same way as with the print versions. [See Illustration 15–6, Figure 2.]

b. *Shepard's PreView.* Shepard's PreView, available exclusively on WESTLAW, contains current citations to cases appearing in the advance sheets of the *National Reporter System.* It allows one to update citations located through the typical online search or through use of the print version. The citing references do not, however, contain history or treatment codes or headnote numbers. When Shepard's completes its analysis of a case, these citing references are incorporated into the online and print versions and the reference to that case in PreView is removed. Shepard's PreView can be updated by use of the Quick*Cite* feature *infra.*

SECTION C. OTHER USES FOR SHEPARD'S CITATIONS—CASES

In addition to the traditional Shepardizing methods discussed *supra,* *Shepard's Citations* have several other important uses common to all versions of these publications:[3]

1. Citations to Articles in Legal Periodicals

The state units of *Shepard's Citations,* in addition to indicating every time a case has been cited, also indicate when the cited case has been mentioned in a legal periodical published within the state or in twenty national legal periodicals.[4]

2. A.L.R. Annotations

When Shepardizing a case citation, the various *Shepard's* units indicate when the case has been cited in an *A.L.R. Annotation,* or when the case has been used as the subject of an *A.L.R. Annotation.* A separate publication, *Shepard's Citations for Annotations,* discussed in Chapter 7–B–4, lists annotations as both citing and cited references.

3. Using Shepard's Citations to Find Parallel Citations

In Chapter 5, it was pointed out how, given a state report citation, the *National Reporter System* regional citations can be found by using the *National Reporter Blue Book. Shepard's Citations* also can be used for this purpose, and in addition, to find the state citation from the regional citation. An entry in *Shepard's* always includes the parallel citation as the first citation under the page number the first time the case is listed.[5] [See Illustrations 15–3, 15–4, and 15–5, Figure 1.] When a case has been reported in one of the *A.L.R.* series, that is also listed.

4. Using Shepard's Citations as Research Aids

Although *Shepard's Citations* are essential research aids, they should not be used to substitute for reading the case intself.

The editors' use of the letter-form abbreviations or symbols to indicate the treatment of cases is intelligently conservative. The essence of a citing case may go beyond its expressed language. The outcome of a case is not identified by the abbreviations unless its expression is clearly stated in the opinion. Therefore, a case that implicitly overrules a cited case will not be marked with the symbol *o* for *overruled.* This can be

---

[3] For a useful article discussing some of the ways *Shepard's* can be utilized, see Adolph J. Levy, *16 More Ways to Use Shepard's Citations,* TRIAL, Feb. 1992, at 69.

[4] These are: *ABA Journal; California Law Review; Columbia Law Review; Cornell Law Review; Georgetown Law Journal; Harvard Law Review; Law and Contemporary Problems; Michigan Law Review; Minnesota Law Review; New York University Law Review; Northwestern University Law Review; Stanford Law Review; Texas Law Review; UCLA Law Review; University of Chicago Law Review; University of Illinois Law Review; University of Pennsylvania Law Review; Virginia Law Review; Wisconsin Law Review;* and *Yale Law Journal.*

[5] Because cases are frequently reported earlier in the units of the *National Reporter System* than in the official reports, the parallel state citation often is not available at the time a citation first appears in a regional *Shepard's.* When a parallel citation is not the first citation under the page number, check the subsequent volumes and pamphlets of the *Shepard's Citations* unit being used. If a parallel citation still does not appear, it is likely that the state citation is from a state that has discontinued its official state reports.

determined only by a careful reading of the case. In other words, although *Shepard's Citations* immeasurably facilitate research, there are no substitutes for reading and "squeezing the juices" from cases.

In addition, cases dealing with the same subject matter, which do not cite each other, are not covered by *Shepard's Citations*. On the other hand, since *Shepard's* are not selective, the citing cases may be so numerous as to create a formidable research problem. A further limitation is that *Shepard's Citations* perpetuate the inaccuracies created by judges who inappropriately cite cases. These, however, are minor defects that the general utility, comprehensiveness, and accuracy of the citators effectively overbalance.

SECTION D.   ILLUSTRATIONS: SHEPARD'S CITATIONS—CASES

Sheperdizing State v. Griffin

[Illustration 15–1]

SECOND PAGE FROM STATE v. GRIFFIN IN WISCONSIN REPORTS 2d

OFFICIAL WISCONSIN REPORTS

State v. Griffin, 131 Wis. 2d 41

---

of firearm by convicted felon and where prosecution did not rely on any recognized exception to justify such warrantless search, but rather, relied on accused's probationary status, court could conclude that, if there was to be such exception to search warrant requirement, its foundation was to be found in nature of probation since neither Wisconsin nor United States Supreme Court has declared such exception.

4. **Constitutional Law § 121*—rights of probationers—role of probation officer.**
    Supreme Court has recognized limits on liberty and privacy interests of probationers based on nature of probation and application of less stringent standard for probation agent's search and seizure coincides with agent's dual role of assisting in rehabilitating probationer and protecting public.

5. **Searches and Seizures § 29*—warrantless search of probationer's residence by probation officer—possibility of police abuse.**
    Probationer's argument on appeal that supreme court should

---

This is the second page of *State v. Griffin*. The Wisconsin Supreme Court has provided a total of ten headnotes for this case in its official *Wisconsin Reports 2d.*

Shepard's Wisconsin Citations—Cases are keyed to these headnotes and will show the treatment of a cited case by a citing case through reference to the headnotes.

---

reasonable search could not be deemed unlawful simply because police were source of information which led to search.

6. **Searches and Seizures § 29*—warrantless search of probationer's residence by probation officer—rights of innocent third persons.**
    In considering propriety of warrantless search of probationer's residence by probation officer, court was unpersuaded by probationer's argument that warrant was necessary to protect rights of innocent third persons who may be living with probationer where court, in creating exception to search warrant requirement which allows probation officers to conduct warrantless search of residences of probationers, court was not

---

*See Callaghan's Wisconsin Digest, same topic and section number.

42

[Illustration 15–2]

FIRST PAGE FROM STATE v. GRIFFIN IN NORTH WESTERN REPORTER 2d

STATE v. GRIFFIN   Wis. **535**

Cite as 388 N.W.2d 535 (Wis. 1986)

131 Wis.2d 41
STATE of Wisconsin,
Plaintiff-Respondent,

v.

Joseph G. GRIFFIN,
Defendant-Appellant-Petitioner.

No. 84–021–CR.

Supreme Court of Wisconsin.

Argued June 4, 1986.

Opinion Filed June 20, 1986.

Defendant was convicted in the Circuit Court, Rock County, J. Richard Long, J., of

> First page of *State v. Griffin* as published in the unofficial *North Western Reporter 2d*. Note that the West editors have prepared four headnotes for this case and that these headnotes differ from those in *Wisconsin Reports 2d*.
>
> *Shepard's Northwestern Reporter Citations* are keyed to these headnotes.

Shirley S. Abrahamson, J., filed dissenting opinion.

Bablitch, J., filed dissenting opinion.

1. Criminal Law �köm982.8

Probation agent who reasonably believes that a probationer is violating the terms of probation may conduct a warrantless search of probationer's residence, and evidence obtained in search may be used at a trial seeking new conviction of the probationer if the search is otherwise reasonable. U.S.C.A. Const.Amends. 4, 14.

2. Criminal Law ⊖982.8

Warrantless search of probationer's residence could be made by probation officer based on "reasonable grounds" to believe that probationer had contraband at

1. Section 941.29(1) and (2), Stats., provides in part:

his residence, where probation officer was informed by police detective that there might be guns in probationer's apartment. U.S.C.A. Const.Amends. 4, 14.

3. Criminal Law ⊖982.8

Reasonable grounds standard contained in administrative code, which was less than probable cause standard needed to obtain warrant, was sufficient for searches and seizures conducted by probation officers of a probationer's residence. U.S.C.A. Const.Amends. 4, 14; W.S.A. 941.-29(2).

4. Criminal Law ⊖982.8

Probation officer had reasonable grounds to make warrantless search of probationer's residence on tip from police detective that there might be guns in probationer's apartment, where search was not a police search, purpose of police officers in going to probationer's residence was for protection of probation officers, and gun was discovered in drawer which was apparently broken in such a way as to allow gun to be seen in unopened drawer. U.S.C.A. Const.Amends. 4, 14; W.S.A. 941.29(2).

Alan G. Habermehl, Madison, argued, for defendant-appellant-petitioner; Kalal & Habermehl, Madison, on brief.

Barry M. Levenson, Asst. Atty. Gen., argued, for plaintiff-respondent; Bronson C. La Follette, Atty. Gen., on brief.

DAY, Justice.

This is a review of a published decision of the court of appeals, *State v. Griffin*, 126 Wis.2d 183, 376 N.W.2d 62 (Ct.App. 1985), affirming the judgment of the circuit court for Rock county, Honorable J. Richard Long, circuit judge, convicting Joseph G. Griffin, (Defendant) of possession of a firearm by a convicted felon contrary to Section 941.29(2), Stats.[1] Defendant was

"941.29 Possession of a firearm. (1) A person is subject to the requirements and penalties of this section if he or she has been: "(a) Convicted of a felony in this state....

[Illustration 15–3]

PAGE FROM SHEPARD'S WISCONSIN CITATIONS: CASE EDITION

WISCONSIN REPORTS, 2d SERIES

Vol. 129

—277— (385NW161) US cert den in107SC148 129Wis2d230 d137Wis2d⁷55	—491— (385NW234)	—230— (387NW98)	—499— (388NW160)	134Wis2d⁵ [361 f135Wis2d⁴ [408 f135Wis2d⁶ [408 135Wis2d498	—416— (388NW652)	—25— (390NW74)	—251— (392NW449)
	—496— (385NW171)	—247— (387NW106) cc122Wis2d [673	—523— (388NW170) s133Wis2d33		—422— (388NW624)	—29— (390NW575)	—262— (392NW97)
—301— (385NW196)	**Vol. 130**	137Wis2d⁴ [208	**Vol. 131**		—435— (389NW49) Cir. 7 819F2d¹822	—62— (390NW79) d133Wis2d [368	—266— (392NW453) cc83Wis2d239
—308— (384NW712)	—1— (385NW509)	—276— (386NW519)	—1— (388NW176)	—189— (388NW553)			—289— (392NW98)
—310— (384NW709)	—4— (386NW53) s125Wis2d224 135Wis2d369 137Wis2d² [231	—285— (387NW118) 132Wis2c ①	—21— (388NW584) s125Wis2d418 f131Wis2d¹⁰ [148	—220— (388NW601) s113Wis2d497 s125Wis2d111 f131Wis2d⁹ [148	—446— (388NW927)	—68— (389NW823) 135Wis2d¹ [226 136Wis2d⁵15 d137Wis2d⁵ [250	—304— (392NW461)
—319— (385NW510)		—291— (387 ① 121) ②			—451— (389NW366)		—310— (392NW104)
—331— (385NW200)	—18— (386NW47) s125Wis2d272	—300— (387NW124)	—41— (388NW535) a107SC3164 a55USLW [5156	134Wis2d⁹ [410 e136Wis2d¹⁰ [480	—459— (389NW359) —477— (389NW54)	j137Wis2d263 —74— (390NW76) 136Wis2d⁸22	—318— (392NW108)
—348— (384NW713) L135Wis2d⁴ [232	—29— (386NW51)	—308— (387NW751) s128 ③ [531	s126Wis2d183 s93LE699 s93LE977 s107SC643 s107SC926 f135Wis2d⁶ [409	—246— (389NW12) cc131Wis2d69 cc131Wis2d [133	—492— (389NW59) —507— (388NW660) 137Wis2d³ [206	137Wis2d⁶ [209 —82— (390NW86) —145— (389NW825)	—335— (392NW469) 133Wis2d² [159
—357— (384NW717)	—34— (387NW55) s83Wis2d601 131Wis2d [242	—313— (387NW128) r136Wis2d37		133Wis2d³ [311			—340— (392NW115)
—362— (384NW719)	134Wis2d² [251	—327— (387NW291)	137Wis2d¹ [183	133Wis2d² [313 e133Wis2d⁹ [314	—515— (389NW73)	—153— (390NW81)	—351— (392NW464)
—373— (385NW514)	—56— (387NW245)	—335— (387NW295)	—69— (389NW1) US cert den in107SC584	137Wis2d¹⁴ [168 Cir. 7	—525— (389NW67)	—164— (389NW828)	—364— (392NW119)
—377— (385NW208)	cc130Wis2d79						—373— (392NW123)

> This Illustration is from a bound Cases volume of *Shepard's Wisconsin Citations*.
>
> 1. Note under 131 Wis.2d 41 (*State v. Griffin*) how the first citation in parentheses, i.e., 388 N.W.2d 535, is to the cited case in another set of court reports. This is a parallel citation for the same case in a different reporter.
>
> 2. Note also that *State v. Griffin* has been affirmed by the Supreme Court of the United States. This case can therefore be cited as good authority.
>
> 3. Assume you are especially interested in knowing if other Wisconsin courts have followed the point of law covered in headnotes 4 and 6. Note that headnote 6 was followed in the case reported in 135 Wis. 2d. The reference to page 409 is a "pinpoint" cite directly to the page on which the reference to headnote 6 appears.
>
> To check for later cases for headnote 6 and to determine if courts have followed the point of law in headnote 4, consult all supplemental pamphlets.

65BRW⁶442 65BRW⁷443	[275 134Wis2d38	(387NW751) j134Wis2d44	—147— (388NW612)	—405— (388NW641)	—18— (390NW572) 135Wis2d² [191	(392NW439)
—478— (386NW59)	—212— (386NW512) r134Wis2d260	j134Wis2d55 61NYL1076	—153— (388NW565) US cert den in107SC583 e134Wis2d¹ [124			—243— (392NW445) Cir. 7 71BRW⁵279

[Illustration 15–4]

PAGE FROM SHEPARD'S NORTHWESTERN REPORTER CITATIONS

NORTHWESTERN REPORTER, 2d SERIES

Vol. 388

> *State v. Griffin* can also be Shepardized in *Shepard's Northwestern Reporter Citations* under its unofficial citation.
>
> 1. Note that the parallel citation is given to the official reports. Note also how citations to all citing cases are to the *North Western Reporter 2d* and other West reporters.
>
> 2. The regional *Shepard's* not only give citations to citing cases within the state of the cited case, but also provide citations from any other states that cite the cited case. In this Illustration, a Massachusetts court has cited *State v. Griffin*.

—257—	**—296—**	416NW562	89Æ7s	**—454—**	64Æ806n	**—525—**	418NW⁴12
(150McA91)	(150McA40)			(222Neb878)	64Æ871n	393NW457	423NW825
404NW677	405NW143	**—336—**	**—385—**		65Æ894n	394NW⁷717	d423NW¹¹
	413NW467	(150McA276)	394NW⁴211	**—458—**	65Æ911n	e394NW721	[825
—259—	417NW¹601	lv app den	394NW²211	(223Neb92)	66Æ430n	j394NW725	d423NW¹826
(150McA97)	428NW327	in428Mch860	430NW⁴230	s382NW576	66Æ436n	403NW⁷423	423NW¹829

(main citation table — multiple columns)

446NW³530	402NW¹95	(150McA294)	410NW⁴413	421NW764	s334NW807	**—535—**	①
31Æ1375s	403NW¹102	lv app den	412NW¹46	424NW¹131	399NW¹796	(131Wis2d41)	(131Wis2d
12Æ1062s	406NW¹225	in426Mch881	d413NW⁸828	424NW⁴131	419NW⁴540	a97LE709	[322)
	408NW¹430	418NW¹⁸719	424NW⁸583	424NW⁴132	e422NW²795	a55USLW	[5156
—274—	413NW¹98	432NW⁸376	438NW⁴677	6Æ1008s	429NW¹729	[5156	s373NW85
(150McA128)	418NW¹417	432NW⁸376	446NW193		431NW²639	s376NW62	432NW²616
lv app den	419NW¹460	f438NW⁴627	89Æ7s	**—477—**	s93LE699	s93LE699	433NW¹3
in425Mch864	421NW¹558	f823F2d⁴992	100Æ1129s	(223Neb139)	444NW⁸326	s93LE977	
395NW¹291	427NW¹581	PLPD§ 4.19		413NW¹301	444NW⁸326	f400NW⁴485	**—584—**
411NW851	428NW¹733	76Æ9s	**—417—**	428NW³507	Tex	404NW74	(131Wis2d21)
446NW300	437NW¹644		412NW791		774SW707	f410NW⁴620	s373NW65
446NW¹486		**—349—**	416NW188	**—479—**		f410NW⁴620	s394NW313
	—306—	(150McA306)		(223Neb142)	**—515—**	444NW435	e859F2d505
—276—	(150McA65)	lv app den	**—421—**	s430NW273	(223L︎⃝ ²92)		859F2d⁴505
(150McA194)		in425Mch882	392NW³346	393NW⁴440	394N ② ⃝	▸ Mass	859F2d⁴506
r414NW706	**—312—**	416NW418	415NW³701	416NW⁸7	402N\ ³	525NE382	647FS902
s364NW284	(150McA78)	436NW⁸727	415NW⁴701	416NW⁸7	416NW510		15COA723§ 7
	s347NW770	10MeLR253	d420NW³244	416NW¹8		**—546—**	SCT§ 5.44
—281—	s377NW703	9PST695§ 39		416NW⁴512	**—516—**	(131Wis2d84)	84Æ322s
(150McA205)	400NW¹⁴716	54Æ273s	**—425—**	434NW⁴308	Case 1	s378NW294	
404NW²728		85Æ889s	392NW²723	442NW⁴863	(223Neb261)	f388NW¹914	**—593—**
Mo	**—315—**		392NW³724	d445NW296		f388NW²915	(131Wis2d
740SW200	(150McA230)	**—355—**	408NW⁸214	d445NW¹296	**—518—**	f427NW133	[101)
	v414NW886	(150McA351)		447NW⁸233	Case 2	433NW²297	s373NW450
—284—	s414NW886	v393NW176	**—429—**		(223Neb273)	433NW³297	407NW318
(149McA394)	s425NW711		s413NW189	**—483—**	388NW¹819	434NW859	f430NW⁴598
v395NW239	391NW³379	**—358—**		(223Neb150)	398NW⁴726	Minn	436NW920
s296NW147	403NW⁷175	(150McA358)	**—432—**	cc246NW594	402NW⁸877	444NW⁴265	f440NW⁴350
s332NW149	405NW⁸118	419NW599	88BRW²963	cc250NW867	423NW³491	444NW³268	
s406NW232	405NW¹⁸393	425NW131		cc303NW490	429NW³369	MFLA§ 4.06	**—601—**
	408NW⁸519	425NW²132	**—434—**	390NW²³532	EDP§ 8.06	12PST475§	(131Wis2d
—287—	408NW¹⁰519		f399NW¹208	391NW²⁸570	56Æ104n	[26	[220)
(150McA212)	411NW⁷821	**—369—**	d401NW¹437	391NW²573	56Æ879n		s335NW376
lv app den	413NW³442	96Æ823s		391NW⁸574	41Æ481s	**—553—**	s370NW827
in426Mch852	413NW³499		**—438—**	394NW⁸641		(131Wis2d	f388NW⁴613
403NW³127	413NW⁴499	**—370—**	(222Neb806)	395NW¹566	**—522—**	[189)	388NW¹⁰615
	431NW⁸64	s364NW900	422NW²549	398NW⁴704	406NW⁸673	s376NW868	397NW⁴150
—291—	q431NW⁸469	403NW²680	74Æ854s	399NW²⁷263	413NW¹307	S D	402NW⁷735
(150McA29)	437NW¹⁸375			399NW⁸264	419NW²168	cc319NW177	e402NW⁴736
401NW¹375	93Æ287s	**—373—**	**—446—**	404NW¹437	419NW²173	413NW643	436NW⁴913
401NW⁴375	64Æ590n	390NW¹829	(222Neb850)	404NW²437	j429NW15	87Æ393s	439NW137
439NW¹271		j390NW833	418NW246	408NW²⁷317	429NW¹447		
444NW²198	**—326—**	414NW²536	419NW⁷156	430NW¹⁰288	432NW874	**—565—**	**—612—**
Pa	(150McA254)	430NW²260	419NW⁸666	442NW¹³200	432NW874	(131Wis2d	(131Wis2d
542A2d165	s418NW94		434NW²340	444NW649	435NW¹702	[153)	[147)
	f408NW¹150	**—376—**	436NW⁸510		436NW¹239	e396NW¹¹162	
—294—	429NW³228	401NW⁸111	442NW¹214	665FS776	437NW¹521	397NW⁸669	**—615—**
(150McA35)	661FS¹310	409NW⁸530	W Va	665FS790	441NW³671	f400NW⁷485	(131Wis2d
58Æ1027s	661FS¹313	Wis	375SE411	Utah	Mich	f400NW⁸485	[301)
	q696FS¹526	j424NW202	31Æ1078s	765P2d898	442NW¹417	401NW180	
	f696FS535	19COA143§	39Æ550s	39Æ550s		406NW⁴403	
	Nebr	[17	43Æ699s	63Æ527n		407NW312	
				64Æ801n		418NW¹12	*Continued*

[Illustration 15–5]

SCREEN PRINTS FROM SHEPARD'S ON LEXIS–NEXIS SHOWING RESTRICTION FEATURES

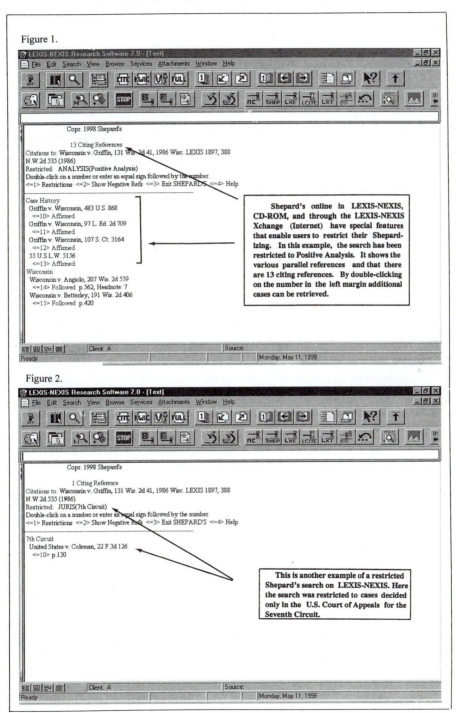

Figure 1.

Figure 2.

[Illustration 15–6]

SCREEN PRINTS FROM SHEPARD'S ON CD–ROM AND LEXIS–NEXIS XCHANGE (INTERNET)SHOWING SIGNAL, UNDERPINNINGS, AND HEADNOTE FEATURES

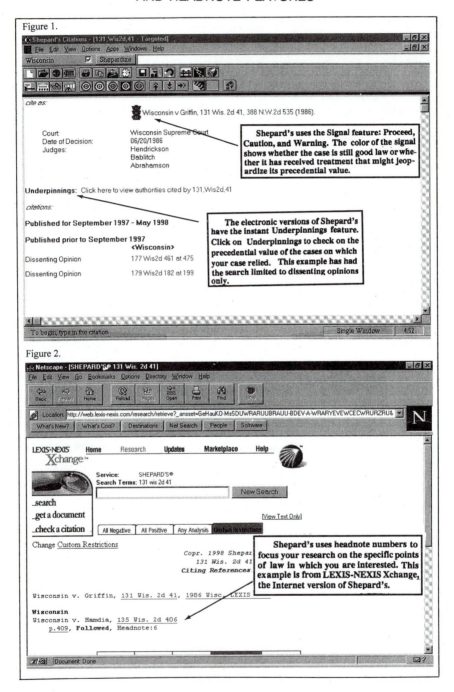

SECTION E. SHEPARD'S STATUTE CITATORS

Statute Editions or Statute sections within multiple units of *Shepard's Citations* cover the various types of legislative enactments and court cases relating to this legislation. *It is important to note that if no reference is given for a particular statutory provision, it means that the provision has not been cited by a court or affected by subsequent legislation.*

1. Statutes

Statutes, both state and federal, are treated by *Shepard's Citations* in a manner similar to cases. The notations cover the form and operation of the law by the legislature and the courts. Its operation is identified by abbreviations (or words or symbols in the electronic versions) denoting legislative changes (amendments, repeals, revisions, reenactments, etc.) and judicial interpretations (constitutional, unconstitutional, invalid, etc.). There are statute citators for the United States and for each state, the District of Columbia, and Puerto Rico. These citators are being added to WESTLAW but, unlike case citators, coverage is by no means complete.

The several volumes in the *Statutes Edition* of *Shepard's United States Citations* provide citations to subsequent legislation and federal court cases for provisions in the U.S. Constitution, all editions of the *United States Code* and the two annotated editions, Tariff Schedules, *U.S. Statutes at Large* (not in the *U.S. Code*), *U.S. Treaties and Other International Agreements,* General Orders in Bankruptcy, and the various federal court rules. A brief examination of the set will reveal its specific arrangement. [See Illustration 15–7 for how to Shepardize the current *U.S. Code* using the print version.] Like the electronic versions for cases, Shepardizing a statute allows one to use a variety of special features. For example, a search can be unlimited, or restricted (customized) to show such things as a statute's legislative history, its constitutionality, or whether other courts have followed it. [See Illustration 15–8, Figures 1 and 2 and Illustration 15–9.] It is worth noting that the *U.S. Statutes at Large* section enables a researcher to locate cases citing statutes no longer in effect or that were never published in the *U.S. Code.*

The format used for publication of state statutes varies, depending on the plan adopted by a jurisdiction. For example, one state may arrange statutes by Title and Section numbers; another by Chapter and Paragraph numbers. The Table of Abbreviations in each state unit of *Shepard's Citations* should be examined specifically to determine the local scheme. In some state *Shepard's* units, especially the supplemental pamphlets, cases and statutes are in separate sections in the same volume; for others, a separate *Statute Edition* may be provided.

The information contained in the state statutes units is presented according to this arrangement: statutory amendments, repeals, etc., are listed first, followed by state and federal court citations and citations in the attorneys general opinions, legal periodicals, and acts of the legislature. [See Illustration 15–10.] There are electronic versions of the state statutory Shepard's which can be searched in a manner similar to Shepardizing federal statutes.

In addition to the statutory coverage provided in the state statute citators, these units cover additional sources, which are described in the remainder of this section.

2. Constitutions

Citations to federal and state constitutions are included in the state *Statute Editions* or Statute sections of *Shepard's Citations*. A Constitution section within the *Statute Editions* or Statute sections is arranged under the articles and amendments to the constitution. Citing sources, from both state and federal courts, are listed under these provisions. [See Illustration 15–11.]

3. Court Rules

Citations to court cases interpreting court rules also are covered by the *Statute Editions* for *Shepard's Citations*. The *Court Rules* section is arranged by court (final, intermediate, and original jurisdiction), and is subdivided by rule number. A separate set, *Federal Rules Citations,* includes citations to the various federal rules, the corresponding state rules of the 50 states and Puerto Rico, as well as every reported state and federal case involving procedural issues.

4. Jury Instructions

A separate section in the *Statute Editions* includes citing references to jury instructions from the particular jurisdiction. Jury instructions are discussed in Chapter 19.

5. City Charters and Ordinances

Municipal charters and ordinances are part of the *Statute Editions*. Reference should be made to the citator of the state in which a city is located for citations to its charter or ordinances.

The sections under *Municipal Charters* in the *Statute Editions* are arranged alphabetically by cities in many state editions and subdivided by topics. The units also have a separate "Index to Municipal Charters." The *Ordinances* section also may be arranged alphabetically by cities and subdivided by topics. It, too, has an "Index to Ordinances." In some citators, the citations to the ordinances of the larger cities are arranged separately. To meet editorial requirements, the citations to ordinances may be indexed by section numbers as well as by topic.

SECTION F.   ILLUSTRATIONS: SHEPARD'S CITATIONS—STATUTES

[Illustration 15–7]

PAGE FROM SHEPARD'S U.S. CITATIONS—STATUTE EDITION

UNITED STATES CODE '88 Ed.

T. 38 § 3404

§ 3404	§ 3504	§ 4010	§ 4063	¶ B	§§ 4105 to 4110	§ 4109	§ 4116
Rn§5904	Rn§6104	Rn§7110	Rn§7263	Cir. Fed.	Cir. 8	Rs105St210	Rs105St210
[105St238	[105St238	[105St238	[105St238	931F2d1544	930F2d1318		59USLW
Cir. 4				933F2d991		§ 4110	[4204
923F2d1086	§ 3505	§ 4051	§ 4064	Subd. 2		Rs105St210	Cir. 10
724FS1209	Rn§6105	Rn§7251	Rn§7264	Cir. Fed.	§ 4105	Cir. 6	906F2d1387
Cir. 9	[105St238	[105St238	[105St238	928F2d391	Rs105St210	760FS630	98 AR F554n
U 778FS1097	Subsec. c	Cir. Fed.		928F2d393	Cir. 2	Cir. 7	Subsec. a
Subsec. a	A105St287	928F2d391	§ 4065	949F2d395	904F2d2	892F2d655	Cir. 1
Cir. 4		928F2d393	Rn§7265		Cir. 6	Cir. 8	745FS26
724FS1213	§ 3511		[105St238	§§ 4096 to	760FS640	930F2d1321	Cir. 10
Subsec. b	Subsec. a	§ 4052		4098	Subsec. a	Cir. 9	906F2d1388
Cir. 4	A105St620	Rn§7252	§ 4066	Ad103St617	Cir. 2	③ 315	
724FS1213		[105St238	Rn§7266		904F2d2	ec. a	§ 4117
Subsec. c	§ 3680	§ 4097	[105St238		Subd. 1	Cir 7	Rs105St210
Cir. 4	Subsec. a	724FS1211	Cir. 4	Subsec. h	Cir 7	892F2d655	
923F2d1086	Subd. 3	Subsec. a	724FS1211	Subd. 1	892F2d654	Subsec. d	§ 4118
724FS1216	A105St622	A105St287	Subsec. b	¶ A		Cir. 7	Rs105St210
724FS1217		Cir. 4	Cir. Fed.	Cl. 1	§ 4106	892F2d658	
Subd. 1	§ 4001		928F2d390	A105St287	Rs105St210		§ 4119
Cir. 4							
724FS1214							
724FS1217							
Subd. 2							
Cir. 4							
724FS1213							
Cir. 9							
778FS1112							
Subsec. d							
Subd. 1							
Cir. 9							
778FS1112							

§ 3405
Rn§5905
[105St238
Cir. 4
923F2d1086
724FS1209
Cir. 9
U778FS1097
1 A 901n

> **Shepardizing *United States Code* Sections.**
>
> This unit gives citations to each case citing the *U.S. Code*. It also indicates when a code section has been repealed or amended, or held constitutional or unconstitutional.
>
> Notice the following:
>
> 1.   § 3405 was held unconstitutional by a federal district court.
>
> 2.   § 3501, Subsec. a was amended by 105 Statutes at Large 286 and was held constitutional by the U.S. Court of Appeals for the First Circuit.
>
> 3.   § 4118 was repealed and superseded by 105 Statutes at Large 210.

	933F2d989	Rn§7255	§ 4083	Subsec. b	§ 4107	Cir. 6	Rn§7331
§ 3501	Subsec. b	[105St238	Rn§7283	Cir. 6	Rs105St210	955F2d437	[105St221
Rn§6101	Subd. 1		[105St238	760FS628	ClCt	760FS629	
[105St238	Cir. Fed.	§ 4056		Subsec. c	23ClC589	Subd. 1	§ 4132
Cir. 1	933 ① 88	Rn§7256	§ 4084	Subd. 1	Cir. 6	Cir. 6	Rn§7332
955F2d101	S c. d	[105St238	Rn§7284	Cir. 6	A104St430	760FS631	[105St221
Subsec. a	Subd. 1		[105St238	760FS628	Subsec. e	¶ A	Cir. 1
A105St286	Cir. Fed.	§ 4061			Subd. 5	904F2d2	770FS63
Cir. 1	928 ② 90	Rn§7261	§ 4085	§ 4102	A104St437	Cir. 6	96 AR F812
C955F2d102		[105St238	Rn§7285	Rs105St210	ClCt	760FS628	
§ 3502	§ 4005A	Subsec. a	[105St238		23ClC589	930F2d1325	§ 4133
Rn§6102	Rn§7105A	Subd. 1		§ 4103	Subsec. g	Subd. 3	Rn§7333
[105St238	[105St238	Cir. Fed.	§ 4091	Rs105St210	A103St2067	¶ A	[105St221
Subsec. a		928F2d391	Rn§7291		Subd. 4	A104St439	§ 4134
A105St286	§ 4006	Subd. 2	[105St238	§ 4104	Subsec. i	Cir. 6	Rn§7334
Subsec. b	Rn§7106	A103St2095		Rs105St210	A103St2067	760FS626	[105St221
A105St286	[105St238	Subd. 3	§ 4092	Cir. 6		¶ C	
		Cir. Fed.	Rn§7292	955F2d437	§ 4108	Rs104St439	§ 4141
§ 3503	§ 4007	928F2d391	Subd. 4	[105St128	Rs105St210	¶ D	Ad104St431
Rn§6103	Rn§7107	Subd. 4	Cir. Fed.	760FS627	Cir. 6	Cir. 6	A & Rn§7451
[105St238	[105St238	Cir. Fed.	937F2d588	Cir. 8	760FS631	760FS631	[105St238
Subsec. a		928F2d391	Subsec. c	890F2d76	Cir. 8	Subsec. b	Subsec. a
Cir. Fed.	§ 4008	Subsec. c	A105St287	Subsec. 1	930F2d1317	Subd. 1	Subd. 3
944F2d869	Rn§7108	A105St287	Cir. Fed.	A104St430	Subsec. a	Cir. 2	A105St208
Subsec. b	[105St238		928F2d391	Cir. 6	Cir. 8	904F2d2	Subsec. d
A105St286		§ 4062	Subsec. d	760FS627	930F2d1318		A105St208
Subsec. e	§ 4009	Rn§7262	Subd. 1	Cir. 8	Subsec. e	§ 4115	§ 4142
Rs105St286	Rn§7109	[105St238	A103St628	890F2d76	Ad103St2067	Rs105St210	Ad104St431
	[105St238		Cir. Fed.			Cir. 6	
			928F2d393			760FS631	
			949F2d395				

Continued

542

[Illustration 15–8]

SCREEN PRINTS FROM SHEPARD'S ON LEXIS–NEXIS SHOWING AN UNRESTRICTED SEARCH AND ONE LIMITED TO NEGATIVE ANALYSIS

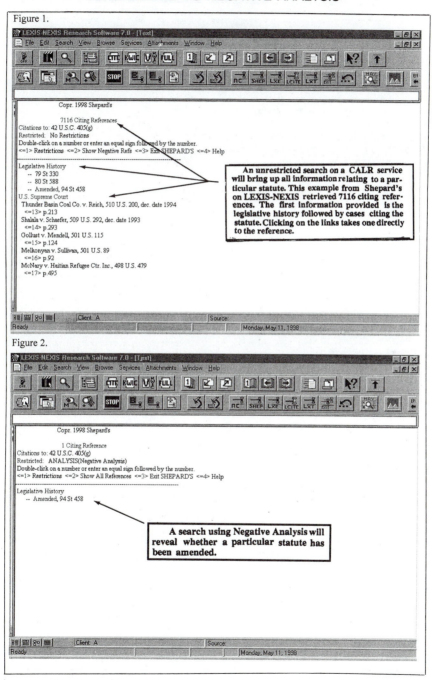

Figure 1.

An unrestricted search on a CALR service will bring up all information relating to a particular statute. This example from Shepard's on LEXIS-NEXIS retrieved 7116 citing references. The first information provided is the legislative history followed by cases citing the statute. Clicking on the links takes one directly to the reference.

Figure 2.

A search using Negative Analysis will reveal whether a particular statute has been amended.

[Illustration 15–9]

SCREEN PRINT FROM SHEPARD'S ON LEXIS–NEXIS XCHANGE (INTERNET) CUSTOMIZED TO SHOW CONSTITUTIONALITY

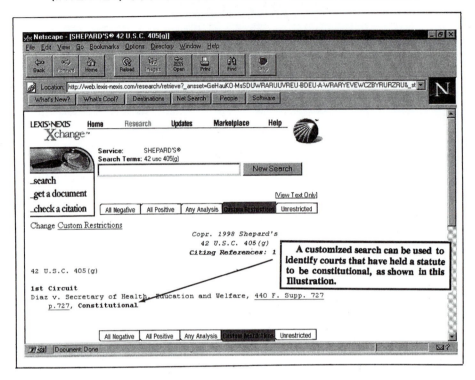

[Illustration 15–10]

PAGE FROM SHEPARD'S WISCONSIN CITATIONS—STATUTES EDITION

WISCONSIN STATUTES—WISCONSIN STATUTES ANNOTATED   1985-86 , 111.70

Sheparding a State Statute.

Notice the following:

1. Wisconsin Statutes § 111.50 was held constitutional by the Wisconsin Supreme Court, but held unconstitutional by the Supreme Court of the United States.

2. Wisconsin Statutes § 111.39, Subsec. 3m was added by the Wisconsin Acts of 1977.

53:

[Illustration 15–11]

PAGE FROM WISCONSIN CONSTITUTION IN SHEPARD'S WISCONSIN CITATIONS—STATUTES EDITION

WISCONSIN CONSTITUTION, 1848

Art. 4

197Wis164	307NW663	**§ 1r**	85NW857	264NW622	**§ 1m**	284NW44	177NW899
198Wis332	36WiAG205	1971p1336	138NW249	267NW433	1965p899	339NW327	184NW683
222Wis69	1950WLR207	**§ 2**	301NW183	277NW687	1967p489	401NW795	186NW729
229Wis151	**§ 34**	200Wis540	19WiAG605	288NW454	1967p493	19WiAG535	187NW830
235Wis530	1959p940	228Wis656	20WiAG1201	289NW662	Ad1967p516	19WiAG598	192NW374
242Wis369	1961p694	228NW903	21WiAG1089	10NW180	1977p2120	29WiAG178	262NW629
265Wis336	Ad1961p737	280NW393	25WiAG480	11NW604	1979p646	31WiAG141	7NW378
34Wis2d191		**§ 3**	27WiAG92	126NW557	RApr3 1979	36WiAG576	13NW580
44Wis2d227	**Art. 5**	1965p868	27WiAG623	182NW482	**§ 1n**	43WiAG226	21NW381
59Wis2d412	70Wis2d867	1967p490	1946WLR283	208NW784	1965p899	61WiAG10	26NW260
61Wis2d555	136Wis2d143	1967p492	1956WLR95	235NW649	1967p489	63WiAG130	49NW415
70Wis2d466	236NW16	A1967p519	1959WLR422	237NW910	1967p493	1970WLR300	60NW353
101Wis2d71	401NW793	200Wis554	**§ 7**	264NW539	Ad1967p516	1974WLR729	98NW394
104Wis2d74	98F350	254Wis 06	1971p1336	28WiAG423	1977p2120	**§ 4**	115NW619
112Wis2d40	600FS765	228 1	1977p2120	29WiAG179	1979p646	1929p1066	182NW460
81NW869	54WiAG15	37N 476	1979p646	30WiAG250	RApr3 1979	A1929p1119	238NW510
84NW246	68WiAG109	48WiAG188	AApr3 1979	41WiAG207	**§ 1p**	1939p1044	263NW219
87NW815	1946WLR283	54WiAG13	228Wis646	43WiAG353	1965p899	1943p1005	291NW618
93NW265	**§ 1**	**§ 4**	242Wis42	52WiAG423	1967p489	1943p1035	292NW822
98NW954	1965p887	148Wis527	280NW393	55WiAG161	1967p493	1945p1144	316NW659
112NW432	1977p2120	170Wis237	7NW375	55WiAG198	Ad1967p517	1947C183	401NW801
121NW889	1979p646	183Wis154	32WiAG206	59WiAG94	1977p2120	1953p599	405NW727
137NW21	AApr3 1979	217Wis540	48WiAG191	60WiAG205	1979p646	1955p817	70US94
140NW79	141Wis628	22Wis2d557	54WiAG14	60WiAG247	RApr3 1979	1957p320	18LE33
142NW502	183Wis154	59Wis2d412	66WiAG185	62WiAG238	1974WLR732	1957p892	752F2d292
147NW226	196Wis493	70Wis2d485	68WiAG109	63WiAG163	**§ 2**	1959p939	769F2d1163
177NW34	228Wis656	71Wis2d131	62MqL538	63WiAG313	1943p1029	1959p949	821F2d451
181NW121	242Wis42	82Wis2d719	1944WLR79	63WiAG346	1945p1157	1961p693	648FS870
187NW218	83Wis2d816	83Wis2d816	**§ 8**	64WiAG20	A1947p1316	1961p727	20WiAG112
201NW385	106Wis2d42	136Wis2d124	1977p2120	66WiAG311	138Wis174	1961p736	21WiAG757
206NW908	111Wis2d180	134NW697	1979p646	70WiAG156	141Wis151	1963p670	22WiAG708

> **Sheparizing a State Constitution.**
>
> Each state *Shepard's* has a part in its statute citators that includes a section on the state's constitution.
>
> Notice the following:
>
> 1. Article 5, § 5 was repealed in 1933.
>
> 2. Article 5, § 7 was amended on April 3, 1979.

235NW650	50WiAG62	47WiAG333	**§ 9**	130NW...	280NW701	131Wis500	45WiAG76
303NW629	54WiAG13	51WiAG4	1929p1085	130NW460	293NW163	132Wis462	45WiAG152
310NW630	34MqL1	61WiAG354	1931p936	401NW793	299NW45	148Wis459	48WiAG188
331NW668	66MqL276	63WiAG129	R1933p1297	20WiAG325	149NW615	154Wis297	48WiAG246
387NW278	1944WLR79	63WiAG238	1933C50	34MqL1	1946WLR283	171Wis521	50WiAG48
194F835	1950WLR234	60MqL886	25Wis2d137	130NW460	19WiAG529	176Wis107	50WiAG65
22WiAG36	1962WLR16	1962WLR16	130NW460	1977WLR941	22WiAG1045	176Wis112	51WiAG202
23WiAG289	1970WLR300	1962WLR330	22WiAG204	**§ 1**	36WiAG205	177Wis295	52WiAG50
26WiAG208	19 /LR940	**§ 5**	**§ 10**	1977p2120	37WiAG84	179Wis407	58WiAG157
26WiAG275	1. 276	1929p1084	1929p1079	1979p646	64WiAG49	177Wis295	60WiAG87
44WiAG152	**§ 1m**	1931p935	A1931p960	AApr3 1979	15MqL191	219Wis132	60WiAG503
52WiAG259	1965p899	R1933p1297	1939p948	101Wis646	1950WLR207	242Wis49	60WiAG117
54WiAG3	1967p489	149Wis86	1979p1845	183Wis154	**§ 3**	245Wis111	61WiAG117
60WiAG109	1967p493	25Wis2d137	160Wis389	248Wis256	101Wis646	248Wis248	61WiAG258
69WiAG154	Ad1967p515	34Wis2d485	183Wis154	254Wis606	102Wis514	250Wis21	61WiAG356
72WiAG138	1977p2120	112Wis2d267	218Wis302	78NW151	136Wis190	259Wis441	61WiAG444
74WiAG169	1979p646	136NW141	220Wis143	197NW832	149Wis86	265Wis3	62WiAG39
56MqL26	RApr3 1979	130NW460	221Wis551	21NW381	248Wis256	8Wis2d121	63WiAG109
1940WLR20	61WiAG46	149NW615	227Wis79	37NW476	19Wis2d577	17Wis2d27	63WiAG225
1944WLR96	**§ 1n**	332NW802	233Wis16	43WiAG226	34Wis2d485	49Wis2d506	63WiAG362
1949WLR312	1965p899	**§ 6**	233Wis442	48WiAG188	63Wis2d260	71Wis2d404	65WiAG134
1949WLR488	1967p489	176Wis539	243Wis459	1950WLR234	91Wis2d710	82Wis2d574	65WiAG247
1964WLR185	1967p493	177Wis303	244Wis8	1970WLR299	115Wis2d35	95Wis2d635	65WiAG294
1964WLR610	Ad1967p515	196Wis556	22Wis2d554	1970WLR	136Wis2d150	96Wis2d676	65WiAG304
57NwL286	1977p2120	200Wis330	49Wis2d320	[1043	78NW151	106Wis2d309	67WiAG3
§ 33	1979p646	2Wis2d240	59Wis2d412	1974WLR729	78NW757	136Wis2d163	67WiAG248
1943p1029	RApr3 1979	29Wis2d122	70Wis2d485	1977WLR947	116NW901	71NW800	67WiAG250
1945p1157		100Wis2d84	71Wis2d119		136NW141	97NW923	68WiAG45
Ad1947p1316		186NW722	82Wis2d679		21NW381	111NW714	68WiAG63
265Wis210		187NW834	152NW437		120NW664	112NW475	68WiAG333
103Wis2d318		221NW611	197NW832		149NW615	134NW690	
60NW765		228NW593	260NW487		217NW259	142NW639	*Continued*

68

SECTION G.   OTHER UNITS OF SHEPARD'S CITATIONS

The *Shepard's Citations* described in the previous sections are all-inclusive; that is, each unit contains all cited cases, statutes, and citing cases irrespective of subject. The following units of *Shepard's Citations* contain citation information relevant only to a specific area or subject of law. This section omits the specialized or subject units previously discussed in this chapter.

1.   Other Specific Shepard's Citators

a. *Acts and Cases by Popular Names, Federal and State.* [See Illustration 9–11.]

b. *Code of Federal Regulations Citations.* Contains citing references from all courts, selected legal periodicals, and annotations for the *Code of Federal Regulations,* Presidential Proclamations, Executive Orders, and reorganization plans.

c. *Federal Law Citations in Selected Law Reviews.* This unit is discussed in Chapter 17.

d. *Law Review Citations.* This unit is discussed in Chapter 17.

e. *Professional and Judicial Conduct Citations.* This unit gives coverage for all citations to the Code of Professional Responsibility, the Model Rules of Professional Conduct, the Code of Judicial Conduct, and the Opinions and Rules of the American Bar Association's Committee on Ethics and Professional Responsibility.

f. *Restatement of the Law Citations.* This unit is discussed in Chapter 18.

2.   Other Shepard's Citators, by Subject

Shepard's publishes numerous citators on particular subjects. New units are added periodically. Occasionally, a new unit will start and then cease abruptly. The listing below represents those of some duration and is not intended to be exhaustive.

a. *Bankruptcy Citations.* This unit includes citations to bankruptcy cases in *American Bankruptcy Reports,* in the various federal reporters, and in looseleaf services such as *Bankruptcy Court Decisions* (LRP), *Bankruptcy Law Reporter* (CCH), and *Collier Bankruptcy Cases* (Matthew Bender).

b. *Criminal Justice Citations.* The American Bar Association has adopted and published the *Standards Relating to the Administration of Criminal Justice* (1968–1973) and the *Revised ABA Standards for Criminal Justice,* 2d ed. (1980). While these *Standards* have no official status, they are frequently cited by courts. *Criminal Justice Citations* lists each of the *Standards* and then gives citations to those cases that have cited sections of the *Standards.*

c. *Employment Law Citations.* This unit covers all U.S. federal and state cases, published and unpublished, reported in BNA's *Federal Employment Practice Cases* and CCH's *Employment Practice Decisions,* as well as employment cases reported in numerous other sources.

d. *Environmental Law Citations (Federal).* This provides a comprehensive set of citations to federal environmental law cases, including the published and unpublished federal cases from the *Environmental Law Reporter,* and also provides statutory and regulatory coverage.

e. *Federal Energy Law Citations.* This unit covers oil and gas, public utilities, natural resources, water, and environmental law. Citing sources include Supreme Court of the United States and lower federal court cases in selected energy cases, decisions and orders of the Federal Power Commission and the Federal Energy Regulatory Commission, and energy provisions in the *United States Code* and *Code of Federal Regulations.* Also included are cross references to reports of the same cases published in CCH's *Energy Management, Oil & Gas Reporter* (Matthew Bender), *Public Utilities Reports,* and CCH's *Utilities Law Reporter,* among others.

f. *Federal Labor Law Citations.* This multi-volume unit contains citations to the decisions and orders of the National Labor Relations Board. It also provides cross-reference tables to citations from labor law looseleaf services. The statutes volumes contain citations to the various federal statutes dealing with labor. A companion set, *Federal Labor Law Case Name Citator,* also is available.

g. *Federal Occupational Safety and Health Citations.* This unit contains citations to the cases of the Supreme Court of the United States and lower federal courts involving safety and health, to decisions of the Federal Occupational Safety and Health Review Commission and its administrative law judges, and to safety and health provisions in the *United States Code* and *Code of Federal Regulations.* Also included are cross references to any reports of the same cases as published in *Occupational Safety and Health Decisions* (CCH) and *Occupational Safety and Health Cases* (BNA).

h. *Federal Tax Citations.* This unit covers tax decisions and is organized in a manner similar to the other *Shepard's Citations* units. It is particularly useful for the cross-reference tables it provides to Commerce Clearing House and other looseleaf service citations. This unit is discussed in Chapter 24.

i. *Immigration and Naturalization Citations.* This unit includes among its citing sources cases of the Supreme Court of the United States as reported in the three series of reporters, cases from the lower federal courts, articles in selected leading law reviews, and the provisions of the *U.S. Statutes at Large.* The cited sources include *Immigration & Nationality Decisions,* immigration and naturalization cases from all federal courts, provisions of the *United States Code,* and the immigration and naturalization parts of the *Code of Federal Regulations.*

j. *Military Justice Citations.* This unit covers citations to cases of the U.S. Court of Military Appeals and the Boards and Courts of Military Review and to the *Uniform Code of Military Justice,* the *Manual for Courts Martial,* and to military court rules and regulations. The citing material includes cases in the *Military Justice Reporter* and in other federal and state reporters, and references to Opinions of the Attorneys General of the United States.

k. *Products Liability Citations.* This citator includes as cited sources not only the usual federal and state court cases from the *National Reporter System,* but all CCH *Products Liability Reporter* cases, products liability provisions of the state statutes, warranty provisions of the U.C.C., and sections of the *Restatement of the Law—Torts.*

l. *Uniform Commercial Code Citations.* This unit is a compilation of citations of the Uniform Commercial Code as adopted by each state. The citing sources include cases from the *National Reporter System,* as well as law reviews and selected legal texts. The citator is arranged by U.C.C. section, then alphabetically by state, with the particular citation given for the U.C.C. section in each state's statutory scheme.

SECTION H.   KEEPING SHEPARD'S CITATIONS CURRENT

1.   Supplementation of Print Versions of Shepard's Citations

As with any set of law books, there must be a method of keeping the set up to date. Because *Shepard's Citations* are used to determine the current status of a case, statute, or administrative regulation or ruling, the method of supplementation is of utmost importance. Nearly every unit of *Shepard's* is published in at least one bound volume. In addition, each unit receives at least one, and sometimes as many as three, pamphlet supplements that cover all the cases since the date of the bound volume.

Typically, the cover of an annual supplement is gold-colored. This annual supplement may then be supplemented by a red cover advance sheet pamphlet that is issued periodically throughout the year. At times, even this red cover pamphlet is supplemented with a thinner pamphlet without a cover. When the next red cover pamphlet is issued, the information from the non-covered pamphlet is incorporated into the red one. At the end of the year a new gold supplement is issued incorporating the existing advance sheets, or alternatively, the gold pamphlet and any other supplements are incorporated into newly-revised bound volumes and the supplementation process begins anew.

The frequency of the issuance of the pamphlet supplements varies among the different units. Some units are updated monthly; others, three times a year; still others, quarterly. Consequently, it is extremely important to ascertain that all bound volumes and pamphlet supplements of the unit being used are available during research. The cover of the latest pamphlet supplement prominently displays *What Your Library Should Contain.* This information should be examined carefully, and all the indicated bound volumes and pamphlet supplements should be consulted.

2. Supplementation of Online Versions of Shepard's Citations

The online CALR versions of *Shepard's Citations* are updated electronically as new print citators are issued. The online display always lists the latest coverage in the CALR service being used. Additional discussion of electronic updating is in Section B–5–a.

3. Shepard's EXPRESS Citations

Shepard's EXPRESS Citations, which is issued monthly or semimonthly depending upon the state, is a blue cover advance sheet supplement to a state's regular citator subscription, and is available for most states. It provides citation information that is more current than the print supplements.

4. Shepard's Citations Telephone Update Service

Subscriber's to *Shepard's Citations* can call the publisher for the latest citations for the set for which a subscription exists. This service provides the most up-to-date information available.

SECTION I. KEYCITE

In 1997, the West Group launched KeyCite, an exciting new addition to the case law citators field and available exclusively on WESTLAW. KeyCite integrates West's editorially-enhanced case law, full-text headnotes, and Topic and Key Numbers into one system for finding cases on point. The same day a case appears on WESTLAW, it is fully represented in KeyCite. In addition to its extensive coverage of reported cases, KeyCite also covers over a million unpublished cases, a service that Shepard's does not offer. Additional discussion of KeyCite is contained in Chapter 22, Section D–7–c.

KeyCite provides the following information about a case:

- Case history—tracing the same case through the appellate process
- Negative indirect history—cases outside the direct appellate line that may have a negative impact on the precedential value of a case
- Citing references—cases that cite or discuss a case
- Citation verification—correct volume and page number for a case
- Secondary source references—secondary sources such as *A.L.R. Annotations* and law review articles that cite your case.

1. Scope and Coverage

The Direct History provided by KeyCite traces the same case through the appellate process and includes both prior and subsequent history. Negative Indirect History is also provided, which consists of cases outside the direct appellate line that may negatively impact the precedential value of a case. Federal Direct and Negative Indirect History are available from 1754 to date and state Direct and Negative Indirect History is from 1879 to date.

Direct History includes related references, which are cases that involve the same parties and facts as the case being researched, whether or not the legal issues are the same. These related references are useful because they give an overview of all procedural and substantive issues involving the parties to a case. KeyCite provides related references from 1983 to date.

Citation verification information, available from 1754 to date for federal cases and from 1879 to date for state cases, provides parallel citations and the correct volume and page numbers for your case.

2. How to Access KeyCite

To access KeyCite the user can click on the **KeyCite** button on the main button palette; click on the **Check a Citation** button from the Welcome to WESTLAW window, then select **KeyCite**; or click the red or yellow case status flag or the blue "H" (status marker) from a displayed case.

3. How to Read a KeyCite Display

When you enter a citation in KeyCite, a screen like the one shown in Illustration 15–12 is displayed. The cases are divided into history categories (direct and negative indirect), enabling the user to see if a case is good law. A red flag adjacent to the name of the case being KeyCited shows that the case is no longer good law for at least one of the points it contains, e.g. Reversed, Vacated, Superseded, Overruled, Abrogated. A yellow flag indicates that the case has some negative history, but it has not been reversed or overruled, e.g., Amended, Modified, Declined to Extend, Holding Limited, Called Into Doubt. A blue "H" means there is some history for the case, e.g., Affirmed, Certiorari Denied, Rehearing Denied, Appeal After Remand. The absence of a flag or an "H" means there is no Direct History or Negative Indirect History for the case.

At the initial screen display, the user is given three ways to look at case history: Show Full History (everything); show Negative History Only; or Omit Minor History (show only the major history). [See Illustration 15–13.] From this screen the user can also select Citations to the Case to retrieve a comprehensive list of cases and secondary sources citing the case, e.g., *A.L.R. Annotations* or law review articles, or use the Edit Limit feature to restrict the citations only to the Headnotes or Topics desired.

When one uses the Citations to the Case feature, the first portion of the display lists all negative cases, followed by a list of other cases citing that case. [See Illustration 15–14.] An extremely valuable part of this feature is that the cases are categorized by the depth of treatment each case gives to the case being KeyCited. The depth of treatment category is represented by a star or stars. A quick glance at the number of stars a case is given can tell the user whether the cited case contains extended discussion of the case being KeyCited, is simply part of a string cite, or something in between. The four depth-of-treatment categories are:

    ****   Examined: The citing case contains an extended discussion of the cited case, usually more than a printed page of text.

    ***   Discussed: The citing case contains a substantial discussion of the cited case, usually more than a paragraph but less than a printed page.

    **   Cited: The citing case contains some discussion of the cited case, usually less than a paragraph.

    *   Mentioned: The citing case contains a brief reference to the cited case, usually in a string citation.

Quotation marks at the end of a citation indicate that this citing case directly quotes the cited case.

4. Restricting Your Results

a. *By Topic and Headnote.* The Limit Citations window can be used to show the user all the headnotes as they appear in the cited case. Next read the headnotes and determine which are relevant to your research. [See Illustration 15–15.] Then check the boxes under Headnotes and Topics on the left side of the screen to restrict the list of citing cases to those that discuss the points of law in the relevant headnotes. KeyCite provides a link to the full text of the headnote allowing the user to quickly see if it is relevant. Alternatively, the user can restrict the citation list to cases that discuss points of law classified under specific Topics.

b. *By Various Other Limits.* A user can also restrict citing references in the following ways: to a specific jurisdiction or West reporter; to cases from a jurisdiction's highest court or its lower courts; to include or exclude citations from *A.L.R.*, law review articles, or other non-case documents; to cases decided before or after a given date, or added to WESTLAW after a given date; and to one or more of the depth-of-treatment star categories.

5. Viewing Citation Counts

The Citation Counts window lists the total number of citing references and the number of citing references by Topic and by Headnote. To view this window, click the **Show Citations Counts** button. An interesting portion of this window is an area near the bottom of the screen that indicates the average citation frequency for cases from the same year and jurisdiction.

SECTION J. ILLUSTRATIONS: KEYCITE

[Illustration 15–12]

READING A KEYCITE DISPLAY: HISTORY OF THE CASE

You can customize your KeyCite result to display different types of case history:

All direct and negative indirect history, including related references

Only negative history (direct and indirect)

Direct history, excluding related references and minor procedural history. Also includes any negative indirect history that may negate the precedential value of a case.

Click to view cases and other materials citing your case.

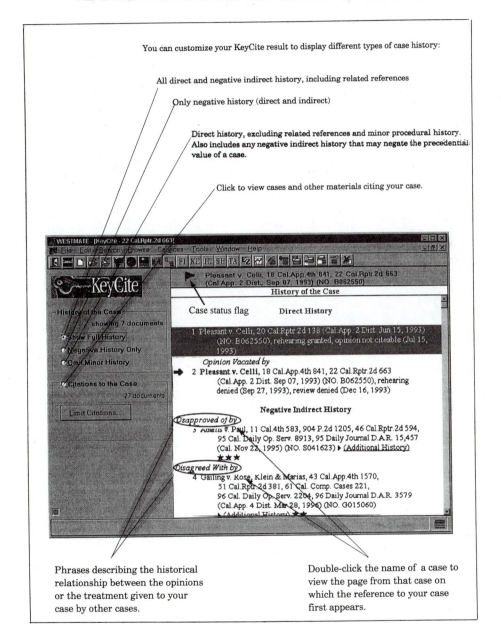

Phrases describing the historical relationship between the opinions or the treatment given to your case by other cases.

Double-click the name of a case to view the page from that case on which the reference to your case first appears.

[Illustration 15–13]

VIEWING CITING REFERENCE THROUGH "CITATIONS TO THE CASE"

Cases citing *Pleasant.*

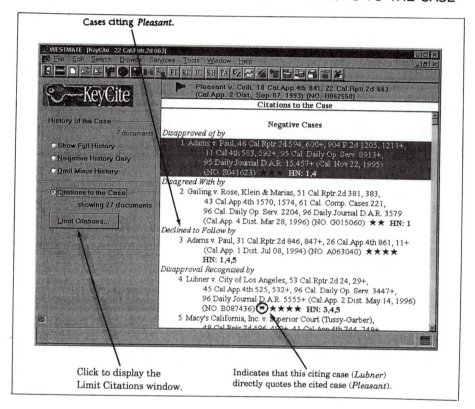

Click to display the
Limit Citations window.

Indicates that this citing case (*Lubner*)
directly quotes the cited case (*Pleasant*).

[Illustration 15–14]

RESTRICTING RESULT BY TOPIC AND HEADNOTE

After selecing **Headnotes** or
Topics, use the check boxes to
restrict citing references to
specific headnotes and click **OK.**

Indicates the number
of cases that cite this
headnote from *Pleasant*.

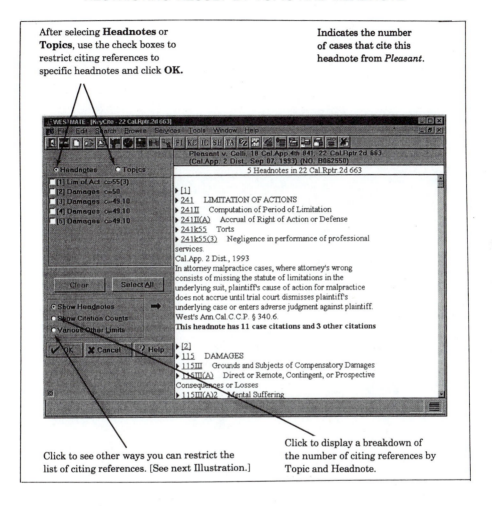

Click to see other ways you can restrict the
list of citing references. [See next Illustration.]

Click to display a breakdown of
the number of citing references by
Topic and Headnote.

[Illustration 15–15]

RESTRICTING RESULT USING VARIOUS OTHER LIMITS

By clicking the **Various Other Limits** from the Limits Citations window, the Various Other Limits window is displayed, which allows the user to restrict the list of citing references in several ways.

Restrict the citing reference to a specific jurisdiction or West publication by entering the jursdiction or publication abbreviation and clicking **Apply Origin**, if necessary.

Restrict the citing references to cases decided before or after a given date, or to cases added to WESTLAW after a given date.

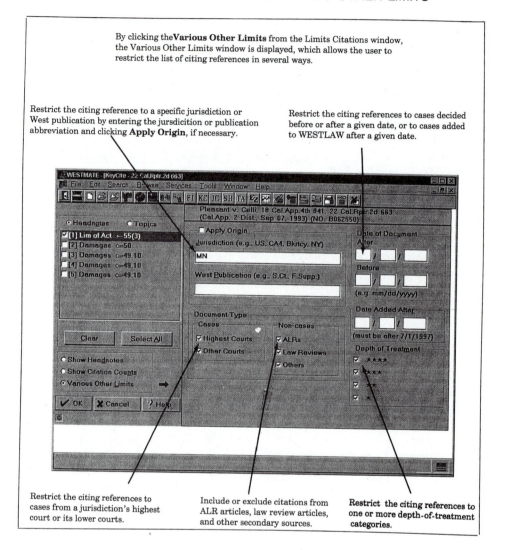

Restrict the citing references to cases from a jurisdiction's highest court or its lower courts.

Include or exclude citations from ALR articles, law review articles, and other secondary sources.

Restrict the citing references to one or more depth-of-treatment categories.

SECTION K.   OTHER CITATORS

Although *Shepard's Citations* are by far the most widely-used and diverse citators, other citators, particularly those available online, can also play an important role in one's research.

1.   Insta–Cite

Insta–Cite, West Group's verification and case history service on WESTLAW, can be accessed at any time during the online research process by entering *ic* and the case citation. It provides precedential history, citation verification, direct history, overruling information, and parallel citations. The direct history and citation verification are comprehensive for federal cases with coverage from 1754, but for state direct history coverage and citation verification is from 1879. [See Illustration 15–16, Figure 1.] References to secondary sources are also retrieved using Insta–Cite.

2. Auto–Cite and LEXCITE

Auto–Cite, on LEXIS–NEXIS, is a citation verification and case history service that can be accessed at any time during the online research process by entering *ac* and the case citation. This service provides the correct name of the case, parallel citations, year of decision, subsequent and prior history, references to cases that have had a negative impact on the precedential value of the case, and citations to *A.L.R.* and *Lawyers' Edition* articles citing the case being researched. [See Illustration 15–16, Figure 2.]

LEXCITE, exclusive to LEXIS–NEXIS, enables a researcher to retrieve the most current cases within LEXIS case law documents that cite your case, including *id* and *supra* references, while automatically searching for all the parallel citations. It also locates references to other documents, such as law review articles and federal agency decisions.

3. WESTLAW and LEXIS–NEXIS as Citators

Both WESTLAW and LEXIS–NEXIS can be used as a citator after accessing a database or file. A search is constructed using information from the case title or statute citation. When this search is run, it retrieves the full text of the citing document. This type of search is particularly useful for retrieving very recent documents not yet covered by *Shepard's Citations.* The Quick*Cite* feature on WESTLAW, accessed by entering *qc,* makes use of WESTLAW as a citator automatic. Quick-*Cite* updates Insta–Cite, Shepard's, and Shepard's PreView. The use of WESTLAW and LEXIS–NEXIS as citators is discussed in more detail in Chapter 22, Section D–7–a.

4. Table of Authorities

While KeyCite and Shepard's list cases *citing* another case, the Table of Authorities service on WESTLAW lists the cases *cited* by another case. It is a useful device for finding hidden weaknesses in your case or in an opponent's case by showing whether the cases on which it relies have significant negative history. The depth-of-treatment markers indicate the extent to which a case discusses the case it cites. [See Illustration 15–17.]

5. Looseleaf Service Citators

A few looseleaf services have citator volumes relating specifically to the subject matter of the service. Specialized looseleaf citators for federal taxation are discussed in Chapter 24.

SECTION L.   ILLUSTRATIONS: AUTO–CITE AND INSTA–CITE; TABLE OF AUTHORITIES

[Illustration 15–16]

SCREEN DISPLAYS FROM INSTA–CITE AND AUTO–CITE

Figure 1. Insta-Cite

```
Insta-Cite        AUTHORIZED FOR EDUCATIONAL USE ONLY      Page    1
                                           Date of Printing: MAY 18,1998


                            INSTA-CITE
     CITATION: 388 N.W.2d 535

                          Direct History

         1 State v. Griffin, 126 Wis.2d 183, 376 N.W.2d 62
              (Wis.App., Sep 12, 1985) (NO. 84-021 CR)
            Review Granted by
         2 State v. Griffin, 127 Wis.2d 569, 383 N.W.2d 62 (Wis., Dec 11, 1985)
              (TABLE, NO. 84-021-CR)
            AND Decision Affirmed by
    =>   3 State v. Griffin, 131 Wis.2d 41, 388 N.W.2d 535 (Wis., Jun 20, 1986)
              (NO. 84-021-CR)
            Certiorari Granted by
         4 Griffin v. Wisconsin, 479 U.S. 1005, 107 S.Ct. 643, 93 L.Ed.2d 699
              (U.S.Wis., Dec 08, 1986) (NO. 86-5324)
            AND Judgment Affirmed by
         5 Griffin v. Wisconsin, 483 U.S. 868, 107 S.Ct. 3164, 97 L.Ed.2d 709,
              55 USLW 5156 (U.S.Wis., Jun 26, 1987) (NO. 86-5324)
              (Additional Negative Indirect History)

                     Negative Indirect History

    Declined to Extend by
         6 In Interest of Angelia D.B., 211 Wis.2d 140, 564 N.W.2d 682,
              118 Ed. Law Rep. 1191 (Wis., Jun 20, 1997) (NO. 95-3104)
              (Additional History)

     (C) Copyright West Group 1998
```

> Both Insta-Cite and Auto-Cite can be used for citation verification and case history. In the two Auto-Cite screens not pictured are references to prior history and *A.L.R. Annotations* citing the case.

Figure 2. Auto-Cite

```
                                                          PAGE    1

     Auto-Cite (R) Citation Service, (c) 1998 LEXIS-NEXIS. All rights reserved.

     131 WIS 2D 41:


     CITATION YOU ENTERED: Auto-Cite Signal:  Caution--check case history

      State v. Griffin, 131 Wis. 2d 41, 388 N.W.2d 535, 1986 Wisc. LEXIS 1897
     (1986)

     SUBSEQUENT APPELLATE HISTORY:

        cert. granted,   Griffin v. Wisconsin, 479 U.S. 1005, 93 L. Ed. 2d
     699, 1986 U.S. LEXIS 5140, 107 S. Ct. 643 (1986)

          mot. granted,  Griffin v. Wisconsin, 479 U.S. 1053, 93 L. Ed. 2d
          977, 1987 U.S. LEXIS 324, 107 S. Ct. 926 (1987)

         and aff'd,   Griffin v. Wisconsin*1, 483 U.S. 868, 97 L. Ed. 2d
      709, 1987 U.S. LEXIS 2897, 107 S. Ct. 3164, 55 U.S.L.W. 5156 (1987)

          (not followed by  Commonwealth v. La France*2, 402 Mass. 789,
          525 N.E.2d 379, 1988 Mass. LEXIS 190 (1988))

          and (not followed as stated in  Commonwealth v. Alexander, 436
          Pa. Super. 335, 647 A.2d 935, 1994 Pa. Super. LEXIS 2832 (1994))
```

[Illustration 15–17]

SCREEN DISPLAY FROM TABLE OF AUTHORITIES ON WESTLAW

While KeyCite and Shepard's list cases citing a case, the Table of Authorities service on WESTLAW lists the cases cited by a case. Access the Table of Authorities by clicking the Table of Authorities button on the main button palette or by choosing Table of Authorities from the Services menu. Depth of treatment markers indicated the extent to which a case discusses the case it cites.

Cited cases with negative history are marked with a red or yellow flag.

Double-click to display the cited case (*Burgess*).

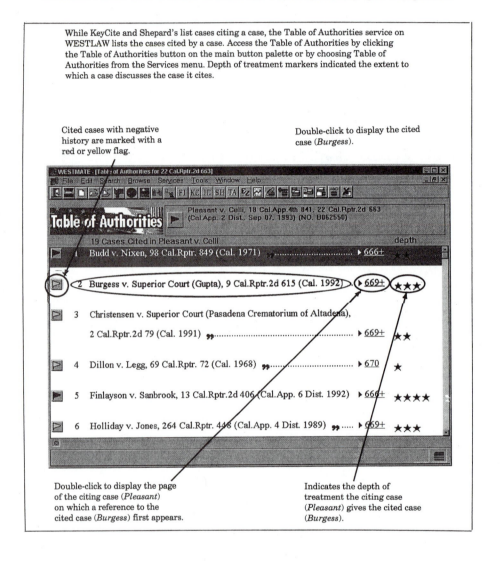

Double-click to display the page of the citing case (*Pleasant*) on which a reference to the cited case (*Burgess*) first appears.

Indicates the depth of treatment the citing case (*Pleasant*) gives the cited case (*Burgess*).

SECTION M. SUMMARY

1. Shepard's Citations—Cases

a. *States*

(1) There is a separate *Shepard's* unit for each of the fifty states, the District of Columbia, and Puerto Rico. In some states, there are separate volumes for cases and statutes; in others, they are combined. *Shepard's* are available in print, CD–ROM, online, and Internet formats.

(2) In the print version of each state unit, all the sets of reports are listed in separate sections. For each state case listed in bold type, the columns thereunder reveal (a) the history of the case in the same or higher courts, and (b) citations to all cases within the state that have cited the cited case. The electronic versions use symbols or words making them easier to understand.

(3) Citations are given to legal periodicals published within the state and to twenty national legal journals.

(4) Citations in state attorneys general opinions are given.

(5) Superscript numbers in a citation key each citing case to the headnotes of the cited case. In the electronic versions, one can click directly on headnote numbers.

b. *National Reporter System*. There is a Shepard's unit in the various formats that corresponds with each of the units of the *National Reporter System*.

Citations to the *National Reporter System* are listed whenever the citation is cited in any unit of the *National Reporter System*.

c. *Shepard's Citations for Federal Cases*.

(1) *United States Citations*. Separate parts for (a) cases of the Supreme Court of the United States, (b) administrative agency decisions, and (3) patents, trademarks, and copyrights.

(2) *Federal Citations*. Separate parts for (a) *Federal Reporter, Federal Reporter 2d*, and *Federal Reporter 3d* and (b) *Federal Supplement, Federal Rules Decisions, Court of Claims Reports*, and *Federal Claims Reporter*.

2. Shepard's Citations—Statutes

a. *States*

(1) Each state unit of Shepard's Citations has either separate volumes or separate sections in which the state constitutions and the current code are listed, with citations to cases that have cited each section.

(2) Reference is also made to any constitutional amendment or statutory clause that has been cited in court cases.

(3) City Charters and Ordinances are in separate parts of the statute volumes or sections of the state units.

(4) Court Rules are in sections in the statute volumes, sections of the state units, and in the electronic versions.

b. *Federal*

Constitutions, statutes, treaties, and court rules are covered in Shepard's United States Citations.

3. Examples of Some Other Units of Shepard's Citations

a. *Acts and Cases by Popular Names*

b. *Bankruptcy Citations*

c. *Code of Federal Regulations Citations*

d. *Criminal Justice Citations*

e. *Federal Circuit Table*

f. *Federal Labor Law Citations*

g. *Federal Law Citations in Selected Law Reviews*

h. *Federal Tax Citations*

i. *Law Review Citations*

j. *Military Justice Citations*

k. *Professional and Judicial Conduct Citations*

l. *Restatement of the Law Citations*

4. Other Uses of Shepard's Citations

a. Indicates when a case is cited in:

(1) *A.L.R. Annotations*

(2) Legal periodical articles

b. Provides parallel citations

5. Keeping Shepard's Current

a. Print versions are kept up-to-date with periodic pamphlet supplements and revised volumes. EXPRESS Citations for cases are more current than the supplemental pamphlets.

b. CD–ROMs are updated through the issuance of new disks. The *Shepard's* units on LEXIS–NEXIS are updated daily. *Shepard's* on WESTLAW is only as current as the latest pamphlet.

6. KeyCite

a. KeyCite, a West Group product, is an electronic case law citator available exclusively on WESTLAW.

b. It provides the following information about a case: case history, negative case history, citing references, citation verification, and secondary source references.

c. Cases are divided into history categories (direct and negative indirect) enabling the user to see if a case is good law.

d. Depth-of-treatment categories use from one to four stars to indicate if a case is Examined, Discussed, Cited, or Mentioned.

e. Inquires can be limited by Topic and Headnote, by specific jurisdiction or West reporter, and to cases from a jurisdiction's highest court or its lower courts, among others.

f. The Citation Counts window lists the total number of citing references and the number of citing references by Topic and Headnote. It also indicates the average citation frequency for cases from the same year and jurisdiction.

7. Other Citators

a. Insta–Cite and Auto–Cite are citation verification and case history services available in WESTLAW and LEXIS–NEXIS, respectively.

b. Both WESTLAW and LEXIS–NEXIS can function as citators.

c. The Table of Authorities feature on both WESTLAW and LEXIS–NEXIS lists the cases cited by another case.

c. Some subject-matter looseleaf services contain citators.

Chapter 16

LEGAL ENCYCLOPEDIAS

SECTION A. INTRODUCTION

In the previous chapters, discussion has focused on the primary sources of the law: court cases; constitutions; statutes; legislative histories; court rules; and various finding and verification aids for these sources: indexes; digests; citators, and other legal materials that enable a researcher to find both the source and status of the law. The mass of primary source materials has reached such voluminous proportions that secondary sources play significant roles in identifying and explaining the law. In this and the next four chapters, discussion will focus on the secondary sources of the law. The secondary sources to be discussed consist of legal encyclopedias, periodicals, treatises, restatements, and other miscellaneous sets of law books. As will be pointed out, it is frequently a much better practice to start one's research with secondary sources rather than initially consulting the sets containing the primary sources studied in some previous chapters.

Sometimes a person beginning a research project will lack even the most rudimentary knowledge necessary to identify and pursue the legal issues involved. At other times, a refresher in broad concepts might be needed. Legal encyclopedias are very useful for objective background information and as sources of leads to other materials.

Legal encyclopedias are written in narrative form, are arranged alphabetically by subject, and contain footnote references to cases on point. In most instances, they are noncritical in approach and do not attempt to be analytical or evaluative. Instead, they simply state the propositions of law, with introductory explanations of an elementary nature. These features make legal encyclopedias popular and useful research tools. However, their usefulness has frequently been exaggerated by both courts and attorneys. In particular, a legal encyclopedia is sometimes cited as an authority rather than as an expository introduction to case authority.

In many research problems, it is necessary to go beyond such rudimentary sources. It is not wise to stop one's research before reading the cases cited in the footnotes, because a summary citation frequently will not fully reflect all aspects of the case, and because the facts of the immediate problem will be distinguishable from those in the cited cases.

These criticisms are not directed at the purpose and function of legal encyclopedias. These publications are excellent introductory guides to the law. As long as this is kept in mind, and legal encyclopedias are not relied upon as the final authority for a legal proposition, they are valuable publications to consult initially. In most instances, the cases cited should be read, analyzed, Shepardized, or KeyCited; and statutory sources must be checked to ascertain whether the rules of law have changed in the particular jurisdiction.

SECTION B.   CURRENT GENERAL ENCYCLOPEDIAS

1.   Corpus Juris Secundum (C.J.S.)

Corpus Juris Secundum has been published by West since 1936 and includes both procedural and substantive law. As its original subtitle indicates, *C.J.S.* was intended initially to be "A Complete Restatement of the Entire American Law As Developed by All Reported Cases." It aimed at citing all reported cases in its footnotes. However, in the mid–1980s, West abandoned its attempt to cite every case and adopted a new subtitle reflecting a different scope of coverage for the revised volumes issued since that time—"A Contemporary Statement of American Law as Derived from Reported Cases and Legislation." This new subtitle indicates that *C.J.S.* is no longer attempting to make reference to every case and that it provides some discussion of federal and local statutory law.

It will take a substantial amount of time before the revision is complete. Until then, the set will consist of volumes reflecting two different editorial philosophies. The volumes reflecting the new philosophy can be identified by the subtitle on the title page, and often by their narrower size and because the labeling of the topics on the volume's spine run horizontally rather than vertically. *C.J.S.* is a massive set consisting of 101 numbered volumes (or over 150 actual volumes considering that some volumes are contained in more than one part) and supersedes its predecessor, *Corpus Juris.*[1]

Over 400 broad topics, which are listed preceding the text of each volume, are covered in *C.J.S.* Each topic is sub-divided into many sections. Preceding each discussion in a section within a topic is a brief summary of the prevailing rule of law. This "black letter" statement is followed by text expounding upon the topic of the section. Footnote references are arranged hierarchically by federal court and then alphabetically by state. [See Illustrations 16–1 through 16–3.]

C.J.S. includes cross references for its titles and sections to corresponding West Topics and Key Numbers, permitting easy entry into the *American Digest System*. The West Topics and Key Numbers and secondary authority sources are noted under "Library References," which precede the text of the section in the *C.J.S.* replacement volumes published since 1961 and in the annual cumulative pocket supplements.

---

[1] Although *Corpus Juris Secundum* supersedes the text of *Corpus Juris,* occasionally the footnotes in *Corpus Juris Secundum* refer to *Corpus Juris* rather than repeating the citations that appear in the older set.

C.J.S. has a multi-volume, soft-cover General Index that is issued annually. Each volume also has a separate, more detailed index to each of the topics contained in it. When a topic is covered in more than one volume, the topic index is at the end of the last volume of the topic.

Research in *C.J.S.* is similar to that described in Chapter 6 for digests. *C.J.S.*'s General Index uses the familiar descriptive-word approach, or, if one knows the Topic, research can commence immediately in the appropriate volume. For example, if one is interested in the law of copyright, the index volumes can be bypassed and the search started immediately by consulting the volume that contains the title *Copyright*. If the broad topic of the law under which the subject is included is not familiar to the researcher, *e.g.*, restrictive covenants, the search should start first in the index volumes. At the beginning of each Topic is an outline and classification for the organization of the Title, which facilitates using the topical approach. [See Illustration 16–1.]

The set is kept up to date by replacement volumes and annual cumulative pocket supplements. The pocket supplements may include rewritten text, citations to cases decided since the publication of the original volumes, and references to secondary sources. Replacement volumes are published when significant sections of the text require rewriting or when the pocket supplements become very extensive and unwieldy. Replacement volumes contain a "Table of Corresponding Sections" that enables one to find where a section in the older volume is discussed in the replacement volume. The four pamphlet volumes covering *Federal Taxation* are issued annually. Because rules, regulations, and new court cases occur so frequently in tax law, the user of these volumes should always check for the most current materials in one of the looseleaf taxation services described in Chapter 24.

Judicial and other definitions of *words and phrases* and *legal maxims* are interfiled alphabetically with the essay topics. They also are listed in each appropriate volume preceding the index, with references to the pages containing the definitions.

2. American Jurisprudence 2d (Am. Jur. 2d)

American Jurisprudence 2d, published by Lawyers Cooperative Publishing until it became a West Group product, is a non-critical, textual statement of substantive and procedural law, arranged under more than 430 topics. It contains 83 numbered volumes and approximately 120 actual volumes and supersedes the earlier edition. The editorial philosophy consistently underlying publication of *Am. Jur. 2d* is for the editors to sift through the legal authorities and then provide discussions of points of law supported by controlling cases that interpret and construe the law. Citations to these selective cases are provided in footnotes, as are citations to *A.L.R. Annotations,* which provide additional access to case law.

Am. Jur. 2d also gives in its footnotes references to treatment of a topic in other sets including *A.L.R.* The publishers describe *Am. Jur. 2d* as giving the law in breadth and *A.L.R.* as giving the law in depth. The former is very useful to obtain a quick answer to a problem that then may be explored in depth in *A.L.R.*

Like *C.J.S., Am. Jur. 2d* can be researched using either a topical or descriptive-word index approach. *Am. Jur. 2d* has a multi-volume, soft cover index that is issued annually with a periodic update as needed and is more inclusive than the entries in the *ALR Index*. Separate indexes arranged by topics, with subheadings under each topic, are at the end of the last volume of the topic.

[See Illustrations 16–4 and 16–5.]

Some other features of *Am. Jur. 2d* are:

a. As compared with *C.J.S.,* greater emphasis is placed on statutory law, federal procedural rules, and uniform state laws. The federal statutory law germane to a topic is covered, while state statutory law is covered in general but without reference to the specific laws of each state. A separate volume, *Table of Statutes, Rules, and Regulations Cited* (2d ed. 1996), covers the *United States Code Service,* the Federal Rules of Procedure, the Federal Rules of Evidence, other federal rules, and uniform and model laws. When a citation to one of these statutes or rules is known, this *Table* can be consulted to find where the subject matter of the citations is discussed in *Am. Jur. 2d.*

b. Federal tax laws are covered in four pamphlet volumes, which are replaced annually. For the most current information, the taxation looseleaf services discussed in Chapter 24 should be consulted.

c. References to definitions of words and phrases are interfiled alphabetically in the index volumes.

d. The set is kept up to date by annual pocket supplements and periodically-revised volumes. In addition, the *American Jurisprudence 2d New Topic Service,* a looseleaf volume started in 1973, covers (1) new topics of law that have developed after the printing of the main volumes and (2) substantial changes in the already published encyclopedic articles. For example, this service contains articles on *Credit Cards and Charge Accounts* and the *Federal Sentencing Guidelines.* The annual index to *Am. Jur. 2d* includes references to this *Service.* There is also an annual cumulative supplement to the new topics. In the process of periodically revising the bound volumes, these new topics are incorporated into the full set and removed from the looseleaf volume. *Am. Jur. 2d* is also available on WESTLAW and LEXIS–NEXIS.

e. The *American Jurisprudence 2d Desk Book,* another feature of *Am. Jur. 2d,* functions as a legal almanac of miscellaneous data and information. It is discussed in more detail in Chapter 19.

3. American Jurisprudence: Related Encyclopedias

Once one has determined the state of the substantive law related to the problem under research, sets related to *Am. Jur. 2d* provide information needed to prepare a case for trial. These sets are:

a. *American Jurisprudence Proof of Facts.* This set, now in its third series, collectively exceeds 125 volumes. The purpose of *Proof of Facts* is to provide a guide for a lawyer in the organization and preparation of materials for trial and in the examination of witnesses. It is designed to assist lawyers in obtaining information from clients, taking depositions, preparing briefs, and in other steps necessary in preparing for trial. Each article contains "Proofs," which are checklists and planning guides designed to assist in the establishment of the facts in issue. A separate soft cover index is provided. The set is kept current through annual pocket supplements and new volumes. A separate one volume *Cyclopedic Medical Dictionary* accompanies the *3d* series.

b. *American Jurisprudence Trials.* This multi-volume set is essentially a treatise on trial practice. The first six volumes cover matters that are common to all types of problems in trial practice. The remaining volumes are called *Model Trials* and deal with the handling of trials for a specific topic. Unlike *Am. Jur. 2d* and the other related sets, *Am. Jur. Trials* is not written by the editorial staff of the publisher. Rather, each topic in the set is written by an experienced trial lawyer. This set has a separate soft cover index and is kept up to date with annual pocket supplements.

c. *American Jurisprudence Legal Forms 2d* and *American Jurisprudence Pleading and Practice Forms Revised.* These two multi-volume sets contain forms needed in the conduct of a trial and for other aspects of a lawyer's practice. Form books are discussed in more detail in Chapter 19.

4. West's Encyclopedia of American Law (WEAL)

This encyclopedia, published by the West Group in 1998, is directed toward the non-lawyer. In 12 volumes and containing over 4,000 entries, *West's Encyclopedia of American Law* replaces *The Guide to American Law: Everyone's Legal Encyclopedia* (1983). Entries in *WEAL* are devoted to terms, concepts, events, movements, cases, and persons significant to U.S. law. Included among the entries are definitions, cross-references, "In Focus" pieces, sidebars, biographies, milestones in the law, graphics, tables and indexes, appendices of historical materials, and bibliographies. Volume 12 contains a dictionary and an index to the set.

SECTION C. ILLUSTRATIONS: ENCYCLOPEDIAS

In earlier chapters, especially those dealing with digests, *A.L.R.*, looseleaf services, and citators, we discussed how these sources can be used for finding cases. Another approach to researching a topic and finding cases and related sources is to start in either *Corpus Juris Secundum* or *American Jurisprudence 2d.*

Problem: Do prescription drug manufacturers have a duty to warn?

Corpus Juris Secundum

American Jurisprudence 2d

[Illustration 16–1]

PAGE FROM C.J.S. TOPIC OUTLINE: DRUGS AND NARCOTICS

The most common method of locating relevant sections in *C.J.S.* is by consulting the General Index volumes. Sometimes it may be easier to take a topical approach. In this instance, by consulting the Topic Outline or "Analysis" for Drugs and Narcotics, it quickly becomes apparent that the matter under research is covered in § 60.

See next Illustration.

See also General Index

[Illustration 16–2]

PAGE FROM TOPIC: DRUGS AND NARCOTICS—28 C.J.S. (1996)

---

§ 59 **DRUGS AND NARCOTICS** 28 C.J.S.

samples [81] or for failure to subject his products to tests under conditions similar to those which they may foreseeably be exposed and which may produce deleterious effects.[82] Premature marketing of a drug without sufficient testing is not justified where there is no epidemic or need warranting the risk and other products are already available to the medical profession which satisfactorily accomplish that which the new drug was designed to do.[83] The public policy favoring the availability of prescription drugs does not provide drug manufacturers with immunity from liability stemming from their failure to conduct adequate research and testing prior to the marketing of their products.[84]

It has been held that the liability of a producer for injury caused by the use of an impure drug does not depend on the manufacturer's knowledge or lack of knowledge of the impurity.[85] On the other hand, under a statute providing that a drug is adulterated if it contains any filthy substance, a

A discussion of cases dealing with the duty of prescription drug manufacturers to warn.

Preceding each discussion in a section within a topic in bold type is a brief summary of the prevailing rule of law, which is followed by "Library References."

C.J.S. **is undergoing revision. This volume 28 was published in 1996 and is said to represent "A Contemporary Statement of American Law As Derived from Reported Cases and Legislation," which is West's current philosophy used in publishing revised** *C.J.S.* **volumes.**

Compare with next Illustration.

U.S.—Tinnerholm v. Parke Davis & Co., D.C.N.Y., 285 F.Supp. 432, affirmed 411 F.2d 48.

87. U.S.—Tinnerholm v. Parke Davis & Co., D.C.N.Y., 285 F.Supp. 432, affirmed 411 F.2d 48.

88. N.Y.—Marcus v. Specific Pharmaceuticals, 77 N.Y.S.2d 508, 191 Misc. 285.

89. U.S.—Plummer v. Lederle Laboratories, Div. of American Cyanamid Co., C.A.2(N.Y.), 819 F.2d 349, certiorari denied 108 S.Ct. 232, 484 U.S. 898, 98 L.Ed.2d 191.

Tinnerholm v. Parke Davis & Co., D.C.N.Y., 285 F.Supp. 432, affirmed 411 F.2d 48—Yarrow v. Sterling Drug, Inc., D.C.S.D., 263 F.Supp. 159, affirmed 408 F.2d 978.

Ill.—Fornoff v. Parke Davis & Co., 434 N.E.2d 793, 61 Ill.Dec. 438, 105 Ill.App.3d 681.

Ind.—Carmen v. Eli Lilly & Co., 32 N.E.2d 729, 109 Ind.App. 76.

La.—Cobb v. Syntex Laboratories, Inc., App. 1 Cir., 444 So.2d 203.

Miss.—Wyeth Laboratories, Inc. v. Fortenberry, 530 So.2d 688.

Mo.—Krug v. Sterling Drug, Inc., 416 S.W.2d 143.

statute.[86] or in not exercising due care in matters not governed by regulations.[87]

A manufacturer may not be held liable for failure to manufacture a product for a particular age group, where injury resulted from administration of an overdose to a young child, on prescription of a physician.[88]

§ 60. **Warning of Dangers**

A drug manufacturer or wholesaler will be liable for injury to a user of the drug distributed by him if he fails to give an adequate warning of the dangers involved in its use.

Library References ◀——

Drugs and Narcotics ⚏17–18.

Generally, a manufacturer or wholesaler of drugs is under a duty to give warning of the dangers incident to using the drugs he sells or distributes.[89] A warning need be given, however, only where the situation calls for it.[90]

The duty to warn applies even where danger threatens only a small number [91] or small percent-

N.Y.—Baker v. St. Agnes Hospital, 421 N.Y.S.2d 81, 70 A.D.2d 400.

Or.—Oksenholt v. Lederle Laboratories, a Div. of American Cyanamid Corp., 656 P.2d 293, 294 Or. 213.

Tex.—Stewart v. Janssen Pharmaceutica, Inc., App.-El Paso, 780 S.W.2d 910, error denied.

Warning of side effects

U.S.—Schenebeck v. Sterling Drug, Inc., C.A.Ark., 423 F.2d 919—Sterling Drug, Inc. v. Cornish, C.A.Mo., 370 F.2d 82.

La.—Miller v. Upjohn Co., App. 1 Cir., 465 So.2d 42, writ denied 467 So.2d 533.

Warning of dangerous side effects and risks

Kan.—Nichols v. Central Merchandise, Inc., 817 P.2d 1131, 16 Kan. App.2d 65, review denied.

Warning of possible adverse reaction

N.Y.—Ullman v. Grant, 450 N.Y.S.2d 955, 114 Misc.2d 220.

Duty not based on theory of "ultra hazardous activity"

Mich.—Reeder v. Hammond, 336 N.W.2d 3, 125 Mich.App. 223.

Inflammability of ointment vapors

N.J.—Martin v. Bengue, Inc., 136 A.2d 626, 25 N.J. 359.

Failure to warn as violation of statute

Failure to provide adequate warnings of known risks associated with normal use of a drug violates the Federal Food, Drug and Cosmetic Act and the New York Education Law.

U.S.—Ezagui v. Dow Chemical Corp., C.A.N.Y., 598 F.2d 727.

90. N.Y.—Glucksman v. Halsey Drug Co., Inc., 1 Dept., 553 N.Y.S.2d 724, 160 A.D.2d 305, 163 A.D.2d 163.

91. Conn.—Tomer v. American Home Products Corp., 368 A.2d 35, 170 Conn. 681.

584

[Illustration 16–3]

PAGE FROM TOPIC: DRUGS AND NARCOTICS— 28 SUPP. C.J.S. (1974)

§§ 56–57   DRUGS & NARCOTICS   28 C. J. S. Supp.

not exercising due care in matters not governed by regulations.[20]

Accordingly, a manufacturer may be liable for his failure to discover harmful side effects of a drug due to his use of inadequate testing procedures and samples[21] or for failure to subject his products to tests under conditions similar to those which they may foreseeably be exposed and which may produce deleterious effects.[22] Premature marketing of a drug without sufficient testing is not justified where there is no epidemic or need warranting the risk and other products are already available to the medical profession which satisfactorily accomplish that which the new drug was designed to do.[23]

It has been held that the liability of a producer for injury caused by the use of an impure drug does not depend on the manufacturer's knowledge or lack of knowledge of the impurity.[24] On the other hand, under a statute providing that a drug is adulterated if it contains any filthy substance, a manufacturer is not liable for jaundice caused by a virus which could not b[e] covered except from its virus was held not to be the statute.[25]

A manufacturer may no[t] to manufacture a produ[ct] group, where injury res[ult] of an overdose to a young

Regulations of National In[stitutes of] Health

U.S.—Tinnerholm v. Parke Co., D.C.N.Y., 285 F.Supp. [. . . af]firmed, C.A., 411 F.2d 48.

20. U.S.—Tinnerholm v. P[arke Da]vis & Co., D.C.N.Y., 285 [F.Supp.] 432, affirmed, C.A., 411 F.2d 48.

Tex.—O. M. Franklin Serum Co. v. C. A. Hoover and Son, Civ.App., 437 S.W.2d 613, reversed on other grounds 444 S.W.2d 596.

21. U.S.—Tinnerholm v. Parke Davis & Co., D.C.N.Y., 285 F.Supp. 432, affirmed, C.A., 411 F.2d 48.

22. U.S.—Tinnerholm v. Parke Davis & Co., D.C.N.Y., 285 F.Supp. 432, affirmed, C.A., 411 F.2d 48.

23. U.S.—Tinnerholm v. Parke Davis & Co., D.C.N.Y., 285 F.Supp. 432, affirmed, C.A., 411 F.2d 48.

24. Tex.—Hoover & Son v. O. M. Franklin Serum Co., 444 S.W.2d 596.

25. U.S.—Merck & Co. v. Kidd, C.A. Tenn., 242 F.2d 592, certiorari denied 78 S.Ct. 15, 355 U.S. 814, 2 L. Ed.2d 31.

physician.[26]

§ 57.   Warning of Dangers

A drug manufacturer or wholesaler will be liable for injury to a user of the drug distributed by him if he fails to give an adequate warning of the dangers involved in its use. In the case of prescription drugs, such warning is sufficient if it is given to the prescribing physician.

Library References

Drugs and Narcotics ⚓17, 18.

Generally, a manufacturer or wholesaler of drugs is under a duty to give warning of the dangers incident to using the drugs he sells or distributes,[27] to persons for whose use the drug is supplied,[28] and the warning must be commensurate with the manufacturer's actual or constructive knowledge of the risk involved.[29] Breach of such duty may give rise to liability to a person injured by use of the drugs, either on the ground of negligence or failure to use due care,[30] and on the theory of strict liability in tort.[31] The fact that there was no negligence in the manufacturing of the drug,[32] and that the manufacturer complied with government regulations and [. . .] manufacture,[33] will not re[lieve it] for failure to give such warn[ing. . .]

[. . .] to give reasonable warning [. . .] and a manufacturer is not re[quired to give] [. . .]est possible warning.[34] The [. . .]quate to disclose the existence [of the] [. . .]isk involved.[35] and the man[u-]

> A discussion of cases dealing with the duty of prescription drug manufacturers to warn.
>
> *C.J.S.* is undergoing revision. This supplement to volume 28 was published in 1974 and was subsequently replaced in 1996. It is said to represent "A Complete Restatement of the Entire American Law As Developed by All Reported Cases." *C.J.S.* once attempted to cite all reported cases in its footnotes. This is no longer the prevailing philosophy.
>
> **Compare with previous Illustration.**

[. . .] C.A., 408 F.2d 978.

Ind.—Carmen v. Eli Lilly & Co., 32 N.E.2d 729, 109 Ind.App. 76.

Mo.—Krug v. Sterling Drug, Inc., 416 S.W.2d 143.

Warning of side effects

U.S.—Schenebeck v. Sterling Drug, Inc., C.A.Ark., 423 F.2d 919—Sterling Drug, Inc. v. Cornish, C.A.Mo., 370 F.2d 82.

Inflammability of ointment vapors

N.J.—Martin v. Bengue, Inc., 136 A. 2d 626, 25 N.J. 359.

28. Pa.—Incollingo v. Ewing, 282 A. 2d 206, 444 Pa. 263, 299.

29. U.S.—Schenebeck v. Sterling Drug, Inc., C.A.Ark., 423 F.2d 919 —O'Hare v. Merck & Co., C.A. Minn., 381 F.2d 286.

Tinnerholm v. Parke Davis & Co., D.C.N.Y., 285 F.Supp. 432, affirmed, C.A., 411 F.2d 48—Yarrow v. Ster[ling]

[. . .]ng Drug, Inc., D.C.S.D., 263 F. [S]upp. 159, affirmed, C.A., 408 F.2d [9]78—Stromsodt v. Parke-Davis & [C]o., D.C.N.D., 257 F.Supp. 991, affirmed, C.A., 411 F.2d 1390.

U.S.—Sterling Drug, Inc. v. Yarrow, C.A.S.D., 408 F.2d 978.

U.S.—McCue v. Norwich Pharmacal Co., C.A.N.H., 453 F.2d 1033.

32. U.S.—Sterling Drug, Inc. v. Yarrow, C.A.S.D., 408 F.2d 978.

N.Y.—Halloran v. Parke, Davis & Co., 289 N.Y.S.2d, 245 App.Div. 727.

33. U.S.—Arman Bros. Farms & Feed Mill, Inc. v. Diamond Laboratories, Inc., C.A.Miss., 437 F.2d 1295.

Stromsodt v. Parke-Davis & Co., D.C.N.D., 257 F.Supp. 991, affirmed. C.A., 411 F.2d 1390.

34. Md.—Nolan v. Dillon, 276 A.2d, 261 Md. 516.

35. **Warning to physician held inadequate**

(1) Manufacturers' warning that hog cholera vaccine should be administered only to "healthy" hogs, without disclosure of existence and extent of risk to hogs, was not adequate to bring vaccine within excep[tion]

[Illustration 16–4]

PAGE FROM INDEX TO AMERICAN JURISPRUDENCE 2d

GENERAL INDEX

PRODUCTS LIABILITY—Cont'd
Unreasonably dangerous products
  design defects, above
  strict liability, above
Unusually susceptible consumers
  generally, Prod Liab § 1453-1473
  complaints, receipt of, Prod Liab § 1461
  definition, Prod Liab § 1456
  express warranty, Prod Liab § 1472, 1473
  fitness, implied warranty of, Prod Liab § 1467, 1468
  foreseeability, Prod Liab § 1459-1464, 1463
  implied warranties, Prod Liab § 1465-1471
  knowledge of consumer of allergy, Prod Liab § 1471
  merchantability, implied warranty of, Prod Liab § 1470
  presumptions and inferences, Prod Liab § 1457
  proximate cause, Prod Liab § 1455
  sealed products,
    ranties, Prod
  warnings, Prod
  warranty princip
    Liab § 1462-1
Used products
  As Is Sales (this
  negligence, above
  parties liable, Prod Liab § 91, 92
  warranties, below
Useful safe life, Prod Liab § 1321, 1322
Vaccines
  market-share liability, Prod Liab § 191
  strict liability, Prod Liab § 605
  warnings, learned-intermediary doctrine, Prod Liab § 1210-1213
Venue *as* Motor vehicles, above
Venue
  Consumer Product Safety Act, recall of imminently hazardous products under, Prod Liab § 2003
  transfer of venue, Prod Liab § 1715
Verdicts
  design defects, enhanced injuries, Prod Liab § 1025
  form, Prod Liab § 1890
Veterinary drugs and vaccines, learned-intermediary doctrine, Prod Liab § 1213
Videotapes and films
  generally, Prod Liab § 1842-1844
  design defects, evidence, Prod Liab § 1088
Virus-Serum-Toxin Act, Prod Liab § 2021
Voluntary dismissals, Prod Liab § 1693
Voluntary safety standards
Volunteers who undertake to warn, Prod Liab § 1135
Vouching in, contribution and indemnity, Prod Liab § 1760-1762
Wages, salaries, and other compensation
Waiver and estoppel
  dismissal, motion for, Prod Liab § 1694
  misuse, Prod Liab § 1412

PRODUCTS LIABILITY—Cont'd
Waiver and estoppel—Cont'd
  statutes of repose, Prod Liab § 1612
  warranties, below
Warnings
  generally, Negl § 392; Prod Liab § 1108-1258
  absence of other accidents, Prod Liab § 1227
  adequacy of warning, questions of law or fact, Prod Liab § 1219
  advertising, Prod Liab § 1239
  alteration of product, Prod Liab § 1149, 1450, 1451
  assumption of risk, Prod Liab § 1398
  blood or blood products, transfusions of, Prod Liab § 1311
  bulk supplier doctrine, dissemination, Prod Liab § 1198
  burden of proof, Prod Liab § 1215, 1240
  causation, Prod Liab § 1171-1173
  Center for Disease Control, learned-
  concurring, intervening and superseding causes, Prod Liab § 1172
  continuing duty to warn. Postsale or continuing duty to warn, below this group
  contraceptives, learned-intermediary doctrine, Prod Liab § 1208, 1209
  contributory negligence and comparative fault, Prod Liab § 1340, 1341
  defect, failure to warn as, Prod Liab § 1124
  defenses, Prod Liab § 1109
  delegation of duty, Prod Liab § 1128
  design defects, Prod Liab § 937, 1073
  discovery, Prod Liab § 1781
  dissemination
    generally, Prod Liab § 1187-1214
    bulk supplier doctrine, Prod Liab § 1198
    component parts, buyers of, Prod Liab § 1199
    distributors and wholesalers, Prod Liab § 1197
    employers, Prod Liab § 1196
    foreseeable users, Prod Liab § 1188
    intermediaries, involvement of, Prod Liab § 1192-1214
    knowledgeable or sophisticated intermediaries, Prod Liab § 1195
    learned-intermediary doctrine, below this group
    physicians. Learned-intermediary doctrine, below this group
    purchasers, Prod Liab § 1189
    Restatement of Torts 2d provisions, Prod Liab § 1187
    ultimate users, Prod Liab § 1190
  distributors and wholesalers, dissemination, Prod Liab § 1197
  documentary evidence, Prod Liab § 1236, 1237

PRODUCTS LIABILITY—Cont'd
Warnings—Cont'd
  drug manufacturers, postsale or continuing duty to warn, Prod Liab § 1167
  duty to warn, Prod Liab § 1123-1170
  economic losses, Prod Liab § 1926
  employers, Prod Liab § 1173, 1196
  evidence
    generally, Prod Liab § 1215-1258
    absence of other accidents, Prod Liab § 1227
    adequacy of warning, questions of law or fact, Prod Liab § 1219
    advertising, Prod Liab § 1239
    burden of proof, Prod Liab § 1215, 1240
    causation, generally, Prod Liab § 1240-1258
    documentary evidence, Prod Liab § 1236, 1237
    expert testimony, Prod Liab § 1221-1223
    foreseeability, questions of law or
     Prod Liab § 1217
    ental standards, Prod Liab § 1234
    standards, Prod
    ns to jury, Prod Liab
  knowledge of defendant, questions of law or fact, Prod Liab § 1217
  knowledge or conduct of plaintiff or other instrumental party, below this group
  obviousness of danger, questions of law or fact, Prod Liab § 1218
  other accidents, Prod Liab § 1224-1227
  presumption that warnings will be read and heeded, Prod Liab § 1241-1244
  professional groups, notice to, Prod Liab § 1239
  questions of law or fact, Prod Liab § 1216-1219, 1245
  rebuttal of presumption that warnings will be read and heeded, Prod Liab § 1244
  recalls, Prod Liab § 1238
  strict liability, subsequent remedial measures, Prod Liab § 1229
  subsequent remedial measures, Prod Liab § 1228-1232
  substantial similarity, other accidents, Prod Liab § 1225
  ultimate issues, expert testimony, Prod Liab § 1223
  expert, manufacturer held to knowledge of, Prod Liab § 1140
  expert testimony, Prod Liab § 1221-1223, 1856
  expression. Form and expression, below this group
  FDA regulations, Prod Liab § 1186, 1203
  foreseeability
    dissemination of warnings, Prod Liab § 1188
    knowledge of defendant, below this group

> The General Index to *Am. Jur. 2d* will lead the researcher to where the topic being researched is covered in *Am. Jur. 2d.*
>
> See next Illustration.

For assistance using this Index, call 1-800-527-0430   963

[Illustration 16–5]

PAGE FROM VOLUME 63A, AMERICAN JURISPRUDENCE 2d

§ 1123   PRODUCTS LIABILITY   63A Am Jur 2d

An adequate warning is one that is reasonable under the circumstances.[56] A warning may be inadequate in factual content, the expression of facts, or in the method by which it is conveyed.[57]

Warnings cases also often involve duties to provide adequate instructions for safe use of a product.[58] A product distributed without adequate warnings or instructions is sometimes said to have a "marketing defect."[59] Failure to provide an adequate warning has also been treated as a design defect.[60]

§ 1124. Failure to warn may render product defective

A manufacturer has a duty to warn with respect to latent dangerous characteristics of the product, even though there is no "defect" in the product itself.[61] A failure to warn of such a latent danger will, without more, cause the product to be unreasonably dangerous as marketed.[62] In such a case, a product, although faultlessly manufactured and designed, may be defective when placed

56. Love v Wolf (3rd Dist) 226 Cal App 2d 378, 38 Cal Rptr 183; Wooderson v Ortho Pharmaceutical Corp., 235 Kan 387, 681 P2d 1038, CCH Prod Liab Rep ¶ 10100, cert den 469 US 965, 83 L Ed 2d 301, 105 S Ct 365; Terhune v A. H. Robins Co., 90 Wash 2d 9, 577 P2...

57. Ameri... F Sup... later p... CCH P... Serv 1... 1419 ... Ackley ... 919 F2d 597, CCH Prod Liab Rep ¶ 12649) (applying Kansas law).

As to the adequacy of warnings, generally, see §§ 1175 et seq.

58. Frey v Montgomery Ward & Co. (Minn) 258 NW2d 782; Andersen v Teamsters Local 116 Bldg. Club (ND) 347 NW2d 309, CCH Prod Liab Rep ¶ 9971.

59. USX Corp. v Salinas (Tex App San Antonio) 818 SW2d 473, CCH Prod Liab Rep ¶ 13028, writ den (Feb 19, 1992) and rehg of writ of error overr (Apr 22, 1992).

60. Byrd v Proctor & Gamble Mfg. Co. (ED Ky) 629 F Supp 602, CCH Prod Liab Rep ¶ 11059 (applying Kentucky law); C & S Fuel, Inc. v Clark Equipment Co. (ED Ky) 552 F Supp 340, CCH Prod Liab Rep ¶ 9664 (applying Kentucky law); Taylor v General Electric Co., 208 NJ Super 207, 505 A2d 190, CCH Prod Liab Rep ¶ 10945, certif den 104 NJ 379, 517 A2d 388.

61. Miles v Olin Corp. (CA5 La) 922 F2d 1221, CCH Prod Liab Rep ¶ 12724, 32 Fed Rules Evid Serv 55, reh den (CA5) 1991 US App LEXIS 4833; Scott v Black & Decker, Inc. (CA5 La) 717 F2d 251, CCH Prod Liab Rep ¶ 9792

(applying Louisiana law); Jackson v Coast Paint & Lacquer Co. (CA9 Mont) 499 F2d 809 (among conflicting authorities noted on other grounds in Prather v Upjohn Co. (CA11 Fla) 797 F2d 923, CCH Prod Liab Rep ¶ 11107); Prince v Parachutes, Inc (Alaska) 685 P2d 83, CCH Prod ... Shore ...3d 594, ...11082, ...tor Co. ...ib Rep ...Ed 2d ...t Light ...56; Rus- ...22 A2d ...iltres v Kidco Exterminating Co., 256 Ga 255, 347 SE2d 568, CCH Prod Liab Rep ¶ 11103; Pettis v Nalco Chemical Co., 150 Mich App 294, 388 NW2d 343, CCH Prod Liab Rep ¶ 1041, app den 426 Mich 881 and (criticized on other grounds in Dewitt v Morgen Scaffolding (CA6 Mich) 1996 US App LEXIS 6111); Streich v Hilton-Davis, Div of Sterling Drug, 214 Mont 44, 692 P2d 440, CCH Prod Liab Rep ¶ 10324, 40 UCCRS 109; Outboard Marine Corp. v Schupbach, 93 Nev 158, 561 P2d 450; Bellotte v Zavre Corp., 116 NH 52, 352 A2d 723; Perfetti v McGhan Medical (App) 99 NM 645, 662 P2d 646, 35 UCCRS 1472, cert den 99 NM 644, 662 P2d 645; Robinson v Reed-Prentice Div. of Package Machinery Co., 49 NY2d 471, 426 NYS2d 717, 403 NE2d 440, CCH Prod Liab Rep ¶ 8658; Harris v Northwest Natural Gas Co., 284 Or 571, 588 P2d 18; Harris v Northwest Natural Gas Co., 284 Or 571, 588 P2d 18; Walton v Avco Corp., 530 Pa 568, 610 A2d 454, CCH Prod Liab Rep ¶ 13227; Ilosky v Michelin Tire Corp., 172 W Va 435, 307 SE2d 603, CCH Prod Liab Rep ¶ 9705

Annotations: Failure to warn as basis of liability under doctrine of strict liability in tort, 53 ALR3d 239

62. Garside v Osco Drug, Inc. (CA1 Mass)

> Notice that *Am. Jur. 2d* contains fewer footnotes than *C.J.S.*, even after the change in *C.J.S.*'s editorial philosophy. But also notice the reference to *A.L.R.* where additional cases can be located. *Am. Jur. 2d* is a useful way to find *A.L.R. Annotations.*
>
> Note: Both *Am. Jur. 2d* and *C.J.S.* include annual pocket supplements. A researcher should always remember to check these supplements for references to later sources.

280

SECTION D.   STATE ENCYCLOPEDIAS

Some states have encyclopedias devoted to their own laws, with most published by the West Group.   These are:

California Jurisprudence 3d

Florida Jurisprudence 2d

Illinois Jurisprudence

Illinois Law and Practice

Indiana Law Encyclopedia

Kentucky Jurisprudence

Maryland Law Encyclopedia

Massachusetts Jurisprudence

Michigan Law and Practice

New York Jurisprudence 2d

Ohio Jurisprudence 3d

Pennsylvania Law Encyclopedia

Texas Jurisprudence 3d

Some of these encyclopedias are modeled after *Am. Jur. 2d.*, while others follow the format of *C.J.S.*. Several of these encyclopedias are available on WESTLAW or LEXIS–NEXIS or both.

Encyclopedias for Georgia, Virginia and West Virginia, and Tennessee are available from other publishers.

SECTION E.   SPECIFIC SUBJECT ENCYCLOPEDIAS

Three smaller legal encyclopedias focus on broad legal subjects that are national in scope.   The four-volume *Encyclopedia of Crime and Justice* (The Free Press, 1983) contains almost 300 topical, encyclopedic essays by named scholars covering the range of issues affecting criminal behavior and society's responses to it.   The *Encyclopedia of the American Judicial System: Studies of the Principal Institutions and Processes of Law* (Charles Scribner's Sons, 1987) is a three-volume work containing 88 encyclopedic essays by named scholars that provide historical accounts and discussions of substantive law, institutions and personnel, the judicial process, and constitutional law.   The *Encyclopedia of the American Constitution* is discussed in Chapter 8, Section A–2.

SECTION F.   SUMMARY

1.   Corpus Juris Secundum

a.   *Scope*

(1) Volumes published prior to the mid–1980s attempt to restate the entire body of American case law, citing all reported cases since publication of *Corpus Juris*.   Where there are earlier cases on point, footnote

references are given to *C.J.* The text of *C.J.S.* supersedes the text of *C.J.*

(2) Volumes published since the mid–1980s do not attempt to provide comprehensive case references, but rather only references of a contemporary nature.

(3) Includes some discussion of federal and state regulatory law.

(4) Definitions of words and phrases and legal maxims are interfiled alphabetically with the essay topics.

b. *Arrangement*

(1) Alphabetically by topic.

(2) Topic outline—delimits and identifies the content of a topic.

(3) Analysis—appears after topic outline giving conceptual breakdown of topic, with each section being preceded by a brief statement of the prevailing rule of law.

c. *Indexes*

(1) General index—arranged alphabetically by broad descriptive and legal terms, and issued annually.

(2) Volume indexes—more detailed subject indexes within the volumes of the set.

d. *Supplementation*

(1) Cumulative annual pocket supplements.

(2) Replacement volumes.

2. American Jurisprudence 2d

a. *Scope*

(1) Textual statement of substantive and procedural law, with selected case references. Available on WESTLAW and LEXIS–NEXIS. Supersedes *American Jurisprudence.*

(2) Greater emphasis on federal statutory law, federal procedural rules, and uniform state laws.

(3) State statutory law is treated broadly.

(4) References to definitions of words and phrases are interfiled alphabetically in the index volumes.

(5) Footnote references to *A.L.R. Annotations* and research aids.

(6) *Table of Statutes, Rules, and Regulations Cited.*

(7) *Desk Book.*

b. *Arrangement*

(1) Alphabetically by topic.

(2) Outlines, cross references, notations to federal aspects of the law. An analysis of the section headings precedes the text pertaining to a topic.

c. *Indexes*

(1) Multi-volume index issued annually with a periodic update possible.

(2) Volume indexes arranged by topics in a volume with subheadings under each topic. The topic index is at the end of the concluding volume of the topic.

d. *Supplementation*

(1) Cumulative annual pocket supplements.

(2) Replacement volumes.

(3) *New Topic Service* in looseleaf binder.

e. *Related Publications*

Several practice-oriented publications that are related to *Am. Jur. 2d* are: *Am. Jur. Proof of Facts; Am. Jur. Trials; Am. Jur. Legal Forms 2d;* and *Am. Jur. Pleading and Practice Forms Revised.*

3. West's Encyclopedia of American Law

a. Directed toward the non-lawyer.

b. Contains over 4,000 entries.

4. State Encyclopedias

Published for approximately one-third of the states, often following the format of either *C.J.S.* or *Am. Jur. 2d.*

5. Subject Matter Encyclopedias

See Section E.

Chapter 17

LEGAL PERIODICALS AND INDEXES

Legal periodicals are extremely valuable secondary sources in legal research. Their value typically lies in the depth to which they analyze and criticize a particular topic and the extent of their footnote references to other sources. During the nineteenth century, they greatly contributed to improving the image of the legal profession in America.[1] With the proliferation of legislation and court cases, legal periodicals in the twentieth century play an increasingly important role in keeping researchers current in developing areas of the law and in providing information on the specialized areas of the law. Today, with the rapid growth of online CALR services and the Internet, access to the information in legal periodicals is increasingly easy. Electronic access is discussed in Section I, *infra*.

The function of a legal periodical has been described as the "recording and criticism of doings of legislators and judges, discussion of current case law, narration of the lives of eminent lawyers, and the scientific study of native and foreign jurisprudence."[2] Legal periodicals can be classified into five types of publications: (1) law school; (2) bar association; (3) subject, special interest, and interdisciplinary (frequently by commercial publishers); (4) legal newspapers; and (5) newsletters.[3] A variety of specialized indexes provide access to these publications.

---

[1] MAXWELL H. BLOOMFIELD, AMERICAN LAWYERS IN A CHANGING SOCIETY, 1776–1876 142–43 (1976). For a brief account of legal periodicals in nineteenth-century America, *see* LAWRENCE M. FRIEDMAN, A HISTORY OF AMERICAN LAW 630–31 (2d ed. 1985). Additional sources that deal with the early history of legal periodicals in the United States include Marion Brainerd, *Historical Sketch of American Legal Periodicals,* 14 LAW LIBR. J. 63 (1921); Roscoe Pound, *Types of Legal Periodical,* 14 IOWA L. REV. 257 (1929); *Digest of American Law Reports and American Legal Periodical,* 23 AM. JURIST. 128 (1840). For an extensive history of law school reviews, *see* Michael I. Swygert & Jon W. Bruce, *The Historical Origin, Founding, and Early Development of Student–Edited Law Reviews,* 36 HASTINGS L.J. 739 (1985).

For a list of legal periodicals of the last century and their dates of publication, *see* LEONARD N. JONES, AN INDEX TO LEGAL PERIODICAL LITERATURE vii-x (1888); 2 *id.* at vii-x (1899). These volumes are part of what is referred to as the *Jones–Chipman Index,* which is discussed in Section B–1.

[2] FREDERICK C. HICKS, MATERIALS AND METHODS OF LEGAL RESEARCH 210 (3d rev. ed. 1942).

[3] For additional breakdowns of categories and for recommendations as to the titles that should be in a broad-based legal periodical collection, *see* Donald J. Dunn, *Law, in* MAGAZINES FOR LIBRARIES 792–813 (Bill Katz & Linda Sternberg Katz eds., 9th ed., 1997).

SECTION A. LEGAL PERIODICALS

1. Law School Reviews/Journals

A periodical published by a law school is most often called a *review,* although *journal* is also widely used, e.g., *Harvard Law Review, Michigan Law Review, Yale Law Journal.* The two terms are used interchangeably. These publications play a unique role in legal research. One distinctive feature is the control of editorial policy and management by student editors. The students forming the membership of law reviews are typically chosen on the basis of their scholarship record, through a writing competition, or a combination of the two. These students "on law review" write articles and edit each other's work, evaluate for potential publication the writings submitted by those outside the school, and then edit those pieces accepted for publication. As one legal scholar has noted:

> There is not so far as I know in the world an academic faculty which pins its reputation before the public upon the work of undergraduate students—there is none, that is, except in the American law reviews.[4]

The typical law review is published quarterly, although some are issued only annually and others as often as eight times a year. It is usually subsidized by its parent institution and sold at a modest cost, with its circulation almost exclusively limited to law libraries, its alumni/ae, and members of the bar within the jurisdiction where it is published.[5] An issue averages around 250 pages.

These publications are generally in two or more sections. The first consists of "lead articles" on various topics, usually written by law professors and occasionally by practitioners or academics from other disciplines. [See Illustration 17–7.] These articles are typically lengthy, scholarly in nature, and may have a substantial impact in changing the law or in charting the course for newly-developing fields of law.[6]

The next section, which is written by law students, is most often called "Notes and Comments," with the former devoted to critical analyses of recent court cases or legislation and the latter to surveys or critiques of selected subjects of contemporary importance. Sometimes these *notes* and *comments* are in two separate sections. Many journals also publish book reviews. In this section are critical, detailed expositions that frequently venture beyond an assessment of the book to include the reviewer's personal opinion about the issues raised in the book. These book reviews are frequently lengthy and extensively documented.

---

[4] KARL N. LLEWELLYN, THE BRAMBLE BUSH 105 (1931).

[5] The *Harvard Law Review* has the largest circulation at approximately 7,500. Most law school law reviews have less than 1,000 subscribers.

[6] *See, e.g.,* Samuel D. Warren & Louis D. Brandeis, *The Right to Privacy,* 4 HARV. L. REV. 193 (1890); William L. Prosser, *The Assault upon the Citadel (Strict Liability to the Consumer),* 69 YALE L.J. 1099 (1960); Donald R. Korobkin, *Rehabilitating Values: A Jurisprudence of Bankruptcy,* 91 COLUM. L. REV. 717 (1991).

A "Commentary" section is appearing with increasing frequency in law reviews.[7] These *commentaries,* which typically undergo little or no student editing and therefore can be published more quickly than other segments in the review, often involve a scholar taking a position on a controversial topic, followed in the same or a subsequent issue with responses from other scholars that challenge those views. Sections like the "Commentary" are sometimes entitled "Essays" or "Correspondence." Frequently, a law review issue will be devoted to a symposium on a particular subject or contain an annual review of the work of a particular court.

Much has changed in the world of law review publishing in recent years. Certainly notable is the proliferation of subject-oriented and interdisciplinary journals. In 1941, the number of reviews published by American law schools totaled 50.[8] Today, students at the more than 180 American Bar Association-accredited law schools publish in excess of 470 titles.[9] Obviously, many schools publish more than one journal, with Harvard leading the way with ten. While it could once be said that law reviews were general in nature with no emphasis on any specific subject, only a law school's so-called "flagship" review or journal typically will be true to the general-interest notion. "Secondary" reviews on specialized subjects, e.g., civil rights, constitutional law, environmental law, international law, and taxation, or reviews that are interdisciplinary in nature, e.g., law and medicine, law and economics, now predominate. A representative listing is set forth in Section I, *infra.*

Also notable is the role of the CALR vendors and the Internet in providing access to legal periodical information. Both WESTLAW and LEXIS–NEXIS have rapidly expanding legal periodical databases. In addition, many law school law reviews have their own home pages containing subscription information, instructions on how to submit articles, the contents of the latest issues, abstracts of articles, and, in some instances, full text. A few law reviews are published exclusively on the Internet, e.g., *Richmond Journal of Technology & Law.*[10] For additional discussion of online access to legal periodicals, see Section A.6, *infra.*

---

[7] For an examination of this practice, *see Commentary,* 24 Conn. L. Rev. 1959 (1991), which contains seven brief articles.

[8] This number is derived from the listing of law reviews in Hicks, *supra* note 1, at 207–09.

[9] This number is obtained from a list of law reviews/journals maintained by the authors of this text.

[10] For a discussion of the role and future of law reviews in an electronic environment, see M. Ethan Katsh, *Law Reviews and the Migration to Cyberspace,* 29 Akron L. Rev. 115 (1996). For an interesting look at the development of the law review and its future in an electronic environment, see Bernard J. Hibbits, *Last Writes? Reassessing the Law Review in the Age of Cyberspace,* 71 N.Y.U. L. Rev. 615 (1996). This article was published on the Internet for comment before making its way into print. See also Shawn G. Pearson, *Hype or Hypertext? A Plan for the Law Review to Move into the Twenty–First Century,* 1997 Utah L. Rev. 765.

Law school reviews have had a high degree of success in providing students with a meaningful research and writing experience[11] while serving as a forum for the foremost legal scholars to contribute articles that have been instrumental in molding the course of many legal doctrines.[12] Increasingly, courts are citing law review articles and student notes and comments.[13] It is interesting that it was not until 1917 that the Supreme Court of the United States began citing legal journal articles in its opinions,[14] while presently most opinions by the Court cite to or quote from these sources.

Today, as a result of the dramatic increase in the number of published journals, it is much less difficult for writers to have their work accepted for publication by a law review somewhere. However, it has become a virtual contest to have one's work published in a source that increases the likelihood that it will be cited and to identify the "best" sources. An increasing amount of literature is being published that attempts to rate the reviews.[15]

There are some notable exceptions to the student-edited law review model—the faculty-edited reviews. These publications are "refereed," *i.e.,* selection of an article for inclusion is based on peer review, often with those participating in the evaluative process not knowing the author of the piece—the so-called "blind" review. These highly-respected journals include *The American Journal of Legal History, Journal of Legal Studies, Journal of Law and Economics, Law and History Review,* and *Law and Society Review.*

[11] *See* articles on *Student–Edited Law Reviews,* 36 J. LEGAL EDUC. 1–23 (1986).

[12] *See, e.g.,* Fred R. Shapiro, *The Most–Cited Law Review Articles,* 73 CAL. L. REV. 1540 (1985); Fred R. Shapiro, *The Most–Cited Articles from* The Yale Law Journal, 100 YALE L.J. 1449 (1991). A book resulted from the first article: FRED R. SHAPIRO, THE MOST-CITED LAW REVIEW ARTICLES (1987), which collects and reprints the 24 law review articles that have been most cited in other law review articles. *See also Symposium: Review of Articles That Shaped the Law,* 21 U. MICH. J.L. REF. 509 (1988).

[13] Richard A. Mann, *The Use of Legal Periodicals by Courts and Journals,* 26 JURIMETRICS J. 400 (1986); Louis J. Sirico, Jr. & Jeffrey B. Margulies, *The Citing of Law Reviews by the Supreme Court: An Empirical Study,* 34 UCLA L. REV. 131 (1986); Louis J. Sirico, Jr. & Beth A. Drew, *The Citing of Law Reviews by the United States Courts of Appeals: An Empirical Analysis,* 45 U. MIAMI L. REV. 1051 (1991).

[14] Chester A. Newland, Comment, *The Supreme Court and Legal Writing: Learned Journals as Vehicles of an Anti–Antitrust Lobby?* 48 GEO. L.J. 105, 127 (1959).

[15] *See, e.g.,* Olavi Maru, *Measuring the Impact of Legal Periodicals,* 1976 Am. B. Found. Res. J. 227; (ranks law reviews by the frequency with which they have been cited); *Chicago–Kent Law Review Faculty Scholarship Survey,* 65 CHIC.-KENT L. REV. 195 (1989) (ranks the leading law reviews based on frequency of citation as well as the productivity of law school faculties in those leading reviews; published annually since 1989); Scott Finet, *The Most Frequently Cited Law Reviews and Legal Periodicals,* LEGAL REFERENCE SERVICES Q., No. 3/4 1989, at 227 (surveys the literature on frequency of citation and then develops a composite listing); James Leonard, *"Seein' the Cites" A Guided Tour of Citation Patterns in Recent American Law Review Articles,* 34 ST. LOUIS U. L.J. 181 (1990) (investigates why some law reviews are cited more often than others as scholarly authority in law reviews). *See also supra* note 12, which includes additional articles frequently used in attempting to rate law reviews.

Although there are numerous virtues to law reviews, they are not without their critics,[16] and the debate as to their relative value continues.[17] The substance of the criticism is usually aimed at their pedantic style, excessive use of footnotes,[18] and their similarity to each other. Indeed, one member of Congress has even attacked law reviews as having an insidious influence on the Supreme Court of the United States.[19] In spite of these criticisms, law school law reviews serve as important vehicles for the publication of significant legal research, as valuable resources for references to additional sources of information, and as incisive and effective teaching tools.

2. Bar Association Periodicals

All fifty states and the District of Columbia have bar associations. In some states, membership is voluntary; in other states, it is a prerequisite to the practice of law within the state. The latter is called an *integrated bar*.[20] In addition, many counties and large cities have their own local bar associations. Most national and state bar associations, sections within these associations, and many local and specialized bar groups publish periodicals. These publications vary in scope from such distinguished periodicals as the *ABA Journal* or the *Record of the Association of the Bar of the City of New York* to those that are little more than newsletters.

The primary purposes of bar association publications are to inform the membership of the association's activities, to comment on pending and recent legislation, and to review current local court cases. When they do publish articles, these tend to stress the more practical aspects of the law, with emphasis on problem solving, rather than the theoretical ones. They are concerned more with the law as it is rather than with what it should be. Thus, bar association publications perform different functions than the law school reviews, where the emphasis is on reform and scholarly legal research. As a consequence, bar association publica-

---

[16] Among the foremost critics was Yale Law Professor Fred Rodell. *See* Fred Rodell, *Goodbye to Law Reviews*, 23 VA. L. REV. 38 (1936); Fred Rodell, *Goodbye to Law Reviews— Revisited*, 48 VA. L. REV. 279 (1962).

[17] *See, e.g.,* Roger C. Cramton, *"The Most Remarkable Institution": The American Law Review*, 36 J. LEGAL EDUC. 1 (1986); Phil Nichols, Note, *A Student Defense of Student Edited Journals: In Response to Professor Roger Cramton*, 1987 DUKE L.J. 1122; E. Joshua Rosenkranz, *Law Review's Empire*, 39 HASTINGS L.J. 859 (1988); Michael Vitiello, *Journal Wars*, 22 ST. MARY'S L.J. 927 (1991); E. Joshua Rosenkranz, *The Empire Strikes Back*, 22 ST. MARY'S L.J. 943 (1991); Max Stier et al., *Law Review Usage and Suggestions for Improvement: A Survey of Attorneys, Professors, and Judges*, 44 STAN. L. REV. 1467 (1992); Rosa Ehrenreich, *Look Who's Editing. The Nation's Law Reviews Are In the Hands of Mere Students. And Some Professors Are Not Amused*, LINGUA FRANCA, Jan.-Feb. 1996, at 58.

[18] The current record is 4,824 established by Arnold S. Jacobs, *An Analysis of Section 16 of the Securities Act of 1934*, 32 N.Y.L. SCH. L. REV. 209 (1987).

[19] 103 CONG. REC. 16,159–62 (1957) (statement of Rep. Patman) (characterizing legal writing as "an organized form of lobbying").

[20] For a complete list of bar associations, see the latest *American Bar Association Directory*, which is published annually.

tions generally have less historical value, but are more useful when researching subjects of current interest to practitioners.

3. Subject, Special Interest, and Interdisciplinary Legal Periodicals

As the literature of the law grows and reflects the increasing complexity of society, it is ever more difficult for lawyers and researchers to keep current not only with the general development of the law but also with their particular legal interests. Concurrent with this law explosion, law practices are increasingly becoming more specialized and legal periodicals are targeting the interest of particular sub-groups within the legal profession. Some of these periodicals are published by law schools, edited by students or faculty members, and follow the format of the traditional law review; others are published by non-profit associations; and still others, in ever-increasing numbers, are published by commercial publishing companies. Another recent development is the publication of periodicals devoted to law and its interaction with some other discipline. These periodicals reflect the increasing emphasis many law schools and legal and non-legal scholars place on integrating the findings of the social and behavioral sciences with the legal process.

a. *Subject Journals.* Journals devoted to one area of law vary in scope from the very practical to the very scholarly.[21] *Taxes: The Tax Magazine* and *Trusts and Estates,* both published by private companies, are examples of periodicals aimed primarily at practicing attorneys specializing in particular fields of law. These contain articles written by well-known practitioners interpreting the impact of recent legislation and court cases, and many contain reviews of books within their subject area. The *American Journal of International Law* and *American Journal of Comparative Law* are examples of periodicals published under the auspices of learned societies, while *Ecology Law Quarterly,* published at the University of California at Berkeley School of Law, and *Review of Litigation,* published at the University of Texas School of Law, are typical of subject journals that are similar in format to traditional law school reviews.

b. *Special Interest Periodicals.* These periodicals are aimed at those members of the legal community who have similar interests and serve as a means to encourage writing and research within the special area of interest. They include such journals as *Catholic Lawyer, Christian Lawyer, Elder Law Journal, Journal of Law & Sexuality, Judges Journal, National Black Law Journal, La Raza Law Journal, Scribes Journal of Legal Writing,* and *Women Lawyers Journal.*

c. *Interdisciplinary Journals.* Perhaps the most distinguished of this group is *Journal of Law and Economics,* published by the faculty of the University of Chicago School of Law. Other representative titles are

---

[21] A few publishers publish annual anthologies consisting of a collection of the best articles written on a particular subject and published over the course of each year. *Advertising Law* is an example of one such annual.

Journal of Law and Health, Journal of Law & Politics, Journal of Law and Religion, Journal of Legal Medicine, Journal of Psychiatry and Law, Law and Psychology Review, and *Yale Journal of Law and the Humanities.*

4. Legal Newspapers

Legal newspapers can be national, state, or local in focus and are frequently available online as well as in print form.[22] There are two weekly legal newspapers that are national in scope—*Legal Times* and *National Law Journal,* both of which began in 1978. These contain articles and regular columns that pertain to a variety of issues and are valuable sources for fast-breaking legal developments. The monthly *American Lawyer,* which commenced in 1979 and is also national in scope, tends to focus on sensational events, although it is also developing a sound reputation for investigative journalism. The *Corporate Legal Times,* launched in 1990, is an example of a monthly, national newspaper with a subject focus. *Lawyers Weekly USA,* started in 1993, is a biweekly national newspaper that places special emphasis on the needs of the smaller law firm.

Legal newspapers are published for many states. These are typically published either weekly or monthly and concentrate on matters of particular importance in the state. They often contain articles of both state and national interest, synopses of cases, and reports of disciplinary proceedings. Examples include *Connecticut Law Tribune, Massachusetts Lawyers Weekly, New Jersey Law Journal,* and *Texas Lawyer.*

In a few larger cities are newspapers devoted to legal affairs of their metropolitan area. These are generally published daily, Monday through Friday, and primarily contain information on court calendars and dockets, changes in court rules, news about recent changes in legislation, new administrative rules, and stories about local judges and lawyers. Some of the larger ones, such as *New York Law Journal* and *Los Angeles Daily Journal,* also publish current court cases and articles on various legal topics.

5. Newsletters

While the number of subject-matter journals has grown rapidly, it is the area of the commercially-published topical newsletter that has expanded most dramatically. As law has become more specialized, subject-matter newsletters have flourished. One would be hard-pressed to find an area of the law that is not served by one, and often many, law-related newsletters on the topic under research. These publications, often quite expensive, are typically issued weekly or monthly, consist of only a few pages, and focus on the most recent trends and developments. Rarely do they contain an index and even more rarely are they indexed by the

---

[22] A complete list of legal newspapers is available in the annual *Gale Directory of Publications* and in a separate volume of the annual *Ulrich's International Periodicals Directory.*

major indexing publications. Their value lies in providing the practitioner with current awareness information.

The best source for identifying these publications is the annual *Legal Newsletters in Print* of Infosources. It contains a Title List of over 2,200 newsletters published in the United States. It also includes a Publisher's Index and a Subject Index with over 300 subject entries.

6. Electronic Access to Legal Periodicals

The full text of many law review articles are available in the LAWREV Library of LEXIS–NEXIS and on WESTLAW in the TP–ALL database (Texts & Periodicals–All Law Reviews, Texts & Bar Journals) and in the JLR database (Journals & Law Reviews). There is also a separate library or database for each title covered. This online access means articles can be searched on both systems using Boolean logic or natural language searches. Since the legal periodical indexes described in the next section cannot capture all the nuances of an article in the subject headings assigned to it, this online access greatly enhances one's ability to locate topics discussed within the articles. Both CALR services have specialized features used for searching these articles. Therefore, the vendors' guides should be consulted for details.

Initially, the philosophies of these two CALR vendors differed as to how legal periodical articles were added to their services. Consistently, LEXIS-NEXIS has identified the specific law review and journal titles it considers most important and added the full text of each issue to its LAWREV Library. Over 400 titles are covered, with the date of coverage varying from the early 1980s to quite recently. From the 1980s until 1994 WESTLAW provided either selective or full-text coverage from law reviews. Beginning with volumes dated 1994 WESTLAW provides the full-text of approximately 600 law reviews, bar journals, and continuing legal education course materials online. Although coverage is not comprehensive in either WESTLAW or LEXIS–NEXIS, both continue to rapidly add law reviews, journals, and related materials to their services. Coverage is by no means limited to the traditional law review, as legal newspapers, bar journals, commercial legal periodicals, and newsletters are also included in the vendors' databases.

The Internet offers great promise for providing electronic access to law review sources. Several law schools, with Duke setting the example, are publishing their journals simultaneously on the Web and in print. This enables users to access these sources electronically without having to rely on the costly CALR services. This trend is likely to continue. Both FindLaw and the WashLaw Web provide excellent links to law review sites. The best source, however, is "Legal Journals on the Web" at the University of Southern California School of Law. The "University Law Review Project," a collaborative effort of online legal information suppliers, has a searchable database and a free service that distributes abstracts of recent law review articles via e-mail.

SECTION B.   COMPREHENSIVE PERIODICAL INDEXES

The usefulness of legal periodicals to legal research depends almost entirely on the researcher's ability to find what articles have been written and where they have been published. Generally, it is necessary to rely on indexes to legal periodical literature for this purpose.

1.   Jones–Chipman Index to Legal Periodicals

This was the first index that attempted to provide a comprehensive and systematic index to English language periodicals. It is in six volumes and covers periodicals published between 1803 to 1937. The first three volumes, which cover to 1908, precede the more extensive *Index to Legal Periodicals* that began in 1908 and is discussed *infra*. Therefore, these first three volumes of the *Jones–Chipman Index* must be consulted to locate articles prior to 1908.

2.   Index to Legal Periodicals & Books (ILP)

The *Index to Legal Periodicals*, which began in 1908, is a product of the H.W. Wilson Company and until 1980 was the only extensive index of legal periodical articles. *ILP* indexes approximately 600 English language legal periodicals published in the United States, Canada, Great Britain, Ireland, Australia, and New Zealand, so long as they regularly publish legal articles of high quality and of permanent reference value.

An advisory committee composed of law librarians and practitioners serves as a consultant to the publisher on editorial policy and content. New periodical titles that meet the criteria for inclusion are added each October. Articles must be at least five pages in length to be included. Biographies, bibliographies, book reviews, and case notes must be at least two pages in length to be indexed. Triennial cumulations were published through 1979. The present publication schedule is monthly, except September, with quarterly and then annual cumulations. A listing of periodicals covered—from the abbreviation used in *ILP* to full title—is included in the front of each issue and each volume.

In 1994, *ILP* began to index books and " *& Books*" was added to the title, although it is still most frequently referred to as *ILP*. Each month, approximately 2,500 law-related titles are extracted from Wilson's *Cumulative Book Index*. Thereafter, subject headings (typically two to three per book) are adapted to those used in *ILP* and then these entries are added at the end of periodical entries for those same subjects. The books indexed are from the same countries as those for periodicals.

ILP has four different access points:

a.   *Author/Subject Index.* Authors and subjects are included in one alphabet. Prior to 1983, the author entry cross references the researcher to the subject(s) under which the author's article is indexed. The cross reference includes the first letter of the title of the article. Under the subject, a full citation to the article, including the title, is provided. Since 1983, authors and subjects include full title and citation under each entry. Beginning in 1982, these citations to the journals are in *Bluebook* form. A list of subject headings used in *ILP* is included in the front of each issue and volume. A separate *Index to Legal Periodicals Thesaurus* (1988), which includes the primary term as well as broader, narrower, and related terms, enables a researcher to focus a search with substantial accuracy.

Commencing in 1994, author entries for books are included in this section. The subject entries for books are at the end of each subject entry for articles.

b. *Table of Cases*. This lists the names of cases (for the time period of the issue or volume) that have had a note or comment written on them. The listing is alphabetical by case name.

c. *Table of Statutes*. This lists statutes by subject under each jurisdiction, with federal laws listed first.

d. *Book Review Index*. This lists by author the books reviewed in the periodicals indexed by *ILP*.

[See Illustrations 17–1 through 17–3 for sample pages from the *Index to Legal Periodicals & Books*.]

The *Index to Legal Periodicals* also is available in a variety of electronic formats. WILSONLINE provides online access, updated twice weekly, to *ILP* from August 1981 and to over twenty other H.W. Wilson Company specialized databases. WILSONLINE is also available to commercial subscribers on both LEXIS–NEXIS and WESTLAW, but not to law schools because of the discounted rates they pay for these two CALR services. WILSONDISC, a CD–ROM product, covers *ILP* from August 1981, is updated and cumulated monthly, and can be accessed without online charges.

3. Current Law Index (CLI), Legal Resource Index (LRI), and **LegalTrac**

These three indexes, produced by Information Access Company, began in 1980 and are published under the auspices of the American Association of Law Libraries (AALL), with an advisory committee of AALL assisting with content selection. As will be described below, the three titles used for these indexes reflect their different formats and, in some instances, their slightly different coverage. These indexes cover substantially more titles than *ILP* and indexing is more extensive.

All titles indexed are in the English language, the exception being those in French from Canada, and coverage is worldwide. All materials of value are indexed without limitation as to the number of pages. Coverage begins with the 1980 imprint for each periodical. Subject headings of the Library of Congress are used. These products are computer-produced and each has the following features:

a. *Subject Index*. The subject heading list, based on Library of Congress Subject Headings and modified as needed, lists entries by subject, personal name (except authors or articles and reviewed works), and other proper names not included elsewhere.

b. *Author/Title Index.* This section lists all articles by author with full title and periodical citation and by title, again with the full bibliographic citation.

c. *Book Reviews.* Book reviews that appear in the periodicals covered by the indexes are listed under both the author and title of the book in the *Author/Title Index* section. An interesting feature is the rating of books from A to F, recording the opinion of the reviewer.

d. *Table of Cases.* Cases that are the subject of case notes are listed under the names of both plaintiff and defendant.

e. *Table of Statutes.* This lists all statutes cited in articles, by both official and popular citation.

(1) *Current Law Index (CLI).* This is a printed index issued monthly with quarterly and annual cumulations. It indexes over 800 periodicals, and each issue contains a list of periodicals indexed with addresses. The first seven volumes are each in single books. Effective with volume 8 (1987), *CLI* is published in two parts: Part A is a subject index; Part B is an index by author/title, cases, and statutes. [See Illustrations 17–4 through 17–6.] A four-volume Cumulative Subject Index covers 1991–1995.

(2) *Legal Resource Index (LRI).* *LRI* is the online counterpart of *CLI.* It includes all titles in *CLI,* plus several major legal newspapers, and articles selected from non-legal periodicals that are law-related. *LRI* is accessible through LEXIS–NEXIS, WESTLAW, and Dialog. It is this online access, updated daily, that greatly facilitates access to legal periodical literature from 1980 forward. It can be searched on LEXIS–NEXIS using Boolean logic, natural language, and segment searches, and on WESTLAW using Boolean logic, natural language, and field searches. In addition, a tape version of *LRI* can be purchased and added to a law library's online catalog.

(3) *LegalTrac.* LegalTrac is a CD–ROM version of the online *LRI,* covering the same time period and same materials as *LRI.* Using a keyboard, a researcher can enter a subject or name and the search will take one to that point in the database. A search can be expanded to include more than one word. For example, entering "assistance," "difference," and "Jones" as an "expanded" search retrieves all citations in which all three words appear in the citation. While rudimentary in terms of search logic and far less sophisticated than online searching of *LRI,* it offers great advantages over the print *CLI.* An attached printer enables a researcher to print out search results, rather than noting them manually. LegalTrac is updated monthly by a newly-issued cumulative disc. A separate program enables subscribers to this product to indicate whether their library subscribes to a periodical indexed in the database.

4. Current Awareness Publications

In-house law library publications designed to alert users to the most recent articles in legal periodicals by reproducing their contents pages are common. A similar type publication, but with a national distribution and especially useful, is *Current Index to Legal Periodicals (CILP)*. Published weekly by the Marian G. Gallagher Law Library of the University of Washington, this index covers articles too new to be in either *Current Law Index* or *Index to Legal Periodicals & Books*. It can be thought of as an advance sheet to the monthly issues of these two publications. *CILP* provides a subject index as well as the contents of the journals indexed. Recent issues are available on WESTLAW in the CILP database.

5. Contents Pages from Law Reviews and Other Scholarly Journals

This service is provided by the Tarlton Law Library at the University of Texas at Austin School of Law, and is made available from the Web site for the Law Library's online catalog, TALLONS. This current awareness tool helps researchers keep up-to-date about articles in the over 750 law reviews received by the Law Library. Tables of contents are scanned as soon as received and subscribers get updates automatically via e-mail. A three-month archive is kept online, after which time the articles are available through the standard law review indexing services. English-language journals are indexed under two categories, U.S. and non-U.S. Simple key word searching is available for the archive. Consult http://tarlton.law.utexas.edu/tallons/content_search.html.

6. Annual Legal Bibliography

Published by the Harvard Law Library from 1961 to 1981, this source indexed both the books and articles the Library received. Over 2,000 periodicals were covered.

SECTION C. ILLUSTRATIONS: LEGAL PERIODICALS AND INDEXES

17–1 to 17–3. Pages from Index to Legal Periodicals & Books
17–4 to 17–6. Pages from Current Law Index
17–7. Page from Volume 19, Western New England Law Review

[Illustration 17–1]

PAGE FROM SUBJECT AND AUTHOR INDEX— INDEX TO LEGAL PERIODICALS & BOOKS

SUBJECT AND AUTHOR INDEX   **17**

Arnold, Scott
See/See also the following book(s):
A complete guide to the Department of Defense Voluntary Disclosure Program; [by] Harvey G. Sherzer, Scott Arnold, David R. Francis. George Washington Univ. Govt. Contracts Program 1996 309p pa
ISBN 0-935165-37-1   LC 96-75727

Arnold, Tom
Twenty-one common mediation errors, and how to avoid them. 8 *Prac. Litig.* 79-88+ Jl '97

Arnopoulos, Paris J.
Public policy planning (general model and case study). 9 *Annals Air & Space L.* 179-99 '84

Arnot, David M.
The honour of the Crown. 60 *Sask. L. Rev.* 339-47 '96

Aronberg, David
Crumbling foundations: why recent judicial and legislative challenges to Title IX may signal its demise. 47 *Fla. L. Rev.* 741-813 D '95

Aronofsky, David
Voters wisely r
eliminate the
333-405 Sum

Arora, Vikas
The Communic
of the "right
'97

Arras, John D.
Physician-assi
Health L. &

Arrest
See also
Bail
Speedy tri

Ashford, Nicholas A.
See/See also the following book(s):
Technology, law, and the working environment; [by] Nicholas A. Ashford, Charles C. Caldart. rev ed Island Press (Covelo) 1996 xxvii,641p il pa
ISBN 1-55963-446-4   LC 96-21826

Asia-Pacific Economic Cooperation (Organization)
APEC and the new regionalism: GATT compliance and prescriptions for the WTO. A. A. Fayé, student author. 28 *Law & Pol'y Int'l Bus.* 175-215 Fall '96

Asian Pacific Economic Cooperation (Organization) *See* Asia-Pacific Economic Cooperation (Organization)

Askin, Frank
The privatization of public space and its impact on free speech. 185 *N.J. Law.* 12-14 Je '97

Asociación Latinoamericana de Libre Comercio
Legal systems of regional economic integration. S. A. Riesenfeld. 20 *Hastings Int'l & Comp. L. Rev.* 539-69 Spr '97

Asprey, Michele M.
See/See also the following book(s):

Federation Press

171
150-

rial countries. Dart-

12

> A page from the *Index to Legal Periodicals & Books.* Assume you are conducting research on assisted suicide.
>
> Note how entries for authors and subjects are in one alphabet.
>
> *ILP* is also available to commercial subscribers on WILSONLINE, LEXIS-NEXIS and WESTLAW, and on WILSONDISC.

Domestic violence as a crime against the state: the need for mandatory arrest in California. M. M. Hoctor, student author. 85 *Cal. L. Rev.* 643-700 My '97

China
Sheltering for examination (shourong shencha) in the legal system of the People's Republic of China. T.-tai Hsia, W. I. Zeldin. 7 *China L. Rep.* 95-128 '92

Great Britain
See/See also the following book(s):
Jason-Lloyd, L. The legal framework of police powers. Cass & Co. 1997 77p il

Northern Ireland
The reasonable suspicion test of Northern Ireland's emergency legislation: a violation of the European Convention on Human Rights. E. Kondonijakos. 3 *Buff. J. Int'l L.* 99-116 Summ '96

Arrest warrants
See also
Arrest

Arriaza, Naomi Roht- *See* Roht-Arriaza, Naomi

Arrigo, Maureen J.
Hierarchy maintained: status and gender issues in legal writing programs. 70 *Temp. L. Rev.* 117-87 Spr '97

Arriola, Elvia R.
LatCrit theory, international human rights, popular culture, and the faces of despair in INS raids. 28 *U. Miami Inter-Am. L. Rev.* 245-62 Wint '96/'97

Arson
See also
Fires and fire prevention
Fighting fire with fire: "reverse bad faith" in first-party litigation involving arson and insurance fraud. C. M. Little. 19 *Campbell L. Rev.* 43-66 Fall '96

Quebec (Province)
La gentrification et l'incendie criminel dans trois quartiers de Montréal. F. Therrien, L. Vallée, S. Dupuis. 63 *Assurances* 83-140 Ap '96

Art, Robert C.
Securitization of state ownership: Chinese securities law; by M. Gu, R. C. Art. 18 *Mich. J. Int'l L.* 115-39 Fall '96

Arthurs, Harry
Understanding labour law: the debate over "industrial pluralism". 38 *Current Legal Probs.* 83-116 '85

Artificial insemination

Great Britain
Life after death. J. Keown. 56 *Cambridge LJ.* 270-2 Jl '97

Arts and law *See* Law and the arts

Asbestos *See* Hazardous substances

Ash, Don R.
Bridge over troubled water: changing the custody law in Tennessee. 27 *U. Mem. L. Rev.* 769-841 Summ '97

nses under Chapter 11 of the Bankruptcy Code. B. N. Raderman, J. W. Murray. 6 *J. Bankr. L. & Prac.* 513-34 Jl/Ag '97

Inventors of the world, unite! A call for collective action by employee-inventors. A. Bartow. 37 *Santa Clara L. Rev.* 673-729 '97

Mortgage loan assignments: a primer in two parts [with form] (Pt. I). J. Stein. 13 *Prac. Real Est. Law.* 67-84 Jl '97

Novation agreements in corporate restructuring: the government's contractual stealth weapon. K. L. Manos. 26 *Pub. Cont. L.J.* 339-52 Spr '97

Assignments for benefit of creditors
See also
Fraudulent conveyances

Assisted suicide
See also
Euthanasia

Assisted suicide and disabled people. S. L. Mikochik. 46 *DePaul L. Rev.* 987-1002 Summ '97

Boot-strapping down a slippery slope in the Second and Ninth Circuits: Compassion in Dying [Compassion in Dying v. Washington, 79 F.3d 790 (9th Cir. 1996)] is neither compassionate nor constitutional. M. P. Miller, student author. 30 *Creighton L. Rev.* 833-54 My '97

Constitutional law—the development of liberty and the right to physician-assisted suicide—Compassion in Dying v. Washington, 49 F.3d 586 (9th Cir. 1995). M. G. Zagrodzky, student author. 38 *S. Tex. L. Rev.* 353-74 Mr '97

The constitutionality of statutes prohibiting and permitting physician-assisted suicide. J. R. Rosenn, student author. 51 *U. Miami L. Rev.* 875-905 Ap '97

Facing the final exit. A. D. Lowe. 83 *A.B.A. J.* 48-52 S '97

The Glucksberg [Washington v. Glucksberg, 117 S. Ct. 2258 (1997)] & Quill [Vacco v. Quill, 117 S. Ct. 2293 (1997)] amicus curiae briefs: verbatim arguments opposing assisted suicide. R. E. Coleson. 13 *Issues L. & Med.* 3-102 Summ '97

Physician-assisted suicide: a tragic view. J. D. Arras. 13 *J. Contemp. Health L. & Pol'y* 361-89 Spr '97

Physician-assisted suicide: symposium. Introduction. Last rights: assisted suicide and the limits of the judicial process. M. Zalman, J. Strate; Death with dignity or unlawful killing: the ethical and legal debate over physician-assisted death. D. A. Pratt, B. Steinbock; Whose life is it: decriminalize assisted suicide and euthanasia? E. Van den Haag. 33 *Crim. L. Bull.* 203-69 My/Je '97

Private uses of lethal force: the case of assisted suicide. R. Hittinger. 43 *Loy. L. Rev.* 151-79 Summ '97

Quarterly Report of the National Legal Center for the Medically Dependent & Disabled, Inc.—2nd quarter 1997. 13 *Issues L. & Med.* v-vii Summ '97

Suicide, Utopia and Saint Thomas More? P. Quirk. 71 *Austl. LJ.* 221-3 Mr '97

[Illustration 17–2]

PAGE FROM TABLE OF CASES—INDEX
TO LEGAL PERIODICALS & BOOKS

316 INDEX TO LEGAL PERIODICALS & BOOKS

Christopher; Lobue v., 893 F. Supp. 65 (D.D.C. 1995)
  15 Dick. J. Int'l L 385-404 Wint '97
  23 New Eng. J. on Crim. & Civ. Confinement 497-528 Summ '97
Chuckleberry Publ'g, Inc.; Playboy Enters., Inc. v. 1996 U.S. Dist. LEXIS 8435 (S.D.N.Y.)
  11 Int'l Rev. L. Computers & Tech. 155-92 Mr '97
Church of Scientology of Toronto; Hill v., [1995] 2 S.C.R. 1130
  8 Sup. Ct. L. Rev.2d 553-75 '97
Church of the New Faith v. Commissioner of Payroll Tax (Victoria), [1983] 154 C.L.R. 120
  14 U.N.S.W. L.J. 332-51 '91
Cie Trust nord-américain; Turmel v. [1994] R.J.Q. 1677
  97 R. du N. 180-218 Ja '95
Cincinnati, Inc.; Gregory v., 538 N.W.2d 325 (Mich. 1995)
  1996 Det. C.L. Rev. 721-65 Fall '96
CIO v. Newcastle City Council, [1996] 9 Austl. & N.Z. Ins. Cas., ¶ 61-301 at 76,356
  1 Newcastle L. Rev. 152-9 '96
Citibank (S.D.), N.A.; Smiley v., 116 S. Ct. 1730 (1996)
  52 Bus. Law. 1065-76 My '97
Citizens For a Better Env't v. Union Oil Co. of Cal., 83 F.3d 1111 (9th Cir. 1996)
  27 Golden Gate U. L. Rev. 43-66 Spr '97
Citizens for Covenant Compliance v. Anderson, 12 Cal. 4th 345 (1996)
  14 Cal. Real Prop. J. 25-30 Spr '96
City & County of Denver; United States v., 100 F.3d 1509 (10th Cir. 1996)
  26 Real Est. L.J. 101-5 Summ '97
City of Eastlake [...] (1976)
  29 Urb. Law. [...]
City of Edmonds [...]
  11 B.Y.U. J. [...]
  70 Temp. L. [...]
City of Linden; [...]
  48 Ala. L. R. [...]
City of Moorpar[...]
  48 Lab. L.J. [...]
  37 Santa Cla[...]
City of Napervill[...]
  85 Ill. B.J. 3 [...]
City of New Yor[...] (1978)
  22 B.C. Envt[...]
City of Niagara [...]
  28 Colum. Hum. Ris. L. Rev. [...]
City of Northlake; O'Hare Truck Serv., Inc. v., 116 S. Ct. 2353 (1996)
  29 Urb. Law. 341-50 Spr '97
City of Oakland; Fuller v., 47 F.3d 1522 (9th Cir. 1995)
  31 U.S.F. L. Rev. 665-701 Spr '97
City of Philadelphia; United Artists' Theater Circuit, Inc. v. 595 A.2d 6 (Pa. 1991)
  22 B.C. Envtl. Aff. L. Rev. 593-622 Spr '95
City of Philadelphia; United Artists' Theater Circuit, Inc. v., 635 A.2d 612 (Pa. 1993)
  22 B.C. Envtl. Aff. L. Rev. 593-622 Spr '95
City of Phoenix; Sabelko v. 68 F.3d 1169 (9th Cir. 1995)
  75 Or. L. Rev. 1297-331 Wint '96
City of Santa Maria; Ruiz v., No. CV-92-4879-JMI (C.D. Cal. Aug. 28, 1996)
  28 Colum. Hum. Ris. L. Rev. 605-28 Spr '97
City of Spokane; Marquis v., 922 P.2d 43 (Wash. 1996)
  72 Wash. L. Rev. 677-708 Ap '97
City of St. Paul; R.A.V. v., 112 S. Ct. 2538 (1992)
  19 Comm. & L. 55-77 Je '97
  72 Notre Dame L. Rev. 1361-89 Jl '97
City of Tigard; Dolan v., 114 S. Ct. 2309 (1994)
  3 Envtl. Law. 725-811 Je '97
  12 J. Land Use & Envtl. L. 303-41 Spr '97
  26 U. West L.A. L. Rev. 451-78 '95
Clary; United States v., 34 F.3d 709 (8th Cir. 1994)
  11 Notre Dame J. L. Ethics & Pub. Pol'y 307-49 '97
Clewis v. State, 922 S.W.2d 126 (Tex. 1996)
  38 S. Tex. L. Rev. 263-80 Mr '97
Clinton; Jones v., 72 F.3d 1354 (8th Cir. 1996)
  30 Creighton L. Rev. 913-47 My '97
Cocco v. Merchants Mortgage Co., 516 A.2d 596 (Md. 1986)
  16 U. Balt. L. Rev. 389-401 Wint '87
Cockatoo Dockyard Pty. Ltd.; Commonwealth v., [1995] 36 N.S.W.L.R. 662
  71 Austl. L.J. 436-58 Je '97
Cockenzie & Port Seton Community Council v. East Lothian D.C., [1996] S.C.L.R. 209
  1997 Jurid. Rev. 250-4 '97

Cohen v. Brown Univ., 879 F. Supp. 185 (D.R.I. 1995)
  23 Empl. Rel. L.J. 93-103 Summ '97
  47 Fla. L. Rev. 741-813 D '95
Collins; R. v. [1987] 1 S.C.R. 265
  39 Crim. L.Q. 435-92 My '97
Colorado Republican Fed. Campaign Comm. v. FEC, 116 S. Ct. 2309 (1996)
  14 Const. Commentary 91-126 Spr '97
  110 Harv. L. Rev. 1573-90 My '97
  81 Minn. L. Rev. 1565-600 Je '97
  75 N.C. L. Rev. 1848-90 Je '97
Columbus Skyline Sec., Inc., In re, 660 N.E.2d 427 (Ohio 1996)
  28 U. Tol. L. Rev. 301-17 Wint '97
Comeau's Sea Foods Ltd. v. Canada, [1997] 142 D.L.R.4th 193
  76 Can. B. Rev. 253-7 Mr/Je '97
Commission v. Belgium, E.C.J., Judgment, Sept. 12, 1996
  22 Eur. L. Rev. 157-65 Ap '97
Commission; Tetra Pak Int'l SA v., [1997] All E.R. (EC) 4
  28 Law & Pol'y Int'l Bus. 549-74 Wint '97
Commission v. United Kingdom, [1994] E.C.R. 2435
  29 Geo. Wash. J. Int'l L & Econ. 803-31 '96
Commissioner; A.E. Staley Mfg. Co. v., 105 T.C. 166 (1995)
  58 Ohio St. L.J. 583-616 '97
Commissioner; Brown Group, Inc. v. 77 F.3d 217 (8th Cir. 1996)
  14 Berkeley J. Int'l L. 239-89 '96
Commissioner; Geisinger Health Plan v., 985 F.2d 1210 (3d Cir. 1993)
  7 Health Matrix 351-80 Summ '97
Commissioner; Indopco, Inc. v. 112 S. Ct. 1039 (1992)

When you know that a particular case deals with the
subject under research, e.g., *Compassion in Dying v.
Washington*, citations to law review notes written about the
case can be located in the Table of Cases section of the *Index
to Legal Periodicals & Books*. Other issues of *ILP* should
be consulted for additional notes on the same case.

Current Law Index also contains a separate Table of
Cases.

  12 Austl. J.L. & Soc'y 1-36 '96
Commonwealth v. Cockatoo Dockyard Pty. Ltd., [1995] 36 N.S.W.L.R. 662
  71 Austl. L.J. 436-58 Je '97
Commonwealth v. Hyatt, 647 N.E.2d 1168 (Mass. 1995)
  23 New Eng. J. on Crim. & Civ. Confinement 529-58 Summ '97
Commonwealth; Langer v., [1996] 70 A.L.J.R. 176
  1 Newcastle L. Rev. 119-27 '96
Commonwealth; Polyukhovich v., [1992] 172 C.L.R. 501
  71 Austl. L.J. 267-93 Ap '97
Commonwealth v. Stoute, 665 N.E.2d 93 (Mass. 1996)
  81 Mass. L. Rev. 163-6 D '96
Compassion in Dying v. Washington, 49 F.3d 586 (9th Cir. 1995)
  35 Duq. L. Rev. 109-24 Fall '96
  38 S. Tex. L. Rev. 353-74 Mr '97
Compassion in Dying v. Washington, 79 F.3d 790 (9th Cir. 1996)
  83 A.B.A. J. 48-52 S '97
  71 Austl. L.J. 221-3 Mr '97
  30 Creighton L. Rev. 833-64 My '97
Compton v. Subaru of Am., 82 F.3d 1513 (10th Cir. 1996)
  1997 B.Y.U. L. Rev. 489-516 '97
Conner; Sandin v., 115 S. Ct. 2293 (1995)
  72 Chi.-Kent L. Rev. 923-47 '97
  7 Geo. Mason U. Civ. Ris. L.J. 25-48 Spr '97
  23 New Eng. J. on Crim. & Civ. Confinement 603-40 Summ '97
Consolidated Rail Corp.; Eckles v., 94 F.3d 1041 (7th Cir. 1996)
  46 DePaul L. Rev. 1043-55 Summ '97
Cooke; Midland Bank plc v., [1995] 4 All E.R. 562
  60 Mod. L. Rev. 420-7 My '97
Coors Brewing Co.; Rubin v. 115 S. Ct. 1585 (1995)
  5 Sup. Ct. Econ. Rev. 81-139 '97
Coppinger v. The County Council of the County of Waterford, unreported, High Ct. Ireland, Geoghegan, J., Mar. 22, 1996
  22 Eur. L. Rev. 173-8 Ap '97

[Illustration 17–3]

PAGE FROM BOOK REVIEWS—INDEX TO
LEGAL PERIODICALS & BOOKS

BOOK REVIEWS

A

Adams, J. N. and Brownsword, R. Key issues in contract. 1995
    11 *Int'l Rev. L. Computers & Tech.* 171-5 Mr '97. J. Wright
Adams on criminal law. 1996
    17 *N.Z.U. L. Rev.* 329-30 Je '97. W. Ball
Ademuni-Odeke. Protectionism and the future of international
    shipping. 1984
    10 *Dalhousie L.J.* 225-8 Je '86. T. L. McDorman
African-American women's health and social issues. 1996
    25 *J.L. Med. & Ethics* 62-4 Spr '97. T. L. Banks
Agresto, J. The Supreme Court and constitutional democracy.
    1984
    4 *Law & Hist. Rev.* 206-9 Spr '86. P. L. Murphy
Albert, S. Les réfugiés bosniaques en Europe. 1995
    9 *Int'l J. Refugee L.* 158-9 Ja '97. J. Thorburn
Ambivalent legacy. 1984
    3 *Law & Hist. Rev.* 451-3 Fall '85. J. R. Wunder
Amerasinghe, C. F. Principles of the institutional law of
    international organizations. 1996
    33 *Stan. J. Int'l L.* 164-5 Wint '97. C. Lyon
Anaya, S. J. Indigenous peoples in international law. 1995
    10 *Harv. Hum. Rts. J.* 333-41 Spr '97. M. Schmidt
Andersen, R. W. Understanding trusts and estates. 1994
    25 *Cap. U. L.*
Angell, M. Science
    17 *B.C. Third*
    18 *J. Legal M*
    32 *Trial* 80-1 |
The Arab-Israeli a
    23 *Syracuse J.*
Arnold, M. S. Une
    4 *Law & Hist. Rev.* 480-1 Fall '86. J. W. McKnight
Atias, C. Épistémologie du droit. 1994
    36 *C. de D.* 549-51 Je '95. B. Melkevik
Atkins, G. P. Latin America in the international political system.
    3rd ed. 1995
    28 *N.Y.U. J. Int'l L. & Pol.* 664-6 Spr '96. E. B. Dominguez

B

Baker, J. H. The order of serjeants at law. 1984
    5 *Law & Hist. Rev.* 293-5 Spr '87. M. E. Kennedy
Ball, S. R. Canadian employment law. 1996
    5 *Can. Lab. & Empl. L.J.* 122-4 '96. T. W. Brooker
Barnett, H. C. Toxic debts and the superfund dilemma. 1994
    13 *Yale L. & Pol'y Rev.* 133-5 '95. S. Sen
Barry, J. M. Rising tide. 1997
    9 *Envtl. Claims J.* 159-68 Summ '97. M. S. Quinn
Bartolomei de la Cruz, H. G. and others. The International
    Labor Organization. 1996
    18 *Comp. Lab. L.J.* 487-91 Spr '97. B. Aaron
Bassiouni, M. C. and Manikas, P. The law of the International
    Criminal Tribunal for the Former Yugoslavia. 1996
    25 *Denv. J. Int'l L. & Pol'y* 429-31 Wint '97. M. Madriz
Beatty, D. M. Constitutional law in theory and practice. 1995
    11 *Can. J. L. & Soc'y* 285-7 Fall '96. D. S. Campbell
Beaulieu, C. L'application de la Charte canadienne des droits et
    libertés au pouvoir judiciaire. 1995
    26 *R.D.U.S.* 209-12 '95. P. Blache
Behrendt, L. Aboriginal dispute resolution. 1995
    21 *Alternative L.J.* 300 D '96. S. Phillips
Bennett, M. J. Community, class, and careerism
    3 *Law & Hist. Rev.* 433-5 Fall '85. B. J. Harris
Bergeron, G. Tout était dans Montesquieu. 1996
    38 *C. de D.* 234-5 Mr '97. B. Melkevik
Bergman, P. and Asimow, M. Reel justice. 1996
    73 *N.D. L. Rev.* 389-93 '97. B. D. Quick
Bernardi, M.-J. Le droit à la santé du foetus au Canada. 1995
    26 *Rev. Gén.* 591-5 '95. J. Rhéaume
Bernier, J. Grèves et services essentiels/strikes and essential
    services. 1994
    26 *Rev. Gén.* 493-501 '95. B. Pelletier
Bertrand, J.-F. L'arrêt des procédures en droit criminel. 1995
    27 *Rev. Gén.* 94-7 '96. P. Kalantzis
The birth of a criminal code. 1995
    76 *Can. B. Rev.* 268-71 Mr/Je '97. W. A. Schabas
Black, C. L. A new birth of freedom. 1997
    83 *A.B.A. J.* 92 S '97. T. E. Baker

Blackshield, T. and others. Australian constitutional law and
    theory. 1996
    25 *Fed. L. Rev.* 205-9 '97. A. Twomey
    1 *Newcastle L. Rev.* 165-6 '96. C. Sneddon
Blouin, R. and Morin, F. Droit de l'arbitrage de grief. 4th ed.
    1994
    26 *Rev. Gén.* 597-603 '95. D. Nadeau
Bohémier, A. Faillite et insolvabilité. 1992
    24 *R.D.U.S.* 219-20 '93. P.-Émile Bilodeau
Bonsignore, J. J. Law and multinationals. 1994
    12 *Austl. J.L. & Soc'y* 195-7 '96. P. von Nessen
Bork, R. H. Slouching towards Gomorrah. 1996
    19 *Campbell L. Rev.* 1-42 Fall '96. A. L. Button
Bork, R. H. The tempting of America. 1990
    14 *U.N.S.W. L.J.* 376-9 '91. E. Handsley
Boulton, M. Torts. 1995
    2 *Deakin L. Rev.* 297-9 '95. M. McInnes
Bourcier, D. La décision artificielle. 1995
    11 *Can. J. L. & Soc'y* 319-25 Fall '96. C. Thomasset
Boussinesq, J. and others. La laïcité française. Mémento
    juridique. 1994
    25 *Rev. Gén.* 637-43 D '94. D. Le Tourneau
Boyce, T. Successful contract administration. 1992
    11 *Int'l Rev. L. Computers & Tech.* 171-5 Mr '97. J. Wright
    1993
                  urneau
                  1996
                  7. N. A. Akers
                  s. 1994
    26 *Rev. Gén.* 588-9 '95. M. Lafontaine
Bright, S. and Gilbert, G. Landlord and tenant law. 1995
    60 *Mod. L. Rev.* 612-14 Jl '97. N. Bamforth
Brock, D. The real Anita Hill. 1993
    5 *Yale J.L. & Feminism* 253-64 Spr '93. J. A. Brown
Brown, D. H. The genesis of the Canadian criminal code of
    1892. 1989
    20 *R.D.U.S.* 215-17 '89. L. Labreche-Renaud
Brown, L. R. Who will feed China? 1995
    28 *N.Y.U. J. Int'l L. & Pol.* 688-91 Spr '96. H. Han
Brun, M. L. and Johnstone, R. The quiet (r)evolution. 1994
    18 *U.N.S.W. L.J.* 566-9 '95. A. Marfording

C

Caenegem, R. C. van. An historical introduction to Western
    constitutional law. 1995
    4 *Griffith L. Rev.* 239-43 '95. T. Rowland
Campbell, R. W. Soviet and post-Soviet telecommunications.
    1995
    28 *N.Y.U. J. Int'l L. & Pol.* 679-82 Spr '96. G. Lumelsky
Caparros, E. Mélanges Germain Brière. 1993
    26 *Rev. Gén.* 159-72 '95. S. Guillemard
Carter, S. L. Integrity. 1996
    27 *Cumb. L. Rev.* 653-80 '96/'97. T. C. Berg
Chanock, M. Law, custom, and social order. 1985
    4 *Law & Hist. Rev.* 474-6 Fall '86. C. J. Greenhouse
Cherniss, C. Beyond burnout. 1995
    11 *Can. J. L. & Soc'y* 317-19 Fall '96. M. Oliver
Chinese women traversing diaspora. 1997
    17 *Loy. L.A. Ent. L.J.* 571-81 '97. M. Chon
Choo, A. L.-T. Hearsay and confrontation in criminal trials.
    1996
    76 *Can. B. Rev.* 282-7 Mr/Je '97. H. Stewart
Christie, A. Integrated circuits and their contents. 1995
    7 *J.L. & Info. Sci.* 240-2 '96. A. Payne
Clinton, B. Between hope and history. 1996
    34 *Harv. J. on Legis.* 617-22 Summ '97. J. F. Brennan
Collins, R. K. L. and Skover, D. M. The death of discourse.
    1996
    13 *J.L. & Pol.* 207-32 Wint '97. N. A. Vitan
Commercial dispute resolution. 1996
    14 *Int'l Constr. L. Rev.* 256-7 Ap '97. H. Lloyd
Comparative studies in construction law. 1995
    14 *Int'l Constr. L. Rev.* 262-4 Ap '97. H. Lloyd
Confronting sexual assault. 1994
    11 *Can. J. L. & Soc'y* 283-5 Fall '96. L. Beaman-Hall

Each issue of ILP has a separate Book Reviews section.
All books that have been reviewed in an issue are in one
alphabet listing the book's author and the book's title.

[Illustration 17–4]

PAGE FROM SUBJECT INDEX—CURRENT LAW INDEX

ASSET-BACKED SECURITIES	SUBJECT INDEX	

Tax facets of FASITs. (financial asset securitization investment trusts) by Haroldene F. Wunder
15 Journal of Taxation of Investments 22-29 Autumn '97

ASSET-LIABILITY management (Banking) *see also*
Bank deposits

ASSETS (Accounting)
Asset-based lending: an overview. by William Barnett
114 Banking

see also
Capital assets

ASSETS, capital *see*
Capital assets

ASSIGNMENTS
Murkiness in group
examples.(United Kingdo
Cor

ASSIGNMENTS for bene
Selling litigation - assi
insolvency office-l der
Fennell   *13 In:*

see also
Fraudulent conveyances

ASSIMILATION (Sociology) *see*
Discrimination
Emigration and immigration
Minorities

ASSISTANCE in emerge
"The Good Samaritan i
broadened duty to aid yo
desire to possess conceal
22 U

ASSISTED living facilitie
Assisted living in M
caring. by Alan S. Goldberg
41 Boston Bar Journal 10(4) Sept-Oct '97

see also
Nursing homes

ASSISTED suicide
Supreme Court upholds state statutes barring physician-assisted suicide. by David M. English
24 Estate Planning 392(5) Oct '97
The right to die: where do we go from here?(Cover Story) by Kenneth Thomas
44 The Federal Lawyer 22(9) Oct '97
Stepping carefully: House of Delegates declines to endorse physician-assisted suicide. (A.B.A) by James Podgers
83 ABA Journal 94(1) Oct '97
A right to physician-assisted suicide? by Erwin Chemerinsky
33 Trial 68(2) Sept '97
→ Assistance in dying: accounting for difference.(Symposium: Physician-Assisted Suicide) by Catherine J. Jones
19 Western New England Law Review 405-420 Spring '97
Natural causes, unnatural results, and the least restrictive alternative.(Symposium: Physician-Assisted Suicide) by Glies R. Schofield
19 Western New England Law Review 317-352 Spring '97
Rationality and injustice in physician-assisted suicide.(Symposium: Physician-Assisted Suicide) by Robert A. Burt
19 Western New England Law Review 353-369 Spring '97
Pleading for physician-assisted suicide in the courts.(Symposium: Physician-Assisted Suicide) by Charles H. Baron
19 Western New England Law Review 371-403 Spring '97

ASSOCIATED corporations *see*
Affiliated corporations

ASSOCIATION, Freedom of *see*
Freedom of association

ASSOCIATION, Right of *see*
Freedom of association

ASSOCIATIONS, institutions, etc. *see also*
Freedom of association
Nonprofit organizations
Religious institutions
Trade and professional associations

ASSOCIATIONS, International *see*
International agencies

ASSOCIATIONS (Law) *see*
Nonprofit organizations

ASSURANCE (Insurance) *see*
Insurance

ASYLUM, Right of
Female genital mutilation: the move toward the recognition of violence against women as a basis for asylum in the United States. by Patricia A. Armstrong
21 Maryland Journal of International Law and Trade 95-122 Spring '97

see also
Extradition
Holy Year

6

-Cases
Prosecuting the persecuted.(Case Note) Rodriguez-Roman v. INS 98 F.3d 416 (9th Cir. 1996) by Andrew Bonavia
22 North Carolina Journal of International Law and Commercial Regulation 1039-1064 Summer '97

ASYLUMS *see also*
Poor

ATHLETIC scholarships *see*
Scholarships

ATHLETICS *see also*
College sports
School sports
Sports

ATM (BANKING) *see*
Automated teller machines

ATM'S (Banking) *see*
Automated teller machines

ATTACHMENT and garnishment
Mareva injunctions in support of foreign proceedings. (United Kingdom) by Andrew Lemon
147 New Law Journal 1234(1236) August 15 '97

ATTEMPT, Criminal *see*
Criminal attempt

ATTEMPTED murder *see*
Criminal attempt

ATTENDANCE, School *see*
School attendance

ATTITUDE (Psychology) *see also*
NIMBY syndrome
Stereotype (Psychology)

ATTORNEY and client
Some expert advice: becoming an expert witness can invoke lawyer-client duties. by Arthur Garwin
83 ABA Journal 84(1) Oct '97
Bearing bad news. by Maureen B. Collins
85 Illinois Bar Journal 499(1) Oct '97
Civility: moving beyond the Code.(Professionalism) by Douglas G. O'Brien
23 Law Practice Management 34(4) Oct '97
Clients who change lawyers; risks for incoming and outgoing firms. (Australia) by Robwyn North
35 Law Society Journal 36(1) August '97
Skewing the results: the role of lawyers in transmitting legal rules. by Donald C. Langevoort and Robert K. Rasmussen
5 Southern California Interdisciplinary Law Journal 375-440 Summer '97

see also
Client development
Clients' funds

ATTORNEYS *see also*
Admission to the bar
Bar associations
Barristers
Corporate counsel
Government attorneys
Law firms
Law offices
Legal assistants
Minority attorneys
Practice of law
Right to counsel
Sole practitioners
Solicitors
Tax consultants
Women attorneys

-Advertising
Playing the marketing game. (attorney advertising) (includes related article on marketing problems) by Jon Newberry
83 ABA Journal 76(5) Oct '97

-Associations and societies
ADA talking about policy procedures: some in association call for limitations on what issues are addressed. by James Podgers
83 ABA Journal 32(2) Oct '97
Defining our work: issues before the House of Delegates should serve justice and the profession. (American Bar Association)(President's Page) by Jerome
83 ABA Journal 8(1) Oct '97

...tudes
...times you'll have to be hard-...ocate. by Mark Melickian
...Student Lawyer 13-2 Nov '97
...Steve Zipperstein lands in the ...on battlefield.(House Counsel)

...lifornia Lawyer S20(4) Oct '97
...nse in legal ethics: sending the ...young lawyers.(Legal ...M. Rice
...rest Law Review 887-933 Fall '97*

...haul in Vietnam. (John Dick)
...ciety Journal 17(1) August '97

...raphy
...a place in history. (Idaho) by ...dvocate (Idaho) 19(5) Oct '97
...riminal trial brought fame to a ...others are thankful for their ...y Michele Marcucci
...alifornia Lawyer 34(7) Oct '97
...Bobb: a profile of integrity & ...Clifford Gately
...1 CBA Record 22(3) Sept '97

...tion systems
Unified messaging. by Erik J. Heels
23 Law Practice Management 64(2) Oct '97

-Conduct of life
Pro bono pays: in positive karma for the law students and lawyers who do it, in justice for society's less-privileged members - and sometimes in publicity and financial rewards for law firms. by Di Mari Ricker
26 Student Lawyer 30-6 Nov '97
Ethics by the numbers: many lawyers have been asked by clients or other lawyers to violate conduct rules, survey suggests.(Brief Article) by Terry Carter
83 ABA Journal 97(1) Oct '97
Northern composure. (attorneys practicing in Aroostook County, Maine)(Cover Story) by Steven Keeva
83 ABA Journal 52(6) Oct '97
When good lawyers go bad. by John Betar Jr.
26 Student Lawyer 30(5) Oct '97
Professionalism, civility, ad the maritime bar: a view from the bench. by Charles L. Brieant
28 Journal of Maritime Law and Commerce 551-554 Oct '97
A life in the balance. by Michael Bryant
23 Law Practice Management 50(2) Oct '97
Balancing autonomy and accountability.(Professionalism) by Gerry Malone
23 Law Practice Management 22(5) Oct '97
Seven practical ways to make professionalism a part of your life. (Michigan)(State of the State Bar) by David L. Haron
76 Michigan Bar Journal 972(2) Sept '97
Hear no evil, see no evil, speak no evil: the intolerable conflict for attorney-mediators between the duty to maintain mediation confidentiality and the duty to report fellow attorney misconduct.(Alternative Dispute Resolution Symposium) by Pamela A. Kentra
1997 Brigham Young University Law Review 715-775 Summer '97

-Contracts
Of counsel and affiliated attorneys can cause disqualifications and vicarious liability. by Ronald E. Mallen and Sherri J. Conrad
23 Law Practice Management 53(2) Oct '97

-Discipline
Executive summary: Colorado lawyer regulation system.
26 Colorado Lawyer 75(2) Oct '97
Nonsanctioned removal brings sanctions. by Norman H. Robbins
20 Family Advocate 6(2) Fall '97
Complaints - the lay member's version. (Scotland) by Matt McManus
42 Journal of the Law Society of Scotland 376-378 Sept '97

-Employment
Alternate paths in law. (Canada) by Gerard V. La Forest
46 University of New Brunswick Law Journal 53-59 Annual '97

-Evaluation
Blaming the lawyer.(United Kingdom) by Robert S. Shiels
Criminal Law Review 740-744 Oct '97

Current Law Index is divided into separate indexes for Subjects and for Author/Title. This Illustration is from Subjects. Note the source indicated by the arrow and then see Illustration 17-7.

Notice how *CLI* uses subdivisions under subject headings.

The full title is given for each case note.

All citations in *CLI*, plus additional citations, are in *Legal Resource Index* and LEGALTRAC. *Legal Resource Index* is available on WESTLAW, LEXIS-NEXIS, and other online services.

[Illustration 17–5]

PAGE FROM AUTHOR/TITLE INDEX—CURRENT LAW INDEX

AUTHOR/TITLE INDEX   **JORDAN, LISA**

IT COULD Happen to Anyone: Why Battered Women Stay. by Ola W. Barnett and Alyce D. LaViolette rev by Dianne Casoni grade=B
39 Canadian Journal of Criminology 483-485 Oct '97

JACKSON, Vicki C.
What judges can learn from gender bias task force studies. by Vicki C. Jackson
81 Judicature 15(9) July-August '97
Seminole Tribe, the Eleventh Amendment, and the potential evisceration of Ex parte Young. by Vicki C. Jackson
72 New York University Law Review 495-546 June '97

JACOB, Anthony J.
Expanding judicial review to encourage employers and employees to enter the arbitration arena. by Anthony J. Jacob
30 John Marshall Law Review 1099-1125 Summer '97

JACOBSON, M.H. Sam
Using the Myers-Briggs Type Indicator to assess learning style: type or stereotype?(Themes in Academic Support for Law Schools) by M.H. Sam Jacobson
33 Willamette Law Review 261-313 Spring '97

JACOBY, Joan E.
The American prosecutor: from appointive to elective status. by Joan E. Jacoby
31 Prosecutor, Journal of the National District Attorneys Association 25(5) Sept-Oct '97

JAMAR, Steven D.
Summer for the Gods: The Scopes Trial and America's Continuing Debate over Science and Religion. by Edward J. Larson rev by Steven D. Jamar grade=A
12 Washington Lawyer, The 47(2) '97

International Monetary Cooperation Since Bretton Woods. by Harold James grade=A
30 George Washington Journal of International Law and Economics 181-182 Fall '96

JAMES, Richard
Delay and abuse of process.(United Kingdom) by Richard James *16 Civil Justice Quarterly 289-294 Oct '97*

JAMESON, J.N. St. C.
The Scots Dimension to Cross-Border Litigation. by R.E. Aird and J.N. St. C. Jameson rev by Kate Cartmell grade=B *13 Insolvency Law & Practice 132-1 July-August '97*

JAMIESON, Robert
Finance leases. (United Kingdom) by Robert Jamieson *139 Taxation 661-664 Sept 18 '97*

JANISCH, H.N.
Administrative Law: Cases, Text, and Materials, 4th ed. by J.M. Evans, H.N. Janisch, David J. Mullan and R.C.B. Risk rev by Margaret Allars grade=B
19 Sydney Law Review 411-420 Sept '97

JAPANESE Corrections: Managing Offenders in an Orderly Society.
by Elmer H. Johnson rev by Frank Keishman grade=A *25 International Journal of the Sociology of the Law 307-309 Sept '97*

JARVIS, Peter R.
Competence and confidentiality in the context of cellular telephone, cordless telephone, and E-mail communications. by Peter R. Jarvis and Bradley F. Tellam *33 Willamette Law Review 467-483 Spring '97*

JARVIS, Robert M.
Law students and the disorder of written expression. by Phyllis G. Coleman, Robert M. Jarvis and Ronald A. Shellow *26 The Journal of Law and Education 1-9 July '97*

JASANOFF, Sheila
Research subpoenas and the sociology of knowledge.(Court-Ordered Disclosure of Academic Research: A Clash of Values of Science and Law) by Sheila Jasanoff *59 Law and Contemporary Problems 95-118 Summer '96*

JAWORSKI, Robert M.
Car leasing developments: a roadmap for bankers. by Robert M. Jaworski *114 Banking Law Journal 726-730 Sept '97*
Car leasing developments require a roadmap. by Robert M. Jaworski *51 Consumer Finance Law Quarterly Report 281-288 Summer '97*

JEFFERS, Michelle
Women who sue; harassment cases against firms on the rise. (California) by Michelle Jeffers *17 California Lawyer 21(2) Oct '97*

JEFFERSON, Jon
Deleting cybercrooks: prosecutors want tough laws to put Internet hackers, scam artists and pedophiles on permanent log off. (includes related article) by Jon Jefferson *83 ABA Journal 68(6)*

JENCKES, Kenyon S.
Protection of foreign copyrights in China: the intellectual property courts and alternative avenues of protection. by Kenyon S. Jenckes *5 Southern California Interdisciplinary Law Journal 551-571 Summer '97*

JENERO, Kenneth A.
Supreme Court rules all employees count toward Title VII threshold. (U.S. Supreme Court) by Kenneth A. Jenero *129-132 Autumn '97*
Validity of FMLA regulatory notice requirements for employers challenged court. (1996 Family and Medical Leave Act) by Kenneth A. Jenero and Mark T. Dabertin *23 Employee Relations Law Journal 115-128 Autumn '97*

JENKINS, Fiona
Philosophia: The Thought of Rosa Luxemburg, Simone Weil and Hannah Arendt. by Andrea Nye rev by Fiona Jenkins grade=A *3 Res Publica 229-237 Autumn '97*

JENNINGS, John M.
Taxpayer Relief Act of 1997 offers significant estate planning opportunities. by James G. Blase and John M. Jennings *52 Taxes: The Tax Magazine 531-538 Oct '97*

JENTZ, Gaylord A.

relief: in re Arndt. by Daniel Joe *50 Tax Lawyer 855-862 Summer '97*

JOELSON, Mark R.
Litigating International Commercial Disputes by Lawrence W. Newman and David Zaslowsky rev by Mark R. Joelson grade=B *30 George Washington Journal of International Law and Economics 159-162 Fall '96*

JOG, Vijay M.
Flowthrough shares: premium-sharing and cost-effectiveness.(Canada) by Vijay M. Jog, Gordon J. Lenjosek and Kenneth J. McKenzie *44 Canadian Tax Journal 1016-1051 August '96*

JOHANSEN, Ingrid M.
Legal issues in school volunteer programs. (part 2) by Ingrid M. Johansen *28 School Law Bulletin 1-15 Summer '97*

JOHN Marshall: Definer of a Nation.
by Jean Edward Smith rev by Christopher C. Faille grade=A *44 The Federal Lawyer 48-51 Sept '97*

JOHNSON, Andrea L.
Distance learning and technology in legal education: a 21st century experiment. by Andrea L. Johnson *7 Albany Law Journal of Science & Technology 213-268 Spring '97*

JOHNSON, Andrew
The Hamburg Rules: From Hague to Hamburg via Visby, 2d ed. by Christof Luddeke and Andrew Johnson rev by Hugh M. Kindred grade=A *28 Journal of Maritime Law and Commerce 681-682 Oct '97*

JOHNSON, Christian A.
Derivatives and rehypothecation failure: it's 3:00 p.m., do you know where your collateral is? by Christian A. Johnson *39 Arizona Law Review 949-1001 Fall '97*

JOHNSON, Don E.
A comment on nonreclamation aspects of SMCRA.(Colloquium on SMCRA: A Twenty Year Review) by Don E. Johnson *21 Southern Illinois University Law Journal 445-448 Spring '97*

JOHNSON, Elmer H.
Japanese Corrections: Managing Offenders in an Orderly Society. by Elmer H. Johnson rev by Frank Keishman grade=A *25 International Journal of the Sociology of the Law 307-309 Sept '97*

JOHNSON, Herbert A.
The Chief Justiceship of John Marshall: 1801-1815. by Herbert A. Johnson rev by Christopher C. Faille grade=A *44 The Federal Lawyer 48-51 Sept '97*

JOHNSON, J. Rodney
The absence of due process in fiduciary accounting: a constitutional concern. (Virginia) by J. Rodney Johnson *23 Virginia Bar Association Journal 11(15) Fall '97*

JOHNSON, Julie
The sanctuary crumbles: the future of clergy malpractice in Michigan. by Julie Johnson *74 University of Detroit Mercy Law Review 493-523 Spring '97*

JOHNSON, Kenneth E.
The Lawyer's Guide to Creating Web Pages. by Kenneth E. Johnson rev by Stuart G. Kern grade=B *23 Law Practice Management 57(2) Oct '97*

JOHNSON-LAIRD, Andy
The anatomy of the Internet meets the body of the law.(Symposium: Copyright Owners' Rights and Users' Privileges on the Internet) by Andy Johnson-Laird *22 University of Dayton Law Review 465-509 Spring '97*

JOHNSON, Michael A.
A gap in the analysis: income tax and gender-based wage differentials. by Michael A. Johnson *85 Georgetown Law Journal 2287-2321 July '97*

JOHNSON, Philip McBride
Honey, they shrunk the accord. by Philip McBride Johnson *17 Futures & Derivatives Law Report 18(2) June '97*

JOHNSON, Walter D.
Economic science and hedonic damage analysis in light of Daubert v. Merrell Dow.(The Daubert Decision and Forensic Economics) by Thomas R. Ireland, Walter D. Johnson and Paul C. Taylor *10 Journal of Forensic Economics 139-156 Spring-Summer '97*

...ications and admissibility: applying the Daubert ... to economic testimony.(The Daubert Decision ...rensic Economics) by Thomas R. Ireland and D. Johnson *10 Journal of Forensic Economics 157-164 Spring-Summer '97*

..., D.
...w of pretext stops since Whren v. United States. ...a Guzaldo Gamrath and D. Johnston *85 Illinois Bar Journal 488(5) Oct '97*

..., Herbert
...ct of certification marks on innovation and the ...market-place. by Roberto Rozas and Herbert ...son *19 EIPR: European Intellectual Property Review 598-602 Oct '97*

JONES, Bryce J., II
Can an operating system vendor have a duty to aid its competitors? by Bryce J. Jones II and James R. Turner *37 Jurimetrics Journal of Law, Science and Technology 355-394 Summer '97*

JONES, Catherine J.
Assistance in dying: accounting for difference.(Symposium: Physician-Assisted Suicide) by Catherine I. Jones *19 Western New England Law Review 405-420 Spring '97*

JONES, Glower W.
Who pays for the unexpected? Recent US subsurface and differing site conditions deicisions. (part 2) by Glower W. Jones *14 The International Construction Law Review 463-485 Oct '97*

JONES, Marzetta
The 1996 Arizona Employment Protection Act: a return to the employment-at-will doctrine. by Marzetta Jones *39 Arizona Law Review 1139-1160 Fall '97*

JONES, Michael A.
The cost of medical negligence.(United Kingdom)(Editorial) by Michael A. Jones *13 Professional Negligence 69-1 Sept '97*

JONES, Nancy Byerly
Programs to help attorneys improve professionalism.(Professionalism) by Nancy Byerly Jones *23 Law Practice Management 28(5) Oct '97*

JONES, Traci L.
Reluctant experts.(Court-Ordered Disclosure of Academic Research: A Clash of Values of Science and Law) by Paul D. Carrington and Traci L. Jones *59 Law and Contemporary Problems 51-65 Summer '96*

JONES, Wendell J.
Lost in cyberspace: intellectual property issues on the Internet. by Wendell J. Jones *22 Thurgood Marshall Law Review 95-120 Fall '96*

JORDAN, Cally
Family resemblances: the family controlled company in Asia and its implications for law reform. by Cally Jordan *8 Australian Journal of Corporate Law 89-104 Oct '97*

JORDAN, Lisa
Deconstructing contingent staffing: flexible work, constrained choice, and union initiatives. by Lisa Jordan *48 Labor Law Journal 512-518 August '97*

135

A typical page from the Author/Title section of *Current Law Index*. This section serves as an index to articles by author and also as an index to book reviews. Note the following:

1. Authors are listed alphabetically with the complete title and citation.

2. Book reviews are listed under both the author and title of the book. Books are rated A–F according to the opinion of the reviewer.

[Illustration 17–6]

PAGE FROM TABLE OF STATUTES—CURRENT LAW INDEX

TABLE OF STATUTES   **RACKETEER INFLUENCED AND CORRUPT**

NORTH American Agreement on Labor Cooperation
The First American case under the North American Agreement for Labor Cooperation.
51 University of Miami Law Review 481-510 Jan '97

NORTH Carolina Limited Liability Company Act
The creation of North Carolina's Limited Liability Corporation Act.(Business Law Symposium: The Revolution of the Limited Liability Entity)
32 Wake Forest Law Review 179-192 Spring '97

NORTH Carolina School Health Education Act
Parental rights and school health: North Carolina's legislation. *28 School Law Bulletin 1-9 Wntr '97*

NORTH Carolina Workers' Compensation Act
A proposal to reform the North Carolina Workers' Compensation Act to address mental-mental claims.
32 Wake Forest Law Review 193-213 Spring '97

NORTHERN Territory. Rights of the Terminally Ill Act 1996
The International Covenant on Civil and Political Rights and euthanasia.(Australia)
20 University of New South Wales Law Journal 170-194 Wntr '97

NUCLEAR Waste Policy Act of 1982
The Winstar precedent and nuclear waste fund claims.
135 Public Utilities Fortnightly (1994) 43(3) May 15 '97

OCCUPATIONAL Safety and Health Act of 1970
Recent court decisions on important OSHA enforcement issues. (Occupational Safety and Health Administration) *22 Employee Relations Law Journal 147-152 Spring '97*

OIL POLLUTION Act of 1990
States' rights and the Oil Pollution Act of 1990: a sea of confusion? *25 Hofstra Law Review 607-637 Winter '96*
Natural resource damage assessm____
Pollution Act of 1990.
3 The Environmental L____

OKLAHOMA Computer Crimes Act
System provider liabili____ keeping.(Symposium: Electron____ Commerce) *50 Consumer Fin____ Report 2____*

OKLAHOMA Feed Yards Act
Environmental law: the Cle____ understanding when a concentrat____ operation should obtain an NPDE____ Pollutant Discharge Elimination Syst____ *49 Oklahoma Law Review 481-509 Fall '96*

OKLAHOMA Governmental Tort Claims Act
Torts: although faculty physicians, resident physicians, and interns face private tort liability for medical malpractice, the state is immune.(Oklahoma)(Case Note) *49 Oklahoma Law Review 537-552 Fall '96*

OMNIBUS Consolidated Rescissions and Appropriations Act of 1996
Constitutional law - Congress imposes new restrictions on use of funds by the Legal Services Corporation.
110 Harvard Law Review 1346-1351 April '97

ONTARIO. Automobile Insurance Rate Stability Act 1996
Walking through the automobile insurance maze.(Ontario)
19 Advocates' Quarterly 1-19 March '97

OREGON Public Employee Collective Bargaining Act
The changing landscape of school district negotiations: a practitioner's perspective on the 1995 amendments to the Oregon Public Employee Collective Bargaining Law. *32 Willamette Law Review 707-783 Fall '96*

PACIFIC Northwest Electric Power Planning and Conservation Act of 1980
Beyond the parity promise: struggling to save Columbia Basin salmon in the mid-1990s.(Symposium on Northwest Water Law)
27 Environmental Law 21-126 Spring '97

PARENTAL Kidnapping Prevention Act of 1980
The Parental Kidnapping Prevention Act: time to reassess.(The 1997 Symposium Edition: Family Law)
33 Idaho Law Review 351-387 Spring '97

PATENT Code
35 U.S.C. 102(b) Reevaluation the geographical limitation of 35 U.S.C. 102(b); policies considered.
22 University of Dayton Law Review 25-53 Fall '96
35 U.S.C. 171 Have trade dress infringement claims gone too far under the Lanham Act?
42 Wayne Law Review 1649-1683 Spring '96

PATENT Cooperation Treaty, 1970
Patent Cooperation Treaty (PCT) national stage commencement and entry in the United States of America. *79 Journal of the Patent and Trademark Office Society 296-304 April '97*

PATIENT Self-Determination Act of 1990
Keeping medical decisions near the end of life in the family. *15 Preventive Law Reporter 23-25 Winter '96*

PENNSYLVANIA Consolidated Statutes
18 Pa. Cons. Stat. 3101-3124 Act 10: remedying problems of Pennsylvania's rape laws or revisiting them?
101 Dickinson Law Review 203-231 Fall '96

PENNSYLVANIA Constitution
Pa. Const. art. 1, s. 28 Pennsylvania's doctrine of necessities: an anachronism demanding abolishment.
101 Dickinson Law Review 233-260 Fall '96

PENNSYLVANIA Land Recycling and Environmental Remediation Standards Act of 1995
The Land Recycling and Environmental Remediation Standards Act: Pennsylvania tells CERCLA enough is enough. *8 Villanova Environmental Law Journal 161-204 Wntr '97*

PENNSYLVANIA Post-Conviction Relief Act
Ineffective assistance of counsel under the Pennsylvania Post Conviction Relief Act.
69 Temple Law Review 1389-1412 Winter '96

PERSONAL Responsibility and Work Opportunity Act of 1996
New responsibilities, old problems: Washington meets the Welfare Reform Act.(Cover Story)
51 Washington State Bar News 19(3) May '97
Two recent acts aim at limiting aliens' access to public welfare. *51 Washington State Bar News 23(3) May '97*
New mechanisms for child support enforcement under the Personal Responsibility and Job Opportunity Reconciliation Act of 1996 (Welfare Reform Act).
9 Divorce Litigation 80-82 April '97
Preserving procedural due process for legal immigrants receiving food stamps in light of the Personal Responsibility Act of 1996.
110 Harvard Law Review 1191-1196 March '97
The family option of the Personal Responsibility and Work Opportunity Reconciliation Act of 1996: interpretation and implementation.(Cover Story)
30 Clearinghouse Review 1079-1100 March-April '97
Child care in the wake of the Federal Welfare Act.
30 Clearinghouse Review 1044-1060 Jan-Feb '97
Legal representation and advocacy under the Personal Responsibility and Work Opportunity Reconciliation Act of 1996. *30 Clearinghouse Review 932-949 Jan-Feb '97*
The impact of the Personal Responsibility and Work Opportunity Reconciliation Act of 1996 on food and nutrition programs.
30 Clearinghouse Review 950-963 Jan-Feb '97
Preserving services for immigrants: state and local implementation of the new welfare and immigration laws. *30 Clearinghouse Review 964-987 Jan-Feb '97*
The family law implications of the 1996 welfare legislation. *30 Clearinghouse Review 988-1007 Jan-Feb '97*
Thrown into the gap: employment discrimination in workfare. *18 Women's Rights Law Reporter 67-78 Fall '96*

PLANT Variety Protection Act of 1970
Guiding the hand that feeds: toward socially optimal appropriability in agricultural biotechnology innovation. *84 California Law Review 1395-1436 Oct '96*

PREGNANCY Discrimination Act of 1978
Only a little bit pregnant: the Pregnancy Discrimination Act from a performer's perspective.
17 Loyola of Los Angeles Entertainment Law Journal 489-515 Spring '97

PRIVACY Act of 1974
Reckless disregard: intentional and willful violations of the Privacy Act's investigatory requirements.
44 The Federal Lawyer 38-44 May '97
Privacy Act record restriction limited by court.
21 News Media & the Law 33-34 Wntr '97

PRIVATE Securities Litigation Reform Act of 1995
The Private Securities Litigation Reform Act of 1995: retroactive application of the RICO amendment.
23 Journal of Legislation 283-305 Summer '97

The coming changes in securities litigation. (part 1)
v8 The Practical Litigator p35(16) May '97
The nonretroactivity of the Private Securities Litigation Reform Act of 1995.
25 Securities Regulation Law Journal 60-86 Spring '97
Proportionate liability, contribution, and indemnification under the Reform Act.
30 Review of Securities & Commodities Regulation 55-63 March 12 '97
Litigation Reform Act precludes RICO claim.
17 Futures & Derivatives Law Report 19(2) March '97
Section 10(B) and the vagaries of federal common law: the merits of codifying the private cause of action under a structuralist approach.
1997 University of Illinois Law Review 71-145 Wntr '97
Has Congress learned its lesson? A plain meaning analysis of the Private Securities Litigation Reform Act of 1995. *71 St. John's Law Review 99-124 Wntr '97*
A practitioner's view of the Private Securities Litigation Reform Act of 1995.
31 University of San Francisco Law Review 283-343 Wntr '97
The Private Securities Litigation Reform Act of 1995: protecting corporations from investors, protectecting investors from corporations, and promoting market efficiency. *31 New England Law Review 655-704 Wntr '97*
Running the gauntlet: a description of the arduous, and now often fatal, journey for plaintiffs in federal securities law actions. (Ninth Annual Corporate Law Symposium: Securities Regulation)
____ University of Cincinnati Law Review 3-41 Fall '96
____sclosure: special problems in public ____looking information, including the ____ a Litigation Reform Act of ____gulation Symposium)
____San Diego Law Review 1027-1076 Summer '96
____ promises kept: the practical ____ivate Securities Litigation Reform ____es Regulation Symposium)
____iego Law Review 845-891 Summer '96
Pleading scienter under Section 21D(b)(2) of the Securities Exchange Act of 1934: motive, opportunity, recklessness, and the Private Securities Litigation Reform Act of 1995.(Securities Regulation Symposium) *33 San Diego Law Review 893-957 Summer '96*
Legislation on a false foundation: the erroneous academic underpinnings of the Private Securities Litigation Reform Act of 1995.(Securities Regulation Symposium)
33 San Diego Law Review 959-1025 Summer '96
Private Securities Litigation Reform Act of 1995 and investors' rights. *65 The Hennepin Lawyer 12(5) March-April '96*
Matsushita and beyond: the role of state courts in class actions involving exclusive federal claims.
Supreme Court Review 219-283 Annual '96

PROFESSIONAL Boxing Safety Act of 1996 (Draft)
Regulating the sport of boxing - Congress throws the first punch with the Professional Boxing Safety Act.
7 Seton Hall Journal of Sport Law 103-127 Wntr '97

PROTOCOL on Blinding Laser Weapons
Blinding laser weapons and Protocol IV: obscuring the humanitarian vision. (Convention on Prohibition or Restrictions on the Use of Certain Conventional Weapons Which May Be Deemed to Be Excessively Injurious or to Have Indiscriminate Effects, Protocol on Blinding Laser Weapons)
15 Dickinson Journal of International Law 237-264 Fall '96

QUEBEC. Youth Protection Act
Le droit de l'enfant a la representation par un avocat en matiere de protection de la jeunesse. (Quebec)
37 Cahiers de Droit 971-994 Dec '96

RACKETEER Influenced and Corrupt Organizations Act
The modern RICO enterprise: the inoperation and mismanagement of Reves v. Ernst & Young.
71 Tulane Law Review 1133-1210 March '97
Margins of the mob: a comparison of Reves v. Ernst & Young with criminal association laws in Italy and France. *20 Fordham International Law Journal 263-322 Nov '96*
Racketeering Influenced Corrupt Organization Act.(The D.C. Circuit Review: September 1994 - August 1995)
64 George Washington Law Review 1441-1449 June-August '96

611

A page from the Table of Statutes of Current Law Index. If the name of a statute is known, this index will lead you to articles dealing with that statute.

The Index to Legal Periodicals and Books contains a similar index.

[Illustration 17–7]

PAGE FROM VOLUME 19—WESTERN NEW ENGLAND LAW REVIEW

Volume 19
Issue 2
1997

WESTERN NEW ENGLAND LAW REVIEW

ASSISTANCE IN DYING: ACCOUNTING FOR DIFFERENCE

CATHERINE J. JONES*

We tend to live—or think we live—in a generically driven society. Sizes are unisex; directions on medicine bottles are written for adults or children (that's as specific as it gets); medical research often is conducted on patient populations that exclude many of the persons most affected by the conditions being studied, often in the name of "protecting" them. Our generic standards are no more generic, t ⌐An example of a lead article from a law school law review.⌐ ·y assertion th └ ┘ dged by a standard of the "man of ordinary prudence."[1] Although Chief Justice Tindal's standard was subsequently interpreted to be gender neutral and generic, my guess is that when he said "man of ordinary prudence" he meant just that.

I believe in making legal the giving of assistance to those who would choose to end their lives by other than natural causes.[2] I am not sure my position on legalization of assisted dying is correct. What I am sure of, however, is that if we frame the question in terms of the so-called generic patient—if we do not consider issues

* Professor of Law, Western New England College School of Law; B.A., Gettysburg College; J.D., Georgetown University Law Center; L.L.M., Yale Law School. This article was originally presented at the Physician-Assisted Suicide Symposium at Western New England College School of Law on October 18, 1996. I have made minor revisions to the text since that time.

My thanks to David Moss, who may give new meaning to the expression "Fools rush in where angels fear to tread." Last spring, when David called to tell me about his plans for the Conference, I was overwhelmed that a new teacher, teaching four new courses in his first year at an institution, would take on such a major task. I knew, however, that David is very competent and I could hear the enthusiasm in his voice, so I encouraged him. The Conference was the result of that competence and enthusiasm. My thanks also to Joan Mahoney who, as Dean of the law school, told David to "Go for it" when he presented her with his ideas. Her support was crucial to the Conference. Finally, I am very grateful to Michele Dill LaRose and Pat Newcombe of the law school's library staff without whose assistance this paper would not have been completed, or even started. Michele's and Pat's work exemplifies what is both routine and best about the law school's superb library staff.

1. Vaughan v. Menlove, 132 Eng. Rep. 490 (C.P. 1837).

2. I prefer the term "assisted dying" rather than "physician-assisted suicide" because of the negative connotations associated with the word "suicide."

SECTION D. OTHER INDEXES TO PERIODICAL LITERATURE

Several other periodical indexes, less comprehensive than those discussed in Section B, can often be useful in legal research.

1. Index to Periodical Articles Related to Law

The *Index to Periodical Articles Related to Law*[23] began in 1958 in recognition of the importance that other disciplines have for the law. It indexes articles of a legal nature in English that, in the judgment of the editors, are of research value and appear in periodicals not covered by the *Index to Legal Periodicals, Index to Foreign Legal Periodicals,* or *Legal Resource Index.* It is issued quarterly and cumulated annually. Citations are arranged alphabetically by subject, with a separate author index. A four-volume, thirty-year cumulation covering 1958–1988 consists of a two-volume subject index and a two-volume author index. A one-volume, five-year cumulation covers 1989–1993.

Since legal subjects are assuming greater prominence in a variety of non-legal journals, this *Index* is particularly valuable in locating timely articles on newly-developing areas that often first appear in non-legal periodicals. With fifteen or more different periodical indexes being brought together in this publication, it is useful as a companion to the comprehensive legal periodical indexes.

2. Index to Foreign Legal Periodicals

The *Index to Foreign Legal Periodicals* began in 1960 and is published under auspices of the American Association of Law Libraries. It indexes over 400 legal and business periodicals from 59 countries as well as collections of essays that deal with public and private international law, comparative law, and the municipal law of all countries of the world other than the United States, the British Isles, and nations of the British Commonwealth whose legal systems are based on the common law. Subject headings are in English, but titles of articles using the Roman alphabet are printed in the language of publication. Titles of articles using a non-Roman alphabet are translated into English, with an indication of the language of publication. Translations of the English language subject headings are provided in separate sections for the French, German, and Spanish languages.

This *Index* is published quarterly. Triennial cumulations were published until 1983; since 1984 annual cumulations have been published. Articles less than four pages and book reviews less than two and one-half pages in length are generally excluded from indexing.

The *Index to Foreign Legal Periodicals* is divided into the following units: (1) subject index; (2) geographical index, grouping—by country or region—the topics of articles listed in the subject index; (3) book review

---

[23] Glanville Publishers, Inc., Dobbs Ferry, NY. 10522. Edited by Roy M. Mersky, J. Myron Jacobstein, and Donald J. Dunn.

index; and (4) author index. The author index entries refer to the subject index where the citations are complete.

3. Index to Canadian Legal Periodical Literature

This index was started by the Canadian Association of Law Libraries in 1961 to cover the growing number of Canadian legal journals and give access to two systems of law, civil and common, in two languages, English and French. This index covering more than 125 titles is published by Index to Canadian Legal Periodical Literature of Montreal in quarterly and since 1986 in annual cumulative volumes. Four cumulative volumes cover 1961–70, 1971–75, 1976–80, and 1981–85.

4. Legal Journals Index

This index, which began in 1986, includes monthly parts and quarterly cumulations, plus an annual cumulative bound volume. It indexes all items in over 300 British legal journals and is published by Legal Information Resources Ltd. of West Yorkshire, England.

5. Index to Indian Legal Periodicals

Since 1963 the Indian Law Institute of New Delhi, India, has issued this publication, which indexes periodicals (including yearbooks and other annuals) pertaining to law and related fields published in India. It is issued semi-annually with annual cumulations.

6. Index to Legal Periodicals in Israel

A single volume published by the Bar Ilan University Law Faculty Library covers from 1976–1996 and includes about 30 periodicals, jubilee volumes, and compilations of essays. Supplements are planned.

7. European Legal Journals Index

Begun in 1993, this monthly publication indexes almost 300 titles that include articles relating to the Council of Europe, European Communities, and the individual European countries. It is published by Legal Information Resources Ltd. of West Yorkshire, England.

8. Legal Information Management Index

This index (Legal Information Services, Newton Highlands, Mass.), published since 1984, is issued bimonthly with an annual cumulation. It indexes approximately 100 periodicals published in the United States and abroad, including journals, newsletters, newspapers, and annuals. Substantive English-language articles, bibliographies, surveys, and reviews relating to legal information management and law librarianship are covered. It includes key word, author, and review indexes.

9. Annuals and Surveys Appearing in Legal Periodicals: An Annotated Listing

Begun in 1987, this looseleaf volume is divided into three sections: state surveys; federal court surveys; and subject-specific surveys. Each listing contains the title of the survey, the name of the publication in which it appears, the author, descriptive notes, and citations. It is supplemented annually and is published by Fred B. Rothman & Company.

SECTION E. INDEXES TO SPECIAL SUBJECTS

Several indexes provide access to periodical articles on particular legal or law-related subjects. These include:

1. Index to Federal Tax Articles

This index, published by Warren, Gorham & Lamont, is a computer-produced bibliography first published in 1975. It covers the literature on federal income, estate, and gift taxation contained in legal, tax, and economic journals, as well as non-periodical publications. Consisting of separate subject and author indexes, entries are arranged in reverse chronological order under author's name. Three volumes provide retrospective coverage from 1913 to 1974. Since 1974 articles are in bound volumes, with the most recent articles in quarterly supplements.

2. Federal Tax Articles

This looseleaf reporter of Commerce Clearing House, Inc. began in 1962 and is updated monthly. It contains summaries of articles on federal taxes (income, estate, gift, and excise) appearing in legal, accounting, business, and related periodicals. Proceedings and papers delivered at major tax institutes are also noted. The contents are arranged by Internal Revenue Code section numbers. Separate author and subject indexes are also provided. Cumulative bound volumes, with coverage dating from 1954, are published periodically to make room for current materials in the looseleaf volume.

3. Criminal Justice Periodical Index

This quarterly index, published by University Microfilms International, covers over 100 criminal justice and law enforcement periodicals published in the United States, England, and Canada. There is an author index and a subject index, which includes case names.

4. Kindex

Subtitled, *An Index to Legal Periodical Literature Concerning Children, Kindex* is published by the National Center for Criminal Justice and is issued six times each year with annual cumulations. The indexers emphasize practical information for those involved in the criminal justice system.

5. Non–Legal Periodical Indexes

Since law impinges on all disciplines, it is sometimes necessary to turn to comprehensive indexes that are non-legal in nature to ascertain general information or to examine legal issues from a non-legal perspective. There are numerous indexes of this type, and they should not be overlooked when exhaustive research is required. For example, H.W. Wilson Company, publisher of *ILP*, also publishes several non-legal indexes, including the following: *Business Periodicals Index; Humanities Index; Reader's Guide to Periodical Literature*, which covers popular magazines; and *Social Science Index*. *PAIS International*, published by Public Affairs Information Service, Inc., focuses on economics and public affairs and includes several law reviews and government publications in its coverage.

The Information Access Company, publisher of *CLI, LRI,* and Le-galTrac, also publishes a number of non-legal indexes, including the following: *Academic Index,* which covers scholarly publications from numerous disciplines; *Magazine Index,* an index somewhat comparable to *Reader's Guide; Business Index,* and *Trade and Industry Index.*

The *U.S. Government Periodicals Index,* which began in 1994 and is issued quarterly, indexes significant articles in approximately 175 U.S. government periodicals from October 1993 forward. This publication of the Congressional Information Service is produced in print, CD–ROM, and MARC tape formats.

SECTION F. PERIODICAL DIGESTS AND ABSTRACTS

1. Criminology and Penology Abstracts

This is a biweekly international abstracting service covering the etiology of crime and juvenile delinquency, the control and treatment of offenders, criminal procedure, and the administration of justice. Former-ly *Excerpta Criminologica* (Volumes 1–8, 1961–68), *Criminology and Penology Abstracts* is prepared by the Criminologica Foundation in cooperation with the University of Leiden, The Hague, Netherlands.

2. Callaghan's Law Review Digest

This bimonthly digest, which began in 1950 and ceased in 1989, contains selected, condensed articles from the legal literature.

3. Monthly Digest of Tax Articles

This monthly periodical by Newkirk Products presents significant current tax articles in abridged form.

SECTION G. OTHER SOURCES

References to legal periodical articles are frequently found in other reference books. Many state codes and the annotated editions of the *United States Code* cite relevant articles in the notes preceding the annotations. Most of the West digests will, under the Topic and Key number, give citations to pertinent law review articles. Similarly, many other West Group sources, including both national legal encyclopedias, provide references to legal periodical articles.

In addition, *Shepard's Citations* provides, through several means, the ability to locate articles cited by courts and other legal periodicals and to locate articles that cite to cases, constitutions, statutes, and rules. These sources are:

1. Shepard's Law Review Citations

This citator, with coverage beginning in 1957, provides citations for almost 200 legal periodicals that have been cited in published reports of the state and federal courts. [See Illustration 17–8.]

2. Federal Law Citations in Selected Law Reviews

This citator lists each time any of the nineteen national law school law reviews covered by *Shepard's Citations*[24] cites to a case in the *U.S. Reports, Federal Reporter* (F., F.2d, F.3d), *Federal Cases, Federal Supplement, Federal Rules Decisions, Bankruptcy Reporter,* and other lower federal court reporters, and each time any of these reviews cites to the U.S. Constitution, any edition of the *United States Code,* or the various federal court rules. It also provides citations to each time any of the nineteen law reviews cites to a review in this group. Coverage is for articles published since 1973. [See Illustration 17–9.]

3. Legal Periodical Citations in Other Units of Shepard's Citations

The individual state citators provide citations to cases, statutes, constitutions, and court rules that have been cited in the law reviews and bar journals of the state unit being used, by the nineteen national law reviews, and by the *ABA Journal. Shepard's United States Citations* and *Shepard's Federal Citations* also provide citations to the *ABA Journal.*

**SECTION H.   ILLUSTRATIONS: LAW REVIEW
CITATIONS IN SHEPARD'S CITATORS**

17–8. Page from Shepard's Law Review Citations
**17–9. Page from Shepard's Federal Law Review Citations in
     Selected Law Reviews**

[24] This list of law reviews is provided in Chapter 15.

[Illustration 17–8]

PAGE FROM SHEPARD'S LAW REVIEW CITATIONS

STANFORD LAW REVIEW					Vol. 35

		Vol. 34	**– 513 –**	17GaL289	83McL1540	**Vol. 35**	132PaL76
36StnL1169	52GW672		32EmJ187	73Geo96	42MdL216		132PaL1309
62TxL1279	52GW703	**– 1 –**	69ILR122	96HLR803	59NYL2	**– 1 –**	17Suf597
63TxL234	95HLR630	32Buf546		69ILR101	36StnL477	741F2d1562	71VaL515
71VaL75	97HLR1355	29CLA72	**– 739 –**	82McL321	17UCD759	40BL105	86WVL1080
7VtL273	21HUL111	32CLA505	83Mch1256	131PaL1351	92YLJ594	50ChL542	
1982WLR	30KLR493	67Cor1039	33Buf729	133PaL550		32CLA457	**– 175 –**
[1071	45LJ526	64MBJ283	63BUR833	133PaL698		84CR1146	38BRW904
1984WLR	80McL1175	12PLR3	49ChL995	58SCL279		19GaL309	1983AzS385
[388	43MdL257	37SLJ1100	30CLA1200	58SCL624		52GW678	64BUR95
94YLJ6	56NYL661	36StnL300	32CLA37	35StnL241		52GW753	50ChL1052
94YLJ8	58NYL947	36StnL611	83CR4	36StnL248		97HLR1363	53FR953
94YLJ827	59NYL279	59TxL705	16Crt600	37StnL4		80McL1175	98HLR1436
	38SLJ863	1981WLR	8Day634	59TuL292		43MdL271	60ILJ78
– 447 –	34SR979	[1126	8Day804	60TxL395		30NYF28	68MnL921
451US635	34StnL776	1983WLR	9Day211	60TxL578		58NYL995	133PaL992
68Lℤ505	35StnL3	[650	10Day810	62TxL1240		59NYL279	36StnL733
101SC2064	35StnL24	94YLJ295	1984DuL	1985UtLR		38SLJ863	
50ChL655	35StnL51	94YLJ512	[104			34SR979	**– 213 –**
52ChL644	36StnL978		17GaL289	29VR674		35StnL23	35Mer841
1982DuL557	70VaL380	**– 113 –**	18GaL167	92YLJ963		35StnL51	37MiL493
46PitL115	35VLR1089	464US519	73Geo96	94YLJ837		36StnL983	69MnL299
14SeH53	28VR55					70VaL654	133PaL550
	91YLJ8					70VaL670	98HLR1175
– 473 –	93YLJ8					35VLR1268	58SCL285
667F2d859						94YLJ271	29StLJ378
71CaL878	**– 97**						70VaL836
7Day313	546FS1					**– 23 –**	
80McL362	1982Az!					741F2d1562	**– 387 –**
15SMJ557	32KLR1					71CaL1100	53USLW
63TxL460	15LoyL					50ChL542	[4407
	132Paℤ					32CLA457	14EnL358
– 591 –	132Paℤ					84CR1147	
562FS398						52GW679	**– 423 –**

This unit of *Shepard's* provides a means for "Shepardizing" law review articles cited since 1957. Through its use, one can find every time a law review article has been cited by another law review or in a court case.

73CaL1094	73CaL1060	78NwL1446	35StnL3	52GW752	Alk
73CaL1192	85CR462	131PaL790	35StnL48	97HLR1363	689P2d478
31CLA1007	23Duq95	133PaL550	35StnL61	59NYL279	NY
85CR901	34FLR369	58SCL76	70VaL614	38SLJ863	462Nℤ1146
34HLJ1035	11JCUL196	58SCL165	28VR65	34SR979	474NYS2d
10Hof742	60NDL631	58SCL279		35StnL3	[428
96HLR563	130PaL613	58SCL566	**– 957 –**	35StnL51	63NbL731
97HLR705	130PaL685	58SCL604	19GaL507	36StnL984	70VaL903
37MiL391	131PaL728	34StnL766	73KLJ476	70VaL654	
68MnL537	132PaL1331	35StnL241	37MiL424	1984WLR	**– 649 –**
130PaL1350	36RLR29	36StnL207	58NYL518	[637	29StLJ1077
131PaL734	55SCL1009	36StnL279	15RLJ26		29StLJ1163
56SCL1192	34StnL64	36StnL490	57SCL562	**– 51 –**	36StnL299
35StnL677	60TxL14	36StnL721	94YLJ10	50ChL542	70VaL1367
36StnL211	62TxL417	36StnL1325		32CLA457	
36StnL255	16UCD926	37StnL2	**– 1017 –**	84CR1147	**– 681 –**
36StnL301	68VaL206	59TuL298	85CR941	19GaL311	85Lℤ439
36StnL427	70VaL55	60TxL392		52GW753	105SC2087
71VaL197	70VaL1236	60TxL497	**– 1133 –**	97HLR1363	53USLW
19WFL357	36VLR1498	60TxL578	105SC3390	80McL1175	[4531
94YLJ6	25W&M190	62TxL1240	105SC3399	59NYL279	125NH64
94YLJ345		62TxL1502	53USLW	38SLJ863	Iowa
	– 275 –	63TxL389	[5091	34SR979	368NW73
– 773 –	693F2d267	29VR672	724F2d1534	35StnL3	NH
16JMR16	92YLJ771	92YLJ678	310NC70	35StnL24	480A2d874
43LJ671		92YLJ1132	NC	36StnL983	NY
12Mem570	**– 385 –**	93YLJ1045	310Sℤ307	37StnL366	489NYS2d
132PaL453	461US490	94YLJ4	33Buf360	70VaL604	[828
24W&M207	76Lℤ90	94YLJ834	53FR393	70VaL654	1984BYU307
10WmM199	103SC1970		15ToI1399	94YLJ271	71VaL4
	693F2d1105	**– 765 –**			93YLJ614
– 819 –	566FS1382	27AzL59	**– 1183 –**	**– 69 –**	
741F2d1560	582FS1144	33Buf729	748F2d163	37AkL567	**– 857 –**
741F2d1562	51USLW	63BUR836	63BUR614	72CaL1045	757F2d169
568FS1547	[4570	30CLA1203	49ChL986	69Cor70	40BL1454
17Akr429	16Pcf106	32CLA37	32CLA496	84CR49	52ChL107
71CaL1120	32SR8ℤ2	83CR4	70Cor822	32DeP269	52ChL645
32CLA457	57TLQ589	84CR1731	34DeP143	34DR390	73KLJ286
70Cor2ℤ	57TuL1295	8Day708	33EmJ718	36FLR707	30NYF16
83CR250	58TuL779	8Day803	52GW278	52FR487	36StnL1007
84CR1147	15UCD841	9Day175	69ILR54	1982IlLRℤ34	70VaL629
1985DuL5		1984DuL	471CP(1)301	59NYL488	*Continued*
19GaL320		[1211	45LJ29		

[Illustration 17–9]

PAGE FROM SHEPARD'S FEDERAL LAW CITATIONS IN SELECTED LAW REVIEWS

UNITED STATES SUPREME COURT REPORTS   **Vol. 494**

1991WLR462	—440—	—781—	100YLJ2319	59ChL203	—265—	—815—	—113—
100YLJ1580	79CaL719	79CaL915	101YLJ189	59ChL480	91McL647	Case 1	93CR312
101YLJ333	58CbL29	105HLR570	101YLJ1208	104HLR1367	140PaL120	91McL117	91McL329
101YLJ999	37CLA657	55LCP(1)30	102YLJ240	105HLR591			87NwL577
	105HLR1005	53LCP(3)200	102YLJ268	106HLR259	—307—	—819—	140PaL840
—223—	105HLR1175	91McL605		1991IlLR927	77Cor728	Case 9	
79CaL740	105HLR1204	139PaL618	—408—	1992IlLR419	90McL612	44StnL934	—152—
37CLA658	86NwL515	71TxL789	77MnL749	90McL517			76MnL1137
93CR340	87NwL128	102YLJ1298	86NwL1	77MnL367	—342—	—820—	87NwL59
101YLJ332	87NwL131			140PaL26	81Geo770	Case 5	87NwL67
	140PaL124	—905—	—469—	140PaL194	141PaL283	70TxL1563	87NwL79
—274—	44StnL396	Case 1	59ChL108	140PaL566	45StnL546		87NwL145
106HLR340	69TxL1095	1991IlLR937	77MnL599	44StnL66		—832—	140PaL1376
70TxL867	69TxL1096		139PaL653	100YLJ1799	—365—	Case 8	44StnL102
	70TxL1074		140PaL2233	102YLJ1615	70TxL1745	102YLJ243	101YLJ987
—324—	70TxL1549	**Vol. 492**	71TxL755				101YLJ1035
92CR549	79VaL72		71TxL791	—905—	—378—	—846—	
80Geo21	1991WLR420	—1—	71TxL800	Case 5	59ChL128	Case 10	—210—
80Geo77	101YLJ405	93CR604		90McL1855	59ChL483	92CR509	92CR1655
91McL882	101YLJ1035	77MnL1017	—490—		90McL518		93CR317
91McL921			79CaL767	—937—	140PaL232	—882—	106HLR215
67NYL493	—490—	—33—	79CaL1538	Case 2	140PaL560	Case 1	76MnL266
	37CLA676	93CR330	80CaL1027	1992IlLR9	79VaL53	86NwL662	
—350—		53LCP(4)155	80CaL1521	1992IlLR37		66NYL1280	—259—
77Cor523	—524—	75MnL1367	81CaL46		—400—		77Cor728
	81CaL132	78VaL1496	59ChL30	**Vol. 493**	80CaL1244	—901—	92CR1690
—376—	59ChL261		59ChL218		92CR1938	Case 5	81Geo561
76MnL1135	77Cor133	—96—	59ChL410	—20—	93CR56	59ChL1296	105HLR1234
77VaL632	55LCP(1)57	80Geo755	38CLA87	1991IlLR683	70TxL1808		91McL943
	55LCP(1)63	101YLJ409	77Cor512			—955—	91McL944
—397—	55LCP(2)						87NwL721
79CaL303	53LCP(3)						141PaL816
79CaL731	140PaL9					446	45StnL963
79CaL841	140PaL2					131	70TxL1745
79CaL867	44StnL92						
58ChL880	1992WLR						—325—
59ChL60	[1					71	77Cor728
59ChL226						39	
59ChL320	—600—					8	—407—
59ChL356	79CaL66						92CR2015
37CLA926	37CLA658	101YLJ1035	91McL635	92CR1124	101TxL1763		77MnL1024
38CLA87	93CR601		91McL665	90McL1062		—1022—	45StnL581
91CR1701	105HLR705	—257—	91McL940	86NwL504	—474—	Case 2	45StnL639
92CR1354	69TxL160	1992IlLR174	91McL968	140PaL817	92CR731	1992WLR	101YLJ333
81Geo302		1992IlLR422	76MnL249	70TxL1559	106HLR245	[1440	
81Geo371		75MnL1358	76MnL253		76MnL1154		—484—
105HLR1208	—617—	77MnL1119	76MnL268	—120—		—1076—	92CR2007
106HLR124	93CR601	77MnL1137	76MnL1174	77Cor9	—521—	Case 7	101YLJ333
106HLR133	104HLR1802	86NwL1130	77MnL1157	77Cor831	80Geo552	80CaL777	
106HLR760	105HLR671	140PaL1254	86NwL582	105HLR850	101YLJ1000		—518—
106HLR946	55LCP(1)239		139PaL574	76MnL1143	101YLJ1035	—1094—	67NYL638
1991IlLR926	76MnL923	—302—	140PaL67	140PaL753		Case 5	70TxL1608
1991IlLR	69TxL160	79CaL749	140PaL1030		—549—	55LCP(2)116	70TxL1633
[1087	70TxL934	92CR2095	141PaL1043	—132—	91McL592	55LCP(2)169	71TxL4
55LCP(1)28		75MnL1443	44StnL262	101YLJ1035	1992WLR368	55LCP(2)192	
55LCP(2)100	—657—	77MnL1042	45StnL31				—696—
53LCP(3)201	140PaL488	45StnL581	71TxL201	—146—	—812—		1991IlLR683
91McL605		45StnL639	71TxL209	Case 1	Case 1	**Vol. 494**	
85NwL471	—701—	78VaL1554	71TxL1091	76MnL1139	70TxL956		—624—
67NYL712	79CaL669	1991WLR936	78VaL1567			—26—	76MnL938
139PaL620	37CLA635	101YLJ189	79VaL1	—165—	—812—	80Geo681	140PaL125
139PaL1351	77Cor190	101YLJ333	79VaL8	1992IlLR59	Case 10	101YLJ1000	
139PaL1369	79Geo1731	102YLJ205	79VaL38	141PaL489	1991IlLR	101YLJ1035	—638—
140PaL25	91McL405	102YLJ228	79VaL46		[1098		101YLJ979
69TxL1005	76MnL1148	102YLJ267	1991WLR853	—182—		—56—	101YLJ987
71TxL781	140PaL757		1991WLR934	59ChL1324	—813—	55LCP(4)255	101YLJ1035
71TxL787	43StnL992	—361—	1992WLR	87NwL606	Case 9	55LCP(4)347	
71TxL1092	69TxL1103	79CaL749	[1417	140PaL8	77MnL755	101YLJ1008	—652—
77VaL868		1992IlLR9	102YLJ1621	71TxL1002	77MnL785		59ChL44
1990WLR	—754—	1992IlLR37		—215—		—83—	59ChL99
[1549	79CaL614	91McL602	—573—	55LCP(1)66		80Geo552	59ChL229
1992WLR725	79CaL741	76MnL1168	80CaL982	1991WLR707		76MnL1143	80Geo1907
100YLJ1405	67NYL270	86NwL1053	80CaL1613				106HLR288
100YLJ2087	101YLJ333	86NwL1057	81CaL294				1992IlLR465
102YLJ1212		45StnL1018	59ChL116				
102YLJ1298		79VaL714	59ChL126				*Continued*

> This unit of *Shepard's* enables one to find when any one of nineteen national law reviews cites to a federal court case, federal statute, federal court rule, or the U.S. Constitution. Coverage began in 1973.

SECTION I.   LISTS OF SUBJECT LEGAL PERIODICALS

1. **Representative Subject Periodicals from American Law Schools**

   Columbia University Law School:

   > *Columbia Business Law Review*
   >
   > *Columbia Human Rights Law Review*
   >
   > *Columbia Journal of Environmental Law*
   >
   > *Columbia Journal of Gender and Law*
   >
   > *Columbia Journal of Law and Social Problems*
   >
   > *Columbia Journal of Transnational Law*
   >
   > *Columbia—VLA Journal of Law & the Arts*
   >
   > *Journal of Chinese Law*
   >
   > *Parker School Journal of East European Law*

   Harvard University Law School:

   > *Harvard BlackLetter Law Journal*
   >
   > *Harvard Civil Rights—Civil Liberties Law Review*
   >
   > *Harvard Environmental Law Review*
   >
   > *Harvard Human Rights Journal*
   >
   > *Harvard International Law Journal*
   >
   > *Harvard Journal of Law and Public Policy*
   >
   > *Harvard Journal of Law & Technology*
   >
   > *Harvard Journal on Legislation*
   >
   > *Harvard Negotiation Law Review*
   >
   > *Harvard Women's Law Review*

   University of California School of Law at Berkeley:

   > *Asian Law Journal*
   >
   > *Berkeley Journal of Employment and Labor Law*
   >
   > *Berkeley Journal of International Law*
   >
   > *Berkeley Technology Law Journal*
   >
   > *Berkeley Women's Law Journal*
   >
   > *Ecology Law Quarterly*
   >
   > *La Raza Law Journal*

   University of Texas School of Law:

   > *American Journal of Criminal Law*
   >
   > *Review of Litigation*
   >
   > *Texas Intellectual Property Law Journal*

   Texas International Law Journal

   Texas Journal of Women & the Law

   Texas Review of Law & Politics

 Yale University Law School:

   Yale Journal of International Law

   Yale Journal of Law & Feminism

   Yale Journal of Law & the Humanities

   Yale Journal on Regulation

   Yale Law & Policy Review

2. International Legal Periodicals from American Law Schools

American University Journal of International Law and Policy

Annual Survey of International & Comparative Law (Golden Gate)

Arizona Journal of International and Comparative Law

Asian Law Journal (University of California at Berkeley)

Boston College International and Comparative Law Review

Boston College Third World Law Journal

Boston University International Law Journal

Brooklyn Journal of International Law

Buffalo Journal of International Law

California Western International Law Journal

Canada–United States Law Journal (Case Western Reserve University School of Law)

Case Western Reserve Journal of International Law

Colorado Journal of International Environmental Law & Policy

Columbia Journal of Transnational Law

Connecticut Journal of International Law

Cornell International Law Journal

Currents: International Trade Law Journal (South Texas College of Law)

Denver Journal of International Law and Policy

Dickinson Journal of International Law

Duke Journal of Comparative & International Law

East European Constitutional Review (University of Chicago)

Emory International Law Review

Florida Journal of International Law

Fordham International Law Journal

George Washington Journal of International Law and Economics

Georgetown International Environmental Law Review

Georgia Journal of International and Comparative Law

Harvard International Law Journal

Hastings International and Comparative Law Review

Houston Journal of International Law

Indiana International & Comparative Law Review (Indianapolis)

Indiana Journal of Global Legal Studies (Bloomington)

International Legal Perspectives (Lewis & Clark)

Journal of Chinese Law (Columbia University School of Law)

Journal of International Law & Policy (U.C. Davis)

Journal of International Law and Practice (Detroit College of Law)

Journal of International Legal Studies (George Mason)

Journal of Space Law (University of Mississippi)

Journal of Transnational Law and Policy (Florida State University College of Law)

Law and Policy in International Business (Georgetown University Law Center)

Loyola of Los Angeles International & Comparative Law Journal

Maryland Journal of International Law and Trade

Michigan Journal of International Law

Minnesota Journal of Global Trade

New England International and Comparative Law Annual

New Europe Law Journal (Yeshiva University, Cardozo Law School)

New York Law School Journal of International and Comparative Law

New York University Journal of International Law and Politics

North Carolina Journal of International Law and Commercial Regulation

Northwestern Journal of International Law & Business

Pace Journal of International and Comparative Law

Pace Yearbook of International Law

Pacific Rim Law & Policy Journal (University of Washington School of Law)

Parker School Journal of East European Law (Columbia University School of Law)

Southwestern Journal of Law and Trade in the Americas

Stanford Journal of International Law

Suffolk University Transnational Law Review

Syracuse Journal of International Law and Commerce

Temple International and Comparative Law Journal

Territorial Sea Journal (University of Maine School of Law)

Texas International Law Journal

Touro International Law Review

Transnational Law & Contemporary Problems (University of Iowa College of Law)

Transnational Lawyer (University of the Pacific, McGeorge School of Law)

Tulane European and Civil Law Forum

Tulsa Journal of Comparative & International Law

UCLA Asian American Pacific Islands Law Journal

UCLA Pacific Basin Law Journal

United States–Mexico Law Journal (University of New Mexico)

University of Miami Inter–American Law Review

University of Miami Yearbook of International Law

University of Pennsylvania Journal of International Business Law

Vanderbilt Journal of Transnational Law

Virginia Journal of International Law

Willamette Bulletin of International Law and Policy

Wisconsin International Law Journal

Yale Journal of International Law

SECTION J.   SUMMARY

1. Legal Periodicals

a. *Law School Reviews/Journals.*   Contain leading articles, notes and comments, and often book reviews and commentary sections.   Over 470 are published.   These publications may be general, subject-oriented, or interdisciplinary in focus.

b. *Bar Association Periodicals.*   Emphasis is more on the practical aspects of the law.

c. *Special Subject Periodicals.*   These are devoted to a single subject, such as labor law or insurance law, or to the relationship of law with another subject, or are published for lawyers in a particular field.

d. *Legal Newspapers.*   These can be national, state, or local in focus.

e. *Newsletters.*   Typically by commercial publishers, most often these are for current awareness purposes.

2. Indexes for Articles in Legal Periodicals

    a.   *Periodical articles published prior to 1908*

    Jones–Chipman Index to Legal Periodicals.   The first three volumes index English language periodicals published prior to 1908.

    b.   *Periodical articles published 1908 through 1979*

    Index to Legal Periodicals.   Indexes articles from most legal periodicals published in Australia, Canada, Great Britain, Ireland, New Zealand, and the United States.

    c.   *Periodical articles published after 1979*

    Index to Legal Periodicals & Books
    Current Law Index
    Legal Resource Index
    LEGALTRAC

    d.   *Articles published in non-legal journals*

    Index to Periodical Articles Related to Law
    Non-legal periodical indexes

    e.   *Current awareness publications*

    Current Index to Legal Periodicals

    f.   *Articles in foreign legal periodicals*

    Index to Foreign Legal Periodicals
    Index to Indian Legal Periodicals
    Index to Canadian Legal Periodical Literature
    Index to Legal Periodicals in Israel
    European Legal Journals Index
    Legal Journals Index

    g.   *Other sources for law-related articles*

    Legal Information Management Index
    Topical looseleaf services, annotated statutes, digests, encyclopedias

    h.   *Locating articles from legal periodicals cited in other articles or in court cases*

    Shepard's Federal Law Citations in Selected Law Reviews
    Shepard's Law Review Citations
    Shepard's State Citators

3. Electronic Research

    Index to Legal Periodicals & Books available online through WILSONLINE, and as a CD–ROM product WILSONDISC.

    Legal Resource Index available online through DIALOG, LEXIS–NEXIS, and WESTLAW, through some online catalogs, and as a CD–ROM product LEGALTRAC.

    Selected legal periodical articles available in full text on LEXIS–NEXIS and WESTLAW.

    Internet access to law reviews is increasing rapidly.

Chapter 18

TREATISES, RESTATEMENTS, UNIFORM LAWS, MODEL CODES, AND INTERSTATE COMPACTS

SECTION A.   TREATISES: IN GENERAL

Legal treatises are another important category of the secondary sources of the law. Treatises can be defined as expositions by legal writers on case law and legislation pertaining to a particular subject and published in book form.[1] This definition, of course, embodies a range of publications, including multi-volume works, textbooks, and shorter monographs. Treatises are usually able to treat a subject in greater depth than a legal encyclopedia, but not to the extent found in a periodical article.

The first treatises were written by legal scholars during the early development of the common law. Since there were few court cases available as precedent during the formative stages of our legal system, writers such as Lord Coke and William Blackstone played significant roles in the development of the law through their thoughtful, detailed *Commentaries*. As the growth of the law resulted in an ever-increasing number of law reports, treatises were needed to organize the diffuse principles of case law. One commentator has noted that treatises were first written because of the lack of precedents and then because there were too many of them.[2]

During the eighteenth and the early nineteenth centuries in the United States, English treatises were an integral part of an American lawyer's library. Gradually, American lawyers and legal scholars, such as James Kent and Joseph Story, began publishing treatises devoted entirely to American law.[3] Moreover, the American system of federalism has resulted in an increasing number of treatises dealing with the law of a particular state.

---

[1] Even this most basic definition is subject to some qualification, as many treatises published in book form are also available in electronic format. In addition, work is underway to publish some legal treatises exclusively in electronic format.

[2] GEORGE PATON, A TEXTBOOK OF JURISPRUDENCE 264 (4th ed. 1972). *See* A.W.B. Simpson, *The Rise and Fall of the Legal Treatise and the Forms of Legal Literature,* 48 U. CHI. L. REV. 632 (1981).

[3] For a discussion of the development and influence of treatises on American law, see LAWRENCE M. FRIEDMAN, A HISTORY OF AMERICAN LAW 624–26 (2d ed. 1985). *See also* Erwin C. Surrency, *The Beginnings of American Legal Literature,* 31 AM. J. LEGAL HIST. 207 (1987).

1. The Nature of Treatises

Treatises can be broadly classified into six types: (1) critical; (2) interpretive; (3) expository; (4) textual (for law students); (5) practitioner-oriented; and (6) law for the layperson. In most instances, however, particular treatises do not fall neatly into such a classification, and they may include some features of all types.

a. *Critical Treatises.* These examine an area of law in depth and constructively criticize, when necessary, rules of law as presently interpreted by the courts. They often include historical analyses in order to show that current rules actually had different meanings or interpretations than those presently given by the courts. The author may include a thoughtful examination of the policy reasons for one or more such rules.[4]

b. *Interpretative Treatises.* These provide an analysis and interpretation of the law. Authors of such works do not attempt to evaluate rules in relation to underlying policy, but rather to explain the terminology and meaning of the rules as they exist. Emphasis is placed upon understanding the law and not upon proposing what the law should be. [See Illustrations 18–1 and 18–2.]

c. *Expository Treatises.* These exist primarily as substitutes for digests and are principally used as case finders. They typically consist of survey-type essay paragraphs arranged under conventional subject headings with profuse footnote citations. Usually minimal analysis and synthesis of conflicting cases are the most a researcher can expect to find in them.

A real danger exists if one relies exclusively upon the expository treatise or encyclopedia article without verifying the writer's synopses of the cases.

d. *Student Textbooks.* These may also be classified as expository because they are usually elementary treatments and omit comprehensive and critical features of other works. In fact, the term *hornbook*[5] *law,* frequently used by a judge to describe simple and well-settled points of law, comes from West's *Hornbook Series* of student treatises. [See Illustrations 18–3 and 18–4.] Student hornbooks, however, are useful as case finders because their references are usually selective and limited to landmark cases.

The titles in West's *Nutshell Series,* another group of student texts, are, as the name implies, unsophisticated books that provide an overview of a topic without detailed analysis or extensive case references. Other leading publishers of student textbooks include The Foundation Press, Inc., Aspen Law and Business, and LEXIS Law Publishing.

---

[4] For example, Professor Richard Powell, in his multi-volume treatise on real property, discussing the interests of a landlord and tenant in a condemnation proceeding, criticizes the current rule as follows: "*This rule is regrettable.* It embodies a rigidly conceptualistic survival of the historical idea that the tenant 'owns the land for the term'...." 2 RICHARD R. POWELL, THE LAW OF REAL PROPERTY ¶ 236[3][A] (1990) (emphasis added).

[5] For the derivation of the word hornbook, see 6 THE NEW ENCYCLOPEDIA BRITANNICA, MACROPEDIA 63–64 (15th ed. 1990).

e. *Practitioner–Oriented Books*. In recent years, continuing education for lawyers has become increasingly important. The American Law Institute and American Bar Association Joint Committee on Continuing Legal Education, the Practising Law Institute, and state bar associations hold seminars and symposia on many current subjects that are directed toward practicing lawyers and intended to keep them up to date on new developments in the law. Many states have their own continuing legal education institutes.[6] It is quite common for such institutes to publish handbooks and texts in conjunction with their programs.

These volumes, as well as a rapidly-increasing number of practice-oriented books by commercial publishers, usually furnish analyses of the law, practical guidance, forms, checklists, and other time-saving aids. Very frequently, these publications deal with such subjects as business transactions, personal injuries, commercial and corporate practice, probate practice, trial practice, and other subjects of primary interest to practicing attorneys. West, for example, has a *Practitioner Treatise Series*.

f. *Law for the Layperson*. Increasingly, non-lawyers are turning to so-called "self-help" books. These publications, which often are met with disdain by the legal community, are intended to enable the lay public to conduct some of their own legal affairs without the aid of an attorney, e.g., preparation of a will.[7] Nolo Press of Berkeley, California, is the leading publisher of books of this genre. Oceana Publications' *Legal Almanac Series* attempts to describe basic legal issues in simple language. The American Civil Liberties Union has also published several titles targeted for the lay audience.

2. The Characteristics of Treatises

The fundamental characteristics of treatises are essentially the same. They typically contain the following elements:

a. *Table of Contents*. The table of contents shows the topical division of the treatise, which is usually arranged by chapters and subdivisions.

b. *Table of Cases*. The table of cases provides references to where cases discussed by the author are cited in the text.

c. *Subject Matter*. The subject matter of the text is contained in the main body of the publication.

d. *Supplementation*. Supplementation of treatises is about evenly split between pocket parts in the back of the volume that indicate recent statutory and case developments, and looseleaf volumes, which provide

---

[6] For a listing of continuing legal education courses, see the bimonthly issues of *The CLE Journal and Register,* published by the ALI/ABA Committee on Continuing Professional Education.

[7] The best source for identifying this type material is FRANK G. HOUDEK, LAW FOR THE LAYMAN: AN ANNOTATED BIBLIOGRAPHY (1991).

for the addition of current material and the removal of that which is obsolete, usually by interfiling. In recent years, treatises are increasingly being published in the looseleaf format.

e. *Index.* The index, embodying an alphabetical arrangement of the topics, sub-topics, descriptive words, and cross references, is the last feature.

3. Locating Treatises

Because of the varied nature and characteristics of treatises, it is important to be able to identify and locate them with ease. Among the more useful sources are the following:

a. *Library Catalog.* The essential starting point in determining whether the library being used has a particular title, or publications on a particular subject, is its catalog. Either containing individual cards or providing information electronically, catalogs enable a researcher to locate materials by author, title, or subject. Most law libraries use the classification system and subject headings established by the Library of Congress. The electronic catalogs typically enable users to also access information by any word in the bibliographic record for that item or to combine two or more words in a search for even more refined results.

b. *New York University, School of Law Library, A Catalogue of the Law Collection of New York University* (Julius Marke ed. 1953). This is an excellent source for older treatises and includes book review annotations.

c. *Law Books Recommended for Libraries; Recommended Publications for Legal Research.* In the 1960s, the Association of American Law Schools (AALS) undertook a massive Library Studies Project designed to identify all published treatises and to provide a listing of those rated either A, B, or C. Arranged under 46 subjects and entitled *Law Books Recommended for Libraries,* these lists were published separately in six notebook volumes during 1967–1970, with supplements issued for 42 of these subjects during 1974 to 1976. Actual coverage of titles extended only to approximately 1970. The project was then discontinued.

Subsequently, *Recommended Publications for Legal Research* (Oscar J. Miller & Mortimer D. Schwartz eds.), published by Fred B. Rothman, began in an effort to fill the gap left by the cessation of the AALS project. A separate volume for each year dating back to 1970 was prepared, and each year a new volume is issued covering titles published during the previous year. This publication also uses the A, B, and C ratings employed in the AALS project.

d. *Law Books in Print; Law Books Published. Law Books in Print,* a multi-volume bibliography first published in 1957, includes law books in the English language from publishers around the world. Separate indexes for author/title, publisher, and subject are included. Each entry includes author, title, edition, publisher, date, pagination, number of volumes, subject, Library of Congress catalog number, and price. The 8th edition, with coverage through 1996, was published in 1997. New editions are issued approximately every three years. This five-volume set, published by Glanville Publishers, Inc., is updated twice per year by cumulative supplements entitled *Law Books Published.*

d. *Catalog of Current Law Titles.* Published bimonthly by Ward and Associates, this source, which began in 1984 as *National Legal Bibliography* and assumed its present title in 1989, lists by subject and jurisdiction the titles cataloged by over sixty law libraries in the country during the intervening two months. A separate section lists those titles cataloged by at least one-fourth of those libraries. Each issue also includes an author index. An annual cumulation is published.

e. *Indexes Covering Treatises.* In 1994, the *Index to Legal Periodicals* added books to the scope of its coverage. Approximately 2,500 titles are included in each issue of *ILP.* Entries are listed under main entry (author or title) and under subject at the end of the subject entries for articles. *PAIS International* indexes some law-related titles, including government publications.

f. *Other Sources.* Numerous other sources provide information pertaining to treatises. Three of the more notable ones are: R.R. Bowker's annual, *Law Books and Serials in Print* and *Books in Print;* and the American Bar Association's *Recommended Law Books* (J.A. McDermott ed. 1986), which is an annotated, subject-arranged listing of books of special value to practitioners.

g. *Library Assistance.* If a source to satisfy your needs is not available in your library, remember to consult a librarian. Librarians likely have access to at least one of the two principal online bibliographic databases, OCLC and RLIN. These databases include millions of records describing published works. This information is merged to form a union catalog. Librarians may also have access to a vast array of other sources, both print and online, all of which can assist in locating materials. Once an item is identified that is not available in your library, it might be possible to obtain that item through interlibrary loan.

SECTION B. TREATISES: RESEARCH PROCEDURE

1. Case Method

If the name of a leading case on point is known, consult the table of cases of an appropriate treatise to ascertain whether this case is discussed in the book. If so, an examination of the cited pages in the text will reveal a discussion of the subject matter, along with additional cases on point.

2. Index Method

Consult the index in the back of the book if the name of a case is not known or if the research is in a particular aspect of a subject. Select an appropriate descriptive word or legal topic to use the index. References will refer to the text of the publication.

3. Topic Method

The Topic method can be used through the table of contents; however, its effectiveness in locating the pertinent text depends on the researcher's understanding of the structural subject subdivisions used in that treatise.

4. Definition Method

The index to the treatise may list words and phrases that are defined and explained in the text.

5. Electronic Format Method

Increasingly, treatises are becoming available in online and CD–ROM formats. This electronic access enables a researcher to use search strategies unavailable in the print versions, and often to hypertext to and from sections in the treatise and perhaps even to sources cited by that treatise. Researchers may want to determine if a treatise is available electronically and use it in that format.

The most noteworthy of these electronic sources is Matthew Bender's *Authority*. *Authority* consists of a series of subject-matter CD–ROM libraries, e.g., Collier's Bankruptcy Library, Federal Practice Library, Environmental Law Library, containing Matthew Bender's many treatise titles. *Authority* libraries allow the user to uplink to the LEXIS–NEXIS database for the most current text.

SECTION C.   ILLUSTRATIONS: TREATISES

[Illustration 18–1]

INDEX PAGE FROM MADDEN, PRODUCTS LIABILITY

INDEX

UNIFORM CONTRIBUTION AMONG TORTFEASORS ACT
Generally, § 17.12

UNREASONABLE DANGER
In negligence, §§ 1.2, 2.2–2.3, 4.2–4.3, 8.2, 10.2
In strict liability,
§§ 519–520, §§ 11.1–11.4
§ 402A, §§ 1.2, 2.12–2.13, 6.11, 10.3
Substantial product hazard, §§ 16.2–16.5

USED PRODUCTS
Alteration affecting liability, § 6.15
Negligence, §§ 3.26, 4.4–4.6, 9.13
Strict tort liability, §§ 3.26, 6.21, 9.13
Warranty, §§ 3.26, 5.19

UNIFORM PRODUCT LIABILITY ACT
Uniform Product Liability Act, §§ 6.16, 8.3, 9.6, 12.3

USERS
Misrepresentation, § 7.5
Negligence, §§ 3.4, 4.2–4.5
Strict tort liability, §§ 3.3, 6.1–6.2, 10.3

> **PROBLEM**
>
> Does a prescription drug manufacturer have a duty to warn?
>
> To locate a discussion of this issue and related cases, consult the Index to Madden, *Products Liability*.

Adequacy, §§ 10.12, 23.13
Allergic user, § 10.10
Causation, §§ 10.10, 14.10
Continuing duty to warn, §§ 10.13, 16.2
Directions distinguished, § 10.1
Drugs, §§ 6.13, 10.10, 23.10–23.14
Duty to warn,
Generally, § 10.1
Manufacturer, §§ 10.2–10.4, 23.10
Negligence, §§ 10.2, 10.9, 10.12
Seller, § 10.8
Strict tort liability, §§ 6.13, 10.1, 10.3, 23.10
Compliance with regulations, § 10.12
Failure to follow, effect, §§ 10.7, 14.4, 14.10
Failure to heed, effect, §§ 10.7, 14.4, 14.10
Instructions, distinguished, § 10.1
Manufacturer, §§ 10.1–10.4, 23.10
Misuse, § 10.6
Necessity of, §§ 10.1–10.3
Obvious danger, § 10.5
Persons to be warned, §§ 10.9, 23.12
Proximate cause, failure to warn as, §§ 10.7, 14.10
Regulations, effect of, §§ 4.12, 10.12, 12.3, 14.11
Seller, § 10.8
Statute, effect of, §§ 4.12, 10.12, 12.3, 14.11
Strict tort liability, §§ 6.13, 10.3, 23.10
Unforeseeable use, §§ 10.6, 14.4, 14.10
Unintended use, §§ 10.6, 14.4, 14.10
Warranty, failure to warn as breach, § 10.4

WARRANTY
See also, Magnuson-Moss Act
Generally, §§ 2.4, 3.2, 3.6, Chapter 5, 5.1, 5.2, 5.6–5.7, 5.11

576

[Illustration 18–2]

PAGE FROM MADDEN, PRODUCTS LIABILITY

Ch. 10 NEGLIGENCE PRINCIPLES § 10.2

the buyer's and the seller's reasonable reciprocal expectations as to product information. This review will demonstrate also that identification of a material disparity in germane safety-related information known to the seller as opposed to that known to the injured claimant will, [...] late warn[...]

Li[...]

> Note that the index leads to a relevant discussion of the issue under research. A typical treatise, such as this one, will contain text and then footnote references to cases and other pertinent materials. If supplementation is provided, as it is with this set, this material should be consulted for later information.

§ 10.2 When a Duty to Warn Arises Under Negligence Principles

At common law, a seller or supplier has a duty to give adequate warnings of any risk involved in the use of a product when the seller "knows of or has reason to know" that in the absence of such warnings the product is likely to be dangerous for the use supplied.[1] This duty to warn under negligence principles is triggered where the potential for harm from the use of the product without warnings or instructions is "significant."[2]

Resolution of the question of whether the risk is significant or unreasonable requires a balancing of the seriousness of harm, and the

§ 10.2

1. Restatement, Second, Torts § 388 provides:

Chattel Known to be Dangerous for Intended Use:

One who supplies directly or through a third person a chattel for another use is subject to liability to those whom the supplier should expect to use the chattel with the consent of the other or to be endangered by its probable use, for physical harm caused by the use of the chattel in the manner for which and by a person for whose use it is supplied, if the supplier

a) knows or has reason to know that the chattel is or is likely to be dangerous for the use for which it is supplied, and

b) has no reason to believe that those for whose use the chattel is supplied will realize its dangerous condition, and

c) fails to exercise reasonable care to inform them of its dangerous condition or the facts which make it likely to be dangerous.

See McKay v. Rockwell Int'l Corp., 704 F.2d 444 (9th Cir.1983), cert. denied 464 U.S. 1043, 104 S.Ct. 711, 79 L.Ed.2d 175 (1984); see also W. Prosser, Handbook on the Law of Torts § 96 (4th ed. 1971); Burch v. Amsterdam Corp., 366 A.2d 1079

(D.C.App.1976) (mastic adhesive with inadequate warnings as to flashpoint and flammability). Courts have given diverse expressions to the standard of actual or constructive knowledge contemplated by the negligent breach of the manufacturer's duty to warn, but they are all materially indistinguishable. E.g., Brocklesby v. United States, 753 F.2d 794 (9th Cir.1985) (duty to warn of defects of which the manufacturer "is or should be aware"); Wood v. Ford Motor Co., 71 Or.App. 87, 691 P.2d 495 (1984), cert. denied 298 Or. 773, 697 P.2d 556 (1985) (duty to warn of a product's dangerous propensities of which the manufacturer or seller "knows or reasonably should know"); Thomas v. Amway Corp., ___ R.I. ___, 488 A.2d 716 (1985) (the defendant seller's duty to warn under negligence theory limited to those dangerous properties of the product the seller "had reason to know about"); Ford Motor Co. v. Stubblefield, 171 Ga.App. 331, 319 S.E.2d 470 (1984) (manufacturer of product must give warning of danger to users of which it has "actual or constructive knowledge").

2. See Suchomajcz v. Hummel Chem. Co., 524 F.2d 19 (3d Cir.1975) (two minors killed and four injured from experimentation with firecracker "kits" ordered by mail from advertisement in Popular Mechanics).

369

[Illustration 18–3]

PAGE FROM PROSSER AND KEETON ON THE LAW OF TORTS, FIFTH EDITION

Chapter 17

PRODUCTS LIABILITY

Table of Sections

> Page from a treatise written primarily for law students. This particular title is part of the West Group's *Hornbook Series.*

§ 95. Theories of Recovery and Types of Losses

Products liability is the name currently given to the area of the law involving the liability of those who supply goods or products for the use of others to purchasers, users, and bystanders for losses of various kinds resulting from so-called defects in those products.

At the very outset, it is important to make a distinction between two types of product conditions that can result in some kind of loss either to the purchaser or a third person. One is a dangerous condition of the product or, if one prefers, a product hazard;[1] the other is the inferior condition or

---

§ 95

1. A recent government estimate placed the number of consumer product injuries (both in and out of the home) at 36 million for 1977. See Prod.Saf. & Liab. Rep. (BNA), June 29, 1979, 511. The total cost of such injuries to the nation has been estimated at $20 billion or more per year. Owen, Punitive Damages in Products Liability Litigation, 1976, 74 Mich.L.Rev. 1258–59 n. 2.

677

[Illustration 18–4]

PAGE FROM PROSSER AND KEETON ON THE LAW OF TORTS, FIFTH EDITION

---

§ 95A   **WARRANTY**   679

and the proper theory or theories of recovery for the resolution of such a claim. Some of the major issues to be resolved in product liability claims are the following: (1) Will fault in the sense of negligence be a necessary basis for recovery? (2) To what extent will a supplier be subject to strict liability? (3) If product defect rather than negligence is the basis or a basis on which liability can be imposed, when is a product to be regarded as defective or unfit in the kind of way that will subject a supplier to liability for the kind of loss suffered? (4) When will a provision to limit liability in some way in the contract of sale or other bargaining transaction be effective as to reduce a seller's or other supplier's liability that would otherwise have been imposed? (5) When, if at all, can the first purchaser called consumer against a seller in than his immedia

> Note the footnote references to court cases and to secondary sources. Note also how this particular volume indicates how to frame an online search for this issue using WESTLAW.

circumstances can a person other than a purchaser bring suit against a seller or other supplier of a defective product? (7) What kind of conduct or misconduct on the part of a purchaser, a user, or a victim will constitute either a defense or a cause of a kind that will be regarded as a superseding cause severing the chain of legal causation? (8) What will be the appropriate statute of limitations applicable to the cause of action and when will the cause of action be regarded as coming into existence? (9) What will be the appropriate conflict of laws rule to apply as between the law of two or more states? (10) What effect, if any, will the failure to give prompt notification to a seller or other supplier of a defect in a product after it was discovered or should have been discovered in

the exercise of ordinary care have on recovery?

🖳 **WESTLAW REFERENCES**

Theories of Recovery and Types of Losses
di product liability
citation(279 +5 443) & court(il)

Warranty and Intangible Economic Losses
topic("product* liability") & caveat emptor"
topic(313a) & express /5 warrant!
topic(313a) & implied /5 warrant!

§ 95A. Warranty and Intangible Economic Losses

The courts in early America adopted the notion of *caveat emptor* so that there was initially no liability of a seller of a product ____ract—on behalf ____ser against his ____ce of fraud, i.e., ____xpress manifestation of an intention to guarantee some specific characteristic or quality of the product that was the subject matter of a sale.[1] This notion came from the celebrated English case of Chandelor v. Lopus.[2] But considerable pressure developed for the protection of the intangible economic interest of those making bargaining transactions. This resulted in the development of the warranty theory of recovery. It came to be recognized that (1) express warranties could result from express statements made amounting to representations or affirmations of fact about the characteristics of goods sold,[3] and (2) implied warranties could result simply as a consequence of the act of selling when the sale was by a merchant.[4] This law that recognized the existence of express warranties flowing from express representa-

---

§ 95A

1. Prosser, The Implied Warranty of Merchantable Quality, 1943, 27 Minn.L.Rev. 117; Horowitz, The Transformation of American Law, 1780–1860, 1977, 167, 180, 330, n. 113.

2. 1603, 79 Eng.Rep. 3.

3. 1 Williston, Sales, Rev.ed.1948, §§ 195, 196. "Any affirmation of fact or any promise by the seller relating to the goods is an express warranty if the nat-

ural tendency of such affirmation or promise is to induce the buyer to purchase the goods, and if the buyer purchases the goods relying thereon." Uniform Sales Act, § 12.

4. Lambert v. Sistrunk, Fla.1952, 58 So.2d 434; Southern Iron & Equipment Co. v. Bamberg, Ehrhardt & Walterboro Railway Co., 1929, 151 S.C. 506, 149 S.E. 271, 278; Lane v. Trenholm Building Co., 1976, 267 S.C. 497, 229 S.E.2d 728, 730.

SECTION D.   RESTATEMENTS OF THE LAW

In the 1920s, prominent American judges, lawyers, and law professors were becoming concerned over two main defects in case law—its growing uncertainty and undue complexity. As a result, in 1923, the American Law Institute (ALI) was founded by a group of these leaders to overcome the weaknesses apparent in case law.[8] The objectives of the ALI focused on reduction of the mass of legal publications that had to be consulted by the bench and bar, on simplification of case law by a clear, systematic restatement of it, and on diminishing the flow of judicial decisions. It was feared that the increasing mass of unorganized judicial opinions threatened to break down the common law system of expressing and developing law.[9]

To remedy these problems, the ALI undertook to produce a clear and precise restatement of the existing common law that would have "authority greater than that now accorded to any legal treatise, an authority more nearly on a par with that accorded the decisions of the courts."[10]

Procedurally, this is accomplished by the engagement of eminent legal scholars to be Reporters for the various subjects that are to be restated. Each Reporter prepares tentative drafts, which are then submitted to and approved by the members of the ALI. Often, numerous tentative drafts, with the work extending over many years, are prepared before final agreement can be reached and a Restatement adopted.

Between 1923 and 1944, Restatements were adopted for the law of agency, conflict of laws, contracts, judgments, property, restitution, security, torts, and trusts. Since 1957, Restatements (Second) have been adopted for agency, contracts, conflict of laws, foreign relations law, judgments, property (landlord & tenant and donative transfers), torts, and trusts, and the process is not yet complete.

In 1986, a third series of the Restatements began with issuance of *Restatement (Third) of the Foreign Relations Law of the United States.* Since then a *Restatement (Third) of Trusts: Prudent Investor Rule, Restatement (Third) of the Law of Unfair Competition, Restatement (Third) Property (Mortgages),* and *Restatement (Third) Suretyship and Guarantee,* have been adopted. In addition, tentative drafts of additional topics for both the second and third series continue to be issued, likely resulting in additional Restatements in the future.

The status of the revision of specific Restatements and of proposed new Restatements can be ascertained from the latest ALI Annual Re-

---

[8] This discussion of the Restatements is based on the following sources: (1) William Draper Lewis, *History of the American Law Institute and the First Restatement of the Law, in* AMERICAN LAW INSTITUTE, RESTATEMENT IN THE COURTS 1–23 (permanent ed. 1945); (2) HERBERT F. GOODRICH & PAUL A. WOLKIN, THE STORY OF THE AMERICAN LAW INSTITUTE, 1923–1961 (1961); (3) AMERICAN LAW INSTITUTE, THE AMERICAN LAW INSTITUTE 50TH ANNIVERSARY (1973); (4) AMERICAN LAW INSTITUTE, ANNUAL REPORTS. *See also The American Law Institute Restatement of the Law and Codifications, in* 3 PIMSLEUR'S CHECKLISTS OF BASIC AMERICAN LEGAL PUBLICA- TIONS § V (Marcia S. Zubrow ed. & comp., looseleaf) [AALL Publication Series No. 4]. This checklist updates all previous checklists and lists all Restatements, including preliminary and tentative drafts.

[9] Lewis, *supra* note 8, at 1.

[10] *Report of the Committee on the Establishment of a Permanent Organization for the Improvement of the Law Proposing the Establishment of the American Law Institute, in* AMERICAN LAW INSTITUTE, THE AMERICAN LAW INSTITUTE 50TH ANNIVERSARY 34 (1973).

ports, which are issued separately and since 1988 are in ALI's annual *Proceedings,* and from its quarterly newsletter, *The ALI Reporter.* ALI's home page also includes the status of its publications along with a variety of other useful information.

It has been recommended that state legislatures be required to approve the Restatement, not as formal legislative enactments, but as aids and guides to the judiciary so that they will feel free to follow "the collective scholarship and expert knowledge of our profession,"[11] but this proposal was not adopted by the ALI membership. Nevertheless, many courts began to give greater authority to the Restatements than that accorded to treatises and other secondary sources. In many instances, an authority is given to the Restatements nearly equal to that accorded to decided cases.[12]

The First Series of the Restatements reflected the desire of the ALI's founders that the Restatements be admired and adopted by the courts. To this end they deliberately omitted the Reporters' citations and reference to the tentative drafts upon which the Restatement rules were based.

With publication of the Second Series of the Restatements, a decision was made to abandon the idea of the Restatements serving as a substitute for the codification of the common law. The Second and Third Series at times indicate a new trend in the common law and attempt to predict what a new rule will or should be.[13] This change in policy is also reflected in the appearance of citations to court cases and to the Notes of the Reporters. Appendices contain citations to and brief synopses of all cases that have cited the Restatements. It should be noted that a new Restatement on the same topic as a existing one, does not supersede the older version. Some courts, in fact, continue to cite the earlier Restatements.

The frequency with which the Restatements are cited by the courts merits their study in legal research. As of April 1, 1997, the Restatements had been cited by the courts 137,732 times.[14] Therefore, they not only provide clear statements of the rules of the common law, which are operative in a great majority of the states, but also provide very valuable sources for finding cases on point.

Moreover, a comparison of the texts of the Restatements and the case law of the several states reveals that there are surprisingly few deviations from the common law as expressed in the Restatements. It has been suggested, therefore, that there is in fact a common law that

---

[11] Alpheus Thomas Mason, *Harlan Fiske Stone Assays Social Justice, 1912–1923,* 99 U. PA. L. REV. 887, 915 (1951) (quoting from a speech given by Stone).

[12] For a discussion of the precedential authority of the Restatements, see James F. Byrne, *Reevaluation of the Restatements as a Source of Law in Arizona,* 15 ARIZ. L. REV. 1021, 1023–26 (1973).

[13] *Id.*

[14] This information is available in the American Law Institute's ANNUAL MEETING PROCEEDINGS and in its CATALOG OF PUBLICATIONS.

transcends state lines and prevails throughout the nation.[15] However, the legal rules may at times be inaccurately and confusingly stated by the various courts. Thus, the objective of the Restatements is to clear away much of the verbal debris and bring the accepted rules to the forefront. To this extent, the Restatements are useful research aids in the law.

Further discussion over the value of the Restatements is best left to others.[16] As a legal researcher, however, one must be familiar with the publications of the American Law Institute and their method of use.

1. The Features of the Restatements

The various Restatements are typically divided broadly into chapters, further subdivided into narrower titles, and then into numbered discrete sections. Each section begins with a "black letter" **(boldface)** restatement of the law, followed by comments that contain hypothetical illustrations. Reporters' Notes are at the end of each section.[17] [See Illustrations 18–6 through 18–8.] These Notes can serve as a legislative history of the section and will, if applicable, give the text of the section or sections of the earlier Restatements that are superseded by this later section. [See Illustration 18–9.]

The following additional features are included in the Restatements, Second and Third Series:

a. *Tables.* These list citations of court cases, statutes, and other authorities included in the Restatement being used.

b. *Conversion Tables.* These enable a user to find where a section in a Tentative Draft is included in the final Restatement.

c. *Cross-references.* These give references to West's *Key Number System* and to *A.L.R. Annotations.*

2. Indexes

a. *Restatements, First Series.* A one-volume index to all the Restatements in the First Series has been published. Each Restatement also has its own subject index.

b. *Restatements, Second Series* and *Third Series.* Some of the older Restatements have their own subject index in each volume and covering only the materials in that volume. More recent Restatements contain an index in the last volume of the Restatement or in a separate volume. [*See*

---

[15] Herbert F. Goodrich, *Restatement and Codification, in* David Dudley Field: Centenary Essays Celebrating One Hundred Years of Legal Reform 241–250 (Allison Reppy ed. 1949).

[16] An exhaustive list of articles on all aspects of the work of the American Law Institute is in the Annual Reports section of the Annual Meeting *Proceedings* under the title *The Institute in Legal Literature, A Bibliography.* This listing is also available on ALI's home page.

[17] For the first three Restatements (Second), namely agency, torts, and trusts, the Reporters' Notes are in the Appendix volumes accompanying these subjects.

Illustration 18–5.] There is not a comprehensive index to all of these Restatements.

3.   The Restatements As Cited By the Courts

As mentioned, the ALI maintains information pertaining to each time the Restatements are cited by the courts. Originally, this was accomplished by a set entitled *Restatements in the Courts.* Issued first as a Permanent Edition covering 1932–1944 and then updated with bound supplements covering from 1945–1975, this set recorded, with annotations, each time a court cited a section of the Restatement.

These annotations were subsequently recompiled and added to the individual Appendix volumes to the current Restatements. New Appendix volumes are published periodically. [See Illustration 18–10.] These Appendices, prior to being cumulated into bound volumes, are updated either by cumulative pocket supplements or separate annual cumulative supplements, and by a semi-annual pamphlet entitled *Interim Case Citations.* This interim pamphlet only contains citations and does not include the case synopses found in the pocket supplements and cumulative volumes.

4.   Online Access to the Restatements

The Restatements, including the current pocket parts, annual supplements, and interim case citation pamphlets, are available on WEST-LAW. All Restatements can be searched by accessing the *Restatements of the Law* database (REST). Each Restatement also is available in its own database. Restatements are available in LEXIS–NEXIS in the RESTAT file of various libraries.

5.   Locating Legal Periodical Articles Concerning the ALI and the Restatements

The *Index to Legal Periodicals, Current Law Index,* and *Legal Resource Index* use the "American Law Institute" as a subject heading. While *ILP* lists articles about the Restatements only under a general subject heading, *CLI* and *LRI* include references by subject as well as under the name of the specific Restatement.

6.   Shepardizing the Restatements

Shepard's Restatement of the Law Citations is devoted entirely to coverage of the Restatements. This set gives citations to all federal court reports, all units of the *National Reporter System,* and all state court reports that cite to a Restatement. It also includes articles citing the Restatements in the nineteen leading law reviews and the *ABA Journal.* [See Illustration 18–11.]

7.   State Annotations

Some states have prepared annotations to court citations to the Restatements, *e.g., The California Annotations to the Restatement of the*

Law of Torts. The law library catalog should be consulted to ascertain if such annotations exist for a particular state.

8. Restatements in the American Law Institute Archive Publications in Microfiche

The *American Law Institute Archive Publications in Microfiche* (William S. Hein & Co.) is the most exhaustive collection of documents on the ALI and its projects and covers from the ALI's founding in 1923 forward. It includes the ALI *Proceedings, Annual Reports,* minutes, the various drafts of the Restatements from inception to completion, the codifications together with their background sources for projects with which the ALI has been associated, and previously unreleased confidential documents. The set is updated either semi-annually or annually, thus covering newly-issued items. At the end of 1992, the collection contained over 2,900 documents. A hard copy guide provides access to these materials.

SECTION E.   ILLUSTRATIONS: RESTATEMENT (SECOND) OF TORTS

Problem: Is a prescription drug manufacturer liable for failure to warn of a dangerous drug?

18–5.   Page from Index to Restatement (Second) of Torts
18–6 to 18–8.   Pages from the Restatement (Second) of Torts
18–9 to 18–10.   Pages from an Appendix volume, Restatement (Second) or torts
18–11.   Page from Shepard's Restatement of the Law Citations

[Illustration 18-5]

PAGE FROM INDEX TO §§ 281 TO 503, RESTATEMENT (SECOND) OF TORTS

LIMITATION OF LIABILITY

The index in each Restatement 2d volume only covers the topics addressed by that volume. Once the appropriate volume is located, typically by reference to the Table of Contents, that volume's index can be used to locate relevant material. In the problem being researched, you will likely consult the heading "Products Liability." In this instance, you are referred to the heading "Manufacturers of Chattels."

See the following Illustrations for examples of how the Restatements are arranged.

[Illustration 18–6]

PAGE FROM RESTATEMENT (SECOND) OF TORTS

Ch. 14 SUPPLIERS OF CHATTELS § **402 A**

C. Neither A nor B is liable to C in an action for negligence.

2. A, a retail dealer, sells to B a hot water bag purchased from a reputable manufacturer. A believes the bag to be in perfect condition, although he has not inspected it, but the bag is defective in that the stopper will not screw in securely. As a result of this defect, C, the minor son of B, is severely scalded by hot water that leaks out of the bag. A is not liable to B or to C in an action for negligence.

e. In many situations the seller who receives his goods from a reputable source of supply receives it with the firm conviction that it is free from defects; and where a chattel is of a type which is perfectly safe for use in the absence of defects, the seller who sells it with the reasonable belief that it is safe for use and represents it to be safe for use does not act negligently. Frequently, the manufacturer's literature and salesmen and his past record of sending the seller perfectly made chattels create a reasonable belief in the seller's mind that the particular chattel he is selling is made perfectly. When the seller reasonably believes that the chattel is safe, his representation in good faith to that effect is neither fraudulent, reckless, nor negligent.

Illustration:

3. A, a retail dealer, sells to B a defective gas heater, obtained from a reputable manufacturer, which A believes to be in perfect condition, although he has not inspected

> The Restatement's "Black Letter" Rules immediately follow the section number.

heater when used emits poisonous fumes, injuring B. A is not liable to B in an action for negligence.

TOPIC 5. STRICT LIABILITY

§ **402 A.** Special Liability of Seller of Product for Physical Harm to User or Consumer

(1) One who sells any product in a defective condition unreasonably dangerous to the user or consumer or to his property is subject to liability for physical harm

See Appendix for Reporter's Notes, Court Citations, and Cross References

[Illustration 18–7]

PAGE FROM RESTATEMENT (SECOND) OF TORTS

§ **402 A**   TORTS, SECOND   Ch. 14

thereby caused to the ultimate user or consumer, or to his property, if

(a) the seller is engaged in the business of selling such a product, and

(b) it is expected to and does reach the user or consumer without substantial change in the condition in which it is sold.

(2) The rule stated in Subsection (1) applies although

(a) the seller has exercised all possible care in the preparation and sale of his product, and

(b) the user or consumer has not bought the product from or entered into any contractual relation with the seller.

See Reporter's Notes.

Caveat:

The Institute expresses no opinion as to whether the rules stated in this Section may not apply

(1) to harm to persons other than users or consumers;

(2) to the seller of a product expected to be processed or otherwise substantially changed before it reaches the user or consumer; or

as

> **Following the "Black Letter" Rule or Rules is a Comment section explaining the purpose of the Rules.**

Comment:

a. This Section states a special rule applicable to sellers of products. The rule is one of strict liability, making the seller subject to liability to the user or consumer even though he has exercised all possible care in the preparation and sale of the product. The Section is inserted in the Chapter dealing with the negligence liability of suppliers of chattels, for convenience of reference and comparison with other Sections dealing with negligence. The rule stated here is not exclusive, and does not preclude liability based upon the alternative ground of negligence of the seller, where such negligence can be proved.

b. *History.* Since the early days of the common law those engaged in the business of selling food intended for human consumption have been held to a high degree of responsibility for their products. As long ago as 1266 there were enacted special criminal statutes imposing penalties upon victualers, vintners,

[Illustration 18–8]

PAGE FROM RESTATEMENT (SECOND) OF TORTS

Ch. 14　　　　　**SUPPLIERS OF CHATTELS**　　　**§ 402 A**

Illustration:

> 1. A manufactures and packs a can of beans, which he sells to B, a wholesaler. B sells the beans to C, a jobber, who resells it to D, a retail grocer. E buys the can of beans from D, and gives it to F. F serves the beans at lunch to G, his guest. While eating the beans, G breaks a tooth, on a pebble of the size, shape, and color of a bean, which no reasonable inspection could possibly have discovered. There is satisfactory evidence that the pebble was in the can of beans when it was opened. Although there is no negligence on the part of A, B, C, or D, each of them is subject to liability to G. On the other hand E and F, who have not sold the beans, are not liable to G in the absence of some negligence on their part.

　　m.　"Warranty."　The liability stated in this Section does not rest upon negligence. It is strict liability, similar in its nature to that covered by Chapters 20 and 21. The basis of liability is purely one of tort.

　　A number of courts, seeking a theoretical basis for the liability, have resorted to a "warranty," either running with the goods sold, by analogy to covenants running with the land, or made directly to the consumer without contract. In some in-

> **Frequently, the Comment section includes hypothetical examples.**

and it is generally agreed that a tort action will still lie for its breach, it has become so identified in practice with a contract of sale between the plaintiff and the defendant that the warranty theory has become something of an obstacle to the recognition of the strict liability where there is no such contract. There is nothing in this Section which would prevent any court from treating the rule stated as a matter of "warranty" to the user or consumer. But if this is done, it should be recognized and understood that the "warranty" is a very different kind of warranty from those usually found in the sale of goods, and that it is not subject to the various contract rules which have grown up to surround such sales.

　　The rule stated in this Section does not require any reliance on the part of the consumer upon the reputation, skill, or judgment of the seller who is to be held liable, nor any representation or undertaking on the part of that seller. The seller is strictly liable although, as is frequently the case, the consumer does not even know who he is at the time of consumption.

See Appendix for **Reporter's Notes, Court Citations, and Cross References**

355

[Illustration 18–9]

PAGE FROM AN APPENDIX VOLUME, RESTATEMENT (SECOND) OF TORTS

Ch. 14　　　　　　　**APPENDIX**　　　　**§ 402**

— injury caused by industrial, business, or farm machinery, tools, equipment, or materials. 78 A.L.R.2d 594.

— injury caused by paint, cement, lumber, building supplies, ladders, small tools, and like products. 78 A.L.R.2d 696.

— injury caused by toys, games, athletic or sports equipment, or like products. 78 A.L.R.2d 738.

— injury caused by drug or medicine sold. 79 A.L.R.2d 301.

— injury caused by medical and health supplies, appliances, and equipment. 79 A.L.R.2d 401.

—injury caused by hair preparations, cosmetics, soaps and other personal cleansers, and the like. 79 A.L.R.2d 431.

— injury caused by domestic or industrial soaps, detergents, cleansers, polishes, and the like. 79 A.L.R.2d 482.

— injury caused by household and domestic machinery, appliances, furnishings, and equipment. 80 A.L.R.2d 598.

— injury caused by firearms, explosives, and flammables. 80 A.L.R.2d 488.

> The Reporter's Notes contain information pertaining to the development of the Restatement and include references to cases and secondary authorities. These notes are in the Appendix volumes for the Restatements (Second) of Agency, Torts, and Trusts. For all other Restatements 2d, these Notes are at the end of each section of the Restatement. Recent Restatements also include WESTLAW references.

or failure to inspect therefor, as affecting liability of dealer for personal injury or property damage to subsequent purchaser or other third person. 164 A.L.R. 371.

Liability of one selling or distributing liquid or bottled fuel gas, for personal injury, death, or property damage. 17 A.L.R.2d 888.

Liability of seller of container (bottle, barrel, drum, tank, etc.) or other packaging material for injury caused thereby. 81 A.L.R.2d 350.

Privity of contract as essential to recovery in action based on theory other than negligence, against seller of product alleged to have caused injury. 75 A.L.R.2d 39.

Privity of contract as essential to recovery in negligence action against seller of product alleged to have caused injury. 74 A.L.R.2d 1111.

§ 402. Absence of Duty to Inspect Chattel.

———▶ REPORTER'S NOTES

In the 1948 Supplement to the first Restatement, this Section was changed by rewriting the Section and Comment *a*, and by adding the other Comments and Illustrations. The Section has been further changed by substituting "liable in an action for negligence" for "subject to liability," and by adding the final limiting clause.

The following is the Reporter's Note in the 1948 Supplement:

Change: The Section Heading, Section and Comment *a* have been rewritten. The other Comments,

Cit.—cited; fol.—followed; quot.—quoted; sup.—support.
A complete list of abbreviations faces page 1.

[Illustration 18–10]

PAGE FROM AN APPENDIX VOLUME, RESTATEMENT (SECOND) OF TORTS

tant to note that the Court purported to follow existing authority rather than to make new law. The Court relied upon (1) Garvey v. Namm, supra, (2) a Louisiana Appeals decision which had been reversed by the Supreme Court of Louisiana in 1930, (3) a Massachusetts decision dealing with the liability of a donor of a chattel known to be dangerous, (4) a decision by the Court of Appeals of Georgia involving the liability of a vendor who, without any knowledge on the subject, made a positive representation of the chattel's safety, and (5) Section 388 of the Restatement of Torts which states the liability of any person who supplies a chattel which he knows to be dangerous for the use for which it is supplied. The only one of these citations which is the

of Phila., 183 S.W.2d 140, 353 Mo. 558, 156 A.L.R. 469 (1944). In the Marhenke case, the Federal Court applied California law and said "A dealer . . . is not under duty to exercise ordinary care to discover whether it is dangerous or not" and added "whether we assume that the defects . . . could have been ascertained by the simple test of filling the bag with water and inverting it after the stopper had been screwed into its socket, the defendant . . . was under no obligation to make such inspection or test." The Reporter believes that this is an accurate statement of the rule of law presently in force in every State which has decided the question, with the exception of Pennsylvania and with the possible exception of New York (in which there is no author-

> The Appendix volumes for the Restatements 2d include a synopsis of each case that has cited a Restatement rule and further indicate whether the court supported or did not support the rule.

sions, there are 27 cases in 20 different Appellate Courts in which vendors who sold, without inspection, defective chattels, which subsequently caused injury to the plaintiff were held not to be liable for such injuries. These cases are reviewed and analyzed in Eldredge, Vendor's Tort Liability (1941), 89 Univ. of Pa. Law Review 306 at pp. 318–323, reprinted in Modern Tort Problems, pages 261–269, and are further discussed in Eldredge, "Vendor's 'Duty' to Inspect Chattels—a Reply" (1941) 45 Dickinson Law Review 269, reprinted in Modern Tort Problems at page 285. The most recent cases are Meyer v. Rich's, Inc., 12 S.E.2d 123, 63 Ga. App. 896 (1940); Sears, Roebuck & Co. v. Marhenke, 121 F.2d 598 (9 Cir. 1941); and Zesch v. Abrasive Co.

ity Supreme Court) and Missouri. In the Zesch case the Supreme Court of Missouri quoted the language of the original § 402 but absolved the vendor from liability on the facts of the case.

[See also, as to opening sealed containers: Kratz v. American Stores Co., 359 Pa. 335, 59 A.2d 138 (1948); Tourte v. Horton Mfg. Co., 108 Cal. App. 22, 290 P. 919 (1930); Outwater v. Miller, 3 Misc. 2d 47, 153 N.Y.S.2d 708 (1956), adhered to on reargument, 3 Misc.2d 51, 155 N.Y.S.2d 357, reversed on other grounds, 3 App. Div. 2d 670, 158 N.Y.S.2d 562; West v. Emanuel, 198 Pa. 180, 47 A. 965, 53 L.R.A. 329 (1901).

As to taking goods apart: Zesch v. Abrasive Co. of Philadelphia, 353 Mo. 558, 183 S.W.2d

Cit.—cited; fol.—followed; quot.—quoted; sup.—support.
A complete list of abbreviations faces page L.

[Illustration 18–11]

PAGE FROM SHEPARD'S RESTATEMENT OF THE LAW CITATIONS

TORTS, SECOND					Sec. 402A
Tex	N Y	782P2d1193		744P2d364	N Y
511SW346	59NY249	786P2d942	Nev	34TxL219	111NYM437
43CaL626	451NE200	Calif	104Nev418	53VaL500	444NYS2d401
67Cor171	464NYS2d442	237CA2d52	760P2d771	1975WLR118	
89PaL317		265CA2d243	N J	79A2320n	**Comment I**
89PaL324	**Comment k**	71CaR314	72NJS174	9A215n	Cir. 4
34TxL219	Cir. 10	Colo	178A2d47		355F2d817
1975WLR118	649FS1515	40CoA418	460A2d207	**Comment a**	Cir. 6
	Ala	576P2d197	N M	Cir. 8	597FS1300
Comment a	335So2d134	761P2d240	97NM201	812FS956	Cir. 7
Ariz		Conn	638P2d413	Cir. 9	
140Az					

> Each Section of the various Restatements and the related Comments, in this Illustration, Sec. 402 of the *Restatement (Second) of Torts*, can be Shepardized using *Shepard's Restatement of the Law Citations*.

Md	673P2d1220	120GuA468	102NCA227	304PaS340	**Comment J**
326Md199		170SE855	186SE202	27DC3d604	Colo
604A2d454	**Sec. 401A**	Haw	372SE899	33DC3d10	809P2d1049
Mo	Pa	6HA655	401SE804		
807SW194	14DC4d4	736P2d443	Ohio	**Comment b**	**Comment k**
		Ill	15OS3d78	Calif	Cir. 6
Comment b	**Sec. 402**	381IlA426	22OA31	1CA4th617	758FS462
Mass		187NE312	62OA3d80	4CaR2d158	
8MaA886	Cir. 1	Ind	257NE764		**Secs. 402a**
393NE417	968F2d120	609NE1200	472NE710	**Comment c**	**to 503**
	Cir. 3	Iowa	Ore	Cir. 7	
Comment c	283FS980	259Ia46	275Ore526	813FS633	Cir. 2
Calif	541FS1386	141NW628	291Ore226	Ill	448F2d489
65CaR815	551FS267	Ky	553P2d373	82IlA1062	
N J	640FS817	281SW917	630P2d352	403NE562	**Sec. 402A**
13NJ334	692FS445	310SW511	Pa	Pa	
99A2d585	708FS711	La	401Pa637	49DC2d491	476US865
Illustration 1	801FS1440	355So2d641	48DC2d198		90LE875
N J	Cir. 5	560So2d892	49DC2d486	**Comment d**	106SC2299
13NJ334	679F2d1206	573So2d525	39DC3d665	Cir. 7	54USLW4651
99A2d585	794F2d1073	Md	41DC3d521	813FS632	50FRD322
	302FS207	326Md198	7DC4d156	Ill	50FRD346
Comment d	Cir. 6	604A2d454	7DC4d430	381IlA427	142FRD553
Calif	260FS277	Mass	165A2d638	187NE312	144FRD439
65CaR815	750FS800	368Mas241	R I	Iowa	Cir. DC
	143FRD164	389Mas338	109RI182	252Ia10	469F2d101
Comment e	Cir. 7	400Mas32	283A2d259	104NW612	543F2d282
Calif	666FS1263	26MaA27	415A2d1044	Md	553F2d143
65CaR815	721FS1029	331NE548	So C	326Md199	567F2d30
N J	813FS632	450NE587	288SoC265	604A2d454	636F2d590
13NJ339	Cir. 8	507NE732	341SE809	N J	637F2d813
99A2d588	797F2d610	Minn	Tenn	72NJS179	757F2d1309
	572FS726	407NW95	664SW692	178A2d49	825F2d453
Comment f	591FS622	441NW132	775SW596	N C	845F2d1072
Calif	788FS1063	Miss	799SW252	53NCA152	851F2d423
65CaR815	Cir. 9	613So2d851	841SW829	280SE514	403FS1174
Mass	901F2d753	Mo	Tex	Wash	559FS345
8MaA886	Cir. 10	361Mo1026	336SW247	39Wsh2d925	637FS738
393NE417	741F2d1581	363Mo418	347SW344	44Wsh2d209	643FS247
Illustration 4	858F2d1439	238SW392	553SW243	57Wsh2d130	663FS1058
Mass	677FS1103	251SW639	728SW849	239P2d849	751FS4
8MaA886	Cir. 11	715SW492	Va	266P2d796	775FS422
393NE417	888F2d803	Mont	5VCO310	356P2d103	95FRD334
	Ala	214Mt52	Wash		Cir. 1
Comment g	554So2d942	692P2d444	39Wsh2d925	**Comment e**	428F2d376
Calif	555So2d92	Nebr	57Wsh2d129	Calif	484F2d1026
65CaR815	Ariz	158Neb548	13WAp55	1CA4th617	494F2d180
	107Az154	163Neb119	49WAp494	4CaR2d164	494F2d370
Comment l	163Az91	64NW97	239P2d849	Md	
Conn	483P2d1393	77NW907	356P2d102	326Md199	
158Ct319			533P2d442	604A2d454	*Continued*
259A2d614					

737

SECTION F. UNIFORM LAWS AND MODEL ACTS

1. Uniform Laws

The Restatements, as mentioned, have as their aim the restating of the common law as developed by the courts. The movement of law reform also has focused on statutory law and the need, in many instances, for uniform statutes among the states. Toward this aim, the American Bar Association passed a resolution recommending that each state and the District of Columbia adopt a law providing for the appointment of Commissioners to confer with Commissioners of other states on the subject of uniformity in legislation on certain subjects. In 1892 the National Conference of Commissioners on Uniform State Laws was organized, and by 1912 each state had passed such a law. According to the National Conference's constitution, its object is to "promote uniformity in state law on all subjects where uniformity is desirable and practical."[18]

The National Conference will designate an act as a *Uniform Act* when it has a reasonable possibility of ultimate enactment in a substantial number of jurisdictions. The Conference meets once a year and considers drafts of proposed uniform laws. When such a law is approved, it is the duty of the Commissioners to try to persuade their state legislatures to adopt it. Of course, adoption by the Conference has no legal effect; only subsequent enactment by a state's legislature can achieve this result. The Conference has approved over 200 acts and over 100 have been adopted by at least one state. Perhaps the most notable example is the *Uniform Commercial Code.*

Laws approved by the National Conference of Commissioners on Uniform State Laws are published in the following forms:

a. As separate pamphlets.

b. In the annual *Handbook* of the National Conference.

c. In *Uniform Laws Annotated, Master Edition.* The multi-volume *Uniform Laws Annotated, Master Edition,* published by West Publishing Company, contains over 160 laws. A law must have been adopted by at least one state to be included in this set. Volumes are revised periodically and pocket supplements and annual pamphlets are issued. [See Illustrations 18–12 through 18–14.]

After each section of a uniform law, pertinent official Comment of the Commissioners is given. This is followed by references to law review articles, related West digest Topics and Key Numbers, and *Corpus Juris*

---

[18] This document is published annually in the HANDBOOK OF THE NATIONAL CONFERENCE OF COMMISSIONERS ON UNIFORM STATE LAWS AND PROCEEDINGS OF THE ANNUAL MEETING. For a more detailed discussion of the National Conference, *see* WALTER P. ARMSTRONG, A CENTURY OF SERVICE: A CENTENNIAL HISTORY OF THE NATIONAL CONFERENCE OF COMMISSIONERS ON UNIFORM STATE LAWS (1991); Richard E. Coulson, *The National Conference of Commissioners on Uniform State Laws and the Control of Law-Making—A Historical Essay,* 16 OKLA. CITY U.L. REV. 295 (1991).

Secundum. In recently-revised volumes and the supplementation WEST-LAW references are also provided. Each volume contains a detailed index to the laws it contains. Tables in both the bound volumes and the supplements list the states that have adopted each uniform law. [See Illustration 18–17.] The *Uniform Laws Annotated, Master Edition* is included in WESTLAW in the ULA database.

d. *National Conference of Commissioners on Uniform State Law Archive Collection in Microfiche.* This collection, prepared by William S. Hein & Co. and containing over 700 documents, includes transcripts of the National Conference's annual meetings and Committee of the Whole meetings, the *Handbooks* from 1892 to date, and successive drafts of uniform laws up to and including the uniform law as adopted. A hard copy index to the set is provided. The collection is updated annually.

2. Model Acts

An act that does not have a reasonable possibility of uniform adoption is designated as a *Model Act.* The expectation of the drafters is that parts, but not necessarily all of the act will be adopted, or modified and then adopted, by various states. The National Conference of Commissioners on Uniform State Laws occasionally drafts some model acts, but this work is most often left to the American Law Institute.[19] Among the more significant of these ALI works are the Model Business Corporation Act and the Model Penal Code. The National Conference and the ALI worked jointly on the Uniform Commercial Code.

3. Locating Uniform Laws and Model Acts and Related Publications

a. *Handbook of the National Conference of Commissioners on Uniform State Laws.* This annual publication includes discussions of pending legislation, as well as the texts of all uniform laws adopted during that year. Through this *Handbook* a researcher can locate a uniform law, even if it has not been adopted by any state. A complete list of acts approved by the National Conference appears each year in the *Handbook's* Appendices. Charts are included that show which states have adopted specific Uniform Laws and Model Acts, and the date of adoption.

b. *Directory of Uniform Acts and Codes.* This annual pamphlet, published as part of the *Uniform Laws Annotated, Master Edition,* shows in which volume of the *Master Edition* a particular law is published. [See Illustration 18–15.] This *Directory* also includes a state-by-state listing showing which laws each state has adopted, a list of the Commissioners by state, and a brief subject index to all acts in the set. [See Illustration 18–16.]

c. *Martindale–Hubbell Law Directory.* One volume of this publication[20] includes, on a selective basis, the unannotated text of uniform laws and model acts.

---

[19] Documents pertaining to the uniform laws and model acts with which the ALI has been associated are contained in the source described in section D–8.

[20] The *Martindale–Hubbell Law Directory* is discussed in Chapter 19.

d. *Legal Periodical Articles.* The *Index to Legal Periodicals, Current Law Index,* and *Legal Resource Index* index under subject the articles written about various uniform laws and model acts. In addition, *ILP* uses a separate heading for "Uniform laws," and *CLI* and *LRI* use the heading "Uniform state laws." These headings enable articles to be grouped collectively. *CLI* and *LRI* also list articles about model codes under the specific name of the act.

SECTION G.   ILLUSTRATIONS: UNIFORM LAWS

[Illustration 18–12]

PAGE FROM VOLUME 9, PART II, UNIFORM
LAWS ANNOTATED, MASTER EDITION

CONTROLLED SUBSTANCES (1994)   **§ 101**

Section

WESTLAW Computer Assisted Legal Research

WESTLAW supplements your legal research in many ways. WESTLAW allows you to

- update your research with the most current information
- expand your library with additional resources
- retrieve direct history, precedential history and parallel citations with the Insta-Cite service

For more information on using WESTLAW to supplement your research, see the WESTLAW Electronic Research Guide following the Explanation.

> **This is the first page of the Uniform Controlled Substances Act (1994).**
> **This is an example of a typical Uniform Law adopted by the National**
> **Conference of Commissioners on Uniform State Laws.**

[ARTICLE] 1

DEFINITIONS

Action in Adopting Jurisdictions

Because of the numerous variations resulting from the frequent amendments made to the corresponding sections of text of this Act by the adopting jurisdictions, it is not feasible to note the differences between the official text of this Act and the counterpart texts in the adopting jurisdictions.

§ 101.   Definitions.

As used in this [Act]:

(1) "Administer," unless the context otherwise requires, means to apply a controlled substance, whether by injection, inhalation, ingestion, or any other means, directly to the body of a patient or research subject by:

(i) a practitioner or, in the practitioner's presence, by the practitioner's authorized agent; or

(ii) the patient or research subject at the direction and in the presence of the practitioner.

(2) "Controlled substance" means a drug, substance, or immediate precursor included in Schedules I through V of [Article] 2.

17

[Illustration 18–13]

PAGE FROM VOLUME 9, PART II, UNIFORM
LAWS ANNOTATED, MASTER EDITION

CONTROLLED SUBSTANCES (1994)   **§ 401**

    (ii) [50] kilograms or more, but less than [100] kilograms, the person is guilty of a crime and upon conviction [may] [must] be imprisoned for not less than [ ] nor more than [ ] and fined not less than [ ];

    (iii) [100] kilograms or more, the person is guilty of a crime and upon conviction [may] [must] be imprisoned for not less than [ ] nor more than [ ] and fined not less than [ ].]

(h) Except as authorized by law, a person may not knowingly or intentionally possess piperidine with intent to manufacture a controlled substance, or knowingly or intentionally possess piperidine knowing, or having reasonable cause to believe, that the piperidine will be used to manufacture a controlled substance contrary to this [Act]. A person who violates this subsection is guilty of a crime and upon conviction may be imprisoned for not more than [ ], fined not more than [ ], or both.

[(i) Except as provided in subsection (j), with respect to an individual who is found to have violated subsection (g), adjudication of guilt or imposition of sentence may not be suspended, deferred, or withheld, nor is the individual eligible for parole before serving the mandatory term of imprisonment prescribed by this section.]

(j) Notwithstanding any other provision of this [Act], the defendant or the attorney for the State   rt to reduce or suspend the sentence of an ind | **After each Section of** | lation of this section and who provides substant | **the Uniform Law the Offi-** | , arrest, or conviction of a person for a violatio | **cial Comment of the Commis-** | give the arresting agency an opportunity to be | **sioners explaining each Sec-** | est. Upon good cause shown, the request m | **tion is given.** | . The judge hearing the motion may reduce or suspend the sentence if the judge finds that the assistance rendered was substantial.

Comment

Except for Section 406, which contains a specific reference to a misdemeanor, criminal penalties throughout the Act are referred to by language "is guilty of a crime and upon conviction may be imprisoned for not more than [ ], fined not more than [ ], or both." States that have a criminal penalty classification system should replace this language with references to their classified penalties, e.g., "is guilty of a class [ ] felony." Actual penalties are not included because it is felt that such a designation is purely a state decision. The penalties imposed under the federal act are found at 21 U.S.C. 841, and additional federal penalties were created by the Anti-Drug Abuse Act of 1986, Public Law 99-570. The criminal penalties in subsection (a) are classified based on the penalties in the federal act, 21 U.S.C. 841(b) as amended by the Anti-Drug Abuse Act of 1986, Public Law 99-570, § 1002 (the "Narcotics Penalties and Enforcement Act of 1986"). In subsection (a)(1) there are no references to amounts of mixtures or substances containing the proscribed controlled substances, and the adopting State should insert amounts appropriate for that State. A reference to an amount is contained in subsection (a)(1)(vii) with respect to marijuana to allow a State that includes this provision to distinguish this provision from subsection (a)(5). Subsections (b), (d), and (e) are based on Florida Statutes Section 893.135. Subsection (c) is based on the offense in the federal act with respect to piperidine, added in 1978 and found in 21 U.S.C. 841(d).

[Illustration 18–14]

PAGE FROM VOLUME 9, PART II, UNIFORM LAWS ANNOTATED, MASTER EDITION

CONTROLLED SUBSTANCES (1994)   **§ 302**
                                                   Note 3

or who prescribe, will be required to register; however, under subsequent sections they may be exempt from the record-keeping requirements. By regi[...] individual dealing with co[...] stances, the State will kno[...] sponsible for a substance and[...] ing in these substances. Th[...] requirements imposed by th[...] designed to eliminate many[...] version, both actual and pote[...] . Common and contract c[...] housemen, ultimate users, [...]

registrants are specifically exempted from the registration requirements since to require otherwise would be extremely bur[...] [...]fford little increase in pro[...] diversion.

[...]ration is called for so that a [...] screened and the registra[...] ed should the need arise. [...] e annual registration re[...] be a form of check on per[...] to deal in controlled sub[...]

> At the end of each Section, references are given to additional research aids.
>
> Also, annotations are provided to all court cases citing the Section.
>
> The supplementation should be checked for later information.

Library References

American Digest System
Drugs and Narcotics ⬥12 to 15, 41, 45.

Encyclopedias
C.J.S. Drugs and Narcotics §§ 2 to 6, 30 to 44, 117 to 133, 158, 163, 269.

WESTLAW Electronic Research

138k[add key number].
See, also, WESTLAW Electronic Research Guide following the Explanation.

Notes of Decisions

Generally   2
Corporations   4
Federal action and requirements   3
Nonresidents   5
Part-time pharmacist   6
Purpose   1
Residents and nonresidents   5
Status of unregistered persons and entities   7

---

1. Purpose

Primary purpose of prohibition against dispensing controlled substances is to require practitioners to register with the Commissioner of Public Health and to keep records and maintain inventories. Com. v. Perry, Mass.1984, 464 N.E.2d 389, 391 Mass. 808;

Overall scheme of Controlled Substances Act reveals legislative intent to place limitations on practitioners. People v. Alford, Mich.App.1977, 251 N.W.2d 314, 73 Mich.App. 604, affirmed 275 N.W.2d 484, 405 Mich. 570.

Legislature, in adopting Uniform Controlled Substances Act, intended to come within scheme of complementary federal-state control of distribution of drugs and to create an "interlocking" trellis" to assure effectiveness of Act. State v. Rasmussen, Iowa 1973, 213 N.W.2d 661.

Regulations relating to licensing of drug distributors and manufacturers had, as their primary purpose, the protection of the public from dangerous drugs and, although the regulations included a license fee to cover administrative costs, the regulations did not impose a tax. Pharmaceutical Mfrs. Ass'n v. New Mexico Bd. of Pharmacy, N.M.App.1974, 525 P.2d 931, 86 N.M. 571.

2. Generally

When viewed in the context of the Controlled Substances Act as a whole, the right to possess drugs incident to professional use is dependent on compliance with the Act's registration requirement. State v. Mann, R.I.1978, 382 A.2d 1319, 119 R.I. 720.

3. Federal action and requirements

Interest of federal authority in issuing licenses to dispense drugs for purpose of controlling drug abuse clearly outweighs any local interest that Iowa might have in allowing only practitioners registered in state to prescribe in Iowa, and for pharmacists in state to fill prescriptions emanating from out-of-state. State v. Rasmussen, Iowa 1973, 213 N.W.2d 661.

Practitioners registered under Federal Comprehensive Drug Abuse Prevention and Control Act, though not registered in Iowa, and not residents of Iowa, are governed solely by Feder-

[Illustration 18–15]

PAGE FROM UNIFORM LAWS ANNOTATED—DIRECTORY OF UNIFORM ACTS AND CODES

DIRECTORY OF UNIFORM ACTS

Title of Act	Uniform Laws Annotated Volume	Page
Reciprocal Enforcement of Support Act (1950 Act)	9B	553
Revised Abortion Act	9, Pt. I	1
Status of Children of Assisted Conception	9B	Pocket Part
Transfers to Minors Act	8B	497
Civil Liability for Support Act	9, Pt. I	333
Class Actions [Act] [Rule] (Model)	12	99
Code of Military Justice	11	71
Commercial Code	1 to 3B	
Commercial Code—Forms	4 and 5	
Common Interest Ownership Act (1994)	7, Pt. I	471
Common Interest Ownership Act (1982)	7, Pt. II	1
Common Trust Fund Act	7, Pt. II	181
Community Property, Disposition of Community Property Rights at Death Act	8A	191
Comparative Fault Act	12	123
Condominium Act	7, Pt. II	199
Conflict of Laws-Limitations Act	12	155
Conservation Easement Act	12	163
Construction Lien Act	7, Pt. II	381
Consumer Credit Code (1974)	7A	1
Consumer Credit Code (1968)	7, Pt. II	475
Consumer Sales Practices Act	7A	231
Contribution Among Tortfeasors Act	12	185
Controlled Substances Act (1994)	9, Pt. II	Pamphlet
Controlled Substances Act (1990)	9, Pt. II	Pamphlet
Controlled Substances Act (1970)	9, Pt. II	1
Conveyances, Fraudulent Conveyance Act	7A	427
Correction or Clarification of Defamation Act	12	291
Corrections, Sentencing and Corrections Act (Model)	10	Pamphlet
Crime Victims Reparations Act	11	55
Crimes and criminals.		

> **This Table lists all Uniform Laws contained in the set and shows in which volume the text of the Uniform Law can be located. Similar information can also be found in the annual *Handbook* of the National Conference of Commissioners on Uniform State Laws.**

Criminal Procedure, Rules of (1974)	10	1
Criminal Statistics Act	11	509
Extradition and Rendition Act	11	523
Insanity Defense and Post Trial Disposition Act (Model)	11A	1
Mandatory Disposition of Detainers Act	11A	47
Military Justice, Code of	11A	71
Model Penal Code	10	433
Model Sentencing and Corrections Act	10	Pamphlet
Motor Vehicle Certificate of Title and Anti-Theft Act	11A	175
Post-Conviction Procedure Act (1980 Act)	11A	247
Post-Conviction Procedure Act (1966 Act)	11A	267
Pretrial Detention Act	11A	407
Rendition of Accused Persons Act	11A	447
Rendition of Prisoners as Witnesses in Criminal Proceedings Act	11A	455
Rules of Criminal Procedure (1987)	10	Pamphlet
Rules of Criminal Procedure (1974)	10	1
Status of Convicted Persons, Act on	11A	467

2

[Illustration 18–16]

PAGE FROM UNIFORM LAWS ANNOTATED—DIRECTORY OF UNIFORM ACTS AND CODES, TABLE (BY JURISDICTIONS) LISTING UNIFORM ACTS ADOPTED

TABLE OF JURISDICTIONS LISTING UNIFORM ACTS ADOPTED

———

List of jurisdictions, in alphabetical order, listing the Uniform Acts or Codes adopted by that particular jurisdiction, and where each may be found in Uniform Laws Annotated, Master Edition.

Each Uniform Act or Code in the Master Edition contains a Table showing the statutory citations of each of the adopting jurisdictions.

———

ALABAMA

Title of Act	Uniform Laws Annotated Volume	Page
Anatomical Gift Act (1968 Act)	8A	63
Attendance of Witnesses From Without a State in Criminal Proceedings, Act to Secure	11	1
Brain Death Act	12	63
Certification of Questions of Law Act	12	49
Child Custody Jurisdiction	9, Pt. I	115
Commercial Code [1]	1 to 3B	
Common Trust Fund Act	7, Pt. II	181
Condominium Act	7, Pt. II	199
Controlled Substances Act (1994)	9, Pt. II	Pamphlet
Controlled Substances Act (1990)	9, Pt. II	Pamphlet
Controlled Substances Act (1970)	9, Pt. II	1
Criminal Extradition Act	11	97
Declaratory Judgments Act	12	309
Disclaimer of Property Interests Act	8A	149
Disposition of Unclaimed Property Act (1966 Act)	8A	207
Division of Income for Tax Purposes Act	7A	331

> **This Table lists all states alphabetically and indicates under each state which uniform laws or model codes have been adopted by the state.**

Fiduciaries Act	7A	391
Fraudulent Transfer Act	7A	639
Guardianship and Protective Proceedings Act	8A	439
Insurers Liquidation Act	13	429
Limited Partnership Act (1976 Act)	6A	1
Mandatory Disposition of Detainers Act	11A	47
Motor Vehicle Certificate of Title and Anti-Theft Act	11A	175
Parentage Act	9B	287
Partnership Act (1994 Act)	6	1
Partnership Act (1914 Act) [2]	6	125
Photographic Copies of Business and Public Records as Evidence Act	14	185
Principal and Income Act (1931 Act)	7B	183
Securities Act (1956 Act)	7B	509
Simplification of Fiduciary Security Transfers Act	7B	689
Simultaneous Death Act (1940 Act)	8B	267
State Administrative Procedure Act (1961) (Model)	15	137
Trade Secrets Act	14	433

9

[Illustration 18–17]

PAGE FROM VOLUME 9, PART II, UNIFORM LAWS ANNOTATED,
MASTER EDITION—TABLE OF JURISDICTIONS ADOPTING
THE UNIFORM CONTROLLED SUBSTANCES ACT

UNIFORM LAWS ANNOTATED

UNIFORM CONTROLLED SUBSTANCES ACT (1994)

1994 ACT

See, also, the 1990 and 1970 Uniform Controlled Substances Acts, infra.

Table of Jurisdictions Wherein Either the 1970, 1990, or 1994 Versions of the Act or a Combination Thereof Has Been Adopted [1]

Jurisdiction	Laws	Effective Date	Statutory Citation
Alabama	1971, No. 140	9–16–1971 *	Code 1975, §§ 20-2-1 to 20-2-190.
Alaska	1982, c. 45	1–1–1983	AS 11.71.010 to 11.71.900, 17.30.010 to 17.30.900.
Arizona	1979, c. 103	7–1–1980	A.R.S. §§ 36–2501 to 36–2553.
Arkansas [2]	1971, No. 590	4–7–1971	A.C.A. §§ 5-64-101 to 5-64-608.
California	1972, c. 1407	3–7–1973	West's Ann.Cal. Health & Safety Code, §§ 11000 to 11651.
Colorado	1981, pp. 707 to 728		West's C.R.S.A. §§ 18-18-101 to 16-18-605.
Connecticut	1967, No. 555	6–21–1967	C.G.S.A. §§ 21a-240 to 21a-308.
Delaware	1972, c. 424	6–13–1972 *	16 Del.C. §§ 4701 to 4796.
District of Columbia	1981, D.C.Law 4-29		D.C.Code 1981, §§ 33-501 to 33-572.
Florida			
Georgia			
Hawaii			
Idaho			
Illinois			
Indiana	1976, P.L. 148	7–1–1977	West's A.I.C. 35-48-1-1 to 35-48-4-15.
Iowa	1971, c. 148	7–1–1971	I.C.A. §§ 124.101 to 124.602.
Kansas	1972, c. 234	7–1–1972	K.S.A. 65-4101 to 65-4164.
Kentucky	1972, c. 226	7–1–1972	KRS 218A.010 to 218A.993.
Louisiana	1972, No. 634	7–26–1972	LSA-R.S. 40:961 to 40:995.
Maine	1975, c. 499	5–1–1976	17-A M.R.S.A. §§ 1101 to 1116.
	1941, c. 251	4–16–1941	22 M.R.S.A. §§ 2383, 2383-A, 2383-B.
Maryland	1970, c. 403	7–1–1970	Code 1957, art. 27, §§ 276 to 303.
Massachusetts	1971, c. 1071	7–1–1972	M.G.L.A. c. 94C, §§ 1 to 48.
Michigan	1978, No. 368	9–30–1978	M.C.L.A. §§ 333.7101 to 333.7545.
Minnesota	1971, c. 937	6–18–1971	M.S.A. §§ 152.01 to 152.20
Mississippi	1971, c. 521	4–16–1971	Code 1972, §§ 41-29-101 to 41-29-185.
Missouri	1971, H.B. No. 69	9–28–1971	V.A.M.S. §§ 195.010 to 195.320.
Montana	1973, c. 412	7–1–1973	MCA 50-32-101 to 50-32-405
Nebraska	1971, LB 326	5–26–1971	R.R.S.1943, § 28-401 et seq.
Nevada	1971, c. 667	1–1–1972	N.R.S. 453.011 et seq.
New Jersey	1970, c. 226	1–17–1971	N.J.S.A. 2C:35-1 to 2C:35-23, 2C:36-1 to 2C:36-9, 24:21-1 to 24:21-53.
New Mexico	1972, c. 84		NMSA 1978, §§ 30-31-1 to 30-31-41
New York	1972, c. 878	4–1–1973 [4]	McKinney's Public Health Law §§ 3300 to 3396
North Carolina	1971, c. 919	1–1–1972	G.S. §§ 90-86 to 90-113.8
North Dakota	1971, c. 235	7–1–1971	NDCC 19-03.1-01 to 19-03.1-43.
Ohio	1975, p. 269	7–1–1976	R.C. §§ 3719.01 to 3719.99.
Oklahoma	1971, c. 119	9–1–1971	63 Okl.St.Ann. §§ 2-101 to 2-610.

> **A Table preceding the start of each Uniform Law indicates the jurisdictions that have adopted Act, its effective date, and where it can be located in the state's code and session laws.**

1

SECTION H. INTERSTATE COMPACTS

The United States Constitution provides that "No State shall, without Consent of Congress . . . enter into any Agreement or Compact with another State . . . ." [23]

In an early interpretation of this clause, the Supreme Court of the United States held that it prohibited all agreements between states unless consented to by Congress.[24] However, in a subsequent case, the Court changed its position and held that Congressional consent was not necessary for agreements or compacts that did not increase the political powers of the states or interfere with the supremacy of the United States.[25] Normally, however, interstate agreements or compacts are formally enacted by the legislatures of the states involved and are then submitted to Congress for its consent.[26]

Until about 1900, most interstate compacts dealt with boundary disputes between states. Since then, the compacts have more commonly been used as a means of cooperation for solving problems common to two or more states, such as flood control, control of pollution, or the establishment of a port authority.

1. Publication of Interstate Compacts

The texts of agreements or compacts are in both the session laws of the respective states and in the *United States Statutes at Large,* since they involve agreements among the states involved and the consent of Congress.[27]

A complete listing of compacts is in *Interstate Compacts and Agencies,* published periodically by the Council of State Governments. It contains the following information:

    a. List of compacts involving boundaries;

    b. Subject arrangement of all other compacts, with short annotations;

    c. Index of defunct or dormant compacts;

    d. Index to compacts.

---

[23] U.S. Const. art. I, § 10, cl. 3.

[24] Holmes v. Jennison, 39 U.S. (14 Pet.) 540 (1840).

[25] Virginia v. Tennessee, 148 U.S. 503, 518 (1893). *See also* United States Steel Corp. v. Multistate Tax Commission, 434 U.S. 452 (1978).

[26] Interstate compacts do not have to be formally enacted. *See* the annotation to Art. 1, § 10, cl. 3, *in* The Constitution of the United States of America: Analysis and Interpretation 433–38 (Libr. of Cong. ed. 1987). *See also* Frederick L. Zimmerman & Mitchell Wendell, The Law and Use of Interstate Compacts (2d ed. 1976); Paul T. Hardy, Interstate Compacts: The Ties That Bind (1982); Kevin J. Heron, *The Interstate Compact in Transition: From Cooperative State Action to Congressionally Coerced Agreements,* 60 St. John's L. Rev. 1 (1985).

[27] For example, the North Dakota–Boundary Agreement is published at 1961 Minn. Laws 399 and 1961 N.D. Laws 517; Congressional consent is given in Pub. L. No. 87–162, 75 Stat. 399 (1961).

Each biennial edition of the *Book of the States,* also published by the Council of State Governments, has a chapter on current developments in interstate compacts, and a selective listing of the more significant ones.

2. Locating Court Cases on Interstate Compacts

a. *Digests.* Digests of cases involving interstate compacts are under *States, Key Number 6* in the West digests and under States § 52 in the *Digest of the United States Supreme Court Reports, Lawyers' Edition.*

b. *Annotated Editions.* The practice of including the text of compacts in state codes varies. The indexes to the codes of the state being researched should be checked.

c. *Citators.* The Statutes volumes or sections of the appropriate *Shepard's Citations* can be used to Shepardize the state code or session law citation, or the *United States Statutes at Large* citation.

SECTION I. SUMMARY

1. Treatises

a. *Scope.*

(1) Expositions, some of which are critical in nature, by legal writers on case law and legislation.

(2) More exhaustive in scope than encyclopedias, but periodical articles are usually more specific.

(3) Functions:

(a) Views of the writer as to what the law ought to be; critically evaluative.

(b) Interpretation of statutory and case law and current developments.

(c) Case finder.

(d) Presents a general view of the principles of a topic.

b. *Arrangement.* Treatises usually include these features:

(1) Table of contents.

(2) Table of cases.

(3) Subject matter—text.

(4) Index.

c. *Supplementation.* The current practice of publishers is to keep treatises current by cumulative pocket supplements or to publish them in looseleaf format. Some treatises also are updated by replacement (revision) volumes.

2. Restatements

a. *Scope.*

(1) Simplify and restate case law on selected subjects.

(2) Originally intended to serve as a substitute for codification of the common law; now treats subject matter antecedently and, at times, prospectively.

b. *Method of Publication, Content, and Supplementation*

(1) Tentative drafts—include Reporter's notes and case discussion.

(2) Restatements (First Series)—text.

(3) Revisions—*Restatements, Second* and *Third.*

(a) Contain "black letter" rule, comment section, illustrations, Reporter's notes, and various finding aids.

(b) Appendix volumes contain annotations for cases citing the Restatement.

(c) Updated by cumulative supplements and *Interim Case Citations.*

c. *Indexes*

(1) *First Series.*

(a) *General Index*—covers the several Restatements.

(b) Each Restatement has an individual index.

(2) *Second* and *Third* series.

(a) Some subjects include an index to the contents to each volume; some subjects include a separate index to the complete Restatement.

(b) There is no comprehensive index to the various Restatements in these two series.

3. Uniform Laws and Model Acts

a. *National Conference of Commissioners on Uniform State Laws.*

(1) Uniform laws adopted by the Conference are published in its annual *Handbook* and in *Uniform Laws Annotated, Master Edition,* the latter being updated annually.

(2) The *Handbook* and *Uniform Laws Annotated, Master Edition* include various tables relating to adoption of these uniform laws.

b. *Model Acts.* Drafted by the National Conference of Commissioners on Uniform State Laws, the American Law Institute, or jointly by both associations.

4. Interstate Compacts

a. Used as a means of cooperation for solving problems common to two or more states; normally require enactment by the states involved and consent of Congress.

b. Listed in *Interstate Compacts and Agencies.*

Chapter 19

OTHER LEGAL AND GENERAL RESEARCH AND REFERENCE AIDS*

Opinions of Attorneys General and the Office of Legal Counsel, Dictionaries, Directories, Abbreviations, Quotations, Form Books, General Legal Reference Sources, Research on the Supreme Court of the United States, Jury Instructions and Verdicts/Settlements, Briefs and Records on Appeal, Professional Responsibility, and Other, Non–Legal Information Sources

This chapter covers a variety of materials that are useful in legal research but do not readily fit into any of the categories discussed in previous chapters. Some are legal, such as opinions of the attorneys general, legal dictionaries, directories, and form books. In addition to primary and secondary legal materials, lawyers have occasion to consult a wide variety of general reference materials that assist in the solution of legal problems. An approach to finding useful materials in other disciplines will be described herein.

SECTION A. OPINIONS OF THE ATTORNEYS GENERAL

The formal opinions of the attorneys general have the characteristics of both primary and secondary authority.[1] As the legal adviser to officials of the executive branch of the government, the attorney general gives requested legal advice to them, generally in the form of written opinions. Although these opinions are official statements of an executive officer, issued according to his or her authority, they are merely advisory and are not mandatory orders. Therefore, the inquirers and other officials are not bound to follow such recommendations and conclusions. However, the opinions are strongly persuasive and are generally followed by executive officers. They also have significant influence on court deliberations.

---

* This chapter was revised and updated by Keith Ann Stiverson, Deputy Law Librarian at the University of Texas at Austin, Jamail Center for Legal Research, Tarlton Law Library.

[1] Formal opinions are those written and signed by the Attorney General. For additional information on the role of attorneys general, *See* Scott M. Matheson, Jr., *Constitutional Status and Role of the State Attorney General*, 6 U. FLA. J.L. & PUB. POL'Y 1 (1993); *State Attorneys General: Powers and Responsibilities* (Lynne M. Ross ed. 1990) (prepared by the National Association of Attorneys General); *200th Anniversary of the Office of the Attorney General* (1989) (i.e., Attorney General of the United States); Peter E. Heiser, Jr., *The Opinion Writing Function of Attorneys General*, 18 IDAHO L. REV. 9 (1982); William N. Thompson, *Transmission or Resistance: Opinions of State Attorneys General and the Impact of the Supreme Court*, 9 VAL. U. L. REV. 55 (1974).

As a general rule, the opinions relate to (1) interpretation of statutes or (2) general legal problems. Some attorneys general limit their advice and will not render opinions as to the constitutionality of proposed legislation.

1. Opinions of the Attorneys General of the United States

The opinions of the Attorneys General of the United States have been published in forty-three volumes covering 1791–1982, with each volume containing opinions that cover a number of years, *e.g.,* volume 43 covers June 10, 1974 to November 30, 1982. Over the years, the number of formal opinions selected for publication has been difficult to predict.[2] Since 1977, opinions of the Attorneys General are included in the annual entitled *Opinions of the Office of Legal Counsel.* This publication is discussed in Section B, *infra.*

The full text of the opinions of the Attorneys General are available on WESTLAW in the USAG database, and on LEXIS–NEXIS in the GENFED Library, USAG file. The *United States Code Annotated* and the *United States Code Service* include digests of U.S. Attorney General opinions in their annotations. Citations are included in the United States and federal units of *Shepard's Citations* when the opinions are cited in a court case.

2. Opinions of State Attorneys General

Almost every state publishes the opinions of its attorney general.[3] They are included in the annotations of many annotated state codes, and the state units of *Shepard's Citations* indicate when a state attorney general's opinion has been cited by a court.

WESTLAW and/or LEXIS–NEXIS also include opinions of state attorneys general, but coverage is not comprehensive, with most of the files beginning in the 1970s.

These vendors' database directories should be checked for the scope of coverage.

Increasingly, state attorney general opinions can be found on the World Wide Web, at the Web site of the particular attorney general's office. At present, the National Association of Attorneys General (NAAG) links to all available Web sites of state attorneys general. Of these sites, not all have the full text of the opinions, but a number of them do.

---

[2] For example, from 1909 through 1912, an average of 58 opinions were published each year. From 1937 through 1940, the average was 37. Only 13 were published from 1970 through 1974, but 40 are included in the latest volume.

[3] A checklist of published opinions of state attorneys general is in 3 PIMSLEUR'S CHECKLISTS OF BASIC AMERICAN LEGAL PUBLICATIONS § III (Marcia S. Zubrow ed. & comp., looseleaf) [AALL Publication Series No. 4]. The present edition [2d.] of *BNA's Directory of State Administrative Codes and Registers* has an appendix that details the availability of opinions of state attorneys general, including U.S. territories and the District of Columbia's Corporation Counsel.

SECTION B. OPINIONS OF THE OFFICE OF LEGAL COUNSEL

Pursuant to 28 U.S.C. § 510, the United States Attorney General has delegated to the Office of Legal Counsel the duties of preparing formal opinions of the Attorney General, rendering informal opinions to the various federal agencies, assisting the Attorney General in the performance of his or her function as adviser to the President, and rendering opinions to the Attorney General and the various organizational units of the Department of Justice.[4]

The *Opinions of the Office of Legal Counsel* have been published annually since 1977 and include the memorandum opinions, which are written by various attorneys in the Office on matters referred to the Office for response, as well as the formal Attorney General Opinions. Only a small portion of the memorandum opinions rendered are actually published, because the addressee of the opinion must agree to publication. The opinions are first published in a paperback preliminary print and are subject to revision until the bound volume is issued. Like the opinions of the Attorney General, the opinions of the Office of Legal Counsel are merely advisory statements and are not mandatory orders. The full text of these opinions is available in WESTLAW's USAG database and on LEXIS–NEXIS in the GENFED library, USAG file.

SECTION C. LAW DICTIONARIES

Law dictionaries are useful for identifying the definitions of words in their legal sense or use. For each word or phrase a short definition is given. Some legal dictionaries also provide a citation to a court case or other reference tracing the source of the word or phrase. The multi-volume set *Words and Phrases,* discussed in Chapter 6, Section L–1, includes digests from court cases in which a word or phrase has been judicially interpreted. *Words and Phrases* can also be used as a dictionary, but because it is limited to those words that were involved in litigation, it is not a true dictionary.[5] Moreover, most dictionaries are much more compact and are published in one or two volumes. Listed below are some of the more commonly-used American and English law dictionaries.

Several law dictionaries are presently available on the World Wide Web and are easily searchable. One way to find them is by going to a Web site that makes links to such resources. Many law school libraries provide an "electronic reference desk" or "virtual library" at their Web site which includes links to a variety of reference materials, including legal dictionaries.

---

[4] *See* 28 C.F.R. § 0.25.

[5] The British counterpart of *Words and Phrases* is the four-volume *Words and Phrases Legally Defined* (3d ed. 1988), which includes both judicial and statutory definitions.

1. American Law Dictionaries

a. *Ballentine's Law Dictionary, with Pronunciations,* 3d ed., Lawyers Cooperative Publishing, 1969, 1429p. This volume often provides citations to *A.L.R. Annotations* and to *American Jurisprudence 2d.*

b. *Black's Law Dictionary,* 6th ed., West Publishing Company, 1990, 1657p. The most widely-used of all law dictionaries, this volume includes a Guide to Pronunciation of Latin Phrases and a Table of Abbreviations. It is on WESTLAW in the DI database. An abridged, paperback version is also available.

c. *Bouvier's Law Dictionary and Concise Encyclopedia* (3d revision), 8th ed., West Publishing Company, 1914, 3 volumes; reprinted in 1984 by William S. Hein & Co., Inc. This edition is out of date in some respects. It is a particularly scholarly work, however, and many of its definitions are encyclopedic in nature. It is still very useful for many historical terms.

d. William C. Burton, *Legal Thesaurus,* 2d ed., Macmillan Publishing Company, 1992, 1011p. This volume consists of legal words, words used by the legal community, and words that will enhance legal communication. It includes "associated concepts" and translations of many foreign words and phrases. An index provides references from secondary words to main words.

e. Bryan Garner, *A Dictionary of Modern Legal Usage,* 2d ed., Oxford University Press, 1995, 953p. Including definitions, spelling rules, and grammar guidelines, this volume is perhaps most valuable for its "authoritative guidance on many matters of usage that are unique to legal writing."[6] This dictionary is available on LEXIS–NEXIS in the LEXREF library, DMLU file.

f. Steven H. Gifis, *Law Dictionary,* 4th ed., Barron's, 1996, 643p. Among the better "pocket" dictionaries, this one includes references to treatises and legal periodical articles.

g. Wesley Gilmer, *The Law Dictionary: Pronouncing Edition: A Dictionary of Legal Words and Phrases with Latin and French Maxims of the Law Translated and Explained,* rev. 6th ed., Anderson Publishing Company, 1986, 426p.

h. David Mellinkoff, *Mellinkoff's Dictionary of American Legal Usage,* West Publishing Company, 1992, 703p. This dictionary provides definitions, which are often followed by illustrative examples of a word's meanings.

i. Daniel Oran, *Oran's Dictionary of the Law,* 2d ed., West Publishing Company, 1991, 500p. Written for a wide audience, the definitions are concise and contemporary. Common abbreviations are identified and explained in the alphabetical arrangement.

---

[6] Charles Alan Wright (reviewing the first edition), Book Review, TOWNES HALL NOTES, Spring 1988, at 5.

j.   Kenneth R. Redden & Gerry W. Beyer, *Modern Dictionary for the Legal Profession,* William S. Hein & Co., 1996, 818p. This volume focuses on modern legal terms and concepts selected from a wide variety of professions.

k.   William P. Statsky, *West's Legal Thesaurus/Dictionary: A Resource Guide for the Writer and Computer Researcher,* West Publishing Company, 1985, 813p. This volume includes in one alphabet definitions as well as alternative words to be used.

2. English Law Dictionaries

a.   William A. Jowitt & Clifford Walsh, *Jowitt's Dictionary of English Law,* 2d ed. edited by John Burke, Sweet & Maxwell, 1977, 2 vols., supplemented periodically.

b.   *Mozley and Whiteley's Law Dictionary,* 11th ed. edited by E.R. Hardy Ivamy, Butterworths, 1993, 296p.

c.   Percy G. Osborn, *Osborn's Concise Law Dictionary,* 8th ed. edited by Leslie Rutherford & Sheila Bone, Sweet & Maxwell, 1993, 392p.

d.   *Stroud's Judicial Dictionary of Words and Phrases,* 5th ed. edited by Frederick Stroud & John S. James, Sweet & Maxwell, 1986, 5 vols., with annual cumulative supplements.

3. Special Law Dictionaries

There are also dictionaries devoted to specific subjects, such as labor law, environmental law, and taxation. These can be located by checking the library's catalog under the subject and its subdivision, *e.g.,* Taxation—United States—Dictionaries. An unusual hybrid is Richard Sloane, *The Sloane–Dorland Annotated Medical–Legal Dictionary,* West Publishing Company, 1987, 787p., which, according to its preface at v, "combines the established definitions of medical terms with judicial interpretations of the same terms." A dictionary that explains the use of Latin terminology with respect to the broader context in which it occurs is Russ VerSteeg, *Essential Latin for Lawyers,* Carolina Academic Press, 1990, 166p. Several bilingual and polyglot law dictionaries are available, such as Portuguese–English, English–Japanese, and English–French– German. These can be identified through the library catalog.

SECTION D.   LAW DIRECTORIES

Law directories vary in their scope of coverage. Some of them attempt to list all lawyers; others are limited to a region, state, municipality, or a practice specialty. Law directories are useful for locating information about a particular lawyer or law firm and are used by lawyers when they have to refer a case to a lawyer in another city.

Increasingly, law directories can be found on the World Wide Web, where they can be kept more up-to-date than an annual printed publication. Sometimes the publisher of the print version of a bound directory also provides a Web site for it. In addition, sometimes the Web site of a particular organization provides access to its member database, which often gives a current address and may provide biographical information as well.

1. General Directories

a. *Martindale–Hubbell Law Directory*. This multi-volume set, consisting of two separate units with different colored bindings, is a very comprehensive directory of lawyers and is published annually in two distinct units.

One unit consists of 17 numbered U.S. volumes, arranged alphabetically by state. Each of these volumes is in three color-coded sections. Practice Profiles (blue pages) consist of two alphabetical lists, one of the cities within each state, and a second of the lawyers or law firms within each city. All lawyers admitted to the bar of any jurisdiction are eligible for a general listing at no charge.

For each listed attorney, information is given regarding date of birth, date of admission to the bar, college and law school attended, American Bar Association membership, and specialty (if any). At the end of this section are Practice Profiles for patent and trademark attorneys. Ratings obtained through confidential inquiries made to members of the bar[7] also are given, which rate legal ability and provide general recommendations. Listings of United States Government Lawyers located in Washington, D.C. are grouped by departments, agencies, commissions, etc. and follow the Practice Profiles for that city.

The second section, Professional Biographies (white pages), is another double alphabetic arrangement, this time by cities within the state and law firms within each city. Each entry may include the address and telephone number of the firm, names and short biographies of its members, representative clients, areas of practice, and references. Because this section requires a fee for inclusion, the list is not comprehensive. Section three, Services and Suppliers (yellow pages), is arranged alphabetically by cities within the state, then by category of service provided, and then by company name.

Volume 17 is devoted to listings for State Bar Association profiles, Corporate Law Departments (which includes a Corporate Geographical Index, Practice Profiles, and a Corporate Professional Biographies section), and Law Schools. The section on law schools includes address, phone number, and key contacts, descriptions of the institution and its academic programs, and professional biographical summaries of the law faculty, but it is not comprehensive.

Two unnumbered volumes complete the first unit. One contains a national, alphabetically-arranged listing of individual names together with the city where they practice, and a national index to the cumulative content for the Services and Suppliers, arranged by category. A separate,

[7] A key to the ratings is included in the preliminary pages of each volume, along with the numeric codes for the List of Colleges, Universities, and Law Schools.

unnumbered volume for "Areas of Practice" requires the payment of a fee for inclusion. The listings are alphabetical by area of practice and within that, alphabetically by states and cities.

Six additional volumes with a contrasting binding comprise the second unit. These volumes consist of: a two-volume Law Digest for the fifty states, the District of Columbia, Puerto Rico, and the Virgin Islands, with the second volume also containing Uniform and Model Acts as well as an American Bar Association Codes section; a Canadian and International Lawyers and Firms volume; an International Law Digest with summaries of selected laws from more than 75 foreign countries and the European Union; a Europe, Asia, Australasia, Middle East & Africa volume; and a North American & The Caribbean and Central & South American volume.

In addition to printed volumes, *Martindale–Hubbell* is available in CD–ROM, on LEXIS–NEXIS in the MARHUB library, and on the World Wide Web.[8]

b. *West's Legal Directory*. This is an online directory available on WESTLAW (WLD) that contains profiles of law firms, branch offices, and biographical records from all states, Puerto Rico, the Virgin Islands, the District of Columbia, and Canada. Numerous topical directories are available within the larger database, all including the same specialized search features. Now comprised of more than 1,000,000 profiles, this directory is available as a CD–ROM product and also is available free on the World Wide Web from West's home page.

c. *Who's Who in American Law*. This biennial compilation contains biographical information on approximately 22,000 attorneys selected for their prominence as judges, educators, or practitioners. Despite the large number of entries, there is no claim to comprehensiveness in any area of the profession. In fact, the content is greatly influenced by one's willingness to complete the paperwork necessary for inclusion. The format is similar to that used in other Marquis *Who's Who* publications.

d. *The American Bar, The Canadian Bar, The International Bar: The Professional Directory of Lawyers of the World*. These are annual biographical directories of ranking United States and foreign lawyers. The first two directories provide sketches of the North American law offices listed and individual biographical data. The third unit is a professional international directory of what the publisher calls "the finest lawyers in the world."

e. *Other International Directories*. Many other companies publish directories that are used to locate an attorney in a particular country to deal with general legal questions. Included in these are *The Canadian Law List, The International Law List, The International Lawyers, The International Lawyers Referral Directory, Kime's International Law Directory,* and *Waterlow's Solicitors' & Barristers' Directory*.

---

[8] For recent discussion about the directory's presence on the Web, see Barry D. Bayer & Benjamin H. Cohen, *Finally, Martindale Makes the Web*, LEGAL TIMES, July 1, 1996, at 26.

f. *Martindale-Hubbell Canadian Law Directory.* This single-volume directory, in a format similar to its American counterpart, is designed as a guide to Canada's legal profession.

2. State and Regional Directories

Many states have directories of the attorneys in their states. Legal Directories Publishing Co.[9] covers all states except New York and Alaska and lists attorneys by county and city. These directories also contain some biographical data.

3. Specialty Directories

Some directories are published that list only the attorneys who practice a particular specialty. These are useful for those who want to find a lawyer in a specific city whose practice includes a particular area of the law. Examples of these directories include *American Bank Attorneys, Lawyer's Register International By Specialties and Fields of Law, Markham's Negligence Counsel, The Probate Counsel,* and Prentice Hall Law & Business's *Directory of Corporate Counsel.* The latter title is available on WESTLAW (CORP–DIR). The *Dispute Resolution Directory* from Martindale–Hubbell is that publisher's first new directory in 78 years.

4. Judicial Directories and Biographies

a. *Directories*

(1) *BNA's Directory of State & Federal Courts, Judges, and Clerks* (Washington, D.C.)

(2) *Judicial Staff Directory* (Congressional Staff Directory, Ltd., Mount Vernon, VA)

(3) *United States Court Directory* (Administrative Office of the U.S. Courts)

(4) *Want's Federal–State Court Directory* (Want Publishing Co., Washington, D.C.)

(5) Iris J. Wildman & Mark J. Handler, *Federal Judges and Justices: A Current Listing of Nominations, Confirmations, Elevations, Resignations, Retirements* (Fred B. Rothman & Co., Littleton, CO)

b. *Biographical Directories*

(1) *Historical*

(a) *Biographical Dictionary of the Federal Judiciary* (covers 1789–1974) (Gale Research Company, Detroit, MI)

(b) *Judges of the United States,* 2d ed., 1983 (Bicentennial Committee of the Judicial Conference of the United States; covers 1780–1982)

(2) *Current*

[9] 9111 Garland Rd., P.O. Box 189000, Dallas, TX 75218–9000.

(a) *The American Bench* (Forster–Long, Inc., Sacramento, CA), annual.

(b) *The Almanac of the Federal Judiciary* (Aspen Law & Business), 2 vols., looseleaf. Also available on WESTLAW, AFJ database.

5. Academic Directories

Certain directories are compiled to serve the academic legal community. The Association of American Law Schools' *AALS Directory of Law Teachers* gives addresses for and biographical information on law school faculty, as well as a listing arranged by teaching specialty. This publication can be searched on WESTLAW (WLD–AALS).

The *Directory of Legal Academia* is an electronic directory presently maintained by the Legal Information Institute at Cornell University; it is accessible from their Web site.

The American Association of Law Libraries' *AALL Directory and Handbook* lists geographically its member law libraries in the United States and Canada and the law librarians employed in them. A separate alphabetical list of law library personnel is also included. This is accessible from AALL's Web site.

SECTION E.   MISCELLANEOUS LEGAL REFERENCE SOURCES

1. Abbreviations

Many of the legal dictionaries and legal research texts contain tables of abbreviations, *see, e.g.,* Appendix A herein. In addition to these sources, the following are especially useful:

a.   Mary Miles Prince, *Bieber's Dictionary of Legal Abbreviations,* 4th ed., William S. Hein & Co., Inc., 1993, 791p. This volume gives the abbreviation followed by the word or words represented by that abbreviation.

b.   Kavass, Igor, ed., *Bieber's Dictionary of Legal Abbreviations Reversed,* Buffalo, NY: William S. Hein & Co., 1995, 660p. A companion to *Bieber's Dictionary of Legal Abbreviations,* 4th ed., 1993, this "reversed" version provides the full meaning followed by the abbreviation.

c.   Mary Miles Prince, *Bieber's Dictionary of Legal Citations,* 5th ed., William S. Hein & Co., 1997, var. pagings. This provides examples of statutes, reporters, and legal periodicals in *Bluebook* form; it includes the full text of the 16th edition of the *Bluebook* (1996).

d.   Donald Raistrick, *Index to Legal Citations and Abbreviations,* 2d ed., Professional Books, 1993, 497p. Although the focus of this publication is British, it also includes references to sources from the United States and other countries.

e.   *World Dictionary of Legal Abbreviations,* Igor I. Kavass & Mary Miles Prince, General Editors, William S. Hein & Co., 1991–(looseleaf). Abbreviations and acronyms from the English, French, Italian, Portuguese, and Spanish legal literature are covered.

2. Quotations

The use of an apt quotation often can enhance a legal document or an oral presentation. A number of sources provide information about law-related quotations. Examples of more recent ones are:

a.   Eugene C. Gerhart, *Quote It! Memorable Legal Quotations,* Clark Boardman Co., 1969, 766p.; Eugene C. Gerhart, *Quote It II: A Dictionary of Memorable Legal Quotations,* William S. Hein & Co., 1988, 553p. Collectively these two volumes contain more than 5,000 quotations arranged by subject. Both include author and word indexes.

b.   Simon James & Chantal Stebbings, *A Dictionary of Legal Quotations,* Macmillan Publishing Company, 1987, 209p. This volume is arranged under 160 key words and includes indexes for authors and sources and for key words.

c.   M. Frances McNamara, *2,000 Classic Legal Quotations,* Aqueduct Books, 1992, 718p. This includes a subject arrangement and a general index.

d.   Suzy Platt, ed. *Respectfully Quoted: A Dictionary of Quotations Requested from the Congressional Research Service,* Library of Congress, 1989, 520p. This volume contains 2,100 statements, a significant number of which are law-related, gathered in response to Congressional inquiries for quotations addressed to the Congressional Research Service.

e.   Fred R. Shapiro, *The Oxford Dictionary of American Legal Quotations,* Oxford University Press, 1993, 582p. The most scholarly of the quotation books, this source contains 3,500 quotations by Americans about law or by non-Americans about law in the United States. It is arranged alphabetically by subject and chronologically within each subject and includes cross references and author and keyword indexes.

f.   David S. Shrager & Elizabeth Frost, *The Quotable Lawyer,* Facts on File Publications, 1986, 373p. In this volume are nearly 2,600 quotations arranged under 140 major subject headings. An author and subject index are included.

g.   Quotations can also be located in WESTLAW and LEXIS–NEXIS, using either the language of the particular quotation sought or through a formulated search strategy.

3. General Legal Reference Sources

Often researchers will need information that is not strictly legal, such as statistics, maps, information on state and federal agencies, compound interest and annuity tables, abbreviations, and addresses and telephone numbers for various groups and organizations. At other times, quick reference may be needed to the U.S. Constitution, the Model Rules of Professional Conduct, correct grammar and usage, biographies, bibliographies, and succinct discussions of legal concepts and legal issues. Although no single resource can respond to all ready-reference needs, those described below collectively fill the most frequent ones.

a. *American Jurisprudence 2d Desk Book,* Lawyers Cooperative Publishing, 2d ed., 1992, 1290p. This volume, with an annual pocket supplement, is in four parts: federal matters; international matters; national and state matters; and research and practice aids. It includes such items as federal agency organization charts, court rules, consumer price indexes, a statute of limitations table by state and subject, medical charts, compound interest and annuity tables, and weights and measures.

b. *Encyclopedia of Legal Information Sources,* Brian L. Baker & Patrick J. Petit eds., 2d ed., Gale Research Inc., 1993, 1083p. This is a bibliographic guide to approximately 29,000 citations for publications, organizations, and other sources of information on 180 law-related subjects.

c. *Law and Legal Information Directory,* Steven Wasserman et al. eds., Gale Research Inc., 9th ed. 1996. This is a guide to national and international legal organizations, services, programs, and other miscellaneous information, including locations for law libraries and information centers.

d. *The Lawyer's Almanac,* Aspen Law & Business, 1980 to date. This annual volume is in five main sections: (1) The Legal Profession, which provides information on the nation's 700 largest law firms, mandatory continuing legal education (CLE) requirements in the 50 states, bar exam statistics, state bar associations, and ABA leadership; (2) The Judiciary; (3) Government Departments and Agencies; (4) Statutory Summaries and Checklists; and (5) Commonly Used Abbreviations. A useful list of online legal research sites on the Internet is included.

e. *Lawyer's Desk Book,* 10th ed., Prentice Hall, 1995, 889p. This volume contains many topical discussions on such matters as commercial paper, landlord and tenant, and estate planning. Its appendices include incorporating fees by state, self-liquidating mortgage payment tables, a garnishment guide, and various tax tables.

f. *Legal Researcher's Desk Reference,* Infosources Publishing, 1990 to date, biennial. This volume includes addresses and phone numbers for agencies, elected officials, clerks, U.S. attorneys, law publishers, etc., plus finding aids to federal laws and regulations and historical tables on presidents and Supreme Court justices.

g. William P. Statsky *et al., West's Legal Desk Reference,* West Publishing Company, 1991, 1564p. This volume combines many types of publications into one source: a dictionary; a style and grammar guide; a bibliography of primary and secondary sources by subject and country; and a collection of litigation documents, plus numerous charts and tables, addresses and telephone numbers, and abbreviations.

h. David M. Walker, *Oxford Companion to Law,* Oxford University Press, 1980, 1366p. Although the focus is primarily British, this one-volume work is a useful combination of dictionary and concise encyclopedia. It elucidates the meaning of words and terms, gives brief biographies for a number of individuals, and includes short histories of the development of various laws and legal systems, often including bibliographical references. Appendices list holders of various offices since 1660 and a list of important bibliographical guides that were used in compiling the volume.

SECTION F. FORMS

Much of a lawyer's time is spent drafting legal documents such as wills, trusts, and leases. To assist lawyers in this aspect of their practice, many different form books have been published to enable lawyers to model documents after examples and to tailor them to their particular needs. Today, most practitioners store electronically the documents that have been created from form books for subsequent revision and reuse. When using form books, it should be kept in mind that they are all general in nature and that before using a form, extreme care should be exercised to make sure that the language is entirely suitable for the purpose for which it is to be used. Books of forms may be classified as follows:

1. General Form Books

General form books provide forms for all aspects of legal practice; coverage varies in one volume and multi-volume sets. They are generally annotated, and each form contains references to cases that have favorably construed provisions within the form. Editorial comment is also frequently given. Examples are:

a. *American Jurisprudence, Legal Forms, 2d* (West Group), 20 numbered volumes in multiple books, with annual pocket supplements. A two-volume soft-cover index provides access to the set. Two separate volumes, *Federal Tax Guide to Legal Forms* serve as a companion to the larger set. This is a part of the publisher's *Total Client–Service Library.*

b. *American Jurisprudence, Pleading and Practice Forms, Revised* (West Group), 25 numbered volumes in multiple books, with annual pocket supplements. A multivolume soft-cover index provides access to the set. This set is part of the publisher's *Total Client–Service Library.*

c. *Nichols Cyclopedia of Legal Forms, Annotated* (Clark Boardman Callaghan), 33 volumes, with annual pocket supplements.

d. Jacob Rabkin & Mark H. Johnson, *Current Legal Forms with Tax Analysis* (Matthew Bender), 34 volumes, looseleaf.

e. *West's Legal Forms, 2d* (West Group), 30 volumes in multiple books, with annual pocket supplements. There is a separate soft-cover annual index.

2. Federal Forms

Bender's Federal Practice Forms, Nichols Cyclopedia of Federal Forms, West's Federal Forms, and *Federal Procedural Forms, Lawyers*

Edition, all of which relate to conducting matters in the federal courts, are discussed in Chapter 12, Section B–7, J. Jacobstein, R. Mersky & D. Dunn, *Fundamentals of Legal Research* (7th ed.).

3. Subject Form Books

Many form books are devoted to a particular subject or to a particular phase of the litigation process. These are similar to the general form books, but contain more forms on the subject covered than will usually be found in those of a general nature. Examples are:

a. *National*

(1) F. Lee Bailey & Kenneth J. Fishman, *Complete Manual of Criminal Forms* (Clark Boardman Callaghan), 3d ed., 3 volumes, looseleaf, 1993–

(2) *Bender's Forms of Discovery* (Matthew Bender), 20 volumes, looseleaf.

(3) *Fletcher Corporation Forms Annotated* (Clark Boardman Callaghan), 21 volumes, with supplements.

(4) Robert P. Wilkins, *Drafting Wills & Trust Agreements*, 3d ed. (Clark Boardman Callaghan), 3 volumes, looseleaf.

b. *State*

Most states also have form books that are keyed to local practice. These are published both by commercial publishers and by state bar associations. They contain the same features as the form books discussed above, but since they are designed for local use, may be more useful for the practitioner. Examples are:

(1) *California Legal Forms: Transaction Guide* (Matthew Bender), multi-volume, looseleaf.

(2) *West's Texas Forms*, 3d ed., 1997–multi-volume.

4. Other Sources of Forms

a. *Forms in Treatises*. Many multi-volume sets of treatises include forms, either integrated into the text or in separate volumes.

b. *State Codes*. Some state codes include both substantive and procedural forms. For a particular state code, consult the general index under *Forms*.

c. *World Wide Web*. A wide variety of Web sites now provide forms, ranging from the Internal Revenue Service and the Copyright Office to state and county officials. There also are many general legal forms on the Web. Look for forms by going to the most direct source first (e.g., the office that generates the form) or check some of the law school or commercial Web sites that offer links to legal materials; many of the sites link to forms.

SECTION G.   JURY INSTRUCTIONS AND VERDICT AND SETTLEMENT AWARDS

1.   Jury Instructions

Before juries begin their deliberations the judge instructs them on the applicable law. Often the attorneys have the opportunity to submit proposed instructions to the judge in advance, tailoring these instructions to the pleadings and evidence in the particular case. It is at the judge's discretion whether to use these instructions or to use his or her own or those from other sources. The instructions given to a jury are often important to the outcome of its deliberations.

A number of publications are available that contain instructions characterized as "pattern" or "model" instructions. Some of these are prepared for use in specific states; others relate to particular subjects, *e.g.*, antitrust, damages in torts, employment discrimination, and medical issues; and still others are for use in the various federal circuits. These federal circuit instructions, both civil and criminal, are published in pamphlet form. The Federal Judicial Center, the Judicial Conference of the United States, and committees of the various circuits are often instrumental in preparing these instructions. These sources can be identified in a library's catalog under "Instructions to Juries."[10] Two commercially-published sets that contain extensive collections of instructions for use in the federal courts, together with commentary and case references, are:

a.   Edward J. Devitt, et al., *Federal Jury Practice and Instructions: Civil and Criminal,* 4th ed., West Group, multi-volume with annual pocket supplements.

b.   Leonard B. Sand, et al., *Modern Federal Jury Instructions,* Matthew Bender, 1985 to date, multi-volume, looseleaf. Both civil and criminal instructions are provided along with commentary and case references.

2.   Verdict and Settlement Awards

It is often instructive to have a sense of the measure of damages that might be awarded in a particular type of case. Having this information available can potentially influence whether to take a case, whether to go to trial and let the case be decided by a judge or jury, or to settle.

The multi-volume *Personal Injury Valuation Handbooks* (Jury Verdict Research, Inc.) are arranged by type of injury, by recovery probabilities, and by psychological factors affecting verdicts. *Jury Verdict and Settlement Summaries* by LRP Publications is available on WESTLAW in the LRP–JV database. These summaries cover, among other things, case type, geographical area, factual information about the case, and the

---

[10] Also useful in locating jury instructions are Cheryl Nyberg & Carol Boast, *Jury Instructions: A Bibliography Part I: Civil Jury Instructions,* Legal Reference Services Q., Spring/Summer 1986, at 5; Cheryl Nyberg et al., *Jury Instructions: A Bibliography Part II: Criminal Jury Instructions,* Legal Reference Services Q., Fall/Winter 1986, at 3.

verdict or settlement amounts. LEXIS–NEXIS has a VERDCT Library with several files containing case information on verdict and settlement amounts, expert witnesses, case summaries, and counsel data.

The National Association of State Jury Verdict Publishers has a Web site with links to their publications and an explanation of methods for subscribing to them. The publications themselves are listed by title and by jurisdiction.

SECTION H. RESEARCHING THE SUPREME COURT OF THE UNITED STATES*

In Chapter 4 we discussed how to research the opinions of the Supreme Court of the United States. In this Section various sources are discussed that help in researching the Court as an institution. No effort has been made to be exhaustive. For general works on the Court and the many biographical works on individual Justices, consult the catalog in your library. In addition, the extensive periodical literature about the Court, none of which is included in this Section, can be found using standard indexes to legal periodicals.

Although many government agencies have created a site on the World Wide Web, the Supreme Court had not yet made available an official Web site at press time. However, The Washington Post newspaper recently created a U.S. Supreme Court site as part of its news site. It contains a wide range of information, including a short history of the Court; biographical information about all of the Justices; summaries of both historical and recent cases; and information about the Court's upcoming term.

1. Biographies and Profiles

Several works provide varying levels of biographical information about the Justices. Perhaps the most comprehensive work is Leon Friedman & Fred L. Israel, *The Justices of the United States Supreme Court: Their Lives and Major Opinions* (Chelsea House, 5 vols., 1969–1978). Henry Flanders' *The Lives and Times of the Chief Justices of the Supreme Court of the United States* (T. & J.W. Johnson & Co., 1881), while dated, is still a good source of information on early Chief Justices.

For briefer entries, one can consult *Men of the Supreme Court: Profiles of the Justices,* by Catherine A. Barnes (Facts on File, 1978) and *The Supreme Court Justices: Illustrated Biographies, 1789–1993,* by Clare Cushman (Congressional Quarterly, 1993). For a more eulogistic treatment of selected Justices, see *Memorials of the Justices of the Supreme Court of the United States,* edited by Roger F. Jacobs (Fred B. Rothman & Co., 1981), which reprints the speeches given at the Bar of the Supreme Court to mark the death of a Justice. Also helpful is *The Supreme Court Justices: A Biographical Dictionary,* by Melvin I. Urofsky (Garland Publishing Co., 1994).

* David Gunn, Head of Reference Services at the University of Texas at Austin, Jamail Center for Legal Research, Tarlton Law Library, assisted with preparation of this section.

2. Nominations

One can gain insight into the ideological and philosophical beliefs of a particular Justice by examining transcripts of the hearings held during the confirmation process. *The Supreme Court of the United States: Hearings and Reports on Successful and Unsuccessful Nominations of Supreme Court Justices by the Senate Judiciary Committee,* compiled by J. Myron Jacobstein & Roy M. Mersky (William S. Hein & Co., Inc., 1975–), is an ongoing, multi-volume set that contains the text of confirmation hearings and any related Committee Reports. Coverage begins with the 1916 nomination of Louis D. Brandeis and runs, to date, through the 1994 nomination of Stephen G. Breyer.

3. Personal Papers

If one needs to research the papers of the Justices, the leading source of information about them is Alexandra K. Wigdor, *The Personal Papers of the Supreme Court Justices: A Descriptive Guide* (Garland Pub., 1986).

4. Ratings and Statistical Studies

The seminal work in this area is Albert P. Blaustein & Roy M. Mersky, *The First One Hundred Justices: Statistical Studies on the Supreme Court of the United States* (Archon Books, 1978). More recently, William D. Pederson and Norman W. Provizer have edited *Great Justices of the U.S. Supreme Court: Ratings and Case Studies* (P. Lang, 1993).

5. History

A large number of histories have been written about the Court. The classic work is Hampton L. Carson's *The Supreme Court of the United States: Its History* (John W. Huber, 1891), written to commemorate the one hundredth anniversary of the Supreme Court. Another important work is Charles Warren's *The Supreme Court in United States History* (rev. ed. 1926), which attempts to put the work of the Court in its historical and political contexts. The most scholarly and complete history of the Court is *The Oliver Wendell Holmes Devise: History of the Supreme Court of the United States,* edited by Paul A. Freund and Stanley Katz (1971–). Nine of the projected fourteen volumes are now available.

An equally impressive work is *The Documentary History of the Supreme Court of the United States, 1789–1800,* under the editorship of Maeva Marcus and James R. Perry (Columbia University Press), which attempts to gather together all the original materials necessary to reconstitute the record of the first eleven years of the Court. Thus far, five volumes of the Documentary History have been published. Bernard Schwartz has written the most current single-volume work, *A History of the Supreme Court* (Oxford University Press, 1993).

For less scholarly, more accessible approaches, consult *The Illustrated History of the Supreme Court of the United States,* by Robert Shnayerson (Harry N. Abrams, 1986), or *The Supreme Court of the United States: Its Beginnings & Its Justices, 1790–1991* (1992), issued by the Commission on the Bicentennial of the United States Constitution.

The *Journal of Supreme Court History,* 1990 to date (formerly the *Yearbook,* 1976–1990), published by the Supreme Court Historical Society, is a good source of interesting articles on former Justices and their Courts. *The Docket,* 1959 to date, which is published quarterly by the Supreme Court's Public Information Office, includes a wealth of Supreme Court trivia and other items on more esoteric aspects of the Court and its work.

6. Reference and Research Guides

Congressional Quarterly, Inc. (CQ) seems to have cornered the market on reference and research guides to the Court. The following titles are all published by CQ. *How to Research the Supreme Court,* by Fenton S. Martin and Robert U. Goehlert (1992) is a good introduction to materials on the Court. These authors have also compiled the invaluable *The U.S. Supreme Court: A Bibliography* (1990), which provides a comprehensive listing of works about the Court. *The Supreme Court A to Z: A Ready Reference Encyclopedia,* edited by Elder Witt (1993), is a single-volume work with typically brief, alphabetical entries. The two-volume *Congressional Quarterly's Guide to the U.S. Supreme Court* (3d ed. 1997), by Joan Biskupic and Elder Witt, provides a narrative overview of the workings of the Court. *The Supreme Court at Work,* is another useful work by Biskupic and Witt (2d ed. 1997). *The Supreme Court Compendium: Data, Decisions, and Developments* (2d ed., 1996), is replete with interesting summary tables on such matters as trends in Supreme Court decision-making, post-confirmation activities of the Court, and the political and legal environments in which the Court must operate.

Other useful works include: *A Reference Guide to the United States Supreme Court,* edited by Stephen P. Elliott (Facts on File, 1986); and *The Supreme Court: A Citizen's Guide,* by Robert J. Wagman (1993). Not to be overlooked is Kermit Hall's wide-ranging *The Oxford Companion to the Supreme Court of the United States* (Oxford University Press, 1992), a single volume, encyclopedic compilation of relatively brief, alphabetical entries, including more than 400 summaries of the most important cases decided by the Court. *Facts about the Supreme Court of the United States* by Lisa Paddock (Facts on File, 1996), has answers to a number of basic questions about the Court.

7. Case Selection and Decisionmaking

For works on the forces that determine Supreme Court decisionmaking, see *Deciding to Decide: Agenda Setting in the United States Supreme Court,* by H.W. Perry, Jr. (Harvard University Press, 1991); *The Transformation of the Supreme Court's Agenda: From the New Deal to the Reagan Administration,* by Richard L. Pacelle, Jr. (1991); *Case Selection in the United States Supreme Court,* by Doris M. Provine (University of

Chicago Press, 1980); and *Supreme Court Decision Making,* by David W. Rohde and Harold L. Spaeth (W.H. Froeman & Co., 1976).

SECTION I. BRIEFS, RECORDS, AND ORAL ARGUMENTS ON APPEAL

After a case has been decided by a trial court or an intermediate court of appeals, the case may be appealed to a higher court. If an appeal is granted, the attorneys for each side submit written briefs in which they set forth the reasons why the appellate court should either affirm or reverse the decision of the lower court. These various briefs contain the theories upon which arguments hinge and discussion and analysis of the law, with citation to authority. At times—but quite often for cases being heard by the Supreme Court of the United States—*amicus curiae* ("friends of the court") briefs are also filed by groups or individuals in support of one side or the other.

Where available, the record of trial court action is submitted with the brief. This record usually contains forms of the preliminary motions and pleadings in the case, examination and cross examination of witnesses, the instructions to the jury, the opinion of the lower court, and various other exhibits.

Briefs and records can potentially provide attorneys who have a similar case with much of their research and a list of arguments that have or have not impressed an appellate court.[11] Oral arguments show the focus of the attorneys and judges during the in-court presentations.

1. Supreme Court of the United States

A small number of libraries receive copies of the briefs and records that are submitted to the Supreme Court of the United States. Most law school libraries and larger bar association libraries also have these briefs and records available in microform.[12] Summaries of some attorneys' briefs are included in the *United States Supreme Court Reports, Lawyers' Edition.*

a. *Computer–Assisted Legal Research.* Briefs and records from the October 1979 Term to the present are available on LEXIS–NEXIS in the GENFED library, BRIEFS file. These same sources are available on WESTLAW in the SCT–BRIEF database, beginning with the 1990 term.

---

[11] For a composite, albeit dated, listing of the locations where the various records and briefs can be located, see the following four articles by Gene Teitelbaum: *United States Supreme Court Records and Briefs: An Updated Union List,* LEGAL REFERENCE SERVICES Q., Fall 1982, at 9; *United States Courts of Appeals Briefs and Records: An Updated Union List,* LEGAL REFERENCE SERVICES Q., Fall 1983, at 67; *State Courts of Last Resort's Briefs and Records: An Updated Union List,* LEGAL REFERENCE SERVICES Q., Summer/Fall 1985, at 187; *Intermediate Appellate State Courts' Briefs and Records: An Updated Union List,* LEGAL REFERENCE SERVICES Q., Spring/Summer 1988, at 159. For an historical account of the appellate brief, see Matthew S. Bewig, *The Emergence of Written Appellate Briefs in the Nineteenth–Century United States,* 38 AM. J. LEGAL HIST. 482 (1994).

[12] The *CIS US Supreme Court Records & Briefs,* a microfiche collection, includes all argued cases since 1987 and, since 1975, all non-argued cases in which one or more Justices wrote a dissent from the *per curiam* decision to deny review.

Records and briefs do not become available in the online services until after the oral argument in the case.

b. *Oral Arguments.*

(1) *Audiotapes.* Oral arguments presented before the Supreme Court have been recorded since 1955. These tapes are available from the National Archives. They will be duplicated at no charge if a tape is provided; otherwise they are available for purchase at a nominal charge.[13]

(2) *Transcripts.* Starting with the 1953 Term, transcripts of oral arguments are available from Congressional Information Service in a microfiche set entitled *Oral Arguments of the U.S. Supreme Court.* The *U.S. Law Week* frequently provides brief excerpts of oral arguments in its weekly releases.

(3) *Oyez Oyez Oyez.* A site on the World Wide Web provides digital audio (RealAudio) of Supreme Court oral arguments in many important cases, for the user who is fortunate enough to have a computer equipped with a sound card. It also includes biographical information on all Supreme Court Justices and a virtual tour of the Supreme Court. There are links to electronic versions of the Court's opinions, which can be searched by subject.

c. *Landmark Briefs and Arguments of the Supreme Court of the United States: Constitutional Law.* This series from University Publications of America covers 1793 to date. The period 1793–1973 is in 80 volumes. Annual supplements published from 1974 forward average approximately eight volumes each. As the title indicates, coverage is selective.

d. *Antitrust Law: Major Briefs and Oral Arguments of the Supreme Court of the United States, 1955 Term–1975 Term.* This 36 volume set, published by University Publications of America, has not been supplemented.

2. Other Courts of Appeals

Most large law libraries receive the briefs and records for the federal court of appeals for the circuit in which they are located. In addition,

---

[13] Until late 1993, tapes were not available until three years after the oral arguments, could only be used for educational or instructional purposes, and could not be copied and disseminated. However, the Supreme Court's policy changed following publication of MAY IT PLEASE THE COURT: THE MOST SIGNIFICANT ORAL ARGUMENTS MADE BEFORE THE SUPREME COURT SINCE 1955 (Peter Irons & Stephanie Guitton eds. 1993). This publication by The New Press consists of a 370 page book and six 100–minute cassettes, which include 23 edited live recordings of oral arguments, with a voice-over narration by Irons. Publication of these materials created a furor, with charges levied by the Supreme Court that one of the editors (Irons) violated contractual arrangements by duplication and dissemination of the tapes. *See, e.g.,* Tony Mauro, *Tapes Project Sparks Clash: Supreme Court to Legal Scholar: Keep Oral Arguments to Yourself,* LEGAL TIMES, at 1, Aug. 16, 1993; Maro Robbins, *"May It Please the Court" Doesn't Please the Court,* NAT'L L.J., at 47, Oct. 11, 1993. Its ultimate result, however, was to cause the Supreme Court to change its existing policy and to make the tapes readily and immediately available to the public through the National Archives. *See* Linda Greenhouse, *Supreme Court Eases Restrictions On Use of Tapes of Its Arguments,* N.Y. TIMES, at A22, col. 1, Nov. 3, 1993.

Microform, Inc. is gradually publishing a microfiche collection of the records and briefs from all circuits. Some law libraries also receive the briefs and records from the state's appellate court or courts. Briefs and records from other circuits and other state appellate courts can frequently be obtained through interlibrary loan.

SECTION J. PROFESSIONAL RESPONSIBILITY

Codes of conduct developed by the American Bar Association have governed the conduct of lawyers since the *Canons of Professional Ethics* was adopted in 1908. The *Canons* was replaced in 1969 by the *Model Code of Professional Responsibility*. The 1969 *Code* was widely-adopted by the states. In 1983, the *Model Rules of Professional Conduct* were promulgated, and it is these *Model Rules* that are supposed to constitute the national standard of conduct for lawyers.[14] The format is similar to that used in the Restatements discussed in Chapter 17.

These *Model Rules* and their related Comments have been amended numerous times since their original promulgation over twenty years ago. It is up to each state to adopt the *Model Rules* as its state standard. While over two-thirds of the states have adopted the *Model Rules,* some have only adopted portions of them, still others follow the 1969 *Code,* and still others have rules specific to the particular state.

The ABA has also promulgated rules of conduct for the judiciary, beginning with the *Canons of Judicial Ethics* in 1922. In 1972 the *Code of Judicial Conduct* was adopted, and in 1990 it was replaced by the *Model Code of Judicial Conduct*. These current codes are published as separate pamphlets and are included in one of the unnumbered volumes of the *Martindale–Hubbell Law Directory.*[15]

Enforcement of these rules and the power to discipline lawyers and judges is the responsibility of the state legislature or the highest court in the state, since the ABA, as a voluntary association, has no such authority. The procedure for the discipline of lawyers varies from state to state. The rules governing discipline can be located by consulting the indexes of the state codes. The common practice is for the highest court of the state to appoint a committee of lawyers to hear complaints and to make recommendations to the court. Disciplinary actions are frequently reported in state legal newspapers and in bar association journals.

1. Opinions on Legal Ethics

The American Bar Association has a Standing Committee on Ethics and Professional Responsibility, which is charged with interpreting the professional standards and recommending appropriate amendments and clarifications. Lawyers and judges can describe to this Committee a

---

[14] For information pertaining to the development of the *Model Rules,* see CENTER FOR PROFESSIONAL RESPONSIBILITY, AMERICAN BAR ASSOCIATION, THE LEGISLATIVE HISTORY OF THE MODEL RULES OF PROFESSIONAL CONDUCT (1987).

[15] An annotated version of the *Model Rules* is available as a separate book, *i.e.,* CENTER FOR PROFESSIONAL RESPONSIBILITY, AMERICAN BAR ASSOCIATION, ANNOTATED RULES OF PROFESSIONAL CONDUCT (2d ed. 1992).

situation they are facing and request an opinion as to the propriety of their action. These opinions interpret the *Model Rules* and the *Model Code of Judicial Conduct,* continuing to include references to the 1969 *Model Code* and the 1972 *Code of Judicial Conduct.*

These opinions are published in *Opinions on Professional Ethics* (1967), the two-volume *Informal Ethics Opinions* (1975), *Formal and Informal Ethics Opinions* (1984), and a current looseleaf service, *Recent Ethics Opinions.* These opinions are also available on WESTLAW (LS–ABAEO) and in LEXIS–NEXIS, in various files in the ETHICS Library. New opinions are published in the *ABA Journal.*

Most state bar associations have committees similar to the ABA Standing Committee. The opinions of these committees, along with other information on professional responsibility, can be located in the following sources:

a. *ABA/BNA Lawyer's Manual on Professional Conduct.* A joint project of the American Bar Association and the Bureau of National Affairs, Inc., this multi-volume looseleaf set is the most comprehensive source for a wide range of materials dealing with the legal profession. It includes court cases on the discipline of lawyers and the text of state ethics opinions.

b. *National Reporter on Legal Ethics and Professional Responsibility* (University Publications of America). This multi-volume looseleaf service includes the full text of court cases on legal ethics and the full text of ethics opinions from state and local bar associations.

c. Eugene M. Wypyski, *Opinions/Committee on Professional Ethics.* Volumes 1–3 contain the opinions of the Association of the Bar of the City of New York and the New York County Bar Association; Volume 4 and subsequent volumes contain the opinions for other states.

d. *State and Local Bar Journals.* These publications often print the new opinions of state and local ethics committees.

e. *State Ethics Sources Online.* WESTLAW has ethics opinions online for some states. These can be searched collectively in the METH–EO database or in separate databases by state. LEXIS–NEXIS has an ETHICS library, which includes state case law relevant to ethical concerns, state codes from all the states, and related ABA publications on professional responsibility.

Some states have published their ethics code and opinions online. See, e.g., the *Texas Electronic Ethics Reporter* available on the World Wide Web. Given the constantly-changing nature of the Web, it is worth looking for a particular set of opinions by accessing the Web site for the state bar association or other appropriate entity.

2. Shepard's Professional and Judicial Conduct Citations

This citator is devoted to coverage of citations by the state and federal courts and secondary sources to the various codes of conduct and the ABA's formal and informal opinions.

SECTION K. OTHER, NON–LEGAL INFORMATION SOURCES: AN APPROACH TO FINDING THEM

The variety of materials that may be useful for solving a lawyer's research and reference questions is infinite, because every area of human endeavor touches and is touched by the law. There is no simple way to summarize all of the useful sources that are available, and the techniques for finding them will vary, depending upon the researcher's expertise and the particular facts of the case. In addition, the research landscape changes daily, now that the Internet is becoming accessible to a wider audience. New resources—both official and unofficial—are appearing daily. What follows, therefore, is a suggested basic approach to finding non-legal information.

One of the most useful general sources covering many fields of inquiry is the *Guide to Reference Books*, now in its 11th ed. (Chicago: American Library Association, 1996). The Guide covers both general and specialized resources in a variety of disciplines and formats and is written by subject specialists. General reference works such as encyclopedias and fact books are described, as well as government publications (international, federal, state, and local). Broad categories included are: humanities; social and behavioral sciences; history and area studies; and science, technology & medicine. Each of these, in turn, is divided into more specific headings; e.g., economics and business is further subdivided into a number of topics such as finance and investment. The researcher would do well to begin with the Guide when venturing into an area of research that is unfamiliar.

Another good resource is fee-based electronic databases. The most readily available to lawyers are LEXIS–NEXIS and WESTLAW, which contain a wide variety of materials on subjects other than law. For instance, WESTLAW has news and information files that include international newspapers and trade publications in such areas as biotechnology, health and medicine, and even travel & tourism in addition to an arrangement of practice-area materials. Lexis has many publications on non-legal subjects too, including accounting, medical, and company information in addition to other categories.

Associations are an important source of information on an infinite variety of subjects. *The Encyclopedia of Associations* (Detroit: Gale, 1998), now in its 33rd edition, serves as a guide to nearly 23,000 national and international organizations in every field. These entities are often a source of original research and statistics of interest to their members, and the Encyclopedia provides contact information, often including email and Web addresses as well as phone and fax numbers. Publications and affiliations are listed.

Using the Internet to find a Web site can often be a fruitful activity. The researcher may be richly rewarded after only a small amount of creative thinking. When the organization, entity, or publication is ascertained, the Web may provide a full-text site.

Chapter 20

INTERNATIONAL LAW*

SECTION A. INTRODUCTION

1. International Law in United States Law

International law is part of our law, and must be ascertained and administered by the courts of justice of appropriate jurisdiction as often as questions of right depending upon it are duly presented for their determination.[1]

International law and international agreements of the United States are law of the United States and supreme over the law of the several States. Cases arising under international law or international agreements of the United States are within the Judicial Power of the United States, and subject to Constitutional and statutory limitations and requirements of justiciability, are within the jurisdiction of the federal courts.[2]

Despite some recently expressed doubts,[3] these quotations, one classic and one contemporary, accurately state the relation between international law and the law of the United States. The Supremacy Clause of the Constitution (Art. VI, § 2) declares:

This Constitution, and the Laws of the United States which shall be made in Pursuance thereof, *and all Treaties made, or which shall be made, under the Authority of the United States,* shall be the supreme Law of the Land; and the Judges in every State shall be bound thereby, any Thing in the Constitution or Laws of any State to the Contrary notwithstanding.[4]

* This chapter was written by Jonathan Pratter, Foreign and International Law Librarian, Tarlton Law Library, Jamail Center for Legal Research, University of Texas School at Austin.

[1] The Paquete Habana, 175 U.S. 677, 700 (1900).

[2] RESTATEMENT (THIRD) OF THE FOREIGN RELATIONS LAW OF THE UNITED STATES §§ 111(1), (2) (1987).

[3] *See generally,* Curtis A. Bradley & Jack L. Goldsmith, *Customary International Law as Federal Common Law: A Critique of the Modern Position,* 110 HARV. L. REV. 815 (1997). The controversy over the Supreme Court's decision in United States v. Alvarez–Machain, 112 S. Ct. 2188 (1992), raises the issue of the application of the rule in The Paquete Habana. *See, e.g.,* Keith Highet *et al., Criminal Jurisdiction, Extradition Treaties, U.S. Government-sponsored Abduction of Mexican Citizen,* 86 AM. J. INT'L L. 811 (1992); Monroe Leigh, *Is the President Above Customary International Law?,* 86 AM. J. INT'L L. 736 (1992); Malvina Halberstam, *In Defense of the Supreme Court Decision in Alvarez–Machain,* 86 AM. J. INT'L L. 736 (1992); Michael J. Glennon, *State Sponsored Abduction: a Comment on United States v. Alvarez–Machain,* 86 AM. J. INT'L L. 746 (1992); Richard Pregent, *Presidential Authority to Displace Customary International Law,* 129 MIL. L. REV. 77 (1990).

[4] Emphasis added.

To give practical impact to these broad statements of law, consider the fact that since 1988 an agreement for the sale of goods (probably the most common of all commercial transactions) between a seller in the United States and a buyer in any of over forty five other countries will be governed by a treaty, the United Nations Convention on Contracts for the International Sale of Goods,[5] unless the parties provide otherwise. In an increasingly transnational world, lawyers practicing anywhere in the United States should consider an understanding of international law and of how to research it to be standard equipment.

2. Definition of International Law

"International law ... consists of rules and principles of general application dealing with the conduct of states and of international organizations and with their relations *inter se,* as well as with some of their relations with persons, whether natural or juridical."[6] Two points arise from this definition. First, the focus is on the legal relations among sovereign states. For this reason the subject is sometimes known as the law of nations, and sometimes as *public* international law. The latter term is often used in contrast to the field known as *private* international law, or more commonly in the United States, conflict of laws. This subject concerns the legal relations of individuals where the law of more than one state may be involved.

The second point to be made about the definition of international law is that sovereign states are not the only actors on the scene. Obviously, international organizations such as the United Nations or the Organization of American States are not nations. But their structure, powers, and relations are a significant topic of international law. Moreover, the individual is by no means excluded from participation, although the understanding of exactly how persons, either natural or legal, participate in international law is not a well-settled question. Nevertheless, it is clear that a topic like international human rights is centrally concerned with the position of the individual.

3. The Sources of International Law

International law lacks the formal machinery for making law that is an obvious characteristic of a national legal system. There is no duly constituted legislature, executive or judiciary, although more or less distant analogs of each of these can be found. In the absence of such a machinery the question of where international law comes from has to receive a lot of attention. This is the question of the *sources* of international law.

Article 38(1) of the Statute of the International Court of Justice[7] is generally considered to be an authoritative statement of the sources of international law. Article 38(1) provides:

---

[5] UN Doc. A/Conf. 97/18 (Annex I) (1980), 52 Fed. Reg. 6262 (1987), *reprinted in* 19 I.L.M. 671 (1980).

[6] RESTATEMENT (THIRD) OF FOREIGN RELATIONS LAW OF THE UNITED STATES § 101 (1987).

[7] 59 Stat. 1055 (1945), T.S. No. 993.

The Court, whose function is to decide in accordance with international law such disputes as are submitted to it, shall apply:

(a) international conventions, whether general or particular, establishing rules expressly recognized by the contesting states;

(b) international custom, as evidence of a general practice accepted as law;

(c) the general principles of law recognized by civilized nations;

(d) ... judicial decisions and the teachings of the most highly qualified publicists of the various nations, as subsidiary means for the determination of rules of law.

We can then identify five main categories of sources:

a. *International Conventions.* This includes treaties and other international agreements of all kinds. ("Convention" here is a synonym for agreement.) It also includes bilateral agreements (between two parties) and multilateral agreements (having three or more parties).

b. *Customary International Law.* These are rules that arise by virtue of the general and consistent practice of states acting out of a sense of legal obligation.

c. *General Principles of Law.* Examples of such general principles "common to the major legal systems" (to use the contemporary formulation) include the doctrine of laches or the passage of time as a bar to a claim, principles of due process in the administration of justice, and the doctrine of *res judicata*.

d. *Judicial Decisions.* This category includes the decisions of international tribunals and of national courts, when the latter deal with questions of international law. An international tribunal covers various kinds of judicial fora, ranging from the International Court of Justice to an ad hoc arbitral panel constituted to decide a particular international dispute.

e. *Writings of International Law Scholars.* This is current usage for the archaic language found in Article 38 ("teachings of the most highly qualified publicists"). This category covers treatises and textbooks of leading scholars, the draft conventions and reports of the International Law Commission of the United Nations, which was formed "for the Purpose of encouraging the progressive development of international law and its codification," and the reports and resolutions of such nongovernmental groups as the American Society of International Law, the International Law Association, and the Institut de Droit International.

Law librarians often use the term "secondary sources" to describe such materials because they are commentaries or discussion of the law rather than formal sources of law. This description is consistent with the usage of Article 38(1), which calls such materials "subsidiary means." The difference comes in the case of judicial decisions, which under

Article 38(1) are also "subsidiary means" rather than primary sources of law.[8]

SECTION B.   INTERNATIONAL AGREEMENTS: UNITED STATES SOURCES

1. Introduction

A treaty is "an international agreement concluded between States in written form and governed by international law ... whatever its particular designation."[9] This basic definition makes the important point that the terminology describing a particular international agreement does not affect its legal status as an agreement binding in international law. There is an entire catalog of terms used in connection with various kinds of international agreement: treaty, convention, protocol, covenant, charter, statute, act, declaration, concordat, exchange of notes, agreed minute, memorandum of agreement, and memorandum of understanding, for example.

The subject is further complicated in the practice of the United States by the frequent use we make of the *executive agreement*. Under the Constitution, the President has the "Power, by and with the Advice and Consent of the Senate, to make Treaties, provided two thirds of the Senators present concur ..."[10] But this formal treaty-making power does not exhaust the President's authority to negotiate international agreements. In fact, there are far more executive agreements in force between the United States and other countries than there are treaties. The difference between the two kinds of agreement is a subject for the substantive course in international law.[11] For our purposes it is enough to know that both constitute binding international agreements.[12]

2. Current Sources

a. *T.I.A.S. and U.S.T.* Since 1945, the State Department has published the international agreements of the United States in a series of pamphlets called *Treaties and Other International Acts Series (T.I.A.S.).* The series began with number 1501 and as of this writing has reached T.I.A.S. 12245, an agreement concluded in September 1995. Since 1950, the State Department has published the agreements that

---

[8] To avoid confusion, the reader should note that in discussions of researching international law the word "sources" can have two different senses. The first sense refers to the formal sources of international law as described in Article 38(1). The other sense refers to published sources, that is, the publications and other resources described in this chapter that make up the documentation of international law.

[9] Vienna Convention on the Law of Treaties, concluded at Vienna, May 23, 1969, art. 2 § 1(a), 1155 U.N.T.S. 331.

[10] U.S. CONST. art. II, § 2.

[11] *See generally,* BARRY E. CARTER & PHILLIP TRIMBLE, INTERNATIONAL LAW 134–208 (1991); LOUIS HENKIN ET AL., INTERNATIONAL LAW: CASES AND MATERIALS 198–240 (3d ed. 1993).

[12] *See* CONGRESSIONAL RESEARCH SERVICE, LIBRARY OF CONGRESS, TREATIES AND OTHER INTERNATIONAL AGREEMENTS: THE ROLE OF THE UNITED STATES SENATE, S. PRT. NO. 103–53 (1993) for a thorough treatment of United States treaty practice.

first appear in *T.I.A.S.* in a series of bound volumes entitled *United States Treaties and Other International Agreements (U.S.T.). U.S.T.* is up to 35 volumes and a volume may have as many as five or six separately bound parts. Volume 35, part 3, the most recently issued as of this writing, ends with T.I.A.S. 10877, an agreement concluded in 1981. *By statute, both U.S.T. and T.I.A.S.* are authoritative sources for the text of agreements published there.[13]

b. *U.S.C., U.S.C.A., U.S.C.S. and Federal Register.* There is a tendency to think that U.S. treaties might be found in one of these places. In general, that is *not* true. *U.S.C.* does not have treaties. The annotated codes, *U.S.C.A.* and *U.S.C.S.,* publish a few treaties of general interest. For example, the United Nations Convention on Contracts for the International Sale of Goods appears in the Appendix volume to Title 15 of *U.S.C.A. U.S.C.S.* has an unnumbered volume titled "International Agreements" containing the text of 23 assorted documents. Strangely, the United States is *not* a party to several of these agreements. That is quite misleading. The *Federal Register* rarely publishes U.S. international agreements. Therefore, research for the text of U.S. international agreements *should not* begin with one of these sources. On the other hand, they *should* be consulted to find implementing legislation and judicial interpretation, as noted below in Section B–7.

c. *Commercial Sources.* The reader should note the substantial delay in the publication of both official series. *T.I.A.S.* has improved slightly in recent years, but *U.S.T.* now runs sixteen years behind! Such delays cause obvious problems for researchers. These are primary sources of law containing binding international agreements of the United States, many of which are *currently in force.* Adding to the difficulty is the fact that *The Bluebook* prefers citation to one of these sources when the U.S. is a party,[14] something that is clearly impossible in the case of more recent international agreements.

Two commercial publishers have services that go some way toward resolving the difficulty. Hein's *United States Treaties and Other International Agreements, Current Microfiche Service* and Oceana's *Consolidated Treaties & International Agreements, Current Service* have made available documents that the State Department has not yet released for publication. At the time of writing, the Oceana series is current to DOS 97–60,[15] and the Hein series, to DOS 97–90. Many of these documents eventually will appear in *T.I.A.S.*

In tandem with the trend toward commercial publication of U.S. international agreements, the commercial suppliers of online legal information, WESTLAW and LEXIS–NEXIS, now offer full-text databases of U.S. treaty documents. WESTLAW rather confusingly contains two different databases devoted to U.S. international agreements. The data-

---

[13] 1 U.S.C. §§ 112a, 113 (1988).

[14] THE BLUEBOOK: A UNIFORM SYSTEM OF CITATION rul. 20.4.5(a)(i) (16th ed. 1996).

[15] The Department of State Number (DOS) is the preliminary number assigned to an international agreement pending publication.

base names are TIA and USTREATIES. [See Illustration 20–1.] The first
is more comprehensive, while the second is more current. LEXIS–NEXIS
has a file called USTRTY in its INTLAW and ITRADE libraries. Regrettably, this file is not available on the educational account.[16]

Given the peculiarities of coverage and access, along with the
difficulties of citation, it is strongly recommended that these databases of
U.S. treaty documentation should be used as supplements to, and not as
substitutes for, the standard printed sources. However, given the time
lag in publication of the official U.S. treaty series, it is fortunate that
both the hard-copy and online commercial products are now available. At
the time of writing, neither the State Department nor another concerned
institution has made use of the Worldwide Web to mount a database of
U.S. international agreements.[17]

3. Earlier Publications

a. *United States Statutes at Large.* Treaties of the United States
were published in *United States Statutes at Large* from volume 8
through volume 64 (1949). Volume 8 collected together treaties entered
into between 1776 and 1845. Beginning with volume 47, executive
agreements were included. Volume 64, part 3 (1950–51) contains an
index of all the agreements in *United States Statutes at Large.*

b. *T.S. and E.A.S.* The current pamphlet series, *T.I.A.S.*, was
preceded by the *Treaty Series (T.S.)* and the *Executive Agreement Series
(E.A.S.).* *Treaty Series* reached number 994 and *Executive Agreement
Series* went to number 506, for a total of 1500. Thus, *T.I.A.S.* begins at
1501.[18]

c. *Bevans.* A useful collection published by the State Department is
*Treaties and Other International Agreements of the United States of
America, 1776–1949,*[19] known as *Bevans* from the name of the compiler.
It collects together in 13 volumes the international agreements of the
United States up to the beginning of *U.S.T.* Multilateral treaties are
arranged chronologically in volumes 1–4. Bilateral treaties are arranged
alphabetically by the name of the other country in volumes 5–12. Volume
13 is a general index. Two other collections published by the State
Department are also known by the names of their respective compilers:
*Treaties, Conventions, International Acts, Protocols, and Agreements
Between the United States of America and Other Powers*[20] (Malloy) and

---

[16] The TIA database on WESTLAW and the USTRTY file on LEXIS–NEXIS are both
derived from the Oceana treaty products mentioned above.

[17] Large amounts are treaty documentation, not limited to agreements to which the U.S.
is a party, are available both on the Worldwide Web and through the commercial online
sources. These are discussed in section C. of this chapter.

[18] For detailed information on these series and on the bibliography of the early publication of United States international agreements, *see* 1 HUNTER MILLER, TREATIES AND OTHER
INTERNATIONAL ACTS OF THE UNITED STATES OF AMERICA 35–138 (1931).

[19] Compiled by Charles I. Bevans (U.S.G.P.O. 1968–1976).

[20] Compiled by William M. Malloy (U.S.G.P.O. 1910–1938).

Treaties and Other International Acts of the United States of America[21] (Miller). For most purposes *Bevans* supersedes both of these earlier collections.

4. United States Treaties in Congressional Documents

a. *Senate Treaty Documents and Senate Executive Reports.* Once a treaty for which the advice and consent of the Senate will be sought has been negotiated and signed, the President submits it to the Senate in a message from the President, with the text of the agreement annexed to it. The proposed treaty is referred to the Committee on Foreign Relations for hearings and a recommendation to the full Senate. Until the 97th Congress (1981–82), the Senate printed the proposed treaty under the name *Senate Executive Document* with a letter designation.

Beginning with the 97th Congress, the printed treaties are called *Treaty Documents* and receive a number, the first part of which corresponds to the relevant session of Congress. For example, the message from the President of July 1997 transmitting the World Intellectual Property Organization Copyright Treaty concluded at Geneva on December 20, 1996, is Treaty Document 105–17. The Committee on Foreign Relations makes its recommendation in a report printed in the numbered series of *Senate Executive Reports.* For example, the committee's report of September 1996 on the Chemical Weapons Convention concluded at Paris on January 13, 1993 is Executive Report 104–33. Again, the first part of the number reflects the relevant session of Congress.

Researchers should note the significance of these congressional treaty documents. The message of transmittal from the President in the Treaty Document series always publishes the text of the agreement in an annex. The report of the Senate Foreign Relations Committee in the Executive Report series reprints the agreement with additional headings ("article-by-article analysis"). Given the serious delay in the standard official publications of U.S. international agreements, these congressional treaty documents often furnish the sole official source of publication for purposes of citation. Moreover, in the case of agreements that have generated disagreement or controversy in the Senate, the Foreign Relations Committee often appends statements of "conditions," "declarations," "understandings," or "provisos" to its recommendation of advice and consent to the full Senate. If the full Senate gives its advice and consent to ratification subject to these conditions, important consequences for the correct understanding of the treaty text and of the legal obligations it imposes will follow, at least from the point of view of the United States. The committee report in the Executive Report series is often the only place to find the text of these appended statements.

Treaty Documents, but not Executive Reports, for the 104th (1995/96) and 105th (1997/98) Congresses are available on the World Wide Web at the home page of the United States Government Printing Office.

[21] Edited by Hunter Miller (U.S.G.P.O. 1931–1948).

Beginning in 1970, the references to both Treaty Documents and Executive Reports, with a descriptive abstract, are found in the annual volumes of *CIS, Abstracts,* under the heading "Senate Committees, Foreign Relations, Executive Reports and Executive Documents" (S384 and S385).[22] The *Monthly Catalog of United States Government Publications* also indexes these documents.

b. *Congressional Index.*[23] Treaties submitted to the Senate for advice and consent can, unlike bills, be held over from year to year. Some international agreements can remain pending in the Senate for a long time. Volume 1 (Senate) of the *Congressional Index* has a "Treaties" tab that is useful for tracking down treaties pending in the Senate. There is a subject index and a section of summaries of all pending treaties with a chronology of actions relating to each one.

5. Other Publications

a. *Unperfected Treaties of the United States, 1776–1976.*[24] This multi-volume set is an annotated collection of the treaties to which the United States was a signatory, but which never went into force.

b. *Extradition Laws and Treaties of the United States.*[25] This looseleaf set contains extradition treaties currently in force between the United States and other countries, arranged alphabetically by the name of the other country. Additional volumes in this set reprint U.S. agreements in the field of international judicial assistance in criminal matters.

c. *Indian Affairs: Laws and Treaties.*[26] Volume 2 contains treaties made by the United States with Indian tribes between 1778 and 1883. It was reprinted under the title *Indian Treaties.*[27] Volume 7 of *United States Statutes at Large* also has a compilation of Indian treaties. Treaties concluded with Indian tribes before the independence of the United States are in *Early American Indian Documents: Treaties and Law, 1607–1789.*[28]

d. *Tax Treaties,*[29] *Federal Tax Treaties.*[30] Both of these looseleaf publications give comprehensive coverage with annotations and background material of the income and estate tax treaties of the United States currently in force and pending ratification. *Treaty Disk: United States International Tax Treaties*[31] is a CD–ROM product containing all tax treaties of the U.S. with their legislative histories.

---

[22] For earlier documents, *see* MARIANA G. MABRY, CHECKLIST OF SENATE EXECUTIVE DOCUMENTS AND REPORTS, 1947–1970 (1970).

[23] (Commerce Clearing House 1938–).

[24] Edited by CHRISTIAN L. WIKTOR (Oceana Publications 1976).

[25] Edited by IGOR I. KAVASS & ADOLPH SPRUDZS (W.S. Hein 1979–).

[26] Compiled and edited by CHARLES J. KAPPLER (U.S.G.P.O. 1903–1941).

[27] (Interland Publishing 1972).

[28] Edited by ALDENT T. VAUGHN (U.P.A. 1979–1989).

[29] (Commerce Clearing House 1952–).

[30] (Prentice–Hall 1958–).

[31] Compiled by J. ROSS MACDONALD (Kluwer Law International 1996).

6. Finding United States International Agreements and Verifying their Status

The process of locating international agreements requires the use of methods with which the researcher will not be familiar from having done research in other U.S. legal materials. In addition, there is an essential second step to take after finding the text of an agreement. International agreements, like other primary sources of law, must be verified as to their current status. Multilateral agreements do not come into force once they are negotiated. A minimum number of countries has to agree to join a multilateral treaty before it becomes binding. That may take years.

Moreover, only those countries that agree to become parties to a multilateral agreement are bound by it, thus making it essential to know who the states party are. States may accede to (join) a multilateral treaty long after it is first negotiated, and as a final complication, they may denounce (terminate) their participation in either a multilateral or bilateral agreement at some time after becoming a party. Obviously then, the process of verification is crucial. The finding tools noted in this section refer to the location of the text of international agreements; they also provide critical additional information for verification.

a.   *Treaties in Force.*[32] The full title is *Treaties in Force: A List of Treaties and Other International Agreements in Force on January 1, 199__.* It is published annually by the State Department, but usually appears several months after the date on the cover. It is divided into bilateral and multilateral sections. The bilateral section is organized alphabetically by the name of the other country and subdivided by subject matter; the multilateral section is organized alphabetically by subject matter and chronologically within each subject heading. Each entry begins with the name of the agreement, followed by the place and date it was concluded, the date it entered into force (if multilateral, the date of entry into force in general and for the United States, in particular), the citation (with parallel citations), a list of the other states party to the agreement (if multilateral), and brief notes regarding such points as whether a state entered a reservation or declaration to a multilateral agreement. [See Illustration 20–2.]

Thus, *Treaties in Force* can answer several questions: a) What international agreements does the United States currently have with a particular country or in a particular subject matter?; b) Is a particular international agreement in force for the United States?; c) Where can the text be found?; and d) What other countries are parties to a multilateral agreement? *Treaties in Force* is current to the date on the cover and needs updating to catch developments that have occurred since it was last issued. The foreword to *Treaties in Force* mentions that further inquiries regarding U.S. international agreements may be made to the Office of Treaty Affairs, Department of State, Washington, DC 20520.

---

[32] (U.S.G.P.O. 1944–).

b. *US Department of State Dispatch.*[33] Since 1939 the State Department has published a journal of information of some kind, either weekly or monthly. Until 1989, it was titled *Department of State Bulletin.* In 1990, after complaints from lawyers and the academic community concerning the termination of the *Bulletin,* the State Department began publication of the weekly *Dispatch.* Every month the *Dispatch* carries a section called "Treaty Actions." This department keeps track of world treaty developments in which the United States participates or which affect the international relations of the United States. By checking the "Treaty Actions" section for the period following the cover date of the current *Treaties in Force,* it is possible to update the status of a U.S. international agreement to within approximately one month to six weeks. *Dispatch* is available on LEXIS–NEXIS (GENFED and INTLAW libraries, among others, DSTATE file), making it possible to search "Treaty Actions" online.

c. *A Guide to the United States Treaties in Force.*[34] This commercial publication contains essentially the same information as that found in *Treaties in Force.* However, as it is more heavily indexed, it can be used to find references to agreements that might be hard to locate in *Treaties in Force.*

d. *United States Treaty Index: 1776–1990 Consolidation.*[35] This is a comprehensive index of all documented international agreements of the United States entered into from 1776 through 1990. It has been updated with "1995 Revision" volumes. The set consists of a "master guide" in numerical order, a chronological guide, a country index, and a subject index. The final volumes are a "geographical subject index," which provides added indexing by country.

e. *Current Treaty Index.*[36] This is the semi-annual supplement to the *United States Treaty Index: 1776–1990 Consolidation.* It is organized along the same lines as the consolidation and updates it to within approximately the last six months. Note that this index takes note of many documents that have not appeared in the official U.S. treaty publications. Therefore, the researcher must use this index in conjunction with one of the commercial sources for recent U.S. international agreements.

7. Implementation and Judicial Interpretation of United States Treaties

a. *U.S.C., U.S.C.A., U.S.C.S., C.F.R., Federal Register.* Often the terms of a U.S. international agreement require implementing legislation to become effective as part of U.S. law. For example, the Convention on the Recognition and Enforcement of Foreign Arbitral Awards[37] is enact-

[33] (U.S.G.P.O. 1990–).

[34] Compiled and edited by IGOR I. KAVASS (W.S. Hein 1983–).

[35] Compiled and edited by IGOR I. KAVASS (W.S. Hein 1991).

[36] Compiled and edited by IGOR I. KAVASS (W.S. Hein 1982–).

[37] 21 U.S.T. 2517, 330 U.N.T.S. 38.

ed as chapter 2 of the Federal Arbitration Act.[38] In addition, when a branch of the federal executive is charged with carrying out various responsibilities of the United States under a treaty and its implementing legislation, then there will be implementing administrative regulations to be found. For example, under the UNESCO Convention on the Means of Prohibiting and Preventing the Illicit Import, Export and Transfer of Ownership of Cultural Property[39] and its implementing legislation,[40] the U.S. Customs Service makes regulations for the emergency restriction on the import of various kinds of cultural property. These regulations are first published in the *Federal Register* and later summarized in a list at 19 C.F.R. § 12.104g. Therefore, when researching a U.S. international agreement, it is essential to check for federal legislation and administrative regulations on point.

b. Finding cases decided under and interpreting U.S. international agreements requires creative research along various lines. Four lines of inquiry are suggested here.

(1) The West digests include a topic, "Treaties," that collects cases involving the interpretation and application of U.S. international agreements.

(2) *U.S.C.S.* has a volume called *"Uncodified: Notes to Uncodified Laws and Treaties,"* which collects case notes to various multilateral, bilateral, and Indian treaties of the United States.

(3) A volume of *Shepard's Federal Statute Citations* has a section collecting cases in federal court citing to U.S. international agreements published in *U.S.T.* and *T.I.A.S.* To find state cases citing U.S. treaties, the various state editions of Shepard's have to be consulted. Note that treaties published before 1950 have to be "shepardized" using the section for *United States Statutes at Large,* where treaties were published up to that time.

(4) The WESTLAW and LEXIS–NEXIS databases are probably the best way to find U.S. cases arising under or interpreting U.S. international agreements. The search query can be formulated by using key words from the formal and popular name of the treaty, e.g., (convention + 3 prevention + 3 pollution + 3 ships) or marpol.[41] When doing thorough research for U.S. cases none of these four avenues of research should be relied upon to the exclusion of the others.

---

[38] 9 U.S.C. §§ 201 *et seq.* (1994).

[39] 823 U.N.T.S. 231.

[40] Convention on Cultural Property Implementation Act, 19 U.S.C. §§ 2601 *et seq.* (1994).

[41] This search will retrieve cases considering the International Convention for the Prevention of Pollution from Ships, 12 I.L.M. 1319 (1973), and its Protocol, 17 I.L.M. 546 (1978). The popular name for these agreements is "MARPOL." A recent example is International Association of Independent Tanker Owners v. Lowry, 947 F. Supp. 1484 (W.D. Wash. 1996), where one issue had to do with the status of MARPOL requirements in U.S. law.

SECTION C. INTERNATIONAL AGREEMENTS: ADDITIONAL SOURCES (OTHER THAN UNITED STATES PUBLICATIONS)

1. General Treaty Collections

a. *United Nations Treaty Series (U.N.T.S.).* Under Article 102 of the United Nations Charter, every member of the UN is required to register its international agreements with the Secretariat, which is required to publish them. The idea of compulsory registration and publication is in part to prevent secret diplomacy. Begun in 1946, *U.N.T.S.* now has well over 1,500 volumes and contains many thousands of agreements. However, *U.N.T.S.* also runs many years behind. Its index volumes also run behind and are difficult to use. The researcher should note that the formal title by which libraries catalog this source is *Treaty Series (United Nations).*

Agreements published in *U.N.T.S.* are now available on the World Wide Web at the website of the United Nations in the section called *United Nations Treaty Collection.* Registration is required to use this site. The user searches for documents according to several options, including date, party, and subject. Summaries are presented with the choice to view the full text. Text is presented in an image format as the document appears in *U.N.T.S.* This has the advantage of authenticity and the disadvantage of being very slow. At the time of writing, the *United Nations Treaty Collection* is a very recent development. Several bugs remain to be worked out.

b. *League of Nations Treaty Series (L.N.T.S.).* This is the predecessor of *U.N.T.S.*, having been published under the auspices of the League of Nations. In 205 volumes covering the period 1920–1946, it published the treaties registered with the Secretariat of the League. The formal title under which the researcher should look in library catalogs is *Treaty Series (League of Nations).*

c. *Consolidated Treaty Series (C.T.S.).* This commercially published series is in 243 volumes covering the period 1648–1919. It is good for locating the text of historically important international agreements. Note that the three treaty series mentioned above (*C.T.S., L.N.T.S.,* and *U.N.T.S.*) cover a continuous period of time from 1648 to the present.

2. Other Treaty Collections

a. *European Treaty Series.* The Council of Europe, an international organization of 25 European nations, has as one of its main purposes the drafting and sponsoring of multilateral agreements on subjects of mutual benefit. The most significant treaty sponsored by the Council of Europe is the European Convention for the Protection of Human Rights and Fundamental Freedoms.[42] The Council of Europe's treaties are first published as individual documents in the *European Treaty Series.* They

---

[42] E.T.S. No. 5, 213 U.N.T.S. 221.

have also been collected and republished (through 1989) in the five volumes of *European Conventions and Agreements.*[43]

b. *International Legal Materials (I.L.M.).* Published since 1962 by the American Society of International Law, this is a leading source for the text of recent international agreements of note. *I.L.M.* appears six times a year and is probably the best place to look for the publication of recent international documents of significance, including international agreements. *I.L.M.* contains many other kinds of documents besides, including judicial decisions, arbitral awards, and the documents of international organizations, for example. It is available online through LEXIS–NEXIS (INTLAW library, ILM file) and WESTLAW (ILM database).

c. *O.A.S. Treaty Series.* Like the Council of Europe, the Organization of American States drafts and sponsors multilateral agreements of mutual interest to member states. These are published in the *O.A.S. Treaty Series.*[44] Its formal title under which it will be cataloged in libraries is *Treaty Series (Organization of American States).*

d. *National Treaty Series.* Like the United States, many other countries publish their international agreements in a special series. Examples are the United Kingdom *Treaty Series* and *Recueil des Traités et Accords de la France.* A useful listing of many of these national collections is compiled at Simone–Marie Kleckner, *Public International Law and Organization: International Law Bibliography* 6–13, which is found in *A Collection of Bibliographic and Research Resources.*[45]

e. *Subject Compilations.* Many publishers, both official and commercial, have put together collections of international agreements. These collections can be very useful because they bring together in one place documents that otherwise are often difficult to find. There are too many of these collections to list comprehensively here, but some leading examples are mentioned.

The Hague Conference on Private International Law publishes its 34 multilateral agreements on various aspects of conflict of laws and international judicial assistance in a one-volume book titled *Collection of Conventions (1951–1996).* The recent explosion of interest in international environmental law has produced several collections of international agreements, including: *Basic Documents of International Environmental Law,*[46] *International Environmental Law: Multilateral Treaties,*[47] and *Basic Documents on International Law and the Environment.*[48] In the field of human rights, another topic of current interest, useful collections

[43] (Council of Europe 1971–).

[44] THE BLUEBOOK, 16th ed., mistakenly continues to use the former title, *Pan-American Treaty Series.*

[45] (Oceana 1984–).

[46] Edited by HARALD HOHMANN (Graham and Trotman 1992).

[47] Edited by W.E. BURHENNE (E. Schmidt 1974–).

[48] Compiled by P.W. Birnie and A.E. Boyle (Oxford 1995).

include: *Basic Documents on Human Rights*[49] and *Human Rights: A Compilation of International Instruments.*[50]

3. Finding and Updating International Agreements (When the United States May Not Be a Party)

In addition to the finding tools mentioned in Section B–6 *supra,* there are several sources that serve to locate international agreements, whether or not the United States is a party.

a. *Multilateral Treaties Deposited With the Secretary–General.* This annual publication from the United Nations tracks the status of 290 international agreements drafted under the auspices of the United Nations and League of Nations. The entry for each treaty gives complete information (as of 31 December) regarding the states party to the treaty and the relevant dates. This is one of the few sources that publishes the text of various declarations and reservations entered by states at the time of becoming a party.

Multilateral Treaties Deposited with the Secretary–General is now available in a frequently-updated version on the World Wide Web on the United Nations home page in the section *United Nations Treaty Collection.* Registration is required. [See Illustration 20–3.]

b. *Multilateral Treaties: Index and Current Status.*[51] This useful volume provides current information on about 1000 treaties. Each entry gives an indication of the date of conclusion, the citation to the location of the text, the date of entry into force, the states party to the treaty, and the states signatory. There is a notes section describing the agreement and making reference to related documents. The latest cumulative supplement brings matters up to 1 January 1994.

c. *World Treaty Index.*[52] The advantage of this five-volume index is that it covers bilateral as well as multilateral agreements. The disadvantage is that it does not go beyond 1980. This limits its usefulness substantially.

4. International Agreements in Electronic Formats

The availability of information in electronic format holds great promise for international legal research. As mentioned at a few points already, substantial information on international agreements is accessible on the Internet. This summarizes the current state of play in this rapidly developing area.

a. *World Wide Web.* A good place to start on the Internet is the site called *ASIL [American Society of International Law] Guide to Electronic Resources for International Law.* There is a section titled "Treaties." [See Illustration 20–4.] Here are found links to some of the major sites

[49] Edited by IAN BROWNLIE (3d ed. Oxford 1992).

[50] (7th ed. United Nations 1994).

[51] Edited by M.J. BOWMAN & D.J. HARRIS (Butterworths 1984).

[52] Edited by PETER H. ROHN (2d ed. ABC–Clio Information Services 1983).

on the World Wide Web dealing with international agreements. Among these is the *United Nations Treaty Collection* containing both the text of international agreements first published in the *United Nations Treaty Series*, as well as a frequently-updated version of the finding tool *Multilateral Treaties Deposited with the Secretary–General*. Also of value as a site for a large general collection of multilateral agreements is the *Multilaterals Project* of the Fletcher School of Law and Diplomacy.

Creative use of Internet browsers will bring up a multitude of other sites reproducing all kinds of international agreements. Subjects covered run the entire range of topics in international law, including international trade, the environment, disarmament, and humanitarian law, etc. A word of caution is in order here. The accuracy and authority of texts reproduced on the World Wide Web varies wildly from site to site. It is dangerous to rely without verifying their accuracy on texts downloaded from Internet sites. Texts as available in official printed sources should be preferred. The value of using the Internet to find the text of international agreements lies in the fact that documents not otherwise available can often be found there.

b. *WESTLAW and LEXIS–NEXIS.* International legal documentation as available via the commercial online legal research services is indicated throughout this chapter. Both LEXIS–NEXIS and WESTLAW carry the text of a fairly wide range of international agreements in several fields, particularly international economic and trade law, international environmental law, and international taxation. This material is scattered throughout several databases/files on both services. Researchers should consult the database directories of both services and should browse their menus for detailed information. The caveat expressed above regarding accuracy and authenticity applies here too.

Treaty information is also available in other digital formats such as CD–ROM. The *ASIL Guide* mentioned above supplies a good overview. As this site is updated regularly, researchers can consult it from time to time to keep up with developments in the publication of international agreements in electronic format.

SECTION D.   CUSTOMARY INTERNATIONAL LAW

1. Introduction

Article 38 of the Statute of the International Court of Justice speaks of "international custom, as evidence of a general practice accepted as law." Several questions arise from this formulation. The first must be, "*Whose* custom?" For those who believe that international law is preeminently the law of *interstate* relations, the focus will be on the custom of state actors and their governmental representatives. For those who believe that international law is *transnational* law, the perspective takes in all actors on the international scene, including international organizations, multinational corporations, and even people. The next question has to be, "*What* is international custom?" The text of Article 38 gives the germ of an answer: "a general practice accepted as law." Customary international law, then, has a dual character. It derives 1) from the general practice of states and other subjects of international law 2) acting from a sense of legal obligation. A leading treatise thus distinguishes customary international law from an international usage because the latter "is a general practice which does *not* reflect a legal obligation."[53]

Unfortunately for research in international law, the definition of international custom simply pushes the difficulty back a step. Now the question becomes, "How does the researcher go about establishing the existence of something that by definition is unwritten and the evidence for which might be found in any number of sources?"

Brownlie suggests the following list of possible documentary sources:

diplomatic correspondence, policy statements, press releases, the opinions of official legal advisers, official manuals on legal questions, e.g., manuals of military law, executive decisions and practices, orders to naval forces, etc., comments by governments on drafts produced by the International Law Commission, state legislation, international and national judicial decisions, recitals in treaties and other international instruments, a pattern of treaties in the same form, the practice of international organs, and resolutions relating to legal questions in the United Nations General Assembly.[54]

This list makes the point that the search for evidence of state practice as an element of customary international law must go forward on several fronts. Despite the difficulties there are some well-established sources with which the researcher can begin the process.

2. Digests of Practice: United States Publications

The United States leads the world in the publication of what are known generally as digests of international law or digests of practice in international law. The first of these was published in 1877.[55] Digests of practice bring together references and quotations from a huge array of sources and organize them according to the main topics of public international law. Sometimes a digest will focus on the practice of a particular nation. However, the digests produced in the United States (under the auspices of the State Department) draw their material from a broad range of international sources.

    a. *Digest of International Law.*[56] Whiteman's is the most recent of the U.S. digests. It is in 14 volumes plus an index volume.

---

[53] IAN BROWNLIE, PRINCIPLES OF PUBLIC INTERNATIONAL LAW 5 (4th ed. Oxford 1990) (emphasis added).

[54] *Id.* (footnotes omitted).

[55] JOHN L. CADWALADER, DIGEST OF THE PUBLISHED OPINIONS OF THE ATTORNEYS-GENERAL, AND OF THE LEADING DECISIONS OF THE FEDERAL COURTS, WITH REFERENCE TO INTERNATIONAL LAW, TREATIES AND KINDRED SUBJECTS (U.S.G.P.O. 1877).

[56] Prepared by MARJORIE M. WHITEMAN (U.S.G.P.O. 1963–1973).

b. *Digest of International Law.*[57] Hackworth's digest, in eight volumes, covers the period 1906–1939.

c. *A Digest of International Law as Embodied in Diplomatic Discussions, Treaties and other International Agreements, International Awards, the Decisions of Municipal Courts, and the Writings of Jurists. . . .* [58] Moore's digest, in eight volumes, set the pattern for its successors and supersedes Wharton's.

d. *A Digest of the International Law of the United States Taken from Documents Issued by Presidents and Secretaries of State, and from Decisions of Federal Courts and Opinions of Attorneys-General.*[59] Wharton's digest in three volumes was the first to adopt a subject arrangement according to the main topics of international law.

e. *Updating the U.S. Digests.* Whiteman's digest completed publication in 1973. The next year the State Department began a new project of preparing an annual *Digest of United States Practice in International Law.*[60] Eight volumes covering the period 1973–1980 are followed by a three-volume set for the years 1981–1988.[61] It is expected that the State Department will publish volumes of the *Digest* for later years. A cumulative index for 1973–1980 has been issued.

Beginning with volume 53 (1959) and continuing to the present, the *American Journal of International Law* has published in each quarterly number a section titled, "Contemporary Practice of the United States Relating to International Law." It follows the arrangement of the annual *Digest of United States Practice in International Law.* In contrast to Whiteman's digest and its predecessors, the focus is on the practice of the United States.

3. Digests of Practice from Other Countries

Several other digests relating to the practice of particular countries in international law are available. Two leading examples are given here.

a. *A British Digest of International Law.*[62] This was to be a major project in two phases. Five volumes of the first phase, covering the years 1860–1914, were published but nothing has appeared since 1967. Fortunately, the *British Yearbook of International Law* carries a section called, "United Kingdom Materials on International Law."

b. *Répertoire de la Pratique Française en Matière de Droit International Publique.*[63] This digest of practice from France can be supplement-

---

[57] Compiled by JOHN B. MOORE (U.S.G.P.O.).

[58] Compiled by JOHN B. MOORE (U.S.G.P.O. 1906).

[59] Edited by FRANCIS WHARTON (U.S.G.P.O. 1886).

[60] (U.S.G.P.O. 1974–).

[61] The last volume was published in 1995.

[62] Edited by CLIVE PARRY (Stevens & Sons 1967–).

[63] Edited by ALEXANDRE C. KISS (C.N.R.S. 1962–1972).

ed with the sections of the *Annuaire Français de Droit International* titled, "Pratique Française du Droit International" and "Chronologie des Faits Internationaux d'Intérêt Juridique."

4. Additional Sources Documenting State Practice

a. *Foreign Relations of the United States.*[64] This multi-volume series prepared by the State Department constitutes the official record of the foreign policy and diplomacy of the United States. Supplemental documents in this series are now published in microform.

b. *American Foreign Policy: Current Documents.*[65] This is an annual series prepared by the State Department since 1956. The last volume published was for 1986. Each volume is organized into topical and regional chapters. These collections published by the government can be supplemented with the privately or commercially-published series, *The United States in World Affairs,*[66] *Documents on American Foreign Relations,*[67] and *American Foreign Relations.*[68]

c. *British and Foreign State Papers.*[69] The British equivalent of *Foreign Relations of the United States,* it covers the period 1812–1968. For the period 1945–1950, *Documents on British Policy Overseas*[70] provides supplemental coverage, as does *Documents on International Affairs*[71] for the period 1926–1963.

d. *United Nations Legislative Series.* This is the overall title for a group of materials published by the United Nations in which are collected national legislation and other elements of state practice in areas of interest to the United Nations. The series includes: *Laws Concerning Nationality; Laws and Regulations Regarding Diplomatic and Consular Privileges and Immunities; Legislative Texts and Treaty Provisions Concerning the Legal Status, Privileges and Immunities of International Organizations; Legislative Texts and Treaty Provisions Concerning the Utilization of International Rivers for Purposes Other than Navigation; Materials on Succession of States; National Legislation and Treaties Relating to the Territorial Sea, the Contiguous Zone, the Continental Shelf, the High Seas, and to Fishing and Conservation of the Living Resources of the Sea; Materials on Succession of States in Respect of Matters other than Treaties; National Legislation and Treaties Relating to the Law of the Sea; Materials on Jurisdictional Immunities of States and their Property.*

[64] (U.S.G.P.O. 1861–).

[65] (U.S.G.P.O. 1956–).

[66] (Council on Foreign Relations 1931–1971).

[67] (Council on Foreign Relations 1939–1970).

[68] (New York University Press 1971–1978).

[69] (H.M.S.O. 1928–1977).

[70] (H.M.S.O. 1984–1989).

[71] (O.U.P. 1929–1973).

e. *Repertory of Practice of United Nations Organs.*[72] In several volumes updated with supplements this is an article-by-article digest of UN practice under the Charter of the United Nations.

SECTION E.   GENERAL PRINCIPLES OF LAW

This source of law, the third main source set out in Article 38 of the Statute of the International Court of Justice, presents some of the same kinds of difficulties as those encountered in researching customary international law. There is no authoritative collection of general principles. The evidence for the existence of a general principle of law has to be developed from a variety of authorities. Some of these may be primary sources, but more likely, the first approach to discovering a general principle will be a discussion of the subject in an authoritative secondary source, such as a leading treatise.

There is a conceptual difficulty that has to be resolved before research can even begin. Does this source have to do with general principles of law as found in *national* legal systems or does it refer to general principles that are peculiar to *international* law? No doubt, there is substantial overlap, for example, where ideas such as good faith in the performance of agreements or the duty to compensate for causing harm are concerned. There is some disagreement, but the prevailing opinion is that the idea refers to those general principles common to the major *domestic* legal systems. Therefore, the phrase has to be distinguished from another one, "general principles of *international* law," which for most purposes are principles derived from customary international law.[73]

Given the emphasis on domestic law, it becomes apparent that someone wanting to do original research on general principles of law would have to know *comparative* law,the comparative study of national legal systems. Fortunately, the secondary literature of international law has already performed a lot of this work with respect specifically to establishing general principles applied in the international arena.[74] However, there is nothing to prevent the researcher from enlisting the assistance of virtually this entire book on the fundamentals of legal research, as part of a project to discover a general principle of law common to the major legal systems, starting with the United States.

SECTION F.   ADJUDICATIONS

States might settle their differences in a variety of hopefully peaceful ways, ranging from diplomatic negotiation to compulsory submission

---

[72] (United Nations 1955–).

[73] *See generally* RESTATEMENT (THIRD) OF THE FOREIGN RELATIONS LAW OF THE UNITED STATES § 102 cmt. 1, reporter's note 7 (1987); IAN BROWNLIE, PRINCIPLES OF PUBLIC INTERNATIONAL LAW 15–19 (4th ed. 1990). *Compare* Herman Mosler, *General Principles of Law, in* II ENCYCLOPEDIA OF PUBLIC INTERNATIONAL LAW 89 (Rudolf Bernhardt ed. 1995).

[74] In addition to the references already noted, *see generally* BIN CHENG, GENERAL PRINCIPLES OF LAW AS APPLIED BY INTERNATIONAL COURTS AND TRIBUNALS (Stevens 1953); Arnold D. McNair, *The General Principles of Law Recognized by Civilized Nations,* 33 BRIT. Y.B. INT'L L. 1 (1957).

of a dispute to the World Court,[75] with such mechanisms as mediation, conciliation, and binding arbitration in between.[76] Article 38 of the Statute of the International Court of Justice accepts "judicial decisions" as a "subsidiary means for the determination of rules of law." The phrase "subsidiary means" does not capture the significance for the contemporary development of international law of the analysis and application of international legal norms in various kinds of international adjudication. Moreover, the phrase "judicial decisions" is too narrow because it does not indicate that the decisions of international arbitral tribunals and the decisions of national courts on international legal questions are also included in the category.[77] This section focuses on the leading documentary sources for the decisions of the main international tribunals. It then discusses the ways of finding United States court cases dealing with questions of international law.

1. International Court of Justice

The International Court of Justice (I.C.J.) is the principal judicial organ of the United Nations. It was founded in 1945 at the same time as the United Nations itself. The seat of the Court is the Peace Palace at the Hague, Netherlands. It is composed of 15 judges elected by the General Assembly and Security Council of the United Nations. Only states may be parties in a proceeding before the I.C.J. The I.C.J. takes jurisdiction of a dispute either by agreement of the parties, or because the parties have made a declaration under Art. 36(2) of the Statute of the International Court of Justice that they accept the "compulsory jurisdiction" of the Court in any legal dispute involving a state that has made the same declaration. The Court also has the authority to give advisory opinions on legal questions to the General Assembly and Security Council. Without a doubt, the judgments of the I.C.J. are the single most significant component of the source of international law known as judicial decisions. The publications of the I.C.J. are described below.

a. *Reports of Judgments, Advisory Opinions and Orders.* The final decisions (judgments on the merits) of the Court are published in this series. The text of a final judgment including separate and dissenting opinions may reach several hundred pages. Judgments appear even longer because the English and French text are printed together on facing pages. Decisions are first published separately; then the collected decisions for each year are published together in a single volume. The researcher should take note that the documents of the I.C.J. as published in this series are available in full text on WESTLAW in the INT–ICJ database. Also, the I.C.J. now has a site on the World Wide Web. [See Illustration 20–5.] It appears that the plan is to make available the full

[75] This is the informal name of the International Court of Justice and of the Permanent Court of International Justice.

[76] *See generally* J.G. MERRILLS, INTERNATIONAL DISPUTE SETTLEMENT (2d ed. Grotius Publications 1991).

[77] *See generally* IAN BROWNLIE, PRINCIPLES OF PUBLIC INTERNATIONAL LAW 19, 20 (4th ed. 1990).

text of documents in this series on this site. However, at the time of writing the text of only three judgments had been loaded.

b. *Pleadings, Oral Arguments, Documents.* Volumes in this series are published after the end of a case, sometimes years after the judgment. They contain the pleadings, the briefs (memorials), the record of oral proceedings, and other documents, such as maps, that may be submitted to the Court. For each case, several volumes may be published in this series.

c. *Acts and Documents Concerning the Organization of the Court.* This is a single volume that has been updated, most recently in 1978. It is a useful place to find the United Nations Charter and the Statute and Rules of Court.

d. *Yearbook.* This annual publication has chapters on the organization of the Court, its work during the year, and useful biographies of the judges.

e. *Bibliography of the International Court of Justice.* Each year the Registry of the Court issues this bibliography listing works relating to the Court.

f. The secondary literature (books and journal articles) on the Court is extensive. It can be researched using the heading "International Court of Justice" in library catalogs and journal indexes. Recent secondary reading on the I.C.J. includes: *The International Court of Justice: Process, Practice and Procedure,*[78] *Precedent in the Word Court,*[79] and *The World Court: What It Is and How It Works.*[80]

g. The predecessor to the I.C.J. was the Permanent Court of International Justice (P.C.I.J.), which was established under the League of Nations. It sat to hear cases from 1922 to early 1940 and was dissolved in 1946 when the I.C.J. was inaugurated. Many decisions of the P.C.I.J. are of continuing significance in international law. The publications of the P.C.I.J. were issued in series much like those of the I.C.J.:

Series A. *Collection of Judgments* (up to 1930);

Series B. *Collection of Advisory Opinions* (up to 1930);

Series A/B. *Judgments, Orders and Advisory Opinions* (after 1930);[81]

Series C. *Acts and Documents Relating to Judgments and Advisory Opinions* (up to 1930)/*Pleadings, Oral Statements and Documents* (after 1930);

Series D. *Acts and Documents Concerning the Organization of the Court;*

---

[78] By D.W. Bowett, et al. (British Institute of International and Comparative Law 1997).

[79] By Mohamed Shahabuddeen (Cambridge University Press 1996).

[80] By Shabtai Rosenne (5th ed. M. Nijhoff 1995).

[81] The judgments of the P.C.I.J. are also available in World Court Reports: A Collection of the Judgments, Orders and Opinions of the Permanent Court of International Justice (Manley O. Hudson ed. Carnegie Endowment for International Peace 1934–1943).

Series E. *Annual Reports;*

Series F. *Indexes.*

2. Digests of I.C.J. and P.C.I.J. Decisions

The use of the digests noted below facilitates research by providing detailed references and extensive excerpts from those parts of often very lengthy I.C.J. and P.C.I.J. judgments dealing with particular points of international law.

a. *The Case Law of the International Court.*[82]

b. *World Court Digest*[83]

c. *A Digest of the Decisions of the International Court.*[84]

3. International Criminal Tribunal for the Former Yugoslavia

The Tribunal was established in 1993 by UN Security Council Resolution 827. The Tribunal sits in The Hague, The Netherlands. The mandate of the Tribunal is to prosecute persons responsible for serious violations of international humanitarian law (including war crimes and genocide) committed in the territory of the former Yugoslavia since 1991.

To date the Tribunal has produced much important documentation as a result of its work, including several judgments. The secretariat of the Tribunal will make documents available on request. The newsletter of the Tribunal, called the *bulletin,* publishes current lists of documentation. Also, substantial amounts of Tribunal documentation and publications have been loaded at the site of the Tribunal on the World Wide Web. It is expected that at some time in the future, a comprehensive edition of the Tribunal's proceedings will be published commercially.

4. International Arbitrations: Collections and Digests of Decisions

Finding published decisions of international arbitral tribunals is notoriously troublesome. Several circumstances contribute to this situation. Most international arbitrations are ad hoc. The tribunal is constituted to resolve the particular dispute, and there is no sponsoring institution to deal with publication.... It has fallen to scholars working in their private capacity to prepare collections and digests. The result is that the documentation in this field is widely scattered.[85]

---

[82] Edited by EDVARD HAMBRO (A.W. Sijthoff 1952–1976).

[83] Prepared by RAINER HOFMANN et al. (Springer 1993–). Before 1993 the title was DIGEST OF THE DECISIONS OF THE INTERNATIONAL COURT OF JUSTICE. Earlier volumes in the series deal with the P.C.I.J.

[84] Edited by KRYSTYNA MAREK (M. Nijhoff 1974–1978).

[85] Jonathan Pratter, Book Review, 26 TEX. INT'L L.J. 597, 603 (1991). On the substantive law of international arbitration, see generally J. GILLIS WETTER, THE INTERNATIONAL ARBITRAL PROCESS: PUBLIC AND PRIVATE (Oceana Publications 1979).

The difficulties of finding international arbitral decisions should not discourage the researcher. The sources noted below and in the following section make the task less frustrating.

a. *Reports of International Arbitral Awards* (R.I.A.A.).[86] Published by the United Nations, this is probably the leading current source for the text of *selected* international arbitral awards. Volume XX, the most recent, was issued in 1994. It contains the text of awards rendered in the 1980s. Each volume is indexed, but there is no overall index or table of cases. This means that R.I.A.A. must be used together with one of the finding tools noted in the next section.

b. *International Law Reports.*[87] Because it contains the reports of many kinds of international adjudications, this series could be mentioned under any of several headings. It appears here because it is particularly valuable for its publication of substantial extracts from arbitral decisions that would be very difficult to find elsewhere.

c. *International Legal Materials* (I.L.M.).[88] Significant arbitral awards often are published first in I.L.M.

d. *History and Digest of the International Arbitrations to which the United States Has Been a Party.*[89] The United States has long been an active participant in the process of international arbitration. In fact, a leading commentator notes that "modern arbitration begins with the Jay Treaty of 1794 between the United States and Great Britain. . . . "[90] In many cases, the government would publish the results of the early arbitrations in which the United States participated. But these books are very difficult to find today. Therefore, Moore's *History and Digest* in six volumes continues to be a valuable source for reports of arbitrations of the United States from the late 18th to the end of the 19th century.

e. *International Adjudications: Ancient and Modern: History and Documents.*[91] This ambitious project never was completed, but six volumes were issued between 1929 and 1936.

f. *The Hague Court Reports*[92] and *The Hague Arbitration Cases.*[93] The title refers to an institution known formally as the Permanent Court of Arbitration. It is not a court, but a mechanism for establishing arbitral panels. Between 1900 and 1932 twenty cases were heard, but

---

[86] (United Nations, 1948–).

[87] (Grotius Publications 1932–). Until 1949 the title was ANNUAL DIGEST AND REPORTS OF PUBLIC INTERNATIONAL CASES and the publisher was Butterworth.

[88] See the main discussion of I.L.M. at Section C.2.B.

[89] By JOHN B. MOORE (U.S.G.P.O. 1898).

[90] IAN BROWNLIE, PRINCIPLES OF PUBLIC INTERNATIONAL LAW 709 (4th ed. 1990). The arbitrations under the Jay Treaty had to do with both boundaries and claims for compensation following the Revolutionary War. The work of the various arbitral commissions is reported in the first volume of MOORE'S HISTORY AND DIGEST.

[91] Edited by JOHN B. MOORE (Oxford University Press 1929–1936).

[92] Edited by JAMES B. SCOTT (Oxford University Press 1916–1932).

[93] Compiled by GEORGE G. WILSON (Ginn 1915).

none since then. The decisions, some of them still significant in international law, are published in these collections.

g. *Iran-United States Claims Tribunal Reports.*[94] Following the resolution of the Iran Hostage Crisis in late 1980, an arbitral tribunal was set up to decide outstanding claims between United States citizens and companies and the government of Iran. Although its work has now wound down, the Iran–United States Claims Tribunal probably has been the most notable arbitral institution in recent years. To date, its decisions are reported in the 28 volumes of this series and on WESTLAW in the INT–IRAN database.[95]

4. Finding Tools for International Arbitrations

Research in international arbitration would be virtually impossible without the use of the finding tools noted here.

a. *Survey of International Arbitrations, 1794–1989.*[96] This book covers approximately 600 international disputes that resulted in an agreement to arbitrate, although in some cases an award was never rendered. The one-page entries for each case give all the critical information, including the parties, a brief description of the dispute, a note on the agreement to arbitrate and where to find it if available, and notes on the disposition with citations to the text of the award if it has been published.

b. *Repertory of International Arbitral Jurisprudence.*[97] This is a comprehensive collection of excerpts from hundreds of arbitral decisions organized according to a detailed outline of international law. Each extract refers to a table of awards where the researcher will find the essential information about the decision, including a citation to the publication of the full text.[98] In three volumes, the *Repertory* covers the period 1794–1988.

5. International Law in U.S. Courts

a. Using the fundamental techniques of legal research introduced in this book, the researcher can find cases of United States courts, usually federal courts, on questions of international law. For example, the West digests have two topics, "International Law" and "Treaties" that collect cases on several points of international law as it is applied in the courts of this country. The first topic is useful for such questions as

---

[94] (Grotius Publications 1983–).

[95] Two collections of arbitral decisions, both in French, deserve mention in a footnote: A. DE LAPRADELLE & N. POLITIS, RECUEIL DES ARBITRAGES INTERNATIONAUX (Pedone 1905–1954); HENRI LA FONTAINE, PASICRISIE INTERNATIONALE: HISTOIRE DOCUMENTAIRE DES ARBITRAGES INTERNATIONAUX (Stämpfli 1902).

[96] Edited by A.M. STUYT (3d ed. M. Nijhoff 1990).

[97] Edited by VINCENT COUSSIRAT-COUSTÈRE & PIERRE M. EISEMANN (M. Nijhoff 1989–1991).

[98] The researcher should be aware that sometimes the text of arbitral awards is never published in completely unabridged form. Instead, for example, lengthy extracts will appear in one of the leading journals of international law.

the sources of international law and its relation to United States law, territorial sovereignty, foreign sovereign immunity, the act of state doctrine, and extraterritoriality. The second topic deals with the negotiation, operation, and interpretation of international agreements in United States law. Another topic on point in a specialized area is "Ambassadors and Consuls."

American Law Reports, Federal (A.L.R. Fed.) offers another example of how to apply the fundamentals of legal research to finding United States cases on international law. Here can be found annotations on subjects such as "Giving United States District Courts Jurisdiction of Action by Alien for Tort Only, Committed in Violation of Law of Nations or Treaty of United States"[99] and "United Nations Resolution as Judicially Enforceable in United States Domestic Courts."[100]

In this area of research, the significance of using WESTLAW and LEXIS–NEXIS cannot be overstated. The fact of the matter is that cases in a United States court raising a question of international law might crop up in almost any field of law. Significant cases having international legal implications could start life as a suit on a bill of lading[101] or promissory note.[102] Obviously, the digests will not deal adequately with this possibility. A well-designed search on WESTLAW or LEXIS–NEXIS is an indispensable step in the research process when looking for cases with an international legal component.

b.　*American International Law Cases.*[103] This set of reports, now in a third series, reprints cases originally published in the West reports.[104]

SECTION G.　SECONDARY SOURCES

Article 38 of the Statute of the International Court of Justice expressly acknowledges secondary sources ("the teachings of the most highly qualified publicists") as means for the "determination of rules of law."[105] A strong case can be made for the view that the researcher in international law, especially the beginner, should *start* work with a good secondary source, such as a leading textbook. The reason is that the beginner has not yet learned what are the significant primary sources of law for a specific question. It is the task of a good secondary source to refer to (with citations) and to analyze the crucial primary sources as

[99] 34 A.L.R. Fed. 388.

[100] 42 A.L.R. Fed. 577.

[101] *See, e.g.,* Banco Nacional de Cuba v. Sabbatino, 376 U.S. 398 (1964) (act of state doctrine).

[102] *See, e.g.,* Gau Shan Co., Ltd. v. Bankers Trust Co., 956 F.2d 1349 (6th Cir. 1992) (injunction against suit in a foreign court and international comity).

[103] (Oceana Publications 1971–).

[104] In-depth discussion of finding international law cases in the national courts of other countries is beyond the scope of this chapter. However, the following English-language sources deserve mention: COMMONWEALTH INTERNATIONAL LAW CASES (Oceana Publications 1974–); DECISIONS OF GERMAN COURTS RELATING TO PUBLIC INTERNATIONAL LAW (Springer 1978–).

[105] *See* the discussion in Section A–3, *supra*.

part of the discussion of an issue. Therefore, a good secondary source can efficiently orient and give direction to research. The secondary literature of international law is massive and expanding rapidly. Moreover, it is multilingual. This section can give only a brief overview of the available resources with indications of specific titles that will be particularly useful to the international law researcher in the United States.

1. Textbooks and Treatises

a.   It is possible to mention only some of the more recent books that discuss general international law. This by necessity excludes the many titles that focus on one aspect of the subject, such as the law of the sea, or the law of treaties. Of course, textbooks and treatises on various aspects of international law are found by consulting the appropriate subject heading in the law library catalog. Mentioned here are four of the most current one-volume introductory texts in English: *Principles of Public International Law* by Ian Brownlie,[106] *An Introduction to International Law* by Mark W. Janis,[107] *International Law* by Malcolm N. Shaw,[108] and *Introduction to International Law* by Joseph G. Starke.[109] Two general, though not comprehensive, works by Louis Henkin, a leading international law scholar in the United States, are *How Nations Behave: Law and Foreign Policy*[110] and *Foreign Affairs and the United States Constitution*.[111] The multi-volume treatise on international law, well-known in France and Germany, is rare in English. An exception is Charles Cheney Hyde's *International Law: Chiefly as Interpreted and Applied by the United States*.[112]

b.   *Restatement of the Law: The Foreign Relations Law of the United States*.[113] Usually known as the *Restatement, Third*, this is probably the secondary source in the United States that can claim the greatest influence and authority in the field of international law. Its "black-letter rules" give a clear and concise statement of the contemporary view of the leading international law scholars in the United States on a wide range of issues. The comments and reporter's notes add background, depth, and copious citations to the primary sources and secondary literature.

c.   *Collected Courses of the Hague Academy of International Law*.[114] Every summer the Hague Academy of International Law offers a series of advanced courses on both public and private international law. This extensive series of collected monographs (lengthy articles devoted to a

---

[106] (4th ed. Oxford University Press 1990).

[107] (2d ed. Little, Brown 1993).

[108] (4th ed. Grotius Publications 1997).

[109] (11th ed. Butterworth 1994). This edition is by I.A. Shearer.

[110] (2d ed. Columbia University Press 1979).

[111] (2d ed. Oxford University Press 1996).

[112] (2d ed. Little, Brown 1945).

[113] (American Law Institute Publishers 1987).

[114] (M. Nijhoff, 1923–).

particular subject) is usually known by its title in French, *Recueil des Cours*. It is true that not all contributions are in English, but many are and they can be valuable secondary sources on many aspects of international law. Unfortunately, the indexing for the *Recueil des Cours* is not current, though some recent volumes contain a listing of article titles back to the last time an index was produced (for the volumes through 1986).

2. Dictionaries and Encyclopedias

a. *Encyclopedia of Public International Law*.[115] Together with the *Restatement, Third*, this encyclopedia offers one of the better starting points for research. Published initially in twelve installments according to broad subjects, it is now being reissued with updated articles in a strictly alphabetical arrangement. To date, the first two volumes (A–D and E–I) of the new edition have appeared.

b. *Encyclopaedic Dictionary of International Law*.[116] There are several dictionaries of international law, some of dubious quality. The one mentioned here is accurate and useful.

3. Journals

There are many journals devoted to international law. The advantage of using journals is that they keep track of the latest developments and of current opinion in the field. Of course, law journal articles are filled with footnotes containing copious citations to primary sources or to other secondary authority on point. The explanation for the proliferation of law journals in international law can be traced in part to the phenomenon of law school publication of student-edited law journals in the United States. There are over 60 of these currently in publication.[117] Leading examples are the *Harvard International Law Journal*,[118] *Columbia Journal of Transnational Law*,[119] and the *Texas International Law Journal*.[120]

The most important journal of international law in the United States is the *American Journal of International Law*[121] published by the American Society of International Law. Also worthy of note is *The International Lawyer*[122] published by the Section of International Law and Practice of the American Bar Association. Of course, many outstanding international law journals are published outside the United States. The leading example in English is the *International and Comparative*

[115] (North–Holland 1992–).

[116] Edited by CLIVE PARRY ET AL. (Oceana Publications 1986).

[117] A listing of these student-edited international law journals is in Chapter 17, Section I–2.

[118] (1967–).

[119] (1961–).

[120] (1965–).

[121] (1907–).

[122] (1966–).

Law Quarterly[123] published by the British Institute of International and Comparative Law.

Quite possibly the most prestigious journals of international law are not published in English. (International law remains one of the few fields in which a working knowledge of more than one language is a valuable asset.) Candidates for the position include the *Journal du Droit International*[124] and the *Zeitschrift für ausländisches öffentliches Recht and Völkerrecht.*[125]

4. Yearbooks

As indicated in the term describing it, the yearbook of international law is an annual publication, generally sponsored and edited by a national association of international law, by a university institute of international law, or by an editorial committee of international law scholars from one country. Unfortunately, no yearbook is produced in the United States. The usual format of a yearbook is to begin with lead articles followed by shorter notes and book reviews. Almost invariably, a yearbook will have sections covering developments in international law in the courts of the country and in the practice of the government. These sections make yearbooks very useful for keeping up with the latest developments as surveyed by the leading scholars. There are roughly 15 yearbooks from various countries. Three of the most prestigious are: *British Yearbook of International Law,*[126] *Annuaire Français de Droit International,*[127] and *German Yearbook of International Law.*[128]

5. Indexes and Bibliographies

The standard periodical indexes in law, *Legal Resources Index* and *Index to Legal Periodicals,* work satisfactorily as far as concerns articles on international law published in the United States. In addition, they will capture a fair percentage of articles on international law published in British law reviews. However, a substantial amount of writing on international law *in English* is done in sources published in Europe, Asia, and other parts of the world not covered by the usual indexes. Therefore, in-depth research requires the use of some creativity and unfamiliar resources.

a.   *Public International Law: A Current Bibliography of Books and Articles.*[129] This is the only source that can make a claim to comprehensive coverage. It is prepared at the Max Planck Institute for Comparative Public Law and International Law in Heidelberg, Germany. References are entered under 26 topics of international law. The bibliography is

---

[123] (1955–).

[124] (Editions Techniques 1874–).

[125] (Kohlhammer 1929–).

[126] (O.U.P. 1921–).

[127] (C.N.R.S. 1956–).

[128] (Duncker & Humblot 1954–).

[129] (Springer 1975–).

published twice a year, but unfortunately is running about two years behind.

b. *Public International Law: A Guide to Information Sources.*[130] This is the most recent book-length guide to the subject. However, it goes into more detail about sources of borderline utility than the average researcher will find beneficial. It is organized in a way that will appeal more to law librarians than to lawyers, and it is not written from the perspective of a practicing lawyer in the United States.

c. *Subject Bibliographies.* There is a large number of bibliographies on particular aspects of international law. The selection given here concentrates on recent titles in selected areas of interest. The researcher should always check to find recent bibliographies on a particular topic; those mentioned here are for illustrative purposes only: *Bibliography of International Humanitarian Law Applicable in Armed Conflicts;*[131] *Bibliography on Peace, Security and International Conflict Management,*[132] *Bibliography on the Peaceful Settlement of International Disputes;*[133] *The Law of the Sea: A Bibliography on the Law of the Sea, 1968–1988: Two Decades of Law–Making, State Practice, and Doctrine;*[134] *Peaceful Settlement of Disputes between States: a Selective Bibliography;*[135] *Public International Law: A Selective Bibliography,*[136] *Selected Bibliography on the Prosecution of International Crimes,*[137] *Sources of International Refugee Law: a Bibliography.*[138]

SECTION H. DOCUMENTS OF INTERNATIONAL ORGANIZATIONS

1. Introduction

The term international organization refers to an association of states established by a treaty. The organization pursues the common aims of its member states as set out in the founding treaty. An international organization has a legal personality separate from its member states and the founding treaty provides for decision-making and administrative structures to allow the organization to carry out its work. There can be "universal" international organizations such as the United Nations. Its purposes are wide-ranging and membership is open to any state. Or there can be international organizations devoted to special purposes, e.g., the World Health Organization, or to particular regions of

---

[130] By ELIZABETH BEYERLY (Mansell 1991).

[131] Prepared by INTERNATIONAL COMMITTEE OF THE RED CROSS & HENRY DUNANT INSTITUTE (2d ed. International Committee of the Red Cross 1987).

[132] (United States Institute of Peace 1993).

[133] By CATHERINE BOULERY (Henry Dunant Institute 1990).

[134] (United Nations 1991).

[135] Prepared by DAG HAMMARSKJÖLD LIBRARY (United Nations 1991).

[136] (United Nations 1995).

[137] 7 TRANSNAT'L L. & CONTEMP. PROBS. 251 (1997).

[138] By Eliza Mason, 8 INT'L J. REFUGEE L. 597 (1996).

the world, e.g., the Organization of American States.[139] The organizations we are concerned with here are sometimes known as international *governmental* organizations (IGOs) to distinguish them from international *non-governmental* organizations (NGOs) such as Amnesty International or Greenpeace.

For our purposes, the significance of international organizations lies in the fact that they produce documents of great interest in international law. Documents of international organizations are interesting because the constitution and law of international organizations, and their methods of deliberation and modes of action, are themselves part of the study of international law. As well, their documentation is significant because the substantive issues international organizations deal with are at the forefront of contemporary international law.

Even experienced researchers have difficulty with the documents of international organizations. There are several reasons for this. First, there is a surprisingly large number of international organizations. Within the UN system alone there are 20 affiliated international organizations known collectively as *specialized agencies,* each autonomous, with its own founding treaty and membership. The *Yearbook of International Organizations*[140] requires three volumes and several thousand pages to catalog and describe all the various international organizations, both IGOs and NGOs, currently in existence. Next, each IGO has its own publishing program and method of organizing its documents. Then, there may be deficiencies in distribution. Finally, libraries may have trouble organizing collections and providing access. Thus, it can be hard to find a particular document of a particular international organization.

The researcher can mitigate frustration by going to work armed with an accurate citation (reference) that includes the name of the document or a clear indication of its subject matter, the document "symbol" or number assigned by the organization, and the date the document was issued. A good overview of issues concerning the use of documents produced by international organizations is *International Information: Documents, Publications, and Information Systems of International Governmental Organizations.*[141]

2. United Nations

a. *Introduction.* The UN carries out its work through a complex organizational structure. The wide range of UN concerns has led to the establishment of an equally wide range of commissions, committees, and conferences, etc. The key to understanding UN documentation is to understand both how the UN is organized and how it carries out its work. This is because most of its documentation is the product of the

---

[139] *See generally* FREDERIC L. KIRGIS, JR., INTERNATIONAL ORGANIZATIONS IN THEIR LEGAL SETTING (2d ed. West 1993); Rudolf L. Bindschedler, *International Organizations, General Aspects,* II ENCYCLOPEDIA OF PUBLIC INTERNATIONAL LAW (North–Holland 1995).

[140] (K.G. Saur 1948–).

[141] Edited by PETER I. HAJNAL (Libraries Unlimited 1988).

UN's official work, combined with the fact that documents are identified with the particular body within the UN structure that produced them. Those unfamiliar with the UN should consult *Everyone's United Nations*,[142] *Basic Facts About the United Nations*,[143] *Guide to United Nations Organization, Documentation & Publishing for Students, Researchers, Librarians*,[144] *Introduction to International Organizations*,[145] and *Encyclopedia of the United Nations and International Agreements*.[146]

b. *United Nations Charter*. The Charter is the constitutive document of the UN, as well as a binding international agreement that is acknowledged to state fundamental principles of international law. The text of the Charter can be found in many places. Likely sources are *Basic Documents in International Law*,[147] *Yearbook of the United Nations*, or any of the documentary supplements to the leading casebooks on international law. There are excellent recent commentaries on the Charter in French[148] and German.[149] The latter is now available in English translation.[150] The other article-by-article commentary in English is somewhat out of date, but still useful.[151]

c. *UN Document Symbols*. The UN uses a system of document symbols to identify and organize its documentation. The ruling idea is the *issuing body*. This means that the symbol is designed to identify the document by its source in the UN hierarchy of organization. Two examples illustrate both the system of document symbols, as well as its range and complexity. A typical symbol is E/C.12/1997/SR.19. The forward slash is a distinguishing characteristic in all UN document symbols. This example is a summary record of the 19th meeting (SR.19) in 1997 of the Committee on Economic, Social and Cultural Rights (C.12) of one of the main UN organs, the Economic and Social Council (E). A less typical example is FCCC/SBI/1997/20. This is the 20th document issued in 1997 by the Subsidiary Body for Implementation (SBI), created under the Framework Convention on Climate Change (FCCC).

The salient components of the system of UN document symbols are:

(1) *Leading elements*, denoting the five major UN organs that use the system (the International Court of Justice does not):

---

[142] (10th ed. United Nations 1986).

[143] (United Nations 1995).

[144] By PETER I. HAJNAL (Oceana 1978). Researchers should also be aware of UNITED NATIONS DOCUMENTATION: A BRIEF GUIDE (UN 1981), available on request from Dag Hammarskjöld Library, United Nations, New York, NY 10017.

[145] Edited by LYONETTE LOUIS-JACQUES & JEANNE S. KORMAN (Oceana 1996).

[146] By EDMUND J. OSMANCZYK (2d ed. Taylor & Francis 1990).

[147] Edited by IAN BROWNLIE (4th ed. O.U.P. 1995).

[148] JEAN-PIERRE COT & ALAIN PELLET, LA CHARTES DES NATIONS UNIES: COMMENTAIRE ARTICLE PAR ARTICLE (Economica 1985).

[149] BRUNO SIMMA, ED., CHARTA DER VEREINTEN NATIONEN: KOMMENTAR (Beck 1991).

[150] BRUNO SIMMA, ED., THE CHARTER OF THE UNITED NATIONS: A COMMENTARY (O.U.P. 1994).

[151] LELAND M. GOODRICH ET AL., CHARTER OF THE UNITED NATIONS: COMMENTARY AND DOCUMENTS (3d ed. Columbia University Press 1969).

A/–	General Assembly
E/–	Economic and Social Council
S/–	Security Council
T/–	Trustee Council
ST/–	Secretariat

(2) *Special leading symbols* have been created for other bodies. Some important examples are:

CCPR/–	Human Rights Committee (under the International Covenant on Civil and Political Rights)
CERD/–	International Convention on the Elimination of All Forms of Racial Discrimination
TD/–	United Nations Conference on Trade and Development (UNCTAD)
UNEP/–	United Nations Environment Programme

(3) Elements denoting the *subsidiary organ:*

–/AC./–	Ad hoc committee
–/C./–	Standing or main sessional committee
–/CN./–	Commission
–/CONF./–	Conference
–/WG./–	Working Group

(4) Elements denoting the *nature of the document:*

–/PV.__	Verbatim records of meetings ("procès verbaux")
–/RES/–	Preliminary text of adopted resolutions
–/SR.__	Summary records of meetings

(5) Elements indicating a *change in an earlier document:*

–/Add.__	Addendum
–/Corr.__	Corrigendum
–/Rev.	Revision

(6) Elements indicating *distribution:*

–/L.__	Limited
–R.__	Restricted

Detailed information on UN document symbols is in *United Nations Document Series Symbols, 1946–1977*[152] and *United Nations Document Series Symbols, 1978–1984.*[153] Updated information is available on a commercial product, *UNBIS Plus on CD–ROM.* Current information on UN document symbols can also be derived from *UN Info Quest* (*UN-I-QUE*), which is available without charge on the UN website (discussed below). Updated information through 1996, when it ceased publication, is available in *UNDOC* (discussed below).

[152] (United Nations 1978).

[153] (United Nations 1986).

d. *UN Working Documents and Official Records*. The various bodies of the UN produce vast amounts of documents relating to their work. Some of these documents receive the name *official records*. The main organs of the UN, the General Assembly and its seven committees, the Security Council, the Economic and Social Council, and the Trusteeship Council, issue official records. Both working documents and official records are issued with a document symbol as described above. A complicating factor is that official records and many working documents come out in both *provisional* and *final* form.

In provisional form, working documents and official records appear individually on plain white paper. Official records are later collected together and republished in bound form, with tan paper covers for the General Assembly, yellow for the Security Council, and light blue for the Economic and Social Council. In final form, official records contain meeting records, annexes, and supplements. Note that significant working documents reappear in the annexes and supplements to the official records.

Obviously, provisional documents appear first. Therefore, they prove more useful for contemporaneous research. The official records in final form are easier to use, but are published late. The experienced researcher doing contemporaneous research learns how to find significant documents by knowing what kind of symbol they are likely to carry.

It should be noted that a comprehensive collection of UN documents is available on microfiche from Readex/Newsbank.

e. *Sales Publications*. The UN has an active publishing program through which it offers a wide array of publications for sale. This includes subscriptions to working documents and official records. However, it also includes many titles in the fields of international relations, population issues, environmental policy, international trade and economics, and statistics. Sales publications receive a sales number, such as, 97.II.F.2, which is used only for ordering and should not be confused with the document symbol.[154]

f. *Tools for Researching UN Documents*.

(1) *UNDOC: Current Index*. This was the main index of UN documents and still must be used for thorough research. *UNDOC* ceased publication with its 1995/96 cumulation. The UN reports that a successor finding tool for UN documentation is forthcoming, but as of the time of writing, it has not appeared.

UNDOC was published quarterly in two parts, a main part of document descriptions with name and title indexes, and a second part containing a subject index. There was an annual cumulation, but since 1984 it is available only on microfiche. Use of *UNDOC* can start with the indexes, or if one knows the UN body or document symbol of interest,

---

[154] The annual UN sales catalog is useful for reference and can be requested free from United Nations Publications, Sales Section, 2 United Nations Plaza, Room DC2–853, New York, NY 10017.

the researcher can go straight to the document descriptions and scan for documents of note. *UNDOC* continued two earlier indexes produced by the UN, *UNDEX*[155] and *United Nations Document Index: Cumulative Index,*[156] which will be of interest for the years before 1979.

(2) *Index to Proceedings of the General Assembly, Index to Proceedings of the Security Council, Index to Proceedings of the Economic & Social Council.* The indexes are not as easy to use as *UNDOC*, but they are valuable resources that would have to be consulted for in-depth research.

(3) *Yearbook of the United Nations.*[157] The *Yearbook* covers the activities of both the UN and the specialized agencies. It is organized in broad subject categories such as Political and Security Questions, Regional Questions, Economic and Social Questions. Under each sub-topic the action of UN organs is summarized and important resolutions are reproduced. Particularly valuable are the references (by document symbol) to UN documents relating to the points discussed.

g.　UN Website. The UN has developed and maintains one of the outstanding websites of any organization, or government, for that matter. It is called simply *United Nations* and has established itself as a chief source of information from and about the UN. The site is divided into five main subject categories: Peace and Security, Economic and Social Development, International Law, Humanitarian Affairs, and Human Rights. Also, there are links for each of the principal organs, links to databases (including the UN Treaty Collection), a sector of selected recent documents of the principal organs in full text, a sector of recent press releases in full text, and links to the many websites throughout the world of the various UN-affiliated organizations. This is just a sampling of the information available. Today, research on the UN must include this website. [See Illustration 20–6.]

3.　European Union

a.　*Introduction.* The European Union (EU) is an international organization of fifteen European countries: Belgium, France, German, Italy, Luxembourg, The Netherlands, Denmark, Ireland, United Kingdom, Greece, Portugal, Spain, Sweden, Finland, and Austria. The EU is sometimes called a *supranational* organization because it has the authority under its founding treaties to make law binding on the member states. A source of confusion is the similarity between the names of the EU and of the Council of Europe, a different organization. The Council of Europe is responsible, among other things, for the administration of the European Convention for the Protection of Human Rights and Fundamental Freedoms.[158] The European Court of Human Rights is an arm of the Council of Europe, *not* of the EU.[159]

[155] (UN 1970–1978).

[156] (UN 1950–1973).

[157] (UN 1947–).

[158] E.T.S. No. 5, 313 U.N.T.S. 221.

[159] *See generally* THE COUNCIL OF EUROPE: A GUIDE (Council of Europe 1986); A.H. ROBERTSON & J.G. MERRILLS, HUMAN RIGHTS IN EUROPE: A STUDY OF THE EUROPEAN CONVENTION ON HUMAN RIGHTS (3d ed. Manchester University Press 1993).

Again, the interest of the EU for our purposes is that it produces a large amount of documents of significance for the study of the EU itself and of subjects with which the EU is concerned. The EU carries out its work through four main institutions, the Council, the Commission, the European Parliament, and the Court of Justice. Of lesser importance for research are the Economic and Social Committee, the Court of Auditors and the newly-created Committee of the Regions. Each institution produces documentation. It can appear in a variety of forms. As in the case of the UN, the researcher will gain by knowing the institutional structure and law-making process of the EU. For this purpose, a leading treatise on the law and institutions of the EU is indispensable.[160]

b. _EU Documents_. There is room in this chapter to touch on only the most notable publications of the EU. Researchers needing in-depth information should consult _The Documentation of the European Communities: a Guide_.[161] Though now somewhat out of date, it is still of use. More current information on conducting EU research will be found in two online guides, "Researching the European Union," and "The European Union—Electronic Information." These guides are found at the website of the Delegation of the European Commission in the U.S., called _The European Union in the US_.

The text of the founding treaties can be located in several places. Likely sources are _European Union: Selected Instruments Taken from the Treaties_,[162] _European Community Law: Selected Documents_,[163] and _Basic Community Laws_.[164] At the time of writing, the text of the latest of the founding treaties, the 1997 Treaty of Amsterdam, can be found in a separate publication from the EU[165] and on the website of the EU, discussed below.

(1) _Official Journal of the European Communities_.[166] The _Official Journal_ is the central gazette of EC legal information. The now somewhat obsolete title continues. The _Official Journal_ is published every business day in all Community languages. The _Official Journal_ has more

---

[160] _See_, e.g., RALPH FOLSOM, EUROPEAN UNION LAW IN A Nutshell (2d ed. West 1995); DOMINIK LASOK, LAW AND INSTITUTIONS OF THE EUROPEAN UNION (6th ed. Butterworths 1994); P.S.R.F. MATHIJSEN, A GUIDE TO EUROPEAN UNION LAW (6th ed. Sweet & Maxwell 1995).

[161] By IAN THOMSON (Mansell 1989).

[162] (Office for Official Publications of the EC 1995–).

[163] Edited by GEORGE A. BERMANN ET AL. (1998 ed. West 1997).

[164] Edited by BERNARD RUDDEN & DERRICK WYATT (6th ed. O.U.P. 1996).

[165] AMSTERDAM EUROPEAN COUNCIL: DRAFT TREATY (Office for Official Publications of the EC 1997).

[166] (1973–). The OFFICIAL JOURNAL was not published in English before 1973. There is an OFFICIAL JOURNAL SPECIAL EDITION (1972–73) of translations of EC law enacted before the UK and Ireland became members.

than one part. Most important are the "L" series (containing final legislative acts such as amendments to the founding treaties, directives, regulations, decisions, opinions, and recommendations) and the "C" series (containing information and notices, including proposals for legislation, European Parliament resolutions, opinions of the Economic and Social Committee, and excerpts from the judgments of the Court of Justice). Every issue of the *Official Journal* is numbered separately. You cannot find something unless you have this number. Thus, a typical reference might be "*OJ* **L291**/10 (1997)." This refers to issue 291 of the L series for 1997, page 10. There are monthly and annual indexes. Many libraries receive the Official Journal on microfiche, rather than paper. It is expected that a version on CD–ROM will be published in the near future.

(2) *Bulletin of the European Union.*[167] Formerly titled *Bulletin of the European Communities*, this is a monthly bulletin that reports on the work of the EU institutions. It is good for starting research on current developments in the EU. There are numerous references to EU documents on point. There is an irregular *Supplement to the Bulletin* that republishes important current documents.

(3) *General Report on the Activities of the European Union.*[168] This is an annual account of the work of the EU. It too is useful for researching current developments across the full range of EU activity. The footnotes refer to documents published in the *Official Journal*.

(4) *Directory of Community Legislation in Force.*[169] EU law as published in the *Official Journal* is *not* later compiled in a set of "statutes in force." Therefore, a research tool like the *Directory* is essential in verifying and updating the status of EC legislation. It is published twice a year, but many libraries in the United States receive it annually in microfiche.

In view of the difficulty of finding current integrated texts of EU primary law, the European Commission recently began publishing a series titled *Collection of Consolidated Texts*. Each booklet contains the updated text of a single piece of EU legislation. However, a warning that accompanies each text advises the reader that the consolidated text is not official in the strict sense and is intended solely to facilitate research.

(5) *Reports of Cases Before the Court.* This is the official name of the reports of the European Court of Justice. However, the informal name is *European Court Reports* and they are often cited *E.C.R.* Several parts are issued each year. Delays caused by the requirement of translating the *Reports* into all community languages have put them behind. Few libraries receive the advance text. Therefore, researchers should know about the commercial editions that appear much faster than *E.C.R.*

[167] (1968–).

[168] (1968–).

[169] (1984–).

These are the *Common Market Law Reports*[170] and *European Community Cases.*[171]

(6) *COM Documents.* The European Commission has what is known as the "right of initiative," *i.e.,* the power to make proposals for EU legislation. Only some of this proposed legislation is published in the "C" series of the *Official Journal,* and even then, without the accompanying report of the Commission. To see much important documentation from the Commission it is necessary to consult it in the form of a COM document, or document from the Commission. These documents are published individually in the hundreds each year. Some libraries, usually EC depository libraries in the United States, will have COM documents available on microfiche. These documents have a title followed (or preceded) by a document number of the type "COM(97)207."

c. *Publications about the EU.* There is a mass of secondary literature about the EU. Much of it deals specifically with legal issues. There is also a large literature on the EU from the perspective of political science and international relations. The more recent Library of Congress subject headings for general works are: "European Union," "Europe—Economic integration", "European Union countries—Politics and government," and "European Federation." Works on EU law in general receive the subject heading "Law—European Union countries." The subject *subheading* used in the last example can be transferred to narrow a search to specific fields of law, e.g., "Antitrust law—European Union countries."

Journal articles on EU law will appear in virtually any of the law reviews published in the United States and Britain. Therefore, research in the standard journal indexes will prove fruitful. There are several English-language journals devoted to EU law: *Common Market Law Review,*[172] *European Law Review,*[173] *Legal Issues of European Integration,*[174] *Columbia Journal of European Law,*[175] and *European Law Journal.*[176] A journal from the perspective of political science is *Journal of Common Market Studies.*[177] Two annuals of interest are *Yearbook of European Law*[178] and *Collected Courses of the Academy of European Law.*[179]

[170] (Sweet & Maxwell 1962–). There is a companion series called C.M.L.R. ANTITRUST REPORTS (Sweet & Maxwell 1991–).

[171] (Commerce Clearing House 1989–).

[172] (Nijhoff 1963–).

[173] (Sweet & Maxwell 1975–).

[174] (Kluwer 1974–).

[175] (Parker School of Foreign & Comparative Law 1994–).

[176] (Blackwell 1995–).

[177] (Blackwell 1962–).

[178] (O.U.P. 1982–).

[179] (Nijhoff 1991–).

d. *EC Information Online.* The latest development in this area is the website of the European Union, called *Europa,* [See Illustration 20–7] along with the associated websites of other institutions of the EU and their divisions. The researcher can reach most of the associated EU websites through links to *Europa. Europa* provides introductory information about the EU, its institutions and its policies, along with the full text of press releases from the institutions and from "RAPID," the general database of EU press releases. [See Illustration 20–7.]

The associated websites of the other institutions cannot be dealt with in detail. Of particular note is the website of the European Commission, with its further links to the websites of each of the Directorates–General of the Commission. Also noteworthy is the website of the European Court of Justice, which provides access to the full text of the Court's judgments. Further information on EU websites is available in the guides to EU information at the website of the Washington delegation of the Commission, mentioned above.

LEXIS–NEXIS maintains a fairly extensive library of legal information relating to the EU. Of particular interest is a version of CELEX available on LEXIS–NEXIS. CELEX is a database of legal information developed by the EU. While not entirely full-text, CELEX does provide the full text of many EU enactments. It also functions as a finding tool and updating tool. On LEXIS–NEXIS the more useful CELEX file is called ECLAW. Also worthy of note is the file called CASES, which contains the full text of the judgments of the European Court of Justice. Confusingly, the judgments of the European Court of Human Rights are also loaded into the CASES file.

WESTLAW formerly carried a version of CELEX, but dropped it. At the time of writing WESTLAW carries no EU primary material. There is a useful online summary of EU law called *European Update* (EURUPDATE). Both LEXIS–NEXIS and WESTLAW have other EU secondary material of use in research. It is necessary to consult the database directories of both systems for current information.

SECTION I. ILLUSTRATIONS

20–1 First Page of Recent U.S. International Agreement As Found In USTREATIES Database on WESTLAW
20–2 Page from Multilateral Section of Treaties in Force
20–3 Page from Multilateral Treaties Deposited with the Secretary–General as found on the United Nations Website
20–4 Page from ASIL Guide to Electronic Resources for International Law As Found on Website of American Society for International Law
20–5 First Page of Recent Judgment of the International Court of Justice as found on the I.C.J. Website
20–6 Home Page of the United Nations Website
20–7 First Page of the Treaty of Amsterdam As Found on EUROPA, the Website of the European Union

[Illustration 20–1]

FIRST PAGE OF RECENT U.S. INTERNATIONAL AGREEMENT AS FOUND IN US TREATIES DATABASE ON WESTLAW

```
                        FOR EDUCATIONAL USE ONLY                    Page    1

Citation                        Found Document    Rank(R) 1 of 1    Database
State Dept. No. 97-157                                              USTREATIES
(Cite as: 1997 WL 734966 (Treaty))

                           Russian Federation

 *1 AGREEMENT BETWEEN THE GOVERNMENT OF THE UNITED STATES OF AMERICA AND THE
 GOVERNMENT OF THE RUSSIAN FEDERATION CONCERNING COOPERATION REGARDING PLUTONIUM
                             PRODUCTION REACTORS

                     Entered into force September 23, 1997
                        Signed at Moscow Sept. 23, 1997

    The Government of the United States of America and the Government of the
  Russian Federation, hereinafter referred to as the Parties,
    Expressing their desire to cooperate with each other to elaborate measures
  designed to prevent the accumulation of excessive stocks of plutonium and to
  reduce them in the future;
    Taking into account the intent of the Government of the Russian Federation to
  take out of operation three presently operating reactors that produce plutonium
```

> The standard official sources for the text of U.S. treaties, T.I.A.S. and U.S.T., run several years behind, making it necessary to use alternate sources. Until this agreement is published in one of the official sources, the "State Dept. No." found in the upper left of the screen will be the only useable form of citation, along with the name of the agreement.

```
  of this Agreement, shall cease by December 31, 2000, their production of non-
  reactor-grade plutonium by undergoing modification. After the completion of
  modifications, these reactors shall permanently cease operation at the end of
  their normal lifetime, consistent with prudent safety considerations.

                                  Article II

    1. The U.S. Party shall provide, subject to the availability of appropriated
  funds for this purpose, and subject to the Agreement between the Department of
  Defense of the United States of America and the Ministry of the Russian
  Federation for Atomic Energy Concerning the Modification of the Operating
  Seversk (Tomsk Region) and Zheleznogorsk (Krasnoyarsk Region) Plutonium
  Production Reactors, which will be governed as specified in Article I, paragraph
  4, of that agreement and overseen as specified in Article VI of that agreement,
  step-by-step funding for cooperative implementation or the reactor modifications
  specified in Article I, paragraph 2, of this Agreement.
    2. Provision of funds as described in paragraph 1 of this Article will be based
  on the achievement of cooperation project milestones to be agreed between the
  U.S. Party and the Russian Party. In the event that the Russian Party should
  fail to achieve an agreed cooperation project milestone or the U.S. Party should
  fail to provide an agreed level of assistance, including funding, to support an
```

[Illustration 20–2]

PAGE FROM MULTILATERAL SECTION OF TREATIES IN FORCE

TREATIES IN FORCE 343

CULTURAL PROPERTY (Cont'd)

NOTES:
[1] See note under ETHIOPIA in bilateral section.
[2] See note under GERMANY, FEDERAL REPUBLIC OF in bilateral section.
[3] See note under UNION OF SOVIET SOCIALIST REPUBLICS in bilateral section.
[4] See note under YUGOSLAVIA in bilateral section.

Convention on the means of prohibiting and preventing the illicit import, export and transfer of ownership of cultural property. Done at Paris November 14, 1970; entered into force April 24, 1972; for the United States December 2, 1983.
TIAS   ; 823 UNTS 231.
States which are parties:
Algeria
Angola
Argentina
Armenia
Australia [1]
Bangladesh

Mali
Mauritania
Mauritius
Mexico
Mongolia
Nepal
Nicaragua
Niger
Nigeria
Oman
Pakistan
Panama
Peru
Poland
Portugal
Qatar
Romania
Russian Fed.
Saudi Arabia
Senegal
Slovak Rep.
Slovenia
Spain
Sri Lanka
Syrian Arab Rep.
Tajikistan
Tanzania
Tunisia
Turkey

Convention concerning artistic exhibitions. Signed at Buenos Aires December 23, 1936; entered into force December 7, 1937.
51 Stat. 206; TS 929; 3 Bevans 383; 188 LNTS 151.
States which are parties:
Brazil
Chile
Colombia
Costa Rica
Dominican Rep.
El Salvador
Guatemala
Haiti
Honduras
Mexico
Nicaragua
Panama
Peru
United States
Venezuela

Convention providing for creation of the Inter-American Indian Institute. Done at Mexico City November 1, 1940; entered into force December 13, 1941.
56 Stat. 1303; TS 978; 3 Bevans 661.
States which are parties:
Bolivia
Brazil

The entry for the UNESCO Cultural Property Convention begins with the formal title near the top of the first column and ends with the notes in the middle column. The citation to T.I.A.S. is blank indicating that this treaty is not published in any official U.S. treaty source. There is a parallel citation to U.N.T.S. The list of states party follows the citation.

Colombia
Costa Rica
Cote d'Ivoire
Croatia
Cuba
Cyprus
Czech Rep.
Czechoslovakia [3]
Dominican Rep.
Ecuador
Egypt
El Salvador
Estonia
Georgia
German Dem. Rep. [4]
Greece
Grenada
Guatemala
Guinea
Honduras
Hungary
India
Iran
Iraq
Italy
Jordan
Korea, Dem. People's Rep.
Korea, Rep.
Kuwait
Kyrgyz Rep.
Lebanon
Libya
Madagascar

[3] See note under CZECHOSLOVAKIA in bilateral section.
[4] See note under GERMANY, FEDERAL REPUBLIC OF in bilateral section.
[5] See note under UNION OF SOVIET SOCIALIST REPUBLICS in bilateral section.
[6] See note under YUGOSLAVIA in bilateral section.

CULTURAL RELATIONS

(See also WORLD HERITAGE)

Treaty on the protection of artistic and scientific institutions and historic monuments. Signed at Washington April 15, 1935; entered into force August 26, 1935.
49 Stat. 3267; TS 899; 3 Bevans 254; 167 LNTS 279.
States which are parties:
Brazil
Chile
Colombia
Cuba
Dominican Rep.
El Salvador
Guatemala
Mexico
United States
Venezuela

United States
Venezuela

Agreement for facilitating the international circulation of visual and auditory materials of an educational, scientific and cultural character, with protocol. (Beirut agreement) Done at Lake Success July 15, 1949; entered into force August 12, 1954; for the United States January 12, 1967.
17 UST 1578; TIAS 6116; 197 UNTS 3.
States which are parties:
Bosnia-Herzegovina
Brazil
Cambodia
Canada
Congo
Costa Rica
Croatia
Cuba [1]
Cyprus
Denmark
El Salvador
Ghana
Greece
Haiti
Iran
Iraq
Jordan
Lebanon
Libya
Madagascar
Malawi

[Illustration 20–3]

PAGE FROM MULTILATERAL TREATIES DEPOSITED WITH THE SECRETARY–GENERAL AS FOUND ON THE UNITED NATIONS WEBSITE

http://www.un.org/Depts...oo/xxvi_boo/xxvi_2.html   http://www.un.org/Depts/Treaty/fina...files/part_boo/xxvi_boo/xxvi_2.html

2. Convention on Prohibitions or Restrictions on the Use of Certain Conventional Weapons which may be deemed to be Excessively Injurious or to have Indiscriminate Effects (and Protocols)

Concluded at Geneva on 10 October 1980

ENTRY INTO FORCE: 2 December 1983, in accordance with article 5, paragraphs 1 and 3.

REGISTRATION: 2 December 1983, No. 22495.

TEXT: United Nations, Treaty Series, vol. 1342, p. 137; depositary notifications C.N.356.1981. TREATIES-7 of 14 January 1982 (procès-verbal of rectification of the Chinese authentic text) and C.N.320.1982. TREATIES-11 of 21 January 1983 (procès-verbal of rectification of the Final Act).

STATUS: Signatories: 51. Parties: 71.

Note: The Convention and its annexed Protocols were adopted by the United Nations Conference on Prohibitions or Restrictions of the Use of Certain Conventional Weapons Which May Be Deemed Excessively Injurious or to Have Indiscriminate Effects, held in Geneva from 10 to 28 September 1979 and from 15 September to 10 October 1980. The Conference was convened pursuant to General Assembly resolutions 32/152 of 19 December 1977 and 33/70 of 14 December 1978. The original of the Convention with the annexed Protocols, of which the Arabic, Chinese, English, French, Russian and Spanish texts are equally authentic, is deposited with the Secretary-General of the United Nations. The Convention was open for signature by all States at United Nations Headquarters in New York for a period of twelve months from 10 April 1981.

Participant	Signature	Ratification, acceptance (A), approval (AA), accession (a), succession (d)	Acceptance pursuant to article 4, paragraphs 3 and 4[1] Protocols		
			I	II	III
Afghanistan	10 Apr 1981				
Argentina	2 Dec 1981	2 Oct 1995	x	x	x
Australia	8 Apr 1982	29 Sep 1983	x	x	x
Austria	10 Apr 1981	14 Mar 1983	x	x	x

The online version of Multilateral Treaties Deposited with the Secretary-General is updated every few weeks-making it an outstanding source for current treaty research.

Benin		27 Mar 1989 a	x		x
Bosnia and Herzegovina		1 Sep 1993 d	x	x	x

[Illustration 20–4]

PAGE FROM ASIL GUIDE TO ELECTRONIC RESOURCES FOR INTERNATIONAL LAW AS FOUND ON WEBSITE OF AMERICAN SOCIETY FOR INTERNATIONAL LAW

ASIL Guide to Electronic Resources for International Law; Treaties   http://www.asil.org/resource/treaty1.htm

TREATIES

This chapter will give you some guidance as to how to go about treaty research, with a particular emphasis on electronic resources. Since there is no such thing as a comprehensive collection of treaties in print or on-line, you will have to conduct your research with a certain amount of creativity, and a lot of perseverance.

This page was last updated March 22, 1998.
The author wishes to thank Paul Zarins and Marci Hoffman for their help and substantive input to this chapter. Please send comments, questions, and requests for additional information to Jill Watson, jwatson@asil1.mhs.compuserve.com - Phone: (202)939-6005.

Table of Contents

- Introduction to Treaty Research
- Texts of Treaties
    1. Internet
    2. Online commercial services
    3. CD-ROM

> **This is the first page of the "Treaties" section of the Guide. It is regularly updated. Use it to find current information on doing treaty research in electronic formats, in particular on the Internet.**

- Treaties by Subject
    1. To Human Rights Chapter of ASIL Guide
    2. Environment
    3. Trade and Finance
    4. Law of the Sea and Maritime
    5. Criminal Law

- Materials about Treaties
    1. Library catalogs
    2. Indexes and articles

Introduction to Treaty Research

The history of treaties stretches back for thousands of years, (a treaty existed between the Hittites and Akkadians, for example). However, it is in the current century that they, and the rules under which they are formed, have become increasingly codified. After drafting efforts in the early 20th century by various

[Illustration 20–5]

FIRST PAGE OF RECENT JUDGMENT OF THE INTERNATIONAL COURT OF JUSTICE AS FOUND ON THE I.C.J. WEBSITE

Judgment HS   http://www.icj-cij.org/idocket/ihs/ihsjudgement/ihsjudcontent.html

INTERNATIONAL COURT OF JUSTICE

YEAR 1997

1997

25 September

General List

No. 92

25 September 1997

CASE CONCERNING THE GABCÍKOVO-NAGYMAROS PROJECT

(HUNGARY/SLOVAKIA)

Treaty of 16 September 1977 concerning the construction and operation of the Gabcíkovo-Nagymaros System of Locks — "Related instruments".

Suspension and abandonment by Hungary, in 1989, of works on the Project — Applicability of the Vienna Convention of 1969 on the Law of Treaties — Law of treaties and law of State responsibility — State of necessity as a ground for precluding the wrongfulness of an act — "Essential interest" of the State committing the act — Environment — "Grave and imminent peril" — Act having to constitute the "only means" of safeguarding the interest threatened — State having "contributed to the occurrence of the state of necessity".

Czechoslovakia's proceeding, in November 1991, to "Variant C" and putting into operation, from October 1992, this Variant — Arguments drawn from a proposed principle of approximate application

Currently, only a few judgments are available in full text at the I.C.J. website, though plans are to expand. An alternative electronic format for I.C.J. documents is the INT-ICJ database on WESTLAW.

Notification by Hungary, on 19 May 1992, of the termination of the 1977 Treaty and related instruments — Legal effects — Matter falling within the law of treaties — Articles 60 to 62 of the Vienna Convention on the Law of Treaties — Customary law — Impossibility of performance — Permanent disappearance or destruction of an "object" indispensable for execution — Impossibility of performance resulting from the breach, by the party invoking it, of an obligation under the Treaty — Fundamental change of circumstances — Essential basis of the consent of the parties — Extent of obligations still to be performed — Stability of treaty relations — Material breach of the Treaty — Date on which the breach occurred and date of notification of termination — Victim of a breach having itself committed a prior breach of the Treaty — Emergence of new norms of environmental law — Sustainable development — Treaty provisions permitting the parties, by mutual consent, to take account of those norms — Repudiation of the Treaty — Reciprocal non-compliance — Integrity of the

[Illustration 20–6]

HOME PAGE OF THE UNITED NATIONS WEBSITE

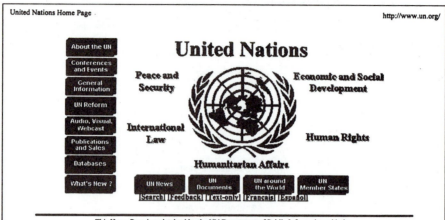

United Nations Home Page   http://www.un.org/

United Nations

About the UN
Conferences and Events
General Information
UN Reform
Audio, Visual, Webcast
Publications and Sales
Databases
What's New ?

Peace and Security   Economic and Social Development

International Law   Human Rights

Humanitarian Affairs

UN News   UN Documents   UN around the World   UN Member States

[Search] [Feedback] [Text-only] [Français] [Español]

This Home Page is maintained by the UN Department of Public Information with the
technical support of the Information Technology Services Division.
© *United Nations 1998*

The United Nations website is an essential source for research on
the UN. The site is divided into five main subject categories:
Peace and Security, Economic and Social Development,
International Law, Humanitarian Affairs. and Human Rights.
Links to databases, recent documents of principal organs, and UN-
affiliated organizations are among the many materials available.

[Illustration 20–7]

FIRST PAGE OF THE TREATY OF AMSTERDAM AS FOUND ON EUROPA, THE WEBSITE OF THE EUROPEAN UNION

Treaty of Amsterdam   http://ue.eu.int/Amsterdam/en/amsteroc/en/treaty/main.htm

■ ■ DE ■ ▶■◀ ■ ■ ■ ■ ■ ■ SV

CONFERENCE OF THE REPRESENTATIVES OF THE GOVERNMENTS OF THE MEMBER STATES

**TREATY OF AMSTERDAM AMENDING
THE TREATY ON EUROPEAN UNION,
THE TREATIES ESTABLISHING THE EUROPEAN COMMUNITIES
AND CERTAIN RELATED ACTS**

TREATY OF AMSTERDAM
Amsterdam, 2 October 1997

SUMMARY

PREAMBLE

PART ONE: SUBSTANTIVE AMENDMENTS

PART TWO: SIMPLIFICATION

PART THREE: GENERAL AND FINAL PROVISIONS

ANNEXES

PROTOCOLS

FINAL ACT

DECLARATIONS

PREAMBLE

HIS MAJESTY THE KING OF THE BELGIANS,
HER MAJESTY THE QUEEN OF DENMARK,
THE PRESIDENT OF THE FEDERAL REPUBLIC OF GERMANY,
THE PRESIDENT OF THE HELLENIC REPUBLIC

Until this treaty is published in a more official form, this version from the Internet
is one of the few places to find the full text of this important EU document.

HER MAJESTY THE QUEEN OF THE NETHERLANDS,
THE FEDERAL PRESIDENT OF THE REPUBLIC OF AUSTRIA,
THE PRESIDENT OF THE PORTUGUESE REPUBLIC,
THE PRESIDENT OF THE REPUBLIC OF FINLAND,
HIS MAJESTY THE KING OF SWEDEN,
HER MAJESTY THE QUEEN OF THE UNITED KINGDOM OF GREAT BRITAIN AND NORTHERN IRELAND,

SECTION J. SUMMARY

This section summarizes the essential sources mentioned in this chapter. References in parentheses are to the sections of this chapter where fuller information will be found.

1. **The Sources of International Law (see Article 38(1) of the Statute of the International Court of Justice) (A.3)**

    a. international agreements

    b. customary international law

    c. general principles of law

    d. judicial decisions

    e. writings of international law scholars (secondary sources)

2. **International Agreements of the United States (B.1–7)**

    a. Current Sources (B.2)

    (1) *Treaties and Other International Acts Series* (T.I.A.S.)

    (2) *United States Treaties and Other International Agreements* (U.S.T.)

    (3) *United States Treaties and Other International Agreements,Current Microfiche Service* (Hein)

    (4) *Consolidated Treaties & International Agreements,Current Service* (Oceana)

    (5) WESTLAW *USTREATIES* database and LEXIS–NEXIS US-TRTY file

    b. Earlier Publications (B.3)

    (1) *United States Statutes at Large* (STAT.), volumes 8 through 64 (1949)

    (2) *Treaty Series* (T.S.) and *Executive Agreement Series* (E.A.S.), the predecessors to T.I.A.S.

    (3) *Treaties and Other International Agreements of the United States of America, 1776–1949* (Bevans)

    c. Finding and Verifying United States International Agreements (B.6)

    (1) *Treaties in Force: A List of Treaties and Other International Agreements in Force on January 1, 199___,* published annually by the State Department

    (2) *US Department of State Dispatch,* "Treaty Actions" section

    (3) *A Guide to the United States Treaties in Force*

    (4) *United States Treaty Index: 1776–1990 Consolidation*

    (5) *Current Treaty Index*

3. **Additional Sources for International Agreements (C.1–4)**

    a. General Treaty Collections (C.1)

(1) *Consolidated Treaty Series,* covering the period 1648–1919

(2) *League of Nations Treaty Series,* covering the period 1920–1946

(3) *United Nations Treaty Series,* covering the period 1946–present

b.   Other Treaty Collections (C.2)

(1) *European Treaty Series*

(2) *International Legal Materials*

(3) *O.A.S. Treaty Series*

c.   Additional Tools for Finding and Verifying International Agreements (C.3)

(1) *Multilateral Treaties Deposited with the Secretary–General*

(2) *Multilateral Treaties: Index and Current Status*

(3) *World Treaty Index,* 2d edition

d.   International Agreements in Electronic Format (C.4)

(1) World Wide Web

(2) *ASIL Guide to Electronic Resources for International Law*

4.   Customary International Law (D.1–4)

a.   Digests of Practice: United States Publications (D.2)

(1) Whiteman, Hackworth, Moore, and Wharton[180]

(2) *Digest of United States Practice in International Law,* eleven volumes covering the period 1973–1980

(3) "Contemporary Practice of the United States Relating to International Law" in each quarterly issue of *American Journal of International Law*

b.   Additional Sources Documenting State Practice (D.4)

(1) *Foreign Relations of the United States*

(2) *American Foreign Policy: Current Documents*

(3) *British and Foreign State Papers*

(4) *United Nations Legislative Series*

5.   General Principles of Law (E)

a.   Consult a leading treatise discussing the idea of general principles of law as it is applied in international law, e.g., Ian Brownlie, *Principles of Public International Law* 15–19 (4th ed. 1990).

b.   Apply the method of comparative law and the fundamental techniques of legal research as described in this book to discover a general principle of law common to the major legal systems.

6.   Adjudications (Judicial Decisions and International Arbitrations) (F.1–5)

a.   International Court of Justice (I.C.J.) (F.1)

---

[180] *See* section D.2, *supra,* for fuller discussion of the U.S. digests of practice, which are informally known by the names of their editors and compilers.

(1) *Reports of Judgments, Advisory Opinions and Orders*

(2) INT–ICJ database on WESTLAW

(3) *Pleadings, Oral Arguments, Documents*

b. Permanent Court of International Justice (P.C.I.J.) (F.1.g)

(1) *Collection of Judgments* (Series A, to 1930)

(2) *Collection of Advisory Opinions* (Series B, to 1930)

(3) *Judgments, Orders and Advisory Opinions* (Series A/B, after 1930)

(4) *Acts and Documents Relating to Judgments and Advisory Opinions* (to 1930); *Pleadings, Oral Statements and Documents* (after 1930) (Series C)

c. International Arbitrations (F.3)

(1) *Reports of International Arbitral Awards* (R.I.A.A.)

(2) *International Law Reports*

(3) *International Legal Materials*

(4) *Survey of International Arbitrations, 1794–1989*

(5) *Repertory of International Arbitral Jurisprudence*

7. Secondary Sources (G.1–5)

a. *Restatement of the Law: the Foreign Relations Law of the United States (Restatement, Third)*

b. *Collected Courses of the Hague Academy of International Law* *("Recueil des Cours")*

c. *Encyclopedia of Public International Law*

d. Journals such as *American Journal of International Law*

e. Yearbooks such as *British Yearbook of International Law*

8. Documents of International Organizations (H.1–3)

a. *Yearbook of International Organizations*

b. United Nations (H.2)

(1) UN website

(2) *Yearbook of the United Nations*

c. European Union (H.3)

(1) *Official Journal of the European Communities*, "L" and "C" series

(2) *Bulletin of the European Union*

(3) *Directory of Community Legislation in Force*

(4) *Reports of Cases Before the Court* (official reports of the European Court of Justice)

(5) *Common Market Law Reports* and *European Community Cases*

(6) EU website, *Europa*

(7) CELEX files on LEXIS–NEXIS (ECLAW).

Chapter 21

ENGLISH LEGAL RESEARCH*

SECTION A. INTRODUCTION

The development of American law from English law was discussed in Chapter One. Even today, English cases are cited as persuasive authority in American courts, and English statutes have served as models for many of our important laws. No book on legal research would be complete without at least an introduction to the methods of finding English primary legal sources. This chapter presents a brief survey of the organization and use of English legal materials.

1. The English Legal System[1]

The United Kingdom of Great Britain and Northern Ireland does not have a single body of law universally applicable within its boundaries. Although there has been a single Parliament since 1707, Scotland has its own distinctive legal system[2] and Northern Ireland also has a distinctive constitutional position and a separate judicial organization.[3] While a common court of last resort and common opinions on broad issues have resulted in a common identity, differences in legal procedure and practice exist in Scotland and Northern Ireland. However, the discussion in this chapter is limited to legal materials of England and Wales.

Perhaps the most fundamental difference between English law and the law of the United States is the lack of a written constitution in England. This difference has been described as follows:

> Since Parliament is the supreme lawmaking body in the United Kingdom, Acts of Parliament are absolutely binding on all

* Revised by Stephen Young, Collection Management Librarian, Tarlton Law Library, Jamail Center for Legal Research, University of Texas at Austin.

[1] See generally, U.K. CENTRAL OFFICE OF INFORMATION, THE LEGAL SYSTEMS OF BRITAIN (1976) (Reference Pamphlet No. 141). For a standard introduction to English law intended for law students in Britain, see GLANVILLE L. WILLIAMS, LEARNING THE LAW (11th ed. 1982). For a lively survey of the administration of justice in England, see MARCEL BERLINS & CLARE DYER, THE LAW MACHINE (3d ed. 1989). For detailed expositions of legal research in England, see GUY HOLBORN, BUTTERWORTHS LEGAL RESEARCH GUIDE (1993) and JEAN DANE & PHILIP A. THOMAS, HOW TO USE A LAW LIBRARY: AN INTRODUCTION TO LEGAL SKILLS (3rd ed. 1996).

[2] See generally DAVID M. WALKER, THE SCOTTISH LEGAL SYSTEM: AN INTRODUCTION TO THE STUDY OF SCOTS LAW (6th ed. 1992) and ENID A. MARSHALL, GENERAL PRINCIPLES OF SCOTS LAW (5th ed. 1991). On legal research in Scotland, see VALERIE STEVENSON, LEGAL RESEARCH IN SCOTLAND (Rev. ed. 1997).

[3] See generally BRICE DICKSON, THE LEGAL SYSTEM OF NORTHERN IRELAND (2d ed. 1989).

courts, taking precedence over all other sources of law; they cannot be *ultra vires* (outside the competence of, in this case Parliament) for, although the principles of natural justice (broadly speaking, rules which an ordinary, reasonable person would consider fair) have always occupied an important position in the British constitution, they have never been defined or codified in the form of guaranteed rights. Thus rights, such as the right of personal freedom, the right of freedom of discussion, and the rights of association and public meeting, which are commonly considered more or less inviolate, are not protected against change by Act of Parliament, and the courts could not uphold them if Parliament decreed otherwise. Acts of Parliament are, in fact, formal announcements of rules of conduct to be observed in the future, which remain in force until they are repealed. *The courts are not entitled to question or even discuss their validity* (emphasis ours), being required only to interpret them according to the wording used or, if Parliament has failed to make its intentions clear, according to certain canons of interpretation....[4]

2. Sources of English Law

There are a number of different sources for English Law; statutes and treaties, case law, custom and convention, The Royal Prerogative, and most recently the European Union. Those sources that can be considered legal include Acts of Parliament (in particular the Magna Carta, The Bill of Rights, the Act of Settlement), reports of decided cases, and the documents and decisions of the European Union. Non-legal sources of the Constitution include the various customs and conventions that have been created over the centuries. Many of these customs relate to the proceedings of Parliament, and despite their unenforceable status they are as much a part of the Constitution as a statute or a decision of the High Court.[5]

SECTION B.   STATUTES

1. The Parliamentary Process

Bills may be introduced in either the House of Commons or the House of Lords. Three classes of bills exist: Public bills, which affect the general public, Private bills which affect either an individual or a company, and Hybrid bills which combine elements of public and private bills. Public bills introduced by a minister are referred to as Government Bills, those introduced by backbenchers are referred to as Private Members' Bill. Government bills usually survive the parliamentary process, however only 10% of private members' bills are able to make it through both houses.

[4] LEGAL SYSTEMS OF BRITAIN, *supra* note 1, at 7.

[5] *See generally* A. W. BRADLEY & K. D. EWING, CONSTITUTIONAL AND ADMINISTRATIVE LAW (11th ed. 1993).

Copies of bills are available from The Stationery Office[6] after an initial reading in Parliament. Select bills are also made available on the Parliament web site shortly after their initial reading. Once introduced bills must then pass through a second reading, a committee (in the Commons it will usually be one of maybe 10 standing committees lettered A–J), a report, and a third reading. The bill is then referred to the other house where it repeats the process before being sent back to the originating house for final approval. If approved the bill is ready for receiving the Royal Assent and becoming an Act of Parliament. Amendments are usually made either after the second reading, in committee, or after being referred to the other house for approval. Bills die if they do not pass through all these stages before the end of the parliamentary session. An exception to this is if the bill is introduced in two successive sessions and approved by the House of Commons but not by the House of Lords (e.g., The War Crimes Act 1991).

Citations to bills include the initials of the House in which the bill had its initial reading, the session of Parliament, and the bill number. A complete overhaul of a bill results in a new bill number being assigned, and a new bill number is also used when it is passed to the other house for approval. *The Weekly Information Bulletin of the House of Commons* is the most complete source for tracing amendments and bill numbers and determining where in the parliamentary process the bill is at any given moment in time.

Legislation can also be traced through the parliamentary process by using *The Official Report of Debates* (*"Hansard"*), or by using the "Progress of Bills" section in *Current Law Monthly Digest. The Weekly Information Bulletin* and *Hansard* are available full-text on the Parliament web site.

2. Acts of Parliament

The acts passed by Parliament are classified as either private and local or public and general acts.[7] Once they have received the Royal Assent they are published individually by Her Majesty's Stationery Office (H.M.S.O.) in a format known as the Queen's Printer's Copy.[8] Full-text Copies are also made available on the H.M.S.O. Web site. Acts passed during the year are then bound together in annual volumes. The public acts have been published annually since 1831 as *The Public General Acts and Measures* and the final volume each year contains an index and other tables listing the acts alphabetically by title, and chronologically. Other tables show *derivations and destinations* of the consolidated acts and the effect of each statute upon earlier measures.

[6] The Stationery Office is a private company formed following the privatization of the HMSO in October 1996.

[7] A more comprehensive treatment of Acts of Parliament is available in Donald Gifford, How to Understand an Act of Parliament (1996).

[8] Commercial editions of selected individual acts are available in the series *Current Law Statutes Annotated* and *Butterworths Annotated Legislation Service.*

Some libraries may have the set *Law Reports: Statutes,* a verbatim reprint published by the Incorporated Council of Law Reporting.

3. Compilations of Statutes

There has not been in England an official codification of all the enactments of Parliament that is comparable to the *United States Code.* There is, however, a current interest in codifying particular branches of the law, such as the criminal law and the law of landlord and tenant. For this purpose and to make recommendations for reform of various areas of the law, a Law Commission for England and Wales has been created. Additionally, from time to time Parliament will pass a consolidated statute in which relevant acts and amendments thereto are consolidated in one act.[9] However there are a number of official and commercial compilations of statutes available to the researcher.

a. *Statutes in Force.*[10] This is the official text published by H.M.S.O. of all acts in force, as amended. It reprints all acts since 1235 that are presently in effect, and it incorporates all amendments that have added to or changed the language of the original act. *Statutes in Force* is published in looseleaf volumes by subject. Each act is in a separate pamphlet that is replaced when repealed or heavily amended.

b. *Halsbury's Statutes of England and Wales, 4th ed.* This commercially published set is a compilation of statutes in force arranged by subject. A valuable feature of this set is its annotations. These follow each section of an act and give references to several kinds of information, including administrative regulations passed under the authority of the act and cases interpreting language used in the act. [See Illustrations 21–1, 21–2, & 21–3.] The fourth edition is made up of the following parts:

(1) The fifty volumes of the main set. Volumes are reissued from time to time to incorporate amendments and additions.

(2) *Cumulative Supplement.* This is issued annually and compiles changes and additions to material in the main volumes.

(3) *Tables and Index volume.* It is issued annually and contains an overall index and an alphabetical and chronological table of statutes.

(4) *Noter-up Service.* This looseleaf volume, used together with the *Cumulative Supplement,* update the main set to within a few months.

(5) *Current Statutes Service Binders.* These looseleaf volumes (lettered A–F) contain the full annotated text of new acts that have not yet been incorporated into the main set.

c. *Current Law Statutes Service*: Originating Full text of all public general and private acts are published once the Royal Assent has been received. Many of the acts are annotated. Acts first appear in a booklet

[9] ALBERT KIRALFY, THE ENGLISH LEGAL SYSTEM 100 (8th ed. 1990).

[10] This set replaces the *Statutes Revised,* 3d ed., which contained all acts in force as of 1948.

format (one month after publication by The Stationery Office) and are filed in the Service File, later the acts for the current year are cumulated and published in annual volumes. The set includes a table of statutes back to 1700 and a table of parliamentary debate going back to 1950.

d. *Butterworth's Annotated Legislation Service*: This is a very selective series that reprints the full-text of a particular act along with extensive annotations and commentary. Individual acts often constitute a single volume. An index volume is produced every two years.

4. In Force Legislation

Unlike American legislation, which usually takes effect once it receives the Presidential signature, an act of Parliament, even though it has received the Royal Assent and has not been repealed, may not be law. An essential component of English legislative research is therefore determining whether the act, either in whole or in part, is currently "in force."

Most acts contain within them a commencement provision. This provision is usually located toward the end of the act alongside the short title and extent information, however it is possible for this information to be spread throughout the act, thereby making research difficult. Section 4 of the Interpretation Act 1978 (c.30)[11] states that this provision may provide a date, either a fixed date or a date after an elapsed period of time (most commonly two months), on which either the whole act or designated sections of the act come into force, or it may allow for a Minister of the Crown to determine when the act or sections of it should be brought into force (this is done through a commencement order). If an act does not provide a commencement provision it is assumed that the entire act comes into force on the date of Royal Assent. However this usually only happens with fairly short or uncomplicated acts.

Determining whether an act or part of an act has been brought into force can therefore be as simple as examining the commencement provision of the original act. However there are other sources that can be utilized that can not only provide information on whether the act is yet in force but also whether it is still in force. Among these the most obvious is the appropriately titled companion volume to *Halsbury's Statutes of England and Wales*, *Is it In Force?* This single volume outlines the status, section by section, of all acts passed in the last 25 years (commencement, amendments and repeals). This 25 year cut off date can present some difficulties to the researcher needing to know whether an act has been repealed, but it is less common that questions regarding the commencement of legislation can not be answered. Obviously, an annual publication like *Is It In Force?* also has another limitation; recent action, commencement, amendment or repeal, is not included. In order to span this gap the researcher must consult the Noter–Up binder to *Halsbury's Statutes*.

---

[11] Interpretation Act, 1978, ch.30 (Eng.).

Current Law's stable of publications does offer the researcher an alternative to *Halsbury's*. *The Monthly Digest* provides a statute citator and a table of commencements. For changes that have been made to legislation prior to the current year researchers need to check the legislation citator volumes (1947–71, 1972–1988, and 1988–1995).

5. Early English Statutes

The early English laws were published in many editions. A few sets are:

a. *Statutes of the Realm.* 12 vols., 1225–1713.

b. *Statutes at Large.* 109 vols., 1225–1869.

c. *Chitty's Statutes of Practical Utility.* 6th ed., 16 vols., 1235–1910, with supplements to 1948.

6. Acts and Ordinances of the Interregnum, 1642–1660

This is a selected three volume integration of the laws enacted during the Interregnum. Volume 3 includes a Chronological Table of Acts and Ordinances, an Index to Subjects, and an Index of Names, Places, and Things.

7. English Statutes on LEXIS–NEXIS

Researchers who have access to LEXIS–NEXIS may use this service to research English statutes. LEXIS–NEXIS has a library of United Kingdom law (UK) that includes all general statutes and statutory instruments in force as well as a bill tracking service.

8. Citation of English Statutes

Prior to 1963, English statutes were cited by name, regnal year (the year of the sovereign's reign spanned by the parliamentary session in which the statute was passed), and chapter, *e.g., National Services Act, 11 & 12 Geo. 6,* c. 64. This method of citation made it necessary to consult a Table to determine the year of passage. As all legal writing on English law prior to 1963 cited to regnal year, a Table of Regnal Years is set forth for convenience.

TABLE OF REGNAL YEARS

Sovereign	Reign Began
William I	Oct. 14, 1066
William II	Sept. 26, 1087
Henry I	Aug. 5, 1100
Stephen	Dec. 26, 1135
Henry II	Dec. 19, 1154
Richard I	Sept. 3, 1189
John	May 27, 1199
Henry III	Oct. 28, 1216
Edward I	Nov. 20, 1272
Edward II	July 8, 1307
Edward III	Jan. 25, 1327

Sovereign	Reign Began
Richard II	June 22, 1377
Henry IV	Sept. 30, 1399
Henry V	Mar. 21, 1413
Henry VI	Sept. 1, 1422
Edward IV	Mar. 4, 1461
Edward V	Apr. 9, 1483
Richard III	June 26, 1483
Henry VII	Aug. 22, 1485
Henry VIII	Apr. 22, 1509
Edward VI	Jan. 28, 1547
Mary	July 6, 1553
Elizabeth I	Nov. 17, 1558
James I	Mar. 24, 1603
Charles I	Mar. 27, 1625
The Commonwealth	Jan. 30, 1649
Charles II	May 29, 1660
James II	Feb. 6, 1685
William & Mary	Feb. 13, 1689
Anne	Mar. 8, 1702
George I	Aug. 1, 1714
George II	June 11, 1727
George III	Oct. 25, 1760
George IV	Jan. 29, 1820
William IV	June 26, 1830
Victoria	June 20, 1837
Edward VII	Jan. 22, 1901
George V	May 6, 1910
Edward VIII	Jan. 20, 1936
George VI	Dec. 11, 1936
Elizabeth II	Feb. 6, 1952

This method of citation was changed by the Acts of Parliament Numbering and Citation Act, 1962 which came into force in 1963. Under it, citation is to the short name of the act and calendar year. Since 1898, each act of Parliament has a section indicating the title of the act under which it is to be cited, *e.g.,* Section 87 of *Highways Acts of 1971* is entitled *Short Titles, Citations, and Commencement and Extent.*

SECTION C. ENGLISH ADMINISTRATIVE LAW

The English equivalent to the rules and regulations that are published in the United States in the *Federal Register* and compiled in the *Code of Federal Regulations* is the *Statutory Instruments* (formerly called *Statutory Rules and Orders*). These are orders, rules, and regulations, known as subordinate or delegated legislation, promulgated by a Minister of the Crown under the authority of a statute. By-laws made by local governmental or other authorities exercising power conferred upon them by Parliament are also included.

1. Publication of Statutory Instruments

Statutory Instrument (or S.I.) is a generic term derived from the Statutory Instrument Act 1946[12], that applies to the four types of

---

[12] Statutory Instruments Act, 9 & 10 Geo. 6, ch. 36 (1946) (Eng.).

delegated legislation (orders, rules, regulations, and by-laws). Prior to 1948 (when the act came into force) S.I.s were referred to as S.R. & O.s (Statutory Rules and Orders), and prior to 1894 orders and proclamations were cited by their title and date (note however that there were very few instruments prior to the middle of the 19th Century). Numerous S.I.s may be published by the Stationery Office on any given week day (over 2,000 per year) and each one is assigned a number based on the order in which it is passed in the calendar year (e.g. S.I. 1993/1068 is the 1,068th S.I. passed in 1993). However, local S.I.s are often not published. A letter may appear in parenthesis after the citation indicating a particular subseries of S.I. (used mainly for ordering from The Stationery Office). The main subseries are C (commencement orders), L (legal matters e.g. court rules), and S (Scottish only). The Northern Ireland series is very different; this constitutes primary legislation from Northern Ireland and is not a Statutory Instrument as such. Actual S.I.s from Northern Ireland are referred to as Northern Ireland Statutory Rules and Orders. Numbered paragraphs within an S.I. can differ depending on the type of S.I.; in an order the paragraph is simply called a paragraph, in a rule or regulation it is called rule or regulation respectively.

a.   Statutory Instruments: S.I.s are first listed in the *Daily List of Government Publications*, and are then made available full-text online on the H.M.S.O.'s web site, and they are also often listed in the major legal periodicals (*Solicitor's Journal, New Law Journal*). S.I.'s will be digested in the monthly issues of *Current Law* and finally appear full-text in running number order in unannotated, annual bound volumes published by HMSO titled simply *Statutory Instruments* (this set extends back to 1946). A monthly, and cumulated annually, publication entitled *List of Statutory Instruments* provides helpful tables and summaries of new SIs.

b.   *Halsbury's Statutory Instruments*: Although this set is selective in providing the full text of delegated legislation, it does offer at least a summary of all the S.I.s currently in force (the closest equivalent to the C.F.R. that exists). This multi-volume work is arranged alphabetically by subject (title) and contains, in addition to the 22 grey base volumes, an index volume, and two looseleaf service binders containing a number of useful tables (list of authorizing statutes, chronological list of S.I.s, commencement orders), changes to the base volumes (an annual supplement to the base volumes and a monthly survey with accompanying key to base volumes), and in volume 2 the full text of selected new S.I.s arranged in numerical order. *Halsbury's Statutory Instruments* is useful in trying to trace delegated legislation on a particular subject , however the set can also be used to trace S.I.s by their title and even their citation (although the annual volumes of *Statutory Instruments* published by HMSO may be more convenient for this). Each S.I. is annotated (with case citations), and an overview is provided at the beginning of each title. Each section also contains a complete list of the S.I.s summarized and a list of S.I.s no longer in force (lapsed, repealed, revoked, superseded, or spent). New reissue volumes come out periodically and may not be indexed by the annual index.

.c. *Table of Government Orders*: This annual publication is a list, in date order, of all instruments passed since 1671. For each it indicates whether the instrument is still in effect or not (by the use of bold type for still in force entries and italics for revoked instruments). The best way to bring this up to date is to use it in conjunction with *Current Law SI Citator*.

d. *Index to Government Orders*: Published biennially by HMSO this two volume set provides a list of all the S.I.s in force at the time of publication and indexes them by subject area. The delay in publication is the major drawback of this set and for this reason it is better to consult Halsbury's.

e. *The Statutory Rules and Orders and Statutory Instruments revised to December 31, 1948*. This set was published in 1949 as the official English administrative compilation. It contains administrative rules of general applicability and a permanent nature. It is now out of date and in need of replacement.

f. *Statutory Instruments on the World Wide Web*. As of January, 1 1997 all Statutory Instruments have been made available full-text on the H.M.S.O. web site. To make access easier a search engine is available.

SECTION D.   COURT REPORTING

1. English Court Organization

Modern organization of English courts began with the *Judicature Act of 1873* and continued with subsequent Parliamentary Acts, the latest being the *Courts Act of 1971*. The present-day court organization is as follows:[13]

a. *House of Lords*. This body, in addition to its legislative function, serves as the supreme court of appeal for the United Kingdom in civil cases and the final court of appeal for criminal cases from England, Wales, and Northern Ireland.

b. *Supreme Court of Judicature*. This is the overall name given to three different courts: the Court of Appeal, the High Court of Justice, and the Crown Court.

(1) Court of Appeal. This court has two divisions: civil and criminal. It hears appeals from the High Court and certain other inferior courts.

(2) High Court. This court[14] now consists of three divisions: the Queen's Bench Division (including the Admiralty Court and Commercial

---

[13] For a more detailed description and history of English courts, see KIRALFY, *supra* note 9, at 128–39.

[14] Prior to the enactment of the *Courts Act of 1971*, the High Court consisted of Queen's Bench Division, Probate, Divorce, and Admiralty Division, and Chancery Division.

Court), the Chancery Division, and the Family Division. In practice, each division acts as a separate court.

(3) Crown Court. This court was created by the *Courts Act of 1971.* It is a criminal court with general jurisdiction. As the main criminal court of England, it tries the more serious criminal cases and hears appeals from the Magistrates' Courts.

c.   *County Courts.* These have limited first instance civil jurisdiction.

d.   *Local and Special Courts.* These are mainly Magistrates' Courts and courts of special jurisdiction such as the Restrictive Practices Court and the Employment Appeal Tribunal.

2.   Development of English Court Reports

The history of court reporting in England is long and confusing.[15] For our purposes, we can divide the reporting of English cases into three periods.

a.   *The Year Books.* 1272–1535. The Year Books are the first available law reports with the original text in *law French.* Their purpose and function are still disputed by legal historians, although it is widely believed that their original purpose was more educational than practical. Other than the fact that they are the sources of modern law reporting, they serve little purpose in most legal research today other than for the study of legal history.

b.   *Nominate Reports.* 1535–1865. During this period there was no officially recognized system of court reporting. Any barrister could publish court reports and over 260 different series were published with many covering the same period of time and the same courts with varying accuracy. It has been customary to refer to these reports by the names of the reporters; hence their generic name, *nominate reports.*

(1) *English Reports, Full Reprint.* This is a reprint of the nominate reports from 1220 to 1865. When there were competing sets of the reports, the editors included only the one they deemed most accurate. There are 176 volumes in this set, including a two-volume Table of Cases, and a chart that lists all of the nominate reports with reference to their location in the *Full Reprint.* Most law libraries have only this set, rather than the original reports.

(2) *The Revised Reports.* The *Revised Reports* are in 149 volumes and cover the period 1785–1865. Although this set largely duplicates the *English Reports, Full Reprint,* its value lies in the fact that the reports were edited by the distinguished legal historian, Sir Frederick Pollock.

---

[15] For detailed treatment of the development of English court reporting, *see* RONALD J. WALKER, THE ENGLISH LEGAL SYSTEM 154–61 (6th ed. 1985). *See also* John H. Baker, *Dr. Thomas Fastoff and the History of Law Reporting,* 45 CAMBRIDGE L.J. 84 (1986). Law students who think reading old English cases is a useless exercise should read David V. Stivison, *The Practical Uses of Legal History,* 33 PRAC. LAW. 27 (1987). The author discusses how some of these cases have come in handy in the current practice of law.

(3) *All England Law Reports Reprint.* This set covers selected cases from 1558 to 1935 and is reprinted from the *Law Journal Reports* in thirty-six volumes plus an index.

c. *The Law Reports.* 1865–. In 1865 the Incorporated Council of Law Reporting for England and Wales was formed. While not an official body, it has quasi-official status. In 1865 the Council started publication of the *Law Reports* and this is the preferred set of reports.

3. Modern Law Reports

As previously mentioned, cases reported before 1865 may be found in the *English Reports, Full Reprint* or *The Revised Reports.* Since 1865 English cases are found in the following sets:

a. The *Law Reports.* This set reports decisions since 1865 and is selective in its reporting, covering decisions of permanent significance of the House of Lords, the Judicial Committee of the Privy Council, the Court of Appeal, and the High Court. In addition to the opinions of the judges, it also includes the legal argument presented to the court. Although originally published in eleven different series, the *Law Reports* are now published in four series: (1) Appeal Cases (includes decisions of the House of Lords and of the Judicial Committee of the Privy Council); (2) Queen's Bench; (3) Chancery; and (4) Family Division. Decisions of the Court of Appeal are published in the last three series.

b. *Weekly Law Reports.* This set is also published by the Incorporated Council of Law Reporting and includes most cases that will ultimately be published in the *Law Reports.* It is issued first in weekly pamphlets and then in bound volumes. It also publishes cases not intended for publication in the *Law Reports.* These appear in the first of the three volumes published each year.

c. *Other Sets of Reports.* Although the Incorporated Council of Law Reporting assumed responsibility for systematizing court reporting, there is no prohibition of private reporting and many such sets are published. The most important of the private reports is the *All England Law Reports.* This set began in 1936, incorporating the *Law Journal Reports* and the *Times Law Reports.* It includes the decisions of the House of Lords, the Court of Appeal, the High Court, and courts of special jurisdiction. The opinions are released in advance sheets and then in bound volumes. [See Illustration 21–4.] It is also worth noting that a great number of cases are only reported in either the daily newspapers or in professional journals. It is therefore not uncommon to see citations to *The Times* or *The Law Society Gazette.*

d. *Electronic Availability of English Cases.* Researchers who have access to LEXIS–NEXIS can use this service to research English case law. LEXIS–NEXIS supplies a library of English cases back to 1945, including all cases from the *All England Law Reports,* the *Law Reports,* and *Lloyd's Reports,* from specialized reporters, and otherwise unreported decisions.[16] Decisions from the House of Lords have also been made available full-text on the World Wide Web within 2 days of the decision having been rendered.[17]

SECTION E. DIGESTS AND ENCYCLOPEDIAS

1. Digests

a. *The Digest: Annotated British, Commonwealth and European Cases.* Prior to 1981, this set was entitled *The English and Empire Digest.* It is a comprehensive digest of English cases reported from the earliest times to date, and is in fifty-six volumes. It also includes cases from the courts of Scotland, Ireland, Canada, and other countries of the British Commonwealth and South Africa. Obsolete cases and cases of only historical interest are excluded from the publication. *The Digest* is arranged topically and has a detailed outline at the beginning of each major subject and an index at the end of each volume. Cases on a particular aspect of a general topic are grouped in chronological order and assigned case numbers.

The Digest is an annotated digest that embodies the citator feature. Each case digest is followed by notes of subsequent cases, if any, showing whether the digested case has been approved, followed, distinguished, overruled, or otherwise mentioned. Under each section or subsection of the digest, cross references and references to pertinent statutes and to *Halsbury's Laws* (an encyclopedia) are given. There is a Consolidated Table of Cases and a Consolidated Index. The *Digest* is updated with replacement volumes, annual cumulative supplements, and quarterly surveys.

2. Encyclopedias

The standard English encyclopedia for both statutory and case law is *Halsbury's Laws of England,* 4th ed. This set should not be confused with *Halsbury's Statutes of England,* a previously described collection of legislation.

Halsbury's Laws of England is alphabetically arranged by topic. Each topic is subdivided into parts, sections, subsections, and paragraphs with appropriate footnote references to cases, statutes, and statutory instruments. [See Illustration 21–5.] *Halsbury's Laws* places great emphasis on statutory law and, unlike its American counterparts, has a Consolidated Table of Cases. Updating is done by an annual cumulative supplement and a looseleaf *Current Service.*

3. Current Law

This set began publication in 1947 and provides a digest of all phases of English law. It is arranged topically and, under each topic, digests cases, statutes, statutory instruments, and recent books and periodical articles. It consists of the following:

---

[16] The UK Library on LEXIS–NEXIS.

[17] House of Lords decisions are available on the Parliament web site.

a. *Current Law Monthly Digest.* A monthly pamphlet advance sheet service which includes a number of useful case, statute, and statutory instrument tables.

b. *Current Law Year Book.* An annual cumulation that includes, among other information, a cumulative subject index, table of cases, tables of statutory instruments and instruments affected, and digests of unreported cases.

c. *Master Volume.* The *Current Law Year Books* were consolidated into a 1947–51 volume; since then, every fifth year, a five-year cumulative Year Book called the *Master Volume* is issued.

d. *Current Law Citators.* These will be discussed in the section on citators.

SECTION F. CITATORS

There is no service precisely similar to *Shepard's Citations* for England. There are, however, several methods of obtaining later citations, or, to use the correct term, *noting up* cases or statutes.

1. Statutes

Citators for statutes are arranged chronologically. For a particular statute, citations are given for each subsequent statute which amends or repeals the cited statute, and for each case which cites the statute. Citators for statutes are contained in:

a. *Chronological Tables of the Statutes.* This publication is a detailed status table of all English statutes giving their status section by section. The reader can tell whether a particular part of a statute of interest has been repealed, amended, or otherwise modified.

b. *Current Law Statute Citator, 1947–1971* and *Current Law Legislation Citator, 1972–1988 and 1989–1995.* Used together, these volumes update legislation between the dates indicated. Citations to cases considering legislation are included. For developments since 1995, use *Current Law Statutes Service.*

c. *All England Law Reports, Consolidated Tables and Index.* The *Tables* volumes contain an extensive listing of statutes considered, with citations to cases in the *All England Law Reports.*

2. Cases

a. *The Digest.* This works as both a tool for finding cases by subject and as a citator. When there are later cases of note, the digest summary of the main case is followed immediately by an Annotations paragraph citing to the later cases which consider the main case.

b. *Current Law Case Citator.* There are three bound volumes covering the years 1947–1995. For developments since 1995, use the issues of *Current Law Monthly Digest* published since the citator volumes. References give both the citation to the main case and to the paragraph of the *Current Law Yearbook* where later cases on point are digested.

c. *All England Law Reports, Consolidated Tables and Index*. Volume 1 contains a cumulative table of cases reported and considered. Cases are listed alphabetically with each case followed by citations to later cases reported in the *All England Law Reports*.

d. *The Index to the Law Reports*. *The Index to the Law Reports* (the popular name is the "Red" and "Pink" index) provides a table of Cases Judicially Considered and a table of Statutes Judicially Considered. [See Illustration 21–6.] It is worth remembering that despite their official title, the "Red" and "Pink" indexes do so much more than just index cases to the *Law Reports*. Also included are references to cases reported in *Industrial Cases, Lloyds Law Reports, Road Traffic Reports, Tax Cases, Criminal Appeal Reports, Local Government Reports*, and the ever-popular *All England Law Reports*. The advance sheets (to use the American terminology) of the *Weekly Law Reports* also include a list of cases judicially considered.

SECTION G. HOW TO FIND ENGLISH STATUTES AND CASES

1. Statutes

a. *Index to the Statutes*. This two-volume set is a detailed alphabetical subject index to United Kingdom legislation. Each main heading begins with references to relevant legislation as found in *Statutes in Force*. Then follow detailed sub-headings with references to sections of relevant legislation cited by year and chapter number.

b. *Halsbury's Statutes of England and Wales, 4th ed*. This commercial edition of statutes arranged by subject is a standard source for current legislation. The researcher selects the right volume by reviewing the subjects listed on the spine or by using the annual index and table of statutes. The advantage to using *Halsbury's Statutes* is its thorough updating, in contrast to the *Index to the Statutes* which runs behind. *Halsbury's Statutes* is comparable in function to *United States Code Service* and *United States Code Annotated*.

2. Cases

a. *The Digest, Annotated British, Commonwealth and European Cases*. This is the most comprehensive English case digest. The following steps are involved in its use:

(1) Consult index volumes for topic under investigation. This will refer to volume, topic name, and *case number* in main set.

(2) Consult *Cumulative Supplement* and *Quarterly Survey* for later citations of cases found through (1) and (2).

Frequently, English legal writing gives only one citation for a case. When that set is not available in the law library being used, check *The Digest* main volumes for complete parallel citations at the place where the case is digested.

b. *All England Law Reports.* There is a *Consolidated Tables and Index* that includes a detailed subject index and a Table of Cases Reported and Considered. Frequent supplements are issued.

c. *Current Law Year Book.* Use indexes in the *Master Year Book* volumes and then subsequent annual volumes. Citations are given to the location of case digests in the *Year Book.*

3. Secondary Sources

It should be mentioned that it is frequently easier in starting research for English law to commence the search with secondary sources. These include:

a. *Halsbury's Laws of England*

b. English treatises

c. English legal periodicals. *Legal Journals Index* exhaustively covers the law journal literature published in the United Kingdom, but goes back only to 1986. For the period before 1986, the U.S. indexes, *Index to Legal Periodicals, Current Law Index,* and *Legal Resource Index* cover several of the leading law reviews published in the United Kingdom. The *Current Index to Commonwealth Legal Periodicals* provided broader coverage, but only up to 1982 when it ceased publication.

SECTION H.   REFERENCE TOOLS

1. Court Rules

Supreme Court Practice (popularly known as "The White Book"). Containing the Rules of the Supreme Court (R.S.C.), this biennial publication is arranged by order and rule number. It is the primary source for court rules and contains annotations and examples where appropriate. Although not the easiest set to use it is an essential tool for the practitioner and a useful reference source for the student.

2. Directories

Waterlow's Solicitors' and Barristers' Directory (Annual). This extensive directory is arranged by geographical location (London first), name of individual and name of firm. Areas of specialization for the law firms are provided. After the listings for Solicitors there are entries for Barristers by chambers (London followed by the provinces) and by name. This is the *Martindale-Hubbel* of British (Scotland is also represented) legal directories.

3. Abbreviations

Index to Legal Citations and Abbreviations (2nd ed, 1993). Now in its second edition, this is the most comprehensive listing of citations and abbreviations in English legal research.

4. Words and Phrases

A number of the English publications include definitions of words and phrases. In addition, several sources exclusively treat judicial interpretations of words and phrases.

a. *Stroud's Judicial Dictionary of Words and Phrases* (5th ed., 1986). This six-volume publication includes not only definitions but also references to cases and statutes from which they are derived. It is kept current by annual supplementation. The Tables volume is a useful addition to the set that can be used to quickly locate a cite to a case.

b. *Words and Phrases Legally Defined* (3d ed., 1988). A revision of Burrow's *Words and Phrases Judicially Defined,* this work has been expanded to include textbook and statutory as well as judicial definitions. A cumulative supplement is published annually.

SECTION I. ENGLAND AND THE EUROPEAN UNION

On January 1, 1973, the United Kingdom became part of the European Communities. As a result, Community law in the form of treaty provisions and secondary legislation became part of English law. Moreover, it became necessary for England to change many aspects of its law to comply with its membership in the European Communities.[18]

Researchers in English law are now faced with the problems of determining when Community law is applicable and of the possible conflict of English law with Community law.[19] The most convenient source of Community legislation is the looseleaf *Encyclopedia of European Community Law.* Volume 50 of *Halsbury's Statutes,* 4th ed., contains Community treaties, while volume 17 has United Kingdom legislation relating to the Community. Decisions of the European Court of Justice can be found in the official *Reports of Cases Before the Court* and in the *Common Market Law Reports.* Volumes 51 and 52 of *Halsbury's Laws of England,* 4th ed., are devoted to European Community law. For fuller details on researching European Community law, see Chapter 20.

---

[18] For a discussion of the European Communities, see Thomas H. Reynolds, *Introduction to the European Economic Community: Its History and Its Institutions,* LEGAL REFERENCE SERVICES Q., Wint. 1988, at 7.

[19] For an explanation of the relationship of English law to the law of the European Communities, see GREAT BRITAIN, CENTRAL OFFICE OF INFORMATION, REFERENCE DIVISION, BRITAIN AND THE EUROPEAN COMMUNITY (Reference Pamphlet No. 137, 1976). *See also* MICHAEL FURMSTON, THE EFFECT ON ENGLISH DOMESTIC LAW OF MEMBERSHIP OF THE EUROPEAN COMMUNITIES AND OF THE RATIFICATION OF THE EUROPEAN CONVENTION ON HUMAN RIGHTS (1983).

SECTION J.   ILLUSTRATIONS: STATUTES, CASES, CITATORS, AND SECONDARY SOURCES

Problem: Are owners liable for injuries caused to others by their dog?

Illustrations

STATUTES

21–1.   Page from Volume 2, Halsbury's Statutes of England and Wales, 4th ed.

21–2.   Page from the 1997 Cumulative Supplement, Halsbury's Statutes of England and Wales, 4th ed.

21–3.   Page from Statutes Service Binder, Halsbury's Statutes of England and Wales, 4th ed.

CASES

21–4.   Page from Volume 3, All England Law Reports 1994.

SECONDARY SOURCES

21–5.   Page from Halsbury's Laws of England, 4th ed.

CITATORS

21–6.   Page from The Law Reports Index.

[Illustration 21-1]

PAGE FROM HALSBURY'S STATUTES OF ENGLAND AND WALES, 4TH ED., VOLUME 2

DANGEROUS DOGS ACT 1991
(1991 c 65)

ARRANGEMENT OF SECTIONS

An Act to prohibit persons from having in their possession or custody dogs belonging to types bred for fighting; to impose restrictions in respect of such dogs pending the coming into force of the prohibition; to enable restrictions to be imposed in relation to other types of dog which present a serious danger to the public; to make further provision for securing that dogs are kept under proper control; and for connected purposes [25 July 1991]

Commencement. This Act came into force or was brought into force in accordance with s 10(4) post and the order made thereunder as noted in the "Commencement" notes throughout.
Northern Ireland. Only s 8 applies; see s 10(5) post.

1 Dogs bred for fighting

(1) This section applies to—

(a) any dog of the type known as the pit bull terrier;

(b) any dog of the type known as the Japanese tosa; and

(c) any dog of any type designated for the purposes of this section by an order of the Secretary of State, being a type appearing to him to be bred for fighting or to have the characteristics of a type bred for that purpose.

(2) No person shall—

(a) breed, or breed from, a dog to which this section applies;

(b) sell or exchange such a dog or offer, advertise or expose such a dog for sale or exchange;

(c) make or offer to make a gift of such a dog or advertise or expose such a dog as a gift;

(d) allow such a dog of which he is the owner or of which he is for the time being in charge to be in a public place without being muzzled and kept on a lead; or

(e) abandon such a dog of which he is the owner or, being the owner or for the time being in charge of such a dog, allow it to stray.

(3) After such day as the Secretary of State may by order appoint for the purposes of this subsection no person shall have any dog to which this section applies in his possession or custody except—

(a) in pursuance of the power of seizure conferred by the subsequent provisions of this Act; or

(b) in accordance with an order for its destruction made under those provisions;

but the Secretary of State shall by order make a scheme for the payment to the owners of such dogs who arrange for them to be destroyed before that day of sums specified in or determined under the scheme in respect of those dogs and the cost of their destruction.

(4) Subsection (2)(b) and (c) above shall not make unlawful anything done with a

[Illustration 21–2]

PAGE FROM HALSBURY'S STATUTES OF ENGLAND AND WALES, 4TH ED., 1997 CUMULATIVE SUPPLEMENT

Vol 2 (1992 Reissue)   **ANIMALS**

PAGE

Badgers Act 1991 (c 36)

534   Whole Act repealed by the Protection of Badgers Act 1992, s 15(2), Schedule, Vol 2, title Animals, and replaced as noted in the destination table thereto.

Deer Act 1991 (c 54)

Section 7

542n   *Sub-s (2): 22.68 grammes (350 grains).* The Units of Measurements Regulations 1986, SI 1986/1082, are amended by SI 1994/2867, regs 3, 4, partly as from 1 October 1995 (reg 4 of the 1994 Regulations, as it amends SI 1986/1082, reg 11, is amended by SI 1995/1804, reg 6).

Section 9

544n   *Standard scale.* The Criminal Justice Act 1982, s 37(2), which sets out the amounts of the standard scale, was substituted by the Criminal Justice Act 1991, s 17(1), Vol 27, title Magistrates, as from 1 October 1992. The scale as so substituted is: level 1: £200; level 2: £500; level 3: £1,000; level 4: £2,500; and level 5: £5,000. (Note that the power to make orders substituting new figures under the Magistrates' Courts Act 1980, s 143, Vol 27, title Magistrates, still exists.)

Section 10

545n   *Summary conviction; standard scale.* As to the standard scale, see the note to s 9 ante.

546–   **Section 11**
547   In sub-s (3), for the words "Part IIIA of the Deer (Scotland) Act 1959", there are substituted the words "section 33 of the Deer (Scotland) Act 1996", by the Deer (Scotland) Act 1996, s 48(2), Sch 4, para 2 (not printed in this work).

     In sub-s (9), the definition "authorised officer" is amended by the Local Government (Wales) Act 1994, s 66(6), Sch 16, para 92, Vol 25, title Local Government.

548n   *Sub-s (8): Summary conviction; standard scale.* As to the standard scale, see the note to s 9 ante.

Section 13

550n   *Summary conviction; standard scale.* As to the standard scale, see the note to s 9 ante.

553   **Section 17** ·

     Sub-s (5) is repealed by the Deer (Scotland) Act 1996, s 48(2), Sch 5 (not printed in this work).

Dangerous Dogs Act 1991 (c 65)

Section 1

560n   *Sub-s (1): This section applies.* This section does not apply only to the breed of dogs known as pit bull terriers, since the word "type" is not synonymous with the word "breed", but applies to a dog having a substantial number or most of the physical characteristics of a pit bull terrier, which is a question of fact for the court; see *R v Crown Court at Knightsbridge, ex p Dunne* [1993] 4 All ER 491, [1994] 1 WLR 296.

     Sub-s (2): Public place. A person having an unmuzzled pit bull terrier in a car which itself is in a public place is a person in charge of the dog in a public place for the purposes of sub-s (2)(d) of this section: see *Bates v DPP* (1993) 157 JP 1004.

     The prohibition contained in sub-s (2)(d) of this section is absolute and accordingly the defence of necessity does not apply; see *Cichon v DPP* [1994] Crim LR 918.

(4)2/45

[Illustration 21–3]

PAGE FROM STATUTES SERVICE BINDER, HALSBURY'S STATUTES OF ENGLAND AND WALES, 4TH ED.

DANGEROUS DOGS (AMENDMENT) ACT 1997

(1997 c 53)

ARRANGEMENT OF SECTIONS

An Act to amend the Dangerous Dogs Act 1991; and for connected purposes

[21 March 1997]

Northern Ireland. This Act does not apply; see s 6(2) post.
Parliamentary debates.
House of Lords:
2nd Reading 12 December 1996: 576 HL Official Report (5th series) col 1234.
Consideration of Commons amendments 20 March 1997: 579 HL Official Report (5th series) col 1139.
House of Commons:
Committee Stage 12 March 1997: HC Official Report, SC E (Dangerous Dogs (Amendment) Bill).

1 Destruction orders

(1) In paragraph (a) of subsection (1) of section 4 (destruction and disqualification orders) of the Dangerous Dogs Act 1991 ("the 1991 Act"), after the words "committed and" there shall be inserted the words ", subject to subsection (1A) below,".

(2) After that subsection there shall be inserted the following subsection—

"(1A) Nothing in subsection (1)(a) above shall require the court to order the destruction of a dog if the court is satisfied—

    (a) that the dog would not constitute a danger to public safety; and

    (b) where the dog was born before 30th November 1991 and is subject to the prohibition in section 1(3) above, that there is a good reason why the dog has not been exempted from that prohibition."

(3) In subsection (2) of that section, the words "then, unless the order is one that the court is required to make" shall cease to have effect.

(4) In subsection (3)(a) of that section, the words ", where the order was not one that the court was required to make" shall cease to have effect.

NOTES

Commencement. See s 6(3) post and the note "Orders under this section" thereto.
General Note. The Dangerous Dogs Act 1991, s 4(1), Vol 2, p 564, requires the court to order the destruction of a dog in the case of conviction of an offence under s 1 (offences relating to dogs breed for fighting) or an aggravated offence under s 3(1) or (3) (injury caused by dogs) of that Act. Sub-s (2) above gives the court a limited discretion not to order the destruction of such a dog if it is satisfied (a) that the dog would not constitute a danger to public safety and (b) where the dog was born before 30 November 1991 and is subject to the prohibition in s 1(3) (prohibition on possession or custody of dogs breed for fighting), that there is a good reason why the dog has not been exempted from that prohibition. Where destruction is not ordered, the provisions of s 4A of the 1991 Act, as inserted by s 2 post apply.
30 November 1991. For the significance of this date, see the General Note to s 2 post.
Dangerous Dogs Act 1991, ss 1, 4. See Vol 2, p 559, 564.

[Illustration 21–4]

PAGE FROM VOLUME 3, ALL ENGLAND LAW REPORTS 1994

964	All England Law Reports	[1994] 3 All ER

R v Bezzina
R v Codling
R v Elvin

a

COURT OF APPEAL, CRIMINAL DIVISION

KENNEDY LJ, WATERHOUSE AND EBSWORTH JJ

2 DECEMBER 1993

b

Animal – Dog – Dangerous dog – Dangerously out of control in public place – Injury to person – Liability of owner – Meaning of 'dangerously out of control' – Whether offence one of strict liability – Dangerous Dogs Act 1991, ss 3(1), 10(3).

c

In the first case, the defendant was exercising his Rottweiler dog off its lead in a small grassy compound and during that time the dog bit one of a group of teenagers. In the second case, the defendant was taking her dog for a walk when it bit the owner of another dog. In the third case, the defendant had left two pit bull terriers in a garage which was inadequately secured, with the result that they escaped and bit a third party. In each case the defendant was charged with being the owner of a dog which was 'dangerously out of control' in a public place and while so out of control injured a person contrary to s 3(1)[a] of the Dangerous Dogs Act 1991. The defendants were convicted of the s 3(1) offence and each appealed, contending that ss 3(1) and 10(1)[b] of the Act, which provided that a dog would be regarded as 'dangerously out of control' if there were grounds for reasonable apprehension that it might injure any person, did not create an offence of strict liability.

d

e

Held – On its true construction, s 3(1) of the 1991 Act imposed strict liability on the owner or handlers of dogs of any breed which were 'dangerously out of control' in public places within the meaning of s 10(3), which served to impose an objective standard of reasonable apprehension that the dog was acting in a way which would injure another person whether or not it actually did so. It was clear that Parliament had not intended to introduce any element of mens rea on the part of the dog owner in ss 3(1) and 10(3) and, accordingly, the fact that the owner had no realisation that his dog might behave in such a manner was immaterial, since the onus was on the owner to take steps which were effective to ensure that it did not cause injury to others. The appeals would therefore be dismissed (see p 966 *g h*, p 968 *j* to p 969 *c h j*, p 970 *b d* and p 971 *a b*, post).

f

g

h

Sweet v Parsley [1969] 1 All ER 347 and *Wings Ltd v Ellis* [1984] 3 All ER 577 applied.

Per curiam. In normal cases there is no room for expert evidence in relation to the primary issue of liability in prosecutions under s 3(1) of the 1991 Act. It may however be admissible in relation to other issues, such as whether the dog, in fact, bit anyone, or the question of sentence if there is a finding of guilt (see p 971 *b*, post).

j

---

a   Section 3, so far as material, is set out at p 966 *b* to *e*, post
b   Section 10, so far as material, is set out at p 966 *f*, post

[Illustration 21–5]

PAGE FROM HALSBURY'S LAWS OF ENGLAND AND WALES, 4TH ED.

6 Control of Dogs Order 1930 art 5, which makes dogs 'animals' for the purposes of the Animal Health Act 1981 ss 60, 63, which relate to the powers of police and of inspectors appointed for the purpose of that Act by the minister or by local authorities: see further paras 511, 512 post; and see also s 66.

372. Worrying of cattle and sheep. With a view to the prevention of worrying of cattle[1], a local authority may make regulations requiring that dogs or any class of dogs shall, during all or any of the hours between sunset and sunrise, be kept under control in the manner prescribed by the regulations[2]. Where a dog is proved to have injured cattle or poultry or chased sheep it may be dealt with as a dangerous dog[3].

Any person committing, or aiding, abetting, counselling or procuring the commission of, any breach of the regulations is liable on summary conviction to a fine not exceeding level 5 on the standard scale or, if the offence is committed with respect to more than ten animals, to a fine not exceeding level 3 on the standard scale for each animal[4].

1 'Cattle' in this context includes horses, mules, asses, sheep, goats and swine: Control of Dogs Order of 1930, SR & O 1930/399, art 2 (2).
2 Ibid art 2 (1). A copy of the regulations, signed and certified by the clerk of the local authority, is prima facie proof of the regulations: art 2 (4) (amended by SR & O 1931/80 and SI 1976/919).
3 Dogs Act 1906 s 1 (4) (amended by the Dogs (Amendment) Act 1928 s 1 (1)); see para 373 post.
4 Control of Dogs Order of 1930 art 6; Animal Health Act 1981 s 75 (1) (a), (b) (amended by virtue of the Criminal Justice Act 1982 ss 38, 46). As to the standard scale see para 232 note 1 ante. At the date at which this volume states the law, levels 3 and 5 on that scale are at £400 and £2,000 respectively. For a dog owner's criminal responsibility for the worrying of livestock on agricultural land under the Dogs (Protection of Livestock) Act 1953 see para 384 post.

(iii) Dangerous Dogs

A. DANGEROUS DOGS GENERALLY

373. Dangerous dogs not under control. On complaint made to a court of summary jurisdiction, the court may order that a dog which appears to it to be dangerous[1] and not kept under proper control[2] be kept by the owner[3] under proper control[4] or destroyed, under penalty of a fine for every day during which the non-compliance continues[5]. Alternatively, if the dog is male and it appears to the court on such a complaint that the dog would be less dangerous if neutered, the court may order it to be neutered[6]. Notice of the penalty must be given to the owner[7]. Where a destruction order is made, the court may also appoint a person to undertake the destruction and require any person having custody of the dog to deliver it up for that purpose, and, if it thinks fit, make an order disqualifying the owner from having a dog for a specified period[8].

A person who fails to comply with a destruction order or to deliver a dog up for destruction as ordered is guilty of an offence and on conviction, in addition to being liable to a fine, may be disqualified from having custody of a dog for a specified period[9].

An order to destroy a dog may be made without giving the owner the option of keeping it under proper control[10]. An order for destruction may be made although the dog has been moved out of the jurisdiction of the court after the offence, unless there has been a bona fide disposal of the dog by its owner[11], in which case an order

[Illustration 21–6]

PAGE FROM THE LAW REPORTS INDEX

724   **Statutes Judicially Considered**

1990 **Social Security Act** (c. 27)
 s. 11(3): Thrells Ltd. v. Lomas [1993] 1 W.L.R. 456
 Human Fertilisation and Embryology Act (c. 37)
 Sch. 3, paras. 1, 5: Reg. v. Human Fertilisation and Embryology Authority, *Ex parte* Blood
  [1996] 3 W.L.R. 1176
 Employment Act (c. 38)
 s. 7(2)(3)(*a*): Newham London Borough Council v. National and Local Government Officers
  Association [1993] I.C.R. 189, C.A.
 s. 7(3)(*b*): Tanks & Drums Ltd. v. Transport and General Workers' Union [1991] I.C.R. 1,
  Rougier J. and C.A.
 Courts and Legal Services Act (c. 41)
 s. 8(1): Rantzen v. Mirror Group Newspapers (1986) Ltd. [1994] Q.B. 670; [1993] 3 W.L.R.
  953, C.A.
 s. 9; Practice Direction (Family Proceedings) [1991] 1 W.L.R. 1178
 s. 15(3)(4): Practice Direction (Enforcement Costs: Recovery) [1991] 1 W.L.R. 1295
 s. 62: Ridehalgh v. Horsefield [1994] Ch. 205; [1994] 3 W.L.R. 462, C.A.
 Broadcasting Act (c. 42)
 s. 92(2)(*a*)(i): Reg. v. Radio Authority, *Ex parte* Bull [1995] 3 W.L.R. 572, D.C.
 Sch. 2, Part I, para. 1(3)(*b*): Reg. v. Radio Authority, *Ex parte* Guardian Media Group Plc.
  [1995] 1 W.L.R. 334
 Environmental Protection Act (c. 43)
 s. 80: Aitken v. South Hams District Council [1995] 1 A.C. 262; [1994] 3 W.L.R. 333, H.L.(E.)
1991 **Child Support Act** (c. 48)
 ss. 1(3), 31(2), 33(2): Department of Social Security v. Butler [1995] 1 W.L.R. 1528, C.A.
 Criminal Justice Act (c. 53)
 ss. 1(2), 3(3), 28(1): Reg. v. Cox [1993] 1 W.L.R. 188, C.A.
 ss. 1(2)(*a*), 2(2)(*a*): Reg. v. Cunningham [1993] 1 W.L.R. 183, C.A.
 ss. 1(2)(*a*)(*b*)(4), 2(2)(*b*), 3(3), 28(1), 29(1), 31(2): Reg. v. Baverstock [1993] 1 W.L.R. 202,
  C.A.
 s. 3(1)(5): Reg. v. Okinikan [1993] 1 W.L.R. 173, C.A.
 s. 8(2)(3)(*c*): Reg. v. Moore (Deborah) [1995] Q.B. 353; [1995] 2 W.L.R. 728, C.A.
 s. 14(1), Sch. 2, para. 8(2)(*b*): Reg. v. Oliver [1993] 1 W.L.R. 177, C.A.
 s. 29(1)(2): Reg. v. Bexley [1993] 1 W.L.R. 192, C.A.
 s. 31(1): Reg. v. Robinson (Kenneth) [1993] 1 W.L.R. 168, C.A.
 ss. 32–40: Practice Statement (Crime: Sentencing) [1992] 1 W.L.R. 948
 s. 34: Practice Direction (Crime: Life Sentences) [1993] 1 W.L.R. 223, C.A.
  Reg. v. Dalton [1995] Q.B. 243; [1995] 2 W.L.R. 377, C.A.
 ss. 34, 35(2), Sch. 12, para. 9: Reg. v. Secretary of State for the Home Department, *Ex parte*
  H. [1995] Q.B. 43; [1994] 3 W.L.R. 1110, C.A.
 ss. 34(3)(6), 35(2), Sch. 12, para. 9: Reg. v. Secretary of State for the Home Department,
  Ex parte T. [1994] Q.B. 378; [1994] 2 W.L.R. 190, D.C.
 ss. 34(4)(*b*), 39(4): Reg. v. Parole Board, *Ex parte* Watson [1996] 1 W.L.R. 906, C.A.
 s. 35: Reg. v. Secretary of State for the Home Department, *Ex parte* Pierson [1996] 3 W.L.R.
  547, C.A.
 s. 52: Reg. v. Hampshire [1996] Q.B. 1; [1995] 3 W.L.R. 260, C.A.
 s. 53, Sch. 6, para. 1(1): Practice Direction (Crown Courts: TV Links) [1992] 1 W.L.R. 838
 Dangerous Dogs Act (c. 65)
 s. 1(1)(*a*): Reg. v. Knightsbridge Crown Court, *Ex parte* Dunne [1994] 1 W.L.R. 296, D.C.
 ss. 3(1), 10(3): Reg. v. Bezzina [1994] 1 W.L.R. 1057, C.A.
 Care of Churches and Ecclesiastical Jurisdiction Measure (No. 1)
 s. 1: *In re* St. Anne's, Wrenthorpe [1994] Fam. 83; [1994] 2 W.L.R. 338
  In re St. Luke the Evangelist, Maidstone [1995] Fam. 1; [1994] 3 W.L.R. 1165
 ss. 1, 17: *In re* St. Barnabas, Dulwich [1994] Fam. 124; [1994] 2 W.L.R. 545
 ss. 12, 13: *In re* West Norwood Cemetery [1994] Fam. 210; [1994] 3 W.L.R. 820
1992 **Social Security Contributions and Benefits Act** (c. 4)
 ss. 33, 34: Graham v. Secretary of State for Social Security (Case C-92/94) [1996] I.C.R. 258,
  E.C.J.
 Social Security Administration Act (c. 5)
 ss. 82(1), 98(1)(*b*): Hassall v. Secretary of State for Social Security [1995] 1 W.L.R. 812, C.A.
 Trade Union and Labour Relations (Consolidation) Act (c. 52)
 s. 5: Government Communications Staff Federation v. Certification Officer [1993] I.C.R. 163,
  E.A.T.
 ss. 49(3), 51(6): Wise v. Union of Shop, Distributive and Allied Workers [1996] I.C.R. 691
 s. 100B (as substituted): National Union of Mineworkers (Yorkshire Area) v. Millward [1995]
  I.C.R. 482, E.A.T.
 s. 137(1): Harrison v. Kent County Council [1995] I.C.R. 434, E.A.T.
 s. 152(1): Speciality Care Plc. v. Pachela [1996] I.C.R. 633, E.A.T.
 s. 188: Reg. v. British Coal Corpn., *Ex parte* Vardy [1993] I.C.R. 720, D.C.
  Reg. v. Secretary of State for Trade and Industry, *Ex parte* Unison [1996] I.C.R. 1003,
  D.C.

SECTION K.   SUMMARY

1.   Statutes

    a.   *Current*

    (1) *The Public General Acts and Measures*

    (2) *Law Reports: Statutes*

    b.   *Compilation*

    (1) *Statutes in Force, Official Revised Edition.* Looseleaf.

    (2) *Halsbury's Statutes of England and Wales,* 4th ed. Multi-volume collection of statutes in force arranged by topic. Most convenient set to locate English statutes.

2.   Administrative Law

    English regulations (delegated, or secondary, legislation) published separately as *Statutory Instruments.* Compiled in *Halsbury's Statutory Instruments.*

    (1) *Index to Government Orders.* Issued biennially.

    (2) Index volume to *Halsbury's Statutory Instruments.*

3.   Courts

    a.   *Court Organization.* Under the *Courts Act of 1971,* English courts *of record* are organized as follows:

    (1) House of Lords

    (2) Supreme Court of Judicature

       (a) Court of Appeal

       (b) High Court

          [1]   Queen's Bench Division

          [2]   Chancery Division

          [3]   Family Division

       (c) Crown Court

    b.   *Court Reporting*

    (1) *Law Reports.* Quasi-official, selective in cases reported.

    (a) *Law Reports, Appeal Cases.* Decisions from House of Lords and Court of Appeal.

    (b) *Law Reports, Queen's Bench Division.*

    (c) *Law Reports, Chancery Division.*

    (d) *Law Reports, Family Division.*

    (2) *Weekly Law Reports.* Decisions from volume 1 are not reprinted in the *Law Reports.*

(3) *All England Law Reports.* Privately published compreher reporting of English cases, began publication in 1936.

4. Digests

a. *The Digest: Annotated British, Commonwealth and European Cases.* A comprehensive digest of English cases with selective digests from Scotland, Ireland, Canada, and other countries of the Commonwealth.

b. *Halsbury's Laws of England,* 4th ed. A comprehensive encyclopedic treatment of English law, cases, and statutes.

c. *Current Law.* Published as the *Monthly Digest* which cumulates into the annual *Yearbook.*

Chapter 22

COMPUTER–ASSISTED LEGAL RESEARCH*

Legal information is published in a variety of formats. This chapter introduces the technologically-advanced formats of computer-assisted legal research (CALR), especially LEXIS–NEXIS, WESTLAW, and CD-ROM products. Included in the discussion is the explosion of law and legally-related information on the Internet.[1] Remember that advances in

---

* Prepared by Robert J. Nissenbaum, Director of the William M. Rains Library and Professor of Law, Loyola Law School, Los Angeles. Professor Nissenbaum is grateful for the assistance of the library staff of the William M. Rains Library in the preparation of this chapter.

[1] M. ETHAN KATSH, THE ELECTRONIC MEDIA AND THE TRANSFORMATION OF LAW (1989), suggests that new electronic research methods will change our perception of the law as a separate and distinct discipline. Application of LEXIS–NEXIS and WESTLAW technology will make our legal system fluid, less structured, and more accessible, reminiscent of law's early oral tradition. Katsh believes the pervasiveness of access to legal precedent fostered by CALR undermines the role of precedent and the application of *stare decisis.* For later views on the role of technology in the legal arena, see CURTIS E.A. KARNOW, FUTURE CODES: ESSAYS IN ADVANCED COMPUTER TECHNOLOGY AND THE LAW (1997), Curtis E.A. Karnow, *Liability for Distributed Artificial Intelligences,* 11 BERKELEY TECH. L.J. 181–92 (computer networks that handle multiple tasks will complicate traditional understandings of proximate cause upsetting established links between human actions and harmful consequences), ETHAN KATSH, LAW IN A DIGITAL WORLD 242 (1995) (" . . . cyberspace is a quite different culture . . . one that will bring its values to bear on all of us as . . . legal tradition increasingly interact with it"), Ethan Katsh, *Law in a Digital World: Computer Networks and Cyberspace,* 38 VILL. L. REV. 403 (1993).

SUSAN W. BRENNER, PRECEDENT INFLATION (1992), believes that "the most logical consequence of putting precedents on-line and using computers to access them is a 'paradigm shift' into a 'quantative conception of precedent'." *Id.* at 265.

This chapter explains how to find legal information in an automated environment that may be relevant to a particular issue. Contrary to Katsh's view, when using computer-assisted legal research, it is important to keep in mind the rules of precedent and how courts interpret binding and persuasive authorities. Artificial intelligence may eventually aid in analysis, but in the interim, CALR provides extensive access to information without eliminating the need for substantive legal analysis. Chapter 1 discusses precedent in some

technology are occurring rapidly. Research technology you read about today may be changed tomorrow as new materials are added to databases, enhancements are made to search strategies, new features are added, additional databases are created, the Internet expands, and new products are developed. Suffice it to say, users of CALR, just as with print sources, should always seek out the latest technological innovations before beginning to research.[2]

SECTION A. INTRODUCTION: THE INTERFACE OF TECHNOLOGY AND LEGAL INFORMATION

Legal research requires the use of many sources—print, electronic, and microforms. Computerized or electronic legal information provides information available in print format with the addition of information and searching capabilities far exceeding traditional legal research methods. With the rise of Internet-based legal research, information never before available in any format is now accessible.

Computerized information is stored in several ways. Storage may be remote, part of a large mainframe computer, accessible through a complicated and sometimes costly telecommunications system. Remotely accessible legal information systems are now available through the Internet, eliminating the need for proprietary network-based telecommunications systems. In addition to the Internet's impact on telecommunications, local storage formats, now available on compact disk, have also reduced the need for large mainframe computers. On the down side, the scope of legal information available on compact disk is severely limited as compared to online mainframe databases such as LEXIS–NEXIS and WESTLAW. The mix of information and technology will likely change dramatically in the next several years. Trends are difficult to predict, but change, innovation, and ingenuity are certain.

SECTION B. EQUIPMENT AND TELECOMMUNICATIONS

The two primary services for computer-assisted legal research are LEXIS–NEXIS, a product of Reed Elsevier, and WESTLAW, a service owned by Thomson Publishing. LEXIS–NEXIS and WESTLAW were recently acquired by off-shore information conglomerates from the Netherlands and United Kingdom respectively. Both services contain almost complete libraries of primary materials and continue to add significant collections of secondary sources.

Access to LEXIS–NEXIS and WESTLAW requires a personal computer and modem or similar telecommunications device. Access is either through a private network that connects to a modem pool or Internet-based access using either dial-up or network connections through an Internet service provider. Both LEXIS–NEXIS and WESTLAW offer

---

detail. *See also* KARL LLEWELLYN, THE BRAMBLE BUSH, Chapters II–IV (1951); RUPERT CROSS, PRECEDENT IN ENGLISH LAW (4th ed. 1991).

[2] For a contrary view of the utility of computerized legal research see Richard Haigh, *What Shall I Wear to the Computer Revolution? Some Thoughts on Electronic Research in Law*, 89 LAW LIBR. J. 245 (1997).

software that interfaces with the Internet and permits their search engines to be compatible with the Internet. LEXIS–NEXIS Internet software is known as LEXIS Exchange, WESTLAW's Internet software is known as Westlaw.com.

Whether using the Internet or other telecommunications provider you will ultimately connect with a large mainframe computer located in Dayton, Ohio for LEXIS–NEXIS or in Eagan, Minnesota for WESTLAW. Depending on the modem speeds in your network or computer and quality of Internet connection, information may be transmitted at speeds up to 56,000 bits of information per second.

SECTION C. THE WESTLAW AND LEXIS–NEXIS DATABASES

Computer-assisted legal research database contents are controlled by the database vendor. Since the development of CALR in the early 1970s, the scope of databases, such as LEXIS–NEXIS and WESTLAW, have grown consistently with the legal profession's acceptance of automated research.

LEXIS–NEXIS and WESTLAW, in their infancy, provided access to case law for the federal and state jurisdictions. At first only LEXIS–NEXIS provided full-text access to case law; WESTLAW followed by providing access to its *National Reporter System*'s synopses and headnotes. WESTLAW eventually expanded to a full-text database for case reporting. Following case law, both vendors concentrated on adding other primary sources of legal information, e.g., administrative regulations and decisions, statutes, attorneys general opinions. Today both databases serve as comprehensive and complex sources of legal information. The databases are constantly undergoing expansion and refinement. In the law school setting, you will find that some databases are not available to the LEXIS–NEXIS or WESTLAW educational subscribers.

Be aware that neither the library nor organization that provides your access to these services controls the database content. You are simply paying to access a database and telecommunications network. The information is not your property or that of the firm, organization, or library of which you are a part. One's interest in the content of the database is defined by the contractual agreement that regulates the conditions of the database's use.

Economic pressures placed on the database vendors' license by proprietary owners of legal information may cause information to be eliminated, with little or no notice to you, by the database vendor. Legal information in its undigested form is widely available; legal information that has been refined through editorial processes has considerable proprietary value. A database vendor may choose to eliminate digested or edited legal information from its database when licensing costs reduce the profitability of placing material in a computerized environment.[3]

---

[3] In 1996 LEXIS–NEXIS merged with Reed–Elsevier, Inc. The following year Thomson Publishing Co. completed the purchase of West Publishing Company including WESTLAW.

This pressure should caution a researcher to evaluate carefully the scope and content of any database before relying on that database as the primary access for legal research information.

Although a particular title or format of legal research materials appears in the database, check the contents for retrospective information carefully. Typically, legal research vendors introduce a particular publication or service on the database, but do not provide a complete historical retrospective file of the collection. Sometimes the vendor retroloads backfiles. A researcher must consistently check those files to know the extent of information currently in the database. Database directories or menu screens on LEXIS–NEXIS and WESTLAW provide instructions for determining the contents of a file. The GUIDE library on LEXIS–NEXIS provides information on the contents of various libraries and files. WESTLAW's SCOPE command permits you to view database information by entering the SCOPE command along with a database identifier.

In some instances, a vendor's license agreement with the proprietary owner of the information in the database prohibits the vendor from placing the most up-to-date releases of information in the database. In those instances, researchers may have an almost complete file of information available to them, but they lack the latest information that is available to the readers of the print, CD–ROM, or Internet version of the publication or service.

The following database content summaries of LEXIS–NEXIS and WESTLAW are fluid, defined by an expanding universe of legal information.

1. LEXIS–NEXIS

LEXIS–NEXIS organizes its database into libraries and sub-libraries known as files. Libraries represent the broadest definition of information in the database and files are the constituent parts of a library. The general legal libraries in LEXIS include: MEGA Library (combined state and federal databases); GENFED Library (general federal court, statutory, and agency information); STATES Library (information from the state jurisdictional level); individual state libraries; CODES Library (federal and state statutory material); INTLAW or International Law Library (U.S. federal and state cases arising under international law including foreign law and the law of the European Communities); LAWREV or Law Reviews Library; and LEXREF or Legal Reference

---

Thomson owned Lawyers–Cooperative Publishing when the purchase of WESTLAW was completed. LEXIS–NEXIS had a licensing agreement with Lawyers Cooperative to make available certain Lawyers Cooperative titles on the LEXIS–NEXIS database. In effect, Thomson found themselves licensing their own products to their competitor LEXIS–NEXIS. Adjustments in the content of both databases is expected overtime as licensing agreements expire. Re-alignment of print materials, as result of the merger, is already taking place. U.S. v. The Thomson Corporation and West Publishing; Proposed Final Judgment and Competitive Impact Statement, 61 Fed. Reg. 35250 (1996), *modified*, U.S. v. Thomson Corp., 949 F. Supp. 907 (D.D.C. 1996), *further modified*, 1997 U.S. Dist. LEXIS 1893, 42 U.S.P.Q. 2d (BNA) 1867; 1997–1 Trade Cas. (CCH) 71,735 (D.D.C.).

Library (legal reference materials including secondary sources for legislative history, indexing sources for legal periodical information, and directories).

In addition to general libraries, LEXIS–NEXIS provides numerous specialized legal libraries. These specialized libraries include such diverse subjects as admiralty and federal transportation. The advantage of these specialized databases is that they more efficiently provide access to the wealth of information available in the overall database. Specialized libraries reduce computer search time and limit the possibility of erroneous results. Noteworthy specialized databases include: CORP or corporate law; ENVIRN or environmental law; HEALTH or health law; LABOR or federal labor law; FEDSEC or federal securities law; and FEDTAX or federal tax law. Nearly 200 specialized libraries are available on LEXIS–NEXIS, including major looseleaf publishers (see Chapter 14).

In 1998, LEXIS–NEXIS added many titles from looseleaf publisher Commerce Clearing House's family of titles. Primarily focused in the tax and business law area, the titles added to LEXIS–NEXIS include electronic versions of Commerce Clearing House looseleaf services in the tax, securities regulation, and banking areas. Commerce Clearing House titles are not available to LEXIS–NEXIS educational contract subscribers.

Other major looseleaf service vendors contributing information to the LEXIS–NEXIS database include the Research Institute of America (RIA) and the Bureau of National Affairs (BNA). Titles contributed by the Bureau of National Affairs include materials from BNA's labor, labor arbitration, and employment services including the *Labor Relations Reporter*, energy and environment services, federal securities, *United States Law Week*, intellectual property, and medical/health care services.

The LEXIS–NEXIS RIA tax library includes *RIA's Tax Citator*, *RIA's Federal Tax Coordinator 2d*, and *Tax Analysts' Tax Notes Today*, along with a variety of tax journals published by Warren Gorham & Lamont.

LEXIS–NEXIS is expanding the scope of its databases devoted to foreign law. Foreign law libraries include: Australia, Dutch, Europe, European Communities, France, Germany, Hong Kong/China, Ireland, Malaysia, Mideast/Africa, Philippine, Singapore, United Kingdom/British Isles, and World. Country specific libraries contain an assortment of primary legal materials. The Europe and World Libraries focus on business and political news, company information, and country reports.

Other LEXIS–NEXIS specialized libraries include: *Shepard's Citations*, an online version of the traditional citator, as described in Chapter 15, located in the CITES or Citation Library; NEWS or News Library, a current awareness news and information service containing over 2,300 world-wide full-text sources from newspapers, magazines, journals, newsletters, wire services and broadcast transcripts; the Business and Financial Library, containing information on businesses and financial institutions; ABA or American Bar Association Library, containing publications of the American Bar Association; ACCTG or the Accounting, Tax & Financial Library; MEDLINE, a medical information service from the National Library of Medicine; LEGIS or Legislation Library, covering state and federal legislation and progress of pending legislation; and ASSETS or Assets Library, providing selective national coverage of real estate assessments and deed transfers.

LEXIS–NEXIS places the full text of over 200 law reviews online and continues to add new titles in the LAWREV or Law Reviews Library. The Law Reviews Library includes full-text of nearly 20 state and local bar journal publications. LEXIS–NEXIS also provides online access to the leading legal periodical indexes—Wilson's *Index to Legal Periodicals* and IAC's *Legal Resource Index* in LEXREF, the Legal Reference Library (see Chapter 17).

LEXIS–NEXIS also provides the *Martindale–Hubbell Law Directory* permitting access to law firm profiles and basic biographical information on lawyers throughout the United States as part of a larger CAREER Library. The Career Library also includes directories of judicial clerkships and government employment along with international position listings.

There are several ways to keep up to date with the contents of LEXIS–NEXIS. Regularly review the libraries and services outlines on the introductory screens when you sign on to LEXIS–NEXIS; use the online bulletin board Guide Library or GUIDE to find out the latest news and enhancements to the database; scan HOTTOPICS, the Hot Topics Library for issues of contemporary importance; and review the annual print or on-line version (available in the GUIDE Library) of the *LEXIS-NEXIS Directory of Online Services*. In addition, LEXIS–NEXIS publishes several newsletters that regularly provide information on new libraries, specialized databases, and search engine features. The most extensive outline of the database is the multi-volume looseleaf *LEXIS-NEXIS Product Guides*.

2. WESTLAW

WESTLAW is organized into a series of databases and sub-databases known as files and operates using WESTMATE, the latest being the 32–bit version, which is compatible with Microsoft's full suite of business applications. On WESTLAW, databases are analogous to LEXIS–NEXIS libraries, and files are similar to LEXIS–NEXIS files. The general divisions in WESTLAW include jurisdictional materials, news and information, practice-area materials, and text and periodicals. You can select a WESTLAW database directly from the main screen if the database identifier is known in advance.

Jurisdictional Materials include primary federal and state legal information including case law, statutes, and administrative materials. The cases in WESTLAW contain not only the actual text of each case, but also all the additional editorial features added in the reporters of the

National Reporter System. These include the synopsis, the headnotes, and the West Key Numbers.

Practice-Area Materials include more than forty unique databases drawn from the primary materials available in the Jurisdictional Materials database and enhanced by specialized information of a secondary nature not available in the Jurisdictional Materials database. This is similar to LEXIS–NEXIS' specialized libraries, which draw on information prepared and digested by other publishers of legal information. For instance, like LEXIS–NEXIS, WESTLAW's labor file in the Practice-Area Materials database includes the *BNA's Labor Relations Reporter.*

A selection of files in the Practice-Area Materials database includes Administrative Law, Communications, First Amendment, Legal Ethics and Professional Responsibility, Securities Regulation, Taxation, and Transportation. Practice-Area Materials databases provide efficient access to the primary materials available in the Jurisdictional Materials database along with specialized primary and secondary resources useful to the specialist practitioner.

WESTLAW also provides a Texts and Periodicals database. WESTLAW offers full text of nearly 600 law reviews. Selective coverage of articles is extended to many more legal periodicals that are not available on LEXIS–NEXIS. Access to online versions of the Wilson's *Index to Legal Periodicals* and IAC's *Legal Resource Index* is available.

Other specialized materials on WESTLAW, many of which are also available on LEXIS–NEXIS, include: materials from the American Bar Association; Billcast, summarizing public bills introduced in Congress; State Net Capitols Report, providing tracking and full text of state legislative bills; and Bureau of National Affairs (BNA) materials, including numerous BNA publications and a BNA Highlights and Contents file providing information from BNA's daily publications covering legislative, judicial, and administrative activities. Some publications of Commerce Clearing House are also available, as are: highlights from Dow Jones News_Retrieval covering the business and financial communities; practitioner-oriented publications of the Practising Law Institute; Standard and Poor's Daily News; MEDLINE, covering medical and health information; and Disclosure, providing financial information on thousands of companies.

WESTLAW'S News and Information database includes information from DIALOG, a vendor of hundreds of databases concentrating in the social sciences; Congressional Quarterly information such as Washington Alert providing the latest information on the events and legislative agenda in Washington, D.C., including the full text of all versions of recent bills and numerous other Congressional documents; and Dun & Bradstreet information providing financial information on millions of companies.

The *West Legal Directory*, available only online, provides information on attorneys, judicial clerkships, and subject specific information throughout the United States. In addition, WESTLAW makes available the National Association of Law Placement's (NALP) *Directory of Legal Employers* consisting of law firm resumes gathered and disseminated by NALP.

WESTLAW provides the WEST's Legal News database designed to keep the user current on breaking legal issues using a jurisdictional and topical approach. WEST's Legal News summarizes cases and other legal news. WEST's Legal News is also available to summarize current legal developments for all states and the Supreme Court of the United States. WEST's Legal News provides topical information and summaries of developments for specific files, such as antitrust, real property, and the United States Supreme Court.

To remain current on the contents of WESTLAW, consult the variety of newsletters WESTLAW publishes and regularly review the database directory for new contents. In addition, West provides an in-print version of the *WESTLAW Database Directory*.

SECTION D.   FORMULATING A SEARCH REQUEST ON LEXIS–NEXIS AND WESTLAW[4]

1.   Costs of Searching the Databases

Mastering search strategy technique is essential to make most efficient use of the power available through online legal research. Pricing for LEXIS–NEXIS and WESTLAW varies, but both vendors have developed price structures that reward efficiency. There are three considerations in the CALR price structure—telecommunications, connect time to the service itself, and variable access charges for using different libraries or databases.

Telecommunication is the cost associated with maintaining a telephone or Internet connection with the vendor's mainframe computer. Depending on one's location, a user accesses LEXIS–NEXIS and WEST-LAW through a proprietary telecommunications network or through widely-available commercial Internet networks. Access to LEXIS–NEXIS and WESTLAW through the Internet may eliminate the telecommunications charge to local phone companies, but additional charges may be incurred from your Internet service provider.

Both LEXIS–NEXIS and WESTLAW maintain a running connect charge to their databases. This charge begins at the moment you sign on to the service and continues until the research session is terminated. Connection charges may vary with the time of day you use the system or with bulk usage agreements.

---

[4] This portion of the chapter is designed as a brief overview for computerized legal research search strategy. LEXIS–NEXIS and WESTLAW produce extensive materials to help you. *See, e.g.,* the latest editions of LEARNING LEXIS: A HANDBOOK FOR MODERN LEGAL RESEARCH and DISCOVERING WESTLAW: THE ESSENTIAL GUIDE, as well as STEVEN L. EMMANUEL, LEXIS–NEXIS FOR LAW STUDENTS (3d ed. 1997). *See also,* THEODORE HERMAN, HOW TO RESEARCH LESS AND FIND MORE: THE ESSENTIAL GUIDE TO COMPUTER-ASSISTED LEGAL RESEARCH (1996) (WESTLAW), and JEAN SINCLAIR McKNIGHT, THE LEXIS COMPANION: A COMPLETE GUIDE TO EFFECTIVE SEARCHING (1995).

Access charges are individually priced based upon the library/file or individual database a user is accessing. This charge begins at the time you instruct the search software to move the research session into a particular database on WESTLAW or when the search begins on LEXIS–NEXIS. Access charges are also subject to different price structures for peak hours versus off-peak hour access. In addition, you are charged per printed line for offline downloading of information to a printer or for moving portions of text found in LEXIS–NEXIS or WESTLAW into a document word processing file. LEXIS–NEXIS and WESTLAW provide an additional pricing option permitting costs to be assessed on an hourly pricing basis. The flat hourly price replaces access charges to individual libraries.

LEXIS–NEXIS and WESTLAW offer price structures that limit a user's access to the database. A user may contract with either company to access only a jurisdictionally specific portion of the database for a substantially reduced cost or even a flat rate. If information is required outside of the contracted databases the user may access non-contracted databases at a higher per use rate.

Charges for both LEXIS–NEXIS and WESTLAW can only be quoted by a representative of each company. Costs vary greatly between subscriptions to the databases in the for-profit sector as opposed to the not-for-profit educational markets. For example, in the law school environment the price to the school is a flat-rate based on the size of student enrollment.

This "educational" subscription enables students, faculty, law librarians, and other qualified individuals at the law school to have unlimited access to these services without the school incurring any additional costs. The educational discount limits law student use of LEXIS–NEXIS and WESTLAW to research associated the curricular and co-curricular elements of the law school program. Using LEXIS–NEXIS or WESTLAW for non-law school related research may result in the law student incurring a charge at the commercial account rate for the use of these services.

Competition in the law school market is so intense that the vendors supply some equipment and supplies, hire law students to assist with the training, and provide software that enables a student to access the services via modem or through the Internet. Although students are trained in proper search techniques and strategies, these educational subscriptions can lead law students to view these services as "free" and to not concentrate on developing efficient, cost-effective search strategies. Students should learn efficient search strategies not only to save non-academic organizations economic resources, but to make their research more timely and productive.

2. Traditional Search Strategies—Words or Terms and Connectors

At the outset of computer assisted legal research, searching on LEXIS–NEXIS and WESTLAW has been accomplished almost exclusively by using words and phrases within a framework of instructions to the database search software. The search strategies employed are similar for both services. LEXIS–NEXIS refers to this technique and the use of "words and connectors;" WESTLAW strategy is called "terms and connectors." In this discussion, "words" and "terms" are used interchangeable. As an alternative to word and term searching, WESTLAW has introduced WIN (**W**estlaw **i**s **N**atural) and LEXIS–NEXIS has introduced FREESTYLE. These newer natural language search techniques are discussed in the next portions of this section, with this portion concentrating on the more traditional words and terms search strategy.

Traditional searching (non-natural language) may be of several types—the computer can be commanded to locate a particular word (term) or phrase or a truncated variation of a word or phrase, to limit the physical area of a document searched to a particular field or segment, or to search based upon Boolean logic connectors.

a. *Plurals, Word Truncation, Universal Character*. Both LEXIS–NEXIS and WESTLAW automatically generate regular plural forms when the word's singular form is searched. For example, dog retrieves dogs.

In addition, words may be truncated. Truncation identifies a particular word root. For example, "tort" and "tortious" may be similar expressions of interest in the documents one is trying to retrieve. A user could choose to place both terms in a search or may wish to capture any expression using the root "tort" followed by the *root expander,* an exclamation point (!). Therefore, "tort!" isolates all these expressions, including tort, tortious, tortiously, and torte. Torte may not have any legal relevance, although it tastes good; but the computer does not understand the legal concept or the idea, rather the search software performs literal search requests.

Some words form plurals irregularly or have variant spellings, for example, woman and women. Women is a plural that would not automatically be retrieved, because the plural is not formed by adding an "s," "es," or "ies." To retrieve both singular and plural forms of the word one may use the *universal character,* an asterisk (*). Using an asterisk as follows, e.g., wom*n, would cause the search software to identify both woman and women. To retrieve variant spellings use the universal character, e.g., "marijuana," "mariguana," and "marihuana" by entering "mari*uana;" or compact dis* to retrieve compact disk or compact disc.

A search request may be enhanced beyond the simple expression of words or phrases, plural forms of words, or variant forms of words using universal characters and truncation. Boolean logic permits a user to express alternative forms of words or phrases with special relationships to one another using a series of Boolean or logical connectors.

b. *Boolean Logic Connectors*. Boolean logic identifies words in particular relationships to one another within a document or within a defined physical area of a document. The following are commonly-used Boolean logic connectors:

The connector AND requires a word or phrase and another word or phrase to be located in the same document. AND does not require the two elements in the search to appear in any particular relationship to each other or in any particular portion of the document. On LEXIS–NEXIS an AND connector may be indicated by typing ''and'' or by typing '' & .'' WESTLAW only recognizes '' & '' as its AND connector. For example, if one wants to locate every appearance of the words cat and dog, including cats and dogs, in a document a search would look like this:

LEXIS: cat and dog   *in the alternative*: cat & dog

WESTLAW: cat & dog

The OR connector requires either or both word or phrase to appear in a document. Again, the words need not appear in any particular relationship to one another.

OR as a connector is commonly used when a word has a synonym or when a phrase may be expressed in several ways. For example, the searches would appear as follows:

LEXIS: dog or canine

WESTLAW: dog canine

The space between dog and canine is understood by the WESTLAW software to imply an OR connector. WESTLAW defines phrases by surrounding the phrase with quotation marks to avoid an implied OR connector. In another example consider these two alternative search strategies on WESTLAW:

1: res ipsa loquitor

2: ''res ipsa loquitor''

In the first, WESTLAW would locate every occurrence of res or ipsa or loquitor. The second example, ''res ipsa loquitor,'' locates only documents where the words *res ipsa loquitor,* the legal phrase appear. On LEXIS–NEXIS the OR connector must be expressed; therefore, quotation marks are not necessary to designate a phrase.

The OR connector can be used to find different expressions used to indicate the same concept. For example, we know that a red traffic light unequivocally expresses the concept to ''stop.'' An individual may also interpret the light to mean ''halt.'' Both words imply the same meaning, but are expressed in different language. However, computers are very literal machines and absent a major thesaurus accompanying the software, they only do what they are asked to do. For example, when searching for ''red light'' as a synonym of ''stop,'' a user may wish to express those terms as ''halt'' or ''stop.'' Similarly, ''dog'' and ''canine'' are equivalent terms, and the document for which one is searching may express the concept in both or either form. Use of the OR connector captures both expressions.

Language also can be idiomatic or metaphorical. The relationship of words and their physical juxtaposition imparts ideas and concepts that the words when expressed independently do not. For instance, an adjective generally precedes a noun, e.g., "reasonable doubt." A researcher examining the jurisprudence of criminal procedure would be interested in documents that place *reasonable* and *doubt* in close proximity to one another. Simply searching the database and all occurrences of *reasonable* and *doubt* in a document using the AND connector would yield a very unwieldy number of irrelevant cases. However, looking for the phrase "reasonable doubt," or *reasonable* and *doubt* within the same sentence or paragraph or within a defined number of words of one another, in a specific order, or in a particular portion of a document, may be helpful. How would a researcher accomplish this using LEXIS–NEXIS and WESTLAW?

c. *Segment or Field Searching.* Electronically-stored documents are broken into identifiable parts, such a citation, date, body, judge, etc. Both LEXIS–NEXIS and WESTLAW enable a user to search these particular predefined portions of a document. LEXIS–NEXIS calls this feature *segment searching.* WESTLAW calls it *field searching.* Searching only a portion of a document can often eliminate the retrieval of irrelevant information.

LEXIS–NEXIS permits a user to search various segments of a document depending on the nature and type of the document. The database indicates what predefined segments are available within the particular library and file a user is searching once a segments screen is accessed.

WESTLAW defines its fields by the physical portions of a document as described in Chapter 3, Section B. Because all *National Reporter System* cases appear in similar formats, the identified structure of the cases as they appear on the written page serves as the defined fields in WESTLAW.

d. *Proximity Connectors.* Besides looking for words or phrases within a certain predefined physical area of a document, both systems permits you to define a physical portion of a document to conduct a search. This is accomplished using *proximity connectors*, for two or more words or phrases within a certain number of words of each other or in a particular order within the defined number of words.

LEXIS–NEXIS lets a user search for words or phrases within the same LEXIS–NEXIS defined segment (w/seg), within a particular number of words of each other (w/n) or (/n) ["n" signifies the number of words], or preceding the next word or phrase by a set number of words or phrases (pre/n) or (+n), with the "n" signifying any number between 1 to 255 words, e.g., emotional distress w/10 damages.

WESTLAW limits its proximity connectors to words or phrases in the same sentence (/s) or paragraph (/p). In addition, words or phrases may be located within a certain number of words of each other (/n [n=the number of words]) or words or phrases may be located sequentially within a certain number of words of each other (+ n), with the "n" signifying any number of words between 1 to 255, e.g., "emotional distress" /p damages; "emotional distress" w/10 damages.

e. *Additional search strategies.* Four additional research tools on LEXIS–NEXIS are capitalization, singular and plural, frequency searching, and FOCUS.

Capitalization permits one to search for terms in all upper or lower case. This is useful when searching for acronyms, country and state abbreviations, agencies, and alphabetical characters in state statutes and codes.

For example:

> caps (doe) retrieves all references to DOE, the common acronym for the United States Department of Energy. The "caps" instruction retrieves any occurrence with one or more capital letters, compared to

> all caps (aids) retrieves all references to the acronym AIDS the disease as opposed to "aids" the verb for assistance. All characters must appear in capital letters. In another example, no caps (anchor) avoids references to a proper name such as Anchor Hocking.

Singular specificity avoids the LEXIS–NEXIS's automatic searching for regular plural forms of words by searching for singular nouns pluralized by adding an "s," "es," or "ies." For example, if one wishes to find references to Dan Connor but not Dan Connors, the search strategy would appear as:

dan w/3 singular (Connor)

Plural specificity is helpful to locate only the plural form of a noun. For example, if one is looking for references to the Cincinnati Reds baseball team, a user may combine plural specificity with capitalization to produce a search request that would appear as:

plural (caps (red))

Finally, frequency searching determines if a particular term appears within a document in a particular number of occurrences. For example, to find a document containing 15 occurrences of the word "redundant," form the search request as:

at least 15 (redundant)

The following are equivalent commands for capitalization and singular and plural designation on LEXIS–NEXIS:

caps: cap

ALLCAPS: allcap, acap, acaps

NOCAPS: nocap, ncap, ncaps

SINGULAR: sing, sng

PLURAL: plur, plr

FOCUS, similar to WESTLAW's LOCATE, permits a user to highlight key words in an initial search request even when those terms were not part of the original query. In effect, one can "focus" on words that were not part of the search strategy, but are relevant to the information retrieved. FOCUS permits the user to select information isolated in the first search request without initiating a new search level. It highlights new search terms, but not the original terms unless it is specifically requested to do so.

Both services have developed menu-driven research systems that enable a novice user to select a database and formulate a search by responding to computer-generated queries step-by-step. This capability is known as Easy Search (the EASY Library) on LEXIS–NEXIS and EZ ACCESS on WESTLAW.

3. Natural Language Searching

a.   *WESTLAW is Natural (WIN).* As an alternative to Boolean logic, WESTLAW introduced in 1992 a natural language search mechanism known as WIN (WESTLAW is Natural). In preparing a natural language search, the WESTLAW database is queried in the simple form of a question. For example, after selecting the appropriate database and file in WESTLAW query the system: *Are universities or colleges liable for injuries to student participating in intramural sports?* (a similar search on WESTLAW using Boolean logic may appear as college universit! /s liab! /3 student /s "intramural sports").

WIN analyzes the natural language query in several ways. First, all the words and phrases are compared to a dictionary developed by the WESTLAW editors. The dictionary serves to identify those words and phrases that have legal significance. Next, the indicated database and file are searched for natural language "hits." A "hit" occurs when the occurrence of words or phrases or roots of words or phrases are compared with a statistical/linguistic algorithm indicating that the "hit" is statistically relevant to the query. The algorithm considers not only the appearance of relevant words or phrases in a document, but the relationship of the words or phrases denoting a relevant meaning consistent with the statistical analysis performed by the algorithm. Finally, the results of the statistical analysis are ranked by frequency of occurrence and statistical weighing using the algorithm.

A WIN search retrieves only twenty documents; however, the researcher may direct the software to rank up to 100 documents. The search is automatically sorted (the SORT command) by "statistical relevance", which displays that part of each of the ranked documents that most closely satisfies the initial query. WIN results may also be sorted in reverse chronology using the AGE command.

To expand the accuracy of a WIN query, WESTLAW provides an on-line legal thesaurus. In effect, the thesaurus permits a user to add words to a natural language search after WIN isolates search concepts and eliminates *stop* words from the natural language query. In the above example, WIN isolated the following search concepts and the thesaurus

augmented those terms by providing the suggestions appearing in parenthesis:

> university (higher education)
>
> liable (accountable)
>
> injury (harm)
>
> student (undergraduate)
>
> sport (athletic competition)

To direct WESTLAW to perform a WIN search, enter "nat" at the
query screen prompt or click on the WIN icon. To request the thesaurus
in WIN, enter "thes" after WIN identifies the search concepts or click on
the thesaurus icon.

Although the ultimate accuracy of WIN is yet to be determined, the
early literature analyzing WIN is mixed.[5] WIN began in WESTLAW's
case-based databases and has been expanded to WESTLAW's text and
periodicals database.

b. *FREESTYLE on LEXIS–NEXIS.* LEXIS–NEXIS has developed
an associative retrieval natural language search protocol known as
FREESTYLE. FREESTYLE is designed to search more conceptual issues, to retrieve information on more complex issues, and to assist the
user in developing a search description with access to an online legal
thesaurus, including a phrase identification system. Unlike WIN, FREE-
STYLE may be used throughout the LEXIS–NEXIS database.

FREESTYLE analyzes one's natural language search strategy, eliminates irrelevant terms, and then ranks in importance the remaining
terms in that strategy. FREESTYLE then provides the user the opportunity to make revisions to the search. FREESTYLE search results are
displayed either by statistical ranking from one to 1,000 documents or a
user may choose to display the search results in reverse chronological
order.

Once a search retrieval has been made, either by statistical ranking
or reverse chronological order, the user may display the text of the
FREESTYLE search in a variety of formats: KWIC (key word in context); FULL document; or in SUPERKWIC. SUPERKWIC displays the
most statistically-relevant portion of one's retrieved document. In addi-

---

[5] Paul Bernstein, *The Natural Way to Search,* TRIAL, June 1993, at 84; Richard A. Leiter,
WIN: "It's the Natural Way," LEGAL INFORMATION ALERT, Nov.–Dec. 1992, at 1; Teresa
Pritchard, *WIN–WESTLAW Goes Natural,* ONLINE, Jan. 1993, at 101–03. *See also* Daniel E.
Harmon, *The New WESTLAW: English–Language Queries and Automatic Analysis of Case
Relevancy,* LAWYER'S PC, Oct. 1992, at 1. *But see* Anthony Aarons, *WIN a Winner?,* CAL. L.
BUS., Nov. 8, 1993, at 8, 29 (... "if any group is to be blamed for WIN's slow start, it is the
librarians ... [who] complain that WIN searches are imprecise and cumbersome."); Sheilla
E. Désert, *Westlaw is Natural v. Boolean Searching: A Performance Study,* 85 LAW LIBR. J.
713 (1993) (complex queries may not be effectively handled by WIN since the system may
not recognize certain legal phrases or terms and the WIN program is oblivious to date of
decision, which may result in inappropriate relevance rankings, the author recommends
the use of both Boolean and natural language techniques to assure accurate and complete
results).

tion, FREESTYLE may be used in conjunction with FOCUS by highlighting important terms in the search results, which may not have been part of the user's initial FREESTYLE query.

FREESTYLE offers additional feedback to assist the user in evaluating search results. The WHERE screen (Figure 1) provides a chart indicating the ranked order of search terms and the document numbers containing each of those terms.

Figure 1.

```
┌─────────────────────────────────────────────────────────────────┐
│       LOCATION OF TERMS IN FIRST 25 DOCUMENTS (.where)            │
│                                                                   │
│ Document numbers are listed across the top of the chart.          │
│ Terms are listed down the side in order of importance.  Asterisks (*) │
│ indicate the existence of terms in documents.  To view a document, enter │
│ the document number.                                              │
│                                                                   │
│                                    1              2               │
│                       1 2 3 4 5 6 7 8 9 0 1 2 3 4 5 6 7 8 9 0 1 2 3 4 5 │
│  ADOPTED CHILDREN                 *         *       *             │
│         BIOLOGICAL    * * * * * *   *     * * * *     *     * * *  │
│             REGAIN    *     *   *   * *             * *         *  │
│           ADOPTION    * * * * * * * *   * * * * * * * * * * * * *  │
│            PARENTS    * * * * * * * * * * * * * * * * * * * * * *  │
│            CUSTODY    * * * * * * * * * * * * * * *   * * * * * *  │
│                                                                   │
│ <=1> Return to browse                                             │
│ <=2> Number of documents with terms  (.why)                       │
└─────────────────────────────────────────────────────────────────┘
```

The WHY screen (Figure 2) shows the level of importance assigned to each term in a user's FREESTYLE query. WHY summarizes the results of a FREESTYLE search indicating the order in which documents were ranked, the total number of retrieved documents containing one's FREESTYLE search terms, the number of documents that match, and the significance assigned each FREESTYLE search term.

Figure 2.

```
┌─────────────────────────────────────────────────────────────┐
│   NUMBER OF DOCUMENTS WITH SEARCH TERMS (.why)              │
│                                                             │
│                    Documents    Documents   Term Importance │
│                    Retrieved    Matched        (1-100)      │
│                                                             │
│   ADOPTED CHILDREN     3           17             31        │
│        BIOLOGICAL     16           88             21        │
│           REGAIN       8          126             19        │
│         ADOPTION      25         1145              8        │
│          PARENTS      23         2204              5        │
│          CUSTODY      23         3487              4        │
│                                                             │
│   Total Retrieved:    25                                    │
│                                                             │
│   <=1> Return to browse                                     │
│   <=2> Location of terms  (.where)                          │
└─────────────────────────────────────────────────────────────┘
```

Other options are available on FREESTYLE not shown in the figures above. For example, FREESTYLE permits a user to require that a term appear in each document retrieved. By entering "=2" when viewing the search option screen one may type those mandatory terms, even terms that were not part of the original description.

By typing "=3" FREESTYLE permits the user to restrict a search by date, a name of a party, or judge, if appropriate to the LEXIS–NEXIS file being searched.

Access to an online legal thesaurus is available by entering "=4." A list of terms in a user's FREESTYLE search having available synonyms appears. The thesaurus provides alternative forms of the terms in one's initial FREESTYLE query and synonyms for terms. At the user's option, one or all of the alternative terms and synonyms may be selected and then added to the FREESTYLE search.

FREESTYLE recognizes legal phrases in a user's search and identifies them with quotation marks, e.g., "directed verdict." Users may also create their own phrases by placing quotation marks around the phrase's words. Phrases are generally given more relevancy for results than single terms.

4. Efficient Query Formulation

In developing a search strategy a user should keep in mind the following steps.

First, select the library and file in LEXIS–NEXIS or the database and file in WESTLAW that is likely to contain the information needed. Remember the structure of courts outline in Chapter 3, Section F [Illustration 1–1] and concepts of precedent as discussed in Chapter 1 in making that determination.

Next, recognizing the ambiguous nature of language, consider all the ways in which the idea trying to be located may be expressed. Remember the TARP analysis (thing, action, relationship, and parties) outlined in Chapter 2 when trying to isolate an appropriate key word using the *National Reporter System.*

Think in terms of the idiomatic nature of language and the use of synonyms. Keep in mind terms of art, or legalese,[6] that are frequently used in legal writing. Try to express a search according to the way the words or phrases may appear in the variety of documents the computer searches and in what relationship, both physical and syntactical, the words and phrases may be used. Recognize that no search strategy is perfect and understand that there is no assurance that every document located satisfies one's personal expression of the idea for which the search strategy was designed.

Structure the search efficiently. Use segments and fields to limit the search to appropriate portions of the physical document. It may be difficult to express the idea one is trying to locate. This is particularly so in emerging areas of the law where no consistent form of expression or "buzz-word" has developed. Recognize that our federal form of government and consequent court structure foster the use of regional and local forms of expression with which the user may not be familiar. There are ways of overcoming the imprecise nature of language using the software capabilities inherent in LEXIS–NEXIS and WESTLAW. When "buzz-words" are not readily available, opting for the use of WESTLAW's WIN or LEXIS–NEXIS' FREESTYLE search method may be helpful.

WESTLAW permits the use of its online thesaurus not only in natural language searching searches, but in terms and connector or Boolean searches too. Use the terms and connectors query editor to access the WESTLAW thesaurus by clicking on the thesaurus button.

Consider using a traditional thesaurus.[7] A thesaurus indicates the variety of ways that one particular concept may be expressed using different words. An example is our canine and dog hypothetical. That example is simplistic, considering the complexity of legal ideas, but a thesaurus may be helpful.

WESTLAW has developed or incorporated features that serve as synthetic thesauri to assist a user in the search expression of a legal principle when formulating a search strategy. These features should be called upon in searches dealing with emerging legal principles, areas of the law where one is unfamiliar with the "buzz-word" language, or documents that may be flavored by regional expressions. These search techniques may augment WESTLAW's WIN thesaurus capabilities.

The Key Number system on WESTLAW, the same used in West's *American Digest System,* is an outline of legal concepts found in American jurisprudence. The breadth of jurisprudence digested by the *National Reporter System* and outlined using West's Key Numbers is formidable (see Chapter 6). Most legal concepts known in our legal system have received an appropriate place within this outline.

---

[6] *See* BRYAN A. GARNER, A DICTIONARY OF MODERN LEGAL USAGE (2d ed. 1995).

[7] WILLIAM C. BURTON, LEGAL THESAURUS (2d ed. 1992).

Including a West Key Number as a component of a search facilitates identifying concepts that defy expression in language with which one is not familiar. The use of Key Numbers as an index is less successful when applied to new legal principles. Once a particular jurisdiction has developed a principle, the Key Number assigned to represent the legal concept should be used by the West Group editors consistently and, hence, can be used in searching the jurisprudence of another jurisdiction. Keep in mind, however, that the Key Number system is not always consistent and the user is relying on the judgment of the West Group editors in assigning the appropriate Key Numbers.

Remember that this application for Key Number searching applies only to material subjected to the West editorial and case analysis process. Obviously, this approach cannot be used when searching the databases containing secondary materials, statutory materials, administrative materials, or unpublished court cases.

The use of Key Numbers does not assure foolproof access to information in the WESTLAW database. Such an approach, however, can be a helpful strategy in developing a search. Future developments of embedded thesauri, such as in WIN or FREESTYLE, and the applications of artificial intelligence[8] to both services promise to enhance the value of both LEXIS–NEXIS and WESTLAW.

5. Manipulating Search Results on LEXIS–NEXIS and WESTLAW

LEXIS–NEXIS and WESTLAW accommodate the ambiguous nature of language through their search strategies and their flexibility in

---

[8] Future enhancements to automation and technology will consider the application of artificial intelligence to the breadth of legal information contained in CALR databases. On the subject of artificial intelligence or "expert" computer systems and legal research and analysis, see generally ANNE VON DER LIETH GARDNER, AN ARTIFICIAL INTELLIGENCE APPROACH TO LEGAL REASONING (1987). Gardner examines legal reasoning through a variety of legal theories including legal realism, legal positivism, and mechanical jurisprudence and attempts to present a framework for computational legal reasoning. Criticism of current CALR software search mechanisms in full-text legal research databases and the need to introduce knowledge-based systems along with artificial intelligence is outlined in RICHARD E. SUSSKIND, EXPERT SYSTEMS IN THE LAW (1987). *See also* PAMELA N. GRAY, ARTIFICIAL LEGAL INTELLIGENCE 202 (1997) (friendliness and the commercial viability of artificial legal intelligence entail an overlap of survival [the study of law as the detail of human survival methods] and technological jurisprudence), Andrew Terrett, *Using Artificial Intelligence to Teach Legal Reasoning*, COMPUTERS & L., Apr./May 1994, at 33, Edwina L. Rissland, *Artificial Intelligence and Law: Stepping Stones to a Model of Legal Reasoning*, 99 YALE L.J. 1957 (1990); Cary G. Debessonet & George R. Cross, *An Artificial Intelligence Application in the Law*, 1 HIGH TECH. L.J. 329 (1986) (describes the application of artificial intelligence to problem solving involving Louisiana's Civil Code); Richard Gruner, *Thinking Like a Lawyer*, 1 HIGH TECH. L.J. 259 (1986) (provides specific artificial intelligence applications to legal problem solving); Christopher C. Metzger, Comment, *Research Pathfinder: Expert Systems and the Law*, 1 HIGH TECH. L.J. 559 (1986) (a complete, but now somewhat outdated bibliography on the literature of artificial intelligence applications to legal reasoning).

A law review that began in 1992, *Artificial Intelligence and the Law,* is directed exclusively to artificial intelligence issues and should be regularly reviewed for issues related to the application of artificial intelligence to legal problem solving.

manipulating one's search results. To determine the success of a user's search request or query, both systems display the number of cases or documents that satisfy a request. If the number of documents or cases is too large to be a manageable amount of information to review, the user may modify the search.

On LEXIS–NEXIS that modification is known as establishing another *search level*. Establish the next level by narrowing the original search request. Do this by adding another word or phrase, preceded by a connector, to the initial search or by adding a restrictive field search preceded by a connector. The additional request is then matched against the already defined set of documents that satisfied the initial inquiry. Those documents that satisfy the amended inquiry are then available for review. A good example of a restrictive field search is instructing the computer to display those cases or documents that were published during a particular time period. Any modification of LEXIS–NEXIS for searching another level of documents must begin with a connector, e.g., AND, OR, in order to tie the two searches together. WESTLAW does not permit modification of search results by establishing another search level.

In lieu of establishing another search level, a user may wish to concentrate on new terms discovered after reviewing the first level. This is the appropriate opportunity to use the LEXIS–NEXIS FOCUS feature to highlight specific terms in documents already retrieved. WESTLAW's LOCATE feature may be used similarly.

You may also use the LEXIS–NEXIS LINK feature to move directly to documents that are cited in a retrieved document to assist you in determining the relevancy to your research of the document you are viewing. LINK is a hypertext feature. Simply type the equal sign "=" followed by the number that appears before the citation in the viewed document. Press ENTER and you will be "linked" to the citation you requested. By pressing ENTER again you will return to your previously retrieved document.

LEXIS–NEXIS permits one to review the documents that satisfy the search request in several ways. The user may review a list of citations to the documents or cases, review the documents or cases in their entirety or FULL format, and also review the documents in KWIC format. The search software highlights term or terms from the search request with twenty-five words on each side of the highlighted term taken from the document that satisfied the initial or modified search request. This permits you to quickly review the results of the search to determine if the research has been satisfactory. That determination is for the user, based on one's level of expertise with the subject area and application of common law precedent analysis. A user's individual analysis should be similar to the TARP analysis engaged in when developing the initial search request.

Considering the pricing factors discussed earlier, a user may wish to review all cases online, download the documents to a disk for off-line review, or simply print a list of citations and use the actual reporters or print form of the document to review the search results in more depth. A clear advantage in using the database in the online mode occurs when LEXIS–NEXIS or WESTLAW is used in conjunction with a personal computer and appropriate word processing software, which allows you to move a portion of the database text into the document being prepared and then return immediately to the database for additional research. Your search skills and own individual desktop automation facilities have to guide one's judgment.

WESTLAW permits you to refine the results of a Boolean search by changing the original search request. WESTLAW also permits one to use the LOCATE function to isolate cases or documents in the already identified search results. LOCATE is a search within a search. LOCATE instructs WESTLAW to look for terms from an initial query or new terms not originally in the initial request. Using LOCATE on WEST-LAW permits you to reduce the number of documents that must be reviewed from the initial search request.

Similar to LEXIS–NEXIS' KWIC display, WESTLAW permits you to display a document by browsing by search term. Term browsing displays only those pages of a document or a case that have a term or terms that satisfy the initial query. The terms are highlighted. LOCATE also provides a similar display.

Like LEXIS–NEXIS, WESTLAW offers a hypertext feature known as JUMP. JUMP permits you to move instantly within a particular document or between documents. JUMP links are easy to identify because they are preceded by a jump marker ">".

LEXIS–NEXIS and WESTLAW can be used to produce a citation list if one wishes to read the identified materials in print format.

Both LEXIS–NEXIS and WESTLAW permit you to quickly locate a document without the need of developing a search strategy. On LEXIS–NEXIS, LEXSEE permits locating a document other than a statute, which requires the LEXSTAT command, assuming you have a valid citation. On WESTLAW, the FIND command retrieves a specific case or statute after you input a valid citation. If you have already searched the databases using a search strategy and are viewing a document identified by that search strategy, using JUMP and LINK avoids the need to use, FIND, LEXSEE, or LEXSTAT to locate a document that is cited in a document one is currently viewing.

6. Using LEXIS–NEXIS and WESTLAW as Citators

LEXIS–NEXIS and WESTLAW both provide methods for using their databases as citators along with access to *Shepard's Citations*. Besides Shepard's, LEXIS–NEXIS and WESTLAW offer their own case history citation systems known as Auto–Cite and KeyCite respectively (see Chapter 15).

a. *LEXIS–NEXIS and WESTLAW Proximity Connectors as Citators*. Proximity connectors serve as a mechanism to locate all occurrences of a particular citation appearing in the LEXIS–NEXIS and WESTLAW databases. This approach can be used for locating references to statutory titles and section numbers. For example, an article appearing in 45 WIDGET L. REV. 123 may have all occurrences of citations to that article's volume and page number searched in LEXIS–NEXIS or WESTLAW.

A suggested search on LEXIS–NEXIS would be:

      45 pre/5 123

On WESTLAW only: 45 pre/5 123 or 45 + 5123

In each example, the search software locates every occurrence where the number 45 (the volume number) precedes the number 123 (the page number) by five words or less. This search, of course, is not perfect as all documents with the same volume and starting page are retrieved.

Make use of proximity connectors, discussed earlier, that require the database to identify references to numbers in a particular sequence. On WESTLAW use the +nor connector; on LEXIS–NEXIS use the pre/n or +n connector.

LEXIS–NEXIS also acts as a citator using its LEXCITE feature. LEXCITE locates references to cases including parallel citations appearing in LEXIS–NEXIS database libraries of cases, law review articles, agencies, and the *Federal Register*. To use LEXCITE, select a library and file and type LEXCITE with the citation in parenthesis.

    b. *Online Versions of Shepard's Citations.* Both LEXIS–NEXIS and WESTLAW provide access to *Shepard's Citations.* The capability exists to shepardize the case viewed on the screen by clicking a Shepard's icon on WINDOWS-based LEXIS–NEXIS or WESTLAW software. The use of Shepard's on WESTLAW is restricted to cases and statutes. On WEST-LAW all citing references to Shepard's are merged into one document instead of retrieving a different Shepard's report for each Shepard's title. When shepardizing on WESTLAW you can restrict your search results and request to only view citations providing specific treatment or history information in Shepard's, view citing references after a certain date or review citations from a specific publication, court or headnote. To retrieve citing references to secondary sources on WESTLAW, such as legal periodicals, use the technique we describe using WESTLAW as a citator.

Shepard's is also available on LEXIS–NEXIS covering a wide variety of legal information including: federal and state case law, federal and state statutory materials, law reviews, federal administrative regulations, patents, and federal rules. You may shepardize a citation by typing "shep" followed by a citation or by clicking on the appropriate tool bar icon. You may then restrict your Shepard's results to negative analysis, positive analysis, any analysis, or to reference to a particular headnote, date, analysis or jurisdiction. You can jump to the actual citing case using LINK markers that appear on the screen. LEXIS–NEXIS maintains a separate CITES library containing its citator services including

Shepard's that you can go directly to after signing-on to begin to check the authority of legal precedent using the Shepard's database.

Both LEXIS–NEXIS and WESTLAW provide their own case history capabilities. LEXIS–NEXIS calls its service Auto–Cite. Auto–Cite permits the user to verify the correct name and official and parallel citations for a case, to check the current validity of a case, and to review a case's prior and subsequent history, including negative indirect history. WEST-LAW's case history service is known as KeyCite.

c. *KeyCite.* WESTLAW recently developed its own citation service to compliment and compete with Shepard's citators. KeyCite provides information regarding a cases' case history including prior and subsequent history, negative indirect history (cases impacting negatively on the cited case, but not within the cited case's appellate history), citing references that cite to and discuss the cited case, verification of the components of a cite and citations from secondary sources citing to the cited case, including law review articles and *American Law Reports.*

KeyCite can be customized so that you view only the treatment of the cited case that interests you. In addition, KeyCite permits you to restrict your search by headnotes and topics that appear in the cited case.

A novel feature of KeyCite is its attempt to analyze the value of the citing case's discussion of the cited case by reference to the length of discussion in the citing cases opinion devoted to the cited case. KeyCite offers four criteria to distinguish the relative value of the citing cases discussion of the cited case:

Examined represented on the KeyCite display by ****

> an extended discussion of the cited case devoted to usually more than one page of printed text

Discussed represented on the KeyCite display by ***

> the cited case contains a substantial discussion of the cited case devoting usually more than a paragraph to the cited case, but less than a page of text

Cited represented on the KeyCite display by **

> the discussion of the cited case is less than a paragraph of text in the citing case

Mentioned represented on the KeyCite display by *

> usually a brief reference to the cited case in the citing case limited sometime to the mere presence of the cited case's citation in a string cite.

Combining KeyCite with the treatment of the case offers a substantial understanding of the relative value of a citing case's discussion of a cited case. For example, if your interest is negative treatment of the cited case, you research will not be efficiently served if you review a case that merely mentions briefly the cited case in a string cite. Your research efficiency is better served if your review of citing cases is limited to more substantive discussion of the negative treatment found in a citing case that meets the "examined" or "discussed" criteria set out above. Key-Cite is discussed more fully in Chapter 15, Sections I and J. [See Illustrations 15–12 through 15–15 for examples of the points made in this section.]

Both LEXIS–NEXIS and WESTLAW have developed customized cite checking software packages. CheckCite, on LEXIS–NEXIS, isolates citations from one's word-processed document and uses Auto–Cite and *Shepard's* online to verify the validity and accuracy of the citation. The results are then printed or saved to disk. LEXIS' Quote Check can be used to verify quotations in a document against the quotation as it appears in the LEXIS database.

Similarly, WESTLAW offers WEST*Check,* which verifies citations using the WESTLAW database, KeyCite, or *Shepard's.* WEST*Check's* latest version extracts quotations from a document and checks them against the documents on WESTLAW containing the quotes. CiteLink is a powerful WESTLAW tool that finds legal citations in a user's Microsoft Word 97 document and creates links to the full text of the documents on the Internet via WestDoc or westlaw.com.

SECTION E. COMPACT DISKS

Compact disk technology, once considered a major technological advance in the storage and retrieval of legal information, is quickly being eclipsed by emerging Internet based technology. One CD–ROM disk is capable of holding 300,000 typed pages. Although the technology requires special equipment for the personal computer—a compact disk drive, an interface board, and special software—the user gains cost efficiency because a modem or a telephone line is not required to access a central database.

On the downside, users of compact disk technology have found the lack of search engine standards frustrating. Two compact disk search engines have emerged as the leaders for accessing compact disk contents-FOLIO and Premise. Neither works well in a networked environment resulting in compact disk users being limited to sole practitioners and the small law office settings. Some larger academic law libraries have experienced greater success with compact disk technology by moving the information from the compact disk onto network servers. Therefore the availability, search software, and format of legal information placed on compact disks will vary greatly among institutions, law firms, and law libraries.

The primary publishers or vendors of CD–ROM products include major looseleaf service vendors-Bureau of National Affairs, Commerce Clearing House, Matthew Bender & Company, Research Institute of America, West Group, LEXIS Law Publishing, and Shepard's.

Indexing services are becoming more prevalent in CD–ROM and online formats. The CD format of the *Index to Legal Periodicals* is known as the *Index to Legal Periodicals and Books.* The search engine is proprietary software known as Wilsondisc. An online version of the product is available through LEXIS–NEXIS and WESTLAW. Updates to the CD–ROM product may also be accomplished on line using WILSON-LINE.

IAC's *Legal Resource Index* is available through a CD–ROM product prepared by Silver Platter Information using a proprietary search engine. The information is also available on the Internet and on LEXIS–NEXIS and WESTLAW.

For United States legislative history research the Congressional Information Services's *Congressional Masterfile 1 & 2* includes all CIS' congressional materials indexes prior to 1969 and abstracts and indexes drawn from the CIS legislative history service since 1970. Both CD–ROM products are available through the CIS web based product CIS Universe, formerly known as the CIS Compass Service. A variety of other sources are available on compact disk. Consulting a directory of CD–ROM products will provide a sense of the scope and content of many additional products.[9]

SECTION F. THE INTERNET[10]

1. General Considerations

The Internet began in the 1960s as an experimental wide-area network run by the U.S. Department of Defense. In its early years, the Internet was used exclusively by the scientific community. The Internet is now the largest computer network in the world. The number of users is now in the hundreds of millions and adding new users at an extraordinary pace.[11] Increasingly the Internet is providing access to vast amounts of legal information. By far the Internet has become the most robust technology for new sources of law and legally-related information. Com-

---

[9] The DIRECTORY OF LAW-RELATED CD–ROMS 1998 (Arlene L. Eis ed. annual), a publication of Infosources Publishing with updates three times a year in a newsletter LAW RELATED CD–ROM UPDATE, lists more than 1200 titles available on CD–ROM. Each CD–ROM product entry provides information on the publisher or distributor of the CD–ROM product, the search engine software required for the product, compatible CD–ROM drives, minimum equipment specifications, the products network capability, site license and network fees, availability of a print equivalent, the language the CD–ROM product is written in, whether the product is also available on the Internet including the products Uniform Resource Locator, update frequency and coverage dates of the product, the number of CD–ROM discs, a description of the CD–ROM's contents and features, citations to published reviews of the CD–ROM product, and the toll-free support telephone number, if available, for the product. This directory is an essential tool to identifying products in the CD–ROM format that meet your information requirements along with providing basic technical information to ascertain the products compatibility with your existing computer environment.

[10] The Internet is creating a new specialty in the practice of law. If you are interested in legal issues involving the Internet see JON A. BAUMGARTEN, BUSINESS & LEGAL GUIDE TO ONLINE INTERNET LAW (1997); GEORGE B. DELTA & JEFFREY H. MATSUURA, LAW OF THE INTERNET (1997); JONATHAN ROSENOER, CYBERLAW: THE LAW OF THE INTERNET (1997); F. LAWRENCE STREET, LAW OF THE INTERNET (1997).

[11] In remarks delivered on March 18, 1998, President Clinton, speaking in Las Vegas, NV, noted, "When I became president, there were 50 Web sites on the Internet. Now 65,000 are being added every hour." LEXIS–NEXIS, FDCH Political Transcripts, March 18, 1998 (Mr. Clinton assumed the presidency in 1993).

prised of millions of individual web sites, the Internet, through the world wide web, offers a seamless electronic highway of information maintained by individuals, for profit and not for profit organizations, and educational institutions.

In recent years, commercial providers of legal information have exploited the Internet as an efficient medium for distributing their products while avoiding the need to maintain costly proprietary network communication systems and the technical difficulties inherent to CD–ROM technology. Once the province of free information, the Internet's future is likely to offer a combination of no-cost and fee for use web sites.

a. *Web Site Addresses or Uniform Resource Locators.* Under Internet protocols, each web site receives a unique address (which must be registered with a central web site registration service such as Network Solutions to avoid duplicate web site addresses) or uniform resource locator, better known as a URL, A URL address permits direct access to a particular web site. A URL is comprised of the web site name and a domain indicating the web site's sponsor and the nature of the sponsoring organization. For example, the address for the web site at the Legal Information Institute at Cornell Law School is:

www.law.cornell.edu

Each element of the address stands for the following:

www	=	world wide web
law	=	the subdivision at the Cornell University web site responsible for maintaining this web site, in this address the subdivision is the university's law school
cornell	=	the web site's sponsoring institution—Cornell University
edu	=	indicates the sponsoring institution is an educational institution

Occasionally you may find, preceding a web site address, the phrase "http://". "Http://" instructs your computer to look for a web site address on the Internet that appears in hyper-text protocol. Hypertext protocol permits the web site to support links to other web sites that compliment or expand upon the information available at the initial web site you accessed. In the Cornell Legal Information web site example the complete URL may be represented as: http://www.law.cornell.edu. As Internet search engines become more sophisticated including "http" in the address is becoming obsolete.

Note that in the Cornell example the address indicated "edu" identifying Cornell University as an educational institution. There are other types of organization indications within world wide web site addresses including "org" for general organizations, "gov" for government agencies, "com" for commercial entities, and "net" for computer-related organizations. You will also find in government-related addresses a further designation for the sponsoring government, for example, "gov. au" indicates the government sponsored site is located in Australia.

b. *Search Engines*. Today you can use any number of search engines to "surf the net" to locate web sites for which you may not have the actual address or URL. These search engines include: Alta Vista, Excite, FindLaw's Law Crawler [See Illustration 22–1], Infoseek [See Illustration 22–2], Lycos, and Yahoo among other. Each search engine will support rather primitive word searches when compared to the Boolean and natural language searching capability of LEXIS–NEXIS and WESTLAW.

Because of web site proliferation and the inadequate search capability of search engines, hits by search engine software are usually too numerous for efficient research. Each search engine will permit some fine tuning of the initial web sites located by the search engine, particularly for search engines that support index searching which permits the researcher to narrow the number of web site hits by adding more restrictive elements to each search. This is similar to level searching on LEXIS–NEXIS.

Some search engines attempt to bring order to the millions of web sites on the world wide web. Aiming to provide structure and guidance, search engines such as Excite, Infoseek and Yahoo, assign web sites to various topic headings. Through the process of reviewing web sites for categorization, those sites that promote illegal activities are eliminated from the search engine topic headings. All web sites, however, are not reviewed for categorization and may remain available through the search engine's term search capabilities or by simply pointing your web browser to the web address.

In addition, search engines provide brief abstracts of the web site contents. Many of these abstracts also prove to be inadequate to experienced researchers. The information provided in the abstract is generally insufficient to determine the value of the site to your research. Further examination of the web site's actual content is generally necessary.

Under the auspices of the American Association of Law Libraries and Aspen Law and Business Research, a search engine specifically designed for law—LIBClient—was developed in 1996.[12] Access to this software is limited to the LIBClient web site. LIBClient is not currently available through commercial search engine providers. LIBClient is specifically designed to search case law, legislation, regulations, and treaties while considering state, federal, and international jurisdictional limitations.

An additional search engine specifically designed for legal materials is LawCrawler. LawCrawler is built on the Alta Vista search engine and is available through the FindLaw web site. LawCrawler permits the

---

[12] Robert C. Vreeland & Bert J. Dempsey, *Toward a Truly Seamless Web: Bringing Order to Law on the Internet*, 88 LAW LIBR. J. 469 (1996) (outlines the need for a search engine specific to legal materials and how the features of LIBClient address those needs).

definition of materials by the researcher restricting searches to materials found on or linked to the LawFind web site including law reviews, government sponsored web sites, the *United States Code*, and opinions of the United States Supreme Court since 1906.

A new generation of search engines will soon provide for Boolean searching and relevancy searching (similar to the natural language searches available on LEXIS–NEXIS and WESTLAW).

Search engines will only search documents that are prepared in HTML format. Some documents, notably documents prepared by government agencies, may be prepared in PDF format or Word 6.0 format. Neither of these protocols are supported by most search engines. Therefore, searching the net for a web site in non-HTML format may result in unsatisfactory search results.

To address the problems researchers encounter when relying solely upon search engines to locate relevant web sites, many experienced researchers initiate their search at an omnibus web site. Omnibus web sites provide links to select web sites. The linked web sites are chosen because of their ability to enhance the scope of information available on the omnibus web site. To access a linked web site point your computer's browser (Netscape Navigator or Microsoft Explorer) to the omnibus web site's link (generally indicated by underlining, boldface type, or a particular graphic) and double click. The hypertext protocol discussed earlier permits the web to immediately locate and make available the linked site.

2. Drawbacks to the Internet[13]

Web sites now come in two varieties: sites that are free and available to the general public and sites that require a license or fee to access. Many non-fee based web sites are maintained by individuals, non-profit organizations, or educational institutions. Researchers will be wise to recognize that information available from such sites may not always provide accurate or timely information. Such non-fee based sites may not include editorial management to assure the researcher appropriate editorial content. Most sites, even non-fee based sites, are maintained with great care and integrity reliably serving your information needs. Particularly educational institutions that make their sites available without a fee provide superb levels of information consistent with the institutions academic integrity.

Fee-based sites rely upon technology to admit only authorized or licensed users to the information contained in the site. Typically, a fee-based site relies upon the internal computer internet protocol address, or IP address, to secure access to their sites. IP addresses uniquely identify the computer accessing the site. Sometimes computers attach to a fee-based site through a network. The network will provide the site with the equivalent of an IP address authorizing those using the network as

---

[13] CLIFFORD STOLL. SILICON SNAKE OIL: SECOND THOUGHTS ON THE INFORMATION HIGHWAY 4 (1995) (" ... the medium is being oversold, our expectations have become bloated.... ").

licensed users of the web site. Keep in mind then that web sites that may be accessible to you through a computer network at your educational institution may not be available to you from your home. However, your educational institution may have made arrangements for you to dial into the institution's network from your home to provide you with access to fee-based sites through the institution's network

Finally, remember the caveats mentioned earlier regarding the distinction between ownership and access to information in the LEXIS–NEXIS and WESTLAW context. Web sites come and go daily, a site useful to your research in previous projects may, without notice, convert to a fee-based site or may simply be removed from the world wide web because the web site owner chooses not to maintain the site. Web site addresses or URLs change frequently requiring a researcher to "surf the web" using a search engine to locate the web site. In effect, the Internet is a flexible creation of technology subject to all the frailties and idiosyncracies we encounter daily in the age of electronic information.

3. Getting to the Internet

To access the Internet you need an Internet Service Provider or ISP. If you are affiliated with an organization that offers a local area network most likely the ISP is available through the network. In a networked environment you may either connect to the ISP through a direct or hard connection from your computer to the network or through dial-up access to the network using a standard telephone line and modem.

If you need to access the Internet in a non-networked setting you may obtain access to the Internet directly through an ISP. Major telecommunications carriers such as AT&T, MCI, Sprint Communications, including local telephone companies, offer Internet access. In addition, Internet-only service is available through many providers including America On–Line and Earthlink. In the non-networked setting your computer will require a modem to access your ISP. Most ISP's support modem speeds up to 56K, a modem capable of transmitting 56,000 bits of information per second.

To access the Internet through your ISP your computer must have software that is able to communicate with the Internet. Many personal computers sold today preload this software into the personal computer. There are two major software providers for this type of software generally referred to as Internet browser software—Netscape Navigator and Microsoft Explorer. Each permit access to the Internet and provide access to several search engines that were discussed earlier. In addition, the browser software provides an address line on their introductory screen. If you know the address of a web site of recurring interest, you can enter the site's address on the address line and the browser will take you directly to the web site. You can maintain a list of frequently-referenced web sites using the Internet browser's bookmark feature. Your Internet browser also supports printing from web sites. You will find the search engine, bookmark, and print features on your browser software's icon tool bar.

4. Noteworthy Law and Law–Related Web Sites

With the proliferation of web sites and the inherent weaknesses in search engines a technological irony has occurred. The best source for locating web sites appropriate to law and law-related research may be to consult a web site print bibliography. Isn't it ironic that we must locate information in a book to find information in cyberspace? A highly-selective print bibliography of law-related Internet sites is contained in Appendix G.

Especially noteworthy law and law related cyber-bibliographies include: Yvonne Chandler's *Guide to Finding Legal and Regulatory Information on the Internet* (Neil–Schuman NetGuide Series, 1998); Don MacLeod, *The Internet Guide for the Legal Researcher* (2d ed., Infosources Publishing, 1997); James Evans, *Law on the Net* (2d ed., Nolo Press, 1997); and *The Legal List: Internet Desk Reference* (Lawyer's Cooperative Publishing, 1996). For references to law-related and non-law web sites consult *Web Site Source Book: A Guide to Major U.S. Businesses, Organizations, Agencies, Institutions, and Other Information Resources on the World Wide Web* (Omnigraphics, 1998) and the *Gale Guide to Internet Databases* (Gale, 1998). If your interest is limited to information distributed on the Internet through the United States Federal Depository Act consider Greg R. Notess' *Government Information on the Internet* (Bernan Press, 1997).

An excellent source of new web sites appearing in the periodical literature is James Evans' "Legal Sites" column in the *California Lawyer*. Each monthly column focuses on particular legal subjects. "Legal Sites" considers free and fee-based web sites. Because this column is a monthly feature it may provide you more timely information on new web sites than some cyber-bibliographies.

Other periodicals and newsletters that may prove helpful in identifying useful law and law-related web sites include: *Internet Connection* (Bernan Press); *Internet Law Researcher* (Glasser Legal Works); *The Internet Lawyer: Navigating the Internet for the Legal Profession* (GoAhead Publications); and *Internet Reference Services Quarterly* (Haworth Press).

Noteworthy among the cyber-bibliographies discussed above is Professor Chandler's *Guide to Finding Legal and Regulatory Information on the Internet*. This guide provides a comprehensive explanation of the technology of the Internet while covering traditional forms of legal information (judicial, administrative, and legislative) on the state and federal jurisdictional levels. The author rounds out her cyber-bibliography by including sources of foreign and international legal materials on the Internet. Not to be missed are Professor Chandler's "Best Bets" recommendations on the research value of numerous sites available on the web.

Although there is a substantial and continuing proliferation of law web sites, it is worthwhile considering several major sites sponsored by academic institutions. By no means is this a comprehensive list. Many academic institutions, notably law schools and their libraries, have launched web sites that provide information and links to other web sites that support their academic programs. Web sites of a more comprehensive nature, sponsored and maintained by law schools include:

Legal Information Institute at *Cornell Law School*. The Legal Information Institute is best known as a site for searchable court opinions, rules, and important uniform and federal statutes. The site includes an e-mail directory of law school faculty and staff. In addition, the site culls through newsworthy items appearing on law-based list servs and distills items of notable content on this site. [See Illustration 4–1.]

Washburn University's WashLaw web site. Considered the best all-round law web site, Washburn offers an enormous array of links to other law and law-related web sites in and outside of academics including law firms, government agencies, and bar associations. WashLaw also offers its own web site search engine supporting Boolean searches. [See Illustration 22–3.]

Center for Information Law and Policy. Provides comprehensive links to federal government and federal court web sites, along with state government and court web sites. The site includes links to international law materials and tax law and law-related materials. The site includes a virtual law library by linking to the Center's own publications. [See Illustration 4–12.]

Government information web sites of note include:

United States Supreme Court. This is in the Cornell site listed above. It includes all decisions of the United States Supreme Court from May 1990 current along with links to web sites containing earlier opinions of the Court. This site also includes the calendar of oral argument and the current term's docket. [See Illustration 4–1.]

Opinions of the United States Circuit Courts of Appeals. Opinions from the federal circuit courts for the most part reside at numerous law school sponsored web sites including: first (Emory University's web site) [See Illustration 4–14], second (Pace and Touro Law Schools' web sites), third (Center for Information Law and Policy), fourth (Emory University's web site), fifth (maintained by the fifth circuit), sixth (Emory University's web site), seventh (Chicago–Kent College of Law's web site), eighth (Washington University's web site), ninth (Center for Information Law and Policy), tenth (Emory University's web site), eleventh (Emory University's web site), federal circuit (Emory University's web site), District of Columbia Circuit (Georgetown University's web site).

Other web sites of note:

FindLaw, developed by the Northern California Association of Law Libraries, and its associated search engine LawCrawler is a web site providing information from law reviews, codes and statutes, legal organizations, and specific legal subjects including constitutional, intellectual property, and labor law along with access to foreign and international resources and law school information. [See Illustration 22–1.]

Web sites sponsored by fee-based organizations:

LOIS. Also known as Law Office Information Systems, Inc., LOIS is a comprehensive web site of federal case law and statutes from the United States Supreme Court, all federal circuit courts, and the *United States Code* along with case law and statutes from selected state courts. The LOIS library offers a citator service permitting you to verify if your case is good law by comparing your cited case to the LOIS database. In addition, LOIS provides links to bar association and other law-related organizations. LOIS also offers a CD–ROM product known as the LOIS Professional Library, which includes caselaw from the United States Supreme Court and the United States Courts of Appeal, the *Code of Professional Responsibility*, and state law libraries including statutes, regulations, and appellate cases for 14 states.

VERSUS LAW. Versus law is a web-based database comprised of federal and state court appellate opinions. Decisions of the United States Supreme Court are available from 1930, while most federal appellate court decisions are available since 1950, with the exception of the eleventh circuit (1981) and the federal circuit (1982). State court appellate decisions go back to 1950 for most states, but for some states the files are limited to decisions starting as late as 1996. Versus Law also provides links from its web site to law school and law-related web sites, legal forms, and state web sites.

5. The Future of the Internet and Cyberspace

The Internet will continue to develop into a strong interactive network, but there is no certainty that investment in the multitude of Internet technology opportunities including infrastructure, browsers, and new standards for telecommunications is anything more than hype.[14] Products in our information age come and go and you must proceed cautiously in your evaluations of new technologies as they are applied to the storage and dissemination of legal information.

We generally know the shortcomings of today's Internet: search engines that do not permit researchers to narrow their search results into manageable quantities of relevant information; ISP's that do not properly gauge the market for their services causing frustration and inefficiency in legal research; and hardware manufacturers along with software developers that require you to replace their personal computers long before your initial investment in the equipment has been recouped. The advent of the next generation of the Internet will undoubtedly have consequences that will be remarkable and frustrating for the legal researcher. Any attempt to predict the Internet environment of the future is generally cast in terms of levity and sarcasm.[15]

---

[14] BILL GATES, THE ROAD AHEAD 259–283 (rev. ed. 1996).

[15] "The Next Generation Internet" in THE HARVARD CONFERENCE ON THE INTERNET & SOCIETY 88, 77–89 (O'Reilly & Associates, eds., 1996) ("I'm going to predict that there will be Internet light bulbs in 2005, When you screw them in, it will use the power wires in the

Although we do not know the ultimate form or standards for the coming ubiquitous world of cyberspace and telecommunications, we do know that technologies impact will be profound. The paradigm or structure that defines our legal research processes will certainly change. Our structural examination of legal research may focus on the role of telespace in the twenty-first century,[16] or our need to set an information technology agenda and its impact on the course of humanity and technology.[17] The economics of underwriting our developing technology[18] and the broadening and unlimited availability of legal and law-related information for our governmental institutions[19] will set boundaries and impose new limits on the applications of technology to the legal process.

We are barely beginning to understand the depths and heights of the Internet culture.[20] While its impact on legal research is already profound, the Internet's future defies ultimate definition.[21] Much as legal research is a process, the development of the Internet and the application of technology to legal research provides unlimited and unimagined possibilities.

SECTION G.   ILLUSTRATIONS OF INTERNET WEB SITES

22–1.   Home Page of FindLaw
22–2.   Home Page of Infoseek Search Engine
22–3.   Home Page of WashLaw Web

house to communicate with the light switch.") (quoting Mario Vecchi, Time–Warner Cable).

[16] LISA MASON, ARACHNE 14, 169 (1997) ("[n]egotiations, deal-making, deal-breaking, dispute resolution, mediation, compliance work, telespace administration ... lawyer[s] doing anything worth doing had to deal with telespace") (telespace was fast becoming the most sophisticated aspect of legal practice ... add[ing] telespace training ... to [the] juris doctorate program.").

[17] MICHAEL L. DERTOUZOS, WHAT WILL BE: HOW THE NEW WORLD OF INFORMATION WILL CHANGE OUR LIVES (1997).

[18] INTERNET ECONOMICS (Lee W. McKnight & Joseph P. Bailey eds., 1997).

[19] LAWRENCE K. GROSSMAN, THE ELECTRONIC REPUBLIC: RESHAPING DEMOCRACY IN THE INFORMATION AGE (1995).

[20] DINTY W. MOORE, THE EMPEROR'S VIRTUAL CLOTHES: THE NAKED TRUTH ABOUT INTERNET CULTURE (1995); INTERNET DREAMS: ARCHETYPES, MYTHS, AND METAPHORS (Mark Stefik, ed., 1996), INTERNET CULTURE XIII (David Porter, ed, 1997) ("[the Internet] give[s] rise to a unique and intriguing form of social space").

[21] MARK DERY, ESCAPE VELOCITY: CYBERCULTURE AT THE END OF THE CENTURY 8 (1996) ("cyberculture is approaching escape velocity, the speed at which a body overcomes the gravitational pull of another body, breaking free from limits of any sort").

[Illustration 22–1]

Home Page of FindLaw

FindLaw: Internet Legal Resources   http://www.findlaw.com/

LegalMinds Community   **Laws** Cases & Codes   **FindLaw** Internet Legal Resources   **LegalNews** Today's News   **LawCrawler** Web Search

US Supreme Court Cases 1893+ Free!

Why Surf When You Can Fly? LEXIS·NEXIS Xchange CLICK HERE

Free Web Sites for Legal Professionals

| Search | FindLaw Guide | ▼ |

[options]

LawCrawler - LegalMinds - Supreme Court Opinions - Law Reviews - Bookstore - Microsoft v. DOJ
Message Boards - Chat - Online CLE - Career Center - Legal Jobs - Legal News

Legal Subject Index
Constitutional, Intellectual Property Labor...

Law Schools
Law Reviews, Outlines, Student Resources...

Professional Development
Career Development, CLE, Employment...

Legal Organizations
National Bars, State Bars, Local Bars ...

Law Firms & Lawyers
Lawyers WWW sites, NLJ 250...

Consultants & Experts

Directories
Government, Yellow Pages, Phone, Maps...

Laws: Cases & Codes
Supreme Court Opinions, Constitution, State Laws...

U.S. Federal Government Resources

State Law Resources
California, New York, Texas...

Foreign & International Resources
Country Pages, Int'l Law, Int'l Trade...

News & Reference
Legal News, Library Information...

Legal Practice Materials
Forms, Publishers, Software & Technology...

LegalMinds - Community
Message Boards, Mailing List Archives, Chat...

FindLaw Wire: Updates, Legal Sites and News

| enter email | Subscribe |

☐ HTML Mail

Free Web Sites for the Legal Community
FindLaw Firms Online

FindLaw User Survey What Do You Want?

FindLaw California | CyberSpace Law Center
Law & Economics | Stanford Copyright and Fair Use Site

Advertising Info | Awards | Disclaimer

Help & Information | Table of Contents | Comments | Add URL
Copyright © 1994-98 FindLaw

[Illustration 22-2]

Home Page of Infoseek Search Engine

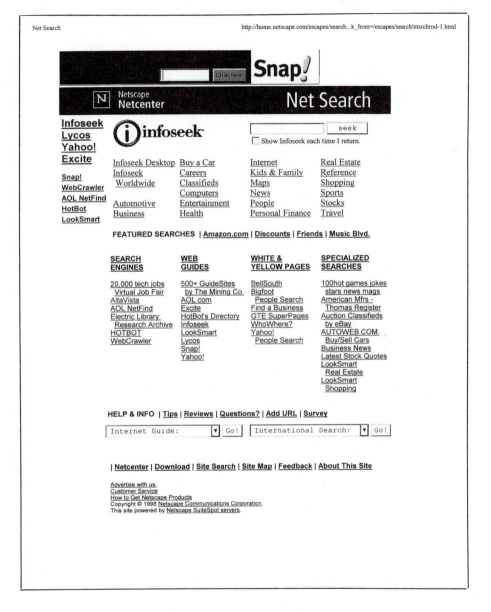

[Illustration 22–3]

Home Page of WashLaw Web

WashLaw WEB -- Washburn University School of Law   http://lawlib.wuacc.edu/washlaw/washlaw.intro.html

Washburn University School of Law
1700 College
Topeka, KS 66621
Phone (913) 231-1088, Fax (913) 232-8087
Add your site? .... TERMS and CONDITIONS .... Old Version

WashLaw WEB links you to law related resources on the Internet. In addition to specialized subject areas, you may access information about Law Schools and Law Libraries. You can search "full text" for the law and law journals, as well as browse law library catalogs. The Law Library hosts many law related web servers and listserv discussion groups. Special collections include the Brown vs Board of Education materials, and Kansas Court Decisions.

● Join a Discussion, ● Subscriber Instructions, ● Listserv Owner Intstructions, ● Table of Contents

Search WashLaw Server? Documentation about making queries is available.

Enter ◉ words describing a concept or ○ keywords:

◄	►	eXcite Search

Search All Local WashlawWeb Servers? Documentation about making queries is available.

Sample Query: montana AND law (note: connectors MUST be capitalized)

| | Harvest Search | Reset |

To use this Harvest Broker, you need a WWW browser that supports the Forms interface.

> **The WashLaw Web of Washburn University School of Law may well be the best site available for beginning law-related research on the Internet. It contains a staggering array of links to legal information and serves as the host site for many law-related listservs.**

Number of spelling errors allowed: [None ▼]

Result Set Options:

☐ Display matched lines

☑ Display object descriptions (if available)

☐ Display links to indexed content summary data for each result

☑ Verbose display

Maximum number of results (or matched lines) allowed: [25 ▼]

Send ✉ Comments to Mark Folmsbee, zzfolm@acc.wuacc.edu

Chapter 23

LEGAL CITATION FORM*

Citation form is required to communicate accurately the results of your legal research efforts. Citations express the location of the information gleaned from your research permitting consumers of that research effort to verify your conclusions. Citation form is the ultimate embodiment of precedent.

The chapter offers an overview of case law citation form referring to sixteenth edition of *The Bluebook: A Uniform System of Citation.* Case law citation form is used to illustrate the overall organizational structure of *The Bluebook.* In addition, a discussion of citation to electronic information in LEXIS–NEXIS and WESTLAW is considered along with suggestions for new citation standards designed to take advantage of legal information available in electronic storage mediums such as compact disk and the Internet (See Chapter 22).

SECTION A. INTRODUCTION TO LEGAL CITATION FORM

Citation form requires consistency. Consistency is imperative for two reasons. Those that rely on your research require efficiency when locating information discovered in that research or when verifying the appropriateness of information you used in reaching particular conclusions. Further, the advent of computer-assisted legal research requires unique forms for each citation in order to take advantage of the literalness of software designed to retrieve information stored in a variety of electronic mediums.

As is discussed in Chapter 22, computers are only able to isolate information expressed in the identical fashion to the request one provides in a search query. Without consistent citation forms, LEXIS–NEXIS and WESTLAW would be unable to locate every instance when a particular citation is used to support a proposition in a legal document, case, statute, or other expression of the proposition.

In the absence of consistent forms of expression, citations could only be located using *Shepard's Citations,*[1] Auto–Cite (LEXIS–NEXIS), Key-Cite (WESTLAW), or proximity connectors in computer-assisted legal research. Although Auto–Cite and KeyCite provide for selected variant forms of citations, a researcher has no way of knowing whether using a

* Prepared by Professor Robert J. Nissenbaum, Director of the William M. Rains Library and Professor of Law, Loyola Law School, Los Angeles. Professor Nissenbaum acknowledges the research assistance of Nadav Ravid, Loyola Law School, Los Angeles, Class of 1997, Joseph P. Buchman, Loyola Law School, Los Angeles, Class of 1990 and Ruth J. Hill, Head of Reference Services, William M. Rains Library, Loyola Law School, Los Angeles.

[1] Note that *Shepard's Citations* uses its own citation form for official and regional reporter cites.

particular citation form will be recognized by either Auto–Cite or Key–Cite. Both services then, despite some flexibility in citation form, thrive on consistency.

Proximity connectors and the LEXSEE and FIND commands can be used to locate all occurrences of citations in the scope of the LEXIS–NEXIS and WESTLAW databases. It is the completeness of both databases that poses the problem. As more information is available electronically, there is a higher incidence of sequential proximity connectors locating citations with identical volume, title and page, and section numbers from print materials.[2] For example, a search for a hypothetical case appearing at 42 U.S. 1983 would also retrieve all instances of citations to the more common statutory section in the *United States Code*. In effect, the electronic advantage of speed and accuracy is undermined by legal writers' inability to develop consistent citation formats.

Our discussion now turns to a system designed to assure uniformity in citation form.

SECTION B. THE ORIGIN OF CITATION FORM

1. The Bluebook: A Uniform System of Citation—Historical Development

Citation form was developed at the outset of the common law system to reflect case law dependency required under the legal system's concept of *stare decisis* and use of precedent.[3] With the development of American legal education during the nineteenth century, law schools provided intensive writing opportunities for their students and began to publish what have become today's law reviews. The editorial boards of the Harvard, Yale, Columbia, and Pennsylvania law reviews produced the first edition of *A Uniform System of Citation* in 1926 in response to the expense of printing their own reviews.[4]

The costs associated with typesetting detailed footnotes were greater than the cost of typesetting the text. By developing a consistent shorthand expression for citation form, these early editors were able to reduce both typesetting costs and the space required for footnotes.

---

[2] Recall from Chapter 22 that on LEXIS–NEXIS a search of:

42 pre/7 1983 or 42 + 7 1983

will locate all instances where the number 42 precedes the number 1983 by 7 words or less. A search on WESTLAW should yield a similar result. Any law review article with those elements in the citation along with any statute, case, or administrative rule would also be identified.

[3] For an excellent historical summary of citation form, *see* Byron D. Cooper, *Anglo–American Legal Citation: Historical Development and Library Implications*, 75 Law Libr. J. 3 (1982). For a general discussion of the advent of the footnote in scholarly and academic writing see Anthony Grafton, The Footnote: A Curious History (1997).

[4] Byron D. Cooper, *Anglo-American Legal Citation: Historical Development and Library Implications*, 75 Law Libr. J. 3, 21 (1982). With the 15th edition, the editors added "The Bluebook" to the *Uniform System's* title to more accurately reflect the common shorthand expression for the citation system.

Over time, *The Bluebook: A Uniform System of Citation,* now in its sixteenth edition,[5] became a widely-used standard. Typically, a first-year law student's right of passage into the legal profession required acquiring a detailed and accurate understanding of the variety of citation rules appearing in this citation manual.

Nevertheless, some jurisdictions and several other law reviews believed their individual jurisdictional citation needs were not adequately addressed by *The Bluebook.* Development of new technologically based sources of legal information using Internet and CD–ROM accessible databases also contributed to alternative citation systems to *The Bluebook.* Proponents of universal citation view their citation system as addressing the inefficiency inherent in having one or two dominant providers of legal information. Known as vendor-neutral citation, this new citation format will be discussed in greater detail later in this chapter. Consequently, alternative citation systems have developed to satisfy these perceived inefficiencies.[6]

2. The Rules of The Bluebook: A Uniform System of Citation[7]

The Bluebook: A Uniform System of Citation is a lengthy (365 pages), complex, and allegedly complete rendition of citation form. *The Bluebook* serves two functions: it acts as a guide to citation form and as a style manual for legal publication. Its periodic revision, including rule

---

[5] THE BLUEBOOK: A UNIFORM SYSTEM OF CITATION (16th ed. 1996) [hereinafter THE BLUEBOOK]. THE BLUEBOOK derives its name from its traditional blue cover.

[6] *The Universal Legal Citation Project: A Draft User Guide to the AALL Universal Statutory Citation,* 90 LAW LIBR. J. 91 (1998)(a draft guide presented for public study and comment to be directed to the American Association of Law Libraries' Committee on Citation Formats), *The Universal Legal Citation Project: A Draft User Guide to the AALL Universal Case Citation,* 89 LAW LIBR. J. 7 (1997)(a draft guide presented for public study and comment to be directed to the American Association of Law Libraries' Committee on Citation Formats).

The University of Chicago Law Review & The University of Chicago Legal Forum, *The University of Chicago Manual of Legal Citation,* 53 U. Chi. L. Rev. 1353 (1986). This *Manual* was subsequently published in 1989 by Lawyers Cooperative Publishing, Bancroft–Whitney Company, and Mead Data Central, Inc. as a 63–page pamphlet with a maroon cover, hence its common name, the MAROON BOOK. The MAROON BOOK eliminates reliance on parallel citation and acted as a catalyst for THE BLUEBOOK to eliminate reliance on parallel citation in its 15th edition. The MAROON BOOK remains more willing to accept LEXIS–NEXIS or WESTLAW database citations. The areas of foreign, international, and comparative law are not handled in the MAROON BOOK. Rather than being a complete guide to citation form, like that provided by THE BLUEBOOK, the MAROON BOOK offers a guiding philosophy of citation form. Editorial discretion, rather than consistent uniform citation form, is the MAROON BOOK's guiding principle. Some law reviews have developed their own particularized style manuals and rules of form.

[7] For a restatement of the rules set out in THE BLUEBOOK, see ALAN DWORSKY, USER'S GUIDE TO THE BLUEBOOK: REVISED FOR THE SIXTEENTH EDITION (rev. ed. 1996). For a training program in citation form designed for assisting legal secretaries and law students, see C. EDWARD GOOD, CITING AND TYPING THE LAW (4th ed. 1997). For a workbook on legal citation form, see MARIA L. CIAMPI, ET AL., THE CITATION WORKBOOK: HOW TO BEAT THE CITATION BLUES (2d ed. 1997). The Consortium of Computer Assisted Legal Instruction also provides computer-based programs offering self directed instruction in the use of *The Bluebook.*

changes, is a frequent source of frustration for those attempting to conform their citation practices with those of the latest edition of *The Bluebook*.[8] The most recent edition is organized into three major parts preceded by an Introduction and Practitioners' Notes.

The Introduction sets out basic principles of citation form along with basic examples. Practitioners' Notes (printed on blue paper) indicate how to adopt *The Bluebook* rules to the style appropriate to court documents and legal memoranda. The first group of rules (numbers 1–9) provides general standards of citation and style. The next group of rules (numbers 10–20) provides specific rules for citation to cases, statutes, books, periodicals, foreign materials, and international materials. The third portion of *The Bluebook* (printed on blue paper) provides tables used in conjunction with the rules. The tables include outlines of United States federal and state jurisdictions with appropriate abbreviations for primary source materials, similar information for foreign nations and intergovernmental organizations, and abbreviations for case names, court names, geographical terms, periodicals, and looseleaf services, among others.

a. *Style and Typeface.* Practitioners' Note 1 and Rule 1.1 deal with typeface conventions and style issues. *The Bluebook* serves both the formalistic legal publication needs of student-edited law reviews and the more pragmatic practitioner-oriented concerns regarding style in legal briefs and memoranda. The typeface conventions were conceived prior to the electronic word processing environment. *The Bluebook* delineates typeface rules for legal memoranda prepared in typescript and alternative rules for law reviews and other publications printed with typeset. In addition, *The Bluebook* does not refer its users to the requirements for style as set out in federal, state, and local court rules or citation manuals. Many legal publications supplement *The Bluebook* by using style manuals designed for the social sciences, arts and humanities, or federal government publications.[9]

For a comprehensive explanation and critique of the sixteenth edition of *The Bluebook* along with suggestions for future editions see A. Darby Dickerson, *An Un–Uniform System of Citation: Surviving with the New* Bluebook, 26 Stetson L. Rev. 53 (1996).

[8] For reviews and other perceptions of citation form and especially for reaction to the latest edition of The Bluebook, see Dickerson, *supra* note 7, Warren D. Rees, *Singing the Bluebook Blues: A Revision of the Sixteenth Edition*, AALL Spectrum, June 1997, at 20, Lawrence Savell, *The Bluebook Blues*, 36 Law Off. Econ. & Mgmt. 514 (1996), Susan E. Thrower, *What's New in the Bluebook, Sixteenth Edition*, 85 Ill. B.J. 137 (1997), Hope Viner Samborn, *What's New in Blue: Citation Guidelines Change along with the Times*, A.B.A. J. Dec. 1996, at 16, Franklin Atwater Weston, *The Bluebook: A Uniform System of Citation, 16th ed.*, Legal Info. Alert, Nov.-Dec. 1996 at 12.

For a general critique of the practice of footnoting, see Arthur Austin, *Footnote Skulduggery and Other Bad Habits*, 44 U. Miami L. Rev. 1009, 1010 (1990) (" ... law students ... have trained to intimidate and confuse the world with a profusion of self-serving, tedious, and lengthy notes") (footnote omitted). Additional discussions of footnotes are in the references in Chapter 17, notes 15–17.

[9] The Chicago Manual of Style (14th rev. ed. 1993), U.S. Government Printing Office Style Manual (1984), and Kate L. Turabian, A Manual For Writers of Term Papers, Theses, and Dissertations (6th ed. 1996) are the manuals most commonly used for this purpose.

b. *Citation Style.* The remainder of *The Bluebook* is devoted to legal citation style. An organizational structure and a variety of finding aids help to locate and clarify the use of the variety of rules set out in *The Bluebook.* The inside front cover provides a basic outline with examples, in legal publication format, of the structure of citation form in *The Bluebook.* The back inside cover provides brief formats for legal memoranda and court documents. The examples are accompanied with references to the appropriate rules, which set out all the nuances, with additional examples, of the particular general rule.

A detailed index at the end of *The Bluebook* provides direct access by subject to very detailed aspects of citation form. On the back cover is a thumb index to each of *The Bluebook* 's basic rules. The rules appear on the back cover in the order that the rules are set out in the inside front and back covers. The thumb index highlights the beginning of a particular rule in the manual's text by providing a darkened page edge parallel to the rule's number on the back cover when the pages are fanned.[10]

c. *Differences Between Editions.* The preface to the sixteenth edition provides a brief discussion of *The Bluebook*'s purpose and includes a listing of the alterations made between it and the fifteenth edition. When you become proficient in *The Bluebook,* this feature will be a welcomed assistant in pointing out the minor alterations that appear between editions. Minute alterations may be made to *The Bluebook* between printings of the same edition.

d. *Priority Within Citations: Citation Structure.* The remainder of *The Bluebook* is arranged according to the perceived value of legal information, going from the primary sources to secondary sources.[11] Each rule begins with a general example, as provided in the inside front covers. *The Bluebook* 's rules and examples then move from left to right covering each element of the general rule's citation form in greater detail.

This perceived value approach to legal information applies to Rules 10 through 17. This technique can be applied to the most common type of citation—cases. The elements of a case citation, moving from left to right, are:

case name

reporter/location information

court and jurisdiction

---

[10] To use the thumb index, hold THE BLUEBOOK's binding in your right hand, closed, and with the back cover under your left thumb. Place your left thumb next to the letter that encompasses the rule to which you want to go. Bend the book and flip the pages out from under your left thumb until you reach a page with a black heading with the letter and subject of the section directly under your left thumb. Slip your thumb into THE BLUEBOOK at this page and open the book to the pre-selected rule.

[11] Notice how Rules 1.3 and 1.4 relate to the order of information within a signal moving from primary to secondary sources of legal information, while the ordering of signals themselves move from direct support of a legal proposition to contradictory sources of legal information.

date and/or year of decision

parenthetical information regarding the case

prior and subsequent case histories

special or unique citation forms

Or as is illustrated by this hypothetical example:

Titan v. JPL, 21 Voy. L. Rep'ts 1 (S.E. Cal. 1993) (Stone, J. dissenting), *aff'd,* No. 94–12345, 1994 U.S. App. LEXIS 1952, at *7 (9th Cir. July 31, 1994).

Look at the elements of this citation and sequence of rules in *The Bluebook* following the basic citation form set out at Rule 10.1.

Titan v. JPL,	case name:	Rule 10.2
21 Voy.L.Rep'ts 1	reporter/location information:	Rule 10.3
(S.D.Cal.1993)	court, jurisdiction, date, year:	Rules 10.4–10.5
(Stone, J. dissenting),	parenthetical information:	Rule 10.6
aff'd,	prior and subsequent histories:	Rule 10.7
Voyager v. JPL, No. 94–12345,	special citation form:	Rule 10.8
1994 U.S. App. LEXIS 1952, at *7		

The special form of citation for unreported cases is followed by repeating court and date information explained in Rules 10.8.1.

e. *Primary and Secondary Sources.* The sequence from general citation form rules through specific exceptions to the general rules is followed throughout *The Bluebook* for primary and secondary sources. Knowing this structure simplifies locating information regarding specific examples and rules needed to construct correct citations.

3. Additional Aids to The Bluebook

Several additional aids have been developed to assist you in understanding all the nuances of *The Bluebook. Bieber's Dictionary of Legal Citations,* published by William S. Hein, is now in its fifth edition.[12] The *Dictionary,* an indispensable aid for citation neophytes, provides an alphabetical list of citation examples prepared according to the rules appearing in the sixteenth edition of *The Bluebook.*

A software program that checks citation form for correctness has been developed for use with standard word processing programs. Cite-Rite, a product of LEXIS–NEXIS, checks a word-processed citation to make sure it conforms with the sixteenth edition of *The Bluebook.*

CiteRite checks for proper underlining, placement of commas, typographical errors, and incorrect or missing parallel citations; federal or state cases reprinted in official or unofficial case reporters; appropriate federal and state statute codifications; and correct citation form for law review articles, federal legislative histories, model codes, and uniform acts.

---

[12] MARY MILES PRINCE, BIEBER'S DICTIONARY OF LEGAL CITATIONS: REFERENCE GUIDE FOR ATTORNEYS, LEGAL SECRETARIES, PARALEGALS AND LAW STUDENTS (5th ed. 1997).

CiteRite is also flexible. It can be customized to specific citation style spelling for individual jurisdictions. CiteRite does not correct the information in the word-processed text; it actually only helps to put the information in correct citation form. The researcher must still be careful to verify all components of a citation, e.g., page number, volume number, and dates.

SECTION C. ONLINE CITATION SYSTEMS— VENDOR–NEUTRAL CITATION SYSTEMS

1. Online Citation Systems.

In the discussion of computer-assisted legal research (see Chapter 22) the advantages and shortcomings of LEXIS–NEXIS and WESTLAW applications were reviewed. The increasing reliance on these databases for legal research is apparent. With continuing enhancements in storage format (for example, Internet-accessible, CD–ROM applications) and the development of artificial intelligence options, computer-*assisted* legal research will soon become *computerized* legal research. Citation directly to computerized legal databases insures intellectual honesty by indicating the precise location of the information that serves as the foundation of legal research. Recall that the editorial work of legal publishers makes each publication of court cases and administrative materials potentially unique. Printed works and electronic publications do not always provide identical sources of legal information. Researchers should cite to the source used in developing their research, not an equivalent, because subtle nuances may imply subtle differences.

In anticipation of the future, both LEXIS–NEXIS and WESTLAW developed online citation systems permitting direct access to the legal information available in their databases. Originally motivated by the difficulty caused in citing to unpublished opinions, both services provided access to the portions of their case law databases that lacked in print distribution or were relegated to the role of slip opinion distribution without precedential value. Both LEXIS–NEXIS and WESTLAW now provide star pagination permitting citation directly to their databases, whether or not an opinion will eventually appear in a print court reporter.

Both LEXIS–NEXIS and WESTLAW provide software searching capability for direct access using star pagination to traditional print reporters or their own unique citation systems. Star pagination indicates the location of page breaks in the traditional bound law reporter along with uniform screen break indications to either LEXIS–NEXIS or WESTLAW as the case would appear on your computer screen. In addition to providing consistent screen numbers for information available in electronic databases, both LEXIS–NEXIS and WESTLAW provide unique identifying codes in individual databases after 1986 which particularly identify the cited case. Locating a specific portion of a case defined by a page number or screen can be accomplished using the LEXSEE instruction on LEXIS-NEXIS and the FIND command on WESTLAW.

References to the print court reporter citation or electronic database citation are found on the running head at the top of the computer screen preceded by the words, "cite as." References to page and screen citations in print court reports and database citations indicate the appropriate reporter's page break or databases screen break by the number of asterisks (*) or stars. [See Illustrations 23–1 and 23–2.]

The Bluebook has adopted the online citation systems developed by LEXIS–NEXIS and WESTLAW in rules 10.8.1 and 10.9(a)(ii). *The Bluebook*, however, permits citation to electronic databases only when a case is unreported and is available on a widely used electronic database. Proponents of vendor-neutral citation systems, discussed below, would encourage citation to an electronic version of a decision, or other electronic formats of legal information, whether or not the information is available in print, regardless of the wide availability of the electronic database or electronic format such as compact disk or Internet-based legal information (see Chapter 22).

a. *LEXIS–NEXIS Database Citations.* A LEXIS–NEXIS electronic database online citation, available from the moment a case is online, offers a precise and permanent uniform method for citing to that case in the LEXIS–NEXIS database. Since most cases are available within 24 to 72 hours after the court's ruling, often LEXIS–NEXIS star pagination citations may be the only available means for referring to information found in the LEXIS–NEXIS database during the editorial and traditional publication process.

A LEXIS database pagination citations consists of:

- name of the case
- document number
- year of decision
- computer database identifier LEXIS
- a unique number identifying the case in the particular database
- jurisdictional information and exact date of decisions

Returning to our previous example, a typical LEXIS–NEXIS star pagination citation may appear as:

Voyager v. JPL, No. 94–12345, 1994 US App LEXIS 3112, at *3 (9th Cir. May 7, 1994).

LEXIS–NEXIS database citations are permanent and remain as an access method to the database even though in print pagination references are available to traditionally-published case and administrative reporters.

b. *WESTLAW Database Citations.* A WESTLAW Cite is comprised of:

- name of the case
- document number
- year of decision
- computer database identifier WL
- a unique number identifying the case in the particular database
- jurisdictional information and exact date of decisions

A WESTLAW Cite would appear as follows:

Voyager v. JPL, No. 94–12345, 1994 WL 78910, at *3 (9th Cir. May 7, 1994).

WESTLAW database citations can be used with WESTLAW's FIND and KeyCite features. Unlike LEXIS–NEXIS, once West assigns a case pagination in the *National Reporter System*, the WESTLAW database citation is eliminated.

c. *Citation to Information on the Internet. The Bluebook* recognizes that information is now available in a variety of formats. Despite the application of new technologies to legal information, *The Bluebook* prefers citation to legal information in print format. A new rule in the sixteenth edition of *The Bluebook*, rule 17.3, deals with electronic sources of separately published documents available in databases and through the Internet. However, even if a document is located through a database search the preferred citation format remains the print format and not the electronic format.

Particular to *the Bluebook* rules for citation to the Internet, because of the transient nature of information available on the Internet, the Internet may only be cited when information is not available in print form or is otherwise difficult to obtain. As more law journals and periodicals proliferate on the Internet as the sole means of publication *The Bluebook*'s rule 17.3.3 will take on greater significance.

When citing to the Internet, rule 17.3.3 requires the following elements:

name of the author (if available)

the title or top-level heading of the cited material

the Uniform Resource Locator (URL)

for a journal or periodicals: give exact date of publication

for other materials: provide the most recent modification date, if no modification date is provided indicate the last date the site was visited

For example, the citation to an article in the web-based *National Journal of Sexual Orientation Law* would appear as:

Mary Coombs, *Transgenderism and Sexual Orientation: More than a Marriage of Convenience*, 3 NAT'L J. SEX. ORIENT. L. 3 (Oct. 1997) <http://sunsite.unc.edu/gaylaw/Issue5/coombs.html>.

2. Vendor–Neutral Citation Systems.

With the advent of legal information in compact disk and Internet-based formats, the economic scale of legal publishing changed significantly. A variety of courts began to report their most recent decisions on electronic bulletin board services. New vendors of legal information realized their entrance to the legal information marketplace was no longer hindered by the monopolistic control of legal information held by LEXIS–NEXIS and WESTLAW and their parent companies Reed–Elsevier and Thomson Publishing Company.

The efforts of the new entrepreneurs of legal information to have their products received in the marketplace was hindered by their inability to have their information sources cited. Reference to parallel citations to official state reporters had been eliminated in the fifteenth edition of *The Bluebook*, yet no provision had been made for non-traditional sources of similar information. In addition, intellectual property restrictions prohibited these new sources of information to parallel cite to similar or identical legal information appearing in publications of the West Group's *National Reporter System*, WESTLAW, or LEXIS–NEXIS.

The dilemma faced by the entrepreneurs of legal information in new formats was further highlighted by the adoption of vendor-neutral citations by the United States Sixth Circuit Court of Appeals and the Supreme Courts of Louisiana and Colorado.[13]

In response to the dilemma of legal information's restriction in availability, the American Association of Law Libraries in 1994 convened a Task Force to address restrictions in legal citation form and the advent of new legal information technologies and vendors. In 1995, the Task Force delivered their report calling for a system of vendor-neutral citation, court decisions should have each paragraph numbered to facilitate the universal adoption of vendor neutral citations and the Task Force made additional recommendations relating to the use of dates in citations for statutes.[14]

a. *Vendor Neutral Citations–Cases.* The basic citation form for vendor neutral citations for cases includes the following elements:

the case name

---

[13] AMERICAN ASSOCIATION OF LAW LIBRARIES, REPORT: TASK FORCE ON CITATION FORMATS 16–17 (1995) (citing Sixth Circuit Electronic Opinion Distribution and Citation Changes Policy (Jan. 1994), Memorandum from Colorado Chief Justice Rovira to all Justices, Judges and Magistrates (May 5, 1994), Order of the Supreme Court of Louisiana (Dec. 17, 1993)).

[14] AMERICAN ASSOCIATION OF LAW LIBRARIES, REPORT: TASK FORCE ON CITATION FORMATS 26 (1995).

the year of decision

the court of decision

the opinion number

a notation indicating if an opinion is unreported (**U**)

a paragraph number if the citation refers to specific text

An example, using our hypothetical case, if the decision were unreported[15]:

Titan v. JPL, 1993 SE Dist CA 1234U ¶ 1

b.   *Vendor Neutral Citations–Statutes.* The basic citation form for vendor neutral citations for statutes includes the following elements for a codification:

the name of the statute if it will be of assistance

standardized code designation

numbering of the code

the date the codification is current through

An example:[16]

California Uniform Testamentary Additions to Trusts Act, CA Prob Code § 6300 (1997 through 12/31)

c.   *Will Vendor Neutral Citations Become a Universal Standard?* *The Bluebook* has enjoyed a dominant role as the standard for legal citation for decades. Any proposed system seeking to unseat *The Bluebook* from its almost universal adoption will take considerable effort and education. Although *The Bluebook* has adopted some elements of vendor neutral citation and citation to compact disk and Internet based sources of information, *The Bluebook* remains deeply attached to print sources of legal information.

Eight states have currently adopted vendor neutral citations.[17] Litigation has curtailed West's assertion of intellectual property rights in

---

[15] American Association of Law Libraries Citation Formats Committee, *User Guide to the AALL Universal Case Citation: Draft Release 5.0*, 89 LAW LIBR. J. 13, 13, 18–20 (1997) (reference to rule 1. basic citation form; abbreviation dictionary part A: geographic abbreviations, part B: court name abbreviations).

[16] American Association of Law Libraries Committee on Citation Formats, *User Guide to the AALL Universal Statutory Citation: Draft Release 3.1*, 90 LAW LIBR. J. 95, 97–99, 102–112 (1998) (elements of statutory code citation, appendix standardized code and session law designations). The user's guide includes formats for non-codified session laws. *Id.* at 97. Use of the term "through" in the date element is the user's guide attempt to identify the version of the code or session law referred to by reference to the last "legislative event" defined as the last activity of the legislature covered in the source consulted. American Association of Law Libraries Committee on Citation Format, *The Universal Legal Citation Project: A Draft User Guide to the AALL Universal Statutory Citation*, 90 LAW LIBR. J. 91, 93 (1998).

[17] Colorado, Louisiana, Maine, Montana, New Mexico, North Dakota, Oklahoma and South Dakota. American Bar Association Standing Committee on Technology and Informa-

their *National Reporter Service*.[18] During the course of the antitrust inquiry into the West Publishing Company and Thomson Publishing merger, West Publishing announced the availability of a free license to the West citation system for small publishers.[19]

The Bluebook has weighed into the controversy by amending its own rule, calling for a vendor neutral citation in legal memoranda and law review citations, along with citing to a regional reporter. The format for the citation is limited *Bluebook* rule 10.8.1 and 17.3.3 discussed earlier.

A study of the available infrastructure issues in state court reporters' offices indicated a host of issues in preparation of opinions for publication consistent with vendor neutral citation[20]

Without greater participation by a variety of jurisdictions in vendor neutral citations along with training to inform court reporters of the new rules for vendor neutral citations, the application of this standard remains in doubt. The West Group's diminished expectation that their compilations of court reports contain information worthy of copyright protection and West's expressed willingness to place their citations in the public domain will not foster the adoption of the vendor neutral citation system.

tion Services, *American Bar Association Official Citation Resolutions* (Apr.10,1998)<http://www.abanet.org/citation/home.html>. The American Bar Association's Standing Committee on Technology and Information Services continues the efforts of the former American Bar Association's Committee on Citation Issues to implement Report No, 107 and a resolution adopted on August 6, 1996 by the American Bar Association's House of Delegates calling for a universal citation system. *Id.*

[18] Matthew Bender v. West Publ'g Co., 42 U.S.P.Q. 2d (BNA) 1930, 25 Media L. Rep. 1856 (S.D. N.Y.1997) (intervenor HyperLaw, a publisher of compact disk based court reports of the United States Supreme Court and various federal courts, copying of reports from the West's reporters does not violate West's copyright when the copying fails to include headnotes, West does not have a copyright in the compilation of their reporters), Matthew Bender v. West Publ'g Co., No. 94 Civ. 0589, 95 Civ. 4496, 1997 U.S. Dist. LEXIS 2710, at 1 (S.D.N.Y. Mar. 11, 1997) (granting summary judgment motion that use of references to page numbers where opinions appear does not violate West's copyright in compilation), Matthew Bender v. West Publ'g Co., 41 U.S.P.Q. 2d (BNA) 1321 (S.D.N.Y. 1996) (compilation copyright on West's case reporters does not protect page numbers and does not infringe on copyright when page numbers are used for star pagination on competitor's compact disk product since page numbers are not an original creation of the compiler West) (declaratory judgment action resulting in summary judgment). *But see* Oasis Publ'g Co. v. West Publ'g Co., 924 F.Supp. 918 (D.Minn. 1996) (upholding West's assertion of copyright in their compilation of court opinions). *But see, e.g.*, U.S. v. Thomson Corp., 949 F. Supp. 907, 926 (D.D.C. 1996) (lack of originality in West's claim of copyright in pagination constitutes a thin claim of copyright).

[19] Anthony Aaron, *Thomson Proposes Free License to West Citation System*, L.A. DAILY J., Feb. 6, 1997, at 5.

[20] A survey conducted by the author in 1997 received 18 responses from a variety of jurisdictions. Concerns in changing to a paragraph numbered system of case citation ranged from personnel expenses, equipment expenses and limitations in hardware and software capable of achieving accurate paragraph numbering. Some courts were concerned with the definition of a paragraph and at what point in the opinion the paragraph numbering would begin. *See also* HyperLaw, Inc., *Comments to Judicial Conference re Citation Reform* (Apr. 29, 1997)<http://hyperlaw.com/jconf.htm>.

The Bluebook remains the standard of legal citation form and will likely enjoy that status for years to come. *The Bluebook's* embrace of some elements of vendor neutral citation and its continued reliance on traditional print sources will elevate *The Bluebook* and its reliance on West Group publications into a synthetic citation system. In effect, West citations will have the ubiquitous role of identifying print and non-print sources of information regardless of the publisher or vendor of the information. Only further development of technological applications for the storage of information will test this hypothesis.

SECTION D.   ILLUSTRATIONS: STAR PAGINATION

23–1.   LEXIS–NEXIS Screen with Star Pagination
23–2.   WESTLAW Screen with Star Pagination

[Illustration 23-1]

LEXIS–NEXIS SCREEN WITH STAR PAGINATION

456 U.S. 305, *318; 102 S. Ct. 1798, **1806;   LEXSEE
1982 U.S. LEXIS 34, ***24; 72 L. Ed. 2d 91   ③

compliance with the Act. The exemption serves a different and   mplementary
purpose, that of permitting noncompliance by federal agencies i extraordinary
circumstances. Executive Order No. 12088, 3 CFR 243 (1979), [***25] which
implements the exemption authority, requires the federal agency requesting such an
exemption to certify that it cannot meet the applicable pollution standards.
"Exemptions are granted by the President only if the conflict between pollution
control standards and crucial federal activities cannot be resolved through the
development of a practical remedial program." Brief for Petitioners 26, n. 30.

   [*319] ① Should the Navy receive a permit here, there would be no need to
invoke the machinery of the Presidential exemption. If not, this course remains open.
The exemption provision would enable the President, believing paramount national
interest so requires, to authorize discharges which the District Court has enjoined.
Reading the statute to permit the exercise of a court's equitable discretion in no way
eliminates the role of the exemption provision in the statutory scheme.

② Like the language and structure of the Act, the legislative history does not suggest
that Congress intended to deny courts their traditional equitable discretion. Congress
[**1807]   passed the 1972 Amendments because it recognized that "the national
effort to abate and control water pollution   [***26]   has been inadequate in every
                                                          ③

The excerpt above, from a LEXIS screen, is from *Weinberger v. Romero-Barcelo*
and shows where the text begins in the (1) *United States Reports* (one *) and in
(2) West's *Supreme Court Reporter* (two **), as well as (3) the LEXIS Cite
(three ***).

[Illustration 23–2]

WESTLAW SCREEN WITH STAR PAGINATION

102 S.Ct. 1798   FOR EDUCATIONAL USE ONLY   **Page 1**
72 L.Ed.2d 91, 17 ERC 1217, 12 Envtl. L. Rep. 20,538
(Cite as: 456 U.S. 305, *306, 102 S.Ct. 1798, **1800
<KeyCite Yellow Flag>

    *   *   *   *   *   *   ①

White, Justice.

The issue in this case is whether the Federal Water Pollution Control Act (1 WPCA or Act) 86 Stat. 816, as amended, 33 U.S.C. ¶ 1251 et seq. (1976 ed. and Supp.IV), requires a district court to enjoin immediately all discharges of pollutants *307 that do not comply with the Act's permit requirements or whether the district court retains discretion to order other relief to achieve compliance. The Court of Appeals for the First Circuit held that the Act withdrew the courts' equitable discretion. Romero-Barcelo v. Brown, 643 F.2d 835 (1981). We reverse.

I

For many years, the Navy has used Vieques Island, a small island of the Puerto Rico coast, for weapons training. Currently all Atlantic Fleet vessels assigned to the Mediterranean Sea and the Indian Ocean are required to complete their training at Vieques because it permits a full range of exercises under conditions similar to combat. During air-to-ground training, however, pilots sometimes miss land-based targets, and ordnance falls into the sea. That is, accidental bombings of the navigable waters and, occasionally, intentional bombings of water targets occur. The District **1801 Court found that these discharges have not harmed the quality of the water.

In 1978, respondents, who include the Governor of Puerto Rico and residents of the island, sued to enjoin the Navy's operations on the island. Their complaint alleged violations of numerous federal environmental statutes and various other Acts.[FN1]

Corp. ℃ West 1998 No Claim to Orig. U.S. Govt. Works

The excerpt above, from a WESTLAW screen, is from *Weinberger v. Romero-Barcelo* and shows where the text begins in the (1) *United States Reports* (one *) and in (2) West's *Supreme Court Reporter* (two **). If a case is so recent as to be printed only in slip opinion form, a WESTLAW Cite is provided.

Chapter 24

FEDERAL TAX RESEARCH*

SECTION A. INTRODUCTION

Many attorneys erroneously believe federal tax research has nothing in common with traditional legal research methods.[1] You can solve problems involving federal taxation using techniques mastered in a basic legal research course, and you can often use traditional materials.[2] However, most library collections include sources, dealing solely with federal taxation, from which you can derive the same solutions with greater ease and in more detail. Whether shelved together in a "tax alcove" or dispersed throughout the collection, they are no more difficult to locate or use than are traditional research tools.

This text discusses primary and secondary sources of federal tax law and presents information about research materials containing these items. It also includes information about the process of evaluating and updating the results of your research. Because so many research tools are available, a library may lack one or more of them, may contain materials omitted here, or may include materials in a different format (*e.g.*, CD–ROM).

Because the publishing industry is consolidating, several formerly-independent companies are now commonly-owned.[3] Some publications described in prior editions have been renamed or dropped. No one can project the extent to which consolidation of publications will follow consolidation of publishers. Because this text focuses on general tax research principles, you should be able to adapt your research strategy to the appearance of new materials and the disappearance of old ones.

---

* This chapter was prepared by Gail Levin Richmond, Associate Dean–Academic Affairs and Professor, Nova Southeastern University Shepard Broad Law Center. An expanded version of this chapter is separately published under the title Federal Tax Research: Guide to Materials and Techniques (5th ed. 1997) (Foundation Press).

[1] *See* Carol A. Roehrenbeck & Gail Levin Richmond, *Three Researchers in Search of an Alcove: A Play in Six Acts*, 84 Law Libr. J. 13 (1992).

[2] This chapter devotes very little space to traditional legal research tools. If the library lacks a tax-oriented tool, researchers may wish to consult traditional materials. References to the appropriate chapters in this text will aid you in locating such materials.

[3] West Publishing, Research Institute of America (RIA), Warren, Gorham & Lamont, Lawyers Cooperative, and Clark Boardman Callahan share Thomson as a common parent; subgroups exist within this group. Reed Elsevier owns Michie, Butterworth, and *LEXIS-NEXIS*; Kluwer, which owned Commerce Clearing House and Aspen, is also part of this group; Aspen has acquired titles formerly published by Little, Brown .. Shepard's is jointly-owned by Reed Elsevier and Times Mirror, the parent of Matthew Bender.

SECTION B.   RESEARCH METHODOLOGY

Tax research begins much the same way as do other types of legal research. Using a set of facts presented in a problem, you must determine the issues these facts raise and ascertain any additional facts that might be relevant. To resolve the issues you isolate, you must locate any governing statutory language. Legislative history or administrative pronouncements would be the next step if you desire guidance in interpreting the statute. If there are administrative pronouncements, courts may have passed upon their validity, so you must locate judicial decisions. In some instances, you may consider constitutional challenges to the statute itself or to an administrative interpretation. If non-U.S. source income or noncitizens are involved, the research expands to include applicable treaties.

If you are familiar with the subject matter involved, you can often locate these items without resort to any secondary authority other than a citator. When you lack such familiarity, you might conduct the research effort in an entirely different manner. Before reading the applicable statute, you may use secondary materials to determine which Code section is involved and to gain understanding of the underlying issues. Looseleaf services, treatises, and periodical articles will be particularly useful in this phase of your research.

SECTION C.   CONSTITUTION

The Constitution contains several specific provisions for taxation. The most commonly-cited are the apportionment clauses (Article I, section 2, clause 3, and Article I, section 9, clause 4), the origination clause (Article I, section 7, clause 1), the uniformity clause (Article 1, section 8, clause 1), and the export clause (Article I, section 9, clause 5). Because the income tax is specifically authorized by the Constitution's sixteenth amendment, it avoids an earlier holding that it was a direct tax subject to apportionment based on population.[4] The estate and gift taxes, on the other hand, are indirect taxes subject only to the requirement that they be uniform throughout the United States.

Because substantive tax research rarely involves the Constitution, tax-oriented research tools are limited. In fact, none of the tax-oriented citators (Section L) includes the Constitution as cited material. Constitutional research is best performed using traditional materials.[5] Alternatively, you can search CD–ROM (Section S) and online tax services (Section T), using either a specific constitutional provision or a common term (*e.g.*, due process). The *Standard Federal Tax Reporter* volume 1

[4] Pollock v. Farmers' Loan & Trust Co., 158 U.S. 601 (1895); *cf.* Springer v. United States, 102 U.S. 586 (1880), concluding the Civil War income tax was indirect.

[5] The most useful materials are annotated constitutions, such as those included in *United States Code Annotated* and *United States Code Service*, and digests. *See* Chapters 6 and 8. 1 BORIS I. BITTKER & LAWRENCE LOKKEN, FEDERAL TAXATION OF INCOME, ESTATES AND GIFTS ch. 1 (2d ed. 1989 & 1997 Cum. Supp.) provides a historical perspective of tax litigation involving constitutional claims.

(Section M) includes materials on litigation involving constitutional claims.

SECTION D. STATUTORY SCHEME

United States Code Title 26, more commonly referred to as the Internal Revenue Code of 1986, contains the vast majority of statutes covering income, estate and gift, excise, and employment taxes. These materials are referred to as the Code throughout this chapter. References to the two previous Codes—1939 and 1954—will include the year.[6]

Some tax-related provisions appear outside the Internal Revenue Code. These include provisions codified elsewhere and uncodified provisions. For example, although many rules affecting retirement benefits appear in Title 26, others appear in Title 29. Rules providing guidance in the employee/independent contractor area are not codified anywhere.[7]

SECTION E. LOCATING CURRENT, REPEALED, AND PENDING LEGISLATION

In researching a tax problem, the time frame involved is quite important. If, for example, the research involves a contemplated transaction, current statutory provisions are certainly important. However, if the current statutory language is of recent vintage, one tool in ascertaining its meaning is the repealed statute it replaced. Moreover, if you ignore pending legislation, you do so at your own peril. A bill changing the tax consequences of a proposed transaction could be enacted before your client negotiates a binding contract.[8]

The following paragraphs discuss sources containing the language of relevant legislative material. You can locate additional information in Section G, Legislative Histories.

1. Current Code—Codifications

Several publishers produce annual versions of the Internal Revenue Code.[9] Those publishing in a looseleaf format regularly integrate new material into the codification volumes. Publishers using hardbound volumes use supplements for new matter. CD–ROM (Section S) and on-line services (Section T) insert new material directly into the relevant

---

[6] Before 1939, tax statutes were reenacted in their entirety, or with necessary changes, on a regular basis. Because many current provisions can be traced back to the 1939 Code or even earlier—I.R.C. § 263, for example, contains language taken almost verbatim from § 117 of the 1864 Act, 13 Stat. 282—cross references to these earlier materials are extremely useful. *See* Section G for materials used to trace statutory language.

[7] Revenue Act of 1978, Pub. L. No. 95–600, § 530, 92 Stat. 2763, 2885, extended indefinitely by the Tax Equity and Fiscal Responsibility Act of 1982, Pub. L. No. 97–248, § 269(c), 96 Stat. 324, 552.

[8] Effective dates for new legislation frequently precede the actual enactment date. However, transactions subject to binding contracts on an act's effective date are often exempted. Notice 90–6, 1990–1 C.B. 304, provides guidance with respect to the existence of a binding contract for purposes of the Revenue Reconciliation Act of 1989.

[9] Nontax-oriented codifications include *United States Code, United States Code Annotated*, and *United States Code Service. See* Chapter 9.

database. The lists below include the format for each looseleaf and hardbound codification.

- *CCH Standard Federal Tax Reporter*[10] and *CCH Federal Tax Service* (Section M) (looseleaf; supplemented during year)

- *RIA United States Tax Reporter*[11] (Section M) (looseleaf; supplemented during year)

- Rabkin & Johnson, *Federal Income, Gift and Estate Taxation* (Section M) (looseleaf; supplemented during year)

- *U.S. Code Congressional & Administrative News—Internal Revenue Code* (Section Q) (hardbound; annual codification)

2. Individual Revenue Acts

Even though looseleaf services integrate the text of recent statutes into their codifications, separate versions of an act are still valuable. These versions may be available more quickly and will include effective dates and congressional instructions to the IRS. Codifications omit this information or reproduced it in relatively small print.

Acts are first published as slip laws and then bound in Public Law number order into the appropriate volume of *United States Statutes at Large.* You can locate these acts in various nontax services[12] and in the tax-oriented materials listed below.

- *Daily Tax Report* (Section P)

- *Internal Revenue Bulletin; Cumulative Bulletin* (Section Q)

- *Internal Revenue Acts—Text and Legislative History* (Section Q)

3. Previous Law

The materials listed in subsection 1 contain the current law. Those listed below provide the previous version of amended sections as well as the text of legislation that has been repealed altogether. Periods covered by each are indicated.

- *RIA Cumulative Changes* (Section Q) (1939 to date)

- *Barton's Federal Tax Laws Correlated* (Section Q) (1913–52)

[10] *Standard Federal Tax Reporter* includes all federal taxes in its two Code volumes but covers only income and employment taxes in the remainder of the set. CCH also publishes *Federal Estate and Gift Tax Reporter* and *Federal Excise Tax Reporter.* Because their formats resemble that of *SFTR,* this text includes few separate references to those services. The Code provisions also appear in each looseleaf service's compilation volumes.

[11] All federal taxes are covered in the two *United States Tax Reporter* Code volumes, but this service is otherwise limited to income and employment taxes. Because *USTR—Estate & Gift Taxes* and *USTR—Excise Taxes* cover their respective subject matters in a similar format, they are rarely referred to separately in this text. The Code provisions also appear in each looseleaf service's compilation volumes.

[12] *U.S. Code Congressional and Administrative News (USCCAN)* and *United States Code Service Advance* are two such sources. *See* Chapter 9.

- *Seidman's Legislative History of Federal Income and Excess Profits Tax Laws* (Section Q) (1861–1953)

- Mertens, *Law of Federal Income Taxation—Code* (Section M) (1954–85)

- *Internal Revenue Acts—Text and Legislative History; U.S. Code Congressional & Administrative News—Internal Revenue Code* (Section Q) (prior years' volumes; these two sets are best used together for this purpose) (1954 to date)

- *Tax Management Primary Sources* (Section Q) (1969 to date)

- *The Internal Revenue Acts of the United States: 1909–1950; 1950–1972; 1973–* (Section Q)

The first three items allow you to trace the language of particular Code and Revenue Act sections through their various permutations. The others use a multivolume format that makes the tracing process tedious.

Eldridge, *The United States Internal Revenue System* (Section Q), provides annotated text for revenue acts prior to 1894. It can be used if *Seidman's* is unavailable, but it does not contain as much information.

4. Pending and Potential Legislation

Even before a bill is introduced, taxpayers may receive hints that it is on the horizon. In presidential election years, for example, party platforms include potential legislative agendas. Presidential budget messages may also serve this function. Items of this nature appear in newsletters (Section P) as well as in many general interest newspapers.[13]

The weekly *CCH Congressional Index* is an excellent source for locating and tracking pending items. This service provides a brief digest of pending bills. It also indicates a bill's progress, listing hearings and other pertinent information.[14]

Although the tax-oriented materials listed below cover pending legislation, only *Daily Tax Report* and *Tax Notes* list a significant number of bills introduced in the current Congress; their descriptions of most items are cursory.

- *CCH Standard Federal Tax Reporter* (Section M)

- *RIA United States Tax Reporter* (Section M)

- *Daily Tax Report* (Section P)

- *Tax Notes* (Section P)

- *Tax Management Primary Sources* (Section Q)

[13] American Law Institute proposals can be harbingers of future bill proposals. *See, e.g.,* H.R. 6261, 98th Cong., 2d Sess. (1984), incorporating ALI proposals on generation skipping taxes. FEDERAL ESTATE AND GIFT TAX PROJECT—STUDY ON GENERATION-SKIPPING TRANSFERS UNDER THE FEDERAL ESTATE TAX (Discussion Draft No. 1, Mar. 28, 1984).

[14] Other useful tools include those published by *Congressional Information Service (CIS)*, which follow a bill's progress through Congress, and the *Weekly Compilation of Presidential Documents. See* Chapter 10.

Online services (Section T) are often the best means for following pending bills.

SECTION F. CITATORS FOR STATUTES

Both *Shepard's Federal Tax Citations* and *Shepard's Federal Statutes Citations* indicate if a federal court determined a statute's constitutionality. These citators are discussed in Section L.

SECTION G. LEGISLATIVE HISTORIES

The process used to enact tax legislation generally parallels that used for other federal laws.[15] Because there are so many steps and groups involved, the number of documents comprising the history of a major tax statute is quite extensive.

The House Committee on Ways and Means and the Senate Committee on Finance have primary jurisdiction over revenue bills. Each committee (or subcommittees thereof) may hold hearings, which will be published, and issue a committee report if a bill is reported out of committee.[16] If House and Senate versions differ, a Conference Committee meets to resolve these differences. This group generates a third committee report, which explains the resolution of House–Senate differences.

Five members each from Ways and Means and from Finance sit on a separate Joint Committee on Taxation (JCT).[17] While proposals and reports may emanate from this committee, it is not charged with drafting legislation and its reports lack the interpretive significance of those issued by the Ways and Means and Finance Committees. In addition to studies for use in the hearings or drafting process, the JCT's staff publishes a post-enactment General Explanation (the "Blue Book"). No Blue Books were published after the one for the 1986 Act until the JCT issued one for 1996 legislation.

Bills reported out by committee are debated on the floor of the appropriate house. Although Senate rules permit more extensive debate and floor amendments than do House procedures, each chamber can change the bill. Discussion of the bill during any congressional debate appears in the *Congressional Record*.[18]

[15] With one constitutional limitation—revenue-raising bills must originate in the House of Representatives—the enactment process follows that described in Chapter 9.

[16] Committee reports can include explanatory language omitted from the act itself. *See, e.g.*, H.R. REP. NO. 101–386, 101ST CONG., 1ST SESS. 653 (1989), discussing items qualifying as authority for avoiding the Code section 6662 substantial underpayment penalty.

[17] I.R.C. §§ 8001–8023. The Committee is charged with investigating the operation and effects of the tax system, its administration, and means of simplifying it. *Id.* § 8022. The Joint Committee also reviews tax refunds exceeding $1,000,000. *Id.* § 6405.

[18] *See, e.g.*, Ashburn v. United States, 740 F.2d 843 (11th Cir. 1984), in which the court referred to committee reports and to congressional debates as evidence of the meaning of a phrase in the Equal Access to Justice Act. *See also* Commissioner v. Engle, 464 U.S. 206 (1984), in which the Court's opinion on the meaning of I.R.C. § 613A cited to testimony at hearings, floor debates, and committee reports.

Unlike treaties, bills die when a Congress's second session ends. Members work under extreme time pressure to complete major legislation by that date. Under these circumstances, a conference report's version of a bill may contain errors, which Congress passes along with the rest of the bill. If both houses agree, a Concurrent Resolution can be used to make necessary changes before the act is enrolled for submission to the President. If they cannot agree, or they find the errors too late, a technical corrections bill is inevitable.[19]

Normally, the President can sign or veto an act in its entirety (or allow it to become law without signing it); Congress can override a veto by a two-thirds vote of each house.[20] After the President signs the act, or it otherwise becomes law, the interpretive process begins. Legislative history includes testimony at hearings, committee reports, and floor debate. It also includes presidential messages, statements of sponsors, and reports by the Joint Committee staff. If no Treasury regulations are available, you can consult legislative history materials to ascertain congressional intent. Even after regulations are issued, you can use these materials to challenge a regulation's validity.[21] Courts vary in the degree of weight accorded to legislative history materials. Do not overlook this fact in doing your research.[22]

The materials below aid you in determining which sections of prior laws to read. These materials are also useful for locating committee reports and other legislative history materials.

1. Cross References to Prior Codes and Revenue Acts

Code cross reference tables provide section cross references between the 1939 and 1954 Codes. However, limitations apply. First, Congress changed section numbers (generally by inserting new subsections and moving old ones) after enacting the 1954 Code and again in the 1986

---

[19] *See, e.g.*, H.R. Con. Res. 328, 98th Cong., 2d Sess. (1984), making technical changes to the Tax Reform Act of 1984. *Compare* H.R. Con. Res. 395, 99th Cong., 2d Sess. (1986), which failed to pass, leaving flaws in the 1986 Act.

[20] A recent attempt was made to allow a President to veto only parts of a piece of legislation when Congress enacted the Line Item Veto Act. However, this act was ruled unconstitutional in *Clinton v. City of New York*, No. 97–1374, 1998 U.S. LEXIS 4215 (June 25, 1998).

[21] *See, e.g.*, United States v. Nesline, 590 F. Supp. 884 (D. Md. 1984), holding invalid a regulation that varied from the plain language of the statute and had no support in the committee reports. *See also* Edward L. Stephenson Trust v. Commissioner, 81 T.C. 283 (1983), later overruled by Congress in the Tax Reform Act of 1984, Pub. L. No. 98–369, § 82(a), 98 Stat. 494, 598 (1984).

[22] The Treasury Department and IRS include legislative history in administrative documents. *See, e.g.*, Rev. Rul. 88–64, 1988–2 C.B. 10, 11, which cites to a statement by Senator Long during floor debate on the Crude Oil Windfall Profit Tax Act of 1980.

Code. Cross reference tables may not reflect these changes. You must determine when each provision received its current section number and try to use tables that are updated regularly. A second limitation is also worth noting. These tables reflect their compilers' opinion as to the appropriate cross references. Different publishers' tables may yield different results.

The services below provide tables cross referencing the 1954 and 1939 Codes.

- *CCH Standard Federal Tax Reporter* (Section M) (Code volume I)

- Rabkin & Johnson, *Federal Income, Gift and Estate Taxation* (Section M) (volume 7B)

- Mertens, *Law of Federal Income Taxation—Code* (Section M) (1954–58 Code volume) (1954 to 1939 only)

- *RIA Cumulative Changes* (Section Q)

- *Barton's Federal Tax Laws Correlated* (Section Q) (looseleaf volume)

- *Seidman's Legislative History of Federal Income and Excess Profits Tax Laws* (Section Q) (1939–53 volume II)

- Joint Committee on Taxation, *Derivations of Code Sections of the Internal Revenue Codes of 1939 and 1954* (JCS–1–92), Jan. 21, 1992, reprinted in DAILY TAX REPORT, Jan. 23, 1992 (Special Supplement).

You can trace back provisions that predate the 1939 Code using *Barton's Federal Tax Laws Correlated* (Section Q); *Seidman's Legislative History of Federal Income and Excess Profits Tax Laws* (Section Q); or the Joint Committee on Taxation report listed above.

[Illustration 24–1]

EXCERPT FROM 1954–1939 CROSS REFERENCE TABLE *STANDARD FEDERAL TAX REPORTER* CODE VOLUME I

101 . . . . 22(b)(1)	265 . . . . . . 23(b), 24(a)(5)	443 . 47(a),(c),(e),(g),146(a)
102 . . . . 22(b)(3)	266 . . . . 24(a)(7)	446 41
103 . . . . 22(b)(4)	267 . . . . 24(b), (c)	451 . . . . 42(a)
104 . . . . 22(b)(5)	268 . . . . 24(f)	453 44
105, 106	269 129	454 . . . . 42(b), (c), (d)
107 . . . . 22(b)(6)	270 130	455 . . . .
108 . . . . . . 22(b)(9), (10)	271 . . . . 23(k)(6)	456 . . . .
109 . . . . 22(b)(11)	272	461 43
110	273 . . . . : . . . . 24(d)	471 . . . . 22(c)
111 . . . . 22(b)(12)	274-279	472 . . . . 22(d)(1)-(5)
112 . . . . 22(b)(13)	281	481 . . . .
113 . . . . 22(b)(14)	301 . . . . 22(e), 115(a), (b),	482 45
114 . . . . 22(b)(16)	(d), (e), (j)	483 . . . .
115 . . . . 116(d), (e)	·302 . . . . . . 115(c), (g)(1)	501 101 except (12) and last
116-119	303 . . . . 115(g)(3)	par. and 165(a), 421
121-123	304 . . . . 115(g)(2)	502 . . . . Last par. 101
141 . . . . 22(aa)(1)	305 . . . . . . 115(f)(1), (2)	503 3813

2. Committee Reports

Major tax legislation involves at least three committee reports. The Conference Committee issues a report in addition to those already issued by the House Ways and Means and Senate Finance Committees. These reports are numbered sequentially by Congress, not by committee, using the issuing house's initials as an identifier.[23]

a. *Citations to Committee Reports.* If you have the citation to a committee report, you can easily locate its text in one of the services discussed in the next paragraph or in the library's government documents (or microform) collection; services such as *CIS Compass* [Illustration 24–2] are also available online. *Bulletin Index–Digest System* and *Barton's Federal Tax Laws Correlated* provide such citations but do not provide the actual text of the reports; each is discussed in Section Q.[24] Only the *Bulletin Index–Digest System* covers the 1986 Code.

[23] The Ways and Means report for the 1986 Act is H.R. REP. No. 426, 99TH CONG., 1ST SESS. (1985). The Senate Finance report for the same act is S. REP. No. 313, 99TH CONG., 2D SESS. (1986). The Conference Committee report is H.R. REP. No. 841, 99TH CONG., 2D SESS. (1986). The Conference report is generally issued only as a House report.

[24] The government itself occasionally prepares citations to legislative history materials. *See, e.g.,* Joint Committee on Taxation, *Listing of Selected Federal Tax Legislation Reprinted in the IRS Cumulative Bulletin, 1913–1990* (JCS–19–91), Dec. 19, 1991. This study appeared as a supplement to *Daily Tax Report* and can also be accessed on the Tax Analysts database in LEXIS–NEXIS. CCH and RIA provide *Cumulative Bulletin* citations to committee reports in their looseleaf services (Section M); *TaxCite* provides this information for commonly-cited statutes enacted between 1913 and 1993.

b. *Text of Committee Reports*. The following services provide at least partial texts of relevant committee reports.

- *CCH Standard Federal Tax Reporter* (Section M) (limited coverage)
- *RIA United States Tax Reporter* (Section M) (limited coverage)
- Rabkin & Johnson, *Federal Income, Gift and Estate Taxation* (Section M) (1954 Code only)
- *Daily Tax Report* (Section P)
- *Cumulative Bulletin* (Section Q)[25]
- *Internal Revenue Acts—Text and Legislative History* (Section Q)
- *Tax Management Primary Sources* (Section Q) (since 1969)
- *Seidman's Legislative History of Federal Income and Excess Profits Tax Laws* (Section Q) (1863–1953)
- *The Internal Revenue Acts of the United States: 1909–1950; 1950– 1972; 1973–* (Section Q)

The Internal Revenue Acts of the United States: 1909–1950; 1950– 1972; 1973– provides full text with original pagination for all materials. Because it begins with 1909, however, you should consult the *Seidman's* set, which includes at least partial texts, for earlier material. Unfortunately, *Seidman's* does not cover estate and gift taxes.

You can also find recent legislative history materials in CD–ROM format (Section S) and online (Section T).

3. Other Documents

a. *Blue Book and Other Staff Documents*. The General Explanation ("Blue Book") issued by the staff of the Joint Committee on Taxation is not an official committee report. As such, it is not covered by materials giving citations to committee reports. The same is true for other Joint Committee staff reports and for reports of subcommittees of legislative committees. The latter reports are published as committee prints. You can find these items online (Section T), in microform collections (Section R), or in the library's government documents section. *Daily Tax Report* prints many of them in its regular issues or as supplements; Tax Analysts includes them in both its microfiche and online databases.

b. *Hearings*. You can locate transcripts of hearings in the government documents section or in microform in most libraries. In addition, their text appears in *The Internal Revenue Acts of the United States:*

---

[25] Committee reports for 1913 through 1938 appear in 1939–1 (pt. 2) C.B. With the exception of the 1954 Code, for which none are included, committee reports for most other acts appear in the *Cumulative Bulletins* as they are issued. William S. Hein & Co., Inc., has issued a one-volume work, *Internal Revenue Code of 1954: Congressional Committee Reports*, covering the 1954 Code's history. In addition, Professor Bernard Reams has compiled a multivolume work containing texts of committee reports, hearings, and debates. This set is available from Hein as part of *The Internal Revenue Acts of the United States* series (Section Q).

1909–1950; 1950–1972; 1973– (Section Q). Excerpts can be located in *Tax Management Primary Sources* (Section Q) (1969 and later) and in *Seidman's Legislative History of Federal Income and Excess Profits Tax Laws* (Section Q) (1863–1953). Transcripts are also available online (Section T). The *CIS Compass* service [Illustration 24–2] provides citations to hearings and an indication of who testified.

c. *Floor Statements.* Floor statements include sponsors' speeches at a bill's introduction and presidential messages accompanying an administration bill. In addition, questions and answers and other statements made during floor debate can illuminate the meaning of an act provision.

The *Congressional Record* includes full text of floor statements. Excerpts appear in *Tax Management Primary Sources* (Section Q) (1969 and later); *Internal Revenue Acts—Text and Legislative History* (Section Q) (since 1954); and *Seidman's Legislative History of Federal Income and Excess Profits Tax Laws* (Section Q) (1863–1953). You can use *Barton's Federal Tax Laws Correlated* (Section Q) as a shortcut for citations to material appearing from 1953 through 1969. You can also obtain citations from a service such as *CIS Compass* [Illustration 24–2].

[Illustration 24–2]

CONGRESSIONAL RECORD STATEMENTS FOR PUB. L. NO. 101–508 FROM *CIS COMPASS* INTERNET DATABASE

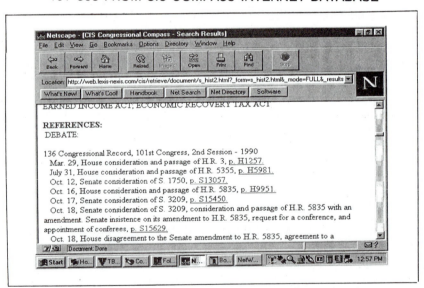

SECTION H. TREATIES

Although United States citizens residing in another country pay United States income tax on both domestic and foreign-source income, they may also be subject to taxation in the foreign country of residence. Congress has enacted several mechanisms to mitigate the resulting double taxation. These include a foreign tax credit, a deduction for foreign taxes, and an exclusion for certain foreign source income.[26] In addition, treaties between the United States and the other country may ameliorate otherwise harsh tax consequences.

In determining which governs a transaction, neither a treaty nor a statute automatically receives preferential treatment by virtue of its status. Article VI, section 2, clause 2 of the Constitution includes both statutes and treaties as the "supreme Law of the Land." However, Congress can decide that treaty provisions will override Code rules governing income earned (or property transferred) abroad by a United States citizen or resident or transactions undertaken in this country by a foreign national.[27] In addition, treaties can be overruled by a later statute, by a later treaty, or by treaty termination.

1. Locating Treaties and Their Histories

Once a treaty goes into force, it is added to the State Department's *Treaties and Other International Acts Series* (T.I.A.S.). T.I.A.S. is the treaty equivalent of *Statutes at Large*; the treaty document equivalent of *United States Code* is *United States Treaties and Other International Agreements* (U.S.T.). Because these treaty compilations are not revised nearly as quickly as their statutory counterparts, you should use other sources to obtain the text of recent treaties.

Although tax treaties and their revising protocols and supplements are published in various places, several are limited to tax treaties. In addition to the sources listed below, online services (Section T) can also be used to find treaty texts and information.

- Tax Analysts Publications (CD–ROM; Microfiche; online)
- *TreatyDisk: United States International Tax Treaties (Kluwer)*[28]
- *Warren, Gorham & Lamont Tax Treaties*
- *Legislative History of United States Tax Conventions* (Roberts & Holland Collection) (William S. Hein & Co., Inc.)
- *CCH Tax Treaties* and *CCH CD–ROM*
- Rhoades & Langer, *U.S. International Taxation and Tax Treaties* (Matthew Bender) (also available on the *Authority* CD–ROM)
- Diamond & Diamond, *International Tax Treaties of All Nations* (Oceana)
- *Federal Tax Coordinator 2d*[29] (Section M)

---

[26] I.R.C. §§ 27, 164(a)(3), 911 & 912.

[27] *See* I.R.C. §§ 894(a) & 7852(d). Disclosure requirements apply to taxpayers who claim that a tax treaty overrules or modifies an internal revenue law. I.R.C. § 6114; Treas. Reg. § 301.6114–1.

[28] Two other CD–ROM sources are *TIARA CD–ROM: Treaties and International Agreements Researchers' Archive* (Oceana) and *Tax Treaties* (International Bureau of Fiscal Documentation).

[29] RIA also includes tax treaties in its *OnPoint* CD–ROM service.

- *Tax Management—Foreign Income* (Section M) (also available in CD–ROM)

- *Daily Tax Report* (Section P)

- *Internal Revenue Bulletin; Cumulative Bulletin*[30] (Section Q)

In addition to treaty texts, these services include the Senate Executive Reports and the Treasury Department Technical Explanations prepared for the Senate. The weekly *Internal Revenue Bulletin* contains the most recent material, which is reprinted in the *Cumulative Bulletin* at six month intervals. These publications are more useful for finding IRS material relating to treaties than for finding the treaties themselves.

2. Citators for Tax Treaties

Shepard's Federal Statutes Citations, discussed in Section L, can be used in locating court decisions involving treaties; you need the U.S.T. and T.I.A.S. citations to use this service. IRS pronouncements can be found in the Service's *Bulletin Index–Digest System*, discussed in Section Q. Looseleaf services (Section M), CD–ROMs (Section S), and online services (Section T) can also be used to find administrative and judicial rulings.

SECTION I.   TREASURY REGULATIONS

Code section 7805(a) authorizes the Secretary of the Treasury to "prescribe all needful rules and regulations for the enforcement" of the tax statutes.[31] Regulations issued pursuant to this authorization are referred to as interpretative (or interpretive). In contrast, there are so-called legislative regulations, issued for Code sections in which Congress has included a specific grant of authority, allowing IRS experts to write rules for highly technical areas.[32] When a regulation is issued or proposed, the transmittal includes a paragraph indicating the Treasury's authority for issuing the regulation, either a specific Code section (legislative) or Code section 7805 (interpretative). Courts uphold interpretative regulations unless they clearly contravene congressional intent; legislative regulations are virtually unassailable.[33]

[30] *Publication 901* contains selected information about treaties, including tax rates and exempt compensation. *See* Joint Committee on Taxation, *Listing of Selected International Tax Conventions and Other Agreements Reprinted in the IRS Cumulative Bulletin, 1913–1990* (JCS–20–91), Dec. 31, 1991, for citations to both treaty documents and administrative guidance.

[31] Regulations are formulated by the IRS and approved by Treasury Department personnel. *See* Procedural Rules of the IRS, § 601.601(a)(1), 26 C.F.R. § 601.601(a)(1).

[32] *See, e.g.,* I.R.C. § 7872(h)(1): "In General—the Secretary shall prescribe such regulations as may be necessary or appropriate to carry out the purposes of this section, including ... adjustments to the provisions of this section will be made to the extent necessary to carry out the purposes of this section...."

[33] *See* Commissioner v. South Texas Lumber Co., 333 U.S. 496 (1948); United States v. Vogel Fertilizer Co., 455 U.S. 16 (1982). Taxpayers may litigate a regulation's status as legislative or interpretative. *See, e.g.,* Newborn v. Commissioner, 94 T.C. 610 (1990).

The type of regulation is apparent from its citation form. A proposed regulation includes "Prop." (*e.g.*, Prop. Treas. Reg. § 1.801–4); a temporary regulation includes a "T" (*e.g.*, Treas. Reg. § 1.71–1T); a final regulation has no special identifier (*e.g.*, Treas. Reg. § 1.106–1). Temporary and final regulations can also be found in title 26 of the *Code of Federal Regulations*.

In the course of a research effort, you may need to locate a current regulation and one or more prior versions. You may also be interested in determining if a regulation is about to be proposed or in reading Preambles that accompanied proposed, temporary, or final regulations.

1. Final and Temporary Regulations

- *CCH Standard Federal Tax Reporter* (Section M)
- *RIA United States Tax Reporter* (Section M)
- *U.S. Code Congressional & Administrative News—Federal Tax Regulations* (Section Q)
- *CCH Federal Tax Service* (Section M)
- Mertens, *Law of Federal Income Taxation—Regulations* (Section M) (includes texts and preambles)
- *Federal Tax Coordinator 2d* (Section M) (*Internal Revenue Bulletin* reprints for proposed and temporary items)
- *Daily Tax Report* (Section P) (includes preambles)
- *Internal Revenue Bulletin; Cumulative Bulletin* (Section Q) (includes preambles)

Online (Section T) and CD–ROM (Section S) materials provide easy access to the language of regulations.

2. Proposed Regulations and Regulations Under Development[34]

Because final and temporary regulations are numbered based on the underlying Code section, they are easy to locate in a tax service or in the *C.F.R.* itself. This is not necessarily true for proposed regulations, which carry project numbers that do not reflect the underlying Code section and which do not appear in *C.F.R.* If you use a service that includes proposed regulations in a separate volume, it generally will have a Code section cross reference table. If you use a CD–ROM (Section S) or online (Section T) service, you can easily locate a proposed regulation by searching for the Code section, project number, or subject matter.

Because Congress enacts new statutes and amends old ones quite frequently, many Code sections lack regulations or have regulations that fail to reflect current law. The *Treasury/IRS Annual Business Plan* indicates projects that should yield regulations during the coming year. The *IRS Semiannual Agenda of Regulations* provides extensive informa-

---

[34] Background memoranda prepared during a regulation's development are relevant if the regulation being litigated is ambiguous. Jewett v. Commissioner, 455 U.S. 305 (1982); *cf.* Deluxe Check Printers, Inc. v. United States, 5 Cl. Ct. 498 (1984).

tion about the status of each item, including its relative priority for the next six months; it appears in the *Federal Register* in April and October. The IRS issues a monthly Regulations Projects Status and Disposition Report to indicate projects it expects will be actively worked on in the near future.[35] The monthly status report is published in the *Daily Tax Report* (Section P). *CCH Standard Federal Tax Reporter* (Section M) also includes a status report. The *Treasury/IRS Business Plan* is available from a variety of sources, including *Tax Notes* (Section P).

3. Prior Regulations

Prior language will often be relevant if you are evaluating recent changes or if your research involves a completed transaction. You can obtain prior language from Mertens, *Law of Federal Income Taxation— Regulations* (Section M) (1954–1985 material); *United States Code Congressional & Administrative News—Federal Tax Regulations* (Section Q); and *RIA Cumulative Changes* (Section Q) (most libraries have the 1954 and 1986 Code versions; some have the 1939 Code version).

If a 1954 Code regulation was originally published before 1960, it was republished that year in T.D. 6498, 6500, or 6516. The *USCCAN* service ignores the original publication in its history notes; *Cumulative Changes* omits the 1960 T.D.s; the Mertens bound volumes cite only the most recent change in a regulation.

4. Citators for Regulations

Regulations rarely keep pace with congressional activity. Whenever a Code section changes, existing regulations may no longer be relevant and may even be totally invalid. If a regulation appears to contradict statutory language, check the date of its most recent T.D. to see if it predates the Code section involved.

When an existing regulation affects a transaction, that regulation's success or failure in previous litigation is quite relevant. The Treasury Department is not bound by adverse decisions in any tribunal other than the Supreme Court. As a result, it will not withdraw a regulation merely because one or more lower courts invalidate it. A citator indicating judicial action on regulations is extremely useful as a tool in gauging the likelihood of taxpayer success in challenging a particular regulation.

The citators listed below, and described further in Section L, follow two basic arrangement patterns: regulations section order or Treasury Decision number order.

- *Shepard's Code of Federal Regulations Citations* (C.F.R. section); *Shepard's Federal Tax Citations* (both C.F.R. section and T.D. number)

- *RIA United States Tax Reporter—Citator* (T.D. number)

- *CCH Standard Federal Tax Reporter—Citator* (T.D. number)

---

[35] Ann. 95–90, 1995–43 I.R.B. 9.

SECTION J.   INTERNAL REVENUE
SERVICE PRONOUNCEMENTS

1.   Types of IRS Pronouncements

There are several methods for categorizing IRS pronouncements. One method looks to the means of publication. The IRS publishes several pronouncements, most notably revenue rulings, revenue procedures, notices, and announcements, in the weekly *Internal Revenue Bulletin*. Most later appear in the semiannual *Cumulative Bulletin*. Other items, including private letter rulings, technical advice memoranda, general counsel memoranda, actions on decisions, and technical memoranda, are not published officially but are available to the public as a result of litigation. Other documents are the subject of Freedom of Information Act (FOIA) litigation as this chapter goes to press.

Another method of categorization involves a document's initial audience. Revenue rulings and other items published in the *Internal Revenue Bulletin* are directed to all taxpayers and their representatives. Private letter rulings, on the other hand, are directed to a specific taxpayer; the IRS makes them available to other readers after deleting identifying material. Still other documents are written for government personnel. Although many of these, such as general counsel memoranda, are publicly available, the IRS resists releasing some other internal documents or releases them with extensive deletions.

2.   Officially–Published IRS Pronouncements

a.   *Revenue Rulings (Rev. Rul.).* The IRS issues rulings designed to apply the law to particular factual situations taxpayers have presented. Rulings fall into two categories—revenue rulings and private letter rulings. If the IRS determines a ruling is of general interest, it publishes it in the *Internal Revenue Bulletin* and *Cumulative Bulletin* as a revenue ruling.[36] Newsletters (Section P) and online systems (Section T) may print the ruling's full text several weeks before the ruling appears in the *Internal Revenue Bulletin*.

Although a revenue ruling is not as authoritative as a Treasury regulation, any taxpayer whose circumstances are substantially the same as those described in the ruling can rely upon it.[37] Revenue rulings constitute authority for avoiding the substantial understatement penalty. Subject to the limitations in Code section 7805(b), rulings can apply retroactively unless their text indicates otherwise. [*See* Illustration 24–3 for a sample revenue ruling.]

[36] The IRS occasionally issued a revenue ruling to indicate it would not follow an adverse appellate court decision. Since 1993, it has used nonacquiescences for this purpose.

[37] The IRS has occasionally issued adverse rulings based upon a set of facts encountered in an audit and then attempted to assert the ruling as authority when the taxpayer litigates. *See* Rev. Rul. 79–427, 1979–2 C.B. 120, discussed in Niles v. United States, 710 F.2d 1391 (9th Cir. 1983).

[Illustration 24–3]

EXCERPT FROM REV. RUL. 87–22, 1987–1 C.B. 146

Rev. Rul. 87-22

ISSUE

        (1) If a taxpayer pays points on the refinancing of a mortgage loan secured by the principal residence of the taxpayer, is the payment deductible in full, under section 461(g)(2) of the Internal Revenue Code, for the taxable year in which the points are paid?

    ...

FACTS

        Situation 1. In 1981, *A* obtained a 16-percent mortgage loan (old mortgage loan) exclusively for the purchase of a principal residence. On August 20, 1986, *A* refinanced the old mortgage loan, which had an outstanding principal balance of $100,000, with a $100,000, 30-year, 10-percent mortgage loan (new mortgage loan) from *L*, a lending institution. The new loan was secured by a mortgage on *A*'s principal residence. Principal and interest payments were due monthly, with the first payment due October 1, 1986, and the last payment due September 1, 2016. In order to refinance, *A* paid 3.6 points ($3,600) to *L* at the loan closing. This points charge was paid from separate funds of *A* that were brought to the loan closing.

    ...

LAW AND ANALYSIS

    ...

        An exception to the general rule of section 461(g)(1) of the Code is set forth in section 461(g)(2). Section 461(g)(2) provides that section 461(g)(1) shall not apply to points paid in respect of any indebtedness incurred in connection with the purchase or improvement of, and secured by, the principal residence of the taxpayer to the extent that such payment of points is an established business practice in the area in which such indebtedness is incurred and the amount of such payment does not exceed the amount generally charged in such area. Therefore, unlike the rule applicable to other instances of prepaid interest, if the requirements of section 461(g)(2) of the Code are satisfied, the taxpayer is not limited to deducting the points over the period of the indebtedness. *Schubel v. Commissioner,* 77 T.C. at 703-04.

    The IRS numbers revenue rulings chronologically.[38] Ruling numbers do not indicate which Code section is involved. The IRS began issuing numbered revenue rulings in 1953 and adopted the current numbering system in 1954. Earlier revenue rulings, with different names [Table 1], were also published in the *Bulletin*.

    Revenue rulings begin with a notation of the regulations section involved; the Code section number also appears. Most recent revenue rulings contain four segments: Issue; Facts; Law and Analysis; and Holding. A fifth segment, Effect on Other Rulings, appears if the current ruling revokes, modifies, obsoletes, or otherwise affects a prior holding. Rulings also include information about the IRS official who drafted them; the *Cumulative Bulletin* omits drafting information included in the *Internal Revenue Bulletin*.

Table 1
Pre–1953 Titles of Cumulative Bulletin Pronouncements

A.R.M.	Committee on Appeals and Review Memorandum
A.R.R.	Committee on Appeals and Review Recommendation
A.T.	Alcohol Tax Unit; Alcohol and Tobacco Tax Division
C.L.T.	Child–Labor Tax Division
C.S.T.	Capital–Stock Tax Division
C.T.	Carriers Taxing Act of 1937; Taxes on Employment by Carriers
D.C.	Treasury Department Circular
Dept.Cir.	Treasury Department Circular

---

[38] Rev. Rul. 98–1 denotes the first revenue ruling issued in 1998. Each week's rulings are numbered sequentially, generally in Code section order. The number of rulings varies from year to year. The IRS issued over 700 in 1955; it released only 65 in 1996.

E.P.C.	Excess Profits Tax Council Ruling or Memorandum
E.T.	Estate and Gift Tax Division or Ruling
Em.T.	Employment Taxes
G.C.M.	Chief Counsel's Memorandum; General Counsel's Memorandum; Assistant General Counsel's Memorandum
I.T.	Income Tax Unit or Division
L.O.	Solicitor's Law Opinion
MS.	Miscellaneous Unit or Division or Branch
M.T.	Miscellaneous Division or Branch
Mim.	Mimeographed Letter; Mimeograph
O.	Solicitor's Law Opinion
O.D.	Office Decision
Op.A.G.	Opinion of Attorney General
P.T.	Processing Tax Decision or Division
S.	Solicitor's Memorandum
S.M.	Solicitor's Memorandum
S.R.	Solicitor's Recommendation
S.S.T.	Social Security Tax and Carriers' Tax; Social Security Tax; Taxes on Employment by Other than Carriers
S.T.	Sales Tax Unit or Division or Branch
Sil.	Silver Tax Division
Sol.Op.	Solicitor's Opinion
T.	Tobacco Division
T.B.M.	Advisory Tax Board Memorandum
T.B.R.	Advisory Tax Board Recommendation
Tob.	Tobacco Branch

b.   *Revenue Procedures (Rev. Proc.) and Procedural Rules.* Revenue procedures are published statements of IRS practices and procedures, numbered chronologically since 1955, and published in the *Internal Revenue Bulletin* and *Cumulative Bulletin*. Procedures of general applicability may be added to the IRS Statement of Procedural Rules and published in the *Code of Federal Regulations*. Revenue procedures constitute authority for avoiding the substantial understatement penalty.

Several regularly-issued revenue procedures are particularly important. The first one issued each year *(e.g.,* Rev. Proc. 98–1) provides procedures for obtaining rulings, determination letters, and closing agreements. It also includes a sample ruling request format and a schedule of user fees. The second revenue procedure each year deals with requests for technical advice, discussed in subsection 3. The third, which is supplemented during the year, contains a cumulative list of areas in which the IRS will not grant rulings.

Revenue procedures include several subdivisions, the exact number of which are determined by the procedure's scope and complexity. The following subdivisions are commonly used: Purpose; Background; Procedure; Effective Date; and Effect on Other Revenue Procedures. Drafting information also appears.

c.   *Notices, Announcements, and Other Items.* The IRS issues notices to provide guidance before revenue rulings and regulations are available. Notices can describe future regulations in a manner that will pass muster under the Code section 7805(b) rules on retroactivity. Notices are numbered by year; their number does not indicate the Code section involved. Notices appear in both the *I.R.B.* and *C.B.* and constitute authority for avoiding the substantial understatement penalty.

Announcements appear in the *I.R.B.* but not the *C.B.* They alert taxpayers to a variety of information but do not have the formality of notices, revenue rulings, or revenue procedures. They are numbered by year and constitute authority for avoiding the substantial understatement penalty.

The *Bulletins* also contain disbarment notices, delegation orders (Del. Order), and IRS acquiescences (and nonacquiescences) in unfavorable court decisions.[39] Non–IRS material includes Treasury regulations, legislative histories, and Supreme Court decisions.

Instructions accompanying tax return forms and explanatory booklets are published on a regular basis. However, they contain few, if any, citations to authority and do not indicate that the IRS position has been disputed. Further, even if they are misleading, taxpayers who rely on them cannot cite them as authority against a contrary IRS position.[40]

3. Publicly–Released Pronouncements

The items discussed below are useful in determining the IRS position on relevant issues. Many of them constitute authority for avoiding the substantial understatement penalty.

a. *Private Letter Rulings (P.L.R.; PLR; Ltr. Rul.; Priv. Ltr. Rul.).* Private letter rulings[41] illustrate IRS policy and often indicate areas where future guidance is likely. The public has access to them subject to the limitations of Code section 6110,[42] but the IRS does not consider itself bound by them in its dealings with other taxpayers.[43] Private letter

---

[39] Although these materials appear in the *Internal Revenue Bulletin*, the *Cumulative Bulletins* include only disbarment information and acquiescences and nonacquiescences. The IRS began including acquiescence notices for all courts beginning with 1993–1 C.B. Previously, it included this information only for Tax Court regular decisions.

[40] *See* Adler v. Commissioner, 330 F.2d 91 (9th Cir. 1964); Manocchio v. Commissioner, 710 F.2d 1400 (9th Cir. 1983). *See also* T.A.M. 83–50–008, involving IRS refusal to allow a taxpayer to claim reliance on a portion of the *Internal Revenue Manual* or on the 1982 version of IRS *Publication 544. But see* Gehl Co. v. Commissioner, 795 F.2d 1324 (7th Cir. 1986) (government decision not to seek *certiorari* explained in A.O.D. 1988–002).

[41] Determination letters are similar to letter rulings but emanate from IRS District Offices. District Offices issue them only if they can be based on well-established rules that apply to the issues presented. Otherwise, the matter is appropriately handled by the National Office.

[42] Access to letter rulings was initially requested under the Freedom of Information Act, 5 U.S.C. § 552. Litigation led to the release of items issued after October 31, 1976, and to the enactment of I.R.C. § 6110. *See* Tax Analysts and Advocates v. Internal Revenue Service, 405 F. Supp. 1065 (D.D.C. 1975). Letter rulings have been released as issued since mid-March 1977. I.R.C. § 6110(h) authorizes inspection of documents issued after July 4, 1967.

[43] *But see* Ogiony v. Commissioner, 617 F.2d 14, 17–18 (2d Cir. 1980) (Oakes, J., concurring). Although commenting that they had no precedential force, the Supreme Court has cited private letter rulings as evidence of IRS inconsistent interpretation. Rowan Cos., Inc. v. United States, 452 U.S. 247, 261 n.17 (1981).

rulings issued after October 31, 1976, constitute authority for avoiding the substantial understatement penalty. As noted above, the IRS may ultimately publish those of general interest as revenue rulings. You can request IRS release of background documents, including IRS-taxpayer correspondence with regard to a particular ruling. The cost of such items can be substantial.[44]

Letter rulings have multi-digit file numbers (*e.g.*, P.L.R. 84–37–084); the first two digits indicate the year, and the next two the week, of release; the remaining numbers indicate the item number for that week. The requesting taxpayer receives a private letter ruling approximately three months before its release to the public. As a result, the actual week of release is later than that shown in the letter. Private letter rulings and technical advice memoranda share a common numbering system. Technical advice memoranda carry the first release numbers each week. Unless you label the document as a P.L.R. or a T.A.M., its identity will not be readily apparent.

b.   *Technical Advice Memoranda (T.A.M.; TAM; Tech. Adv. Mem.).* Technical advice memoranda share several characteristics with private letter rulings. They are issued by the IRS National Office, which does not consider them precedential for other taxpayers, and they are available subject to the limitations of Code section 6110. Technical advice memoranda are issued in response to IRS requests arising out of tax return examinations; private letter ruling requests focus on proposed transactions.

c.   *Actions on Decisions (A.O.D.; AOD).* A.O.D.s indicate the reasoning behind the Service's recommendation whether or not to appeal an adverse decision by a trial or appellate court[45] and whether to acquiesce or nonacquiesce in that decision.[46] A.O.D.s are numbered sequentially by year (*e.g.*, A.O.D. 1984–022); the numbering provides no information about the underlying case name or issue. A.O.D.s were made available after FOIA litigation.[47] Taxpayers can use those issued after March 12, 1981, as authority for avoiding the substantial understatement penalty.

d.   *General Counsel Memoranda (G.C.M.; Gen. Couns. Mem.).* These memoranda emanate from the Office of Chief Counsel.[48] They indicate the reasoning and authority used in revenue rulings, private letter

---

[44] *See* I.R.C. § 6110. The IRS imposes a search fee and a per page fee for the effort in deleting identifying and other confidential information from background documents. Rev. Proc. 95–15, 1995–1 C.B. 523.

[45] Even the IRS has a sense of humor. *See* A.O.D. 1984–022 for a poetic rejoinder to the Tax Court's "Ode to Conway Twitty" footnote in Jenkins v. Commissioner, 47 T.C.M. (CCH) 238, 247 n.14 (1983).

[46] The IRS originally issued notices of acquiescence and nonacquiescence only for Tax Court regular decisions. Beginning with 1993–1 C.B., it now issues these notices for decisions by other courts as well. A.O.D.s were never limited to Tax Court decisions.

[47] G.C.M.s, A.O.D.s, and T.M.s became available only after a second round of litigation. *See* Tax Analysts v. Internal Revenue Service, 49 A.F.T.R.2d 82–421 (D.D.C. 1981).

[48] Do not confuse current G.C.M.s with revenue rulings issued before 1953, which were also called G.C.M.s. *See* Table 1.

rulings, and technical advice memoranda. The IRS does not consider them precedential, but IRS personnel can use them as guides in formulating positions. Taxpayers can use those issued after March 12, 1981, as authority for avoiding the substantial understatement penalty.

These documents are numbered sequentially (*e.g.*, G.C.M. 39278). The numbering system does not indicate the year of issue, the Code section involved, or the document about which they supply information. The number of issued has declined significantly in recent years.

e. *Technical Memoranda (T.M.; Tech. Mem.).* Technical memoranda provide background information on regulations that are in the process of being promulgated. Much of their content is reflected in the preamble to each regulation.

f. *Internal Revenue Manual (I.R.M.).* In many instances a tax problem will require knowledge of IRS operating policies. Thus, you may desire information about IRS procedures for compliance with the Privacy Act of 1974, the audit procedures applied to stock brokers, or the Associate Chief Counsels' functions. The *Internal Revenue Manual (I.R.M.)* is the best source of such information.

g. *Field Service Advice (F.S.A.).* IRS field attorneys, revenue agents, and appeals officers may request national office advice if a case presents a significant legal question of first impression and no guidance exists as to the Chief Counsel's legal position or policy.[49] The auditor may seek field service advice instead of requesting a technical advice memorandum and may do so without the taxpayer's knowledge.

So-called field service advice is issued in formal and informal modes. Although the IRS has released several informal field service advice memoranda, FOIA litigation to gain access to formal field service advice memoranda was ongoing as this chapter went to press.[50]

h. *Litigation Guideline Memoranda (L.G.M.).* Litigation guideline memoranda are prepared by attorneys assigned to two Assistant Chief Counsel offices (Field Service and General Litigation). These memoranda discuss variations on fact patterns and tactical approaches that might be used. Unlike field service advice, they are not drafted for a specific case being litigated. Some were released after an FOIA request was filed.[51]

i. *Industry Specialization Program (I.S.P.); Market Segment Understandings (M.S.U.).* The industry specialization program is designed to provide coordinated examination and litigation efforts in a variety of industries; the goal is consistency in result after allowing for differences in facts. The Examination Division and Chief Counsel select industries for inclusion in the program. Coordinated Issue Papers are designed to enhance the audit process by assuring that key issues will be covered in

---

[49] I.R.M. (35)(19)41 (Apr. 8, 1992).

[50] Tax Analysts v. Internal Revenue Service, 117 F.3d 607 (D.C. Cir. 1997). The IRS recently announced a new type of guidance, Service Center Advice, which is being disclosed.

[51] Tax Analysts filed suit to have these released. TAX NOTES, Oct. 7, 1996, at 7.

a consistent manner within an industry. Other industry-specific programs include Market Segment Understandings. These involve IRS agreements with representatives of a particular industry on how to handle a specific issue.

j. *Legal Memoranda (L.M.).* These memoranda provide the IRS position on issues that will be covered in a revenue ruling. The IRS has severely redacted many of the memoranda released to the public.

k. *Tax Litigation Bulletins (T.L.B.).* Issued by the Office of Chief Counsel, the bulletins summarize recent court decisions and briefs and publish recommendations for appellate action and IRS recommendations to the Justice Department. Several of these have been released, but with significant deletions.

4. Unreleased Documents

Technical Assistance Memoranda provide internal guidance on a variety of requests for information. Among other matters, they can cover on-going litigation, ruling requests, and research projects. Closing Agreements memorialize the agreement regarding specific IRS-taxpayer disputes. The IRS has forced publication of certain agreements with exempt organizations but has otherwise resisted releasing these agreements to the public. Advance Pricing Agreements (APA) are made between taxpayers and the IRS regarding income allocation between commonly-controlled entities. They are important for companies that segment their operations between countries with different tax rates.

5. Locating And Evaluating IRS Pronouncements

a. *Internal Revenue Bulletin Items–Citations and Texts.* Because IRS materials do not carry numbers that correspond to the Code sections they discuss, CD–ROM (Section S) and online (Section T) services are excellent sources for finding these items; you can search each database by topic, Code or regulations section, or prior ruling. You can also use digests and looseleaf services (Section M) to locate appropriate rulings and procedures.

The following publications can also be used to locate and read relevant items.

- *CCH Standard Federal Tax Reporter* (Section M)
- *RIA United States Tax Reporter* (Section M)
- *Federal Tax Coordinator 2d* (Section M)
- Mertens, *Law of Federal Income Taxation* (Section M) (does not print text of notices and announcements) [*See* Illustration 24–4.]
- Rabkin & Johnson, *Federal Income, Gift and Estate Taxation* (Section M)
- *CCH Federal Tax Service* (Section M) (does not print texts)
- *Tax Management Portfolios* (Section M) (does not print texts)
- *Tax Notes* (Section P) (does not print texts)

- *Daily Tax Report* (Section P)
- *Bulletin Index–Digest System* (Section Q) [*See* Illustration 24–5.]; full texts appear in *Internal Revenue Bulletin* and *Cumulative Bulletin.*

[Illustration 24–4]

EXCERPT FROM MERTENS CODE–RULINGS TABLE

Code Sec.	Rev. Rul. or Rev. Proc.	Code Sec.	Rev. Rul. or Rev. Proc.
441(d)	85-22, 87-57	446	57-166, 57-379, 57-510
	Rev. Proc. 85-15, 87-32		57-588, 58-78, 58-474
441(e)	57-51, 85-15, 87-57		59-272, 59-285, 60-24
	Rev. Proc. 85-15, 87-32		60-31, 60-60, 60-85
441(f)	55-10, 85-22, 87-57		60-133, 60-145, 60-191
	89-13		60-243, 63-57, 64-148
	Rev. Proc. 85-15. 87-32		64-278, 68-35, 68-83

[Illustration 24–5]

EXCERPT FROM IRS *BULLETIN INDEX–DIGEST SYSTEM*

Allowances

they are not ordained, commissioned, or licensed as ministers of the gospel. §1.107-1. (Sec. 22(b), '39 Code; Sec. 107, '86 Code.)
　　Rev. Rul. 59-270, 1959-2 C.B. 44.

22.40　Rental; minister; personal residence purchased. An ordained minister, who purchases his own home and has his church designate his entire compensation as a rental allowance, may exclude from gross income as rental allowance only an amount equal to the fair rental value of the acquired home plus the cost of utilities. §1.107-1. (Sec. 107, '86 Code.)
　　Rev. Rul. 71-280, 1971-2 C.B. 92.

22.47　Rental; minister; traveling evangelist. An ordained minister, who performs evangelistic services at churches located away from the community in which he maintains his permanent home may exclude from gross income rental allowances paid to him by such churches, as part of his compensation, to the extent used by him to maintain his permanent home. §1.107-1. (Sec. 107, '86 Code.)
　　Rev. Rul. 64-326, 1964-2 C.B. 37.

22.48　Rental; minister; utilities. A minister of the gospel who is provided a home rent-free by his church, but pays for his utilities, may not deduct

nished by the National Guard to officers and enlisted personnel while on active duty is not includible in the gross income of the recipients. §1.61-2. (Sec. 61, '86 Code.)
　　Rev. Rul. 60-65, 1960-1 C.B. 21.

22.55　Subsistence; ROTC students. Amounts received as subsistence allowances by students participating in advanced ROTC training are not includible in the gross income of the recipients. §1.61-2. (Sec. 61, '86 Code.)
　　Rev. Rul. 66-3, 1966-1 C.B. 19.

22.56　Subsistence; state police officers. Procedures are set forth for state police officers

Mertens and the *Cumulative Bulletin* cumulate prior years' rulings in bound volumes. Because it contains only rulings and procedures, Mertens may be slightly easier to use for a project involving multiple years. However, its coverage from 1954 until 1987 is limited to the income tax.

b.   *Forms and Publications.* IRS forms and accompanying instructions appear in *CCH Federal Tax Forms*, *RIA Federal Revenue Forms*, *RIA Tax Action Coordinator*, and *Tax Management IRS Forms*. The *Tax Management Portfolios* (Section M) also reproduce a significant number of forms. Forms are also available in CD–ROM (Section S) and online (Section T) services, including the IRS website. IRS publications designed to guide taxpayers in preparing returns and keeping records are published in *CCH IRS Publications* and *RIA Publications of the IRS*. They are also available in CD–ROM and online.

c.   *Other IRS Documents.*

(1) *Private Letter Rulings and Technical Advice Memoranda.* Every week the IRS releases these documents for inspection and copying. Although IRS personnel do not include headnotes or summaries, several commercial services do. You can use these commercial services to compile lists of documents to read. Many of these services also contain digests or full texts. In some instances, you can even use a service as a citator for these items. These various functions are discussed in the following lists.

Online (Section T) and CD–ROM (Section S) services are excellent sources for finding private letter rulings and technical advice memoranda. Other sources include:

- *CCH IRS Letter Rulings Reports* (full text service)
- *CCH Standard Federal Tax Reporter* (Section M) (finding lists)
- *RIA United States Tax Reporter* (Section M) (finding lists)
- *Daily Tax Report* (Section P) (digests)
- *Tax Notes* (Section P) (digests); *Tax Analysts Letter Rulings Service* (full text)

In addition to citations to private letter rulings in their compilation volumes, you can use the citator volumes of *CCH Standard Federal Tax Reporter* and *RIA United States Tax Reporter* to locate letter rulings construing revenue rulings, T.D.s, and judicial decisions.

(2) *General Counsel Memoranda, Actions on Decisions, and Technical Memoranda.* Digests of these internal documents appear in both *Daily Tax Report* and *Tax Notes* (Section P). Full texts are available in CD–ROM (Section S) and online services (Section T), and in *CCH IRS Positions*. *CCH IRS Positions* prints the full text of G.C.M.s, A.O.D.s, and T.M.s issued since December 24, 1981. The CCH introduction to each document gives cross references to the location of related documents in other CCH services.

(3) *Internal Revenue Manual.* The workings of the IRS are compiled in the *Internal Revenue Manual*. Commerce Clearing House publishes

those portions released to the public in two looseleaf services. The Administrative volumes contain the text of policies, procedures, instructions, and guidelines involved in the organization, functions, administration, and operations of the Service. The Audit volumes contain policies and other information relating to the Service's audit function. The volumes are updated whenever the IRS finalizes a change in existing policies.

(4) *Other Internal Documents.* Other documents available to the public can be found online (Section T), on CD–ROM services (Section S), and excerpted in newsletters (Section P).

6. Citators for IRS Materials

The IRS reviews revenue rulings and procedures for continued relevance. In addition, some rulings have been subjected to judicial scrutiny. The status of these items can be determined from CD–ROM (Section S) and online (Section T) services and from the following materials. [*See* Illustration 24–6.]

- *Shepard's Federal Tax Citations* (Section L)
- *RIA United States Tax Reporter—Citator* (Section L)
- *CCH Standard Federal Tax Reporter—Citator* (Section L)
- Mertens, *Law of Federal Income Taxation—Rulings* (Section M)
- *Bulletin Index–Digest System* (Section Q)

The last two items exclude judicial action from their coverage. The *RIA* and *Shepard's Federal Tax* citators also provide citations to letter rulings.

[Illustration 24–6]

EXCERPT FROM MERTENS RULINGS STATUS TABLE

RULINGS STATUS TABLE

1997 TO DATE

Use this Table to determine if there has been any subsequent action taken on previously published Rulings or Procedures during the period 1997 to date.

To use this Table refer to the **Previous Ruling** (left-hand) column to see if the ruling which you have previously relied upon has been Modified by a subsequent action. If the ruling you have been relying upon has been changed, you will see by the designation in the **Action** column what change has been made and you will then be referred in the **Current Ruling** column to the Revenue Ruling or Procedure that is presently controlling.

Previous Ruling	**Action**	**Current Ruling**
Rev. Rul. 92-19	Supplemented	Rev. Rul. 97-2

SECTION K. JUDICIAL REPORTS

1. Court Organization

Four courts serve as trial courts for tax disputes: District Courts; the Court of Federal Claims; the Tax Court; and Bankruptcy Courts.

a. *United States District Courts.* Because District Courts are courts of general jurisdiction, their judges rarely develop as high a level of expertise on tax law questions as do judges of the Tax Court or even of the Court of Federal Claims. Taxpayers must pay the amount in dispute and sue for a refund before litigating in District Court, the only tribunal where a jury trial is available.

b. *United States Court of Federal Claims.* Although the Court of Federal Claims does not hear tax cases exclusively, the percentage of such cases it hears is greater than that heard in the average District Court. As in the District Court, a taxpayer must first pay the disputed amount before bringing suit. Prior to October 1, 1982, this court was called the United States Court of Claims. Trials were conducted by a trial judge (formerly called a commissioner), whose decisions were reviewed by Court of Claims judges; only the Supreme Court had jurisdiction over appeals from its decisions. Between October 1, 1982, and October 29, 1992, this court was called the United States Claims Court.

c. *United States Tax Court.* Because Tax Court judges hear only tax cases, their expertise is substantially greater than that of judges in the other trial courts. Tax Court cases are tried by one judge, who submits an opinion to the chief judge for consideration. The chief judge can allow the decision to stand or refer it to the full court for review. The published decision will indicate if it has been reviewed; dissenting opinions, if any, will be included. In some instances, special trial judges will hear disputes and issue opinions.

There are two types of Tax Court decisions:[52] the court publishes decisions presenting important legal issues (regular decisions); other publishers print decisions involving well-established legal issues (memorandum decisions). A taxpayer can sue in the Tax Court without paying the amount in dispute prior to litigating. Taxpayers also had this privilege in the Tax Court's predecessor, the Board of Tax Appeals.

d. *United States Bankruptcy Court.* In addition to deciding priority of liens and related matters, United States Bankruptcy Courts may also issue substantive tax rulings. District Court judges review Bankruptcy Court decisions.[53]

e. *Appellate Review.* When your research uncovers conflicting decisions at the trial court level, you should trace those decisions to the appellate court level. If no appeals have been taken, the Tax Court's specialized knowledge may cause you to accord greater weight to its decisions than to decisions from the other trial courts.[54] In addition, if a court has ruled against the government and the IRS has issued a notice of acquiescence, the precedential value of the decision is further enhanced.[55]

Decisions of District Courts and the Tax Court are appealed to the Court of Appeals for the taxpayer's geographical residence[56] and from there to the Supreme Court. Decisions of the Court of Federal Claims are appealed to the Court of Appeals for the Federal Circuit. Because the Supreme Court reviews so few Court of Appeals decisions, the Court of Federal Claims–Federal Circuit route offers a forum-shopping opportuni-

---

[52] The Tax Court also has a Small Cases division that taxpayers can elect to use for disputes of $10,000 or less. Decisions in such cases are not appealable, cannot be used as precedents, and are not published in any reporter service. I.R.C. § 7463(a) & (b).

[53] *See, e.g.,* Michaud v. United States, 97–1 U.S.T.C. ¶ 50,292 (D.N.H. 1997), upholding the result in *In re* Michaud, 199 B.R. 248 (Bankr. D.N.H. 1996).

[54] *But see* Clougherty Packing Co. v. Commissioner, 811 F.2d 1297, 1299 (9th Cir. 1987) ("Although the Tax Court's judgments in its field of expertise are accorded a presumption that they correctly apply the law, we do not apply a rule of special deference to its decisions.").

[55] You should always check the A.O.D.s (Chapter 9) to learn the rationale for an IRS decision about appealing or acquiescing.

[56] From 1924 to 1926, decisions of the Board of Tax Appeals (the Tax Court's predecessor) were appealed to District Court. Revenue Act of 1924, ch. 234, § 900(g), 43 Stat. 253, 336; Revenue Act of 1926, ch. 27, § 1001(a), 44 Stat. 9, 109.

ty to taxpayers living in circuits where appellate court decisions involving similar issues are adverse.[57]

2. Locating Decisions

a. *Finding Lists.* If you need decisions involving a particular statute, treaty, regulation, or ruling, you can compile a preliminary reading list using the looseleaf servicees discussed in Section M. You can also use the following services for that purpose:[58]

- *Shepard's Citations; Shepard's Federal Tax Citations* (Section L)

- *RIA United States Tax Reporter—Citator* (Section L)

- *CCH Standard Federal Tax Reporter—Citator* (Section L)

- *Bulletin Index–Digest System* (Section Q)

b. *Texts of Decisions.*[59] Federal court decisions involving taxation appear in the sets listed below. You can also locate them online (Section T), in microform (Section R), and in CD–ROM format (Section S). Various newsletters (Section P) also print texts or digests.

(1) *Supreme Court (since 1796): United States Reports (U.S.)* (official); *United States Supreme Court Reports, Lawyers' Edition (L. Ed.; L. Ed. 2d)* ; *Supreme Court Reporter (S. Ct.)* (since 1882); *American Federal Tax Reports*; *U.S. Tax Cases* (since 1913); *Internal Revenue Bulletin (I.R.B.); Cumulative Bulletin (C.B.)* (since 1920).

(2) *Courts of Appeals* (since 1880): *Federal Reporter (F.; F.2d; F.3d)*; *American Federal Tax Reports*; *U.S. Tax Cases* (since 1915).

(3) *District Courts* (since 1882): *Federal Supplement (F. Supp.)* (since 1932); *Federal Reporter* (from 1882 until 1932); *American Federal Tax Reports*; *U.S. Tax Cases* (since 1915).

(4) *Court of Federal Claims* (since 1884): *U.S. Court of Claims Reports (Ct. Cl.)* (official) (until October 1, 1982); *Federal Reporter* (from 1929 until 1932; from 1960 until October 1, 1982); *Federal Supplement* (between 1932 and 1960); *United States Claims Court Reporter (Cl. Ct.)* (from October 1, 1982, until October 29, 1992); *United States Court of Federal Claims Reporter (Fed. Cl.)* (since October 30, 1992); *American Federal Tax Reports*; *U.S. Tax Cases* (since 1924).

(5) *Tax Court* (since 1942): *Tax Court of the United States Reports; United States Tax Court Reports (T.C.)* (official); *CCH Tax Court Report-*

---

[57] *See* Ginsburg v. United States, 184 Ct. Cl. 444, 449, 396 F.2d 983, 986 (1968), for a discussion of this phenomenon in the court's predecessor, the Court of Claims.

[58] *See* Table 2 (Section L) for an indication of each service's coverage. None uses every source as cited material.

[59] Relevant dates of coverage are indicated for each court. Separate indications are noted for unofficial reports if their coverage dates are different. Early *Cumulative Bulletins* included lower federal court decisions either as Court Decisions (Ct. D.) or as Miscellaneous Rulings. Because the disparate labels make these items virtually impossible to locate, they are omitted from these lists. *See* Chapter 4, for an extensive discussion of case reports.

er ; *RIA Tax Court Reports* (formerly *P-H*); *CCH Tax Court Memorandum Decisions*; *RIA Tax Court Memorandum Decisions* (formerly *P-H.*)

(6) *Board of Tax Appeals* (between 1924 and 1942; memorandum decisions between 1928 and 1942): *Board of Tax Appeals Reports (B.T.A.)* (official); *P-H B.T.A. Memorandum Decisions*.

(7) *Bankruptcy Courts* (since 1979): *West's Bankruptcy Reporter (B.R.)*; *American Federal Tax Reports*; *U.S. Tax Cases*.

3. Tax–Oriented Case Reporter Services

Most of the sets listed above are published by the Government Printing Office or by West Group and are used the same way for tax research as for non-tax research. The sets published by Research Institute of America and Commerce Clearing House differ enough from the others to warrant further discussion.

a. *A.F.T.R.* and *U.S.T.C.* The use of these sets can be coordinated with the use of each publisher's looseleaf reporting service, *A.F.T.R.* with *RIA United States Tax Reporter* and *U.S.T.C.*[60] with *CCH Standard Federal Tax Reporter*. Each service publishes decisions from all courts except the Tax Court, and each includes "unpublished" decisions omitted from *Federal Supplement* and *Federal Reporter*. Each first includes these decisions in an Advance Sheets volume of the related looseleaf reporting service. This initial publication in conjunction with the looseleaf services results in recent decisions being available in hard copy on a weekly basis. While both services are supplemented weekly, each occasionally prints decisions before the other does.

These cases also appear in the listings of new material in the services' update volumes (Recent Developments for *RIA United States Tax Reporter*; New Matters for *CCH Standard Federal Tax Reporter*). The listings appear in Code section order and are cross referenced to discussions in the services' compilation volumes. As a result, you can locate a recent case when you know the Code section involved but not the taxpayer's name, and you can immediately find a discussion of the topic involved in the compilation volumes. The daily newsletters (Section P), which are probably the only more current print source of these cases, print only partial texts and lack a weekly index.

When using these reporter services, note the reference method being used. *U.S.T.C.* uses paragraph numbers for cross references to the Advance Sheets and bound volumes (*e.g.*, 88–1 U.S.T.C. ¶ 9390). RIA cites decisions in the *A.F.T.R.* Advance Sheets and bound volumes by page number (*e.g.*, 62 A.F.T.R.2d 88–5228).

The bound volumes include all types of tax cases—income, estate and gift, and excise; the individual Advance Sheets volumes do not. The

---

[60] The earliest volumes of this service print all Supreme Court decisions and those lower court decisions of "genuine precedent value.... " *Foreword* to 1 U.S.T.C. (1938). When CCH began issuing two volumes per year, it expanded coverage to all decisions.

different types of cases appear in Advance Sheets sections accompanying each publisher's looseleaf service for the particular area of tax law.

b. *Tax Court Reports*. Both CCH and RIA publish looseleaf Tax Court reporters.

The *RIA Tax Court Reports* prints the full texts of both regular and memorandum decisions in a single looseleaf volume. References are given to *RIA United States Tax Reporter*. The weekly Report Bulletin contains case digests arranged by Code section. There is also an alphabetical Table of Decisions.

The *CCH Tax Court Reporter* has three looseleaf volumes. Volume 1 contains memorandum decisions and Volume 2 contains regular decisions. Volume 3, which is discussed below, contains case digests and information about pending litigation. Volume 1 has an alphabetical Table of Decisions, while Volume 2 provides cross references from the reporter service to CCH case numbers.

4. Pending Litigation, Briefs, and Petitions

You can use either the *RIA United States Tax Reporter* Tables volume or the *CCH Standard Federal Tax Reporter* New Matters volume to determine if appeals have been filed in recent tax cases. *United States Tax Reporter* has an alphabetical Table of Cases in which appeals are noted; the *SFTR* version is the current year's Case Table.

Cases pending decision by the Tax Court appear in volume 3 of the *CCH Tax Court Reporter*, which contains digests of petitions. These digests identify cases whose eventual outcome might affect the results of a current research effort. CCH arranges cases by docket numbers; these numbers appear in the alphabetical Petitioners Table and the topical Petitions Index. The *CCH Tax Court Reporter* also contains Motion and Trial Calendars and a section for New Tax Disputes. The Disputes section contains explanations of newsworthy petitions—*e.g.*, those presenting novel theories or involving previously unexplored areas of the Code. A Docket Disposition Table covers final action on each petition. Updating is weekly.

Because the IRS often indicates its recommendation about appealing adverse decisions in actions on decisions (Section J), you should also research these documents before deciding if appeals are likely in cases of interest.

Tax Analysts covers pending litigation in the Court Petitions and Reviewed Briefs sections of *Tax Notes* (Section P); its online version prints the full text of taxpayer petitions and government briefs for Tax Court cases (Section T).

5. Citators for Decisions

There are four commonly-used citators for judging the relative authority of any tax decision, and many libraries own all of them. Although there is substantial overlap in their coverage, each citator contains some information the others lack. All four are discussed in Section L. CD–ROMs (Section S) and online services (Section T) also include access to citators.

- *Shepard's Citations (Bankruptcy; Federal; United States)*

- *Shepard's Federal Tax Citations*

- *RIA United States Tax Reporter—Citator*

- *CCH Standard Federal Tax Reporter—Citator*

IRS action with regard to cases it has lost can be located in the *Bulletin Index–Digest System* (Section Q) or in one of the internal document services discussed in Section J.

SECTION L. CITATORS

You can use four citator services to judge whether a particular statute, treaty, regulation, ruling, or judicial decision has been criticized, approved, or otherwise commented upon in a more recent proceeding. The material being evaluated is referred to as the *cited* item; any later material that refers to it is a *citing* item. The four services are *Shepard's Citations*; *Shepard's Federal Tax Citations*; *RIA United States Tax Reporter-Citator*; and *CCH Standard Federal Tax Reporter-Citator*. *Shepard's*, *CCH*, and *RIA* all make their citators available in a variety of formats: traditional print versions; CD–ROM; and online. You can also do CD–ROM and online searches without using traditional citators by using the case you are interested in as a search term.

The *Shepard's* and *RIA* citators use syllabus numbers to indicate issues and letter symbols to indicate judicial or other commentary; *CCH* does neither. Although many users prefer *Shepard's* and *RIA* because they do provide this information, misleading results can occur. [*See* Illustrations 24–7 through 24–9.]

Shepard's is arranged by numerical reporter citations. *CCH* and *RIA* arrange cited cases by taxpayer name. You should note the taxpayer's first name to make your search easier, particularly if the taxpayer has a common surname.

CCH uses fewer citing cases than do the others. *CCH* also divides its citator service to correspond to its separate income, estate and gift, and excise tax services. The other two do not and thus appear much larger.

Mertens, *Law of Federal Income Taxation* (Section M) and the IRS *Bulletin Index–Digest System* (Section Q) also have citator features, but these are limited to IRS action on revenue rulings and procedures.

Table 2
Comparison of Selected Citator Features

	Shepard's	Shepard's Tax	RIA	CCH	Bulletin Index–Digest	Mertens
Cited Material						
Constitution	x					
Statutes	x	x			x	x
Treaties	x				x	
Regulations						
C.F.R. §	x	x			x	
T.D.		x	x	x		
IRS						
Rev. Rul.		x	x	x	x	x
P.L.R.		x	x			
Decisions	x	x	x	x		
Citing Material						
IRS Materials						
Rev. Rul.		x	x	x	x	x
P.L.R.		x	x	x		
Decisions	x	x	x	x		
References to Topical Discussion						
Articles		x				
Treatises or Looseleafs				x		
Case Citations by Case Name			x	x		
Reporter Page	x	x				
Syllabus Issue Indicated	x	x	x			
Grouped Together			x			
Symbols for Result	x	x	x			

[Illustration 24–7]

EXCERPT FROM *SHEPARD'S FEDERAL TAX CITATIONS*

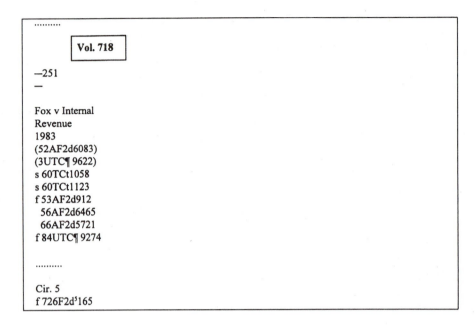

→ *Shepard's* now indicates the case name the first time it includes the main case.

→ *Shepard's* includes citations to *A.F.T.R.* and *U.S.T.C.* for citing material directly after listing the main case. Citations to citing material in the *Federal Reporter* and *Federal Supplement* are organized by circuit. As a result, the citation to *Oelze* appears twice directly under *Fox* (*A.F.T.R.* and *U.S.T.C.*) and once under Cir. 5 (*F.2d*).

→ *Shepard's A.F.T.R.* and *U.S.T.C.* listings indicate that *Oelze* followed *Fox* but do not list a syllabus number. Its *F.2d* listing indicates that *Oelze* followed syllabus number 5 in *Fox*.

[Illustration 24–8]

EXCERPT FROM *RIA UNITED STATES TAX REPORTER—CITATOR*

FOX, GEORGE J. v COMM., 52 AFTR2d 83-6083, 718 F2d 251 (USCA 7, 10-6-83)

e—Figura, Donald W., 1984 P-H TC Memo 84-2304 [See 52 AFTR2d 83-6086]

q-l—Oelze, Richard E. v Comm., 53 AFTR2d 84-913, 726 F2d 165 (USCA 5)

→ *RIA* provides both the *A.F.T.R.* and *F.2d* citations in the same section.

→ *RIA* indicates that *Oelze* questioned issue 1 in *Fox*. This is based on the syllabus numbers assigned by RIA, not those assigned by West in *F.2d*. *A.F.T.R.* assigned only one number to *Fox*.

[Illustration 24–9]

EXCERPT FROM *CCH STANDARD FEDERAL TAX REPORTER—CITATOR*

Fox, George
• CA-7—(aff'g unreported TC), 83-2 USTC ¶ 9622; 718 F2d 251
Cited in:
Oelze, 84-1 USTC ¶ 9274, 726 F2d 165
Dusha, Dec. 41,123, 82 TC 592

→ *CCH* provides both *U.S.T.C.* and *F.2d* citations in the same section.

→ *CCH* does not indicate how *Oelze* treated *Fox*; it indicates only that it cited *Fox*. In addition, it does not include syllabus numbers.

SECTION M. LOOSELEAF SERVICES, ENCYCLOPEDIAS, AND TREATISES

You may wish to consult explanatory materials early in the research effort, perhaps even before you read the relevant statutes. The texts described in this chapter often provide insight into the problem being researched, and you can draw upon their liberal use of citations for a preliminary reading list of cases and administrative pronouncements. Each is updated at frequent intervals, and most have at least one related newsletter (Section P).

While general research texts would list some of these materials as looseleaf services and others as legal encyclopedias or treatises,[61] those classifications are less significant in this context than are classifications based upon their formats. Most of them take a subject matter approach, but two of the best-known services are arranged in Code section order.

Before using a looseleaf service, you should familiarize yourself with its format for designating materials; cross references to updating items will use that format.

1. Code Section Arrangement

The *Standard Federal Tax Reporter*[62] and the *United States Tax Reporter*[63] looseleaf services take essentially the same approach. Compilation volumes provide the full texts of Code sections and Treasury regulations along with editorial explanations. An annotation section listing cases and rulings follows each section. Users wanting ready access to the text of the law while they are reading explanations of it will appreciate this format.

Because of the arrangement described above, however, problems involving multiple Code sections do not receive comprehensive discussion in the Code compilations. The publishers solve this problem in two ways: pamphlets containing in-depth discussions and special sections devoted to tax planning, problems of specific businesses, and other materials involving several Code sections.

Although each service is arranged in Code section order, all materials are assigned paragraph numbers; *USTR* uses the Code sections in its paragraph numbering system. A "paragraph" can be several pages long or the size of a traditional paragraph. Each service cross references between paragraph numbers, not between page numbers. New developments are indexed according to the paragraph in the main compilation to which they relate, *i.e.*, in Code section order. Both services provide information about pending litigation, proposed regulations, and other matters of interest to researchers.

Libraries often carry both of these services in either looseleaf or CD–ROM format, and users eventually develop a preference for one or the other. As each service's annotations are editorially selected, use of both can reduce the risk of missing a valuable annotation although it may substantially increase research time. The extra material obtained rarely justifies the additional time involved.

[61] *See* Chapters 14, 16, and 18, for further discussion of these research tools. The annotated law reports discussed in Chapter 7 also provide textual material.

[62] *CCH Standard Federal Tax Reporter* (income tax); *CCH Federal Estate and Gift Tax Reporter*; *CCH Federal Excise Tax Reporter*. CCH also publishes subject matter format services (*e.g.*, *CCH Federal Tax Service*).

[63] *United States Tax Reporter—Income Taxes*; *United States Tax Reporter—Estate & Gift Taxes*; *United States Tax Reporter—Excise Taxes*. RIA also publishes subject matter format services (*e.g.*, *Federal Tax Coordinator 2d*).

These services contain the following features. In addition, each has a variety of other useful tables and finding lists.

a. *Code Volumes*. These volumes print, in Code section order, all provisions involving income, gift and estate, employment, and excise taxes as well as procedural provisions. *SFTR's* Code volume I includes a table cross referencing Code sections to each other. As the Code itself is not fully cross referenced, the value of this table, particularly for researching an unfamiliar area, cannot be overstated. Unfortunately, there will be many situations in which Code sections do not refer to each other. *SFTR* also contains tables providing cross references between the 1939 and 1954 Codes.

b. *Compilation Volumes*. These volumes contain, in Code section order, the full text of the Code, proposed, temporary, and final regulations, and digest-annotations to technical advice memoranda, letter rulings, revenue rulings, revenue procedures, and judicial decisions. [*See* Illustration 24–10.]

[Illustration 24–10]

EXCERPT FROM *STANDARD FEDERAL TAX REPORTER*

EXPENSES—TAX-EXEMPT INCOME— §265 [¶14,050]   29,551

Expenses incurred by a corporate officer in connection with a wrongful discharge claim were not deductible. The settlement payments attributable to the wrongful discharge tort claim were tax exempt; thus the fees allocable to the action were not deductible.

B.E. McKay, Jr., 102 TC 465, Dec. 49,736. Vac'd and rem'd on another issue, *per curiam*, CA-5 (unpublished opinion), 96-1 USTC ¶50,279

Legal expenses incurred in order to collect a nontaxable lump-sum payment, the nontaxability of which the taxpayer did not dispute, were not deductible.

G. Nehus, 68 TCM 1503, Dec. 50,308(M), TC Memo. 1994-631

When two sons purchased their mother's life interest (that included a power to sell) in stock, they acquired the entire interest in an intangible asset, the stock, that had an unlimited useful life. Accordingly, the sons were not entitled to deductions for the exhaustion of the interest they acquired from their mother.

Sohosky, 57 TC 403, Dec. 31,116

→ These annotations appear at ¶¶ 14,054.0396 & 14,054.0397 of *SFTR*. You can update your research by cross referencing from them to the New Matters volume.

c. *Updating Volumes*. Recent material is indexed in the New Matters volume (*SFTR*) or Recent Developments volume (*USTR*). [*See* Illustration 24–11.] Because these materials are arranged according to the paragraph numbers used in the Compilation volumes, it is very easy to use the updating volumes to find recent rulings and decisions in any area of interest. These volumes also cover pending legislation. The updating volumes print full text of recent IRS materials.

d. *Advance Sheets Volumes*. These volumes contain the texts of income tax decisions rendered by courts other than the Tax Court. Recent court decisions involving estate and gift taxes or excise taxes appear in the CCH and RIA services covering those topics. Court decisions covering all taxes will later be issued in hardbound volumes as part of the *U.S.T.C.* and *A.F.T.R.* reporter services discussed in Section K.

e. *Citator Volumes.* The CCH and RIA citators, which cover both judicial decisions and IRS materials, are discussed in Section L. The RIA citator is more comprehensive than its CCH counterpart.

[Illustration 24–11]

ILLUSTRATION FROM UNITED STATES TAX REPORTER

CROSS REFERENCE TABLE		
From ¶ **To ¶/page**		**Listed in Code Section Order**
60,135.05(12) 4.18		Peterson: Innocent spouse relief; knowledge of ex-husband's embezzlement income. TCMem
60,135.05(14) 97-1122		Stiteler aff: Innocent spouse relief properly denied; equity. CA
IRC §6050I		**Reporting Cash Received**
60,50I5 86,114		Cash receipts reporting requirements for mobile home sales. Ltr-Rul 9710001

→ Note the three types of cross reference: 4.18 is a paragraph reference to *Weekly Alert* newsletter; 97–1122 is an *A.F.T.R.* page; 86,114 is a *USTR* paragraph.

2. Subject Matter Arrangement—Multiple Topics

The materials described in this section cover a wide range of topics using a subject matter arrangement. If you use several services, you will get quicker access to relevant items in the second (or later) service by using tables for cases and other primary sources. Once you have obtained these items from one service, you can use them to locate relevant discussion in the other service. If the second service lacks these tables,[64] you would enter it from a topical or Code section index.

a. *Federal Tax Coordinator 2d (Research Institute of America).* This biweekly service contains excellent discussions of all areas of taxation, with minimal coverage of employment taxes. The text volumes are arranged by chapters using a subject matter approach. Discussions in each chapter include liberal use of citations, cross references to topics of potential relevance discussed in other chapters, and analysis of as yet unresolved matters.

Each chapter has the following arrangement: a Detailed Reference Table for topics included; discussion of each topic, including footnote

---

[64] For example, *Tax Management Portfolios* lack case and rulings tables. They have excellent Code and topical indexes.

annotations; and text of Code and regulations sections applicable to the chapters being discussed. [*See* Illustration 24–21, from the *OnPoint* CD–ROM version of this service.] Chapters are further subdivided into topics, and then into "paragraphs."

The service has an extensive Topical Index and cross reference tables for discussions of primary source material. A variety of practice aids, such as IRS Service Center addresses and annuity tables, are also included.

Volume 20 contains the texts of United States tax treaties and lists of signatory countries in addition to textual material dealing with the treaties. Volumes 27 and 27A contain proposed regulations reproduced in the order in which they were issued, along with preambles and *Federal Register* citations. Volume 28 contains reprints of the weekly *Internal Revenue Bulletin* (Section Q).

b. *Tax Management Portfolios (Bureau of National Affairs)*. BNA issues five series of *Tax Management Portfolios*: *U.S. Income; Foreign Income; Estates, Gifts, and Trusts; Real Estate;* and *Compensation Planning*. Each series is subdivided into several softbound *Portfolios* that cover narrow areas of tax law in great depth.[65]

In addition to a Table of Contents, each *Portfolio* includes a Detailed Analysis section with extensive footnoting (including references to IRS letter rulings); a Working Papers section, which includes checklists, forms that can be used as models in drafting documents, and texts of relevant IRS materials; and a Bibliography and References section, which includes citations to regulations, legislative history, and court decisions as well as digests of rulings. Books and articles are listed by year of publication.

BNA supplements the *Portfolios* with Changes and Analysis of New Developments sheets, or completely revises them, as warranted by new developments. In addition, *Tax Management Weekly Report* includes updating material before it is added to the *Portfolios*.

BNA provides several methods for locating relevant *Portfolios*. The looseleaf Portfolio Index includes the Classification Guides, lists of *Portfolios* in each series arranged by major category (such as Life Insurance), and a more detailed Key Word Index. A Code section index covers all series.[66] IRS forms are cross referenced numerically and alphabetically to appropriate *Portfolios*.

c. *Mertens, Law of Federal Income Taxation (Clark Boardman Callaghan)*. The original Mertens service contained four sets of volumes: treatise; Code; regulations; and rulings. Although the revised service

---

[65] Subdivisions are so narrow that several *Portfolios* may cover any one Code section; for example, § 2622 is covered in *Portfolios* 201, 301, 800, and 850.

[66] The *Tax Management Weekly Report* also includes weekly and cumulative Code section indexes. Because *Portfolios* are not updated this frequently, the *Weekly Report* is a useful supplementary tool.

includes only treatise, regulations, and rulings, the Code materials are still useful for historical research.

(1) *Treatise.* The treatise volumes closely resemble general encyclopedias such as *Am. Jur. 2d* and *C.J.S.* in format.[67] Material is presented by subject matter with extensive footnoting. Each chapter contains cross references to relevant materials found elsewhere in the service. Discussions include extensive historical background information. A section summarizing revenue rulings and IRS acquiescences appears at the end of each chapter. This material is divided by topic.

Two Tables Volumes (with main and supplementary sections) contain tables indicating where primary source materials are discussed. IRS materials include items printed in the *Cumulative Bulletin* and letter rulings, technical advice memoranda, and general counsel memoranda.

The Index Volume contains a detailed subject matter index. Treatise materials are supplemented monthly; the supplement is cumulated semiannually.

(2) *Code.* Each Code volume contains all income tax provisions enacted or amended during a particular time period (one or more years). Textual notations (diamond shapes and brackets) indicate additions and deletions. A historical note indicates Act, section, and effective date and can be used to reconstruct the prior language. The subject matter index in the looseleaf current volume cross references each topic to applicable Code sections. This material does not cover the 1986 Code.

Looseleaf volumes of Code Commentary provide useful short explanations of statutory provisions as well as cross references to the discussions in the treatise materials. The commentary materials are still being updated.

(3) *Regulations.* Hardbound volumes include the texts of all income tax regulations issued or amended during a particular time period (two or more years). Publication is made in Code section order. Looseleaf volumes cover proposed and final regulations since 1985, printing them in Code section order. A Regulations Status Table indicates where in this set regulations adopted in prior years appear. The IRS *Semiannual Agenda of Regulations*, indicating proposals under development within the Service, is also included.

Textual notations indicate deletions, additions, and other changes in amended regulations. Historical notes allow you to determine the regulation's prior wording. Sections reproducing the Preamble to the Treasury Decision or Notice of Proposed Rulemaking announcing each proposed and final regulation appear in separate looseleaf volumes (and at the back of the hardbound volumes).

(4) *Rulings.* The Rulings volumes in this service contain the texts of revenue rulings and procedures as well as those of less formal IRS pronouncements, such as news releases. Internal memoranda are exclud-

---

[67] *See* Chapter 16. Although each of them covers a wide variety of topics, discussions of taxation appear in separate volumes within each service and are thus quite accessible.

ed. Each volume covers a particular time period and includes rulings in numerical order, followed by procedures in numerical order. Mertens adds current items monthly.

The looseleaf current volume has a Code–Rulings Table [see Illustration 24–4], which provides a chronological listing of every revenue ruling and procedure involving income tax Code sections or subsections. In addition, a Rulings Status Table [see Illustration 24–6] lists the most recent revenue ruling or procedure affecting the validity of a previously published item. Mertens indicates the effect on the earlier item (*e.g.*, modified, revoked). A separate section includes *Cumulative Bulletin* citations for this material.

d. *Rabkin & Johnson, Federal Income, Gift and Estate Taxation (Matthew Bender).* This service has three segments: treatise; Code and Congressional Reports; and Regulations. Two additional volumes contain the text of the 1986 Code. Subscribers also receive Tax Planning pamphlets and a Year in Review pamphlet. Supplementation is monthly, with New Matter pages appearing near the beginning of each volume in text section number order.

While discussions are thorough, they do not purport to cover all types of authority. Letter rulings are rarely discussed and are not cited as authority "[b]ecause they lack precedential value."[68]

e. *CCH Federal Tax Service.* First published in 1989 by Matthew Bender, this service is authored by tax practitioners, who are identified at the beginning of the chapters each authored. This service is updated semimonthly; more frequent updating material appears in the *Federal Tax Weekly* newsletter, which is cross referenced to the looseleaf service. The service is also available in a CD–ROM format (Section S).

3. Subject Matter Arrangement—Limited Scope

Various publishers issue textual materials discussing a limited number of Code sections, such as those covering S corporations. These texts are extremely useful for research involving very complex areas of tax law. In recent years the number of topics and related texts have grown explosively. You can locate at least one text on almost any topic, from tax problems of the elderly to estate planning for farmers. Although these materials are periodically supplemented, their updating is rarely as frequent as that for the looseleaf services in subsections 1 and 2.

SECTION N.   LEGAL PERIODICALS

Commentary on particular tax problems appears in various legal periodicals, several of which focus on taxation.[69] This group includes such offerings as *Journal of Taxation, Tax Lawyer, Taxation for Law-*

---

[68] 1A Rabkin & Johnson, Federal Income, Gift and Estate Taxation § G 1.03[6], at G–11 (1996) (Rel. 641–1/96).

[69] While not technically periodicals, annual Institutes, such as those given at New York University (taxation) and the University of Miami (estate planning), are extraordinarily useful sources of information and are covered in several periodical indexes.

yers, TAXES—The Tax Magazine, and *Tax Law Review*. Many publications adopt a narrower focus within taxation, *e.g., Journal of Partnership Taxation.*

While the materials discussed in Section M include selected citations to periodical literature, you can obtain a more extensive list through use of periodical indexes. Many general legal periodical indexes contain lists of relevant articles,[70] but *CCH Federal Tax Articles* and *Index to Federal Tax Articles* provide an even wider selection of readings. Their focus is exclusively on taxation, and they cover periodicals the general indexes omit.

1. CCH Federal Tax Articles

This monthly looseleaf reporter contains summaries of articles on federal taxes appearing in legal, accounting, business, and related periodicals. Proceedings and papers delivered at major tax institutes are also noted. The contents appear in Code section order; each item receives a paragraph cross reference number. [*See* Illustration 24–12.]

There are main and current topical and author indexes. Hardbound volumes cover materials since 1954; the looseleaf volume contains the most recent material. Many researchers will prefer this index because of its format, scope, and frequent supplementation.

---

[70] You can also locate citations to law review articles in various units of *Shepard's Citations. Shepard's Federal Law Citations in Selected Law Reviews* indicates if a constitutional provision, statute, regulation, or case (other than Tax Court) has been cited in a law review article; this set does not cover specialized tax periodicals. Even *Shepard's Federal Tax Citations* covers few tax-oriented periodicals. *See* Chapter 17 for a discussion of periodical indexes.

[Illustration 24–12]

EXCERPT FROM *CCH FEDERAL TAX ARTICLES*

| 2374 | 1996 Article Summaries-Reports 401-406 | 407 7-96 |

¶ 2981   Alternative minimum tax imposed (Code Sec. 55)

.074 Repeal of AMT Depreciation. Bruce H. Barnett. 47 Tax Executive, November/ December 1995, p. 471.

Presents the proposed legislation that would require use of the same deprecia-tion method for regular tax purposes and for alternative minimum tax (AMT) purposes. Observes that compliance with the proposal would be difficult, and notes that the depreciation rules have been amended many times. Believes that the AMT should be repealed in its entirety. Suggests ways for taxpayers to comply with the provision if it is enacted.

¶ 2982   Adjusted gross income defined (Code Sec. 62)

.026 Accountable Plans Can Cut the Tax on Reimbursements. Richard Gore and Jack R. Petralia, Jr. 55 Taxation for Accountants, September 1995, pp. 132-137.

Contrasts the tax benefits of an expense reimbursement plan that qualifies as an "accountable plan" with the less favorable treatment of a nonaccountable plan. States that unreimbursed employee business expenses are subject to the two percent of adjusted gross income limitation of Code Sec. 67 unless the plan satisfies three tests sets forth in IRS Reg. § 1.62-2: (1)business connection; (2) substantiation; and (3) return of excess. Describes with illustrative examples the application of these tests. Touches upon other issues, including arrangements with multiple employees.

2. Index to Federal Tax Articles (Warren, Gorham & Lamont)

This multivolume work covers the literature on federal income, gift, and estate taxation contained in legal, specialized tax, accounting, and economics journals, as well as in nonperiodical publications. There is very comprehensive coverage of non-tax oriented journals.

Coverage begins with 1913, making this the index of choice for discussions of pre–1954 Code developments. Current material appears in the quarterly cumulative supplement volume. There are separate topical and author indexes but no Code section index. The most recent entry appears first in each listing of articles. [*See* Illustration 24–13.]

[Illustration 24–13]

EXCERPT FROM *INDEX TO FEDERAL TAX ARTICLES*

Self-employed Taxpayers—*Cont'd*	(1992)
Retirement Plans—*Cont'd*	**Sham Transactions**—*Cont'd*
The Impact of Retirement Plans on Medicaid Eligibility, William J. Browning, 19 Estate Planning No. 6, 362 (1992)	The Separate Tax Status of Loan-Out Corporations, Mary LaFrance, 48 Vanderbilt Law Review No. 4, 879 (1995)
Estate Planning with Retirement Accounts: Top Tax Tips and Traps for the Estate Planner, Robert B. Wolf, 63 Pennsylvania Bar Association Quarterly No. 2, 87 (1992)	Sham Transaction Test Should Include an Analysis of After-Tax Cash Flow, James A. Doering, 11 Journal of Taxation of Investments No. 2, 196 (1994)
Protect Retirement Assets—Implement a Qualified Plan, William F. Hall, 6 Probate and Property No. 5, 34	The Rule of *Sheldon v. Commissioner*: Is it an Economically Efficient Evolution of the Sham Transaction Doctrine? Paul J. Dona-hue, 13 Virginia Tax Review No. 1, 187 (1993)

3. Current Law Index; Legal Resource Index; LegalTrac (Information Access Company)

The *Current Law Index* is the most convenient print-based general periodical index for federal tax research. Although its subject matter listing is not geared to Code sections, its Table of Statutes includes a separate heading for "Internal Revenue Code." This section lists articles in Code section order. In addition to indexing by statutes, this service also indexes articles by subject, author/title, and case name. It covers several tax-oriented periodicals.

The *Legal Resource Index* can be accessed online through both LEXIS–NEXIS and WESTLAW; LegalTrac is a cumulative CD–ROM version. These services cover material since 1980.

4. Index to Legal Periodicals; WILSONLINE; WILSONDISC (H.W. Wilson Company)

Index to Legal Periodicals includes tax articles in its subject matter listings. Because it arranges articles about statutes by act, it is not Code section accessible. *ILP* indexes articles by subject/author, case name, and act name. It indexes somewhat fewer publications than *Current Law Index* does, and it imposes page minimums for indexed material. Because *ILP* began publication in 1908, it is better than the *Current Law Index* for extensive historical research.

WILSONLINE is available online, and *ILP* is carried on LEXIS–NEXIS and WESTLAW; *WILSONDISC* is a CD–ROM product. Both cover material indexed since mid–1981.

5. Tax Management Portfolios (Bureau of National Affairs)

The Bibliography & References section of each *Portfolio* contains articles listings, arranged by year of publication. Updating material appears in each *Portfolio's* Changes & Analysis section; this section includes cross references to the Bibliography & References materials. The *Portfolios* are discussed further in Section M.

6. Mertens, Law of Federal Income Taxation (Clark Boardman Callahan)

Mertens lists current articles by topic in the Literature Review section of its monthly *Highlights* newsletter. Although Mertens is an income tax service, the lists include articles on estate planning. Mertens is discussed further in Section M.

7. NYU Institute on Federal Taxation (Matthew Bender)[71]

Although limited to the NYU Institute in their scope, this set's Consolidated Indexes offer ready access to numerous significant articles. The indexes are arranged by subject, author, title, cases, statutes, regulations, and rulings.

8. Tax Notes (Tax Analysts)

The weekly Tax Bibliography section indexes articles by Code section and by topic. *Tax Notes*, which is also available online, is discussed further in Section P.

9. Tax Policy in the United States: A Selective Bibliography with Annotations (1960–84)

Published by the Vanderbilt Law School Library in cooperation with the ABA Section of Taxation, this looseleaf provides retrospective coverage of articles, books, and government documents dealing with tax policy. Each item is explained briefly. This service includes both author and subject indexes.

10. Monthly Digest of Tax Articles (Newkirk Associates)

This periodical presents significant current tax articles in abridged form. Its descriptions of these articles are far more detailed than are the summaries given in *CCH Federal Tax Articles*; because of this detail, however, fewer articles receive coverage.

11. WG & L Tax Journal Digest (Warren, Gorham & Lamont)

Previously published as the *Journal of Taxation Digest*, this service currently covers articles published in the *Journal of Taxation, Taxation for Accountants, Taxation for Lawyers, Estate Planning, Journal of International Taxation, Journal of Tax Exempt Organizations, Journal of Taxation of Employee Benefits*, and *Journal of Limited Liability Companies*. Coverage begins with 1977; early volumes cover only the

---

[71] Other Institutes also have useful consolidated indexes.

first three listed journals. The digests are arranged by topic; the most recent items appear first. Cross references are given to relevant articles digested under other topical headings. Each annual volume has a Code section index and a subject index.

SECTION O. FORM BOOKS

There are several form books available to aid lawyers in drafting documents in situations where tax consequences may be determined by the drafter's choice of language. In addition, the IRS occasionally publishes prototype language in revenue procedures and notices. Many form books are available as CD–ROMs; users can download and customize the forms for their clients' needs.

Available form books include Bittker, Emory & Streng, *Federal Income Taxation of Corporations and Shareholders: Forms* (Warren, Gorham & Lamont); Mancoff, *Qualified Deferred Compensation Plans—Forms* (Clark Boardman Callaghan); and *Murphy's Will Clauses* (Matthew Bender).

SECTION P. NEWSLETTERS

Researchers in any area must update their findings or risk citing obsolete sources. When the research involves taxation, the odds of change are higher than in most fields and the number of sources to be consulted may appear endless.

Newsletters are convenient tools for keeping up with changes in the law. While they are no substitute for updating with a citator or the new matter section of a looseleaf service, they offer the opportunity for a leisurely review of changes occurring during a predetermined time period.

1. Daily Tax Report (BNA)

This newsletter, published five times each week, is an invaluable aid in locating current developments in tax law.[72] [*See* Illustration 24–14.] Each separately paginated issue begins with a section describing congressional activity, including bills passed and introduced, committee hearings, and committee reports.

The *Daily Tax Report* prints texts of Supreme Court decisions and full or partial texts of decisions rendered by other courts; full texts of most revenue rulings and procedures; summaries of other IRS materials such as private letter rulings; and texts of statutes and of proposed, temporary, and final regulations. Texts of bills and excerpts from hearings and committee reports also appear when the editors deem the material significant. *Daily Tax Report* prints the IRS Status of Regulations Projects report each month.

The indexes follow a subject matter format and cite to the report number and page where each item appears. Because the indexes never

---

[72] BNA also publishes a weekly newsletter, *Tax Management Weekly Report*.

cover more than a two-month period, you may find *Daily Tax Report* easier to search online if you are using it for retrospective research.

[Illustration 24–14]

EXCERPT FROM *DAILY TAX REPORT*

DTR   NO. 7   •   WASHINGTON, D.C.   FRIDAY, JANUARY 10, 1997

HIGHLIGHTS

IRS Issues Rules Package On Defining, Amortizing Intangibles — IRS issues package of proposed, temporary, and final rules governing how to define an intangible asset under statutory provisions allowing 15-year amortization of intangibles, and how to allocate the purchase price of intangibles under Code Sections 1060 and 338 . . . . **G-9, Special Supplement**

Tax-Cut Expectations Running High This Year; Budget Deal Possible — Expectations are high among Capitol Hill watchers that 1997 will be the "Year of the Great Tax-Cut Compromise" between President Clinton and the GOP-led Congress, with both sides saying they want to negotiate. Congress and the White House also appear ready to make a deal on a balanced budget package. Meanwhile, IRS faces the challenge of trying to put out important domestic and international tax guidance while it is under close scrutiny from lawmakers and an independent commission charged with coming up with ways to restructure the agency . . . . **Special Report**

→ Items listed on the cover are reported on within the issue itself or in Special Reports received by subscribers.

2. Tax Notes (Tax Analysts)

This weekly newsletter contains a comprehensive collection of recent tax-oriented material.[73] In addition, it is readily accessible through quarterly indexes. These are divided in highly usable fashion into categories covering the various types of information printed in *Tax Notes*.

Tax Notes includes digests of revenue rulings and procedures; other IRS documents; court opinions; and briefs and petitions. *Tax Notes* includes summaries of committee reports, testimony at hearings, bills, and statements in *Congressional Record*. It also includes information about public hearings on regulations and summaries of comments received on proposed regulations. [*See* Illustration 24–15.]

Recent tax articles are listed in Code section or subject order. In addition to all of the above information, *Tax Notes* includes several policy-oriented articles in each issue.

Tax Notes is virtually complete in itself for most readers' purposes. What distinguishes it from other newsletters is its usefulness for research involving prior years' events. Full text information, such as statements at hearings on legislation and regulations, texts of tax articles, and even the IRS *Cumulative Bulletin* are included in the *Tax Notes Microfiche Database* (Section R) and in *Tax Notes Today*, an on-line service (Section T). Document cross references in *Tax Notes* allow you to retrieve full text from these other sources.

---

[73] Tax Analysts also publishes a daily newsletter, *Highlights & Documents*.

[Illustration 24–15]

EXCERPT FROM TAX NOTES

IRS TECHNICAL ADVICE MEMORANDUMS

Section 61 — Gross Income Defined

PER CAPITA PAYMENTS UNDER THE IGRA ARE INCOME. The Service has ruled in technical advice that per capita payments made under the Indian Gaming Regulatory Act (IGRA), which are equal payments to tribal members that are not based on the personal situations of the recipients, are includable in gross income.

The tribe, a federally recognized Indian tribe, conducts gaming operations on tribal land under IGRA and makes equal payments to tribal members out of a portion of its revenues from class II and class III gaming activities. The Service concluded that because the payments actually made to tribal members were equal, per capita payments of net revenues from gaming activities and were made regardless of financial status, health, educational background, or employment status, no portion of the payments was excludable from gross income under the general welfare doctrine.

Full Text Citations: *LTR 9717007; Doc 97-11607 (6 pages); LTRServ,* May 5, 1997, p. 1415

→ To read the full text of this technical advice memorandum, you would find Doc 97–11607 in the *Microfiche Database* or in *Tax Notes Today*.

SECTION Q.   COLLECTIONS OF PRIMARY SOURCE MATERIALS

The materials described below, which have been referred to at various points in this chapter, print several types of material necessary for tax research. Except as indicated in the following paragraphs, these sets contain no textual discussion of the materials presented.

1.   Internal Revenue Bulletin; Cumulative Bulletin; Bulletin Index–Digest System

The three IRS-generated series contain the text of almost every nonjudicial primary authority and provide the means to locate included material. As the discussion below indicates, the *Bulletin Index–Digest System (Index–Digest)* is invaluable as an aid to using the other two series. The primary source materials printed in these volumes are also available in microform (Section R), CD–ROM (Section S), and online (Section T) services offered by a variety of vendors.

a.   *Internal Revenue Bulletin.* The weekly *Internal Revenue Bulletin* is divided into four parts. Part I prints all revenue rulings, final regulations, and Supreme Court tax decisions issued during the week; publication is in Code section order. Part II does likewise for treaties, including Treasury Department Technical Explanations (Subpart A), and for tax legislation, including committee reports (Subpart B). Part III contains notices and revenue procedures, while Part IV, "Items of General Interest," is varied in content. Its coverage ranges from disbarment notices to announcements of proposed regulations. *Federal Register* dates and comment deadlines are provided in addition to the preambles and text of proposed regulations. The *Bulletin* also indicates IRS acquiescence or nonacquiescence in judicial decisions decided against its position.

Although the *Bulletin* has indexes, they are unwieldy. Every issue contains a cumulative Numerical Finding List for each type of item, listing each in numerical order; these Finding Lists lack any tie-in to Code sections. The Finding List of Current Action on Previously Published Rulings indicates IRS, but not judicial, action. Subject matter indexes cover only one month's material.[74] Because of its index format, the *Bulletin* is best used to locate material for which you already have a citation or as a tool for staying abreast of recent developments.

b. *Cumulative Bulletin.* Every six months the material in the *Internal Revenue Bulletin* is republished in a hardbound *Cumulative Bulletin.* The *Cumulative Bulletin* format follows that of the weekly service with three exceptions.[75] First, major tax legislation and committee reports generally appear in a third volume rather than in the two semiannual volumes.[76] Second, only disbarment notices and proposed regulations appear from Part IV. Finally, rulings appear in the *Cumulative Bulletin* in semiannual Code section order; this bears no relation to their numerical order. The *Cumulative Bulletin* indexes are as difficult to use as are their counterparts in the *Internal Revenue Bulletin.*

The *Cumulative Bulletin* has been published since 1919. Volumes initially were given Arabic numerals (1919–1921); the IRS adopted a Roman numeral system in 1922. Since 1937, volumes have been numbered by year (*e.g.*, 1937–1). There have been two volumes annually (with occasional extra volumes for extensive legislative history material) since 1920; the–1,–2 numbering system for each year began in 1922. The *Cumulative Bulletin's* format differed slightly from the above description until the 1974–2 volume. Proposed regulations, which appear as a separate category, were added in the 1981–1 volume.

c. *Bulletin Index–Digest System.* The IRS issues the *Index-Digest* in four services: Income Tax; Estate and Gift Tax; Employment Tax; and Excise Tax. The Income Tax service, which is the focal point for this discussion, is supplemented quarterly; the other services receive semiannual supplementation. New softbound cumulations generally are issued every two years.

You can use the *Index-Digest* to obtain *Internal Revenue Bulletin* or *Cumulative Bulletin* citations for revenue rulings and procedures, Supreme Court and adverse Tax Court decisions, Public Laws, Treasury Decisions, and treaties. In addition, it digests the rulings, procedures, and court decisions.

---

[74] There are also quarterly and semiannual cumulations. The indexes are subdivided by type of tax.

[75] Although the *Cumulative Bulletin* includes preambles, it does not print drafting information.

[76] Committee reports for 1913 through 1938 appear in 1939–1 (pt. 2) C.B. Committee reports for the 1954 Code's enactment never appeared in the *Cumulative Bulletin.*

The following paragraphs explain using the *Index-Digest* to locate citations and digests.

(1) *Statutes and Regulations.* You can locate specific Code and regulations sections that have been added or amended in the Finding Lists for Public Laws and Treasury Decisions. A *Cumulative Bulletin* citation is given for the first page of each Public Law and regulation involved.

Still another Finding List, "Public Laws Published in the Bulletin," is useful for locating committee report citations and popular names for the various revenue acts. It is in Public Law number order.

(2) *Rulings and Procedures.* The Finding Lists for Revenue Rulings, Revenue Procedures, and other Items can be used in various ways to locate relevant rulings and procedures. These items appear in Code and regulations section order in the "Internal Revenue Code of 1986" section, and in ruling and procedure number order in the "Revenue Rulings" and "Revenue Procedures" sections of these Lists. The *Index-Digest* lists revenue rulings and procedures involving treaties by country in the "Revenue Rulings and Revenue Procedures under Tax Conventions" section.

Finding Lists omit *Cumulative Bulletin* citations but cite to a digest of each item in the *Index-Digest* itself; the *Cumulative Bulletin* citation follows the digest. Although you must take an extra step to obtain the citation, the format frequently saves time; a glance through the digest may indicate the item is not worth reading in full text.[77] [*See* Illustration 24–5.]

Because the digests are arranged by subject matter, you can locate pertinent rulings even if you do not know the underlying Code or regulations section. In fact, the subject matter divisions are so numerous that the same item may be digested under several different headings.

If you want to know if a particular ruling or procedure has been modified or otherwise affected by subsequent IRS action, you can obtain this information from the "Actions on Previously Published Revenue Rulings and Revenue Procedures" section of the Finding Lists. Judicial decisions affecting a ruling are not indicated, however. Whenever a subsequent ruling affects an earlier item, a *Cumulative Bulletin* citation is given for the updating material.

(3) *Judicial Decisions.* The Finding Lists for Revenue Rulings, Revenue Procedures, and Other Items can be used to locate all Supreme Court decisions and those Tax Court decisions adverse to the government in which the IRS has acquiesced or nonacquiesced.

Supreme Court decisions appear alphabetically in the "Decisions of the Supreme Court" section of the Finding Lists. The *Index-Digest* also lists them by the IRS-assigned Court Decision (Ct. D.) number in the

---

[77] Because the digest may omit a pertinent holding, exclusive use of the digest would yield inadequate results. You run this risk whenever you rely on an editor's view of an item's significance.

"Internal Revenue Code of 1986" materials, arranged according to the applicable Code and regulations sections. Tax Court decisions are listed alphabetically in the "Decisions of the Tax Court" section of the Finding Lists; they are listed by T.C. citation in the "Internal Revenue Code of 1986" materials.

As with rulings and procedures, references to Supreme Court decisions in the Finding Lists give only the digest number.[78] The official and *Cumulative Bulletin* citations follow the digest.

2. U.S. Code Congressional & Administrative News—Federal Tax Regulations; Internal Revenue Acts—Text and Legislative History; U.S. Code Congressional & Administrative News—Internal Revenue Code (West Group)

These three West series can be used in researching the texts and histories of the Code and regulations sections.

The annual *Federal Tax Regulations* volumes contain the text of all income, estate and gift, and employment tax regulations in force on the first day of the year. These materials include references to the T.D. number, date, and *Federal Register* publication for both original promulgation and all amendments. However, *Federal Tax Regulations* omits T.D. numbers for original promulgation of pre-existing regulations republished in 1960 in T.D. 6498, 6500, or 6516. The final volume for each year contains a subject matter index.

Internal Revenue Acts, issued each year in pamphlet form, prints the full text of currently enacted statutes in chronological order. Hardbound volumes cumulate the material in one or more years' pamphlets. Texts of selected committee reports and *Congressional Record* statements appear in the second section of each *Internal Revenue Acts* pamphlet. Each pamphlet includes a subject matter index; tables indicate Code sections affected and cross reference Public Law section numbers to pages in *Statutes at Large*. The cross reference table lists acts by name. This series is excerpted from the general *U.S. Code Congressional & Administrative News (USCCAN)* service and cross references to material printed there but omitted here.

The *Internal Revenue Code* volume issued each year contains the text of all existing Code sections. Dates, Public Law numbers, and *Statutes at Large* citations appear in the brief history of enactment and amendment following each section. Editorial notes indicate effective dates but do not indicate how a particular amendment modified an existing section. Each volume contains a subject matter index.

3. Tax Management Primary Sources (Bureau of National Affairs)

Primary Sources is an excellent tool for locating significant proposed legislation and deriving the legislative history of existing Code sections. It also covers the Employee Retirement Income Security Act (ERISA).

---

[78] Tax Court citations appear in the finding lists and the digests. The finding lists indicate acquiescences; the digests provide citations for the acquiescences.

The Current Congress binders of this looseleaf service contain the text of major bills[79] and other related material. Once a bill appears in this service, the editors also include its progress through Congress. Available documents include the introduced version; press releases or *Congressional Record* statements accompanying the introduction; administration testimony at hearings; committee reports; and other significant documents. In addition, a "Background Materials" section prints other important materials related to tax legislation. Cross reference to these is provided from each bill to which they relate.

A "Legislative Calendar" allows you to determine what progress each bill has made in Congress to date. This service is updated monthly. Bills appear in numerical order. Subscribers can file materials for bills that do not pass in an Unenacted Legislation storage binder. *Primary Sources* incorporates materials connected with enacted bills into the volumes described in the next paragraph.

Extensive legislative histories for selected Code sections comprise the remainder of this service. The sections chosen for inclusion in the historical binders are traced back to their original 1954 Code versions;[80] all changes are presented. [*See* Illustration 24–16.] Materials presented for each Code section include presidential messages, committee reports, Treasury Department testimony at hearings, and discussion printed in *Congressional Record*.

The legislative histories are published in several series, each of which covers several years. Within each series, material appears in Code section order. Each Series contains a Master Table of Contents in Code section order. *Primary Sources* limits its coverage to Code sections affected by the Tax Reform Act of 1969 or by subsequent legislation.

[79] *Primary Sources* selects bills for printing "(1) according to probability of Congressional consideration; (2) overall importance to the business community; and (3) relative timeliness of the subject." Series V, V–27, at 5.

[80] Series I also includes the 1939 Code version for each section covered.

[Illustration 24–16]

EXCERPT FROM *TAX MANAGEMENT PRIMARY SOURCES*

IV-26   §168 [1981] pg.(i)

SEC. 168 — ACCELERATED COST RECOVERY SYSTEM

Table of Contents

Page

---

4. RIA Cumulative Changes

This multivolume looseleaf service allows you to track changes in the Code and Treasury regulations. There are series for the 1939, 1954, and 1986 Codes and regulations; many libraries lack the 1939 Code series. *Cumulative Changes* covers employment taxes but not excise taxes.

The Code and regulations materials appear separately, arranged in Code section order. There are parallel citation tables for the 1939 and 1954 Codes.

a. *Internal Revenue Code.* A chart for each Code section indicates its original effective date. The chart includes the Public Law number, section, enactment and effective dates of each amendment, and the act section prescribing the effective date. The chart is particularly useful because it covers Code section subdivisions (subsections, paragraphs, and even smaller subdivisions). It does not include *Statutes at Large* citations. [*See* Illustration 24–17.]

The pages following each chart reproduce each version (except the current one) since the provision's original introduction in the relevant Code. The current version can be found in the *RIA United States Tax Reporter* Code and compilation volumes (Section M).

b. *Treasury Regulations.* Tables of amendments cover all regulations sections for each tax; individual sections do not have their own charts. The table indicates the original and all amending T.D. numbers and filing dates and provides a *Cumulative Bulletin* or *Internal Revenue Bulletin* citation. Cross references to *RIA United States Tax Reporter* are also given. A final table, in T.D. number order, indicates the purpose, date and *Cumulative Bulletin* or *I.R.B.* citation for each regulation issued under each Code.[81]

Because the tables list temporary regulations after final regulations, the numerical sequence is not absolute. The editors include tables for regulations that have been redesignated or replaced.

Immediately following the tables, the editors print each regulation in all of its versions except the current one. They note changes in italics and use footnotes to indicate stricken language. *Cumulative Changes* includes the T.D. number and the dates of approval and of filing for each version.

[Illustration 24–17]

EXCERPT FROM *RIA CUMULATIVE CHANGES*

4-4-83				§ 104—p. 1

SEC. 104 COMPENSATION FOR INJURIES OR SICKNESS

DATES given are effective dates
t.y.b.a. = Taxable years beginning after.

                                                                         t.y.e.a. = Taxable years ending after
                                                                     e.a. = Ending after.

SECTION (§) NUMBERS are those of amending Act; star (*) indicates
                section prescribing effective date.

Subsections in heavy black boxes are in I.R.C. as last amended.

SEC. 104	SUBSECTIONS			
	(a)		(b)(1)	(b)(2)
Original I.R.C.	t.y.b.a. 12-31-53 and e.a. 8-16-54		t.y.b.a. 12-31-53 and e.a. 8-16-54	t.y.b.a. 12-31-53 and e.a. 8-16-54
Amending Acts				
Pub. Law 86-723	§51 §56(e)* t.y.e.a.			

5. Barton's Federal Tax Laws Correlated (Federal Tax Press, Inc.)

The six volumes of this set trace income, estate, and gift tax

---

[81] Although T.D. 6500, a 1960 republication of existing income tax regulations is not formally included, *Cumulative Changes* does list the original pre–1960 T.D. A cautionary note warns the user to remember that pre–1960 regulations were republished in T.D. 6500. T.D. 6498 (procedure and administration) and T.D. 6516 (withholding tax) receive similar treatment. None of these T.D.s appears in the *Cumulative Bulletin*.

provisions from the Revenue Act of 1913[82] through the Tax Reform Act of 1969.

The five hardbound volumes reproduce in Code or act section order the text of the various tax acts through 1952. Because the acts are lined up in several columns on each page, you can read across a page and see every enacted version of a particular section for the period that volume covers.[83] Whenever possible, *Barton's* uses different typefaces to highlight changes.

The first two volumes provide a citation to *Statutes at Large* for each act. Volume 1 includes case annotations, and each volume has a subject matter index. The volumes following the 1939 Code include tables indicating amending acts and effective dates for 1939 Code sections. Volume 5 has a retrospective table cross referencing sections to pages in the four previous volumes.

The looseleaf sixth volume does not print the text of Code sections. Instead it consists of Tables that provide citations to primary sources where desired material appears. Tables A–D are in Code section order; Table E is in Public Law Number order.

Table A provides the history of the 1954 Act. It indicates *Statutes at Large* page; House, Senate, and Conference report page (official and *U.S. Code Congressional & Administrative News*); 1939 Code counterpart; Revenue Act where the provision originated; and relevant pages in volumes 1–5. Table C is similar to Table A, but it covers the 1939 Code. It gives the 1954 Code section; the origin of the 1939 Code provision; and cross references to volumes 1–5.

Table B covers amendments to the 1954 Code. For each section it provides Public Law number, section, and enactment date; *Statutes at Large* citation; House, Senate, and Conference report numbers and location in the *Cumulative Bulletin*; comment (*e.g.*, revision, amendment); and effective date information. Table D is the same as Table B, but it covers post–1953 changes to the 1939 Code.

Table E provides citations to legislative history for all acts from 1953 through 1969. Table E provides the following information provided for each act: Public Law number; date of enactment; congressional session; *Statutes at Large*, *Cumulative Bulletin*, and *USCCAN* citations for the act; congressional sessions, dates, and *Cumulative Bulletin* and *USCCAN* citations for House, Senate, and Conference report numbers; and *Congressional Record* citations for floor debate. Acts are not cited by popular name.

---

[82] The original Second Edition (vol. 1) also contained the text of the income tax laws from 1861 through 1909. This section was omitted in the Reproduced Second Edition.

[83] Volume 1 covers 1913–1924; volume 2 covers 1926–38; volume 3 covers 1939–43; volume 4 covers 1944–49; volume 5 covers 1950–52.

6. Seidman's Legislative History of Federal Income and Excess Profits Tax Laws[84] (Prentice–Hall)

Although *Seidman's* stops in 1953, it remains useful for determining the legislative history of those provisions that originated in the 1939 Code or even earlier.[85] This series follows each act in reverse chronological order, presenting the text of Code sections, followed by relevant committee reports and citations to hearings[86] and the *Congressional Record*.[87] Because Seidman's uses different type styles, you can easily ascertain where in Congress a provision originated or was deleted. [*See* Illustration 24–18.]

[Illustration 24–18]

EXCERPT FROM *SEIDMAN'S LEGISLATIVE HISTORY OF FEDERAL INCOME TAX LAWS*

---

for key to statute type]	1934 ACT	381

SEC. 164 DIFFERENT TAXABLE YEARS.   Sec. 164

      If the taxable year of a beneficiary is different from that of the estate or trust, the amount which he is required, under section 162 (b), to include in computing his net income, shall be based upon the income of the estate or trust for any taxable year of the estate or trust (whether beginning on, before, or after January 1, 1934) ending within his taxable year.

Committee Reports

Report—Ways and Means Committee (73d Cong., 2d Sess., H. Rept. 704).—Section 164. Different taxable years: The present law requires a beneficiary of an estate or trust to include in his income amounts allowed as a deduction to the estate or trust under section 162 (b). In order to continue this policy, it is necessary in view of the policy adopted in section 1 to add additional language to provide for cases where the estate or trust has a taxable year beginning in 1933 and ending in 1934 (p.32) **Report—Senate Finance Committee** (73d Cong., 2d Sess., S. Rept. 558).—Same as Ways and Means Committee Report. (p.40)

SEC. 166 REVOCABLE TRUSTS.   Sec. 166

      Where at any time (96) <del>during the taxable year</del> the power to revest in the grantor title to any part of the corpus of the trust is vested—

Seidman's prints proposed sections that were not enacted along with relevant history explaining their omission. Such information can aid you in interpreting those provisions Congress actually adopted. Although its coverage has great breadth, *Seidman's* does not print every

---

[84] The two volumes covering 1939 through 1953 include both taxes. Separate volumes for the income tax and the excess profits tax were used for the earlier materials, covering 1861 through 1938 and 1917 through 1947, respectively.

[85] I.R.C. § 263, for example, contains language taken almost verbatim from § 117 of the 1864 Act. *See* 13 Stat. 282.

[86] *Seidman's* cites relevant page numbers in the hearings and indicates appearances by Treasury representatives.

[87] *Seidman's* cites to relevant pages and reproduces the text itself in some instances.

Code section. It omits provisions with no legislative history, items lacking substantial interpretative significance, and provisions the editor considered long outmoded. *Seidman's* does not cover gift, estate, or excise taxes.

Seidman's has three indexes and a Code cross reference table. The Code section index lists each section by act and assigns it a key number. The same key number is assigned to corresponding sections in subsequent acts. The key number index indicates every act, by section number and page in the text, where the item involved appears. A subject index lists key numbers by topic. Volume II of the 1939–1953 set contains a table cross referencing 1953 and 1954 Code sections covered in *Seidman's*.

7. The Internal Revenue Acts of the United States: 1909–1950; 1950–1972; 1973–(William S. Hein & Co., Inc.)

a. *Original Series.* This set, edited by Bernard D. Reams, Jr., provides the most comprehensive legislative histories of all materials discussed in this section. In addition to each congressional version of revenue bills, the 144 original volumes (1909–1950) contain the full texts of hearings, committee reports, Treasury studies, and regulations. Official pagination is retained for relevant documents. In addition to income and excise taxes, this set includes estate and gift, social security, railroad retirement, and unemployment taxes. This set is available in hard copy and microfiche.

An Index volume contains several indexes that you can use in locating relevant materials. [*See* Illustration 24–19.] The longest index, which is chronological, lists each act and every item comprising its legislative history. A volume reference is given for each item. Other indexes cover Miscellaneous Subjects, such as hearings on items that did not result in legislation; Treasury studies; Joint Committee reports; regulations; congressional reports; congressional documents; bill numbers; and hearings. Unfortunately, there is neither a Code section nor a subject matter index.

[Illustration 24–19]

EXCERPT FROM *THE INTERNAL REVENUE ACTS OF THE UNITED STATES*

REVENUE ACT OF 1916	
	Volume
BILL IN ITS VARIOUS FORMS	
Passed Senate, 64th Cong., 1st session,	
H.R. 16763. In the House of Representatives.	
September 6, 1916. Ordered to be printed	
with the amendments of the Senate numbered	61
SLIP LAW	
Public No. 271, 64th Cong., (H.R. 16763),	
an act to increase the revenue, and for	
other purposes. Approved September 8, 1916	
39 Stat. 756	91
REPORTS	
To increase the revenue, and for other	
purposes, report, H.Rpt. 64-922, July 5, 1916	93

Full text materials appear by type of document rather than by the act involved. All hearings are printed together, as are all bills, laws (accompanied by committee reports), studies, and regulations. You will need to use several volumes to assemble all materials for a particular law or provision. This is by no means a substantial drawback to using this set; assembling the same materials from elsewhere in the collection (assuming they are all available) would be far more difficult.

b. *Subsequent Series.* Professor Reams subsequently compiled materials to extend this set's coverage to later years. The later volumes are similar in coverage and format to the 1909–50 materials, although hearings receive less attention.

The 1954 volumes include committee reports, hearings, debates, and the final act. Revenue bills and Treasury studies do not appear. Because the IRS *Cumulative Bulletins* do not cover the 1954 Act, these materials are particularly valuable. A two-volume update published in 1993 includes fifty House and Senate bills missing from the original volumes.

Additional sets cover 1950–51, 1953–72, 1969, 1971, 1975, 1976, 1978, 1980, 1984, 1986, 1988, 1990, and 1993. Several of these sets are currently available only in microfiche.

8. *Eldridge, The United States Internal Revenue System (Hein)*

This reprint of early legislative materials is a useful complement to *Internal Revenue Acts of the United States*, discussed *supra*. It includes texts of revenue acts passed through 1894. There is extensive textual material as well as annotations for the various acts. It also contains a descriptive history of the various acts.

SECTION R. MICROFORMS

As primary and secondary source materials proliferate, many libraries seek alternatives to bound volumes. Microforms provide one option for expanding the collection within space limitations. In addition, libraries may be limited to microform acquisitions for out-of-print materials. Because so many items are available in this format, you should always check the library microform file before abandoning your search for a particular item.

If the library contains the *Tax Analysts Microfiche Database*, you have access to virtually all primary sources as well as to selected commentary. The weekly service includes full texts of *Tax Notes* and other *Tax Analysts* publications in addition to primary source materials. This service began including treaties and their background documents in 1996; earlier treaty documents can be found in the *Tax Notes International Microfiche Database*. Tax Analysts' print publications provide document numbers allowing you easy access to the *Microfiche Database*.

CCH publishes the following materials in ultrafiche: *U.S. Tax Cases, Tax Court Reports, Tax Court Memorandum Decisions,* and *Board of Tax Appeals Reports* (Section K); and the IRS *Cumulative Bulletin* (Section Q).

Several government publications are available in microform. These include *Congressional Record, Federal Register,* and *Code of Federal Regulations.* Many libraries include briefs filed with the United States Supreme Court in their microform collections.

Several sets include legislative histories. These include Congressional Information Service's *CIS/Microfiche Library*; Information Handling Services' *Legislative Histories Microfiche Program*; Commerce Clearing House's *Public Laws—Legislative Histories on Microfiche*; *Micro-Mini Prints* (William S. Hein & Co.); and *CIS Legislative History Service*. A service remains valuable for historic research even after the publisher stops adding new material.

Several series of *Internal Revenue Acts of the United States* (Section Q) are available in microform format. *Tax Management Primary Sources—Series I* (Section Q) is available in ultrafiche as well as in hard copy.

SECTION S.   CD–ROM

Compact discs store significant amounts of information yet require little storage space. Because you can access them at various points, much like the online services described in Section T, they offer another means for libraries to maintain large amounts of data in a small area. The ability to network CD–ROM services is a particularly attractive feature for many libraries. In many areas of research, CD–ROM has supplanted microform as an alternative to print materials.

1. Tax Analysts

Tax Analysts' *OneDisc* is available in both Windows and DOS versions. Subscribers can select among monthly, quarterly, and annual update options. In addition to primary source materials, the *OneDisc* includes Little, Brown treatises, explanations of recent legislation, and useful tables of IRS information. Another recent addition is the *Treasury/IRS Business Plan*, which Tax Analysts supplements with progress reports.

Court Opinions Reference discs include full text opinions for since 1942; current year material is on the *OneDisc*. An *IRS Letter Rulings and Technical Advice Memorandums* disc includes full text rulings since 1980. Tax Analysts plans to add legislative histories during 1998.

Tax Analysts also publishes a *Worldwide Treaty Disc* (Section H), an *Exempt Organization Master List*, and a *Tax Directory* in CD–ROM. The *Tax Directory* provides contact information for tax professionals in government and the private sector.

2. Commerce Clearing House

The *CCH CD–ROM* service (previously called *CCH ACCESS CD–ROM*) includes both primary source and textual material. You can customize an order to include various combinations of materials.

3. Shepard's Citations on CD–ROM

This CD–ROM can be integrated with *Shepard's Daily Update* using the Internet.

4. Bureau of National Affairs

BNA publishes *Tax Management Portfolios*, an interactive IRS forms service, and *Tax Practice Series* in CD–ROM format.

5. OnPoint System (RIA)

OnPoint System includes a variety of available discs. Subscribers can customize their order. Materials covered include primary source, citator, and looseleaf service, and treatise materials. [See Illustrations 24–20 and 24–21.]

[Illustration 24–20]

TABLE OF CONTENTS

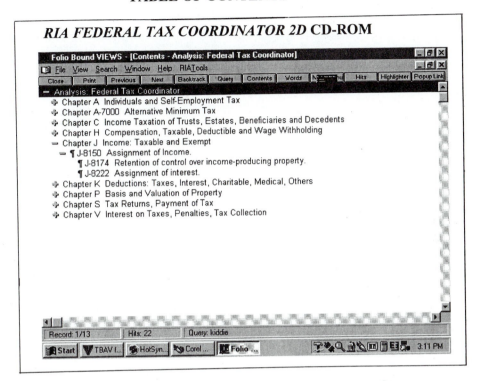

→ A + sign indicates additional subheadings in the table of contents; click to reach them. A − sign indicates there are no additional subheadings.

→ If you double click on a paragraph in the table of contents, you jump to descriptive text, as shown in Illustration 24–21. From there, you can jump to additional explanatory material or to primary source material. The "next," and "previous," and "backtrack" buttons allow you to retrace your steps at any time during the research session.

[Illustration 24–21]

TEXTUAL DISCUSSION

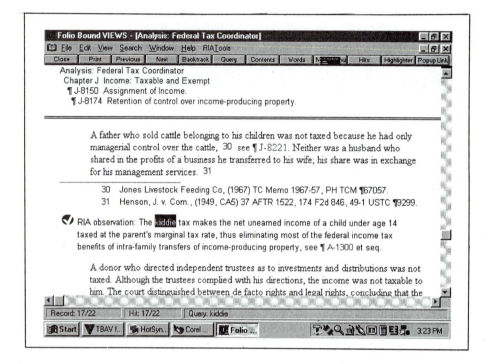

6. West

West's *Federal Tax Library* includes a variety of primary source materials and offers an optional link to WESTLAW. As is true for many of the services discussed in this chapter, subscribers can select among a variety of options.

7. Authority (Matthew Bender)

The *Authority* CD–ROM service can be customized to include a wide variety of titles. The Tax and Estate Planning Library in *Authority* focuses primarily on secondary source materials, including annual Institutes and Bender treatises. Rabkin & Johnson, *Current Legal Forms with Tax Analysis*, is part of the Business Law Library in *Authority*.

8. Warren, Gorham & Lamont

Warren, Gorham & Lamont offers several CD–ROM series featuring subject-specific WG & L treatises.

9. Other CD–ROM Sources

The Internal Revenue Service makes tax forms available in CD–ROM. Both *Index to Legal Periodicals* and *Current Law Index* (Section

N) are available. *ILP's* version is *WILSONDISC*; *CLI's* is *LegalTrac*. Potomac Publishing has a *Statutes at Large* disc (and Internet option). *Kleinrock's Tax Library* includes a variety of primary source material.

SECTION T. ONLINE LEGAL RESEARCH

Online legal research systems have several useful features. First, they bring the research materials together in one readily accessible location. Libraries with tax alcoves require several rows of shelves to house the relevant information; libraries without this arrangement may shelve relevant items on several floors. An online system requires only a computer, modem, and printer.

More important than the time saved in gathering the material is the ability to do searches that are virtually impossible to accomplish using print materials. Because the service responds to queries based on words appearing or not appearing in its database, you could easily use an on-line system to compile a list of all opinions by a particular judge. Likewise, the computer can quickly locate all decisions rendered in 1997, at every court level, involving the innocent spouse defense. Although CD–ROM searches can yield similar results, an online service generally includes far more material than does a single CD–ROM disc.

Online commercial services include a variety of sources in their master databases. Internet sites may include data from a variety of sources or may focus on a single type of information.

1. On–Line Commercial Services

Two online services, LEXIS–NEXIS and WESTLAW, have extensive tax databases.[88] In addition, both Commerce Clearing House (*Internet Tax Research NetWork*) and Research Institute of American (*On-Point*) provide online access to a variety of primary and secondary source materials. Tax Analysts includes an online connection to its *OneDisc* (Section S).

These services include a variety of primary source materials–Code, treaties, regulations, IRS material, judicial decisions. They may include legislative histories. Secondary source materials include citators, loose-leaf services, law reviews, and newsletters. Services frequently expand the number of sources covered and the time periods covered.

Each of these services differs slightly in its coverage and in the search terms you would use while online. All allow you to specify particular words that must appear or be absent in a document; if the words must be in a desired proximity, you can include that limitation. You can use these systems to locate decisions involving damages within five words of the term personal injury, or for decisions involving damages that do not involve personal injury.

---

[88] Chapter 22 includes extensive coverage of these services.

Before formulating a search query, you should become familiar with the search term symbols used on the system being accessed. In addition to each service's explanatory texts, other guides are available.

DIALOG Information Retrieval Service offers a significant number of databases that can be searched for abstracts of journal articles or references to relevant texts. Databases likely to be of interest include Business/Economics; Law and Government; and Bibliography—Books and Monographs. The Bibliography database includes the *Legal Resource Index* (Section N). *Tax Notes Today* is also available. *DIALOG* can also be accessed through WESTLAW.

2. The Internet

The Internet provides a means for communicating both text and graphics anywhere in the world; with appropriate equipment, you can even receive audio transmissions. Internet services include e-mail, online discussion groups, and websites that provide primary source material, commentary, and general news.

There are a variety of useful websites available. Some provide primary source material directly; others provide hypertext links to a variety of other websites. Unfortunately, websites often change address or cease to exist altogether. You are likely to find that many of your searches lead you to at least a few nonexistent sites.[89]

The following list, which includes a sampling of these sites, includes the URL for each site.

- Internal Revenue Service—forms and publications.[90]

(http://www.irs.ustreas.gov/prod/forms_pubs/index.html)

- House of Representatives—search full text and digests of bills by key word. The site indicates if a bill has passed one or both houses; it includes *Congressional Record* and committee reports.

(http://thomas.loc.gov)

- Frank McNeil's TaxSites—links to tax-related net sites.

(http://www2.best.com/?ftmexpat/html/taxsites.html)

- TaxWeb—links to tax publishers, discussion groups, and other information.

(http://www.taxweb.com/resear2.html)

---

[89] By the time you use this text, some of these addresses may be incorrect. In that case, you might find the correct address using one of the search engines described previously.

[90] You may need special software, such as Adobe Acrobat, to convert the online materials to a form you can use.

Appendix A *

TABLE OF LEGAL ABBREVIATIONS

Even the legal scholar may occasionally encounter an abbreviation whose complete title is difficult to identify. He or she may have to consult a specialized source such as William H. Bryson's *Dictionary of Sigla and Abbreviations to and in Law Books Before 1607* (Buffalo: William S.Hein 1996), Mary Miles Prince's *Bieber's Dictionary of Legal Abbreviations* (Buffalo: William S. Hein, 4th ed. 1993), *World Dictionary of Legal Abbreviations,* edited by Igor I. Kavass and Mary Miles Prince (Buffalo: Hein, 1991), or Donald Raistrick's *Index to Legal Citations and Abbreviations* (London: Bowker-Saur, 2d ed. 1993). Australian abbreviations are contained in Colin Fong's *Finding the Law: Guide to Australian Secondary Sources of Legal Information* (Sydney: Legal Information Press, 1990). One of the largest listings of periodical abbreviations, including legal periodicals, is *Periodical Title Abbreviations* (Detroit: Gale Research, 1993).

As primary and secondary legal materials continue to proliferate each year, it is virtually impossible to include in one place all their abbreviations and titles. Appendix A is restricted primarily to the English language periodicals, court reports, and looseleaf services that one could expect to find in a large American law school library as of January 1, 1994. In addition, Appendix A includes many esoteric and historical citations. This Appendix is not presumed to be authoritative in any official sense, but to reflect acceptable usage by most members of the legal community. Superseded titles have been retained because they are never out of date as possible citations.

A

A.	Atlantic Reporter	A. & E.Enc.	American & English
A.2d	Same, Second Series	L. & Pr.	Encyclopedia of
A. & E.	Adolphus & Ellis		Law and Practice
	Queen's Bench	A. & E.Ency.	American & English
	(Eng.)		Encyclopedia of
A. & E.Ann.	American & English		Law
Cas.	Annotated Cases	A. & E.Ency.	Same
A. & E.Anno.	Same	Law	
A. & E.Cas.	Same	A. & E.P. & P.	American & English
A. & E.Corp.	American & English		Pleading and Prac-
Cas.	Corporation Cases		tice
A. & E.Corp.	Same, New Series	A. & E.R.Cas.	American & English
Cas. (N.S.)			Railroad Cases

* Revised for this edition by Daniel W. Martin, Director of the Pepperdine University Law Library, and Kevin Slatum.

A. & E.R.Cas. (N.S.)	Same, New Series	AIDS Litigation Rep.	AIDS Litigation Reporter
A. & E.R.R. Cas.	American & English Railroad Cases	A.I.L.C.	American International Law Cases 1783–1968
A. & E.R.R. Cas. (N.S.)	Same, New Series	A.K.Marsh.	A.K. Marshall (Ky.)
A.B.	Anonymous Reports at end of Benloe, or Bendloe (1661) (Eng.)	A.L.I.	American Law Institute
		ALI–ABA CLE Rev.	American Law Institute—American Bar Association—Continuing Legal Education Review
A.B.A.J.	American Bar Association Journal		
A.B.A.Rep.	American Bar Association Reports	A.L.R.	American Law Reports
A.B.A.Sect. Ins.N. & C. L.Proc.	American Bar Association Section of Insurance, Negligence and Compensation Law Proceedings	A.L.R.2d	Same, Second Series
		A.L.R.3d	Same, Third Series
		A.L.R.Fed.	American Law Reports Federal
		A.L.Rec.	American Law Record
A.B.C.Newsl.	International Association of Accident Boards and Commissions Newsletter	A.L.Reg. (N.S.)	American Law Register, New Series
		A.L.Reg. (O.S.)	American Law Register, Old Series
A.B.F.Res.J.	American Bar Foundation Research Journal	A.M. & O.	Armstrong, Macartney & Ogle Nisi Prius (Ir.)
A.B.F.Research Reptr.	American Bar Foundation Research Reporter	A.M.C.	American Maritime Cases
A.C.	Law Reports Appeal Cases (Eng.)	A.O.C.Newsl.	Administrative Office of the Courts Newsletter
	Appeal Cases (Can.)	APLA Q.J.	American Patent Law Association Quarterly Journal
	Advance California Reports		
A.C.A.	Advance California Appellate Reports	A.P.R.	Atlantic Provinces Reports, 1975–
A.C.L.U.Leg. Action Bull.	American Civil Liberties Union Legislative Action Bulletin	A.R.	Alberta Reports, 1977–
		A.R.C.	American Ruling Cases
A.C.R.	American Criminal Reports	A.R.M.	Appeals & Review Memorandum Committee (I.R.B.)
A.D.	American Decisions		
A/E Legal Newsl.	A/E Legal Newsletter	A.R.R.	Appeals & Review Recommendation (I.R.Bull.)
AELE Legal Liab.Rep.	AELE Legal Liability Reporter	A.S.A.Newsl.	Association for the Study of Abortion Newsletter
A.F.L.Rev.	Air Force Law Review		
AFTR	American Federal Tax Reports	ASILS Int'l L.J.	Association of Student International Law Society's International Law Journal
A.I.D.	Accident/Injury/Damages		
AIDS L. Rep.	AIDS Law Reporter		
AIDS L.Rev. Q.	AIDS Law Review Quarterly	A.S.R.	American State Reports

A.T.	Alcohol Tax Unit (I.R.B.)	Ad.Ct.Dig.	Administrative Court Digest
A.T.L.A.J.	American Trial Lawyers Association Journal	Ad.L.	Pike and Fircher, Administrative Law
		Ad.L.2d	Same, Second Series
ATLA L.J.	Journal of the Association of Trial Lawyers of America	Ad.L.Bull.	Administrative Law Bulletin
		Ad.L.News	Administrative Law News
AbN.	Abstracts, Treasury Decisions, New Series	Ad.L.Newsl.	Administrative Law Newsletter
Abb.	Abbott (U.S.)	Ad.L.Rev.	Administrative Law Review
Abb.Adm.	Abbott's Admiralty (U.S.)	Adams	Adams (Me.)
Abb.App.Dec.	Abbott's Appeal Decisions (N.Y.)	Add.	Adams (N.H.) Addison (Pa.)
Abb.Dec.	Abbott's Decisions (N.Y.)	Add.Eccl.Rep.	Addams' Ecclesiastical Reports (Eng.)
Abb.Dict.	Abbott's Dictionary	Add.Penn.	Addison (Pa.)
Abb.N.Cas.	Abbott's New Cases (N.Y.)	Add.Rep.	Same
		Adel.L.Rev.	Adelaide Law Review
Abb.Prac.	Abbott's Practice (N.Y.)	Adm. & Ecc.	Admiralty & Ecclesiastical (Eng.)
Abb.Prac. N.S.	Same, New Series	Admin. L.J.	Administrative Law Journal
Abb.R.P.S.	Abbott's Real Property Statutes (Wash.)	Admin.L.J. Am.U.	Administrative Law Journal of the American University
A'Beck.Res. Judgm.	A'Beckett's Reserved Judgments (Vict.)		
Abogada Int'l	Abogada Internacional	Admin.L.Rev.	Administrative Law Review
Abs.	Abstracts, Treasury Decisions	Advocates' Q.	Advocates' Quarterly
		Afr. J. Int'l L.	African Journal of International Law
	Ohio Law Abstract	Afr.L.Dig.	African Law Digest
Abstr.Crim. & Pen.	Abstracts on Criminology and Penology	Afr.L.R.	African Law Reports
		Afr.L.R., Mal. Ser.	African Law Reports, Malawi Series
Acad.Pol.Sci. Proc.	Academy of Political Science Proceedings	Afr.L.R., Sierre L.Ser.	African Law Reports, Sierre Leone Series
		Afr.L.Stud.	African Law Studies
Acct. for L. Firms	Accounting for Law Firms	Agric.Dec.	Agriculture Decisions
Act.	Acton Prize Cases, Privy Council (Eng.)	Agric.L.J.	Agriculture Law Journal
		Aik.	Aikens (Vt.)
		Air & Space L.	Air and Space Law
Acta Cancelariae	English Chancery Reports	Air L.	Air Law
		Air L.Rev.	Air Law Review
Acta Crim.	Acta Criminologica	Akron L.Rev.	Akron Law Review
Acta Jur.	Acta Juridica	Akron Tax J.	Akron Tax Journal
Acton	Acton Prize Cases, Privy Council (Eng.)	Ala.	Alabama Reports
		Ala.App.	Alabama Court of Appeals
Ad. & El.	Adolphus & Ellis, Queen's Bench (Eng.)	Ala.L.J.	Alabama Law Journal
		Ala.L.Rev.	Alabama Law Review
Ad. & El. (N.S.)	Same, New Series	Ala.Law.	The Alabama Lawyer
		Ala.Sel.Cas.	Alabama Select Cases

Ala.St.B. Found.Bull.	Alabama State Bar Foundation Bulletin	Am. & Eng. Eq.D.	American & English Decisions in Equity
Alaska	Alaska Reports	Am. & Eng. Pat.Cas.	American & English Patent Cases
Alaska B.Brief	Alaska Bar Brief	Am.Acad. Matri.Law. J.	American Academy of Matrimonial Lawyers Journal
Alaska B.J.	Alaska Bar Journal		
Alaska L.J.	Alaska Law Journal		
Alaska L.Rev.	Alaska Law Review	Am.B.Found. Res.J.	American Bar Foundation Research Journal
Alb.L.J.	Albany Law Journal		
Alb.L.J.Sci. & Tech.	Albany Law Journal of Science and Technology	Am.B.News	American Bar News
		Am.B.R. (N.S.)	American Bankruptcy Reports, New Series
Alb.L.Rev.	Albany Law Review		
Albany L.Rev.	Same	Am.Bankr. L.J.	American Bankruptcy Law Journal
Albuquerque B.J.	Albuquerque Bar Journal	Am.Bankr. Reg.	American Bankruptcy Register
Alc. & N.	Alcock & Napier, King's Bench (Ir.)	Am.Bankr. Rep.	American Bankruptcy Reports
Alc.Reg.Cas.	Alcock Registry Cases (Ir.)	Am.Bankr. Rev.	American Bankruptcy Review
Alcohol. Treat.Q.	Alcoholism Treatment Quarterly	Am.Bus.L.J.	American Business Law Journal
Ald.	Alden's Condensed Reports (Pa.)	Am.Corp.Cas.	American Corporation Cases
Aleyn	Aleyn, King's Bench (Eng.)	Am.Cr.	American Criminal Reports
Alison Pr.	Alison Practice (Scot.)	Am.Crim. L.Q.	American Criminal Law Quarterly
All E.R.	All England Law Reports	Am.Crim. L.Rev.	American Criminal Law Review
All India Crim. Dec.	All India Criminal Decisions	Am.Dec.	American Decisions
		Am.Elect. Cas.	American Electrical Cases
All India Rptr.	All India Reporter		
All N.L.R.	All Nigeria Law Reports	Am.Fed.Tax R.	American Federal Tax Reports
All Pak.Leg. Dec.	All Pakistan Legal Decisions	Am.Fed.Tax R.2d	Same, Second Series
Allen	Allen (Mass.)	Am.For.L. Ass'n Newsl.	American Foreign Law Association Newsletter
Allen N.B.	Allen (N.B.)		
Allinson	Allinson, Pa. Superior District Courts	Am.Hist.Rev.	American Historical Review
Alta.	Alberta Law Reports	Am. Ind.J.	American Indian Journal
Alta.L.	Alberta Law		
Alta.L.Q.	Alberta Law Quarterly	Am.Ind.L. Newsl.	American Indian Law Newsletter
Alta.L.Rev.	Alberta Law Review	Am.Indian L.Rev.	American Indian Law Review
Am. & E. Corp.Cas.	American & English Corporation Cases	Am.Insolv. Rep.	American Insolvency Reports
Am. & E. Corp.Cas. (N.S.)	Same, New Series	Am.J.Comp. L.	American Journal of Comparative Law
Am. & E.R. Cas.	American & English Railroad Cases	Am.J.Crim. L.	American Journal of Criminal Law
Am. & E.R. Cas. (N.S.)	Same, New Series	Am.J.Fam. L.	American Journal of Family Law
Am. & Eng. Ann.Cas.	American & English Annotated Cases		

Am.J.For. Psych.	American Journal of Forensic Psychiatry	Am.Mar.Cas.	American Maritime Cases
Am.J.Int'l Arb.	American Journal of International Arbitration	Am.Negl.Cas.	American Negligence Cases
Am.J.Int'l	American Journal of International Law	Am.Negl.Rep.	American Negligence Reports
Am.J.Juris.	American Journal of Jurisprudence	Am.Notary	American Notary
		Am.Pol.Sci. Rev.	American Political Science Review
Am.J.L. & Med.	American Journal of Law and Medicine	Am.Pr.Rep.	American Practice Reports (D.C.)
Am.J.Legal Hist.	American Journal of Legal History	Am.Prob.	American Probate Reports
Am.J.Police Sci.	American Journal of Police Science	Am.Prob. (N.S.)	Same, New Series
Am.J.Tax Pol'y	American Journal of Tax Policy	Am.R.	American Reports
		Am.R. & Corp.	American Railroad Corporation
Am.J.Trial Advoc.	American Journal of Trial Advocacy	Am.R.Rep.	American Railway Reports
Am.Jur.	American Jurisprudence	Am.Railw. Cas.	American Railway Cases (Smith & Bates)
	American Jurist		
Am.Jur.2d	American Jurisprudence, Second Series	Am.Rep.	American Reports
		Am.Ry.Rep.	American Railway Reports
Am.L.Ins.	American Law Institute	Am.Soc'y Int'l L.Proc.	American Society of International Law Proceedings
Am.L.J.	American Law Journal (Ohio)		
	American Law Journal (Pa.)	Am.St.R.	American State Reports
		Am.St.R.D.	American Street Railway Decisions
Am.L.J. (N.S.)	Same, New Series		
Am.L.Mag.	American Law Magazine	Am.St.Rep.	American State Reports
Am.L.Rec.	American Law Record (Ohio)	Am.Tr.M. Cas.	American Trademark Cases (Cox)
Am.L.Reg.	American Law Register	Am.Trial Law.J.	American Trial Lawyers Journal
Am.L.Reg. (N.S.)	Same, New Series	Am.Trial Law. L.J.	American Trial Lawyers Law Journal
Am.L.Reg. (O.S.)	Same, Old Series	Am.U.Intra. L.Rev.	American University Intramural Law Review
Am.L.Rev.	American Law Review		
Am.L.Sch. Rev.	American Law School Review	Am.U.J. Gender & L.	American University Journal of Gender and the Law
Am.L.T. Bankr.	American Law Times Bankruptcy Reports	Am.U.J.Int'l L. & Pol'y	American University Journal of International Law and Policy
Am.Lab.Leg. Rev.	American Labor Legislation Review	Am.U.L.Rev.	American University Law Review
Am.Law.	American Lawyer		
Am.Law Rec.	American Law Record (Ohio)	Amb.	Ambler, Chancery (Eng.)
Am.Law Reg.	American Law Register	Ames	Ames (Minn.)
			Ames (R.I.)

Ames K. & B.	Ames, Knowles & Bradley (R.I.)	Annals Air & Space	Annals of Air and Space Law
Amicus	Amicus (South Bend, Ind.)	Annaly	Annaly's Hardwicke King's Bench (Eng.)
	Amicus (Thousand Oaks, Cal.)	Anst.	Ansthruther, Exchequer (Eng.)
An.B.	Anonymous Reports at end of Benloe, or Bendloe (1661) (Eng.)	Anth.N.P.	Anthon's Nisi Prius (N.Y.)
And.	Anderson, Common Pleas (Eng.)	Antitrust Bull.	Antitrust Bulletin
		Antitrust L. & Econ.Rev.	Antitrust Law and Economics Review
Andr.	Andrews, King's Bench (Eng.)	Antitrust L.J.	Antitrust Law Journal
Ang.	Angell (R.I.)	Antitrust L.Sym.	Antitrust Law Symposium
Ang. & Dur.	Angell & Durfee (R.I.)	App.	Appleton (Me.)
Anglo-Am.L. Rev.	Anglo-American Law Review	App.Cas.	Law Reports, Appeal Cases (Eng.)
Animal Rights L.Rep.	Animal Rights Law Reporter	App.Cas.2d	Same, Second Series
Ann.	Annaly's Hardwicke King's Bench (Eng.)	App.Court Ad. Rev.	Appellate Court Administration Review
Ann.Cas.	American Annotated Cases	App.D.C.	Appeal Cases (D.C.)
Ann.Dig.	Annual Digest and Reports of International Law Cases	App.Div.	Appellate Division (N.Y.)
		App.Div.2d	Same, Second Series
		App.N.Z.	Appeal Reports (N.Z.)
		App.R.N.Z.	Same, Second Series
Ann.Indus. Prop.L.	Annual of Industrial Property Law	App.Rep.Ont.	Ontario Appeal Reports
Ann.L.Reg. U.S.	Annual Law Register of the United States	Arb.J.	Arbitration Journal
		Arb.J. (N.S.)	Same, New Series
		Arb.J. (O.S.)	Same, Old Series
Ann.Leg. Forms Mag.	Annotated Legal Forms Magazine	Arb.L.Dig.	Arbitration Law: A Digest of Court Decisions
Ann.Rev.Int'l Aff.	Annual Review of International Affairs	Archer	Archer (Fla.)
Ann.Surv. Afr.L.	Annual Survey of African Law	Archer & H.	Archer & Hogue (Fla.)
Ann.Surv. Am.L.	Annual Survey of American Law	Argus L.R.	Argus Law Reports (Austl.)
Ann.Surv. Banking L.	Annual Survey of Banking Law	Ariz.	Arizona Reports
Ann.Surv. Colo.L.	Annual Survey of Colorado Law	Ariz.App.	Arizona Appeals Reports
		Ariz.B.J.	Arizona Bar Journal
Ann.Surv. Commonw. L.	Annual Survey of Commonwealth Law	Ariz.J.Int'l & Comp.L.	Arizona Journal of International and Comparative Law
Ann.Surv. Ind.L.	Annual Survey of Indian Law	Ariz.L.Rev.	Arizona Law Review
		Ariz.Law.	Arizona Lawyer
Ann.Surv. S.Afr.L.	Annual Survey of South African Law	Ariz.St.L.J.	Arizona State Law Journal
Ann.Tax Cas.	Annotated Tax Cases	Ark.	Arkansas Reports
Annals	Annals of the American Academy of Political and Social Science	Ark.Just.	Arkley's Justiciary (Scot.)
		Ark.L.J.	Arkansas Law Journal

Ark.L.Rev.	Arkansas Law Review	Aust.L.T.	Australian Law Times
Ark.Law.	The Arkansas Lawyer	Austl. & N.Z. J.Crim.	Australian and New Zealand Journal of Criminology
Ark.Law.Q.	Arkansas Lawyer Quarterly	Austl.Argus L.R.	Australian Argus Law Reports
Armour	Queen's Bench, Manitoba Tempere Wood, by Armour	Austl.Bankr. Cas.	Australian Bankruptcy Cases
Arms.Con. Elec.	Armstrong's Contested Elections (N.Y.)	Austl.Bus. L.Rev.	Australian Business Law Review
Army Law.	Army Lawyer	Austl.Com.J.	Australian Commercial Journal
Arn.	Arnold, Common Pleas (Eng.)	Austl.Convey. & Sol.J.	Australian Conveyancer and Solicitors Journal
Arn. & H.	Arnold & Hodges, Queen's Bench (Eng.)	Austl.Current L.Rev.	Australian Current Law Review
Arnold	Arnold, Common Pleas (Eng.)	Austl.J.For. Sci.	Australian Journal of Forensic Sciences
Art & L.	Art and the Law	Austl.J.L. Soc'y	Australian Journal of Law and Society
Ashm.	Ashmead (Pa.)	Austl.Jr.	Australian Jurist
Asian Comp. L.Rev.	Asian Comparative Law Review	Austl.L.J.	Australian Law Journal
Asian Pac. Comm.Law.	Asian Pacific Commercial Lawyer	Austl.L.J. Rep.	Australian Law Journal Reports
Aspin.	Aspinall's Maritime Cases (Eng.)	Austl.L. Times	Australian Law Times
Ass'n Trial Law.Am. Newsl.	Association of Trial Lawyers of America Newsletter	Austl.Law.	Australian Lawyer
Ateneo L.J.	Ateneo Law Journal	Austl.Tax	Australian Tax Decisions
Atk.	Atkyns, Chancery (Eng.)	Austl.Tax Rev.	Australian Tax Review
Atl.	Atlantic Reporter		
Atom.Energy L.J.	Atomic Energy Law Journal	Austl.Y.B. Int'l L.	Australian Yearbook of International Law
Att'y Gen.	Attorney General		
Att'y Gen.L.J.	Attorney General's Law Journal	Austr.C.L.R.	Commonwealth Law Reports, Australia
Att'y Gen.Rep.	United States Attorneys General's Reports	Auto.Cas.	Automobile Cases
		Auto.Cas.2d	Same, Second Series
		Auto.L.Rep.	Automobile Law Reporter (CCH)
Atty.Gen.	Attorney General		
Atwater	Atwater (Minn.)	Av.Cas.	Aviation Cases
Auckland U.L.Rev.	Auckland University Law Review	Av.L.Rep.	Aviation Law Reporter (CCH)
Aust.Jur.	Australian Jurist		

B

B.	Weekly Law Bulletin	B. & Ald.	Barnewall & Alderson, King's Bench (Eng.)
B. & A.	Barnewall & Alderson, King's Bench (Eng.)		
B. & Ad.	Barnewall & Adolphus, King's Bench (Eng.)	B. & Arn.	Barron & Arnold, Election Cases (Eng.)

B. & Aust.	Barron & Austin Election Cases (Eng.)	B.C. Int'l & Comp. L. Rev.	Boston College International and Comparative Law Review
B. & B.	Ball & Beatty's Chancery (Ir.) Broderip & Bingham, Common Pleas (Eng.)	B.C.L. Notes	British Columbia Law Notes
B. & C.	Barnewall & Cresswell's King's Bench (Eng.)	B.C.L.Rev.	Boston College Law Review
B. & C.R.	Reports of Bankruptcy & Companies Winding up Cases (Eng.)	B.C. Third World L.J. B.D. & O.	Boston College Third World Law Journal Blackham, Dundas & Osborne, Nisi Prius (Ir.)
B. & D.	Benloe & Dalison, Common Pleas (Eng.)	B.Exam. B.Exam.J.	Bar Examiner Bar Examination Journal
B. & F.	Broderip & Freemantle's Ecclesiastical (Eng.)	B.I.C.I.L. Newsl.	British Institute of International and Comparative Law Newsletter
B. & H.Cr. Cas.	Bennet & Heard's Criminal Cases (Eng.)	B.I.L.C.	British International Law Cases
B. & H.Crim. Cas.	Same	B.Leader B.Mon. BNA	Bar Leader Ben Monroe (Ky.) Bureau of National Affairs
B. & Macn.	Brown & Macnamara, Railway Cases (Eng.)	BNA Banking Rep.	BNA's Banking Report
B. & P.	Bosanquet & Puller, Common Pleas (Eng.)	BNA Sec.Reg.	Securities Regulation & Law Report
B. & P.N.R.	Bosanquet & Puller's New Reports (Eng.)	B.R. (Army)	Board of Review (Army)
B. & S.	Best & Smith, Queen's Bench (Eng.)	B.R.C. B.R.–J.C. (Army)	British Ruling Cases Board of Review and Judicial Council of the Army
B.Bull.	Bar Bulletin	B.T.A.	Board of Tax Appeals Reports
B.C.	British Columbia		
B.C.Branch Lec.	Canadian Bar Association, British Columbia Branch Meeting Program Reports	B.U.Int'l L.J.	Boston University International Law Journal
		B.U.J.Tax L.	Boston University Journal of Tax Law
B.C.C.	Bail Court Cases (Eng.)	B.U.L.Rev.	Boston University Law Review
B.C.Envtl. Aff.L.Rev.	Boston College Environmental Affairs Law Review	B.U.Pub.Int. L.J.	Boston University Public Interest Law Journal
B.C.Indus. & Com.L.Rev.	Boston College Industrial and Commercial Law Review	B.W.C.C.	Butterworths Workmen's Compensation Cases (Eng.)
B.C.Int'l & Comp.L.J.	Boston College International and Comparative Law Journal	B.Y.U.J.L. & Educ.	Brigham Young University Journal of Law and Education
		BYU J.Pub.L.	Brigham Young University Journal of Public Law

B.Y.U.L.Rev.	Brigham Young University Law Review	Bar. & Aust.	Barron & Austin, Election Cases (Eng.)
Bac.Abr.	Bacon's Abridgment (Eng.)	Barb.	Barber (Ark.)
Bag. & Har.	Bagley & Harman (Cal.)		Barbour (N.Y.)
Bagl.	Bagley (Cal.)	Barb.Ch.	Barbour's Chancery (N.Y.)
Bagl. & H.	Bagley & Harman (Cal.)	Barber	Barber (N.Y.)
Bail Ct.Cas.	Lowndes & Maxwell, Bail Court Cases (Eng.)	Barn.	Barnardiston, King's Bench (Eng.)
Bail.Eq.	Bailey's Equity (S.C.)	Barn. & Ad.	Barnewall & Adolphus, King's Bench (Eng.)
Baild.	Baildon's Select Cases in Chancery (Eng.)	Barn. & Ald.	Barnewall & Alderson, King's Bench (Eng.)
Bailey	Bailey's Law (S.C.)	Barn. & C.	Barnewall & Cresswell, King's Bench (Eng.)
Bal.Ann. Codes	Ballinger's Annotated Codes & Statutes (Wash.)	Barn. & Cress.	Same
Bal.Pay't Rep.	Balance of Payments Reports (CCH)	Barn.Ch.	Barnardiston, Chancery (Eng.)
Baldw.	Baldwin (U.S.)	Barnes	Barnes, Practice Cases (Eng.)
Balf.Pr.	Balfour's Practice (Scot.)	Barnes' Notes	Barnes' Notes (Eng.)
Ball & B.	Ball & Beatty, Chancery (Ir.)	Barnet	Barnet, Common Pleas (Eng.)
Balt.L.T.	Baltimore Law Transcript	Barr	Barr (Pa.)
Ban. & A.	Banning & Arden, Patent Cases (U.S.)	Barr.Ch.Pr.	Barroll, Chancery Practice (Md.)
Bank. & Ins.R.	Bankruptcy & Insolvency Reports (Eng.)	Barr.MSS.	Barradall, Manuscript Reports (Va.)
Bank.Cas.	Banking Cases	Barrister	Barrister (Chicago)
Bank.Ct.Rep.	Bankrupt Court Reports		Barrister (Coral Gables, Fla.)
Banking L.J.	Banking Law Journal		Barrister (Davis, Cal.)
Banking L. Rev.	Banking Law Review		Barrister (Fort Lauderdale, Fla.)
Bankr.B.Bull.	Bankruptcy Bar Bulletin		Barrister (Toronto)
Bankr.Dev.J.	Bankruptcy Developments Journal	Bart.Elec. Cas.	Bartlett's Election Cases
Bankr.L.Rep.	Bankruptcy Law Reporter (CCH)	Bates Ch.	Bates, Chancery (Del.)
Bankr.Reg.	National Bankruptcy Register (N.Y.)	Batty	Batty, King's Bench (Ir.)
Banks	Banks (Kan.)	Baxt.	Baxter (Tenn.)
Bann.	Bannister's Common Pleas (Eng.)	Bay	Bay (Mo.)
			Bay (S.C.)
Bann. & A.	Banning & Arden, Patent Cases (U.S.)	Baylor L.Rev.	Baylor Law Review
		Beasl.	Beasley (N.J.)
Bann. & Ard.	Same	Beav.	Beavan, Rolls Court (Eng.)
Bar. & Arn.	Barron & Arnold, Election Cases (Eng.)	Beav. & W. Ry.Cas.	Beavan & Walford's Railway & Canal Cases (Eng.)
		Beav.R. & C.Cas.	Beavan, Railway & Canal Cases (Eng.)

Beaw.Lex Mer.	Beawes Lex Mercatoria (Eng.)	Benl.Old	Benloe, Old English Common Pleas
Bee	Bee's (U.S.)	Benn.	Bennett (Cal.)
Bee Adm.	Bee's Admiralty, United States District Court (S.C.)		Bennett (Dakota)
			Bennett (Mo.)
Bee C.C.R.	Bee's Crown Cases Reserved (Eng.)	Bent.	Bentley's Chancery (Ir.)
Behav.Sci. & L.	Behavioral Sciences and the Law	Berkeley Women's L.J.	Berkeley Women's Law Journal
Belg.Rev.Int'l L.	Belgian Review of International Law	Berry	Berry (Mo.)
		Bibb	Bibb (Ky.)
Bell.	Bellewe, King's Bench (Eng.)	Bibl.Cott.	Cotton Manuscripts.
		Bick.	Bicknell (Nev.)
Bell App.Cas.	Bell's Appeal Cases, House of Lords (Scot.)	Bick. & H.	Bicknell & Hawley (Nev.)
		Big.Ov.Cas.	Bigelow's Overruled Cases
Bell C.C.	Bell's Crown Cases Reserved (Eng.)	Bill Rights J.	Bill of Rights Journal
Bell Cas.	Bell's Cases (Scot.)	Bill Rights Rev.	Bill of Rights Review
Bell.Cas.t.H. VIII	Bellewe, King's Bench, tempore Henry VIII (Eng.)	Bing.	Bingham, New Cases, Common Pleas (Eng.)
Bell.Cas.t.R. II	Same, tempore Richard II (Eng.)	Binn.	Binney (Pa.)
Bell Comm.	Bell's Commentaries (Eng.)	Biss.	Bissell (U.S.)
		Bitt.Rep. in Ch.	Bittleson's Reports, Queen's Bench (Eng.)
Bell Cr.C.	Bell's Crown Cases Reserved (Eng.)		
Bell H.L.	Bell's Appeal Cases, House of Lords (Scot.)	Bitt.W. & P.	Bittleson, Wise & Parnell Practice Cases (Eng.)
Bell P.C.	Bell's Parliament Cases (Scot.)	Bk.	Black (U.S.)
		Bl.	William Blackstone's King's Bench (Eng.)
Bell Sc.Cas.	Bell's Scotch Court of Sessions Cases		
Bell Ses.Cas.	Same	Bl.H.	Henry Blackstone's Common Pleas (Eng.)
Bellewe (Eng.)	Bellewe, King's Bench		
Ben.	Benedict (U.S. District Court)	Bl.W.	William Blackstone's King's Bench (Eng.)
Ben. & H.L.C.	Bennett & Heard, Leading Criminal Cases (Eng.)	Bla.	Same
		Bla.H.	Henry Blackstone's Common Pleas (Eng.)
Bendl.	Bendloe's English Common Pleas		
Bened.	Benedict (U.S. District Court)	Bla.W.	William Blackstone's King's Bench (Eng.)
Benl.	Benloe's Common Pleas (Eng.)	Black	Black (Ind.)
Benl.	Benloe's King's Bench (Eng.)		Black (U.S.)
		Black L.J.	Black Law Journal
Benl. & D.	Benloe & Dalison, Common Pleas (Eng.)	Black.	William Blackstone's King's Bench (Eng.)
Benl. & Dal.	Same		
Benl.K.B.	Benloe's King's Bench (Eng.)	Black.Cond.	Blackwell's Condensed Reports (Ill.)

Black.Cond. Rep.	Same	Bos.Pol.Rep.	Boston Police Reports
Black.D. & O.	Blackham, Dandas & Osborne, Nisi Prius (Ir.)	Bost.L.R.	Boston Law Reporter
		Boston B.J.	Boston Bar Journal
		Bosw.	Boswell (Scot.)
Black.H.	Henry Blackstone's Common Pleas (Eng.)		Bosworth, Superior Court (N.Y.)
		Bott Poor Law Cas.	Bott's Poor Laws Settlement Cases (Eng.)
Black.Jus.	Blackerby's Justices' Cases (Eng.)		
Black L.J.	Black Law Journal	Bott's Set. Cas.	Same
Blackf.	Blackford (Ind.)		
Blackst.R.	William Blackstone's King's Bench (Eng.)	Bould.	Bouldin (Ala.)
		Bouv.	Bouvier Law Dictionary
Blackw.Cond.	Blackwell's Condensed Reports (Ill.)	Bov.Pat.Cas.	Bovill's Patent Cases
		Boyce	Boyce (Del.)
		Br. & B.	Broderip & Bingham, Common Pleas (Eng.)
Blair Co.	Blair County Law Reports (Pa.)		
Blake	Blake (Mont.)	Br. & Col.	British & Colonial Prize Cases
Blake & H.	Blake & Hedge (Mont.)		
		Br. & F.Ecc.	Broderick & Freemantle's Ecclesiastical Cases (Eng.)
Bland	Bland's Chancery (Md.)		
Blatchf.	Blatchford (U.S.)		
Blatchf. & H.	Blatchford & Howland (U.S. District Court)	Br. & Gold.	Browndow & Goldesborough's Common Pleas (Eng.)
Blatchf.Prize Cas.	Blatchford's Prize Cases (U.S.)	Br. & L.	Brownlow & Lushington's Admiralty Cases (Eng.)
Bleckley	Bleckley (Ga.)		
Bli.	Bligh, House of Lords (Eng.)	Br. & Lush.	Same
		Br.N.C.	Brooke's New Cases, King's Bench (Eng.)
Bli. (N.S.)	Same, New Series		
Bligh	Same		
Bligh (N.S.)	Same, New Series	Br.N.Cas.	Same
Bliss	Bliss, Delaware County Reports (Pa.)	Bract.	Bracton De Legibus et Consuetudinibus Angliae (Eng.)
Blue Sky L.Rep.	Blue Sky Law Reporter (CCH)	Bracton L.J.	Bracton Law Journal
		Bradf.	Bradford (Iowa)
Bluett	Bluett's Isle of Man Cases	Bradf.Surr.	Bradford's Surrogate Court (N.Y.)
Bombay L.J.	Bombay Law Journal	Bradl.	Bradley (R.I.)
Bond	Bond (U.S.)	Bradw.	Bradwell (Ill.)
Book of Judg.	Book of Judgments (Eng.)	Brame	Brame (Miss.)
		Branch	Branch (Fla.)
Boor.	Booraem (Cal.)	Brantly	Brantly (Md.)
Bos.	Bosworth, Superior Court (N.Y.)	Brayt.	Brayton (Vt.)
		Breese	Breese (Ill.)
Bos. & P.	Bosanquet & Puller, Common Pleas (Eng.)	Brev.	Brevard (S.C.)
		Brew.	Brewer (Md.)
			Brewster (Pa.)
Bos. & P. N.R.	Same	Brews.	Brewster (Pa.)
Bos. & Pul.	Same	Bridg.	J. Bridgmore, Common Pleas (Eng.)

Bridg.J. — Sir J. Bridgman, Common Pleas (Eng.)

Bridg.O. — Sir Orlando Bridgman, Common Pleas (Eng.)

Bridgeport L.Rev. — Bridgeport Law Review

Brightly — Brightly (Pa.)

Brightly El. Cas. — Brightly's Leading Election Cases (Pa.)

Brisb. — Brisbin (Minn.)

Brit.Cr.Cas. — British Crown Cases

Brit.J.Ad.L. — British Journal of Administrative Law

Brit.J. Criminol. — British Journal of Criminology

Brit.J.Law & Soc'y — British Journal of Law and Society

Brit.Prac. Int'l L. — British Practice in International Law

Brit.Ship.L. — British Shipping Laws (Stevens)

Brit.Tax Rev. — British Tax Review

Brit.Y.B.Int'l L. — British Year Book of International Law

Bro. & F. — Broderick & Freemantle's Ecclesiastical (Eng.)

Bro. & Fr. — Same

Bro. & Lush. — Browning & Lushington's Admiralty (Eng.)

Br.Eccl. — Brown's Ecclesiastical (Eng.)

Bro.Just. — Brown's Justiciary (Scot.)

Brock. — Brockenbrough (U.S.)

Brock. & Hol. Cas. — Brockenbrough & Holmes' Cases (Va.)

Brock.Cas. — Brockenbrough's Cases (Va.)

Brod. & F. Ecc.Cas. — Broderick & Freemantle's Ecclesiastical Cases (Eng.)

Brod. & Fr. Ecc.Cas. — Same

Brodix Am. & El.Pat.Cas. — Brodix's American & English Patent Cases

Brook Abr. — Brook's Abridgment (Eng.)

Brook. Barrister — Brooklyn Barrister

Brook.J.Int'l L. — Brooklyn Journal of International Law

Brook.L.Rev. — Brooklyn Law Review

Brook N.Cas. — Brook's New Cases, King's Bench (Eng.)

Brooks — Brooks (Mich.)

Brown — Brown (Miss.)
Brown (Mo.)
Brown (Neb.)

Brown & MacN. — Brown & MacNamara, Railway Cases (Eng.)

Brown & R. — Brown & Rader (Mo.)

Brown A. & R. — Brown's United States District Court Admiralty & Revenue Cases

Brown Adm. — Brown's Admiralty (U.S.)

Brown Ch. — Brown's Chancery (Eng.)

Brown Dict. — Brown's Law Dictionary

Brown Ecc. — Brown's Ecclesiastical (Eng.)

Brown N.P. — Brown's Nisi Prius (Mich.)

Brown P.C. — Same

Brown Parl. Cas. — Brown's House of Lords Cases (Eng.)

Brown. & L. — Browning & Lushington, Admiralty (Eng.)

Browne — Browne (Mass.)
Browne, Common Pleas (Pa.)

Browne & G. — Browne & Gray (Mass.)

Browne & H. — Browne & Hemingway (Miss.)

Browne Bank Cas. — Browne's National Bank Cases

Brownl. & G. — Brownlow & Goldesborough, Common Pleas (Eng.)

Bruce — Bruce (Scot.)

Brunn.Coll. Cas. — Brunner's Collected Cases (U.S.)

Bt. — Benedict (U.S.)

Buck — Buck (Mont.)
Buck, Bankrupt Cases (Eng.)

Buck. — Bucknill's Cooke's Cases of Practice, Common Pleas (Eng.)

Buck.Dec.	Buckner's Decisions (in Freeman's Chancery Reports) (Miss.)	Bulstr.	Bulstrode, King's Bench (Eng.)
		Bunb.	Bunbury, Exchequer (Eng.)
Buff.L.Rev.	Buffalo Law Review	Burf.	Burford (Okla.)
Bull.	Weekly Law Bulletin	Burgess	Burgess (Ohio)
Bull.Am. Acad.Psych. & L.	Bulletin of the American Academy of Psychiatry and the Law	Burk	Burk (Va.)
		Burlesque Rep.	Skillman's New York Police Reports
		Burnett	Burnett (Ore.)
Bull.Can. Welfare L.	Bulletin of Canadian Welfare Law		Burnett (Wis.)
Bull.Copyright Soc'y	Bulletin of the Copyright Society of the United States of America	Burr.	Burrow, King's Bench (Eng.)
		Burr.S.Cases	Burrow's Settlement Cases (Eng.)
		Burr.t.M.	Burrow's Reports, tempore Mansfield (Eng.)
Bull.Czech.L.	Bulletin of Czechoslovak Law		
Bull.Int'l Fiscal Doc.	Bulletin for International Fiscal Documentation	Bus. & L.	Business and Law
		Bus.L.J.	Business Law Journal
Bull.L.Science & Tech.	Bulletin of Law, Science and Technology	Bus.L.Rev.	Business Law Review (Eng.)
			Business Law Review (U.S.)
Bull.Legal Devel.	Bulletin of Legal Developments	Bus.Law.	The Business Lawyer
Bull.Waseda U.Inst. Comp.L.	Bulletin, Waseda University Institute of Comparative Law	Bus.Reg.L. Rep.	Business Regulation Law Report
		Busb.Eq.	Busbee, Equity (N.C.)
		Busb.L.	Busbee, Law (N.C.)
Buller N.P.	Buller's Nisi Prius (Eng.)	Bush	Bush (Ky.)
		Buxton	Buxton (N.C.)

C

C.	Cowen (N.Y.)	C. & E.	Cababe & Ellis, Queen's Bench (Eng.)
C. & A.	Cooke & Alcock, King's Bench and Exchequer (Ir.)		
		C. & F.	Clark & Finelly, House of Lords (Eng.)
C. & C.	Case and Comment Colemand & Caines' Cases (N.Y.)		
		C. & J.	Crompton & Jervis, Exchequer (Eng.)
C. & D.	Corbett & Daniel's Election Cases (Eng.)	C. & K.	Carrington & Kirwan, Nisi Prius (Eng.)
	Crawford & Dix's Abridged Cases (Ir.)	C. & L.	Connor & Lawson's Chancery (Ir.)
C. & D.A.C.	Crawford & Dix's Abridged Cases (Ir.)	C. & L.C.C.	Caines & Leigh, Crown Cases (Eng.)
C. & D.C.C.	Crawford & Dix's Circuit Cases (Ir.)	C. & M.	Carrington & Marshman's Nisi Prius (Eng.)
	Crawford & Dix's Criminal Cases (Ir.)		Crompton & Meeson's Exchequer (Eng.)

C. & Marsh.	Carrington & Marshman's Nisi Prius (Eng.)	CCH Fed.Federal Banking L.Rep.	Banking Law Reporter (CCH)
C. & N.	Cameron & Norwood's North Carolina Conference	CCH Fed.Sec. L.Rep.	Federal Securities Law Reporter (CCH)
C. & P.	Carrington & Payne's Nisi Prius (Eng.)	CCH Inh.Est. & Gift Tax Rep.	Inheritance, Estate, and Gift Tax Reporter (CCH)
	Craig & Phillips, Chancery (Eng.)	CCH Lab. Arb.Awards	Labor Arbitration Awards (CCH)
C. & R.	Cockburn & Rowe's Election Cases	CCH Lab.Cas.	Labor Cases (CCH)
C. & S.	Clarke & Scully's Drainage Cases (Ont.)	CCH Lab.L. Rep.	Labor Law Reporter (CCH)
[ ] C.A.	Recueils de Jurisprudence du Quebec, Cour d'appel. 1970	CCH Stand. Fed.Tax Rep.	Standard Federal Tax Reporter (CCH)
C.A.A.	Civil Aeronautics Authority Reports	CCH State Tax Cas.Rep.	State Tax Cases Reporter (CCH)
C.A.B.	Civil Aeronautics Board Reports	CCH State Tax Rev.	State Tax Review (CCH)
C.A.D.	Customs Appeals Decisions	CCH Tax Ct. Mem.	Tax Court Memorandum Decisions (CCH)
C.B.	Cumulative Bulletin (Internal Revenue)	CCH Tax Ct. Rep.	Tax Court Reporter (CCH)
	Manning, Granger & Scott, Common Bench (Eng.)	C.C.L.T.	Canadian Cases on the Law of Torts (1976–)
C.B. (N.S.)	Manning, Granger & Scott, Common Bench (New Series) (Eng.)	C.C.P.A.	Court of Customs & Patent Appeals (U.S.)
CBA Rec.	Chicago Bar Association Record	C.C.Supp.	City Court Reports Supplement (N.Y.)
C.B.C.	Collier's Bankruptcy Cases	C.D.	Commissioner's Decisions, United States Patent Office
C.B.R.	Canadian Bankruptcy Reports		Ohio Circuit Decisions
C.C.	Ohio Circuit Court Reports		United States Customs Court Decisions
C.C. (N.S.)	Same, New Series	CEB	Continuing Education of the Bar (Cal.)
C.C.A.	Circuit Court of Appeals (U.S.)		
C.C.C.	Canadian Criminal Cases (1893–1962)	C.E.Gr.	C.E. Greene's Equity (N.J.)
	Canadian Criminal Cases (1963–)	C.E.Greene	Same
CCF	Federal Contract Cases (CCH)	C.F.R.	Code of Federal Regulations
CCH	Commerce Clearing House	C.I.L.C.	Commonwealth International Law Cases
CCH Atomic En.L.Rep.	Atomic Energy Law Reporter (CCH)	C.I.L.J.S.A.	Comparative and International Law Journal of Southern Africa
CCH Comm. Mkt.Rep.	Common Market Reporter (CCH)		

C.J.	Corpus Juris	C.P.R.	Canadian Patent Reporter
C.J.Ann.	Corpus Juris Annotations	C.P.Rep.	Common Pleas Reporter (Pa.)
C.J.S.	Corpus Juris Secundum	C.R.	Criminal Reports (Canada)
C.L.A.I.T.	Constitutions and Laws of the American Indian Tribes (Scholarly Resources)	C.R.A.C.	Canadian Reports, Appeal Cases
		C.R.C.	Canadian Railway Cases
C.L.A.S.	Criminal Law Audio Series	C.R.T.C.	Canadian Railway & Transport Cases
C.L.Chambers	Chambers' Common Law (Upper Can.)	C.Rob.	Christopher Robinson's Admiralty (Eng.)
CLE J. & Reg.	Continuing Legal Education Journal and Register	C.S.C.R.	Cincinnati Superior Court Reporter
C.L.L.C.	Canadian Labour Law Cases	C.S.T.	Capital Stock Tax Division (I.R.B.)
C.L.L.R.	Canadian Labor Law Reports (CCH)	C.T.	Carrier's Taxing Ruling (I.R.B.)
C.L.R.	Common Law Reports (Eng.)	C.T.C.	Canada Tax Cases
	Commonwealth Law Reports (Austl.)	C.T.L.J.	California Trial Lawyers Journal
	Cyprus Law Reports	C.T.S.	Consolidated Treaty Series
C.L.Rec.	Cleveland Law Record	C.W.Dud.	C.W. Dudley's Law or Equity (S.C.)
C.L.Reg.	Cleveland Law Register	C.W.Dudl.Eq.	C.W. Dudley's Equity (S.C.)
C.L.Rep.	Cleveland Law Reporter	Cab. & E.	Cababe & Ellis, Queen's Bench (Eng.)
C.L.S.R.	Computer Law Service Reporter	Cahiers	Les Cahiers de Droit
CLU J.	Chartered Life Underwriter Journal	Cai.	Caines (N.Y.)
		Cai.Cas.	Caines' Cases
C.L.W.	Commercial Laws of the World (Oceana)	Cai.R.	Caines' Reports
		Cal.	California Reports
C.M. & R.	Crompton, Meeson & Roscoe, Exchequer (Eng.)	Cal.2d	Same, Second Series
		Cal.3d	Same, Third Series
		Cal.App.	California Appellate
C.M.A.R.	Canadian Court Martial Appeal Reports (1957–)	Cal.App.2d	Same, Second Series
		Cal.App.3d	Same, Third Series
		Cal.App.Dec.	California Appellate Decisions
C.M.R.	Court-Martial Reports	Cal.Dec.	California Decisions
C.M.R. (Air Force)	Court-Martial Reports of the Judge Advocate General of the Air Force	Cal.Ind. Acci.Dec.	California Industrial Accidents Decisions
		Cal.Jur.	California Jurisprudence
C.P.C.	Carswell's Practice Cases (1976–)	Cal.Jur.2d	Same, Second Edition
		Cal.L.Rev.	California Law Review
C.P.Coop.	C.P. Cooper, Chancery (Eng.)	Cal. Law.	California Lawyer
		Cal.Leg.Rec.	California Legal Record
C.P.D.	Law Reports, Common Pleas Division (Eng.) (1865–1880)	Cal.Prac.	California Practice

Cal.Reg.L. Rep.	California Regulatory Law Reporter	Can.App.Cas.	Canadian Appeal Cases
Cal.Rptr.	West's California Reporter	Can.B.A.J.	Canadian Bar Association Journal
Cal.Rptr.2d	Same, Second Series	Can.B.Ass'n Y.B.	Canadian Bar Association: Year Book
Cal.St.B.J.	California State Bar Journal	Can.B.J.	Canadian Bar Journal
Cal.Unrep. Cas.	California Unreported Cases	Can.B.R.	Canadian Bar Review
Cal.W.Int'l L.J.	California Western International Law Journal	Can.B.Rev.	Same
		Can.Bankr. Ann.	Canadian Bankruptcy Reports Annotated
Cal.W.L.Rev.	California Western Law Review	Can.Bankr. Ann. (N.S.)	Same, New Series
Calcutta W.N.	Calcutta Weekly Notes	Can.Bus.L.J.	Canadian Business Law Journal
Cald.	Caldecott's Magistrate's and Settlement Cases (Eng.) Caldwell (W.Va.)	Can.Com.L. Rev.	Canadian Communications Law Review
Cald.J.P.	Caldecott's Magistrate's and Settlement Cases (Eng.)	Can.Com.R.	Canadian Commercial Law Reports
Cald.M.Cas.	Same	Can.Community L.J.	Canadian Community Law Journal
Cald.Mag. Cas.	Same	Can.Cr.Cas.	Canadian Criminal Cases
Cald.S.C.	Same	Can.Crim.	Criminal Reports (Can.)
Cald.Sett. Cas.	Same	Can.Crim. Cas. (N.S.)	Canadian Criminal Cases, New Series
Call	Call (Va.)		
Calthr.	Calthrop, King's Bench (Eng.)	Can.Crim. Cas.Ann.	Canadian Criminal Cases Annotated
Cam.	Cameron's Privy Council Decisions	Can. Env.L.News	Canadian Environmental Law News
Cam. & N.	Cameron & Norwood's Conference Reports (N.C.)	Can.Exch.	Canadian Exchequer
		Can.Green Bag	Canadian Green Bag
		Can.Hum. Rts.Advocate	Canadian Human Rights Advocate
Cam.Cas.	Cameron's Cases (Can.)		
Cambrian L.Rev.	Cambrian Law Review	Can.Human Rights Rep.	Canadian Human Rights Reporter
Cambridge L.J.	Cambridge Law Journal	Can. J. Admin. L. & Prac.	Canadian Journal of Administrative Law & Practice
Cameron	Cameron's Supreme Court Cases	Can.J.Correction	Canadian Journal of Correction
Cameron Pr.	Cameron's Practice (Can.)	Can.J.Crim & Corr.	Canadian Journal of Criminology and Corrections
Camp	Camp (N.D.)		
Campaign L.Rep.	Campaign Law Reporter	Can.J.Fam.L.	Canadian Journal of Family Law
Campb.	Campbell (Neb.) Campbell's Nisi Prius (Eng.)	Can. J. L. & Juris.	Canadian Journal of Law and Jurisprudence
Campb.L.G.	Campbell's Legal Gazette (Pa.)	Can.L.J.	Canadian Law Journal
Campbell L.Rev.	Campbell Law Review	Can.L.J. (N.S.)	Same, New Series

Can.L.R.B.R.	Canadian Labour Relations Board Reports (1974–)	Cardozo Arts & Entertainment L.J.	Cardozo Arts & Entertainment Law Journal
Can.L.Rev.	Canadian Law Review	Cardozo L.Rev.	Cardozo Law Review
		Carolina L.J.	Carolina Law Journal
Can.L.T. Occ.N.	Canadian Law Times Occasional Notes	Carolina L.Repos.	Carolina Law Repository
Can.L.Times	Canadian Law Times	Carp.	Carpenter (Cal.)
Can.Lab.	Canadian Labour	Carp.P.C.	Carpmael, Patent Cases (Eng.)
Can.Law.	Canadian Lawyer		
Can.Legal Stud.	Canadian Legal Studies	Carribean L.J.	Carribean Law Journal
Can.Mun.J.	Canadian Municipal Journal	Caribbean L.Libr.	Caribbean Law Librarian
Can.Native L.Rep.	Canadian Native Law Reporter	Cart.B.N.A.	Cartwright's Constitutional Cases (Can.)
Can.Oil & Gas	Canadian Oil and Gas (Butterworths)	Carter	Carter (Ind.) Carter, Common Pleas (Eng.)
Can.Pub.Ad.	Canadian Public Administration		
Can.R.Cas.	Canadian Railway Cases	Carth.	Carthew, King's Bench (Eng.)
Can.Ry.Cas.	Same	Cartwr.Cas.	Cartwright's Cases (Can.)
Can.S.C.	Canada Supreme Court	Cary	Cary Chancery (Eng.)
Can.S.Ct.	Canada Supreme Court Reports	Cas.C.L.	Cases in Crown Law (Eng.)
Can.Tax App. Bd.	Canada Tax Appeal Board Cases	Cas.t.Hardw.	Cases tempore Hardwicke, King's Bench (Eng.)
Can.Tax Cas. Ann.	Canada Tax Cases Annotated	Cas.t.Holt	Cases tempore Holt, King's Bench (Eng.)
Can.Tax Found.Rep. Proc.Tax Conf.	Canadian Tax Foundation Report of Proceedings of the Tax Conference	Cas.t.King	Cases tempore King, Chancery (Eng.)
Can.Tax J.	Canadian Tax Journal	Cas.t.Northington	Cases tempore Northington, Chancery Reports (Eng.)
Can.Tax News	Canadian Tax News		
Can.-U.S.L.J.	Canada-United States Law Journal	Cas.t.Talb.	Cases tempore Talbot, Chancery (Eng.)
Can.Wel.	Canadian Welfare		
Can.Y.B.Int'l L.	Canadian Yearbook of International Law	Cas.t.Wm. III	Cases tempore William III (Eng.)
Cane & L.	Cane & Leigh's Crown Cases Reserved (Eng.)	Cas.Tak. & Adj. Cases	Taken and Adjudged (Report in Chancery, First Edition) (Eng.)
Cap.U.L.Rev.	Capital University Law Review	Case & Com.	Case & Comment
Car. & K.	Carrington & Kirwan, Nisi Prius (Eng.)	Case W.Res. J.Int'l L.	Case Western Reserve Journal International Law
Car. & P.	Carrington & Payne, Nisi Prius (Eng.)	Case W.Res. L.Rev.	Case Western Reserve Law Review
Car.H. & A.	Carrow, Hamerton & Allen, New Sessions Cases (Eng.)	Casey	Casey (Pa.)
		Cass.Prac. Cas.	Cassels' Practice Cases (Can.)

Cass.S.C.	Cassels' Supreme Court Decisions	Chi.Leg.N.	Chicago Legal News
Cates	Cates (Tenn.)	Chic.L.T.	Chicago Law Times
Cath.Law.	Catholic Lawyer	Chicago L.B.	Chicago Law Bulletin
Cath.U.L.Rev.	Catholic University of America Law Review	Chicago L.J.	Chicago Law Journal
		Chicago L.Rec.	Chicago Law Record
		Chicano L.Rev.	Chicano Law Review
Cent.Dig.	Century Digest	Chicano–Latino L.Rev.	Chicano–Latino Law Review
Centr.L.J.	Central Law Journal	Chin.L. & Gov't	Chinese Law and Government
Ceylon L.Rev.	Ceylon Law Review		
Ch.	Law Reports, Chancery (Eng.)	China L.Rev.	China Law Review
		Chip.	Chipman (N.Bruns.)
Ch.Cal.	Calendar of Proceedings in Chancery (Eng.)		Chipman (Vt.)
		Chit.	Chitty's Bail Court (Eng.)
Ch.Cas.	Cases in Chancery (Eng.)	Chit.B.C.	Same
		Chitt.	Same
Ch.Chamb.	Chancery Chambers (Upper Can.)	Chitty's L.J.	Chitty's Law Journal
		Choyce Cas. Ch.	Choyce's Cases in Chancery (Eng.)
Ch.Col.Op.	Chalmers' Colonial Opinions	Chr.Rep.	Chamber Reports (Upper Can.)
Ch.D.	Law Reports, Chancery Division (Eng.)	Chr.Rob.	Christopher Robinson's Admiralty (Eng.)
Ch.D.2d	Same, Second Series		
Ch.Prec.	Precedents in Chancery	Chy.Chrs.	Upper Canada Chancery Chambers Reports
Ch.R.	Upper Canada Chambers Reports		
		Cin.B.Ass'n J.	Cincinnati Bar Association Journal
Ch.R.M.	R.M. Charlton (Ga.)		
Ch.Rep.	Chancery Reports (Eng.)	Cin.L.Rev.	Cincinnati Law Review
	Chancery Reports (Ir.)	Cin.Law Bull.	Weekly Law Bulletin (Ohio)
Ch.Sent.	Chancery Sentinel (N.Y.)	Cin.Mun.Dec.	Cincinnati Municipal Decisions
Ch.T.U.P.	T.U.P. Charlton (Ga.)	Cin.R.	Cincinnati Superior Court Reporter
Cha.App.	English Law Reports, Chancery Appeal Cases		
		Cin.S.C.R.	Same
		Cin.S.C.Rep.	Same
Chamb.Rep.	Chancery Chambers (Ont.)	Cinc.L.Bul.	Cincinnati Law Bulletin
Chandl.	Chandler (N.H.) Chandler (Wis.)	Cinc.Sup.Ct. Rep.	Cincinnati Superior Court Reporter
Chaney	Chaney (Mich.)	Cincinnati Law Bull.	Weekly Law Bulletin (Ohio)
Charley Pr. Cas.	Charley's Practice Cases (Eng.)		
Charlt.	R.M. Charlton (Ga.)	Cir.Ct.Dec.	Circuit Court Decisions (Ohio)
	T.U.P. Charlton (Ga.)	City Ct.R.	City Court Reports (N.Y.)
Chase	Chase (U.S.)		
Chest.Co.	Chester County (Pa.)	City Ct.R. Supp.	Same
Chev.Ch.	Cheves' Chancery (S.C.)	City Hall Rec.	City Hall Recorder (N.Y.)
Chev.Eq.	Same		
Cheves	Cheves' Law (S.C.)	City Hall Rep.	City Hall Reporter, Lomas (N.Y.)
Chi.B.Record	Chicago Bar Record		
Chi.-Kent L.Rev.	Chicago-Kent Law Review	Civ. & Mil. L.J.	Civil and Military Law Journal

Civ.Just.Q.	Civil Justice Quarterly	Cliff.	Clifford (U.S.)
Civ.Lib.	Civil Liberty	Clif.South.El. Cas.	Clifford, Southwick Election Cases
Civ.Lib.Dock.	Civil Liberties Docket	Clk's Mag.	Clerk's Magazine (London)
Civ.Lib.Rev.	Civil Liberties Review		Clerk's Magazine (R.I.)
Civ.Lib.Rptr.	Civil Liberties Reporter		Clerk's Magazine (Upper Can.)
Civ.Litigation Rep.	Civil Litigation Reporter (CEB)	Co.Ct.Cas.	County Court Cases (Eng.)
Civ.Proc.R.	Civil Procedure Reports (N.Y.)	Co.Ct.Ch.	County Court Chronicle (Eng.)
Civ.Rights Dig.	Civil Rights Digest	Co.Ct.Rep.	Pennsylvania County Court Reports
Cl. & F.	Clark & Finnelly, House of Lords (Eng.)	Co.Inst.	Coke's Institutes (Eng.)
Clark	Clark (Ala.) Clark (Pa.)	Co.Litt.	Coke on Littleton (Eng.)
Clark & F.	Clark & Finnelly, House of Lords (Eng.)	Co.Mass.Pr.	Colby Massachusetts Practice
Clark & F. (N.S.)	Same, New Series	Co.P.C.	Coke Pleas of the Crown (Eng.)
Clark App.	Clark, Appeals Cases House of Lords (Eng.)	Cobb	Cobb (Ala.) Cobb (Ga.)
Clark Col.Law	Clark Colonial Law	Cochr.	Cochran (Nova Scotia)
Clarke	Clarke (Iowa) Clarke (Mich.)	Cockb. & R.	Cochrane (N.D.) Cockburn & Rowe's Election Cases (Eng.)
Clarke & S. Dr.Cas.	Clarke & Scully's Drainage Cases (Ont.)	Cocke	Cocke (Ala.) Cocke (Fla.)
Clarke Ch.	Clarke, Chancery (N.Y.)	Code Rep.	Code Reporter (N.Y.)
Class Act. Rep.	Class Action Reports	Code Rep. (N.S.)	Same, New Series
Clayt.	Clayton's Reports York Assizes (Eng.)	Coff.Prob.	Coffey's Probate (Cal.)
Clearinghouse Rev.	Clearinghouse Review	Coke	Coke, King's Bench (Eng.)
Clemens	Clemens (Kan.)	Col.	Coleman (Ala.)
Clev.Bar Ass'n J.	Cleveland Bar Association Journal	Col. & C.Cas.	Coleman & Caine's Cases (N.Y.)
Clev.Mar.L. Rev.	Cleveland Marshall Law Review	Col.Cas.	Coleman's Cases (N.Y.)
Clev.St.L. Rev.	Cleveland State Law Review	Col.Int'l Dr. Comp.	Colioque International de Droit Compare
Cleve.L.Rec.	Cleveland Law Record (Ohio)		
Cleve.L.Reg.	Cleveland Law Register (Ohio)	Col.L.Rev.	Columbia Law Review
Cleve.L.Rep.	Cleveland Law Reporter (Ohio)	Cold.	Coldwell (Tenn.)
Cleve.Law R.	Same	Coldw.	Same
Cleve.Law Rec.	Cleveland Law Record (Ohio)	Cole	Cole (Ala.) Cole (Iowa)
Cleve.Law Reg.	Cleveland Law Register (Ohio)	Cole. & Cai. Cas.	Coleman & Caines' Cases
		Cole.Cas.	Coleman's Cases

Coll.	Collyer's Chancery (Eng.)	Com. & L.	Communications and the Law
Coll. & E. Bank	Collier's & Eaton's American Bankruptcy Reports	Com. & Mun. L.Rep.	Commercial & Municipal Law Reporter
Coll.L.Bull.	College Law Bulletin	Com.B.	Manning, Granger & Scott, Common Bench (Eng.)
Coll.L.Dig.	College Law Digest		
Colles	Colles Cases in Parliament (Eng.)		
Colo.	Colorado Reports	Com.Cas.	Commercial Cases Since 1895 (Eng.)
Colo.App.	Colorado Appeals	Com.Dec.	Commissioners' Decisions (Patent)
Colo.J. Int'l Envtl.L. & Pol'y	Colorado Journal of International Environmental Law and Policy	Com.L.	Commercial Law (Can.)
		Com.L.J.	Commercial Law Journal
Colo.Law Rep.	Colorado Law Reporter	Com. L. Rep.	Commercial Law Report
Colo.Law.	Colorado Lawyer		
Colombo L.Rev.	Colombo Law Review (Ceylon)	Com.P.Reptr.	Common Pleas Reporter (Scranton, Pa.)
Colonial Law.	Colonial Lawyer		
Coltm.	Coltman Registration Appeal Cases (Eng.)	Comb.	Comberbach, King's Bench (Eng.)
Colq.	Colquit (Modern) (Eng.)	Comm.B.	Manning, Granger & Scott, Common Bench (Eng.)
Colum.Bus.L. Rev.	Columbia Business Law Review	Comm.Cause	Common Cause
Colum.Hum. Rts.L.Rev.	Columbia Human Rights Law Review	Comm. Mkt.L.R.	Common Market Law Reports
Colum.J. Envtl.L.	Columbia Journal of Environmental Law	Commodity Futures L.Rep.	Commodity Futures Law Reporter (CCH)
Colum.J.Gender & L.	Columbia Journal of Gender and Law	Common Mkt. L.Rev.	Common Market Law Review
Colum.J.Int'l Aff.	Columbia Journal of International Affairs	Community Prop.J.	Community Property Journal
		Commw.Arb.	Commonwealth Arbitration Reports
Colum.J.L. & Arts	Columbia Journal of Law and the Arts	Commw.L.R.	Commonwealth Law Reports
Colum.J.L. & Soc.Probs.	Columbia Journal of Law and Social Problems	Comp.Dec.	United States Comptroller of Treasury Decisions
Colum.J. Transnat'l L.	Columbia Journal of Transnational Law	Comp.Gen.	United States Comptroller General Decisions
Colum.L.Rev.	Columbia Law Review		
Colum.Soc'y Int'l L.Bull.	Columbia Society of International Law Bulletin	Comp.Jurid. Rev.	Comparative Juridical Review
		Comp.L.J.	Company Law Journal
Colum.Survey Human Rights L.	Columbia Survey of Human Rights Law	Comp.Lab.L.J.	Comparative Labor Law Journal
Colum.–VLA J.L. & Arts	Columbia Volunteer Lawyers for the Arts Journal of Law & the Arts	Comparisons in L. & Monet.Com.	Comparisons in Law and Monetary Comments
		Compleat Law.	Compleat Lawyer

Comptr. Treas.Dec.	United States Comptroller of Treasury Decisions	Const. Nations	Constitutions of Nations (Nijhoff)
Computer L. & Prac.	Computer Law & Practice	Const.Rep.	Constitutional Reports (S.C.)
Computer L. & Tax	Computer Law and Tax Report	Const.Rev.	Constitutional Review
Computer L.J.	Computer Law Journal	Const.World	Constitutions of the Countries of the World (Oceana)
Computers & L.	Computers and Law	Consumer Fin. L.Q. Rep.	Consumer Finance Law Quarterly Report
Comst.	Comstock, Appeals (N.Y.)	Consumer Prod.Saf'y Guide	Consumer Product Safety Guide (CCH)
Comyns	Comyn's King's Bench and Common Pleas (Eng.)	Contemp. Drug Prob.	Contemporary Drug Problems
Comyns Dig.	Comyn's Digest (Eng.)	Conv. & Prop. Law	Conveyancer and Property Lawyer
Con.B.J.	Connecticut Bar Journal	Convey.	Conveyancer
Condit.Sale— Chat.Mort. Rep.	Conditional Sale— Chattel Mortgage (CCH)	Convey. (N.S.)	Conveyancer & Property Lawyer, New Series
Conf.	Conference Reports (N.C.)	Cook Vice- Adm.	Cook's Vice-Admiralty (Lower Can.)
Conf.Teach. Int'l L.	Conference of Teachers of International Law	Cooke	Cooke, Cases of Practice, Common Pleas (Eng.)
Cong.Dig.	Congressional Digest		Cooke (Tenn.)
Cong.Rec.	Congressional Record (U.S.)	Cooke & A.	Cooke & Alcock, King's Bench (Ir.)
Conn.	Connecticut Reports	Cooley L.Rev.	Cooley Law Review
Conn.B.J.	Connecticut Bar Journal	Coop.	Cooper (Fla.)
Conn.Cir.Ct.	Connecticut Circuit Court Reports		Cooper's Chancery (Eng.)
Conn.J.Int'l L.	Connecticut Journal of International Law		Cooper's Chancery (Tenn.)
Conn.L.Rev.	Connecticut Law Review	Coop.C. & P.R.	Cooper's Chancery Practice Reporter (U.S.)
Conn.Prob. L.J.	Connecticut Probate Law Journal	Coop.Pr.Cas.	Cooper's Practice Cases (Eng.)
Conn.Supp.	Connecticut Supplement	Coop.t. Brough.	Cooper's Cases tempore Brougham, Chancery (Eng.)
Conn.Surr.	Connolly's Surrogate (N.Y.)	Coop.t.Cott.	Cooper's Cases tempore Cottenham, Chancery (Eng.)
Conov.	Conover (Wis.)		
Const.	Constitution	Coop.t.Eldon	Cooper's Reports tempore Eldon, Chancery (Eng.)
Const. Afr.States	Constitutions of African States (Oceana)		
		Cope	Cope (Cal.)
Const. Commentary	Constitutional Commentary	Copp Min. Dec.	Copp's Mining Decisions (U.S.)
Const.Dep. & Sp.Sov.	Constitutions of Dependencies and Special Sovereignties	Copp's Land Owner	Copp's Land Owner
		Copy.	Copyright
		Copy.Bull.	Copyright Bulletin

Copyright L.Sym. — Copyright Law Symposium (American Society of Composers, Authors, and Publishers)

Corb. & D. — Corbett & Daniels Election Cases (Eng.)

Cornell Int'l L.J. — Cornell International Law Journal

Cornell J.L. & Pub.Pol'y — Cornell Journal of Law and Publicity

Cornell L.F. — Cornell Law Forum

Cornell L.J. — Cornell Law Journal

Cornell L.Q. — Cornell Law Quarterly

Cornell L.Rev. — Cornell Law Review

Corp.Couns. Rep. — Corporate Counsel Reporter

Corp.Counsel Rev. — Corporate Counsel Review

Corp.J. — Corporation Journal

Corp.L.Rev. — Corporation Law Review

Corp.Pract. Comment. — Corporate Practice Commentator

Corp.Pract. Rev. — Corporate Practice Review

Corp.Reorg. — Corporate Reorganizations

Corp.Reorg. & Am.Bank. Rev. — Corporate Reorganization & American Bankruptcy Review

Coup. — Couper's Justiciary (Scot.)

Court. & MacL. — Courtenay & MacLean (Scot.)

Coutlea — Coutlea's Supreme Court Cases

Cow. — Cowen (N.Y.)

Cow.Cr. — Cowen's Criminal (N.Y.)

Cowp. — Cowper King's Bench (Eng.)

Cowp.Cas. — Cowper (Eng.)

Cox — Cox (Ark.)

Cox & Atk. — Cox & Atkinson, Registration Appeals (Eng.)

Cox Am.T. Cas. — Cox's American Trademark Cases

Cox C.C. — Cox's Criminal Cases (Eng.)

Cox Ch. — Cox's Chancery (Eng.)

Cox Crim. Cas. — Cox's Criminal Cases

Cox Eq. — Cox's Equity

Cox J.S.Cas. — Cox's Joint Stock Cases (Eng.)

Coxe — Coxe (N.J.)

Cr. & M. — Crompton & Meeson, Exchequer (Eng.)

Cr. & Ph. — Craig & Phillips, Chancery (Eng.)

Cr.App. — Criminal Appeals (Eng.)

Cr.App.R.(S.) — Criminal Appeal Reports (Sentencing)

Cr.Cas.Res. — Law Reports, Crown Cases Reserved (Eng.)

Crabbe — Crabbe (U.S.)

Craig & Ph. — Craig & Phillips, Chancery (Eng.)

Cranch — Cranch (U.S.)

Cranch C.C. — Cranch's Circuit Court (U.S.)

Cranch Pat. Dec. — Cranch's Patent Decisions (U.S.)

Crane — Crane (Mont.)

Craw. — Crawford (Ark.)

Crawf. & D. Abr.Cas. — Crawford & Dix's Abridged Cases (Ir.)

Crawf. & Dix — Crawford & Dix Circuit Cases (Ir.)
Crawford & Dix Criminal Cases (Ir.)

Creighton L.Rev. — Creighton Law Review

Crim. — Criminologie

Crim. & Soc. Just. — Crime and Social Justice

Crim.App. — Criminal Appeal Reports

Crim.App. Rep. — Cohen's Criminal Appeals Reports (Eng.)

Crim.Case & Com. — Criminal Case and Comment

Crim.Def. — Criminal Defense

Crim.Just. — Criminal Justice

Crim.Just. & Behav. — Criminal Justice and Behavior

Crim.Just. Ethics — Criminal Justice Ethics

Crim.Just.J. — Criminal Justice Journal

Crim.Just. Newsl. — Criminal Justice Newsletter

Crim.Just.Q. — Criminal Justice Quarterly

Crim.Just. Rev.	Criminal Justice Review	Crosw.Pat. Cas.	Croswell's Collection of Patent Cases (U.S.)
Crim.L.Bull.	Criminal Law Bulletin	Crounse	Crounse (Neb.)
Crim.L.F. Int'l J.	Criminal Law Forum: An International Journal	Crumrine	Crumrine (Pa.)
		Ct.Cl.	Court of Claims (U.S.)
Crim.L.J.	Criminal Law Journal	Ct.Cust & Pat. App.	Court of Customs & Patent Appeals
Crim.L.Mag.	Criminal Law Magazine (N.J.)	Ct.Cust.App.	Court of Customs Appeals (U.S.)
Crim.L.Mag. & Rep.	Criminal Law Magazine and Reporter	Ct.Rev.	Court Review
Crim.L.Q.	Criminal Law Quarterly	Cum.Bull.	Cumulative Bulletin
		Cum.L.Rev.	Cumberland Law Review
Crim.L.Rec.	Criminal Law Recorder	Cum.Sam.L. Rev.	Cumberland-Samford Law Review
Crim.L.Rep.	Criminal Law Reporter	Cumb.L.Rev.	Cumberland Law Review
Crim.L.Rev.	Criminal Law Review (Manhattan)	Cummins	Cummins (Idaho)
		Cunn.	Cunningham King's Bench (Eng.)
Crim.L.Rev. (Eng.)	Criminal Law Review (Eng.)	Cur.Leg. Thought	Current Legal Thought
Crim.L.Rptr.	Criminal Law Reporter	Current Com. & Leg.Mis.	Current Comment and Legal Miscellany
Crim. Prac. L. Rev.	Criminal Practice Law Review	Current L.	Current Law
Crim.Rep. (N.S.)	Criminal Reports, New Series	Current L. & Soc.Prob.	Current Law and Social Problems
Crime & Delin'cy	Crime & Delinquency	Current L.Y.B.	Current Law Yearbook
Crime & Delin'cy Abst.	Crime and Delinquency Abstracts	Current Legal Prob.	Current Legal Problems
Crime & Delin'cy Lit.	Crime and Delinquency Literature	Current Med. for Atty's	Current Medicine for Attorneys
Cripp Ch.Cas.	Cripp's Church & Clergy Cases	Currents: Int'l Trade L.J.	Currents: International Trade Law Journal
Critch.	Critchfield (Ohio St.)		
Cro.	Croke's King's Bench (Eng.)	Curry	Curry (La.)
		Curt.	Curtis, Circuit Court (U.S.)
Cro.Car.	Croke tempore Charles I (Eng.)	Curt. Eccl.	Curtis, Ecclesiastical (Eng.)
Cro.Eliz.	Croke tempore Elizabeth (Eng.)	Cush.	Cushing (Mass.)
Cro.Jac.	Croke tempore James I, King's Bench (Eng.)	Cust.App.	United States Customs Appeals
		Cust.Ct.	Custom Court Reports (U.S.)
Cromp.	Star, Chamber Cases (Eng.)	Cyc.	Cyclopedia of Law & Procedure
Cromp. & J.	Crompton & Jervis, Exchequer (Eng.)	Czech.J. Int'l L.	Czechoslovak Journal of International Law
Cromp. & M.	Crompton & Meeson, Exchequer (Eng.)		
Cromp.M. & R.	Crompton, Meeson & Roscoe, Exchequer (Eng.)	Czech.Y.B. Int'l L.	Czechoslovak Yearbook of International Law

D

D.	Disney (Ohio)	D. & War.	Drewry & Warren's Chancery (Ir.)
D. & B.	Dearsley & Bell's Crown Cases (Eng.)	D.B.	Domesday Book
		D.B. & M.	Dunlop, Bell & Murray (Scot.)
D. & B.C.C.	Same		
D. & C.	Deacon & Chitty's Bankruptcy Cases (Eng.)	D.C.	District of Columbia Treasury Department Circular (I.R.B.)
	Dow & Clark's Parliamentary Cases (Eng.)	D.C.A.	Dorion's Queen's Bench (Can.)
D. & Ch.	Same	D.C.App.	District of Columbia Appeals
D. & Chit.	Same		
D. & E.	Dwinford & East's King's Bench, Term Reports (Eng.)	D.C.B.J.	District of Columbia Bar Journal
		D.C.Cir.	District of Columbia Court of Appeals Cases
D. & J.	De Gex & Jones, Chancery (Eng.)	D.C.L.Rev.	District of Columbia Law Review
D. & J.B.	De Gex & Jones, Bankruptcy (Eng.)	D.Chip.	D. Chipman (Vt.)
		D.Chipm.	Same
D. & L.	Dowling & Lowndes, Bail Court (Eng.)	D.D.C.	District Court, District of Columbia
D. & M.	Davison & Merivale's Queen's Bench (Eng.)	D.Dec.	Dix's School Decisions (N.Y.)
D. & P.	Denison & Pearce's Crown Cases (Eng.)	D.I.L. (Hack.)	Digest of International Law (Hackworth)
D. & R.	Dowling & Ryland's King's Bench (Eng.)	D.I.L. (Moore)	Digest of International Law (Moore)
D. & R.M.C.	Dowling & Ryland's Magistrates' Cases (Eng.)	D.I.L. (White.)	Digest of International Law (Whiteman)
		D.L.R.	Dominion Law Reports (Can.) (1912–1922)
D. & R.Mag. Cas.	Same		
D. & R.N.P.	Dowling & Ryland's Nisi Prius Cases (Eng.)	D.L.R.	Same (1923–1955)
		D.L.R.2d	Same, Second Series (1956–1968)
D. & R.N. P.C.	Same	D.L.R.3d	Same, Third Series (1969–present)
D. & S.	Deane & Swabey's Ecclesiastical (Eng.)	D.P.R.	Decisiones de Puerto Rico
	Drewry & Smale's Chancery (Eng.)	D.Rep.	Ohio Decisions Reprint
D. & Sm.	Drewry & Smale's Chancery (Eng.)	D.Repr.	Same
		D.T.C.	Dominion Tax Cases
D. & Sw.	Deane & Swabey Ecclesiastical (Eng.)	Dak.	Dakota
		Dak.L.Rev.	Dakota Law Review
D. & W.	Drewry & Walsh's Chancery (Ir.)	Dal.C.P.	Dallson's Common Pleas (Eng.)
	Drewry & Warren's Chancery (Ir.)	Dale	Dale (Okla.)
		Dale Ecc.	Dale's Ecclesiastical (Eng.)

Dale Eccl.	Same		Deane & Swabey's
Dale Leg.Rit.	Dale's Legal Ritual (Eng.)		Probate & Divorce (Eng.)
Dalhousie L.J.	Dalhousie Law Journal	Deac.	Deacon, Bankruptcy (Eng.)
Dall.	Dallam (Tex.)	Deac. & C.	Deacon & Chitty, Bankruptcy (Eng.)
	Dallas (Pa.)		
	Dallas (U.S.)	Deac. & Chit.	Same
Dal. in Keil.	Dallison in Keilway's	Deacon & C.	Same
	King's Bench (Eng.)	Deacon, Bankr.Cas.	Deacon, Bankruptcy (Eng.)
Dalr.	Dalrymple's Decisions (Sc.)	Deady	Deady, United States Circuit and District Courts (Cal. & Ore.)
Daly	Daly (N.Y.)		
Dan.	Daniell's Exchequer & Equity (Eng.)	Deane	Deane (Vt.)
Dana	Dana (Ky.)		Deane & Swabey's Probate & Divorce (Eng.)
Dane Abr.	Dane's Abridgment of American Law (Eng.)	Deane & S.Eccl.Rep.	Deane & Swabey's Ecclesiastical (Eng.)
Dann	Dann (Ariz.)		
	Dann (Cal.)	Deane & Sw.	Same
Dann.	Danner (Ala.)	Deane Ecc.	Same
Dans. & L.	Danson & Lloyd's Mercantile Cases (Eng.)	Deane Ecc. Rep.	Same
		Dears.	Dearsley & Bell, Crown Cases (Eng.)
Dans. & Lld.	Same		
D'Anv.Abr.	D'Anver's Abridgment (Eng.)	Dears. & B.	Same
		Dears. & B.C.C.	Same
Dass.Ed.	Dassler (Kan.)		
Dauph.Co.	Dauphin County (Pa.)	Dears.C.C.	Same
Dav. & M.	Davison & Merivale, Queen's Bench (Eng.)	Deas & A.	Deas & Anderson (Scot.)
		Deas & And.	Same
Dav. & Mer.	Same	Dec.Com.Pat.	Decisions of Commissioner of Patents
Daveis	Daveis (Ware) (U.S.)		
Davies	Davis, King's Bench (Ir.)	Dec.Dig.	Decennial Digest
		Dec.Rep.	Ohio Decisions Reprint
Davis	Daveis (Ware) (U.S.)		
	Davis (Haw.)	Dec.U.S. Compt.Gen.	Decisions of United States Comptroller General
	Davis, King's Bench (Ir.)		
Davys	Davys, King's Bench	Decalogue	Decalogue Journal
Day	Day (Conn.)	Def. Couns. J.	Defense Counsel Journal
Dayton	3 Ohio		
Dayton T.R.	Same	Def.L.J.	Defense Law Journal
Dayton Term Rep.	Iddings' Term Reports (Ohio)	De G. & J.	De Gex & Jones, Chancery (Eng.)
Dea.	Deady, United States Circuit & District Courts (Cal. & Ore.)	De G. & Sm.	De Gex & Smale, Chancery (Eng.)
		De G.F. & J.	De Gex, Fisher & Jones, Chancery (Eng.)
Dea. & Chit.	Same		
Dea. & Sw.	Deane & Swabey's Ecclesiastical (Eng.)	De G.J. & S.	De Gex, Jones & Smith, Chancery (Eng.)

De G.M. & G.	De Gex, Macnaghten & Gordon, Chancery (Eng.)	Detroit Coll L Rev	Detroit College of Law Review
		Detroit L.Rev.	Detroit Law Review
De Gex	De Gex, Bankruptcy (Eng.)	Dev.	Devereux's Equity (N.C.)
Del.	Delaware Reports		Devereux's Law (N.C.)
Del.Ch.	Delaware Chancery		
Del.Co.	Delaware County (Pa.)		Devereux's United States Court of Claims
Del.County	Delaware County Reports	Dev. & B.	Devereux & Battle's Equity (N.C.)
Del.Cr.Cas.	Delaware Criminal Cases		Devereux & Battle's Law (N.C.)
Del.J.Corp.L.	Delaware Journal of Corporate Law	Dev.Ct.Cl.	Devereux's Court of Claims (U.S.)
Dem.	Demarest's Surrogate (N.Y.)	Dew.	Dewey (Kan.)
Dem.Surr.	Same	De Witt	De Witt (Ohio)
Den.	Denio (N.Y.)	Di.	Dyer's King's Bench (Eng.)
	Denis (La.)		
Den. & P.	Denison & Pearce's Crown Cases (Eng.)	Dice	Dice (Ind.)
		Dick.	Dickens' Chancery (Eng.)
Den. & P.C.C.	Same		
Den.C.C.	Denison's Crown Cases (Eng.)		Dickinson's Equity (N.J.)
Den.J. Int'l L. & Policy	Denver Journal of International Law and Policy	Dick.J.Envtl. L. & Pol'y	Dickinson Journal of Environmental Law and Policy
Den.L.J.	Denver Law Journal	Dick.J.Int'l L.	Dickinson Journal of International Law
Den.L.N.	Denver Legal News		
Den.U.L.Rev.	Denver University Law Review	Dick.L.Rev.	Dickinson Law Review
Denio	Denio (N.Y.)	Dick. Law.	Dickinson Lawyers
Denis	Denis (La.)	Dicta	Dicta of Denver Bar Association
Denning L.Rev.	Denning Law Review		
Denv.J.Int'l L. & Pol'y	Denver Journal of International Law and Policy	Dig.C.L.W.	Digest of Commercial Law of the World (Oceana)
Denv.U.L.Rev.	Denver University Law Review	Dill.	Dillon, Circuit Court (U.S.)
DePaul Bus. L.J.	DePaul Business Law Journal	Dirl.Dec.	Direlton's Decisions (Scot.)
DePaul L.Rev.	DePaul Law Review	Disn.	Disney (Ohio)
Dept.State Bull.	Department of State Bulletin, United States	Disney	Same
		Dispute Res.N.	Dispute Resolution Notes
Des.	Dessaussure's Equity (S.C.)	Docket	Docket (Lebanon, Pa.)
Desaus.Eq.	Same		Docket (St. Paul, Minn.)
Dess.	Same		
Dessaus.	Same	Dod.	Dodson's Admiralty (Eng.)
Det.C.L.Rev.	Detroit College of Law Review	Dod.Adm.	Same
Det.L.J.	Detroit Law Journal	Dods.	Same
Det.L.Res.	Detroit Law Review	Dom.L.R.	Dominion Law Reports (Can.)
Det.Leg.N.	Detroit Legal News		

Donaker	Donaker (Ind.)
Dona.	Donnelly's Chancery (Eng.)
	Donnelly's Irish Land Cases
Donnelly	Donnelly's Chancery
Dorion	Dorion (Lower Can.)
Doshisha L.Rev.	Doshisha Law Review
Doug.	Douglas (Mich.)
	Douglas' King's Bench (Eng.)
Dougl.	Douglas (Mich.)
Dougl.El.Cas.	Douglas, Election Cases (Eng.)
Dougl.K.B.	Douglas, King's Bench (Eng.)
Dow	Dow's House of Lords Parliamentary Cases (Eng.)
Dow & Cl.	Dow & Clark's House of Lords Cases (Eng.)
Dow.	Dowling's Practice Cases (Eng.)
Dow. & L.	Dowling & Lowndes' Bail Court (Eng.)
Dowl. & Lownd.	Dowling & Lowndes' Practice Cases (Eng.)
Dowl. & R.	Dowling & Ryland's King's Bench (Eng.)
	Dowling & Ryland's Queen's Bench & Magistrates' Cases (Eng.)
Dowl.P.C. (N.S.)	Dowling, Practice Cases, New Series (Eng.)
Dowl.Pr.Cas.	Dowling, Practice Cases (Eng.)
Down. & Lud.	Downton & Luder's Election Cases (Eng.)
Drake L.Rev.	Drake Law Review
Draper	Draper (Upper Can.)
Drew	Drew (Fla.)
Drew.	Drewry's Chancery (Eng.)
Drew. & S.	Drewry & Smale's Chancery (Eng.)
Drinkw.	Drinkwater Common Pleas (Eng.)

Drug Abuse L.Rev.	Drug Abuse Law Review
Drug L.J.	Drug Law Journal
Drury	Drury's Chancery (Ir.)
Dublin U.L.J.	Dublin University Law Journal
Dublin U.L.Rev.	Dublin University Law Review
Dudl.	Dudley (Ga.)
	Dudley's Equity (S.C.)
	Dudley's Law (S.C.)
Duer	Duer's Superior Court (N.Y.)
Duke B. Ass'n J.	Duke Bar Association Journal
Duke Envtl. L. & Pol'y F.	Duke Environmental Law and Policy Forum
Duke J.Comp. & Int'l L.	Duke Journal of Comparative & International Law
Duke L.J.	Duke Law Journal
Duke's Charitable Uses	Duke's Charitable Uses (Eng.)
Dunc.Ent. Cas.	Duncan Entail Cases (Scot.)
Dunc.N.P.	Duncombe, Nisi Prius
Dunl.	Dunlop, Bell & Murray (Scot.)
Dunl.B. & M.	Same
Dunlop	Dunlop (Scot.)
Dunn.	Dunning's King's Bench (Eng.)
Duq.L.Rev.	Duquesne Law Review
Duq.U.L.Rev.	Duquesne University Law Review
Durf.	Durfee (R.I.)
Durfee	Same
Durie	Durie (Scot.)
Durn. & E.	Durnford & East's King's Bench, Term Report (Eng.)
Dutch.	Dutcher's Law (N.J.)
Duv.	Duval's Reports (Can.)
	Duval's Supreme Court (Can.)
Dy.	Dyer's King's Bench (Eng.)
Dyer	Same

E

E.	East's King's Bench (Eng.)	E.E.R.	English Ecclesiastical Reports
E. & A.	Grant Error & Appeal Reports (Upper Can.)	E.G.L.	Encyclopedia of Georgia Law
	Spink's Ecclesiastical & Admiralty (Eng.)	E.L. & Eq.	English Law & Equity Reports
E. & B.	Ellis & Blackburn's Queen's Bench (Eng.)	E.L.R.	Eastern Law Reporter (Can.)
E. & E.	Ellis & Ellis' Queen's Bench (Eng.)	E.P.D.	Employment Practices Decisions (CCH)
E. & I.	English & Irish Appeals, House of Lords (Eng.)	E.R.	East's King's Bench (Eng.)
E.A.S.	Executive Agreement Series (U.S.)	E.R.C.	English Ruling Cases
E.A.W.R.	Employment-At-Will Reporter		Environmental Reporter Cases
E.Afr.L.J.	East African Law Journal	E.School L.Rev.	Eastern School Law Review
E.Afr.L.R.	East Africa Law Reports	E.T.	Estate Tax Division (I.R.B.)
E.Afr.L.Rev.	Eastern Africa Law Review	E.T.R.	Estates & Trusts Reports (1977–)
E.B. & E.	Ellis, Blackburn & Ellis' Queen's Bench (Eng.)	Ea.	East's King's Bench (Eng.)
E.B. & S.	Ellis, Best & Smith's Queen's Bench (Eng.)	Eag. & Y.	Eagle & Young's Tithe Cases (Eng.)
E.C.	English Chancery	Eag.T.	Eagle's Commutation of Tithes (Eng.)
E.C.L.	English Common Law	Earth L.J.	Earth Law Journal
E.C.L.R.	European Competition Law Review	East	East's King's Bench (Eng.)
E.C.R.	Reports of Cases before the Court of Justice of the European Communities	East P.C.	East's Pleas of the Crown (Eng.)
		East.	Eastern Reporter (U.S.)
		East.J.Int'l L.	Eastern Journal of International Law
		East.L.R.	Eastern Law Reporter (Can.)
E.D.S.	E.D. Smith (N.Y.)	East.Rep.	Eastern Reporter (U.S.)
E.D.Smith	Same		
E.E.	English Exchequer	East.T.	Eastern Term (Eng.)
E.E.C.J.O.	Official Journal of the European Communities	East. U.S. Bus.L.Rev.	Eastern United States Business Law Review
E.E.C.L.	Encyclopedia of European Community Law (Bender)	Ebersole	Ebersole (Iowa)
		Eccl. & Adm.	Spink's Ecclesiastical & Admiralty (Upper Can.)
E.E.O.C.Compliance Manual	Equal Employment Opportunity Commission Compliance Manual (CCH)	Eccl.R.	Ecclesiastical Reports (Eng.)
		Eccl.Rep.	Same
		Ecology L.Q.	Ecology Law Quarterly

Ed.	Eden's Chancery (Eng.)	Elect.Cas. (N.Y.)	Election Cases, Armstrong, New York
Ed.Ch.	Edward's Chancery (N.Y.)	Elect.Rep.	Election Reports (Ont.)
Eden	Eden's Chancery (Eng.)	Ell. & Bl.	Ellis & Blackburn's Queen's Bench (Eng.)
Edg.	Edgar (Scot.)		
Edinb.L.J.	Edinburgh Law Journal	Ell.Bl. & Ell.	Ellis, Blackburn & Ellis' Queen's Bench (Eng.)
Edm.Sel.Cas.	Edmond's Select Cases (N.Y.)	Els.W.Bl.	Elsley's Edition of William Blackstone's King's Bench (Eng.)
Edw.	Edwards (Mo.) Edward's Chancery (N.Y.)		
Edw.Abr.	Edward's Abridgment, Prerogative Court Cases Edward's Abridgment, Privy Council	Em.App.	Emergency Court of Appeals (U.S.)
		Emory Int'l L.Rev.	Emory International Law Review
		Emory J. Int'l Disp.Resol.	Emory Journal of International Dispute Resolution
Edw.Adm.	Edward's Admiralty (Eng.)		
Edw.Ch.	Edward's Chancery (N.Y.)	Emory L.J.	Emory Law Journal
		Empl.Rel.L.J.	Employee Relations Law Journal
Edw.Lead. Dec.	Edward's Leading Decisions in Admiralty	Empl.Saf'y & Health Guide	Employment Safety and Health Guide (CCH)
Edw.Pr.Cas.	Edward's Prize Cases, Admiralty (Eng.)	Enc.Pl. & Pr.	Encyclopedia of Pleading & Practice
Edw.Pr.Ct. Cas.	Edward's Abridgement of Prerogative Court Cases	Enc.U.S.Sup. Ct.Rep.	Encyclopedia of United States Supreme Court Reports
Efird	Efird (S.C.)		
El.	Elchie's Decisions (Scot.)	Energy Controls	Energy Controls (P–H)
El. & B.	Ellis & Blackburn's Queen's Bench (Eng.)	Energy L.J.	Energy Law Journal
		Eng.	English (Ark.)
		Eng.Adm.	English Admiralty
El. & Bl.	Same	Eng.Adm.R.	Same
El. & El.	Ellis & Ellis, Queen's Bench (Eng.)	Eng.C.C.	English Crown Cases
		Eng.C.L.	English Common-Law Reports
El.B. & E.	Ellis, Blackburn & Ellis' Queen's Bench (Eng.)	Eng.Ch.	Condensed English Chancery
El.B. & El.	Same		English Chancery
El.B. & S.	Ellis, Best & Smith's Queen's Bench (Eng.)	Eng.Com.L.R.	English Common Law Reports
		Eng.Cr.Cas.	English Crown Cases
El.Bl. & El.	Ellis, Blackburn & Ellis' Queen's Bench (Eng.)	Eng.Ecc.R.	English Ecclesiastical Reports
		Eng.Eccl.	Same
El.Cas.	Election Cases	Eng.Exch.	English Exchequer
El Paso Trial Law.Rev.	El Paso Trial Lawyers Reviews	Eng.Hist. Rev.	English Historical Review
Elchies'	Elchies' Decisions (Scot.)	Eng.Ir.App.	Law Reports English & Irish Appeals

Eng.Judg.	English Judges (Scot.)	Est.Plan.	Estate Planning
Eng.L. & Eq.	English Law & Equity Reports	Est.Plan.Rev.	Estate Planning Review (CCH)
Eng.L. & Eq.R.	Same	Euer	Euer Doctrina Placitandi (Eng.)
Eng.Rep.	English Reports, Full Reprint	Eur.Consult. Ass.Deb.	Council of Europe Consultative Assembly, Official Report of Debates
Eng.Rep.R.	Same		
Eng.Ry. & C.Cas.	English Railway and Canal Cases		
Eng.Sc.Ecc.	English & Scotch Ecclesiastical Reports	Eur.L.Dig.	European Law Digest
		Eur.L.Newsl.	European Law Newsletter
Entertainment & Med.L.	Entertainment & Media Law	Eur.L.Rev.	European Law Review
Entertainment L.J.	Entertainment Law Journal	Eur.Parl. Deb.	Debates of the European Parliament
Envir.L.	Environmental Law	Eur.Parl. Docs.	European Parliament Working Documents
Env't Rptr.	Environment Reporter (BNA)		
Envtl.Affairs	Environmental Affairs	Eur.Tax.	European Taxation
		Eur.Trans.L.	European Transport Law
Envtl.F.	Environmental Forum		
Envtl.L.	Environmental Law	Eur.Y.B.	European Yearbook
Envtl.L.J.	Environmental Law Journal	Eurolaw Com.Intel.	Eurolaw Commercial Intelligence
Envtl.L.Rev.	Environmental Law Review	Europ.T.S.	European Treaty Series
Envtl.L.Rptr.	Environmental Law Reporter	Evans	Evans, Washington Territory Reports
Envtl.Pol'y & L.	Environmental Policy and Law	Ex.	Exchequer Reports (Eng.)
Eq.Cas.Abr.	Equity Cases Abridged (Eng.)	Ex.C.R.	Exchequer Court Reports (Can.) (1923–present)
Eq.Rep.	Harper's Equity (S.C.)		
Equity Rep.	English Chancery Appeals	Ex.D.	Law Reports, Exchequer Division (Eng.) (To 1880)
	Gilbert, Equity (Eng.)		
	Harper's Equity (S.C.)	Ex.Div.	Same
		Examiner	Examiner (N.Y.)
Err. & App.	Error & Appeals (Upper Can.)		Examiner (Que.)
Ersk.	Erskine (U.S. Circuit Court)	Excerpta Crim.	Excerpta Criminologica
Esp.	Espinasse's Nisi Prius (Eng.)	Exch.	Exchequer (Scot.)
			Welsby, Hurlstone & Gordon, Exchequer (Eng.)
Esp.N.P.	Same	Exch.Can.	Exchequer Reports (Can.)
Est. & Tr.J.	Estates & Trusts Journal		
Est. & Tr.Q.	Estates and Trusts Quarterly	Exch.Cas.	Exchequer Cases (Scot.)
		Exch.Rep.	Exchequer Reports
Est. Gifts & Tr.J.	Estates, Gifts & Trusts Journal	Exec.Order	Executive Order
		Eyre	Eyre's King's Bench (Eng.)

F

F.	Federal Reporter (U.S.)	Fac.L.Rev.	Faculty of Law Review (Toronto)
F. (Ct.Sess.)	Fraser's Court of Sessions Cases (Scot.)	Fairf.	Fairfield (Me.)
F.2d	Federal Reporter, Second Series (U.S)	Falc.	Falconer's Court of Sessions Cases (Scot.)
F.3d	Same, Third Series	Falc. & F.	Falconer & Fitzherbert's Election Cases (Eng.)
F. & F.	Foster & Finlason, Nisi Prius (Eng.)		
F.A.D.	Federal Anti-Trust Decisions	Fam.L. Commtr.	Family Law Commentator
F.B.C.	Fonblanque's Bankruptcy Cases (Eng.)	Fam.L. Newsl.	Family Law Newsletter
FBILEB	Federal Bureau of Investigation Law Enforcement Bulletin	Fam.L.Q.	Family Law Quarterly
		Fam.L.Rep.	Family Law Reporter (BNA)
F.C.	Faculty Collection of Decisions (Scot.)	Fam.L.Rev.	Family Law Review
F.C.	Canada Federal Court Reports (1971–)	Far East. L.Rev.	Far Eastern Law Review
		Far.	Farresley's King's Bench (Eng.)
F.C.A.	Federal Code Annotated	Fed.	Federal Reporter (U.S.)
F.C.C.	Federal Communication Commission Reports	Fed.B.A.J.	Federal Bar Association Journal
F.Carr.Cas.	Federal Carriers Cases (CCH)	Fed.B.J.	Federal Bar Journal
		Fed.B.News	Federal Bar News
F.D.Cosm.L. Rep.	Food, Drug, Cosmetic Law Reporter (CCH)	Fed.Carr. Rep.	Federal Carriers Reporter (CCH)
		Fed.Cas.	Federal Cases (U.S.)
F.E.P.Cas.	Fair Employment Practice Cases	Fed.Com.B.J.	Federal Communications Bar Journal
F.H.L.	Fraser, House of Lords (Scot.)	Fed.Com.L.J.	Federal Communications Law Journal
F.L.J.	Forum Law Journal (U. of Baltimore)	Fed.Crim.L. Rep.	Federal Criminal Law Report
F.L.P.	Florida Law and Practice	Fed.Ct.Rep.	Federal Court Reports (Aust.)
F.M.C.	Federal Maritime Commission Reports	Fed.Est. & Gift Tax Rep.	Federal Estate and Gift Tax Reporter (CCH)
F.O.I.Dig.	Freedom of Information Digest	Fed.Juror	Federal Juror
F.O.I.C.R.	Freedom of Information Center Reports	Fed.L.Rep.	Federal Law Reports
		Fed.L.Rev.	Federal Law Review
		Fed.Prob.	Federal Probation
F.P.C.	Federal Power Commission Decisions	Fed.Reg.	Federal Register
		Fed.Rules Serv.	Federal Rules Service
FR	Federal Register		
F.R.D.	Federal Rules Decisions	Fed.Rules Serv.2d	Same, Second Series
F.Supp.	Federal Supplement	Fed'n Ins. Counsel Q.	Federation of Insurance Counsel Quarterly
F.T.C.	Federal Trade Commission Decisions		

Ferg.Cons.	Fergusson's Consistory, Divorce (Scot.)	Fordham Envtl.L.Rep.	Fordham Environmental Law Report
Fergusson	Fergusson (of Kilkeran) (Scot.)	Fordham Int'l L.F.	Fordham International Law Forum
Fin.Tax. & Comp.L.	Finance Taxation and Company Law (Pak.)	Fordham Int'l L.J.	Fordham International Law Journal
Finch	Finch's Chancery (Eng.)	Fordham L.Rev.	Fordham Law Review
Fire & Casualty Cas.	Fire and Casualty Cases (CCH)	Fordham Urb. L.J.	Fordham Urban Law Journal
Fish.Pat.Cas.	Fisher's Patent Cases (U.S.)	Form.	Forman (Ill.)
		Forr.	Forrest's Exchequer (Eng.)
Fish.Pat.R.	Fisher's Patent Reports (U.S.)	Forrester	Forrester's Chancery Cases Tempore Talbot (Eng.)
Fish.Prize Cas.	Fisher's Prize Cases (U.S.)	Fort.L.J.	Fortnightly Law Journal
Fitzh.	Fitzherbert's Abridgment (Eng.)	Fortesc.	Fortescue's King's Bench (Eng.)
Fitzh.N.Br.	Fitzherbert's Natura Brevium (Eng.)	Forum	The Forum
Fla.	Florida Reports	Fost.	Foster (Haw.)
Fla. & K.	Flanagan & Kelly, Rolls (Ir.)		Foster (N.H.)
			Foster's Crown Cases (Eng.)
Fla.B.J.	Florida Bar Journal		
Fla.Int'l L.J.	Florida International Law Journal		Foster's Legal Chronicle Reports (Pa.)
Fla.J.Int'l L.	Florida Journal of International Law	Found.L.Rev.	Foundation Law Review
Fla.Jur.	Florida Jurisprudence	Fount.Dec.	Fountainhall's Decisions (Scot.)
Fla. L.J.	Florida Law Journal	Fox	Fox's Registration Cases (Eng.)
Fla. L. Rev.	Florida Law Review		
Fla.St.U. L.Rev.	Florida State University Law Review		Fox's Decisions (Me.)
Fla.Supp.	Florida Supplement	Fox & S.	Fox & Smith's King's Bench (Ir.)
Flan. & Kel.	Flanagan & Kelly, Rolls (Ir.)	Fox Pat.C.	Fox's Patent, Trade Mark, Design and Copyright Cases
Fletcher F. World Aff.	Fletcher Forum of World Affairs	Fran.Coll.L.J.	Franciso College Law Journal
Flipp.	Flippin (U.S.)		
Fogg	Fogg (N.H.)	France	France (Colo.)
Fonbl.	Fonblanque's Bankruptcy (Eng.)	Franchise L. Rev.	Franchise Law Review
Food Drug Cosm.L.J.	Food, Drug, Cosmetic Law Journal	Fraser	Fraser, Court of Session Cases (Scot.)
For.Sci.	Forensic Science	Freem.	Freeman (Ill.)
For.Tax Bull.	Foreign Tax Law Bi-Weekly Bulletin	Freem.Ch.	Freeman's Chancery (Miss.)
Fordham Ent.Media & Intell. Prop.L.F.	Fordham Entertainment Media & Intellectual Property Law Forum	Freem.K.B.	Freeman's King's Bench (Eng.)
		French	French (N.H.)
		Fuller	Fuller (Mich.)

G

G. & D.	Gale	Geld. & M.	Geldart & Maddock's Chancery (Eng.)
G. & G.	Goldsmith & Guthrie (Mo.)	Geld. & O.	Geldert & Oxley (Nova Scotia)
G. & J.	Gill & Johnson (Md.)	Geo.Immigr. L.J.	Georgetown Immigration Law Journal
	Glyn & Jameson's Bankruptcy (Eng.)	Geo.Int'l Envtl. L.Rev.	Georgetown International Environmental Law Review
G. & R.	Geldert & Russell (Nova Scotia)		
GA	Decisions of General Appraisers (U.S.)	Geo.J.Legal Ethics	Georgetown Journal of Legal Ethics
G.C.M.	General Counsel's Memorandum (I.R.B.)	Geo.L.J.	Georgetown Law Journal
G.Coop.	G. Cooper's Chancery (Eng.)	Geo.Mason L. Rev.	George Mason Law Review
G.S.R.	Gongwer's State Reports (Ohio)	Geo.Mason U.Civ.Rts. L.J.	George Mason University Civil Rights Law Journal
Ga.	Georgia		
Ga.App.	Georgia Appeals	Geo.Mason U.L.Rev.	George Mason University Law Review
Ga.B.J.	Georgia Bar Journal		
Ga.Bus.Law.	Georgia Business Lawyer	Geo.Wash.J. Int'l L. & Econ.	George Washington Journal of International Law and Economics
Ga.Dec.	Georgia Decisions		
Ga.J.Int'l & Comp.L.	Georgia Journal of International & Comparative Law		
Ga.L.J.	Georgia Law Journal	Geo.Wash. L.Rev.	George Washington Law Review
Ga.L.Rep.	Georgia Law Reports	George	George (Miss.)
Ga.L.Rev.	Georgia Law Review	Gibb.Surr.	Gibbon's Surrogate (N.Y.)
Ga.St.B.J.	Georgia State Bar Journal		
Ga.St.U. L.Rev.	Georgia State University Law Review	Gibbs	Gibbs (Mich.)
		Giff.	Giffard's Chancery (Eng.)
Ga.Supp.	Lester, Supplement (Ga.)	Giff. & H.	Giffard & Hemming's Chancery (Eng.)
Galb.	Galbraith (Fla.)		
Galb. & M.	Galbraith & Meek (Fla.)	Gil.	Gilman (Ill.)
		Gilb.	Gilbert's Chancery (Eng.)
Gale	Gale's Exchequer (Eng.)		
Gale & D.	Gale & Davison's Queen's Bench (Eng.)	Gilb.C.P.	Gilbert's Common Pleas (Eng.)
		Gilb.Cas.	Gilbert's Cases, Law & Equity (Eng.)
Gale & Dav.	Same		
Gall.	Gallison (U.S. Circuit Court)	Gilb.Exch.	Gilbert's Exchequer (Eng.)
Gard.N.Y. Reptr.	Gardenier's New York Reporter	Gildr.	Gildersleeve (N.M.)
		Gilf.	Gilfillan (Minn.)
Garden.	Gardenhire (Mo.)	Gill	Gill (Md.)
Gaz.	Gazette	Gill & J.	Gill & Johnson (Md.)
	Weekly Law Gazette (U.S.)	Gill & Johns.	Same
		Gilm.	Gilmer (Va.)
Gaz.Bankr.	Gazette of Bankruptcy	Gilm. & Falc.	Gilmour & Falconer (Scot.)
Gaz.L.R.	Gazette Law Reports	Gilp.	Gilpin (U.S.)

Gl. & J.	Glyn & Jameson's Bankruptcy Cases (Eng.)	Gov't Cont. Rep.	Government Contracts Reporter (CCH)
Glanv.	Glanville De Legibus et Consuetudinibus Angliae (Eng.)	Gow	Gow's Nisi Prius (Eng.)
Glanv.El.Cas.	Glanville's Election Cases (Eng.)	Gr.	Grant, Chancery Reports (Upper Can.)
Glasc.	Glascock (Ir.)	Granger	Granger (Ohio)
Glendale L.Rev.	Glendale Law Review	Grant	Grant's Cases (Pa.)
Glenn	Glenn (La.)	Grant Err. & App.	Grant's Error & Appeal (Upper Can.)
Glyn & J.	Glyn & Jameson's Bankruptcy Cases (Eng.)	Gratt.	Grattan (Va.)
		Gray	Gray (Mass.)
Glyn & Jam.	Same		Gray (N.C.)
Godb.	Godbolt's King's Bench (Eng.)	Green	Green (Okla.)
			Green (R.I.)
			Green Equity (N.J.)
			Green Law (N.J.)
Godson	Godson, Mining Commissioner's Cases (1911–1917)	Green Cr.	Green's Criminal Law (Eng.)
Goebel	Goebel's Probate (Ohio)	Greene	Greene (Iowa)
			Greene's Annotated Cases (N.Y.)
Gold. & G.	Goldsmith & Guthrie (Mo.)	Greenl.	Greenleaf (Me.)
		Greenl.Ov. Cas.	Greenleaf's Overruled Cases
Golden Gate L.Rev.	Golden Gate Law Review	Grein.Pr.	Greiner, Practice (La.)
Golden Gate U.L.Rev.	Golden Gate University Law Review	Griffith	Griffith (Ind.)
Gonz.L.Rev.	Gonzaga Law Review	Gris.	Griswold (Ohio)
Gonz.Pub. Lab.L.Rep.	Gonzaga Special Report: Public Sector Labor Law	Griswold	Same
		Group Legal Rev.	Group Legal Review
Gottschall	Gottschall (Ohio)	Guild Prac.	Guild Practitioner
Gouldsb.	Gouldsborough's King's Bench (Eng.)	Guthrie	Guthrie (Mo.)
		Gwill.T.Cas.	Gwillim's Tithe Cases (Eng.)

H

H.	Handy (Ohio)	H. & J.	Harris & Johason (Md.)
H. & B.	Hudson & Brooke's King's Bench (Ir.)		Hayes & Jones' Exchequer (Ir.)
H. & C.	Hurlstone & Coltman's Exchequer (Eng.)	H. & J.Ir.	Hayes & Jones' Exchequer (Ir.)
H. & D.	Hill & Denio, Lalor's Supplement (N.Y.)	H. & M.	Hemming & Miller's Vice Chancery (Eng.)
H. & G.	Harris & Gill (Md.)		Hening & Munford (Va.)
	Hurlstone & Gordon's Exchequer (Eng.)		
H. & H.	Harrison & Hodgin's Municipal Reports (Upper Can.)	H. & M.Ch.	Hemming & Miller's Vice Chancery (Eng.)
	Horn & Hurlstone's Exchequer (Eng.)	H. & McH.	Harris & McHenry (Md.)

H. & N.	Hurlstone & Norman's Exchequer (Eng.)	Halst.	Halsted's Equity (N.J.)
			Halsted's Law (N.J.)
H. & R.	Harrison & Rutherford's Common Pleas (Eng.)	Ham.	Hammond (Ga.)
			Hammond (Ohio)
		Ham. & J.	Hammond & Jackson (Ga.)
H. & S.	Harris & Simrall (Miss.)		
		Ham.A. & O.	Hamerton, Allen & Otter, New Session Cases (Eng.)
H. & T.	Hall & Twell's Chancery (Eng.)		
H. & W.	Harrison & Wollaston's King's Bench (Eng.)	Hamlin	Hamlin (Me.)
		Hamline J.Pub.L. & Pol'y	Hamline Journal of Public Law and Policy
	Hurlstone & Wahnsley's Exchequer (Eng.)	Hamline L.Rev.	Hamline Law Review
H.Bl.	Henry Blackstone's Common Pleas (Eng.)	Hammond	Hammond (Ohio)
		Han.	Handy (Ohio)
		Han.N.B.	Hannay's Reports (N.B.)
H.C.L.M.	Health Care Labor Manual		
		Hand	Hand (N.Y.)
H.L.Cas.	House of Lords Cases (Eng.)	Handy	Handy (Ohio)
		Hans.	Hansbrough (Va.)
H.L.N.R.	Health Lawyers News Report	Har.	Harrington (Del.)
			Harrington's Chancery (Mich.)
H.R.L.J.	Human Rights Law Journal		Harrison (La.)
H.W.Gr.	H.W. Green's Equity (N.J.)		Harrison's Chancery (Mich.)
Ha.	Hare's Vice-Chancery (Eng.)	Harc.	Harcarse, Decisions (Scot.)
Ha. & Tw.	Hall & Twell's Chancery (Eng.)	Hard.	Hardesty, Term Reports (Del.)
Had.	Hadley (N.H.)	Hardes.	Same
Hadd.	Haddington Manuscript Reports (Scot.)	Hardin	Hardin (Ky.)
		Hardres	Hardres' Exchequer (Eng.)
Hadl.	Hadley (N.H.)	Hare	Hare's Vice-Chancery (Eng.)
Hagan	Hagan (Utah)		
Hagans	Hagans (W.Va.)	Hare & W.	American Leading Cases, Hare & Wallace
Hagg.Adm.	Haggard's Admiralty (Eng.)		
Hagn. & M.	Hagner & Miller (Md.)	Harg.	Hargrove (N.C.)
		Harp.	Harper's Equity (S.C.)
Hailes Dec.	Hailes' Decisions (Scot.)		Harper's Law (S.C.)
Hale	Hale (Cal.)	Harper	Harper's Conspiracy Cases (Md.)
	Hale's Common Law (Eng.)	Harr.	Harrington
Hale P.C.	Hale's Pleas of the Crown (Eng.)		Harrison (Ind.)
			Harrison (N.J.)
Hall	Hall (N.H.)	Harr. & H.	Harrison & Hodgins' Municipal Reports (Upper Can.)
	Hall's Superior Court (N.Y.)		
Hall & Tw.	Hall & Twell's Chancery (Eng.)	Harr. & Hodg.	Same
Hall.	Hallett (Colo.)	Harr. & J.	Harris & Johnson (Md.)

Harr. & M.	Harris & McHenry (Md.)	Hastings Int'l & Comp.L. Rev.	Hastings International and Comparative Law Review
Harr. & R.	Harrison & Rutherford's Common Pleas (Eng.)	Hastings L.J.	Hastings Law Journal
Harr. & W.	Harrison & Wollaston's King's Bench (Eng.)	Hastings Women's L.J.	Hastings Women's Law Journal
Harr.Ch.	Harrison's Chancery (Eng.)	Havil.	Haviland (P.E.I.)
Harris	Harris (Pa.)	Haw.	Hawaii Reports
Harris & G.	Harris & Gill (Md.)	Hawaii	Same
Harris & S.	Harris & Simrall (Miss.)	Hawaii B.J.	Hawaii Bar Journal
Hart.	Hartley (Tex.)	Hawk.	Hawkins' Louisiana Annual
Hart. & H.	Hartley & Hartley (Tex.)	Hawk.P.C.	Hawkins' Pleas of the Crown
Harv.Blackletter J.	Harvard Blackletter Journal	Hawks	Hawks (N.C.)
		Hawl.	Hawley (Nev.)
Harv.Bus.Rev.	Harvard Business Review	Hay & H.	Hay & Hazelton (U.S.)
Harv.C.R.—C.L.L.Rev.	Harvard Civil Rights—Civil Liberties Law Review	Hay & M.	Hay & Marriott's Admiralty (Eng.)
Harv. Envtl.L.Rev.	Harvard Environmental Law Review	Hay.	Haywood (N.C.) Haywood (Tenn.)
		Hayes	Hayes (Scot.) Hayes' Exchequer (Ir.)
Harv.Hum. Rts.J.	Harvard Human Rights Journal	Hayes & J.	Hayes & Jones' Exchequer (Ir.)
Harv.Int'l L.J.	Harvard International Law Journal	Hayw.	Haywood (N.C.) Haywood (Tenn.)
Harv.J.L. & Pub.Pol'y	Harvard Journal of Law and Public Policy	Haz.Reg.	Hazard's Register (Pa.)
		Head	Head (Tenn.)
Harv. J. L. & Tech.	Harvard Journal of Law & Technology	Health Matrix: J.L.–Med.	Health Matrix: Journal of Law–Medicine
Harv.J. on Legis.	Harvard Journal on Legislation	Heath	Heath (Me.)
Harv.L.Rev.	Harvard Law Review	Hedges	Hedges (Mont.)
Harv.L.S. Bull.	Harvard Law School Bulletin	Heisk.	Heiskell (Tenn.)
		Helm	Helm (Nev.)
Harv.W.Tax Ser.	Harvard World Tax Series (CCH)	Hem. & M.	Heming & Miller's Vice-Chancery (Eng.)
Harv.Women's L.J.	Harvard's Women's Law Journal	Heming.	Hemingway (Miss.)
Hasb.	Hasbrouck (Idaho)	Hemp.	Hempstead U.S. (Circuit Court)
Hask.	Haskell's Reports for United States Courts in Maine (Fox's Decisions)	Hempst.	Same
		Hen. & M.	Hening & Munford (Va.)
Hast.	Hastings (Me.)	Henn.Law.	Hennepin Lawyer (Minn.)
Hastings Comm. & Ent.L.J.	Hastings Communications and Environmental Law Journal	Henning CLE Rep.	Henning Continuing Legal Education Reporter
		Hepb.	Hepburn (Colo.)
Hastings Const.L.Q.	Hastings Constitutional Law Quarterly	Het.	Hetley's Common Pleas (Eng.)
		Hibb.	Hibbard (N.H.)

High Tech. L.J.	High Technology Law Journal	Hope Dec.	Hope's Decisions (Scot.)
Hight	Hight (Iowa)	Hopk.	Hopkins' Chancery
Hil.T.	Hilary Tenn (Eng.)		(N.Y.)
Hill	Hill (Ill.)	Hopk.Dec.	Hopkinson's Admiralty Decisions
	Hill (N.Y.)		(Pa.)
	Hill's Equity (S.C.)		
	Hill's Law (S.C.)	Hopw. & C.	Hopwood & Coltman's Registration
Hill & D.	Hill & Denio (N.Y.)		Appeal Cases
Hillyer	Hillyer (Cal.)		(Eng.)
Hilt.	Hilton (N.Y.)		
Hines	Hines (Ky.)	Hopw. & P.	Hopwood & Philbrick's Registration
Hitotsubashi J.L. & Pol.	Hitotsubashi Journal of Law and Politics		Appeal Cases (Eng.)
Hob.	Hobart's Common Pleas & Chancery	Horner	Horner (S.D.)
	(Eng.)	Horw.Y.B.	(Horwood) Year Book of Edward I
Hobart	Hobart's King's Bench (Eng.)	Hosea	Hosea (Ohio)
Hod.	Hodges' Common Pleas (Eng.)	Hoskins	Hoskins (N.D.)
		Houghton	Houghton (Ala.)
Hodg.El.	Hodgin's Election (Upper Can.)	Hous.J.Int'l L.	Houston Journal of International Law
Hodges	Hodges' Common Pleas (Eng.)	Hous.L.Rev.	Houston Law Review
Hoffm.	Hoffman's Chancery (N.Y.)	Hous.Law.	Houston Lawyer
	Hoffman's Land Cases (U.S.)	Housing & Devel.Rep.	Housing and Development Reporter (BNA)
Hofstra L.Rev.	Hofstra Law Review	Houst.	Houston (Del.)
Hofstra Lab. L.F.	Hofstra Labor Law Forum	Houst.Cr.	Houston, Criminal Cases (Del.)
Hofstra Lab. L.J.	Hofstra Labor Law Journal	Houst.L.Rev.	Houston Law Review
Hofstra Prop. L.J.	Hofstra Property Law Journal	Houston Law.	Houston Lawyer
Hog.	Hogan's Rolls Court (Ir.)	Hov.	Hovenden's Supplement, Vesey's Chancery (Eng.)
Hogue	Hogue (Fla.)	How.	Howard (Miss.)
Holl.	Holligshead (Minn.)		Howard (U.S.)
Holmes	Holmes (Ore.)		Howell (Nev.)
	Holmes (U.S.)	How. & Beat.	Howell & Beatty (Nev.)
Holt Adm.	Holt's Admiralty Cases (Eng.)	How. & N.	Howell & Norcross (Nev.)
Holt Eq.	Holt's Equity (Eng.)	How.A.Cas.	Howard's Appeal Cases (N.Y.)
	Holt's Vice Chancery (Eng.)	How.Ch.	Howard's Chancery (Ir.)
Holt K.B.	Holt's King's Bench (Eng.)	How.L.J.	Howard Law Journal
Holt N.P.	Holt's Nisi Prius (Eng.)	How.N.P.	Howell's Nisi Prius (Mich.)
Home	Home Manuscript, Decisions, Court of Sessions (Scot.)	How.Pr.	Howard's Practice (N.Y.)
		How.Pr. (N.S.)	Same, New Series
Hong Kong L.J.	Hong Kong Law Journal	How.St.Tr.	Howell's State Trials (Eng.)
Hook.	Hooker (Conn.)	Howard L.J.	Howard Law Journal

Hubb.	Hubbard (Me.)	Hume	Hume's Decisions (Scot.)
Hud. & B.	Hudson & Brooke's King's Bench (Ir.)	Humph.	Humphrey
Hughes	Hughes (Ky.)	Humphr.	Humphrey's (Tenn.)
	Hughes (U.S.)	Hun	Hun (N.Y.)
Hum.Rts.	Human Rights	Hung.L.Rev.	Hungarian Law Review
Hum.Rts.J.	Human Rights Journal	Hunt.Torrens	Hunter's Torrens Cases
Hum.Rts.L.J.	Human Rights Law Journal	Hurl. & G.	Hurlstone & Gordon's Exchequer (Eng.)
Hum.Rts.Q.	Human Rights Quarterly		
Hum.Rts.Rev.	Human Rights Review	Hurl. & W.	Hurlstone & Wahnsley's Exchequer (Eng.)
Hum.Rts. U.S.S.R.	Human Rights in Union of Soviet Socialist Republics	Hutch.	Hutcheson (Ala.)
		Hutt.	Hutton's Common Pleas (Eng.)

I

I. & N.Dec.	Immigration and Nationality Decisions	I.R.	Internal Revenue Decisions
I.A.C.	Immigration Appeal Cases (1970–)	I.R.B.	Internal Revenue Bulletin
ICC	Interstate Commerce Commission	I.R.C.	Internal Revenue Code
I.C.C.Pract.J.	Interstate Commerce Commission Practitioners' Journal	I.R.R.Newsl.	Individual Rights and Responsibilities Newsletter
I.C.J.	International Court of Justice Reports	ISL L.Rev.	International School of Law Law Review
I.C.J.Y.B.	Yearbook of the International Court of Justice	I.T.R.	Ridgeway, Lapp & Schoaler, Term Reports (Ir.)
I.D.	Interior Department Decisions, Public Land	Idaho	Idaho Reports
		Idaho L.J.	Idaho Law Journal
		Idaho L.Rev.	Idaho Law Review
IIC	International Review of Industrial Property and Copyright Law	Idd.T.R.	Idding's Term Reports (Dayton, Ohio)
		Idding	Same
		Iddings T.R.D.	Same
I.L.C. Newsl.	International Legal Center Newsletter	Ill.	Illinois Reports
		Ill.2d	Same, Second Series
I.L.E.	Indiana Law Encyclopedia	Ill.App.	Illinois Appellate Court
I.L.P.	Illinois Law and Practice	Ill.App.2d	Same, Second Series
		Ill.App.3d	Same, Third Series
I.L.R.	Insurance Law Reporter (Can.)	Ill.B.J.	Illinois Bar Journal
		Ill.Cir.	Illinois Circuit Court
	International Law Reports	Ill.Cont.L.Ed.	Illinois Continuing Legal Education
I.L.W.	Investment Laws of the World (Oceana)	Ill.Cont.Legal Ed.	Same
I.O.C.C.Bull.	Interstate Oil Compact Commission Bulletin	Ill.Ct.Cl.	Illinois Court of Claims Reports
		Ill.L.B.	Illinois Law Bulletin

Ill.L.Q.	Illinois Law Quarterly	Indus.L.Rev.	Industrial Law Review
Ill.L.Rev.	Illinois Law Review	Indus.Rel.L.J.	Industrial Relations Law Journal
Immig.B.Bull.	Immigration Bar Bulletin		
		Inequal.Ed.	Inequality in Education
Immig. L. & Bus.News	Immigration Law & Business News	Ins.Counsel J.	Insurance Counsel Journal
Immig.Newsl.	Immigration Newsletter	Ins.L.J.	Insurance Law Journal (Pa.)
Ind.	Indiana Reports		
Ind. & Intell. Prop.Austl.	Industrial and Intellectual Property in Australia	Ins.L.Rep.	Insurance Law Reporter (CCH)
		Ins.Liability Rep.	Insurance Liability Reporter
Ind. & Lab. Rel.Rev.	Industrial and Labor Relations Review	Inst.Ad.Legal Stud.Ann.	Institute of Advanced Legal Studies Annual
Ind.Advocate	Indian Advocate		
Ind.App.	Indiana Appellate Court Reports	Inst.Est.Plan.	Institute on Estate Planning (U. of Miami)
Ind.Cl.Comm.	Indian Claims Commission Decisions		
Ind.Int'l & Comp.L. Rev.	Indiana International & Comparative Law Review	Inst.Lab.Rel. Bull.	Institute for Labor Relations Bulletin
		Inst.Min.L.	Institute on Mineral Law (La.State University)
Ind.J. Int'l L.	Indian Journal of International Law		
Ind.L.J.	Indiana Law Journal	Inst. on Fed. Tax'n	Institute on Federal Taxation
Ind.L.Q.Rev.	Indian Law Quarterly Review	Inst.Plan. & Zoning	Institute on Planning and Zoning
Ind.L.Rev.	Indian Law Review	Inst.Plan. Zoning & E.D.	Institute on Planning, Zoning and Eminent Domain
	Indiana Law Review		
Ind.L.Stud.	Indiana Law Student		
Ind.Legal F.	Indiana Legal Forum		
Ind.Prop.	Industrial Property	Inst.Sec.Reg.	Institute on Securities Regulation (PLI)
Ind.Prop.Q.	Industrial Property Quarterly		
Ind.Rel.J. Econ. & Soc.	Industrial Relations: Journal of Economy and Society	Int.Rev.Bull.	Internal Revenue Bulletin
		Int.Rev.Code	Internal Revenue Code
Ind.S.C.	Indiana Superior Court	Int.Rev.Code of 1954	Internal Revenue Code of 1954
Ind.Y.B.Int'l Aff.	Indian Yearbook of International Affairs	Int.Rev.Rec.	Internal Revenue Record
India Crim.L. J.R.	India Criminal Law Journal Reports	Intell.Prop. L.Rev.	Intellectual Property Law Review
India S.Ct.	India Supreme Court Reports	Inter-Am. L.Rev.	Inter-American Law Review
Indian Cas.	Indian Cases	Interior Dec.	United States Interior Department Decisions
Indian L.J.	Indian Law Journal		
Indian L.R.	Indian Law Reports		
Indian Rul.	Indian Rulings	Int'l & Comp. L.Bull.	International and Comparative Law Bulletin
Indian Terr.	Indian Territory Reports		
Indus. & Lab. Rel.Rev.	Industrial and Labor Relation Review	Int'l & Comp. L.Q.	International and Comparative Law Quarterly
Indus.L.J.	Industrial Law Journal	Int'l Aff.	International Affairs

Int'l Arb. Awards	Reports of International Arbitral Awards	Int'l L.News	International Law News
Int'l Arb.J.	International Arbitration Journal	Int'l L.Persp.	International Law Perspective
Int'l B.J.	International Bar Journal	Int'l L.Q.	International Law Quarterly
Int'l Bus. & Trade L.Rep.	International Business & Trade Law Reporter	Int'l L.Stud.	International Law Studies
Int'l Bus. Lawyer	International Business Lawyer	Int'l Lab.Rev.	International Labour Review
Int'l Bus.Ser.	International Business Series (Ernst & Ernst)	Int'l Law.	The International Lawyer
		Int'l Legal Ed. Newsl.	International Legal Education Newsletter
Int'l Concil.	International Conciliation	Int'l Legal Materials	International Legal Materials
Int'l Crim. Pol.Rev.	International Criminal Police Review	Int'l Prop. Inv.J.	International Property Investment Journal
Int'l Dig. Health Leg.	International Digest of Health Legislation	Int'l Rev.Ad. Sci.	International Review of Administrative Sciences
Int'l Encycl. Comp.L.	International Encyclopedia of Comparative Law	Int'l Rev. Crim.Policy	International Review of Criminal Policy
Int'l J.	International Journal	Int'l Rev.L. & Econ.	International Review of Law and Economics
Int'l J.Crim. & Pen.	International Journal of Criminology and Penology	Int'l Soc'y of Barr.Q.	International Society of Barristers Quarterly
Int'l J. L. & Fam.	International Journal of Law and the Family	Int'l Surv.L. D.L.L.	International Survey of Legal Decisions on Labour Laws
Int'l J.L. & Psych.	International Journal of Law and Psychiatry	Int'l Sym. Comp.L.	International Symposium on Comparative Law
Int'l J.L.Lib.	International Journal of Law Libraries	Int'l Tax & Bus.Law.	International Tax & Business Lawyer
Int'l J.Legal Res.	International Journal of Legal Research	Int'l Tax J.	International Tax Journal
Int'l J.Off. Ther. & Comp.Crim.	International Journal of Offender Therapy and Comparative Criminology	Int'l Trade L.J.	International Trade Law Journal
		Int'l Woman Law.	International Woman Lawyer
Int'l J.Pol.	International Journal of Politics	Intramural L.J.	Intramural Law Journal
Int'l J.Soc.L.	International Journal of the Sociology of the Law	Intramural L.Rev.	Intramural Law Review
Int'l J.World Peace	International Journal on World Peace	Iowa	Iowa Reports
Int'l Jurid. Ass'n Bull.	International Juridical Association Monthly Bulletin	Iowa L.B.	Iowa Law Bulletin
		Iowa L.Rev.	Iowa Law Review
		Ir.	Law Reports (Ir.)
Int'l L. & Trade Persp.	International Law & Trade Perspective	Ir.C.L.	Irish Common Law
		Ir.Ch.	Irish Chancery
		Ir.Cir.	Irish Circuit Reports
Int'l L.Doc.	International Law Documents	Ir.Eccl.	Irish Ecclesiastical Reports

Ir.Eq.	Irish Equity	Ired.	Iredell's Law (N.C.)
Ir.Jur.	Irish Jurist	Ired.Eq.	Iredell's Equity
Ir.L. & Eq.	Irish Law & Equity		(N.C.)
Ir.L.T.R.	Irish Law Times Reports	Irv.Just.	Irvine's Justiciary (Scot.)
Ir.R.	Irish Reports	Israel L.Rev.	Israel Law Review
Ir.R.C.L.	Irish Reports Common Law	Israel Y.B. Human Rights	Israel Yearbook on Human Rights
Ir.R.Eq.	Irish Reports Equity	Issues Crim.	Issues in Criminology
Ir.Soc'y for Lab.L.J.	Irish Society for Labor Law Journal	Iustitia	Iustitia

J

J. & C.	Jones & Cary's Exchequer (Ir.)		Chartered Life Underwriters
J. & H.	Johnson & Hemming's Chancery (Eng.)	J.Art & Ent.L.	Journal of Art and Entertainment Law
J. & L.	Jones & La Touche's Chancery (Ir.)	J.Arts Mgmt.L. Soc'y	Journal of Arts Management, Law and Society
J. & La. T.	Same		
J. & S.	Jones & Spencer's Superior Court (N.Y.)	J.Ass'n L.Teachers	Journal of the Association of Law Teachers
J. & W.	Jacob & Walker's Chancery (Eng.)	J.B.Ass'n D.C.	Journal of the Bar Association of the District of Columbia
JAG Bull.	Judge Advocate General Bulletin, United States Air Force	J.B.Ass'n St. Kan.	Journal of the Bar Association of the State of Kansas
JAG J.	Judge Advocate General Journal	J.B.Moore	J.B. Moore's Common Pleas (Eng.)
JAG L.Rev.	Judge Advocate General Law Review, United States Air Force	J.Beverly Hills B.Ass'n	Journal of the Beverly Hills Bar Association
JAMA	Journal of the American Medical Association	J.Bridg.	Sir John Bridgman's Common Pleas (Eng.)
J.Accountancy	Journal of Accountancy	J.Bridgm.	Same
J.Afr.L.	Journal of African Law	J.Bus.L.	Journal of Business Law
J.Agr.Tax'n & L.	Journal of Agricultural Taxation and the Law	J.C.	Johnson's Cases (N.Y.)
J.Agric.Tax. & L.	Same	J.C. & U.L.	Journal of College & University Law
J.Air L. & Com.	Journal of Air Law and Commerce	J.C.N.P.S.	Journal of Collective Negotiations in the Public Sector
J.Am.Acad. Matrim. Law.	Journal of American Academy of Matrimonial Lawyers	J.C.R.	Johnson's Chancery (N.Y.)
J.Am.Jud. Soc'y	Journal of the American Judicature Society	J.Can.B. Ass'n	Journal of the Canadian Bar Association
J.Am.Soc'y C.L.U.	Journal of the American Society of	J.Ceylon L.	Journal of Ceylon Law

J.Ch.	Johnson's Chancery (N.Y.)	J.Energy & Devel.	Journal of Energy and Development
J. Chinese L.	Journal of Chinese Law	J.Energy L. & Pol'y	Journal of Energy Law & Policy
J.Church & St.	Journal of Church and State	J.Envtl.L. & Litig.	Journal of Environment Law and Litigation
J.Coll. & U.L.	Journal of College and University Law	J.Eth.L.	Journal of Ethiopian Law
J.Comm.Mt. Stud.	Journal of Common Market Studies	J.Fam.L.	Journal of Family Law
J.Comp.Leg. & Int'l L.3d	Journal of Comparative Legislation and International Law, Third Series	J.For.Med.	Journal of Forensic Medicine
		J.For.Med. Soc'y	Journal of the Forensic Medicine Society
J.Confl.Res.	Journal of Conflict Resolution	J.For.Sci.	Journal of the Forensic Sciences
J.Cons.Affairs	Journal of Consumer Affairs	J.For.Sci. Soc'y	Journal of the Forensic Science Society
J.Const. & Parl.Stud.	Journal of Constitutional and Parliamentary Studies	J.Health Pol. Pol'y & L.	Journal of Health, Politics, Policy & Law
J.Contemp. Health L. & Pol'y	Journal of Contemporary Health Law and Policy	J.Ind.L.Inst.	Journal of the Indian Law Institute
J.Contemp.L.	Journal of Contemporary Law	J.Int'l Aff.	Journal of International Affairs
J.Contemp. Legal Issues	Journal of Contemporary Legal Issues	J.Int'l Arb.	Journal of International Arbitration
J.Contemp. R.D.L.	Journal of Contemporary Roman-Dutch Law	J.Int'l Comm. Jur.	Journal of the International Commission of Jurists
J.Copyright Entertainment Sports L.	Journal of Copyright Entertainment and Sports Law	J.Int'l L. & Dipl.	Journal of International Law and Diplomacy
J.Corp.L.	Journal of Corporation Law	J.Int'l L. & Econ.	Journal of International Law and Economics
J.Corp.Tax'n	Journal of Corporate Taxation	J.Int'l L. & Pol.	Journal of International Law and Politics
J.Crim.Just.	Journal of Criminal Justice	J.Int'l L. & Prac.	Journal of International Law and Practice
J.Crim.L. (Eng.)	Journal of Criminal Law (Eng.)		
J.Crim.L. & Criminology	Journal of Criminal Law and Criminology	J.Ir.Soc. Lab.L.	Journal of the Irish Society for Labour Law
J.Crim.L., C. & P.S.	Journal of Criminal Law, Criminology and Police Science	J.Islam. & Comp.L.	Journal of Islamic and Comparative Law
J.Crim.Sci.	Journal of Criminal Science	J.J.Mar. J.J.Marsh. (Ky.)	J.J. Marshall (Ky.) Same
J.D.	Juris Doctor		
J.Denning L.Soc'y	Journal of the Denning Law Society	J.Juris.	Journal of Jurisprudence
J. Disp.Resol.	Journal of Dispute Resolution	J.Juv.L.	Journal of Juvenile Law

J.Kan.B. Ass'n	Journal of the Kansas Bar Association	J.Marshall L.Rev.	John Marshall Law Review
J.L.	Journal of Law	J.Min.L. & Pol'y	Journal of Mineral Law and Policy
J.L. & Com.	Journal of Law and Commerce	J.Mo.Bar	Journal of the Missouri Bar
J.L. & Econ.	Journal of Law & Economics	J.P.	Justice of the Peace (Eng.)
J.L. & Educ.	Journal of Law and Education	J.P.Sm.	J.P. Smith's King's Bench (Eng.)
J.L. & Pol.	Journal of Law and Politics	J.Pat. & Trademark Off.Soc.	Journal of the Patent and Trademark Office Society
J.L. & Religion	Journal of Law and Religion	J.Pat.Off. Soc'y	Journal of the Patent Office Society
J.L. & Tech.	Journal of Law and Technology	J.Pension Plan. & Compliance	Journal of Pension Planning & Compliance
J.L.Soc'y	Journal of the Law Society of Scotland	J.Plan. & Env.L.	Journal of Planning and Environment Law
J.Land & P.U.Econ.	Journal of Land and Public Utility Economics	J.Pol.Sci. & Admin.	Journal of Police Science and Administration
J.Land Use & Envtl.L.	Journal of Land Use & Environmental Law	J.Prod. & Toxics Liab.	Journal of Products and Toxics Liability
J.Law & Econ.	Journal of Law and Economics	J.Prod.Liab.	Journal of Products Liability
J.Law & Econ. Dev.	Journal of Law and Economic Development	J.Psych. & L.	Journal of Psychiatry and Law
J.Law & Health	Journal of Law and Health	J.Publ.L.	Journal of Public Law
J.Law, Econ. & Org.	Journal of Law, Economics and Organization	J.Quantitative Criminology	Journal of Quantitative Criminology
J.Law Reform	Journal of Law Reform	J.R.	Johnson (N.Y.)
J.Legal Educ.	Journal of Legal Education	J.Radio L.	Journal of Radio Law
J.Legal Hist.	Journal of Legal History	J.Real Est. Tax.	Journal of Real Estate Taxation
J.Legal Med.	Journal of Legal Medicine	J.Reprints Antitrust L. & Econ.	Journal of Reprints for Antitrust Law and Economics
J.Legal Prof.	Journal of the Legal Profession	J.S.Gr. (N.J.)	J.S. Green (N.J.)
J.Legal Stud.	Journal of Legal Studies	J.Soc.Welfare L.	Journal of Social Welfare Law
J.Legis.	Journal of Legislation	J.Soc'y Comp. Leg.	Journal of the Society of Comparative Legislation
J.Mar.J.Prac. & Proc.	John Marshall Journal of Practice and Procedure	J.Soc'y Pub. Tchrs.L.	Journal of the Society of Public Teachers of Law
J.Mar.L. & Com.	Journal of Maritime Law and Commerce	J.Space L.	Journal of Space Law
J.Mar.L.J.	John Marshall Law Journal	J.St.Tax'n	Journal of State Taxation
J.Mar.L.Q.	John Marshall Law Quarterly	J.Tax'n	Journal of Taxation

J.Transnat'l L. & Pol'y	Journal of Transnational Law and Policy	Johns. & H.	Johnson & Hemming's Chancery (Eng.)
J.World Trade L.	Journal of World Trade Law	Johns. & Hem.	Same
Jac.	Jacob's Chancery (Eng.)	Johns.Cas.	Johnson's Cases (N.Y.)
Jac. & W.	Jacob & Walker's Chancery (Eng.)	Johns.Ch.	Johnson's Chancery (Md.)
Jac. & Walk.	Same		Johnson's Chancery (N.Y.)
Jac.L.Dict.	Jacob's Law Dictionary	Johns.Ct.Err.	Johnson's Court of Errors (N.Y.)
Jack.	Jackson (Ga.)	Johns.Dec.	Johnson's Chancery Decisions (Md.)
Jack. & L.	Jackson & Lumpkin (Ga.)	Johns.N.Z.	Johnson's New Zealand Reports
Jack.Tex. App.	Jackson's Texas Appeals	Johns.U.S.	Johnson's United States Circuit Court Decisions
James	James' Reports (Nova Scotia)		
James. & Mont.	Jameson & Montagu's Bankruptcy (Eng.)	Jon. & L.	Jones & La Touche's Chancery (Ir.)
		Jon. & La T.	Same
Jap.Ann.Int'l L.	Japanese Annual of International Law	Jones	Jones (Ala.) Jones (Mo.)
Japan Ann.L. & Pol.	Japan Annual of Law and Politics		Jones (Pa.) Jones, T., King's Bench (Eng.)
Jebb	Jebb's Crown Cases (Ir.)		Jones, W., King's Bench (Eng.)
Jebb & B.	Jebb & Bourke's Queen's Bench (Ir.)		Jones' Exchequer (Ir.)
Jebb & S.	Jebb & Symes' Queen's Bench (Ir.)		Jones' Law or Equity Jones' Reports (Upper Can.)
Jebb & Sym.	Same		
Jebb C.C.	Jebb's Crown Cases (Ir.)	Jones & C.	Jones & Cary's Exchequer (Ir.)
Jeff.	Jefferson (Va.)		
Jenk.	Jenkins' Exchequer (Eng.)	Jones & L.	Jones & La Touche's Chancery (Ir.)
Jenk.Cent.	Same	Jones & La T.	Same
Jenks	Jenks (N.H.)	Jones & McM.	Jones & McMurtrie
Jenn.	Jennison (Mich.)	(Pa.)	(Pa.)
Jew.Y.B.Int'l L.	Jewish Yearbook of International Law	Jones & S.	Jones & Spencer's Superior Court (N.Y.)
Jo. & La T.	Jones & La Touche's Chancery (Ir.)	Jud.Conduct Rep.	Judicial Conduct Reporter
John.	Johnson (N.Y.)	Judd	Judd (Haw.)
	Johnson's Vice-Chancery (Eng.)	Judge Advoc.J.	Judge Advocate Journal
John Mar.J. Prac. & Proc.	John Marshall Journal of Practice and Procedure	Judges' J.	Judges' Journal
		Judge's J.	Judge's Journal
John Marsh. L.J.	John Marshall Law Journal	Judicature	Journal of the American Judicature Society
John Marsh. L.Q.	John Marshall Law Quarterly		Judicature
Johns.	Johnson (N.Y.)	Jur.	Jurist (Eng.)
	Johnson's Vice-Chancery (Eng.)	Jur. (N.S.)	Same, New Series
		Jurid.Rev.	Juridical Review

Jurimetrics J.	Jurimetrics Journal	Just.Syst.J.	Justice System Journal
Juris.	Jurisprudence		
Jurist	Jurist (Wash., D.C.)	Juv. & Fam.	Juvenile and Family
Just.Cas.	Justiciary Cases	Courts J.	Courts Journal
Just.L.R.	Justice's Law Reporter (Pa.)	Juv.Ct.J.	Juvenile Court Journal
Just.P.	Justice of the Peace and Local Government Review	Juv.Ct.Judges J.	Juvenile Court Judges Journal
		Juv.Just.	Juvenile Justice

K

K. & G.	Keane & Grant's Registration Appeal Cas	Keb.	Keble's King's Bench (Eng.)
K. & G.R.C.	Same	Keen	Keen's Rolls Court (Eng.)
K. & Gr.	Same	Keil.	Keilway's King's Bench (Eng.)
K.B.	Law Reports King's Bench (Eng.)	Kel.C.C.	Kelyng's Crown Cases (Eng.)
K.Counsel	King's Counsel	Kel.W.	Kelyng's Chancery (Eng.)
K.L.R.	Kenya Law Reports		
Kames Dec.	Kames' Decisions (Scot.)	Kellen	Kellen (Mass.)
Kames Elucid.	Kames' Elucidation (Scot.)	Kelly	Kelly (Ga.)
		Kelly & C.	Kelly & Cobb (Ga.)
Kames Rem. Dec.	Kames' Remarkable Decisions (Scot.)	Kenan	Kenan (N.C.)
Kames Sel. Dec.	Kames' Select Decisions (Scot.)	Keny.	Kenyon (Lord) King's Bench (Eng.)
Kan.	Kansas Reports		Kenyon's Notes of King's Bench Reports (Eng.)
Kan.App.	Kansas Appeals		
Kan.B.Ass'n J.	Kansas Bar Association Journal	Keny.Ch.	Kenyon's Chancery (Eng.)
Kan.C.L.Rep.	Kansas City Law Reporter	Kenya L.R.	Kenya Law Reports
Kan.City L.Rev.	Kansas City Law Review	Kerala L.J.	Kerala Law Journal
		Kern	Kern (Md.)
Kan.J.L. & Pub. Pol'y	Kansas Journal of Law and Public Policy	Kern.	Kernan (N.Y.)
		Kerr	Kerr (Ind.)
			Kerr (N.B.)
Kan.L.J.	Kansas Law Journal		Kerr's Civil Procedure (N.Y.)
Kan.L.Rev.	University of Kansas Law Review	Keyes	Keyes (N.Y.)
Kan.St.L.J.	Kansas State Law Journal	Kilk.	Kilkerran's Decisions (Scot.)
Karachi L.J.	Karachi Law Journal (Pak.)	Kilkerran	Same
Kay	Kay's Vice-Chancery (Eng.)	King	King's Civil Practice Cases (Colo.)
Kay & J.	Kay & Johnson's Chancery (Eng.)		King's Louisiana Annual
Ke.	Keen's Rolls Court (Eng.)	Kingston L.Rev.	Kingston Law Review
Keane & G.R.C.	Keane & Grant's Registration Appeal Cases (Eng.)	Kirby	Kirby (Conn.)
		Kn.P.C.	Knapp's Privy Council (Eng.)
Keane & Gr.	Same	Knapp	Same

Knapp & O.	Knapp & Ombler's Election Cases (Eng.)	Kulp	Kulp (Pa.)
Knight's Ind.	Knight's Industrial Reports	Kwansei Gak. L.Rev.	Kwansei Gaknin Law Review
Knowles	Knowles (R.I.)	Ky.	Kentucky Reports
Knox	Knox (N.S.W.)	Ky.Bench & B.	Kentucky Bench and Bar
Knox & F.	Knox & Fitzhardinge (N.S.W.)	Ky.Comment'r	Kentucky Commentator
Kobe U.L.Rev.	Kobe University Law Review	Ky.Dec.	Kentucky Decisions
Korea L.Rev.	Korea Law Review	Ky.L.J.	Kentucky Law Journal
Korean J.Comp.L.	Korean Journal of Comparative Law	Ky.L.R.	Kentucky Law Reporter
Korean J.Int'l L.	Korean Journal of International Law	Ky.L.Rptr.	Same
Korean L.	Korean Law	Ky.Op.	Kentucky Opinions
Kreider	Kreider (Wash.)	Ky.St.B.J.	Kentucky State Bar Journal
Kress	Kress (Pa.)	Kyoto L.Rev.	Kyoto Law Review

L

L. & B.Bull.	Weekly Law and Bank Bulletin (Ohio)	L.A.J.P.E.L.	Latin American Journal of Politics, Economics and Law
L. & C.	Lefroy and Cassels' Practice Cases (Ont.)	L.Advertiser	Law Advertiser
	Leigh & Cave's Crown Cases Reserved (Eng.)	L.Am.Soc'y	Law in American Society
		L.Book Adviser	Law Book Adviser
L. & Computer Tech.	Law and Computer Technology	L.C.	Lower Canada
L. & E.	English Law & Equity Reports (Boston)	L.C.D.	Ohio Lower Court Decisions
L. & E.Rep.	Law & Equity Reporter (N.Y.)	L.C.Jur.	Lower Canada Jurist
		L.C.L.J.	Lower Canada Law Journal
L. & Just.	Law and Justice	L.C.R.	Land Compensation Reports (1971–)
L. & Leg. GDR	Law and Legislation in the German Democratic Republic	L.C.Rep. S.Qu.	Lower Canada Reports Seignorial Questions
		L.Chron.	Law Chronicle
L. & Lib.	Law and Liberty	L.Chron. & L.Stud.Mag.	Law Chronicle and Law Students' Magazine
L. & M.	Lowndes & Maxwell, Bail Cases (Eng.)		
L. & Order	Law and Order	L.Chron. & L.Stud.Mag., (N.S.)	Same, New Series
L. & Psych. Rev.	Law and Psychology Review		
L. & Soc.Inquiry: J. Am. B. Found.	Law and Social Inquiry: Journal of the American Bar Foundation	L.Coach	Law Coach
		L.Comment'y	Law Commentary
		L.D.	Land Office Decisions (U.S.)
L.A.B.J.	Los Angeles Bar Journal	L.D.L.R.	Land Development Law Reporter
L.A.C.	Labour Arbitration Cases	L.East.Eur.	Law in Eastern Europe
L.A.G.Bull.	Legal Act Group Bulletin	L.Ed.	Lawyers' Edition, United States Su-

	preme Court Reports
L.Ed.2d	Same, Second Series
L.G.	Law Glossary
L.Gaz.	Law Gazette
L.Guard.	Law Guardian
L. in Soc'y	Law in Society
L. in Trans.Q.	Law in Transition Quarterly
L.Inst.J.	Law Institute Journal
L.Inst.J.Vict.	Law Institute Journal of Victoria
L.J.Adm.	Law Journal, Admiralty (Eng.)
L.J.Bankr.	Law Journal, Bankruptcy (Eng.)
L.J.C.P.	Law Journal, Common Pleas (Eng.)
L.J.C.P. (O.S.)	Same, Old Series
L.J.Ch.	Law Journal, Chancery, New Series (Eng.)
L.J.Ch.(O.S.)	Same, Old Series
L.J.Eccl.	Law Journal, Ecclesiastical (Eng.)
L.J.Exch.	Law Journal, Exchequer, New Series (Eng.)
L.J.Exch. (O.S.)	Same, Old Series
L.J.H.L.	Law Journal House of Lords, New Series (Eng.)
L.J.K.B.	Law Journal, King's Bench, New Series (Eng.)
L.J.M.C.	Law Journal, Magistrate Cases, New Series (Eng.)
L.J.M.C. (O.S.)	Same, Old Series (Eng.)
L.J.Mag.	Law Journal, New Series Common Law, Magistrates Cases
L.J.N.C.	Law Journal, Notes of Cases (Eng.)
L.J.O.S.	Law Journal, Old Series (1822–1830)
L.J.P. & M.	Law Journal, Probate & Matrimonial (Eng.)
L.J.P.C.	Law Journal, Privy Council (Eng.)
L.J.P.C. (N.S.)	Same, New Series

L.J.P.D. & Adm.	Law Journal, Probate, Divorce & Admiralty (Eng.)
L.J.Q.B.	Law Journal, Queen's Bench, New Series (Eng.)
L.Japan	Law in Japan
L.L.J.	Law Library Journal
L.Lib.	Law Librarian
L.Libr.J.	Law Library Journal
L.M. & P.	Lowndes, Maxwell & Pollock's Bail Cases (Eng.)
L.M.C.L.Q.	Lloyd's Maritime and Commercial Law Quarterly
L.Mag. & Rev.	Law Magazine and Review
L.N.T.S.	League of Nations Treaty Series
L.Notes Gen. Pract.	Law Notes for the General Practitioner
L.Off.Econ. & Mgt.	Law Office Economics and Management
L.Q.	Law Quarterly
L.Q.Rev.	Law Quarterly Review
L.R.	Law Recorder (Ir.)
	Law Reports (Eng.)
	Ohio Law Reporter
L.R. (N.S.)	Irish Law Recorder, New Series
L.R.A.	Lawyers' Reports Annotated (U.S.)
L.R.A. & E.	Law Reports, Admiralty & Ecclesiastical (Eng.)
L.R.A. (N.S.)	Lawyers' Reports Annotated, New Series (U.S.)
L.R.App.Cas.	Law Reports, House of Lords Appeal Cases (Eng.)
L.R.C.C.	Law Reports, Crown Cases (Eng.)
L.R.C.C.R.	Law Reports, Crown Cases Reserved (Eng.)
L.R.C.P.	Law Reports, Common Pleas Cases (Eng.)
L.R.C.P.D.	Law Reports, Common Pleas Division (Eng.)

L.R.Ch.	Law Reports, Chancery Appeal Cases (Eng.)	L.T.R. (N.S.)	Law Times, Reports, New Series (Eng.)
		L.T.Rep.N.S.	Same
L.R.Ch.D.	Law Reports, Chancery Division (Eng.)	L.Teacher	Law Teacher
		L.Trans.Q.	Law in Transition Quarterly
L.R.Eq.	Law Reports, Equity Cases (Eng.)	La Raza L.J.	La Raza Law Journal
		La.	Louisiana Reports
L.R.Exch.	Law Reports, Exchequer Cases (Eng.)	La.Ann.	Louisiana Annual
		La.App.	Louisiana Appeals
L.R.Exch.D.	Law Reports, Exchequer Division (Eng.)	La.App. (Orleans)	Court of Appeal, Parish of Orleans
		La.B.J.	Louisiana Bar Journal
L.R.H.L.	Law Reports, House of Lords (English & Irish Appeal Cases)	La.L.J.	Louisiana Law Journal
		La.L.Rev.	Louisiana Law Review
L.R.H.L.Sc.	Law Reports, House of Lords (Scotch Appeal Cases)	La.T.R.	Martin's Louisiana Term Reports
L.R.Indian App.	Law Reports, Indian Appeals (Eng.)	Lab.	Labatt's District Court (Cal.)
L.R.Ir.	Law Reports (Ir.)	Lab. & Auto. Bull.	Labor and Automation Bulletin
L.R.N.S.W.	Law Reports, New South Wales	Lab.Arb.	Labor Arbitration Reports (BNA)
L.R.P. & D.	Law Reports, Probate & Divorce (Eng.)	Lab.L.J.	Labor Law Journal
L.R.P.C.	Law Reports, Privy Council (Eng.)	Lab.Law.	Labor Lawyer
		Lab.Rel.L.Letter	Labor Relations Law Letter
L.R.Q.B.	Law Reports, Queen's Bench (Eng.)	Lab.Rel.Rep.	Labor Relations Reporter
L.R.Q.B.Div.	Law Reports, Queen's Bench Division (Eng.)	Lack.Jur.	Lackawanna Jurist (Pa.)
		Lack.Leg.N.	Lackawanna Legal News (Pa.)
L.R.R.	Labor Relations Reporter	Lack.Leg.Rec.	Lackawanna Legal Record (Pa.)
L.R.R.M.	Labor Relations Reference Manual (BNA)	Lackawanna B.	Lackawanna Bar
L.R.S.A.	Law Reports, South Australia	Ladd	Ladd (N.H.)
		Lalor	Lalor's Supplement to Hill & Denio (N.Y.)
L.Record.	Law Recorder		
L.Rev.Dig.	Law Review Digest		
L.S.G.	Law Society Gazette (Eng.)	Lamar	Lamar (Fla.)
		Lamb	Lamb (Wis.)
L.Stud.Helper	Law Student's Helper	Lanc.Bar	Lancaster Bar (Pa.)
		Lanc.L.Rev.	Lancaster Law Review (Pa.)
L.Stud.J.	Law Students' Journal	Land & Water L.Rev.	Land and Water Law Review
L.T.	Law Times (Pa.)		
L.T. (N.S.)	Law Times, New Series (Eng.)	Land Dec.	Land Decisions (U.S.)
L.T. (O.S.)	Same, Old Series (Eng.)	Land Use & Env.L.Rev.	Land Use and Environment Law Review
L.T.G.F.Newsl.	Lawyers' Title Guaranty Funds Newsletter	Lane	Lane's Exchequer (Eng.)
		Lans.	Lansing (Mich.)

Latch	Latch's King's Bench (Eng.)	Law.Am.	Lawyer of the Americas
Lath.	Lathrop (Mass.)	Lawasia	Lawasia, Journal of the Law Association for Asia and the Western Pacific
Law & Bk. Bull.	Weekly Law and Bank Bulletin (Ohio)		
Law & Computer Tech.	Law and Computer Technology	Lawr.	Lawrence (Ohio)
Law & Contemp.Probs.	Law and Contemporary Problems	Lawrence	Same
		Lawyer & Banker	Lawyer and Banker and Central Law Journal
Law & Housing J.	Law and Housing Journal		
Law & Hum. Behav.	Law and Human Behavior	Lawyer's Med.J.	Lawyer's Medical Journal
Law & Phil.	Law & Philosophy	Ld.Raym.	Lord Raymond's King's Bench (Eng.)
Law & Pol'y Int'l Bus.	Law and Policy in International Business		
		Lea	Lea (Tenn.)
		Leach C.C.	Leach's Crown Cases, King's Bench (Eng.)
Law & Pol'y Q.	Law and Policy Quarterly		
Law & Psych. Rev.	Law and Psychology Review	League of Nations Off.J.	League of Nations Official Journal
Law & Soc. Ord.	Law and the Social Order, Arizona State Law Journal	Learn. & L.	Learning and the Law
		Lect.L.S.U.C.	Special Lectures of the Law Society of Upper Canada
Law & Soc'y Rev.	Law and Society Review		
Law Cases	Law Cases, William I to Richard I (Eng.) (Placita Anglo-Normannica)	Lee	Lee (Cal.)
		Lee Eccl.	Lee's Ecclesiastical (Eng.)
		Lee t.Hardw.	Lee tempore Hardwicke, King's Bench (Eng.)
Law.Committee News	Lawyers Committee News		
Law Inst.J.	Law Institute Journal	Leese	Leese (Neb.)
		Leg. & Ins.R.	Legal & Insurance Reporter (Pa.)
Law Libr.J.	Law Library Journal	Leg.Chron.	Legal Chronicle (Pa.)
Law.Med.J.	Lawyer's Medical Journal	Leg.Gaz.	Legal Gazette Reports (Pa.)
Law Notes	Law Notes	Leg.Int.	Legal Intelligencer (Pa.)
Law Q.Rev.	Law Quarterly Review		
Law Rep.	Law Reporter (Mass.) Law Reports (Eng.) (1865–1875)	Leg.Op.	Legal Opinions (Pa.)
		Leg.Rec.	Legal Record (Pa.)
		Leg.Rep.	Legal Reporter (Tenn.)
Law Rep. (N.S.)	Law Reports, New Series (N.Y.)	Leg.Rev.	Legal Review (Eng.)
Law Rev.J.	Law Review Journal	Legal Aspects Med.Prac.	Legal Aspects of Medical Practice
Law Soc'y Gaz.	Law Society Gazette (Toronto) Law Society's Gazette (London)	Legal Med. Ann.	Legal Medicine Annual
		Legal Med.Q.	Legal Medical Quarterly
Law Soc'y J.	Law Society Journal (Boston) Law Society Journal (N.S.W.)	Legal Obser.	Legal Observer
		Legal Res.J.	Legal Research Journal
Law.	Lawyer	Legal Resp. Child Adv. Protection	Legal Response: Child Advocacy and Protection
Law. & Magis.Mag.	Lawyer's and Magistrate's Magazine		

Legal Stud.Fo-rum	Legal Studies Forum	Ll.L.Rep.	Lloyd's List Reports (Eng.)
Legal Video Rev.	Legal Video Review	Lloyd's L.Rep.	Lloyd's Law Reports
Lehigh Co. L.J.	Lehigh County Law Journal (Pa.)	Lloyds Mar. & Com.L.Q.	Lloyds Maritime and Commercial Law Quarterly
Lehigh Val. L.R.	Lehigh Valley Law Reporter (Pa.)	Lloyd's Rep.	Lloyd's List Law Reports Admiralty
Leigh	Leigh (Pa.)	Local Ct. & Mun.Gaz.	Local Courts and Municipal Gazette
Leigh & C.	Leigh & Cave's Crown Cases (Eng.)	Local Gov't	Local Government and Magisterial Reports
Leigh & C.C.C.	Same		
Leo.	Leonard, King's Bench, Common Pleas, Exchequer (Eng.)	Local Gov't R.Austl.	Local Government Reports of Australia
Leon.	Same	Lock.Rev.Cas.	Lockwood's Reversed Cases (N.Y.)
Lester	Lester (Ga.)	Lofft	Lofft's King's Bench (Eng.)
Lester & B.	Lester & Butler's Supplement (Ga.)	Lois Rec.	Lois Recentes du Canada
Lev.	Leving, King's Bench, Common Pleas (Eng.)	London L.Rev.	City of London Law Review
Lew.C.C.	Lewin's Crown Cases (Eng.)	Long & R.	Long & Russell's Election Cases (Mass.)
Lewis	Lewis (Mo.)		
	Lewis (Nev.)	Long Beach B.Bull.	Long Beach Bar Bulletin
	Lewis' Kentucky Law Reporter	Longf. & T.	Longfield & Townsend's Exchequer (Ir.)
Lex & Sci.	Lex et Scientia		
Ley	Ley, King's Bench (Eng.)	Louisville Law.	Louisville Lawyer
	Common Pleas (Eng.)	Low.Can. Jurist	Lower Canada Jurist
	Exchequer (Eng.)		
	Court of Wards (Eng.)	Low.Can.L.J.	Lower Canada Law Journal
	Court of Star Chamber (Eng.)	Low.Can.R.	Lower Canadian Reports
Liberian L.J.	Liberian Law Journal	Lowell	Lowell (U.S.)
Life Cas.	Life, Health & Accident Cases (CCH)	Lower Ct.Dec.	Lower Court Decisions (Ohio)
Life Cas.2d	Same, Second Series	Loy.Cons. Prot.J.	Loyola of Los Angeles Consumer Protection Journal
Lincoln L.Rev.	Lincoln Law Review		
Liquor Liab.J.	Liquor Liability Journal	Loy. Consumer L. Rep.	Loyola of Los Angeles Consumer Law Reporter
Litig.	Litigation		
Livingston's M.L.Mag.	Livingston's Monthly Law Magazine	Loy.Dig.	Loyola Digest
Ll. & G.t.Pl.	Lloyd & Goold tempore Plunkett, Chancery (Ir.)	Loy. Ent.L. J.	Loyola of Los Angeles Entertainment Law Journal
Ll. & G.t.S.	Lloyd & Goold tempore Sugden, Chancery (Ir.)	Loy.L.A.Int'l & Comp.L.Ann.	Loyola of Los Angeles International & Comparative Law Annual
Ll. & W.	Lloyd & Welsby Mercantile Cases (Eng.)	Loy.L.A. Int'l & Comp.L.J.	Loyola of Los Angeles International and

	Comparative Law Journal	Lutw.	Lutwyche's Common Pleas (Eng.)
Loy.L.A.L. Rev.	Loyola of Los Angeles Law Review	Lutw.Reg.Cas.	Lutwyche's Registration Cases (Eng.)
Loy.L.Rev.	Loyola Law Review (New Orleans)	Luz.L.J.	Luzerne Law Journal (Pa.)
Loy.Law.	Loyola Lawyer	Luz.L.T.	Luzerne Law Times (Pa.)
Loy.U.Chi. L.J.	Loyola University of Chicago Law Journal	Luz.Leg.Obs.	Luzerne Legal Observer (Pa.)
Loy.U.L.J.	Same	Luz.Leg.Reg.	Luzerne Legal Register (Pa.)
Ludd.	Ludden (Me.)		
Lump.	Lumpkin (Ga.)	Lynd.	Lyndwoode, Provinciale (Eng.)
Lush.	Lushington's Admiralty (Eng.)	Lyne	Lyne's Chancery (Ir.)

M

M. & A.	Montagu & Ayrton's Bankruptcy Reports (Eng.)		Manning & Ryland's King's Bench (Eng.)
M. & Ayr.	Same		Moody & Robinson's Nisi Prius (Eng.)
M. & B.	Montague & Bligh's Bankruptcy (Eng.)	M. & R.M.C.	Manning & Ryland's Magistrates' Cases, King's Bench (Eng.)
M. & C.	Montague & Chitty's Bankruptcy (Eng.) Mylne & Craig's Chancery (Eng.)	M. & Rob.	Moody & Robinson's Nisi Prius (Eng.)
M. & Cht. Bankr.	Montague & Chitty's Bankruptcy (Eng.)	M. & S.	Manning & Scott's Common Pleas (Eng.)
M. & G.	Maddock & Geldhart's Chancery (Eng.) Manning & Granger's Common Pleas (Eng.)		Maule & Selwyn's King's Bench (Eng.) Moore & Scott's Common Pleas (Eng.)
M. & Gel.	Maddock & Geldhart's Chancery (Eng.)		
M. & Gord.	Macnaghten & Gordon's Chancery (Eng.)	M. & Scott	Moore & Scott's Common Pleas (Eng.)
M. & H.	Murphy & Hurlstone's Exchequer (Eng.)	M. & W.	Meeson & Welsby's Exchequer (Eng.)
M. & K.	Mylne & Keen's Chancery (Eng.)	M. & W.Cas.	Mining & Water Cases Annotated (U.S)
M. & M.	Moody & Malkin's Nisi Prius (Eng.)	M. & Y.	Martin & Yerger (Tenn.)
M. & McA.	Montague & McArthur's Bankruptcy (Eng.)	M.A.L.C.M.	Mercantile Adjuster and the Lawyer and Credit Man
M. & P.	Moore & Payne's Common Pleas & Exchequer (Eng.)	M.C.C.	Mixed Claims Commission Motor Carriers' Cases (I.C.C.)
M. & R.	Maclean & Robinson's Appeal Cases (Scot.)	M.C.J.	Michigan Civil Jurisprudence

M.C.R.	Montreal Condensed Reports (1854 & 1884)	McBride	McBride (Mo.)
		McC.	McCahon (Kan.)
		McCah.	Same
M.D.	Master's Decisions (Patents)	McCarter	McCarter's Chancery (N.J.)
M.F.P.D.	Modern Federal Practice Digest	McCartney	McCartney's Civil Procedure (N.Y.)
M.L.Dig. & R.	Monthly Digest & Reporter (Que.) (1892–1893)	McClell.	McClelland's Exchequer (Eng.)
		McClell. & Y.	McClelland & Younge's Exchequer (Eng.)
M.L.E.	Maryland Law Encyclopedia		
M.L.P.	Michigan Law and Practice	McCook	McCook (Ohio)
		McCord	McCord's Chancery (S.C.)
M.L.R.	Military Law Reporter		
		McCork.	McCorkle (N.C.)
M.L.R. (Q.B.)	Montreal Law Reports, Queen's Bench	McCrary	McCrary (U.S.)
		MacFarl.	MacFarlane, Jury Court (Scot.)
M.L.R. (S.C.)	Montreal Law Reports, Superior Court	McG.	McGloin (La.)
		McGill L.J.	McGill Law Journal
		Mackey	Mackey
M.P.L.R.	Municipal and Planning Law Reports (1976–)	MacL.	MacLean (U.S. Circuit Court)
		MacL. & R.	MacLean & Robinson's House of Lords (Eng.)
M.P.R.	Maritime Province Reports		
M.P.T.M.H.	Major Peace Treaties of Modern History (1648–1967)	McLean	McLean (U.S. Circuit Court)
		McMul.	McMullan's Chancery (S.C.)
M.V.R.	Motor Vehicle Reports (1978–)		McMullan's Law (S.C.)
Mac.	Macnaghten's Chancery (Eng.)	Macn. & G.	Macnaghten & Gordon's Chancery (Eng.)
Mac. & G.	Macnaghten & Gordon's Chancery (Eng.)		
		Macph.	Macpherson, Court of Sessions (Scot.)
Mac. & Rob.	Maclean & Robinson's Appeals, House of Lords (Scot.)	Macph.L. & B.	Macpherson, Lee & Bell (Scot.)
		Macph.S. & L.	Macpherson, Shireff & Lee (Scot.)
MacAll.	MacAllister (U.S.)		
MacAr.	MacArthur (D.C.) MacArthur's Patent Cases (D.C.)	Macq.	Macqueen's Scotch Appeal Cases
		Macr.	Macrory's Patent Cases (Eng.)
MacAr. & M.	MacArthur & Mackey's District of Columbia Supreme Court	McWillie	McWillie (Miss.)
		Madd.	Maddock (Mont.)
			Maddock's Chancery (Eng.)
MacAr. & Mackey	Same		
		Madd. & B.	Maddock & Back (Mont.)
MacAr.Pat. Cas.	MacArthur's Patent Cases (D.C.)	Madd.Ch.Pr.	Maddock's Chancery Practice (Eng.)
MacArth.	MacArthur (D.C.) MacArthur's Patent Cases (D.C.)	Madras L.J.	Madras Law Journal
		Madras L.J. Crim.	Madras Law Journal Criminal
MacArth. & M.	MacArthur & Mackey (D.C.)	Mag.	Magruder (Md.)

Mag. & Const.	Magistrate and Constable	Marq.L.Rev.	Marquette Law Review
Mag.Cas.	Magisterial Cases	Marq. Sports	Marquette Sports
Mag.Mun.	Magistrate and Municipal and Parochial Lawyer	L.J.	Law Journal
Par.Law.		Mars.Adm.	Marsden's Admiralty (Eng.)
Maine L.Rev.	Maine Law Review	Marsh.	Marshall (U.S.)
Mal.L.J	Malayan Law Journal		Marshall (Utah)
Mal.L.Rev.	Malaya Law Review		Marshall, A.K. (Ky.)
Malloy	Malloy's Chancery (Ir.)		Marshall, J.J. (Ky.)
Malone	Malone's Heiskell (Tenn.)		Marshall's Common Pleas (Eng.)
Man.	Manitoba Law	Mart. & Y.	Martin & Yerger (Tenn.)
	Manning (Mich.)	Martin	Martin (Ga.)
Man. & G.	Manning & Granger's Common Pleas (Eng.)		Martin (Ind.)
			Martin (La.)
Man. & Ry.	Manning & Ryland's		Martin (U.S.)
Mag.	Magistrates' Cases (Eng.)		Martin's Decisions (Law) (N.C.)
		Martin Mining	Martin Mining Cases
Man. & S.	Manning & Scott's Common Bench (Old Series) (Eng.)		Martin's New Series (La.)
		Marv.	Marvel (Del.)
Man.B.News	Manitoba Bar News	Mason	Mason (U.S.)
Man.G. & S.	Manning, Granger & Scott's Common Bench (Eng.)	Mass.	Massachusetts Reports
		Mass.App.	Massachusetts Appellate Decisions
Man.Gr. & S.	Same	Dec.	
Man.L.J.	Manitoba Law Journal	Mass.App.	Massachusetts Appellate Division Reports
		Div.	
Man.t.Wood	Manitoba tempore Wood	Mass.App.	Massachusetts Appeals Court Reports
Man.Unrep.	Manning's Unreported Cases (La.)	Rep.	
Cas.		Mass.L.Q.	Massachusetts Law Quarterly
Mann.	Manning (Mich.)		
Mann. & G.	Manning & Granger's Common Pleas (Eng.)	Mass.L.Rev.	Massachusetts Law Review
Mansf.	Mansfield (Ark.)	Mathews	Mathews (W.Va.)
Manson	Manson's Bankruptcy (Eng.)	Matson	Matson (Conn.)
		Md.	Maryland Reports
Mar.L.Cas.	Maritime Law Cases, New Series	Md.App.	Maryland Appellate Reports
(N.S.)			
Mar.Law.	Maritime Lawyer	Md.B.J.	Maryland Bar Journal
Mar.N. & Q.	Maritime Notes and Queries		
		Md.Ch.	Maryland Chancery
Mar.Prov.	Maritime Provinces Reports (Can.)	Md.J.	Maryland Journal of Contemporary Legal Issues
		Contemp. Legal Issues	
March	March's King's Bench (Eng.)	Md. J. Int'l L.	Maryland Journal of International Law and Trade
Marijuana	Marijuana Review	& Trade	
Rev.			
Maritime L.J.	Maritime Law Journal	Md.L.F.	Maryland Law Forum
Mark's &	Mark's & Sayre's (Ala.)	Md.L.Rec.	Maryland Law Record
Sayre's			

Md.L.Rep.	Maryland Law Reporter	Mich.St.B.J.	Michigan State Bar Journal
Md.L.Rev.	Maryland Law Review	Mich.T.	Michaelmas Term (Eng.)
Me.	Maine Reports	Michie's Jur.	Michie's Jurisprudence of Va. and W.Va.
Me.L.Rev.	Maine Law Review		
Mean's	Mean's Reports (Kan.)	Mid.East L.Rev.	Middle East Law Review
Med.L. & Pub. Pol.	Medicine, Law and Public Policy	Mil.L.Rev.	Military Law Review
Med.-Legal Crim.Rev.	Medico-Legal and Criminological Review	Miles	Miles (Pa.) Miles' Philadelphia District Court
Med.-Legal J.	Medico-Legal Journal	Mill Const.	Mill's Constitutional Reports (S.C.)
Med.-Legal Soc'y Trans.	Medico-Legal Society Transactions	Mill.Dec.	Miller's Decisions (U.S.)
Med.Sci. & L.	Medicine, Science and the Law	Mills	Mills, Surrogate (N.Y.)
Med.Trial Tech.Q.	Medical Trial Technique Quarterly	Milw.	Milward's Ecclesiastical (Ir.)
Medd.	Meddaugh (Mich.)	Min.	Minor (Ala.)
Media L.Notes	Media Law Notes	Minn.	Minnesota Reports
Medico-Legal J.	Medico-Legal Journal	Minn.Cont. L.Ed.	Minnesota Continuing Legal Education
Meg.	Megone Company Cases (Eng.)		
Meigs	Meigs (Tenn.)	Minn.Cont.Legal Ed.	Same
Melanesian L.J.	Melanesian Law Journal (Papua N.G.)	Minn.L.Rev.	Minnesota Law Review
Melb.U.L. Rev.	Melbourne University Law Review	Misc.	Miscellaneous (N.Y.)
		Misc.Dec.	Ohio Miscellaneous Decisions
Mem.L.J.	Memphis Law Journal (Tenn.)	Miss.	Mississippi Reports
Mem.St.U.L. Rev.	Memphis State University Law Review	Miss.C.L.Rev.	Mississippi College Law Review
Menken	Menken's Civil Procedure (N.Y.)	Miss.Dec.	Mississippi Decisions (Jackson)
Mercer Beasley L.Rev.	Mercer Beasley Law Review	Miss.L.J.	Mississippi Law Journal
Mercer L.Rev.	Mercer Law Review	Miss.St.Cas.	Mississippi State Cases
Meridith Lect.	W.C.J. Meredith Memorial Lectures	Mister	Mister (Mo.)
Meriv.	Merivale's Chancery (Eng.)	Mitchell's Mar. Reg.	Mitchell's Maritime Register
Met.	Metcalf (Ky.) Metcalf (Mass.)	Ml.	Miller (Law) (Md.)
		Mo.	Missouri Reports
Metc.	Same	Mo.A.R.	Missouri Appellate Reporter
Miami L.Q.	Miami Law Quarterly		
Mich.	Michigan Reports	Mo.App.	Missouri Appeals
Mich.App.	Michigan Court of Appeals Reports	Mo.B.J.	Missouri Bar Journal
		Mo.Dec.	Missouri Decisions
Mich. J. Int'l L.	Michigan Journal of International Law	Mo.J.Dispute Res.	Missouri Journal of Dispute Resolution
Mich.L.Rev.	Michigan Law Review	Mo.L.Rev.	Missouri Law Review
		Moak	Moak (Eng.)
Mich.N.P.	Michigan Nisi Prius	Mod.	Modern (Eng.)

Mod.L. & Soc'y	Modern Law and Society		Moore (Ark.)
			Moore (Tex.)
Mod.L.Rev.	Modern Law Review	Moore & S.	Moore & Scott's Common Pleas (Eng.)
Mod.Pract. Comm.	Modern Practice Commentator		
Moll.	Molloy's Chancery (Ir.)	Moore & W.	Moore & Walker (Tex.)
Mon.	B. Monroe (Ky.) T.B. Monroe (Ky.)	Moore B.B.	Moore's King's Bench (Eng.)
Monash U.L. Rev.	Monash University Law Review	Moore C.P.	Moore's Common Pleas (Eng.)
Mont.	Montana Reports	Moore Indian App.	Moore's Indian Appeals (Eng.)
Mont. & Ayr.	Montagu & Ayrton's Bankruptcy (Eng.)	Moore P.C.C.	Moore's Privy Council Cases (Eng.)
Mont. & M.	Montagu & McArthur's Bankruptcy (Eng.)	Morg.	Morgan's Chancery Acts & Orders (Eng.)
Mont.L.Rev.	Montana Law Review	Morr.	Morrill's Bankruptcy Cases (Eng.)
Mont.Super.	Montreal Law Reports (Superior Court)	Morris (Cal.)	
		Morris (Iowa)	
Month.Dig. Tax Articles	Monthly Digest of Tax Articles	Morris (Miss.)	
Month.L.J.	Monthly Journal of Law (Wash.)	Morr.St.Cas.	Morris State Cases (Miss.)
Month.L.Mag.	Monthly Law Magazine (London)	Morr.Trans.	Morrison's Transcript United States Supreme Court Decisions
Month.L.Rep.	Monthly Law Reporter (Boston) Monthly Law Reports (Can.)		
		Morris.	Morrissett (Ala.)
Month.L.Rev.	Monthly Law Review	Morrow	Morrow (Ore.)
Month.Leg. Exam.	Monthly Legal Examiner (N.Y.)	Morse Exch. Rep.	Morse's Exchequer Reports (Can.)
Month.West. Jur.	Monthly Western Journal (Bloomington, Ind.)	Mosely	Mosely's Chancery (Eng.)
Montr.Cond. Rep.	Montreal Condensed Reports	Moult.Ch.	Moulton's Chancery Practice (N.Y.)
Montr.Leg.N.	Montreal Legal News	Mun.	Munford (Va.)
Montr.Q.B.	Montreal Law Reports, Queen's Bench	Mun.Att'y	Municipal Attorney
		Mun.Corp. Cas.	Municipal Corporation Cases
Moo.C.C.	Moody's Crown Cases Reserved (Eng.)	Mun.L.Ct. Dec.	Municipal Law Court Decisions
Moo.P.C.	Moore, Privy Council	Mun.L.J.	Municipal Law Journal
Moo.P.C. (N.S.)	Moore, New Series	Mun.Ord. Rev.	Municipal Ordinance Review
Mood. & Mack.	Moody & Mackin's Nisi Prius (Eng.)	Mun.Rep.	Municipal Reports (Can.)
Mood. & Malk.	Moody & Malkin's Nisi Prius (Eng.)	Munf.	Munford (Va.)
Mood. & Rob.	Moody & Robinson's Nisi Prius (Eng.)	Munic. & P.L.	Municipal & Parish Law Cases (Eng.)
Moody Cr.C.	Moody's Crown Cases Reserved (Eng.)	Mur.	Murray's New South Wales Reports
Moon	Moon (Ind.)		Murray's Scotch Jury Court Reports
Moore	Moore (Ala.)		

Mur. & H.	Murphy & Hurlstone's Exchequer (Eng.)	Myer Fed. Dec.	Myer's Federal Decisions
Mur. & Hurl.	Same	Myl. & C.	Mylne & Craig's Chancery (Eng.)
Murph.	Murphy (N.C.)	Myl. & Cr.	Same
Murph. & H.	Murphy & Hurlstone's Exchequer (Eng.)	Myl. & K.	Mylne & Keen's Chancery (Eng.)
Murr.	Murray's Scotch Jury Court Reports	Mylne & K.	Same
		Myr.	Myrick's Probate (Cal.)
Murr.Over. Cas.	Murray's Overruled Cases	Myr.Prob.	Same
		Myrick (Cal.)	Same
		Mysore L.J.	Mysore Law Journal

N

N. & H.	Nott & Huntington's U.S. Court of Claims	N.C.J.Int'l L. & Com. Reg.	North Carolina Journal of International Law and Commercial Regulation
N. & Dr.	Neville & Manning's King's Bench (Eng.)	N.C.L.Rev.	North Carolina Law Review
N. & Mc.	Nott & McCord (S.C.)	N.C.T.Rep.	North Carolina Term Reports
N. & McC.	Same		
N. & Macn.	Nevile & Macnamara Railway & Canal Cases (Eng.)	N.Cent. School L.Rev.	North Central School Law Review
		N.Chipm.	North Chipman (Vt.)
N. & P.	Nevile & Perry's King's Bench (Eng.)	N.D.	North Dakota Reports
NACCA L.J.	National Association of Claimant's Compensation Attorneys Law Journal	N.D.J.Legis.	North Dakota Journal of Legislation
		N.D.L.Rev.	North Dakota Law Review
N.Atlantic Reg.Bus. L.Rev.	North Altantic Regional Business Law Review	N.E.	North Eastern Reporter
N.B.	New Brunswick	N.E.2d	Same, Second Series
N.B.Eq.	New Brunswick Equity	N.Eng.J.Prison L.	New England Journal on Prison Law
N.B.Rep.	New Brunswick Reports	N.Eng.L.Rev.	New England Law Review
N.Benl.	New Benloe, King's Bench (Eng.)	N.H.	New Hampshire Reports
N.C.	North Carolina Reports	N.H.B.J.	New Hampshire Bar Journal
N.C.App.	North Carolina Court of Appeals Reports	N.I.M.L.O. Mun.L.Rev.	N.I.M.L.O. Municipal Law Review
N.C.C.	New Chancery Cases (Eng.)	N.Ill.U.L. Rev.	Northern Illinois University Law Review
N.C.C.A.	Negligence & Compensation Cases Annotated	N.Ir.L.Q.	Northern Ireland Legal Quarterly
		N.Ir.L.R.	Northern Ireland Law Reports
N.C.Cent.L.J.	North Carolina Central Law Journal	N.J.	New Jersey Reports
		N.J.Eq.	New Jersey Equity
N.C.Conf.	North Carolina Conference Reports	N.J.L.	New Jersey Law
		N.J.L.J.	New Jersey Law Journal

N.J.L.Rev.	New Jersey Law Review	N.S.Wales L.R.Eq.	New South Wales Law Reports Equity
N.J.Law	New Jersey Law Reports	N.W.	North Western Reporter
N.J.Misc.	New Jersey Miscellaneous Reports	N.W.2d	Same, Second Series
N.J.St.B.J.	New Jersey State Bar Journal	N.W.T.L.R.	North West Territories Law Reports
N.J.Super.	New Jersey Superior Court and County Court Reports	N.W.Terr.	Northwest Territories Supreme Court Reports
N.Ky.L.Rev.	Northern Kentucky Law Review	N.Y.	New York Reports
N.Ky.St.L.F.	Northern Kentucky State Law Forum	N.Y.2d	New York Court of Appeals Reports, Second Series
NLADA Brief.	National Legal Aid and Defendant's Association Brief-case	N.Y.Anno. Cas.	New York Annotated Cases
		N.Y.Anno. Dig.	New York Annotated Digest
N.L.R.B.	National Labor Relations Board Reports	N.Y.App.Div.	New York Supreme Court Appellate Division Reports
N.M.	New Mexico Reports	N.Y.Cas.Err.	New York Cases in Error (Claim Cases)
N.M.L.R.	Nigerian Monthly Law Reports		
N.M.L.Rev.	New Mexico Law Review	N.Y.Ch.Sent.	Chancery Sentinel (N.Y.)
NOLPE Sch. L.J.	National Organization on Problems of Education School Law Journal	N.Y.City Ct.	New York City Court
		N.Y.City Ct. Supp.	New York City Court Supplement
NOLPE School L. Rep.	National Organization on Problems of Education School Law Reporter	N.Y.City H.Rec.	New York City Hall Recorder
		N.Y.Civ.Pro.	New York Civil Procedure
N.P.	Ohio Nisi Prius Reports	N.Y.Civ. Pro.R. (N.S.)	Same, New Series
N.P. (N.S.)	Same, New Series	N.Y.Civ.Proc.	New York Civil Procedure
N.P. & G.T. Rep.	Nisi Prius & General Term Reports (Ohio)	N.Y.Civ.Proc. (N.S.)	Same, New Series
N.R.A.B. (4th Div.)	National Railroad Adjustment Board Awards	N.Y.Code Rep.	New York Code Reporter
		N.Y.Code Rep. (N.S.)	New York Code Reports, New Series
N.R.	National Reporter (1974–)	N.Y.Cond.	New York Condensed Reports
N.S.	Nova Scotia	N.Y.Cont. L.Ed.	New York Continuing Legal Education
N.S.Dec.	Nova Scotia Decisions		
N.S.R.	Nova Scotia Reports	N.Y.Cont. Legal Ed.	Same
N.S.W.	New South Wales State Reports	N.Y.County Law. Ass'n B.Bull.	New York County Lawyers Association Bar Bulletin
N.S.W.St.R.	New South Wales State Reports	N.Y.Cr.	New York Criminal
N.S.Wales	New South Wales	N.Y.Crim.	New York Criminal Reports
N.S.Wales L.	New South Wales Law		

N.Y.Daily L.Gaz.	New York Daily Law Gazette	N.Y.St.	New York State Reporter
N.Y.Daily L.Reg.	New York Daily Law Register	N.Y.St.B.J.	New York State Bar Journal
N.Y.Dep't R.	New York Department Reports	N.Y.Super.	New York Superior Court
N.Y.Elec.Cas.	New York Election Cases	N.Y.Supp.	New York Supplement
N.Y.Jud. Repos.	New York Judicial Repository	N.Y.U.Conf. Charitable	New York University Conference on Charitable Foundations Proceedings
N.Y.Jur.	New York Jurisprudence		
	New York Jurist	N.Y.U.Conf. Lab.	New York University Conference on Labor
N.Y.L.Cas.	New York Leading Cases		
N.Y.L.F.	New York Law Forum	N.Y.U. Envtl. L.J.	New York University Environmental Law Journal
N.Y.L.J.	New York Law Journal	N.Y.U. Inst. on Fed. Tax.	New York University Institute on Federal Taxation
N.Y.L.Rec.	New York Law Record		
N.Y.L.Rev.	New York Law Review	N.Y.U.Intra.L.Rev.	New York Intramural Law Review
N.Y.L.Sch. Int'l L.Soc'y J.	New York Law School International Law Society Journal	N.Y.U.J.Int'l L. & Pol.	New York University Journal of International Law and Politics
N.Y.L.Sch.J. Int'l & Comp.L.	New York Law School Journal of International and Comparative Law	N.Y.U.L.Center Bull.	New York University Law Center Bulletin
		N.Y.U.L.Q. Rev.	New York University Law Quarterly Review
N.Y.L.Sch.J. Hum.Rts.	New York Law School Journal of Human Rights	N.Y.U.L.Rev.	New York University Law Review
N.Y.L.Sch. L.Rev.	New York Law School Law Review	N.Y.U.Rev.L. & Soc. Change	New York University Review of Law and Social Change
N.Y.Leg.N.	New York Legal News	N.Y.Wkly. Dig.	New York Weekly Digest
N.Y.Leg.Obs.	New York Legal Observer	N.Z.L.J.	New Zealand Law Journal
N.Y.Misc.	New York Miscellaneous Reports	N.Z.L.R.	New Zealand Law Reports
N.Y.Misc.2d	Same, Second Series	N.Z.U.L.Rev.	New Zealand Universities Law Review
N.Y.Month. L.Rep.	New York Monthly Law Reports	Napt.	Napton (Mo.)
N.Y.Mun. Gaz.	New York Municipal Gazette	Napton	Same
N.Y.P.R.	New York Practice Reports	Narcotics Control Dig.	Narcotics Control Digest
N.Y.Pr.Rep.	Same	Narcotics L.Bull.	Narcotics Law Bulletin
N.Y.Rec.	New York Record		
N.Y.S.	New York Supplement	Nat.Bankr. Reg.	National Bankruptcy Register (U.S.)
N.Y.S.2d	Same, Second Series	Nat.Corp. Rep.	National Corporation Reporter
N.Y.Sea Grant L. & Pol'y J.	New York Sea Grant Law and Policy Journal	Nat. Jewish L. Rev.	National Jewish Law Review

Nat.L.F.	Natural Law Forum	Negotiation J.	Negotiation Journal
Nat.L.Rep.	National Law Reporter	Negro.Cas.	Bloomfield's Manumission (N.J.)
Nat.Munic. Rev.	National Municipal Review	Nels.	Nelson's Chancery (Eng.)
Nat.Reg.	National Register (Mead)	Nels.Abr.	Nelson's Abridgment (Lag.)
Nat.Resources & Env't	Natural Resources & Environment	Neth.Int'l L.Rev.	Netherlands International Law Review
Nat.Resources J.	Natural Resources Journal	Neth.Y.B. Int'l.Law	Netherlands Yearbook of International Law
Nat.Resources L.Newsl.	Natural Resources Law Newsletter	Nev.	Nevada Reports
		Nev. & P.	Neville & Perry's King's Bench (Eng.)
Nat.Resources Law.	Natural Resources Lawyer	Nev.St.Bar J.	Nevada State Bar Journal
Nat'l Black L.J.	National Black Law Journal	New Eng.L. Rev.	New England Law Review
Nat'l Civic Rev.	National Civic Review	New Eng.J. Prison L.	New England Journal of Prison Law
Nat'l Income Tax Mag.	National Income Tax Magazine	New L.J.	New Law Journal
Nat'l J.Crim. Def.	National Journal of Criminal Defense	New Rep.	New Reports in All Courts (Eng.)
Nat'l Legal Mag.	National Legal Magazine	New Sess. Cas.	New Session Cases (Eng.)
Nat'l Mun. Rev.	National Municipal Review	New Yugo.L.	New Yugoslav Law
		New Zeal.L.	New Zealand Law
		New.	Newell (Ill.)
Nat'l Prison Project J.	National Prison Project Journal	Newb.Adm.	Newberry's Admiralty (U.S.)
Nat'l School L.Rptr.	National School Law Reporter	Newf.S.Ct.	Newfoundland Supreme Court Decisions
Nat'l Taiwan U.L.J.	National Taiwan University Law Journal	Newfoundl.	Newfoundland
		Nfld. & P.E.I.R.	Newfoundland and Prince Edward Island Reports (1971)
Nat'l Tax J.	National Tax Journal		
Neb.	Nebraska Reports		
Neb. (Unoff.)	Nebraska Unofficial Reports	Nfld.R.	Newfoundland Reports
Neb.L.Bull.	Nebraska Law Bulletin	Nfld.Sel.Cas.	Tucker's Select Cases (Nfld.) (1817–1828)
Neb.L.Rev.	Nebraska Law Review	Nigeria L.R.	Nigeria Law Reports
		Nigerian Ann. Int'l L.	Nigerian Annual of International Law
Neb.St.B.J.	Nebraska State Bar Journal	Nigerian L.J.	Nigerian Law Journal
Negl. & Comp. Cas. Ann.	Negligence & Compensation Cases Annotated	Noise Reg. Rep.	Noise Regulation Reporter (BNA)
Negl. & Comp. Cas. Ann. (N.S.)	Same, New Series	Nolan	Nolan, Magistrate Cases (Eng.)
Negl. & Comp. Cas. Ann.3d	Same, Third Series	Norc.	Norcross (Nev.)
		Norris	Norris (Pa.)
		North	North (Ill.)
		North & G.	North & Guthrie (Mo.)
Negl.Cas.	Negligence Cases (CCH)	North.	Northington's Chancery (Eng.)
Negl.Cas.2d	Same, Second Series		

North.Co.   Northampton County Legal News (Pa.)

Northrop U.L.J.Aerospace Energy & Env.   Northrop University Law Journal of Aerospace, Energy and the Environment

Northumb. Co.Leg. News   Northumberland County Legal News (Pa.)

Northumb. Legal J.   Northumberland Legal Journal

Notes of Cas.   Notes of Cases (Eng.)

Notre Dame Int'l & Comp. L.J.   Notre Dame International and Comparative Law Journal

Notre Dame J.L.Ethics & Pub.Pol'y   Notre Dame Journal of Law, Ethics & Public Policy

Notre Dame L. Rev.   Notre Dame Law Review

Notre Dame Law.   Notre Dame Lawyer

Nova L.J.   Nova Law Journal

Nova L.Rev.   Nova Law Review

Noy   Noy, King's Bench (Eng.)

Nuclear L.Bull.   Nuclear Law Bulletin

Nuclear Reg. Rep.   Nuclear Regulation Reporter (CCH)

Nw.J.Int'l L. & Bus.   Northwestern Journal of International Law & Business

Nw.U.L.Rev.   Northwestern University Law Review

O

O.   Ohio
Oklahoma
Oregon

O.A.   Ohio Appellate Report

O.A.R.   Same
Ontario Appeal Reports

O.App.   Ohio Appellate

O.B. & F.N.Z.   Olliver, Bell & Fitzgerald's New Zealand Reports

O.Ben.   Old Benloe, Common Pleas (Eng.)

O.Benl.   Same

O.Bridgm.   Orlando Bridgman, Common Pleas (Eng.)

O.C.A.   Ohio Courts of Appeals Reports

O.C.C.   Ohio Circuit Court Decisions
Ohio Circuit Court Reports

O.C.C. (N.S.)   Ohio Circuit Court Reports, New Series

O.C.D.   Ohio Circuit Decisions

O.C.S.   Office of Contract Settlement Decisions

O.D.   Office Decisions (I.R.B.)
Ohio Decisions

O.D.C.C.   Ohio Circuit Decisions

O.D.N.P.   Ohio Decisions, Nisi Prius

O.Dec.Rep.   Ohio Decisions Reprint

O.E.M.   Office of Emergency Management

O.F.D.   Ohio Federal Decisions

O.G.   Official Gazette, United States Patent Office

O.G.Pat.Off.   Same

O.L.A.   Ohio Law Abstract

O.L.B.   Weekly Law Bulletin (Ohio)

O.L.D.   Ohio Lower Court Decisions

O.L.J.   Ohio Law Journal

O.L.Jour.   Same

O.L.N.   Ohio Legal News

O.L.R.   Ohio Law Reporter
Ontario Law Reports (1901–1930)

O.L.R.B.   Ontario Labour Relations Board Monthly Report

O.L.Rep.   Ohio Law Reporter

O.Legal News   Ohio Legal News

O.Lower D.   Ohio (Lower) Decisions

O.M.B.R.   Ontario Municipal Board Reports (1973–)

O.N.P.	Ohio, Nisi Prius	Oh.L.Bull.	Ohio Law Bulletin
O.N.P. (N.S.)	Same, New Series	Oh.L.Ct.D.	Ohio Lower Court
O.O.	Ohio Opinions		Decisions
O.R.	Ontario Reports	Oh.L.J.	Ohio Law Journal
	(1882–1900)	Oh.L.Rep.	Ohio Law Reporter
	Same (1931 to present)	Oh.Leg.N.	Ohio Legal News
		Oh.N.P.	Ohio Nisi Prius
O.S.	Ohio State Reports	Oh.N.P. (N.S.)	Same, New Series
O.S.C.D.	Ohio Supreme Court	Oh.Prob.	Ohio Probate
	Decisions (Unreported Cases)	Oh.S. & C.P.	Ohio Superior & Common Pleas Decisions
O.S.H.Dec.	Occupational, Safety, and Health Decisions (CCH)	Oh.S.C.D.	Ohio Supreme Court Decisions (Unreported Cases)
O.S.H.Rep.	Occupational, Safety, and Health Reporter (BNA)	Oh.St.	Ohio State Reports
		Ohio	Ohio Reports (1821–1852)
O.S.L.J.	Ohio State Law Journal	Ohio (N.S.)	Same, New Series
O.S.U.	Ohio Supreme Court Decisions, Unreported Cases	Ohio App.	Ohio Appellate Reports
		Ohio App.2d	Same, Second Series
O.St.	Ohio State Reports	Ohio Bar	Ohio State Bar Association Reports
O.Su.	Ohio Supplement		
O.W.N.	Ontario Weekly Notes (1909–1932)	Ohio C.A.	Ohio Courts of Appeals Reports
	Same (1933–1962)	Ohio C.C.	Ohio Circuit Court Reports
O.W.R.	Ontario Weekly Reporter	Ohio C.C.R.	Same
Obiter Dictum	Obiter Dictum	Ohio C.C.R. (N.S.)	Same, New Series
Ocean Dev. & Int'l L.J.	Ocean Development and International Law Journal	Ohio C.Dec.	Ohio Circuit Decisions
Odeneal	Odeneal (Ore.)	Ohio Cir.Ct.	Ohio Circuit Court Decisions
Off.Brev.	Officina Brevium		
Off.Gaz.	Official Gazette, United States Patent Office	Ohio Cir.Ct. (N.S.)	Ohio Circuit Court Reports, New Series
Officer	Officer (Minn.)	Ohio Cir.Ct.R.	Ohio Circuit Court Reports
Official Rep. Ill.Courts Commission	Official Reports: Illinois Courts Commission	Ohio Cir.Ct.R. (N.S.)	Same, New Series
Ogd.	Ogden (La.)	Ohio Ct.App.	Ohio Courts of Appeals Reports
Oh.	Ohio Reports (1821–1852)		
		Ohio Dec.	Ohio Decisions
Oh.A.	Ohio Court of Appeals	Ohio Dec. Repr.	Same, Reprint
Oh.Cir.Ct.	Ohio Circuit Court	Ohio F.Dec.	Ohio Federal Decisions
Oh.Cir.Ct. (N.S.)	Same, New Series		
Oh.Cir.Dec.	Ohio Circuit Decisions	Ohio Fed.Dec.	Same
		Ohio Jur.	Ohio Jurisprudence
Oh.Dec.	Ohio Decisions	Ohio Jur.2d	Same, Second Edition
Oh.Dec. (Reprint)	Same (Reprint)	Ohio L.Abs.	Ohio Law Abstract
		Ohio L.B.	Weekly Law Bulletin (Ohio)
Oh.F.Dec.	Ohio Federal Decisions	Ohio L.J.	Ohio Law Journal
Oh.Jur.	Ohio Jurisprudence	Ohio L.R.	Ohio Law Reporter

Ohio Law Abst.	Ohio Law Abstract	(Sw.Legal Fdn.)	(Southwestern Legal Foundation)
Ohio Law Bull.	Weekly Law Bulletin (Ohio)	Oil & Gas Rptr.	Oil and Gas Reporter
Ohio Law J.	Ohio Law Journal	Oil & Gas Tax Q.	Oil and Gas Tax Quarterly
Ohio Law R.	Ohio Law Reporter	Okla.	Oklahoma Reports
Ohio Leg.N.	Ohio Legal News	Okla.B.Ass'n J.	Oklahoma Bar Association Journal
Ohio Legal N.	Same		
Ohio Lower Dec.	Ohio Lower Court Decisions	Okla.City U.L.Rev.	Oklahoma City University Law Review
Ohio Misc.	Ohio Miscellaneous Reports	Okla.Cr.	Oklahoma Criminal
Ohio Misc. Dec.	Ohio Miscellaneous Decisions	Okla.Crim.	Oklahoma Criminal Reports
Ohio N.P.	Ohio Nisi Prius Reports	Okla.L.J.	Oklahoma Law Journal
Ohio N.P. (N.S.)	Same, New Series	Okla.L.Rev.	Oklahoma Law Review
Ohio N.U. L.Rev.	Ohio Northern University Law Review	Okla.S.B.J.	Oklahoma State Bar Journal
Ohio Op.	Ohio Opinions	Olcott	Olcott (U.S.)
Ohio Op.2d	Same, Second Series	Oliv.B. & L.	Oliver, Beavan & Lefroy, English Railway & Canal Cases
Ohio Prob.	Goebel's Ohio Probate Reports		
Ohio R.Cond.	Ohio Reports Condensed	Olliv.B. & F.	Olliver, Bell & Fitzgerald (New Zealand)
Ohio S. & C.P.Dec.	Ohio Superior & Common Pleas Decisions	O'M. & H.El. Cas.	O'Malley & Hardcastle, Election Cases (Eng.)
Ohio S.U.	Ohio Supreme Court Decisions (Unreported Cases)	Ont.	Ontario Reports
		Ont.A.	Ontario Appeals
		Ont.El.Cas.	Ontario Election Cases
Ohio St.	Ohio State Reports		
Ohio St. (N.S.)	Same, New Series	Ont.Elec.	Same
Ohio St.2d	Same, Second Series	Ont.L.	Ontario Law
Ohio St.J. on Disp.Resol.	Ohio State Journal on Dispute Resolution	Ont.L.J.	Ontario Law Journal
		Ont.L.J. (N.S.)	Same, New Series
		Ont.L.R.	Ontario Law Reports
		Ont.Pr.	Ontario Practice
Ohio St.L.J.	Ohio State Law Journal	Ont.W.N.	Ontario Weekly Notes
Ohio Sup. & C.P.Dec.	Ohio Decisions	Ont.W.R.Op.	Ontario Weekly Reporter Opinions of Attorneys General (U.S.)
Ohio Supp.	Ohio Supplement		
Ohio Tax Rev.	Ohio Tax Review		
Ohio Unrep. Jud.Dec.	Pollack's Ohio Unreported Judicial Decisions Prior to 1823	Op.Att'y Gen.	Opinions of the Attorney General, United States
		Op.Sol.Dept.	Opinions of the Solicitor, U.S. Department of Labor
Ohio Unrept. Cas.	Ohio Supreme Court Decisions, Unreported Cases		
		Ops.Atty. Gen.	Opinions of Attorneys General (U.S.)
Oil & Gas Compact Bull.	Oil and Gas Compact Bulletin	Or.	Oregon Reports
Oil & Gas Inst.	Oil and Gas Institute	Or.L.Rev.	Oregon Law Review
Oil & Gas J.	Oil and Gas Journal	Orange County B.J.	Orange County Bar Journal
Oil & Gas L. & Tax.Inst.	Oil & Gas Law & Taxation Institute	Ore.	Oregon Reports

Ore.App.	Oregon Court of Appeals Reports	Otago L.Rev.	Otago Law Review
		Ottawa L.Rev.	Ottawa Law Review
Ore.L.Rev.	Oregon Law Review	Otto	Otto (U.S.)
Ore.St.B. Bull.	Oregon State Bar Bulletin	Out.	Outerbridge (Pa.)
		Outerbridge	Same
Ore.Tax Ct.	Oregon Tax Court Reports	Over.	Overton (Tenn.)
		Overt.	Same
Orleans' App.	Orleans' Appeals (La.)	Overton	Same
		Ow.	Owen's King's Bench (Eng.)
Orleans Tr.	Orleans Term Reports (La.)		
		Ow.	Owen's Common Pleas (Eng.)
Ormond	Ormond (Ala.)		
Osaka Pref. Bull.	University of Osaka Prefecture Bulletin	Owen	Same
Osaka U.L. Rev.	Osaka University Law Review	Oxford Law.	Oxford Lawyer
		Oxley	Oxley, Young's Vice Admiralty Decisions (Nova Scotia)
Osgoode Hall L.J.	Osgoode Hall Law Journal		

P

P.	Law Reports Probate, Divorce & Admiralty Division, Third Series		tice Annual Reports
		P.Coast L.J.	Pacific Coast Law Journal
	Pacific Reporter Pickering (Mass.) Probate	P.D.	Law Reports, Probate, Divorce & Admiralty Division, Second Series Division
P.2d	Pacific Reporter, Second Series		
P. & B.	Pugsley & Burbridge's Reports (N.B.)		Pension and Bounty (U.S. Dept. of Interior)
P. & C.	Prideaux & Cole's New Sessions Cases (Eng.)	P.Div.	Law Reports, Probate Division (Eng.)
P. & D.	Perry & Davison's Queen's Bench (Eng.)	PEAL	Publishing, Entertainment, Advertising and Allied Fields Law Quarterly
P. & F.Radio Reg.	Pike & Fischer's Radio Regulation Reporter	P.E.I.	Haszard & Warburton's Reports (Prince Edward Island)
P. & H.	Patton & Heath (Va.)		
P. & K.	Perry & Knapp, Election Cases (Eng.)		
P. & W.	Penrose & Watts (Pa.)	P.F.Smith	P.F. Smith (Pa.)
		P–H	Prentice-Hall
P.C.	Price Control Cases (CCH)	P–H Am.Lab. Arb.Awards	American Labor Arbitration Awards (P–H)
P.C.I.J.	Permanent Court of International Justice Advisory Opinions, Cases, Judgments, Pronouncements	P–H Am.Lab. Cas.	American Labor Cases (P–H)
		P–H Corp.	Corporation (P–H)
		P–H Est. Plan.	Estate Planning (P–H)
P.C.I.J. Ann.R.	Permanent Court of International Jus-	P–H Fed. Taxes	Federal Taxes (P–H)

P–H Fed. Wage & Hour	Federal Wage and Hour (P–H)	Pa.C.Pl.	Pennsylvania Common Pleas
P–H Ind. Rel.Lab. Arb.	Industrial Relations, American Labor Arbitration (P–H)	Pa.Cas.	Sadler (Penn.)
		Pa.Co.Ct.	Pennsylvania County Court
P–H Ind. Rel.Union Conts.	Industrial Relations, Union Contracts and Collective Bargaining (P–H)	Pa.D. & C.	Pennsylvania District & County Reporter
		Pa.D. & C.2d	Same, Second Series
P–H Soc.Sec. Taxes	Social Security Taxes (P–H)	Pa.Dist.	Pennsylvania District Reporter
P–H State & Local Taxes	State and Local Taxes (P–H)	Pa.Fid.Reporter	Pennsylvania Fiduciary
P–H Tax Ct. Mem.	Tax Court Memorandum Decisions (P–H)	Pa.L.J.	Pennsylvania Law Journal
		Pa.L.J.R.	Clark's Pennsylvania Law Journal Reports
P–H Tax Ct. Rep. & Mem. Dec.	Tax Court Reported and Memorandum Decisions (P–H)	Pa.L.Rec.	Pennsylvania Law Record
P.L.E.	Pennsylvania Law Encyclopedia	Pa.Misc.	Pennsylvania Miscellaneous Reports
PLI	Practising Law Institute	Pa.State	Pennsylvania State Reports
P.L.Mag.	Pacific Law Magazine	Pa.Super.	Pennsylvania Superior Court Reporter
P.L.Rep.	Pacific Law Reporter	Pac.	Pacific Reporter
P.Jr. & H.	Patton, Jr., & Heath (Va.)	Pac. Basin Int'l L.J.	Pacific Basin International Law Journal
P.R.	Parliamentary Reports		
	Practice Reports (Ont.)	Pac.L.J.	Pacific Law Journal
		Pac.Rim.L. & Pol'y J.	Pacific Rim Law & Policy Journal
	Probate Reports	Pace Envtl. L.Rev.	Pace Environmental Law Review
	Puerto Rico Supreme Court Reports	Pace J.Int'l & Corp.L.	Pace Journal of International and Comparative Law
P.R. & D.El. Cas.	Power, Rodwell & Dew's Election Cases (Eng.)		
		Pace L. Rev.	Pace Law Review
P.R.H.	Puerto Rico Federal Reports	Pace Y.B. Int'l L.	Pace Yearbook of International Law
P.R.R.	Puerto Rico Reports	Paige	Paige's Chancery (N.Y.)
P.T.	Processing Tax Division (I.R.B.)	Paine	Paine (U.S.)
P.U.Fort.	Public Utilities Fortnightly	Pak.Crim. L.J.	Pakistan Criminal Law Journal
P.U.R.	Public Utilities Reports	Pak.L.R.	Pakistan Law Reports
P.U.R. (N.S.)	Same, New Series	Palm.	Palmer (N.H.)
P.U.R.3d	Same, Third Series		Palmer (Vt.)
P.Wms.	Peere-Williams, Chancery (Eng.)		Palmer, King's Bench & Common Pleas (Eng.)
Pa.	Pennsylvania Reports		
Pa.B.A.Q.	Pennsylvania Bar Association Quarterly	Pan-Am.T.S.	Pan-American Treaty Series
Pa.B.Brief	Pennsylvania Bar Brief	Papua & N.G.	Papua and New Guinea Law Reports
Pa.C.P.	Common Pleas Reporter		
		Papy	Papy (Fla.)

Park.	Parker's Exchequer (Eng.)	Penn.B.A.Q.	Pennsylvania Bar Association Quarterly
Park.Cr.	Parker's Criminal Reports (N.Y.)	Penn.Del.	Pennewill (Del.)
Park.Cr.Cas.	Same	Pennyp.	Pennypacker (Pa.)
Park.Ins.	Parker's Insurance	Pennyp.Col. Cas.	Pennypacker's Colonial Cases
Parker	Parker (N.H.)	Penr. & W.	Penrose & Watts (Pa.)
Parker Cr.Cas.	Parker's Criminal Reports (N.Y.)	Pension Plan. & Tax'n	Pension Planning and Taxation
Pars.Dec.	Parson's Decisions (Mass.)	Pension Rep.	Pension Reporter (BNA)
Pars.Eq.Cas.	Parsons' Select Equity Cases (Pa.)	Pepp.L.Rev.	Pepperdine Law Review
Pasch.	Paschal (Tex.)		
Pat. & T.M.Rev.	Patent & Trade Mark Review	Pepperdine L.Rev.	Same
Pat. & Tr. Mk.Rev.	Same	Perry & K.	Perry & Knapp's Election Cases (Eng.)
Pat.Cas.	Reports of Patent, Design and Trade Mark Cases	Pers.Finance L.Q.	Personal Finance Law Quarterly Report
Pat.L.Rev.	Patent Law Review	Pers.Inj. Comment'r	Personal Injury Commentator
Pat.Off.Rep.	Patent Office Reports		
Pat.T.M. & Copy.J.	Patent, Trademark & Copyright Journal	Pers.Inj. Def.Rep.	Personal Injury Defense Reporter
Pater. Ap. Cas.	Paterson's Appeal Cases (Scot.)	Pet.	Peters (U.S)
Paton App. Cas.	Paton's Appeal Cases (Can.)	Pet.Ab.	Petersdorf's Abridgment
Patr.Elec. Ca.	Patrick, Contested Elections (Ont.) (1824–1849)	Pet.Adm.	Peters' Admiralty (U.S.)
		Pet.Br.	Petit (Or Little) Brook (Brooke) New Cases King's Bench (Eng.)
Patt. & H.	Patton & Heath (Va.)		
Peab.L.Rev.	Peabody Law Review		
Peake N.P.	Peake's Nisi Prius (Eng.)	Pet.C.C.	Peters' Circuit Court (U.S.)
Peake N.P. Add.Cas.	Peake, Additional Cases, Nisi Prius (Eng.)	Peters	Peters (U.S.)
		Pheney Rep.	Pheney's New Term Reports (Eng.)
Pearce C.C.	Pearce's Reports in Dearsley's Crown Cases (Eng.)	Phil.	Phillips' (Ill.) Phillips' Chancery (Eng.)
Pearson	Pearson, Common Pleas (Pa.)		Phillips' Equity (N.C.)
Peck	Peck (Ill.) Peck (Tenn.)		Phillips' Law (N.C.)
Peck.El.Cas.	Peckwell's Election Cases (Eng.)	Phil.El.Cas.	Phillips Election Cases (Eng.)
Peeples	Peeples (Ga.)	Phil.Int'l L.J.	Philippine International Law Journal
Peeples & Stevens	Peeples & Stevens (Ga.)	Phil.L.J.	Philippine Law Journal
Peere Williams	Peere Williams' Chancery (Eng.)	Phila.	Philadelphia (Pa.)
Peere Wms.	Same	Philanthrop.	Philanthropist
Pen.	Pennington's Law (N.J.)	Phillim.	Phillimore Ecclesiastical (Eng.)
Pen. & W.	Penrose and Watts (Pa.)	Pick.	Pickering (Mass.)
		Pickle	Pickle (Tenn.)

Pig. & R.	Pigott & Rodwell's Registration Cases (Eng.)	Poph.	Popham, King's Bench (Eng.) Chancery (Eng.) Common Pleas (Eng.)
Pike	Pike (Ark.)		
Pin.	Pinney (Wis.)	Port.	Porter (Ala.)
Pinn.	Same		Porter (Ind.)
Pipe Roll Soc'y	Publications of the Pipe Roll Society	Portia L.J.	Portia Law Journal
		Portland U.L.Rev.	Portland University Law Review
Pipe Roll Soc'y (N.S.)	Same, New Series	Porto Rico Fed.	Porto Rico Federal Reports
Pitblado Lect.	Isaac Pitblado Lectures on Continuing Legal Education	Posey	Posey (Tex.)
		Posey Unrep. Cas.	Posey's Unreported Commissioner Cases (Tex.)
Pitts.L.J.	Pittsburgh Legal Journal	Post	Post (Mich.) Post (Mo.)
Pitts.Leg.J. (N.S.)	Same, New Series	Potomac L.Rev.	Potomac Law Review
Pitts.Rep.	Pittsburgh Reports (Pa.)	Potter	Potter (Wyo.)
Pittsb.	Pittsburgh (Pa.)	Pow.Surr.	Power's Surrogate (N.Y.)
Pittsb.Leg.J.	Pittsburgh Legal Journal (Pa.)	Pr.	Price, Exchequer (Eng.)
Pittsb.R. (Pa.)	Pittsburgh Reporter (Pa.)	Pr.Edw.Isl.	Prince Edward Island
Pl.Ang.-Norm.	Placitca Anglo-Normannica Cases (Bigelow)	Pr.Reg.B.C.	Practical Register, Bail Court (Eng.)
Plan. & Comp.	Planning and Compensation Reports	Pr.Reg.C.P.	Practical Register, Common Pleas (Eng.)
Plan.Zoning & E.D.Inst.	Planning, Zoning & Eminent Domain Institute	Pr.Reg.Ch.	Practical Register, Chancery (Eng.)
Plowd.	Plowden, King's Bench (Eng.)	Pr.Rep.	Practice Reports (Eng.)
Pol.	Pollack's Ohio Unreported Judicial Decisions Prior to 1823		Practice Reports (Upper Can.)
		Prac.Law.	Practical Lawyer
	Pollexfen, King's Bench (Eng.)	Prac.Real Est. Law.	Practical Real Estate Lawyer
Pol.Sci.Q.	Political Science Quarterly	Prec.Ch.	Precedents in Chancery (Eng.)
Pol.Y.B.Int'l L.	Polish Yearbook of International Law	Preview	Preview of United States Supreme Court Cases
Police J.	Police Journal	Price	Price, Exchequer (Eng.)
Police L.Q.	Police Law Quarterly		
Poll.Contr. Guide	Pollution Control Guide (CCH)		Price's Mining Commissioner's Cases (Ont.)
Pollution Abs.	Pollution Abstracts		
Pollexf.	Pollexfen, King's Bench (Eng.)	Price Pr.Cas.	Price's Notes of Practice Cases (Eng.)
Poly L.Rev.	Poly Law Review	Prick.	Prickett (Idaho)
Pomeroy	Pomeroy (Cal.)	Prin.Dec.	Sneed's Printed Decisions (Ky.)
Poor L. & Local Gov't	Poor Law and Local Government Magazine	Prison L.Reptr.	Prison Law Reporter

Priv.Counter- feit. & Infr- ing.Rep.	Privacy, Counterfeit- ing & Infringement Report
Prob. & Prop.	Probate and Property
Prob.L.J.	Probate Law Journal
Prob.Law.	Probate Lawyer
Prob.Rep.	Probate Reports (Ohio)
Probation & Parole L.Rep.	Probation and Parole Law Reports
Probation & Parole L.Sum.	Probation and Parole Law Summaries
Prod.Liab. Int'l	Product Liability In- ternational
Prod.Safety & Liab.Rep.	Product Safety and Liability Reporter (BNA)
Prop. & Comp.	Property and Com- pensation Reports
Prop.Law.	Property Lawyer
Prouty	Prouty (Vt.)
Pub.Ad.Rev.	Public Administra- tion Review
Pub.Cont. L.J.	Public Contract Law Journal

Pub.Cont. Newsl.	Public Contract Newsletter
Pub.Em- ployee Rel. Rep.	Public Employee Re- lations Reports
Pub. Interest L.J.	Public Interest Law Journal
Pub.Int'l L.	Public International Law
Pub.L.	Public Law
Pub.Land & Res.L.Dig.	Public Land and Re- sources Law Digest
Pub.Util. Fort.	Public Utilities Fort- nightly
Pugs.	Pugsley (N.B.)
Pugs. & B.	Pugsley & Burbridge (N.B.)
Pugs. & T.	Pugsley & Truenian (N.B.)
Puls.	Pulsifer (Me.)
Pulsifer	Same
Pyke	Pyke (Lower Can.) Pyke's Reports, King's Bench (Que.)

Q

Q.B.	Law Reports, Queen's Bench
Q.B.D.	Law Reports, Queen's Bench Di- vision
Q.B.L.C.	Queen's Bench (Low- er Can.)
Q.B.U.C.	Queen's Bench (Up- per Can.)
Q.Intramural L.J.	Queen's Intramural Law Journal
Q.L.	Quebec Law
Q.L.J.	Queen's Law Journal
Q.L.R.	Quebec Law Reports
Q.L.Rev.	Quarterly Law Re- view
Q.Newsl.- Spec.Comm. Env.L.	Quarterly Newslet- ter-Special Com- mittee on Environ- mental Law
Que.B.R.; Que.C.S.	Quebec Rapports Judicaires Officiels (Banc de la Reine; Cour superieure)
Que.C.A.	Quebec Official Re- ports (Court of Ap- peal) (1970–)
Que.K.B.	Quebec Official Re- ports, King's Bench

Que.L.	Quebec Law
Que.L.R.	Quebec Law Reports
Que.Pr.	Quebec Practice
Que.Prac.	Quebec Practice Re- ports
Que.Q.B.	Quebec Official Re- ports, Queen's Bench
Que.Rev.Jud.	Quebec Revised Judi- cial
Que.S.C.	Quebec Official Re- ports, Superior Court (1892–1941) Same (1942 to pres- ent)
Que.Super.	Quebec Reports Su- perior Court
Queens B.Bull.	Queens Bar Bulletin
Queensl.	Queensland Reports
Queensl.J.P.	Queensland Justice of the Peace
Queensl.J.P. Rep.	Queensland Justice of the Peace Re- ports
Queensl.L.	Queensland Law
Queensl.L.J.	Queensland Law Journal
Queensl.L. Soc'y L.	Queensland Law So- ciety Journal

Queensl.Law.	Queensland Lawyer	Queensl.W.N.	Queensland Weekly
Queensl.	Queensland Supreme		Notes
S.C.R.	Court Reports	Quincy	Quincy (Mass.)
Queensl.	Queensland State Re-	Quis Cust.	Quis Custodiet?
St.Rep.	ports		

R

R.	Rawle (Pa.)	R.M.C.C.	Ryan & Moody's
	The Reports, Coke's		Crown Cases
	King's Bench		(Eng.)
	(Eng.)	R.M.C.C.R.	Same
R. & C.	Russell & Chesley	R.M.Charlt.	R.M. Charlton (Ga.)
	(Nova Scotia)	R.P.	Rapports des Pra-
R. & Can.	Railway & Canal		tique de Que-
Cas.	Cases (Eng.)		bec/Quebec Prac-
R. & Can.	Railway & Canal		tice Reports (1898)
Tr.Cas.	Traffic Cases	R.P.C.	Reports of Patent
	(Eng.)		Cases
R. & M.	Russell & Mylne's	R.P. & W.	Rawle, Penrose &
	Chancery (Eng.)		Watt (Pa.)
R. & M.C.C.	Ryan & Moody's	R.P.R.	Real Property Re-
	Crown Cases		ports (1977–)
	(Eng.)	R.P.W.	Rawle, Penrose &
R. & N.L.R.	Rhodesia and Nyasa-		Watt
	land Law Reports	R.R.	Pike & Fischer Radio
R. & R.	Russell & Ryan,		Regulation Revised
	Crown Cases		Reports
	(Eng.)	R.R.2d	Same, Second Series
R. 1 Cro.	Croke, Elizabeth	Race Rel.L.	Race Relations Law
R. 2 Cro.	Croke, James I.	Rep.	Reporter
R. 3 Cro.	Croke, Charles I.	Rac.Rel.L.	Race Relations Law
R.A.C.	Ramsay's Appeal	Survey	Survey
	Cases (Que.)	Rader	Rader (Mo.)
R.C.L.	Ruling Case Law	Rand	Rand (Ohio)
R.D.F.Q.	Recueil de droit fiscal	Rand.	Randall (Ohio)
	Quebecois (1977–)		Randolph (Kan.)
R.D.T.	Revue de Droit du		Randolph (Va.)
	Travail (1963)	Rand.Ann.	Randolph Annual
R. de D.	Revue de Droit De		(La.)
McGill	McGill	Raney	Raney (Fla.)
R.E.D.	Russell's Equity De-	Rawle	Rawle (Pa.)
	cisions (Nova Sco-	Raym.	Raymond (Iowa)
	tia)	La Raza L.J.	La Raza Law Journal
R.I.	Rhode Island Reports	Real Est.Fin.	Real Estate Finance
R.I.B.J.	Rhode Island Bar	L.J.	Law Journal
	Journal	Real Est.L.J.	Real Estate Law
R.J.R.Q.	Quebec Revised Re-		Journal
	ports	Real Est.	Real Estate Law Re-
R.L. & S.	Ridgeway, Lapp &	L.Rep.	port
	Schoales, King's	Real Est.Rev.	Real Estate Review
	Bench (Ir.)	Real Prop.	Real Property, Pro-
R.L. & S.	Robert, Leaming &	Prob. & Tr.J.	bate and Trust
	Wallis County		Journal
	Court (Eng.)	Reap.Dec.	U.S. Customs Court
R.L.B.	United States Rail-		Reappraisement
	road Labor Board		Decisions
	Decisions		

Rec.L.	Recent Law	Rev.Bar.	Revue du Barreau
Rec.Laws	Recent Laws in Canada	Rev.Barreau Que.	Revue de Barreau de Quebec
Record of N.Y.C.B.A.	Record of the Association of the Bar of the City of New York	Rev.C.Abo. Pr.	Revista de Derecho del Colegio de Abogados de Puerto Rico
Recueil des Cours	Recueil des Cours	Rev.Contemp.L.	Review of Contemporary Law
Redf. & B.	Redfield & Bigelow's Leading Cases (Eng.)	Rev.Crit.	Revue Critique (Can.)
		Rev.D.P.R.	Revista de Derecho Puertorriqueno
Redf.Surr.	Redfield's Surrogate (N.Y.)	Rev.D.U.S.	Revue de Droit Universite de Sherbrooke
Reding.	Redington (Me.)		
Reese	Reese, Heiskell's (Tenn.)	Rev. de Legis.	Revue de Legislation (Can.)
Reeve Eng.L.	Reeve's English Law	Rev.Gen.D.	Revue Generale de Droit
Ref.J.	Referees' Journal (Journal of National Association of Referees in Bankruptcy)	Rev.Ghana L.	Review of Ghana Law
		Rev. Int'l Bus. L.	Review of International Business Law
Regent U.L. Rev.	Regent University Law Review	Rev.Int'l Comm.Jur.	Review of the International Commission of Jurists
Rel. & Pub. Order	Religion and the Public Order		
Remy	Remy (Ind.)	Rev., Jud., & Police J.	Revenue, Judicial, and Police Journal
Rep.Atty. Gen.	Attorneys General's Reports (U.S.)	Rev.Jur.U. Inter.P.R.	Revista Juridica de law Universidad Interamericana de Puerto Rico
Rep.Pat.Cas.	Reports of Patent Cases (Eng.)		
Rep.Pat.Des. & Tr.Cas.	Reports of Patents Designs & Trademark Cases	Rev.Jur.U. P.R.	Revista Juridica de la Universidad de Puerto Rico
Reports	Coke's King's Bench (Eng.)	Rev.L. & Soc. Change	Review of Law and Social Change
Reprint	English Reports, Full Reprint	Rev.Leg.	Revue Legale (Can.)
Rept.t.Finch	Cases tempore Finch, Chancery (Eng.)	Rev.Leg. (N.S.)	Same, New Series
		Rev.Leg. (O.S.)	Same, Old Series
Rept.t.Holt	Cases tempore Holt, King's Bench (Eng.)	Rev.Legale	Revue Legale (Can.)
		Rev.Litig.	Review of Litigation
		Rev.Not.	Revue de Notariat
Res Ipsa	Res Ipsa Loquitur		Revue du Notariat
Res Judic.	Res Judicatae	Rev.P.R.	Revista de Derecho Puertorriqueno
Res. & Eq. Judgm.	Reserved & Equity Judgments (N.S.W.)	Rev.Pol.L.	Review of Polish Law
		Rev.R.	Revised Reports (Eng.)
Res.L. & Econ.	Research in Law and Economics	Rev.Rep.	Same
Res.L. & Soc.	Research in Law and Sociology	Rev.Sec. & Commodities Reg.	Review of Securities and Commodities Regulation
Restric.Prac.	Reports of Restrictive Practices Cases	Rev.Sec.Reg.	Review of Securities Regulation
Rettie	Rettie, Crawford & Melville's Session Cases (Scot.)	Rev.Sel.Code Leg.	Review of Selected Code Legislation

Rev.Soc.L.	Review of Socialist Law		Robinson (Nev.) Robinson (Upper Can.)
Rev.Stat.	Revised Statutes		Robinson (Va.)
Rev. Tax'n for Indiv.	Review of Taxation for Individuals		Robinson's Annual (La.)
Revised Rep.	Revised Reports (Eng.)	Rob. & J.	Robard & Jackson (Tex.)
Reyn.	Reynolds (Miss.)		
Rhodesian L.J.	Rhodesian Law Journal		Robertson & Jacob's Marine Court (N.Y.)
Rice	Rice's Equity (S.C.) Rice's Law (S.C.)	Rob.Adm.	Robinson, Admiralty (Eng.)
Rich.	Richardson (N.H.)		
	Richardson's Equity (S.C.)	Rob.Eccl.	Robertson's Ecclesiastical (Eng.)
	Richardson's Law (S.C.)	Rob.L. & W.	Robert, Leaming & Wallis' County Court (Eng.)
Rich. & H.	Richardson & Hook's Street Railway Decisions	Robb Pat. Cas.	Robb's Patent Cases (U.S.)
Rich. & W.	Richardson & Woodbury (N.H.)	Robert.App. Cas.	Robertson's Appeal Cases (Scot.)
Rich.C.P.	Richardson's Practice, Common Pleas (Eng.)	Robin.App. Cas.	Robinson's Appeal Cases, House of Lords (Scot.)
Rich.Ct.Cl.	Richardson's Court of Claims	Rocky Mt. L.Rev.	Rocky Mountain Law Review
Ridg.Ap.	Ridgeway's Appeals Parliament Cases (Ir.)	Rocky Mt. Min.L. Inst.	Rocky Mountain Mineral Law Institute
Ridg.App.	Same	Rocky Mt. Min.L. Newsl.	Rocky Mountain Mineral Law Newsletter
Ridg.L. & S.	Ridgeway, Lapp & Schoales' King's Bench (Ir.)		
Ridg.P.C.	Ridgeway's Parliamentary Cases (Ir.)	Rocky Mt. Miner.L. Rev.	Rocky Mountain Mineral Law Review
Ridg.t.Hardw.	Ridgeway tempore Hardwicke, Chancery, King's Bench	Rodm.	Rodman (Ky.)
		Rogers	Rogers Annual (La.)
		Roll.	Rolle, King's Bench (Eng.)
Ried.	Riedell (N.H.)		
Riley	Riley (W.Va.)	Rolle	Same
	Riley's Equity (S.C.)	Rolle Abr.	Rolle's Abridgment (Eng.)
	Riley's Law (S.C.)		
Ritchie	Ritchie's Equity (Can.)	Rom.Cas.	Romilly's Notes of Cases (Eng.)
Rob.	Robard (Mo.)	Root	Root (Conn.)
	Robard, Conscript Cases (Tex.)	Rose	Rose, Bankruptcy (Eng.)
	Robert's Louisiana Annual	Rose's Notes (U.S.)	Rose's Notes on United States Reports
	Robertson (Hawaii)	Ross Lead. Cas.	Ross's Leading Cases (Eng.)
	Robertson's Marine Court (N.Y.)		
	Robertson's Superior Court (N.Y.)	Rot.Chart.	Rotulus Chartarum (The Charter Roll)
	Robinson (Calif.)		
	Robinson (Colo.)	Rot.Claus.	Rotuli Clause (The Close Roll)
	Robinson (La.)	Rot.Parl.	Rotulae Parliamentarum

Rot.Pat.	Rotuli Patenes	Russ.Eq.Cas.	Russell's Equity Cases (Nova Scotia)
Rot.Plac.	Rotuli Placitorum		
Rotuli Curiae Reg.	Rotuli Curiae Regis (Eng.)	Russ.t.Eld.	Russell's Chancery tempore Eldon (Eng.)
Rowe	Rowe, Parliament & Military Cases (Eng.)		
		Russell	Russell's Chancery (Eng.)
Rowell	Rowell (Vt.)		
Rowell El.Cas.	Rowell, Election Cases (U.S.)	Rut.Cam.L.J.	Rutgers-Camden Law Journal
Rucker	Rucker (W.Va.)	Rutgers Computer & Tech. L.J.	Rutgers Computer and Technology Law Journal
Ruff. & H.	Ruffin & Hawks (N.C.)		
Runn.	Runnell (Iowa)	Rutgers J. Computers Tech. & L.	Rutgers Journal of Computers, Technology and the Law
Rus.	Russell's Election Cases (Nova Scotia)		
		Rutgers J. Computers & Law	Rutgers Journal of Computers and the Law
Rus. & C.Eq. Cas.	Russell & Chesley's Equity Cases (Nova Scotia)		
		Rutgers L.J.	Rutgers Law Journal
		Rutgers L.Rev.	Rutgers Law Review
Russ. & Geld.	Russell & Geldert (Nova Scotia)	Rutgers U.L.Rev.	Rutgers University Law Review
Russ. & M.	Russell & Mylne, Chancery (Eng.)	Ry. & M.	Ryan & Moody's Nisi Prius (Eng.)
Russ. & Ry.	Russell & Ryan, Crown Cases (Eng.)	Ry.M.C.C.	Ryan & Moody's Crown Cases (Eng.)
Russ.El.Cas.	Russell's Election Cases (Mass.)	Ryan & M.	Ryan & Moody's Nisi Prius (Eng.)
	Russell's Election Reports (Can.)	Ryde	Ryde's Rating Appeals (Eng.)

S

S.	Shaw, Dunlop & Bell, Court of Sessions (Scot.)	S. & M.	Smedes & Maclean's Appeal Cases, House of Lords (Scot.)
	Shaw's Appeal Cases, House of Lords (Scot.)		
			Smedes & Marshall (Miss.)
	Southern Reporter	S & M.Ch.	Smedes & Marshall's Chancery (Miss.)
S.A.G.	Sentencis arbitrales de griefs (Que.) (1970–)		
		S. & Mar.	Smedes & Marshall (Miss.)
SALT News	Strategic Arms Limitation Treaty News	S. & Mar.Ch.	Smedes & Marshall's Chancery (Miss.)
S. & B.	Smith & Batty's King's Bench (Ir.)	S. & R.	Sergeant & Rawle (Pa.)
S. & C.	Saunders & Cole's Bail Court (Eng.)	S. & S.	Sausse & Scully's Rolls Court (Ir.)
S. & C.P.Dec.	Ohio Decisions		
S. & D.	Shaw, Dunlop & Bell, Court of Sessions, 1st Series (Scot.)		Simons & Stuart's Vice Chancery (Eng.)
S. & L.	Schoales & Lefroy's Chancery (Ir.)	S. & Sc.	Sausse & Scully's Rolls Court (Ir.)

S. & Sm.	Searle & Smith's Probate & Divorce Cases (Eng.)	S.D.	South Dakota Reports
S. & T.	Swabey & Tristram's Probate & Divorce Cases (Eng.)	S.D.L.Rev.	South Dakota Law Review
		S.D.St.B.J.	South Dakota State Bar Journal
S.Afr.J.Hum. Rts.	South African Journal on Human Rights	S.E.	South Eastern Reporter
		S.E.2d	Same, Second Series
S.Afr.L.J.	South African Law Journal	S.E.C.	United States Securities and Exchange Commission Decisions
S.Afr.L.R.	South African Law Reports		
S.Afr.L.R. App.	South African Law Reports Appellate	S.F.L.J.	San Francisco Law Journal
S.Afr.L.Rev.	South African Law Review	S.Ill.U.L.J.	Southern Illinois University Law Journal
S.Afr.L.T.	South African Law Times	S.Ill.U.L.Rev.	Southern Illinois University Law Review
S.Afr.Tax Cas.	South African Tax Cases		
S.Aust.L.	South Australian Law	S.L.C.	Stuart's Appeal Cases (Lower Can.)
S.Austl.	South Australia State Reports	S.L.J.R.	Sudan Law Journal and Reports
S.Austl.L.R.	South Australian Law Reports	SLU LJ	Saint Louis University Law Journal
S.B.J.	State Bar Journal (Cal.)	S.M.	Solicitor's Memorandum (Treasury) (I.R.B.)
S.C.	Court of Session Cases (Scot.) South Carolina Reports	SMU L.Rev.	Southern Methodist University Law Review
S.C.Cas.	Cameron's Supreme Court (Can.)	S.Pac.L.Rev.	South Pacific Law Review
S.C.Eq.	South Carolina Equity	S.R.	Solicitor's Recommendation (I.R.B.)
S.C.L.Q.	South Carolina Law Quarterly	S.R. & O. and S.I.Rev.	Statutory Rules & Orders and Statutory Instruments Revised
S.C.L.Rev.	South Carolina Law Review		
S.C.R.	Supreme Court Reports (Can.) (1876–1922)	S.S.L.R.	Selective Service Law Reporter
	Same (1923 to present)	S.S.T.	Social Security Tax Ruling (I.R.B.)
		S.T.	Sales Tax Division (I.R.B.)
S.Cal.L.Rev.	Southern California Law Review	S.Tex.L.J.	South Texas Law Journal
S.Calif.Law Rev.	Same	S.Tex.L.Rev.	South Texas Law Review
S.Cal.Rev.L. & Women's Stud.	Southern California Review of Law and Women's Studies	S.U.L.Rev.	Southern University Law Review
S.Ct.	Supreme Court Reporter (U.S.)	S.W.	South Western Reporter
		S.W.2d	Same, Second Series
S.Ct.Rev.	Supreme Court Review	S.W.L.J.	South Western Law Journal (Nashville)

Sadler	Sadler's Cases (Pa.)	Sc.St.Crim.	Scandinavian Studies in Criminology
Sal.	Salinger (Iowa)		
Salk.	Salkeld, King's Bench, Common Pleas & Exchequer (Eng.)	Sc.St.L.	Scandinavian Studies in Law
		Scam.	Scammon (Ill.)
		Sch. & Lef.	Schoales & Lefroy, Equity (Ir.)
Samoan P.L.J.	Samoan Pacific Law Journal	Scher.	Scherer's Miscellaneous Reports (N.Y.)
San Diego L.Rev.	San Diego Law Review	Schm.L.J.	Schmidt's Law Journal (New Orleans)
San Fern.V. L.Rev.	San Fernando Valley Law Review	Schuyl.L.Rec.	Schuylkill Legal Record (Pa.)
San Fran.L.J.	San Francisco Law Journal	Scot.Jur.	Scottish Jurist
Sand.I.Rep.	Sandwich Islands Reports (Haw.)	Scot.L.J.	Scottish Law Journal and Sheriff Court Record
Sandf.	Sandford's Superior Court (N.Y.)	Scot.L.Mag.	Scottish Law Magazine and Sheriff Court Reporter
Sandf.Ch.	Sandford, Chancery (N.Y.)		
Sanf.	Sanford (Ala.)	Scot.L.Rep.	Scottish Law Report
Santa Clara Computer & High Tech. L.J.	Santa Clara Computer and High Technology Law Journal	Scot.L.Rev.	Scottish Law Review and Sheriff Court Report
		Scot.L.T.	Scottish Law Times
Santa Clara L.Rev.	Santa Clara Law Review	Scots L.T.R.	Scots Law Times Reports
Santa Clara Law.	Santa Clara Lawyer	Scott	Scott, Common Pleas (Eng.)
Santo Tomas L.Rev.	University of Santo Tomas Law Review	Scott N.R.	Scott's New Reports, Common Pleas (Eng.)
Sar.Ch.Sen.	Saratoga Chancery Sentinel	Scr.L.T.	Scranton Law Times (Pa.)
Sask.	Saskatchewan Law Reports	Sea Grant L. & Pol'y J.	Sea Grant Law and Policy Journal
Sask.B.Rev.	Saskatchewan Bar Review	Sea Grant L.J.	Sea Grant Law Journal
Sask.L.	Saskatchewan Law	Sec.L.Rev.	Securities Law Review
Sask.L.Rev.	Saskatchewan Law Review		
Sau. & Sc.	Sausee & Scully, Rolls Court (Ir.)	Sec.Reg. & Trans.	Securities Regulation and Transfer Report
Sauls.	Saulsbury (Del.)		
Saund.	Saunders, King's Bench (Eng.)	Sec.Reg.L.J.	Securities Regulation Law Journal
Saund. & Cole	Saunders & Cole, Bail Court (Eng.)	Sel.Cas.	Yates' Select Cases (N.Y.)
Sav.	Savile, Common Pleas & Exchequer (Eng.)	Sel.Cas.Ch.	Select Cases in Chancery (Eng.)
		Sel.Serv. L.Rptr.	Selective Service Law Reporter
Sawy.	Sawyer, Circuit Court (U.S.)	Seld.	Selden's Notes (N.Y.)
Sax.	Saxton's Chancery (N.J.)	Selden	Selden's Court of Appeals (N.Y.)
Say.	Sayer, King's Bench (Eng.)	Selw.N.P.	Selwyn's Nisi Prius (Eng.)
Sc.Sess.Cas.	Scotch Court of Sessions Cases	Senior Law.	Senior Lawyer
		Seoul L.J.	Seoul Law Journal

Serg. & R.	Sergeant & Rawle (Pa.)	Shaw, D. & B.Supp.	Shaw, Dunlop & Bell's Supplement, House of Lords Decisions (Scot.)
Sess.Ca.	Sessions Cases, King's Bench (Eng.)		
Sess.Cas.	Court of Sessions Cases (Scot.)	Shaw Dec.	Shaw's Decisions in Scotch Court of Sessions (1st Series)
	Sessions Cases King's Bench (Eng.)	Shaw, Dunl. & B.	Shaw, Dunlop & Bell's Sessions Cases (Scot.)
Sess.Laws	Session Laws		
Seton Hall Const.L.J.	Seton Hall Constitutional Law Journal	Shaw, W. & C.	Shaw, Wilson & Courtnay, House of Lords (Scot.)
Seton Hall J. Sport L.	Seton Hall Journal of Sport Law	Shep.	Shepherd (Ala.)
Seton Hall L.Rev.	Seton Hall Law Review	Shep.Abr.	Sheppard's Abridgment
Seton Hall Legis.J.	Seton Hall Legislative Journal	Shep.Sel.Cas.	Shepherd's Select Case (Ala.)
Sex.L.Rep.	Sexual Law Reporter		
Sex Prob.Ct. Dig.	Sex Problems Court Digest	Sher.Ct.Rep.	Sheriff Court Reports (Scot.)
Shad.	Shadford's Victoria Reports	Shingle	The Shingle, Philadelphia Bar Association
Shan.	Shannon (Tenn.)		
Shand	Shand (S.C.)	Shipp	Shipp (N.C.)
Shand Pr.	Shand Practice, Court of Sessions (Scot.)	Shirl.	Shirley (N.H.)
		Shirl.L.C.	Shirley's Leading Crown Cases (Eng.)
Shaw	Shaw (Vt.)		
	Shaw, Appeal Cases, English House of Lords from Scotland	Show.	Shower, King's Bench (Eng.)
		Show.P.C.	Shower's Parliamentary Cases (Eng.)
	Shaw, Scotch Justiciary Cases	Sick.	Sickel's Court of Appeals (Eng.)
	Shaw, Scotch Teind Reports, Court of Sessions	Sid.	Siderfin, King's Bench (Eng.)
Shaw & D.	Shaw & Dunlop (Scot.)	Sil.	Silver Tax Division (I.R.B.)
		Silv.A.	Silvernail's Appeals (N.Y.)
Shaw & Dunl.	Same		
Shaw & M.	Shaw & McLean, Appeals, House of Lords (Scot.)	Silv.Sup.	Silvernail's Supreme Court (N.Y.)
		Silv.Unrep.	Silvernail's Unreported Cases (N.Y.)
Shaw & Macl.	Same		
Shaw App.	Shaw Appeal Cases	Sim.	Simmons (Wis.)
Shaw Crim. Cas.	Shaw's Criminal Cases Justiciary Court (Scot.)		Simon's Vice-Chancery (Eng.)
		Sim. (N.S.)	Simon's Vice-Chancery, New Series (Eng.)
Singapore L.Rev.	Singapore Law Review		
Shaw, D. & B.	Shaw, Dunlop & Bell's Court of Sessions (1st Series) (Scot.)	Sim. & C.	Simmons & Conover (Wis.)
		Sim. & St.	Simons & Stuart's Vice-Chancery (Eng.)
	Shaw, Dunlop & Bell's Session Cases (Scot.)	Skill.Pol.Rep.	Skillman's Police Reports (N.Y.)

Skin.	Skinner, King's Bench (Eng.)	Sneed Dec.	Sneed's Kentucky Decisions
Skink.	Skinker (Mo.)	Snow	Snow (Utah)
Sm. & M.	Smedes & Marshall (Miss.)	So.	Southern Reporter
		So.2d	Same, Second Series
Sm. & M.Ch.	Smedes & Marshall, Chancery (Miss.)	So.Calif. L.Rev.	Southern California Law Review
Sm. & S.	Smith & Sager's Drainage Cases (Ont.) (1901–1917)	So.Car.Const.	South Carolina Constitutional Reports
		So.Car.L.J.	South Carolina Law Journal
Smale & G.	Smale & Gifford's Vice-Chancery (Eng.)	So.L.J.	Southern Law Journal (Nashville)
Small Bus. Tax'n	Small Business Taxation	So.L.Q.	Southern Law Quarterly
Smith	Smith (Calif.)	So.L.Rev.	Southern Law Review (Nashville)
	Smith (Eng.)		Southern Law Review (St. Louis)
	Smith (Ind.)		
	Smith (Me.)		
	Smith (Mo.)	So.L.Rev. (N.S.)	Southern Law Review, New Series (St. Louis)
	Smith (N.H.)		
	Smith (S.D.)		
	Smith (Wis.)	So.Law T.	Southern Law Times
	Smith, E.B. (Ill.)	So.Tex.L.J.	South Texas Law Journal
	Smith, E.D., Common Pleas (N.Y.)		
	Smith, E.H., Court of Appeals (N.Y.)	So.U.L.Rev.	Southern University Law Review
	Smith, E.P., Court of Appeals (N.Y.)	Soc. & Lab. Bull.	Social and Labour Bulletin
	Smith, P.F. (Pa.)	Soc.Action & L.	Social Action and the Law
Smith & B.	Smith & Batty, King's Bench (Ir.)	Soc.Just.	Social Justice
Smith & B.R.C.	Smith & Bates, American Railway Cases	Soc.Sec.Bull.	Social Security Bulletin
		Software L.J.	Software Law Journal
Smith & G.	Smith & Guthrie (Mo.)	Sol.	Solicitor
		Sol.J.	Solicitor's Journal (Eng.)
Smith & H.	Smith & Heiskell (Tenn.)	Sol.Op.	Solicitor's Opinions (I.R.B.)
Smith C.C.M.	Smith, Circuit Courts-Martial (Me.)	Sol.Q.	Solicitor Quarterly
		Solar L.Rep.	Solar Law Reporter
Smith Cond.	Smith's Condensed Alabama Reports	Somerset L.J.	Somerset Legal Journal
Smith K.B.	Smith's King's Bench (Eng.)	Southard	Southard (N.J.)
		Southwestern L.J.	Southwestern Law Journal
Smith L.J.	Smith's Law Journal		
Smith Lead. Cas.	Smith's Leading Cases (Eng.)	Soviet Jewry L.Rev.	Soviet Jewry Law Review
Smith Reg. Cas.	Smith's Registration Cases (Eng.)	Soviet L. & Gov't.	Soviet Law and Government
Smy.	Smythe, Common Pleas (Ir.)	Soviet Stat. & Dec.	Soviet Statutes and Decisions
Smythe	Same	Soviet Y.B. Int'l L.	Soviet Year-Book of International Law
Sneed	Sneed (Tenn.)		
	Sneed's Decisions (Ky.)	Spaulding	Spaulding (Me.)
		Spear	Spear's Law (S.C.)

Spear Ch.	Spear's (or Speer) Chancery (S.C.)	Stan.J.L. Gender & Sex. Orient.	Stanford Journal of Law, Gender & Sexual Orientation
Spear Eq.	Spear's Equity (S.C.)	Stan.L. & Pol'y Rev.	Stanford Law & Policy Review
Speer	Spear's Law (S.C.)		
Spenc.	Spencer (Minn.) Spencer, Law (N.J.)	Stan.L.Rev.	Stanford Law Review
Spencer	Spencer, Law (N.J.)	Stan.Pa.Prac.	Standard Pennsylvania Practice
Spinks	Spinks, Ecclesiastical and Admiralty (Eng.)	Stant.	Stanton (Ohio)
		Stanton	Same
Spinks Eccl. & Adm.	Same	Star Ch.Cas.	Star Chamber Cases (Eng.)
Spoon.	Spooner (Wis.)	Stark.	Starkie's Nisi Prius (Eng.)
Spooner	Same		
Spott.	Spottiswoode (Scot.)	Stat.	Statutes at Large (U.S.)
Spott.C.L. & Eq.Rep.	Common Law & Equity Reports published by Spottiswoode		
		Stat. at L.	Same
		State Court J.	State Court Journal
		State Gov't	State Government
Spottis.Eq.	Spottiswoode's Equity (Scot.)	State Tr.	State Trials (Eng.)
		Stath.Abr.	Statham's Abridgment
Sprague	Sprague, District Court Admiralty (U.S.)	Stetson L.Rev.	Stetson Law Review
		Stev. & G.	Stevens & Graham (Ga.)
St. John's J. Legal Comment.	St. John's Journal of Legal Commentary	Stew.	Stewart (Ala.) Stewart (S.D.) Stewart's Reports (N.S.)
St. John's L.Rev.	St. John's Law Review		
St. Louis L.Rev.	St. Louis Law Review	Stew. & P.	Stewart & Porter (Ala.)
St. Louis U.L.J.	St. Louis University Law Journal	Stew.Admr.	Stewart's Admiralty (N.S.)
St. Louis U.Pub.L.F.	St. Louis University Public Law Forum	Stew.Eq.	Stewart's Equity (N.J.)
St. Louis U.Pub.L.Rev.	St. Louis University Public Law Review	Stewart	Stewart's Vice-Admiralty Reports (N.S.)
St. Mary's L.J.	St. Mary's Law Journal	Stiles	Stiles (Iowa)
		Still.Eccl.Cas.	Stillingfleet's Ecclesiastical Cases (Eng.)
St.Rep.	State Reporter	Stiness	Stiness (R.I.)
St.Rep.N. S.W.	State Reports (N.S.W.)	Stockett	Stockett (Md.)
		Stockt.	Stockton's Equity (N.J.)
St. Thomas L.Rev.	St. Thomas Law Review	Stockt.Vice-Adm.	Stockton's Vice-Admiralty (N.B.)
Stafford	Stafford (Vt.)	Stockton	Same
Stair	Stair (Scot.)	Story	Story (U.S.)
Stan.Envt'l L.Ann.	Stanford Environmental Law Annual	Story Eq.Jur.	Story on Equity Jurisprudence
Stan.Envtl.L.J.	Stanford Environmental Law Journal	Str.	Strange's King's Bench (Eng.)
		Stra.	Same
		Strahan	Strahan (Ore.)
Stan.J.Int'l L.	Stanford Journal of International Law	Straits L.J. & Rep.	Straits Law Journal and Reporter
Stan.J.Int'l Stud.	Stanford Journal of International Studies	Stratton	Stratton (Ore.)
		Stringf.	Stringfellow (Mo.)

Strob.	Strobhart's Law (S.C.)	Sup.Ct.Rep.	Supreme Court Reporter (U.S.)
Strob.Eq.	Strobhart's Equity (S.C.)	Sup.Ct.Rev.	Supreme Court Review
Stu.M. & P.	Stuart, Milne & Peddie (Scot.)	Susq.Leg. Chron.	Susquehanna Legal Chronical (Pa.)
Stu.Mil. & Ped.	Same	Sw.L.J.	Southwestern Law Journal
Stuart	Stuart's King's Bench (Lower Can.)	Sw.U.L.Rev.	Southwestern University Law Review
Stuart Vice-Adm.	Stuart's Vice-Admiralty (Lower Can.)	Swab.	Swabey's Admiralty (Eng.)
Stud.Int'l Fiscal L.	Studies on International Fiscal Law	Swab. & Tr.	Swabey's & Tristram, Probate & Divorce (Eng.)
Stud.L. & Econ.Dev.	Studies in Law and Economic Development	Swan	Swan (Tenn.)
		Swanst.	Swanston, Chancery (Eng.)
Student Law.	Student Lawyer	Sween.	Sweeney's Superior Court (N.Y.)
Student Law. J.	Student Lawyer Journal	Swin.	Swinton's Registration Appeal Cases (Scot.)
Style	Style, King's Bench (Eng.)	Swiss Rev.Int'l Competition L.	Swiss Review of International Competition Law
Suffolk Transnat'l L.J.	Suffolk Transnational Law Journal	Sydney L.Rev.	Sydney Law Review
Suffolk U.L. Rev.	Suffolk University Law Review	Syme	Syme's Justiciary Cases (Scot.)
Summerfield	Summerfield (Nev.)	Symposium Jun.B.	Symposium l'Association de jeune Barreau de Montreal
Sumn.	Sumner, Circuit Court (U.S.)		
Sup. & C.P. Dec.	Ohio Decisions	Syn.Ser.	Synopsis Series of Treasury Decisions (U.S.)
Sup.Ct.	Superior Court (Pa.)		
Sup.Ct.Hist. Soc'y Q.	Supreme Court Historical Society Quarterly	Syracuse J. Int'l L. & Com.	Syracuse Journal of International Law and Commerce
Sup.Ct.Hist. Soc'y Y.B.	Supreme Court Historical Society Yearbook	Syracuse L.Rev.	Syracuse Law Review

T

T.	Tappan (Ohio) Tobacco Division (I.R.B.)	T. & R.	Turner & Russell's Chancery (Eng.)
		T.B. & M.	Tracewell, Bowers & Mitchell, Comptroller's Decisions (U.S.)
T. & C.	Thompson & Cook, Supreme Court (N.Y.)		
T. & G.	Tyrwhitt & Granger's Exchequer (Eng.)	T.B.M.	Tax Board Memorandum (I.R.B.)
		T.B.Mon.	T.B. Monroe (Ky.)
T. & M.	Temple & Mew's Crown Cases (Eng.)	T.B.R.	Advisory Tax Board Recommendation (I.R.B.)
T. & P.	Turner & Phillips' Chancery (Eng.)	T.B.R.	Tariff Board Reports (1937–1962)

T.C.	Tax Court of the United States Reports	Tam.	Tamlyn, Rolls Court (Eng.)
		Taml.	Same
TCR	Tribal Court Reporter	Tamlyn	Tamlyn's Chancery (Eng.)
T.D.	Treasury Decisions	Tamlyn Ch.	Same
T.Holt	Holt, Modern Cases (Eng.)	Taney	Taney, Circuit Court (U.S.)
T.I.A.S.	Treaties and Other International Acts Series (U.S.)	Tann.	Tanner (Ind.)
		Tanner	Same
		Tapp.	Tappan (Ohio)
T.I.Agree.	Treaties and Other International Agreements of the United States of America (1776–1949)	Tappan	Same
		Tasm.	Tasmanian State Reports
		Tasm.L.R.	Tasmania Law Reports
		Tasm.U.L. Rev.	Tasmania University Law Review
T.I.F.	Treaties in Force	Taun.	Taunton, Common Pleas (Eng.)
T.Jones	Thomas Jones, King's Bench and Common Pleas (Eng.)	Taunt.	Same
		Tax A.B.C.	Canada Tax Appeal Board Cases
T.L.R.	Times Law Reports (Eng.)	Tax Adm'rs News	Tax Administrators News
T.M.Bull.	Trade Mark Bulletin (U.S.)	Tax Cas.	Tax Cases (Eng.)
		Tax Counsel-or's Q.	Tax Counselor's Quarterly
T.M.Bull. (N.S.)	Same, New Series	Tax L.Rep.	Tax Law Reporter
T.M.M.	Tax Management Memorandum (BNA)	Tax L.Rev.	Tax Law Review
		Tax Law.	The Tax Lawyer
T.M.Rep.	Trade Mark Reporter	Tax Mag.	Tax Magazine
T. Marshall L.J.	Thurgood Marshall Law Journal	Tax Mgmt. Est.Gifts & Tr.J.	Tax Management Estates, Gifts and Trusts Journal
T. Marshall L.Rev.	Thurgood Marshall Law Review	Tax Pract. Forum	Tax Practitioners Forum
T.N.E.C.	Temporary National Economic Committee	Tax. for Law.	Taxation for Lawyers
		Tax.R.	Taxation Reports
T.R.	Durnford & East, Term Reports, King's Bench (Eng.)	Taxes	Taxes, The Tax Magazine (CCH)
		Tay.	Taylor's Carolina Reports (N.C.)
T.Raym.	Thomas Raymond, King's Bench (Eng.)		Taylor's King's Bench (Can.)
T.S.	Treaty Series (U.S.)		Taylor's Term Reports (N.C.)
T.T.	Jurisprudence de droit de Travail (1970–)	Taylor	Same
		Taylor, U.C.	Taylor, King's Bench (Ont.)
T.U.P.Charlt.	T.U.P. Charlton (Ga.)	Tel-Aviv U.Stud.L.	Tel-Aviv University Studies in Law
Tait	Tait's Manuscript Decisions (Scot.)	Temp.	tempore
Tal.	Cases tempore Talbot, Chancery (Eng.)	Temp. & M.	Temple & Mew, Crown Cases (Eng.)
Talb.	Same		

Temp.Envtl. L. & Tech.J.	Temple Environmental Law and Technology Journal	Terr.L.R.	Territories' Law Reports (N.W.T.)
		Tex.	Texas Reports
Temp.Geo.II	Cases in Chancery tempore Geo. II. (Eng.)	Tex.A.Civ. Cas.	White & Wilson's Civil Cases (Tex.)
		Tex.A.Civ. Cas. (Wilson)	Texas Court of Appeal Civil Cases
Temp.Int'l & Comp. L.J.	Temple International and Comparative Law Journal	Tex.App.	Texas Civil Appeals Cases
Temp.L.Q.	Temple Law Quarterly		Texas Court of Appeals Cases
Temp.L.Rev.	Temple Law Review	Tex.B.J.	Texas Bar Journal
Temp.Pol. & Civ.Rts. L.Rev.	Temple Political and Civil Rights Law Review	Tex.Civ.App.	Texas Civil Appeals
		Tex.Civ.Rep.	Same
		Tex.Com. App.	Texas Commission Appeals
Temp.Wood	Manitoba Reports tempore Wood (Can.)	Tex.Cr.App.	Texas Criminal Appeals
Temple & M.	Temple & Mew, Crown Cases (Eng.)	Tex.Cr.R.	Same
		Tex.Crim.	Texas Criminal Reports
Temple L.Q.	Temple Law Quarterly	Tex.Ct. App.R.	Texas Court of Appeals Reports
Tenn.	Tennessee Reports	Tex.Dec.	Texas Decisions
Tenn.App.	Tennessee Appeals	Tex.Int.L. Forum	Texas International Law Forum
Tenn.App. Bull.	Tennessee Appellate Bulletin	Tex.Int'l L.F.	Same
Tenn.B.J.	Tennessee Bar Journal	Tex.Int'l L.J.	Texas International Law Journal
Tenn.C.C.A.	Tennessee Court of Civil Appeals	Tex.J. Women & L.	Texas Journal of Women and the Law
Tenn.Cas.	Shannon's Tennessee Cases	Tex.Jur.	Texas Jurisprudence
Tenn.Ch.	Cooper, Chancery (Tenn.)	Tex.Jur.2d	Same, Second Series
		Tex.L.J.	Texas Law Journal
Tenn.Ch. App.	Tennessee Chancery Appeals	Tex.L.Rev.	Texas Law Review
Tenn.Civ. App.	Tennessee Court of Civil Appeals	Tex.Law.	Texas Lawman
		Tex.Lawyer	Texas Lawyer
Tenn.Crim. App.	Tennessee Criminal Appeals Reports	Tex. Oil & Gas L.J.	Texas Oil and Gas Journal
Tenn.L.Rev.	Tennessee Law Review	Tex.Real Est. L.Rep.	Texas Real Estate Law Reporter
Tenn.Leg. Rep.	Tennessee Legal Reporter	Tex.S.Ct.	Texas Supreme Court Reporter
Term	Durnford & East, Term Reports, King's Bench (Eng.)	Tex.So.U. L.Rev.	Texas Southern University Law Review
		Tex.Supp.	Texas Supplement
		Tex.Tech L.Rev.	Texas Tech Law Review
Term N.C.	Taylor, Term Reports		
Term R.	Durnford and East, Term Reports, King's Bench (Eng.)	Tex.Unrep. Cas.	Posey Unreported Cases (Tex.)
		Th. & C.	Thompson & Cook's (N.Y.) Supreme Court (N.Y.)
Term.Rep.	Same		
Terr.	Terrell (Tex.)	Thatcher Cr.	Thatcher's Criminal Cases (Mass.)
Terr. & Wal.	Terrell & Walker (Tex.)	Thayer	Thayer (Ore.)

Themis	La Revue Juridique Themis	Tread. Const.	Treadway's Constitutional Reports (S.C.)
Thom.	Thomson's Reports (Nova Scotia)	Treas.Dec.	Treasury Decisions (U.S.)
Thomas & Fr.	Thomas & Franklin Chancery (Md.)	Trem.P.C.	Tremaine, Pleas of Crown (Eng.)
Thomp.	Thompson (Cal.)		
Thomp.Tenn. Cas.	Thompson's Unreported Tennessee Cases	Trends L. Libr. Mgmt. & Tech.	Trends in Law Library Management and Technology
Thompson & C.	Thompson & Cook, Supreme Court (N.Y.)	Trent L.J.	Trent Law Journal
		Trial	Trial
Thomson	Thomson's Reports (Nova Scotia)	Trial Advoc.Q.	Trial Advocate Quarterly
Thor.	Thorington (Ala.)	Trial Law. Forum	Trial Lawyers Forum
Thorpe	Thorpe's Louisiana Annual	Trial Law. Guide	Trial Lawyer's Guide
Thur.Marsh. L.J.	Thurgood Marshall Law Journal	Trial Law.Q.	Trial Lawyers' Quarterly
Tiff.	Tiffany, Court of Appeals (N.Y.)	Trial Prac. Newsl.	Trial Practice Newsletter
Tiffany	Same	Trin.T.	Trinity Term (Eng.)
Till.	Tillman (Ala.)	Tripp	Tripp (Dak.Terr.)
Tillman	Same	Tru.	Trueman's Equity Cases (N.B.)
Timber Tax J.	Timber Tax Journal		
Tinw.	Tinwald (Scot.)	Trust Bull.	Trust Bulletin
Tobey	Tobey (R.I.)	Trust Terr.	Trust Territory Reports
Tort L.Rev.	Tort Law Review		
Toth.	Tothill's Chancery (Eng.)	Tuck.	Tucker (Mass.)
Touro J. Transnat'l L.	Touro Journal of Transnational Law	Tuck. & C.	Tucker & Clephane (D.C.)
Touro L.Rev.	Touro Law Review	Tuck.Dist. of Col.	Tucker's Appeals (D.C.)
Tr. & Est.	Trusts & Estates		
Tr. & H.Pr.	Troubat & Haly's Practice (Pa.)	Tuck.Sel.Cas.	Tucker's Select Cases (Nfld.)
Trace. & M.	Tracefell & Mitchell, Comptroller's Decisions (U.S.)	Tuck.Surr.	Tucker's Surrogate (N.Y.)
Trade Cas.	Trade Cases (CCH)	Tul.Civ.L.F.	Tulane Civil Law Forum
Trade Reg. Rep.	Trade Regulation Reporter (CCH)	Tul.Envtl.L. J.	Tulane Environmental Law Journal
Trade Reg. Rev.	Trade Regulation Review	Tul.L.Rev.	Tulane Law Review
Trademark Rep.	Trade-Mark Reporter	Tul.Mar.L.J.	Tulane Maritime Law Journal
Trans. & Wit.	Transvaal & Witswatersrand Reports	Tul.Tax Inst.	Tulane Tax Institute
		Tulane L.Rev.	Tulane Law Review
Transc.A.	Transcript Appeals (N.Y.)	Tulsa L.J.	Tulsa Law Journal
		Tupp.App.	Tupper's Appeal Reports (Ont.)
Transit L.Rev.	Transit Law Review	Turn.	Turner (Ark.)
Transnat'l L.Contemp. Probs.	Transnational Law & Contemporary Problems		Turner (Ky.)
			Turner & Russell's Chancery (Eng.)
Transp.L.J.	Transportation Law Journal	Turn. & P.	Turner & Phillips' Chancery (Eng.)
Trauma	Trauma	Turn. & Ph.	Same

Turn. & R.	Turner & Russell's Chancery (Eng.)	Tutt. & Carp.	Same
		Tyler	Tyler (Vt.)
Turn. & Rus.	Same	Tyng	Tyng (Mass.)
Turn. & Russ.	Same	Tyrw.	Tyrwhitt, Exchequer (Eng.)
Tutt.	Tuttle (Cal.)		
Tutt. & C.	Tuttle & Carpenter (Cal.)	Tyrw. & G.	Tyrwhitt & Granger, Exchequer (Eng.)

U

U.Ark.Little Rock L.J.	University of Arkansas at Little Rock Law Journal	U.C.Chan.	Upper Canada Chancery Reports
U.B.C.L.Rev.	University of British Columbia Law Review	U.C.Davis L.Rev.	University of California at Davis Law Review
U.B.C.Notes	University of British Columbia Legal Notes	U.C.E. & A.	Upper Canada Error & Appeals Reports
		U.C.Err. & App.	Same
U.Balt.J. Envtl.L.	University of Baltimore Journal of Environmental Law	U.C.I.S.	Unemployment Compensation Interpretation Service, Benefit Series
U.Balt.L.F.	University of Baltimore Law Forum		Unemployment Compensation Interpretation Service, Federal Series
U.Balt.L.Rev.	University of Baltimore Law Review		Unemployment Compensation Interpretation Service, State Series
U.Bridgeport L.Rev.	University of Bridgeport Law Review		
U.C.	Upper Canada	U.C.Jur.	Upper Canada Jurist
U.C. (O.S.)	Upper Canada Queen's Bench Reports, Old Series	U.C.K.B.	Upper Canada King's Bench Reports, Old Series
U.C.App.	Upper Canada Appeal Reports		
U.C.App.Rep.	Same		
U.C.C.	Uniform Commercial Code	UCLA	University of California Los Angeles
U.C.C.L.J.	Uniform Commercial Code Law Journal	UCLA–Alaska L.Rev.	UCLA Alaska Law Review
U.C.C.Law Letter	Uniform Commercial Code Law Letter	UCLA Intra.L.Rev.	UCLA Intramural Law Review
U.C.C.P.	Upper Canada Common Pleas Reports	UCLA J.Envtl.L. & Pol'y	UCLA Journal of Environmental Law & Policy
U.C.C.P.D.	Upper Canada Common Pleas Division Reports (Ont.)	UCLA L.Rev.	UCLA Law Review
		UCLA Pac. Basin L.J.	UCLA Pacific Basin Law Journal
U.C.C.Rep. Serv.	Uniform Commercial Code Reporting Service	UCLA Women's L.J.	UCLA Women's Law Journal
U.C.Ch.	Upper Canada Chancery Reports	U.C.L.J.	Upper Canada Law Journal
U.C.Ch.Rep.	Same	U.C.L.J. (N.S.)	Same, New Series
U.C.Cham.	Upper Canada Chamber Reports	U.C.P.R.	Upper Canada Practice Reports
U.C.Chamb. Rep.	Same	U.C.Pr.	Same

U.C.Q.B.	Upper Canada Queen's Bench Reports	U.Miami L.Rev.	University of Miami Law Review
U.C.Q.B. (O.S.)	Same, Old Series	U.Miami Y.B.Int'l L.	University of Miami Yearbook of International Law
U.C.R.	Same	U.Mich.J. L.Ref.	University of Michigan Journal of Law Reform
U.C.Rep.	Upper Canada Reports		
U.Chi.L.Rec.	University of Chicago Law School Record	U.Mo.Bull. L.Ser.	University of Missouri Bulletin Law Series
U.Chi.L.Rev.	University of Chicago Law Review		
U.Chi.Legal F.	University of Chicago Legal Forum	U.N.	United Nations Law Reports
U.Cin.L.Rev.	University of Cincinnati Law Review	U.N.B.L.J.	University of New Brunswick Law Journal
U.Colo.L.Rev.	University of Colorado Law Review		
U.Dayton L.Rev.	University of Dayton Law Review	U.N.Comm. Int'l Trade L.Y.B.	United Nations Commission on International Trade Law Yearbook
U.Det.J. Urb.L.	University of Detroit Journal of Urban Law	U.N.Doc.	United Nations Documents
U.Det.L.J.	University of Detroit Law Journal	U.N.ECOSOC	United Nations Economic and Social Council Records
U.Det.L.Rev.	University of Detroit Law Review	U.N.GAOR	United Nations General Assembly Official Records
U.Det.Mercy L.Rev.	University of Detroit Mercy Law Review		
U.East.L.J.	University of the East Law Journal	U.N.Jur.Y.B.	United Nations Juridical Yearbook
U.Fla.J.L. & Pub.Pol'y	University of Florida Journal of Law and Public Policy	U.N.M.T.	United Nations Multilateral Treaties
U.Fla.L.Rev.	University of Florida Law Review	U.N.R.I.A.A.	United Nations Reports of International Arbitral Awards
U.Ghana L.J.	University of Ghana Law Journal		
U.Hawaii L.Rev.	University of Hawaii Law Review	U.N.Res., Ser. I	United Nations Resolutions, Series I
U.I.L.R.	University of IFE Law Reports (Nigeria)	U.N.SCOR	United Nations Security Council Official Records
U.Ill.L.F.	University of Illinois Law Forum	U.N.T.S.	United Nations Treaty Series
U.Ill.L.Rev.	University of Illinois Law Review	U.New S.Wales L.J.	University of New South Wales Law Journal
U.Kan.City L.Rev.	University of Kansas City Law Review	U.Newark L.Rev.	University of Newark Law Review
U.Kan.L.Rev.	University of Kansas Law Review	U.Pa.J.Int'l Bus.L.	University of Pennsylvania Journal of International Business Law
U.Miami Ent. & Sports L.Rev.	University of Miami Entertainment and Sports Law Review		
U.Miami Inter-Am. L.Rev.	University of Miami Inter-American Law Review	U.Pa.L.Rev.	University of Pennsylvania Law Review

U.Pitt.L.Rev.	University of Pittsburgh Law Review	U.S.L.Rev.	United States Law Review
U.Puget Sound L.Rev.	University of Puget Sound Law Review	U.S.L.W.	United States Law Week
U.Queensl. L.J.	University of Queensland Law Journal	U.S.L.Week	Same
		U.S.Law.Ed.	United States Supreme Court Reports, Lawyers' Edition
U.Rich. L.Rev.	University of Richmond Law Review		
U.S.	United States Reports	U.S.M.C.	United States Maritime Commission
U.S. & Can.Av.	United States and Canadian Aviation Reports	U.S.M.L.Mag.	United States Monthly Law Magazine
U.S.App.	United States Appeals	U.S.P.Q.	United States Patent Quarterly
U.S.Av.R.	Aviation Reports (U.S.)	U.S.S.B.	United States Shipping Board
U.S.Aviation	Same	U.S.S.C.Rep.	United States Supreme Court Reports
U.S.C.	United States Code		
U.S.C. (Supp.)	Same		
U.S.C.A.	United States Code Annotated	U.S.Sup.Ct. Rep.	United States Supreme Court Reporter (West)
U.S.C.Govt'l Rev.	University of South Carolina Governmental Review	U.S.T.	United States Treaties and Other International Agreements
U.S.C.M.A.	United States Court of Military Appeals		
U.S.C.S.	United States Code Service	U.S.T.D.	United States Treaty Development
U.S.Code Cong. & Ad. News	United States Code Congressional & Administrative News	U.S.Tax Cas.	United States Tax Cases (CCH)
		U.S.V.A.A.D.	United States Veterans Administration Administrator's Decisions
U.S.Ct.Cl.	United States Court of Claims Reports		
U.S.D.C.	United States District Court	U.S.V.B.D.D.	United States Veterans Bureau Directors Decisions
U.S.F.L.Rev.	University of San Francisco Law Review	U.San Fernando V.L.Rev.	University of San Fernando Valley Law Review
U.S.F.Mar. L.J.	University of San Francisco Maritime Law Journal	U.So. Cal.1955 Tax Inst.	University of Southern California Tax Institute
U.S.I.C.C. V.R.	United States Interstate Commerce Commission Valuation Reports	U.Tasm. L.Rev.	University of Tasmania Law Review (or Tasmania University Law Review)
U.S.Jur.	United States Jurist (D.C.)		
U.S.L.Ed.	United States Supreme Court Reports, Lawyers' Edition	U.Tol.L.Rev.	University of Toledo Law Review
		U.Tor.Fac. L.Rev.	University of Toronto Faculty of Law Review
U.S.L.J.	United States Law Journal	U.Tor.L.Rev.	University of Toronto School of Law Review
U.S.L.Mag.	United States Law Magazine		

U.Toronto Fac. L.Rev.	University of Toronto Faculty of Law Review	Unempl.Ins. Rep.	Unemployment Insurance Reporter (CCH)
U.Toronto L.J.	University of Toronto Law Journal	Unif.L.Conf. Can.	Uniform Law Conference of Canada
U.Toronto Sch. L.Rev.	University of Toronto School of Law Review	Unific.L.Y.B.	Unification of Law Yearbook
U.W.Austl. L.Rev.	University of Western Australia Law Review	Uniform L.Rev.	Uniform Law Review
		Unof.	Unofficial Reports
		Up.Can.L.J.	Upper Canada Law Journal
U.W.L.A. L.Rev.	University of West Los Angeles Law Review	Urb.L. & Pol'y	Urban Law and Policy
U.Wash. L.Rev.	University of Washington Law Review	Urb.L.Ann.	Urban Law Annual
		Urb.Law.	Urban Lawyer
U.West L.A. L.Rev.	University of West Los Angeles Law Review	Urban Affairs Rep.	Urban Affairs Reporter (CCH)
		Urban L.Rev.	Urban Law Review
		Utah	Utah Reports
U.Windsor L.Rev.	University of Windsor Law Review	Utah 2d	Same, Second Series
		Utah L.Rev.	Utah Law Review
Udal	Fiji Law Reports	Util.L.Rep.	Utilities Law Reporter (CCH)
Uganda L.Foc.	Uganda Law Focus		
Un.Prac.News	Unauthorized Practice News	Util.Sect. Newsl.	Utility Section Newsletter

V

V.C.Rep.	Vice Chancellor's Reports (Eng.)	Va.L.J.	Virginia Law Journal
V.I.	Virgin Islands Reports	Va.L.Reg.	Virginia Law Register
V.I.B.J.	Virgin Islands Bar Journal	Va.L.Reg. (N.S.)	Same, New Series
VJNRL	Virginia Journal of Natural Resources Law	Va.L.Rev.	Virginia Law Review
		Va.R.	Gilmer's Virginia Reports
V.R.	Valuation Reports, Interstate Commerce Commission	Val.R. (I.C.C.)	Interstate Commerce Commission Valuation Reports
Va.	Virginia Reports	Val.U.L.Rev.	Valparaiso University Law Review
Va.Bar News	Virginia Bar News		
Va.Cas.	Virginia Cases	Van K.	Van Koughnett's Common Pleas (Upper Can.)
Va.Ch.Dec.	Chancery Decisions (Va.)		
Va.Dec.	Virginia Decisions	Van Ness Prize Cas.	Van Ness, Prize Cases (U.S.)
Va.Envtl.L.J.	Virginia Environmental Law Journal	Vand.J.Transnat'l L.	Vanderbilt Journal of Transnational Law
		Vand.L.Rev.	Vanderbilt Law Review
Va.J.Int'l L.	Virginia Journal of International Law	Vaug.	Vaughan, Common Pleas (Eng.)
Va.J.Nat.Resources L.	Virginia Journal of Natural Resources Law	Vaugh.	Same
		Vaughan	Same
Va.J.Soc. Pol'y & L.	Virginia Journal of Social Policy and the Law	Vaux	Vaux, Decisions (Pa.) Vaux, Recorder's Decisions (Pa.)

Ve.	Vesey, Chancery Reports (Eng.)	Vez.	Vezey, (Vesey) Chancery (Eng.)
	Vesey, Senior, Chancery (Eng.)	Vict.	Victoria
Ve. & B.	Vesey & Beames, Chancery (Eng.)	Vict.Admr.	Victorian Admiralty
		Vict.Eq.	Victorian Equity
Veaz.	Veazey (Vt.)	Vict.L.	Victorian Law
Veazey	Same	Vict.L.R.	Victorian Law Reports
Vent.	Ventris, Common Pleas (Eng.)	Vict.L.R.Min.	Victorian Law Mining Reports
	Ventris, King's Bench (Eng.)	Vict.L.T.	Victorian Law Times
Ventr.	Ventris, King's Bench (Eng.)	Vict.Rev.	Victorian Review
		Vict.St.Tr.	Victorian State Trials
Ver.	Vermont	Vict.U.L.Rev.	Victoria University Law Review
Vern.	Vernon's Cases (Eng.)	Vict.U.Well. L.Rev.	Victoria University of Wellington Law Review
Vern. & S.	Vernor & Scriven, King's Bench (Ir.)		
Vern. & Sc.	Same	Vil. & Br.	Vilas & Bryant's Reports (Wis.)
Vern. & Scr.	Same	Vilas	Vilas' Criminal Reports (N.Y.)
Vern. & Scriv.	Same		
Vern.Ch.	Vernon's Chancery (Eng.)	Vill.Envtl. L.J.	Villanova Environmental Law Journal
Ves.	Vesey, Chancery (Eng.)		
	Vesey, Senior, Chancery (Eng.)	Vill.L.Rev.	Villanova Law Review
Ves. & B.	Vesey & Beames' Chancery (Eng.)	Vin.Abr.	Viner's Abridgment (Eng.)
Ves. & Bea.	Same	Vin.Supp.	Same, Supplement
Ves. & Beam.	Same	Vir.	Virgin (Me.)
Ves.Jr.	Vesey, Junior, Chancery (Eng.)	Virgin	Same
		Virgin Is.	Virgin Islands
Ves.Jun.	Same	Vr.	Vroom's Law Reports (N.J.)
Ves.Jun. Supp.	Same		
Ves.Sen.	Vesey, Senior, Chancery (Eng.)	Vroom	Same
		Vroom (G.D.W.)	G.D.W., Vroom (N.J.)
Ves.Sr.	Same		
Ves.Supp.	Vesey, Senior Supplement, Chancery (Eng.)	Vroom (P.D.)	P.D., Vroom (N.J.)
		Vt.	Vermont Reports
		Vt.L.Rev.	Vermont Law Review

W

W.	Wandell (N.Y.)	W. & M.	Woodbury & Minot, Circuit Court (U.S.)
	Watts (Pa.)		
	Wheaton's Supreme Court (U.S.)	W. & S.	Watts & Sergeant (Pa.)
	Wright (Ohio)		
W.A'B. & W.	Webb, A'Beckett & Williams (Vict.)		Wilson & Shaw's Appeal Cases (Scot.)
W.A.C.A.	Selected Judgments of the West African Court of Appeals	W. & W.	White & Webb's Victorian Reports
W. & C.	Wilson & Courtenay's Appeal Cases	W. & W.Vict.	Wyatt & Webb's Victorian Reports

W.Afr.App.	West African Court of Appeal Reports	Western Law Reporter
W.Austl.Ind. Gaz.	Western Australia Industrial Gazette	Women Law Reporter
W.Austl.J.P.	Western Australia Justice of the Peace	W.L.T. — Western Law Times and Reports
W.Austl.L.R.	Western Australia Law Reports	W.N. — Weekly Notes (Eng.)
W.Bl.	Sir William Blackstone's King's Bench & Common Pleas (Eng.)	W.New Eng. L.Rev. — Western New England Law Review
W.Bla.	Same	W.Ont.L.Rev. — Western Ontario Law Review
W.C.C.	Washington's Circuit Court (U.S.)	W.R. — Weekly Reports
	Workmen's Compensation Cases	W.Res.L.Rev. — Western Reserve Law Review
W.C.Ins.Rep.	Workmen's Compensation & Insurance Reports	W.Rob. — William Robinson's Admiralty (Eng.)
W.C.Rep.	Workmen's Compensation Reports	W.St.U. L.Rev. — Western State University Law Review
W.Coast Rep.	West Coast Reporter	W.Va.Crim. Just.Rev. — West Virginia Reports Criminal Justice Review
W.F.P.D.2d	West's Federal Practice Digest, Second Series	W.Va.L.Q. — West Virginia Law Quarterly
W.H. & G.	Welsby, Hurlstone & Gordon's Exchequer (Eng.)	W.Va.L.Rev. — West Virginia Law Review
W.H.Cases	Wage & Hour Cases	W.W. & D. — Willmore, Wollaston & Davison, Queen's Bench (Eng.)
W.H.Man.	Wages & Hours Manual	
W.H.R.	Wage & Hour Reporter	W.W. & H. — Willmore, Wollaston & Hodges' Queen's Bench (Eng.)
W.Jo.	William Jones King's Bench, Common Pleas, House of Lords and Exchequer (Eng.)	W.W.D. — Western Weekly Digests (1975–)
		W.W.Harr. — W.W. Harrington (Del.)
W.Jones	Same	W.W.R. — Western Weekly Report (Can.)
W.Kel.	William Kellynge, King's Bench & Chancery (Eng.)	W.W.R.(N.S.) — Same, New Series, (1951–1955)
		Wa. — Wage and Hour Reporter
W.L.A.C.	Western Labour Arbitration Cases (1966–)	Wage & Hour Cas. — Wage and Hour Cases (BNA)
		Watts (Pa.)
W.L.Bull.	Weekly Law Bulletin	Wage & Hour Rep. — Wage & Hour Reporter
W.L.G.	Weekly Law Gazette (Ohio)	Wage-Price L. & Econ.Rev. — Wage-Price Law and Economics Review
W.L.Gaz.	Same	Wake For. L.Rev. — Wake Forest Law Review
W.L.J.	Western Law Journal	Wake Forest Intra.L.Rev. — Wake Forest Intramural Law Review
W.L.Jour.	Weekly Law Journal	Wake Forest L.Rev. — Wake Forest Law Review
W.L.M.	Western Law Monthly (Ohio)	Wal.By L. — Wallis, Irish Chancery (By Lyne)
W.L.R.	Weekly Law Reports (Eng.)	Wal.Jr. — Wallace Junior (U.S.)

Walk.	Walker (Ala.) (Miss.) (Pa.) (Tex.)	temp.L.	ban and Contemporary Law
	Walker (Miss.)	Wash.U.L.Q.	Washington University Law Quarterly
	Walker (Pa.)		
	Walker (Tex.)	Washb.	Washburn (Vt.)
Walk.Ch.	Walker's Chancery (Mich.)	Washburn L.J.	Washburn Law Journal
Walk.Ch.Cas.	Same	Watts	Watts (Pa.)
Wall.	Wallace (U.S.) (Philadelphia)		Watts (W.Va.)
		Watts & S.	Watts & Sergeant (Pa.)
	Wallis (Phila.)		
Wall.C.C.	Wallace, Circuit Court (U.S.)	Watts & Ser.	Same
		Watts & Serg.	Same
Wall.Jr.	Wallace, Junior (U.S.)	Wayne L.Rev.	Wayne Law Review
		Webb	Webb (Kans.)
Wall.Rep.	Wallace, The Reporters		Webb (Tex.)
			Webb's Civil Appeals (Tex.)
	Wallace's Supreme Court Reports (U.S.)	Webb & D.	Webb & Duval (Tex.)
		Webb & Duval	Same
Wall.Sr.	Wallace Senior (U.S.)	Webb, A'B. &	Webb, A'Beckett &
Wallis	Wallis' Chancery (Ir.)	W.	Williams' Reports (Austl.)
Wallis by L.	Wallis, Irish Chancery (By Lyne)	Webs.Pat.	Webster's Patent
		Cas.	Cases (Eng.)
Walsh	Walsh's Registry Cases (Ir.)	Week.Cin.	Weekly Law Bulletin
		L.B.	(Ohio)
Ward.	Warden (Ohio)	Week.Dig.	Weekly Digest (N.Y.)
Ward. & Sm.	Warden & Smith (Ohio)	Week.Jur.	Weekly Jurist (Ill.)
		Week.L.Gaz.	Weekly Law Gazette (Ohio)
Warden's Law & Bk.Bull.	Weekly Law & Bank Bulletin (Ohio)		
Ware	Ware, District Court (U.S.)	Week.L.Rec.	Weekly Law Record
		Week.Law	Weekly Law Bulletin
Wash.	Washington Reports	Bull.	(Ohio)
	Washington Reports (Va.)	Week.Law	Weekly Law Gazette
		Gaz.	(Ohio)
Wash.2d	Washington Reports, Second Series	Week.Notes	Weekly Notes of
		Cas.	Cases (London)
Wash.App.	Washington Appellate Reports		Weekly Notes of Cases (Pa.)
Wash. & Haz. P.E.I.	Washburton & Hazard's Reports (P.E.I.)	Week.Rep.	Weekly Reporter (Eng.)
		Week.Trans.	Weekly Transcript
Wash. & Lee L.Rev.	Washington & Lee Law Review	Rep.	Reports (N.Y.)
		Weekly L.R.	Weekly Law Reports (Eng.)
Wash.C.C.	Washington Circuit Court (U.S.)	Welfare L.Bull.	Welfare Law Bulletin
Wash.L.Rep.	Washington Law Reporter (D.C.)	Welfare	Welfare Law News
		L.News	
Wash.L.Rev.	Washington Law Review	Welsb.H. & G.	Welsby, Hurlstone & Gordon's Exchequer (Eng.)
Wash.Terr.	Washington Territory		
		Welsby H. &	Same
Wash. Terr.(N.S.)	Same, New Series	G.	
		Welsh (Ir.)	Welsh's Registry Cases
Wash.Ty.	Same		
Wash.U.J. Urb. & Con-	Washington University Journal of Ur-	Wend.	Wendell (N.Y.)
		Wenz.	Wenzell (Minn.)

Wes.C.L.J.	Westmoreland County Law Journal	
West	West Publishing or West Group	
West Ch.	West's Chancery (Eng.)	
West Va.	West Virginia	
West.	Weston (Vt.)	
West.Austl.	Western Australian Reports	
West.Jur.	Western Jurist (Des Moines, Iowa)	
West.L.Gaz.	Western Law Gazette (Ohio)	
West.L.J.	Western Law Journal	
West.L.M.	Western Law Monthly (Ohio)	
West.L.Mo.	Same	
West.L. Month.	Same	
West.L.R.	Western Law Reporter (Can.)	
West.L.Rev.	Western Law Review	
West.Law J.	Western Law Journal	
West.Law M.	Western Law Monthly (Ohio)	
West.Legal Obser.	Western Legal Observer	
West.R.	Western Reporter	
West.School L.Rev.	Western School Law Review	
West.St.U. L.Rev.	Western State University Law Review	
West t.Hardw.	West tempore Hardwicke, Chancery (Eng.)	
West.Week. Rep.	Western Weekly Reports (Can.)	
West.Wkly.	Western Weekly (Can.)	
Western Res. L.Rev.	Western Reserve Law Review	
Westm.	State of Westminster (Eng.)	
Westm.L.J.	Westmoreland Law Journal (Pa.)	
Wethey	Wethey's Queen's Bench (Upper Can.)	
Whart.	Wharton (Pa.)	
Whart.Law Dict.	Wharton's Law Lexicon	
Whart.St.Tr.	Wharton's State Trials (U.S.)	
Wheat.	Wheaton (U.S.)	
Wheel.	Wheeler's Criminal Cases (N.Y.)	

	Wheelock (Tex.)
Wheeler Abr.	Wheeler's Abridgment
Wheeler C.C.	Wheeler's Criminal Cases (N.Y.)
Whit.Pat.Cas.	Whitman's Patent Cases (U.S.)
White	White (Tex.)
	White (W.Va.)
	White's Justiciary Cases (Scot.)
White & T. Lead.Cas. Eq.	White & Tudor's Leading Cases in Equity (Eng.)
White & W.	White & Wilson (Tex.)
Whitm.Lib. Cas.	Whitman's Libel Cases (Mass.)
Whitt.	Whittlesey (Mo.)
Whittier L.Rev.	Whittier Law Review
Widener J.Pub.L.	Widener Journal of Public Law
Wight	Wight's Section Cases (Scot.)
Wight.	Wightwick, Exchequer (Eng.)
Wightw.	Same
Wilc.	Wilcox (Ohio)
Wilc.Cond.	Wilcox, Condensed Ohio Reports
Wilcox	Wilcox (Ohio)
	Wilcox (Pa.)
Wilcox Cond.	Wilcox, Condensed Ohio Reports
Wilk.	Wilkinson (Austl.)
	Wilkinson, Court of Appeals and Civil Appeals (Tex.)
Will.	Williams (Mass.)
	Willson (Tex.)
Will.L.J.	Willamette Law Journal
Will.Woll. & Dav.	Willmore, Wollaston & Davison, Queen's Bench (Eng.)
Will.Woll. & H.	Willmore, Wollaston & Hodges' Queen's Bench (Eng.)
Will.Woll. & Hodg.	Same
Willamette L.J.	Willamette Law Journal
Willamette L.Rev.	Willamette Law Review

Willes	Willes, King's Bench & Common Pleas (Eng.)	Wis.B.T.A.	Wisconsin Board of Tax Appeals Reports
Williams	Peere-Williams' English Chancery Reports	Wis.Int'l L.J.	Wisconsin International Law Journal
	Williams (Mass.)	Wis.L.N.	Wisconsin Legal News
	Williams (Utah)	Wis.L.Rev.	Wisconsin Law Review
	Williams (Vt.)		
Williams & Bruce Ad.Pr.	Williams & Bruce's Admiralty Practice	Wis.Law.	Wisconsin Lawyer
		Wis.Multi-Cultural L.J.	Wisconsin Multi–Cultural Law Journal
Williams P.	Peere-Williams' English Chancery Reports	Wisc.Stud. B.J.	Wisconsin Student Bar Journal
Williams-Peere	Same	Wis.Tax App.C.	Wisconsin Tax Appeals Commission Reports
Willm.W. & D.	Willmore, Wollaston & Davison's Queen's Bench (Eng.)	Wis.Women's L.J.	Wisconsin Women's Law Journal
		Withrow	Withrow (Iowa)
		Wkly.Dig.	Weekly Digest (N.Y.)
Willm.W. & H.	Willmore, Wollaston & Hodges' Queen's Bench (Eng.)	Wkly.L.Bul.	Weekly Law Bulletin (Ohio)
		Wkly.L.Gaz.	Weekly Law Gazette (Ohio)
Willson	Willson, Civil Cases (Tex.)	Wkly.Law Bull.	Weekly Law Bulletin (Ohio)
Willson, Civ. Cas.Ct.App.	Same	Wkly.N.C.	Weekly Notes of Cases (Pa.)
Wilm.	Wilmot's Notes (Eng.)	Wkly.Rep.	Weekly Reporter (Eng.)
Wils.	Wilson (Cal.)		
	Wilson (Minn.)	Wm. & Mary Bill Rts.J.	William and Mary Bill of Rights Journal
	Wilson (Ore.)		
	Wilson, Superior Court (Ind.)	Wm. & Mary J.Envtl.L.	William & Mary Journal of Environmental Law
	Wilson's King's Bench & Common Pleas (Eng.)	Wm. & Mary L.Rev.	William & Mary Law Review
Wils. & S.	Wilson & Shaw, House of Lords (Scot.)	Wm. & Mary Rev.Va.L.	William and Mary Review of Virginia Law
Wils.C.P.	Wilson's Common Pleas (Eng.)	Wm.Mitchell L.Rev.	William Mitchell Law Review
Wils.Ch.	Wilson's Chancery (Eng.)	Wol.	Wolcott's Chancery (Del.)
Wils.Exch.	Wilson's Exchequer (Eng.)		Wollaston's English Bail Court Reports (Eng.)
Wils.K.B.	Wilson's King's Bench (Eng.)		
Wils.P.C.	Wilson's Privy Council (Eng.)	Wolf. & B.	Wolferstan & Bristow's Election Cases (Eng.)
Winch	Winch, Common Pleas (Eng.)	Wolf. & D.	Wolferstan & Dew's Election Cases (Eng.)
Winst.	Winston (N.C.)		
Wis.	Wisconsin Reports	Woll.	Wollaston's English Bail Court Reports
Wis.2d	Same, Second Series		
Wis.B.Bull.	Wisconsin Bar Bulletin	Woll.P.C.	Same

Woman Of-fend.Rep.	Woman Offender Report		Woolworth, Circuit Court (U.S.)
Women & L.	Women and Law	Workmen's	Workmen's Compensation Law Review
Women Law.J.	Women Lawyer's Journal	Comp. L.Rev.	
Women's Rights L.Rptr.	Women's Rights Law Reporter	World Jurist	World Jurist
		World Pol.	World Polity
Wood.	Woodbury & Minot, Circuit Court (U.S.)	Wright	Wright (Ohio) Wright (Pa.)
		Wy. & W.	Wyatt & Webb (Vict.)
Wood. & M.	Same	Wy.W. &	Wyatt, Webb &
Woodb. & M.	Same	A'Beck	A'Beckett (Vict.)
Woods	Woods, Circuit Court (U.S.)	Wyo.	Wyoming Reports
		Wyo.L.J.	Wyoming Law Journal
Woodw.	Woodward's Decisions (Pa.)		
Woolw.	Woolworth (Neb.)	Wythe	Wythe's Chancery (Va.)

Y

Y.	Yeates (Pa.)	Y.B.P.1, Edw. II	Year Books, Part 1, Edward II
Y. & C.	Younge & Collyer's Chancery (Eng.)	Y.B.S.C.	Year Books, Selected Cases
Y. & C.C.C.	Same		
Y. & J.	Younge & Jervis' Exchequer (Eng.)	Y.B.U.N.	Yearbook of the United Nations
Y.A.D.	Young's Admiralty Decisions (Nova Scotia)	Y.B.World Pol.	Yearbook of World Polity
Y.B.	Year Book, King's Bench (Eng.)	Yale J.Int'l L.	Yale Journal of International Law
Y.B. (Rolls Series)	Year Books, Rolls Series (Eng.)	Yale J.L. & Feminism	Yale Journal of Law & Feminism
Y.B. (Sel. Soc.)	Year Books, Selden Society (Eng.)	Yale J.L. & Humanities	Yale Journal of Law & the Humanities
Y.B.A.A.A.	Yearbook of the Association of Attenders and Alumni of the Hague Academy of International Law	Yale J.L. & Lib.	Yale Journal of Law & Liberation
		Yale J. on Reg.	Yale Journal on Regulation
		Yale J.World Pub.Ord.	Yale Journal of World Public Order
Y.B.A.S.L.	Yearbook of Air and Space Law	Yale L. & Pol'y Rev.	Yale Law & Policy Review
Y.B.Ed. I	Year Books, Edward I	Yale L.J.	Yale Law Journal
Y.B.Eur. Conv. on Human Rights	Yearbook of the European Convention on Human Rights	Yale Rev.Law & Soc.Act'n	Yale Review of Law and Social Action
Y.B.Human Rights	Yearbook on Human Rights	Yale Stud. World Pub. Ord.	Yale Studies in World Public Order
Y.B.Int'l L.Comm'n	Yearbook of the International Law Commission	Yates Sel. Cas.	Yates' Select Cases (N.Y.)
Y.B.Int'l Org.	Yearbook of International Organizations	Yea.	Yeates (Pa.)
		Yearb.	Year Book, King's Bench (Eng.)
Y.B.League	Yearbook of the League of Nations	Yearb.P.7, Hen.VI	Year Books, Part 7, Henry VI
		Yeates	Yeates (Pa.)

Yel.	Yelverton, King's Bench (Eng.)	Young Naut. Dict.	Young's Nautical Dictionary
Yelv.	Same	Younge	Younge's Exchequer (Eng.)
Yerg.	Yerger (Tenn.)		
York Leg. Rec.	York Legal Record (Pa.)	Younge & C. Ch.Cas.	Younge & Collyer's Chancery or Exchequer Equity (Eng.)
Yorke Ass.	Clayton Reports, Yorke Assizes		
You.	Younge's Exchequer (Eng.)	Younge & C. Exch.	Younge & Collyer's Exchequer Equity (Eng.)
You. & Coll. Ch.	Younge & Collyer's Exchequer (Eng.)	Younge & Coll. Ex.	Same
You. & Coll. Ex.	Same	Younge & J.	Younge & Jervis, Exchequer (Eng.)
You. & Jerv.	Younge & Jervis, Exchequer (Eng.)	Younge & Je.	Same
Young	Young (Minn.)	Younge Exch.	Younge, Exchequer (Eng.)
Young Adm.	Young, Admiralty (N.S.)		
		Younge M.L. Cas.	Younge, Maritime Law Cases (Eng.)
Young Adm. Dec.	Same	Yugo.L.	Yugoslav Law

Z

Zab.	Zabriskie (N.J.)	Zane	Zane (Utah)
Zambia L.J	Zambia Law Journal		

Appendix B

STATE GUIDES TO LEGAL RESEARCH

As discussed in Chapter 1, the United States consists of 51 major legal systems, one for each state and the federal government. While the state systems have much in common, each is the product of a unique history and legal background. Methods of legislating, codifying, and court reporting vary from state to state. Where possible, a researcher should take the time to learn the unusual aspects of legal research in each state's materials in which extended research is conducted.

In many states, law librarians and others who are familiar with legal research, have written guides detailing the history and organization of their states. The list below is a compilation of these guides. It includes books as well as shorter bibliographic sources from the American Association of Law Libraries (AALL) Occasional Papers Series, but excludes sources that may appear in legal periodicals. A researcher contemplating or beginning any research in one of the states listed below is advised to consult the guides first. Such a first step could save much time and effort in the endeavor. For a description of the many various state legal research guides available, see Nancy Adams Deel & Barbara G. James, *An Annotated Bibliography of State Legal Research Guides,* LEGAL REFERENCE SERVICES Q., No. 1/2, 1994, at 23.

Alabama	George D. Schrader, *Alabama Law Bibliography* (Barrister Press, 1990).
	Hazel L. Johnson & Timothy L. Coggins, *Guide to Alabama State Documents and Selected Law–Related Materials* (AALL, 1993).
Alaska	Aimee Ruzicka, *Alaska Legal and Law–Related Publications: A Guide for Law Libraries* (AALL, 1984).
Arizona	Kathy Shimpock–Vieweg & Marianne Sidorski Alcorn, *Arizona Legal Research Guide* (Hein, 1992).
	Richard Teenstra et al., *Survey of Arizona Law–Related Documents* (AALL, 1984).
Arkansas	Lynn Foster, *Arkansas Legal Bibliography: Documents and Selected Commercial Titles* (AALL, 1988).
California	Karla Castetter, *Locating the Law: A Handbook for Non–Librarians,* 2d ed. (Southern California Association of Law Libraries, 1989).
	Larry D. Dershem, *California Legal Research Handbook* (Fred B. Rothman & 1997).
	John K. Hanft, *Legal Research in California,* 2d ed. (Bancroft/Whitney, 1996).
	Verona Mackay & Laura Peritore, *California Government Publications and Legal Resources* (AALL, 1991).
	Daniel Martin ed., *Henke's California Law Guide,* 3d ed. rev. (Michie Butterworth, 1995).

Colorado	Gary Alexander et al., *Colorado Legal R(* *Annotated Bibliography* (AALL, 1987).
Connecticut	Shirley R. Bysiewicz, *Sources of Connectic(* worth, 1987). Lawrence G. Cheeseman & Arlene C. Bielefield, (...) *cut Legal Research Handbook* (Connecticut Law B(...) Company, 1992). David R. Voisinet et al., *Connecticut State Legal Documents: A Selective Bibliography* (AALL, 1985).
District of Columbia	Carolyn P. Ahearn et al., *Selected Information Sources for the District of Columbia,* 2d. ed. (AALL, 1985). Chanin, Leah F., et al., *Legal Research in the District of Columbia, Maryland, and Virginia* (William S. Hein & Co., Inc., 1995).
Florida	Harriet L. French, *Research in Florida Law,* 2d ed. (Oceana, 1965). Mark E. Kaplan, *Guide to Florida Legal Research,* 3d ed. (Florida Bar, 1992). Niki L. Martin, *Florida Legal Research and Source Book* (D & S Publishers, 1990). Carol A. Roehrenbeck, *Florida Legislative Histories: A Practical Guide to Their Preparation and Use* (D & S Publishers, 1986). Betsy L. Stupski, *Guide to Florida Legal Research,* 4th ed. (Florida Bar, Continuing Legal Education, 1994).
Georgia	Leah F. Chanin & Suzanne L. Cassidy, *Guide to Georgia Legal Research and Legal History* (Harrison Company, 1990). Rebecca Simmons Stillwagon, *Georgia Legal Documents: An Annotated Bibliography* (AALL, 1991).
Hawaii	Jerry Dupont & Beverly D. Keever, *The Citizens Guide: How to Use Legal Materials in Hawaii* (1983). Richard F. Kahle, *How to Research Constitutional Legislative and Statutory History in Hawaii* (Hawaii Legislative Reference Bureau, 1986).
Idaho	Patricia A. Cervenka et al., *Idaho Law–Related State Documents* (AALL, 1989).
Illinois	Bernita J. Davies & Francis J. Rooney, *Research in Illinois Law* (Oceana, 1954). Roger F. Jacobs et al., *Illinois Legal Research Sourcebook* (Illinois Institute for Continuing Legal Education, 1977). Cheryl R. Nyberg et al., *Illinois State Documents: A Selective Annotated Bibliography for Law Librarians* (AALL, 1986). Laurel Wendt, *Illinois Legal Research Manual* (Butterworth, 1988).
Indiana	Linda K. Fariss & Keith A. Buckley, *An Introduction to Indiana State Publications for the Law Librarian* (AALL, 1982).
Iowa	Angela K. Secrest, *Iowa Legal Documents Bibliography* (AALL, 1990).
Kansas	Fritz Snyder, *A Guide to Kansas Legal Research* (Kansas Bar Association, 1986).

	Martin E. Wisneski, *Kansas State Documents for Law Libraries: Publications Related to Law and State Government* (AALL, 1984).
Kentucky	Paul J. Cammarata, *Kentucky State Publications: A Guide for Law Librarians* (AALL, 1990).
	Wesley Gilmer, Jr., *Guide to Kentucky Legal Research 2d: A State Bibliography* (State Law Library, 1985).
Louisiana	Win–Shin S. Chiang, *Louisiana Legal Research,* 2d ed. (Butterworth, 1990).
	Madeline Hebert, *Louisiana Legal Documents and Related Publications* (AALL, 1990).
	Kate Wallach, *Louisiana Legal Research Manual* (LSU Law School, 1972).
Maine	William W. Wells, Jr., *Maine Legal Research Guide* (Tower Publishing, 1989).
Maryland	Lynda C. Davis, *An Introduction to Maryland State Publications* (AALL, 1981).
	Michael S. Miller, *Ghost Hunting: Finding Legislative Intent in Maryland* (Maryland State Law Library, 1984).
Massachusetts	Margot Botsford et al., *Handbook of Legal Research in Massachusetts,* rev. ed. (Massachusetts Continuing Legal Education, Inc., 1988).
	Anthony J. Burke & Mary McLellan, *Guide to Massachusetts Legislative and Government Research* (Legislative Service Bureau, 1981).
	Leo McAuliffe & Susan Z. Steinway, *Massachusetts State Documents Bibliography* (AALL, 1985).
Michigan	Richard L. Beer & Judith J. Field, *Michigan Legal Literature: An Annotated Guide,* 2d ed. (Hein, 1991).
	Nancy L. Bosh, *Research Edge: Finding Law and Facts Fast* (Institute of Continuing Legal Education, 1993).
	John Doyle, *Michigan Citation Manual* (Hein, 1986).
	Michigan Association of Law Libraries, *Legal Research Guide for Michigan Libraries* (1982).
	Stuart D. Yoak & Margaret A. Heinen, *Michigan Legal Documents: an Annotated Bibliography* (AALL, 1982).
Minnesota	Marsha L. Baum & Mary Ann Nelson, *Guide to Minnesota State Documents and Selected Law–Related Publications* (AALL, 1985).
	Arlette M. Soderberg & Barbara L. Golden, *Minnesota Legal Research Guide* (Hein, 1985).
Mississippi	Ben Cole, *Mississippi Legal Documents and Related Publications: A Selected Annotated Bibliography* (AALL, 1987).
Missouri	Mary Ann Nelson, *Guide to Missouri State Documents and Selected Law–Related Materials* (AALL, 1991).
Montana	Stephen R. Jordan, *Bibliography of Selective Legal and Law Related Montana Documents* (AALL, 1990).
Nebraska	Mitchell J. Fontenot et al., *Nebraska State Documents Bibliography* (AALL, 1988).
	Paul F. Hill, *Nebraska Legal Research and Reference Manual* (Mason, 1983).
Nevada	Katherine Henderson, *Nevada State Documents Bibliography* (AALL, 1984).

New Jersey   Cameron Allen, *A Guide to New Jersey Legal Bibliography and Legal History* (Rothman, 1984).

Paul Axel–Lute, *New Jersey Legal Research Handbook*, 2d ed. (New Jersey Institute for Continuing Legal Education, 1996).

Christina M. Senezak, *New Jersey State Publications, A Guide for Law Libraries* (AALL, 1984).

New Mexico   Arie W. Poldervaart, *Manual for Effective New Mexico Legal Research* (Univ. of New Mexico Press, 1955).

Patricia Wagner & Mary Woodward, *Guide to New Mexico State Publications,* 2d ed. (AALL, 1991).

New York   Robert Allan Carter, *New York State Constitution: Sources of Legislative Intent* (Rothman, 1988).

Susan L. Dow & Karen L. Spencer, *New York Legal Documents: A Selective Annotated Bibliography* (AALL, 1985).

Ellen M. Gibson, *New York Legal Research Guide* (Hein, 1988).

North Carolina   Igor I. Kavass & Bruce A. Christensen, *Guide to North Carolina Legal Research* (Hein, 1973).

Jean Sinclair McKnight, *North Carolina Legal Research Guide* (Rothman 1994).

Thomas M. Steele & Donna Diprisco, *Survey of North Carolina State Legal and Law–Related Documents* (AALL, 1987).

Ohio   Christine A. Corcas, *Ohio Legal and Law–Related Documents* (AALL, 1986).

David M. Gold, *A Guide to Legislative History in Ohio* (Ohio Legislative Service Commission, 1985).

Ohio Regional Association of Law Libraries, *Ohio Legal Resources—An Annotated Bibliography and Guide,* 4th ed. (1996).

Melanie K. Putnam & Susan M. Schaefgen, *Ohio Legal Research Guide* (William S. Hein & Co., 1996).

Susan Schaefgen & Melanie K. Putnam, *Ohio Legal Research* (Professional Education Systems, 1988).

Oklahoma   Christine A. Corcas, *Oklahoma Legal and Law–Related Documents and Publications: a Selected Bibliography,* (AALL, 1983).

Oregon   Leslie Ann Buhman et al., *Bibliography of Law Related Oregon Documents* (AALL, 1984).

Pennsylvania   Joel Fishman, *Bibliography of Pennsylvania Law: Secondary Sources* (Pennsylvania Legal Resources Institute, 1992).

Joel Fishman, *An Introduction to Pennsylvania State Publications for the Law Librarian* (AALL, 1985).

Caroll C. Moreland & Erwin C. Surrency, *Research in Pennsylvania Law,* 2d ed. (Oceana, 1965).

Rhode Island   *Legal Research in Rhode Island* (Rhode Island Law Institute, 1989).

South Carolina   Paula Gail Benson & Deborah Ann Davis, A *Guide to South Carolina Legal Research and Citation* (South Carolina Bar, Continuing Legal Education Division, 1991).

Robin K. Mills & Jon S. Schultz, *South Carolina Legal Research Handbook* (Hein, 1976).

South Dakota	Delores A. Jorgensen, *South Dakota Legal Documents: A Selective Bibliography* (AALL, 1988).
	Delores A. Jorgensen, *South Dakota Legal Research Guide* (Hein, 1988).
Tennessee	Lewis L. Laska, *Tennessee Legal Research Handbook* (Hein, 1977).
	D. Cheryn Picquet & Reba A. Best, *Law and Government Publications of the State of Tennessee: A Bibliographic Guide* (AALL, 1988).
Texas	Malinda Allison & Kay Schleuter, *Texas State Documents for Law Libraries* (AALL, 1983).
	Lydia M.V. Brandt, *Texas Legal Research: An Essential Lawyering Skill* (Texas Lawyer Press, 1995).
	Karl T. Gruben & James E. Hambleton, *A Reference Guide to Texas Law and Legal History,* 2d ed. (Butterworth, 1987).
	Paris Permenter & Susan F. Ratliff, *Guide to Texas Legislative History* (Legislative Reference Library, 1986).
Vermont	Virginia Wise, *A Bibliographic Guide to the Vermont Legal System,* 2d ed. (AALL, 1991).
Virginia	John D. Eure et al. eds., *A Guide to Legal Research in Virginia,* 2d ed. (Committee on Continuing Legal Education of the Virginia Law Foundation, 1994).
	Jacqueline Lichtman & Judy Stinson, *A Law Librarian's Introduction to Virginia State Publications* (AALL, 1988).
Washington	Scott F. Burson, *Washington State Law–Related Publications: A Selective Bibliography with Commentary* (AALL, 1984).
	Gallagher Law Library, *Washington Legal Researcher's Deskbook,* 2d ed. (1996).
West Virginia	Sandra Stemple et al., *West Virginia Legal Bibliography* (AALL, 1990).
Wisconsin	Richard A. Danner, *Legal Research in Wisconsin* (University of Wisconsin, Extension Law Department, 1980).
	Janet Oberla, *An Introduction to Wisconsin State Documents and Law Related Materials* (AALL, 1987).
Wyoming	Nancy S. Greene, *Wyoming State Legal Documents: An Annotated Bibliography with Commentary* (AALL, 1985).

Appendix C

LEGAL RESEARCH IN TERRITORIES OF THE UNITED STATES*

The United States exercises sovereignty, in varying degrees, over a small number of places outside the fifty states and the District of Columbia. These are all island jurisdictions found in either the Caribbean or the Pacific. These jurisdictions can usefully be grouped as either territories or possessions of the United States on the one hand, or as states in free association with the United States on the other hand. For comprehensive discussion of the political and legal status of these jurisdictions the researcher should consult the recent book, *The Law of United States Territories and Affiliated Jurisdictions*.[1]

Each of the jurisdictions discussed in this appendix has substantial local autonomy and lawmaking power. Therefore, legal research in these jurisdictions requires the use of the locally published materials described in this appendix, in conjunction with research in the applicable federal law as described elsewhere in this book.

I. TERRITORIES OF THE UNITED STATES

"Incorporated" or "unincorporated," and "organized" or "unorganized" denote two sets of ideas used to describe the political status of territories of the United States. The first set refers to the application of the United States Constitution. Given that by definition a territory does not have the status of a state, it is also thought not to be fully a part of the United States, with the further consequence that the federal Constitution is held not to apply there fully. Territories are said to be unincorporated. The second set of terms refers to the existence of an "organic act" passed by Congress for the governance of a territory. Where Congress has passed such an organic act, the territory is said to be organized.[2]

AMERICAN SAMOA

American Samoa is an unincorporated and unorganized territory of the United States. The United States gained sovereignty over American Samoa by a treaty of 1899 with Germany and Great Britain,[3] and by cessions of 1900 and 1904 from the indigenous Samoans. American

---

* For his assistance in revising and updating Appendix C, the authors thank Jonathan Pratter, Foreign and International Law Librarian, University of Texas School of Law.

[1] By Stanley K. Laughlin, Jr. (Lawyers Cooperative Publishing 1995).

[2] *See id.* at 79–104.

[3] Convention on Adjustment of Jurisdiction in Samoa, 31 Stat. 1878, T.S. 314, 1 Bevans 276.

Samoa's status as a territory was confirmed by statute in 1929.[4] The Department of the Interior is responsible for the administration of American Samoa.[5]

While American Samoa does not have an organic act, it does have a Constitution of 1967 approved by the voters and by the Secretary of the Interior. The text of the Constitution as amended can be found in volume 10 of *Constitutions of Dependencies and Special Sovereignties*[6] and at the beginning of the *American Samoa Code Annotated*. The Constitution provides American Samoa with a legislature, a judiciary, and an executive, so that American Samoa enjoys substantial local lawmaking authority.

Statutes

American Samoa Code Annotated. Seattle: Book Publishing Co., 1981–.

The code is organized in 46 titles. It is in looseleaf format and is supposed to be updated annually with replacement pages. It appears however that updates have not been issued for several years.

Court Reports

American Samoa Reports. Orford, NH: Equity Pub. Corp., 1977–.

Complete in four volumes and a digest, this series reports the decisions of the High Court of American Samoa from 1900 to 1975.

American Samoa Reports, 2d series. Pago Pago, American Samoa: The Court, 1983–.

Originally published biennially, this series became annual, but the last volume issued appears to be volume 25 of 1993/94. It contains decisions of the Trial, Land and Titles, and Appellate Divisions of the High Court of American Samoa.

Administrative Regulations

American Samoa Administrative Code. Seattle: Book Publishing Co., 1981–.

The administrative code is in looseleaf format and is supposed to be updated annually, although it appears that the last update was issued in 1991.

GUAM

Guam was ceded to the United States by treaty following the Spanish–American War.[7] Guam is an unincorporated but organized

---

[4] Act of Feb. 20, 1929, ch. 281, 45 Stat. 1253 (1929), codified as amended at 48 U.S.C. § 1661 (1994).

[5] Exec. Order No. 10,264, 16 Fed. Reg. 6419 (1951).

[6] Albert P. Blaustein, ed. (Oceana Publications, 1975–).

[7] Treaty of Peace, Spain–U.S., December 10, 1898, 30 Stat. 1754, T.S. 343, 11 Bevans 615.

territory of the United States. Guam received its organic act in 1950.[8] The act establishes a legislature, judiciary, and executive for Guam. In addition to territorial courts, there is a United States District Court of Guam from which appeal lies to the United States Court of Appeals for the Ninth Circuit. Negotiations with Congress and successive administrations on commonwealth status have been underway for a decade.

Statutes

Guam Code Annotated. Agana, Guam: Guam Law Revision Commission: 1993–.

In 1993 the code was published in a new edition with amendments. There are 22 titles in 19 looseleaf volumes.

Public Laws and Executive Orders. Agana, Guam: Guam Law Revision Commission, 1979–.

Published in hardcopy as a looseleaf, the session laws are available in the microfiche collection of state session laws published by William S. Hein & Co.

Administrative Regulations

Administrative Rules and Regulations of the Government of Guam. Agana, Guam: Office of Compiler of Laws, 1975–1983.

This set is currently undergoing revision. A partial update was published on microfiche in 1990.

Computer Databases

WESTLAW has a database (GU–CS) that carries decisions from both the Supreme Court of the Territory of Guam and the U.S. District Court of Guam. *Guam Code Annotated* is searchable in databases with the identifiers GU–ST and GU–ST–ANN. Additional WESTLAW databases with relevant material can be found using the IDEN database.

NORTHERN MARIANA ISLANDS

This island group in the Pacific north of Guam was part of the Trust Territory of the Pacific Islands created in 1947 by the United Nations and administered by the United States. Negotiations on status led to the signing in 1975 of the Covenant to Establish a Commonwealth of the Northern Mariana Islands in Political Union with the United States of America, approved by Congress in 1976.[9] Under the Covenant the Northern Mariana Islands are a self-governing Commonwealth "in political union with and under the sovereignty of the United States." The Commonwealth exercises authority of local self-government while the United States retains sole responsibility for defense and foreign affairs.

---

[8] Act of Aug. 1, 1950, ch. 512, 64 Stat. 384, codified as amended at 48 U.S.C. § 1421 *et seq.* (1994).

[9] Act of March 24, 1976, P.L. 94–241, 90 Stat. 263.

Under section 105 of the Covenant, general federal legislation applies in the Northern Mariana Islands.

The Covenant calls for the drafting and approval of a Constitution, which was promulgated in 1977. It establishes a legislature, judiciary, and executive. The text of the Constitution can be found in volume X of *Constitutions of Dependencies and Special Sovereignties* and at the beginning of the *Commonwealth Code*. An annotated text of the Constitution, published as a separate in 1995, is available from the Commonwealth Law Revision.

The Covenant establishes a United States District Court of the Northern Mariana Islands the jurisdiction of which tracks that of its counterpart for Guam. Appeal lies to the Ninth Circuit.

Statutes

Commonwealth Code (1997 Revision). Saipan, Northern Mariana Islands: Commonwealth Law Revision Commission, 1997–.

A four-volume looseleaf publication, this is the official codification of legislation enacted by the Northern Mariana Islands Legislature. It is also available on CD–ROM.

Court Reports

Northern Mariana Islands Reporter. Saipan, Northern Mariana Islands: Commonwealth Law Revision Commission, 1991–.

Currently in four volumes, this series reports the decisions of the Commonwealth Supreme Court from the time of its establishment in 1989 through June 1996. A separately published digest and citator covering volumes 1–4 of the reporter is available.

Commonwealth Reporter. Saipan, Northern Mariana Islands: Commonwealth Law Revision Commission, 1987–1989.

This three-volume set in looseleaf format reports the decisions of the Commonwealth Superior Court (formerly the Trial Court) and of the District Court of the Northern Mariana Islands from 1978 to 1989. There is an associated digest.

The rules of court for the Commonwealth courts are available as separate publications from the Commonwealth Law Revision Commission.

Computer Databases

The MP–CS database on Westlaw contains decisions of both the Commonwealth Supreme Court and the District Court of the Northern Mariana Islands. Additional WESTLAW databases with relevant material can be found using the IDEN database.

PUERTO RICO[10]

Puerto Rico is the largest of the territories associated with the United States, both in terms of land area and population (over 3.6 million in 1993). The United States acquired Puerto Rico from Spain following the Spanish–American War. The law governing Puerto Rico's current political status is found in federal legislation,[11] the Constitution of Puerto Rico,[12] and judicial decisions, both federal and territorial. In its Constitution, Puerto Rico is denominated a Commonwealth. Puerto Rico exercises a degree of sovereignty approaching that of a state of the United States. In addition to a fully developed Commonwealth judiciary, there is a United States District Court for Puerto Rico from which appeals lie to the United States Court of Appeals for the First Circuit.

Statutes

Leyes de Puerto Rico/Laws of Puerto Rico. San Juan, Puerto Rico: Michie Co., 1900–.

The session laws are published in separate Spanish and English series. They are also available on microfiche in the William S. Hein & Co. series of state session laws. Because of the substantial delay in the publication of bound session law volumes, private publishers have started advance session law services. There are currently three competing services: *Servicio Legislativo de Puerto Rico and Leyes Selladas,* both published by Michie Co. and *Leyes Aprobadas* published by Consulta Legislativa, Inc.

Laws of Puerto Rico Annotated. San Juan, Puerto Rico: Michie Co., 1965–.

This is the standard English-language compilation of the Puerto Rican statutes. It is updated with pocket parts and replacement supplements. The annotations include not only court cases but also cross-references to *Rules and Regulations of Puerto Rico*. There are historical notes to trace the development of various sections. *Laws of Puerto Rico Annotated* is published in separate English and Spanish editions, as both languages are official.

Court Reports

Puerto Rico Reports. San Juan, Puerto Rico: Michie Co., vols. 1–100, 1900–1972.

This English-language set includes all cases from the Supreme Court of Puerto Rico from 1900–1972. The English version suspended publication with volume 100. The decisions of the Supreme Court since 1972 are available in translation, but unpublished, from the Court. Certified or

---

[10] The authors thank María M. Otero, Esq., Head, Reference Department, University of Puerto Rico Law Library, for her assistance in updating the Puerto Rico section of Appendix C.

[11] *See generally 48 U.S.C. §§ 731* et seq. (1994)

[12] The current text in English is found in Title 1, *Laws of Puerto Rico*.

plain copies of translations prepared by the Court can be requested from Secretaría del Tribunal Supremo, Negociado de Traducciones, Apartado 2392, San Juan, Puerto Rico 00902–2392, phone (787) 723–6033.

Decisiones de Puerto Rico. San Juan, Puerto Rico: Michie Co., 1900–.

The Spanish version of the reports of the Supreme Court of Puerto Rico continues to be published, but there is approximately a two-year delay before a volume of decisions is published.

Jurisprudencia del Tribunal Supremo de Puerto Rico. San Juan, Puerto Rico: Publicaciones JTS, 1977–.

These are weekly advance sheets of the decisions of the Supreme Court, published only in Spanish, with quarterly indexes and case tables.

Opiniones Avanzadas del Tribunal Supremo. San Juan, Puerto Rico: Colegio de Abogados de Puerto Rico, 1963–.

The Puerto Rico Bar Association publishes these advance sheets of the decisions of the Supreme Court of Puerto Rico. Includes annual index.

Decisiones del Tribunal de Circuito de Apelaciones de Puerto Rico. San Juan, Puerto Rico: Publicaciones JTS, 1995–.

These advance sheets of the decisions of the Puerto Rico Appellate Circuit Court are published twice monthly in Spanish. They include annual indexes.

Digests

Digesto de Puerto Rico. San Juan, Puerto Rico: Michie Co., 1974–.

This is the topical digest to the decisions of the Supreme Court of Puerto Rico. It is published in Spanish only. Organization is analogous to the West digests. Updating is by cumulative annual pocket parts.

Administrative Regulations

Catalog of Regulations of Puerto Rico. San Juan, Puerto Rico: Michie, Co., 1991–.

This is a looseleaf compilation of Puerto Rican administrative regulations in force. It contains an abstract of the regulation. Updating is by replacement pages.

Reglamentos del Estado Libre Asociado de Puerto Rico. San Juan, Puerto Rico: Michie Co., 1995–

This new publication contains the code of administrative regulations of the governmental agencies in Puerto Rico. This set is not complete and currently there are 10 volumes published, representing 30% of the regulations. Updating is twice annually.

Rules and Regulations of Puerto Rico. San Juan, Puerto Rico: Commonwealth of Puerto Rico, Department of State, 1957–1972.

This looseleaf service contained the English-language codification of all regulations adopted by the executive branch of Puerto Rico. This set is no longer published.

Puerto Rico Register. San Juan, Puerto Rico: Commonwealth of Puerto Rico, Department of State, 1957–1982.

This looseleaf service was published periodically (about seven times a year), and contained new regulations and amendments to existing regulations, thus keeping the *Rules and Regulations of Puerto Rico* up to date. It is not currently published in either Spanish or English.

Executive Opinions

Opiniones del Secretario de Justicia de Puerto Rico. San Juan, Puerto Rico: Puerto Rico Department of Justice, 1903–.

The *Opiniones* are more or less equivalent to state attorneys general opinions. They come out irregularly but are kept up to date. They are published in the William S. Hein & Co. microfiche set of attorneys general opinions.

Law Reviews

Revista de Derecho Puertorriqueño. Quarterly publication of the Universidad Católica de Puerto Rico, School of Law, Ponce, Puerto Rico, 1961–.

Revista del Colegio de Abogados de Puerto Rico. Quarterly publication of the Colegio de Abogados de Puerto Rico, San Juan, Puerto Rico, 1939–.

Revista Jurídica de la Universidad de Puerto Rico. Quarterly publication of the Escuela de Derecho de la Universidad de Puerto Rico, Río Piedras, Puerto Rico, 1932–.

Revista Jurídica de la Universidad Interamericana de Puerto Rico. A triannual publication of the Universidad Interamericana de Puerto Rico, Santurce, Puerto Rico, 1964–.

Citation Index

Shepard's Puerto Rico Citations. Colorado Springs, Colo.: Shepard's, 1968–.

This is a complete citation system showing all citations by the Puerto Rico and federal courts to the Puerto Rico cases reported in the various series of Puerto Rico reports and all citations by the Puerto Rico and federal courts to the Constitution of the Commonwealth of Puerto Rico, the Organic Acts, and codes and laws, acts, ordinances, and court rules. All citations by the Puerto Rico courts to the United States Constitution and federal statutes are also shown.

Computer Databases

WESTLAW has a Puerto Rico database that contains the Puerto Rico statutes (PR–ST–ANN), the rules of court, and a legislative service that purports to have the text of recently passed laws, though it does not appear to contain anything more recent than the other statutory databases. There is another database of decisions from the 1st Circuit and from the U.S. District Court for the District of Puerto Rico. It contains many decisions from the District Court that are not published in the *Federal Supplement*. Westlaw recently added the decisions of the Supreme Court of Puerto Rico, in Spanish, since 1989 to the database (PRS–CS). For additional information on these and other Puerto Rico databases, the researcher should consult the current edition of the WESTLAW *Database Directory*.

LEXIS–NEXIS has a Puerto Rico library that contains a file for the annotated statutes and a file that purports to have the text of recently passed laws, though it does not appear to contain anything more recent than the other statutory databases. There is a separate cases file which contains the decisions of the Supreme Court of Puerto Rico, in Spanish, since 1948.

Neither LEXIS–NEXIS nor WESTLAW carries the complete decisions of the Puerto Rico Supreme Court since its first volume in 1899.

Compuclerk/LPRA. West Group, 1992–.

This is a database in CD–ROM format containing the full text in Spanish of *Leyes de Puerto Rico Anotadas (Laws of Puerto Rico Annotated)*.

Compuclerk/DPR. West Group, 1989–.

This is the only database containing the full text of the decisions, in Spanish, of the Supreme Court of Puerto Rico, from 1899 to the present. It is in CD–ROM format.

Microjuris. San Juan, Puerto Rico: Microjuris, Inc. 1989–.

This database is available through the World Wide Web on a subscription basis. It contains the opinions of the Supreme Court of Puerto Rico since1949 and the Appellate Circuit Court of Puerto Rico since 1995. It also includes the *Laws of Puerto Rico Annotated* and a database for legislative information which contains the acts approved daily. Some regulations of various government agencies are also included.

Michie's Puerto Rico Law on Disc. Michie Co., 1995–.

This database in CD–ROM format contains the opinions of the Supreme Court of Puerto Rico since 1948, the opinions of the Appellate Circuit Court of Puerto Rico since 1995, the *Laws of Puerto Rico Annotated*, and a file containing the regulations of Puerto Rico organized by government agency. A file containing the latest bills signed into law is included also.

Pronline. Michie Co., 1989–.

This is the only database in Puerto Rico which contains an abstract of the bills and resolutions introduced in the Legislative Assembly of Puerto Rico since 1985. It includes information about the history of the bills, organized by subject, bill number, and other indexes. It also includes abstracts of the government regulations organized by subject, agency names and other indexes. The information is in English and Spanish and is updated on a daily basis.

Legal Research Guides

Carlos I. Gorrín Peralta. *Fuentes y Proceso de Investigación Jurídica.* Orford, NH: Butterworth Legal Publishers, Equity Publishing Division, 1991.

Luis Muñiz Arguelles & Migdalia Fraticelli Torres. *La Investigación Jurídica en el Derecho Puertorriqueño: Fuentes Puertorriqueñas, Norteamericanas y Españolas.* 2d ed. San Juan, Puerto Rico: Centro Gráfico del Caribe, 1995.

VIRGIN ISLANDS

The United States Virgin Islands were acquired by purchase from Denmark in 1916.[13] The Virgin Islands are an unincorporated, organized territory. The organic act was adopted in 1936[14] and amended in various ways since.[15] There is a unicameral legislature, an elected governor and a Territorial Court of the Virgin Islands. The United States District Court of the Virgin Islands exercises jurisdiction along the lines of other territorial federal courts, but in addition hears appeals from the Territorial Court. In 1976 Congress authorized the adoption of a constitution, but two attempts to do so failed with the voters, as did a 1993 referendum on political status.

Statutes

Session Laws of the Virgin Islands. Charlotte Amalie, Virgin Islands: Law Revision Commission, 1955–.

Published annually, the session laws contain the text of laws and resolutions enacted by the legislature and approved by the governor. The session laws are also published in the series of state session laws produced in microfiche by William S. Hein & Co.

Virgin Islands Code Annotated. Charlottesville, Va.: Michie Co., 1970–.

Annotated and updated annually with pocket parts and replacement volumes, this is the standard commercial edition of the Virgin Islands statutes in compiled form. Unnumbered index and tables volumes, a volume of court rules, and an advance session law service complete the set.

Court Reports

Virgin Islands Reports. Charlottesville, Va.: Michie, 1959–.

[13] Convention on Cession of Danish West Indies, Denmark–U.S., Aug. 4, 1916, 39 Stat. 1706, T.S. 629, 7 Bevans 56.

[14] Act of June 22, 1936, ch. 699, 49 Stat. 1807, codified as amended at 48 U.S.C. §§ 1405 *et seq.* (1994).

[15] Amendments are reflected in the codified version of the organic act.

Covering the period from 1917, and now in 36 volumes, this is the standard series of reports for the courts of the Virgin Islands. It publishes the decisions of the Territorial Court, the District Court and the United States Court of Appeals for the Third Circuit.

Digests

Virgin Islands Digest. Charlottesville, Va.: Michie, 1991–.

In six volumes, including a descriptive-word index and table of cases, this set gives topical access to decisions published in *Virgin Islands Reports*. Coverage in the bound volumes is through 1990 and updating is done by means of pocket parts.

Administrative Regulations

Virgin Islands Rules and Regulations. Orford, N.H.: Equity, 1959–.

Current information indicates that this compilation of Virgin Islands administrative regulations is no longer published. Michie publishes a *Virgin Islands Zoning, Building and Housing Laws and Regulations*.

Attorney General Opinions

Opinions of the Attorney General of the Virgin Islands. Charlottesville, Va.: Michie, 1965–.

In ten volumes, covering the period from 1935–1986, this series is not currently published.

II.   STATES IN FREE ASSOCIATION WITH THE UNITED STATES

The freely associated states are the Federated States of Micronesia, Palau, and the Republic of the Marshall Islands, all in the western Pacific. The fundamental distinction between a territory and a freely associated state is that in international law the latter has the status of a sovereign nation. Each of the freely associated states is a member of the United Nations.

The freely associated states formerly were part of the Trust Territory of the Pacific Islands created by the United Nations in 1947 and administered by the United States. Negotiations on political status led to the signing and approval of Compacts of Free Association with the United States in the 1980s.[16] The compacts are in the nature of international agreements. The freely associated states have much of the status of independent sovereign states. Under the compacts the United States takes on responsibility for military security and defense and receives exclusive military authority. However, in consultation with the United States, the freely associated states retain the authority to conduct their foreign affairs.

---

[16] For the Marshall Islands and Micronesia, see 48 U.S.C. § 1901. For Palau, see 48 U.S.C. § 1931. The texts of the Compacts of Free Association will be found in the notes following these sections in the annotated editions of U.S.C.

FEDERATED STATES OF MICRONESIA

Statutes

Federated States of Micronesia Code Annotated. Kolonia, Pohnpei, FM: Pacific Island Planning Consultants, 1995–.

In two looseleaf volumes of 58 titles, this compilation is updated annually. It is annotated with casenotes and source notes. The text of the constitution is found at the beginning.

Court Reports

Federated States of Micronesia Supreme Court Reports. Kolonia, Pohnpei, FM: The Court, [1997?-].

Formerly called the *Interim Reports*, this reporter has been reissued in hardbound format. It contains the decisions of the Supreme Court of the Federated States of Micronesia from 1982 as well selected decisions from the state supreme courts. New volumes are supposed to be produced approximately annually.

PALAU

Statutes

Palau National Code Annotated: PNCA. Koror, Palau: Orakiruu Corp., 1995–.

In two looseleaf volumes of 42 titles and index, with a third volume of tables and appendices, this edition of the statutes is authorized by the Palau National National Code Commission. It is annotated with case citations and source notes. Update pages were issued in 1996. The text of the constitution is found at the beginning.

Court Reports

Courts of the Republic of Palau Interim Reporter. Koror, Palau: The Court, 1987–.

This series contains the decisions of the Supreme Court, Appellate Division and selected decisions of the lower courts.

REPUBLIC OF THE MARSHALL ISLANDS

Marshall Islands Revised Code. Majuro, Marshall Islands: The Republic, 1988–.

In two looseleaf volumes, this is the current edition of the statutes.

Marshall Islands Law Reports. Majuro, Marshall Islands: Supreme Court, 1993–.

These are the reports of the decisions of the Supreme Court of the Marshall Islands. Volumes are supposed to be issued annually, with volume one covering cases from 1982 to 1993.

Appendix D

STATE REPORTS

A. YEAR OF FIRST REPORTED CASE DECIDED IN THE STATES' APPELLATE COURTS

Many of the states were territories or colonies at the time of their first appellate decision. Pennsylvania was a commonwealth. In 1840, what is now the state of Texas was an independent republic.

While printing began in the Colonies in 1638, the first case reported appears to be the *Trial of Thomas Sutherland* for murder, printed in 1692. About 30 of the 150 English reports were being used in this country prior to the American Revolution as the written case law, because only about 35 to 40 legal books or pamphlets had been printed here.

Connecticut was the first state to publish an official law report after a 1784 statute entitled *An Act Establishing the Wages of the Judges of the Superior Court* was passed requiring judges of the supreme and superior courts to file written opinions. The first volume, known as *Kirby's Reports,* was published in 1789 by Ephraim Kirby in Litchfield, Connecticut, and includes as its first case one from 1785. In 1790 came Dallas' *Pennsylvania Cases;* in 1792 followed Hopkinson's *Admiralty Reports;* and Chipman's *Vermont Reports* in 1793. Through the early 1800s reports followed in North Carolina, Virginia, Kentucky, New Jersey, Maryland, Louisiana, New York, and Tennessee. Some of these early reports gathered and published cases much older than the publication date of the reporter. For example, the *Harris & McHenry Reports* from the General Court of Maryland contains a case decided in 1658.

State	Date	State	Date
Alabama	1820	Indiana	1817
Alaska	1869	Iowa	1839
Arizona	1866	Kansas	1858
Arkansas	1837	Kentucky	1785
California	1850	Louisiana	1809
Colorado	1864	Maine	1820
Connecticut	1785	Maryland	1658
Delaware	1792	Massachusetts	1804
District of Columbia	1801	Michigan	1805
Florida	1846	Minnesota	1851
Georgia	1846	Mississippi	1818
Hawaii	1847	Missouri	1821
Idaho	1866	Montana	1868
Illinois	1819	Nebraska	1860

State	Date	State	Date
Nevada	1865	Rhode Island	1828
New Hampshire	1796	South Carolina	1783
New Jersey	1789	South Dakota	1867
New Mexico	1852	Tennessee	1791
New York	1791	Texas	1840
North Carolina	1778	Utah	1855
North Dakota	1867	Vermont	1789
Ohio	1821	Virginia	1729
Oklahoma	1890	Washington	1854
Oregon	1853	West Virginia	1864
Pennsylvania	1754	Wisconsin	1839
		Wyoming	1870

B. STATES THAT HAVE DISCONTINUED PUBLISHING OFFICIAL STATE REPORTS

State	Last Published Volume	Year	First Volume Only in National Reporter System
Alabama	295	1976	331 So. 2d
Ala. App.	57	1976	331 So. 2d
Colorado	200	1980	616 P.2d
Colo. App.	44	1980	616 P.2d
Delaware	59	1966	220 A.2d
Florida	160	1948	37 So. 2d
Indiana	275	1981	419 N.E.2d
Ind. App.	182	1979	366 N.E.2d
Iowa	261	1968	158 N.W.2d
Kentucky	314	1951	237 S.W.2d
Louisiana *	263	1972	270 So. 2d
Maine	161	1965	215 A.2d
Minnesota	312	1977	254 N.W.2d
Mississippi	254	1966	183 So. 2d
Missouri	365	1956	295 S.W.2d
Mo. App.	241	1952	274 S.W.2d
North Dakota	79	1953	60 N.W.2d
Oklahoma	208	1953	265 P.2d
Okla. Crim.	97	1953	265 P.2d
Rhode Island	122	1980	501 A.2d
South Dakota	90	1976	245 N.W.2d
Tennessee	225	1972	476 S.W.2d
Tenn. App.	63	1971	480 S.W.2d
Tenn. Crim. App.	4	1970	475 S.W.2d
Texas *	163	1962	358 S.W.2d
Tex. Crim. App.*	172	1963	363 S.W.2d
Tex. Civ. App.*	63	1911	134 S.W.
Utah (2d Series)	30	1974	519 P.2d
Wyoming	80	1959	346 P.2d

* These states have discontinued their official reports, but have not adopted the *National Reporter System* Reports as official. Alaska has used the *Pacific Reporter* as its official reporter since being admitted to statehood.

Appendix E

COVERAGE OF THE NATIONAL
REPORTER SYSTEM

The entire system, with its beginning year of coverage and its jurisdictional coverage is outlined below:

Reporter	Began in	Jurisdictional Coverage (start date varies by state)
Atlantic Reporter	1885	Conn., Del., Me., Md., N.H., N.J., Pa., R.I., Vt., and D.C.
California Reporter	1959	Calif. Sup. Ct., Courts of Appeal and Appellate Department of the Superior Court.
Illinois Decisions	1976	Ill. (all state appellate courts).
New York Supplement	1888	N.Y. (all appellate courts to 1932). Since 1932, the N.Y. Court of Appeals opinions are published here as well as in the North Eastern Reporter.
North Eastern Reporter	1885	Ill., Ind., Mass., N.Y., and Ohio.
North Western Reporter	1879	Iowa, Mich., Minn., Neb., N.D., S.D., and Wis.
Pacific Reporter	1883	Alaska, Ariz., Cal. to 1960, Calif. Sup. Ct. since 1960, Colo., Hawaii, Idaho, Kan., Mont., Nev., N.M., Okla., Or., Utah, Wash., and Wyo.
South Eastern Reporter	1887	Ga., N.C., S.C., Va., and W.Va.
South Western Reporter	1886	Ark., Ky., Mo., Tenn., and Tex.
Southern Reporter	1887	Ala., Fla., La., and Miss.
Supreme Court Reporter	1882	Supreme Court of the United States.
Federal Reporter	1880	From 1880 to 1911: United States Circuit Court (abolished in 1912). From 1880 to 1932: District Courts of the United States (coverage transferred to Federal Supplement). 1891 to date: United States Court of Appeals (formerly U.S. Circuit Court of Appeals). 1911 to 1913: Commerce Court of the United States (abolished in 1913). 1929 to 1932 and 1960 to 1982: United States Court of Claims (abolished in 1982). 1929 to 1982: United States Court of Customs and Patent Appeals.[1] 1943 to 1961: United States Emergency Court of Appeals.

[1] Since 1983, jurisdiction of the U.S. Court of Customs and Patent Appeals and the appellate division of the U.S. Court of Claims transferred to U.S. Court of Appeals for the Federal Circuit.

Reporter	**Began in**	**Jurisdictional Coverage (start date varies by state)**
		1972 to date: Temporary Emergency Court of Appeals.
Federal Supplement	1932	1932 to 1993: United States District Courts.
		1932 to 1960: United States Court of Claims.
		1954 to 1980: United States Customs Court (replaced by United States Court of International Trade).
		1980 to date: United States Court of International Trade.
		1968 to date: Judicial Panel on Multidistrict Litigation.
		1974 to date: Special Court under the Regional Rail Reorganization Act of 1973.
Federal Claims Reporter	1982	1982 to 1992: formerly United States Claims Court Reporter through vol. 26, covering United States Claims Court.[2]
		1992 to date: United States Court of Federal Claims. Commences with vol. 27.
Federal Rules Decisions	1939	1939 to date: District Courts of the United States construing Federal Rules of Civil (1939 to date) and Federal Rules of Criminal Procedure (1946 to date).
Military Justice Reporter	1975	1975 to date: U.S. Court of Appeals for the Armed Forces (formerly the Court of Military Appeals) and Courts Criminal Appeals (formerly Courts of Military Review) for the Army, Navy, Marine Corps, Air Force, and Coast Guard.
Bankruptcy Reporter	1979	1979 to date: Bankruptcy cases from U.S. Bankruptcy Courts, U.S. District Courts dealing with bankruptcy matters (cases not printed in Federal Supplement), U.S. Courts of Appeals (reprinted from Federal Reporter), and U.S. Supreme Court (reprinted from Supreme Court Reporter).
Veterans Appeals Reporter	1989	1989 to date: Veterans appeals cases from the United States Court of Veterans Appeals, U.S. District Courts, U.S. Courts of Appeals, and U.S. Supreme Court (in review of the Court of Veterans Appeals).

[2] This court changed its name in 1992 to the United States Court of Federal Claims.

Appendix F *

FUNDAMENTAL LAWYERING SKILLS
§ 3 LEGAL RESEARCH

In order to conduct legal research effectively, a lawyer should have a working knowledge of the nature of legal rules and legal institutions, the fundamental tools of legal research, and the process of devising and implementing a coherent and effective research design:

3.1 *Knowledge of the Nature of Legal Rules and Institutions.* The identification of the issues and sources to be researched in any particular situation requires an understanding of:

(a) The various sources of legal rules and the processes by which these rules are made, including:

(i) Caselaw. Every lawyer should have a basic familiarity with: (A) The organization and structure of the federal and state courts of general jurisdiction; general concepts of jurisdiction and venue; the rudiments of civil and criminal procedure; the historical separation between courts of law and equity and the modern vestiges of this dual court system; (B) The nature of common law decisionmaking by courts and the doctrine of *stare decisis;* (C) The degree of "authoritativeness" of constitutional and common law decisions made by courts at the various levels of the federal and state judicial systems;

(ii) Statutes. Every lawyer should have a basic familiarity with: (A) The legislative processes at the federal, state, and local levels, including the procedures for preparing, introducing, amending, and enacting legislation; (B) The relationship between the legislative and judicial branches, including the power of the courts to construe ambiguous statutory language and the power of the courts to strike down unconstitutional statutory provisions;

(iii) Administrative regulations and decisions of administrative agencies. Every lawyer should have a basic familiarity with the rudiments of administrative law, including: (A) The procedures for administrative and executive rulemaking and adjudication; (B) The relationship between the executive and judicial branches, including the power of the courts to construe and pass on the validity and constitutionality of administrative regulations and the actions of administrative agencies;

(iv) Rules of court;

* Reprinted by permission of the American Bar Association.

    (v) Restatements and similar codifications (covering non-official expositions of legal rules that courts tend to view as authoritative);

(b) Which of the sources of legal rules identified in § 3.1(a) *supra* tend to provide the controlling principles for resolution of various kinds of issues in various substantive fields;

(c) The variety of legal remedies available in any given situation, including: litigation; legislative remedies (such as drafting and/or lobbying for new legislation; lobbying to defeat pending legislative bills; and lobbying for the repeal or amendment of existing legislation); administrative remedies (such as presenting testimony in support of, or lobbying for, the adoption, repeal, or amendment of administrative regulations; and lobbying of an administrator to resolve an individual case in a particular way); and alternative dispute-resolution mechanisms (formal mechanisms such as arbitration, mediation, and conciliation; and informal mechanisms such as self-help);

3.2   *Knowledge of and Ability to Use the Most Fundamental Tools of Legal Research:*

(a) With respect to each of the following fundamental tools of legal research, a lawyer should be generally familiar with the nature of the tool, its likely location in a law library, and the ways in which the tool is used:

    (i) Primary legal texts (the written or recorded texts of legal rules), including: caselaw reporters, looseleaf services, and other collections of court decisions; codifications of federal, state, and local legislation; collections of administrative regulations and decisions of administrative agencies;

    (ii) Secondary legal materials (the variety of aids to researching the primary legal texts), including treatises, digests, annotated versions of statutory compilations, commentaries in looseleaf services, law reviews, and Shepard's Compilations of citations to cases and statutes;

    (iii) Sources of ethical obligations of lawyers, including the standards of professional conduct (the Code of Professional Responsibility and the Model Rules of Professional Conduct), and collections of ethical opinions of the American Bar Association and of state and local bar associations;

(b) With respect to the primary legal texts described in § 3.2(a)(i) *supra,* a lawyer should be familiar with:

    (i) Specialized techniques for reading or using the text, including:

        (A) Techniques of reading and analyzing court decisions, such as: the analysis of which portions of the decision are holdings and which are *dicta;* the identification of narrower and broader possible formulations of the holdings of the case; the evaluation of a case's relative precedential value; and the reconciliation of doctrinal inconsistencies between cases;

(B) Techniques of construing statutes by employing well-accepted rules of statutory construction or by referring to secondary sources (such as legislative history);

(ii) Specialized rules and customs permitting or prohibiting reliance on alternative versions of the primary legal texts (such as unofficial case reporters or unofficial statutory codes);

(c) With respect to the secondary legal materials described in § 3.2(a)(ii) *supra*, a lawyer should have a general familiarity with the breadth, depth, detail and currency of coverage, the particular perspectives, and the relative strengths and weaknesses that tend to be found in the various kinds of secondary sources so that he or she can make an informed judgment about which source is most suitable for a particular research purpose;

(d) With respect to both the primary legal materials described in § 3.2(a)(i) *supra*, and the secondary legal materials described in § 3.2(a)(ii) *supra*, a lawyer should be familiar with alternative forms of accessing the materials, including hard copy, microfiche and other miniaturization services, and computerized services (such as LEXIS and WESTLAW);

3.3 *Understanding of the Process of Devising and Implementing a Coherent and Effective Research Design:* A lawyer should be familiar with the skills and concepts involved in:

(a) Formulating the issues for research:

(i) Determining the full range of legal issues to be researched (*see* Skill § 2.1 *supra*);

(ii) Determining the kinds of answers to the legal issues that are needed for various purposes;

(iii) Determining the degree of confidence in the answers that is needed for various purposes;

(iv) Determining the extent of documentation of the answers that is needed for various purposes;

(v) Conceptualizing the issues to be researched in terms that are conducive to effective legal research (including a consideration of which conceptualizations or verbalizations of issues or rules will make them most accessible to various types of search strategies);

(b) Identifying the full range of search strategies that could be used to research the issues, as well as alternatives to research, such as, in appropriate cases, seeking the information from other people who have expertise regarding the issues to be researched (for example, other attorneys or, in the case of procedural issues, clerks of court);

(c) Evaluating the various search strategies and settling upon a research design, which should take into account:

(i) The degree of thoroughness of research that would be necessary in order to adequately resolve the legal issues (*i.e.,* in order to find an answer if there is one to be found, or, in cases where the issue is still open, to determine to a reasonable degree of certainty that it is still unresolved and gather analogous authorities);

(ii) The degree of thoroughness that is necessary in the light of the uses to which the research will be put (*e.g.,* the greater degree of thoroughness necessary if the information to be researched will be used at trial or at a legislative hearing; the lesser degree of thoroughness necessary if the information will be used in an informal negotiation with opposing counsel or lobbying of an administrator);

(iii) An estimation of the amount of time that will be necessary to conduct research of the desired degree of thoroughness;

(iv) An assessment of the feasibility of conducting research of the desired degree of thoroughness, taking into account:

   (A) The amount of time available for research in the light of the other tasks to be performed, their relative importance, and their relative urgency;

   (B) The extent of the client's resources that can be allocated to the process of legal research; and

   (C) The availability of techniques for reducing the cost of research (such as, for example, using manual research methods to gain basic familiarity with the relevant area before using the more expensive resource of computerized services);

(v) If there is insufficient time for, or the client lacks adequate resources for, research that is thorough enough to adequately resolve the legal issues, a further assessment of the ways in which the scope of the research can be curtailed with the minimum degree of risk of undermining the accuracy of the research or otherwise impairing the client's interests;

(vi) Strategies for double-checking the accuracy of the research, such as using different secondary sources to research the same issue; or, when possible, conferring with practitioners or academics with expertise in the area;

(d) Implementing the research design, including:

(i) Informing the client of the precise extent to which the scope of the research has been curtailed for the sake of time or conservation of the client's resources (*see* § 3.3(c)(v) *supra*); the reasons for these curtailments; and the possible consequences of deciding not to pursue additional research;

(ii) Monitoring the results of the research and periodically considering:

   (A) Whether the research design should be modified;

(B) Whether it is appropriate to end the research, because it has fully answered the questions posed; or, even though it has not fully answered the questions posed, further research will not produce additional information; or the information that is likely to be produced is not worth the time and resources that would be expended;

(iii) Ensuring that any cases that will be relied upon or cited have not been overruled, limited, or called into question; and that any statutes or administrative regulations that will be relied upon or cited have not been repealed or amended and have not been struck down by the courts.

––––––––

In 1989 the American Bar Association Section of Legal Education and Admissions to the Bar created the Task Force on Law Schools and the Profession: Narrowing the Gap. Its purpose was to study and improve the processes by which new members of the profession are prepared for the practice of law. In August 1992, the Task Force issued its final report, *Legal Education and Professional Development—An Educational Continuum.* That report includes within it a "Statement of Fundamental Skills and Values," identifying "Legal Research" as one of the ten fundamental skills a lawyer should possess. The Task Force was chaired by former ABA President Robert MacCrate. We are grateful to Mr. MacCrate and to the American Bar Association for granting permission to reprint § 3 Legal Research.[1]

JMJ
RMM
DJD

[1] For additional information on § 3 Legal Research of the Task Force report, see Donald J. Dunn, *Legal Research: A Fundamental Lawyering Skill,* 1 PERSPECTIVES: TEACHING LEGAL RES. & WRITING 2 (1992); Donald J. Dunn, *Are Legal Research Skills Essential? "It Can Hardly Be Doubted ...",* 1 PERSPECTIVES: TEACHING LEGAL RES. & WRITING 34 (1993).

Appendix G

SELECTED LAW–RELATED INTERNET SOURCES

The tremendous growth of the Internet has spawned an enormous number of law-related Web sites. The highly selective list that follows represent those the authors believe are among the best sources for use in locating various types of legal information. While several of these sites are discussed in the text, others in this list are provided for additional reference.[1]

ABA Network

[http://www.abanet.org]

Provides a variety of information about the American Bar Association and its activities and publications.

AltaVista

[http://www.altavista.digital.com]

A great search engine using Infoseek. Boolean searching is available.

American Association of Law Libraries

[http://aallnet.org]

An extremely valuable resource for learning about the workings of the professional association for law librarians.

American Law Resources On–Line

[http://www.lawsource.com/also]

Includes links to all states and to Canadian and Mexican law materials.

Bureau of Labor Statistics

[http://stats.bls.gov]

An excellent source for learning about the American work force.

Center for Information Law and Policy

[http://www.law.vill.edu]

Perhaps the most comprehensive site for almost anything law related. Extremely valuable for finding state materials. Houses the "State

---

[1] For additional information on law related sources on the Internet, see JAMES EVANS, LAW ON THE NET, Nolo Press (2d ed. 1997), and DON MACLEOD, THE INTERNET GUIDE FOR THE LEGAL RESEARCHER, Infosources Publishing (2d ed. 1997). Both publications were extremely helpful in developing this Appendix.

Web Locator," "Federal Court Locator," and "International Law Locator," among many others.

Code of Federal Regulations

[http://www.access.gpo.gov/nara/cfr/cfr-table-search.html]

A searchable text, title by title, of the *Code of Federal Regulations*. A part of the U.S. House's "Internet Law Library."

Constitution of the United States of America

[http://www.access.gpo.gov/congress/senate/constitution/toc.html]

The complete text of the Library of Congress' *Constitution of the United States of America: Analysis and Interpretation; Annotations of Cases Decided by the Supreme Court of the United States to June 29, 1992*. Also includes the latest supplement.

CourtTV

[http://www.courttv.com]

A terrific source for background documents relating to high-profile cases.

Federal Courts Finder

[http://www.law.emory.edu/FEDCTS]

Located at Emory University School of Law, this is probably the best site for finding links to the decisions of the various federal circuit courts.

Federal Court Locator

[http://www.law.vill.edu/Fed–Ct/fedcourt.html]

Provides links to all United States courts of appeals sites and sources for decisions of the U.S. Supreme Court.

Federal Register

[http://www.access.gpo.gov:80/su_docs/aces/aces140.html]

Contains the *Federal Register* since 1994. Searchable in various ways.

FedWorld

[http://www.fedworld.gov]

A good source for locating federal documents, with over half a million available.

FindLaw

[http://www.findlaw.com]

A great source for locating Supreme court cases, state law resources, subject-matter coverage, law reviews, and information about law schools and legal organizations. It also has a powerful search engine known as "Law Crawler."

GPO Access

[http://www.access.gpo.gov]

The home page of the Government Printing Office, this site covers more than 70 government databases and includes, among many others, bills, the *CFR*, *Federal Register*, and *U.S. Code*.

Hieros Gamos

[http://www.hg.org]

An enormous resource with links to just about everything imaginable that is law related.

Human Rights Library

[http://www.umn.edu/humanrts]

Developed at the University of Minnesota Law School, this is a wonderful site for locating the most important international human rights sources.

Hytelnet

[http://www.law.indiana.edu/law/v-lib/law schools.html]

Provides access to hundreds of law library electronic catalogs worldwide. The best site is at Indiana University School of Law at Bloomington at the URL provided.

Infoseek

[http://www.infoseek.com]

A great search engine with a directory-style design.

Internet Law Library

[http://law.house.gov]

A great source for statutory materials. This one is especially valuable for the alphabetical listing of laws from other nations and for treaties and international law sources.

Internet Legal Research Guide

[http://www.ilrg.com]

A categorized index of over 3100 select web sites in 238 nations, islands, and territories, as well as more than 850 locally stored web pages and other files.

Law Journal EXTRA!

[http://www.ljextra.com]

A great source for legal news.

Law Lists

[http:www.lib.uchicago.edu/?llou/lawlists/info.html]

An effort to index all law-related discussion groups.

Lawyers Weekly

[http://www.lweekly.com]

This is a national newspaper with national legal news. It contains links to its seven state legal newspapers.

Legal Domain Network

[http://www.kentlaw.edu/lawnet/lawnet.html]

Hosted by Chicago–Kent Law School, this site maintains archives for many law-related listservs.

Legal Information Institute (Cornell)

[http://www.law.cornell.edu]

The pioneer in providing legal information via the Internet. Especially useful for U.S. Supreme Court cases and for court rules.

Library of Congress

[http://www.loc.gov]

A truly wonderful source. In addition to the searchable catalogs, the links and descriptions of other resources are as good as they get.

Martindale-Hubbell Lawyer Locator

[http:www.martindale.com]

The online version of the *Martindale-Hubbell Law Directory*. Includes lawyers' e-mail addresses and firm Web sites.

National Center for State Courts

[http://www.ncsc.dni.us/ncsc.htm]

An especially valuable source for finding information on court statistics, juries, and caseloads.

Office of Management and Budget

[http://www2.whitehouse.gov/WH/EOP/html/ombhome.html]

Includes the annual budget of the federal government.

Office of the President

[http://www.whitehouse.gov]

A very fine resource, especially for the general public. Even an online tour of the White House is available.

State Court Locator

[http://www.law.vill.edu]

Contains state court decisions and information on the judges and the courts.

Thomas

[http://thomas.loc.gov]

This is the legislative server of the Library of Congress and is the best source for legislative information on the Internet, e.g., bills, legislative histories, *Congressional Record*.

U.S. Census Bureau

[http://www.census.gov]

The best source for locating vital statistics of the United States.

U.S. Department of Justice

[http://www.usdoj.gov]

Learn about the organizational structure of the DOJ, including links to its various divisions.

U.S. Department of Labor

[http://www.dol.gov]

Includes statutory and regulatory information and various types of labor-related data.

U.S. Department of State

[http://www.state.gov]

Valuable in locating international policy positions and travel advisories. Includes a listing of the countries of the world.

U.S. Department of the Treasury

[http://www.ustreas.gov]

Includes "IRS Search" for use in finding tax forms or regulations.

U.S. Environmental Protection Agency

[http://www.epa.gov]

A huge, well-designed site that includes regulations and links to thousands of titles.

U.S. Federal Judiciary

[http://www.uscourts.gov]

Maintained by the Administrative Office of the U.S. Courts, it serves as a clearinghouse for information about the judicial branch of the U.S. government.

U.S. Federal Trade Commission

[http://www.ftc.gov]

The best source for materials on antitrust.

U.S. House of Representatives

[http://www.house.gov]

A terrific source for legislative activity, including a weekly schedule of bills, resolutions, and legislative issues. Includes almost 9,000 links to law resources on the Internet.

U.S. Internal Revenue Service

[http://www.irs.ustreas.gov]

In addition to IRS tax forms, its a public relations bonanza for this agency in the amount of information it provides.

U.S. Patent and Trademark Office

[http:www.uspto.gov]

This site can actually be used to search for information on patents and to download forms.

U.S. Securities and Exchange Commission

[http://www.sec.gov]

Using the EDGAR database for corporate information, this is the place to locate SEC filings on public companies.

U.S. Senate

[http://www.senate.gov]

Provides a wealth of information about legislative activities and committees.

WashLaw Web

[http://lawlib.wuacc.edu]

Just about the most all-inclusive site available. Hosts many law related listservs.

West's Legal Directory

[http://www.wld.com]

An online directory that can be used to locate individuals as well as law firm Web sites.

World Wide Web Virtual Library: Law

[http://www.law.indiana.edu/law/lawindex.html]

An outstanding site for use in finding sources by organization and by topic. Especially useful for locating law schools and libraries, law journals on the Web, law firms, and publishers and vendors.

Yahoo!

[http://www.yahoo.com]

Perhaps one of the better known search engines as a result of its catchy name, it is best for non-law research.

Appendix H

CHART ON LEGAL RESEARCH PROCEDURE

RESEARCH PROBLEM	GENERAL BACKGROUND	MORE CRITICAL & DETAILED STUDIES	ANNOTATIONS	TEXT OF LAW OR CASE	LEGISLATIVE HISTORY	INTERPRETATION	SHEPARDIZING	ADDITIONAL CASES	OTHER
CASE LAW									
1. Federal	1. C.J.S. 2. Am. Jr. 2d	1. Treatises 2. *Periodicals:* Index Leg. Per.; Leg. Res. Index; Cur. Law Index; LegalTrac 3. Restatements	ALRs	1. *S. CT.:* U.S. Rpts; U.S. Sup. Ct. Rpts (L. Ed.); Sup. Ct. Rptr. (West) 2. Fed. Rptr.; F.2d; F.3d 3. Fed. Supp.			1. Shepard's U.S. & Fed. Citator	1. U.S. Sup. Ct. Digest 2. West's various sets of lower court federal digest 3. Looseleaf Services	1. WESTLAW 2. LEXIS 3. Records & Briefs, if available
2. State	1. State Ency. 2. C.J.S. or Am. Jr. 2d	1. Treatises 2. *Periodicals:* Index Leg. Per.; Leg. Res. Index; Cur. Law Index; LegalTrac	ALRs	1. National Reporter System 2. State Reports			1. Shepard's State or Regional Citator 2. Nat'l Rpr. Blue Book	1. Am. Dig. System 2. National Reporter Blue Book	1. WESTLAW 2. LEXIS 3. Records & Briefs, if available 4. Restatements
STATUTORY LAW									
1. Federal	C.J.S. or Am. Jr. 2d	1. Treatises 2. *Periodicals:* Index Leg. Per.; Leg. Res. Index; Cur. Law Index; LegalTrac	1. ALRs 2. L. Ed.	1. U.S.C. 2. U.S.C.A. 3. U.S.C.S.	1. *Pre-1970:* See Chap. 10 2. *Post-1970:* C.I.S. 3. Pub. Legis. Histories	1. U.S.C.A 2. U.S.C.S. 3. U.S. Att'y Gen. Opinions	1. *Provisions & Cases:* U.S. 2. *Cases:* Fed. 3. *Provisions:* State or Regional Citator	1. U.S. Sup. Ct. Digests 2. West's various sets of lower court federal digests 3. Looseleaf Services	1. WESTLAW 2. LEXIS
2. State	1. State Ency. or 2. C.J.S. or Am. Jr. 2d	1. State Treatises 2. *Periodicals:* Index Leg. Per.; Leg. Res. Index; Cur. Law Index; LegalTrac	ALRs	1. State Code 2. State Code Annotated	1. *Citations:* State 2. *Intent:* See Chap. 11	1. State Code Annotated 2. State Att'y Gen. Opinions	*Provisions & Cases:* State or Regional Citator	1. State or Regional Digests 2. Other State Codes Annotated 3. Uniform Laws Annotated	1. WESTLAW 2. LEXIS 3. Legal research guide for the state, where available
3. Local		Treatises		1. Mun. Code 2. Mun. Ordinances 3. Appropriate city official		State Digest	*Provisions & Cases:* State Citator	Shepard's Ordinance Law Annotations	1. WESTLAW 2. LEXIS

RESEARCH PROBLEM	GENERAL BACKGROUND	MORE CRITICAL & DETAILED STUDIES	ANNOTATIONS	TEXT OF LAW OR CASE	LEGISLATIVE HISTORY	INTERPRETATION	SHEPARDIZING	ADDITIONAL CASES	OTHER
CONSTITUTIONAL LAW 1. Federal	1. C.J.S 2. Am. Jr. 2d	1. Treatises 2. *Periodicals:* Index Leg. Per.; Leg. Res. Index; Cur. Law Index; LegalTrac 3. Restatements	1. ALR Fed. 2. U.S. Sup. Ct. Rpts. L. Edition 3. LC Const.	1. U.S.C. 2. U.S.C.A. 3. U.S.C.S.	1. Citations: U.S.C.A., U.S.C.S, Shepard's U.S., U.S.C. Stat. at Large 2. *Intent:* Federalist, etc.	1. U.S.C.A. 2. U.S.C.S. 3. LC Constitution 4. U.S. Att'y Gen. Opinions	1. *Provisions:* U.S., State 2. *Cases:* Fed., U.S., State	1. U.S. Sup. Ct. Dige. 2. West's various sets of lower court federal digests 3. Am. Dig. System	1. WESTLAW 2. LEXIS 3. Records & Briefs, if available
2. State	1. State Ency. 2. C.J.S. or Am. Jr. 2d	1. *Periodicals:* Index Leg. Per. Leg. Res. Index Cur. Law Index LegalTrac	ALRs	1. State Code 2. State Code Annotated	1. State Const. Convention a. Proceedings b. Reports 2. Locally pub'd legis. rpts, H. & S. Jrnals, etc.	1. State Code Annotated 2. State Digest 3. State Att'y Gen. Opinions	1. *Provisions:* State Citator 2. *Cases:* State or Regional Citator	1. Am. Dig. System 2. Constitution of the U.S. National and State, Index	1. WESTLAW 2. LEXIS 3. Records & Briefs, if available
ADMINISTRATIVE LAW 1. Federal	C.J.S. or Am. Jr. 2d	1. Pike & Fischer 2. Treatises 3. *Periodicals:* Index Leg. Per.; Leg. Res. Index; Cur. Law Index; LegalTrac	1. ALRs 2. L. Ed.	1. *Fed. Regt. & CFR:* Rules & Decisions 2. *Agency Rpts:* Decisions 3. *Looseleaf Services:* Rules & Decisions		1. Looseleaf Services 2. U.S. Sup. Court Digests 3. West's various sets of lower ct. federal digests	1. *CFR.* Citator 2. *Agency Cases:* U.S. Admin. Citator 3. *Court Cases:* U.S. & Fed. Citator		1. WESTLAW 2. LEXIS
2. State	State Ency.	1. State Treatises 2. *Periodicals:* Index Leg. Per.; Leg. Res. Index; Cur. Law Index; LegalTrac	ALRs	1. Adm. Code, if published 2. Register of agency reg. & rulings, if pub. 3. Agency: Rules & Decisions 4. Looseleaf service, if available		1. State or Regional Dig. 2. State Atty. Gen. Ops.	*Cases:* State or Regional Citator	1. Other state or regional digests 2. American Digest System	
3. Local				1. Local Adm. Dept. 2. Pamphlets		State Digest	*Cases:* State Citator	Other state digests	1. WESTLAW 2. LEXIS

[G5.795]

INDEX*

References are to Pages; italic type indicates Titles of Publications

* Prepared by Bonnie L. Koneski-White, Director of the Law Library, Western New England College, School of Law.

INDEX

INDEX

INDEX

INDEX

INDEX

INDEX

INDEX

Looseleaf Services
Generally, 304
Digests, 113
Electronic format, 321–322
Features, 316–317
Interfiled, 318
Newsletter, 318
Federal administrative agencies
Rules and regulations, 274
Federal laws, recent, 157–158
In LEXIS–NEXIS and WESTLAW, 321–322
Publishers, 317–318
State statutes, 241–242
Summary, 333
Use, 318–321

Majority Opinion, 26

Malloy's Treaties, 480–481

Mandatory Authority, 2

Memorandum Opinion, 27

Military Justice Citations (Shepard's), 359

Military Justice Reporter, 51

Miller's Treaties, 481
Model Acts, 442
Finding aids, 442–443

Model Code of Judicial Conduct, 472

Model Rules of Professional Conduct, 472

Monthly Catalog of United States Government Publications, 197

Monthly Digest of Tax Articles, 410

Multilateral Treaties Deposited with the Secretary–General, 488

Multilateral Treaties: Index and Current Status, 488

Municipal Legislation
Citators, 245, 349
Codes, 244
Judicial interpretation of, 244–245
Ordinances, 245
Indexes to, Illustrated, 247
Summary, 249–250

Named Reporters
Citation form, 78
English, 533
Supreme Court of the United States, 43–44

National Conference of Commissioners on Uniform State Laws, 441
Archive collection, 442
Handbook, 441–442

National Conference of Commissioners on Uniform State Laws Archive Collection in Microfiche, 442

National Law Journal, 394

National Reporter Blue Book, 78
Illustrated, 81

INDEX

National Reporter System
Generally, 28, 72
Advance sheets, 75
Current awareness features, 75
Citations, 77–78
Components, 73–74
Coverage, Appendix E, 770–771
Cross-reference tables, 78–79
Features, 74–75
History, 72–73
Map, 76
Star pagination, 79
Summary, 84
Ultra Fiche edition, 74
West's Key Number Digests, relation to, 75
Words and phrases, 75, 113–114

National Survey of State Laws, 242

Newsletters
See Legal Periodicals

Newspapers
See Legal Periodicals

Nominative Reporters
See Named Reporters

Non–Legal Sources, 474

Obiter Dictum
See Dictum

Official Publications, 12, 27

Official Reports, 27, 71–72

Offprint Reporters, 73–74

Opinions of the Office of Legal Counsel, 455
See Also Attorneys General Opinions, United States

Oral Arguments
Generally, 470–471
Supreme Court of the United States, 471
Antitrust law, 471
Audiotapes, 471
Constitutional law, 471
Internet, 471
Transcripts, 471

Ordinance
See Municipal Legislation

Ordinance Law Annotations (Shepard's), 243, 349

Organization of American States Treaty Series, 487

Parallel Citations
Auto–Cite, 79
Illustrated, 82
Cross-reference tables, 78–79
Insta–Cite, 79
Illustrated, 82
National Reporter Blue Book, 78
Illustrated, 81
State *Blue and White Book,* 78

804

INDEX

INDEX

ISBN 1–56662–613–7

9 781566 626132

90000